FLORIDA EDITION

McDougal Littell

Science

GRADE 7

Earth's Waters

Human Biology

Life Over Time

Electricity and Magnetism

Space Science

Earth's Surface

Printed in the U.S.A.

ISBN-13: 978-0-618-57128-4

ISBN-10: 0-618-57128-0   3 4 5 6 7 8 VJM 09 08 07 06

Internet Web Site: http://www.mcdougallittell.com

Science Consultants

Chief Science Consultant

James Trefil, Ph.D. is the Clarence J. Robinson Professor of Physics at George Mason University. He is the author or co-author of more than 25 books, including *Science Matters* and *The Nature of Science*. Dr. Trefil is a member of the American Association for the Advancement of Science's Committee on the Public Understanding of Science and Technology. He is also a fellow of the World Economic Forum and a frequent contributor to *Smithsonian* magazine.

Rita Ann Calvo, Ph.D. is Senior Lecturer in Molecular Biology and Genetics at Cornell University, where for 12 years she also directed the Cornell Institute for Biology Teachers. Dr. Calvo is the 1999 recipient of the College and University Teaching Award from the National Association of Biology Teachers.

Kenneth Cutler, M.S. is the Education Coordinator for the Julius L. Chambers Biomedical Biotechnology Research Institute at North Carolina Central University. A former middle school and high school science teacher, he received a 1999 Presidential Award for Excellence in Science Teaching.

Instructional Design Consultants

Douglas Carnine, Ph.D. is Professor of Education and Director of the National Center for Improving the Tools of Educators at the University of Oregon. He is the author of seven books and over 100 other scholarly publications, primarily in the areas of instructional design and effective instructional strategies and tools for diverse learners. Dr. Carnine also serves as a member of the National Institute for Literacy Advisory Board.

Linda Carnine, Ph.D. consults with school districts on curriculum development and effective instruction for students struggling academically. A former teacher and school administrator, Dr. Carnine also co-authored a popular remedial reading program.

Donald Steely, Ph.D. serves as principal investigator at the Oregon Center for Applied Science (ORCAS) on federal grants for science and language arts programs. His background also includes teaching and authoring of print and multimedia programs in science, mathematics, history, and spelling.

Sam Miller, Ph.D. is a middle school science teacher and the Teacher Development Liaison for the Eugene, Oregon, Public Schools. He is the author of curricula for teaching science, mathematics, computer skills, and language arts.

Vicky Vachon, Ph.D. consults with school districts throughout the United States and Canada on improving overall academic achievement with a focus on literacy. She is also co-author of a widely used program for remedial readers.

Content Reviewers

Safety Consultant

Juliana Texley, Ph.D.
Former K–12 Science Teacher and School Superintendent
Boca Raton, FL

English Language Advisor

Judy Lewis, M.A.
Director, State and Federal Programs for reading proficiency
and high risk populations
Rancho Cordova, CA

Teacher Panel Members

Carol Arbour
Tallmadge Middle School,
Tallmadge, OH

Patty Belcher
Goodrich Middle School,
Akron, OH

Gwen Broestl
Luis Munoz Marin Middle School,
Cleveland, OH

Al Brofman
Tehipite Middle School,
Fresno, CA

John Cockrell
Clinton Middle School,
Columbus, OH

Jenifer Cox
Sylvan Middle School,
Citrus Heights, CA

Linda Culpepper
Martin Middle School,
Charlotte, NC

Melvin Figueroa
New River Middle School,
Ft. Lauderdale, FL

Doretha Grier
Kannapolis Middle School,
Kannapolis, NC

Robert Hood
Alexander Hamilton Middle School,
Cleveland, OH

Scott Hudson
Covedale Elementary School,
Cincinnati, OH

Loretta Langdon
Princeton Middle School,
Princeton, NC

Carlyn Little
Glades Middle School,
Miami, FL

Ann Marie Lynn
Amelia Earhart Middle School,
Riverside, CA

James Minogue
Lowe's Grove Middle School,
Durham, NC

Kathleen Montagnino-DeMatteo
Jefferson Davis Middle School,
West Palm Beach, FL

Joann Myers
Buchanan Middle School,
Tampa, FL

Barbara Newell
Charles Evans Hughes Middle School,
Long Beach, CA

Anita Parker
Kannapolis Middle School,
Kannapolis, NC

Greg Pirolo
Golden Valley Middle School,
San Bernardino, CA

Laura Pottmyer
Apex Middle School,
Apex, NC

Lynn Prichard
Williams Middle Magnet School,
Tampa, FL

Jacque Quick
Walter Williams High School,
Burlington, NC

Stacy Rinehart
Lufkin Road Middle School,
Apex, NC

Robert Glenn Reynolds
Hillman Middle School,
Youngstown, OH

Theresa Short
Abbott Middle School,
Fayetteville, NC

Rita Slivka
Alexander Hamilton Middle School,
Cleveland, OH

Marie Sofsak
B F Stanton Middle School,
Alliance, OH

Nancy Stubbs
Sweetwater Union Unified School District,
Chula Vista, CA

Sharon Stull
Quail Hollow Middle School,
Charlotte, NC

Donna Taylor
Bak Middle School of the Arts,
West Palm Beach, FL

Sandi Thompson
Harding Middle School,
Lakewood, OH

Lori Walker
Audubon Middle School & Magnet Center,
Los Angeles, CA

Teacher Lab Evaluators

Andrew Boy
W.E.B. DuBois Academy,
Cincinnati, OH

Jill Brimm-Byrne
Albany Park Academy,
Chicago, IL

Gwen Broestl
Luis Munoz Marin Middle School,
Cleveland, OH

Al Brofman
Tehipite Middle School,
Fresno, CA

Michael A. Burstein
The Rashi School,
Newton, MA

Trudi Coutts
Madison Middle School,
Naperville, IL

Jenifer Cox
Sylvan Middle School,
Citrus Heights, CA

Larry Cwik
Madison Middle School,
Naperville, IL

Jennifer Donatelli
Kennedy Junior High School,
Lisle, IL

Melissa Dupree
Lakeside Middle School,
Evans, GA

Carl Fechko
Luis Munoz Marin Middle School,
Cleveland, OH

Paige Fullhart
Highland Middle School,
Libertyville, IL

Sue Hood
Glen Crest Middle School,
Glen Ellyn, IL

William Luzader
Plymouth Community Intermediate School,
Plymouth, MA

Ann Min
Beardsley Middle School,
Crystal Lake, IL

Aileen Mueller
Kennedy Junior High School,
Lisle, IL

Nancy Nega
Churchville Middle School,
Elmhurst, IL

Oscar Newman
Sumner Math and Science Academy,
Chicago, IL

Lynn Prichard
Williams Middle Magnet School,
Tampa, FL

Jacque Quick
Walter Williams High School,
Burlington, NC

Stacy Rinehart
Lufkin Road Middle School,
Apex, NC

Seth Robey
Gwendolyn Brooks Middle School,
Oak Park, IL

Kevin Steele
Grissom Middle School,
Tinley Park, IL

 ## Florida Teacher Panel Members

Colleen Doulk
West Hernando Middle School,
Brooksville, FL

Maya D. Edgar
Henry D. Perry Middle School,
Miramar, FL

Melvin Figueroa
New River Middle School,
Fort Lauderdale, FL

Carlyn Little
Glades Middle School,
Miami, FL

Kathleen Montagnino-DeMatteo
Jefferson Davis Middle School,
West Palm Beach, FL

Joann Myers
Buchanan Middle School,
Tampa, FL

Lynn Prichard
Williams Middle Magnet School,
Tampa, FL

Donna Taylor
Bak Middle School of the Arts,
West Palm Beach, FL

Kim Zenon
Braden River Middle School,
Bradenton, FL

 ## Florida Teacher Reviewers

Julie K. Ball
Coleman Middle School,
Tampa, FL

Jane Gucciardo
Martinez Middle School,
Lutz, FL

Melanie Musolino
Hoover Middle School,
Indialantic, FL

Kathy Poe
Fletcher Middle School,
Jacksonville Beach, FL

Richard M. Regan
Stone Middle School,
Melbourne, FL

Guytri Still
McNair Magnet School,
Cocoa, FL

Karrie Wikman
Punta Gorda Middle School,
Punta Gorda, FL

Introducing Science   FL26

Unifying Principles of Science   FL30
Florida Student Handbook   FL36

1 The Nature of Science   2

1 Basic tools of science are universal.   5
    CONNECTING SCIENCES *The Science of Clean Water*   13

2 Scientific ideas are based on evidence.   14
    CHAPTER INVESTIGATION *Using a Filter*   22

3 Scientists belong to a world community.   24
    MATH IN SCIENCE *Making Bar Graphs*   31

FLORIDA CONNECTIONS

Saving Coral   42

Florida's Sinkholes   190

Animatronics   334

The Ultimate Fish   450

A Place in the Sun   564

Cape Canaveral: Step to the Stars   666

Student Resources

Florida Resources   809
    Florida Content Review/Preview   811
    FCAT Science Reference   823
    Appendix   825
Student Resource Handbooks   R1
    Scientific Thinking Handbook   R2
    Lab Handbook   R10
    Math Handbook   R36
    Note-Taking Handbook   R45
Glossary   R52
Index   R74
Acknowledgments   R117

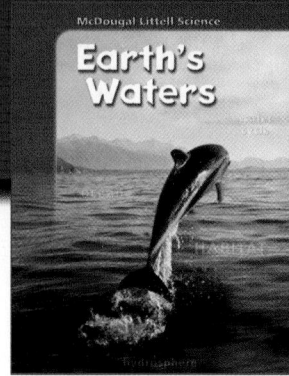

eEdition

Unit Features

SCIENTIFIC AMERICAN **FRONTIERS IN SCIENCE** *Exploring the Water Planet*   38

🌴 **FLORIDA CONNECTION** *Saving Coral*   42

TIMELINES IN SCIENCE *Exploring the Ocean*   146

2 The Water Planet   46

the **BIG** idea

Water moves through Earth's atmosphere, oceans, and land in a cycle.

1. **Water continually cycles.**   49
   THINK SCIENCE *Does Mars Have a Water Cycle?*   55

2. **Fresh water flows and freezes on Earth.**   56
   MATH IN SCIENCE *Multiplying Fractions and Whole Numbers*   63

3. **Fresh water flows underground.**   64
   CHAPTER INVESTIGATION *Water Moving Underground*   72

3 Freshwater Resources   78

the **BIG** idea

Fresh water is a limited resource and is essential for human society.

1. **Fresh water is an essential resource.**   81
   MATH IN SCIENCE *Volume of Rectangular Prisms*   89

2. **Society depends on clean and safe water.**   90
   CHAPTER INVESTIGATION *Monitoring Water Quality*   98

3. **Water shortages threaten society.**   100
   SCIENCE ON THE JOB *Water and Farming*   107

In what ways do you depend on water? page 78

What causes these waves? page 112

4 Ocean Systems 112

(the **BIG** idea)

The oceans are a connected system of water in motion.

1 The oceans are a connected system. 115
  MATH IN SCIENCE *Plotting Coordinates* 123

2 Ocean water moves in currents. 124

3 Waves move through oceans. 129
  CHAPTER INVESTIGATION *Wave Movement* 134

4 Waters rise and fall in tides. 136
  CONNECTING SCIENCES *Tidal Energy* 141

5 Ocean Environments 150

(the **BIG** idea)

The ocean supports life and contains natural resources.

1 Ocean coasts support plant and animal life. 153
  MATH IN SCIENCE *Making a Double Bar Graph* 160

2 Conditions differ away from shore. 161
  EXTREME SCIENCE *Undersea Hot Spots* 169

3 The ocean contains natural resources. 170
  CHAPTER INVESTIGATION *Population Sampling* 178

Visual Highlights

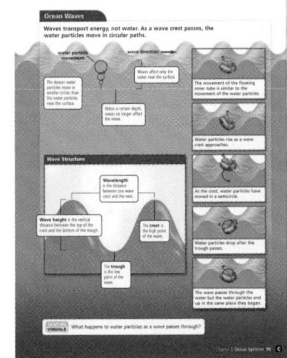

Springs and Wells 69
Sources of Water Pollution 95
The Ocean Floor 120
Ocean Waves 131
Intertidal Zone 155
Coral Reefs 163
Life in the Open Ocean 167

UNIT 2
Earth's Surface

Unit Features

SCIENTIFIC AMERICAN **FRONTIERS IN SCIENCE** *Remote Sensing* — 186

FLORIDA CONNECTION *Florida's Sinkholes* — 190

TIMELINES IN SCIENCE *History of the Earth System* — 292

6 Views of Earth Today — 194

the **BIG** idea

Modern technology has changed the way we view and map Earth.

1 **Technology is used to explore the Earth system.** — 197

2 **Maps and globes are models of Earth.** — 203
   MATH IN SCIENCE *Using Proportions* — 211

3 **Topographic maps show the shape of the land.** — 212
   CHAPTER INVESTIGATION *Investigate Topographic Maps* — 216

4 **Technology is used to map Earth.** — 218
   THINK SCIENCE *Which Site Is Best for an Olympic Stadium?* — 223

7 Weathering and Soil Formation — 228

the **BIG** idea

Natural forces break rocks apart and form soil, which supports life.

1 **Mechanical and chemical forces break down rocks.** — 231
   MATH IN SCIENCE *Surface Area of a Prism* — 237

2 **Weathering and organic processes form soil.** — 238
   CHAPTER INVESTIGATION *Testing Soil* — 246

3 **Human activities affect soil.** — 248
   SCIENCE ON THE JOB *Soil, Water, and Architecture* — 253

How is rock related to soil? page 228

Erosion and Deposition 258

the BIG idea

Water, wind, and ice shape Earth's surface.

1. **Forces wear down and build up Earth's surface.** 261
2. **Moving water shapes land.** 266
   CHAPTER INVESTIGATION *Creating Stream Features* 272
3. **Waves and wind shape land.** 274
   CONNECTING SCIENCES *Life on Dunes* 280
4. **Glaciers carve land and move sediments.** 281
   MATH IN SCIENCE *Creating a Line Graph* 287

Natural Resources 296

the BIG idea

Society depends on natural resources for energy and materials.

1. **Natural resources support human activity.** 299
   CONNECTING SCIENCES *Got Oil Spills?* 307
2. **Resources can be conserved and recycled.** 308
   MATH IN SCIENCE *Comparing Decimals* 312
3. **Energy comes from other natural resources.** 313
   CHAPTER INVESTIGATION *Wind Power* 322

How do people obtain energy from Earth's resources? page 296

Visual Highlights

Mechanical Weathering 233
World Soil Types 241
Organisms and Soil Formation 243
Types of Glaciers and Movement 283
Natural Resources 301

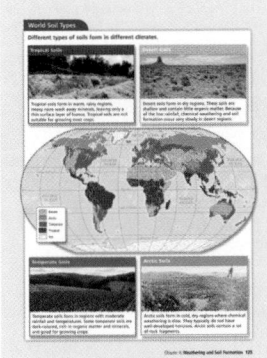

McDougal Littell Science

Electricity and Magnetism

eEdition

UNIT 3
Electricity and Magnetism

Unit Features

SCIENTIFIC AMERICAN **FRONTIERS IN SCIENCE** *Electronics in Music*　330

FLORIDA CONNECTION *Animatronics*　334

TIMELINES IN SCIENCE *The Story of Electronics*　404

10 Electricity　338

the **BIG** idea

Moving electric charges transfer energy.

1　Materials can become electrically charged.　341
　CONNECTING SCIENCES *Electric Eels*　349

2　Charges can move from one place to another.　350
　CHAPTER INVESTIGATION *Lightning*　358

3　Electric current is a flow of charge.　360
　MATH IN SCIENCE *Using Variables*　367

11 Circuits and Electronics　372

the **BIG** idea

Circuits control the flow of electric charge.

1　Charge needs a continuous path to flow.　375
　SCIENCE ON THE JOB *The Science of Electrical Work*　382

2　Circuits make electric current useful.　383
　MATH IN SCIENCE *Solving Percent Problems*　388

3　Electronic technology is based on circuits.　389
　CHAPTER INVESTIGATION *Design an Electronic Communication Device*　398

How can circuits control the flow of charge? page 372

What force is acting on this compass needle?
page 408

12 Magnetism 408

the BIG idea

Current can produce magnetism, and magnetism can produce current.

1 **Magnetism is a force that acts at a distance.** 411
THINK SCIENCE *Can Magnets Heal People?* 419

2 **Current can produce magnetism.** 420

3 **Magnetism can produce current.** 427
CHAPTER INVESTIGATION *Build a Speaker* 432

4 **Generators supply electrical energy.** 434
MATH IN SCIENCE *Using Significant Figures* 439

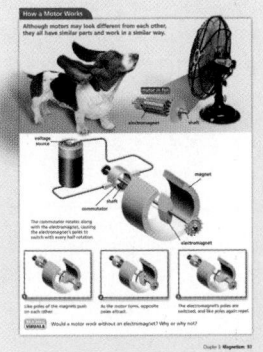

Visual Highlights

How a Photocopier Works 347
How Lightning Forms 353
Batteries 365
How a PC Works 394
How Magnets Differ from Other Materials 415
How a Motor Works 425

UNIT 4
Life Over Time

eEdition

Unit Features

SCIENTIFIC AMERICAN **FRONTIERS IN SCIENCE** *Life by Degrees* — 446

FLORIDA CONNECTION *The Ultimate Fish* — 450

TIMELINES IN SCIENCE *Life Unearthed* — 520

13 Views of Earth's Past

454

the BIG idea

Rocks, fossils, and other types of natural evidence tell Earth's story.

1 Earth's past is revealed in rocks and fossils. — 457
   CONNECTING SCIENCES *Could* T. Rex *Win a Race?* — 464

2 Rocks provide a timeline for Earth. — 465
   MATH IN SCIENCE *Interpreting Graphs* — 472

3 The geologic time scale shows Earth's past. — 473
   CHAPTER INVESTIGATION *Geologic Time* — 480

What does this footprint tell you about the animal that left it? page 454

How do scientists learn about the history of life on Earth? page 486

14 The History of Life on Earth — 486

the BIG idea

Living things, like Earth itself, change over time.

1 Earth has been home to living things for about 3.8 billion years. — 489
  MATH IN SCIENCE *Using Proportions* — 496

2 Species change over time. — 497
  CHAPTER INVESTIGATION *Modeling Natural Selection* — 506

3 Many types of evidence support evolution. — 508
  THINK SCIENCE *How Did the Deep-Sea Angler Get Its Glow?* — 515

15 Population Dynamics — 524

the BIG idea

Populations are shaped by interactions between organisms and the environment.

1 Populations have many characteristics. — 527
  MATH IN SCIENCE *Finding Averages* — 535

2 Populations respond to pressures. — 536
  SCIENCE ON THE JOB *Studying the Schools* — 543

3 Human populations have unique responses to change. — 544
  CHAPTER INVESTIGATION *Sustainable Resource Management* — 552

Visual Highlights

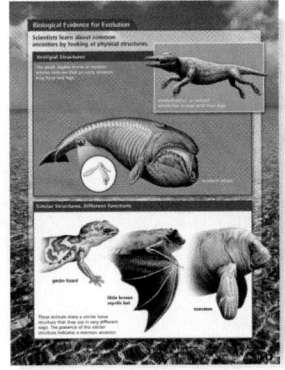

Fossils in Rocks — 461
Radioactive Breakdown — 470
Natural Selection — 503
Biological Evidence for Evolution — 511

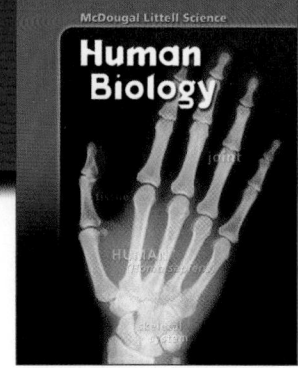

McDougal Littell Science
Human Biology
eEdition

UNIT 5
Human Biology

Unit Features

SCIENTIFIC AMERICAN **FRONTIERS IN SCIENCE** *Surprising Senses* — 560

FLORIDA CONNECTION *A Place in the Sun* — 564

TIMELINES IN SCIENCE *Seeing Inside the Body* — 624

16 Systems, Support, and Movement — 568

the **BIG** idea

The human body is made up of systems that work together to perform necessary functions.

1 **The human body is complex.** — 571
THINK SCIENCE *What Does the Body Need to Survive?* — 575

2 **The skeletal system provides support and protection.** — 576
MATH IN SCIENCE *Comparing Rates* — 583

3 **The muscular system makes movement possible.** — 584
CHAPTER INVESTIGATION *A Closer Look at Muscles* — 590

What materials does your body need to function properly? page 596

Red blood cells travel through a blood vessel. How do you think blood carries materials around your body? page 628

17 Absorption, Digestion, and Exchange 596

(the **BIG** idea)

Systems in the body obtain and process materials and remove waste.

1 **The respiratory system gets oxygen and removes carbon dioxide.** 599
   SCIENCE ON THE JOB *Breathing and Yoga* 606

2 **The digestive system breaks down food.** 607
   MATH IN SCIENCE *Choosing Units of Length* 613

3 **The urinary system removes waste materials.** 614
   CHAPTER INVESTIGATION *Modeling a Kidney* 618

18 Transport and Protection 628

(the **BIG** idea)

Systems function to transport materials and to defend and protect the body.

1 **The circulatory system transports materials.** 631
   CHAPTER INVESTIGATION *Heart Rate and Exercise* 638

2 **The immune system defends the body.** 640
   MATH IN SCIENCE *Making a Line Graph* 648

3 **The integumentary system shields the body.** 649
   EXTREME SCIENCE *Artificial Skin* 655

Visual Highlights

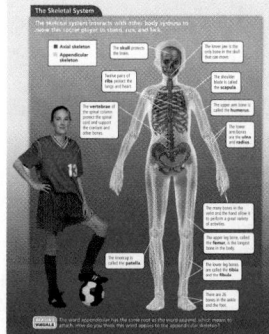

The Skeletal System   579
Muscle Tissue   587
Respiratory System   603
Digestive System   611
Circulatory System   634

McDougal Littell Science

Space Science

UNIVERSE

electromagnetic radiation

eEdition

UNIT 6
Space Science

Unit Features

SCIENTIFIC AMERICAN **FRONTIERS IN SCIENCE** *Danger from the Sky* 662

FLORIDA CONNECTION *Cape Canaveral: Step to the Stars* 666

TIMELINES IN SCIENCE *The Story of Astronomy* 736

19 Exploring Space 670

the BIG idea

People develop and use technology to explore and study space.

1 **Some space objects are visible to the human eye.** 673

2 **Telescopes allow us to study space from Earth.** 679
   CHAPTER INVESTIGATION *Observing Spectra* 684

3 **Spacecraft help us explore beyond Earth.** 686
   MATH IN SCIENCE *Using Exponents* 694

4 **Space exploration benefits society.** 695
   CONNECTING SCIENCES *How Earth's Gravity Affects Plants* 699

20 Earth, Moon, and Sun 704

the BIG idea

Earth and the Moon move in predictable ways as they orbit the Sun.

1 **Earth rotates on a tilted axis and orbits the Sun.** 707
   CHAPTER INVESTIGATION *Modeling Seasons* 714

2 **The Moon is Earth's natural satellite.** 716
   MATH IN SCIENCE *Making Line Graphs* 722

3 **Positions of the Sun and Moon affect Earth.** 723
   SCIENCE ON THE JOB *Astronomy in Archaeology* 731

What would you see if you looked at the Moon with a telescope? page 704

This image shows Jupiter with one of its large moons. How big are these objects compared with Earth? page 740

21 Our Solar System 740

the BIG idea

Planets and other objects form a system around our Sun.

1 **Planets orbit the Sun at different distances.** 743
  MATH IN SCIENCE *Using Percentages* 748

2 **The inner solar system has rocky planets.** 749
  THINK SCIENCE *What Shapes the Surface of Mars?* 757

3 **The outer solar system has four giant planets.** 758

4 **Small objects are made of ice and rock.** 764
  CHAPTER INVESTIGATION *Exploring Impact Craters* 770

22 Stars, Galaxies, and the Universe 776

the BIG idea

Our Sun is one of billions of stars in one of billions of galaxies in the universe.

1 **The Sun is our local star.** 779
  CHAPTER INVESTIGATION *Temperature, Brightness, and Color* 784

2 **Stars change over their life cycles.** 786
  MATH IN SCIENCE *Interpreting a Scatter Plot* 793

3 **Galaxies have different sizes and shapes.** 794
  EXTREME SCIENCE *When Galaxies Collide* 798

4 **The universe is expanding.** 799

Visual Highlights

Structures in the Universe 675
Seasons 711
Lunar Phases 725
Objects in the Solar System 744
Features of Rocky Planets 751
Layers of the Sun 781
Life Cycles of Stars 791

Features

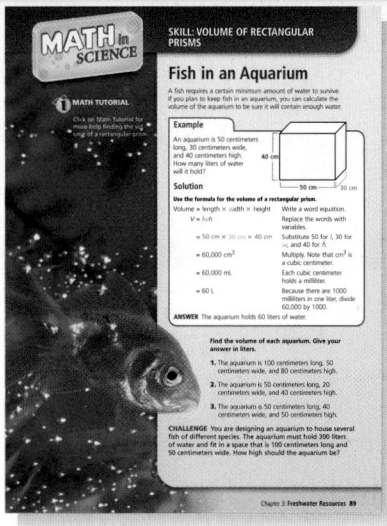

Math in Science

NATURE OF SCIENCE
Making Bar Graphs — 31

EARTH'S WATERS
Multiplying Fractions and Whole Numbers — 63
Volume of Rectangular Prisms — 89
Plotting Coordinates — 123
Making a Double Bar Graph — 160

EARTH'S SURFACE
Using Proportions — 211
Surface Area of a Prism — 237
Creating a Line Graph — 287
Comparing Decimals — 312

ELECTRICITY AND MAGNETISM
Using Variables — 367
Solving Percent Problems — 388
Using Significant Figures — 439

LIFE OVER TIME
Interpreting Graphs — 472
Using Proportions — 496
Finding Averages — 535

HUMAN BIOLOGY
Comparing Rates — 583
Choosing Units of Length — 613
Making a Line Graph — 648

SPACE SCIENCE
Using Exponents — 694
Making Line Graphs — 722
Using Percentages — 748
Interpreting a Scatter Plot — 793

Think Science

EARTH'S WATERS
Determining Relevance — 55

EARTH'S SURFACE
Interpreting Data — 223

ELECTRICITY AND MAGNETISM
Evaluating Conclusions — 419

LIFE OVER TIME
Evaluating Hypotheses — 515

HUMAN BIOLOGY
Inferring — 575

SPACE SCIENCE
Forming Hypotheses — 757

Connecting Sciences

NATURE OF SCIENCE
Physical Science and Earth Science — 13

EARTH'S WATERS
Earth Science and Physical Science — 141

EARTH'S SURFACE
Earth Science and Life Science — 208
Earth Science and Life Science — 307

ELECTRICITY AND MAGNETISM
Physical Science and Life Science — 349

LIFE OVER TIME
Earth Science and Life Science — 464

SPACE SCIENCE
Earth Science and Life Science — 699

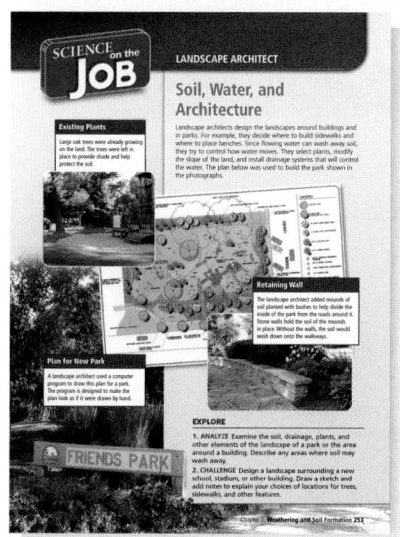

Science on the Job

EARTH'S WATERS
Water and Farming 107

EARTH'S SURFACE
Soil, Water, and Architecture 253

ELECTRICITY AND MAGNETISM
The Science of Electrical Work 382

LIFE OVER TIME
Studying the Schools 543

HUMAN BIOLOGY
Breathing and Yoga 606

SPACE SCIENCE
Astronomy in Archaeology 731

Extreme Science

EARTH'S WATERS
Undersea Hot Spots 169

HUMAN BIOLOGY
Artificial Skin 655

SPACE SCIENCE
When Galaxies Collide 798

Frontiers in Science

EARTH'S WATERS
Exploring the Water Planet 38

EARTH'S SURFACE
Remote Sensing 186

ELECTRICITY AND MAGNETISM
Electronics in Music 330

LIFE OVER TIME
Life by Degrees 446

HUMAN BIOLOGY
Surprising Senses 560

SPACE SCIENCE
Danger from the Sky 662

Florida Connections

EARTH'S WATERS
Saving Coral 42

EARTH'S SURFACE
Florida's Sinkholes 190

ELECTRICITY AND MAGNETISM
Animatronics 334

LIFE OVER TIME
The Ultimate Fish 450

HUMAN BIOLOGY
A Place in the Sun 564

SPACE SCIENCE
Cape Canaveral: Step to the Stars 666

Timelines in Science

EARTH'S WATERS
Exploring the Ocean 146

EARTH'S SURFACE
History of the Earth System 292

ELECTRICITY AND MAGNETISM
The Story of Electronics 404

LIFE OVER TIME
Life Unearthed 520

HUMAN BIOLOGY
Seeing Inside the Body 624

SPACE SCIENCE
The Story of Astronomy 736

Internet Resources @ ClassZone.com

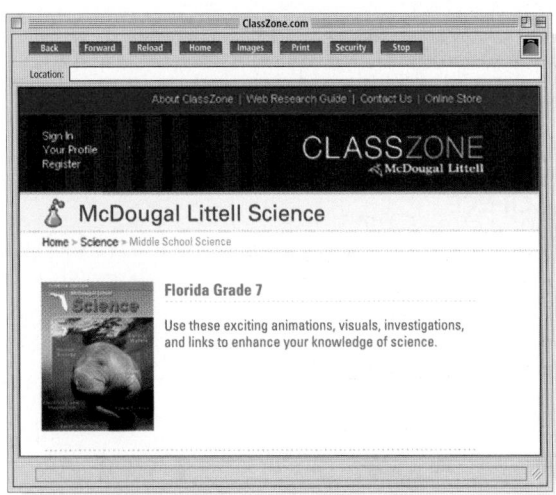

Simulations

EARTH'S WATERS
Aquifers   66
Limits of an Aquifer   79
The Ocean Floor   113
Ocean Life and Environments   151

EARTH'S SURFACE
Topographic Maps and Surface Features   215
Nuclear Power Plant   315

ELECTRICITY AND MAGNETISM
Static Electricity   339
Ohm's Law   361
Circuits   373
Electromagnets   409

LIFE OVER TIME
Matching Finch Beaks to Food   487

HUMAN BIOLOGY
Human Body Systems   569
Assemble a Skeleton   578

SPACE SCIENCE
Levels of the Universe   671
Sun at Different Wavelengths   780

Visualizations

EARTH'S WATERS
The Water Cycle   53
Water Treatment Plant   92
Daily Tides   137
Life at Hydrothermal Vents   168

EARTH'S SURFACE
Latitude and Longitude   206
Soil Formation   229
Chemical Weathering   234
Wind Erosion   259
Cave Formation   270
Hydrogen Fuel Cell   320

ELECTRICITY AND MAGNETISM
Hard Drive   395
Motor   424

LIFE OVER TIME
Molten Rock in Sedimentary Layers   467
Fossil Formation   490
Response to Environmental Change   534

HUMAN BIOLOGY
Lung and Diaphragm Movement   597
Peristalsis   608
Heart Pumping Blood   629
Skin Healing   653

SPACE SCIENCE
Night Sky throughout the Year   676
Exploring Seasons   705
Lunar Phases   724
Virtual Flight through the Solar System   741
Shapes of Galaxies   777

Career Centers

Oceanography   41
Mineralogy   189
Music and Computer Science   333
Paleontology   449
Neurobiology   563
Astronomy   665

Resource Centers

NATURE OF SCIENCE
Resources for the following topics may be found at ClassZone.com: *Ethics; Prions; Technology and Its Consequences; Aquifers and Purification.*

EARTH'S WATERS
Resources for the following topics may be found at ClassZone.com: *Florida's Coral Reefs; Water; Evidence of a Water Cycle on Mars; Frozen Fresh Water; Geysers and Hot Springs; Ocean Currents; Ocean Waves; Ocean Tides; Ocean Research; Coral Reefs; Hydrothermal Vents; Ocean Pollution and Pollution Prevention.*

EARTH'S SURFACE
Resources for the following topics may be found at ClassZone.com: *Sinkholes; Satellite Mapping; Map Projections; GIS; Weathering; Soil; Mudflows; Rivers and Erosion; Glaciers; Earth System Research; Natural Resources; Pollution-Digesting Microbes; Renewable Energy Resources.*

ELECTRICITY AND MAGNETISM
Resources for the following topics may be found at ClassZone.com: *Amusement Park Animatronics; Lightning and Lightning Safety; Electrochemical Cells; Electrical Safety; Electronics; Electronic and Computer Research; Magnetism; Dams and Electricity; Energy Use and Conservation.*

LIFE OVER TIME
Resources for the following topics may be found at ClassZone.com: *Sharks; Evidence of an Event in Earth's Past; Fossils; Finding the Ages of Rocks; Mass Extinctions; Natural Selection; Evidence Supporting Evolution; Current Fossil and Living Fossil Finds; Population Dynamics; Human Population Growth; Introduced Species in the United States.*

HUMAN BIOLOGY
Resources for the following topics may be found at ClassZone.com: *Skin and the Sun; Shackleton's Expedition; Skeletal System; Muscles; Respiratory System; Urinary System; Current Medical Imaging Techniques; Circulatory System; Blood Types; Lymphatic System; Skin.*

SPACE SCIENCE
Resources for the following topics may be found at ClassZone.com: *Cape Canaveral; Telescopes; Space Exploration; Seasons; Tides; Advances in Astronomy; Impact Craters; Moons of Giant Planets; Life Cycles of Stars; Galaxies; Galaxy Collisions.*

Math Tutorials

NATURE OF SCIENCE
Bar Graphs — 31

EARTH'S WATERS
Multiplying Fractions and Whole Numbers — 63
Volume of a Rectangular Prism — 89
Coordinates and Line Graphs — 123
Bar Graphs — 160

EARTH'S SURFACE
Solving Proportions — 211
Surface Area of a Rectangular Prism — 237
Making a Line Graph — 287
Comparing Decimals — 312

ELECTRICITY AND MAGNETISM
Equations — 367
Percents and Proportions — 388
Rounding Decimals — 439

LIFE OVER TIME
Reading Line Graphs and Multiplying Whole Numbers — 472
Writing and Solving Proportions — 496
Finding the Mean — 535

HUMAN BIOLOGY
Unit Rates — 583
Measuring Length — 613
Making Line Graphs — 648

SPACE SCIENCE
Powers and Exponents — 694
Line Graphs — 722
The Percent Equations — 748
Scatter Plots — 793

NSTA SciLinks

Codes for use with the NSTA SciLinks site may be found on every chapter opener.

Florida Review

There is a content review and FCAT practice for every chapter at ClassZone.com.

Explore the Big Idea

Chapter Opening Inquiry

Each chapter opens with hands-on explorations that introduce the chapter's Big Idea.

Nature of Science

Reproducing a Result; Effects of Changes   3

Earth's Waters

Where Can You See Water?
  Does the Ice Float?   47
How Much Water Do You Drink? What
  Happens When Salt Water Evaporates?   79
What Makes Things Float or Sink? How
  Does Moving Air Affect Water?   113
It's Alive! Beneath the Surface   151

Earth's Surface

Earth's Changing Surface; Using
  Modern Maps   195
Ice Power; Getting the Dirt on Soil   229
Where Has Water Been? How Do
  Waves Shape Land?   259
Sunlight as an Energy Source; Saving
  Water as You Brush   297

Electricity and Magnetism

How Do the Pieces of Tape Interact?
Why Does the Water React Differently?   339
Will the Flashlight Still Work?
  What's Inside a Calculator?   373
Is It Magnetic? How Can You Make
  a Chain?   409

Life Over Time

How Do You Know What Happened?
  How Long Has That Been There?   455
What Can Rocks Show About Earth's
  History? Which One of These Things
  Is Not Like the Others?   487
How Does Population Grow? How Do
  Populations Differ?   525

Human Biology

How Many Bones Are in Your Hand?
  How Does It Move?   569
Mirror, Mirror; Water Everywhere   597
Blood Pressure; Wet Fingers   629

Space Science

Why Does the Sun Appear to Move Around
  Earth? What Colors Are in Sunlight?   671
How Do Shadows Move? What Makes the
  Moon Bright?   705
How Big Is Jupiter? How Round Is an Orbit?   741
How Can Stars Differ? How Do Galaxies
  Move Apart?   777

Chapter Investigations

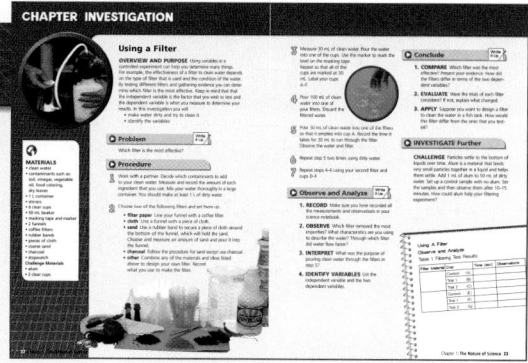

Full-Period Labs

The Chapter Investigations are in-depth labs that let you form and test a hypothesis, build a model, or sometimes design your own investigation.

Nature of Science

Using a Filter	22

Earth's Waters

Water Moving Underground *Design Your Own*	72
Monitoring Water Quality	98
Wave Movement	134
Population Sampling	178

Earth's Surface

Investigate Topographic Maps	216
Testing Soil	246
Creating Stream Features	272
Wind Power	322

Electricity and Magnetism

Lightning	358
Design an Electronic Communication Device *Design Your Own*	398
Build a Speaker	432

Life Over Time

Geologic Time	480
Modeling Natural Selection	506
Sustainable Resource Management	552

Human Biology

A Closer Look at Muscles	590
Modeling a Kidney	618
Heart Rate and Exercise	638

Space Science

Observing Spectra	684
Modeling Seasons	714
Exploring Impact Craters *Design Your Own*	770
Temperature, Brightness, and Color	784

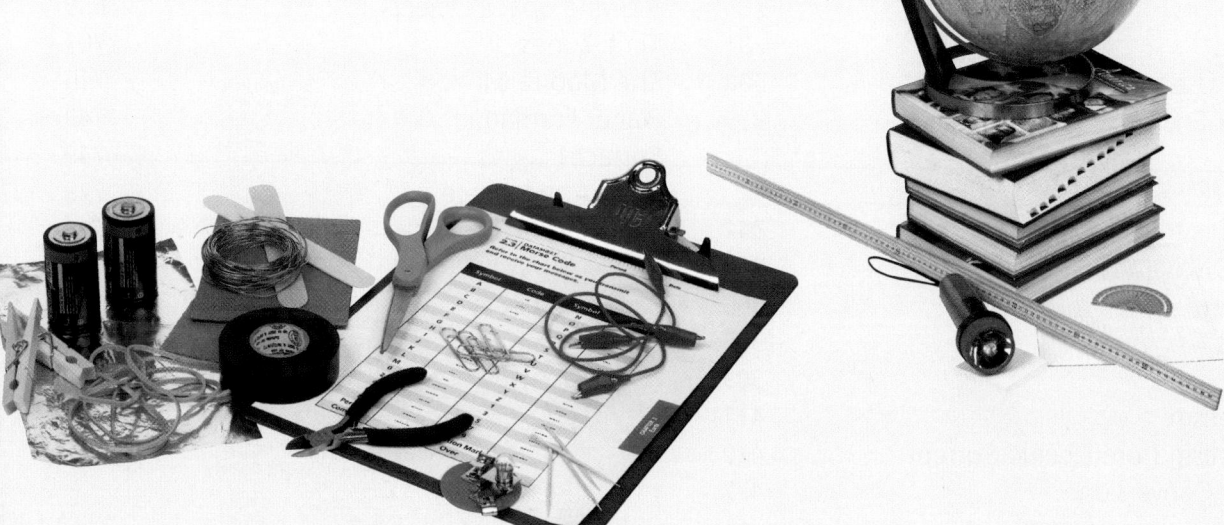

Explore

Introductory Inquiry Activities

Most sections begin with a simple activity that lets you explore the Key Concept before you read the section.

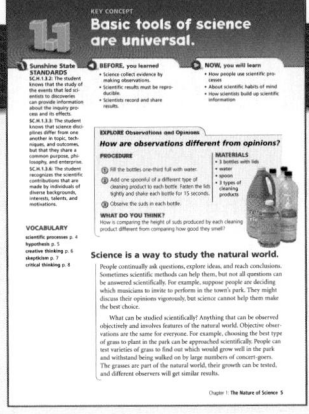

Nature of Science

Observations and Opinions	5
Effects of Changes in Procedures	14

Earth's Waters

Water Vapor	49
Water Collection	56
Flow of Water	64
Concentration	90
The Value of Fresh Water	100
Density	115
Currents	124
Waves	129
Air Bladders	161
Ocean Pollution	170

Earth's Surface

Mapping	203
Topographic Maps	212
Mechanical Weathering	231
Soil Composition	238
Divides	266
Glaciers	281
Energy Use	308
Nuclear Energy	313

Electricity and Magnetism

Static Electricity	341
Static Discharge	350
Current	360
Circuits	375
Codes	389
Magnetism	411
Magnetism from Electric Current	420
Energy Conversion	427

Life Over Time

Rocks	457
Time Scales	473
Fossils	489
Evidence	508
Population Density	536
Population Change	544

Human Biology

Levers	576
Muscles	584
Breathing	599
Digestion	607
Waste Removal	614
The Circulatory System	631
Membranes	640
The Skin	649

Space Science

Distance	673
Distortion of Light	679
Viewing Space Objects	686
Time Zones	707
The Moon's Motion	716
Planet Formation	743
Surfaces	749
Solar Atmosphere	779
Characteristics of Stars	786
The Milky Way	794
Large Numbers	799

Investigate

Skill Labs

Each Investigate activity gives you a chance to practice a specific science skill related to the content that you're studying.

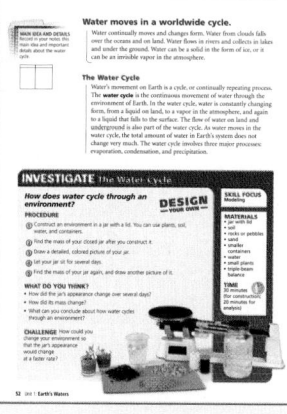

Nature of Science

Solving Problems	*Design Your Own*	9
Ethics	*Judging*	28

Earth's Waters

The Water Cycle	*Design Your Own*	52
Icebergs	*Calculating*	61
Aquifer Filtration	*Making Models*	67
Water Usage	*Analyzing Data*	83
Water Conservation	*Measuring*	103
Density	*Predicting*	118
Currents	*Observing*	127
Tides	*Making Models*	138
Coastal Environments	*Design Your Own*	156
Floating	*Design Your Own*	165

Earth's Surface

Geosphere's Layers	*Modeling*	201
Map Projections	*Modeling*	208
Satellite Imaging	*Modeling*	220
Chemical Weathering	*Identifying Variables*	234
Soil Conservation	*Making Models*	251
Erosion	*Design Your Own*	262
Longshore Drift	*Observing*	276
Kettle Lake Formation	*Design Your Own*	285
Fossil Fuels	*Modeling*	305
Conservation	*Design Your Own*	310

Electricity and Magnetism

Making a Static Detector	*Inferring*	346
Conductors and Insulators	*Interpreting Data*	354
Electric Cells	*Inferring*	363
Fuses	*Making Models*	380
Circuits	*Inferring*	386

Digital Information	*Making Models*	391
Earth's Magnetic Field	*Inferring*	417
Electromagnets	*Observing*	422
Electric Current	*Inferring*	430
Power	*Making Models*	437

Life Over Time

Learning from Tree Rings	*Observing*	462
Relative and Absolute Age	*Making Models*	468
Fossil Records	*Analyzing*	491
Genes	*Sequencing*	513
Limiting Factors	*Design Your Own*	540
Population	*Graphing data*	548

Human Biology

Systems	*Predicting*	572
Movable Joints	*Observing*	581
Lungs	*Making models*	601
Chemical Digestion	*Making models*	609
Antibodies	*Making models*	645
Skin Protection	*Observing*	651

Space Science

Constellation Positions	*Analyzing*	677
Launch Planning	*Identifying Variables*	689
Weathering	*Predicting*	697
Rotation	*Making Models*	708
Moon Features	*Inferring*	719
Phases of the Moon	*Making Models*	726
Distances	*Using Models*	746
Layers	*Using Models*	752
Giant Planets	*Observing*	761
Parallax	*Measuring*	787
Galaxy Shapes	*Classifying*	795
Galaxies	*Measuring*	802

Introducing Science

Scientists are curious. Since ancient times, they have been asking and answering questions about the world around them. Scientists are also very suspicious of the answers they get. They carefully collect evidence and test their answers many times before accepting an idea as correct.

In this book you will see how scientific knowledge keeps growing and changing as scientists ask new questions and rethink what was known before. The following sections will help get you started.

Unifying Principles of Science   FL30

These pages introduce unifying principles that will give you a big picture of science.

Florida Student Handbook   FL36

This section provides an overview of the Sunshine State Standards in this book. It also previews the four types of items you will find on the Florida Comprehensive Achievement Test (FCAT), which you will take in grade 8, and gives you strategies for answering each type.

Chapter 1 The Nature of Science   2

This chapter introduces you to the scientific habits of mind common to scientists in many different fields of study. You will read about different ways of thinking that are useful when doing science, different types of observations scientists make, and different ways in which science and scientists both affect and are affected by society.

What Is Science?

Science is the systematic study of all of nature, from particles too small to see to the human body to the entire universe. However, no individual scientist can study all of nature. Therefore, science is divided into many different fields. For example, some scientists are biologists, others are geologists, and still others are chemists or astronomers.

All the different scientific fields can be grouped into three broad categories: life science, earth science, and physical science.

- Life science focuses on the study of living things; it includes the fields of cell biology, botany, ecology, zoology, and human biology.
- Earth science focuses on the study of our planet and its place in the universe; it includes the fields of geology, oceanography, meteorology, and astronomy.
- Physical science focuses on the study of what things are made of and how they change; it includes the fields of chemistry and physics.

Even though science has many different fields, all scientists have similar ways of thinking and approaching their work. For example, scientists use instruments as well as their minds to look for patterns in nature. Scientists also try to find explanations for the patterns they discover. As you study each unit, you will in part focus on the patterns that scientists have found within that particular specialized branch. At the same time, as you move from one unit to another, you will be blending knowledge from the different branches of science together to form a more general understanding of our universe.

McDougal Littell Science, Grade 7

This course presents concepts from the life, earth/space, and physical sciences and describes some of their applications to everyday life. It begins by describing the processes all scientists use to conduct investigations in a safe and effective way, showing that all scientists share a common purpose and philosophy. The next chapters describe Earth's waters (oceans, rivers, and lakes) and the kinds of life they support. The course then focuses on Earth's surface, identifying a few of the forces that shape it and the resources living things can get from it. Unit 4 explores the history of life on Earth and the factors that shape their populations. Unit 5 looks closely at the unique biology of human beings, and Unit 6 describes Earth's place in the universe.

Unifying Principles

As you learn, it helps to have a big picture of science as a framework for new information. McDougal Littell Science has identified unifying principles from each of the three broad categories of science: life science, earth science, and physical science. These unifying principles are described on the following pages. However, keep in mind that the broad categories of science do not have fixed borders. Earth science shades into life science, which shades into physical science, which shades back into earth science.

the BIG idea

Each chapter begins with a big idea. Keep in mind that each big idea relates to one or more of the unifying principles.

What Is Life Science?

Life science is the study of the great variety of living things that have lived or now live on Earth. Life science includes the study of the characteristics and needs that all living things have in common. It is also a study of changes—both daily changes and those that take place over millions of years. Probably most important, in studying life science you will explore the many ways that all living things—including you—depend on Earth and its resources.

Living things, such as these birds, have certain characteristics that distinguish them from nonliving things. One important characteristic is the ability to grow. If all goes well, these warbler chicks will grow to become adult birds that can feed and take care of themselves.

UNIFYING PRINCIPLES of Life Science

All living things share common characteristics.

Despite the variety of living things on Earth, there are certain characteristics common to all. The basic unit of life is the **cell.** Any living thing, whether it has one cell or many, is described as an **organism.** All organisms are characterized by

- organization—the way that an organism's body is arranged
- growth—the way that an organism grows and develops over its lifetime
- reproduction—the way that an organism produces offspring like itself
- response—the ways an organism interacts with its surroundings

All living things share common needs.

All living things have three basic needs: energy, materials, and living space. Energy enables an organism to carry out all the activities of life. The body of an organism needs water and other materials. Water is important because most of the chemical reactions in a cell take place in water. Organisms also require other materials. Plants, for example, need carbon dioxide to make energy-rich sugars, and most living things need oxygen. Living space is the environment in which an organism gets the energy and materials it needs.

Living things meet their needs through interactions with the environment.

The **environment** is everything that surrounds a living thing. This includes other organisms as well as nonliving factors, such as rainfall, sunlight, and soil. Any exchange of energy or materials between the living and nonliving parts of the environment is an **interaction.** Plants interact with the environment by capturing energy from the Sun and changing that energy into chemical energy that is stored in sugar. Animals can interact with plants by eating the plants and getting energy from the sugars that the plants have made.

The types and numbers of living things change over time.

A **species** is a group of living things so closely related that they can produce offspring together that can also reproduce. Scientists have named about 1.4 million different species. The great variety of species on Earth today is called **biodiversity.** Different species have different characteristics, or **adaptations,** that allow the members of that species to get their needs met in a particular environment. Over the millions of years that life has existed on Earth, new species have come into being and others have disappeared. The disappearance of a species is called **extinction.** Fossils of now extinct organisms is one way that scientists have of seeing how living things have changed over time.

What Is Earth Science?

Earth science is the study of Earth's interior, its rocks and soil, its oceans, its atmosphere, and outer space. For many years, scientists studied each of these topics separately. They learned many important things. More recently, however, scientists have looked more and more at the connections among the different parts of Earth—its oceans, atmosphere, living things, and rocks and soil. Scientists have also been learning more about other planets in our solar system, as well as stars and galaxies far away. Through these studies they have learned much about Earth and its place in the universe.

When a wolf eats a rabbit, matter and energy move from one living thing into another. When a wolf drinks water warmed by the Sun, matter and energy move from Earth's waters into one of its living things.

UNIFYING PRINCIPLES of Earth Science

Heat energy inside Earth and radiation from the Sun provide energy for Earth's processes.

Energy is the ability to cause change. All of Earth's processes need energy to occur. Earth's interior is very hot. This heat energy moves up to Earth's surface, where it provides the energy to build mountains, cause earthquakes, and make volcanoes erupt. Earth also receives energy from the Sun as **radiation**—energy that travels across distances in the form of certain types of waves. Energy from the Sun causes winds to blow, ocean currents to flow, and water to move from the ground to the atmosphere and back again.

Physical forces, such as gravity, affect the movement of all matter on Earth and throughout the universe.

What do the stars in a galaxy, the planet Earth, and your body have in common? For one thing, they are all made of matter. **Matter** is anything that has mass and takes up space. Rocks are matter. You are matter. Even the air around you is matter. Everything in the universe is also affected by the same physical forces. A **force** is a push or a pull. Forces affect how matter moves everywhere in the universe.

Matter and energy move among Earth's rocks and soil, atmosphere, waters, and living things.

Think of Earth as a huge system, or an organized group of parts that work together. Within this system, matter and energy move among the different parts. The four major parts of Earth's system are the

- **atmosphere,** which includes all the air surrounding the solid planet
- **geosphere,** which includes all of Earth's rocks and minerals, as well as Earth's interior
- **hydrosphere,** which includes oceans, rivers, lakes, and every drop of water on or under Earth's surface
- **biosphere,** which includes all the living things on Earth

Earth has changed over time and continues to change.

Events are always changing Earth's surface. Some events, such as the building or wearing away of mountains, occur over millions of years. Others, such as earthquakes, occur within seconds. A change can affect a small area or even the entire planet

What Is Physical Science?

Physical science is the study of what things are made of and how they change. It combines the study of both physics and chemistry. Physics is the study of matter, energy, and forces, and it includes such topics as motion, light, and electricity and magnetism. Chemistry is the study of the structure and properties of matter. It focuses especially on how substances change into different substances.

The force of the rushing water pushes the rafts forward, while the force from the people paddling helps to steer the rafts.

UNIFYING PRINCIPLES of Physical Science

Matter is made of particles too small to see.

The tiny particles that make up all matter are called **atoms.** Just how tiny are atoms? They are far too small to see even through a powerful microscope. In fact, an atom is about a million times smaller than the period at the end of this sentence. There are more than 100 basic kinds of matter called **elements.** The atoms of any element are all alike but different from the atoms of any other element. Everything around you is made of atoms and combinations of atoms.

Matter changes form and moves from place to place.

You see objects moving and changing all around you. All changes in matter are the result of atoms moving and combining in different ways. Regardless of how much matter may change, however, under ordinary conditions it is never created or destroyed. Matter that seems to disappear merely changes into another form of matter.

Energy changes from one form to another, but it cannot be created or destroyed.

All the changes you see around you depend on energy. Energy, in fact, means the ability to cause change. Using energy means changing energy. But energy is never created or destroyed, no matter how often it changes form. This fact is known as the **law of conservation of energy.** The energy you may think you've lost when a match has burned out has only been changed into other forms of energy that are less useful to you.

Physical forces affect the movement of all matter on Earth and throughout the universe.

A **force** is a push or a pull. Every time you push or pull an object, you are applying a force to that object, whether or not the object moves. There are several forces—several pushes or pulls—acting on you right now. All these forces are necessary for you to do the things you do, even sitting and reading. **Gravity** keeps you on the ground. Gravity also keeps the Moon moving around Earth, and Earth moving around the Sun. **Friction** is the force that opposes motion. The friction between the bottoms of your shoes and the floor makes it possible for you to walk without slipping. Too much friction between a heavy box and the floor makes it hard to push the box across the floor.

Florida Student Handbook

The Sunshine State Standards

Florida has established standards for science. These standards define what you should know about science as you progress through school. The knowledge described in the standards is tested by the Florida Comprehensive Assessment Test, or FCAT. You will next take the science portion of the FCAT in eighth grade.

About the Standards

The Sunshine State Standards are organized into eight different strands. These strands define important science topics. Beneath each strand are detailed descriptions of what you need to know, beginning with standards. The standards are broken up into benchmarks. The state of Florida uses a numbering system to identify strands, standards, and benchmarks. The example below shows how a benchmark is identified.

SC.A.1.3.1: The student identifies various ways in which substances differ (e.g., mass, volume, shape, density, texture, and reaction to temperature and light).

S C . A . 1 . 3 . 1

Subject Area	Strand	Standard	Level	Benchmark
The SC indicates that this is a science benchmark.	The A identifies the strand. This benchmark is in strand A.	This is the standard number within strand A.	This is the grade-level cluster. Grades 6–8 are level 3.	This is the benchmark number.

What You'll Learn

The major topics defined by the strands are the following:

A. The Nature of Matter,
B. Energy,
C. Force and Motion,
D. Processes That Shape the Earth,
E. Earth and Space,
F. Processes of Life,
G. How Living Things Interact with Their Environment, and
H. The Nature of Science.

Each year, you will gain knowledge and skills related to these topics. Your knowledge will build as you advance from sixth grade to eighth grade. Although the Florida benchmarks are not all taught in any one grade, you will cover all of the Benchmarks by the end of eighth grade.

Each section of your science textbook identifies the Sunshine State Benchmarks you will be studying. It also lists important vocabulary that you need to know for the FCAT.

At the end of each chapter, you'll find a page of FCAT practice questions. These questions are in the same formats you'll see on the FCAT test—multiple choice (MC), short response (SR), extended response (ER), and gridded response (GR). You are probably familiar with the first three question formats. Gridded response, however, may be new to you. For these questions, you solve a problem and then record your answer in a special grid, shown here. Throughout this book you will be given practice in answering all four types of questions.

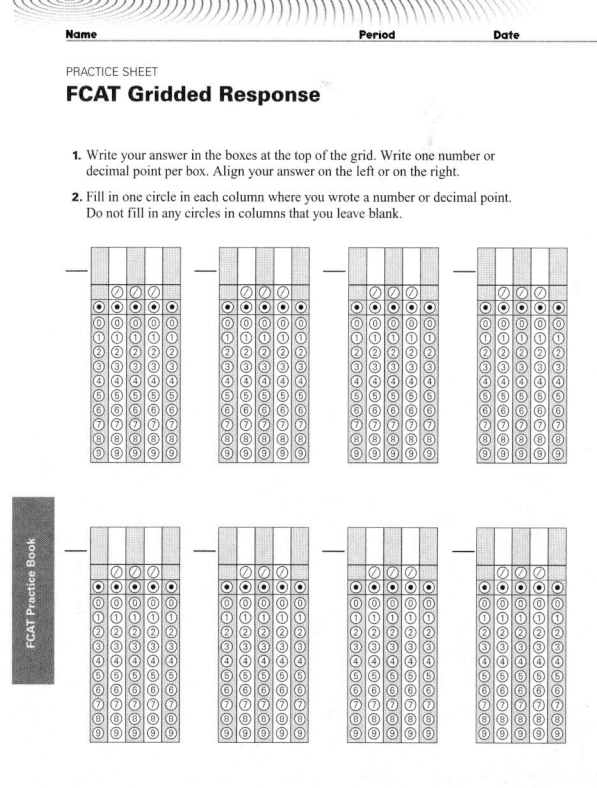

KEY CONCEPT

1.2 Scientific ideas are based on evidence.

Sunshine State STANDARDS
SC.H.1.3.3: The student knows that science disciplines differ from one another in topic, techniques, and outcomes, but that they share a common purpose, philosophy, and enterprise.
SC.H.1.3.5: The student knows that a change in one or more variables may alter the outcome of an investigation.
SC.H.1.3.7: The student knows that when similar investigations give different results, the scientific challenge is to verify whether the differences are significant by further study.

BEFORE, you learned
• Different sciences focus on different topics but have a common approach
• Scientific methods can be used to analyze information, solve problems, and evaluate conclusions

NOW, you will learn
• About variables and controls in scientific experiments
• About four different types of scientific inquiries
• How new evidence can change widely accepted ideas

EXPLORE Effects of Changes in Procedures
How many drops of water can a coin hold?

PROCEDURE
1. Put two different types of coins on a paper towel.
2. Use an eyedropper to put drops of water on the coins. Count how many drops each coin can hold before the water overflows.

MATERIALS
• 2 different coins
• paper towel
• eyedropper
• water

WHAT DO YOU THINK?
• Does it matter what type of coin you use or which side of the coin you use? Does it matter how far the eyedropper is above the coin?
• How would keeping detailed records help others reproduce your results?

FCAT VOCABULARY
independent variable p. 15
dependent variable p. 15

VOCABULARY
experimental group p. 15
control group p. 15
model p. 16
theory p. 19

REMINDER
You can find detailed information about different units and unit conversions on pages R20–R21.

Observations provide scientific evidence.

Observations are a way of learning about the world. You continually make observations with your senses as you see, hear, touch, smell, and taste things. You can increase your ability to observe by using equipment, such as a magnifying glass. When you keep records, you can compare observations made at different times or places.

A measurement is an observation expressed as a number and a unit. Suppose some bicyclists tell you they normally bike a distance of 15. This information is meaningless because a unit, such as kilometers or miles, is missing. In the United States, many people use nonmetric units of measurement, such as inches and quarts. Scientists usually use units of the metric system, such as centimeters and liters. The formal name of the standard scientific system is the International System of Units, or SI.

14 Chapter 1: **The Nature of Science**

FCAT Practice

For FCAT practice, go to :
FLORIDA REVIEW
CLASSZONE.COM

Analyzing Data

In an experiment to study the effect of heating on evaporation, identical pans of water were placed for two hours under different types of lights. The temperature of the air just above each pan was measured with a thermometer every 30 minutes. The amount of evaporation was determined by subtracting the amount of water in the pan at the end of two hours from the amount that was in the pan at the beginning. The data table shows the results. Study the data and answer the questions below.

Pan	Description	Average Air Temperature Above the Water	Evaporation
1	under regular light	22°C (72°F)	30 mL (10 oz)
2	under heat lamp on low	25°C (78°F)	40 mL (14 oz)
3	under heat lamp on high	28°C (83°F)	50 mL (17 oz)

FCAT TIP
When analyzing a data table, read the title above each column of data. This will help you identify the data that you need to answer specific questions.

GRIDDED RESPONSE
1. If the air temperature averaged 27°C (80°F), about how much water would evaporate in two hours?

2. The evaporation from pan 1 to pan 3 increased by 20 milliliters. By how many degrees Celsius did the temperature increase from pan 1 to pan 3?

MULTIPLE CHOICE
3. What is the relationship between the air temperature and the evaporation rate?
A. There is no relationship between the temperature and the rate.
B. As the temperature increases, the rate decreases.
C. As the temperature increases, the rate stays the same.
D. As the temperature increases, the rate increases.

4. Which is the most important reason that placing a pan in a refrigerator would not be a good way to test for the influence of heat in this experiment?
F. The refrigerator would be cold.
G. The refrigerator is a closed space.
H. The refrigerator is an appliance.
I. The refrigerator may have other objects in it.

5. The dependent variable in an experiment is the factor that is measured to gather results. Which is the dependent variable in this experiment?
A. the amount of evaporation
B. the amount of water in each pan in the beginning
C. the type of light
D. the air temperature

6. Which change would make the results of this experiment more reliable?
F. conducting the experiment for four hours
G. decreasing the amount of water in the pans
H. increasing the air temperature for one pan
I. using a fan to blow air on one of the pans

EXTENDED RESPONSE
Answer the two questions below in detail. Include some of the terms shown in the word box. In your answers, underline each term you use.

low	eutrophication	meadow
water table	saturation zone	

7. Kori notices that a pond at his summer camp is filled with more soil and plants each year. Explain how this change fits into the pattern of how ponds change over time.

8. Juanita's family gets water from a well on their ranch. Each time a well has gone dry, they have had to dig a new one that was deeper than the old one. Explain why they have needed to go deeper.

Chapter 2: **The Water Planet 77**

Name **Period** **Date**

PRACTICE SHEET
FCAT Gridded Response

1. Write your answer in the boxes at the top of the grid. Write one number or decimal point per box. Align your answer on the left or on the right.

2. Fill in one circle in each column where you wrote a number or decimal point. Do not fill in any circles in columns that you leave blank.

FCAT Practice Book

Sunshine State Standards

As you read and study your science book this year, you'll be learning many of the ideas described the Florida Sunshine State Standards. The Benchmarks that you will concentrate on in seventh grade are listed here.

Following each Benchmark is an explanation of what it means and how you will learn about it. References to chapters tell you where content about the Benchmark is emphasized. You'll also find information on how each Benchmark is tested on the Science FCAT that you'll take next year.

Many Benchmarks reference several chapters. That's because you will have to read and study information presented in several chapters to really understand a Benchmark. In fact, you'll be applying information you learned in sixth grade as you develop a deeper understanding of the Benchmarks. By the end of eighth grade, you will have learned the content in *all* the Benchmarks, and thus all the Sunshine State Standards.

Benchmark SC.A.1.3.1	What It Means to You
The student identifies various ways in which substances differ (e.g., mass, volume, shape, density, texture, and reaction to temperature and light).	Matter has different properties. You will learn about mass (a measure of how much matter an object contains), volume (the amount of space an object takes up), shape, density (the amount of mass per unit of volume), texture, and how different kinds of matter react to changes in temperature and light. **(Chapters 2 and 4)** **On the FCAT** This benchmark is tested as multiple choice, gridded response, or short response.

Benchmark SC.A.1.3.5	
The student knows the difference between a physical change in a substance and a chemical change.	You will learn two main ways that matter can be changed. During a physical change, the physical properties of a substance change but the kind of substance stays the same. During a chemical change, a new kind of substance forms. **(Chapter 7)** **On the FCAT** This benchmark is tested in multiple-choice form.

Benchmark SC.A.2.3.1	
The student describes and compares the properties of particles and waves.	Particles can be neutral or they can have a positive charge or a negative charge. You will learn that charged particles attract or repel each other. You will also learn about the basic properties of waves. A wave is a disturbance that transfers energy from one place to another. Frequency is the number of waves that pass a fixed point in a given amount of time and is directly related to the energy of a wave. Amplitude is a measure of how great the disturbance is, and wavelength is the distance from one wave peak to the next. **(Chapters 4 and 10)** **On the FCAT** This benchmark is tested in multiple-choice form.

Benchmark SC.A.2.3.2	What It Means to You
The student knows the general properties of the atom (a massive nucleus of neutral neutrons and positive protons surrounded by a cloud of negative electrons) and accepts that single atoms are not visible.	The basic particles that make up matter are called atoms. Atoms are so small that you cannot see them. Each atom has a nucleus surrounded by negatively charged particles called electrons. The nucleus contains neutral particles called neutrons and positively charged particles called protons. **(Chapter 10)** **On the FCAT** This benchmark is tested in multiple-choice form.

Benchmark SC.B.1.3.1	
The student identifies forms of energy and explains that they can be measured and compared.	Energy is the capacity to do work—that is, the capacity to make matter move. There are many different forms of energy, including solar, nuclear, electrical, mechanical, and heat energy. You will learn how energy can be converted from one form to another, and some of the ways that these different forms of energy are used. **(Chapters 10, 11, and 12)** **On the FCAT** This benchmark may be tested in any of the formats: multiple choice, gridded response, short response, or extended response.

Benchmark SC.B.1.3.2	
The student knows that energy cannot be created or destroyed, but only changed from one form to another.	Energy is neither created nor destroyed, but energy can be converted from one form to another. For example, your muscles convert chemical energy to mechanical energy when you move. **(Chapters 4, 9, and 11)** **On the FCAT** This benchmark may be tested in any of the formats.

Benchmark SC.B.1.3.3	
The student knows the various forms in which energy comes to Earth from the Sun (e.g., visible light, infrared, and microwave).	The Sun is the major source of energy on Earth. You will learn about the forms of energy that come from the Sun, such as visible light, infrared radiation, and ultraviolet radiation. **(Chapter 9)** **On the FCAT** This benchmark may be tested in any of the formats: multiple choice, gridded response, short response, or extended response.

Benchmark SC.B.1.3.4	
The student knows that energy conversions are never 100% efficient (e.g., some energy is transformed to heat and is unavailable for further useful work).	There are many ways that energy can change from one form to another. Every time energy changes form, some of it changes into heat that is not available for further useful work. **(Chapter 9)** **On the FCAT** This benchmark is tested in either multiple-choice or gridded-response form.

Benchmark SC.B.2.3.2	What It Means to You
The student knows that most of the energy used today is derived from burning stored energy collected by organisms millions of years ago (e.g., nonrenewable fossil fuels).	Most of the consumer energy that people use today comes from fossil fuels, which include coal, oil, and natural gas. You will learn that the energy stored in these fuels comes from organisms that lived long ago. **(Chapters 5 and 9)** **On the FCAT** This benchmark is tested in multiple-choice form.

Benchmark SC.C.2.3.1	
The student knows that many forces (e.g., gravitational, electrical, and magnetic) act at a distance (e.g., without contact).	A force is a push or a pull. Some forces act only when one object touches another—such as when your hand pushes on a box. You will learn that other forces, including gravity, electrical force, and magnetic force act even when the objects are not in contact. A magnet, for example, can attract an iron nail even when the magnet and the nail are not touching. **(Chapters 4, 10, and 12)** **On the FCAT** This benchmark is tested in multiple-choice form.

Benchmark SC.C.2.3.3	
The student knows that if more than one force acts on an object, then the forces can reinforce or cancel each other, depending on their direction and magnitude.	When more than one force acts on an object, the forces have a combined effect. You will learn how forces add together or cancel each other, and how to describe their combined effect on the object. **(Chapter 4)** **On the FCAT** This benchmark is tested in either multiple-choice, gridded-response, or short-response form.

Benchmark SC.C.2.3.7	
The student knows that gravity is a universal force that every mass exerts on every other mass.	Gravity is the force that gives objects weight and causes objects to fall to Earth. Every mass exerts a pull of gravity on every other mass. You will learn that the more mass an object has, the greater its gravity. **(Chapters 4, 8, and 19)** **On the FCAT** This benchmark is tested in multiple-choice form.

Benchmark SC.D.1.3.1	
The student knows that mechanical and chemical activities shape and reshape the Earth's land surface by eroding rock and soil in some areas and depositing them in other areas, sometimes in seasonal layers.	You will learn that weathering, erosion, and deposition constantly change Earth's surface. During weathering, rock is broken down into smaller pieces or dissolved. Erosion is a process in which gravity, ice, wind, or water picks up and moves rock or soil. Deposition occurs when these pieces of rock and soil are laid down. **(Chapters 7, 8, and 9)** **On the FCAT** This benchmark is tested in multiple-choice form.

Benchmark SC.D.1.3.2	What It Means to You
The student knows that over the whole Earth, organisms are growing, dying, and decaying as new organisms are produced by the old ones.	Fossils are remains or traces of ancient plants or animals that are preserved in rock. Fossils provide evidence that living things have been growing, dying, and decaying for millions of years. You will learn about different kinds of fossils and how scientists use them. **(Chapters 13 and 14)** **On the FCAT** This benchmark is tested in multiple-choice form.

Benchmark SC.D.1.3.3

The student knows how conditions that exist in one system influence the conditions that exist in other systems.	A system is a set of parts that work together as a whole. The Earth system has four major parts: the solid Earth, the air around the planet, the water on the planet, and all of the life on Earth. You will learn how the parts of Earth's system are connected and how conditions in one of them may affect another. **(Chapters 2, 3, 4, 19, 20, 21, and 22)** **On the FCAT** This benchmark is tested in multiple-choice form.

Benchmark SC.D.1.3.4

The student knows the ways in which plants and animals reshape the landscape (e.g., bacteria, fungi, worms, rodents, and other organisms add organic matter to the soil, increasing soil fertility, encouraging plant growth, and strengthening resistance to erosion).	You will learn some ways that plants, animals, fungi, and bacteria affect the landscape. For example, bacteria and fungi enrich soil by breaking down dead plant and animal matter. Plants that then grow in the rich soil help prevent erosion. **(Chapters 7 and 8)** **On the FCAT** This benchmark is tested in multiple-choice form.

Benchmark SC.D.1.3.5

The student understands concepts of time and size relating to the interaction of Earth's processes (e.g., lightning striking in a split second as opposed to the shifting of the Earth's plates altering the landscape, distance between atoms measured in Angstrom units as opposed to distance between stars measured in light-years).	You will learn that time and distance can be incredibly short or amazingly long. For example, the distances between the atoms in a substance are extremely small. But the distances between stars are immense. **(Chapters 4, 6, 8, 10, and 22)** **On the FCAT** This benchmark is tested in either multiple-choice or gridded-response form.

Benchmark SC.D.2.3.2	What This Means to You
The student knows the positive and negative consequences of human action on the Earth's systems.	Everything people do affects the Earth system and its ability to provide the things people need. You will learn some of the positive ways and some of the negative ways human activities affect the environment. You will also learn about people who work to protect the environment. **(Chapters 3, 5, 7, 9, and 15)**
	On the FCAT This benchmark is tested in either multiple-choice or short-response form.

Benchmark SC.E.1.3.1	
The student understands the vast size of our Solar System and the relationship of the planets and their satellites.	You will learn how the motions of Earth and the Moon produce moon phases, tides, and eclipses. Earth is one of many objects orbiting the Sun, including nine planets and the moons orbiting them. The solar system is huge—about 10,000 Earths could fit between Earth and the Sun, which is itself about 100 Earths across. **(Chapters 20 and 21)**
	On the FCAT This benchmark is tested in multiple-choice, gridded-response, or short-response form.

Benchmark SC.F.1.3.1	
The student understands that living things are composed of major systems that function in reproduction, growth, maintenance, and regulation.	A system is a set of parts that work together as a whole. Plants, animals, and other multicellular living things have systems that perform the functions that enable them to live, grow, and reproduce. You will learn about many of these systems—including the skeletal system, the muscle system, the circulatory system, and the digestive system—and how they interact to enable living things to respond to their environment. **(Chapters 16, 17, and 18)**
	On the FCAT This benchmark is tested in either multiple-choice or short-response form.

Benchmark SC.F.1.3.2	
The student knows that the structural basis of most organisms is the cell and most organisms are single cells, while some, including humans, are multicellular.	All living things are made of cells, the basic unit of structure and function. Despite the great variety found in living things, there are basic structures common to all cells. Some organisms are unicellular—made up of a single cell. Other organisms are multicellular, having many different types of cells that work together to perform the functions of life. **(Chapters 14 and 16)**
	On the FCAT This benchmark is tested in multiple-choice form.

Benchmark SC.F.1.3.3	What This Means to You
The student knows that in multicellular organisms cells grow and divide to make more cells in order to form and repair various organs and tissues.	You will learn about how cells in multicellular organisms go through a cycle in which they grow, mature, and then divide. This cycle of growth and division allows the organism itself to grow and mature. Cell division also allows an organism's body to repair damage to tissues and organs. **(Chapter 18)**
	On the FCAT This benchmark is tested in multiple-choice form.

Benchmark SC.F.1.3.4	
The student knows that the levels of structural organization for function in living things include cells, tissues, organs, systems, and organisms.	Cells are organized in ways that enable living things to function. You will learn how similar cells form tissues, how different tissues form organs, and how different organs make up the systems found in multicellular organisms. **(Chapters 16, 17, and 18)**
	On the FCAT This benchmark is tested in multiple-choice form.

Benchmark SC.F.1.3.5	
The student explains how the life functions of organisms are related to what occurs within the cell.	All cells perform the basic functions that support life. Their functions are similar to the functions of systems in multicellular organisms. For example, cells take in nutrients and water and expel waste products. Each cell, in turn, contributes to the life function of the entire organism. **(Chapter 18)**
	On the FCAT This benchmark is tested in multiple-choice form.

Benchmark SC.F.1.3.6	
The student knows that the cells with similar functions have similar structures, whereas those with different structures have different functions.	Multicellular organisms—those with many cells—have specialized cells that contain structures that enable them to perform specific functions. You will learn that cells with similar structures perform similar functions and cells with different structures perform different functions. **(Chapter 18)**
	On the FCAT This benchmark is tested in multiple-choice form.

Benchmark SC.F.1.3.7	
The student knows that behavior is a response to the environment and influences growth, development, maintenance, and reproduction.	Living things have different behaviors that enable them to interact with their environment. Some of the different stimuli that living things respond to include light, temperature, pressure, and moisture. You will learn that different behaviors affect how living things grow, develop, and reproduce. **(Chapter 16)**
	On the FCAT This benchmark is tested in multiple-choice form.

Benchmark SC.F.2.3.3	What This Means to You
The student knows that generally organisms in a population live long enough to reproduce because they have survival characteristics.	Organisms survive if they have characteristics that enable them to meet their needs and avoid danger. Organisms that survive long enough to reproduce pass those characteristics on to their off-spring. Different species have different characteristics that have enabled the species to survive. **(Chapters 14 and 15)** **On the FCAT** This benchmark is tested in multiple-choice form.

Benchmark SC.F.2.3.4	
The student knows that the fossil record provides evidence that changes in the kinds of plants and animals in the environment have been occurring over time.	You will learn about fossils and how they provide evidence of how plant and animal species have changed over time. Fossils can provide a record of how a species changed in response to changes in the environment during the early history of life on Earth. **(Chapters 13 and 14)** **On the FCAT** This benchmark is tested in multiple-choice form.

Benchmark SC.G.1.3.2	
The student knows that biological adaptations include changes in structures, behaviors, or physiology that enhance reproductive success in a particular environment.	Species survive when individuals within the species have characteristics that enable them to meet their needs and avoid danger. When conditions in an environment change, individuals with characteristics better suited to the new environment will more likely survive and pass on those characteristics. This is how biological adaptations occur, adaptations that include different structures and behaviors. **(Chapters 5, 14, and 15)** **On the FCAT** This benchmark is tested in multiple-choice form.

Benchmark SC.G.1.3.4	
The student knows that the interactions of organisms with each other and with the non-living parts of their environments result in the flow of energy and the cycling of matter throughout the system.	An ecosystem is made of biotic factors—the living things in an area—and abiotic factors—the physical surroundings. You will learn that matter and energy are transferred through ecosystems as living things interact with other living things and with their surroundings. Food chains show how energy and matter move from one organism to another. Food webs show the interaction of many food chains and how they affect the amount of food energy of an ecosystem. Also important to an ecosystem are different cycles, such as the water cycle and the carbon cycle. **(Chapters 2, 3, and 5)** **On the FCAT** This benchmark is tested in either multiple-choice or short-response form.

Benchmark SC.G.2.3.1	What This Means to You
The student knows that some resources are renewable and others are nonrenewable.	Resources that can never be used up are called renewable resources. Resources that are being used faster than they can form are nonrenewable resources. You will learn why it is important to understand how to best use renewable and nonrenewable resources. **(Chapters 3 and 9)** **On the FCAT** This benchmark is tested in multiple-choice form.

Benchmark SC.G.2.3.2	
The student knows that all biotic and abiotic factors are interrelated and that if one factor is changed or removed, it impacts the availability of other resources within the system.	Abiotic (nonliving) and biotic (living) factors interact in an ecosystem. A change to one part of an ecosystem can affect the other parts of an ecosystem. For example, draining a pond not only kills fish and water plants, it also affects other populations of living things that depend on those fish and plants for energy. **(Chapters 5 and 15)** **On the FCAT** This benchmark is tested in either multiple-choice or gridded-response form.

Benchmark SC.G.2.3.3	
The student knows that a brief change in the limited resources of an ecosystem may alter the size of a population or the average size of individual organisms and that long-term change may result in the elimination of animal and plant populations inhabiting the Earth.	You will learn how a short-term decrease in resources may temporarily affect the size of a population in an area, and even the size of the individuals in that population. However, a long-term change may threaten a population and possibly contribute to the extinction of a species. **(Chapter 15)** **On the FCAT** This benchmark is tested in either multiple-choice or gridded-response form.

Benchmark SC.G.2.3.4	
The student understands that humans are a part of an ecosystem and their activities may deliberately or inadvertently alter the equilibrium in ecosystems.	Like other living things, humans are a part of the ecosystems in which they live, and human actions sometimes affect these ecosystems. You will learn that some changes are made deliberately, as when a forest is cleared for farming. Other changes may be unintentional, as when residues from chemical fertilizers move into ponds or streams. **(Chapters 5 and 15)** **On the FCAT** This benchmark is tested in either multiple-choice or short-response form.

Benchmark SC.H.1.3.1	What This Means to You
The student knows that scientific knowledge is subject to modification as new information challenges prevailing theories and as a new theory leads to looking at old observations in a new way.	Scientific knowledge is always changing. As scientists ask questions, gather more information, and think about ideas differently, they revise old theories. One source of new information is improved technology for observing the world. Just as new information leads scientists to reevaluate old theories, revised theories lead them to look at old data in new ways. **(Chapters 7, 9, and 21)** **On the FCAT** This benchmark is tested in either multiple-choice or short-response form.

Benchmark SC.H.1.3.2	
The student knows that the study of the events that led scientists to discoveries can provide information about the inquiry process and its effects.	Scientists use careful, systematic procedures to test ideas. You will improve your understanding of the scientific process by studying how important discoveries were made. **(Chapters 1, 2, 13, and 14)** **On the FCAT** This benchmark is tested in multiple-choice form.

Benchmark SC.H.1.3.3	
The student knows that science disciplines differ from one another in topic, techniques, and outcomes but that they share a common purpose, philosophy, and enterprise.	There are many different sciences, each about a different subject. For example, biology is the study of life, geology is the study of Earth, and physics is the study of physical interactions of matter. You will learn that although different sciences have different techniques and topics, all sciences are based on the same basic methods. All sciences also share the same purpose: to understand the world in which we live. **(Chapters 1, 11, and 13)** **On the FCAT** This benchmark is tested in multiple-choice form.

Benchmark SC.H.1.3.6	
The student recognizes the scientific contributions that are made by individuals of diverse backgrounds, interests, talents, and motivations.	You will learn about scientists from different backgrounds with varied talents, interests, and accomplishments—for example, Jacques Cousteau, the undersea explorer who helped develop underwater breathing gear. **(Chapter 13 and Timelines following Chapters 4, 8, 11, 14, 17, and 20)** **On the FCAT** This benchmark is not tested on the FCAT.

Benchmark SC.H.2.3.1	What This Means to You
The student recognizes that patterns exist within and across systems.	Most natural events occur in repeating, predictable patterns. You will understand how recognizing patterns—such as tides, seasons, and repeating types of weather—allows scientists to predict and prepare for natural events. **(Chapters 4, 15, and 20)** **On the FCAT** This benchmark is tested in multiple-choice form.

Benchmark SC.H.3.3.1	
The student knows that science ethics demand that scientists must not knowingly subject coworkers, students, the neighborhood, or the community to health or property risks.	Scientific research can be hazardous. You will learn some of the precautions scientists are required to take to make sure their activities do not cause harm to people or property. **(Chapters 1 and 2)** **On the FCAT** This benchmark is tested in multiple-choice form.

Benchmark SC.H.3.3.4	
The student knows that technological design should require taking into account constraints such as natural laws, the properties of the materials used, and economic, political, social, ethical, and aesthetic values.	You will learn about some of the many factors designers of new technology must consider as they develop new products. Designers must consider the limitations imposed by the laws of nature and the limitations of the materials they use. Designers must also consider whether their products are useful, attractive, and cost effective. **(Chapters 9, 10, 11, and 12)** **On the FCAT** This benchmark is tested in multiple-choice form.

In eighth grade you will take the science FCAT. This test is designed to show what you have learned about science in sixth through eighth grades. There are four types of questions: multiple choice, gridded response, short response, and extended response. On the following pages, you'll learn more about each type and how to approach it.

Multiple Choice

Multiple-choice questions are worth 1 point each. Plan to spend about 1 minute on each question. You will have four answers to choose from. The answers will be labeled **A, B, C,** and **D** or **F, G, H,** and **I.** Choose the best answer and record it on your answer sheet.

Strategies for Multiple-Choice Questions

1. **Read the question carefully.** Try to answer the question before you read the answer choices. If you need to make a calculation, make it before you choose an answer.

2. **Read all the answer choices before you choose one.** Make sure you choose the answer that best answers the question.

3. **Make sure you understand what is being asked.** If your answer is not among the choices, read the question again.

4. **If you are not sure of an answer,** begin by using your science knowledge to eliminate choices that you know are wrong.

Example Question

 About twice a month, high tides are higher and low tides are lower than usual. These tides are called spring tides. When do spring tides occur?

A. when Earth is on the same side of the Sun as Jupiter

B. when Earth, the Moon, and the Sun are lined up

C. when the Moon is at first or third quarter

D. when Earth and the Moon are closest together

Tips for Answering the Question

This question asks you to apply your understanding of the cause of tides. Start by reviewing what you know about the cause of tides. Then eliminate answers you know are wrong.

- Choice **A** is wrong. The Moon and Sun produce tides on Earth, but Jupiter does not.

- Choice **D** is wrong. Tides are not produced by a change in the distance between Earth and the Moon.

This leaves **B** and **C.** The question says the higher and lower (stronger) tides occur twice a month. Both **B** and **C** describe situations that occur about twice a month, because the Moon takes about a month to orbit Earth and go through a cycle of phases. You know that the gravity of the Moon and Sun cause tides. Think about when the gravitational pull of these space objects would most affect tides on Earth. You may find it useful to make a quick sketch to work this out.

- Choice **C** is wrong. Reread this choice. When the Moon is at first or third quarter, the Sun, Earth, and the Moon form a right angle. The bulges of water on Earth due to the Sun's pull would reduce those due to the Moon's pull.

- The correct answer is **B.** Before recording your final choice on your answer sheet, think through why it would be correct. When the Moon, Earth, and the Sun are lined up, the Sun and the Moon produce bulges of water along the same line.

Short Response

Short-response items are marked with an icon like the one shown on the right. You will write your answer to a short-response item in a few sentences. You will receive 2 points for a complete and correct answer and 1 point for a partially correct answer. Plan to spend 3–5 minutes on each short-response question.

Strategies for Short-Response Questions

1. **Read the question carefully.** Be sure you know exactly what information you need to include.

2. **Look carefully at any illustrations, charts, or graphs.**

3. **Plan your answer before you start to write.** If you need to, make a list of key points to include.

4. **Write clearly and concisely.** Use complete sentences and correct spelling and grammar. Answer the question as fully as you can.

5. **Read over your answer.** Make sure it answers the question completely and correctly.

Example Question

**Read
Inquire
Explain**

2 When a person's kidneys stop working, that person may be treated with dialysis. The person is hooked up to a machine that serves the same function as the kidneys. What is that function? What would happen to the person if dialysis were not available?

The kidneys filter the blood, taking out waste products and excess water. The filtered blood goes back into the body. The kidneys then send the waste products and water to the bladder to be removed from the body. If a person's kidneys stopped working and the person didn't get dialysis, the blood would not be purified. Toxins and wastes would build up in the blood. This would poison the body and make it harder for body cells to carry out their functions.

Tips for Answering the Question

First, identify the information you need to provide. This question asks for two pieces of information: what the kidneys do, and what would happen to a person if the kidneys stopped working and were not replaced by dialysis.

Second, outline the key points you want to include.

I. Function of the kidneys
 A. filtering wastes and toxins from the blood
 B. sending water and waste products to the bladder to be removed

II. What would happen without the kidneys?
 A. Toxins would build up in the blood.
 B. The toxins would harm body functions and poison the body.

Finally, write your answer. Use complete sentences and write clearly and concisely.

Gridded Response

Gridded-response questions are marked with an icon like the one shown on the right. They are worth one point each. You should plan to spend about a minute and a half on each question. The answer will always be a number. It may be a decimal. You will first write your answer, and then fill out a grid to show your answer.

Strategies for Gridded-Response Questions

1. **Perform calculations carefully.** You may need to get information from a chart or graph. Check your reference sheet for any formulas you need.

2. **Check your work.** Before you enter your answer on the grid, check your calculation.

3. **Write your answer in the boxes at the top of the grid.** You may align your answer on the left or on the right. Write one number or decimal point per box.

4. **Fill in the grid carefully.** Fill in only one circle in each column where you wrote a number or decimal point. Do not fill in any circles in columns that you leave blank.

The grid you will use looks like this:

- answer boxes
- fraction bar
- decimal point
- number bubbles

Examples of answers with no decimal points

OR

Examples of answers with decimal points

OR

Example Question

3

A cube of a sample material has a volume of 27 cm³. Elena measures its mass and finds it is 62.1 g.

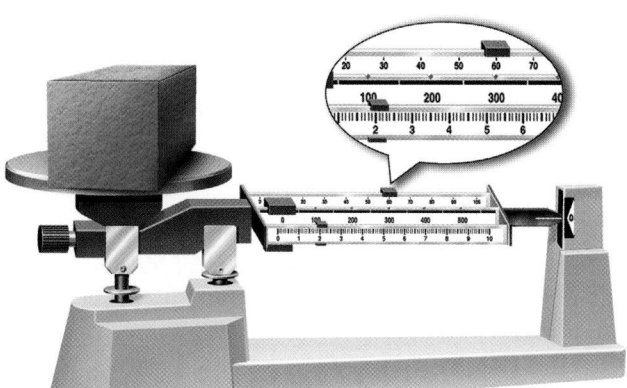

What is the density of the material in g/cm³?

Tips for Answering the Question

First, decide what question you need to answer. You need to find the density of the material.

Then identify the information you need from the question and illustration. The mass of the cube is 62.1 grams, and its volume is 27 cm³.

Make your calculation. To find the density, divide the mass by the volume. The density is 2.3 g/cm³.

Record your answer in your grid. Write one number or decimal point per box and fill in the matching circle. Do not leave any blank spaces in the middle of your number. Both of these are acceptable ways to fill in the grid.

Extended Response

Extended-response questions require longer answers than short-response items. They are marked with an icon like the one shown on the right. You can receive 0, 1, 2, 3, or 4 points, depending on how complete and correct your answer is. Plan to spend 10–15 minutes on each of these questions.

Read
Inquire
Explain

Strategies for Extended-Response Questions

1. **Read the question carefully before you answer it.** Be sure you know what you are being asked.

2. **Examine any illustrations, charts, and graphs carefully.** Note any information you need from them.

3. **Plan your answer before you start to write.** You may want to make a brief outline.

4. **Answer the question completely.** Make sure you identify all the parts that need answering.

5. **Reread your answer.** Make sure it says what you wanted it to say, and that you have answered all parts of the question.

Example Question

 4 Martin conducted an experiment on the growth of plants and recorded the results in a table. He used four plants of the same type and size and measured their growth after one month.

Read
Inquire
Explain

Plant	Amount of Fertilizer	Frequency of Fertilizer Use	Fertilizer Brand	Growth After 1 Month
1	2 mL	Once per week	Brand A	3 cm
2	2 mL	Three times per week	Brand A	4 cm
3	2 mL	Once per week	Brand B	2 cm
4	2 mL	Twice per week	Brand B	6 cm

Part A Identify the possible variables in Martin's experiment. Tell whether each variable was controlled. Also identify the dependent variable observed.

The variables are plant type, amount of fertilizer, frequency of fertilizer use, brand of fertilizer, and how much the plant grew. Plant type and amount of fertilizer were controlled. Plant growth is the dependent variable.

Part B Explain what is wrong with Martin's experiment. What could he change to allow for better conclusions to be drawn?

Martin's experiment has too many uncontrolled variables. There is no way to tell whether the frequency of fertilizer use or the brand of fertilizer caused the differences in plant growth, or whether some combination of the two caused it. Martin could improve his experiment by choosing just one variable to test. He might use the same fertilizer and change how often he uses it, or use different fertilizers and keep the frequency the same.

Extended Response *continued*

Tips for Answering the Question

First, read the question carefully, and identify the information you are asked to provide.

- *Part A* asks you to list the possible variables, say whether each is controlled, and identify the dependent variable.
- *Part B* asks you to identify problems with the experiment and suggest how to improve it.

Second, think about what you know about variables and constants. Make a list or an outline to help you plan your answer. Your plan might look like this.

Part A

List of variables: plant type, amount of fertilizer, frequency of fertilizer use, brand of fertilizer, plant growth; plant type and amount of fertilizer are controlled, and plant growth is the dependent variable

Part B

I. What problems are there?

- too many uncontrolled variables
- can't tell which change is causing the change in growth

II. How to improve it?

- choose only one variable to test
- hold all other variables constant

Finally, write your answer in the space provided.

Other Things to Keep in Mind

- Sometimes you'll be asked to fill in blanks on a diagram before writing a paragraph. You'll need to use those responses to answer the rest of the question. Read over each part of your answer before moving on to the next part to be sure the information you are using is as accurate as possible.
- Partial answers count. Try to be as complete as possible, but if you can't answer the entire question, answer the part that you can.

The Nature of Science

the **BIG** idea

All sciences use similar processes and tools.

Growers sometimes spray water on oranges in cold weather. How did they figure out that this could help protect the fruit?

Key Concepts

SECTION

1 **Basic tools of science are universal.**
Learn why different sciences have a common approach.

SECTION

2 **Scientific ideas are based on evidence.**
Learn how different kinds of scientific inquiries are used to gather evidence.

SECTION

3 **Scientists belong to a world community.**
Learn how science and society interact with each other.

FCAT Practice

Prepare and practice for the FCAT
• Section Reviews, pp. 12, 21, 30
• Chapter Review, pp. 32–34
• FCAT Practice, p. 35

CLASSZONE.COM
• Florida Review: Content Review and FCAT Practice

EXPLORE (the BIG idea)

Reproducing a Result

Using only a cup of water and a table-tennis ball, find a way to make the ball float so that it does not touch the cup. Write down your procedure.

Observe and Think
Why is it important to keep detailed records of a procedure?

Effects of Changes

Use a plastic straw, paper strips, and tape to make a glider like the one shown in the photograph. Hold the glider with the smaller loop of paper in front. Throw the glider several times and measure how far it flies each time. Then change the sizes of the loops or use different shapes for them. Test the glider's flight after each change.

Observe and Think How did each change affect the flight of your glider?

Internet Activity: Ethics

Go to **ClassZone.com** to learn more about ethics and scientific study.

Observe and Think
What are some of the ethical questions scientists face? Is there always one right answer to an ethical question?

NSTA
scilinks.org
SCiLINKS

Technology and Society **Code: MDL069**

CHAPTER 1

Getting Ready to Learn

◀ CONCEPT REVIEW

- Science is a continuous process of asking questions and seeking answers.
- Scientists are observant and creative.
- Technology is used to advance scientific inquiry.

◀ VOCABULARY REVIEW

See Glossary for definitions.

data, experiment, qualitative, quantitative, reproducible, variable

FLORIDA REVIEW
CLASSZONE.COM

Content Review and FCAT Practice

▶ TAKING NOTES

MAIN IDEA WEB

Write each new blue heading—a main idea—in a box. Then, in boxes around that box, write important terms and the main details about that idea.

SCIENCE NOTEBOOK

exploration of questions and ideas	Not all questions can be answered scientifically.

Science is a way to study the natural world.

objective observations	Results should be reproducible.

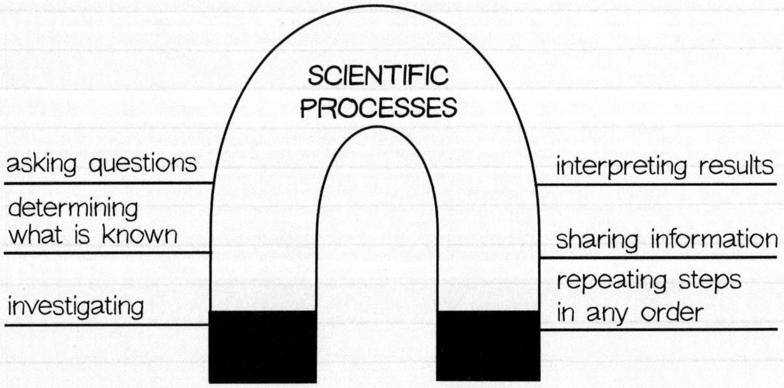

VOCABULARY STRATEGY

For each vocabulary term, make a **magnet word** diagram. Around the term, write other terms or ideas related to it.

SCIENTIFIC PROCESSES

asking questions

determining what is known

investigating

interpreting results

sharing information

repeating steps in any order

See the Note-Taking Handbook on pages R45–R51.

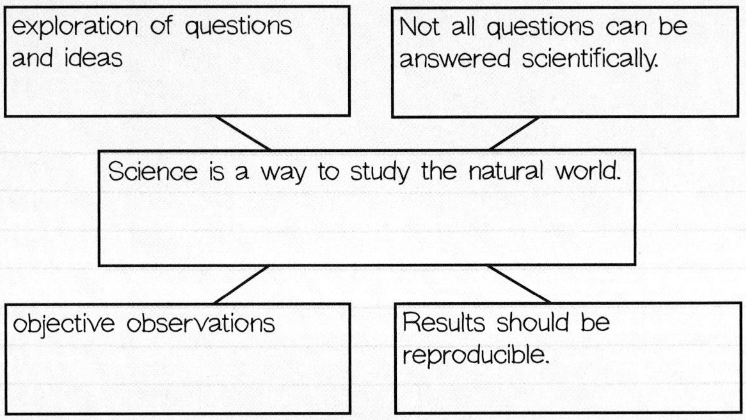

Basic tools of science are universal.

VOCABULARY

scientific processes p. 6
hypothesis p. 7
creative thinking p. 8
skepticism p. 9
critical thinking p. 10

◁ BEFORE, you learned

- Scientists collect evidence by making observations
- Scientific results must be reproducible
- Scientists record and share results

▷ NOW, you will learn

- How people use scientific processes
- About scientific habits of mind
- How scientists build up scientific information

EXPLORE Observations and Opinions

How are observations different from opinions?

PROCEDURE

1. Fill the bottles one-third full with water.

2. Add one spoonful of a different type of cleaning product to each bottle. Fasten the lids tightly and shake each bottle for 15 seconds.

3. Observe the suds in each bottle.

MATERIALS

- 3 bottles with lids
- water
- spoon
- 3 types of cleaning products

WHAT DO YOU THINK?

How is comparing the heights of suds produced by the cleaning products different from comparing how good they smell?

Science is a way to study the natural world.

People continually ask questions, explore ideas, and reach conclusions. Sometimes scientific methods can help them, but not all questions can be answered scientifically. For example, suppose people are deciding which musicians to invite to perform in the town's park. They may discuss their opinions vigorously, but science cannot help them make the best choice.

What can be studied scientifically? Anything that can be observed objectively and that involves features of the natural world. Objective observations are the same for everyone. For example, choosing the best type of grass to plant in the park can be approached scientifically. People can test varieties of grass to find out which would grow well in the park and withstand being walked on by large numbers of concert-goers. The grasses are part of the natural world, their growth can be tested, and different observers will get similar results.

Different sciences use similar processes.

FLORIDA
Content Review

Remember what you learned in grade 6 about scientific thinking. See pages R2–R9 for a reminder.

READING TiP

The word *inquiry* means a search for information or truth.

Suppose you asked a group of scientists to describe in one word what they study. Each person would probably name a specific area of science. Because science is the study of the natural world, you could get as many answers as there are aspects of the universe. The pictures below show a few of the many types of science.

All scientists, no matter what topics they study, use the same processes when they make their scientific inquiries. As you will read in Section 2, inquiries can include experiments and other ways of gathering data. An inquiry usually involves these **scientific processes:**

- asking questions
- determining what is known
- investigating
- interpreting results
- sharing information

Some of the Types of Science

A scientific study can often be classified as life science, physical science, or earth science. Some types of studies fall into two or more categories.

Geology is the study of Earth's surface and interior. This scientist examines glowing molten rock from a volcano.

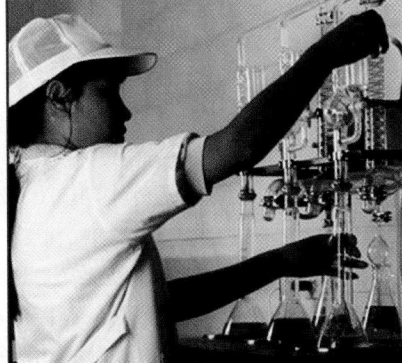

Chemistry is the study of the properties and interactions of substances. This scientist has purified a liquid by removing certain substances from it.

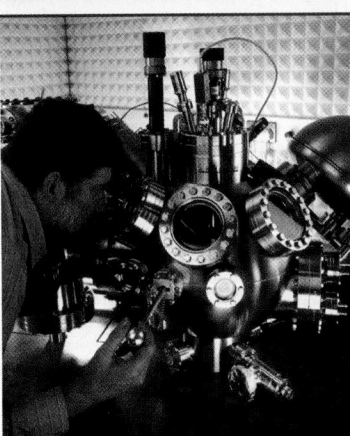

Physics is the study of energy and matter. This scientist uses three special microscopes to understand and change the surface of a material.

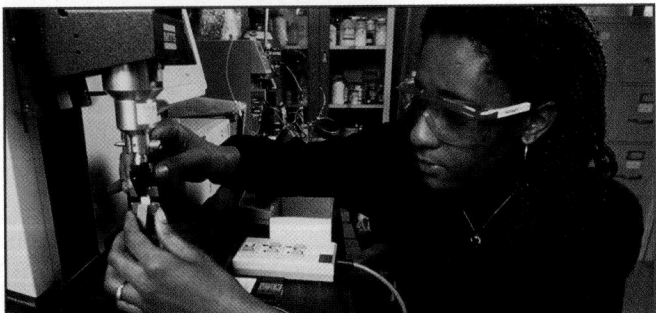

Biology is the study of living things. This scientist tests materials that can be useful in human organ transplants.

The list of processes may look like a simple, logical series of steps. However, science seldom follows such a rigid format. Results often lead to new questions. An investigation may include several cycles of observing, thinking of possible explanations, and making new observations to test the explanations. Steps can occur in any order, and some may be repeated many times during a scientific inquiry.

For example, suppose you want to identify a beetle like the one shown below. You might first observe the beetle. Investigating usually includes observing, or gathering data. You can use instruments and tools as well as your senses to gather data. You can make measurements to get quantitative data. Perhaps you estimate the size of the beetle and record its color.

REMINDER
Quantitative data are observations that include a number or an amount.

CHECK YOUR READING How are measurements related to observations?

To identify the beetle, you need to compare your observations with what is already known. You might use the descriptions and illustrations in a field guide. You will likely need to make more observations and comparisons before you can identify the beetle. The descriptions in the guide might lead you to questions about the beetle's life cycle or its usual food. Often an answer to one question leads to new questions.

Investigating also means thinking about observations. Scientists commonly develop and test several hypotheses. A **hypothesis** is a tentative explanation for a set of observations. A hypothesis can be written in the form of an "If . . . , then . . . , because . . ." statement—for example, "If I drop a book, it will fall to the ground, because gravity acts on it." The first part of the statement describes a possible process or event: dropping a book. The second part states a prediction that can be tested by observation: the book will fall. The third part explains why the predicted event should occur: gravity acts on the book. The explanation may state a cause and effect, or it may just describe a general pattern, such as "Clearer nights are colder." Often, scientists need to make observations and apply what they know before they can develop and test hypotheses.

An important part of a scientist's inquiry is the sharing of methods, results, and conclusions. Scientific results must be reproducible—possible to repeat. Other people need to be able to duplicate the process and get similar outcomes. Results and conclusions are accepted into the body of scientific knowledge only when many people have tested them. For example, scientists had to observe the same characteristics in many beetles of a certain type before the information could be put into a field guide.

Scientists develop certain habits of mind.

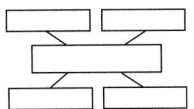

MAIN IDEA WEB
Record in your notebook important information about scientific habits of mind.

Anyone can take a scientific approach to a question. People who conduct scientific inquiries develop certain habits of mind. They learn to be observant, curious, creative, and skeptical. They think critically.

Being Observant and Curious

Observant people pay attention to the world around them. They think and ask questions about what they observe. Curiosity leads people to explore different questions. Scientific questions are sometimes called problems. Used in this way, the word *problem* refers to something to be solved, like a puzzle. Curious people solve problems.

For example, Jocelyn Bell and Anthony Hewish were studying radio waves from space. They were using a huge pattern of wires held in place on poles. In 1967 Bell was collecting and looking at data. She needed to find the parts of the data that came from space. To do this, she needed to identify and eliminate signals from human activities.

Bell was looking at data in the form of a graph, like the line on a heartbeat monitor. Different types of signals had different shapes. Bell compared the data with the shapes of sources she knew. She observed something odd. One signal was a repeating group of fast pulses, or bursts. It was similar to some familiar signals from human activities. However, Bell found differences. She was curious about the differences and not sure that the signals came from human activity. She decided to keep investigating what the source was.

Jocelyn Bell and Anthony Hewish strung wires on poles in order to detect radio waves from space. They discovered pulsars, stars that seem to pulse as they spin.

Being Creative

You may not usually think of scientists as creative, but creative thinking is an important source of ideas, questions, and explanations. **Creative thinking** is a way to play with ideas to solve problems. For example, Bell had to think of different possible sources for the radio pulses, as well as ways to test her ideas.

Creative thinking takes practice. People think creatively by combining and expanding ideas in fresh ways. The more they know, the more easily they can find the ideas to put together. Sometimes people get together and share the ideas they have. Most of the ideas are later rejected, but one wild idea may inspire a useful inquiry. This process is called brainstorming. At other times, a person keeps a problem in mind while doing other things. New ideas can come from seeing something ordinary in a new way.

Being Skeptical

Scientists accept uncertainty. They often work on problems to which nobody yet knows the answers. Scientists think of many ideas, but they don't trust their ideas right away. **Skepticism** is the refusal to accept an idea that is not backed up by evidence. Skeptical people doubt and question. They learn to be comfortable with not knowing for sure. They are willing to test their own ideas, to draw tentative conclusions, and to change their minds. Sometimes people think that a skeptic refuses to believe anything. Actually, a skeptic evaluates ideas and accepts them if the evidence is good enough. A skeptic requires unusual ideas or claims to have strong supporting evidence before putting trust in them.

 When is a skeptic willing to accept an idea?

For example, Bell had doubts that the radio pulses came from human activity. She was skeptical. Eventually she and Hewish determined that the signal came from a location in space. Could the signal be a communication from aliens? Bell and Hewish didn't believe it could be. They would have needed a great deal of evidence to convince themselves. However, they tested the data to be sure. When they analyzed their results, they became confident enough to reject the idea of aliens as the source.

READING **TiP**

The words *skepticism* and *skeptic* both come from the Greek word *skeptikos,* which means "to examine." A skeptic is a person who displays skepticism.

INVESTIGATE Solving Problems

PROCEDURE

DESIGN —YOUR OWN— EXPERIMENT

1. Study the photograph. It shows a paper clip that appears to be floating in air, held only by a thread attached to its bottom.

2. Brainstorm ideas to explain why the paper clip seems to be floating in air.

3. Use skepticism to eliminate some possible explanations. Use your best ideas to determine how you might reproduce the setup in the photograph.

4. Request materials you need from your teacher, and test your ideas.

WHAT DO YOU THINK?

- How did you use creative thinking and skepticism?
- How many ideas did you test? How many people contributed to the process?

CHALLENGE Brainstorm another way to reproduce the setup in the photograph.

SKILL FOCUS
Evaluating

MATERIALS
- paper clip
- thread
- other materials as needed

TIME
20 minutes

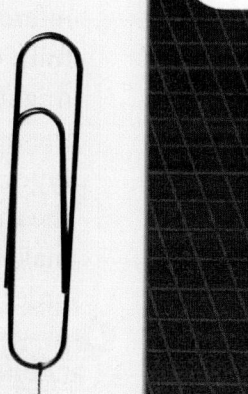

Thinking Critically

Skepticism is one part of critical thinking. **Critical thinking** is a method of analysis that depends on logic, or correct reasoning. It includes different skills that can help you find answers.

Analyze and Relate Big problems are often made of small, solvable parts. You analyze something when you break it down into smaller parts and examine how the parts are related. Bell analyzed her data by breaking it into signals from different sources.

Compare and Contrast Many problems are similar to other problems. You can look for similarities to problems that have already been solved. Differences between problems can alert you to differences in their answers. Bell compared the pulses with signals from sources on Earth. The differences made her look for a new source.

Connect and Apply Some problems are solved by connecting two or more pieces of knowledge that, at first, may not seem related. Often, you must take general knowledge and apply it to a specific situation. Hewish connected the idea of Earth's motion to the radio signals. He applied his knowledge to figure out how the pulses would be different if they had come from a source on Earth.

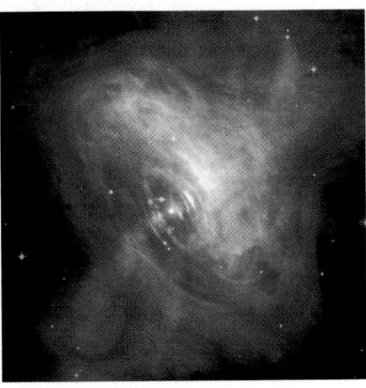

This pulsar image combines data from two different telescopes. The jet at the lower left shows where the pulsar gives off a narrow beam of energy. Observers can detect pulses of energy as the star spins.

Infer and Hypothesize When you have several related examples, you can sometimes infer a general rule. Or you might be able to use logic to combine pieces of information to infer new information. Bell thought she saw a second signal similar to the first. She used existing data to infer the timing of the repeating signal. She used this as a hypothesis and tested it by looking for the signal at the right time. She found it.

Evaluate and Conclude Different parts of a problem, such as evidence, inferences, and possible actions, should be examined and judged carefully, or evaluated. With enough reasons or convincing evidence, you might draw a conclusion. Bell evaluated two more sets of signals. When she had enough evidence, she concluded that they were from the same types of things. She did not have enough information to know what the things were. You will often use several skills together. You might make a general hypothesis and then apply it to a particular situation in order to predict an outcome. You might use other combinations.

CHECK YOUR READING What are some critical-thinking skills? Make a list.

Scientists build on previous knowledge.

While scientists are still working on problems, they may share their work with other scientists. They may talk about their results and ideas informally or present them at scientific conferences. The scientists might give talks—perhaps multimedia presentations—or make posters showing their early results. Other scientists can ask questions or challenge the methods being used. These actions often lead to new ideas and better approaches to the problems.

When Bell and Hewish thought they had enough information, they shared their results. Other scientists made additional observations, which led to an explanation—a cause that accounted for the observed effect. Bell and Hewish had discovered pulsars, which are stars that give off narrow beams of energy, including radio waves. The energy is detected in pulses because the stars rotate. The beams sweep around like flashing lights on emergency vehicles. Scientists later connected the beams of energy with other features, such as the jets in the image on page 10.

Scientists get together at conferences to share their work. Results may also be reported in the news or may be used to develop new laws.

Changing Ideas

Scientists have to be willing to change their ideas. Many problems are solved by challenging assumptions—ideas accepted as true without evidence. For example, someone might assume that it would be foolish to coat oranges with ice to protect them from frost. However, when the air temperature drops to slightly below freezing, spraying water on crops such as oranges can save them from frost damage. As water freezes, it releases heat energy into the fruit. The ice also protects the fruit from colder air.

Spraying fruit with water during cold weather may seem strange at first. However, it makes sense when you understand how energy is transferred.

Evaluating Conclusions

Scientists can build on one another's work only when that work is shared. Papers are evaluated by other scientists before being published in scientific journals.

Scientists evaluate one another's work. When scientists finish an inquiry, they write a scientific paper describing their methods, results, and conclusions. They send the paper to a scientific journal. The journal's editors send the paper to other scientists for review. Only when the work has been checked and corrected does the journal publish the paper.

A scientist relies on experience and training to evaluate the information and conclusions in a scientific paper. As part of everyday life, you evaluate conclusions too. You use your personal experience to figure out whether they are trustworthy. You might ask whether a conclusion was reached by someone who understands the topic. You might judge how well the evidence supports the conclusion. You would be skeptical if no evidence were presented. You might also doubt a conclusion presented by someone who would benefit from the acceptance of it. For example, a study in favor of a certain product might not be trustworthy if paid for by a manufacturer who wanted to sell that product.

Scientific conclusions can be supported by evidence, but they are never considered to be proved. Science is an ongoing process. Some amount of uncertainty is always present. Any conclusion can be overturned if new evidence clearly shows it to be wrong. This ability to change is a great strength of science. When scientists make mistakes or their understanding is not complete, the work of other scientists sooner or later corrects the ideas and expands the body of scientific knowledge.

1.1 Review

KEY CONCEPTS

1. What processes do scientists use?

2. Choose one of the habits of mind that scientists develop and explain how it is useful in an inquiry.

3. How is new scientific information checked and evaluated?

CRITICAL THINKING

4. **Compare and Contrast** How are creative thinking and critical thinking similar? How are they different?

5. **Infer** Why do scientists need to learn to be comfortable with uncertainty?

⬤ CHALLENGE

6. **Provide Examples** Choose two of the critical-thinking skills and show how you have already used them in your everyday life.

CONNECTING SCIENCES

The Science of Clean Water

Scientists continually work to find the best methods to make water clean enough to drink. Their inquiries build on the work of other scientists who research ways to maintain and protect sources of clean water. Some drinking water comes from rivers and lakes, but about half of the drinking water in the United States is pumped from wells. Well water comes from aquifers—underground layers of sediment or rock containing interconnected spaces through which water flows.

Removing and Adding Chemicals

The water in a river or lake is not pure. It contains solid particles and dissolved chemicals. This water becomes cleaner underground. As water flows through sediment and rock, particles are filtered from it. Clay minerals absorb some chemicals from the water. Acids can be removed by minerals that are common in limestone. But scientists have discovered that many chemicals cannot be completely removed by natural processes. Therefore, it is important to properly dispose of things like used motor oil and batteries so that they do not contaminate water sources.

Sediment and rock can add chemicals to water as well as remove them. Some minerals dissolve in water as it flows underground. Many of these substances are harmless.

Copying Earth

aquifer

Before drinking water arrives at your home, it may pass through a water-treatment plant that removes harmful materials. Also, water that has been used by people may be cleaned by water-treatment plants before it is returned to the environment. Water-treatment plants copy some of the natural cleaning processes of Earth. Water is filtered through beds of sand and gravel, and certain chemicals are added to remove other, harmful chemicals.

EXPLORE

1. **INFER** How can human activity affect an aquifer?
2. **CHALLENGE** Use the Internet or call your local water company to find the source of your drinking water. Find out what dissolved chemicals are most common in your drinking water.

RESOURCE CENTER
CLASSZONE.COM

Learn more about aquifers and water purification.

KEY CONCEPT

1.2 Scientific ideas are based on evidence.

Sunshine State STANDARDS

SC.H.1.3.3: The student knows that science disciplines differ from one another in topic, techniques, and outcomes, but that they share a common purpose, philosophy, and enterprise.

SC.H.1.3.5: The student knows that a change in one or more variables may alter the outcome of an investigation.

SC.H.1.3.7: The student knows that when similar investigations give different results, the scientific challenge is to verify whether the differences are significant by further study.

BEFORE, you learned

- Different sciences focus on different topics but have a common approach
- Scientific methods can be used to analyze information, solve problems, and evaluate conclusions

NOW, you will learn

- About variables and controls in scientific experiments
- About four different types of scientific inquiries
- How new evidence can change widely accepted ideas

FCAT VOCABULARY
independent variable p. 15
dependent variable p. 15

VOCABULARY
experimental group p. 15
control group p. 15
model p. 16
theory p. 19

REMINDER
You can find detailed information about different units and unit conversions on pages R20–R21.

EXPLORE Effects of Changes in Procedures

How many drops of water can a coin hold?

PROCEDURE

1. Put two different types of coins on a paper towel.

2. Use an eyedropper to put drops of water on the coins. Count how many drops each coin can hold before the water overflows.

MATERIALS
- 2 different coins
- paper towel
- eyedropper
- water

WHAT DO YOU THINK?
- Does it matter what type of coin you use or which side of the coin you use? Does it matter how far the eyedropper is above the coin?
- How would keeping detailed records help others reproduce your results?

Observations provide scientific evidence.

Observations are a way of learning about the world. You continually make observations with your senses as you see, hear, touch, smell, and taste things. You can increase your ability to observe by using equipment, such as a magnifying glass. When you keep records, you can compare observations made at different times or places.

A measurement is an observation expressed as a number and a unit. Suppose some bicyclists tell you they normally bike a distance of 15. This information is meaningless because a unit, such as kilometers or miles, is missing. In the United States, many people use nonmetric units of measurement, such as inches and quarts. Scientists usually use units of the metric system, such as centimeters and liters. The formal name of the standard scientific system is the International System of Units, or SI.

An inquiry is a way to gather evidence.

A laboratory experiment is one type of scientific inquiry. You will read about other types later in this section. In a laboratory, scientists have more control over factors in experiments. Scientists can get clearer results as they test their ideas about cause-and-effect relationships.

Variables and Controls

In an experiment, each repetition of a procedure is called a trial. A factor that changes or can be changed in a trial is called a variable.

Suppose you are testing how salt affects the freezing temperature of water. Variables include the amounts of water and salt as well as temperature. A controlled variable is one that you keep constant in all trials. You use the same amount of water in each trial, so it is a controlled variable. A factor that you change individually is an **independent variable.** In your experiment, you change the amount of salt used in each trial. The amount of salt used is an independent variable. A factor that depends on another factor is a **dependent variable.** The temperature at which the water freezes is a dependent variable, because it depends on the amount of salt used.

An experiment may have variables that are uncontrolled. These variables can change by chance. If one part of your freezer is sometimes colder than another part, your experiment has an uncontrolled variable. To decrease the effects of uncontrolled variables on your results, you can make several, or multiple, trials in which the same value is used for the independent variable. You could make multiple trials for each amount of salt used.

Some experiments, such as tests on living organisms, have many uncontrollable variables. Suppose you want to test the effect of a new fertilizer. Because plant seeds are slightly different from one another, you might plant a number of seeds in pots that contain the new fertilizer. Each seed becomes a trial. You have made an **experimental group**—a set of trials with the same value of the independent variable.

But how can you know whether the new fertilizer is better than the one you have been using? Make a **control group,** a group used for comparison in an experiment. Add the currently used fertilizer to some pots, then put seeds in them. This group is the control group. The control group and the experimental group are treated equally except for the fertilizer used. Therefore, any change in plant growth is likely to be caused by the difference in fertilizers.

VOCABULARY
Add magnet word diagrams for *independent variable, dependent variable, experimental group,* and *control group* to your notebook.

This scientist is studying how changes in the amount of light and water affect experimental groups of plants and insects.

 **CHECK YOUR READING** How is a control group different from an experimental group?

Types of Scientific Inquiries

Doing science does not always require laboratory equipment. Indeed, many types of scientific inquiries cannot take place in a lab. Some common types of inquiries are described below and on the next page.

1 **Laboratory Experiments** In a laboratory, scientists can regulate most conditions. Variables are easier to control, and uncontrolled variables are easier to reduce or correct for. The subject of a laboratory experiment can be tiny, such as an inquiry into the arrangement of a substance's atoms. Or it can be huge, such as an inquiry into tree growth in a field enclosed by a greenhouse.

2 **Fieldwork** Inquiries that are done outside a laboratory are called fieldwork. Variables are more difficult to control, or they may not be controlled at all. Scientists do fieldwork when, for example, they want to investigate animal behavior in the wild. Some subjects—such as relationships among rock layers in a mountain—are too large to be studied without doing fieldwork.

3 **Surveys** A survey involves examining a part of a group and then using the results to draw conclusions about the whole group. This type of survey requires data from direct observations, not from asking questions of people. For example, scientists might want to know the numbers of organisms in the soil of an area. It is not possible to count all the organisms without destroying the area. Instead, the scientists could examine samples of the soil at different locations. They would infer that the rest of the soil held similar numbers of organisms.

4 **Models** Some things are too large, are too small, are too far away, or take too long to study directly. Other things are too dangerous or too expensive to test directly. For example, scientists cannot study directly how stars form. Such things are often studied by using **models,** which are representations of objects or processes. In a computer model, mathematical equations and techniques are used to represent the behavior of things like stars or volcanic eruptions. In a physical model, objects are used to represent other objects—ones that are difficult or impossible to work with directly. A physical model might be used to test a design for a new aircraft.

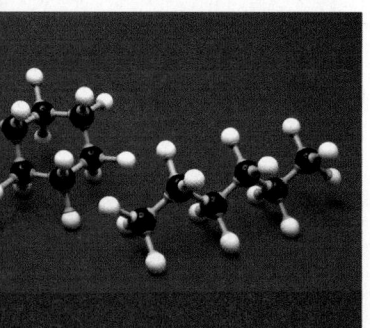

In this physical model, spheres are used to represent atoms in a molecule.

Scientists often use several types of inquiries together. A survey might be part of a larger program of fieldwork. Data from several types of inquiries might be used to build a model. Then scientists can control variables in the model that would be impossible to control in real life. The results might suggest new effects to look for in fieldwork or might suggest new experiments to design.

 **CHECK YOUR READING** What questions do you have about different types of scientific inquiries?

Scientific Inquiries

The type of inquiry scientists choose to use depends on the topic they are investigating. Often, scientists use more than one type of inquiry as they study different aspects of a topic.

① Laboratory Experiments

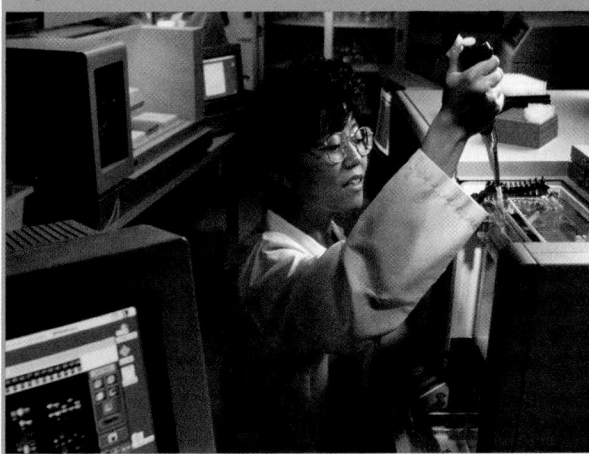

When scientists do a laboratory experiment, they can more easily change just one variable at a time, so they get clearer results. The photograph shows a scientist using laboratory equipment to analyze a substance.

② Fieldwork

Scientist Jane Goodall began fieldwork in 1960 to study chimpanzees. At that time, scientists thought that only humans used tools. Goodall's observations of chimpanzees in their natural habitat showed that they use tools too.

③ Surveys

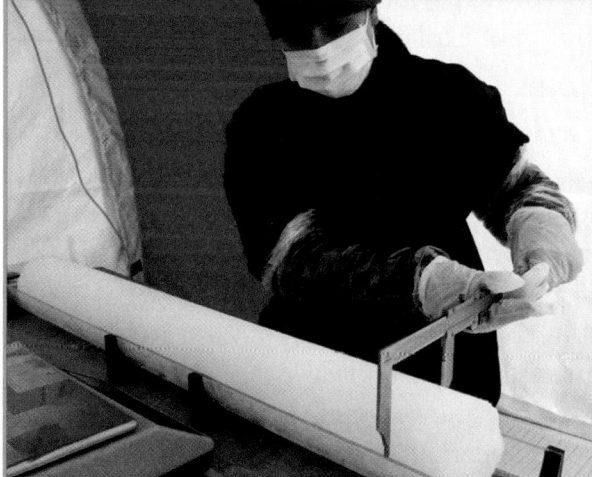

This researcher is working with an ice core collected in Antarctica. Each core gives information about what climatic conditions were like when the ice formed.

④ Models

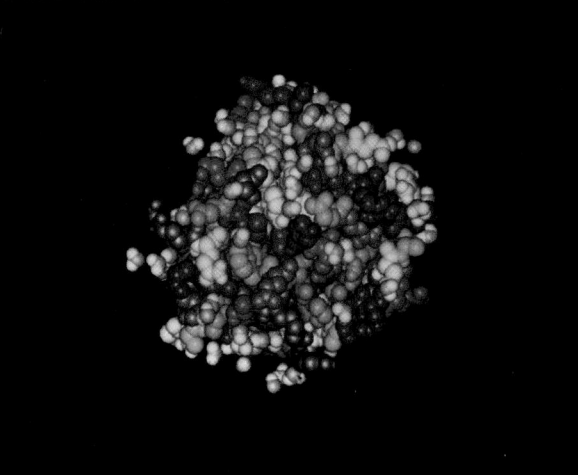

This computer model represents a protein molecule. The model, which is much larger than the actual molecule, allows scientists to study the structure of the molecule in detail.

READING VISUALS Why might scientists who are studying the formation of tornadoes in thunderstorms do fieldwork and use models?

New evidence can change scientific ideas.

Scientists make various types of inquiries as they explore a topic. They develop, test, and either discard or improve hypotheses. Scientists look for relationships among different types of evidence and develop ideas that account for as much of the evidence as possible.

Science is always an ongoing process. If new evidence is discovered that does not support an idea or if scientists begin to think about old evidence in a new way, then the idea can be overturned. An example is how scientific understanding of the solar system has changed.

In the mid-1900s, scientists thought that the solar system was stable and unchanging. They understood the motions of planets and moons very well. Scientists did not think that small objects in the solar system could cause large changes to moons or planets, including Earth.

At one time, scientists used models such as this one to study the solar system. Now, scientists realize that such models do not represent many important processes.

New Evidence

Over time, different types of scientists made observations that seemed inconsistent with the idea of an unchanging solar system. Major challenges to this idea developed from inquiries into topics that seemed unrelated, including

- circular features on the Moon
- rock layers on Earth
- the extinction of the dinosaurs

Together, these inquiries provided evidence that the accepted idea could not explain.

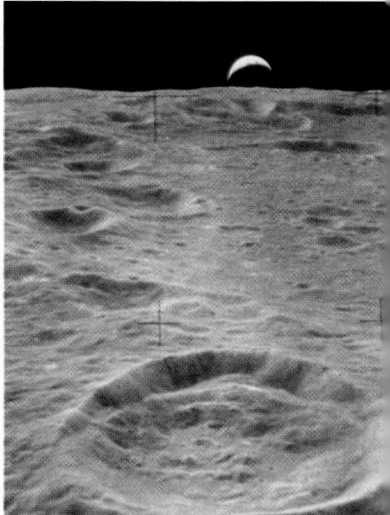

The Moon's surface shows many circular features created by the impact of small objects.

Scientists studying Earth's moon noticed circular features on its surface. They did not know if the features were caused by volcanoes or by collisions of smaller objects with the Moon. Then, astronauts exploring the Moon brought back samples of rock that showed that the features were from collisions, or impacts. Most of the impacts had taken place a very long time ago. Spacecraft showed that other planets and moons had been hit many times by small objects. By comparison, evidence of impacts on Earth's surface seemed rare. Just a few circular features on Earth were shown to be caused by impacts.

Meanwhile, scientists studying rock layers on Earth found an element—iridium (ih-RIHD-ee-uhm)—in a thin layer that formed about 65 million years ago. Iridium is more common in rocks from space than in rocks formed on Earth. The scientists developed a hypothesis that a huge rock from space hit Earth 65 million years ago. They suggested that the impact destroyed the rock and threw huge amounts of iridium-rich dust into the atmosphere. The dust spread around the world before settling on Earth's surface.

Models of nuclear explosions suggested that large clouds of dust would make the weather cooler by reflecting some of the sunlight that warms Earth's surface. The scientists suspected that dust from the impact could suddenly have produced cooler weather on Earth. Scientists who study the patterns of life on Earth already knew that many species, including dinosaurs, had become extinct about 65 million years ago. Perhaps the extinctions were related to the impact.

The scientists who were studying impact features added information about the age of the iridium layer and the timing of the extinctions to their knowledge. At first, the hypothesis that a rock from space had hit Earth 65 million years ago seemed unlikely to many scientists, because they held the idea that the solar system was stable and unchanging.

The extinction of the dinosaurs is now thought to be related to the impact of a space object with Earth about 65 million years ago.

Building a New Idea

Part of the work scientists did to test the new hypothesis involved looking for an iridium layer in other 65-million-year-old rocks. The scientists found the layer in locations around the world. They also looked for and found evidence of additional impacts. By the late 1980s, many scientists accepted that large numbers of small objects had hit and changed Earth, other planets, and moons. They realized that more impacts are likely in the future. Scientists now think that the solar system is dynamic and changing.

The hypothesis that an impact of a space rock with Earth occurred 65 million years ago developed into a theory. A **theory** is a well-tested explanation that brings together many sets of scientific observations. Theories are the big ideas of science. Details of a theory can change as more evidence is discovered. More rarely, a theory is overturned by new evidence and eventually replaced with a new theory.

CHECK YOUR READING   How do scientific ideas change?

Results and conclusions may be challenged.

Scientists must accurately describe the work that led to the results and conclusions they report. Such openness allows other scientists to judge the work's credibility and to reproduce the work if they want to. If a report lacks this information, scientists often reject the results or conclusions. If a report is complete, then any scientist can decide whether or not to accept the results.

Sometimes scientists accept the results of an inquiry but not the conclusions. Even when scientists think that results are valid, they might think that the conclusions are not supported by enough evidence. The conclusion that a space object collided with Earth 65 million years ago was not widely accepted until many types of evidence were discovered that all supported the same conclusion.

When scientists report that they have discovered evidence that challenges a widely accepted idea, their results may lead to controversy. A period of uncertainty and argument may follow while scientists try to confirm or disprove the results. If further results and other evidence support the challenge, more and more scientists begin to reject the accepted idea.

READING TiP

The word *controversy* refers to a dispute between people holding opposite views. If people agree, a subject is noncontroversial, but if they disagree, it is controversial.

Controversial Results

Many factors can lead to controversy. A new result can be controversial at first. If a new result does not support earlier results or theories, scientists first test whether the new result can be reproduced. Then they try to understand how it fits with what they already know. Sometimes, a new result or idea changes how scientists think about an entire aspect of the natural world.

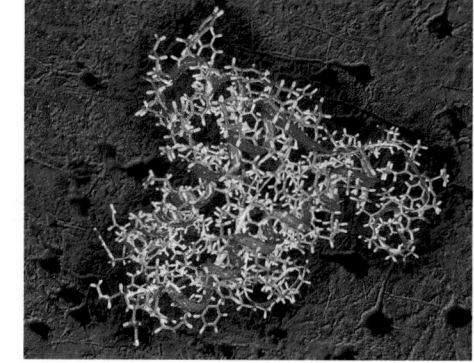

Prions, such as the one shown in this computer model, are proteins that can multiply and cause diseases by causing normal proteins to change their shapes.

The hypothesis that prions (PREE-ahnz), a type of protein, can cause infectious diseases was very controversial. Prions are now thought to cause infections such as mad cow disease, a fatal disorder that affects the structure of cows' brains. A form of the disease can be passed to people when they eat meat from infected cows.

Most scientists at first did not accept that prions could multiply and cause infections. Unlike bacteria or viruses, prions cannot reproduce because they have no genetic material. Therefore, scientists did not believe that a few prions passed to an organism could cause an infection. In 1982, however, a U.S. scientist named Stanley Prusiner hypothesized that prions can cause the shape of normal proteins to

RESOURCE CENTER
CLASSZONE.COM

Learn more about special proteins known as prions.

change, making new prions. Although some scientists are still skeptical about Prusiner's hypothesis, he was awarded the Nobel prize in medicine in 1997.

Some controversies occur when groups of scientists get different results when doing similar inquiries. For example, teams at two laboratories might analyze the same substance but find different materials. A controversy could result over which results are correct. The controversy ends if an explanation is found. Perhaps some samples of the substance were contaminated, or a procedure was performed incorrectly.

Controversies can also be the result of bias. Scientists can be biased if they become too attached to particular ideas. They may unknowingly choose data, design inquiries, or make assumptions that support these ideas. People are more likely to suggest the possibility of bias when results are personally unfavorable to them. For example, research showing that a material is harmful may be challenged by a manufacturer that uses the material.

READING **TiP**

The word *bias* comes from the French word *biais*, meaning "slant." A biased person might not consider an idea fairly or might not consider all possibilities.

 **CHECK YOUR READING** Give two reasons why scientific results might be controversial.

Noncontroversial Results

Results that can be easily reproduced are rarely controversial. For example, a chemist might analyze a substance with common equipment and accepted methods. The results of the analysis are noncontroversial because scientists who question them can repeat the analysis themselves. Results that are similar to previous results or that confirm a theory in a new way are likely to be noncontroversial.

1.2 Review

KEY CONCEPTS

1. What is the purpose of controlled variables in an experiment?

2. Briefly describe four common types of scientific inquiries.

3. How can a widely accepted theory be replaced with a new theory?

CRITICAL THINKING

4. **Apply** What types of inquiries would be most appropriate for studying how mountains form? Explain.

5. **Synthesize** How can a scientific controversy help advance understanding of the natural world?

⬥ CHALLENGE

6. **Identify Limits** What sorts of problems might be associated with using models to represent actual features or processes?

CHAPTER INVESTIGATION

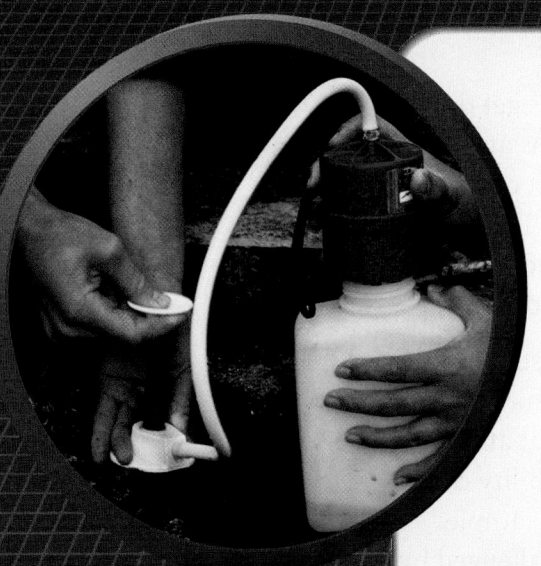

Using a Filter

OVERVIEW AND PURPOSE Using variables in a controlled experiment can help you determine many things. For example, the effectiveness of a filter in cleaning water depends on the type of filter that is used and the condition of the water. By testing different filters and gathering evidence, you can determine which filter is the most effective. Keep in mind that the independent variable is the factor that you wish to test and the dependent variable is what you measure to determine your results. In this investigation you will

- make water dirty and try to clean it
- identify the variables

▶ Problem

Write It Up

Which of two filters is more effective?

▶ Procedure

MATERIALS
- clean water
- contaminants, such as soil, vinegar, vegetable oil, food coloring, dry leaves
- 1 L container
- stirrers
- 6 clear cups
- 50 mL beaker
- masking tape and marker
- 2 funnels
- coffee filters
- rubber bands
- pieces of cloth
- coarse sand
- charcoal
- stopwatch
for Challenge:
alum
2 clear cups

1. Work with a partner. Decide which contaminants to add to your clean water. Measure and record the amount of each ingredient that you use. Mix your water thoroughly in a large container. You should make at least 1 L of dirty water.

2. Choose two of the following filters and set them up:

   - **filter paper** Line a funnel with a coffee filter.
   - **cloth** Line a funnel with a piece of cloth.
   - **sand** Use a rubber band to secure a piece of cloth around the bottom of a funnel, which will hold the sand. Choose and measure an amount of sand and pour it into the funnel.
   - **charcoal** Follow the procedure for sand but use charcoal.
   - **other** Combine any of the materials listed above to design your own filter. Record what you use to make the filter.

3 Measure 30 mL of clean water. Pour the water into one of the cups. Use the marker to mark the level on the masking tape. Repeat so that all of the cups are marked at 30 mL. Label your cups A–F.

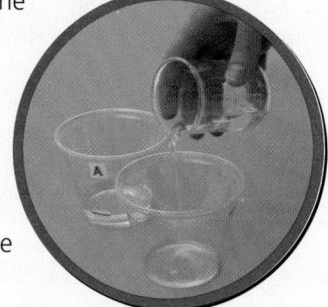

4 Pour 100 mL of clean water through one of your filters. Discard the filtered water.

5 Pour 50 mL of clean water into one of the filters so that it empties into cup A. Record the time it takes for 30 mL to run through the filter. Observe the water and the filter.

6 Repeat step 5 two times, using dirty water.

7 Repeat steps 4–6, using your second filter and cups D–F.

Observe and Analyze

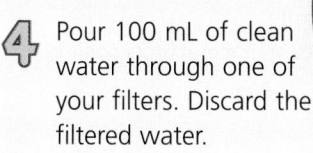

1. **RECORD** Make sure you have recorded all the measurements and observations in your science notebook.

2. **OBSERVE** Which filter removed more impurities? What characteristics are you using to describe the water? Through which filter did water flow faster?

3. **INTERPRET** What was the purpose of pouring clean water through the filter in step 5?

4. **IDENTIFY VARIABLES** List the independent variable and the two dependent variables.

Conclude

1. **COMPARE** Which filter was more effective? Present your evidence. How did the filters differ in terms of the two dependent variables?

2. **EVALUATE** Were the trials of each filter consistent? If not, explain what changed.

3. **APPLY** Suppose you wanted to design a filter to clean the water in a fish tank. How would this filter differ from the ones you tested?

INVESTIGATE Further

CHALLENGE Particles settle to the bottom of liquids over time. Alum is a material that binds very small particles together in a liquid and helps them settle. Add 1 mL of alum to 50 mL of dirty water. Set up a control sample with no alum. Stir the samples and then observe them after 10–15 minutes. How could alum help your filtering experiment?

Using a Filter
Observe and Analyze
Table 1. Filtering Test Results

Filter Material	Cup		Time	Observations
	Control	(A)		
	Trial 1	(B)		
	Trial 2	(C)		
	Control	(D)		
	Trial 1	(E)		
	Trial 2	(F)		

Scientists belong to a world community.

Sunshine State STANDARDS

SC.H.3.3.1: The student knows that science ethics demand that scientists must not knowingly subject coworkers, students, the neighborhood, or the community to health or property risks.

SC.H.3.3.2: The student knows that special care must be taken in using animals in scientific research.

SC.H.3.3.3: The student knows that in research involving human subjects, the ethics of science require that potential subjects be fully informed about the risks and benefits associated with the research and of their right to refuse to participate.

◁ BEFORE, you learned

- Scientists try to change just one variable at a time
- Different sciences use scientific methods in different ways
- New evidence can change scientific ideas

▷ NOW, you will learn

- How society affects the way science is done
- About special rules needed for experiments using animals or people
- How science affects society

THINK ABOUT

How do events in society influence science?

Many discoveries in science occur as people try to meet the needs of society, such as the needs that occur when a society is at war. Based on earlier work by a British physicist, scientists developed radar in the 1930s as a way to use radio waves to detect enemy airplanes. Although radar was first used for tracking planes, it has many other applications in today's society. Some applications, such as aircraft traffic control, benefit society. Other applications benefit science, such as the use of radar to explore underground tombs remotely or to detect radio waves from outer space.

VOCABULARY

technology p. 25
ethics p. 27
informed consent p. 29

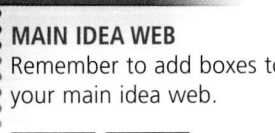

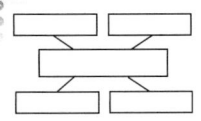

MAIN IDEA WEB
Remember to add boxes to your main idea web.

Scientists interact with society.

Scientists are part of the society they live in, and their work both affects and is affected by that society. The opportunities to do research, the topics investigated, and even some of the methods of science depend on the larger society.

Scientific research uses resources, including the time of scientists and others. A society concerned about war or national defense may put its resources into the development of weapons, defenses, and technologies that help the society survive and win. A society concerned about famine may encourage research that can lead to greater food production. When a society is hit by a disease, its resources might be used to look for a cure, help the sufferers, and prevent the disease from spreading.

Society affects scientific research.

Society, science, and technology are interconnected—each one affects the others. **Technology** is the use of science to solve a problem or need that society has. Science can lead to new discoveries that make new technologies possible. New technologies can also make new discoveries in science possible. Society can direct and control both science and technology, while new advances in science or technology can have a deep and lasting impact on society.

Science generally focuses on understanding how the world works. While applications may arise from the study of science, those applications are not the primary goal of science. Technology is the specific application of science to create a device or process. While science and technology have different purposes, many times people will pursue one in hopes of making advances in the other. When the scientists working for the British government were developing the first radar system, research showed that radio waves should be able to detect aircraft. The British military, however, were less interested in the scientific theory than in a working model of the device.

Society often encourages scientists to do research that will lead to new technologies. For instance, a large part of medical research focuses on finding ways to cure diseases and to improve people's health. A government might encourage scientists to develop computer models showing how infectious diseases spread or to develop vaccines.

A society with long-range goals might encourage scientific research even if there is no obvious goal. History has shown that many technological advances occur by accident as scientists pursue their research. Some scientific fields, such as space science and the study of dinosaurs, capture the imagination of the public and create an interest in science and technology.

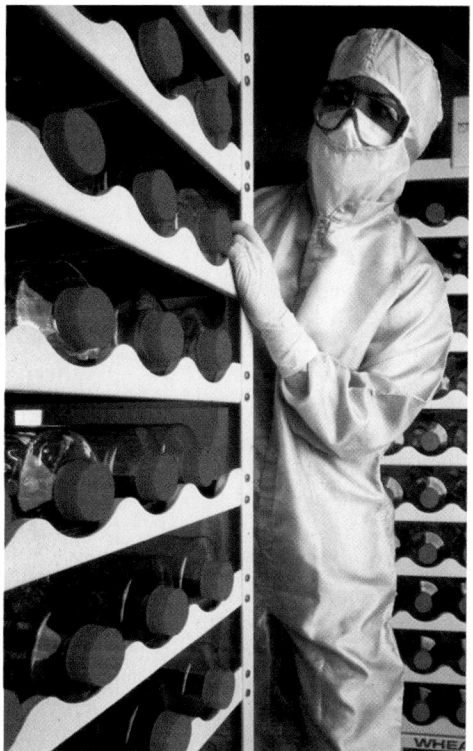

The bottles shown in this photograph contain cells used for making chickenpox vaccine. Vaccines protect societies against the spread of diseases.

 **CHECK YOUR READING** How do a society's resources and needs affect what scientists do?

The science and technology developed in one society may have effects on other societies. Useful technologies tend to spread and eventually become commonplace. The computer and the Internet are an example. When each technology was first developed, it was concentrated in just a few countries. Now both technologies are available worldwide.

Science affects society.

Just as society affects science, so science affects society. Science can affect society through advances in technology that accompany many scientific discoveries. Cars, airplanes, televisions, and computers have caused major shifts in how people do things and how they think. New communications technologies, such as cell phones and the Internet, have changed the ways in which people interact with one another.

Scientific findings can change people's behavior in other ways. As people gain more knowledge about the world around them, they can better understand the consequences of choices they make. As scientists find more evidence to support the idea that fruits and vegetables can help fight certain diseases, people are more likely to increase the amount of fruits and vegetables they eat.

Benefits, Risks, and Costs

Scientific and technological advances can greatly benefit society, as when a better, less wasteful, or safer method is found to accomplish something. However, science research and new technologies may have unintended or negative consequences. Some advances have known risks and costs. Risks are disadvantages that might occur, and costs are disadvantages that will definitely occur. Costs are not only the amounts of money spent to make things. They also include any negative effects of the technologies.

APPLY Why might companies develop hydrogen fuel cell cars even though the costs are currently greater than the benefits?

Society must compare the benefits of an advance with the known risks and costs. For example, using hydrogen fuel cells in cars would reduce the pollution from cars on the road and provide an alternative to burning fossil fuels. However, the current technology for producing the hydrogen used by the cells requires using existing fuel sources, including fossil fuels. Unless a better technology for producing hydrogen is found, the environmental costs of using hydrogen fuel cells will be greater than the benefit society would receive by switching to hydrogen fuel.

Unintended Consequences

Many scientific decisions and advances have unintended consequences. Science is an ongoing process, and new discoveries are continually being made. While scientists base their decisions on the knowledge currently available to them, things may not always turn out as they expect.

One example of unintended consequences can be seen in the story of wolves in Yellowstone National Park. In the 1920s, the wolves in the park area were considered a menace to the people and livestock that lived in the area. Wolf hunting was deliberately encouraged to protect ranchers and their livestock, and eventually no wolves remained in Yellowstone. In the 1990s, scientists reintroduced wolves, now an endangered species, into the Yellowstone area. Scientists expected that the wolves would keep down the elk population, but they were surprised to find that this was not the only consequence of reintroducing the wolves.

Since the wolves were reintroduced, there have been significant changes in the ecosystem. Cottonwood and aspen trees have started regrowing, and beavers have begun moving back into rivers. Although some scientists think milder winters may in part be responsible for these effects, many scientists see them as direct results of the wolves' being returned to the ecosystem.

Scientists think that once the wolves were gone, the elk population had no natural predators. The number of elk in Yellowstone exploded. The elk were eating most of the young tree shoots. Beavers vanished from the area as the trees they needed disappeared. Reintroducing the wolves produced changes throughout the entire food web. The effect on the ecosystem was far greater than scientists had imagined.

This wolf walks through snow in Yellowstone National Park. How did the reintroduction of wolves to the park affect the food chain there?

RESOURCE CENTER
CLASSZONE.COM

Explore another use of technology and its consequences.

Society's values shape scientific ethics.

A system of **ethics** deals with distinctions between right and wrong. Scientific ethics are rules that help scientists protect themselves, society, and the natural world. What scientists do affects both society and the world around them. Therefore, they must be careful to minimize any dangerous consequences their studies might have.

Scientists are also affected by society's values. Many societies have rules about the procedures scientists can use when working with people or animals. Societies that value the environment will put limits on the types of technologies that can be developed or used. Scientists must also be aware of how the research they do could impact society. Scientists studying a rare disease, for example, must be careful to ensure that the disease is confined to the laboratory.

Inquiries That Affect People

Scientists must not knowingly put other people at risk. Scientists must also not put people's property or their environment at risk. The environment that must be protected includes work areas such as classrooms and neighborhoods. For example, in a classroom, you must properly dispose of any hazardous chemicals you use so that they do not harm other students.

Sometimes scientists can easily see and understand the effects of their actions. Leaving a dangerous chemical that has spilled on the counter has obvious consequences—someone might get hurt. At other times, the consequences are more complex. A scientist working on a new vaccine may not be aware of all its side effects. In many cases, scientists have legal guidelines to help them decide how to handle specific situations.

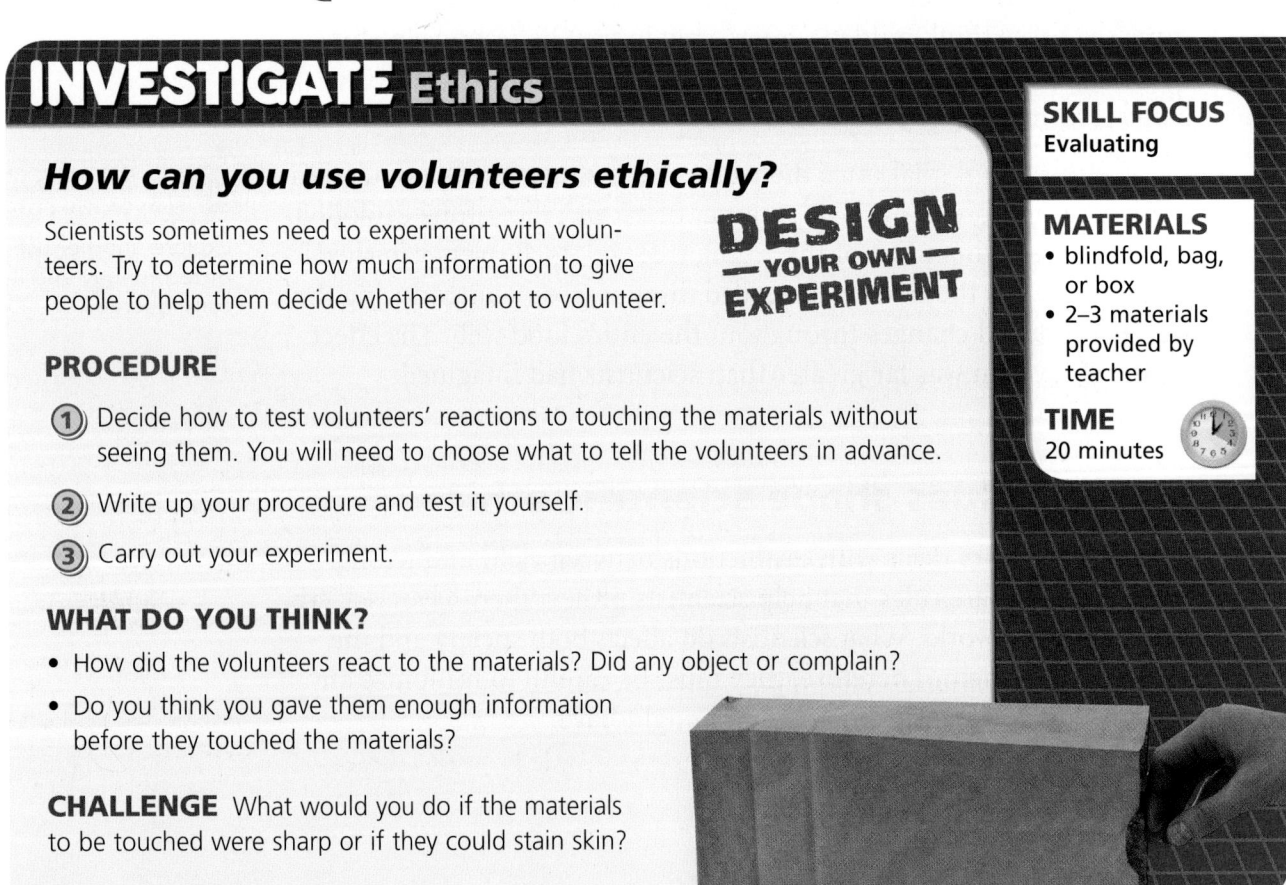

INVESTIGATE Ethics

How can you use volunteers ethically?

Scientists sometimes need to experiment with volunteers. Try to determine how much information to give people to help them decide whether or not to volunteer.

DESIGN
— YOUR OWN —
EXPERIMENT

PROCEDURE

1. Decide how to test volunteers' reactions to touching the materials without seeing them. You will need to choose what to tell the volunteers in advance.

2. Write up your procedure and test it yourself.

3. Carry out your experiment.

WHAT DO YOU THINK?

- How did the volunteers react to the materials? Did any object or complain?
- Do you think you gave them enough information before they touched the materials?

CHALLENGE What would you do if the materials to be touched were sharp or if they could stain skin?

SKILL FOCUS
Evaluating

MATERIALS
- blindfold, bag, or box
- 2–3 materials provided by teacher

TIME
20 minutes

Informed Consent

What if someone wants to test people's reactions to a situation or determine how effective a new medicine is? Some experiments have to put people at risk. Scientific ethics require that experiments involving people must be done only on people who have given their informed consent. **Informed consent** is a person's voluntary agreement to be part of an experiment after being told about the experiment's purpose and procedures as well as any risks and benefits. The benefits may include payment or other rewards that are not part of the experiment. Even after giving consent, people can leave an experiment at any time and for any reason.

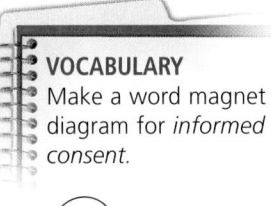

VOCABULARY
Make a word magnet diagram for *informed consent.*

 **CHECK YOUR READING** Why is it important to get informed consent before doing an experiment that involves people?

Inquiries That Affect Animals

When scientists make field studies of animals, they must take care not to harm the animals or change their environment. In most studies, scientists take care not to touch or even disturb the animals. Scientists must also frequently evaluate the methods that they use to be sure no harm is being done.

A common way of studying animals is by tagging them and then releasing them. The tags make it possible to recognize the animals later. Scientists have recently discovered that placing tags on some birds, such as penguins, can seriously interfere with the birds' life cycle. In the case of the penguins, the tags slow the penguins down when they are swimming. This causes a serious disruption in the penguins' normal life cycle. Tags have also caused injury in some animals. Animal researchers are switching to very lightweight transmitters under the skin, which does not interfere as much with the animals' movements.

These king penguins, like all penguins, cannot fly through the air. Instead, they use their flippers to "fly" through seawater.

Scientists also study animals in laboratory experiments. Sometimes the purpose is to learn more about the animals. In addition, scientists often use animals to develop medical treatments for humans. Unlike humans, animals cannot give informed consent. Scientific ethics require that animals used in experiments be treated properly and that they be harmed as little as possible. People have developed many guidelines for experiments that involve animals.

Ethics and safety can be practiced in the classroom.

This student is taking care to do laboratory work safely. Goggles help protect his eyes.

When you do laboratory experiments or science-fair experiments, it is important to be aware of ethical and safety issues. Some science investigations may involve working with equipment and procedures that can be dangerous if proper care is not taken. It is not enough to mean no harm. Scientific ethics require you to think about possible harm and prevent it.

You will find laboratory safety rules on pages R10–R11. There may be additional safety rules posted in your laboratory. Some lab instructions have reminders to use safety equipment, such as goggles. Remember that other students will be working at the same time you are, so you must take care not to endanger them or yourself. Use equipment the way it was meant to be used, so that it does not break or cause injury. Practice the scientific habit of being safe consistently, even if it takes extra time.

If you are doing an experiment that involves people, make sure they understand the experiment and agree to participate. Follow any guidelines your school or the science-fair organizers have about informed consent. If you are doing experiments involving animals or plants, make sure you understand and follow any guidelines about experimenting on living things.

Rules about the use of people and animals in science come from the values of the society in which the science is done. In the United States, there are many guidelines for experiments involving people and animals. In science fairs, there are often guidelines about using plants as well. Whenever possible, scientists should try to minimize any disruption to the environment around them.

1.3 Review

KEY CONCEPTS

1. How do a society's resources affect science?
2. Why do scientists need to get informed consent from volunteers?
3. Give an example of how scientific results can affect society.

CRITICAL THINKING

4. **Infer** Can a scientist usually pursue any research she or he wishes? Explain.
5. **Apply** Large experimental and control groups can help scientists be more sure of the results of an experiment. How might scientific ethics limit the number of animals used in an experiment?

○ CHALLENGE

6. **Predict** Suppose scientists develop a bacterium that kills crop-destroying insects. List at least three possible effects on society.

Graphing Fire Damage

Fires can be dangerous—even deadly. They can destroy homes and property. In order to protect people and property, scientists need to understand why fires start. The table below shows some of the causes of fires in Florida in 1996–2000. Fires are often started by lightning, especially during droughts. Incendiary fires are ones that people set on purpose. Other causes of fires include out-of-control campfires and discarded cigarettes. A bar graph can make these data easier to compare.

MATH TUTORIAL

Click on Math Tutorial for more help with bar graphs.

Area Burned by Fires in Florida

Year	Lightning Caused Fires (km²)	Incendiary Fires (km²)	Other Fires (km²)
1996	55	70	254
1997	131	280	181
1998	1625	155	271
1999	412	132	893
2000	295	161	397

Source: Florida Department of Agriculture and Consumer Services

Example

Create a bar graph that shows causes of fires and total areas burned in Florida during each year from 1996 to 2000.

(1) Show the years on the horizontal axis. Each year will have three bars.

(2) Show the area burned on the vertical axis. Use the height of a bar to indicate a numerical value.

(3) Use a different color for each cause of fires. Display the causes in the same order for each year.

ANSWER

Florida Fires, 1996–2000

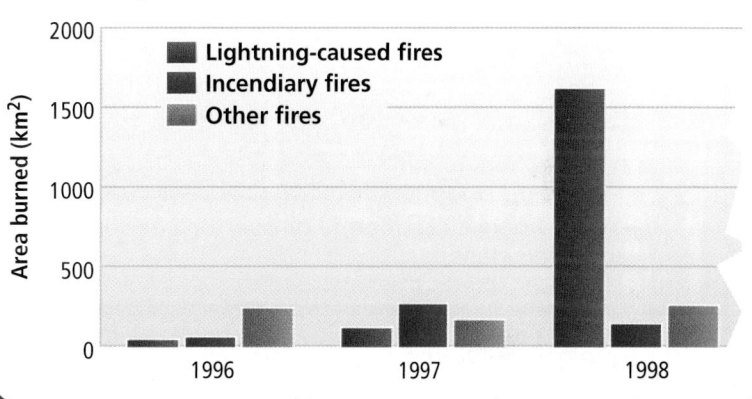

Answer the following questions.

1. Copy the bar graph and complete to show the causes of fires and the areas burned in 1996–2000.

2. In the graph, which cause of fire has the tallest bar? the shortest bar?

CHALLENGE Choose one year and make a circle graph showing the causes of fires during that year. (**Hint:** First convert the values for areas burned into percentages of total area burned in that year.)

Chapter Review

the **BIG** idea

All sciences use similar processes and tools.

FLORIDA REVIEW
CLASSZONE.COM

Content Review and
FCAT Practice

◀ KEY CONCEPTS SUMMARY

1 **Basic tools of science are universal.**

Types of Science

physics   geology   chemistry   biology

Scientific processes include asking questions, investigating,
interpreting results, and sharing information.

VOCABULARY
scientific processes p. 6
hypothesis p. 7
creative thinking p. 8
skepticism p. 9
critical thinking p. 10

2 **Scientific ideas are based on evidence.**

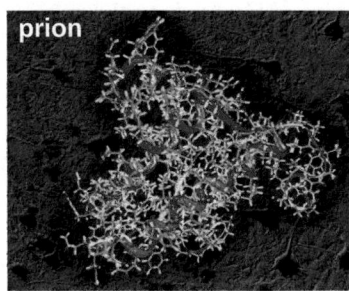
prion

Stanley Prusiner was
awarded a Nobel
prize for his research
on prions.

New evidence can modify or overturn existing
scientific ideas.

VOCABULARY
independent variable
p. 15
dependent variable
p. 15
experimental group
p. 15
control group p. 15
model p. 16
theory p. 19

3 **Scientists belong to a world community.**

SCIENCE		SOCIETY

• research
• advances in
  technology
• ethics
	affects →
	 ← *affects*
		• funding of
		  research
		• use of technology
		• values

VOCABULARY
technology p. 25
ethics p. 27
informed consent
p. 29

Reviewing Vocabulary

Copy and complete the chart below. In the middle column, briefly describe how each term is used in science. In the right-hand column, give an opposite or a nonexample of the term.

Term	Use in Science	Opposite or Nonexample
Example skepticism	requiring evidence	accepting assumptions
1. creative thinking		
2. hypothesis		
3. independent variable		
4. control group		
5. model		
6. theory		
7. technology		
8. ethics		
9. informed consent		

Reviewing Key Concepts

Multiple Choice *Choose the letter of the best answer.*

10. Which of these questions can be answered scientifically?
    a. Which of these foods tastes best?
    b. Which of these crops grows best here?
    c. How good is this piece of music?
    d. How attractive is this flower?

11. People are most likely to make new observations when they are
    a. being curious
    b. drawing conclusions
    c. using evidence
    d. evaluating results

12. Which ideas does a skeptic accept?
    a. only his or her own ideas
    b. only ideas from scientists
    c. only ideas supported by evidence
    d. only ideas published in books

13. Which situation is most likely to produce controversy about the results of an experiment?
    a. Other scientists repeat the experiment and get the same results.
    b. Scientists publish their results in a scientific journal.
    c. The results support a widely accepted theory.
    d. The results seem to be affected by bias.

14. A society is most likely to use a technology when the
    a. costs are greater than the benefits
    b. benefits are more important than the costs
    c. technology has unintended consequences
    d. technology conflicts with the society's ethics

15. Which type of scientific inquiry is best suited to determining the kinds of soil in an area?
    a. fieldwork
    b. laboratory experiment
    c. physical model
    d. computer model

Short Response *Write a short answer to each question.*

16. Why is creativity important in science?

17. Why must someone give informed consent before being a subject in an experiment?

18. What is the difference between technology and science?

This photograph shows a researcher studying laundry detergents. A cloth is stained with various substances and then washed to see how well a detergent removes the stains. Use the photograph to answer the next six questions.

19. IDENTIFY VARIABLES Suppose the researcher makes trials to compare how well different detergents remove the same type of stain. What is the dependent variable being tested?

20. PROVIDE EXAMPLES Give three examples of variables the researcher might control during trials of a particular detergent.

21. ANALYZE Why might a researcher wash a stained cloth in water without using a detergent?

22. APPLY Why might a researcher make several trials to examine the effects of a detergent?

23. IDENTIFY LIMITS How useful is a detergent that removes all stains but also damages some types of cloth?

24. INFER Why might the researcher combine different detergents during some trials?

25. APPLY Pablo reads the history of an important scientific inquiry. He finds it hard to match the steps the scientists took with common descriptions of the scientific method. What should he know about how scientists really work?

26. INFER Why is a control group used in an experiment that tests the effects of a new medication on people?

27. COMPARE AND CONTRAST Think about an idea you once held firmly but later abandoned. What changed your mind? How was the way you altered your thinking similar to or different from the way scientists change their ideas?

28. INFER Why might one scientist ask another to criticize his or her work?

29. APPLY List possible clues that a claim might be unreliable.

30. ANALYZE Why would it be difficult to design a laboratory experiment to find out how big a squirrel's territory typically is?

31. ANALYZE Makers of science textbooks update their books every few years. Why do you think this is necessary?

32. PROVIDE EXAMPLES Give three examples of ways that science and society affect one another.

the BIG idea

33. APPLY Look again at the photograph of ice on oranges on pages 2–3. Think about how you first answered the question about how growers figured out that spraying water on oranges in cold weather might help protect the fruit. How would you answer the question now?

34. SYNTHESIZE Identify similarities in approach between an inquiry into methods to protect fruit from frost damage and an inquiry into the formation of sinkholes.

Analyzing Tables

A layer of enamel protects our teeth. When this enamel is broken down, cavities and decay occur. Jonathan wants to find out which liquids break down the enamel on teeth the fastest. He decides to do an experiment using four baby teeth that he has saved.

FCAT TiP

When answering multiple choice questions, don't just pick the first answer choice you think could be right.

He sets up four glass containers. He fills each container with the same amount of liquid. He fills one with carbonated beverage, one with pure water, one with orange juice, and one with milk. He places one of his baby teeth in each of the containers. After four weeks, he removes all of the teeth and observes the changes. The following table lists his observations.

Changes to Teeth

Data	Carbonated Beverage	Pure Water	Orange Juice	Milk
Tooth Before	Surface: hard Color: white	Surface: hard Color: white	Surface: hard Color: white	Surface: hard Color: white
Tooth After Four Weeks	Surface: very soft Color: brownish-black	Surface: hard Color: white	Surface: soft Color: yellow-brown	Surface: hard Color: off-white

MULTIPLE CHOICE

1. Based on Jonathan's observations, which liquid produced the most change to the teeth?
   A. carbonated beverage   C. orange juice
   B. pure water   D. milk

2. What two types of observations did Jonathan record?
   F. mass and color
   G. size and mass
   H. color and surface strength
   I. surface strength and mass

3. Jonathan's friend Sam decides to do the same experiment, except he keeps the teeth in the liquids for ten weeks instead of four. Which of the following predictions can you make about Sam's experiment?
   A. Only the enamel on the teeth in the pure water will change color.
   B. Only the enamel on the teeth in the orange juice will change color.
   C. Only the enamel on the teeth in the carbonated beverage, orange juice, and milk will change color.
   D. Only the enamel on the teeth in pure water and milk will change color.

SHORT RESPONSE

4. What else could Jonathan measure to help understand his results?

5. Suppose that Jonathan thinks that the more sugar found in a liquid the faster the tooth will decay. What else will Jonathan need to determine to see if he is correct?

EXTENDED RESPONSE

6. Jonathan decides to test his liquids to determine their acidity. The acidity levels are shown below.

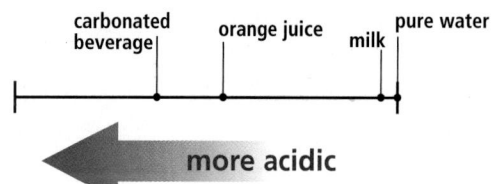

Part A: Write a hypothesis for the relationship between the liquid's acidity and tooth decay.

Part B: Describe one way you could test this hypothesis.

UNIT 1

Earth's Waters

water cycle

ocean

HABITAT

hydrosphere

Contents Overview

Frontiers in Science
Exploring the Water Planet   38

Florida Connection
Saving Coral   42

Timelines in Science
Exploring the Ocean   146

Chapter 2 The Water Planet   46
Chapter 3 Freshwater Resources   78
Chapter 4 Ocean Systems   112
Chapter 5 Ocean Environments   150

Exploring the Water Planet

Technology allows scientists to see far below the ocean's surface, making exploration easier than ever before.

SCIENTIFIC AMERICAN FRONTIERS

View the video segment "Into the Deep" to learn how scientists explore mid-ocean ridges and deep-sea vents.

A crab encounters a research submersible.

Earth's Least-Known Region

What is the least-explored region on Earth? You might guess it's a small area where few things live, perhaps in a vast desert or in high mountains. But this region covers more than 50 percent of the planet and contains almost 98 percent of its living space. It is the deep sea, the part of the ocean sunlight cannot reach, where no plants grow. The deep sea was once thought to be of little interest. Now researchers are studying the organisms living in the deep sea and mapping the resources of the sea floor. Other parts of the ocean are getting more attention, too. For example, researchers are studying how surface water carries nutrients to new areas and how the ocean affects Earth's climate.

As people explore the ocean more thoroughly, they frequently discover new organisms. Many of these organisms are being found in the deep sea. Some, though, are being found in water that is only a few meters deep. One octopus that lives in shallow tropical water was first described in 1998. This brown octopus avoids being eaten by predators by mimicking the appearances and colors of poisonous organisms. For example, the octopus slips six of its arms and much of its body into a hole on the sea floor. Then it waves its other two arms in opposite directions, which makes it look like a banded sea snake. The octopus's colors change to yellow and black, matching the snake's bands. Another organism the octopus mimics is a multicolored lionfish with its poisonous fins spread out.

An octopus (above) changes its colors and hides most of its body and all but two arms to mimic a poisonous sea snake (right).

These scale worms, first described in 1988, live only around deep-sea vents and are thought to feed on the larger tubeworms.

Exploring Deep-Sea Vents

Deep-sea vents support astonishing life forms. These organisms depend on materials dissolved in scalding hot vent water, not on sunlight, for their ultimate source of energy. The superheated vent water contains many dissolved minerals. The minerals become solid as the vent water mixes with cold ocean water. Earth's richest deposits of minerals like copper, silver, and gold may be around some of these vents. To study the minerals that lie beneath thousands of meters of water, researchers use remotely operated devices to collect data and samples.

Exploring the Ocean and Climate

The ocean moves large amounts of heat energy between areas of Earth, affecting the atmosphere and climate. Consider that even though some parts of Alaska and Great Britain are equally close to the North Pole, Great Britain is warmer. Air over the Atlantic Ocean gains heat energy from a warm ocean current, and winds carry this warmth toward Great Britain. In addition to moving across the surface, water also mixes vertically in the ocean. The ocean contains many layers of water, with the warmest generally at the top. But the middle layers of the ocean may now be heating up quickly. Researchers are working to understand how the mixing of water in the ocean affects Earth's atmosphere and climate.

View the "Into the Deep" segment of your *Scientific American Frontiers* video to learn how scientists are exploring the deep sea.

IN THIS SCENE FROM THE VIDEO ▶ a deep-sea vent spews out superheated water that is rich in dissolved minerals.

THE DEEPEST DIVES Robert Ballard has made dozens of expeditions in *Alvin,* a three-person submarine. This small vessel can dive deep below the surface to underwater mountain ranges called mid-ocean ridges. Ballard's photographs helped prove that the mountains in a mid-ocean ridge are volcanoes.

While exploring a valley that runs along the top of a mid-ocean ridge, Ballard discovered deep-sea vents. Water that flows out of the vents is very hot and rich in minerals. Ballard was also one of the first scientists to see the giant clams, tubeworms, and other animals that live around the vents. Such life forms are unusual because they depend on energy from within Earth instead of energy from the Sun.

Exploring Ocean Nutrients

Some water masses move in circular or spiral patterns, as you can see in the photograph below. These spinning water masses are called eddies. Water in eddies mixes slowly with the surrounding water. An eddy that contains nutrient-rich water can drift great distances, mixing with nutrient-poor water over a long time, sometimes years. The added nutrients allow populations of tiny plantlike organisms to grow quickly. These organisms are the base of the ocean food chain, and almost all other ocean organisms depend on them. Researchers are studying how changes in the sizes and numbers of eddies affect ocean organisms. Nutrient-rich eddies may be important to fish, such as salmon, that many people eat.

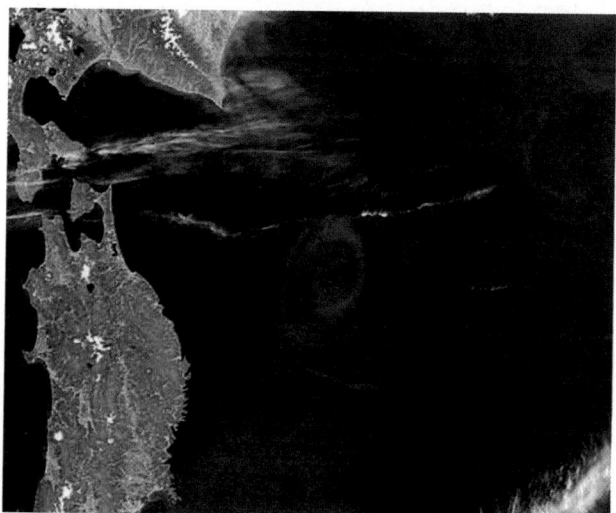

Eddies are mixing seawater from the coast of Japan with water farther from shore.

UNANSWERED Questions

Scientists who study the ocean know that much of it is yet to be explored and that many questions remain.

- How many, and what types of, ocean organisms will be discovered in the next decades?

- How do changes in ocean surface temperatures affect weather?

- What is the best way to maintain populations of fish that people depend on for food?

UNIT PROJECTS

As you study this unit, work alone or with a group on one of the projects listed below.

Track a Drop of Water

Suppose you could follow a drop of surface water as it journeys from your hometown to the ocean.

- Find out which rivers and lakes the drop would travel through, and which ocean it would join.

- Present your findings. You might make a travelogue, a map, or both.

Life in the Water

Investigate the different life forms that live in the water in your area.

- Collect water samples from different sources, such as indoor taps, fountains, puddles, marshes, lakes, and streams.

- Examine a drop from each sample under a microscope. Sketch any living organisms you see.

- Write a lab report to present your findings about the water samples.

Ocean News Report

Imagine that you are part of a news group assigned to report on major discoveries made about the world's oceans over the past 25 years.

- Research the most important or unusual facts uncovered about the oceans. Note what technology was used to gather the data.

- Prepare a special TV or Web-site report about your investigation. Where possible, include photographs or illustrations.

CAREER CENTER
CLASSZONE.COM

Learn more about careers in oceanography.

Saving Coral

🔲 Sunshine State Standards

In "Saving Coral" you'll read how organisms called polyps grow, die, and decay, leaving skeletons that form coral reefs. **(SC.D.1.3.2)**

Slight changes in a reef ecosystem can have long-term effects on population size. **(SC.G.2.3.3)**

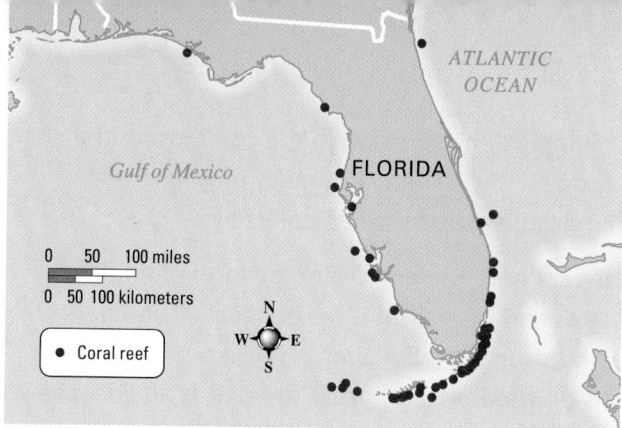

The Coral Below

Which U.S. state has the only living barrier reefs in North America? If you said Florida, you're correct. Approximately 6000 coral reefs lie off the coast of Florida. Most of the reefs are located about 10 kilometers (6 mi) offshore and parallel to the Florida Keys, islands that are themselves the remains of coral reefs that are now above water.

A coral reef is a marine, or ocean-water, ecosystem with biological diversity. Florida's coral reefs contain about 110 species of coral and more than 500 species of tropical fish. Hard corals, soft corals, sponges, fish, crustaceans, worms, snails, sea turtles, sharks, rays, algae, and many other organisms live in the reef community. A reef provides shelter, a hiding place, and food for its inhabitants.

Formation of Coral Coral reefs are the largest structures on Earth created by living creatures. Who are these creatures and how do they do it? Millions of tiny animals called polyps (PAHL-ihps) form reefs. These soft-bodied creatures use calcium carbonate from seawater to build protective skeletons. Thousands of these skeletons connected together become a coral formation. A reef is made up of corals that form side by side and on top of one another.

Orange cup coral polyps extend their tentacles to feed on plankton.

Coral formations may look like domes, branching trees, or tiny organ pipes. Healthy living coral is usually brightly colored in shades of red, orange, yellow, and purple. The color comes from single-celled algae that live in polyp tissues and provide the animal with food for growth.

The water off the coast of Florida is ideal for coral reefs. For reefs to form, the water can be no deeper than 70 meters (230 ft) and the temperature no lower than 18°C (63°F). The Florida Current, made up of warm Gulf Stream water, plays an important role in keeping reefs healthy. It brings clean, clear, warm water to the area. Clear water is important because large amounts of sand can cover coral and smother it.

An Undersea Treasure Why are reefs important to Florida? One benefit is protection of the shore. The underwater structures help protect the mainland by absorbing the impact of violent waves from storms, including hurricanes.

Florida's reefs are also a tourist attraction, and the economy of the Florida Keys depends on tourism. More than three million scuba divers, snorkelers, fishers, boaters, and sightseers are drawn to the beauty of Florida's coral reefs each year. The reefs also attract scientists and students from around the world to study the reefs' living and nonliving parts. Commercial fishing is the second most important economic factor in the keys. Reefs provide shelter, food, and breeding grounds for species that are popular food items, such as lobsters, shrimp, grouper, and snapper.

Natural and Human Threats to Reefs

Florida's coral reefs have thrived for more than 5000 years, but in the last 30 years much damage has been done to them. A healthy reef has 30 to 40 percent coral cover—that is, the amount of living coral growing on its surface. In 2002 the Florida Marine Research Institute recorded only 7.4 percent coral cover on the Florida reefs. Scientists and environmentalists report a number of causes for rapidly shrinking numbers of living coral polyps.

Overfishing If too many fish that eat algae are taken from the ocean by the fishing industry, algae build up on reefs. Too many algae can smother polyps and prevent young corals from attaching to the reef. In some areas, commercial fishers use dynamite and chemicals to stun fish. These methods can destroy the structure of a reef.

Pollution Older sewer and septic systems allow human waste to seep into the water. Currents may carry the wastes to the reefs. Chemicals in fertilizers, pesticides, and wastes stimulate the growth of algae that compete for space with coral polyps. The algae reduce the oxygen concentration in the water. Solid waste such as plastic-foam cups, aluminum cans, plastic bags, fishing line, six-pack connectors, and cigarette butts kill or entangle animals, including coral polyps. Engine exhaust and oil from boat engines can keep sunlight from reaching below the surface of the water to the coral.

Changes in Water Temperature Changing sea-surface temperatures affect both the polyps and the algae that provide them with nutrients. A rise of only 1°C above the normal monthly average temperature can result in the coral losing their food supply. When corals die, they lose their color in a process called bleaching.

Divers and Boaters Diving or snorkeling near reefs can be a thrilling experience. But divers who touch coral or break off pieces, or stand or sit on the reefs, do great harm. It is against the law to collect, harvest, or sell Florida coral.

Boaters should be very careful when near reefs. Running into a reef with a boat can destroy corals that are hundreds of years old. Dropping an anchor into a reef can do even more damage.

Predators Several types of fish—such as parrotfish and butterfly fish—eat coral, skeletons and all. The red boring sponge attacks corals by burrowing inside and starting to grow. Other predators include sea snails and slugs.

One species of brown seaweed can suffocate coral. In some areas, the seaweed covers 30 to 70 percent of the reefs. The thick weeds can smother and kill sponges and coral. The weed spreads by producing chemicals that keep fish from grazing on it.

SPOTLIGHT ON Life-Saving Coral

Some scientists have studied corals to determine how they have adapted to survive long-term ultraviolet (UV) radiation. UV radiation from the Sun can penetrate shallow reef waters. Polyps emit a clear substance that helps protect them from this radiation. Scientists in Australia have synthesized the protective chemicals in this substance. They hope to market it as a type of coral sunscreen for humans. They believe that the new sunscreen could replace the UVB blockers now widely used. Because the chemicals can be synthesized, or produced by humans in a laboratory, no harm is done to coral reefs.

Coral is also being recommended as graft material, a substitute for bone in reconstructive surgery. Doctors can use coral to repair a bone fracture or fill in an area where a bone tumor has been removed. Usually these bone grafts are taken from the patients themselves. Now, specially treated coral is often effective as bone graft material because of its

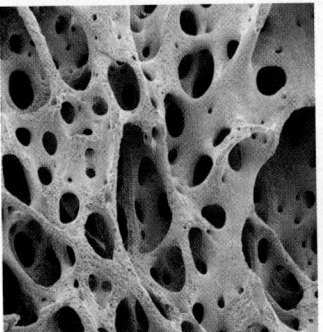
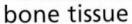
bone tissue

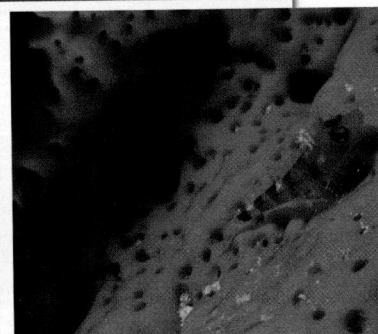
coral

porous structure. The interconnected holes allow living bone to send new blood vessels and bone tissue into the coral openings. This creates a strong bond of new bone. Only a small amount of coral is needed to grow new bone, so this procedure does not threaten the health of the world's coral reefs. One coral with a mass of 68–90 kilograms (weighing 150–200 lb) provides enough material for hundreds of grafts.

Natural Events Hurricanes and other natural events can harm coral reefs overnight. High winds cause pounding surf, which can in turn cause extensive damage to reefs. Winds also carry dust across the ocean from Africa. A soil fungus in the dust can kill sea fans, part of a coral reef community.

For the most part, reefs have adapted to cope with natural events. But frequent hurricanes cause damage that may be permanent.

Land-Based Activities Shore development, channel dredging, landfilling, seawall construction, farming, and mining can place stress on the ecological balance of a reef. Such activities churn up silt from the bottom of the ocean. The silt turns the water a milky color and interferes with photosynthesis in sea grasses and algae inside coral polyps. Heavy loads of sediment may bury corals, killing them or preventing their growth.

Florida has a specialty license plate that says "Protect Our Reefs." The $25 additional fee for this plate goes to reef restoration efforts.

Protecting Reefs

Local, regional, and global efforts are underway to reverse reef damage. Here are some things you can do to help ensure the continued health of Florida's coral reefs:

• Volunteer for a reef cleanup if you live near a reef or will be vacationing near one.

• When you visit a reef, follow all posted guidelines and regulations.

• If you're diving near a reef, don't touch it. Take photographs instead. Stay off the ocean floor because stirred-up sediment can settle on coral and smother it.

• Don't put garbage or other wastes in the water or leave trash on the beach.

• If you're boating over a reef, never drop anchor there. Tie your boat to a buoy instead.

ASKING Questions

• What questions do you have about how corals form?

• What questions do you have about Florida's coral reefs?

RESOURCE CENTER

Visit **ClassZone.com** for more information on coral reefs.

WRITING ABOUT SCIENCE

Use facts from this article to create a brochure that encourages tourists to visit Florida's coral reefs. Include the history of the reefs, why they are worth visiting, and tips for how to enjoy the reefs without harming them.

Writing Tips

Plan, draft, and revise your writing using the tips below.

• Skim the article to review facts about how reefs are formed.

• Use examples and details to show why Florida's reefs are a remarkable underwater ecosystem.

• If possible, use a word-processing or page-layout computer program to make your brochure appealing.

• Revise your brochure to make it as persuasive as possible.

CHAPTER

The Water Planet

the BIG idea

Water moves through Earth's atmosphere, oceans, and land in a cycle.

In what forms does water exist on Earth?

Key Concepts

SECTION
Water continually cycles.
Learn about how water on Earth moves in a world-wide system.

SECTION
Fresh water flows and freezes on Earth.
Learn about fresh water in rivers, lakes, and ice.

SECTION
Fresh water flows underground.
Learn about water under the land surface and how it is used.

FCAT Practice

Prepare and practice for the FCAT
• Section Reviews, pp. 54, 62, 71
• Chapter Review, pp. 74–76
• FCAT Practice, p. 77

CLASSZONE.COM
• Florida Review: Content Review and FCAT Practice

Where Can You See Water?

Look in your home or school for examples of frozen and liquid water. Go outside and look for the same, plus evidence of water in the air. Record your observations.

Observe and Think
What did you find inside? outside? Did you see evidence of water in the air?

Does the Ice Float?

Place an ice cube in a glass of tap water. Does it float at all? Now add two spoonfuls of salt to the water and stir it in. What happens to the ice cube?

Observe and Think What might the salt do to the water that affects the way the ice cube floats?

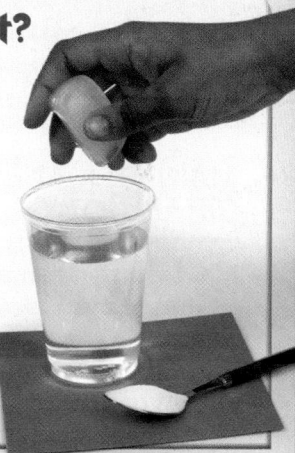

Internet Activity: Water

Go to **ClassZone.com** to learn what different forms of water exist on Earth and how water is a part of Earth's systems.

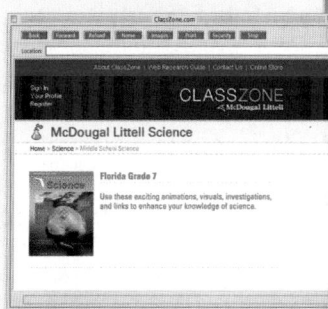

Observe and Think What are the different ways that water exists on Earth?

scilinks.org

Water Cycle **Code: MDL018**

CHAPTER 2

Getting Ready to Learn

◀ CONCEPT REVIEW

- Events such as flooding that take place on Earth change Earth's features.
- Water is essential for life.
- Water built up on Earth's surface over time.

◀ VOCABULARY REVIEW

See Glossary for definitions.

atmosphere

glacier

system

FLORIDA REVIEW
CLASSZONE.COM

Content Review and FCAT Practice

▶ TAKING NOTES

MAIN IDEA AND DETAIL NOTES

Make a two-column chart. Write the main ideas, such as those in the blue headings, in the column on the left. Write details about each of those main ideas in the column on the right.

VOCABULARY STRATEGY

Write each new vocabulary term in the center of a **four-square** diagram. Write notes in the squares around the term. Include a definition, some characteristics, and some examples. If possible, write some things that are not examples.

See the Note-Taking Handbook on pages R45–R51.

SCIENCE NOTEBOOK

MAIN IDEAS	DETAIL NOTES
1. Water is a unique substance.	1. Only substance in three forms at normal temperatures 1. Can be solid, liquid, gas 1. As liquid, can fit any container

Definition	Characteristics
Water that is not salty	Little or no taste, color, or smell

FRESH WATER

Examples	Nonexamples
Liquid in rivers, lakes	Liquid in oceans

Water continually cycles.

Sunshine State STANDARDS

SC.D.1.3.3: The student knows how conditions that exist in one system influence the conditions that exist in other systems.

SC.G.1.3.4: The student knows that the interactions of organisms with each other and with the non-living parts of their environments result in the flow of energy and the cycling of matter throughout the system.

SC.G.1.3.5: The student knows that life is maintained by a continuous input of energy from the sun and by the recycling of the atoms that make up the molecules of living organisms.

BEFORE, you learned

- The force of running water causes erosion
- Water can be solid

NOW, you will learn

- What makes water important
- How much of Earth's water is salt water
- How water moves throughout Earth and its atmosphere

EXPLORE Water Vapor

Where does the water come from?

PROCEDURE

(1) Put the ice in the glass and fill it with water.

(2) Observe what happens to the outside of the glass.

MATERIALS
- clear glass
- ice
- water

WHAT DO YOU THINK?
- Where did the water on the outside of the glass come from?
- What does this activity tell you about the air surrounding you? What conclusion can you draw?

FCAT VOCABULARY
water cycle p. 52
evaporation p. 53
condensation p. 53

VOCABULARY
fresh water p. 51
salt water p. 51
precipitation p. 53

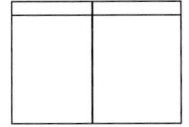

MAIN IDEA AND DETAILS
Make a two-column chart to start organizing information about water.

Water is a unique substance.

Seen from outer space, Earth glistens like a beautiful blue and white marble. Welcome to the "water planet," the only planet in our solar system with a surface covered by a vast amount of liquid water. Because of water, a truly amazing substance, life can exist on Earth.

What is so amazing about water? In the temperature ranges we have on Earth, it exists commonly as a solid, a liquid, and a gas. At a low temperature, water freezes. It becomes a solid, which is ice. At a higher temperature, it flows easily in liquid form. Liquid water can become a gas, especially at higher temperatures. If you have ever noticed how something wet dries out in the hot sunlight, you have observed the effect of liquid water changing into a gas. The gas form is the invisible water vapor in our atmosphere.

Liquid water can fit any container. It can hold its shape in a raindrop, then merge with other drops to flow down a hill or slow down and sit for centuries in a lake.

Water covers most of Earth.

Earth looks bluish from space because most of Earth's surface is ocean. If you look at a globe or a world map, you will see the names of four oceans—Atlantic, Pacific, Indian, and Arctic. If you look more closely or trace the four named oceans with your finger, you will see that they are connected to one another. Together they form one huge ocean. Any part of this ocean is called the sea.

The global ocean covers 71 percent, or almost three-quarters, of Earth's surface. Most of the ocean is in the Southern Hemisphere. The ocean is, on average, 3.8 kilometers (2.4 mi) deep. Although most of the water covering Earth is ocean, water also covers some land areas, as rivers, lakes, and ice.

 **CHECK YOUR READING** Where is most of Earth's water?

Water-to-Land Ratio

Almost three-quarters of Earth's surface is covered by water.

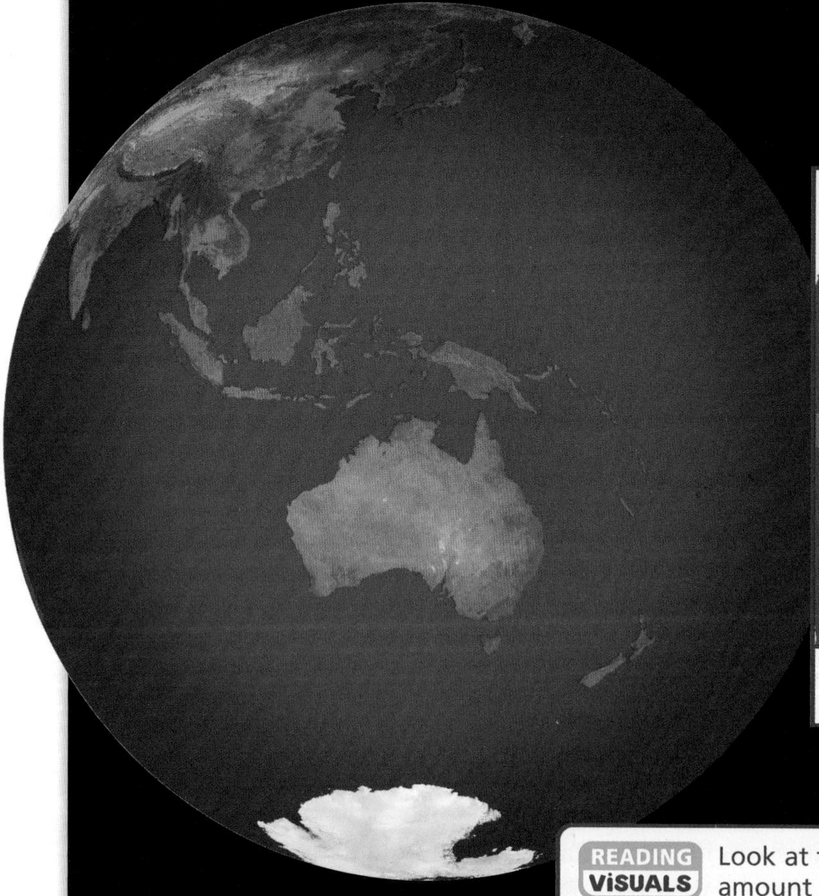

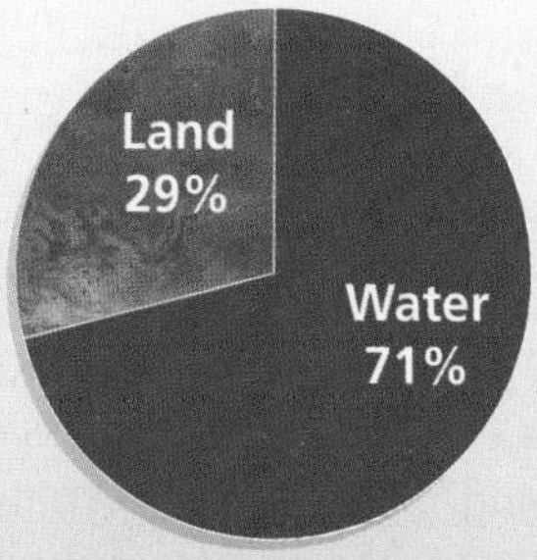

Land 29%

Water 71%

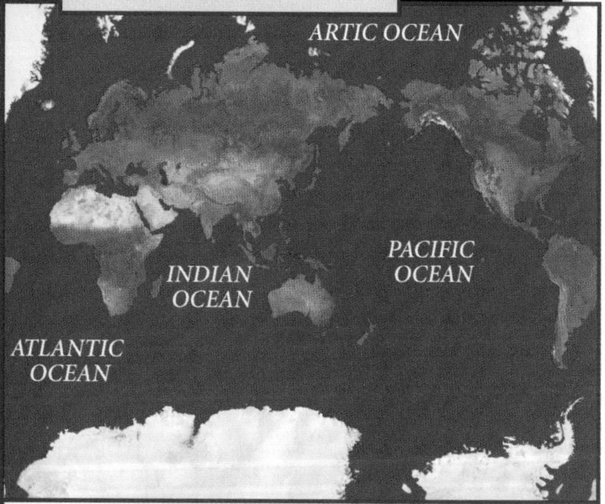

ARTIC OCEAN

PACIFIC OCEAN

INDIAN OCEAN

ATLANTIC OCEAN

A flat map can make the percentage of land on Earth appear greater than it is.

READING VISUALS Look at the globe and the map. Where is the amount of land most exaggerated on the map?

Water and Life

Without water, nothing would live on Earth. Living things need water to function. Your own body is two-thirds water. In your body, your blood—which is mostly water—carries nutrients that give you energy and flushes wastes away. Many forms of life live in water. Oceans, lakes, and rivers are home to fish, mammals, plants, and other organisms. Even a single drop of water may contain tiny forms of life.

Fresh Water and Salt Water

When you hear the word *water,* you might imagine a cool drink that quenches your thirst. The water that you drink and depend on for survival is fresh water. **Fresh water** is water that is not salty and has little or no taste, color, or smell. Most rivers and lakes are fresh water.

The water in the ocean is salt water. **Salt water** is water that contains dissolved salts and other minerals. Human beings and most other land animals cannot survive by drinking salt water, although many other forms of life can live in salt water.

VOCABULARY
Remember to write the terms *fresh water* and *salt water* in four-square diagrams in your notebook.

You may be surprised to learn that even though fresh water is important for life, fresh water is actually scarce on Earth. Because most of Earth's water is in the ocean, most of the water on Earth is salt water. The illustration below compares the amounts of fresh water and salt water on Earth. Almost all—about 97 percent—of Earth's water is salt water in the ocean. Only about 3 percent of Earth's water, at any given time, is fresh water.

⚠ **CHECK YOUR READING** What is the difference between fresh water and salt water?

Salt Water vs. Fresh Water

Most water on Earth is salt water.

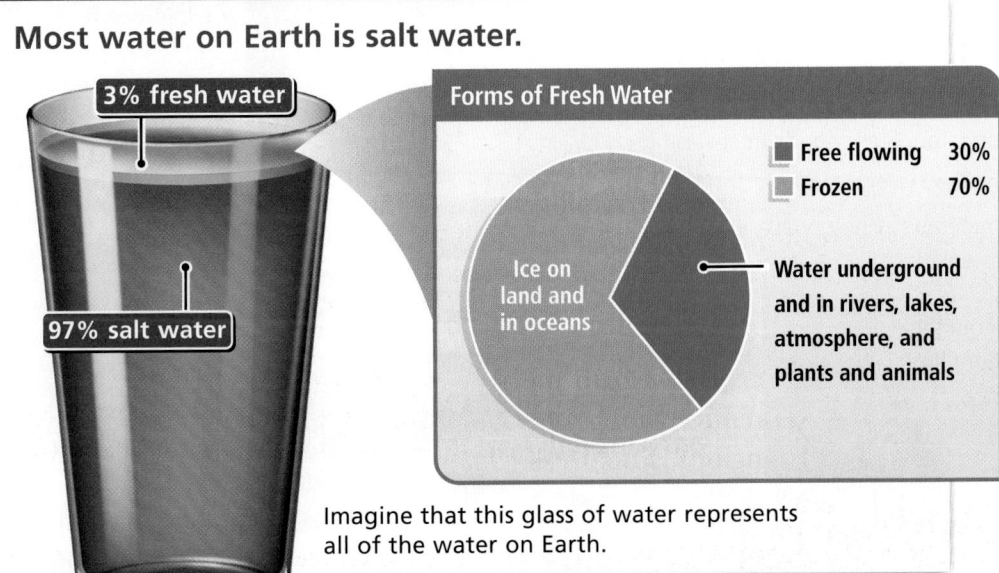

3% fresh water

97% salt water

Forms of Fresh Water

◼ Free flowing 30%
◼ Frozen 70%

Ice on land and in oceans

Water underground and in rivers, lakes, atmosphere, and plants and animals

Imagine that this glass of water represents all of the water on Earth.

Water moves in a worldwide cycle.

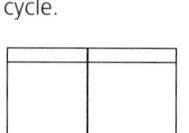

MAIN IDEA AND DETAILS
Record in your notes this main idea and important details about the water cycle.

Water continually moves and changes form. Water from clouds falls over the oceans and on land. Water flows in rivers and collects in lakes and under the ground. Water can be a solid in the form of ice, or it can be an invisible vapor in the atmosphere.

The Water Cycle

Water's movement on Earth is a cycle, or continually repeating process. The **water cycle** is the continuous movement of water through the environment of Earth. In the water cycle, water is constantly changing form, from a liquid on land, to a vapor in the atmosphere, and again to a liquid that falls to the surface. The flow of water on land and underground is also part of the water cycle. As water moves in the water cycle, the total amount of water in Earth's system does not change very much. The water cycle involves three major processes: evaporation, condensation, and precipitation.

INVESTIGATE The Water Cycle

How does water cycle through an environment?

DESIGN —YOUR OWN—

PROCEDURE

1. Construct an environment in a jar with a lid. You can use plants, soil, water, and containers.

2. Find the mass of your closed jar after you construct it.

3. Draw a detailed, colored picture of your jar.

4. Let your jar sit for several days.

5. Find the mass of your jar again, and draw another picture of it.

WHAT DO YOU THINK?

- How did the jar's appearance change over several days?
- How did its mass change?
- What can you conclude about how water cycles through an environment?

CHALLENGE How could you change your environment so that the jar's appearance would change at a faster rate?

SKILL FOCUS
Modeling

MATERIALS
- jar with lid
- soil
- rocks or pebbles
- sand
- smaller containers
- water
- small plants
- triple-beam balance

TIME
30 minutes (for construction; 20 minutes for analysis)

The Water Cycle

Water on Earth moves in a continual cycle.

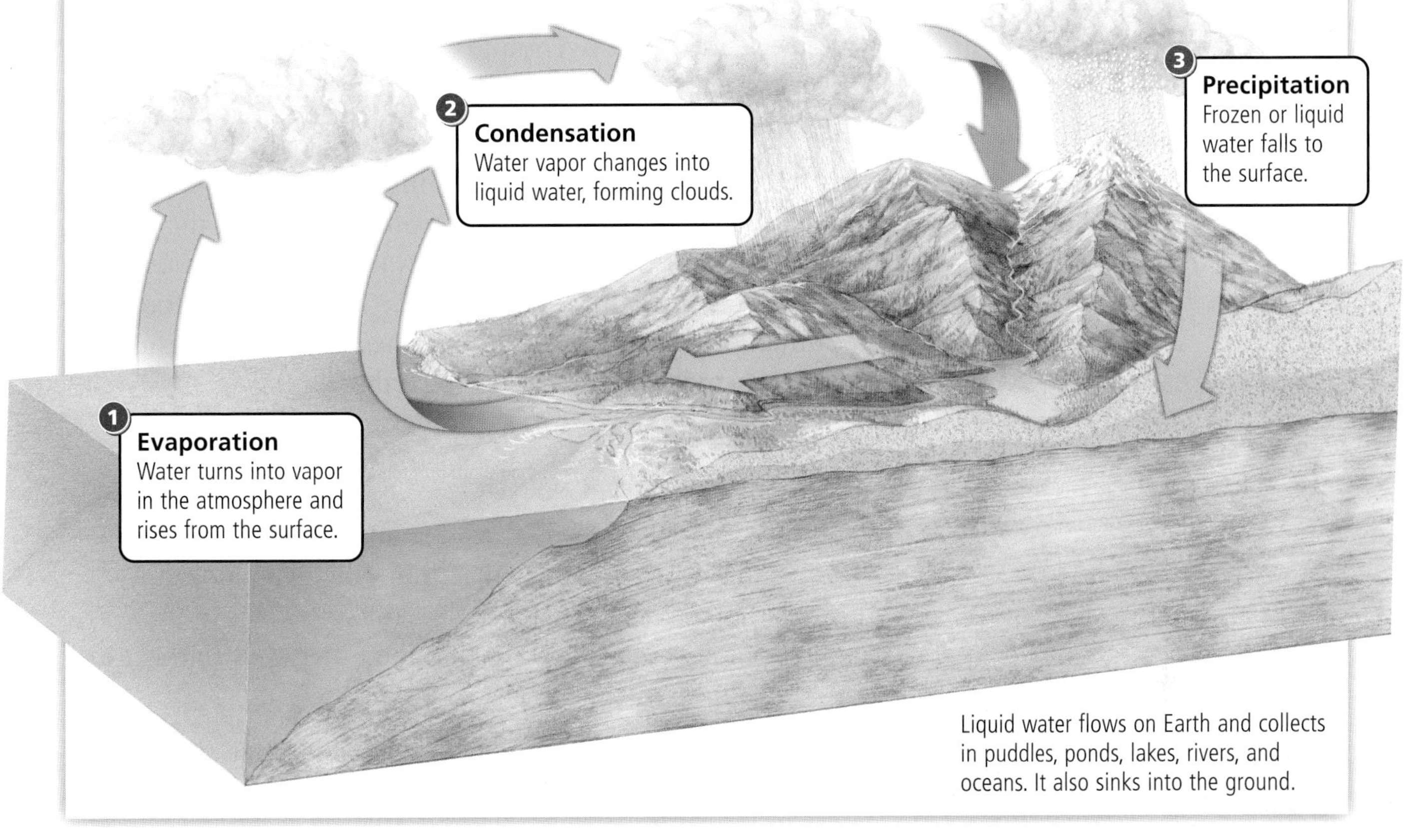

2 Condensation
Water vapor changes into liquid water, forming clouds.

3 Precipitation
Frozen or liquid water falls to the surface.

1 Evaporation
Water turns into vapor in the atmosphere and rises from the surface.

Liquid water flows on Earth and collects in puddles, ponds, lakes, rivers, and oceans. It also sinks into the ground.

① The process in which water changes from liquid to vapor is called **evaporation.** Heat energy from the Sun warms up the surface of the ocean or another body of water. Some of the liquid water evaporates, becoming invisible water vapor, a gas.

② The process in which water vapor in the atmosphere becomes liquid is called **condensation.** Condensation occurs as air cools. Because cold air can have less water vapor than warm air, some of the vapor condenses, or turns into droplets of liquid water. These droplets form clouds. At high altitudes clouds are made of ice crystals. Unlike water vapor, clouds are visible evidence of water in the atmosphere.

③ Water that falls from clouds is **precipitation.** Inside a cloud, water droplets bump together and merge into larger droplets. They finally become heavy enough to fall as precipitation—such as rain or sleet. The water from precipitation sinks into the soil or flows into streams and rivers in the process called runoff. The force of gravity pulls the flowing water downward and, in most cases, eventually to the ocean.

VISUALIZATION
CLASSZONE.COM

See how water moves through Earth's system in the water cycle.

 **CHECK YOUR READING** Why does water vapor in air condense into liquid droplets?

Most of the water that evaporates on Earth—85 percent of it—evaporates from the ocean. (About 75 percent of this condenses into cloud droplets and falls right back into the ocean.) The remaining 15 percent of evaporating water comes from such sources as damp ground, lakes, wet sidewalks, rivers, and sprinklers. Plants are also part of the water cycle. They pull up water from the ground and then release much of it into the air through their leaves.

Even though the water that evaporates into the atmosphere comes from both the salty ocean and from fresh water on land, all the precipitation that falls back to the surface is fresh water. When salt water evaporates, the salt is left behind. Through the water cycle the ocean water that human beings cannot drink becomes a source of fresh water for human beings and other life on Earth.

INDIA

The Impact of the Water Cycle

The action of the water cycle is easy to spot. When it rains or snows, you can see precipitation in action. When you look at a flowing stream, you see the water cycle returning water to the sea. When a stream dries up, you know that the water cycle in the area has slowed down for a while.

Wet weather can fill reservoirs with drinking water and pour needed water on crops. Wet weather can also bring too much rain. For example, during the wet season in India, winds blow moist air inland from the Indian Ocean. Tremendous rains fall over the land for months. The rain is usually welcome after a long and hot dry season. However, these seasonal rains frequently cause devastating floods, covering acres and acres of land with water.

Flooding usually occurs during India's annual rainy season.

2.1 Review

KEY CONCEPTS

1. Name three things about water that make it unique or important.

2. How much of Earth's water is fresh water?

3. Explain the three processes that make up the water cycle.

CRITICAL THINKING

4. **Apply** How can a drop of salt water once have been a drop of fresh water?

5. **Compare and Contrast** What are two differences between salt water and fresh water?

● CHALLENGE

6. **Infer** In 1996, the *Galileo* space probe sent back photographs that showed ice on the surface of one of the moons of Jupiter. Scientists suspected there was water under the ice. Why did this discovery excite some people who thought there was a chance of finding life on that moon?

Does Mars Have a Water Cycle?

Mars once had water flowing on its surface. Today, it is a frozen desert. Most astronomers think that there has been no liquid water on Mars for the past 3.9 billion years. Others, though, think that Mars has had flowing water recently—in the last 10 million years. They suggest that Mars may have a multimillion-year water cycle. According to their hypothesis, occasional volcanic activity melts ice, releasing floods of water. After the water evaporates, condenses, and falls as rain, it becomes ice again. And if Mars does have a water cycle, it could have something else that goes with water on Earth: life.

▶ Issues

For Mars to have a water cycle, it would need several features.

- a source of energy for melting ice into water
- conditions for water to evaporate
- conditions for water vapor to condense

▶ Observations

Astronomers have observed several facts about Mars.

- Mars has water ice at its north and south poles.
- Mars has had very large volcanoes in the past, although it seems to have no active volcanoes today.
- Mars takes about 687 Earth days to orbit the Sun.
- Mars is the fourth planet from the Sun.
- Mars has an atmosphere that is 100 times thinner than the atmosphere of Earth.
- Mars has an average surface air temperature of -55°C (-67°F).
- Mars has features that look like ones shaped by water on Earth: ocean shorelines, river valleys, and gullies.
- Mars has many visible craters—unlike Earth, where most craters get washed away, filled with water, or covered up.

▶ Determine the Relevance of Each Observation

On Your Own Decide whether each observation is relevant in determining whether Mars has a water cycle.

As a Group Discuss the relevance of each observation to the idea of a water cycle on Mars. List other information that might be helpful.

CHALLENGE Research information about Mars. Identify facts that support or oppose the idea of a Martian water cycle.

Mars has features that appear to be like those created by water on Earth.

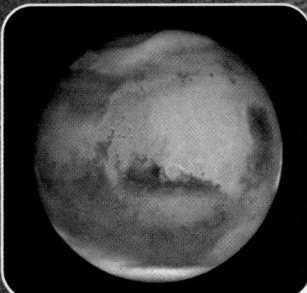

Icecaps cover the poles of Mars.

RESOURCE CENTER

Learn more about evidence that Mars may or may not have a water cycle.

2.2 Fresh water flows and freezes on Earth.

BEFORE, you learned

- Water covers most of Earth's surface
- Water continually cycles
- Water falls to Earth's surface as precipitation

NOW, you will learn

- How fresh water flows and collects on land
- How surface water forms lakes
- How frozen water exists on Earth

VOCABULARY

divide p. 57
drainage basin p. 57
turnover p. 59
eutrophication p. 60
iceberg p. 62

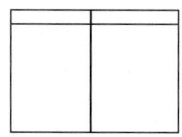

MAIN IDEA AND DETAILS
Record in your notebook this main idea and details about it.

EXPLORE Water Collection

How does water flow and collect?

PROCEDURE

1. With the open egg carton on a level tray, pour water slowly into the center of the carton until the cups are three-quarters full.

2. Empty the carton. Tip it slightly, as shown in the photograph, and pour water into the higher end. Stop pouring when the carton is about to overflow.

WHAT DO YOU THINK?

- How did the water flow when you poured it into the level carton? into the tilted carton? Where did it collect in the carton? Where did it not collect?
- What might your observations tell you about how water flows when it falls on land?

MATERIALS
- plastic-foam egg carton
- tray or pan
- plastic bottle
- water

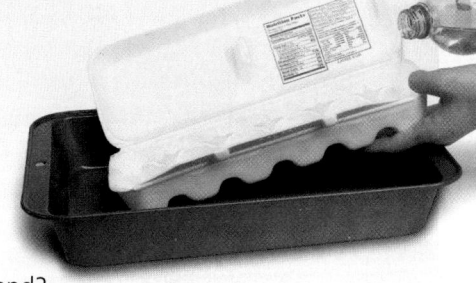

Water flows and collects on Earth's surface.

Imagine you are in a raft on a river, speeding through whitewater rapids. Your raft splashes around boulders, crashing its way downriver. Then the raft reaches a lake. You glide across the surface, slowing down. At the end of the lake, your raft enters a river again and floats down it.

In your raft you are following the path a water drop might take on its way to the ocean. All over the planet, the force of gravity pulls water downhill. Fresh water flows downhill in a series of streams and rivers, collects in lakes and ponds, and eventually flows into the ocean. All of this water flows between high points called divides, in areas called drainage basins.

Divides and drainage basins affect the way water flows on land. A **divide** is a ridge, or continuous line of high land, from which water flows in different directions. If you were on a skateboard and began at the top of a hill, you would ride in one general direction down the hillside. On the other side of the hill, you would ride downhill in a completely different direction. The top of the hill is like a divide. A divide can be a continuous ridge of high mountains. On flatter ground, a divide can simply be the line of highest ground.

A **drainage basin,** or watershed, is an area into which all of the water on one side of a divide flows. If you pour water into the basin of your bathroom sink, it will flow down the side from high points to low, and eventually down the drain, which is at the lowest point. In mountainous areas, hills and mountains form the sides of basins, and valleys form the low points. Flatter regions also have basins. The basins may not be obvious in these regions, but they still drain water.

When it rains in a drainage basin, the water forms streams and rivers or sinks into the ground. Every stream, river, and lake is in a basin. In most places, the water eventually flows to the sea. In a bowl-shaped basin, the water may collect at the bottom of the basin or evaporate.

Divides and Drainage Basins

Divides separate drainage basins.

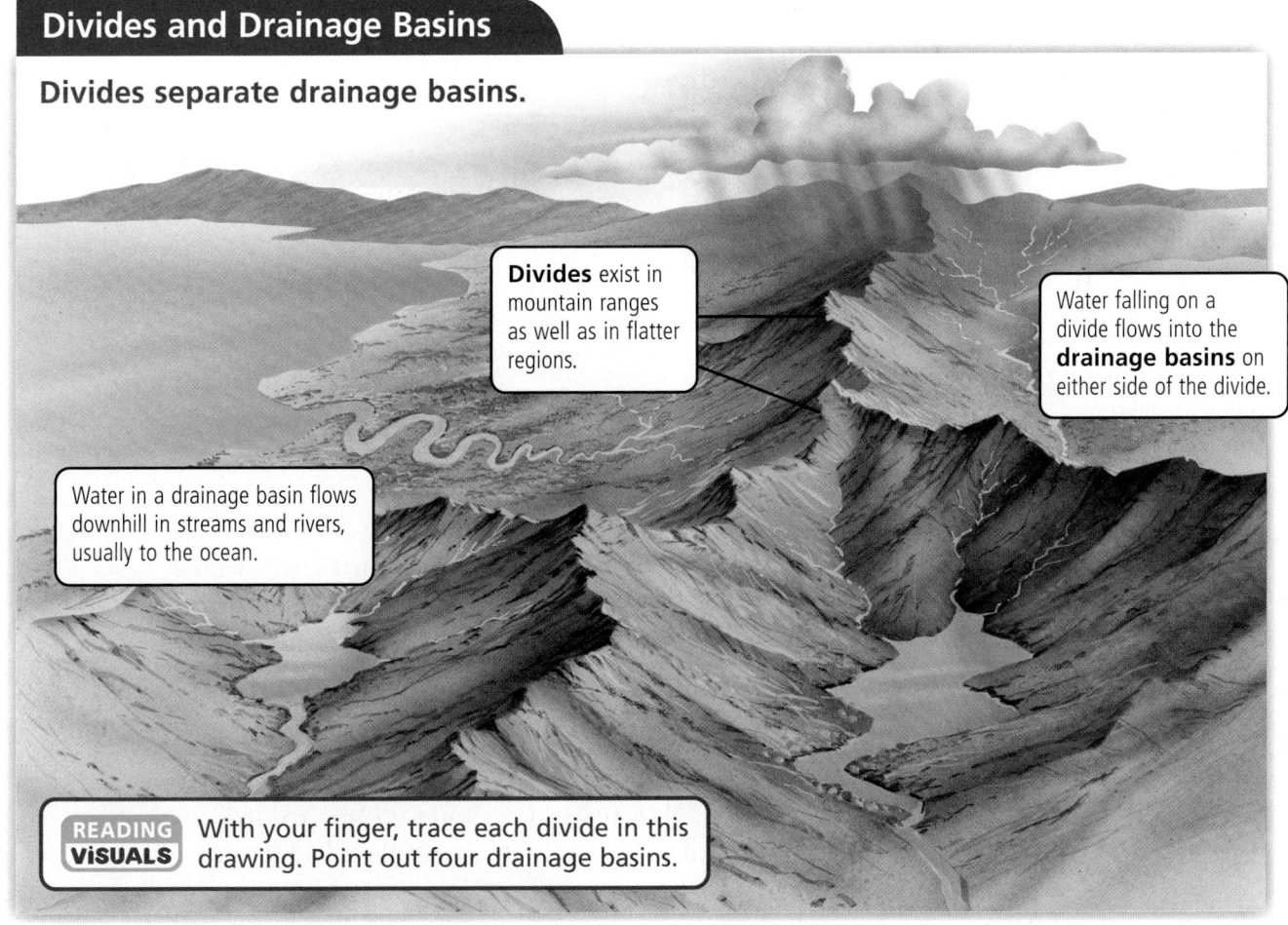

Divides exist in mountain ranges as well as in flatter regions.

Water falling on a divide flows into the **drainage basins** on either side of the divide.

Water in a drainage basin flows downhill in streams and rivers, usually to the ocean.

READING VISUALS With your finger, trace each divide in this drawing. Point out four drainage basins.

Surface water collects in ponds and lakes.

Lakes and ponds form where water naturally collects in low parts of land. Some lakes were formed during the last ice age. For example, the Great Lakes were formed when huge sheets of ice scraped out a series of giant depressions. Other lakes, such as Crater Lake in Oregon, were formed when water collected inside the craters of inactive volcanoes.

Water can fill a lake in several ways. Where the land surface dips below the level of underground water, the low land area fills with water. Rainfall and other precipitation contribute water to all lakes. Water may flow through a lake from a stream or river. Water may also flow away from a lake through a stream running downhill from the lake. Many lakes maintain fairly steady levels because of the balance of flow in and flow out.

The main difference between a pond and a lake is in their overall size. A pond is smaller and shallower than a lake, and there are many plants, such as water lilies and cattails, rooted in its muddy bottom. A lake may have water so deep that sunlight can't reach the bottom. In the deeper part of the lake, plants can't take root, so they grow only around the lake's edges. Ponds and lakes provide homes for many kinds of fish, insects, and other wildlife. They also provide resting places for migrating birds.

CHECK YOUR READING Name two differences between a pond and a lake.

Chicago, Illinois, at the southwest corner of Lake Michigan, is the largest city on a Great Lake. Note that the lake is so wide that from Chicago you cannot see Michigan on the other side.

Lake Michigan

Chicago

Lake Michigan is the third largest of the five Great Lakes, which border eight states and Canada's Ontario province.

Lake Turnover

The water in a lake is not as still as it might appear. The changing temperatures of the seasons affect the water and cause it to move within the lake in a yearly cycle.

In a place with cold winters, ice may form on a lake, so that the wind cannot ruffle the surface. The water temperature in the lake remains steady, and the water stops moving. The water just below the surface ice is near freezing, so the fish move to the bottom, where the water is a bit warmer.

In many lakes the water temperatures at different levels vary as the seasons change. In the spring and summer, sunlight can warm a layer of water at the top of a lake. Because the colder water beneath the top layer is denser than the warmer water above it, the water levels do not mix easily. The warm water contains more oxygen, so fish may be more plentiful in the upper part of the lake.

READING TiP

Cold water is denser than (has more mass than the same amount of) warm water.

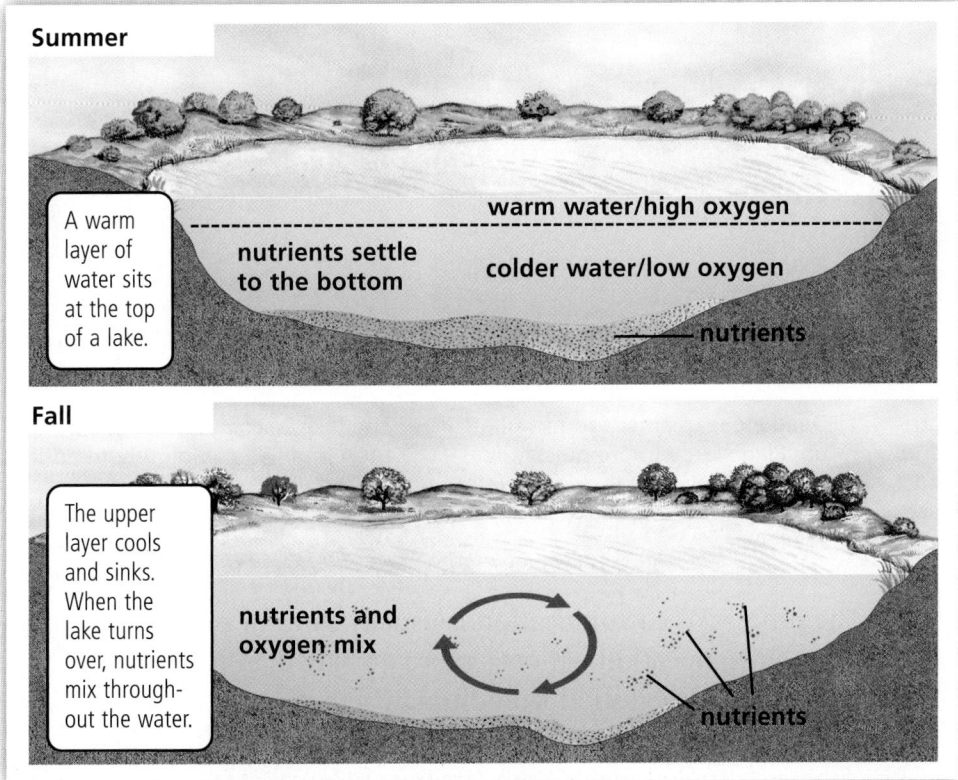

Summer

A warm layer of water sits at the top of a lake.

warm water/high oxygen

nutrients settle to the bottom

colder water/low oxygen

nutrients

Fall

The upper layer cools and sinks. When the lake turns over, nutrients mix throughout the water.

nutrients and oxygen mix

nutrients

In the fall, days cool and the surface water cools too. The upper layer becomes heavy and sinks, so that the lake water "turns over." Nutrients from minerals and from dead plants and organisms are stirred up from the bottom. These nutrients are used by many life forms in the lake. The rising and sinking of cold and warm water layers in a lake is called **turnover.** Turnover occurs twice each year as the seasons change.

CHECK YOUR READING What happens to surface water when the weather cools in the fall?

Eutrophication

A lake does not remain a lake forever. Through natural processes that take thousands of years, most lakes eventually are filled in and become meadows—fields covered with grass and other plants. A lake can become filled in as sediments, including the remains of dead fish, plants, and other organisms, pile up on the bottom.

READING TiP

Eutrophication comes from the Greek word *eutrophos,* meaning "well-nourished."

The activity of life in a lake is affected by nutrients. Nutrients are the foods and chemicals that support living things. When the amounts of such nutrients as phosphorus and nitrogen in a lake increase, algae and other organisms in the water grow more rapidly. An increase of nutrients in a lake or pond is called **eutrophication** (yoo-TRAHF-ih-KAY-shuhn). As eutrophication occurs, algae form a thick scum on the water. The amount of oxygen in the water decreases, until fish and other organisms that require oxygen cannot survive. The illustration below shows what happens to a lake when nutrient levels increase.

When the amounts of such nutrients as nitrogen and phosphorus increase, algae grow faster and form a scum layer at the surface.

Dead algae, plants, and fish pile up. Plants grow more quickly, leaving more debris as they die. Water evaporates, and the lake becomes shallower.

The lake becomes a soggy marsh, then finally a completely filled-in meadow.

The process of eutrophication is usually slow. In some cases, however, eutrophication happens more quickly than it normally would because of pollution from human activities. Nitrogen in fertilizers used on farms and gardens may be washed into lakes. Phosphates from laundry detergents may be present in wastewater that reaches lakes. The extra nutrients cause algae and plants in lakes to grow faster and more thickly than they normally would grow. Eutrophication from pollution causes clear lakes to become clogged with algae and plants.

How does human activity contribute to eutrophication?

Most fresh water on Earth is frozen.

If you want fresh water, take a trip to Greenland or the South Pole. Two-thirds of the world's fresh water is locked up in the ice covering land near the poles.

The ice sheet that covers Antarctica is almost one and a half times as big as the United States and is in places more than a kilometer thick. Ice on Earth's surface contains more than 24 million cubic kilometers of fresh water. Just how much water is that? Imagine that you have three glasses of lemonade. If you take one sip from one of the glasses of lemonade, you have drunk the water in all the lakes and rivers on Earth. The rest of the glass represents liquid ground water. The other two glasses of lemonade represent all the frozen water on the planet.

Ice on Land

In Earth's coldest regions—near both poles and in high mountains—more snow falls each year than melts. This snow builds up to form glaciers. A glacier is a large mass of ice and snow that moves over land. There are two types of glaciers. The ice sheets of Antarctica and Greenland are called continental glaciers because they cover huge landmasses. The other type of glacier is a valley glacier, which builds up in high areas and moves slowly down between mountains.

RESOURCE CENTER
CLASSZONE.COM

Find out more about frozen fresh water.

INVESTIGATE Icebergs

Why do icebergs float?
PROCEDURE

1. Find the masses of the empty graduated cylinder and the ice cube.

2. Add 200 mL of water to the cylinder. Find the volume of the ice cube by measuring how much water it displaces. Make sure the water is extremely cold to prevent the ice cube from melting. Use the point of a paper clip to completely submerge the ice.

3. Remove the water and let the ice melt in the cylinder.

4. Calculate the density (Density = mass/Volume) of the ice cube. Now find the mass and volume of the liquid water from the melted ice and calculate its density.

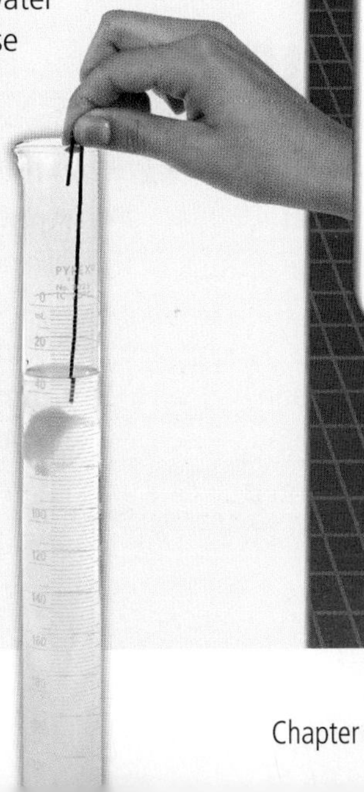

WHAT DO YOU THINK?
• What was the density of the ice cube? the water?
• Why do icebergs float?

CHALLENGE Float a cork in water. How does its behavior compare with that of floating ice?

SKILL FOCUS
Calculating

MATERIALS
• balance
• ice cube
• water
• 250 mL graduated cylinder
• paper clip
• calculator
for Challenge:
• cork

TIME
30 minutes

Icebergs

An **iceberg** is a mass of ice floating in the ocean. An iceberg starts out as part of a glacier. In places such as Antarctica and Greenland, glaciers form ice shelves that extend out over the ocean. When a large chunk of a shelf breaks off and floats away, it becomes an iceberg.

Thousands of icebergs break off from ice sheets each year. In the Northern Hemisphere, ocean currents push icebergs south into the warmer Atlantic Ocean. It may take an iceberg two to three years to float down to the area off the coast of Canada. In that region, it breaks apart and melts in the sea. A North Atlantic iceberg sank the *Titanic*.

Icebergs are masses of frozen fresh water floating in the salt water of the world's oceans.

How big is an iceberg? One iceberg that recently broke off an Antarctic ice shelf was the size of Connecticut. Off the coast of eastern Canada, some icebergs tower 46 meters (150 ft) above the surface of the ocean. This is impressive, because most of a floating iceberg is below the surface. Only about one-eighth of the total weight and volume of the iceberg can be seen above the surface of the sea. When people say "It's only the tip of the iceberg," they mean that a lot of something is unrevealed.

The water in an iceberg may have been frozen for 15,000 years. However, the ice in the center, if melted, can be clean, clear drinking water. And an iceberg can hold a lot of water. An iceberg as big as a city block holds enough drinking water to supply a city of 50,000 people for about ten years. Unfortunately, no one knows how to cheaply move icebergs to cities in order to use the frozen water.

  **CHECK YOUR READING**   How much of an iceberg is below the surface?

2.2 Review

KEY CONCEPTS

1. Why is it important that fresh water flows over Earth's surface?

2. Explain the relationship between a drainage basin and a divide.

3. Where and in what form is most of the fresh water on Earth?

CRITICAL THINKING

4. **Apply** If you were going on a fishing trip in a northern state, why would you want to know about lake turnover?

5. **Connect** Explain the connection between living things in a lake and eutrophication.

CHALLENGE

6. **Synthesize** How is the water in icebergs involved in the water cycle on Earth?

MATH TUTORIAL

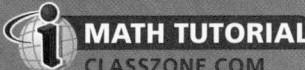

CLASSZONE.COM

Click on Math Tutorial for help multiplying fractions and whole numbers.

How Big Is an Iceberg?

In salt water, the part of an iceberg that is visible above water is only 1/8 of the whole iceberg. The remaining 7/8 of the iceberg is hidden under the water's surface. You can use fractions to estimate how much ice is underwater.

Example

An iceberg is made of 1000 cubic meters of ice. How much of the ice is underwater?

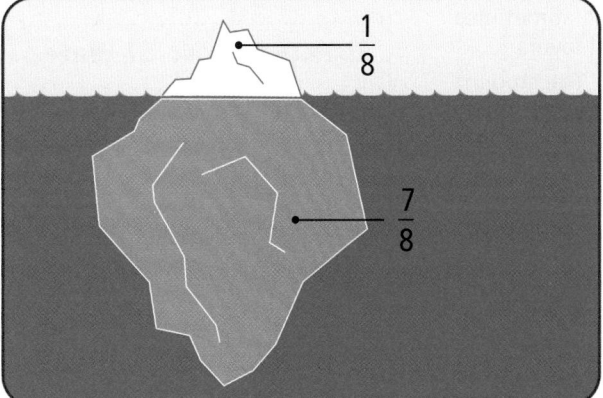

Solution

(1) Write a word equation.

$$\text{Volume of ice underwater} = \text{volume of iceberg} \cdot \text{fraction underwater}$$

(2) Substitute.

$$\text{Volume of ice underwater} = 1000 \text{ m}^3 \cdot \frac{7}{8}$$

(3) Multiply the numerator by the total volume.

$$= \frac{1000 \text{ m}^3 \cdot 7}{8}$$

(4) Calculate and simplify.

$$= \frac{7000 \text{ m}^3}{8} = 875 \text{ m}^3$$

ANSWER About 875 cubic meters of ice are underwater.

Calculate how much ice is underwater.

1. The iceberg is made of 1600 cubic meters of ice.

2. The iceberg is made of 1800 cubic meters of ice.

3. The iceberg is made of 12,000 cubic meters of ice.

CHALLENGE About 500 cubic meters of an iceberg is visible above the water. Estimate the total volume of the iceberg.

2.3 Fresh water flows underground.

Sunshine State STANDARDS

SC.D.1.3.1: The student knows that mechanical and chemical activities shape and reshape the Earth's land surface by eroding rock and soil in some areas and depositing them in other areas, sometimes in seasonal layers.

SC.D.2.3.1: The student understands that quality of life is relevant to personal experience.

BEFORE, you learned

- Water flows in river systems on Earth's surface
- Water collects in ponds and lakes on Earth's surface

NOW, you will learn

- How water collects and flows underground
- How underground water reaches the surface in springs and by wells

VOCABULARY

groundwater p. 64
permeable p. 64
impermeable p. 65
water table p. 65
aquifer p. 66
spring p. 68
artesian well p. 68

EXPLORE Flow of Water

What does water flow through?

PROCEDURE

① Fill the cup with water.

② Have a partner hold the filter open over a sink, bucket, or pan while you pour water into it.

WHAT DO YOU THINK?

- Why did the water remain in the cup before you poured it?
- What route did the water take to pass through the filter?

CHALLENGE What other materials might hold water? allow water to flow through?

MATERIALS
- water
- cup
- paper coffee filter
- bucket, dishpan, or sink

Water fills underground spaces.

After a rainstorm, water does not stay on the ground for long. What happens to this water? It flows along Earth's surface into a river or reservoir, evaporates, or sinks into the soil. Plants use some of the water that sinks into the ground, and the rest of it sinks deeper into Earth. Water held underground is called **groundwater.** The ground under your school may seem too solid to hold water, but it is likely that groundwater sits or moves under the surface.

To understand how groundwater collects, you need to know the difference between permeable and impermeable materials. The ground beneath your feet is made of both permeable and impermeable materials.

A **permeable** substance is a substance that liquids can flow through. Liquids flow through a coffee filter because the filter is permeable. Soil,

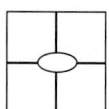

VOCABULARY
In your notebook make four-square diagrams for the terms *groundwater* and *permeable.*

sand, and gravel are permeable because there are spaces between the particles. Water flows into and through these spaces. The bigger the particles, the more easily water can flow. Gravel and larger rocks have large spaces between them, so water flows quickly through. Sandy soil also has many pores, or spaces. Some rocks, such as sandstone, are permeable although the spaces in these rocks are extremely small.

An **impermeable** substance is a substance that liquids cannot flow through. A drinking glass holds orange juice because the material of the glass is impermeable. Rocks such as granite are impermeable. Unless granite has cracks, it has no spaces for water to go through. Many impermeable materials are hard, but not all of them. Clay is soft, but it is nearly impermeable. Water can get between its particles, but the overlapping of the particles stops the water from flowing through.

How does groundwater collect? Gravity causes rainwater to sink into the soil. If it rains heavily, all the spaces in the soil fill with water. Eventually the water reaches impermeable rock. There it is held in place or forced to flow in a different direction.

Even when the soil on Earth's surface is dry, huge amounts of groundwater may be stored below. The top of the region that is saturated, or completely filled with water, is called the **water table.** The saturated region below the water table is called the saturation zone.

READING TiP

The prefix *im* in *impermeable* means "not."

CHECK YOUR READING What prevents groundwater from sinking farther down?

Groundwater

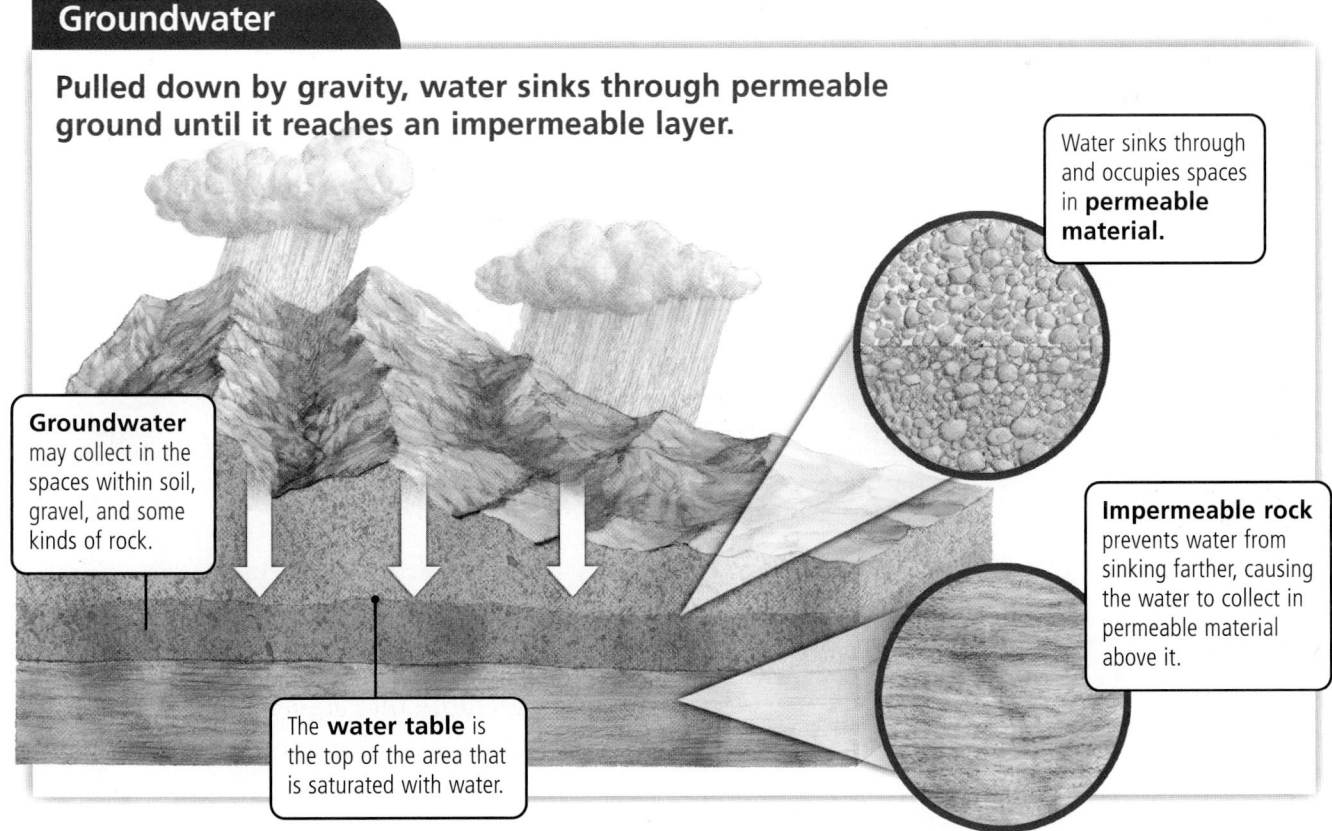

Pulled down by gravity, water sinks through permeable ground until it reaches an impermeable layer.

Water sinks through and occupies spaces in **permeable material.**

Groundwater may collect in the spaces within soil, gravel, and some kinds of rock.

Impermeable rock prevents water from sinking farther, causing the water to collect in permeable material above it.

The **water table** is the top of the area that is saturated with water.

Aquifers

An **aquifer** is an underground layer of permeable rock or sediment that contains water. Some aquifers lie deep under layers of impermeable rock. Other aquifers lie just beneath the topsoil.

SIMULATION
CLASSZONE.COM

Explore how groundwater fills in aquifers.

Aquifers can be found all over the world. They lie under deserts as well as wet regions. As the map below shows, they are found in many areas of the United States. An aquifer might be a bed of sand or gravel only a few meters thick. Or it might be an enormous layer of sandstone, several hundred meters thick, holding water in countless pore spaces. The Ogallala Aquifer is the largest aquifer in North America. It covers 450,000 square kilometers (176,000 mi^2), from South Dakota to Texas.

For an aquifer to form, three things are needed:

- A layer of permeable material holds the water. Groundwater is stored in the pore spaces of gravel, sand, or rock.
- A neighboring area of impermeable rock keeps the water from draining away. Sometimes impermeable rock lies both above and below an aquifer.
- A source of water replenishes or refills the aquifer. Like any body of water, an aquifer can be emptied.

You know that fresh water on land flows toward the ocean. Water that is underground acts like slow-motion streams, rivers, and lakes. Underground water moves slowly. The water is under pressure

Aquifers

Water collects underground in layers of permeable material.

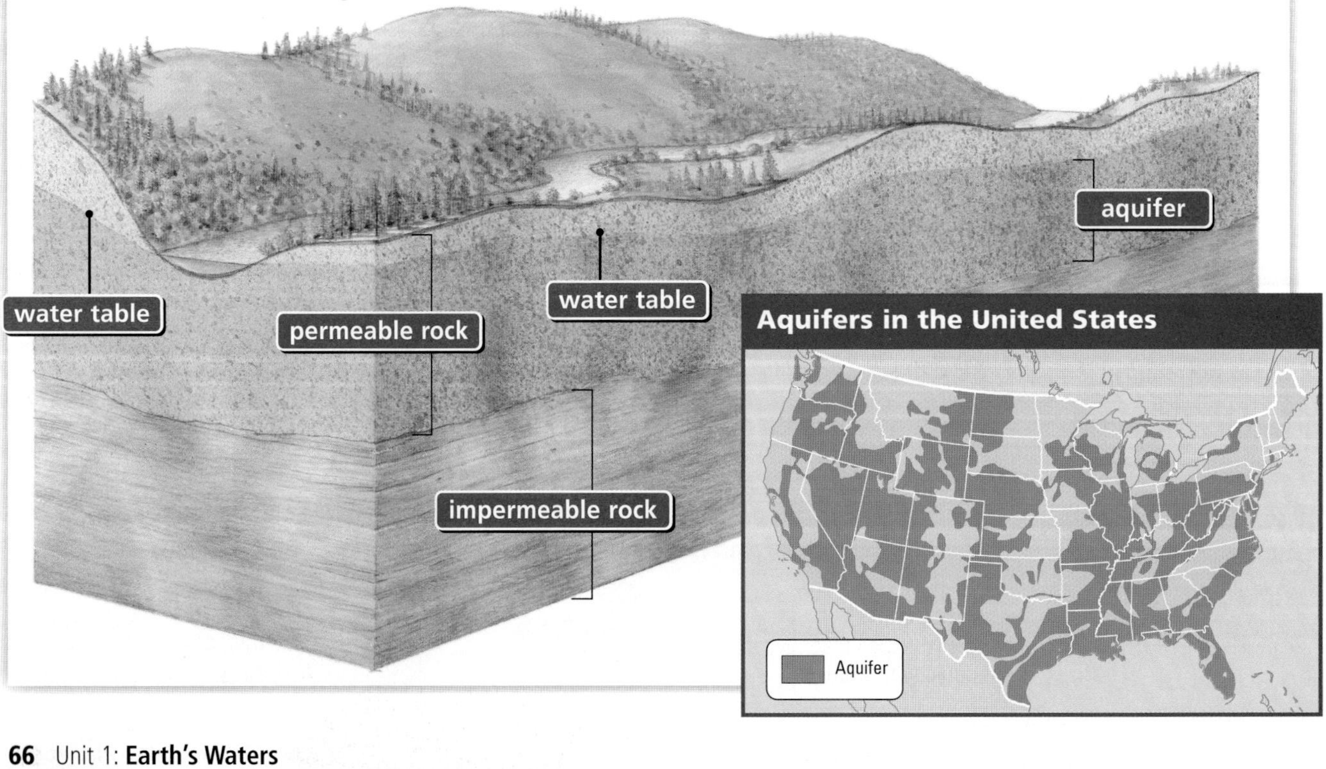

aquifer

water table

permeable rock

water table

impermeable rock

Aquifers in the United States

Aquifer

from all sides, and it must go around endless tiny corners and passageways in rock. Unlike the water in an aboveground river, groundwater moves sideways, down, and even up. In some areas, groundwater is pushed upward so that it flows from a hillside. Because it moves so slowly, much of the water in an aquifer may have been there for thousands of years.

The Importance of Aquifers

When water sinks into land, the ground acts like a giant filter. Stones and sand in the ground can filter out bacteria and other living organisms. This ground filter also removes some harmful chemicals and minerals. The filtering process can make groundwater clear and clean and ready to drink. If it is not polluted, groundwater may not need expensive treatment. It is one of our most valuable natural resources.

Many big cities collect water from rivers and store it in reservoirs above the ground. However, about one-fifth of the people in the United States get their fresh water from underground. Most people who live in rural areas pump groundwater from wells. In many desert regions people depend on sources of underground water.

INVESTIGATE Aquifer Filtration

How can the ground filter water?

PROCEDURE

1. Cap the top of the bottle. Invert it and add to it a layer of gravel, then a layer of sand, then a layer of soil.

2. Slowly pour water onto the soil until a water table becomes visible in the sand beneath it.

3. Add the pollutants pepper, cocoa, and food coloring to the bottle top. Slowly unscrew the cap so that water trickles into the bucket.

4. Observe the water that filtered through.

5. Pour more water onto the soil and let water trickle out.

WHAT DO YOU THINK?

- Which pollutants were filtered out before reaching the "aquifer"? Which ones reached the aquifer?

- What effect does pollution have on drinking water that comes from aquifers?

CHALLENGE What could you do to clean up an aquifer?

SKILL FOCUS
Making models

MATERIALS
- water
- 1L plastic bottle with bottom cut off
- gravel
- sand
- soil
- pepper
- cocoa
- food coloring
- bottle bottom or bucket

TIME
30 minutes

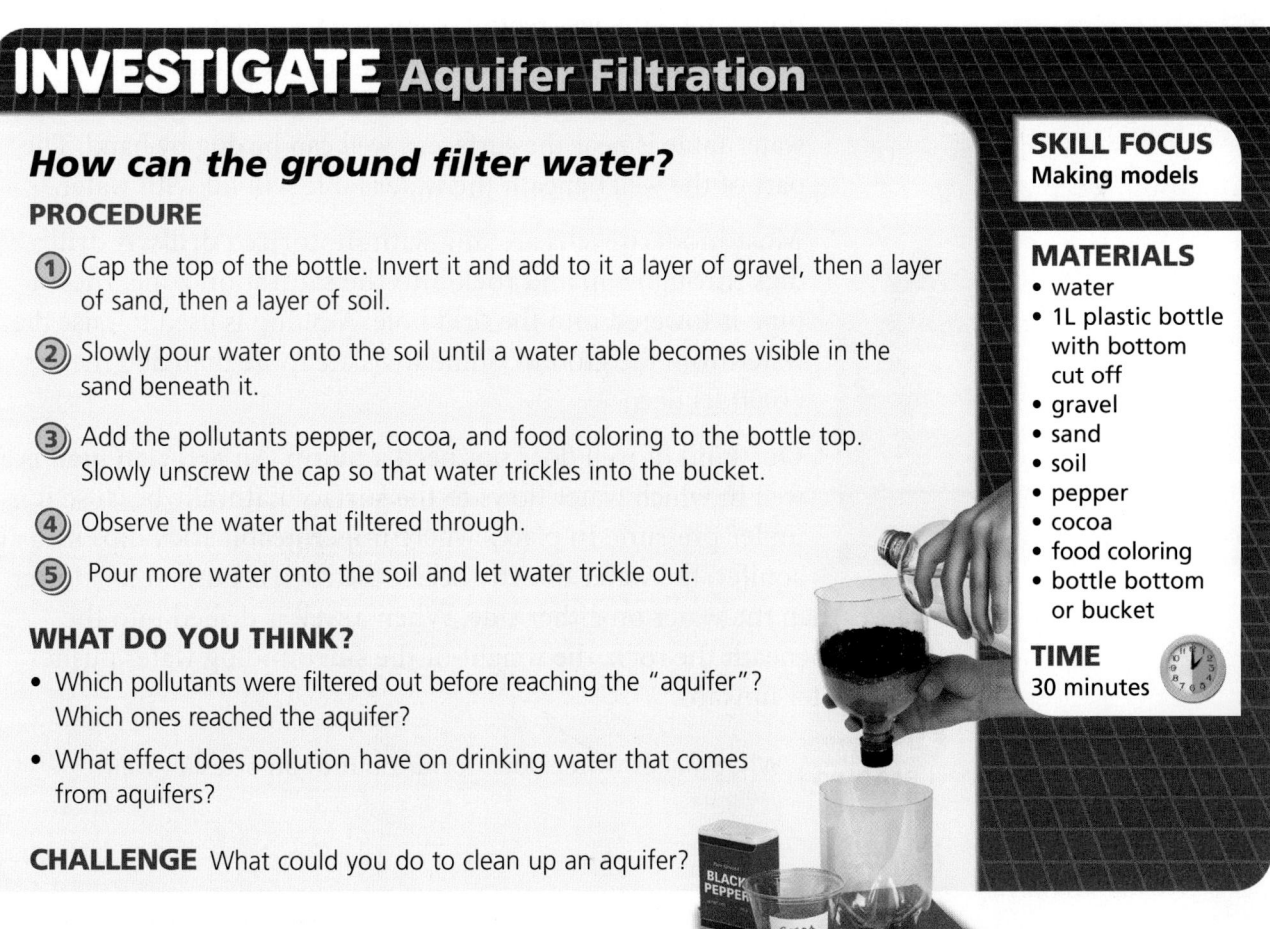

Underground water can be brought to the surface.

MAIN IDEA AND DETAILS
In your notebook, fill out a chart for this main idea.

If you had lived in colonial America or in ancient Greece, your daily chore might have been to haul water home from a well. You would have lowered a bucket into a pit until it reached the water table, then pulled the filled bucket up with a rope. Or you might have worked at digging a well, hacking away at the ground with a shovel until water flowed into the hole you dug.

Today's technology makes it easier to bring groundwater to the surface. Powerful drills bore through rock, and motors pump groundwater to the surface and to kitchen sinks. Scientists study the sizes and areas of aquifers. They know where to get water and how much to expect.

Springs and Wells

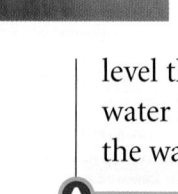

Underground pressure causes this artesian well to shoot water 18 meters (60 ft) into the air.

Groundwater can be collected from springs and wells. A **spring** is a flow of water from the ground at a place where the surface of the land dips below the water table. In some springs, the water bubbles up, then sinks back into the soil. In others, the water flows into a stream or lake. Spring water has a fresh clean taste, and many water companies bottle this water to sell.

A well is a hole in the ground that reaches down to the saturation zone—the wet region below the water table. Usually, a pump is used to draw the water out of the ground, and a screen is used to filter out particles of sand and gravel. If the water table is near the surface, a well can be dug by hand. The part of the well beneath the water table will fill with water.

Most modern wells are dug with motorized drills. A drill digs through soil and rock into the saturation zone; then a pipe is lowered into the drill hole. A pump is used to raise the water from the ground. Some wells are more than 300 meters (1000 ft) deep.

One kind of well does not need a pump. An **artesian well** is a well in which water flows to the surface naturally because it is under pressure. In places where impermeable rock dips into an aquifer, the water directly below the rock is pushed to a lower level than the water on either side. When a well is drilled into the water beneath the rock, the weight of the surrounding water pushes the water upward.

CHECK YOUR READING What makes water flow upward out of an artesian well?

Springs and Wells

Water is brought up from the ground in various ways.

Water flows from an **artesian well** because the water underground is under pressure.

A **spring** occurs where the water table meets the ground surface.

well dug for home

water table

aquifer

How to Make a Well

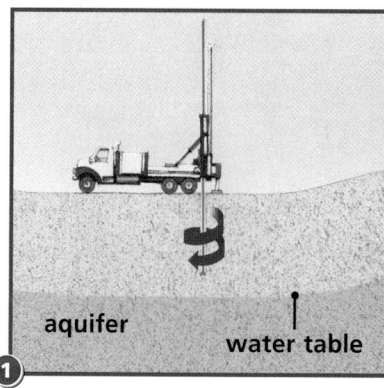

aquifer

water table

1 Drill into the ground with special machinery.

2 When the drill hole reaches below the water table, lower a pipe into it.

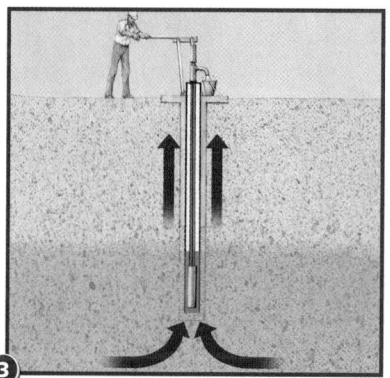

3 At the top of the well, install a pump powered by a motor or human effort to pull up water.

READING VISUALS Look at the top illustration. What would happen if the water table dropped below the bottom end of the well?

The depth of the water table in a particular place can vary from season to season, depending on how much rain falls and how much water is used. When water is taken from an aquifer, the water table might drop. When it rains or snows, some of the water filters back into the aquifer, replacing what has been taken. If water is used faster than it is replaced, wells may run dry. Low groundwater levels can also cause the ground to settle and damage the environment.

As more and more people live on Earth, the amounts of groundwater used to irrigate crops increase. In some states where crops are grown in dry areas, as much as 70 percent of all the groundwater brought to the surface is used for irrigation. Water used for irrigation is recycled back into the water cycle. In some places it sinks back into the ground and filters into aquifers. In other regions much of the water evaporates or flows away, and the groundwater levels are lowered.

Hot Springs

Yellowstone National Park sits atop the remains of an ancient volcano. The rain and melted snow that sink into the ground there eventually reach depths of more than 3000 meters (10,000 feet), where the rocks are extremely hot. The water heats up and reaches the boiling point. Then it becomes even hotter while remaining liquid because it is under such great pressure from the rocks pushing on it from all sides.

The hot water deep underground is like water in an enormous boiling pot—with a lid 3000 meters thick. The water expands the only way that it can, by pushing upward through weak places in the rocks. A place where the water surfaces is a hot spring. A hot spring has a continual flow of hot water.

Vapor rises from these hot springs in Yellowstone National Park in Wyoming.

① In a geyser, water heats underground. The diagram shows the underground "plumbing" of a geyser in Iceland.

② Hot water and steam are pushed up to the surface where they erupt.

A geyser is a kind of hot spring. The illustrations above show how a geyser works. Beneath the surface, there are underground channels in the rock. The rising hot water is forced to travel through these narrow passages. Like water in a garden hose, the water moves with force because it is under pressure. When it finally reaches Earth's surface, the pressure makes it burst out. It shoots into the air as a dramatic fountain of water and steam. In Yellowstone National Park there are more than 300 geysers. One of the largest, Old Faithful, shoots a jet of hot water and steam about 20 times a day. The eruptions last from 1.5 to 5 minutes, and reach heights of 30 to 55 meters (106 to 184 ft).

 **CHECK YOUR READING** Why does water shoot out of Old Faithful with such great force?

FLORIDA Content Preview

Pressure in fluids acts in all directions. You will learn more about pressure in grade 8.

RESOURCE CENTER CLASSZONE.COM

Learn more about geysers and hot springs.

2.3 Review

KEY CONCEPTS

1. Draw a diagram that shows how water collects underground.

2. What is the difference between a spring and a well?

3. What causes water to rise out of the ground in hot springs and geysers?

CRITICAL THINKING

4. **Connect** Is a T-shirt permeable or impermeable? How about a raincoat? Explain why.

5. **Infer** Would you expect to find a spring on the very top of a hill? Why or why not?

◆ CHALLENGE

6. **Sequence** On a blank sheet of paper, draw a cartoon strip that shows how aquifers collect and store water and how people bring the water to the surface. Show at least five steps in the process. Write captions for your drawing to explain the steps.

CHAPTER INVESTIGATION

Water Moving Underground

OVERVIEW AND PURPOSE

Many people rely on underground aquifers for their drinking water. Some aquifers are small and localized. Others can supply water to huge regions of the United States. Perhaps your own drinking water comes from an underground aquifer. In this investigation you will

- design an experiment to determine what types of materials best hold and transport water
- infer which types of Earth materials make the best aquifers

DESIGN — YOUR OWN — EXPERIMENT

▶ Problem

Write It Up

What types of materials will best hold and transport water?

▶ Hypothesize

Write It Up

Write a hypothesis that answers the problem question in "If . . . , then . . . , because . . ." form.

▶ Procedure

1. Design a procedure to test the materials samples to determine which will best hold and transport water. Your procedure should be designed to identify both which material absorbed the most water and which material absorbs water the fastest.

2. Record your procedure in your **Science Notebook.**

MATERIALS

- granite sample
- sandstone sample
- sand
- square piece of cotton muslin or cotton knit, measuring 30 cm per side
- rubber band
- golf ball
- scale
- large jar
- water

WATER

3 Create a data table to organize the data you will collect.

4 Be sure that you make both qualitative and quantitative observations.

5 Be sure to include a calculations section in your **Science Notebook.**

▶ Observe and Analyze   Write It Up

1. **RECORD OBSERVATIONS** Draw a diagram of your experimental setup.

2. **CALCULATE** Which item absorbed the most water?

3. **SCIENTIFIC METHOD** How did you use the golf ball? What did it represent?

▶ Conclude   Write It Up

1. **INTERPRET** Answer the problem question.

2. **COMPARE** Compare your results with your hypothesis. Do your data support your hypothesis?

3. **IDENTIFY LIMITS** In what ways was this activity limited in demonstrating how water moves underground? How might your experimental setup lead to incorrect conclusions?

4. **APPLY** Look over your data table. Your results should indicate both which material absorbed the most water and which material absorbed water the fastest. How do these two characteristics compare in terms of their importance for an aquifer?

5. **INFER** Which types of Earth materials make the best aquifers?

▶ INVESTIGATE Further

CHALLENGE The data you gathered in this investigation reflect the permeability of each Earth material tested. What qualities and characteristics determine their permeabilities?

Water Moving Underground
Problem What types of materials will best hold and transport water?
Hypothesize
Procedure
Observe and Analyze
Table 1.

Conclude

FLORIDA REVIEW
CLASSZONE.COM

Content Review and
FCAT Practice

the BIG idea

Water moves through Earth's atmosphere, oceans, and land in a cycle.

◀ KEY CONCEPTS SUMMARY

1 Water continually cycles.
Water moves through Earth's environment in a continuous cycle.

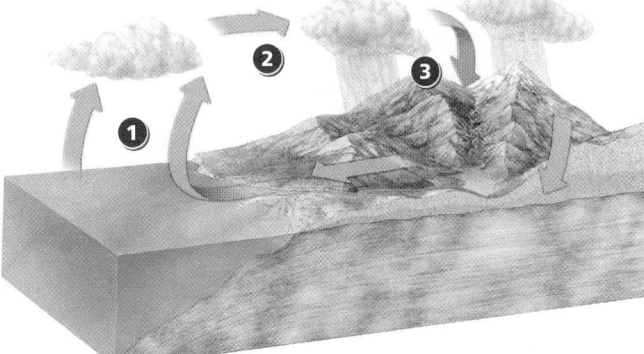

1 Evaporation Water becomes vapor.

2 Condensation Vapor changes into liquid.

3 Precipitation Water falls to the surface.

VOCABULARY
fresh water p. 51
salt water p. 51
water cycle p. 52
condensation p. 53
evaporation p. 53
precipitation p. 53

2 Fresh water flows and freezes on Earth.

Water on land collects and flows in rivers and lakes. Much of Earth's fresh water is frozen.

drainage basins

divide

VOCABULARY
divide p. 57
drainage basin p. 57
turnover p. 59
eutrophication p. 60
iceberg p. 62

3 Fresh water flows underground.
Water collects and moves beneath the land surface.

Gravity pulls water down through **permeable** materials until it reaches an impermeable layer.

The **impermeable** layer prevents water from sinking farther down.

Water collects in open spaces in soil, gravel, or rock.

VOCABULARY
groundwater p. 64
permeable p. 64
impermeable p. 65
water table p. 65
aquifer p. 66
spring p. 68
artesian well p. 68

Reviewing Vocabulary

Use the terms in the box below to answer the next nine questions.

evaporation	precipitation	water cycle
turnover	eutrophication	artesian
iceberg	groundwater	permeable

1. Which word describes an increase in nutrients in a lake or pond?

2. Which kind of well does not need a pump?

3. Which term describes a seasonal change in a lake?

4. Which term describes a substance through which water can pass?

5. Which term names the continuous movement of water through Earth's environment?

6. What is the name for an enormous chunk of floating ice?

7. What word means the turning of liquid water into a gas?

8. What is the name of water stored in an aquifer?

9. What word is another name for rain, snow, sleet, and hail?

Reviewing Key Concepts

Multiple Choice *Choose the letter of the best answer.*

10. What are the three forms of water on Earth?
    a. groundwater, lakes, and clouds
    b. liquid water, frozen water, and water vapor
    c. gas, steam, and vapor
    d. groundwater, oceans, and ice

11. How much of Earth's water is fresh water?
    a. almost all
    b. about half
    c. very little
    d. none

12. Which process forms clouds?
    a. evaporation
    b. precipitation
    c. condensation
    d. dehydration

13. What ice formation covers Greenland and Antarctica?
    a. iceberg
    b. landmass
    c. valley glacier
    d. continental glacier

14. Which is a characteristic of a pond?
    a. rooted plants covering the entire bottom
    b. plants only near shore
    c. a layer of impermeable rock
    d. water heated by underground rock

15. How are glaciers like rivers?
    a. They are made of liquid water.
    b. Their water sinks into the ground.
    c. They flow downhill.
    d. They are a mile thick.

16. How is water stored in an aquifer?
    a. in an open underground lake
    b. in cracks and spaces in rocks
    c. in impermeable rock
    d. in wells and springs

Short Response *Write a short response to each question.*

17. Explain why most of the water cycle takes place over the ocean.

18. How does an iceberg form?

19. Why are aquifers valuable?

20. What is the difference between a valley glacier and a continental glacier?

Thinking Critically

Use the photograph to answer the next four questions. There are four liters of water in the jug. The hose has been overflowing for about ten seconds.

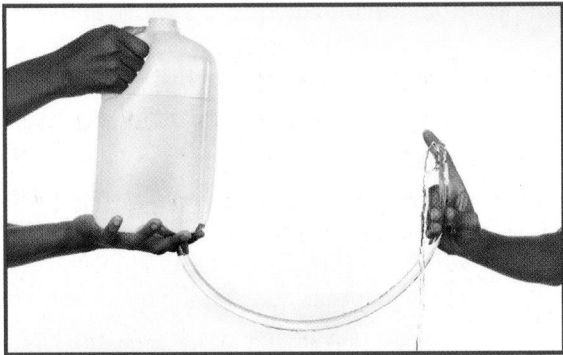

21. OBSERVE Describe what the water in the hose is doing.

22. IDENTIFY EFFECTS Explain what effect the water in the jug has on the water in the hose. Why does the water rise in the hose?

23. PREDICT When will the water stop flowing from the hose? Why?

24. COMPARE AND CONTRAST How is what is happening in the hose like and unlike what happens in an artesian well?

25. EXPLAIN Explain why the water cycle matters to humans and animals.

26. CONNECT In a mountainous area, temperatures are lower at higher altitudes. Explain the connection between this fact and the existence of valley glaciers.

27. COMPARE AND CONTRAST Explain the difference between clouds and water vapor in the atmosphere.

28. INFER Explain why water in a bowl-shaped drainage basin does not eventually flow to the ocean.

29. APPLY Name at least two things that you think people could do to lessen eutrophication caused by pollution.

30. APPLY Explain why even though evaporation draws water but not salt from the ocean, the ocean does not become saltier.

PREDICT Fill in the chart with predictions of how water will collect under the stated conditions.

Conditions	Prediction
31. A bed of permeable rock lies atop a bed of impermeable rock; rainfall is plentiful.	
32. Heavy snows fall in a region that has year-round freezing temperatures.	
33. A large depression is left in impermeable rock by a glacier.	
34. Water from farm fields and gardens runs off into ponds.	

the BIG idea

35. SYNTHESIZE Explain why a raindrop that falls on your head may once have been water in the Pacific Ocean.

36. MODEL Draw a diagram of two drainage basins, showing how water flows and collects on the surface of Earth. Label the divide, as well as the bodies of water into which water flows.

UNIT PROJECTS

If you are doing a unit project, make a folder for your project. Include in your folder a list of the resources you will need, the date on which the project is due, and a schedule to keep track of your progress. Begin gathering data.

FCAT Practice

Analyzing Data

In an experiment to study the effect of heating on evaporation, identical pans of water were placed for two hours under different types of lights. The temperature of the air just above each pan was measured with a thermometer every 30 minutes. The amount of evaporation was determined by subtracting the amount of water in the pan at the end of two hours from the amount that was in the pan at the beginning. The data table shows the results. Study the data and answer the questions below.

Pan	Description	Average Air Temperature Above the Water	Evaporation
1	under regular light	22°C (72°F)	30 mL (1.0 oz)
2	under heat lamp on low	25°C (78°F)	40 mL (1.4 oz)
3	under heat lamp on high	28°C (83°F)	50 mL (1.7 oz)

FCAT TiP

When analyzing a data table, read the title above each column of data. This will help you identify the data that you need to answer specific questions.

GRIDDED RESPONSE

1. If the air temperature averaged 27°C (80°F), about how much water would evaporate in two hours?

2. The evaporation from pan 1 to pan 3 increased by 20 milliliters. By how many degrees Celsius did the temperature increase from pan 1 to pan 3?

MULTIPLE CHOICE

3. What is the relationship between the air temperature and the evaporation rate?
   A. There is no relationship between the temperature and the rate.
   B. As the temperature increases, the rate decreases.
   C. As the temperature increases, the rate stays the same.
   D. As the temperature increases, the rate increases.

4. Which is the most important reason that placing a pan in a refrigerator would not be a good way to test for the influence of heat in this experiment?
   F. The refrigerator would be cold.
   G. The refrigerator is a closed space.
   H. The refrigerator is an appliance.
   I. The refrigerator may have other objects in it.

5. The dependent variable in an experiment is the factor that is measured to gather results. Which is the dependent variable in this experiment?
   A. the amount of evaporation
   B. the amount of water in each pan in the beginning
   C. the type of light
   D. the air temperature

6. Which change would make the results of this experiment more reliable?
   F. conducting the experiment for four hours
   G. decreasing the amount of water in the pans
   H. increasing the air temperature for one pan
   I. using a fan to blow air on one of the pans

EXTENDED RESPONSE

Answer the two questions below in detail. Include some of the terms shown in the word box. In your answers, underline each term you use.

low	eutrophication	meadow
water table	saturation zone	

7. Kori notices that a pond at his summer camp is filled with more soil and plants each year. Explain how this change fits into the pattern of how ponds change over time.

8. Juanita's family gets water from a well on their ranch. Each time a well has gone dry, they have had to dig a new one that was deeper than the old one. Explain why they have needed to go deeper.

CHAPTER

3 Freshwater Resources

the **BIG** idea

Fresh water is a limited resource and is essential for human society

Key Concepts

SECTION

(1) Fresh water is an essential resource. Learn how water is needed for life and how water is used for human activities.

SECTION

(2) Society depends on clean and safe water. Learn how water is made safe for drinking and how wastewater is treated.

SECTION

(3) Water shortages threaten society. Learn about the causes of water shortages and about ways to conserve water.

In what ways do you depend on water?

FCAT Practice

Prepare and practice for the FCAT
- Section Reviews, pp. 88, 97, 106
- Chapter Review, pp. 108–110
- FCAT Practice, p. 111

CLASSZONE.COM
- Florida Review: Content Review and FCAT Practice

How Much Water Do You Drink?

From the time you get up to when you finish dinner, keep a list that notes each time you drink a liquid—including water, juice, milk, and soda. Write down what you drank and how much you think you drank.

Observe and Think
How many times did you drink something? From your list, estimate in numbers of medium glassfuls the total amount you drank.

What Happens When Salt Water Evaporates?

Dissolve a spoonful of salt in a cup of water. Put the cup in a warm place, such as a sunny windowsill. Leave it there until the water completely evaporates.

Observe and Think Examine the cup. If you could capture the water that evaporated, would that water be salty? Explain your answer.

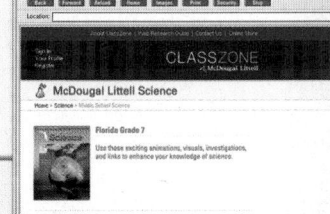

Internet Activity: Aquifers

Go to **ClassZone.com** to explore the limits of an aquifer. Review past water usage and try to determine how long the water in an aquifer will last.

Observe and Think
What can be done to slow the use of underground water?

NSTA
scilinks.org

SCiLINKS

Water Pollution Code: MDL019

Getting Ready to Learn

◀ CONCEPT REVIEW

- Water can be a solid, a liquid, or a gas.
- Water continually cycles on Earth.
- Water flows underground.

◀ VOCABULARY REVIEW

fresh water p. 51

water cycle p. 52

groundwater p. 64

aquifer p. 66

FLORIDA REVIEW
CLASSZONE.COM

Content Review and FCAT Practice

▶ TAKING NOTES

SUPPORTING MAIN IDEAS

Make a chart to show main ideas and the information that supports them. Write each blue heading from the chapter in each box. In boxes below it, add supporting information, such as reasons, explanations, and examples.

VOCABULARY STRATEGY

Place each vocabulary term at the center of a **description wheel**. Write some words describing it on the spokes.

See the Note-Taking Handbook on pages R45–R51.

SCIENCE NOTEBOOK

Fresh water supports life.

→ The human body is more than one-half water.

→ Living cells need water.

→ Water is a limited resource.

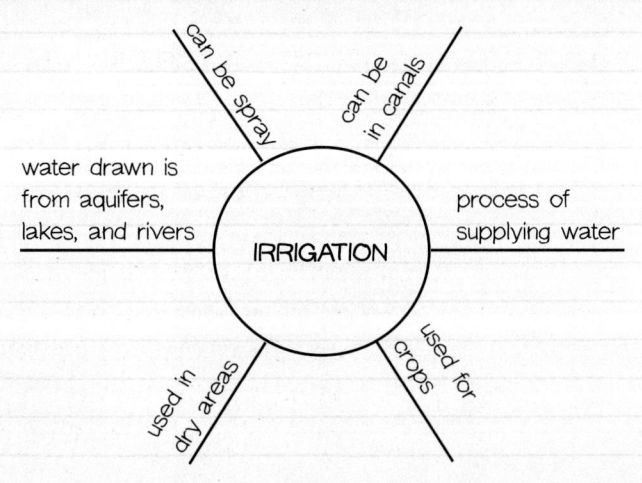

IRRIGATION

- can be spray
- can be in canals
- process of supplying water
- used for crops
- used in dry areas
- water drawn is from aquifers, lakes, and rivers

KEY CONCEPT

Fresh water is an essential resource.

Sunshine State STANDARDS

SC.D.2.3.1: The student understands that quality of life is relevant to personal experience.

SC.G.2.3.1: The student knows that some resources are renewable and others are nonrenewable.

SC.H.3.3.4: The student knows that technological design should require taking into account constraints such as natural laws, the properties of the materials used, and economic, political, social, ethical, and aesthetic values.

VOCABULARY

irrigation p. 83
aquaculture p. 85
dam p. 86
lock p. 86

◀ **BEFORE, you learned**

• Fresh water is found on Earth's surface and underground
• People use wells to bring ground water to the surface

▶ **NOW, you will learn**

• How water is required for life
• How water is used for many human activities

THINK ABOUT

How valuable is water?

In the United States, fresh water seems plentiful. When you want water for a drink or to wash, you can go to a drinking fountain or turn on the tap to get all the water you want. In some parts of the world, water is scarce and difficult to get. In Port-au-Prince, Haiti, this girl is getting her bucket filled with fresh water so that she can take water home. If you had to get your water this way, how might that change the way you think of water? Would you use water differently than you do now?

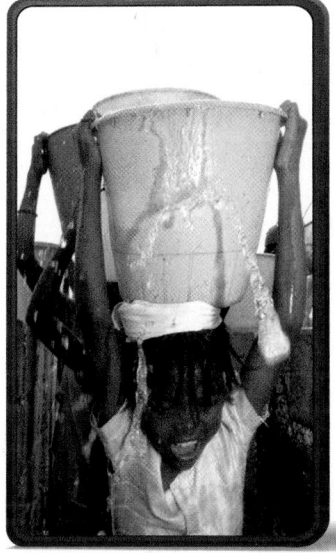

Fresh water supports life.

Close your eyes and imagine a beautiful place in nature that is full of life. Maybe you think of trees, flowers, and a waterfall and pools where animals come to drink. Water is important in any scene that involves life.

People have always lived near clean, fresh water. Why is water so important to humans? One reason is that our bodies are more than one-half water. Without the water in your blood, your cells would not receive the nutrients they need. Your skin and tissues hold water in your body, but some water is lost every day. As a result, you get thirsty and drink water or something that contains mostly water, such as milk or juice. Without water, a person cannot live for more than a few days. And without water, people wouldn't be able to grow food.

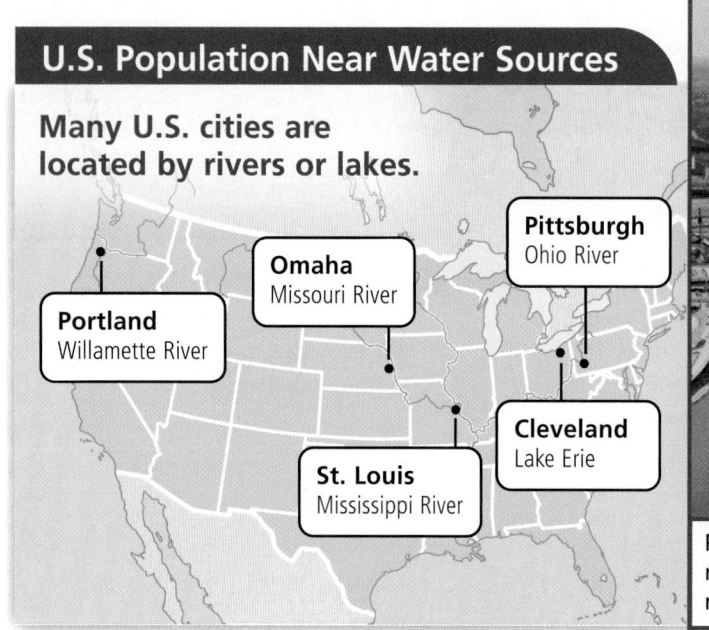

U.S. Population Near Water Sources

Many U.S. cities are located by rivers or lakes.

Portland
Willamette River

Omaha
Missouri River

Pittsburgh
Ohio River

St. Louis
Mississippi River

Cleveland
Lake Erie

Pittsburgh, Pennsylvania, is one of many cities by rivers. Here the Allegheny and the Monongahela rivers come together to form the Ohio River.

You have read that fresh water on Earth is a limited resource. A fixed amount cycles through the atmosphere, flows in rivers, is held in lakes and glaciers, and is stored in aquifers deep under the ground. As more and more people live on the planet every year, our water sources become more precious. If too much water is taken from aquifers, the supply will eventually run out. If the water in rivers and lakes becomes polluted, we can no longer use it.

 **CHECK YOUR READING** What can happen to water as the world population grows?

Most human activities require water.

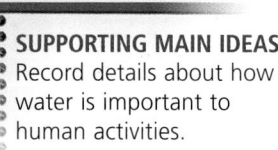
SUPPORTING MAIN IDEAS
Record details about how water is important to human activities.

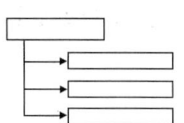

Almost everything you do requires water. When you take a shower or brush your teeth, you use water. Your dishes and clothes are washed with water. You might exercise in water at a pool.

Some of the ways you use water might surprise you. Let's say you do your homework after school. You grab a slice of pizza from the refrigerator, switch on the light, and sit down to read a book in your favorite chair. Have you used any water so far? The answer is yes, many gallons of water.

On farms water was needed to grow the tomatoes and wheat for your pizza. The cheese topping came from a cow that drank water and ate grain grown with water. The paper in your book was produced at a paper plant that used vast amounts of water to wash and mix wood pulp. When you switch on a light, you are probably using energy that was generated by some form of moving water. And the metal in the lamp was mined from underground, using—you guessed it—water.

How much water do you use in a week?

PROCEDURE

1. Write down all the ways you use water in a day. Start with the time you get up in the morning. Include things such as brushing your teeth, flushing the toilet, using ice, and taking a shower.

2. Look at the Water Use sheet, and from it, identify other ways that you and others in your household use water.

3. Add up how many liters of water you use in a day, and multiply that by 7. This is how much water you use in a week.

WHAT DO YOU THINK?

- Which of your activities used the most water?
- What are some ways that you could reduce the amount of water you use weekly?

CHALLENGE Based on your weekly water usage, how much water is used by the United States annually? **Hint:** Find the population of the United States in a reference source.

SKILL FOCUS
Analyzing data

MATERIALS
- Water Use sheet
- calculator

TIME
30 minutes

Farming

In the United States, about 40 percent of the water that is used goes to growing crops and raising livestock. Any kind of farm depends on water to grow plants for food and to raise animals. To grow oranges, a farm needs about 0.25 centimeters (0.1 in.) of rainfall a day. To produce one hamburger can require 5000 liters (1300 gal.) of water or more because animals not only drink water but also eat grass and grain that use water.

In many areas, rainfall does not provide enough water to support crops and animals. In these drier areas, farmers draw water from aquifers, rivers, or lakes to grow crops. The process of supplying water to land to grow crops is **irrigation.**

A common method of irrigation pours water through canals and waterways so that it flows through the fields. A little more than half of U.S. farms that are irrigated use this method, which is called flood irrigation. Most of the other farms that irrigate use spray irrigation, which sprays water onto the fields. You can think of lawn sprinklers as an example of spray irrigation for grass. On farms, the water often is delivered by metal structures that roll around entire fields.

These green irrigated fields are circular because the metal sprinklers move like clock hands from a center point

Industry

The industries that make our cars, notebooks, jeans, sneakers, skateboards, and TVs are major water users. The manufacture of just about any item you can name probably uses water. Consider these examples.

- The process of making one car can require about 50 times the car's weight in water. This process begins with the mining of minerals and ends with the final washing as the car rolls out of the factory.
- In many industries, huge amounts of water are used to cool down machines.
- In a coal mine, water is used to separate chunks of coal from other clumps of dirt and rock.
- A paper mill uses 100 to 300 metric tons of water to manufacture one ton of paper.

Water used in industry can be used again. Factories can clean the water they use and return most of it to lakes and rivers.

 **CHECK YOUR READING** How is water used in industry?

A paper mill uses large quantities of water to process wood pulp.

Transportation and Recreation

Since the earliest times, rivers and lakes have helped people visit their neighbors and trade food and goods. In the United States, major rivers and the Great Lakes provide an efficient way to transport goods, especially cargo that is bulky and heavy, such as coal. For example, on the Great Lakes, large ships carry iron ore from Minnesota to cities where it is used to make steel. On the Mississippi River, barges haul grain to ports, where the grain may be processed or placed on ships to go overseas.

Great Lakes

This freighter carries cargo on the Great Lakes.

People also use rivers and lakes for recreation. Whitewater rafting, canoeing, and kayaking are popular activities. Many people also like to camp, picnic, swim, and fish along the shores of freshwater rivers and lakes.

Not every section of a river can be navigated by boat. A river may flow too fast or be too shallow for safe travel. To make water transportation easier, people dig channels called canals that bypass rough spots and connect waterways. For example, a 376-kilometer (234-mi) canal lets boats travel between the Tennessee and Tombigbee rivers in Mississippi and Alabama. In Canada, west of Buffalo, New York, the Welland Canal connects two Great Lakes, Ontario and Erie. It is part of the waterway known as the St. Lawrence Seaway, which connects the Great Lakes to the Atlantic Ocean.

Fisheries and Aquaculture

Fresh water is full of life—from tiny one-celled organisms to small shrimp and worms, to trout and salmon. Rivers and lakes provide fish for our food, a living resource that people depend upon. They also provide food for frogs, insects, birds, and larger animals.

When people talk about livestock, do you think of fish? Probably not, but fish farming is a thriving business all over the world. **Aquaculture** is the science and business of raising and harvesting fish in a controlled situation. Freshwater fish farms provide a cheap, ready source of catfish, trout, and salmon. However, aquaculture also causes some problems. The farms can cause excess nutrients and pollution to flow into rivers and lakes.

To help maintain the population of fish in rivers and lakes, fish hatcheries are used to raise fish to release into lakes and rivers. Hatcheries give people who fish something to catch and also help threatened species survive.

READING TiP

You can use word parts to help remember vocabulary terms. *Aqua-* comes from the Latin word for water.

An aquaculture worker tends to a fish farm in Nepal.

NEPAL

Energy

Not so long ago, water wheels could be seen dotting the rivers of America. The force of the river turned the water wheel, which powered machinery in factories such as grain mills. In dams, electricity is generated in a similar way. A **dam** is a structure that holds back and controls the flow of water in a river or other body of water.

At a hydroelectric dam built across a river, water rushing through the dam turns machines called turbines, generating electricity. Even electric plants that are not powered by rivers use water. For example, many plants use coal or nuclear power to heat water, creating steam that turns the turbines. Nuclear power stations also use water to cool the system.

At a hydroelectric plant, water flowing through a dam spins turbines to produce electricity.

FLORIDA
Content Review

You learned how humans impact ecosystems in grade 6. Building dams is another example.

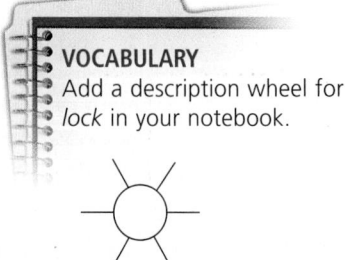

VOCABULARY
Add a description wheel for *lock* in your notebook.

Dams and other structures alter rivers.

When a dam is built on a river, the landscape and the shape of a river are greatly changed. Below the dam, the speed and volume of water flow may change, making a new ecosystem. Behind the dam, water may collect and form a lake covering what once had been a river valley.

In some locations, a lake behind a dam is used as a source of fresh water. A lake that is used to store water is called a reservoir (REHZ-uhr-VWAHR). Some dams are built solely for the purpose of creating a reservoir, and many communities rely on reservoirs for their water needs. Some reservoirs provide opportunities for boating and other recreational activities.

Dams have purposes in addition to providing hydroelectric power and forming reservoirs. Dams may also be built to control rivers that flow too fast or too unpredictably for boats to use them. These dams might separate a river into sections of different elevations, like steps in a staircase. To allow boats to climb or descend these steps and move to the next river section, locks are built at the dams. A **lock** is a section of waterway, closed off by gates, in which the water level is raised or lowered to move ships through.

In addition to rivers with dams, locks are used in canals and rivers that connect lakes of different elevations. Locks are also used in canals that slope upward and then downward, such as the Panama Canal. The Panama Canal is dug into a strip of land between the Atlantic and Pacific oceans, allowing ships a handy shortcut.

CHECK YOUR READING Why do ships need to use locks?

In some cases dams cause problems as well as solve them. For example, in Egypt's Nile valley the giant Aswan Dam stopped floods that happened every year. However, the dam also blocked the flow of rich soil to the valley below the dam. The soil in the Nile valley was fertile for more than 4000 years. Yet today farmers need to add chemical fertilizers to grow their crops.

Dams can also cause problems for fish. When a dam blocks a river, salmon and steelhead cannot reach their breeding grounds. People have tried to solve this problem by installing fish ladder structures along dams that allow fish to climb up the river.

Learn more about dams.

Locks and Dams

Locks and dams control the flow of rivers and allow boats to pass through.

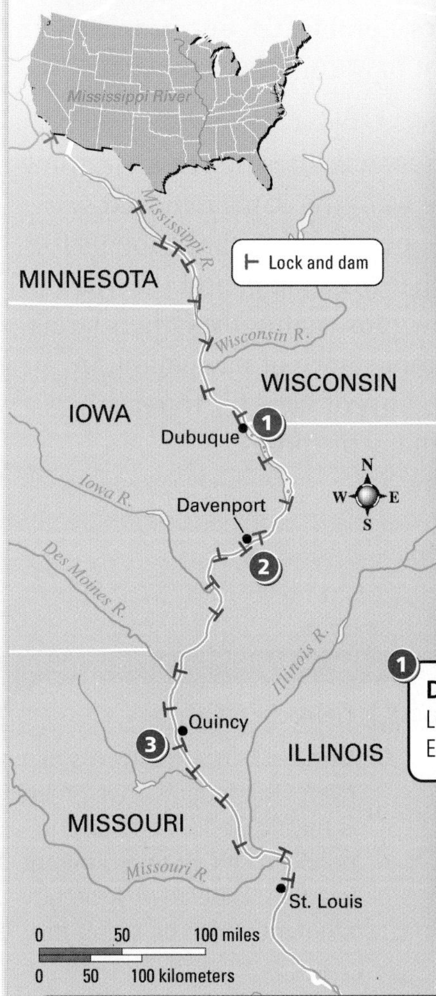

⊢ Lock and dam

MINNESOTA

Mississippi R.

Wisconsin R.

WISCONSIN

IOWA

① Dubuque

Iowa R.

Davenport

②

Des Moines R.

Illinois R.

③ Quincy

ILLINOIS

MISSOURI

Missouri R.

St. Louis

N W E S

0   50   100 miles

0   50   100 kilometers

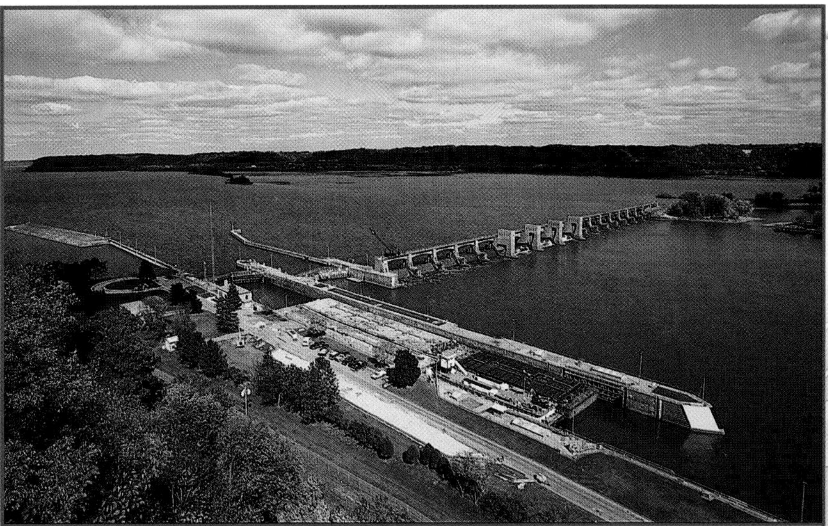

Locks and dams on the upper Mississippi River have divided the river into a series of sections that flow downhill like a staircase. This is Lock and Dam #11 near Dubuque, Iowa.

Mississippi River Locks and Dams

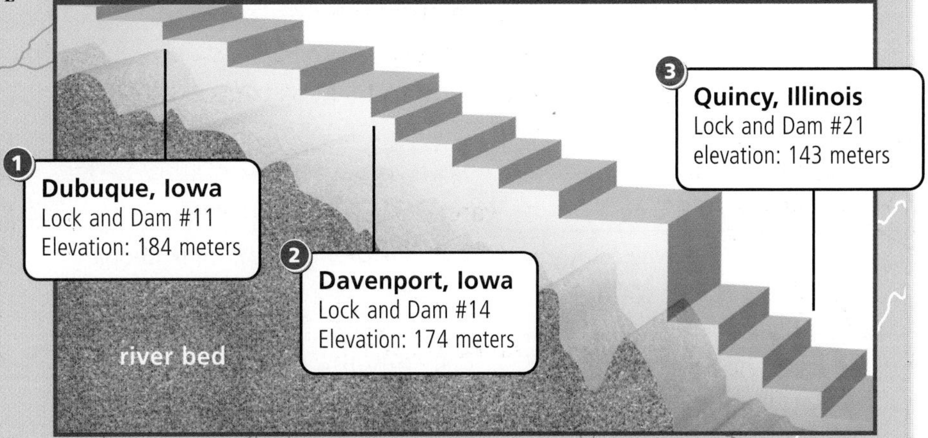

③ Quincy, Illinois
Lock and Dam #21
elevation: 143 meters

① Dubuque, Iowa
Lock and Dam #11
Elevation: 184 meters

② Davenport, Iowa
Lock and Dam #14
Elevation: 174 meters

river bed

READING VISUALS Which gates are open in the lock shown in the photograph? Which gates are closed?

This dammed-up waterway in Texas spilled around its dam during a flood. It formed a new channel that flows to the left of the dam.

Other changes to rivers can have unwanted effects. The placement of locks and the digging of a channel into a river bottom force a river to follow a constant path. In nature, however, a river changes its path depending on how much water it is carrying. It regulates itself by flooding during the wet season. As people alter rivers and build their homes closer to them, flooding becomes a problem. Some people argue that changing the natural flow makes it hard for a river to regulate itself, causing even more flooding.

People have different opinions about structures on rivers. In some places with hydroelectric dams, people want the dams removed so that salmon can swim upstream. Some people think that habitats for wildlife would be improved on the upper Mississippi and the Missouri rivers if the waters were allowed to flow more naturally. Others stress the value of hydroelectricity and the importance of navigation. In many cases the people with differing points of view try to reach compromises so that rivers can serve many purposes.

3.1 Review

KEY CONCEPTS

1. What are three ways that you directly use fresh water daily?

2. Identify a benefit and a possible disadvantage of aquaculture.

3. Explain why dams are both helpful to people and harmful to a river.

CRITICAL THINKING

4. **Predict** Do you think people will need more or less fresh water in the future? Why?

5. **Provide Examples** Explain how water is used in the manufacture of three products that you use every day.

⬥ CHALLENGE

6. **Connect** In some towns near rivers, the federal government is buying houses and paying people to move to a different location. Explain why the government might be doing this.

 MATH TUTORIAL
CLASSZONE.COM

Click on Math Tutorial for more help finding the volume of a rectangular prism.

Fish in an Aquarium

A fish requires a certain minimum amount of water to survive. If you plan to keep fish in an aquarium, you can calculate the volume of the aquarium to be sure it will contain enough water.

Example

An aquarium is 50 centimeters long, 30 centimeters wide, and 40 centimeters high. How many liters of water will it hold?

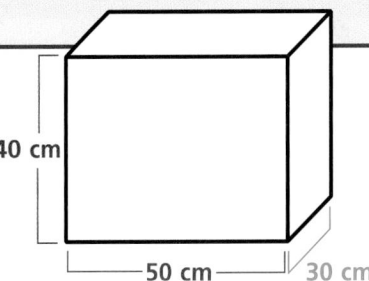

40 cm
50 cm
30 cm

Solution

Use the formula for the volume of a rectangular prism.

Volume = length × width × height	Write a word equation.
$V = lwh$	Replace the words with variables.
= 50 cm × 30 cm × 40 cm	Substitute 50 for l, 30 for w, and 40 for h.
= 60,000 cm³	Multiply. Note that cm³ is a cubic centimeter.
= 60,000 mL	Each cubic centimeter holds a milliliter.
= 60 L	Because there are 1000 milliliters in one liter, divide 60,000 by 1000.

ANSWER The aquarium holds 60 liters of water.

Find the volume of each aquarium. Give your answer in liters.

1. The aquarium is 100 centimeters long, 50 centimeters wide, and 80 centimeters high.

2. The aquarium is 50 centimeters long, 20 centimeters wide, and 40 centimeters high.

3. The aquarium is 50 centimeters long, 40 centimeters wide, and 50 centimeters high.

CHALLENGE You are designing an aquarium to house several fish of different species. The aquarium must hold 300 liters of water and fit in a space that is 100 centimeters long and 50 centimeters wide. How high should the aquarium be?

3.2 Society depends on clean and safe water.

Sunshine State STANDARDS

SC.D.2.3.2: The student knows the positive and negative consequences of human action on the Earth's systems.

◀ BEFORE, you learned

- Water supports life
- Water is used in many ways

▶ NOW, you will learn

- How drinking water and wastewater are treated
- How fresh water can become polluted
- How water pollution can be prevented

VOCABULARY

concentration p. 91
sewage system p. 93
septic system p. 94
point-source pollution p. 94
nonpoint-source pollution p. 94

EXPLORE Concentration

What is one part per million?

PROCEDURE

1. Pour 50 mL of water into the graduated cylinder. This is equal to 1000 drops of water.

2. Add one drop of food coloring to the water in the cylinder. This represents one drop of food coloring to 1000 drops of water, or one part per thousand.

3. Fill the eyedropper from the cylinder.

4. Empty the cylinder and pour 50 mL of new water into the cylinder. Add one drop from the eyedropper to the cylinder. The mixture now contains one part food coloring per thousand thousand parts water, or one part per million (ppm).

MATERIALS

- water
- graduated cylinder
- eyedropper
- food coloring

WHAT DO YOU THINK?

The amount of sodium found in clean spring water is five parts per million. How would you conduct this experiment to make a mixture of food coloring in water of five parts per million?

Treatment makes water safe for drinking.

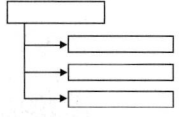

SUPPORTING MAIN IDEAS
Remember to start a new chart for each main idea.

When you wash your face or brush your teeth, do you ever wonder where the water comes from? It depends on where you live. In many places, water is pumped from a nearby well dug into an underground aquifer. If you live in a big city such as New York City or San Francisco, the water may travel a great distance to arrive at your sink. It is piped to the city from reservoirs that may be many miles away. Then it is stored in tanks or in a local reservoir before flowing through pipes to your home.

Water comes from many different sources, so it may contain impurities or organisms that cause disease. For this reason, drinking water in larger systems is cleaned, or treated, before people can drink it.

Quality Standards

Fresh water can contain a variety of harmful substances and organisms. Certain substances and organisms may be present naturally, but others get into water because of pollution from human activity. Some of the impurities in water are safe for humans to drink in small quantities. However, when impurities reach high concentrations, they can harm people. A **concentration** is the amount of a substance that is in another substance. For example, soft drinks have a high concentration of sugar in water. Concentrations are often expressed in parts per million.

A government agency called the Environmental Protection Agency (EPA) sets standards for safe, clean drinking water. The EPA standards are guidelines for the protection of our natural water sources and the quality of the water that reaches our homes. Government agencies in states and local communities enforce laws based on the EPA standards.

The EPA lists standards for harmful organisms that can cause disease. It also lists safe levels for copper and certain other metals that can be found in water. In addition, the EPA checks for a variety of chemicals and harmful radioactive materials.

Your local water provider regularly tests the water to make sure it meets the EPA requirements. If any concentrations are higher than the EPA standards, the water must be treated. As a result, the United States has one of the safest, cleanest water supplies in the world.

CHECK YOUR READING How does a water provider know that it must treat water?

Students test river water in West Virginia for pollutants.

EPA Standards for Substances in Water		
Substance	**Common Source**	**Maximum Allowed, in Parts per Million**
Copper	Natural deposits; household pipes	1.3
Cyanide	Various factories	0.2
Lead	Natural deposits; household pipes	0.015
Mercury	Natural deposits; refineries and factories; landfills; crop fields	0.002
Nitrite	Water running off fertilized fields; sewage leaks; natural deposits	1

Treatment of Drinking Water

VISUALIZATION
CLASSZONE.COM

See a water treatment plant in action.

In a water treatment plant, thousands of gallons of water flow through a series of tanks, where the water is filtered and treated with chemicals to remove harmful substances and kill organisms. The major steps are chemical disinfection and the removal of dirt.

Water Treatment and Distribution

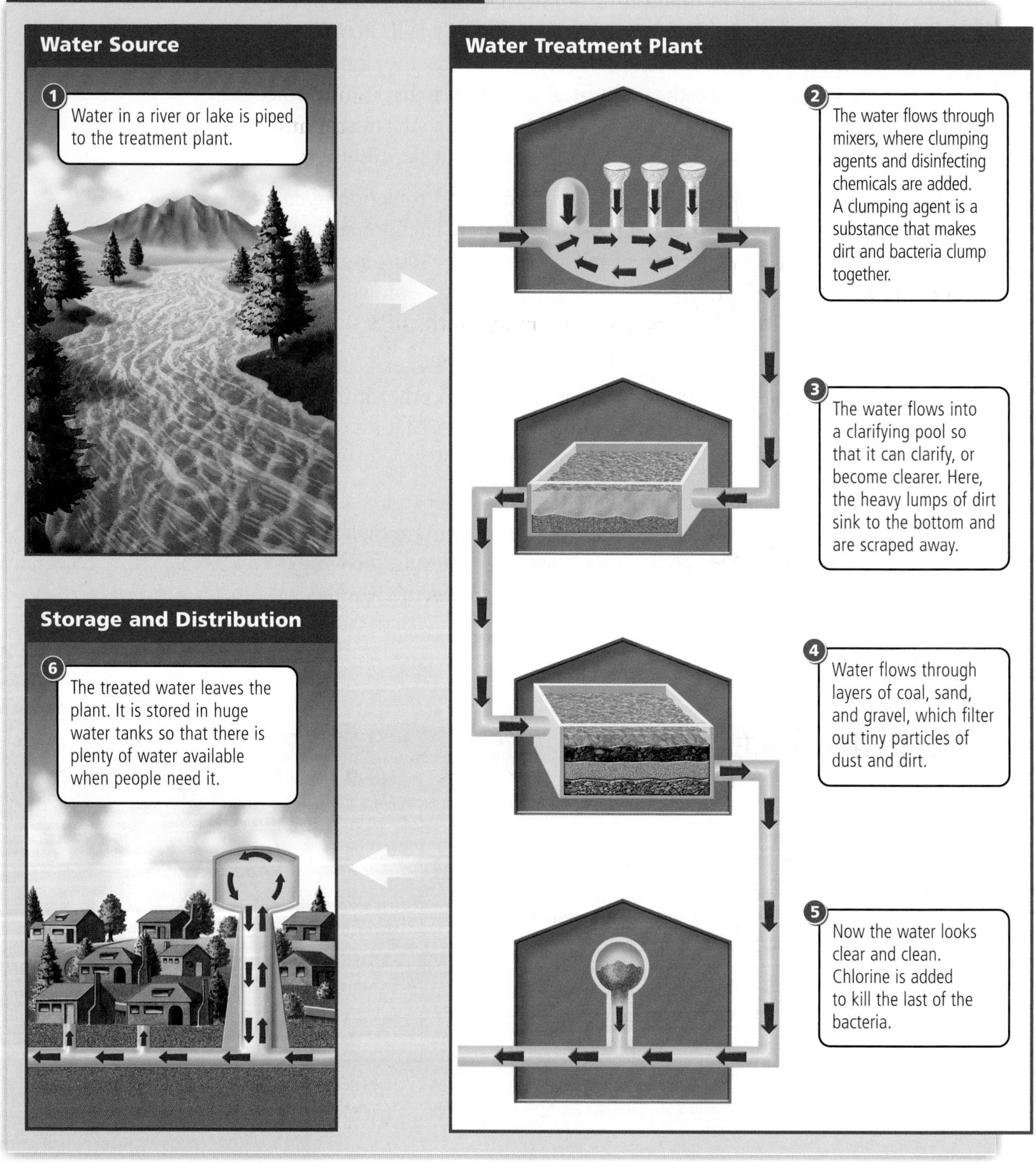

Water Source

1 Water in a river or lake is piped to the treatment plant.

Water Treatment Plant

2 The water flows through mixers, where clumping agents and disinfecting chemicals are added. A clumping agent is a substance that makes dirt and bacteria clump together.

3 The water flows into a clarifying pool so that it can clarify, or become clearer. Here, the heavy lumps of dirt sink to the bottom and are scraped away.

4 Water flows through layers of coal, sand, and gravel, which filter out tiny particles of dust and dirt.

5 Now the water looks clear and clean. Chlorine is added to kill the last of the bacteria.

Storage and Distribution

6 The treated water leaves the plant. It is stored in huge water tanks so that there is plenty of water available when people need it.

Wastewater is treated and released.

Wastewater is the water that runs down the drain. Before wastewater can be released back into the environment, it needs to be treated. Sewage and septic systems are two ways of treating wastewater.

Sewage System

A **sewage system** is a system that collects and treats wastewater from a city or a town. Sewage pipes carry wastewater from homes and businesses to a water treatment plant.

In the first part of treatment, wastewater is strained to remove large objects. Then the water is pumped into a tank, where it sits until the heaviest sludge sinks to the bottom. The sludge is taken away to decompose in another tank. Then chlorine is added to the water to kill the harmful bacteria. This process removes about half of the pollutants.

During the second part of the process, extra oxygen is pumped into the wastewater. The oxygen causes certain kinds of bacteria to grow in great numbers. These bacteria consume much of the sludge and oil that is still in the water. In other words, these tiny organisms help clean the water. More sludge also settles out, and grease is skimmed off the top. Chemicals clean the water one more time and remove any extra chlorine.

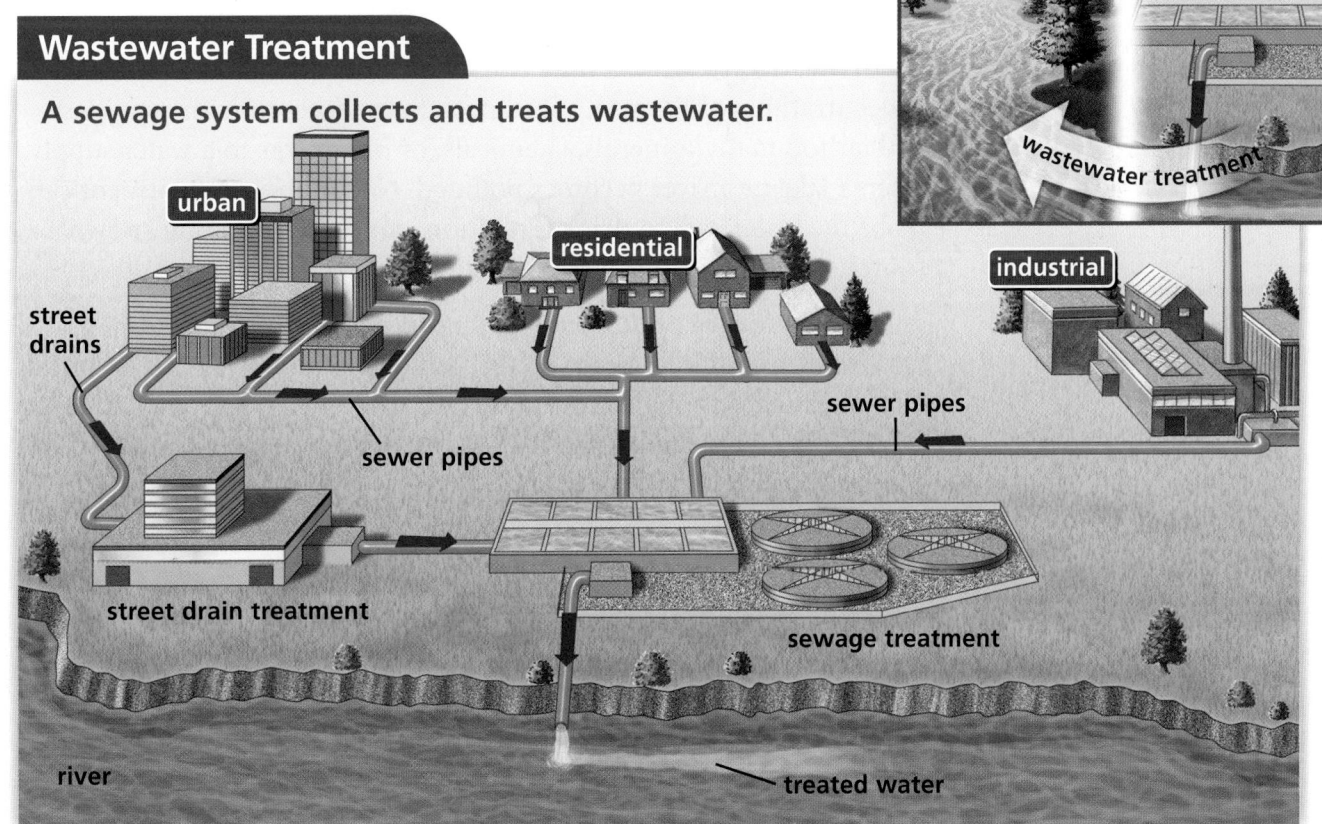

Water Use Cycle

water treatment

wastewater treatment

Wastewater Treatment

A sewage system collects and treats wastewater.

urban

residential

industrial

street drains

sewer pipes

sewer pipes

street drain treatment

sewage treatment

river

treated water

Septic System

A **septic system** is a small wastewater system used by a home or a business. Septic systems are more common in lightly populated areas that do not have central sewage treatment centers. In a house with a septic system, wastewater is carried out through a pipe to an underground tank away from the house. The sludge, or thicker material, in the wastewater settles to the bottom. Much of this sludge is consumed naturally by bacteria, just as in the large sewage treatment plants. Sludge that remains has to be removed from the tank every few years.

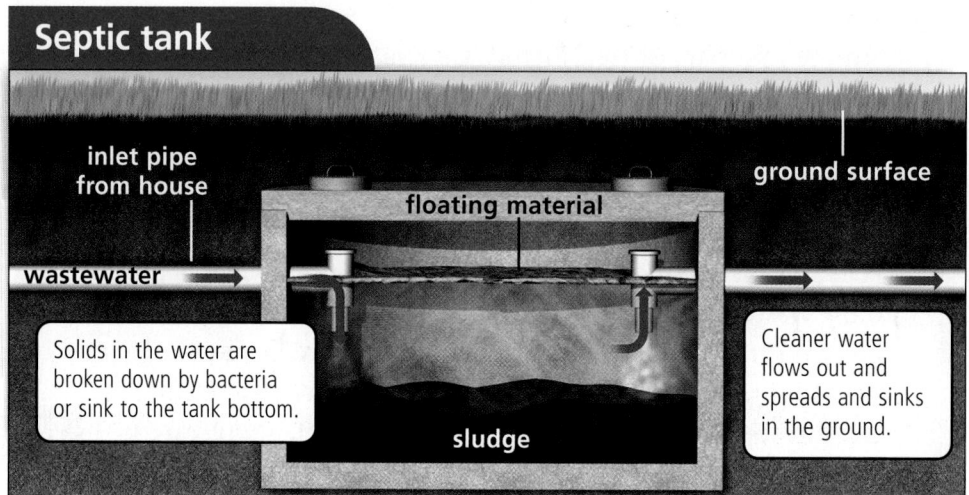

Septic tank

inlet pipe from house

floating material

ground surface

wastewater

Solids in the water are broken down by bacteria or sink to the tank bottom.

Cleaner water flows out and spreads and sinks in the ground.

sludge

Water pollution comes from many sources.

You have learned how fresh water is treated before we drink it. Unfortunately, treatment only works for water that has fairly low concentrations of harmful substances. Sometimes human activities add far too many minerals, chemicals, or organisms to a water supply. Then a lake or a river becomes polluted. No amount of treatment can make the water safe to drink. Pollution can come from one known source, or point, or it can come from many points.

VOCABULARY
Add a description wheel for *point-source pollution* to your notebook.

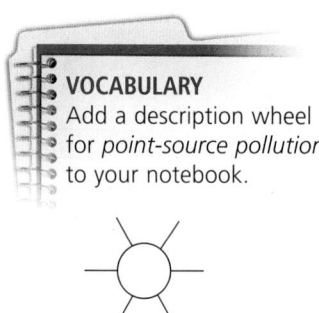

- **Point-source pollution** is pollution that enters water from a known source. It might be sewage flowing from a pipe or chemicals spewing out of a factory. This pollution is easy to spot, and laws can be enforced to stop it.

- **Nonpoint-source pollution** is pollution whose source is hard to find or is scattered. Rain and gravity cause water to wash off streets, lawns, construction sites, and farms. This water, called runoff, can carry oil, gas, pesticides, chemicals, paints, and detergents into storm drains or over land and then to rivers and lakes. If you don't know exactly where pollution comes from, it is hard to enforce laws against it. For this reason, nonpoint-source pollution causes most water pollution.

Sources of Water Pollution

Human activity can pollute the water supply.

Homes

- Improper disposal of household batteries, chemicals, and motor oil
- Use of fertilizers and pesticides
- Poorly functioning septic systems

Cities

- Illegal dumping of toxic chemicals
- Water and pollutants running off from streets
- Unsafe disposal of motor oil and other products

Sewage

- Improper disposal of factory wastewater
- Poorly functioning sewage systems
- Dumping of raw wastewater when sewage systems cannot handle heavy rainfall

Farms

- Heavy use of fertilizers and pesticides
- Leaks and spills of animal waste
- Animals grazing near rivers and lakes

Shipping, Boating, and Oil Transport

- Spills of oil or other cargo from barges and ships
- Fuel spills and leakage from small boats
- Illegal dumping
- Illegal release of sewage

READING VISUALS Identify three examples of point-source pollution.

Water pollution can be prevented.

Water pollution is a serious problem because water is a limited resource. When water is polluted, there is less water available for use. Water pollution can also endanger people's health. People and businesses can do a number of things to prevent or reduce pollution of water.

Industry and Transportation Operators of factories and of vehicles that haul cargo can take a number of steps to prevent or reduce water pollution. For example, factories can maintain their pipelines and equipment to ensure that harmful chemicals are not leaking into the ground and contaminating groundwater. Transportation companies can inspect and repair their trucks, planes, and ships to prevent oil and fuels from leaking onto pavement or into water.

Industry can prevent or reduce pollution by reducing the amount of toxic waste it generates. Factories can reuse and recycle chemicals and materials used in manufacturing. Companies can also provide ways for their customers to recycle or return certain products—such as used motor oil or batteries—that can pollute water if they are disposed of improperly.

In the construction industry, builders can design their projects to reduce the pollution that new construction can cause. Builders can use less pavement when they build parking areas for malls and office buildings. Less pavement reduces the amount of water that may run off and carry pollutants from cars and other sources to rivers and lakes. And measures to preserve open land, especially wetland areas, can protect a natural water cleansing system and reduce runoff.

READING TiP

A toxic substance is one that is capable of causing harm to health.

CHECK YOUR READING How does pavement contribute to water pollution?

Pollution can make a lake or river dangerous or unusable. In many places, people are cleaning up and restoring freshwater resources.

Agriculture Farming generates chemical and natural waste that can contaminate water. Farmers can follow practices that prevent or reduce pollution from agriculture. On farms with livestock, pastures used by cows and other grazing animals can be fenced off to keep animals away from streams and lakes. Keeping livestock away from water reduces pollution from animal waste. Farms that keep animals in structures can keep waste out of the water supply by storing and disposing of manure properly.

New techniques in farming can reduce pollution. Many farmers grow food without pesticides, which can be toxic and pollute water. The farmers fight insects and other pests by bringing in their natural enemies, such as ladybugs. To fertilize soil, the use of natural substances and the planting of certain crops can take the place of manufactured chemicals. Farming that does not use such chemicals is known as organic.

At home There are a number of things most people can do in their daily lives to prevent or reduce water pollution. People can take their old household chemicals to hazardous waste collection sites. Toxic chemicals should not be poured down the drain or onto the ground. Proper disposal and recycling of electronic devices such as computers can prevent toxic metals contained in them from reaching the water supply.

In shopping for food, consumers can choose organic products to support farming methods that don't use toxic pesticides. People can try to use nontoxic products in their homes. They can also stop using toxic pesticides and weed killers, as well as chemical fertilizers, on lawns and gardens.

These farmers in Vermont use organic methods to produce milk and ice cream.

3.2 Review

KEY CONCEPTS

1. How are EPA standards used to ensure a clean, safe supply of water?

2. What are two ways that wastewater is treated before it can be released?

3. What is the difference between point-source pollution and nonpoint-source pollution?

CRITICAL THINKING

4. **Compare and Contrast** How are sewage systems and septic systems alike? How are they different?

5. **Categorize** Categorize the following as point- or non-point-source pollution: small boat leaking oil; fish farm releasing wastes into a river; person dumping motor oil onto the ground.

CHALLENGE

6. **Compare** What parts of sewage and septic systems are similar to the way water is naturally cleaned by Earth's water cycle?

CHAPTER INVESTIGATION

Monitoring Water Quality

OVERVIEW AND PURPOSE Water pollution in some amount seems to happen wherever people live. That's why water for home drinking is almost always treated. Proper water treatment depends on knowing what forms of pollution water contains. This two-part activity models the process of monitoring for water quality. In this investigation you will

- perform systematic testing procedures similar to those used to test the water supply
- test known samples for common "pollutants," and then identify unknown water samples based on those tests

▶ Procedure

PART ONE

1 Make a data table for Part One like the one shown on the sample **Science Notebook** page on page 99.

2 Test the three different known contaminated water samples with the three types of indicator strips. Dip one of each strip into the solution and instantly remove it. A positive result causes a color change. Make your observations of color changes exactly 30 seconds after dipping the strip. Observe and note the results in your table so you know what a positive result looks like for each contaminant. Do not reuse test strips. You need fresh strips for each water sample.

3 Test the pure distilled water with the three types of indicator strips and note your results.

step 2

PART TWO

1 A water-testing company has mixed up four water samples taken from the following locations: a runoff stream from an agricultural field, a river near a factory, a pond on a dairy farm, and a mountain stream. You will test the four unknown samples using the same procedures as above to determine which sample has which contaminant. You will then determine which location the sample most likely came from.

MATERIALS
- 8 each of three types of indicator strips
- watch with second hand
- "pesticide-contaminated" water sample
- "bacteria-contaminated" water sample
- "chemical-contaminated" water sample
- pure distilled water sample
- 4 unknown water samples

2. Make a data table for Part Two like the one shown on the sample **Science Notebook** below.

3. Test each water sample as in step 2, Part One. Record your observations as you test each unknown sample with each indicator strip. Note all color changes you observe.

4. Consult the chart you completed in Part One as you perform tests to determine which type of contaminant each unknown sample contains. From this information determine which location the sample probably came from.

Observe and Analyze

1. **IDENTIFY CONTROLS** Why was it necessary to test the distilled water in Part One?

2. **IDENTIFY** Use what you have learned in this chapter to determine which location corresponds to the types of pollution you learned to identify in Part One.

3. **ANALYZE** Compare your testing results from the unknown water samples with your testing results from the known water samples. Are your results similar?

Conclude

1. **COMPARE** How did your results in Part One compare with your results in Part Two?

2. **EVALUATE** What part of this investigation was the most difficult? Why?

3. **IDENTIFY LIMITS** What limitations does this type of testing pose for real-life water-quality technicians?

4. **APPLY** A runoff pool is contaminated with bacteria, chemicals, and pesticides. How would your water-testing results appear for a sample from this pool?

▶ INVESTIGATE Further

CHALLENGE Design a procedure to test unknown water samples that have numerous contaminants.

Monitoring Water Quality

Table 1. Positive Test Results of Known Water Samples

	Pure distilled water	Chemical-contaminated water	Bacteria-contaminated water	Pesticide-contaminated water
Indicator A				
Indicator B				
Indicator C				

Table 2. Test Results of Unknown Samples with Probable Locations

	Unknown #1	Unknown #2	Unknown #3	Unknown #4
Indicator A				
Indicator B				
Indicator C				
Type of Contaminant				
Location				

KEY CONCEPT

Water shortages threaten society.

Sunshine State STANDARDS

SC.D.1.3.1: The student knows how conditions that exist in one system influence the conditions that exist in other systems.

SC.D.2.3.1: The student understands that quality of life is relevant to personal experience.

◀ **BEFORE, you learned**

- Water is treated for drinking
- Wastewater is treated and released
- Pollutants contaminate the water supply

▶ **NOW, you will learn**

- How overuse causes water shortages
- How water can be conserved
- How governments and organizations manage water use

VOCABULARY

drought p. 101
desalination p. 106

EXPLORE The Value of Fresh Water

Does water cost more than gasoline?

PROCEDURE

1. Find out the current price of a liter of bottled water.

2. Find out the current price of a gallon of gasoline.

3. To calculate the price of gasoline in liters, multiply the price per gallon by 0.26.

WHAT DO YOU THINK?

- How do the prices of bottled water and gasoline compare?
- What do your results tell you about the value of drinking water?

MATERIALS
calculator

Water shortages are a global problem.

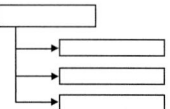

SUPPORTING MAIN IDEAS
Support the main idea of global water shortages with details and examples.

Most nations in the deserts of northern Africa and in the Middle East have severe water shortages. These are some of the driest regions on Earth, but their populations require more and more water as cities grow. Water that could be used to grow food is piped instead to the growing cities, where it is needed in homes and factories.

So how do people in these regions grow enough food? For the most part, they cannot. There is simply not enough water. Jordan imports, or brings in from other countries, about 91 percent of its grain. Israel imports about 87 percent, and Egypt, once a center of agriculture, imports 40 percent.

All over the world, the water supply is dwindling. Populations are growing everywhere, and people must be fed. Farmers draw water from underground aquifers faster than the water can be replaced.

Even places that normally get regular rainfall can face water shortages. **Drought** (drowt) is a long period of abnormally low rainfall. Drought can destroy crops and dry up water supplies. Usually, trees can survive a dry period because their roots reach into the ground for water. However, severe drought can dry out entire forests. Dry trees are more vulnerable to disease, and wildfires are harder to control.

Overuse can cause water shortages.

As the world's population grows, usable fresh water is becoming scarcer in many places. Agriculture uses two-thirds of the world's available fresh water. Unfortunately, only half of that water reaches the roots of the plants. The other half is lost to evaporation and runoff.

Overuse of underground water can cause an aquifer to be depleted, or consumed faster than its water is replaced. In most places where crops require irrigation, farmers water their fields with groundwater. India is using twice as much water from its aquifers as can be replaced. In the United States, farmers are taking so much water that they are draining the huge Ogallala Aquifer. The problem is that underground stores of water can take thousands of years to refill. Draining an aquifer can also destroy it. When water is removed, the ground may settle and close up the storage space.

River water is also being overused in many places. So much water is being taken out that many major rivers now run dry for a large part of the year. These rivers include the Ganges River in South Asia, the Indus River in Pakistan, and the Colorado River in the southwestern United States. People in seven western states use water from the Colorado. As cities in these states have grown, the demand for the river water has increased.

A bridge stands over a dried-out part of a reservoir during a drought in Maryland.

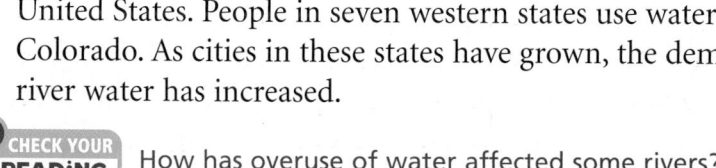

CHECK YOUR READING How has overuse of water affected some rivers?

Fresh water can be conserved.

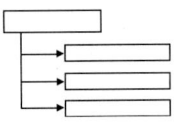
Although water shortages are a serious problem, the situation is not entirely hopeless. Conserving can solve a big part of the problem. Conservation is action taken to protect and preserve the natural world. To conserve water means to use less of it.

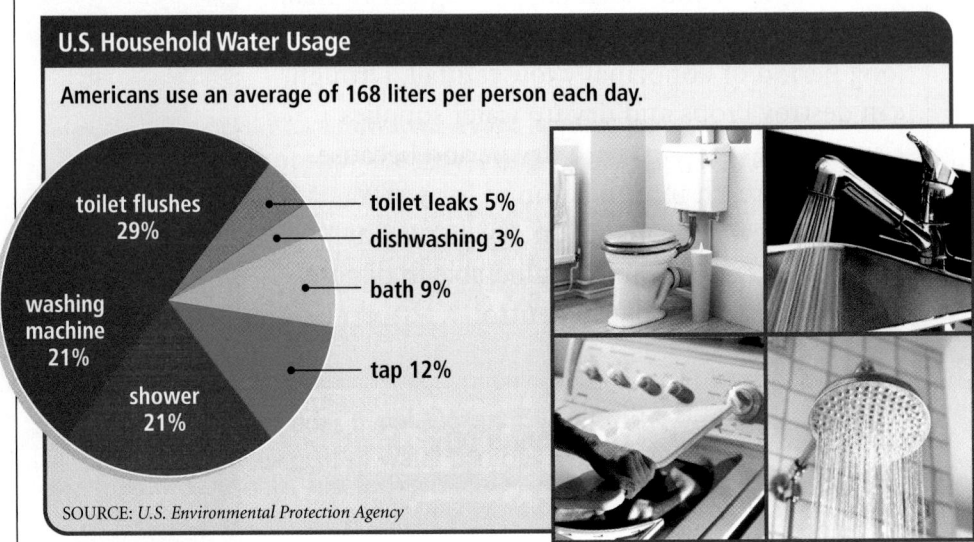

U.S. Household Water Usage

Americans use an average of 168 liters per person each day.

- toilet flushes 29%
- washing machine 21%
- shower 21%
- toilet leaks 5%
- dishwashing 3%
- bath 9%
- tap 12%

SOURCE: *U.S. Environmental Protection Agency*

The chart above shows how Americans use water each day. The amount that each American uses on average—168 liters—is higher than in most parts of the world. Note that 5 percent of the amount—more than 8 liters—is wasted by leaking toilets.

The Need for Conservation

Think about what you already know about the water cycle. When aquifers, lakes, and rivers are depleted—or used up faster than the water in them can be replaced naturally—available fresh water from those water supplies decreases. Because water supplies in many regions are being depleted, conservation is an urgent issue.

Much of the western United States is mostly desert, and yet the population in dry parts of the West is growing each year. What will happen if the aquifers and rivers that supply this region with water dry up? The less water that people use today, the more water there will be to use in the future.

Water shortages are an increasing problem around the world as the population grows in many regions. About half a billion people in 31 countries—mostly in the Middle East and Africa—currently face water shortages. By 2025, the number of people without enough water will increase five times, to about 2.8 billion people.

These water-catching devices are used to collect and store rainwater in Hawaii.

Conservation Practices

People conserve water in three ways. The first way is to use less water. Some cities conserve their supply of water simply by repairing leaks in underground pipes. The second way is to reuse water. Many cities reuse treated wastewater for landscaping. The third method is to recycle water, or use water again for the same purpose.

RESOURCE CENTER
CLASSZONE.COM
Learn more about water conservation.

Farmers can conserve water by using drip irrigation instead of spraying water. They can change the grooves in their fields so the water stays in the soil longer. Most industries can use water at least twice before returning it to a river or lake. For example, water used to cool machines can be recycled back through the same system.

At home, people can change their plumbing and their habits. Low-flow toilets and showerheads can cut water use in half. People conserve water by turning off the faucet while brushing their teeth, taking shorter showers, and running the dishwasher only when it is full. Leaking pipes and dripping faucets in homes cause huge amounts of water to be wasted. Repair and maintenance of plumbing systems would reduce water use greatly.

CHECK YOUR READING   What are the three main ways in which people conserve water?

INVESTIGATE Water Conservation

How much water does a dripping faucet use?

1. Adjust a faucet so that water drips slowly.

2. Set a container under the faucet and collect the dripping water for five minutes.

3. Turn off the faucet. Use the graduated cylinder to measure how much water dripped. Record your results in milliliters.

4. Multiply the amount by 12 to determine how much water would drip in an hour. Then divide that number by 1000 to convert your result to liters.

WHAT DO YOU THINK?

- How much water would one leaky faucet waste in a day?

- In a town with 2000 houses with one leaky faucet in each, how much water would be wasted each day?

CHALLENGE How could you combine your results with those of your classmates to make the results more reliable?

SKILL FOCUS
Measuring

MATERIALS
- water faucet
- container
- funnel
- 100 mL graduated cylinder

TIME
20 minutes

Chapter 3: Freshwater Resources **103**

People can balance water needs and uses.

People around the world have different views about how water should be used. Americans in the hot Southwest might want water for swimming pools and lawns. Developing countries need water to prevent disease and grow food. In some places, farmers use river water before it can reach others downstream. Some industries want water to make products.

As water becomes scarcer, the arguments become more serious. Public officials and experts can help manage water use and enforce fair laws. For example, what happens when a river flows from one state into another or across a national border? In such a situation, people must agree to share the water rights.

The Rio Grande flows through two states and then between Texas and Mexico. The water in this river is an international issue. In 1939 a legal agreement was made between the states of Colorado, New Mexico, and Texas, and between the United States and Mexico. It listed how much water each region could take.

In the past, water from the Rio Grande was used for farming. However, cities along the river are growing rapidly. All the cities need more water from the Rio Grande, and every year they will need more. The international agreement no longer solves this urgent problem. American and Mexican officials are looking for new solutions.

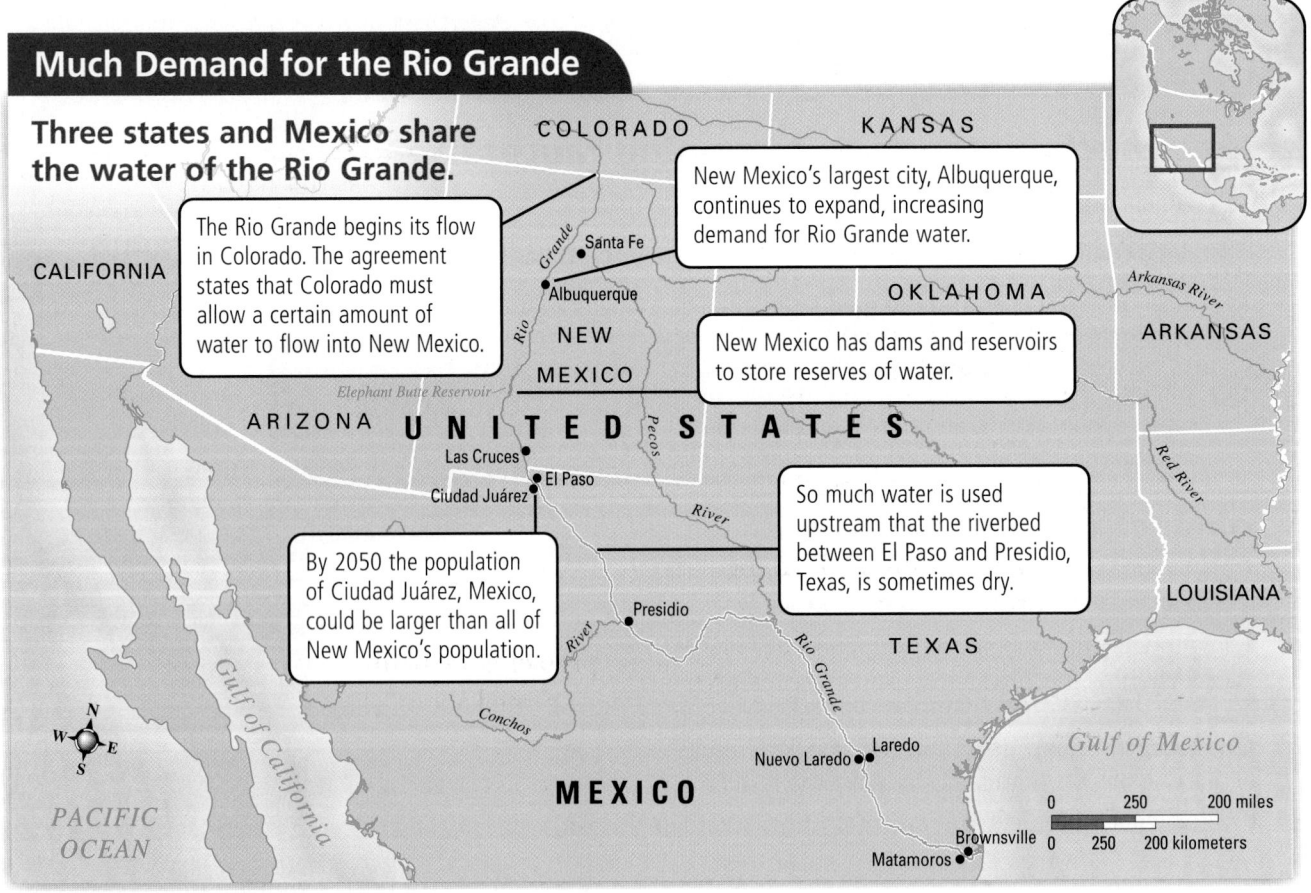

Much Demand for the Rio Grande

Three states and Mexico share the water of the Rio Grande.

The Rio Grande begins its flow in Colorado. The agreement states that Colorado must allow a certain amount of water to flow into New Mexico.

New Mexico's largest city, Albuquerque, continues to expand, increasing demand for Rio Grande water.

New Mexico has dams and reservoirs to store reserves of water.

So much water is used upstream that the riverbed between El Paso and Presidio, Texas, is sometimes dry.

By 2050 the population of Ciudad Juárez, Mexico, could be larger than all of New Mexico's population.

Shortages

When there is not enough water, crops will not grow. And when the crops fail to grow, there is not enough food to eat. The Middle East countries that import most of their grain are, in a way, importing water. Billions of tons of water are used to grow the imported grain.

International organizations help out countries where drought and floods have destroyed the crops. For example, in 2002 the World Food Programme alerted the world to a serious lack of food in southeast Africa. The United Nations agencies arranged for food aid. The shrinking of Lake Chad has also caused hardship for many Africans.

In the future, people may solve some of the problems by sharing water around the world. The governor of Alaska has suggested an undersea pipeline. This line would be between 2200 kilometers (1360 mi) and 3400 kilometers (2100 mi) long. Through this pipe, thousands of liters of fresh water would flow from Alaska to California. Some people have also suggested selling Great Lakes water to Japan. Many people in states and Canadian provinces around the lakes have strongly objected, because they think removing water could damage the lakes.

 **CHECK YOUR READING** How can Alaska help solve a water shortage in California?

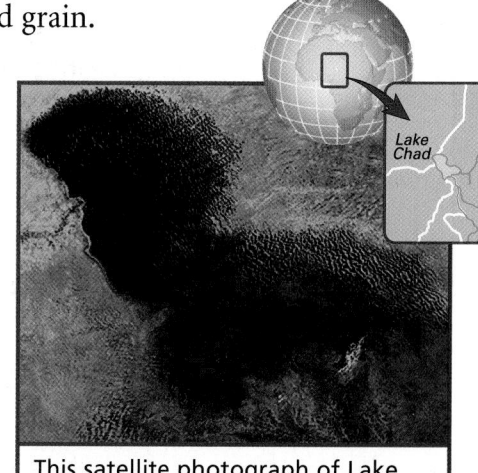

This satellite photograph of Lake Chad in Africa was taken in 1973.

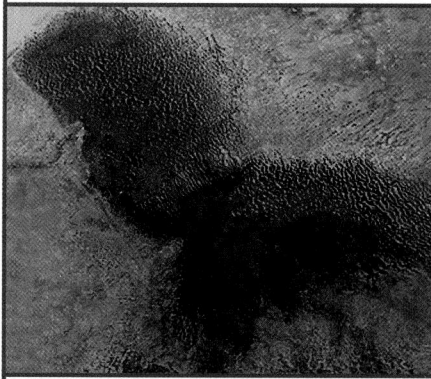

A recent photograph shows how much the lake has shrunk.

Pollution

Where water flows across the boundaries of nations, pollution can flow across as well. One example of this problem is the Danube River in Europe. This river begins in the Black Forest in Germany. It empties into the Black Sea on the coast of Romania. As it flows through the cities of Vienna, Budapest, and Belgrade, more and more pollution is added to the water. Seventeen countries border either the Danube River or the Black Sea. To protect the river and the sea, as well as to manage use of the river water, 11 nations made an agreement among themselves and the European Union. They agreed to cooperate to prevent pollution of the water and to conserve and use water from the Danube sensibly. They also agreed to conserve and protect groundwater.

Some national and international water pollution problems are hard to solve. States in the northeastern United States are concerned about acid rain. Particle pollution from factories to the west is collected in clouds. Then the wind blows the clouds across the Eastern states, and acid rain falls in lakes and rivers that are far from the source. The acid rain can kill plants, as well as fish and other animals.

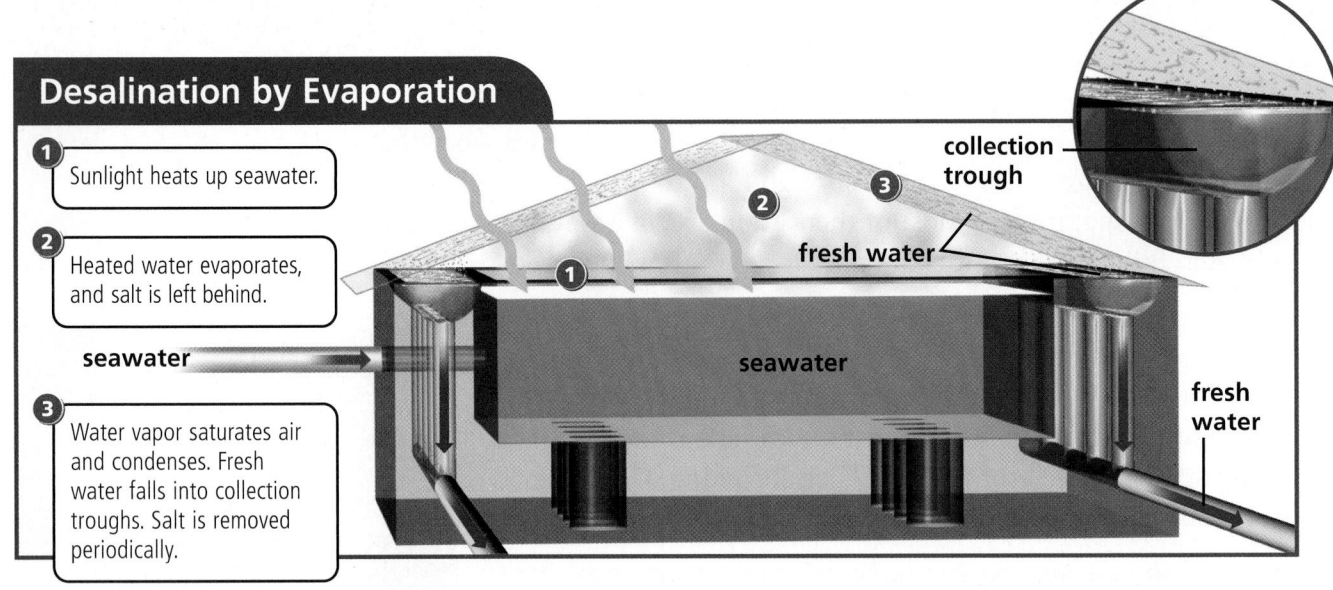

Desalination by Evaporation

1 Sunlight heats up seawater.

2 Heated water evaporates, and salt is left behind.

3 Water vapor saturates air and condenses. Fresh water falls into collection troughs. Salt is removed periodically.

collection trough

fresh water

seawater

seawater

fresh water

New Sources

Can people find new sources of fresh water? The answer, at first, seems obvious. Just remove the salt from seawater. In dry regions, such as Israel, Lebanon, and some coastal towns in California and Florida, people are trying to obtain fresh water this way. The process of removing salt from ocean water is called **desalination** (dee-SAL-ih-NAY-shun). Some treatment plants use a method similar to the natural water cycle. Salt water is evaporated, and salt is left behind. Then water vapor is condensed, or returned to liquid form, as fresh water.

If this process were easy and inexpensive, water shortages might never happen. However, desalination can cost five times as much as normal water treatment. Therefore, it is not a solution that will work for most countries. As technology improves, the cost may go down.

Another possible source of fresh water is icebergs. Icebergs contain millions of liters of fresh water. However, the process of towing an iceberg to a city before it melts is too expensive to be practical.

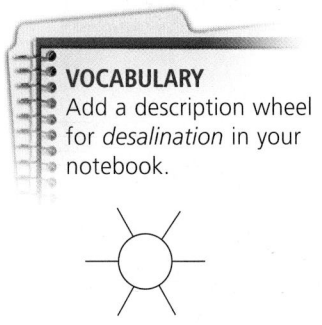

VOCABULARY
Add a description wheel for *desalination* in your notebook.

3.3 Review

KEY CONCEPTS

1. What is drought and what problems does it cause?

2. How are aquifers and rivers being depleted?

3. Name two ways to help prevent water shortages.

CRITICAL THINKING

4. **Connect** Draw up a plan that suggests three ways to conserve water at your school. Be sure your ideas are practical, and explain how you might convince people to make the changes.

5. **Infer** Why do you think some people object to building a water pipeline from Alaska to California?

◆ CHALLENGE

6. **Synthesize** Think about what you have learned about national and international water issues. Then think about what you know about aquifers. What usage problems might occur when one aquifer lies under two countries? How might people solve any problems that arise?

Water and Farming

Farmers have used irrigation, the process of supplying water to crops, for at least 7000 years. Today, about 60 percent of the fresh water used in the world goes for irrigation. However, about one-third of this water does not reach the crops. Some of it runs off the field. By building ditches and ponds, farmers can capture runoff water and pump it back into a field.

Irrigation water can also evaporate before crops can use it. Farmers can reduce this loss by understanding how changes in air temperature, relative humidity, and wind speed affect the evaporation rate. Then farmers can adjust when and how much they irrigate.

Spray Irrigation

In some systems, sprinklers as much as 400 meters (1300 ft) long spray water on crops. Since the water is sprayed into the air, evaporation loss can be high. Spray irrigation is used for many crops in the western United States. Spraying at night can reduce evaporation loss.

Flood Irrigation

Many farmers send water through small ditches between rows of crops, or sometimes farmers flood entire fields. Compared with other systems, flooding results in higher losses from runoff. Flooding is commonly used by rice farmers in eastern Asia.

Drip Irrigation

In drip irrigation, water bubbles out of pipes lying on or just above the ground throughout a field or orchard. The water reaches the ground quickly and in small amounts, so little is lost to runoff or evaporation. Farmers growing fruits and vegetables frequently use this system.

EXPLORE

1. **ANALYZING** Compare the amounts of labor, machinery, and water used in each irrigation system. Which system uses water most efficiently? In what climate regions is this most important? Why would farmers choose a system that uses water less efficiently?

2. **CHALLENGE** Create a model of a flood irrigation system. Use dirt in a pan, with toothpicks to represent crops. Make ditches that send water evenly throughout the "field." As you pour water into your system, note any soil loss that may occur. How can you fix this problem?

3 Chapter Review

the **BIG** idea

Fresh water is a limited resource and is essential for human society.

KEY CONCEPTS SUMMARY

1 Fresh water is an essential resource.
Fresh water is essential for life and is used for many human activities.

fresh water

- farming
- industry
- transportation and recreation
- fisheries and aquaculture
- energy
- living organisms

VOCABULARY
irrigation p. 83
aquaculture p. 85
dam p. 86
lock p. 86

2 Society depends on clean and safe water.
Water is treated for safe drinking. Pollution can harm the water supply.

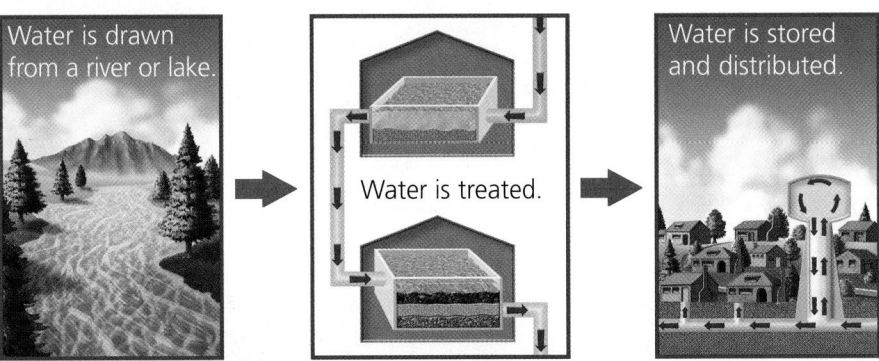

Water is drawn from a river or lake. → Water is treated. → Water is stored and distributed.

VOCABULARY
concentration p. 91
sewage system p. 93
septic system p. 94
point-source pollution
  p. 94
nonpoint-source
  pollution p. 94

3 Water shortages threaten society.
Drought and overuse can cause water shortages.

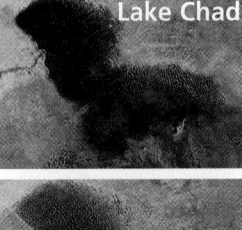
Lake Chad

Americans use an average of 168 liters per person each day.

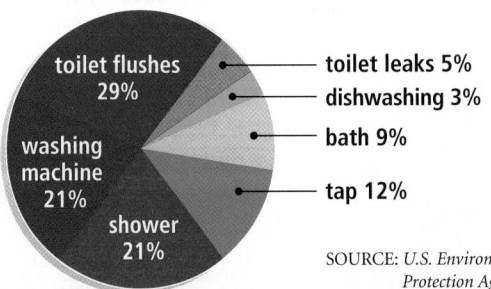

toilet flushes 29%
washing machine 21%
shower 21%
toilet leaks 5%
dishwashing 3%
bath 9%
tap 12%

SOURCE: *U.S. Environmental Protection Agency*

VOCABULARY
drought p. 101
desalination p. 106

Use words from the box below to answer the next nine questions.

septic system	nonpoint-source pollution	desalination
concentration	sewage system	point-source pollution
aquaculture	drought	irrigation

1. Which word means "fish farming"?

2. What is the term for a method farmers use to bring water to their fields from rivers and aquifers?

3. Which term can be used to describe the amount of a harmful substance in fresh water?

4. Which term would be used for waste flowing from a factory pipe?

5. Select the term for what a city uses to collect and treat wastewater.

6. Which term would describe oil running off from a parking lot during a rainstorm?

7. What word describes a period when there is little or no rainfall?

8. What process is used to obtain fresh water from seawater?

9. Which term describes a method for treating home wastewater in an underground tank?

Reviewing Key Concepts

Multiple Choice Choose the letter of the best answer.

10. Which type of irrigation pours water through canals and waterways?
　a. flood irrigation　　**c.** drip irrigation
　b. spray irrigation　　**d.** reservoir irrigation

11. A channel dug to allow boats to travel from one river to another is an example of a
　a. canal　　**c.** reservoir
　b. lake　　**d.** sewage system

12. A section of a waterway in which ships are raised or lowered is called a
　a. turbine　　**c.** dam
　b. fish ladder　　**d.** lock

13. Concentrations of substances are often expressed as
　a. whole parts
　b. parts per million
　c. parts per thousand
　d. parts per hundred

14. In a sewage plant, sludge and oil are consumed by
　a. chlorine　　**c.** bacteria
　b. sand　　**d.** filters

15. In a sewage system, what is added to kill harmful bacteria?
　a. chlorine　　**c.** bacteria
　b. sand　　**d.** soap

16. The term for pollution that can be traced to a specific location is
　a. water pollution
　b. point-source pollution
　c. nonpoint-source pollution
　d. runoff pollution

Short Response Write a short response to each question.

17. How are aquifers depleted?

18. How are EPA standards used to protect fresh water?

19. How does the practice of organic farming help prevent water pollution?

20. What problems do people have sharing water from the Rio Grande?

Thinking Critically

Use the map to answer the next five questions.

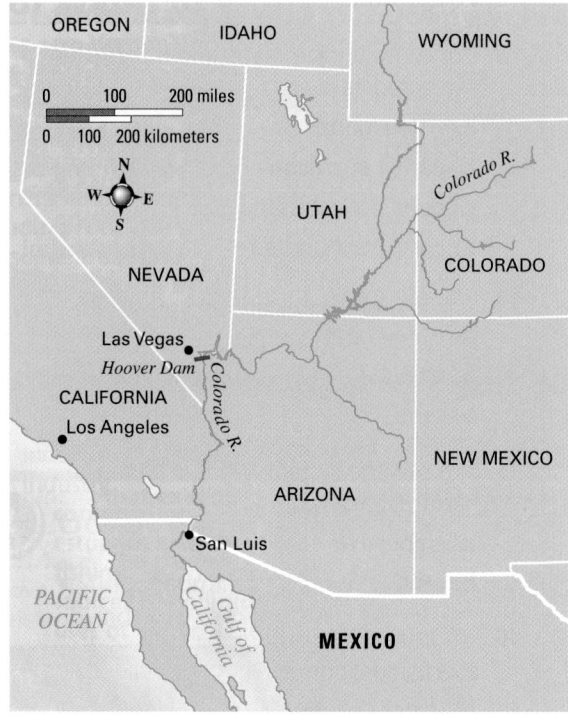

The Colorado River runs from Colorado to the Gulf of California. In California water is needed for 17 million people and also to irrigate 3642 square kilometers (900,000 acres) of farmland. The Colorado provides 60 percent of this water.

21. OBSERVE Through which states and countries does the Colorado River flow?

22. EXAMPLES What are three ways in which water from the Colorado is probably used?

23. INFER What conflicts probably exist between the states of California and Arizona?

24. PREDICT As populations grow in Las Vegas, southern California, and San Luis, Mexico, what problems will arise? How can they be solved?

25. CONNECT Do you think states should receive equal shares of the water in the Colorado River? Explain your answer.

26. IDENTIFY CAUSE Copy the concept map below, and complete it by adding two causes of, and two solutions to, the problem of the water level of an aquifer sinking.

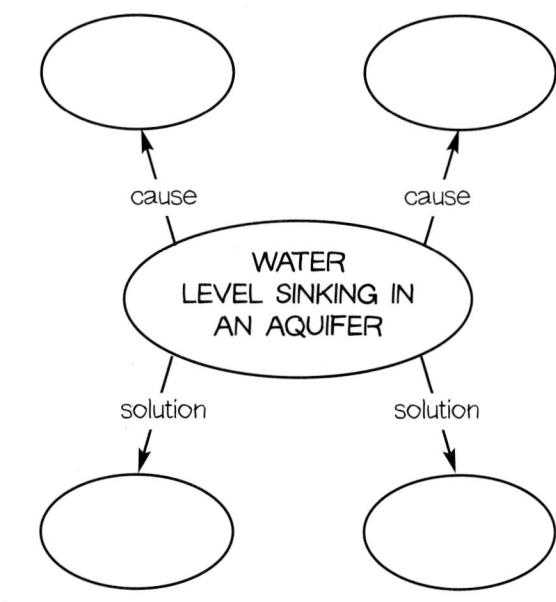

the BIG idea

27. PROVIDE EXAMPLES Look again at the photograph on pages 78–79. Now that you have finished the chapter, how would you change your response to the question on the photograph?

28. SEQUENCE Draw a diagram of the path that fresh water travels before and after humans use it. Show where freshwater comes from, how it is treated, how it arrives at our homes, how it leaves our homes as wastewater, how it is treated again, and how it reenters the water cycle.

UNIT PROJECTS

If you need to do an experiment for your unit project, gather the materials. Be sure to allow enough time to observe results before the project is due.

Analyzing a Graph

The line graph below shows the amount of a chemical found in a stream. During the period shown, a factory opened and released water into the stream. Later, a wastewater treatment plant opened and treated water from the factory before it entered the stream. Study the graph and use it to answer the first six questions below.

> **FCAT TiP**
>
> When analyzing a line graph, be sure to read the labels on the x-axis and y-axis. This will help you understand the relationship between the two types data shown on the graph.

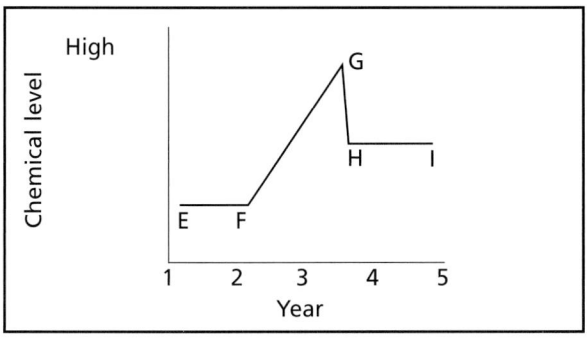

MULTIPLE CHOICE

1. Which word or phrase best describes the concentration of the chemical at Point E?
   - **A.** low
   - **B.** medium
   - **C.** somewhat high
   - **D.** very high

2. A new factory opens during year 2. What immediately happens to the concentration of the chemical?
   - **F.** It does not change.
   - **G.** It decreases sharply.
   - **H.** It decreases slightly.
   - **I.** It increases sharply.

3. Which point probably marks when a new wastewater treatment plant opened?
   - **A.** E
   - **B.** F
   - **C.** G
   - **D.** I

4. Point-source pollution comes from a known source. Which amount is point-source pollution?
   - **F.** the difference between E and F
   - **G.** the difference between F and G
   - **H.** the difference between G and H
   - **I.** the difference between H and I

SHORT RESPONSE

5. In which year did the wastewater treatment plant most likely open? What effect did it have on data for later years?

6. How could you explain that the overall concentration in year 5 was higher than in year 1?

EXTENDED RESPONSE

Answer the two questions below in detail. Include some of the terms shown in the word box. Underline each term you use in your answers.

evaporate	condense	precipitation
groundwater	irrigation	rain

7. Describe the parts of the water cycle that are involved at a desalination plant.

8. For a science fair project, Anthony compared the growth of plants that got their water in different ways. One group grew in soil that he kept moist by providing water through a tube under the surface. For a second group, he poured water on top of the soil each day. In the third group, he sprayed water from a bottle on the plants. How are the three methods Anthony used similar to ways that farmers irrigate crops?

Ocean Systems

the **BIG** idea

The oceans are a connected system of water in motion.

Key Concepts

SECTION
1 The oceans are a connected system.
Learn about ocean water and the ocean floor.

SECTION
2 Ocean water moves in currents.
Learn about currents and how they interact with climate and weather.

SECTION
3 Waves move through oceans.
Learn how waves form and move through the ocean.

SECTION
4 Waters rise and fall in tides.
Learn how tides are related to the Sun and the Moon.

FCAT Practice

Prepare and practice for the FCAT
• Section Reviews, pp. 122, 128, 133, 140
• Chapter Review, pp. 142–144
• FCAT Practice, p. 145

CLASSZONE.COM
• Florida Review: Content Review and FCAT Practice

What causes these waves?

EXPLORE the BIG idea

What Makes Things Float or Sink?

Fill two clear cups with water. Add a heaping spoonful of salt to one cup and stir until it dissolves. Gently squeeze two drops of food coloring into each cup.

Observe and Think What happened to the drops of food coloring in each cup?

How Does Moving Air Affect Water?

Fill a pan with water. Use a straw to blow over the surface of the water.

Observe and Think What happened to the water when you blew on it? Draw a diagram to show what happened.

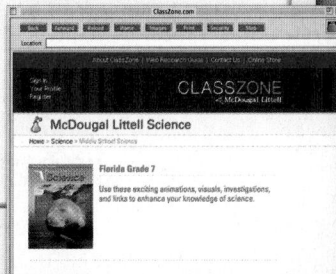

Internet Activity: The Ocean Floor

Go to **ClassZone.com** to expose the ocean floor by draining all of the water out of the ocean.

Observe and Think How are the features of the ocean floor similar to features on land? How are they different?

NSTA
scilinks.org

SCI LINKS

Exploring Earth's Oceans Code: MDL020

Getting Ready to Learn

◀ CONCEPT REVIEW

- Water covers most of Earth.
- Earth's waters circulate in the water cycle.
- The water in the oceans is salt water.

◀ VOCABULARY REVIEW

salt water p. 51

water cycle p. 52

evaporation p. 53

desalination p. 106

ⓘ FLORIDA REVIEW
CLASSZONE.COM

Content Review and FCAT Practice

▶ TAKING NOTES

OUTLINE

As you read, copy the headings into your notebook in the form of an outline. Then add notes in your own words that summarize what you read.

VOCABULARY STRATEGY

Draw a **word triangle** for each new vocabulary term. At the bottom, write and define the term. Above that, write a sentence in which you use the term correctly. At the top, draw a small picture to represent the term.

See the Note-Taking Handbook on pages R45–R51.

SCIENCE NOTEBOOK

OUTLINE

I. The oceans are a connected system.

  A. Ocean water covers much of Earth.

  B. Ocean water contains salts and gases.

    1.

    2.

  C. Ocean temperatures vary.

    1.

    2.

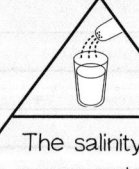

The salinity of ocean water is about 35 grams of salt per 1000 grams of water

salinity: a measure of the saltiness of water

4.1 The oceans are a connected system.

① **Sunshine State STANDARDS**

SC.D.1.3.3: The student knows how conditions that exist in one system influence the conditions that exist in other systems.

◁ **BEFORE, you learned**

- Most water on Earth is salt water
- The ocean plays an important role in the water cycle

▷ **NOW, you will learn**

- What ocean water contains
- What the ocean floor looks like
- How people explore the ocean

① **FCAT VOCABULARY**

density p. 116

VOCABULARY

salinity p. 116
continental shelf p. 120
sonar p. 122

EXPLORE Density

Why do liquids form layers?

PROCEDURE

① Insert the straw into one of the solutions. Cover the top of the straw with your finger and then remove the straw from the solution. The liquid should stay in the straw.

② Using this technique, try to layer the three liquids in your straw so that you can see three distinct layers.

③ Experiment with the order in which you place the liquids into the straw. Between trials, empty the contents of the straw into the waste cup.

WHAT DO YOU THINK?
Did it matter in what order you layered the liquids? If so, can you explain why?

MATERIALS
- 3 solutions—A, B, and C—provided by your teacher
- clear straw
- waste cup

Ocean water covers much of Earth.

As land animals, we naturally think of our planet as a rocky and solid place. We even named our planet Earth, which means "land" or "soil." But look at a globe and you will see that oceans cover most of Earth. In fact, 71 percent of Earth is covered in seawater.

Looking at a map of the world, you can see the seven continents spread over our planet. These landmasses divide Earth's global ocean into connected sections. Different sections of the ocean have different names, such as Atlantic, Indian, and Pacific. However, all the sections are connected.

OUTLINE
Remember to start an outline for this section.

I. Main idea
  A. Supporting idea
    1. Detail
    2. Detail
  B. Supporting idea

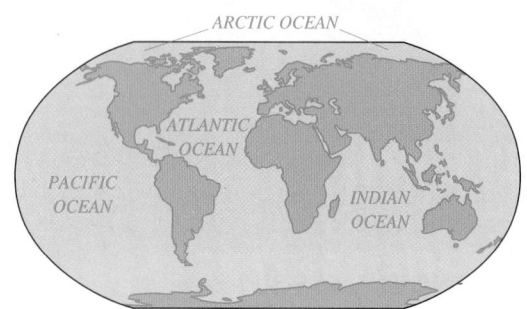
The global ocean is one connected body of water, divided into sections by the continents.

How did Earth become covered by an ocean? Scientists have several theories. The most commonly accepted explanation has to do with how Earth formed. Earth formed about 4.6 billion years ago as a ball of molten rock. Heavier materials sank to the core, and lighter materials floated toward the surface—the same way oil and vinegar in salad dressing separate into layers. Water vapor, a very light substance, rose to the cooler surface. By about 4 billion years ago, Earth had cooled enough for the water vapor to become liquid. At that time, the vapor condensed—just as water vapor condenses into droplets on a cool glass of lemonade—forming liquid water that became the ocean.

Ocean water contains salts and gases.

Despite its name, the salt water that fills the ocean is much more than just salt and water. Ocean water contains many different dissolved substances. Sodium chloride, which is the same compound as ordinary table salt, is the most plentiful of these substances. The ocean also contains other dissolved solids, as well as dissolved molecules of the same gases found in the atmosphere. In fact, the ocean contains all 92 elements that occur in nature, although most are in very tiny amounts.

Salts

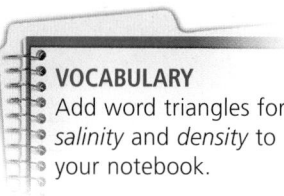

VOCABULARY
Add word triangles for *salinity* and *density* to your notebook.

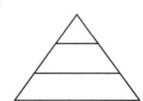

One taste will convince you that ocean water is salty. Every 1000 grams of seawater contains an average of 35 grams of salt. **Salinity** (suh-LIHN-ih-tee) is a measure of the amount of dissolved salt contained in water. The ocean contains many different kinds of salts. However, sodium chloride accounts for most of the ocean's salinity.

The elements that make up salts are found in rocks and minerals. Over time, rain and rivers wash some of these elements into the sea. The elements that make up salts also enter the ocean when underwater volcanoes erupt. Natural processes also remove salt from the ocean. Because salt is added as well as removed, the ocean's overall salinity does not change much over time. The ocean's salinity has stayed constant for the past 1.5 billion years.

Water that contains dissolved solids, such as salts, is heavier than the same amount of water with no dissolved solids. In other words, salt water has a greater density than fresh water. **Density** is a measure of the amount of matter packed into a given volume.

The higher water's salt content, the greater its density. The denser the water, the more easily things float in it. As you can see in the photograph on page 117, the Dead Sea is so salty (and dense) that people can float easily on the surface.

Salinity and Density

Salt water has a greater density than fresh water.

Fresh Water	Ocean Water	Dead Sea Water
 dissolved solids		
Fresh water has fewer dissolved solids than salt water, so it is less dense than salt water.	Ocean water is more dense than fresh water because it has more dissolved solids.	The Dead Sea is about ten times saltier than the ocean, so Dead Sea water is more dense than ocean water.

Located between Israel and Jordan, the Dead Sea is actually a salty lake and not part of the ocean. Its high salinity, and therefore high density, allows people to float more easily in it than in fresh water or in the ocean.

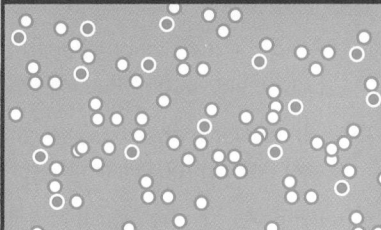

Dead Sea

Some parts of the ocean are saltier than others. When water evaporates from the ocean, the salts are left behind, causing the remaining water to become even saltier. Ocean water is especially salty in places where water evaporates quickly, such as in shallow areas and warm climates. Salinity is also higher in very cold areas, where the ocean water freezes. When ice forms on the ocean, the salt is left in the water below.

Salinity is lower in areas where the ocean is diluted by fresh water. For example, seawater has lower salinity in places where rivers empty into the ocean. Similarly, the ocean's salinity is lower in areas where a lot of rain falls.

CHECK YOUR READING How are salinity and density related?

INVESTIGATE Density

How does dense water move?

PROCEDURE

1. Read the instructions below and predict what will happen in steps 3 and 4 before you begin. Record your predictions.

2. Fill one jar with tap water and color it blue. Fill another jar with salt water and color it red. Place an index card over the top of the jar of red salt water.

3. With your hand over the index card, turn the jar over and place it on top of the jar with the blue tap water. Pull out the index card and observe the water movement, if any.

4. Repeat steps 2 and 3, but with the blue tap water on the top.

WHAT DO YOU THINK?

- Describe any ways in which your observations differed from your predictions. On what did you base your predictions?

- Explain why the water moved, if it did, in each of the two setups.

CHALLENGE How do you think water in the ocean might be layered?

Oxygen and Other Gases

Fish, like other animals, need oxygen to live. Oxygen and other gases dissolve in water, just as sugar dissolves in tea. The ocean contains the same gases as the air, including oxygen, nitrogen, and carbon dioxide. Dissolved gases are essential to ocean life.

You know that when you breathe, you use oxygen and exhale carbon dioxide. Ocean animals also take in oxygen and give off carbon dioxide. Oxygen and carbon dioxide get mixed into the ocean from the air above the ocean surface. Oxygen is also added to the ocean by plants and algae that live near the surface. Plants and algae use sunlight to convert carbon dioxide and water into food, and release oxygen into the water. Besides being used by plants to make food, carbon dioxide is a building block of ocean animals' shells.

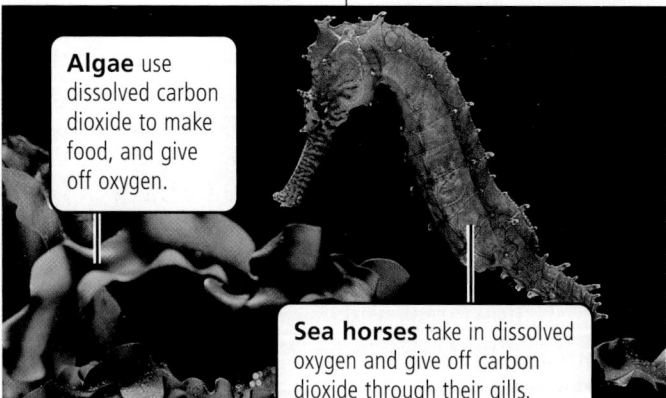

Algae use dissolved carbon dioxide to make food, and give off oxygen.

Sea horses take in dissolved oxygen and give off carbon dioxide through their gills.

CHECK YOUR READING Where does the oxygen in the ocean come from? Name two sources.

Ocean temperatures vary.

Oceanographers—people who study the ocean—divide ocean water into three layers on the basis of temperature.

1 **The surface layer,** heated by the Sun and mixed by winds and waves, is the warmest layer. Warm water is less dense than cold water, so the heated water stays at the surface.

2 **The thermocline** (THUR-muh-KLYN) lies below the surface layer. The temperature of the water in the thermocline drops fast with depth.

3 **The deep water** is cold all year. Almost anywhere on the globe—even in the tropics—the temperature of the water at the ocean's bottom is around 0°C–3°C (32°F–37°F), at or barely above freezing.

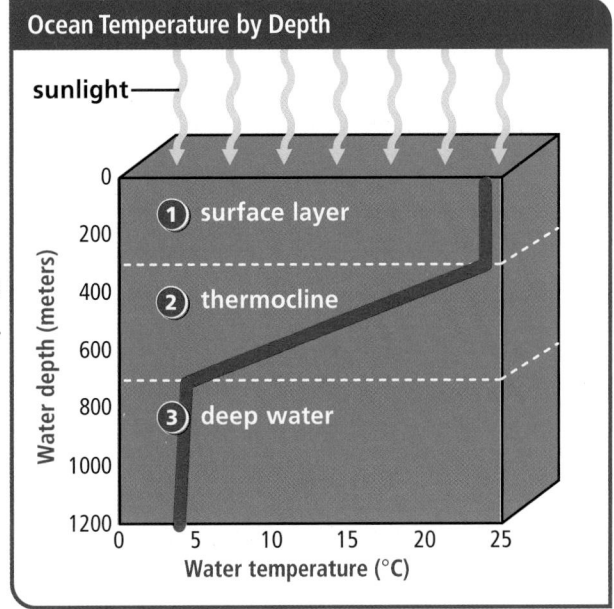

Ocean Temperature by Depth

sunlight

1 surface layer

2 thermocline

3 deep water

Water depth (meters)

Water temperature (°C)

The temperature of the water at the surface of the ocean varies by location and season. As you can see in the map of satellite data below, the surface layer is warmer near the equator than near the poles. Over much of Earth, the surface layer is warmer in the summer and cooler in the winter.

CHECK YOUR READING Why doesn't the warm water at the ocean's surface sink to the bottom?

Surface Temperature

The temperature of the ocean's surface varies by location.

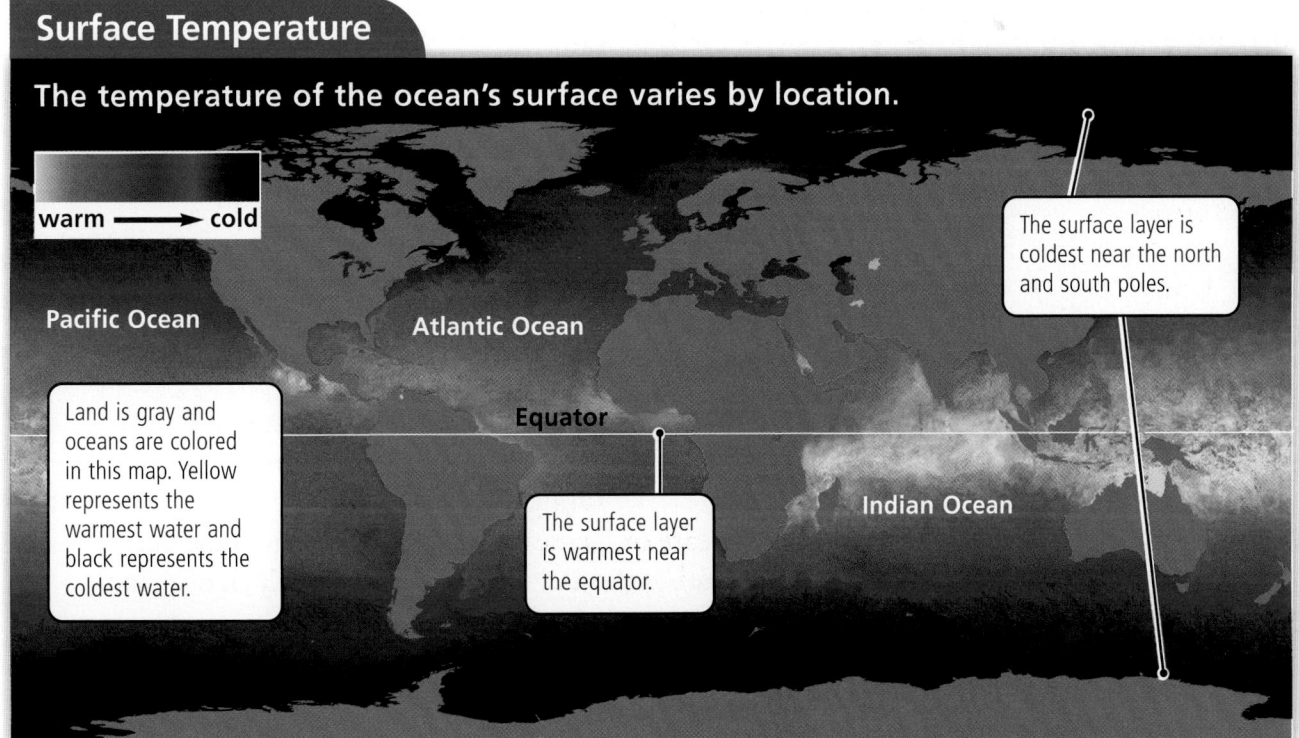

warm ——→ cold

Pacific Ocean

Atlantic Ocean

Land is gray and oceans are colored in this map. Yellow represents the warmest water and black represents the coldest water.

Equator

The surface layer is warmest near the equator.

Indian Ocean

The surface layer is coldest near the north and south poles.

The ocean floor has many features.

People have sailed the ocean for thousands of years. However, the landscape of most of the ocean floor remained a mystery until the 1950s. Since then, exploration and improvements in mapping techniques have revealed many spectacular features on the ocean floor, including the tallest mountains and deepest canyons on Earth.

A **continental shelf** is the flat or gently sloping land that lies submerged around the edges of a continent and that extends from the shoreline out to a continental slope. Huge submarine canyons, some similar in size to the Grand Canyon, slice through continental shelves and slopes. Farther out, ocean trenches cut deep into the ocean floor. With a bottom over 11,000 meters (36,000 ft) below sea level, the Mariana Trench is the deepest place in the world. Flat abyssal (uh-BIHS-uhl) plains cover huge portions of the deep-ocean floor. Seamounts are undersea mountains. Tall volcanoes that poke above the surface are volcanic islands. Mid-ocean ridges, the world's longest mountain range, run throughout Earth's ocean like the seams on a baseball.

READING TiP

Abyss means "a very deep place." Abyssal plains are on the deep-ocean floor.

The Ocean Floor

The ocean floor has canyons, mountains, and many other features.

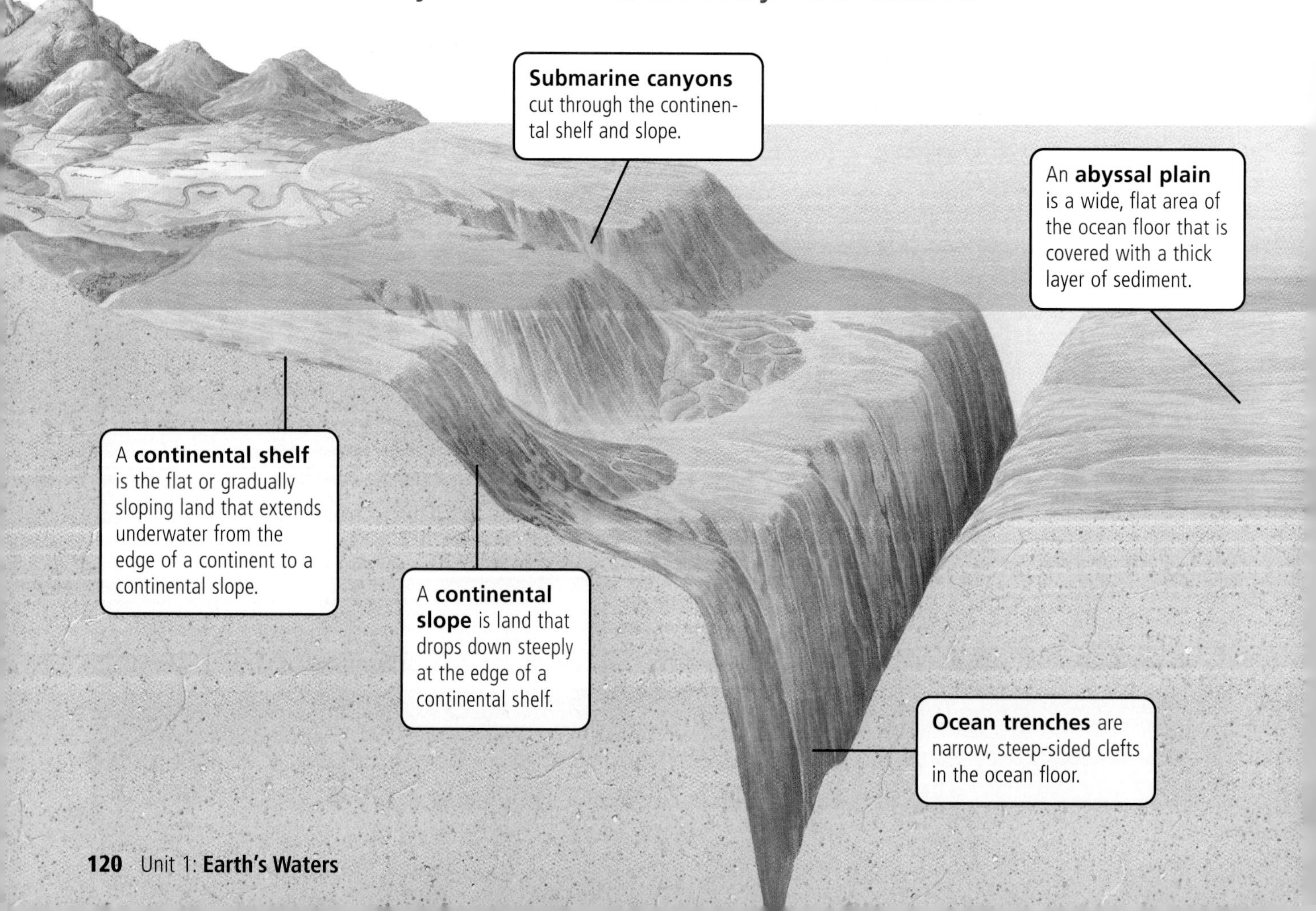

Submarine canyons cut through the continental shelf and slope.

An **abyssal plain** is a wide, flat area of the ocean floor that is covered with a thick layer of sediment.

A **continental shelf** is the flat or gradually sloping land that extends underwater from the edge of a continent to a continental slope.

A **continental slope** is land that drops down steeply at the edge of a continental shelf.

Ocean trenches are narrow, steep-sided clefts in the ocean floor.

Ocean Exploration

Because the majority of Earth's surface is underwater, until recently it remained largely unexplored. If your ears have ever hurt when you dived to the bottom of a pool, you have felt the effects of water pressure. That pressure is multiplied hundreds of times deep in the ocean. The deeper down you go, the more crushing the weight of the water.

Despite the pressure, darkness, lack of air, chilling cold, and other obstacles to ocean exploration, scientists have developed tools that help them discover what lies beneath the surface. Scuba equipment allows a diver to spend about an hour underwater, breathing air carried in a tank on his or her back. Scuba divers can safely reach depths as great as 40 meters (130 ft). To go even deeper, people use small submarines, such as the one pictured here. Robots equipped with cameras offer views of areas too deep or difficult for humans to reach.

Small submarines carry researchers to depths as great as 6500 meters (21,300 ft).

 **CHECK YOUR READING** What is one obstacle to ocean exploration?

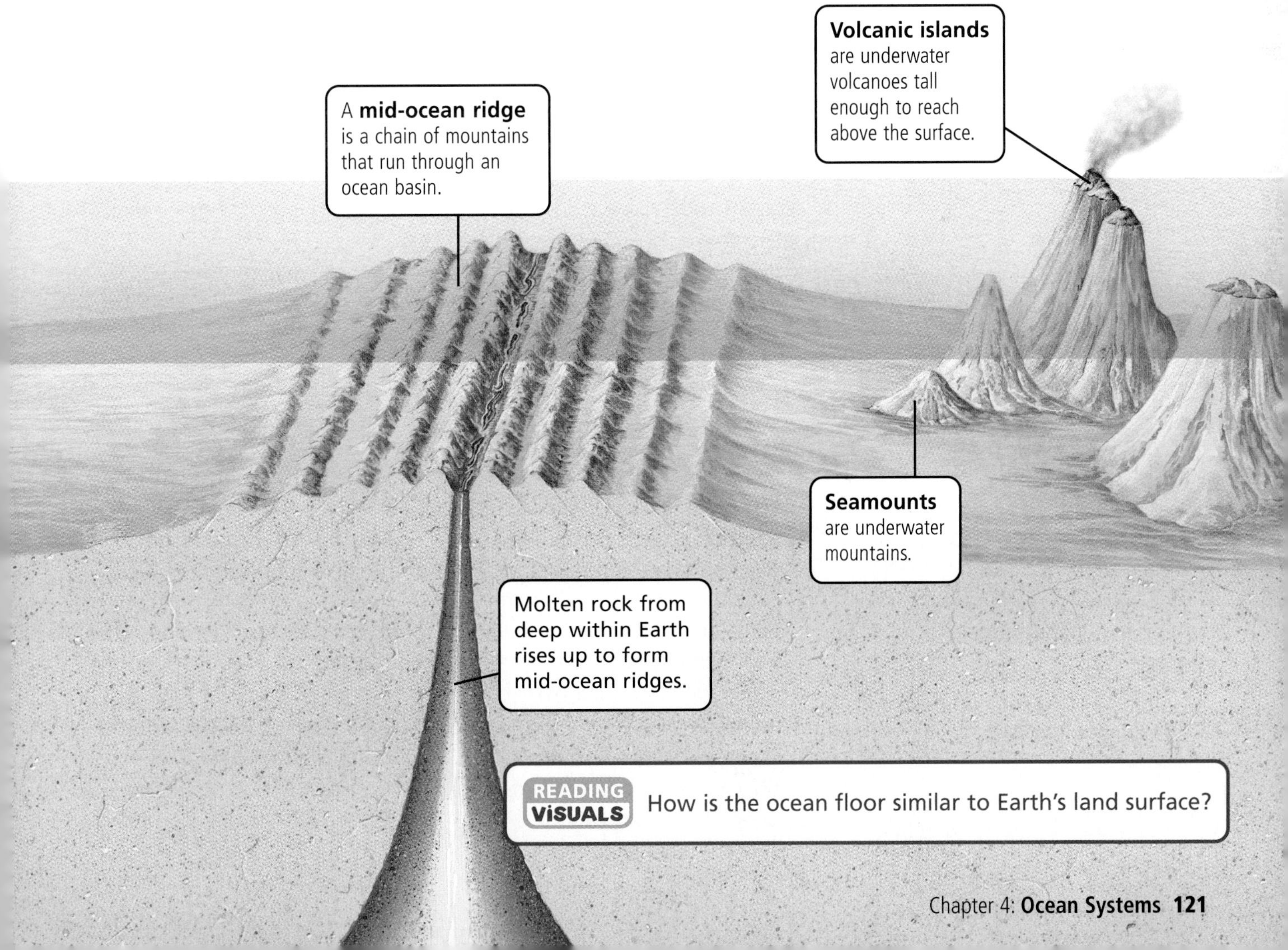

A **mid-ocean ridge** is a chain of mountains that run through an ocean basin.

Volcanic islands are underwater volcanoes tall enough to reach above the surface.

Seamounts are underwater mountains.

Molten rock from deep within Earth rises up to form mid-ocean ridges.

READING VISUALS How is the ocean floor similar to Earth's land surface?

Mapping the Ocean Floor

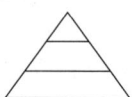
VOCABULARY Add a word triangle for *sonar* to your notebook.

Today's detailed maps of the ocean floor would amaze early scientists and sailors, who tested sea-floor depths by dropping weighted lines overboard. Now sailors find depths with **sonar,** a system that uses sound waves to measure distances and locate objects. Ships aim sound waves at the ocean's bottom and measure the time it takes to receive the echo. A fast echo means the bottom is shallow; a slow echo means the bottom is deep.

In shallow areas sonar is reflected more quickly than in deep areas.

① To measure sea-floor depth, ships aim sound waves at the ocean floor.

② The time it takes for the echo to return depends on the depth of the ocean floor.

FLORIDA
Content Preview

Sound waves are used a great deal to explore the ocean. You'll learn more about how sound waves work in grade 8.

Sonar can provide detailed images of small areas of the ocean floor. For mapping large areas, satellite imaging is much more efficient. Satellites can detect tiny bumps and dips in the ocean's height. These small surface differences reveal the shape of the ocean floor. For example, water levels are slightly higher over seamounts and lower over trenches. Because of its vast size and the challenges of exploring it, the ocean still holds many secrets. Exploration continues to bring new discoveries of geological formations and events.

CHECK YOUR READING What are two methods used in mapping the ocean floor?

4.1 Review

KEY CONCEPTS

1. What substances are contained in ocean water?

2. Describe or draw five features of the ocean-floor landscape.

3. Describe three kinds of technology or equipment used to explore the ocean.

CRITICAL THINKING

4. **Predict** A shallow pan and a deep bowl hold equal amounts of salt water. If you left both containers in the sun for a day and then measured the salinity of the water in each, which would be saltier? Why?

5. **Analyze** Where in the ocean do you think water pressure is greatest? Explain why.

CHALLENGE

6. **Synthesize** If you wanted to design a submarine to obtain the most information possible during a research voyage, what features would you include and why? First think about what types of information you would like to collect.

MATH in SCIENCE

MATH TUTORIAL
CLASSZONE.COM

Click on Math Tutorial for more help with coordinates and line graphs.

Mapping the Ocean Floor

Before sonar and satellites, scientists used weighted lines to map the ocean floor. They tied a weight to a cable and dropped the weight overboard. When the weight landed on the ocean floor, the length of the cable indicated the depth of the ocean at that point. By combining many measurements, scientists could make approximate maps of sections of the ocean floor.

The table on the right gives depths at eight positions in the ocean off a coast. The positions are at regular intervals along a straight line. Depths are given as negative numbers.

Ocean-Floor Depths	
Position	Depth
1	−293
2	−302
3	−381
4	−485
5	−593
6	−624
7	−517
8	−204

Example

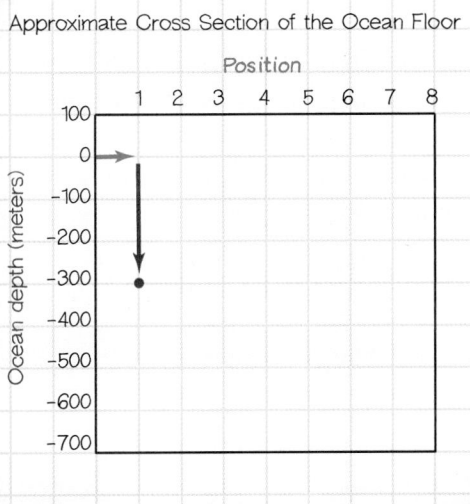

You can draw an approximate cross section of part of the ocean floor by making a line graph of the data. To graph the data, think of each column in the table as an ordered pair: **(Position, Depth).**

(1) Copy the axes and labels.

(2) Graph each point. The first point has been graphed as an example.

(3) Connect the points with line segments.

Follow the steps above to graph points 2 through 8. Use the data and your graph to answer the following questions.

1. How deep is the ocean at position 2?

2. Which position is the deepest, and what is the depth there?

3. Shade the part of the graph that is underwater.

CHALLENGE Does your graph accurately represent the ocean floor between positions 5 and 6? Explain your reasoning.

The continents are shown in black and the ocean floor is colored in this satellite image. High points are orange and yellow, and the lowest points are deep blue-purple.

4.2 Ocean water moves in currents.

🌴 Sunshine State STANDARDS

SC.D.1.3.3: The student knows how conditions that exist in one system influence the conditions that exist in other systems.

BEFORE, you learned

- The ocean is explored with sonar and satellite imaging
- The ocean floor is a varied landscape
- The ocean contains dissolved salts and gases

NOW, you will learn

- What causes ocean currents
- How currents distribute heat around the globe
- How currents interact with climate and weather

VOCABULARY

ocean current p. 124
downwelling p. 126
upwelling p. 126
El Niño p. 128

EXPLORE Currents

How does cold water move?

PROCEDURE

1. Stir together cold water, ice, and 3 drops of food coloring in the paper cup. Tape the cup to one inside corner of the plastic box.

2. Fill the plastic box with enough room-temperature water to submerge the bottom of the cup.

3. Use a toothpick to carefully poke a hole in the bottom of the cup. Observe the movement of water.

WHAT DO YOU THINK?

How do you know the water is moving? What do you think is the reason for this movement?

MATERIALS

- cold water
- ice cubes
- food coloring
- paper cup
- masking tape
- clear plastic box
- toothpick
- room-temperature water

The oceans have major currents.

Would you ever want to go rafting on the ocean? Thor Heyerdahl of Norway did it in 1947 to demonstrate how early people might have migrated around the world. He floated on a wood raft from South America to Polynesia, without motor or paddles, powered only by an ocean current. An **ocean current** is a mass of moving water. There are many different currents that move water through the ocean. As they move water, ocean currents distribute heat and nutrients around the globe.

RESOURCE CENTER
CLASSZONE.COM

Learn more about the different types of ocean currents.

Surface Currents

Strong winds blowing over the ocean are set in motion by the uneven heating of Earth's surface. These winds cause surface currents to flow. The currents extend only about 100 to 200 meters (300–500 ft) down into the ocean, but they cover large areas. The map below shows the major surface currents.

Earth's rotation curls surface currents into giant clockwise whirlpools in the Northern Hemisphere. In the Southern Hemisphere, currents curl counterclockwise because of Earth's rotation. The shapes of continents also affect the paths of surface currents.

Use your finger to trace a few of the surface currents on the map. Surface currents carry warm water away from the equator and cool water away from the poles. In this way, surface currents moderate global temperatures.

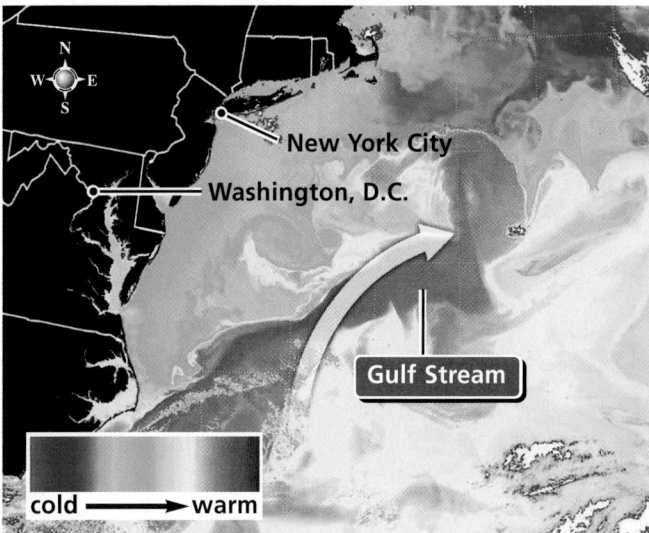

This satellite image shows the Gulf Stream, a surface current that flows along the eastern coast of the United States. The colors indicate the temperature of the water.

CHECK YOUR READING What causes surface currents?

Global Surface Currents

Surface currents are caused by winds. They move warm water away from the equator and cool water away from the poles.

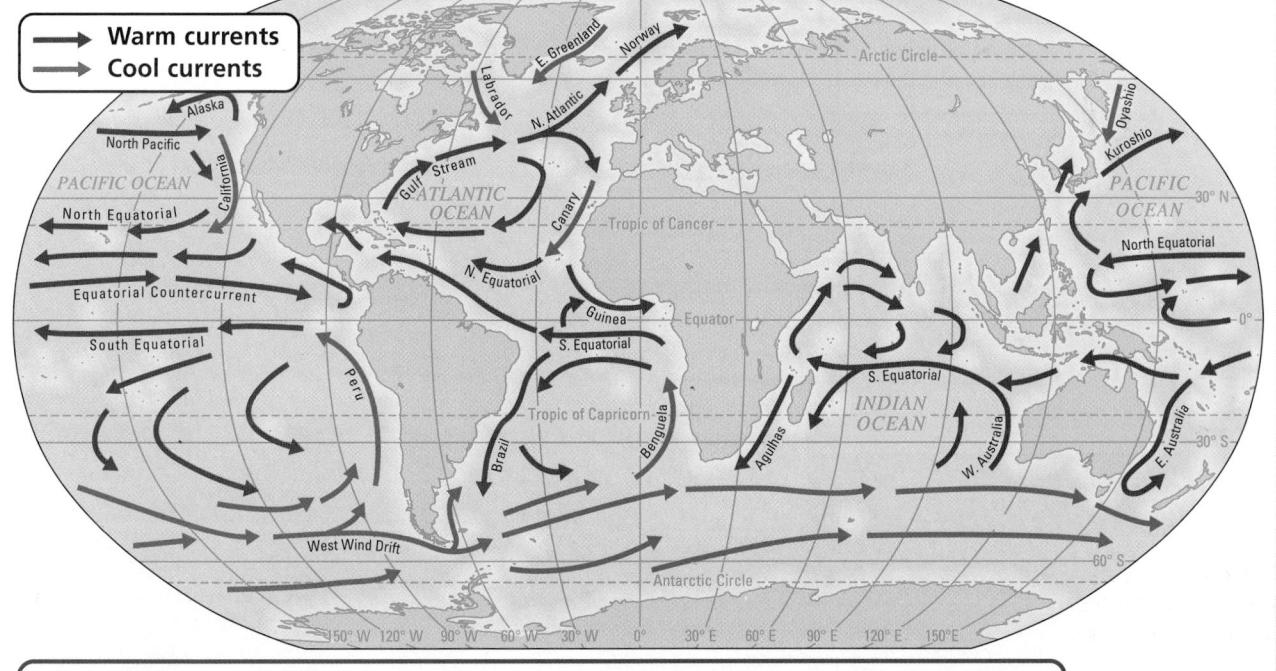

READING VISUALS Which currents could be used for sailing east across the Atlantic Ocean?

Deep Currents

In addition to surface currents, there are also currents flowing deep in the ocean. Deep currents are driven by differences in water density. Dense water sinks in the ocean the same way that dense chocolate syrup sinks in a glass of milk.

Seawater can become more dense because of cooling, an increase in salinity, or both. The densest water is found in the polar regions. For example, as sea ice forms near Antarctica, the salinity of the cold water beneath the ice increases. The highly dense water sinks down the continental slope of Antarctica and then moves slowly across the ocean floor. It may take 1000 years for water from this current to resurface near the equator. Another deep current flows out from the Arctic Ocean.

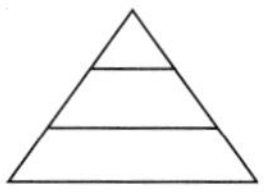

The movement of water in deep currents involves two processes important to ocean life. **Downwelling** is the movement of water from the surface to greater depths. As the water sinks, it carries oxygen down from the surface. The oxygen allows animals to live in the deep ocean. **Upwelling** is the movement of water up to the surface. Because this process brings up nutrients from the deep ocean, large numbers of ocean animals live in areas where upwelling occurs.

VOCABULARY
Add word triangles for *downwelling* and *upwelling* to your notebook.

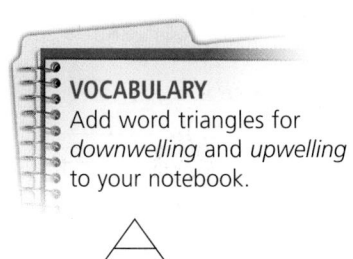

How Upwelling Affects Ocean Life

Upwelling provides nutrients that support animals and plants in surface waters.

surface water

1 Wind moves water away from the shore.

2 Upwelling occurs as deeper water rises to replace the surface water that has moved away.

The water rising to the surface is rich in nutrients. Many fisheries are located in areas of upwelling because ocean animals thrive there.

SEA BRING

INVESTIGATE Currents

What happens where bodies of water meet?

PROCEDURE

1. Divide the box into two compartments, using masking tape and aluminum foil.

2. Pour one solution into one side of the box while a partner pours the other solution into the opposite side. Be sure you and your partner pour at the same time in order to keep the barrier from breaking.

3. Sprinkle pepper on the high-salinity side.

4. Use the pencil to poke two holes in the aluminum foil—one just below the water surface and another near the bottom of the box. Observe for 10 minutes.

WHAT DO YOU THINK?

• What did you observe in the box? Did you expect this?

• What forces drove any movements of water you observed?

CHALLENGE Compare what you observed with what you have learned about the actual movements of water in the ocean. How could you change the experiment to better model actual ocean currents?

SKILL FOCUS
Observing

MATERIALS
• clear plastic box
• aluminum foil
• masking tape
• high-salinity water
• low-salinity water
• pepper
• sharp pencil

TIME
30 minutes

Currents interact with climate and weather.

Imagine mixing red and blue paint in a cup by blowing through a straw. You can move some paint around, but you cannot predict exactly what pattern will result. Similarly, the ocean and the atmosphere interact in unpredictable ways. Moving air produces movement in the water while the water changes the air above it.

Remember that windblown surface currents help distribute heat around the globe by moving warm water away from the equator and cool water away from the north and south poles. The Gulf Stream, for example, is a surface current that moves warm water northeast-ward toward Great Britain and Europe. Because of the warm Gulf Stream waters, the British climate is mild. No polar bears wander the streets of Great Britain, as they might in places in Canada that are just as far north.

> **FLORIDA**
> **Content Review**
>
> Recall what you learned about climate in grade 6. Notice here how the temperature of ocean currents affects the climate of an area.

CHECK YOUR READING How does the Gulf Stream affect Great Britain?

La Scie, Newfoundland

Fowey, England

ATLANTIC OCEAN

La Scie   Fowey

READING VISUALS **COMPARE AND CONTRAST** These two towns are at about the same latitude, or distance from the equator. Ice can be found off the coast of La Scie, Newfoundland. Ice is never found off the coast of Fowey, England, which has mild weather year-round. What might explain this difference? **Hint:** the answer has to do with the Gulf Stream.

A change in even one of Earth's surface currents can result in huge changes in weather patterns. Most years, winds blow westward across the tropical Pacific Ocean. Every three to seven years, however, these winds do not blow as strongly as usual. Without the winds, the movement of currents in the Pacific is disrupted. These changes in air and water movements cause a global weather event called **El Niño,** which may last for 12 to 18 months.

During El Niño years, weather patterns change around the planet. Some places get more or less rain or snow than usual. Temperatures may be warmer or cooler than in other years. By using satellite readings of ocean temperatures and floating measurement devices to study conditions in the Pacific, scientists can often predict when El Niño will occur and how severe, or strong, it will be.

VOCABULARY
Remember to make a word triangle for *El Niño*.

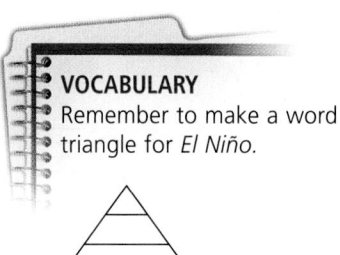

4.2 Review

KEY CONCEPTS

1. What are two causes of currents in the ocean?

2. How do currents distribute heat around the globe?

3. How are climate and weather related to currents? Give two examples.

CRITICAL THINKING

4. **Infer** Describe at least two ways in which upwelled water might differ from the water around it.

5. **Infer** What factor do you think might cause a surface current to change direction?

○ CHALLENGE

6. **Predict** What would happen if all ocean currents suddenly came to a halt? Describe some effects this change would have.

Waves move through oceans.

Sunshine State STANDARDS

SC.B.1.3.6: The student knows the properties of waves (e.g., frequency, wavelength, and amplitude); that each wave consists of a number of crests and troughs; and the effects of different media on waves.

SC.B.2.3.1: The student knows that most events in the universe (e.g., weather changes, moving cars, and the transfer of a nervous impulse in the human body) involve some form of energy transfer and that these changes almost always increase the total disorder of the system and its surroundings, reducing the amount of useful energy.

BEFORE, you learned

- Currents are masses of moving water
- Surface currents are driven mainly by winds
- Deep currents are driven mainly by differences in density

NOW, you will learn

- How waves form
- How waves move energy through water
- How wave action changes near the shore
- How waves can cause currents near the shore

VOCABULARY
longshore current p. 132
rip current p. 132

EXPLORE Waves

How does wave motion change with depth?

PROCEDURE

① Fill an aquarium or another clear rectangular container about three-fourths full of water.

② Tie several metal washers to each of four corks to make them float at different heights, as shown in the photograph.

③ Using your hand or a piece of cardboard, make steady waves in the water. Experiment with a variety of waves—some small and some large. Observe the cork movements.

WHAT DO YOU THINK?
How does the movement of the corks change with depth?

MATERIALS
- aquarium or clear container
- corks
- string
- metal washers
- water

OUTLINE
Remember to start an outline for this section.

I. Main idea
  A. Supporting idea
    1. Detail
    2. Detail
  B. Supporting idea

Waves form in the open ocean.

If you have ever blown across the surface of hot chocolate, you may have noticed ripples. Each of these ripples is a small wave. A wave is an up-and-down motion along the surface of a body of water. The vast ocean surface is covered with waves of various sizes, which are usually caused by winds. Moving air drags across the water's surface and passes energy to the water, causing waves. Other disturbances—such as earthquakes, landslides, and underwater volcanic eruptions—can also cause waves.

 **CHECK YOUR READING** What can cause waves to form in the ocean?

Wave Action at the Water's Surface

READING TiP

As you read about wave action at the water's surface, look at the illustrations on page 131.

RESOURCE CENTER
CLASSZONE.COM

Explore ocean waves.

A wave in the ocean has the same basic shape as many other waves.

- The **crest** is the high point of the wave.
- The **trough** (trawf) is the low point of the wave.
- **Wave height** is the vertical distance between the top of the crest and the bottom of the trough.
- **Wavelength** is the distance between one wave crest and the next.

You have read that currents move water from one place to another. In contrast, waves do not transport water. Waves move energy. They move through water, but the water stays more or less in the same place. Follow the drawings on page 131 to see how water particles move in a circle as a wave passes through. If waves do not transport water, how do surfers zip toward shore on waves? Surfers are powered by the energy traveling in the waves. Waves transport energy, not water.

Most waves affect only the water near the surface of the ocean. Water particles farther down move in smaller circles than particles near the surface. Below a certain depth, the waves no longer affect the water.

Wave Action near Shore

Waves may pass through the ocean for hundreds or thousands of kilometers before moving into shallow water. Then the waves lose speed and eventually topple over, losing their energy as they break on shore.

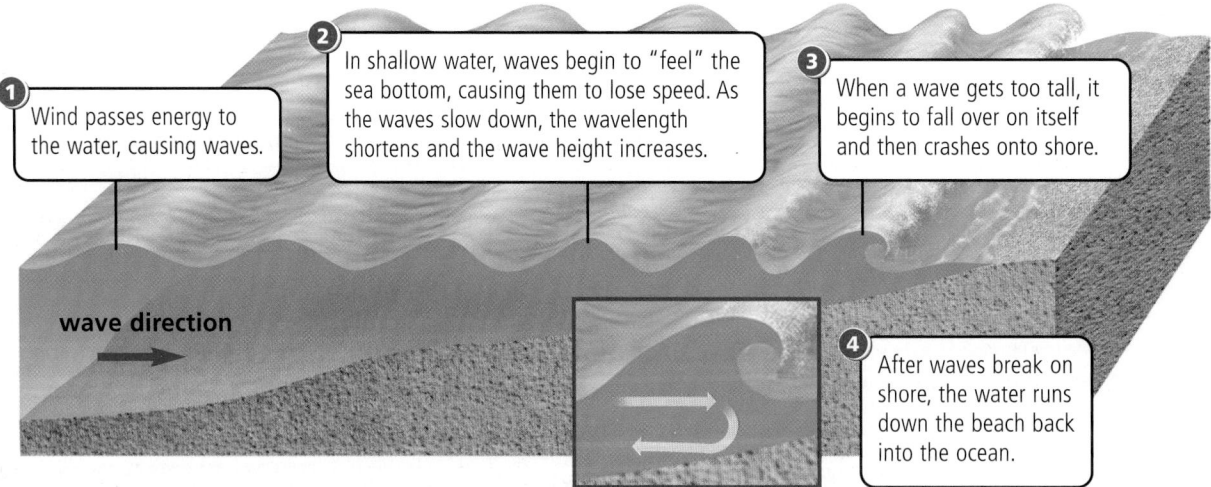

1 Wind passes energy to the water, causing waves.

2 In shallow water, waves begin to "feel" the sea bottom, causing them to lose speed. As the waves slow down, the wavelength shortens and the wave height increases.

3 When a wave gets too tall, it begins to fall over on itself and then crashes onto shore.

4 After waves break on shore, the water runs down the beach back into the ocean.

wave direction

When waves break on a beach, the water runs back down the sand into the ocean. If the shore is steeply sloped toward the water, the water may rush back to sea forcefully. An undertow is the pull of the water as it runs back to sea. Undertows may be dangerous. Some are strong enough to knock a person off his or her feet and into the waves.

Ocean Waves

Waves transport energy, not water. As a wave crest passes, the water particles move in circular paths.

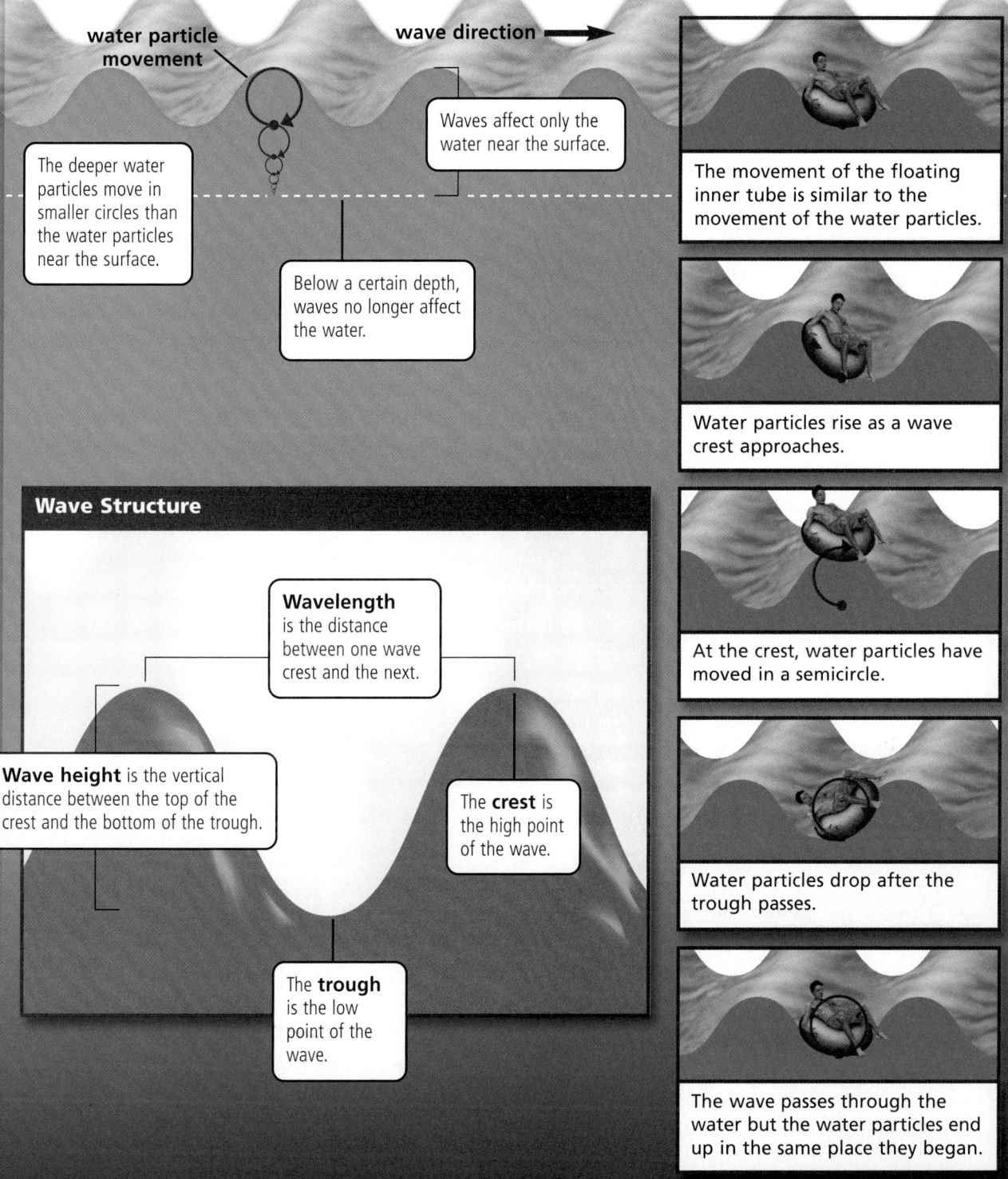

water particle movement

wave direction →

Waves affect only the water near the surface.

The deeper water particles move in smaller circles than the water particles near the surface.

Below a certain depth, waves no longer affect the water.

The movement of the floating inner tube is similar to the movement of the water particles.

Water particles rise as a wave crest approaches.

At the crest, water particles have moved in a semicircle.

Water particles drop after the trough passes.

The wave passes through the water but the water particles end up in the same place they began.

Wave Structure

Wavelength is the distance between one wave crest and the next.

Wave height is the vertical distance between the top of the crest and the bottom of the trough.

The **crest** is the high point of the wave.

The **trough** is the low point of the wave.

READING VISUALS What happens to water particles as a wave passes through?

Waves cause currents near shore.

Sometimes swimmers notice that without trying, they have drifted far down a beach. Their drifting is due to a **longshore current,** which moves water parallel to the shore. Longshore currents occur in places where waves meet the land at an angle rather than head-on. Since waves rarely meet the land exactly head-on, or perpendicular to the shore, there is a longshore current along almost every shore. The waves hit the shore at an angle and then wash back straight down the beach into the ocean. This zigzag motion moves sand along the beach, piling it up at one end.

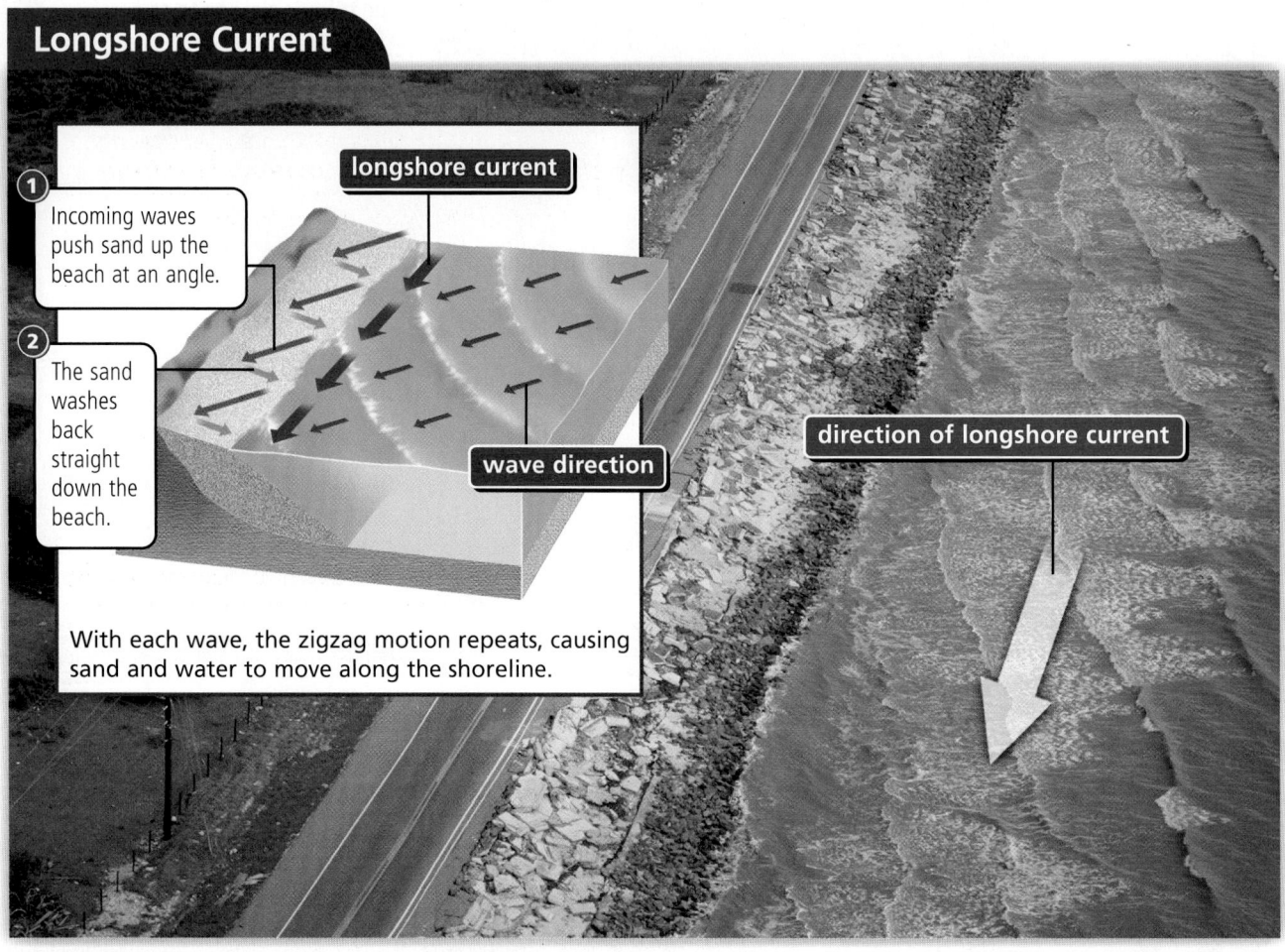

Longshore Current

longshore current

1 Incoming waves push sand up the beach at an angle.

2 The sand washes back straight down the beach.

wave direction

direction of longshore current

With each wave, the zigzag motion repeats, causing sand and water to move along the shoreline.

The movement of waves and longshore currents can build up sandbars in the waters near a shore. Sandbars are long ridges or piles of sand that can form parallel to the coastline. As waves wash over the sandbars and onto shore, water may collect behind the sandbars. Eventually, the pooled water will break through. **Rip currents** are narrow streams of water that break through sandbars and drain rapidly back to sea. Rip currents occur when high winds or waves cause a larger-than-usual amount of water to wash back from the shore.

○ CHECK YOUR READING   What role does a sandbar play in the formation of a rip current?

Rip Current

Signs such as this one on a beach in Hawaii warn swimmers of dangerous currents.

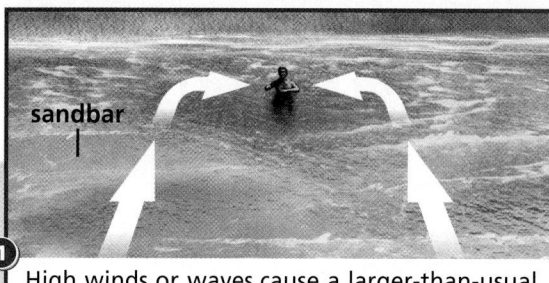

1 High winds or waves cause a larger-than-usual amount of water to collect behind a sandbar.

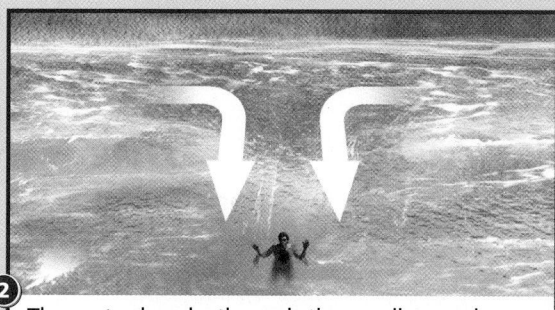

2 The water breaks through the sandbar and washes rapidly out to sea in a rip current.

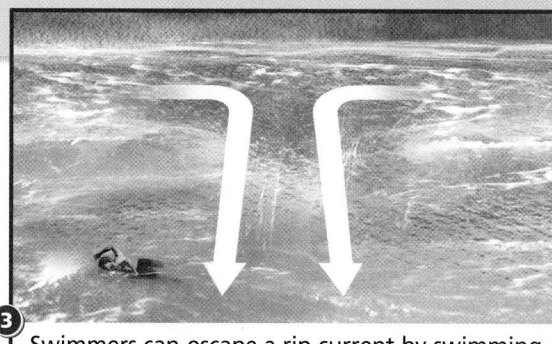

3 Swimmers can escape a rip current by swimming parallel to shore, out of the narrow current.

sandbar

Like undertows, rip currents can be dangerous for swimmers. In the United States, around 100 people drown in rip currents each year. Most rescues made by lifeguards on U.S. beaches involve swimmers caught in rip currents.

Rip currents are too strong to swim against, but as you can see in the diagram, they are narrow. Swimming parallel to the shore is the best way to escape a rip current. Of course, it is better to avoid rip currents altogether! Many beaches offer daily rip-current forecasts based on information about wind and wave conditions.

4.3 Review

KEY CONCEPTS

1. How does moving air form waves in water?

2. Describe the movement of a water particle as a wave passes through.

3. What happens to waves near shore?

4. Name and describe two kinds of currents that wave action can cause near shore.

CRITICAL THINKING

5. **Compare and Contrast** Describe the similarities and differences between surface currents and waves.

6. **Apply** Imagine you find a piece of wood on the beach. The next day, the wood is 100 meters farther north. How might it have moved? Your answer should refer to currents.

⬥ CHALLENGE

7. **Infer** Some coastlines are more steeply sloped than others. How might wave action on a steeply sloped coastline differ from that on a gently sloped coastline?

CHAPTER INVESTIGATION

Wave Movement

OVERVIEW AND PURPOSE The particles in liquid water are constantly moving. Surfers, boaters, and people in inner tubes enjoy the effects of this motion—even though they never see what is happening at the particle level. How do water particles move in waves? In this investigation you will

- observe the movements of a floating object as waves pass through water
- use your observations to draw conclusions about how water particles move in waves

▶ Problem

What does the motion of a floating object reveal about the movement of water particles in a passing wave?

▶ Hypothesize

Write a hypothesis to explain what the motion of a floating object might reveal about how water particles move in a wave. Your hypothesis should take the form of an "If . . . , then . . . , because . . ." statement.

▶ Procedure

MATERIALS
- small aquarium or clear, shoebox-size container
- water
- small plastic dropping bottle or plastic spice container, with cap
- salt

1. Fill the aquarium or clear container with cold tap water until it is three-quarters full.

2. Make the small bottle float with its top just below the surface of the water. You can accomplish this in several ways. First, try adding warm water to the bottle, then securely capping it without air bubbles. See if it will float. You can add salt to the bottle to move the bottle lower in the water. If the bottle is too low, you can trap a small air bubble under the cap to move the bottle higher in the water. Adjust these factors until you successfully float the bottle. The investigation will also work if the top of the bottle just touches the water's surface.

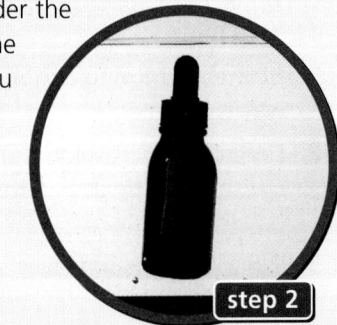
step 2

3. Remove the bottle from the water. Make sure the cap is tightly sealed.

4 Push your hand back and forth in the water at one end of the aquarium for about 30 seconds, to produce waves.

5 Gently place the small bottle back into the center of the aquarium. With your eyes level with the water surface, observe the motion of the waves and the bottle. Repeat as many times as needed until you notice the bottle behaving the same way with each passing wave.

▶ Observe and Analyze   Write It Up

1. RECORD Make a diagram showing the aquarium setup, including the water, the waves, and the small bottle. Use arrows to show how the bottle moved as waves passed. Or you may draw several diagrams of the aquarium, showing the bottle at different locations as waves passed. Label the various parts of the waves.

2. ANALYZE Did the bottle travel with the wave? Why or why not?

▶ Conclude   Write It Up

1. INTERPRET Compare your results with your hypothesis. Do your data support your hypothesis?

2. INTERPRET Answer the problem question.

3. INFER What do your observations tell you about particle movement in waves? Did the results surprise you? Explain.

4. EVALUATE Why was it necessary to float the bottle just under the surface of the water rather than letting it float right on top?

5. IDENTIFY PROBLEMS What problems, if any, did you encounter in carrying out the procedure?

6. IDENTIFY LIMITS In what ways was this experiment limited in showing particle movement? Identify possible sources of error.

7. PREDICT How do you think particle motion in a wave with a tall wave height might differ from that in a wave with a short wave height?

8. SYNTHESIZE In this lab you made waves with your hand. In the ocean, most waves are caused by wind. Earthquakes, landslides, and other events also cause waves in the ocean. What do earthquakes, landslides, wind, and your hand have in common that allows all of them to make waves?

▶ INVESTIGATE Further

CHALLENGE Redesign this experiment in a way you think will better demonstrate the particle motion in a water wave. You need not limit yourself to the materials you used in this lab. Why will your version of the experiment work better?

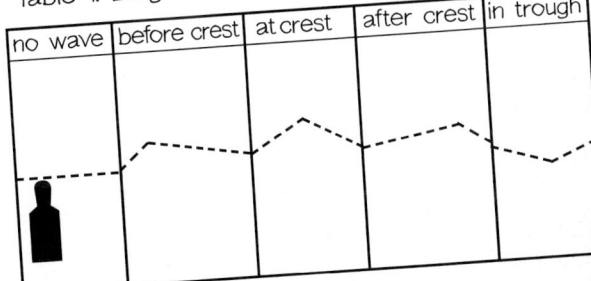

Wave Movement

Problem What does the motion of a floating object reveal about the movement of water particles in a passing wave?

Hypothesize

Observe and Analyze

Table 1. Diagram of Setup

no wave	before crest	at crest	after crest	in trough

Conclude

Waters rise and fall in tides.

 Sunshine State STANDARDS

SC.C.2.3.7: The student knows that gravity is a universal force that every mass exerts on every other mass.

◁ **BEFORE, you learned**

- Wind provides the energy to form waves in the ocean
- Ocean waves change near shore
- The ocean is a global body of water

▷ **NOW, you will learn**

- What causes tides
- How tides affect coastlines
- How tides can be used to generate electricity

FCAT VOCABULARY
spring tide p. 139
neap tide p. 139

VOCABULARY
tide p. 136
tidal range p. 138

THINK ABOUT

What causes water levels to change in the ocean?

These two photographs were taken on the same day at the boat harbor in Lympstone, England. The change in water level in the harbor occurs every day on a regular and predictable basis. What forces cause shifts in such huge volumes of water? How can we explain the clocklike regularity of the flow?

Coastal waters rise and fall each day.

Have you ever spent a day at a beach along the ocean? Perhaps you placed your blanket and beach chairs in the sand close to the water's edge. An hour later, you may have needed to move your blanket and chairs to keep the advancing waves from washing them away. The water level on coastlines varies with the time of day. This periodic rising and falling of the water level of the ocean is called the **tide.** The water level along a coast is highest at high tide, submerging parts of the coastline. The water level is lowest at low tide, exposing more of the coastline.

What in the world could cause such dramatic changes in the ocean's level? The answer is, nothing in this world. Read on to find out how out-of-this-world objects cause tides.

VOCABULARY
Add a word triangle for *tide* to your notebook.

 **CHECK YOUR READING** How does the water level along a coast differ at high tide and at low tide?

The gravity of the Moon and the Sun causes tides.

Over 2000 years ago, people knew that the Moon and the tide were related. But 1700 years passed before the connection was explained in the terms of modern science. In 1687, Sir Isaac Newton developed his theories of gravity and linked the tide to the Moon's gravitational pull. Gravity is a force of attraction between objects. Earth's gravity pulls things toward its center—including you.

The gravity of the Sun and the gravity of the Moon also pull on objects on Earth. In response to the Moon's gravitational pull, Earth's water bulges on the side facing the Moon. The Moon's gravity also pulls on Earth itself. Earth gets pulled toward the Moon, leaving a second bulge of water on the side of Earth facing away from the Moon. The Sun's gravity pulls too, but with less effect because the Sun is so far away.

Daily Tides

The diagram below shows the two bulges of ocean water: one on the side of Earth closest to the Moon, and the other on the opposite side of Earth. At these bulges, it is high tide. Between the two bulges are dips. At these dips, it is low tide. As Earth rotates, different parts of it pass through the bulges and the dips. As a result, most places experience two high tides and two low tides each day.

VISUALIZATION
CLASSZONE.COM
Watch daily tides in action.

Daily Tides

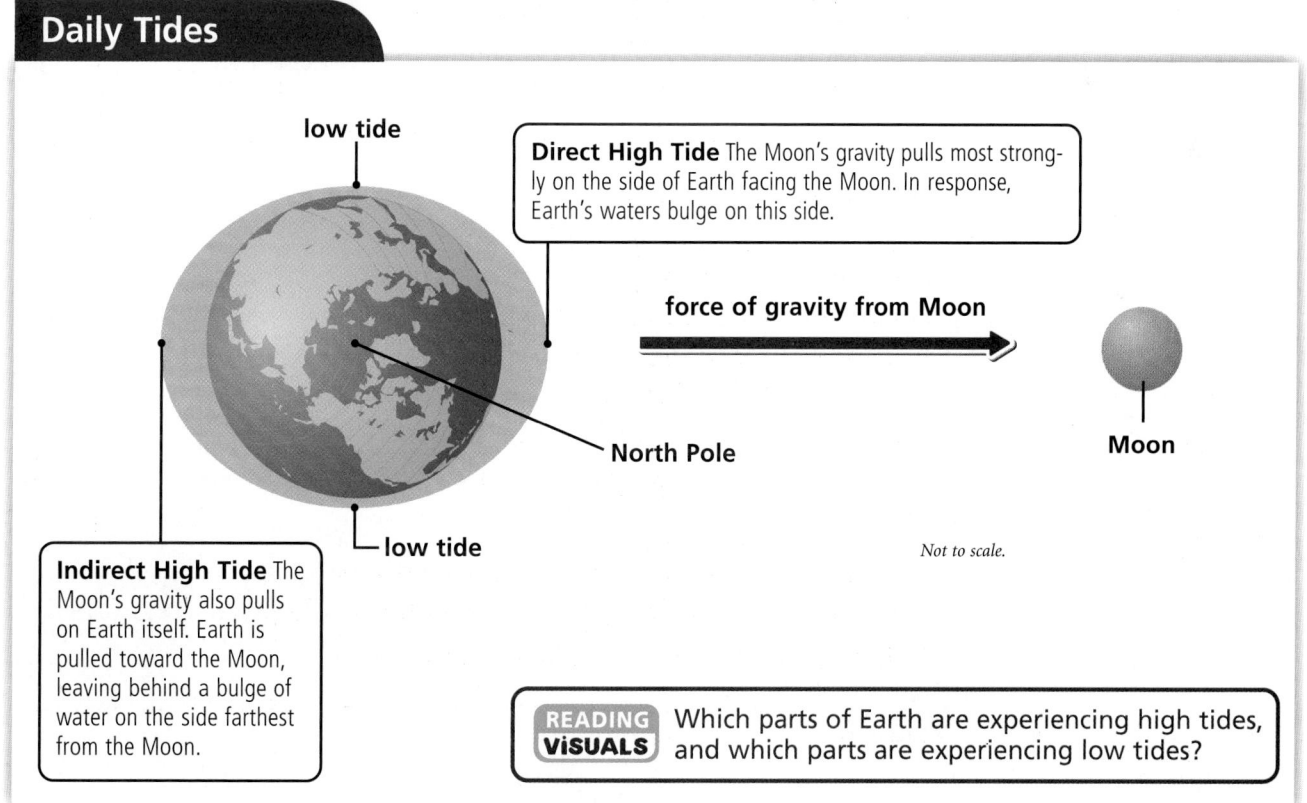

low tide

Direct High Tide The Moon's gravity pulls most strongly on the side of Earth facing the Moon. In response, Earth's waters bulge on this side.

force of gravity from Moon

North Pole

Moon

Indirect High Tide The Moon's gravity also pulls on Earth itself. Earth is pulled toward the Moon, leaving behind a bulge of water on the side farthest from the Moon.

low tide

Not to scale.

READING VISUALS Which parts of Earth are experiencing high tides, and which parts are experiencing low tides?

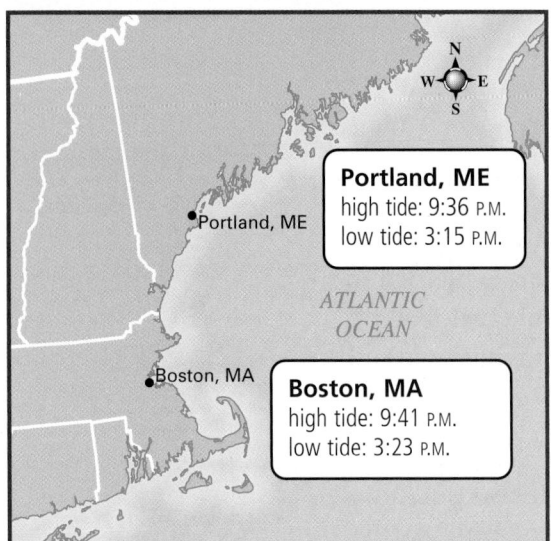

Portland, ME
high tide: 9:36 P.M.
low tide: 3:15 P.M.

ATLANTIC OCEAN

Boston, MA
high tide: 9:41 P.M.
low tide: 3:23 P.M.

A place farther east along a coastline experiences high and low tides earlier in the day, because it passes through the tidal bulge first. Times for high and low tides change daily.

The timing of high and low tides at one location on a coast may differ from the timing at other locations along that coast. As you can see on the map of the coastline of New England, the tides occur later as you move west along the coastline. As Earth rotates, the easternmost points on a coastline will pass through the tidal bulge before places farther west on the same coastline.

The timing of high and low tides is not the only way that tides can differ along a coastline. Some places experience higher high tides and lower low tides than other places. The shape of the land above and below the water affects tidal ranges. A **tidal range** is the difference in height between a high tide and the next low tide. The tidal range is greater in a narrow bay than on a wide-open shore. For example, the narrow harbor of Lympstone, England, shown in the photographs on page 136, has a very large tidal range. A coastline with a steeply sloped ocean floor has a larger tidal range than a coastline with a gradually dropping floor. For example, the coasts of Texas and western Florida have very small tidal ranges because of the gradual slope of the ocean floor there.

CHECK YOUR READING — In what two ways does the shape of the land affect the tidal range? What sentences tell you this?

INVESTIGATE Tides

How does the Moon make tides?

PROCEDURE

1. Cut the Tides datasheet in two, along the dotted line. Cut out the map of Earth on the bottom half of the sheet.
2. Use a paper fastener to connect the two pieces as shown in the photograph.
3. Now you are ready to model the tides. Rotate Earth one full turn in the direction of the arrow. One full turn is equal to one day.

WHAT DO YOU THINK?

- How does the model demonstrate the Moon's role in tides?
- How many times does each place in the ocean experience high tide and low tide each day?

CHALLENGE One full rotation of Earth takes place in a day, or 24 hours. About how much time passes between one high tide and the next high tide at any location on Earth?

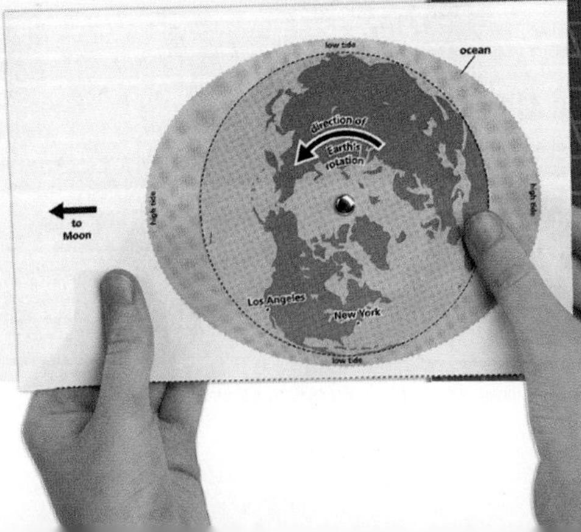

SKILL FOCUS
Making models

MATERIALS

- Tides datasheet
- scissors
- brass paper fastener

TIME
15 minutes

Monthly Tides

The Moon is the main cause of tides, but the Sun affects tides as well. The Moon takes about a month to move around Earth. Twice during this month-long journey—at the new moon and the full moon—the Moon, the Sun, and Earth line up. The gravity of the Sun and the gravity of the Moon combine to pull Earth's waters in the same directions. The result is an extra-high tidal bulge and an extra-low tidal dip, called a **spring tide.**

During first- and third-quarter moons, the Sun and the Moon are not lined up with Earth. The gravity of each pulls from a different direction. The result is a smaller tidal bulge and tidal dip, called a **neap tide.** During a neap tide, high and low tides are less extreme.

Changes in the timing and the height of tides occur in a regular cycle. The timing of tides may be important to people who live near a coast or use coasts for fishing or boating. In many coastal communities, tide tables printed in newspapers give the exact times and heights of the tides.

RESOURCE CENTER
CLASSZONE.COM
Find out more about ocean tides.

READING **TiP**
Spring tides occur twice a month all year long, not just in spring. This use of the word *spring* is related to its meaning "to jump."

Monthly Tides

Spring Tide

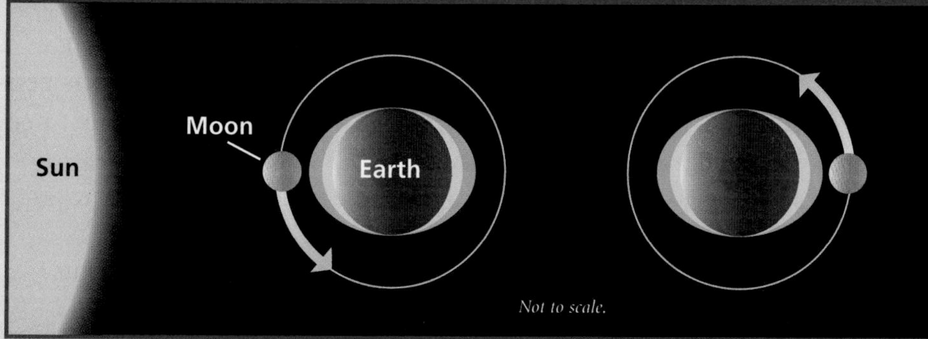

Sun | Moon → | Earth

Not to scale.

At new moon and full moon, Earth, the Moon, and the Sun are lined up. The gravity of the Sun and the gravity of the Moon pull Earth's waters in the same direction. As a result high tides are extra high and low tides are extra low.

Neap Tide

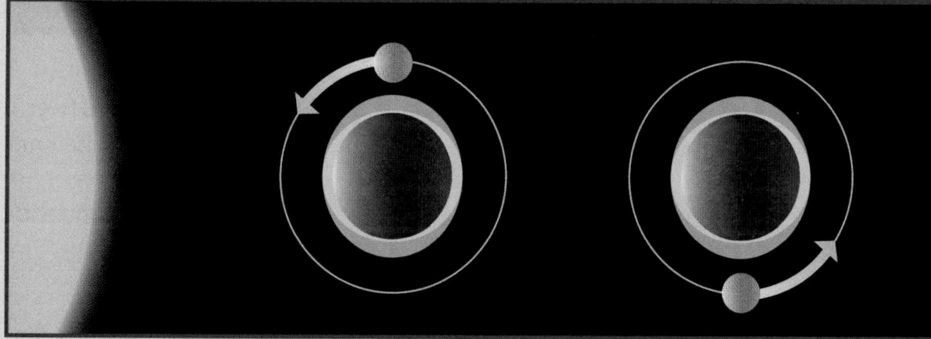

At first- and third-quarter moons, Earth, the Moon, and the Sun are not lined up. The gravity of the Sun pulls in a different direction from that of the Moon. As a result, high and low tides are less extreme.

READING VISUALS How are Earth, the Moon, and the Sun positioned during spring tides? How are they positioned during neap tides?

Tides can be used to generate electricity.

The energy of tides can be used to generate electricity. A tidal dam is built near a coast in the path of tidal waters. The water flows in during high tide and is trapped behind the gates of the dam. Then, when the tide is low, the gates open and the trapped water rushes out. As the water flows out, it spins turbines that power electric generators.

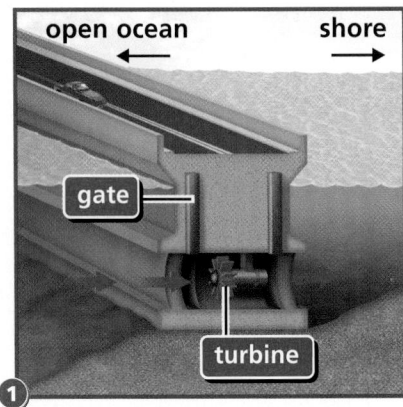

The dam's gates are open as the tide rises. Notice that the water level is the same on both sides.

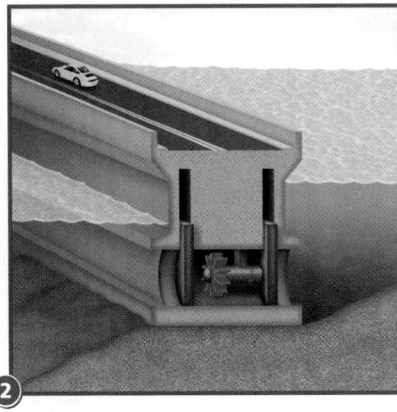

When the tide begins to lower, the gates close, trapping water behind the dam.

At low tide, the gates open and the water rushes out, spinning turbines that generate electricity.

Tidal dams cause much less pollution than many other methods of generating electricity. Also, tides are a renewable source of energy; the tides are not used up in the process. However, tidal dams have some drawbacks. Few places in the world are actually suitable for such dams. Another problem is that the times of day when tidal dams generate electricity might not be the times of day when people most need electricity. Tidal dams also sometimes block the paths of migrating fish and might hurt marine life by altering the regular flow of water.

 **CHECK YOUR READING** What are the benefits and drawbacks of tidal power plants?

 **Review**

KEY CONCEPTS

1. Describe the appearance of tidal changes at a coastline.
2. Explain the difference between the Sun's role and the Moon's role in creating tides.
3. How are tides used to generate electricity?

CRITICAL THINKING

4. **Synthesize** Contrast the daily and monthly patterns of tides. What role does the Moon's orbit around Earth play in both?
5. **Compare** Tidal range is the daily difference in high and low water levels. Compare the tidal ranges of neap and spring tides.

⬤ CHALLENGE

6. **Draw Conclusions** How would the tides be different if the Moon revolved around Earth twice a month instead of once a month?

The first and largest tidal energy plant in the world is in northern France, where the Rance River enters the English Channel. The plant opened in 1966.

Tidal Energy

Tidal power plants can work only in a few locations in the world. The best locations for tidal energy plants are ones with large differences between high and low tides. Why can't tides make electricity just anywhere?

Under Pressure

Each of these jugs contains the same amount of water. Water sprays out of the hole at the bottom of each—but why does it spray farther out of the narrow jug? The water pressure is greater in the tall, narrow jug because the water is deeper. The width of the jug does not matter—just the depth. The deeper the water, the greater the water pressure. The higher the water pressure, the faster the water comes out of the hole—and the farther the water sprays.

From Pressure to Power

Tidal dams use moving water to turn turbines that power generators. Turning turbines requires work. Work is the use of force to move an object. In this case, the force of the water is doing work on the turbines. The faster the water moves, the more work it can do.

Location, Location, Location

Think again about the two jugs. The water moves faster out of the hole in the tall, narrow jug—the one with the higher water pressure. Tidal power plants work best in places where high water pressure moves the water fast enough to turn the turbines. Remember that deeper water makes for higher water pressure. So tidal power plants work best in places with a large tidal range—the difference between high and low tide.

EXPLORE

1. **APPLY** When the water trapped behind a dam is released, it is channeled through openings in the dam and spins the turbines. From what you've learned about water pressure, where do you think the openings are, toward the top of the dam or toward the bottom? Explain your reasoning.
2. **CHALLENGE** Make a model of a tidal-energy plant. Use the side of a milk jug as a base, modeling clay to make the basin, and pieces of plastic for the dam and gates. Try different shapes for your basin and different sizes of gates to see how fast you can get the water to flow.

Chapter Review

the BIG idea

The oceans are a connected system of water in motion.

FLORIDA REVIEW
CLASSZONE.COM

Content Review and
FCAT Practice

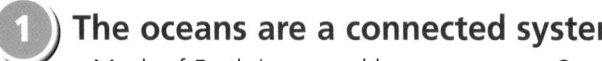

◀ KEY CONCEPTS SUMMARY

1 The oceans are a connected system.

- Much of Earth is covered by ocean water, which contains dissolved salts and gases.

- Ocean temperatures decrease with depth.

- The ocean floor has canyons, mountains, and many other features.

VOCABULARY
salinity p. 116
density p. 116
continental shelf p. 120
sonar p. 122

---

2 Ocean water moves in currents.

- Surface currents are set in motion by winds and carry heat around the globe.

- Deep currents are caused by differences in water density. Dense water sinks at the poles and very slowly flows toward the equator.

VOCABULARY
ocean current p. 124
upwelling p. 126
downwelling p. 126
El Niño p. 128

---

3 Waves move through oceans.

- Ocean waves transport energy, not water. When a wave passes, water particles end up in the same places they began.

- Longshore currents occur when waves hit shores at angles.

- Rip currents are narrow streams of water that break through sandbars.

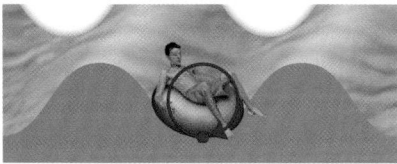

VOCABULARY
longshore current p. 132
rip current p. 132

---

4 Waters rise and fall in tides.

The Moon's gravity pulls Earth's waters into bulges and dips. As Earth rotates, its movement through these bulges and dips causes tides.

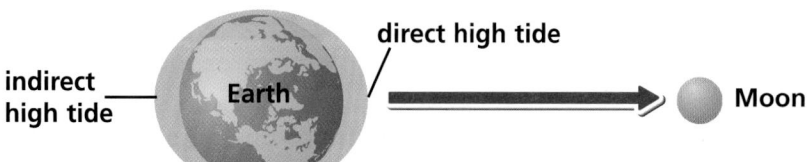

indirect high tide — Earth — direct high tide → Moon

VOCABULARY
tide p. 136
tidal range p. 138
spring tide p. 139
neap tide p. 139

Reviewing Vocabulary

Make a description wheel like the one below for each of the following terms. Write the term in the circle. On the spokes, write words or phrases that describe the term.

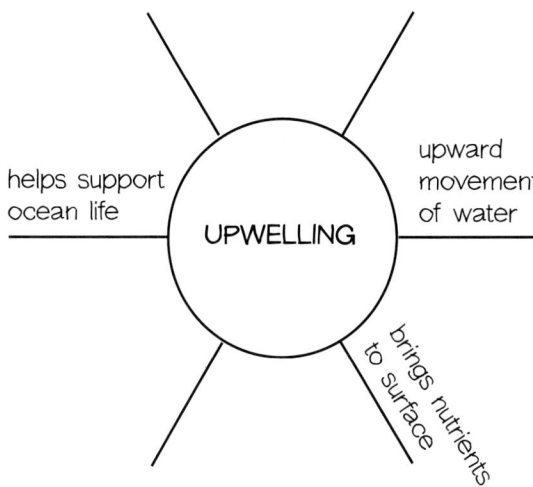

helps support ocean life

upward movement of water

UPWELLING

brings nutrients to surface

1. El Niño

2. longshore current

3. rip current

Reviewing Key Concepts

Multiple Choice *Choose the letter of the best answer.*

4. Warm water stays at the ocean surface because
  a. it is less dense than cold water
  b. it is more dense than cold water
  c. it is saltier than cold water
  d. it has more carbon dioxide than cold water

5. Sonar measures ocean depth by means of
  a. weighted lines   **c.** sound waves
  b. light waves   **d.** magnets

6. Surface currents are caused by
  a. waves   **c.** density
  b. winds   **d.** heat

7. El Niño is caused by changes in
  a. wave speed   **c.** salinity
  b. currents   **d.** tides

8. Deep currents are caused by differences in
  a. location   **c.** depth
  b. wind speed   **d.** density

9. Tides are caused by the gravitational pull of
  a. Earth and the Sun
  b. the Sun and the Moon
  c. Earth alone
  d. Earth and the Moon

10. What does wave action involve?
  a. the transfer of water molecules across the ocean surface
  b. the transfer of energy across the ocean surface
  c. oscillations generated by tides
  d. rip currents

Short Response *Write a short response to each question.*

11. What is the connection between salinity and density?

12. Explain why Earth's oceans are actually parts of one connected body of water.

13. Describe the relationship between ocean temperature and depth.

14. What are the characteristics of a wave? Copy the drawing below onto your paper, and label each part.

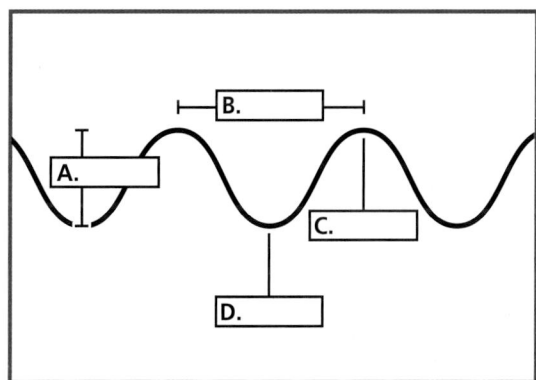

Thinking Critically

15. **SYNTHESIZE** One of these cups contains salt water, and the other contains fresh water. Without tasting the water, how could you figure out which sample is which? Describe two methods. You may specify tools or materials you would need to carry out the two methods. **Hint:** Think about the water cycle and density when considering the two methods.

16. **INFER** After the development of sonar, oceanographic researchers discovered much about the features of the ocean floor. How would the sonar readings of a research ship be affected as it passes above a mid-ocean ridge?

17. **COMPARE AND CONTRAST** How are space exploration and ocean exploration similar? How are they different?

18. **PROVIDE EXAMPLES** How could a change in the direction of a surface current in the ocean affect weather? Give examples of the weather in an area before and after the change.

19. **INFER** If global winds were to change, which ocean motions would be affected?

20. **APPLY** During a violent storm that causes huge waves to form on the ocean's surface, a submarine glides deep underwater, unaffected by the waves above. Explain why.

21. **COMPARE AND CONTRAST** Copy and fill in the Venn diagram below. In the overlapping section, list at least one characteristic that is shared by waves and tides. In the outer sections, list characteristics that are not shared. Then write a short summary of the information in the Venn diagram.

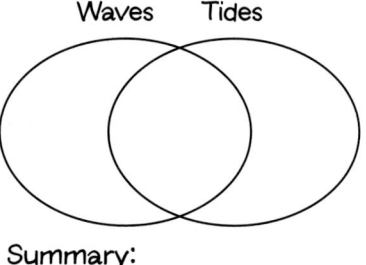

Summary:

22. **APPLY** Maria and her friends like to play soccer on a beach. Sometimes the water is very low at low tide, and there is plenty of room to play. At other times, the water does not get as low at low tide, and there is not enough room to play. What does Maria need to know about monthly tidal cycles so that she can plan to have the soccer games when there is plenty of room on the beach?

the BIG idea

23. **IDENTIFY CAUSE AND EFFECT** Look again at the photograph on pages 112–113. Now that you have finished the chapter, explain what is causing the waves in the photograph. Also explain what might cause the water level to rise and cover the area where the surfer is standing.

24. **SYNTHESIZE** One system can interact with another system. The oceans are a connected system of water in motion. The solar system is the Sun and its family of orbiting planets, moons, and other objects. Describe a connection between the solar system and the ocean system.

UNIT PROJECTS

Check your schedule for your unit project. How are you doing? Be sure that you have placed data or notes from your research in your project folder.

Analyzing a Table

The table below shows the times of high and low tides at a location on the Atlantic Ocean coast. Use the table to answer the questions below.

FCAT TiP

When answering multiple-choice questions, try to eliminate answer choices you know are not correct.

	Low Tide	High Tide	Low Tide	High Tide
Monday	12:01 A.M.	5:33 A.M.	11:58 A.M.	5:59 P.M.
Tuesday	12:57 A.M.	6:33 A.M.	12:51 P.M.	6:54 P.M.
Wednesday	1:51 A.M.	7:30 A.M.	1:45 P.M.	7:48 P.M.
Thursday	2:43 A.M.	8:25 A.M.	2:38 P.M.	8:40 P.M.

GRIDDED RESPONSE

1. What was the time difference in minutes between the first low tide on Monday and the second low tide on Wednesday?

2. What was the time difference in minutes between the first high tide on Wednesday and the second high tide on Wednesday?

MULTIPLE CHOICE

3. On which day was there a high tide at 7:48 P.M.?
   - **A.** Monday
   - **B.** Tuesday
   - **C.** Wednesday
   - **D.** Thursday

4. Low tide is a good time to find shells along the beach. What time would be best for finding shells on Wednesday?
   - **F.** 8:00 A.M.
   - **G.** 10:00 A.M.
   - **H.** noon
   - **I.** 2:00 P.M.

5. What was happening to the water level along the beach between 12:00 A.M. and 5:33 A.M. on Monday?
   - **A.** The water level was getting higher.
   - **B.** The water level was getting lower.
   - **C.** The water level was at its lowest.
   - **D.** The water level was at its highest.

6. Which of the following graphs best represents the tides during one day?

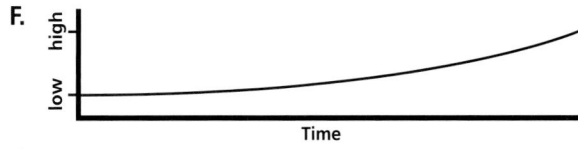

F.

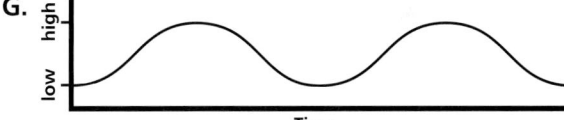

G.

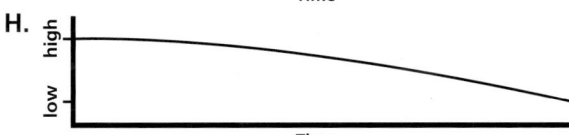

H.

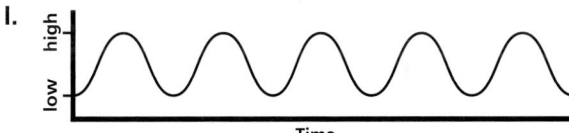

I.

EXTENDED RESPONSE

Answer the two questions below in detail.

7. How could you use a cork and a tank of water to demonstrate that waves transport energy, not water? You may include a diagram as part of your response if you wish.

8. The beaker contains both salt water and fresh water. Why do the two liquids form layers? Use the words *salinity* and *density* in your response.

fresh water
salt water

TIMELINES in Science

EXPLORING THE OCEAN

People have been studying ocean waves and currents at least since Egyptians sailed in the Mediterranean Sea more than 5000 years ago. Almost 3000 years ago, Phoenicians in the Mediterranean and Polynesians in the South Pacific understood enough to sail the open sea with confidence. More than 2000 years ago, people developed special gear to provide divers with oxygen so that they could explore the undersea world.

The timeline shows some historical events in the study of the ocean. The boxes below the timeline show how technology has made this study possible and useful.

345 B.C.

Alexander Goes Undersea?
According to legend, Macedonia's powerful ruler Alexander the Great has himself lowered into the ocean in a glass ball so that he can explore what lies underwater.

Events

360 B.C.   320 B.C.

APPLICATIONS AND TECHNOLOGY

APPLICATION

Measuring Ocean Depth

Around 85 B.C., the Greek philosopher Posidonius used a simple method to answer a simple question. He wanted to know the depth of the Mediterranean Sea. So he and a crew sailed out into the sea near Italy. There, they dropped a weight tied to a very long rope into the water. When the weight struck bottom, they measured how much rope they had let out. It was almost 2 kilometers (about 1 mi). This was the standard method for measuring depth for almost 2000 years. Today, instruments on ships emit sound waves that bounce off the sea floor. The instruments then calculate depth according to how long the sound waves take to return to the surface.

A sailor in 1916 prepares to lower a weight on a rope to measure the ocean's depth.

1775
Submarines Allow Undersea Travel

Connecticut inventor David Bushnell designs and builds a wooden submarine. It holds enough air for a person to stay underwater for 30 minutes. The *Turtle*, as his vessel is known, is among the first to allow people to travel underwater.

1797
Explorer Designs First Diving Suit

German mechanic Karl Heinrich Klingert combines waterproof clothes and a helmet with two tubes, one for inhaling and one for exhaling. He calls his outfit a diving machine. It allows people to stay underwater for longer periods than ever before.

1876
Expedition Surveys the Oceans

The sailing ship *Challenger* completes one of the great scientific research efforts of the 1800s, and returns home to Great Britain. In 362 locations around the world, the crew recorded data on ocean depth, currents, temperature, and water chemistry. They identified more than 4000 previously unknown species of plants and animals.

A.D. **1760**   **1800**   **1840**   **1880**

APPLICATION

Charting the Ocean Floor

In the 1800s, sailors began recording measurements of the deep Atlantic Ocean floor. The U.S. Navy lieutenant Matthew Maury collected 200 of these measurements and created the first chart showing water depths in such a large region. His chart, completed in 1855, provided the first evidence of mountains in the middle of the Atlantic. A decade later, Maury's studies of the ocean floor guided those who were laying the first telegraph cable connecting the United States and Europe.

1943

Explorer Breathes Underwater

In 1943, Jacques Cousteau, the most famous of 20th-century undersea explorers, helps develop scuba—a *s*elf-*c*ontained *u*nderwater *b*reathing *a*pparatus. The breathing gear allows divers to explore depths of 30 meters and beyond without having to wear heavy suits and metal helmets.

1938

Fish with Elbows Caught

Among the day's catch of the South African fisherman Hendrick Goosen is an odd five-foot-long fish with joints in its fins, like elbows and knees. Surprised scientists identify it as a coelacanth, a creature they thought had been extinct for 60 million years. The catch spurs people's imaginations about what else the ocean might contain.

1951

Exploration as Entertainment

Improvements in underwater breathing gear in the 1940s make recreational scuba diving possible. Then, a 1951 movie about scuba-wearing soldiers, *The Frogmen*, spurs popular interest in the activity. The movie inspires more people than ever before to start exploring the underwater world for themselves.

1953

Robotic Probe Searches Ocean

POODLE, the first remote operated vehicle (ROV), is invented. Since ROVs carry no people, they allow more research to be done in deep areas that are difficult for people to travel to.

1900	1920	1940	1960	1980

TECHNOLOGY

Sonar

In 1914, Reginald Fessenden developed the first practical instrument for using the echo of a sound to measure distances underwater. This technique, later named sonar, for "*so*und *na*vigation and *r*anging," allows scientists to study the undersea world without the expense and danger of going underwater. Sonar has been a valuable tool for measuring the depth of the ocean and the landforms along the bottom. Because temperature and salt concentration affect how sound travels, oceanographers can use sonar to measure these properties as well. One of sonar's most important early uses was to help sailors spot icebergs. Today, industry uses sonar to identify schools of fish, places likely to have oil, and other features.

This sonar image, recorded in October 1999, shows a shipwreck at the bottom of Delaware Bay.

1998

Aquarius *Keeps Researching*

After renovation, the 12-year-old *Aquarius* lab settles on the ocean floor in the Florida Keys. Its crew is investigating a nearby coral reef. They have studied the impact of sewage, the effects of ultraviolet radiation, and chemicals produced by organisms in the reef.

1994

Life Thrives Under Ocean

The discovery of microorganisms thriving in rock pulled up from 500 meters (1600 ft) below the ocean floor raises new questions for scientists. How did the bacteria get there? How do they survive? How many are there? Scientists call the region the deep biosphere.

RESOURCE CENTER
CLASSZONE.COM

Learn more about exploring the ocean.

2000

TECHNOLOGY

Ocean Buoys

Starting in 2000, scientists scattered in the ocean 3000 buoys equipped with the latest developments in floating technology. These Argo floats then started collecting information on water temperature and salinity. They transmitted data by satellite every 15 days. With this more detailed information about ocean water, scientists may be able to make weather predictions more accurate than ever before.

INTO THE **FUTURE**

Over the past 5000 years, people have learned more and more about the ocean. This knowledge has helped scientists understand how ocean systems work, how Earth has changed, and what factors influence the weather. Continuing research is expanding knowledge in these areas. New findings could be just as surprising as the previous discovery of a fish considered extinct or of microorganisms deep under the ocean floor.

People will probably continue to catch fish and to drill for oil in the ocean for many decades. In addition, people might find it profitable to use other ocean resources. For example, they might mine gold or manganese. Or they might use the tremendous energy in ocean tides or waves—or in the winds that blow over the ocean—to generate electricity. The ocean is so large that many possibilities for using its resources remain.

ACTIVITIES

Mapping the Sea Floor

Suppose you are in a boat that is traveling in a straight line. You take a sonar reading every one-half minute. Your readings, which show how long sound waves take to reach bottom and return to the surface, are as follows:

1. 2 seconds   **3.** 3 seconds
2. 0.5 second   **4.** 3 seconds

Sound travels at about 1500 meters per second (4900 ft/s) in seawater.

From this information, draw what the sea floor looks like under the path of your boat.

Writing About Science

Technology has been used for centuries to study the ocean. Trace the history of one piece of technology, such as a submarine, diving gear, sonar, or a depth gauge. Write a short history of that device.

CHAPTER

Ocean Environments

the BIG idea

The ocean supports life and contains natural resources.

Key Concepts

SECTION

1 Ocean coasts support plant and animal life. Learn about conditions in coastal environments and about the plants and animals that live there.

SECTION

2 Conditions differ away from shore. Learn how conditions change as you move away from the shore and deeper into the ocean.

SECTION

3 The ocean contains natural resources. Learn about the ocean's living and nonliving resources and how pollution affects the ocean.

FCAT Practice

Prepare and practice for the FCAT
• Section Reviews, pp. 159, 168, 177
• Chapter Review, pp. 180–182
• FCAT Practice, p. 183

CLASSZONE.COM
• Florida Review: Content Review and FCAT Practice

How is the deep ocean different from the shore?

EXPLORE the BIG idea

It's Alive!

Carefully observe a fish in a fish tank. Pay attention to all of the fish's movements. Record what the fish does and what the fish's environment is like.

Observe and Think All animals, including fish, need oxygen to live. Where does the fish get its oxygen?

Beneath the Surface

What forms of life would you expect to see underwater in the ocean near shore? Draw a picture to show your ideas.

Observe and Think What do you need to know in order to make your picture more accurate? Write five questions you have about the ocean environment near shore.

Internet Activity: Ocean Environments

Go to **ClassZone.com** to learn more about organisms in the ocean. See which plants and animals live in different ocean environments.

Observe and Think What factors or conditions might affect the kinds of organisms that can live in each part of the ocean?

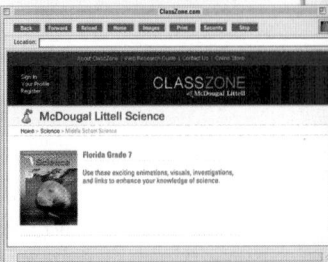

NSTA
scilinks.org

*SCI*LINKS

Ocean Resources **Code: MDL021**

Getting Ready to Learn

◀ CONCEPT REVIEW

- The ocean contains oxygen and other gases.
- Deep currents carry oxygen from the surface to the ocean floor.
- Upwelling carries nutrients from the bottom of the ocean to the surface.

◀ VOCABULARY REVIEW

point-source pollution p. 94
nonpoint-source pollution p. 94
continental shelf p. 120
ocean current p. 124

FLORIDA REVIEW
CLASSZONE.COM
Content Review and FCAT Practice

▶ TAKING NOTES

MAIN IDEA WEB

Write each new blue heading—a main idea—in a box. Then put notes with important terms and details into boxes around the main idea.

CHOOSE YOUR OWN STRATEGY

Take notes about new vocabulary terms, using one or more of the strategies from earlier chapters—**four square, description wheel,** or **word triangle.** Feel free to mix and match the strategies, or use an entirely different vocabulary strategy.

See the Note-Taking Handbook on pages R45–R51.

SCIENCE NOTEBOOK

| Different parts of the ocean have different characteristics. | Almost 95 percent of the ocean is still unexplored. |

Ocean waters contain many environments.

| | Swimmers, floaters, and bottom dwellers are three groups of ocean life. |

Four Square
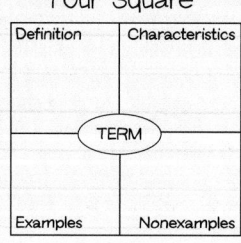

Description Wheel
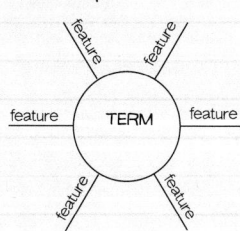

Word Triangle
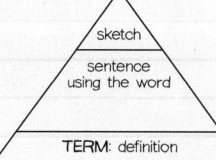

Ocean coasts support plant and animal life.

Sunshine State STANDARDS

SC.G.1.3.2: The student knows that biological adaptations include changes in structures, behaviors, or physiology that enhance reproductive success in a particular environment.

SC.G.1.3.4: The student knows that the interactions of organisms with each other and with the non-living parts of their environments result in the flow of energy and the cycling of matter throughout the system.

SC.G.2.3.4: The student understands that humans are a part of an ecosystem and their activities may deliberately or inadvertently alter the equilibrium in ecosystems.

FCAT VOCABULARY
habitat p. 154

VOCABULARY
intertidal zone p. 154
estuary p. 156
wetland p. 156

MAIN IDEA WEB
Remember to start a main idea web in your notebook for this blue heading.

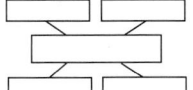

BEFORE, you learned

- Ocean water contains gases such as oxygen
- Salinity is a measure of the amount of salt in water
- Coastal waters rise and fall each day because of tides

NOW, you will learn

- What the intertidal zone is
- What coastal environments exist where fresh water and salt water meet
- How human activity affects shoreline environments

THINK ABOUT

What are the characteristics of shoreline environments?

This map shows the migration route of the osprey, a type of bird. Each fall ospreys fly south to warmer weather. In the spring they fly north. Each dot on the map represents a place where ospreys stop along the way. What do you notice about where the birds stop? What resources might shoreline environments provide for birds?

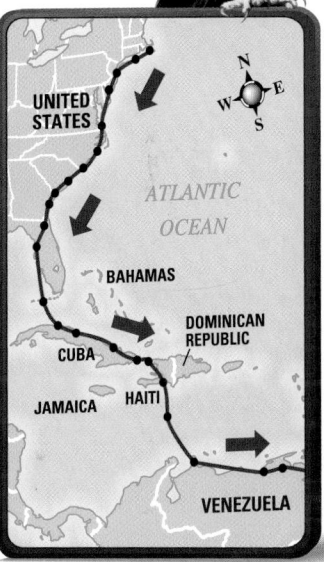

Ocean waters contain many environments.

Where on Earth can you find a living animal that is larger than the largest dinosaur that ever lived? Where can you find birds that use their wings to fly underwater, or animals that can eject their internal organs—and grow another set? Where can you find warm tropical zones thick with plants, or cold, empty plains where no plant can grow? The ocean contains all these and more.

Like the land, the ocean contains many different environments, each with its own special characteristics. Although scientists have learned a lot about the ocean and its environments, almost 95 percent of the ocean remains unexplored. It is possible that many millions more species of ocean life are yet to be discovered.

The many known ocean organisms are organized in three groups according to the way the organisms live. Bottom dwellers include plantlike organisms called algae (AL-jee) and other organisms that live on the ocean bottom—for example, seaweeds, crabs, corals, starfish, and shellfish. Swimmers are animals such as fish, dolphins, whales, and octopuses that swim in the ocean. Floaters are organisms that do not swim but float at or near the ocean surface. Some floaters, such as jellyfish, are large, but most are so small you need a microscope to see them. These tiny living things include plants, animals, bacteria, and single-celled organisms called protists (PROH-tihsts).

CHECK YOUR READING What are the three groups of ocean life?

The shoreline supports many plants and animals.

READING TiP

Word parts can help you remember the meaning of *intertidal zone.* The prefix *inter-* means "between." The root *tidal* means "relating to the tides." The *intertidal zone* is the area between high and low tides.

An environment that has all the necessary requirements for an organism to live is called a **habitat.** In this chapter you will explore some of the many different ocean habitats. Your journey begins on the coastline, where the ocean meets the land. The habitat at the edge of the ocean is the **intertidal zone** (IHN-tuhr-TYD-uhl)—the narrow ocean margin between the high tide mark and the low tide mark. The conditions constantly change in the intertidal zone. Organisms that live here must be able to survive both wet and dry periods. Plants and animals must also withstand the force of waves that constantly crash onto shore.

1. At **low tide,** the intertidal zone is dry and exposed to direct sunlight. Organisms must be able to live out of water. They must also be able to tolerate the air temperature, which may differ from the temperature of the water.

2. At **high tide,** the intertidal zone is covered with water, so it is not exposed to direct sunlight. Organisms must be able to live completely underwater and tolerate the temperature of the water.

Tidal pools are areas along the shore where water remains at low tide. Plants and animals that live in tidal pools must survive drastic changes in salinity, or salt content. When sunlight causes water to evaporate, the salinity increases. When rain falls, the salinity decreases.

Organisms have different ways of surviving the conditions of the intertidal zone. For example, crabs can move around and seek cover in the sand or in between rocks. Mussels attach themselves to rocks and close their shells to keep from drying out during low tide. Some seaweeds dry out at low tide but are able to regain moisture at high tide.

Intertidal Zone

The intertidal zone is the area along the coastline between the high tide mark and the low tide mark.

intertidal zone

① Low Tide

At low tide, the intertidal zone is exposed to the air.

Tidal pools are areas where water remains at low tide.

Some seaweeds can dry out during low tide and absorb water at high tide.

At low tide, mussels close their shells tightly to keep from drying out.

② High Tide

At high tide, the intertidal zone is covered with water.

Plants and animals must survive the constant crashing of waves against the shore.

At high tide, mussels open their shells to eat and take in oxygen.

READING VISUALS What organisms can you see in the photograph of low tide?

INVESTIGATE Coastal Environments

How do mussels survive?

Most intertidal zone organisms require water to survive, and they must endure long dry periods during low tides. Mussels close their shells tightly during low tide and open them during high tide.

PROCEDURE

DESIGN —YOUR OWN— EXPERIMENT

1. Using the materials listed, design an experiment to demonstrate why mussels close their shells during low tide.

2. Write up your procedure.

3. Test your experiment.

WHAT DO YOU THINK?

- How does your experiment demonstrate why mussels close their shells?

- What were the variables in your experiment?

CHALLENGE How could you redesign your experiment to better model what happens during low tide? What other variables would you include?

SKILL FOCUS
Designing experiments

MATERIALS
- small plastic containers with lids
- sponges
- water

TIME
30 minutes

Fresh water and salt water meet on coasts.

This aerial photograph shows the Pawcatuck River estuary in the northeastern United States. Fresh water from the river mixes with salt water from the ocean.

You have read that rivers flow to the sea. What happens when they get there? The fresh water from rivers mixes with salt water from the ocean in shoreline areas called **estuaries** (EHS-choo-EHR-eez), which include bays, inlets, and harbors. The water in estuaries is not as salty as ocean water, nor as fresh as river water. The salinity changes as the tide flows in and out. Sometimes the water at the surface is fresh, while denser salt water remains below.

Estuaries are bursting with life. Plants and animals thrive on nutrients washed in by rivers. Worms and shellfish live along the bottom. Plants and animals too small to see without a microscope float in the water. Many different kinds of birds and sea animals breed in estuaries. Roots and grasses offer protection for young fish and other animals. These small fish and other animals are an important food source for larger fish and for birds.

Coastal wetlands form along the edges of estuaries. As the name suggests, **wetlands** are wet, swampy areas that are often flooded with water. There are two kinds of coastal wetlands. Away from the equator, in cooler regions, coastal wetlands are salt marshes. Closer to the equator, in tropical regions, coastal wetlands are mangrove forests.

CHECK YOUR READING How are coastal wetlands related to estuaries?

Salt Marshes

Away from the equator, in cooler regions, grassy salt marshes are found along the edges of estuaries. In the United States, salt marshes are found along the coasts of the Atlantic and Pacific oceans and the Gulf of Mexico. Salt marshes help keep the shoreline from washing away. They also provide an important habitat for fish, birds, and other wildlife.

The rivers that flow into estuaries carry nutrient-rich soil. When the rivers reach the sea, they drop the soil. This rich soil supports thick grasses. The grasses form a protective barrier against waves, tides, and storms. Thick root systems hold the muddy bottom together. Tiny organisms decompose, or break down, dead grasses and return the nutrients the grasses contained to the marsh.

Crabs, snails, and minnows thrive among the grasses. Ospreys and other fish-eating birds find food in salt marshes. Birds that migrate use salt marshes as rest stops when they fly back and forth each season.

In the past, people did not understand the importance of wetlands. Over the last 200 years, about half of all wetlands in the United States were destroyed. Many were drained or filled in with soil to provide solid ground to build on or to farm. In the 1970s, people started working to protect and restore coastal wetlands.

CHECK YOUR READING Why are grasses an important part of the salt marsh environment?

VIRGINIA

Marsh grasses have thick root systems that help hold the muddy soil together.

Many small fish and other animals live in the sheltered areas among the marsh grasses.

Fish-eating birds find plenty to eat in salt marshes.

This is an underwater view of mangrove roots.

INFER This photograph shows mangrove plants along the coast of Florida. How do the roots brace the mangroves against waves and storms?

Mangrove Forests

In tropical regions, the main coastal wetland is the mangrove forest. In the United States, mangrove forests are found along the coast of southern Florida. A mangrove forest is a thick group of mangrove shrubs and trees. The mangrove plants' roots brace them against storms and waves. Without the protection of these plants, shorelines in tropical areas would be drastically changed by heavy storms.

The sheltered mangrove forest is home to many living things. Fiddler crabs may live in the shallow waters among the mangrove roots. You may find seaweeds, oysters, shrimp, and snails. You may even see tree-climbing fish! These fish, called mudskippers, climb mangrove roots to catch insects and crabs.

MAIN IDEA WEB
Remember to start a main idea web in your notebook for this blue heading.

Human activity affects shorelines.

Coastal environments are home not only to many plants and animals, but to many humans as well. About half of the world's population lives within 80 kilometers (50 mi) of a coastline. Big cities and important commercial ports are often located where rivers meet the sea. Many people use coastlines and estuaries for recreation, such as boating, swimming, and fishing.

Human activity can harm the estuary environment. For example, some coastal wetlands are cleared for shrimp farms and for raising crops. Other areas are filled in to make new land for houses and other development. Industry and shipping can disturb wildlife and alter the estuary habitat. In some places, human waste and other sewage drains directly into the water.

About half of the world's population lives near a coastline, such as this one in Mexico.

Even pollution that occurs far away from the shore can affect the coast. The rivers that empty into estuaries pass through farms and cities. Along the way, the rivers may pick up pollutants such as pesticides, fertilizers, oil, and other chemicals. Pollution that washes into the river—even kilometers away from the shore—will eventually end up in the estuary.

Governments, local organizations, and individuals work to protect and preserve shoreline environments in many states. Improved sewage treatment plants reduce the amount of human waste that ends up in shoreline environments. Laws that restrict dumping help reduce pollution along shorelines. Many states have shoreline sanctuaries where plants and animals are protected.

 **CHECK YOUR READING** What are three ways shorelines are protected?

5.1 Review

KEY CONCEPTS

1. Describe the characteristics of the intertidal zone.

2. Name and describe two coastal environments that border estuaries.

3. What human activities are harmful to shoreline environments?

CRITICAL THINKING

4. **Compare and Contrast** What similarities exist between salt marshes and mangrove forests? How are they different?

5. **Infer** Sometimes estuaries are called nursery areas. Why do you think estuaries may have been given that name?

⏷ CHALLENGE

6. **Identify Cause** A salinity meter placed in a tidal pool shows a dramatic decrease in salinity between 2 A.M. and 3 A.M. This decrease is followed by a gradual rise in salinity from 11 A.M. until 4 P.M. the next day. What might explain these changes?

MATH in SCIENCE

SKILL: MAKING A DOUBLE BAR GRAPH

MATH TUTORIAL
CLASSZONE.COM
Click on Math Tutorial for more help with bar graphs.

Machines mounted on boats drill down into the ocean floor to collect sediment cores.

This tube contains a sediment core.

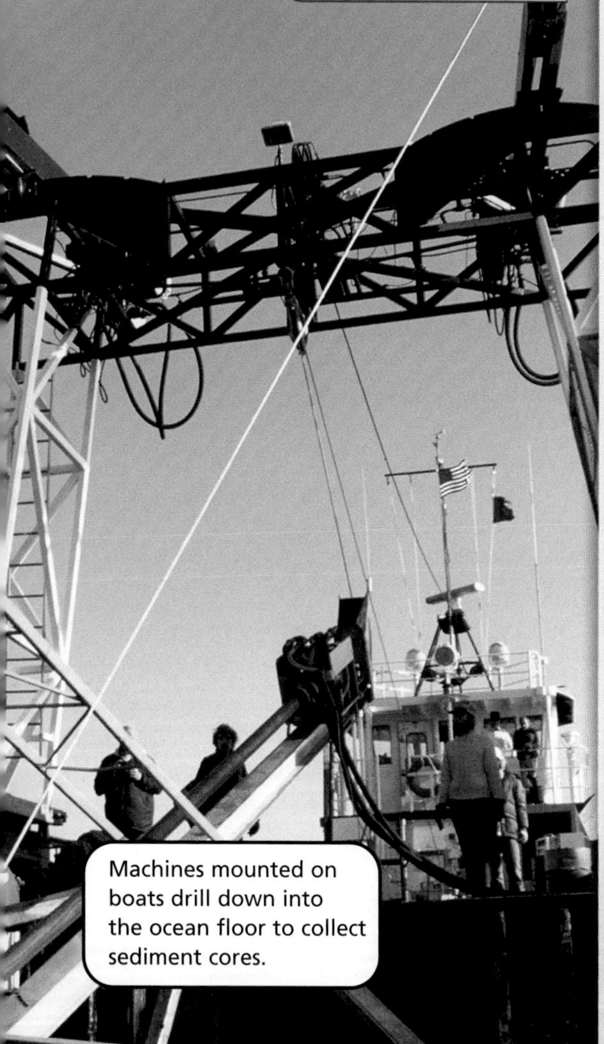

Tracking Contaminants

The layered sediments at the bottom of the ocean have formed over time. The particles in the deeper layers settled to the floor long ago, while those in the top layers settled out of the water more recently. By studying the amounts of pollutants in different layers of sediment, scientists can see how the water quality has changed over time. In 1991, scientists collected sediment cores north of Dash Point in Puget Sound. The table below shows levels of two pollutants, lead and arsenic, in the sediment layers for 1880, 1960, and 1990. The levels are measured in milligrams per kilogram dry weight (mg/kg d.w.).

Levels of Lead and Arsenic in Sediments

Year	Lead (mg/kg d.w.)	Arsenic (mg/kg d.w.)
1880	10	6
1960	62	22
1990	45	17

You can use a double bar graph to analyze the data. A double bar graph shows two sets of data on the same graph. The first two bars of the graph are drawn for you below.

Example

(1) Copy the axes and labels.

(2) Draw bars for the lead data. Use the scale to determine the height of each bar, as shown.

(3) Draw the arsenic bars next to the lead bars.

(4) Shade the bars in different colors. Include a key.

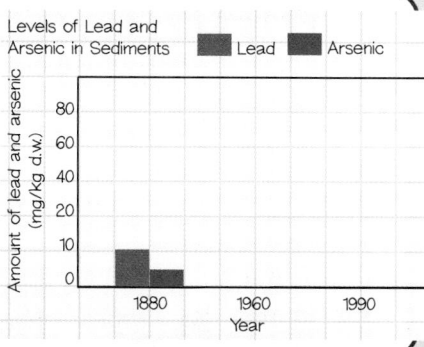

Make a double bar graph of the data by following the steps above. Use your graph to answer the following questions.

1. What happened to the levels of lead and arsenic between 1880 and 1960?

2. What happened to the levels of lead and arsenic between 1960 and 1990?

CHALLENGE Because lead can be harmful to humans, the use of leaded gasoline in new cars was banned in 1975 and the sale of lead-based paint was banned in 1978. How might these bans have affected the amount of lead in Puget Sound? Use evidence from your graph to support your answer.

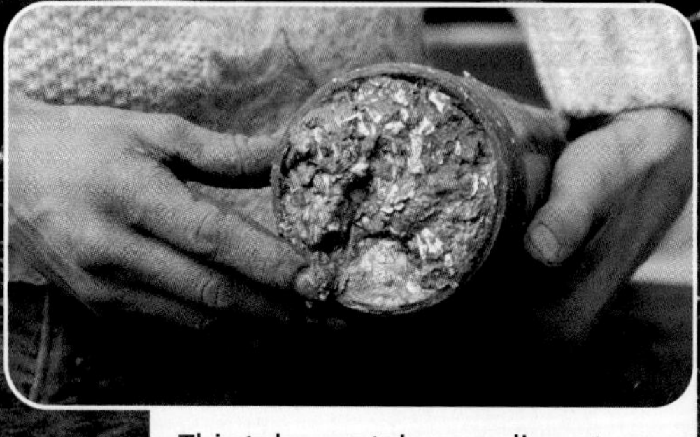

KEY CONCEPT

Conditions differ away from shore.

Sunshine State STANDARDS

SC.G.1.3.4: The student knows that the interactions of organisms with each other and with the non-living parts of their environments result in the flow of energy and the cycling of matter throughout the system.

SC.G.2.3.2: The student knows that all biotic and abiotic factors are interrelated and that if one factor is changed or removed, it impacts the availability of other resources within the system.

SC.G.2.3.4: The student understands that humans are a part of an ecosystem and their activities may deliberately or inadvertently alter the equilibrium in ecosystems.

BEFORE, you learned

- Coasts support plants and animals
- Estuaries and intertidal zones are coastal environments

NOW, you will learn

- About ocean environments away from the coast
- How ocean environments change with depth
- How hydrothermal vents support life in the ocean

EXPLORE Air Bladders

How can air make things float?

PROCEDURE

1. Fill the container halfway with soda water.
2. Add raisins to the container, one by one.
3. Observe for 5 minutes. Record your observations.

MATERIALS
- clear container
- soda water
- 5 raisins

WHAT DO YOU THINK?
- How did the air bubbles control the movement of the raisins?
- Many ocean fish have an air-filled organ called an air bladder. The fish can control the amount of air in the bladder. How might the amount of air in the bladder change as a fish dives from the ocean surface to the bottom and then returns to the surface?

VOCABULARY

coral reef p. 162
kelp forest p. 164
phytoplankton p. 166
hydrothermal vent p. 168

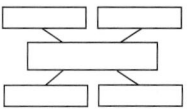

MAIN IDEA WEB
Remember to start a main idea web in your notebook for the blue heading.

Ocean environments change with depth and distance from shore.

Your journey through ocean environments continues as you leave the intertidal zone and move farther out into the ocean. First, you will visit the habitats found in the waters near shore. Next you will move out into the open ocean.

Near shore—in the waters over the continental shelf—sunlight reaches most of the way to the ocean bottom. Nutrients wash in from land. Temperature and salinity are nearly constant from the surface to the bottom. These conditions support many kinds of living things.

 **CHECK YOUR READING** What are some characteristics of the environment near shore?

Chapter 5: **Ocean Environments** **161**

The waters near shore support diverse life forms.

More kinds of ocean life live in the waters near shore than in any other ocean environment. Microscopic organisms including bacteria, protists, plants, and animals live there. They share the waters near shore with plants as tall as ten-story buildings and animals larger than elephants. Each organism is part of a delicate and complex food web. You become part of this food web when you eat a fish from the waters near shore. In fact, most of the world's fish are caught in this ocean environment.

Two important habitats near shore are the kelp forest and the coral reef. Kelp forests are found in cooler waters, and coral reefs are found in tropical warm waters.

Coral Reefs

VOCABULARY
A four square diagram would be a good choice for taking notes about the term *coral reef*.

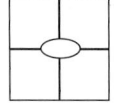

In warm, tropical regions of the globe, the waters near shore support coral reefs. **Coral reefs** are built-up limestone deposits formed by large colonies of ant-sized organisms called corals. Corals produce a hard limestone covering that remains after the corals die. New generations of corals grow on top of older limestone coverings. Although individual corals are small, coral reefs can be huge. Australia's Great Barrier Reef is about 2000 kilometers (1250 mi) long—as long as the distance from Chicago, Illinois, to San Antonio, Texas.

Corals rely on a special relationship with a kind of algae for almost all of their food needs. Tiny algae live inside individual corals. Like plants, the algae use sunlight to produce food through photosynthesis. The food algae produces provides the coral with most of its nutrition. In return, the coral provides some nutrients to the algae. Because the algae need sunlight to survive, coral reefs exist only in the ocean environment near shore, where sunlight reaches all the way to the ocean floor.

Coral reefs, which contain over 25 percent of all of the species of ocean life, help protect shorelines from wave and storm damage.

Coral Reefs

The nutrient-rich, sunlit waters near shore support a greater variety of life than any other part of the ocean.

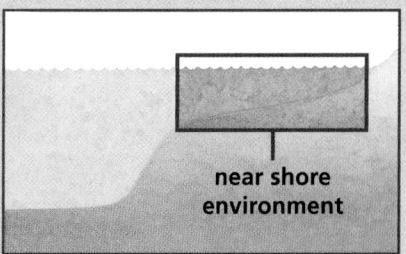

near shore environment

The **anemone** can paralyze most fish with its stinging tentacles.

The **anemone fish** (also called the clown fish) is covered by mucus that protects it from the anemone. The anemone shelters the fish from predators. The anemone benefits by eating bits of food that the fish drops.

The **parrotfish** uses its hard teeth to chew on coral. It eats the algae that live in and on the coral. The hard coral skeletons get ground into sand as they pass through the parrotfish's digestive system.

The **moray eel** spends days hidden in cracks or holes in the reef. At night the eel comes out to hunt.

The **nudibranch** is related to snails but has no shell. It contains bad-tasting or poisonous chemicals that discourage fish from eating it.

The **giant clam** can grow to be over 1 meter (3 ft) long. It feeds by filtering tiny organisms from the water. Like corals, the giant clam gets some of its nutrients from algae that live within its own tissues.

READING VISUALS Which organisms in the diagram appear to be using nooks in the reef for shelter?

RESOURCE CENTER
CLASSZONE.COM

Explore coral reefs.

The huge amount and variety of life found at coral reefs compares with that found in rain forests. In fact, coral reefs contain over 25 percent of all the species of ocean life. Some reef inhabitants use nooks and crannies in the reef for shelter. Other inhabitants eat corals or feed on seaweed that grows on the corals. Clown fish, sea anemones, (uh-NEHM-uh-neez), sea urchins, starfish, giant clams, and parrotfish are some of the many colorful reef inhabitants.

Coral reefs are now endangered habitats. Pollution that drains off land or that is dumped directly into the water harms coral reefs. Some fishing practices also harm corals and other life at reefs.

 Why are coral reefs endangered?

Kelp Forests

In cold waters, a seaweed called kelp attaches itself to the ocean floor and grows as tall as 40 meters (130 ft)—about the length of an airline jet. Air-filled bulbs on the seaweed's stalks help it to float up toward the surface and remain upright underwater. Large communities of this seaweed form **kelp forests.** Like plants, kelps use sunlight to produce food. Because kelps need sunlight and grow in the ocean, kelp forests

Kelp forests, such as this one in California, provide food and shelter for many living things.

Kelp is an ingredient in many common products including ice cream. Kelp can grow up to 33 cm (13 in) each day.

A sea otter off the coast of California wraps itself in kelp.

are found only in the waters near shore, where sunlight reaches to the ocean floor. Thick kelp forests provide habitats for many organisms. Worms, starfish, lobsters, crabs, abalones, and octopuses are some of the animals that live among the crowded stands of kelp. Fish find shelter and food there. Sea otters dining on sea urchins anchor themselves to the thick mats that the kelps form on the surface.

 **CHECK YOUR READING** Why are kelp forests found only in waters near shore?

INVESTIGATE Floating

How do plankton float?

DESIGN
— YOUR OWN —

Plankton are microscopic organisms that drift in the ocean, where they are moved about by wind, waves, and currents. They must stay near the sunlit surface in order to live. Because plankton have no muscles, they cannot swim to stay afloat. In this lab, you will construct different-shaped clay models to determine how shape helps plankton stay near the ocean surface.

PROCEDURE

1. Fill the clear container with tap water.
2. Use the clay to make several different shapes that you think will stay afloat.
3. One by one, place your clay models on the surface of the water. Time how long each piece takes to reach the bottom. Record your observations.

WHAT DO YOU THINK?

• What were the characteristics of the clay shape that sank the slowest?

• What factors affected how fast your clay shape sunk?

CHALLENGE Some kinds of floating organisms release oil droplets or air bubbles to help them stay afloat. How could oil or air help them float?

SKILL FOCUS
Modeling

MATERIALS
• clear container
• water
• modeling clay
• watch with a second hand

TIME
30 minutes

Environments in the open ocean change with depth.

Out in the open ocean, conditions are different from these found in the waters near shore. Sunlight reaches through only the very top part of the open ocean. Nutrients sink down to the dark depths. There are no rocks, reefs, or big plants to provide shelter from predators. The open ocean covers a huge area but contains fewer living things than the waters near shore. Life is more spread out in the open ocean.

Surface Zone

The surface zone of the open ocean is the sunlit top 200 meters (650 ft). Microscopic floating organisms called **phytoplankton** (FY-toh-PLANGK-tuhn) live at or near the sunlit surface. Like plants, phytoplankton convert sunlight and carbon dioxide into food and oxygen. In fact, phytoplankton convert about as much carbon dioxide into oxygen as all land plants combined. Phytoplankton are an important source of the oxygen that you are breathing right now. Tiny floating animals called zooplankton eat phytoplankton. Zooplankton and phytoplankton then become food for fish, squids, and ocean mammals, such as whales.

Inhabitants of the surface zone must keep from sinking. To stay afloat, phytoplankton bodies have big surface areas and may use air bubbles or oil droplets to stay near the ocean surface. Many fish have an air-filled organ called an air bladder that helps the fish change depth. Changing the amount of air in the bladder allows these fish to move up and down in the water. When the bladder fills with air, the fish floats up toward the surface. Releasing air from the bladder allows the fish to dive down into deeper water.

Deep Zone

The dark and cold deep zone of the open ocean lies under the surface zone. Because sunlight does not reach the deep zone, no plants can live there. Without plants for food, many deep-sea animals must either eat each other or rely on food drifting down from above.

The anglerfish in the photograph on page 167 has many of the common features of deep-sea animals. Its huge mouth and sharp teeth are typical of predators—animals that hunt and eat other animals. Many deep-sea animals glow in the dark, as fireflies do. A glowing extension sticks out from the head of the anglerfish and acts as bait to attract prey. Animals of the deepest waters often have small eyes—and some have no eyes at all. Among the animals found in the deep zone are lantern fish, squids, octopuses, and shrimp.

Life in the Open Ocean

The open ocean consists of a sunlit surface zone and a dark deep zone.

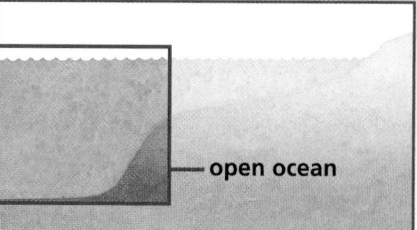
open ocean

dolphin

The **surface zone** is the top 200 meters of the ocean.

Many kinds of phytoplankton and zooplankton live in the surface zone.

zooplankton

jellyfish

The **deep zone** is the part of the ocean beneath the surface zone all the way to the ocean floor.

phytoplankton

No sunlight reaches below this line.

Sperm whales need to breathe air at the surface but may dive down hundreds of meters to hunt giant squid.

lantern fish

hatchet fish

mid-water shrimp

This extension glows in the dark and attracts prey.

The gulper eel's huge jaws can open wide enough to swallow animals as large as itself.

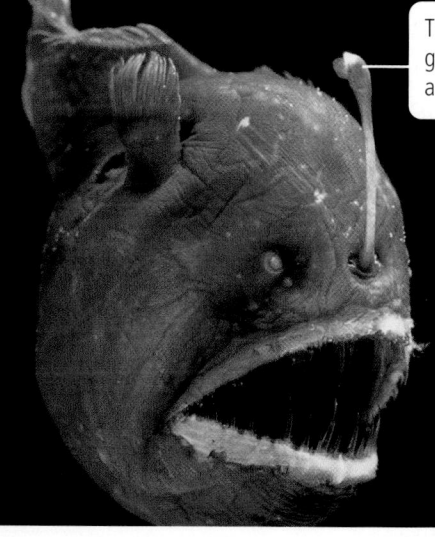
The anglerfish is a predator that lives in the deep zone.

Scientists estimate there are about 20 billion rattail fish in the ocean—over three times the number of people on Earth.

giant squid

The **deep zone** continues to the ocean floor.

Open ocean inhabitants shown here are not drawn to scale.

READING VISUALS Which are bigger, phytoplankton or zooplankton? How can you tell?

New discoveries about ocean life continue.

VISUALIZATION
CLASSZONE.COM

Examine the life found at hydrothermal vents.

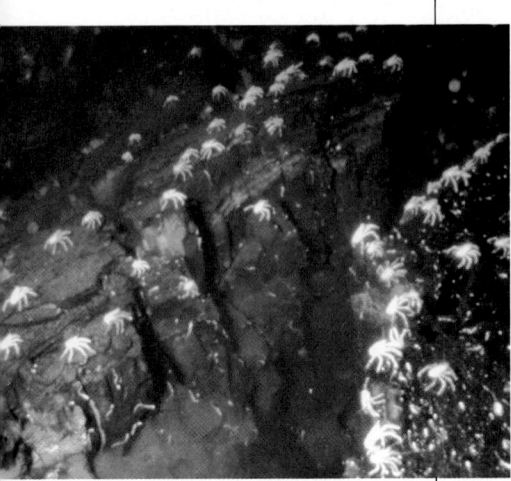

Hydrothermal vents support many kinds of life, including clams, crabs, fish, tubeworms, and bacteria.

While investigating deep-sea sediments in 1977, scientists got quite a surprise. On the deep-ocean floor they found thriving communities of crabs, fish, mussels, shrimp, giant clams, and tubeworms. These animals live near openings in Earth's crust called **hydrothermal vents**. Cold ocean water that seeps into cracks in the ocean floor gets heated deep underground by hot magma. The heated water then rises up and gushes out into the ocean, forming hydrothermal vents.

Before the discovery of animal communities near vents, most scientists thought life was impossible on the dark ocean floor. On land, life depends on plants, which use sunlight to produce food. Without sunlight, how could these deep sea animals live?

Scientists found that animals at hydrothermal vents depend on a special type of bacteria. Instead of making food from sunlight and carbon dioxide, like plants, these bacteria make food from chemicals released by the vents. The bacteria thus form the base of the food chain at the vents. Some of the animals living there eat the bacteria. Other animals, such as tubeworms, have the bacteria living within their bodies. Tubeworms do not eat and have no digestive system—they absorb all their food directly from the bacteria.

Because of its crushing pressure, darkness, and huge size, the deep ocean remains mostly unexplored. The discovery of animal communities at hydrothermal vents is a reminder that life may be possible even in seemingly impossible places. In fact, more recent explorations have even found life deep within the sediments of the ocean floor.

CHECK YOUR READING Why were scientists surprised to find life at hydrothermal vents?

5.2 Review

KEY CONCEPTS

1. What are two environments in the waters near shore? Describe the characteristics of each.

2. How does the surface zone of the open ocean differ from the deep zone?

3. How do hydrothermal vents support life on the deep-ocean floor?

CRITICAL THINKING

4. **Predict** How might a change in the amount of phytoplankton in the ocean affect the world's atmosphere?

5. **Evaluate** Suppose you are seeking a site for a submarine station where scientists could live for months at a time. Which ocean environment would you choose, and why?

CHALLENGE

6. **Apply** Diatoms are tiny ocean organisms that convert carbon dioxide to oxygen. Describe the depth at which diatoms live and where they fit into the ocean food chain.

(magnified 200x)

EXTREME SCIENCE

Undersea Hot Spots

Deep within Earth, volcanic activity heats up water. When this water shoots out through a crack in the ocean floor, it forms a hydrothermal vent. These vents are among the world's strangest environments.

- The pressure of the ocean water is so high that the water emerging from the vents does not boil—even though it is as hot as 400°C (750°F).
- The water from the vents is so filled with minerals, particularly hydrogen sulfide, that it would poison most animals.
- Sunlight is so dim that the vents exist in near total darkness. However, they often glow slightly, perhaps due to heat radiation.

Home Sweet Home

Organisms that live anywhere else on Earth would not be able to survive the combination of pressure, heat, poisonous water, and darkness that exists near vents. Yet scientists have identified 300 species living near vents.

- Bacteria convert the sulfur in the water into energy. This is one of the few places on Earth where the living things at the base of a food chain get energy from chemicals rather than from sunlight.
- Tubeworms that grow up to 3 meters (10 ft) long and oversized clams thrive on the sulfur-eating bacteria.
- Crabs with gigantic legs that make them look like enormous spiders from a horror movie survive by eating the worms and other creatures.

Life Far Away

Organisms that live around the vents are like no others on Earth. However, could a different planet with a sulfur-rich environment support similar life forms? As scientists explore the possibility of life on other planets, they will look to hydrothermal vents for lessons on unusual life.

EXPLORE

1. **SEQUENCE** Create a diagram showing the relationship on the hydrothermal vent food chain between bacteria, crabs, and tubeworms.
2. **CHALLENGE** In 1997 scientists discovered features on Jupiter's moon Europa that look like icebergs floating on an ocean. Why did this discovery suggest that life might exist on Europa?

RESOURCE CENTER
CLASSZONE.COM

Learn more about hydrothermal vents.

When the hot water from the vent hits the nearly freezing ocean water, it cools rapidly. The minerals dissolved in the water settle out, sometimes creating a chimney around the vent. Some chimneys are as tall as 15-story buildings.

Tubeworms may grow up to 3 meters (10 ft) in length.

5.3 The ocean contains natural resources.

Sunshine State STANDARDS

SC.B.2.3.2: The student knows that most of the energy used today is derived from burning stored energy collected by organisms millions of years ago (e.g., nonrenewable fossil fuels).

SC.D.2.3.2: The student knows the positive and negative consequences of human action on the Earth's systems.

SC.G.2.3.4: The student understands that humans are a part of an ecosystem and their activities may deliberately or inadvertently alter the equilibrium in ecosystems.

BEFORE, you learned

- The waters near shore support diverse life forms
- The ocean environment changes with depth

NOW, you will learn

- What living resources the ocean contains
- What mineral, energy, and other resources the ocean contains
- How pollution affects the ocean

VOCABULARY

overfishing p. 171
by-catch p. 172

EXPLORE Ocean Pollution

How do oil spills affect birds?

PROCEDURE

1. Fill the bowl with water.
2. Carefully place the feather on top of the water in the bowl.
3. Holding the end of the feather, blow on it to try to make the feather rise up out of the bowl. Record your observations.
4. Remove the feather and place three spoonfuls of oil into the bowl.
5. Repeat steps 2 and 3.

MATERIALS
- bowl
- water
- feather
- spoon
- cooking oil

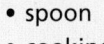

WHAT DO YOU THINK?
- How did the oil in the water affect the feather?
- Based on your findings, how do you think oil spills might affect birds?

The ocean supports living resources.

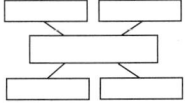

MAIN IDEA WEB
Remember to start a main idea web in your notebook for the blue heading.

The ocean's many algae and animals are important food sources for people in many areas of the world, including the United States. In fact, the United States is the third largest consumer of seafood in the world. The ocean also supports living resources you do not eat for dinner. You have already read about phytoplankton, tiny ocean organisms. Phytoplankton are a very important resource because they produce much of the oxygen in Earth's air. Chemicals from other ocean organisms are used in medicines—including some that treat cancer. As research continues, scientists may find even more useful chemicals in ocean organisms.

Seafood and Algae

Across the United States, supermarkets sell ocean fish and shellfish. Most people, whether they realize it or not, eat seaweeds, too. These ocean algae are commonly used to thicken cheese, ice cream, and pudding. Seaweeds are also ingredients in nonfood products such as shaving cream and pesticides.

When you think of fishing, you might think of a person with a fishing pole catching one fish at a time. This method of fishing, however, is far too slow and inefficient for the commercial fishing industry to use. Instead, the fishing industry uses huge nets bigger than football fields or lines of fishing hooks kilometers long to catch large amounts of fish at a time. As you read this sentence, tens of thousands of nets and fishing lines trail in the ocean. The fishing industry uses sonar, satellites, airplanes, and other technology to find areas in the ocean that contain large numbers of fish.

Overfishing and By-Catch

Over the years, people have noticed that there are fewer and fewer fish than there once were. The main cause of the decrease in fish populations is **overfishing,** or catching fish at a faster rate than they can reproduce. Cod is one popular food fish that was nearly killed off by overfishing. Cod were once common in the North Atlantic, but now the cod population is very small. All of the world's fisheries, or main fishing areas of the ocean, are either overfished or very close to being overfished. Overfishing is a major threat to ocean environments.

VOCABULARY
You can use a description wheel to take notes about the term *overfishing.*

Overfishing

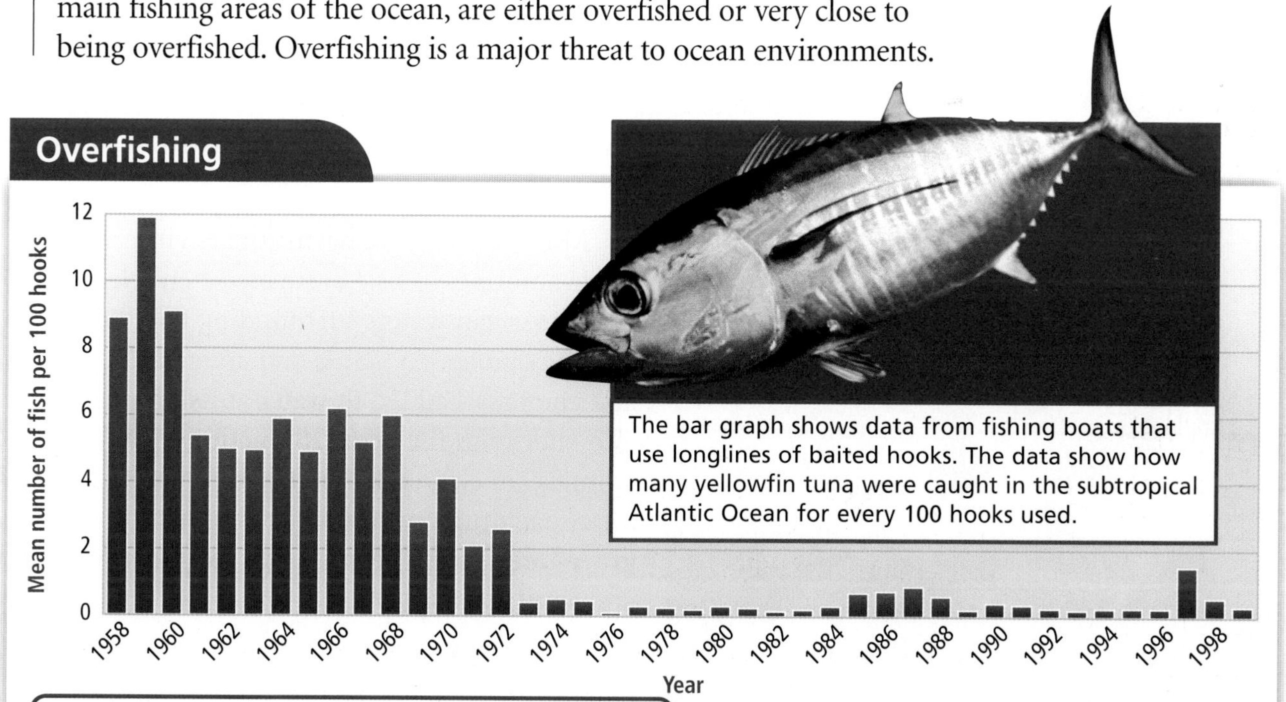

The bar graph shows data from fishing boats that use longlines of baited hooks. The data show how many yellowfin tuna were caught in the subtropical Atlantic Ocean for every 100 hooks used.

Mean number of fish per 100 hooks (y-axis: 0, 2, 4, 6, 8, 10, 12)

Year (x-axis: 1958, 1960, 1962, 1964, 1966, 1968, 1970, 1972, 1974, 1976, 1978, 1980, 1982, 1984, 1986, 1988, 1990, 1992, 1994, 1996, 1998)

READING VISUALS What can you conclude about the number of yellowfin tuna left by 1999?

SOURCE: *Census of Marine Life*

Everything except the shrimp will be thrown away as by-catch from this boat in the Gulf of Mexico.

Fishing nets catch nearly everything in their path. A net that is being used to catch shrimp, for example, may also catch fish, turtles, sharks, dolphins, and other sea animals. The extra catch—everything besides the shrimp—gets tossed back into the ocean either dead or dying. **By-catch,** or by-kill, is the portion of animals that are caught in a net and then thrown away. Sometimes the by-catch is greater than the portion of fish or other animals the net is meant to catch.

To help reduce by-catch, fisheries started using nets designed to prevent animals such as turtles and dolphins from getting caught. Although these efforts have lessened the number of turtles and dolphins caught in fishing nets, fisheries worldwide still throw away about 30 percent of the fish they catch.

CHECK YOUR READING   What harm does overfishing cause?

Saltwater Aquaculture

As you read in Chapter 3, aquaculture is the farming of both freshwater and ocean organisms. Saltwater farmers may raise fish, oysters, mussels, shrimp, seaweeds, or other organisms.

Most aquaculture harms the environment. Huge amounts of fish waste are often released into the ocean waters surrounding fish farms, causing damage to plants and animals. Nutrients and chemicals added to water at fish farms may also end up in the ocean. Sometimes plants and animals are cleared from an area to make space for aquaculture. About half of the world's mangrove forests have been cleared for shrimp farms and similar uses.

Some methods of aquaculture cause more damage than others. For 4000 years, farmers in China have raised fish without causing much harm. Chinese fish farms are often small, so they release less waste than larger farms.

A shrimp farm extends out into the water off the island of Bora Bora in French Polynesia.

SOCIETY ISLANDS, FRENCH POLYNESIA

The ocean contains nonliving resources.

Ocean water itself is a valuable resource for people living in regions with little fresh water. As you read in Chapter 3, desalination is the process by which salt is removed from seawater. Desalinated seawater is a major portion of the fresh water used by many Middle Eastern countries, such as Saudi Arabia.

Many of the natural resources found on land are also found in the ocean. It is often less expensive to remove resources from the land than from the ocean, so many of the ocean's resources are not currently mined. However, as resources on land are used up and new technology makes ocean exploration and mining easier, ocean mining may increase.

Energy Resources

Oil and gas form from the remains of living organisms. In the ocean, organisms are concentrated in the waters over the continental shelf. Oil deposits, therefore, are found near shore. Oil and gas are pumped from the continental shelf of every continent but Antarctica. About 30 percent of the world's oil is pumped from deposits under the ocean floor.

Huge anchored platforms serve as artificial islands that house workers and the necessary equipment for drilling offshore oil wells. The platforms are built to withstand ocean currents, tides, and weather conditions such as storms. Underwater pipelines carry the oil to shore.

Oil is pumped from the ocean floor at huge anchored platforms such as this one in the North Sea.

Offshore Drilling

Oil and natural gas are pumped up to the platform, separated, and then pumped down to storage tanks on the sea floor.

Tankers load oil and gas at buoys.

Oil and gas are piped to shore.

storage tanks

natural gas reservoir

oil reservoir

Minerals and Rocks

When rivers empty into the sea, sediments carried by the rivers drop to the bottom. These sediments may contain phosphorite, iron, copper, lead, gold, tin, diamonds, and other minerals. Because these minerals wash into the ocean from land, most of them are found in areas near shore. It is currently too expensive to mine many of these minerals.

Nodules are found away from the coast on the deep-ocean floor.

Some minerals are found away from shore. Nodules (NAHJ-oolz) are lumps of minerals that are scattered across the deep-ocean floor. The nodules are small at first, but they can build up over millions of years to a size of as much as a meter across. Nodules contain valuable manganese, iron, and cobalt, which are used to make metals such as steel. Nodules are not mined because it would be very expensive to remove them from the ocean floor. In the future, however, nodules may be removed—perhaps with giant vacuums.

The Ocean's Energy and Mineral Resources

The ocean floor contains valuable energy and mineral resources.

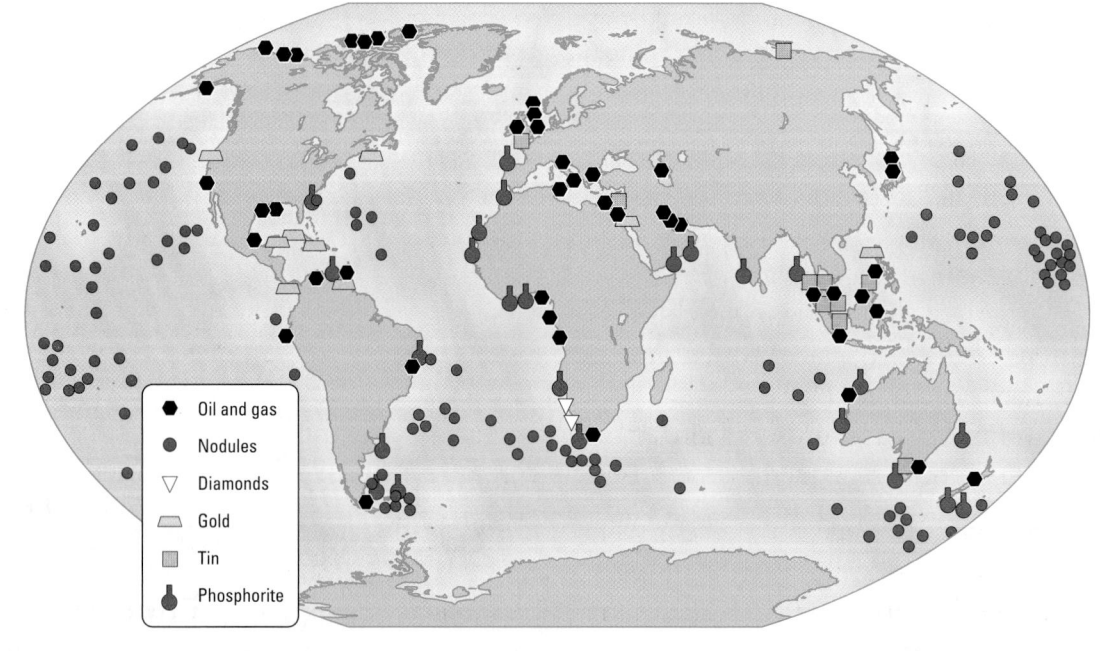

Legend:
- Oil and gas
- Nodules
- Diamonds
- Gold
- Tin
- Phosphorite

READING VISUALS Which ocean environment contains most of the known energy and mineral resources?

When ocean water evaporates, salt is left behind.

Each of these mounds is a pile of salt harvested from ocean water in Thailand.

A mineral you eat is also removed from the ocean. About one-third of the world's table salt comes from the ocean. Ocean water is left to evaporate in flat, shallow areas. As the water evaporates, salts are left behind.

Sand and gravel might not be the first things you think of when you think of important resources. However, they are building materials used in concrete and cement. Sand and gravel are currently scraped off the sea floor in many locations near shore.

Pollution affects the ocean.

Every part of the ocean is polluted. Solid waste—such as plastic garbage, tar balls, and hypodermic needles—is a visible form of pollution along ocean shorelines. Trash washes up on beaches worldwide, even on the beaches of remote islands. Sea animals may mistake trash for food and eat plastic that can block their digestive systems. Animals also get tangled in and even strangled by plastic waste.

Although you may not see this much garbage on every beach, trash washes up on beaches all over the world—even on remote islands.

Most ocean pollution is harder to see than solid waste. Chemical pollutants, nuclear wastes, and heavy metals like mercury and lead are found in all parts of the ocean. These pollutants are known to harm and kill ocean life. They are also harmful to humans. Pregnant women are sometimes advised not to eat tuna and other fish because the fish may contain low levels of toxic mercury. Although the small amounts of mercury may not harm an adult, they could damage the developing child.

Human waste, sewage, and fertilizers have caused dead zones in the ocean—areas where no plants or animals can live. These pollutants contain nutrients and cause a huge increase in the amount of algae that live in an area. When the algae die, bacteria consume them. The large numbers of bacteria use up all the oxygen in an area of ocean. Without oxygen, the animals in the area cannot survive.

Sources of Ocean Oil Pollution

- Runoff from land 44%
- Air pollution 33%
- Shipping and oil spills 12%
- Ocean dumping 10%
- Offshore drilling 1%

SOURCE: *Joint Group of Experts on the Scientific Aspects of the Marine Environment, The State of the Marine Environment, UNEP Regional Seas Reports and Studies No. 115 (Nairobi: U.N. Environment Programme, 1990)*

Oil spills are dramatic and disastrous events. However, most oil pollution in the ocean is washed in from land.

Some pollutants are dumped directly into the ocean. Many other pollutants wash from the land into the ocean or into rivers that flow into the ocean. Although oil spills are dramatic events that kill many animals, they account for only a small percentage of the oil pollution in the ocean. More oil enters the ocean by washing off the land than by being spilled. In addition to oil, pesticides, fertilizers, and many other pollutants wash into the ocean from land.

CHECK YOUR READING What is the source of most of the ocean's oil pollution?

Preventing Ocean Pollution

RESOURCE CENTER
CLASSZONE.COM

Find out more about ocean pollution and pollution prevention.

Ocean pollution can be prevented or reduced. In 1988, for example, the United States government restricted the use of a harmful chemical that had been used in ship paint. As a result, levels of the chemical dropped in certain areas of the ocean, and the health of some types of sea life, such as oysters, improved. Government organizations have also banned the dumping of some chemicals into the ocean. These bans have successfully reduced some kinds of pollution.

Individuals can help prevent or reduce ocean pollution. Many people may not realize that oil or other chemicals dumped in a drain or sewer or on the ground can end up in the ocean. The proper disposal of household chemicals and other toxic substances could reduce ocean pollution. The Environmental Protection Agency (EPA) has information about the proper disposal of many common chemicals.

Some oyster populations recovered after the use of a toxic chemical in ship paint was restricted. This photo shows an oyster farm in Washington State.

oyster

Global Pollution Problems

Remember that the ocean is a connected global body of water. Ocean currents circulate water around the globe and carry pollutants to all parts of the ocean. Pollution that occurs in any part of the world can affect the whole ocean.

The United Nations, through its 1994 Law of the Sea, attempts to manage ocean resources and to conserve ocean environments. The law calls on all countries to enforce pollution controls. It also sets pollution rules for ships operating in international waters, regulates fishing, and attempts to divide rights to undersea resources. This international law is an important step toward protecting the ocean and its resources for future generations.

 Why is ocean pollution a global problem?

 **Review**

KEY CONCEPTS

1. Describe one living resource contained in the ocean and how its use affects the ocean environment.

2. Describe one nonliving resource contained in the ocean and how its use affects the ocean environment.

3. How does pollution affect the ocean?

CRITICAL THINKING

4. **Connect** How could ocean pollution affect your life?

5. **Sequence** Describe how oil from a car many miles away from the shore could reach the ocean.

◯ CHALLENGE

6. **Evaluate** Most of the ocean does not belong to any country or government. Who do you think should be responsible for limiting pollution in areas outside country borders? Who should be able to claim ownership of resources in these areas?

CHAPTER INVESTIGATION

Population Sampling

OVERVIEW AND PURPOSE Scientists have found that overfishing is decreasing the population of many organisms. They have also found that the population of some other organisms are increasing. How do scientists know this? They count the number of individuals in a small measured area, called a quadrat, then estimate from their counts how many organisms live in a larger area. Repeated samplings over time allow them to determine whether populations are growing or decreasing. In this investigation you will

- count the number of items in a "population" using a quadrat technique
- use small and large quadrats to form two different estimates for the size of a "population"

MATERIALS
- calculator
- removable tape

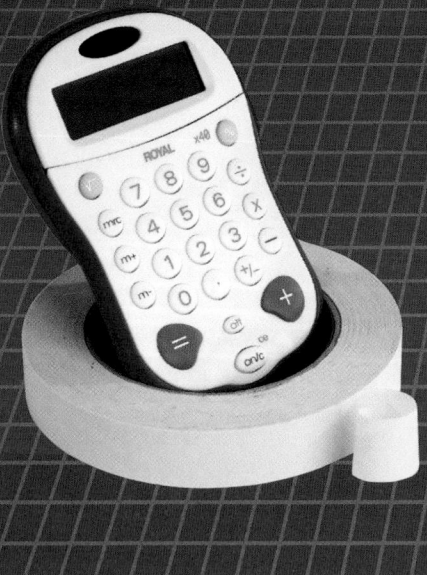

▶ Procedure

1. As a class, brainstorm some objects that you might find in your classroom—for example: pencil, protractor, calculator, or ball cap. Choose one of those objects to count. You will estimate the population at your school of this object.

2. Remove all of the objects that your class decided to count from bags and drawers. For example, if your class is counting pencils, everyone should remove all of their pencils from their bags and place them on their desks.

3. Divide your classroom into four equal-sized pieces. Use removable tape to mark the boundaries of each quadrat. Label the quadrats A, B, C, and D.

4. Count the items in one of the quadrats—either A, B, C, or D. Record the number of objects in your **Science Notebook.**

5. Find the total classroom population of your object by combining your data with the data from groups who counted other quadrats. Record the total classroom population.

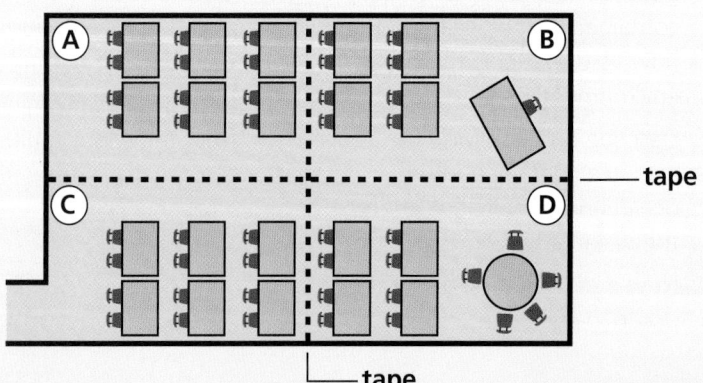

Observe and Analyze

 *Write It Up*

1. **RECORD** Make a data table like the one in the notebook.

2. **CALCULATE** Multiply the number of each item you counted in your quadrat by four. This will give you an estimate of the number of each item in your classroom. Record your answer.

3. **CALCULATE** For this investigation, assume that each classroom in your school is the same size as your classroom. Your teacher will provide you with the number of classrooms in your entire school. Multiply your answer from question 2 by the number of classrooms in your school. This will give you an estimate of the number of each item in your school. Record your answer.

4. **CALCULATE** Now estimate the population of the object in the whole school using the total count from the classroom. Multiply the total classroom population by the number of classrooms in your school. This will give you a second estimate for the population of each item in your school. Record your answer.

Conclude

 *Write It Up*

1. **COMPARE** How does your school population estimate based on your small quadrat count compare with your school population estimate based on your total classroom estimate?

2. **INFER** If there was a difference between your two total population estimates, what do you think could explain the difference?

3. **INFER** Do you think your total population estimate for your object in the school is accurate? Explain.

4. **COMPARE** How would your population estimate compare to one done the same way ten years ago? ten years from now? Explain your reasoning.

5. **IDENTIFY LIMITS** What possible limitations or sources of error could have affected your results?

6. **CONNECT** How would you need to change your procedure if you were sampling an ocean fish population? Give at least two examples.

INVESTIGATE Further

CHALLENGE Suppose your quadrat size was one square meter. How would this have affected your accuracy? Imagine that you were given a wooden frame measuring one square meter in size. How would you change your procedure to best sample the school "population" using this smaller quadrat?

Population Sampling
Observe and Analyze
Table 1. Population Data

Quadrat	Number of Items	Classroom Population Estimate	School Population Estimate (No. in classroom × No. of classrooms in school)
A	7	7 × 4 = 28	
B			
C			
D			
Total: classroom count			

Chapter Review

the BIG idea

The ocean supports life and contains natural resources.

◀ KEY CONCEPTS SUMMARY

1 Ocean coasts support plant and animal life.

Organisms in the intertidal zone are covered by water during high tide and exposed to the air during low tide.

high tide mark

low tide mark

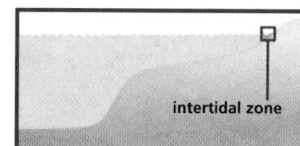

intertidal zone

- Fresh water and salt water mix in estuaries.
- Salt marshes and mangrove forests form along coasts.

VOCABULARY
habitat p. 154
intertidal zone p. 154
estuary p. 156
wetland p. 156

---

2 Conditions differ away from shore.

near shore environment

open ocean

Life in the open ocean is more spread out. The surface zone is lit by the Sun. The deep zone is dark.

The waters near shore support more life than any other part of the ocean.

VOCABULARY
coral reef p. 162
kelp forest p. 164
phytoplankton p. 166
hydrothermal vent p. 168

---

3 The ocean contains natural resources.

Living ocean resources include seafood and algae. Overfishing and pollution threaten ocean environments.

Nonliving ocean resources include oil, natural gas, and minerals.

VOCABULARY
overfishing p. 171
by-catch p. 172

Reviewing Vocabulary

Copy and complete the chart below. In the middle column, list characteristics of each environment. In the last column, list examples of organisms that live in each environment.

Vocabulary Term	Characteristics	Organisms
1. intertidal zone		
2. estuary		
3. coral reef		
4. kelp forest		
5. hydrothermal vent		

Reviewing Key Concepts

Multiple Choice *Choose the letter of the best answer.*

6. An environment that contains all the necessary requirements for an organism to live is called
   a. the surface zone   c. a habitat
   b. a nodule   d. an estuary

7. Where would you expect to find ocean organisms that are able to survive out of water and withstand drastic changes in salinity?
   a. the intertidal zone   c. the open ocean
   b. a coral reef   d. a hydrothermal vent

8. Two kinds of wetlands that border estuaries are
   a. coral reefs and mangrove forests
   b. salt marshes and mangrove forests
   c. tidal pools and salt marshes
   d. mangrove forests and tidal pools

9. Tiny plantlike organisms that float at the surface of the ocean are called
   a. phytoplankton   c. corals
   b. kelps   d. bottom dwellers

10. Where are hydrothermal vents located?
    a. in the intertidal zone
    b. on the deep-ocean floor
    c. on coral reefs
    d. in kelp forests

11. The bacteria that form the base of the food chain at hydrothermal vents convert
    a. dim sunlight that filters down into food
    b. heat from the vents into food
    c. phytoplankton that drift down into food
    d. chemicals released by the vents into food

12. Overfishing is best described as catching
    a. more fish than people can eat
    b. fish at a faster rate than they can reproduce
    c. other kinds of fish than the ones intended
    d. fish with huge nets and long lines of hooks

13. Why are 30 percent of the fish that are caught by commercial fishing boats thrown away?
    a. Fishing nets catch everything in their path.
    b. Smaller fish are thrown back into the ocean.
    c. Oil pollution has damaged many of the fish.
    d. Large phytoplankton interfere with nets and lines.

Short Response *Write a short response to each question.*

14. How does human activity affect shoreline environments?

15. Name the three categories of ocean life, and give an example of an organism for each category.

16. What resources does the ocean contain?

17. What kinds of pollution are found in the ocean?

18. Why is ocean pollution a global problem?

Thinking Critically

Use the maps shown below to answer the next three questions.

Catch per Hundred Hooks, 1958

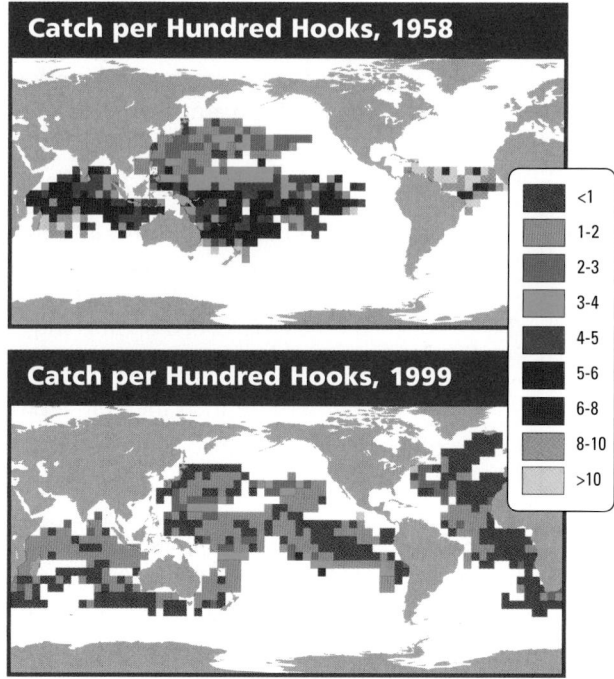

Catch per Hundred Hooks, 1999

Legend:
- <1
- 1-2
- 2-3
- 3-4
- 4-5
- 5-6
- 6-8
- 8-10
- >10

SOURCE: *Census of Marine Life*

These maps show data from Japanese fishing boats of the total numbers of fish that were caught in 1958 and 1999. The color code shows the number of fish caught per 100 hooks on longlines.

19. INTERPRET What do these data show about how ocean fish populations have changed between 1958 and 1999?

20. INFER The data for 1999 were collected over a wider area than were the data for 1958. What might explain the wider area for the 1999 data?

21. PREDICT What would you expect a map with data for the current year to look like? Describe it in terms of color and the extent of the data.

22. COMPARE AND CONTRAST What similarities exist between kelp forests and coral reefs? How are they different?

23. INFER It is believed that life on Earth first appeared in the oceans. In which ocean zone might life have first appeared? Explain your reasoning.

24. APPLY The sargassum frogfish lives among sargassum algae, a type of algae that grows attached to the ocean floor. In which ocean zones could this species of frogfish possibly live? In which could it not live? Explain.

25. SYNTHESIZE A marine sanctuary is an area of the ocean that is protected from fishing and most human use. An environmental organization is trying to decide whether to establish a marine sanctuary. Based on what you have learned, write a short letter telling the organization whether you think a marine sanctuary is a good idea and in which ocean zone the sanctuary should be established.

the BIG idea

26. COMPARE AND CONTRAST Look again at the photograph on pages 150–151. Now that you have finished the chapter, make a Venn diagram to answer the question on the photograph in more detail. For information about Venn diagrams, see page R49.

27. PROVIDE EXAMPLES What types of habitats and resources does the ocean contain? To answer, copy the concept map below into your notebook and add to it. For information about concept maps, see page R49.

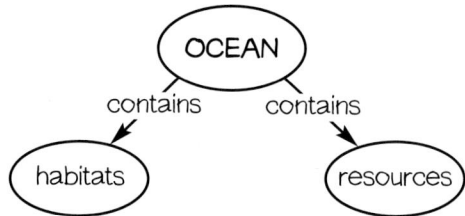

UNIT PROJECTS

Evaluate all the data, results, and information from your project folder. Prepare to present your project. Be ready to answer questions posed by your classmates about your results.

FCAT Practice

For FCAT practice, go to . . .
FLORIDA REVIEW
CLASSZONE.COM

Analyzing a Diagram

The diagram below shows a side view of part of the ocean. Use the diagram to answer the questions below.

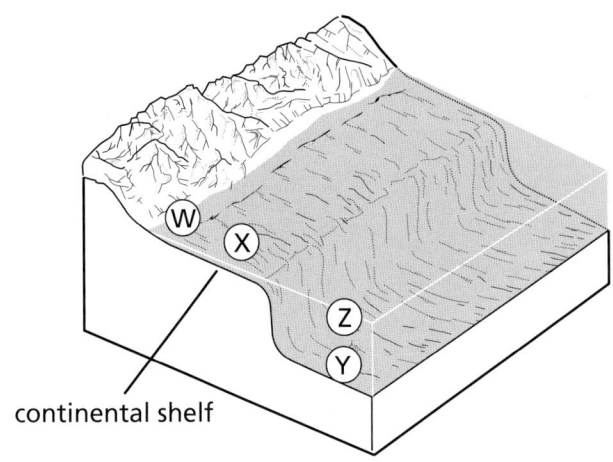

continental shelf

FCAT TiP

Some short-response questions have multiple parts. When answering short-response questions, read the question carefully and make sure that you answer everything the question asks for.

MULTIPLE CHOICE

1. Which area is most affected by tides?
   - **A.** W
   - **B.** X
   - **C.** Y
   - **D.** Z

2. Where is water the coldest?
   - **F.** W
   - **G.** X
   - **H.** Y
   - **I.** Z

3. Which trait is most useful for fish in position Z as they try to escape predators?
   - **A.** the ability to hide in rocks
   - **B.** the ability to blend in with plants
   - **C.** the ability to swim very fast
   - **D.** the ability to swim without sunlight

4. A limpet is an ocean snail whose flat shape allows it to remain attached to rocks even when waves are pounding against the rocks. Where does the limpet probably live?
   - **F.** W
   - **G.** X
   - **H.** Y
   - **I.** Z

SHORT RESPONSE

5. Study the diagram. Determine which point on the diagram shows an area where kelps, which are plantlike algae, could live and grow. Explain your answer.

6. The anglerfish lives in area Y. Use what you know about life in the deep zone to name characteristics that help the anglerfish survive there.

EXTENDED RESPONSE

The illustration below shows part of an ocean food web. Use the illustration to answer the next two questions in detail.

7. Describe how the killer whale, salmon, and zooplankton in the illustration are linked.

8. What would happen if overfishing caused herring to be removed from the food web? Describe how the other organisms would be affected.

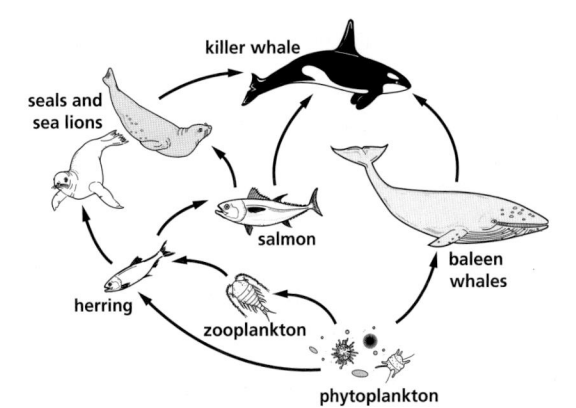

Chapter 5: **Ocean Environments** 183

UNIT 2

Earth's Surface

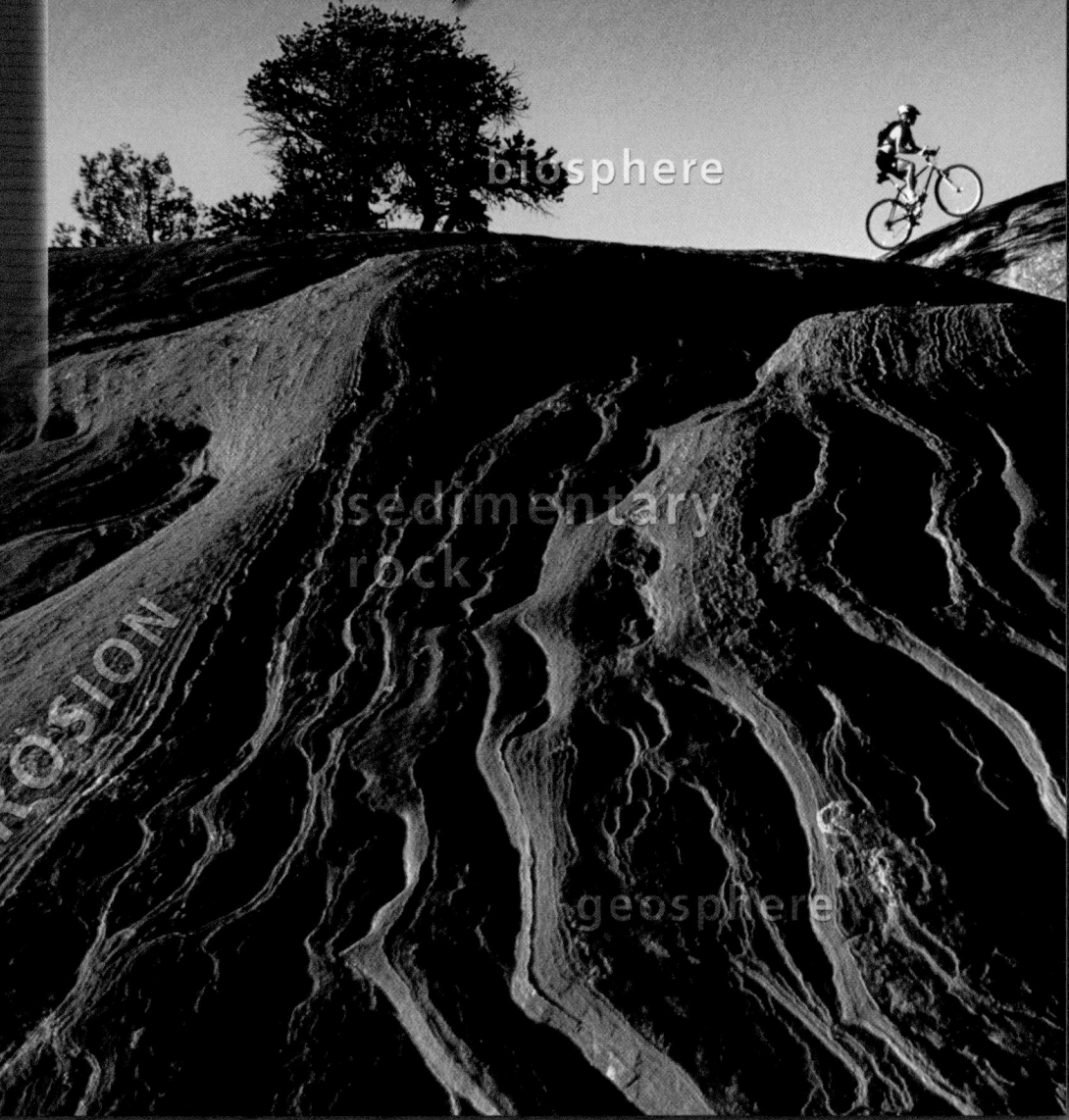

biosphere

sedimentary rock

EROSION

geosphere

Contents Overview

Frontiers in Science
Remote Sensing   186

Florida Connection
Florida's Sinkholes   190

Timelines in Science
History of the Earth System   292

Chapter 6 Views of Earth Today   194

Chapter 7 Weathering and
             Soil Formation   228

Chapter 8 Erosion and Deposition   258

Chapter 9 Natural Resources   296

REMOTE SENSING

Technology high above Earth's surface is giving scientists a whole new look at our planet. This image is of Jasper Ridge, near Palo Alto, California.

SCIENTIFIC AMERICAN FRONTIERS

View the video segment "All That Glitters" to learn how explorers use remote sensing and other methods to find valuable materials.

This research jet aircraft carries instruments to study Earth's land surface, ocean, and atmosphere. It flies at high altitudes, allowing it to collect data and images over large areas during a single flight.

Mapping Earth

You're probably familiar with images of gold prospectors in the Old West. Maybe you've seen them in old movies or read about them in history books. Prospectors wandered through the mountains, looking for signs of ores or gemstones, going here and there in response to rumors or stories, pitching camp in remote canyons on a hunch. People still prospect for minerals today, but they're more likely to fly in airplanes than to ride mules. And stories of fabled mines are just stories and fables. Today's prospectors rely on scientific evidence from remote sensing.

Remote sensing—the use of instruments to gather data from a distance—has two great advantages. The first is that sensors mounted in satellites and airplanes can collect vast amounts of detailed information over large areas. The second is that the sensors can easily collect information about the same area again and again.

For example, scientists use remote sensing to make better and more detailed maps of Earth and to track changes over time. Thanks to remote sensing, scientists now know that Mount Everest, the highest point on Earth, is actually getting higher by about 1 centimeter (0.4 in.) per year. Remote sensors on satellites are also mapping global ocean temperatures and showing how they change over the course of a year.

Uncut diamond

Detecting Minerals from Above

One of the many uses of remote sensing is to find new sources of valuable minerals, such as diamonds. To detect minerals from airplanes or satellites, remote sensors make use of the energy in sunlight. Sunlight reaches Earth as radiation, which travels in the form of waves. All objects absorb some types of radiation and reflect others. The particular wavelengths absorbed or reflected depend upon the materials that make up the objects. Each kind of material has a unique "fingerprint" of the wavelengths it absorbs and the wavelengths it reflects.

When sunlight strikes Earth's surface, some of it is reflected back into the sky. Some of the radiation is absorbed by rocks and other objects and then emitted, or given off, in a different form. Remote sensors in airplanes and satellites collect the reflected and emitted radiation and analyze it to determine which types of rocks and minerals lie on the surface. The remote sensing

Energy from the Sun reflects at different wavelengths from materials at Earth's surface. Instruments on the jet analyze the reflected energy and map the surface.

systems collect so much data that computer processing and analysis are difficult and expensive. Still, the data are usually clear enough to show the types of minerals located in the regions scanned. However, minerals that are buried cannot be detected by remote sensing from aircraft or satellites. The sensors receive only energy from or near the surface.

SCIENTIFIC AMERICAN FRONTIERS

View the "All that Glitters" segment of your *Scientific American Frontiers* video to see how finding certain common minerals can indicate the presence of a valuable mineral like diamond.

IN THIS SCENE FROM THE VIDEO ◉ a mineral prospector searches for diamonds in a cylinder of rock drilled from beneath Earth's surface.

SEARCHING FOR DIAMONDS People used to think that North America did not have many diamonds. However, northern Canada is geologically similar to the world's major diamond-producing areas: southern Africa, Russia, and Australia. A few diamond prospectors kept searching, using remote sensing and other techniques. The prospectors looked for more common minerals that form under the same conditions as diamonds. They made maps showing where these minerals were most plentiful and used the maps to search for diamond-rich rock. Once the prospectors realized that the glaciers of the last ice age had moved the minerals, they looked for and found diamonds farther northward. Canada is now a big producer of diamonds.

Remote sensing can show the presence of minerals that occur with diamonds, but people must still use older methods to collect samples for further analysis.

Prospecting for Diamonds

One of the major regions of mineral exploration in which remote sensing is used is in the Northwest Territories of Canada, where the first diamond mine began operating in 1998. The Canada Centre for Remote Sensing has helped develop sensing equipment that can fit easily onto light airplanes and computer equipment to analyze results quickly. The sensing equipment is used to detect certain types of minerals that are often found along with diamonds.

Using remote sensing to locate minerals associated with diamonds or valuable ores is only a beginning. The data cannot show how far the minerals or ores extend underground. Prospectors must still explore the area and take samples. However, remote sensing gives mineral prospectors an excellent idea of where to start looking.

? UNANSWERED Questions

As scientists use remote sensing to study Earth's land surface, ocean, and atmosphere, they work to answer new questions.

- Can remote sensing be used to locate sources of iron, platinum, or gold in areas that are difficult to explore on foot?

- How do changes in water temperature at the ocean surface affect long-range weather patterns and the health of ocean organisms?

- How do different types of clouds affect the amount of sunlight reaching Earth's surface and the average temperature of the surface?

UNIT PROJECTS

As you study this unit, work alone or with a group on one of the projects listed below.

Hiker's Guide Video

Like prospectors, wilderness hikers must be able to read maps that show the shape of the land. Prepare a video to teach hikers how to choose hiking and camping areas by reading maps.

- Obtain a topographic map of a wilderness area in a national or state park.

- Write a script outlining what you will teach and how you will videotape it.

- Present your video and display the maps you used.

Diamond Mine Model

Diamonds can be carried toward Earth's surface by kimberlite pipes. Show how diamonds are mined from kimberlite.

- Build a model of a diamond-mine tunnel that passes through kimberlite.

- Present your model to your class. Explain the relationship between kimberlite and diamonds.

Glacier Photo Essay

Make a photo essay showing how glaciers reshape Earth's surface as they move and melt.

- Find images of areas that are or have been affected by glaciers. Write captions for them.

- Present the images as a photo essay on a poster or in a portfolio.

 **CAREER CENTER**
CLASSZONE.COM

Learn more about careers in mineralogy.

Florida's Sinkholes

Sunshine State Standards

In "Florida's Sinkholes" you'll learn how mechanical and chemical activities shape and reshape Earth's surface to form aquifers, caverns, and sinkholes. (SC.D.1.3.1)

Human activities, such as pumping too much ground water from wells, may cause sinkholes to form. (SC.G.2.3.4)

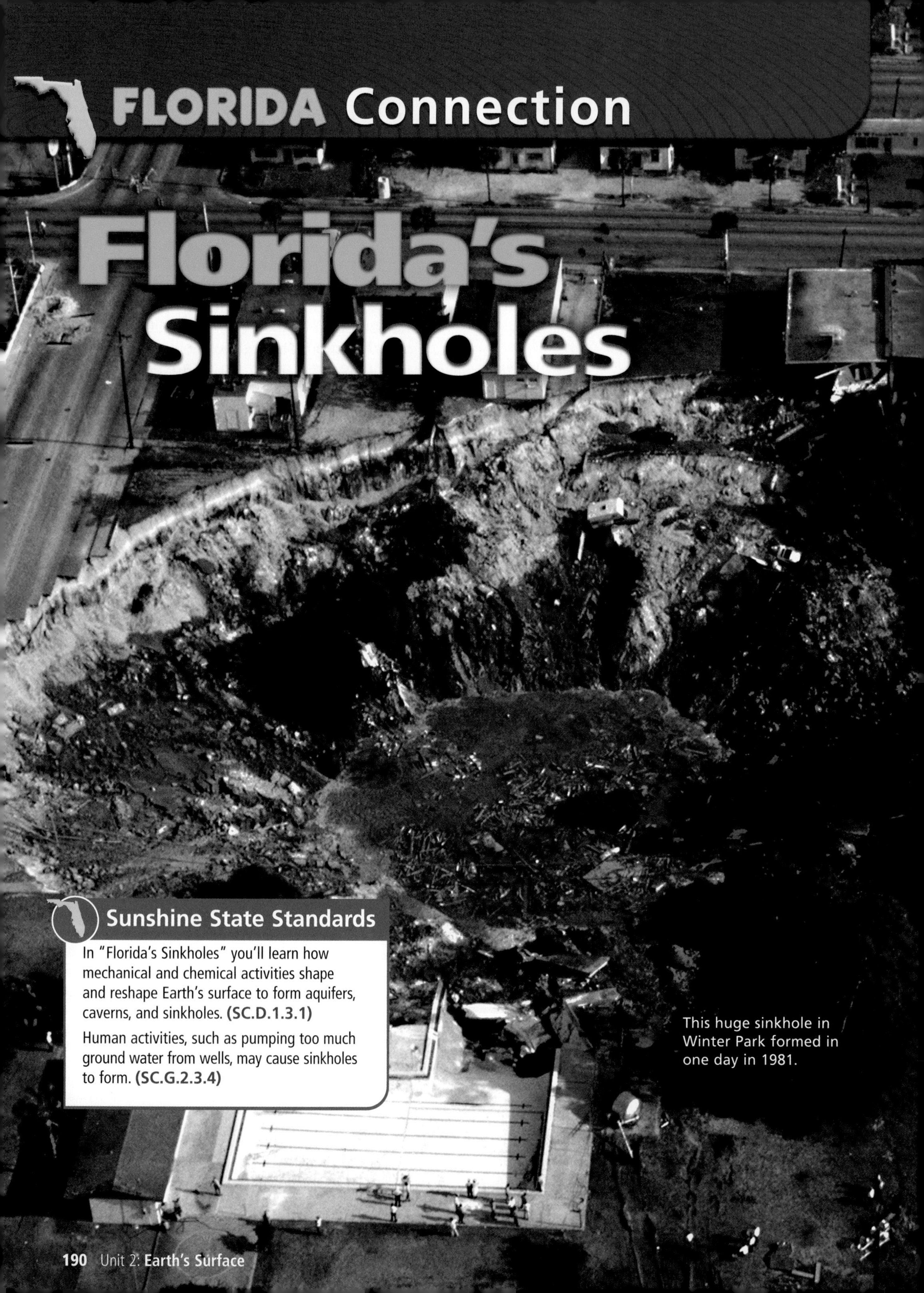

This huge sinkhole in Winter Park formed in one day in 1981.

Highest concentration of sinkholes

The Sinkhole That Swallowed a City Block

In 1981 a resident of Winter Park, near Orlando, was astonished to see a tree suddenly disappear. It had been swallowed up by a sinkhole that continued to grow rapidly. A day later, the hole had consumed 118,520 cubic meters (160,000 cu yd) of land, including a house, an auto repair shop, a laundromat, five cars, and a swimming pool. The resulting hole was more than 100 meters (330 ft) wide and 38 meters (125 ft) deep.

The hole filled with water. The city of Winter Park eventually sealed the bottom of the hole, landscaped the area around it, and built a playground and recreation center nearby. Now the sinkhole is a popular tourist attraction.

What caused this amazing hole to appear? To understand sinkholes, it's important to know something about the geology of Florida.

That Sinking Feeling

What's underneath your feet? If you're outdoors, you may be standing on a thin layer of clay and sand, but what's underneath that? The answer in Florida is carbonate rocks, mostly limestone and dolomite. Carbonate rocks are often porous, or full of holes. As rain falls through the atmosphere, it dissolves carbon dioxide and other gases and becomes slightly acidic. When the rain falls on the ground and moves through decaying plants, it becomes more acidic. This acidic rainwater sinks into porous limestone, dissolving some of the stone and carrying it away. Over time, small holes can become big holes. Big holes can become caverns.

This type of erosion has created underground caverns throughout Florida, like those in Florida Caverns State Park in Marianna. When the roof of a shallow underground cavern becomes so thin that it collapses, a sinkhole is formed. Regions in which erosion has produced sinkholes, springs, underground streams, and caverns are said to have karst topography. The landscape of northern Florida contains almost eight sinkholes per square kilometer.

Underground Cavern

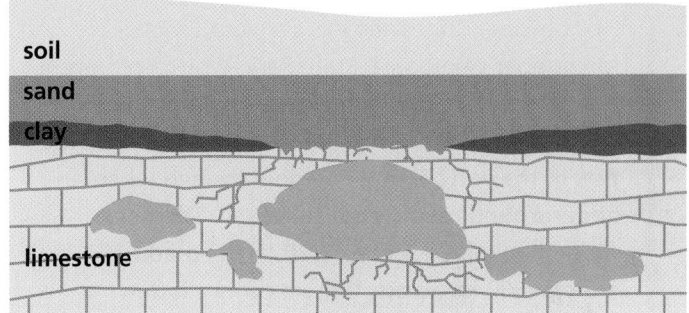

When erosion dissolves underlying limestone, cavities form. Over time, the cavities can grow into large caverns.

Collapse Sinkhole

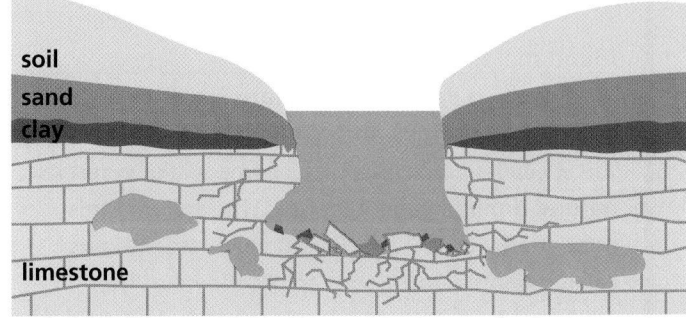

When the roof of a cavern becomes thin and weak, it can cave in, forming a type of sinkhole called a collapse sinkhole.

Types of Sinkholes

Sinkholes are a fact of life in Florida, thanks to the porous rock under its surface. There are three general types of sinkholes.

Collapse Collapse sinkholes are the most common type of sinkhole in Florida. They usually occur where the surface of the ground is made up of thick soil and heavy clay. When the roof of an underground cavern grows thinner and becomes weak, it may fall in suddenly. This often leaves a deep hole with steep sides.

Solution Solution sinkholes form slowly over a long period of time. They occur where limestone is exposed at the surface or is covered by only a thin layer of soil and sand. Surface materials are broken down by erosion from wind and surface water, forming a bowl-shaped hole. Water may collect in this hole, forming a lake.

Subsidence A subsidence sinkhole forms where the ground cover is a thin layer made up mostly of sand. Individual grains of sand slowly subside, or settle down, into an underground cavern. Subsidence sinkholes are usually only a few feet in diameter and depth.

Dangers from Sinkholes

Sinkholes in Florida can appear suddenly and cause threats to life and property. Roads and building foundations can be damaged, and trees may be uprooted. A sinkhole in a streambed can divert all of the stream's flow, causing what is called a disappearing stream.

Sinkholes also pose a major threat to drinking water. Pollutants at the surface, such as farm and lawn fertilizers and wastes from leaking septic tanks, can get into ground water by traveling

SPOTLIGHT ON Sinkhole Sightseeing

Just outside Gainesville you can visit Devil's Millhopper Geological State Park, which contains a sinkhole that is 20 million years old. It became a popular destination for curious tourists and scientists in the early 1880s. The hole formed when an underground cavern roof collapsed. The bowl-shaped hole is 37 meters (120 ft) deep and 153 meters (500 ft) across. Visitors can walk down a 232-step stairway to the bottom.

The sinkhole got its name because its funnel-like shape reminded farmers of hoppers used to hold grain at mills. Marine shells and fossils can be found in the sinkhole. Much of Florida's natural history has been revealed by studying fossils of shark teeth and remains of extinct land animals found there.

Nearby is Paynes Prairie State Preserve, which is also an enormous round sinkhole. Several times this 21,000-acre prairie has become a lake when its natural drain became blocked. The last time this happened was in 1871. For 20 years, steamboats carried people and goods across the lake. Then in 1891 the drain suddenly became unblocked, and the lake drained in less than two weeks!

The Devils Mill Hopper. Near Gainesville. Fla.

Sinkhole diving is a popular recreational activity for experienced divers.

though sinkholes. Underground aquifers provide more than 80 percent of the drinking water in the state. When ground water is polluted, it is difficult to remove the pollutants and make the water suitable for drinking.

As many as 150 new sinkholes are reported each year in Florida. Forecasting where they will occur is difficult and expensive. Geologists and geotechnical engineering consultants attempt to locate underground cavities by using drilling machinery and radar surveys. Weather conditions can give clues to potential sinkholes. Dry weather followed by large amounts of rainfall can lead to more sinkholes.

Signs of potential sinkholes include

- trees and fence posts that are slumping or falling
- cracked building foundations
- cracked or bare soil
- exposed parts of building foundations or tree roots
- doors and windows of buildings not closing properly
- circular areas of wilting vegetation

Even though sinkholes are common in Florida, most sinkholes are not catastrophic or even harmful. Don't worry that the ground might give way beneath your feet at any moment. The best course of action is learning about the geology of your area and knowing what signs to look for. If you suspect that a sinkhole may be forming, notify the landowner and the local water management district.

 ASKING Questions

- What questions do you have about sinkholes and their effect on Florida's landscape?
- What questions do you have about other karst landforms?

RESOURCE CENTER

Visit ClassZone.com for more information on sinkholes.

WRITING ABOUT SCIENCE

Small streams and waterfalls run down the sides of the Devil's Millhopper sinkhole, described on page 192. Where does this water come from? Since the hole doesn't fill with water and become a lake, where does the water go? Write two paragraphs explaining this process.

Writing Tips

Plan, draft, and revise your writing using the tips below.

- Think about what you know about the water cycle.
- Skim the article to review how sinkholes form.
- Make connections to explain the process.
- Be sure that each paragraph has a topic sentence.
- Revise your paragraphs to make them as clear as possible.

CHAPTER
6 Views of Earth Today

the **BIG** idea

Modern technology has changed the way we view and map Earth.

Key Concepts

SECTION
1 Technology is used to explore the Earth system.
Learn how technology has changed people's view of Earth.

SECTION
2 Maps and globes are models of Earth.
Learn how to locate any place on Earth and how Earth's sphere is portrayed on flat maps.

SECTION
3 Topographic maps show the shape of the land.
Learn about representing the features of Earth's surface on flat maps.

SECTION
4 Technology is used to map Earth.
Learn how satellites and computers are used to provide more detailed maps of Earth.

FCAT Practice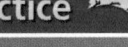

Prepare and practice for the FCAT
- Section Reviews, pp. 202, 210, 215, 222
- Chapter Review, pp. 224–226
- FCAT Practice, p. 227

CLASSZONE.COM
- Florida Review: Content Review and FCAT Practice

What do all these views show about Earth?

Swirling clouds over North and South America: NASA Terra satellite data

Warm and cool ocean-surface
temperatures: NASA satellite image

Chlorophyll levels (green) on land
and sea: SeaStar spacecraft image

Earth's rocky surface without the
oceans: NASA satellite data

EXPLORE (the BIG idea)

Earth's Changing Surface

Go outside and find evidence
of how wind, water, or living
things change the surface of
Earth. You might look in alley-
ways, parks, wooded areas, or
backyards. For example, you
might find a path worn through
a grassy area near a parking lot.

Observe and Think What
changes do you observe? What
do you think caused the changes?

Using Modern Maps

Find a map of a city, a bus or
rail system, or a state. Study
the names, colors, and
symbols on the map and
any features of interest.

Observe and Think Which
direction on the map is
north? What do the symbols
mean? How do you measure
the distance from one point
to another?

Internet Activity: Mapping

Go to **ClassZone.com** to learn more about
mapping Earth from space. Find out about a
NASA mission to develop the most accurate
map of Earth ever made.

Observe and Think
Why do you think
scientists need different
maps produced from
satellite data?

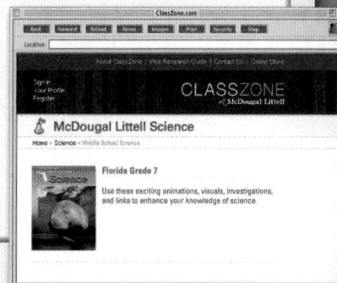

NSTA
scilinks.org
SCiLINKS

Earth's Spheres **Code: MDL013**

Getting Ready to Learn

◐ CONCEPT REVIEW

- Earth, like all planets, is shaped roughly like a sphere.
- Earth supports a complex web of life.
- The planet consists of many parts that interact with one another.

◐ VOCABULARY REVIEW

See Glossary for definitions.

energy

matter

planet

satellite

FLORIDA REVIEW
CLASSZONE.COM

Content Review and FCAT Practice

▶ TAKING NOTES

MAIN IDEA AND DETAIL NOTES

Make a two-column chart. Write the main ideas, such as those in the blue headings, in the column on the left. Write details about each of those main ideas in the column on the right.

VOCABULARY STRATEGY

Draw a **word triangle** diagram for each new vocabulary term. On the bottom line write and define the term. Above that, write a sentence that uses the term correctly. At the top, draw a picture to show what the term looks like.

See the Note-Taking Handbook on pages R45–R51.

SCIENCE NOTEBOOK

MAIN IDEAS	DETAIL NOTES
1. The Earth system has four main parts.	1. Atmosphere = mixture of gases surrounding Earth 1. Hydrosphere = all waters on Earth

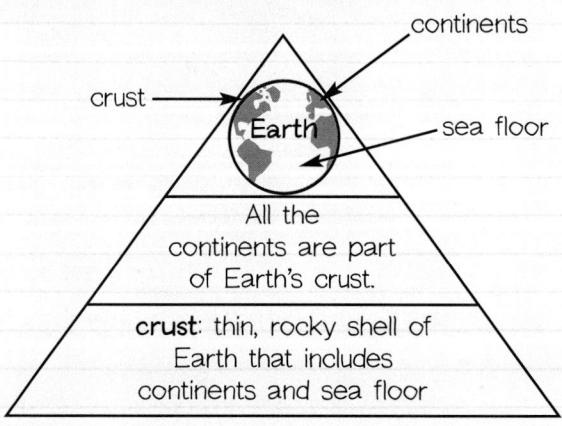

crust → Earth ← continents, sea floor

All the continents are part of Earth's crust.

crust: thin, rocky shell of Earth that includes continents and sea floor

6.1 Technology is used to explore the Earth system.

 BEFORE, you learned

- Earth has a spherical shape and supports a complex web of life
- Earth's environment is a system with many parts

▷ **NOW,** you will learn

- About the Earth system and its four major parts
- How technology is used to explore the Earth system
- How the parts of the Earth system shape the surface

THINK ABOUT

How do these parts work together?

Look closely at this terrarium. Notice that the bowl and its cover form a boundary between the terrarium and the outside world. What might happen to the entire terrarium if any part were taken away? What might happen if you placed the terrarium in a dark closet?

FCAT VOCABULARY
system p. 197
atmosphere p. 198

VOCABULARY
hydrosphere p. 198
biosphere p. 199
geosphere p. 200

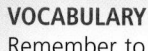

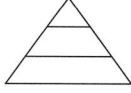

VOCABULARY
Remember to draw a word triangle in your notebook for each vocabulary term.

The Earth system has four major parts.

A terrarium is a simple example of a **system** —an organized group of parts that work together to form a whole. To understand a system, you need to see how all its parts work together. This principle is true for a small terrarium, and it is true for planet Earth.

Both a terrarium and Earth are closed systems. They are closed because matter, such as soil or water, cannot enter or leave. However, energy can flow into or out of the system. Just as light and heat pass through the glass of the terrarium, sunlight and heat enter and leave the Earth system through the atmosphere.

Within the Earth system are four connected parts: the atmosphere (Earth's air), the hydrosphere (Earth's waters), the biosphere (Earth's living things), and the geosphere (Earth's interior and its rocks and soils). Each of these parts is an open system because both matter and energy move into and out of it. The four open systems work together to form one large, closed system called Earth.

Atmosphere

READING TIP

The names of the Earth system's four parts contain Greek prefixes. *Atmo-* refers to vapor or gas. *Hydro-* refers to water. *Bio-* refers to life, and *geo-* refers to earth.

The **atmosphere** (AT-muh-SFEER) is the mixture of gases and particles that surrounds and protects the surface of Earth. The most abundant gases are nitrogen (about 78%) and oxygen (nearly 21%). The atmosphere also contains carbon dioxide, water vapor, and a few other gases.

Before the 1800s, all studies of the atmosphere had to be done from the ground. Today, scientists launch weather balloons, fly specially equipped planes, and view the atmosphere in satellite images. The data they collect show that the atmosphere interacts with the other parts of the Earth system to form complex weather patterns that circulate around Earth. The more scientists learn about these patterns, the more accurately they can predict local weather.

Hydrosphere

The **hydrosphere** (HY-druh-SFEER) is made up of all the water on Earth in oceans, lakes, glaciers, rivers, and streams and underground. Water covers nearly three-quarters of Earth's surface. Only about 3 percent of the hydrosphere is fresh water. Nearly 70 percent of Earth's fresh water is frozen in glaciers and polar ice caps.

Parts of the Earth System

Atmosphere

Over 400 cones make this weather balloon more stable as it gathers data about the atmosphere.

Hydrosphere

Scientists need special diving equipment to study Earth's oceans.

In the past 50 years, scientists have used deep-sea vehicles, special buoys, satellite images, and diving suits, such as the one shown on page 198, to study the world's oceans. They have discovered that the oceans contain several layers of cold and warm water. As these layers circulate, they form cold and warm ocean currents. The currents interact with wind patterns in the atmosphere and affect Earth's weather.

 **CHECK YOUR READING** How does the hydrosphere affect the atmosphere?

Biosphere

The **biosphere** (BY-uh-SFEER) includes all life on Earth, in the air, on the land, and in the waters. The biosphere can be studied with a variety of technologies. For example, satellite photos are used to track yearly changes in Earth's plant and animal life. As the photograph below shows, special equipment allows scientists to study complex environments, such as rain forests, without damaging them.

Scientists have learned a lot about how the biosphere interacts with the other parts of the Earth system. For example, large forests act as Earth's "lungs," absorbing carbon dioxide and releasing oxygen into the atmosphere. When dead trees decay, they return nutrients to the soil.

 **CHECK YOUR READING** Name one way the biosphere and the atmosphere interact.

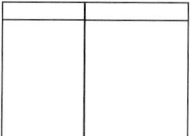

MAIN IDEA AND DETAILS
As you read this section, use this strategy to take notes.

Biosphere

These platforms, built in the treetops, are used to observe forest plants and animals.

Geosphere

In mines dug deep underground, scientists can explore Earth's minerals and rocks.

Geosphere

The **geosphere** (JEE-uh-SFEER) includes all the features on Earth's surface—the continents, islands, and sea floor—and everything below the surface. As the diagram illustrates, the geosphere is made up of several layers: crust, mantle, and outer and inner core.

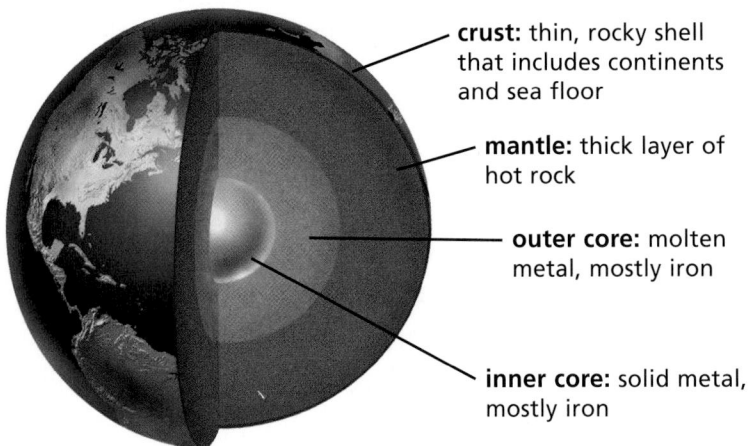

crust: thin, rocky shell that includes continents and sea floor

mantle: thick layer of hot rock

outer core: molten metal, mostly iron

inner core: solid metal, mostly iron

People have studied the surface of the geosphere for centuries. Not until the 1900s, however, were people able to study Earth from space or to explore deep within the planet. Today, scientists use satellite images, sound waves, and computer modeling to develop accurate pictures of features on and below Earth's surface. These images show that Earth constantly changes. Some changes are sudden—a volcano explodes, releasing harmful gases and dust into the air. Other changes, such as the birth of new islands, happen over millions of years.

Earth's continents have many unique landforms such as these rock towers in Cathedral Valley, Utah.

CHECK YOUR READING Give an example of matter moving from the geosphere to the atmosphere.

INVESTIGATE Geosphere's Layers

How can you model the geosphere's layers?

PROCEDURE

(1) To model the layers of the geosphere, you will be using a quarter of an apple that your teacher has cut. Note: NEVER eat food in the science classroom.

(2) Hold the apple slice and observe it carefully. Compare it with the diagram of the geosphere's layers on page 200.

(3) Draw a diagram of the apple and label it with the names of the layers of the geosphere.

WHAT DO YOU THINK?

• What are the four parts of the apple slice?

• What major layer of the geosphere does each part of the apple resemble?

CHALLENGE What other object do you think would make a good model of the geosphere's layers? What model could you build or make yourself?

SKILL FOCUS
Modeling

MATERIALS
apple slice

TIME
15 minutes

All four parts of the Earth system shape the planet's surface.

Earth's surface is worn away, built up, and reshaped every day by the atmosphere, the hydrosphere, the biosphere, and the geosphere. Here are some of the ways they affect the surface.

Atmosphere and Hydrosphere Not even the hardest stone can withstand wind and water. Over millions of years, rain, wind, and flowing water carve huge formations such as the Grand Canyon in Arizona or the rock towers of Utah, shown on page 200.

Geosphere Landmasses pushing together have set off earthquakes and formed volcanoes and mountain ranges around the world.

Biosphere Plants, animals, and human beings have also changed Earth's surface. For instance, earthworms help make soils more fertile. And throughout human history, people have dammed rivers and cleared forests for farmland.

You are part of this process, too. Every time you walk or ride a bike across open land, you are changing Earth's surface. Your feet or the bike's tires dig into the dirt, wearing away plants and exposing soil to sunlight, wind, and water. If you take the same route every day, over time you will wear a path in the land.

READING **TiP**

Landmass is a compound word made up of the words *land* and *mass*. Landmass means "a large area of land."

Chapter 6: **Views of Earth Today 201**

Mudslide in California

Atmosphere and Hydrosphere
Heavy winter rains soak the ground until it cannot absorb any more water.

Biosphere People who build on fragile hillsides remove plants whose roots help hold the soil in place.

Geosphere With nothing to hold the water-soaked ground, it slides downhill, leaving a deep trench.

The photograph above shows a good example of how the four parts can suddenly change Earth's surface. A mudslide like this one can happen in a matter of minutes. Sometimes the side of a mountain may collapse, becoming a river of mud that can bury an entire town.

The four parts of the Earth system continue to shape the surface with every passing year. Scientists will continue to record these changes to update maps and other images of the planet's complex system.

CHECK YOUR READING Find three examples on pages 201 and 202 that show how the parts of the Earth system shape the planet's surface.

 Review

KEY CONCEPTS

1. Define *system*. Compare an open and a closed system.

2. Name the four parts of the Earth system. List one fact about each part that scientists learned through modern technology.

3. Give two examples of how the Earth system's four parts can interact with each other.

CRITICAL THINKING

4. **Apply** One day you see that plants are dying in the class terrarium. What part might be missing from its system?

5. **Infer** You visit a state park and see a thin rock wall with a hole, like a window, worn through it. Which of the four parts of the Earth system might have made the hole? Explain.

CHALLENGE

6. **Predict** Imagine that a meteorite 200 meters wide strikes Earth, landing in a wooded area. Describe one way that this event would affect the biosphere or the geosphere. **Hint:** A meteorite is traveling several thousand kilometers per hour when it strikes the ground.

Maps and globes are models of Earth.

Sunshine State STANDARDS

SC.H.3.3.4: The student knows that technological design should require taking into account constraints such as natural laws, the properties of the materials used, and economic, political, social, ethical, and aesthetic values.

BEFORE, you learned

- The Earth system has four main parts: atmosphere, hydrosphere, biosphere, and geosphere
- Technology is used to study and map the Earth system
- The Earth system's parts interact to shape Earth's surface

NOW, you will learn

- What information maps can provide about natural and human-made features
- How to find exact locations on Earth
- Why all maps distort Earth's surface

FCAT VOCABULARY

equator p. 206

VOCABULARY

relief map p. 204
map scale p. 205
map legend p. 205
latitude p. 206
prime meridian p. 207
longitude p. 207
projection p. 208

EXPLORE Mapping

What makes a good map?

PROCEDURE

MATERIALS
- paper
- pencil or pen

① Draw a map to guide someone from your school to your home or to a point of interest, such as a park, statue, or store, near your school.

② Trade maps with a classmate. Is his or her map easy to understand? Why or why not?

③ Use feedback from your partner to revise your own map.

WHAT DO YOU THINK?
What visual clues make a map easy to understand and use?

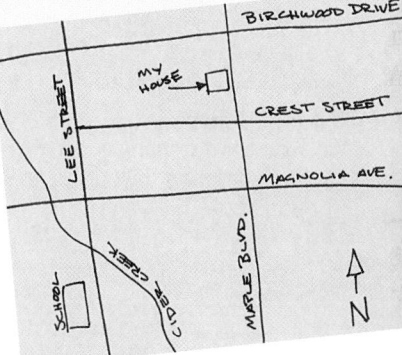

Maps show natural and human-made features.

Have you ever drawn a map to help someone get to your home? If so, your map is actually a rough model of your neighborhood, showing important streets and landmarks. Any map you use is a flat model of Earth's surface, showing Earth's features as seen from above.

On the other hand, a globe represents Earth as if you were looking at it from outer space. A globe is a sphere that shows the relative sizes and shapes of Earth's land features and waters.

In this section you will learn how maps and globes provide different types of information about Earth's surface. They can show everything from city streets to land features to the entire world.

 **CHECK YOUR READING** How are maps and globes alike? How are they different?

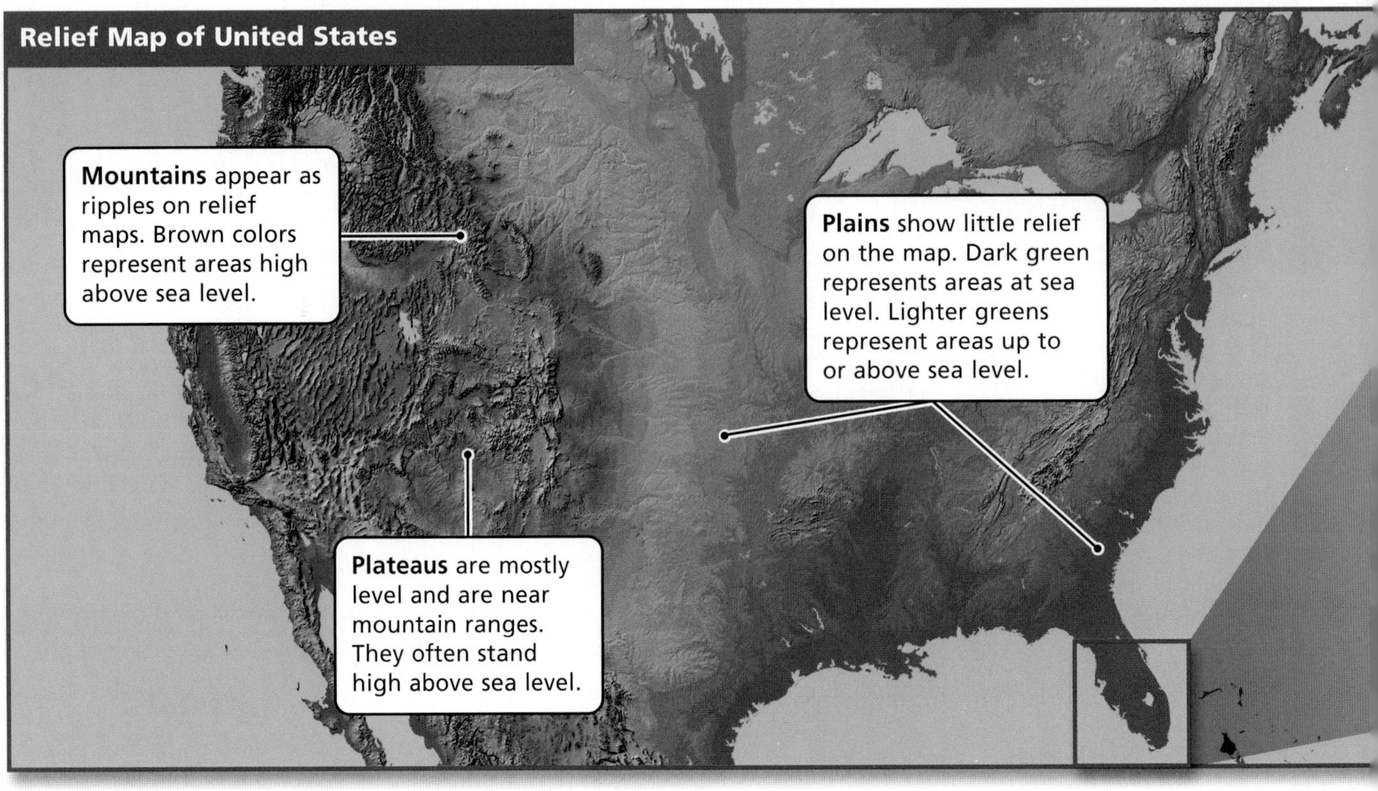

Relief Map of United States

Mountains appear as ripples on relief maps. Brown colors represent areas high above sea level.

Plains show little relief on the map. Dark green represents areas at sea level. Lighter greens represent areas up to or above sea level.

Plateaus are mostly level and are near mountain ranges. They often stand high above sea level.

Land Features on Maps

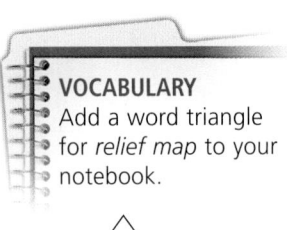

VOCABULARY
Add a word triangle for *relief map* to your notebook.

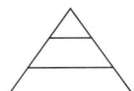

When scientists or travelers want to know what the landscape of an area actually looks like, they will often use a relief map. A **relief map,** such as the one above, shows how high or low each feature is on Earth. A mapmaker uses photographs or satellite images to build a three-dimensional view of Earth's surface. A relief map shows three main types of land features: mountains, plains, and plateaus.

Mountains stand higher than the land around them. A mountain's base may cover several square kilometers. A group of mountains is called a mountain range. Mountain ranges connected in a long chain form a mountain belt. The Rocky Mountains in the United States are part of a huge mountain belt that includes the Canadian Rockies and the Andes Mountains in South America.

Plateaus have fairly level surfaces but stand high above sea level. Plateaus are often found near large mountain ranges. In the United States, the Colorado Plateau is about 3350 meters (11,000 ft) above sea level. This plateau includes parts of Arizona, Colorado, New Mexico, and Utah.

Plains are gently rolling or flat features. The United States has two types of plains—coastal plains near the eastern and southeastern shores, and interior plains in the center of the nation. The interior Great Plains cover the middle third of the United States.

CHECK YOUR READING   How is a plateau different from either a mountain or a plain?

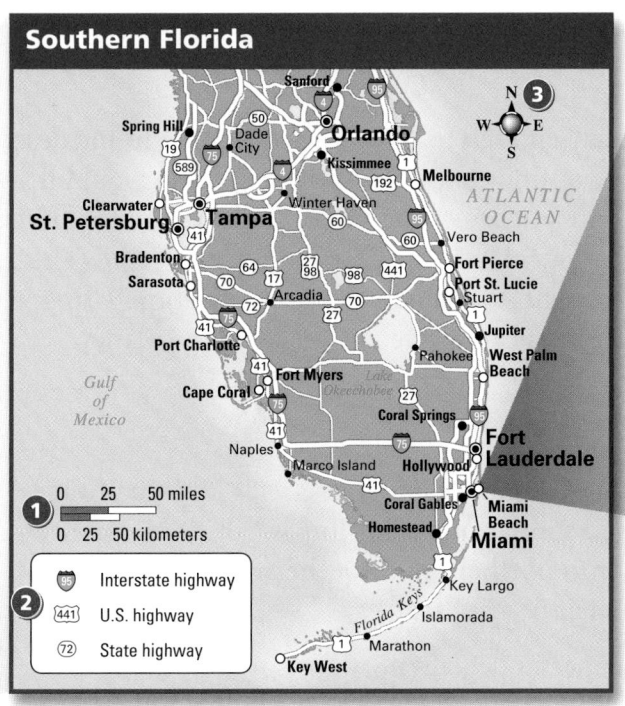

Southern Florida

0 25 50 miles
0 25 50 kilometers

Interstate highway
U.S. highway
State highway

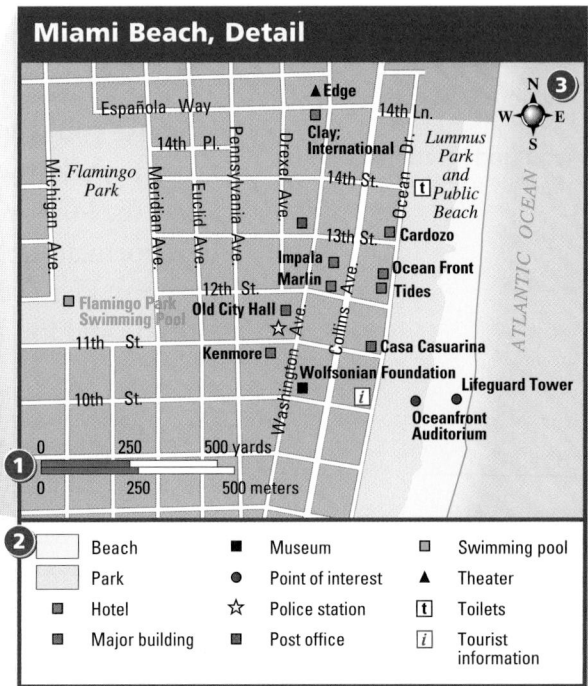

Miami Beach, Detail

0 250 500 yards
0 250 500 meters

Beach   ■ Museum   □ Swimming pool
Park   ● Point of interest   ▲ Theater
■ Hotel   ☆ Police station   t Toilets
■ Major building   ■ Post office   i Tourist information

Scale and Symbols on Maps

The maps most people use are road and city maps like the ones above. These maps provide information about human-made features as well as some natural features. To use these maps, you need to know how to read a map scale and a map legend, or key.

❶ A **map scale** relates distances on a map to actual distances on Earth's surface. Notice that on the map of southern Florida above, the scale is in kilometers and miles. On the Miami Beach map, the scale is in meters and yards. The smaller the area a map shows, the more detail it includes.

The scale can be expressed as a ratio, a bar, or equivalent units of distance. For example, a ratio of 1:25,000 means that 1 centimeter on the map represents 25,000 centimeters (0.25 kilometer) on Earth.

Three Types of Map Scale

Ratio   1:25,000
Bar scale   0 1 2 3 km
Equivalent-units scale   1 cm = 1 km

❷ A **map legend,** also called a key, is a chart that explains the meaning of each symbol used on a map. Symbols can stand for highways, parks, and other features. The legend on the Miami Beach map shows major points of interest for tourists.

❸ A map usually includes a compass rose to show which directions are north, south, east, and west. In general, north on a map points to the top of the page.

READING TiP

As used here, *legend* does not refer to a story. It is based on the Latin word *legenda*, which means "to be read."

CHECK YOUR READING   What information do map scales and map legends provide?

Latitude and longitude show locations on Earth.

Suppose you were lucky enough to find dinosaur bones in the desert. Would you know how to find that exact spot again? You would if you knew the longitude and latitude of the place. Latitude and longitude lines form an imaginary grid over the entire surface of Earth. This grid provides everyone with the same tools for navigation. Using latitude and longitude, you can locate any place on the planet.

Latitude

Latitude is based on an imaginary line that circles Earth halfway between the north and south poles. This line is called the **equator,** and it divides Earth into northern and southern hemispheres. A hemisphere is one half of a sphere.

Latitude is a distance in degrees north or south of the equator, which is 0°. A degree is 1/360 of the distance around a full circle. If you start at one point on the equator and travel all the way around the world back to that point, you have traveled 360 degrees.

The illustration below shows that latitude lines are parallel to the equator and are evenly spaced between the equator and the poles. Also, latitude lines are always labeled north or south of the equator to

Latitude and Longitude

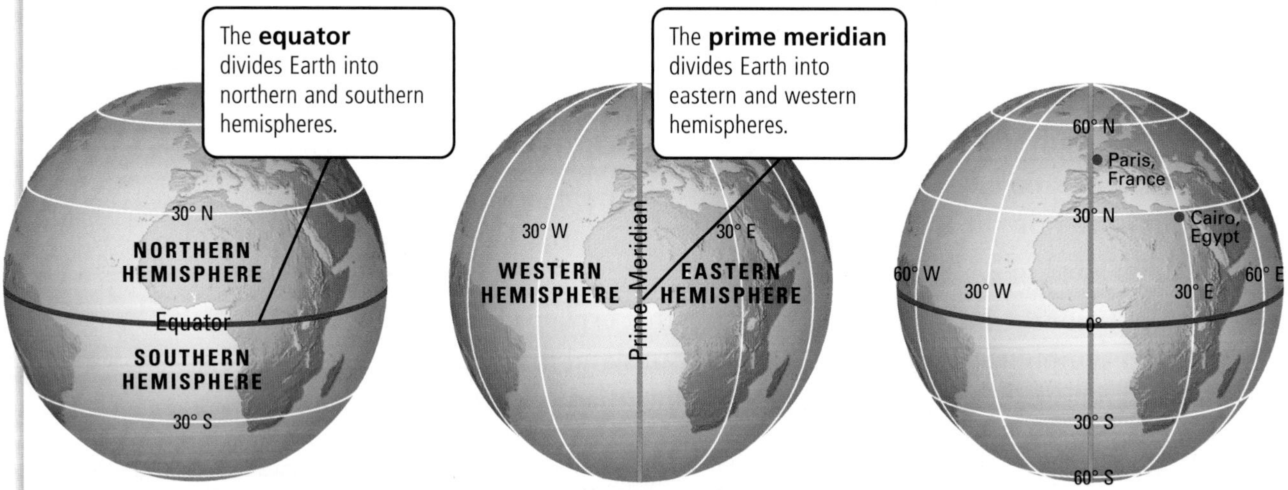

The **equator** divides Earth into northern and southern hemispheres.

30° N
NORTHERN
HEMISPHERE
Equator
SOUTHERN
HEMISPHERE
30° S

The **prime meridian** divides Earth into eastern and western hemispheres.

30° W   30° E
WESTERN   EASTERN
HEMISPHERE HEMISPHERE
Prime Meridian

60° N
Paris, France
30° N
Cairo, Egypt
60° W   60° E
30° W   30° E
0°
30° S
60° S

Latitude is a distance in degrees north or south of the equator.

Longitude is a distance in degrees east or west of the prime meridian.

You can find a location by noting where latitude and longitude lines cross.

READING
VISUALS   What are the approximate latitudes and longitudes of Cairo, Egypt, and Paris, France?

show whether a location is in the northern or southern hemisphere. For instance, the North Pole is 90° north, or 90°N, while the South Pole is 90° south, or 90°S. Latitude, however, is only half of what you need to locate any spot on Earth. You also need to know its longitude.

FLORIDA
Content Review

Recall what you learned about location and position in grade 6. Latitude and longitude are another way of describing position.

Longitude

Longitude is based on an imaginary line that stretches from the North Pole through Greenwich, England, to the South Pole. This line is called the **prime meridian.** Any place up to 180° west of the prime meridian is in the Western Hemisphere. Any place up to 180° east of the prime meridian is in the Eastern Hemisphere.

Longitude is a distance in degrees east or west of the prime meridian, which is 0°. Beginning at the prime meridian, longitude lines are numbered 0° to 180° west and 0° to 180° east.

Longitude lines are labeled east or west to indicate whether a location is in the eastern or western hemisphere. For example, the longitude of Washington, D.C., is about 78° west, or 78°W. The city of Hamburg, Germany, is about 10° east, or 10°E. If you understand latitude and longitude, you can find any spot on Earth's surface.

READING TiP

There is an easy way to remember the difference between latitude and longitude. Think of longitude lines as the "long" lines that go from pole to pole.

CHECK YOUR READING Why do all cities in the United States have a north latitude and a west longitude?

Global Positioning System

The Global Positioning System (GPS) is a network of satellites that are used to find the latitude, longitude, and elevation, or height above sea level, of any site. Twenty-four GPS satellites circle Earth and send signals that are picked up by receivers on the surface. At least three satellites need to be above the horizon for GPS to work. A computer inside a receiver uses the satellite signals to calculate the user's exact location—latitude, longitude, and elevation. GPS is an accurate, easy method for finding location.

GPS devices are used by many people, including pilots, sailors, hikers, and map makers. Some cars now have GPS receivers and digital road maps stored in their computers. A driver types in an address, and the car's computer finds the best way to get there.

Never be lost again. This hiker turns on his GPS unit to find out his current latitude and longitude. He then locates these data on his map to pinpoint his exact location.

CHECK YOUR READING Explain how GPS can help someone find their exact location.

Map projections distort the view of Earth's surface.

The most accurate way to show Earth's surface is on a globe. A globe, however, cannot show much detail, and it is awkward to carry. People use flat maps for their detail and convenience. A **projection** is a way of representing Earth's curved surface on a flat map. Mapmakers use different types of projections, all of which distort, or misrepresent, Earth's surface in different ways.

Cylindrical Projection

The Mercator projection shows Earth as if the map were a large cylinder wrapped around the planet. The outlines of the landmasses and seas are then drawn onto the map. As shown in the diagram on page 209, the cylinder is unrolled to form a flat map. Latitude and longitude appear as straight lines, forming a grid of rectangles.

The Mercator projection is useful for navigating at sea or in the air. It shows the entire world, except for regions near the poles, on one map. Sailors and pilots can draw a straight line from one point to

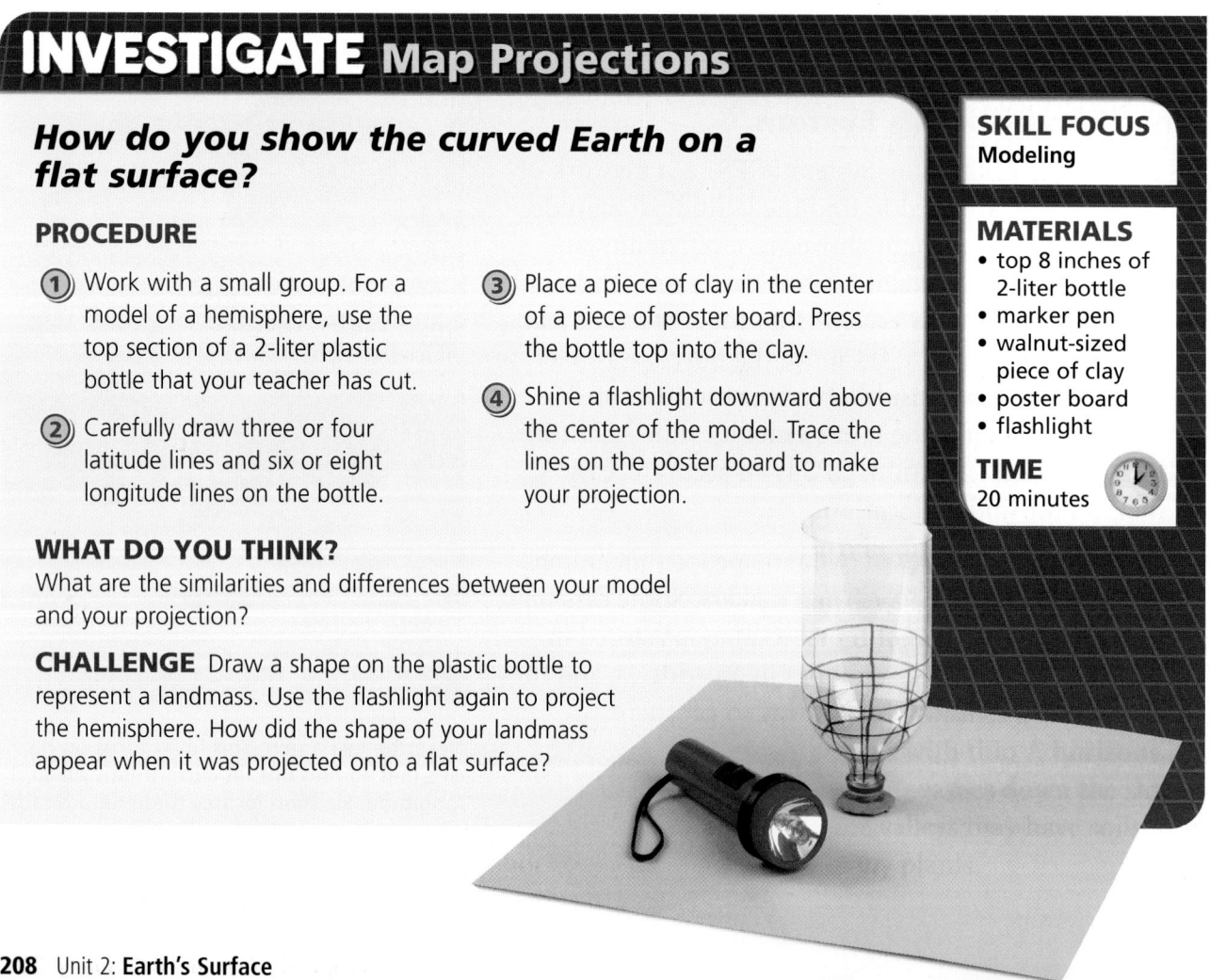

INVESTIGATE Map Projections

How do you show the curved Earth on a flat surface?

PROCEDURE

1. Work with a small group. For a model of a hemisphere, use the top section of a 2-liter plastic bottle that your teacher has cut.

2. Carefully draw three or four latitude lines and six or eight longitude lines on the bottle.

3. Place a piece of clay in the center of a piece of poster board. Press the bottle top into the clay.

4. Shine a flashlight downward above the center of the model. Trace the lines on the poster board to make your projection.

WHAT DO YOU THINK?
What are the similarities and differences between your model and your projection?

CHALLENGE Draw a shape on the plastic bottle to represent a landmass. Use the flashlight again to project the hemisphere. How did the shape of your landmass appear when it was projected onto a flat surface?

SKILL FOCUS
Modeling

MATERIALS
- top 8 inches of 2-liter bottle
- marker pen
- walnut-sized piece of clay
- poster board
- flashlight

TIME
20 minutes

another to plot a course. The problem with Mercator maps is that areas far away from the equator appear much larger than they really are. On the map below, Greenland looks bigger than South America. In reality, South America is about eight times larger than Greenland.

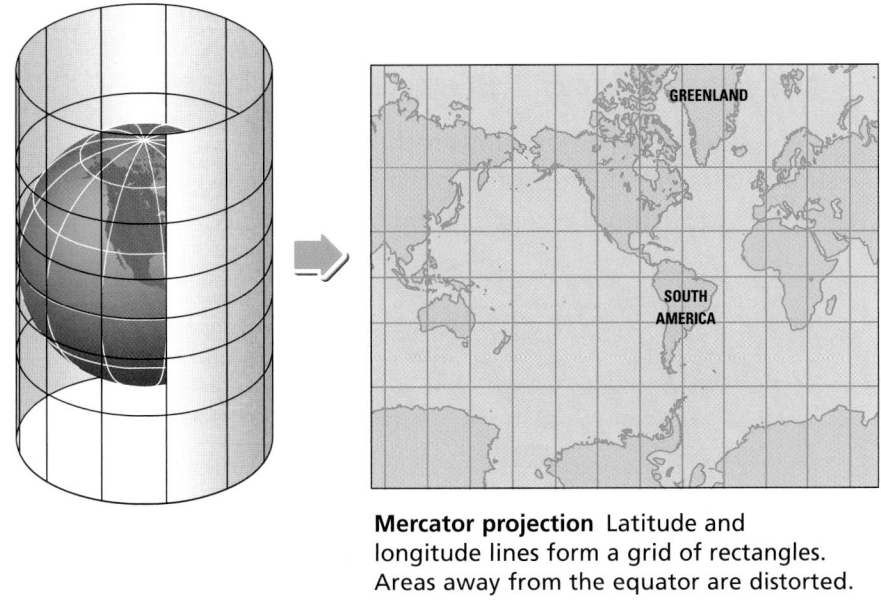

Mercator projection Latitude and longitude lines form a grid of rectangles. Areas away from the equator are distorted.

Conic Projections

Conic projections are based on the shape of a cone. The diagram below shows how a cone of paper might be wrapped around the globe. The paper touches the surface only at the middle latitudes, halfway between the equator and the North Pole.

When the cone is flattened out, the latitude lines are curved slightly. The curved lines represent the curved surface of Earth. This allows the map to show the true sizes and shapes of some landmasses.

Conic projections are most useful for mapping large areas in the middle latitudes, such as the United States. However, landmasses near the equator or near the north or south pole will be distorted.

CHECK YOUR READING What are the main uses of Mercator and conic projections?

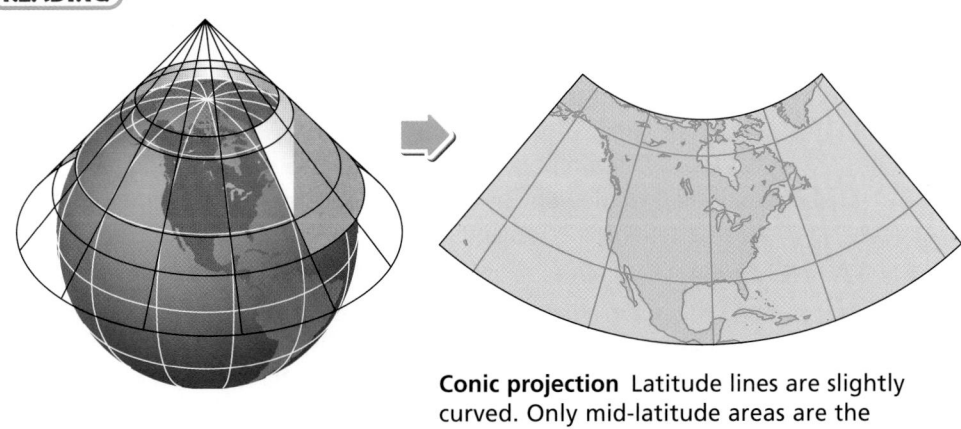

Conic projection Latitude lines are slightly curved. Only mid-latitude areas are the correct size and shape.

Planar Projections

Planar projections were developed to help people find the shortest distance between two points. They are drawn as if a circle of paper were laid on a point on Earth's surface. As you look at the diagram below, notice how the shape of the sphere is transferred to the flat map. When a planar map represents the polar region, the longitude lines meet at the center like the spokes of a wheel.

A planar map is good for plotting ocean or air voyages and for showing the north and south polar regions. However, landmasses farther away from the center point are greatly distorted.

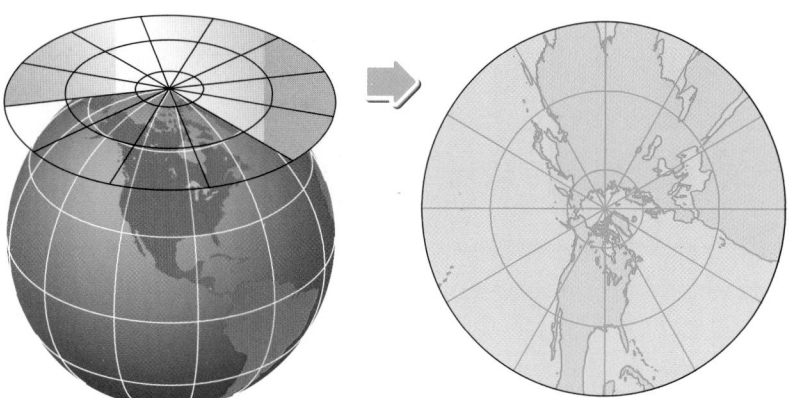

Planar projection Only areas near the center point are the correct size and shape.

The Mercator, conic, and planar projections are all attempts to solve the problem of representing a curved surface on a flat map. Each projection can show certain areas of the world accurately but distorts other areas.

CHECK YOUR READING What areas does the planar projection show accurately?

Review

KEY CONCEPTS

1. What natural and human-made features can maps show? Give two examples of each.

2. Explain how latitude and longitude can help you locate any place on Earth.

3. Why do all flat maps distort Earth's surface?

CRITICAL THINKING

4. **Provide Examples** Imagine that your family is on a long car trip. What symbols on a road map would you pay the most attention to? Explain.

5. **Apply** Use a world map to find the approximate latitudes and longitudes of Moscow, Russia; Tokyo, Japan; Denver, Colorado; and La Paz, Bolivia.

CHALLENGE

6. **Apply** Working with a partner or with a small group, select the shortest airline route from Chicago to London, using a globe and a Mercator map. **Hint:** Notice that as you go farther north on the globe, the longitude lines become closer together.

SKILL: USING PROPORTIONS

How Far Is It?

A science class is visiting Chicago and is using the map on the left to walk to the lakefront museums. Remember, a map scale shows how distances on the map compare to actual distances on the ground.

Buckingham Fountain

MATH TUTORIAL
CLASSZONE.COM
Click on Math Tutorial for more help with solving proportions.

Example

In this case, the map scale indicates that 1 centimeter on the map represents 300 meters on the ground. The map scale shows this as equivalent units. By using these units to write a proportion, you can use cross products to determine actual distances.

What distance does 3 cm on the map represent? Set up the problem like this:

$$\frac{1 \text{ cm}}{300 \text{ m}} = \frac{3 \text{ cm}}{x}$$

(1) $\quad 1 \text{ cm} \cdot x = 3 \text{ cm} \cdot 300 \text{ m}$

(2) $\quad\quad\quad x = 3 \cdot 300 \text{ m}$

(3) $\quad\quad\quad x = 900 \text{ m}$

ANSWER 3 centimeters on the map represents 900 meters on the ground.

Use cross products and a metric ruler to answer the following questions.

1. The science class divides into two groups. Each group starts at Buckingham Fountain. How far, in meters, will one group walk to get to the Adler Planetarium if they follow the red dotted line?

2. How far, in meters, will the other group walk to get to the end of Navy Pier if they follow the blue dotted line?

3. The group that walked to Adler decides to take a boat to join the other group at Navy Pier. How far, in meters, is their boat ride along the red dotted line?

CHALLENGE What is the total distance, in kilometers, that the two groups traveled? Set up the problem as a proportion. **Hint:** There are 1000 meters in a kilometer.

0   150   300 meters

1 cm = 300 m

6.3 Topographic maps show the shape of the land.

BEFORE, you learned

- Different maps provide information about natural and human-made features
- Latitude and longitude are used to find places on Earth
- All flat maps distort Earth's surface

NOW, you will learn

- How contour lines show elevation, slope, and relief
- What rules contour lines follow
- What common symbols are used on topographic maps

FCAT VOCABULARY
topography p. 212

VOCABULARY
contour line p. 213
elevation p. 213
slope p. 213
relief p. 213
contour interval p. 214

EXPLORE Topographic Maps

How can you map your knuckles?

PROCEDURE

1. Hold your fist closed, knuckles up, as shown in the photo.

2. Draw circles around the first knuckle. Make sure the circles are the same distance from each other.

3. Flatten out your hand. Observe what happens. Write down your observations.

WHAT DO YOU THINK?

- How does the height of your knuckles change when you clench your fist, then flatten out your hand?
- What do you think the circles represent?

MATERIAL
washable colored pen

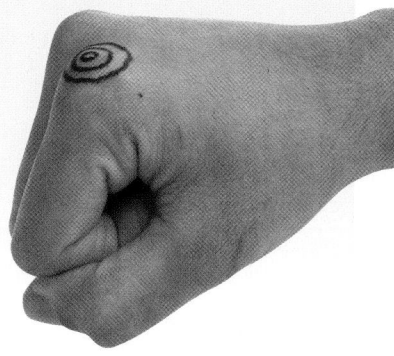

Topographic maps use contour lines to show features.

VOCABULARY

Add a word triangle for *topography* to your notebook.

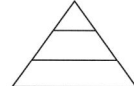

Imagine you are on vacation with your family in a national park. You have a simple trail map that shows you where to hike. But the map does not tell you anything about what the land looks like. Will you have to cross any rivers or valleys? How far uphill or downhill will you have to hike?

To answer these questions, you need to know something about the topography of the area. **Topography** is the shape, or features, of the land. These features can be natural—such as mountains, plateaus, and plains—or human-made—such as dams and roads. To show the topography of an area, mapmakers draw a topographic map.

A topographic map is a flat map that uses lines to show Earth's surface features. Distance and elevation can be given in feet or meters. Take a look at the topographic map of Mount Hood on this page. The wiggly lines on the map are called **contour lines,** and they show an area's elevation, slope, and relief.

1 The **elevation** of a place is how high above sea level it is. An area can range from a few meters to several thousand meters above sea level. The numbers on the contour lines show the elevations of different points in the Mount Hood area.

2 The **slope** of a landform or area is how steep it is. The more gradual the slope, the farther apart the contour lines on the map. The steeper the slope, the closer together the contour lines.

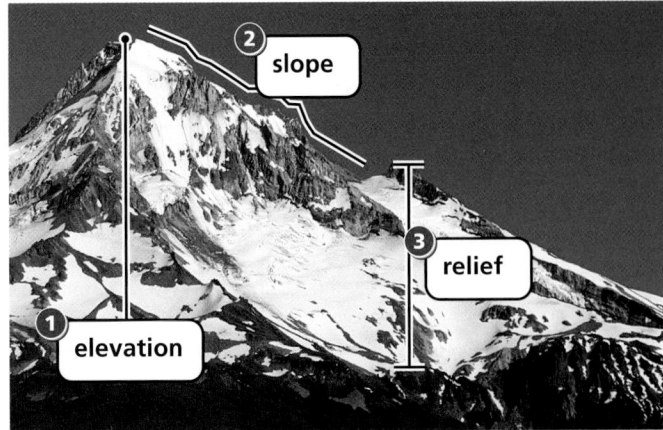

3 The **relief** of an area is the difference between its high and low points. For example, subtracting the lowest elevation on the map from the highest gives you a measure of the area's relief.

CHECK YOUR READING What is the difference between elevation and slope?

Mount Hood Topographic Map

A topographic map shows the land as if you were above the land looking down on it.

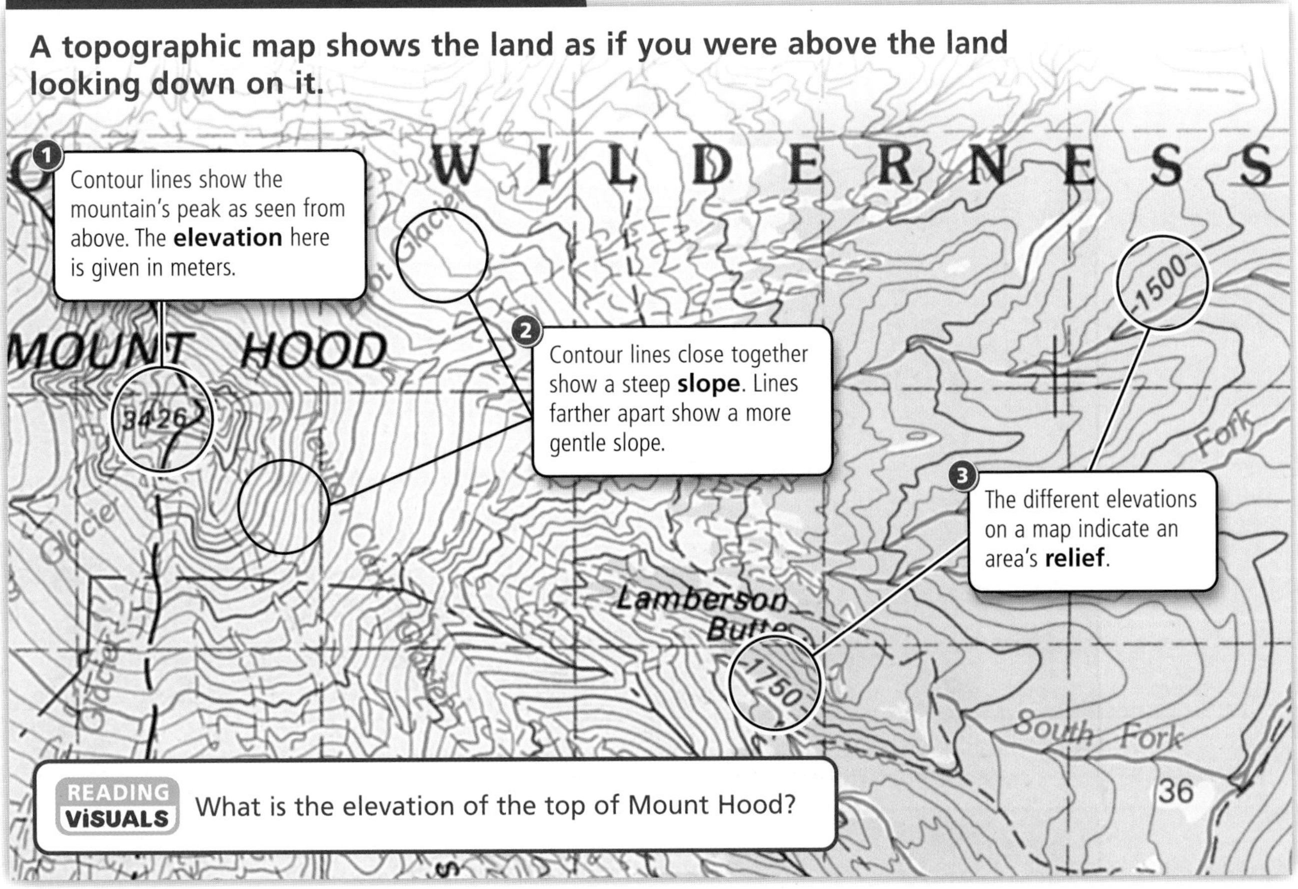

1 Contour lines show the mountain's peak as seen from above. The **elevation** here is given in meters.

2 Contour lines close together show a steep **slope**. Lines farther apart show a more gentle slope.

3 The different elevations on a map indicate an area's **relief**.

WILDERNESS

MOUNT HOOD

3426

-1500-

Lamberson Butte

1750

South Fork

Fork

36

READING VISUALS What is the elevation of the top of Mount Hood?

Chapter 6: **Views of Earth Today** 213

Contour lines follow certain rules.

MAIN IDEA AND DETAILS
Use your main idea and details chart to take notes on the rules for reading a topographic map.

Contour lines on topographic maps can help you visualize landforms. Think of the following statements as rules for reading such maps:

- **Lines never cross.** Contour lines never cross, because each line represents an exact elevation.

- **Circles show highest and lowest points.** Contour lines form closed circles around mountaintops, hilltops, and the centers of depressions, which are sunken areas in the ground. Sometimes, the elevation of a mountain or hill is written in meters or feet in the middle of the circle.

- **Contour interval is always the same on a map.** The **contour interval** is the difference in elevation from one contour line to the next. For example, the contour interval on the map below is 10 feet. This means that the change in elevation between contour lines is always 10 feet. The contour interval can differ from map to map, but it is always the same on a particular map.

Ely, Minnesota, Topographic Map

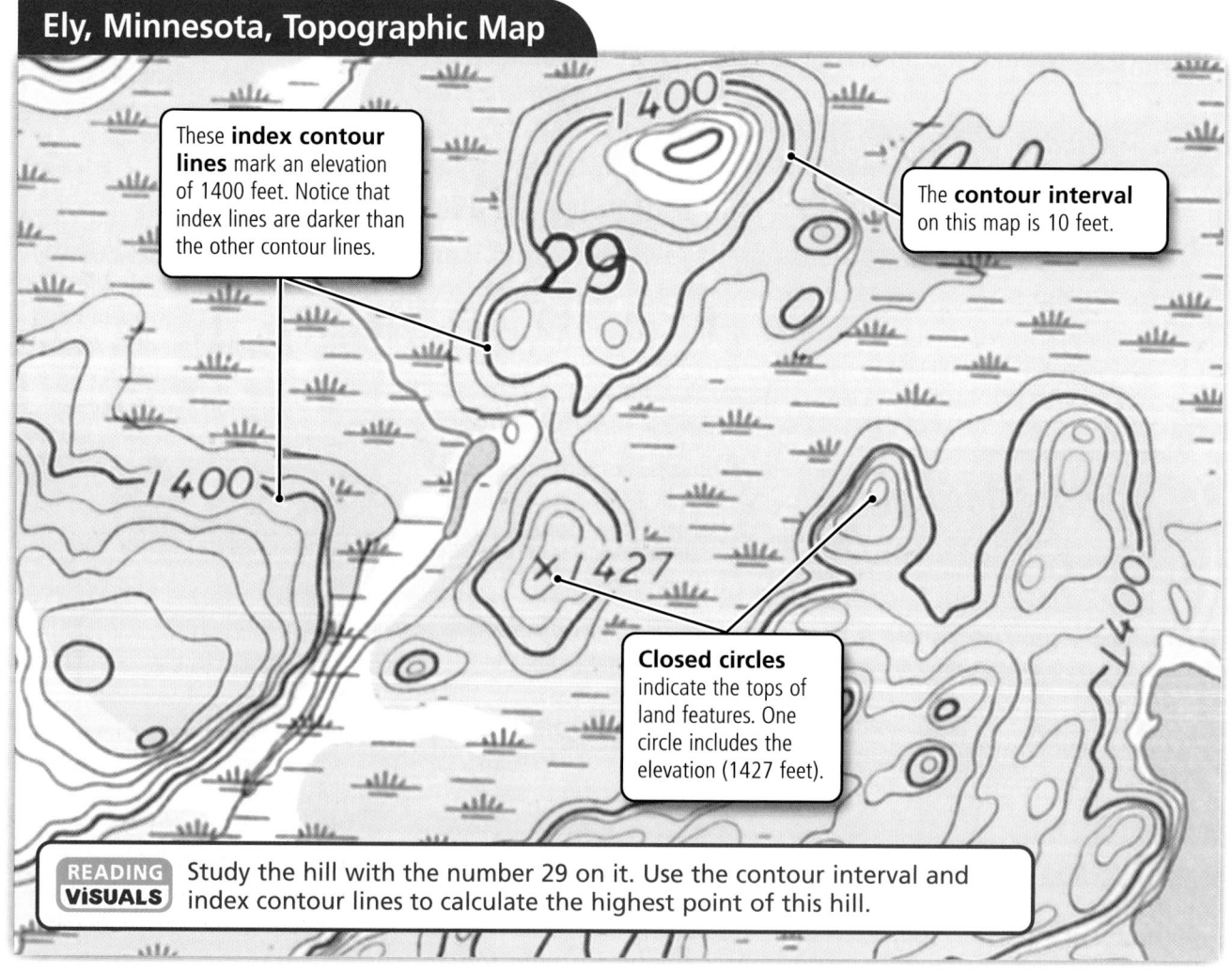

These **index contour lines** mark an elevation of 1400 feet. Notice that index lines are darker than the other contour lines.

The **contour interval** on this map is 10 feet.

Closed circles indicate the tops of land features. One circle includes the elevation (1427 feet).

READING VISUALS Study the hill with the number 29 on it. Use the contour interval and index contour lines to calculate the highest point of this hill.

- **Index contour lines mark elevations.** The darker contour lines on a map are called index contour lines. Numbers that indicate elevations are often written on these lines. To calculate higher or lower elevations, simply count the number of lines above or below an index line. Then multiply that number by the contour interval. For instance, on the Ely map, one index line marks 1400 feet. To find the elevation of a point three lines up from this index line, you would multiply 10 feet (the contour interval) by 3. Add the result, 30, to 1400. The point's elevation is 1430 feet.

SIMULATION
CLASSZONE.COM
Discover the relationship between topographic maps and surface features.

CHECK YOUR READING   What information do index contour lines provide?

Besides contour lines, topographic maps also contain symbols for natural and human-made features. Below are some common map symbols that the United States Geological Survey (USGS) uses on its topographic maps.

Topographic Map Symbols

⸿ Marsh or swamp		↶ Hiking trail	
Vegetation		⌁ Stream	
⌒ Lake or pond		╫ Railroad tracks	

The USGS provides topographic maps for nearly every part of the United States. These maps cover urban, rural, and wilderness areas. Hikers and campers are not the only ones who use topographic maps. Engineers, archaeologists, forest rangers, biologists, and others rely on them as well.

 **Review**

KEY CONCEPTS

1. How do contour lines show elevation, slope, and relief?

2. Why do contour lines never cross on a topographic map?

3. How would you show the top of a hill, an area of vegetation, or a hiking trail on a topographic map?

CRITICAL THINKING

4. **Apply** For an area with gently sloping hills and little relief, would you draw contour lines close together or far apart? Explain why.

5. **Compare and Contrast** How would a road map and a topographic map of the same area differ? What information would each provide?

CHALLENGE

6. **Synthesize** Work with a group to make a topographic map of the area around your school. First decide how big an area you will include. Then choose a contour interval, a map scale, and symbols for buildings, sports fields, and other features. Let other students test the map's accuracy.

CHAPTER INVESTIGATION

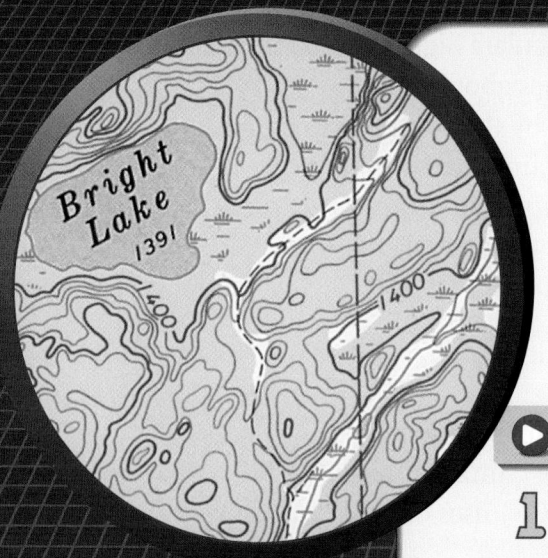

Bright Lake 1391

Investigate Topographic Maps

OVERVIEW AND PURPOSE Topographic maps show the shape of the land. In this lab you will use what you have learned about how Earth's three-dimensional surface is represented on maps to
- make a terrain model out of clay
- produce a topographic map of the model

▶ Procedure

MATERIALS
- half-gallon cardboard juice container
- scissors
- modeling clay
- clear plastic sheet (transparency or sheet protector)
- cellophane tape
- ruler
- water
- food coloring
- box of spaghetti
- erasable marker pen

1 Build a simple landscape about 6–8 cm high from modeling clay. Include a variety of land features. Make sure your model is no taller than the sides of the container.

2 Place your model into the container. Stand a ruler upright inside the container and tape it in place.

3 Lay the clear plastic sheet over the container and tape it on one side like a hinge. Carefully trace the outline of your clay model.

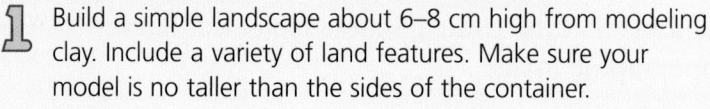

step 3

4 Add 2 cm of colored water to the container.

5 Insert spaghetti sticks into the model all around the waterline. Place the sticks about 3 cm apart. Make sure the sticks are vertical and are no taller than the sides of the container.

6 Lower the plastic sheet back over the container. Looking straight down on the container, make a dot on the sheet wherever you see a spaghetti stick. Connect the dots to trace the contour line accurately onto your map.

7 Continue adding water, 2 cm at a time. Each time you add water, insert the sticks into the model at the waterline and repeat step 6. Continue until the model landscape is underwater. Carefully drain the water when finished.

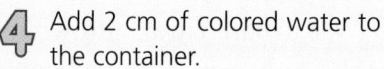

step 5

▶ Observe and Analyze

1. Compare your topographic map with the three-dimensional model. Remember that contour lines connect points of equal elevation. What do widely spaced or tightly spaced contour lines mean? What does a closed circle mean?

2. Make a permanent record of your map to keep in your **Science Notebook** by carefully tracing the contour lines onto a sheet of white paper. To make reading the map easier, use a different color for an index contour line.

3. What is the contour interval of your model landscape? For example, each 2 centimeters might represent 20 meters in an actual landscape. Record the elevation of the index contour line on your map.

▶ Conclude

1. **INFER** How would you determine the elevation of a point located halfway between two contour lines?

2. **EVALUATE** Describe any errors that you may have made in your procedure or any places where errors might have occurred.

3. **APPLY** Explain how you would use a topographic map if you were planning a hiking trip or a cross-country bike race.

▶ INVESTIGATE Further

CHALLENGE Choose one feature on a topographic map—such as the map on page 214—to translate into a cross-sectional diagram.

1. Lay a piece of ruled paper across the center of the topographical feature.

2. Mark each of the contour lines on the ruled paper and label each mark with the elevation.

3. Mark the same elevations on the side of the paper, as shown in the example.

4. Use a ruler to draw a straight line down from each mark to the matching elevation on the side of the paper.

5. Connect the points to draw a profile of the landform.

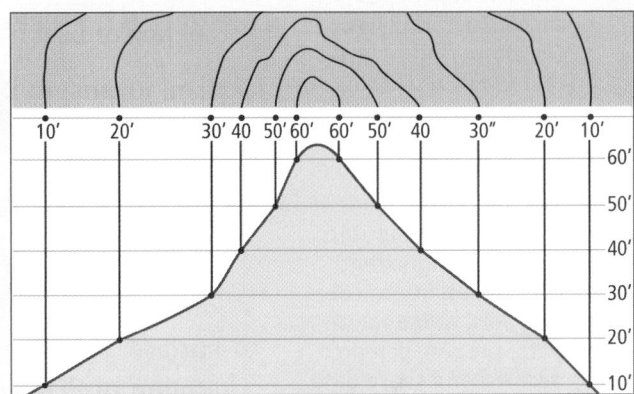

INVESTIGATE TOPOGRAPHIC MAPS

Observe and Analyze

Figure 1. Topographic Map of Model

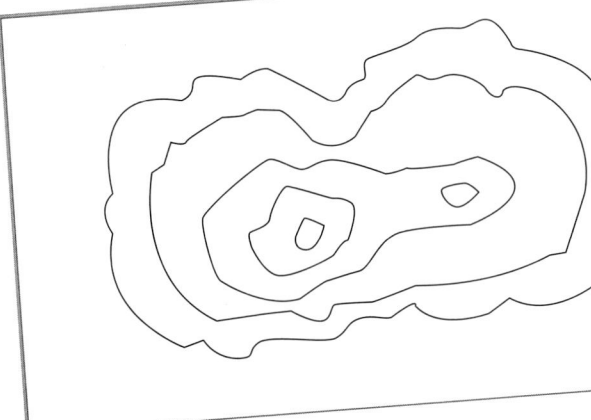

Conclude

Technology is used to map Earth.

Sunshine State STANDARDS

SC.H.3.3.4: The student knows that technological design should require taking into account constraints such as natural laws, the properties of the materials used, and economic, political, social, ethical, and aesthetic values.

SC.H.3.3.7: The student knows that computers speed up and extend people's ability to collect, sort, and analyze data; prepare research reports; and share data and ideas with others.

BEFORE, you learned

- Contour lines are used on topographic maps to show elevation, slope, and relief
- Contour lines follow certain rules
- Map symbols show many natural and human-made features

NOW, you will learn

- How remote-sensing images can provide detailed and accurate information about Earth
- How geographic data can be displayed in layers to build maps

VOCABULARY

remote sensing p. 218
sensor p. 219
false-color image p. 220
geographic information systems p. 221

THINK ABOUT

What can you see in this image?

Satellites can record all types of information about Earth's surface. This image shows a section of Washington, D.C. The satellite that collected the data is 680 kilometers (420 mi) above Earth. What familiar items can you see in the picture? How might images like this be useful to scientists, mapmakers, and engineers?

Remote sensing provides detailed images of Earth.

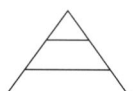

VOCABULARY
Add a word triangle for *remote sensing* to your notebook.

If you have ever looked at an object through a pair of binoculars, you have used remote sensing. **Remote sensing** is the use of scientific equipment to gather information about something from a distance. Remote-sensing technology can be as simple as a camera mounted on an airplane or as complex as a satellite orbiting Earth.

To get an idea of how important remote sensing is, imagine you are a mapmaker in the 1840s. You have been asked to draw a map of a state, but you have no cameras, no photographs from airplanes, and no satellites to help you. To get a good view of the land, you have to climb to the highest points and carefully draw every hill, valley, river, and landform below you. It will take you months to map the state.

Today, that same map would take far less time to make. Modern mapmakers use remote-sensing images from airplanes and satellites to develop highly detailed and accurate maps of Earth's surface.

Airplane cameras use film to record data, but satellites use sensors to build images of Earth. A **sensor** is a mechanical or electrical device that receives and responds to a signal, such as light. Satellite sensors detect far more than your eyes can see. They collect information about the different types of energy coming from Earth's surface. The satellites then send that information to computers on Earth.

The computers turn the information into images, as shown in the illustration below. Satellite data can be used to build an image of the entire planet, a single continent, or a detail of your area. For example, the image on the right shows a closeup of the Jefferson Memorial in Washington, D.C.

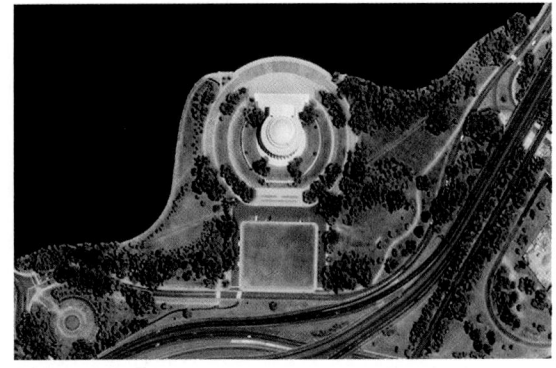

This satellite image includes the Jefferson Memorial, walkways, and roads. See if you can find the memorial in the image on page 218.

CHECK YOUR READING Explain how remote sensing is used to gather information about Earth.

Satellite Imaging

Objects on Earth reflect or emit different types of energy. Satellite sensors can detect and record these energies.

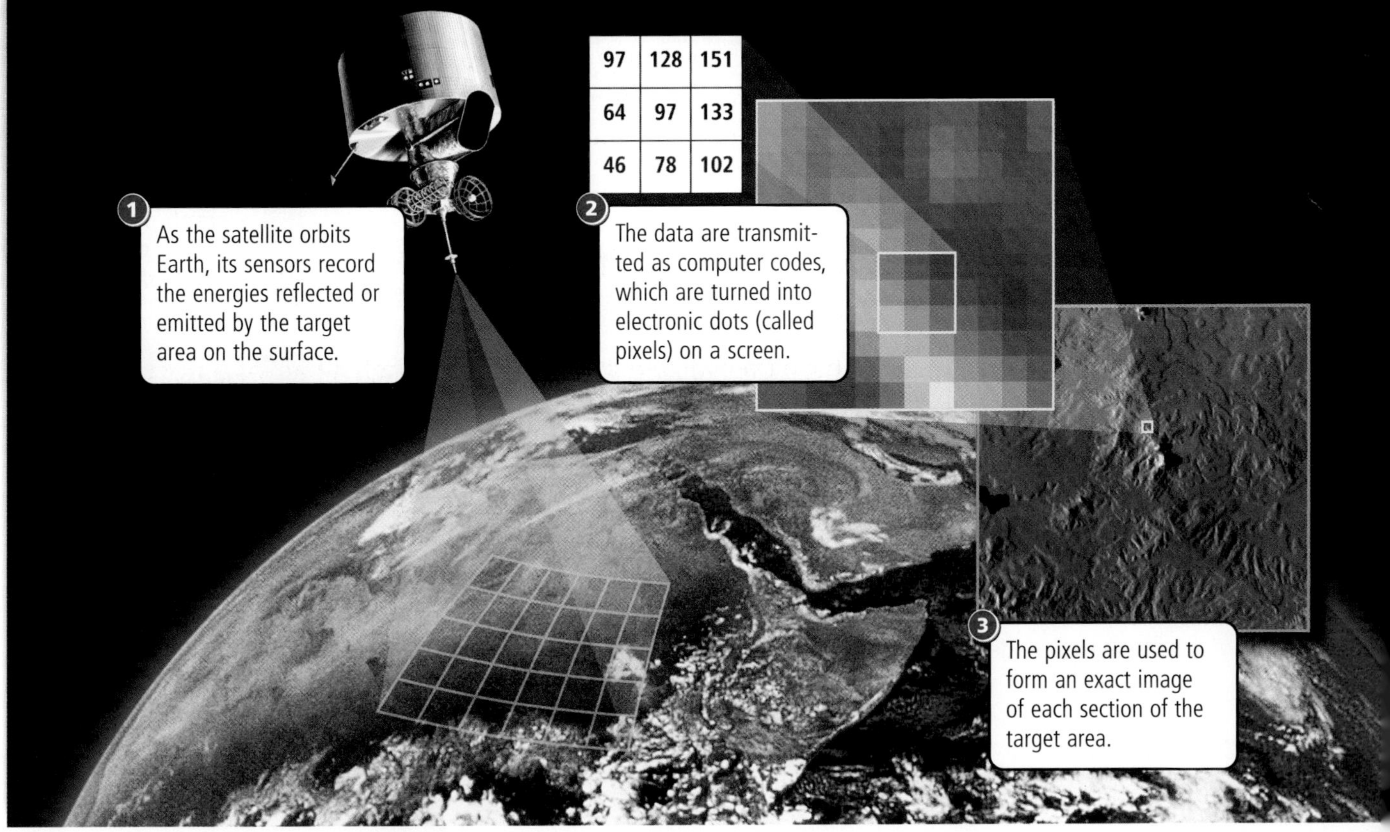

97	128	151
64	97	133
46	78	102

1 As the satellite orbits Earth, its sensors record the energies reflected or emitted by the target area on the surface.

2 The data are transmitted as computer codes, which are turned into electronic dots (called pixels) on a screen.

3 The pixels are used to form an exact image of each section of the target area.

One of the ways scientists study changes is by using false-color images. In one type of **false-color image,** Earth's natural colors are replaced with artificial ones to highlight special features. For example, fire officials used false-color images like the ones below to track the spread of a dangerous wildfire in southern Oregon.

July 21, 2002

Small fires break out.

In this false-color image, vegetation is bright green, burned areas are red, fire is bright pink, and smoke is blue.

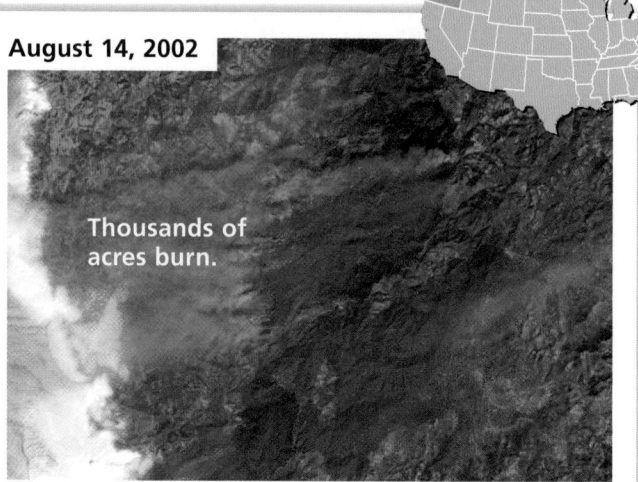

August 14, 2002

Thousands of acres burn.

Three weeks later, as this false-color image clearly shows, the fires had spread over a large area.

OREGON

INVESTIGATE Satellite Imaging

How do satellites send images to Earth?

PROCEDURE

1. Work with a partner. One of you will be the "sensor," and the other will be the "receiving station."

2. The sensor draws the initials of a famous person on a piece of graph paper. The receiving station does NOT see the drawing.

3. The sensor sends the picture to the receiving station. For blank squares, the sensor says "Zero." For filled-in squares, the sensor says "One." Be sure to start at the top row and read left to right, telling the receiving station when a new row begins.

4. The receiving station transfers the code to the graph paper. At the end, the receiver has three tries to guess whose initials were sent.

SKILL FOCUS
Modeling

MATERIALS
- graph paper
- pen or pencil
- *for Challenge:* colored pens or pencils

TIME
25 minutes

WHAT DO YOU THINK?

- What would happen if you accidentally skipped or repeated a row?

- If you increased or decreased the number and size of the squares, how would this affect the picture?

CHALLENGE Use a variety of colors to send other initials or an image. Your code must tell the receiver which color to use for each square.

Geographic information systems display data in layers.

RESOURCE CENTER
CLASSZONE.COM
Find out more about how GIS is used.

Any good city map will show you what is on the surface—buildings, streets, parks, and other features. But suppose you need to know about tunnels under the city. Or maybe you want to know where the most students live. An ordinary map, even one based on remote-sensing images, will not tell you what you want to know.

Instead, you would turn to geographic information systems. **Geographic information systems** (GIS) are computer systems that can store and arrange geographic data and display the data in many different types of maps. Scientists, city planners, and engineers all use GIS maps to help them make decisions. For example, suppose your city wants to build a new airport. It must be away from populated areas and near major highways. The illustration below shows how city officials might use GIS to pick the best site.

Geographic Information Systems

GIS can be used to produce maps that help people make decisions.

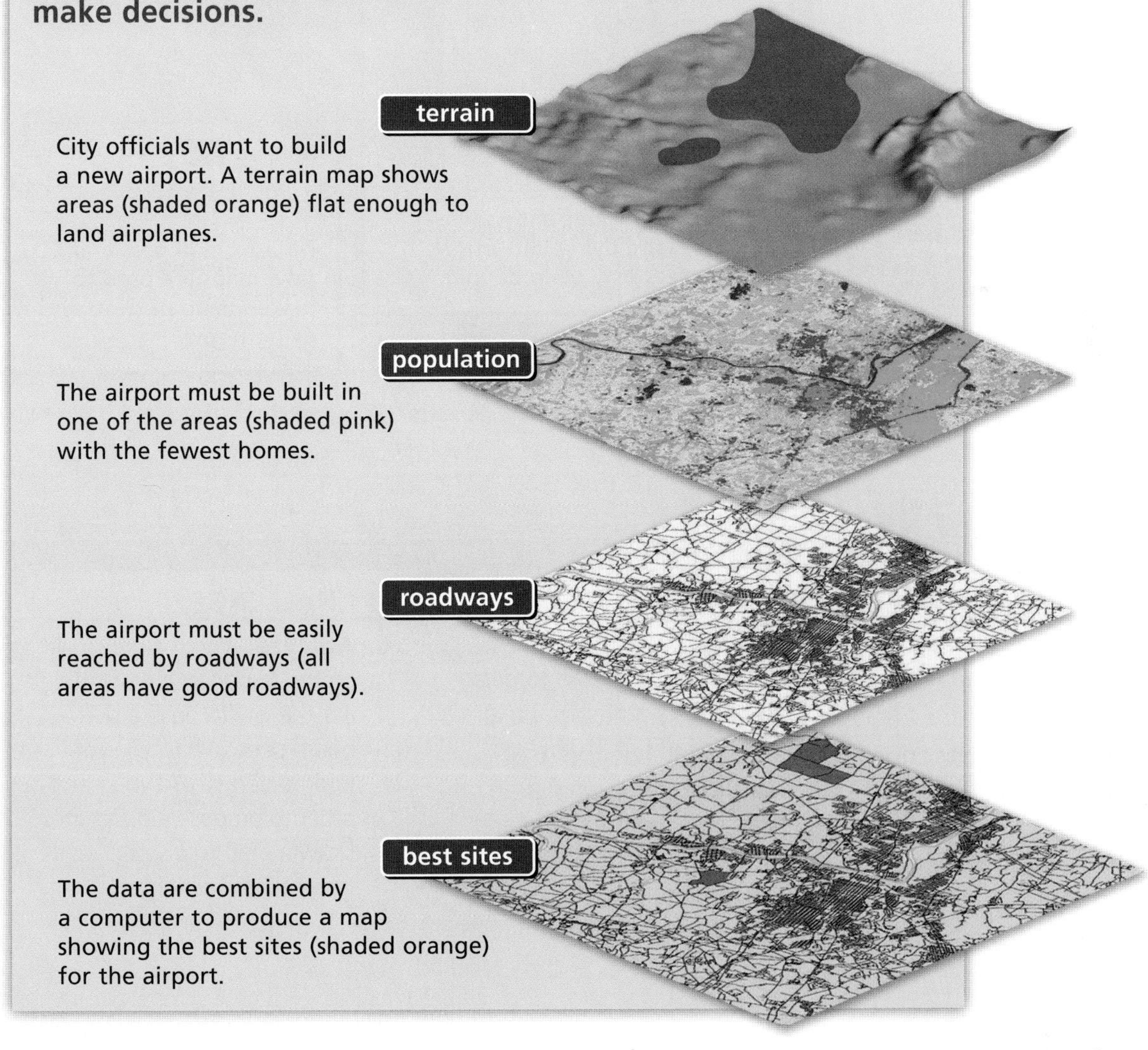

City officials want to build a new airport. A terrain map shows areas (shaded orange) flat enough to land airplanes.

terrain

The airport must be built in one of the areas (shaded pink) with the fewest homes.

population

The airport must be easily reached by roadways (all areas have good roadways).

roadways

The data are combined by a computer to produce a map showing the best sites (shaded orange) for the airport.

best sites

Any geographic information can be entered into GIS and converted into a map. These systems are especially useful in displaying information about changes in the environment.

For example, near Long Valley in California, the volcano known as Mammoth Mountain began giving off carbon dioxide, or CO_2. As the gas rose through the soil, it began killing the roots of trees nearby. Scientists measured the flow of CO_2 around Horseshoe Lake and other areas. They used computer software to build the maps shown below.

CHECK YOUR READING Summarize the ways GIS maps can be helpful to engineers, city planners, and scientists.

Mammoth Mountain

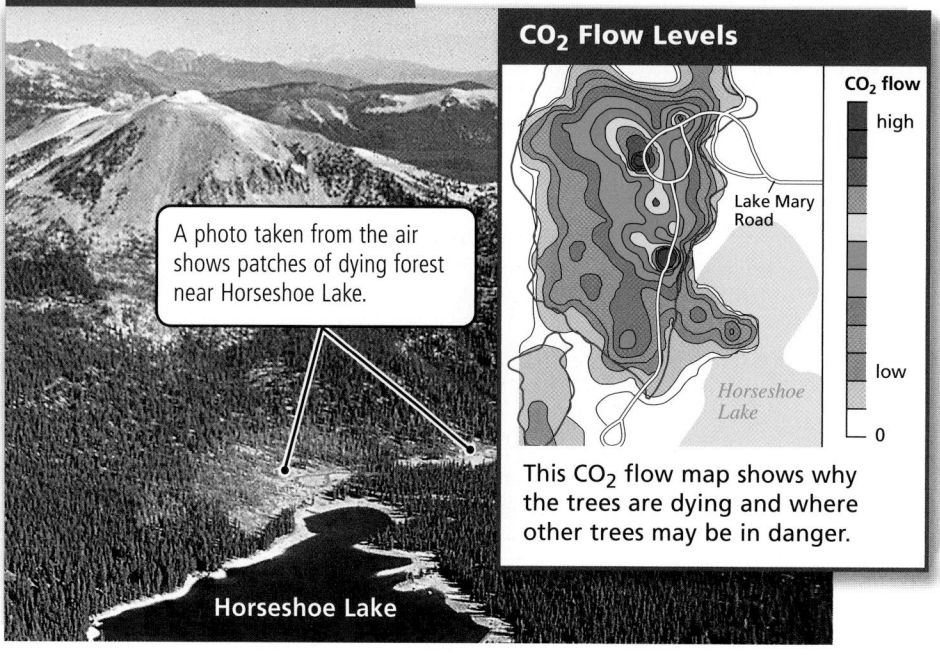

A photo taken from the air shows patches of dying forest near Horseshoe Lake.

Horseshoe Lake

CO_2 Flow Levels

CO_2 flow
high

low

0

Lake Mary Road

Horseshoe Lake

This CO_2 flow map shows why the trees are dying and where other trees may be in danger.

Area Map

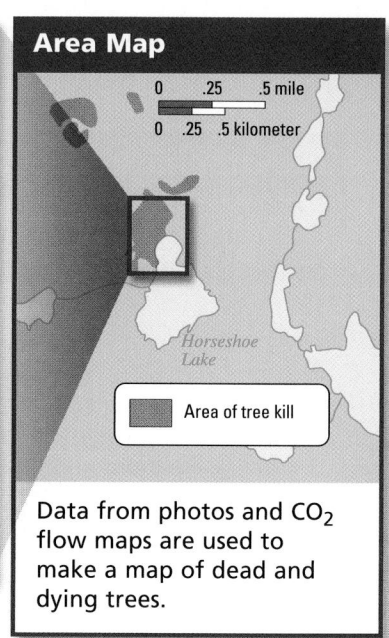

0   .25   .5 mile
0   .25   .5 kilometer

Horseshoe Lake

Area of tree kill

Data from photos and CO_2 flow maps are used to make a map of dead and dying trees.

6.4 Review

KEY CONCEPTS

1. How are satellites used to make images of Earth from outer space?

2. What are some of the types of information obtained by remote sensing?

3. Explain in your own words what a GIS map is.

CRITICAL THINKING

4. **Infer** Explain how satellite images might be used to predict what a natural area might look like in 50 or 100 years.

5. **Evaluate** If you wanted to compare a region before and during a flood, how could false-color images help you?

◯ CHALLENGE

6. **Analyze** Work with a small group. Suppose you wanted to ask the city to build a skateboard park. What types of information would you need in order to propose a good site? Draw a map to display each type of information.

Think SCIENCE

Which Site Is Best for an Olympic Stadium?

Imagine you live in a city that has been chosen to host the Summer Olympics. The only question is where to build the Olympic stadium—in the center of town, in the suburbs, or on the site of an old baseball park. The city government has developed maps to help them decide which is the best site. The planners know that thousands of people will come to see the games. Therefore, they reason, the stadium should be (1) easy to reach by car, (2) close to mass-transit stops, and (3) near restaurants and shops.

▶ Analyzing Map Data

As you study the maps, keep these requirements in mind.

1. Which site(s) is/are easiest to reach by car?
2. Which site(s) is/are closest to bus and train lines?
3. Which site(s) is/are close to shopping areas?

▶ Interpreting Data

In your **Science Notebook,** create a chart like the one below to help you interpret the data displayed on the maps. As you fill in the chart, think about which site offers the greatest benefits to all the people who will attend the Olympic Games.

	Site Ⓐ		Site Ⓑ		Site Ⓒ	
	Yes	No	Yes	No	Yes	No
Near mass transit						
Near highways and roads						
Near shopping areas						

As a group Choose the best site based on your interpretation of the data. Discuss your choice with other groups to see if they agree.

CHALLENGE Once the site is chosen, the planners will start building the stadium. What types of information about the site will they need? Sketch maps displaying the information. **Hint:** The stadium will need electricity, water, and delivery of supplies.

Trains and Bus Lines
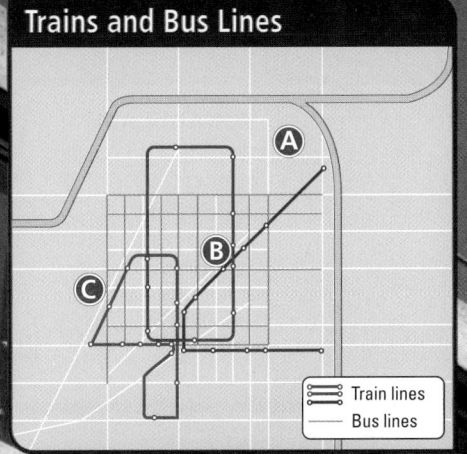
Train lines
Bus lines

Streets and Freeways
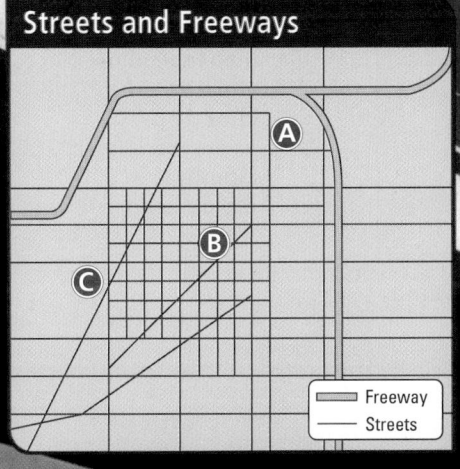
Freeway
Streets

Restaurants and Shopping

Shops and restaurants

6 Chapter Review

the **BIG** idea

Modern technology has changed the way we view and map Earth.

FLORIDA REVIEW
CLASSZONE.COM

Content Review and
FCAT Practice

 KEY CONCEPTS SUMMARY

---

1 **Technology is used to explore the Earth system.**

The atmosphere, hydrosphere, biosphere, and geosphere work together to form one large system called Earth.

VOCABULARY
system p. 197
atmosphere p. 198
hydrosphere p. 198
biosphere p. 199
geosphere p. 200

---

2 **Maps and globes are models of Earth.**

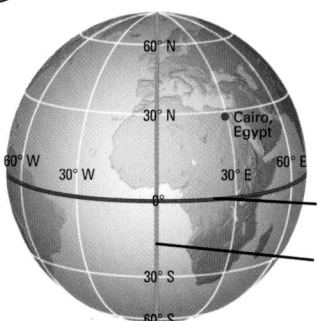

Latitude and longitude are used to locate any point on Earth.

— **equator**

— **prime meridian**

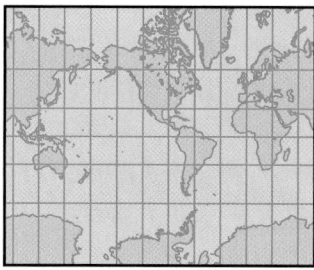

All map projections distort Earth's surface.

VOCABULARY
relief map p. 204
map scale p. 205
map legend p. 205
equator p. 206
latitude p. 206
prime meridian p. 207
longitude p. 207
projection p. 208

---

3 **Topographic maps show the shape of the land.**

Contour lines show elevation, slope, and relief.

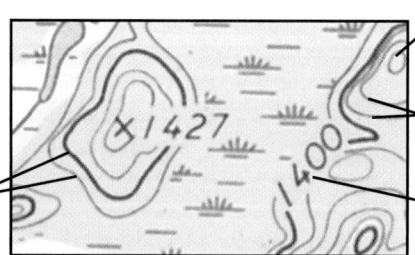

Contour lines never cross.

Closed circles represent hilltops.

Contour lines show steepness of slope.

Index contour lines show elevation.

VOCABULARY
topography p. 212
contour line p. 213
elevation p. 213
slope p. 213
relief p. 213
contour interval p. 214

---

4 **Technology is used to map Earth.**

Remote-sensing technology gathers accurate data about Earth.

Geographic information systems are computer programs used to merge layers of information.

VOCABULARY
remote sensing p. 218
sensor p. 219
false-color image p. 220
geographic information systems p. 221

Reviewing Vocabulary

Copy and complete the chart below, using vocabulary terms from this chapter.

Term	Use	Appearance
map legend	to explain map symbols	chart of symbols
1. latitude	to show distance from the equator	
2. longitude		lines going from pole to pole
3.	to show land features	rippled and smooth areas
4. map scale	to represent distances	
5. equator		line at 0° latitude
6. prime meridian	to separate east and west hemispheres	
7.	to show height above sea level	line showing elevation
8. false-color image	to highlight information	

Reviewing Key Concepts

Multiple Choice *Choose the letter of the best answer.*

9. Which Greek prefix is matched with its correct meaning?
   a. *hydro* = life
   b. *atmo* = gas
   c. *bio* = earth
   d. *geo* = water

10. What portion of Earth is covered by water?
    a. one-quarter
    b. one-half
    c. three-quarters
    d. nine-tenths

11. The continents and ocean basins are part of Earth's
    a. crust
    b. mantle
    c. outer core
    d. inner core

12. Which Earth system includes humans?
    a. atmosphere
    b. biosphere
    c. hydrosphere
    d. geosphere

13. One way the atmosphere shapes Earth's surface is by
    a. winds
    b. floods
    c. earthquakes
    d. tunnels

14. How are the major parts of the Earth system related to each other?
    a. They rarely can be studied together.
    b. They often are in conflict.
    c. They usually work independently.
    d. They continually affect each other.

15. A flat map shows Earth's curved surface by means of
    a. elevation
    b. topography
    c. relief
    d. projection

16. People use latitude and longitude lines mostly to identify
    a. map scales
    b. country names
    c. exact locations
    d. distances

17. The most accurate way to show Earth's surface is a
    a. globe
    b. conic projection
    c. cylindrical projection
    d. planar projection

18. One example of remote sensing is the use of
    a. contour lines
    b. projections
    c. GIS
    d. binoculars

Short Response *Write a short response to each question.*

19. How does the Global Positioning System work? In your answer use each of the following terms. Underline each term in your answer.

24 satellites	computer	longitude
receiver	latitude	elevation

20. How do Mercator maps distort the view of Earth's surface?

21. How do people use sensors in making maps?

Use the topographic map below to answer the next seven questions.

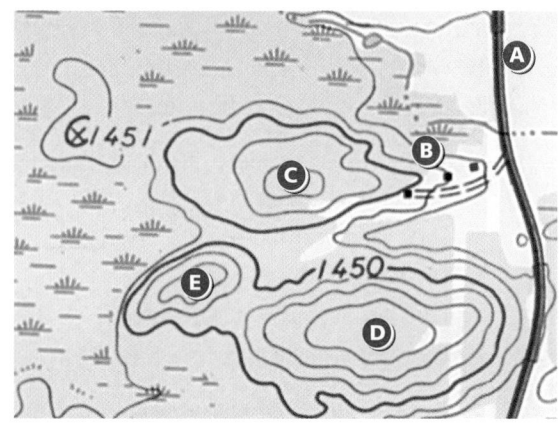

⨇ marsh	road
■ ■ buildings	unpaved road

22. APPLY Imagine you are hiking through this area. Which hill—*C, D,* or *E*—has the steepest slope? How do you know?

23. ANALYZE What is the topography of the land through which the curved road *A* goes?

24. IDENTIFY CAUSE The squares at *B* represent buildings. Why do you think the buildings were placed here instead of somewhere else in the area?

25. APPLY The contour interval is 10 meters. What is the elevation of the highest point on the map?

26. SYNTHESIZE Sketch the two hills *D* and *E*. What would they look like to someone on the ground?

27. INFER Suppose someone wanted to build a road through the terrain on the far left side of the map. What are the advantages and disadvantages of such a route?

28. EVALUATE Do you think this area would be a good place to ride mountain bikes? Why or why not?

CHART INFORMATION *On a separate sheet of paper, write a word to fill each blank in the chart.*

Feature	Shown on Topographic Maps?	Belongs to Which Major System?
rivers	*yes*	*hydrosphere*
29. slope		
30. winds		
31. plants		
32. lakes		
33. relief		

the **BIG** idea

34. APPLY Look again at the photographs on pages 194–195. Now that you have finished the chapter, reread the question on the main photograph. What would you change in or add to your answer?

35. SYNTHESIZE Describe some of the types of information that new technology has provided about Earth.

36. DRAW CONCLUSIONS What type of technology do you think has done the most to change the way people view and map Earth? Explain your conclusion.

UNIT PROJECTS

If you are doing a unit project, make a folder for your project. Include in your folder a list of the resources you will need, the date on which the project is due, and a schedule to track your progress. Begin gathering data.

FCAT Practice

Analyzing a Diagram

This diagram shows the four major parts of the Earth system. Use it to answer the questions below.

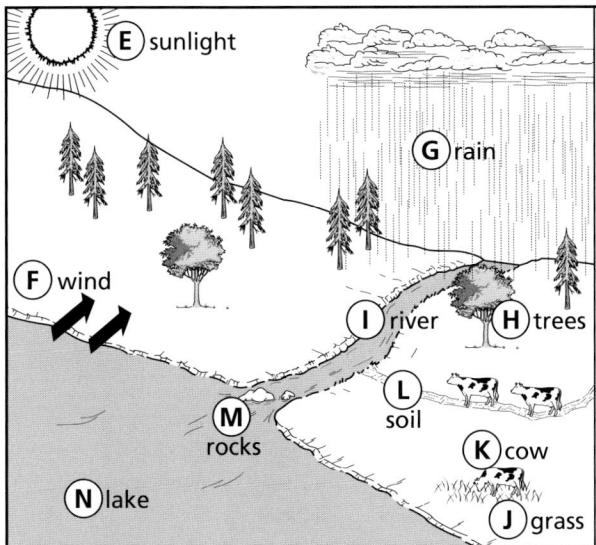

FCAT TiP

If you don't know the answer to a short-response question, finish the rest of the test and then come back to it. Other questions on the test may give you hints that will help you make an educated guess.

MULTIPLE CHOICE

1. Where is the main source of energy for the Earth system?
   A. E
   B. F
   C. G
   D. L

2. Where is the biosphere shaping the geosphere?
   F. E
   G. F
   H. L
   I. M

3. Where is matter moving from one part of the hydrosphere to another?
   A. I to N
   B. G to H
   C. J to H
   D. N to M

4. Which items belong to the geosphere?
   F. F and G
   G. H and J
   H. I and N
   I. M and L

5. Which process is occurring at M, where water is running over rocks?
   A. The geosphere is shaping the atmosphere.
   B. The atmosphere is shaping the biosphere.
   C. The hydrosphere is shaping the geosphere.
   D. The biosphere is shaping the geosphere.

6. Where is matter moving from the atmosphere to the biosphere?
   F. E and F
   G. F and M
   H. G and H
   I. I and G

SHORT RESPONSE

7. Study the diagram and describe what is taking place at K. Then explain what kind of movement in the Earth system is represented at K.

8. Study the diagram and identify a point that shows how the hydrosphere is supported by the geosphere. Explain why.

EXTENDED RESPONSE
Answer the two questions below in detail. Include some of the terms shown in the word box. In your answers, underline each term you use.

| geosphere | surface | system |
| atmosphere | hydrosphere | biosphere |

9. Rain falls and soaks into the soil. Plants and animals use some of the water. More of the water drains into a river, then enters the ocean. Describe this process as movements among the major parts of the Earth system.

10. Describe an example of how people can shape the surface of the geosphere.

Chapter 6: **Views of Earth Today** 227

CHAPTER

Weathering and Soil Formation

the BIG idea

Natural forces break rocks apart and form soil, which supports life.

How is rock related to soil?

Key Concepts

SECTION

1 Mechanical and chemical forces break down rocks.
Learn about the natural forces that break down rocks.

SECTION

2 Weathering and organic processes form soil.
Learn about the formation and properties of soil.

SECTION

3 Human activities affect soil.
Learn how land use affects soil and how soil can be protected and conserved.

FCAT Practice

Prepare and practice for the FCAT
• Section Reviews, pp. 236, 245, 252
• Chapter Review, pp. 254–256
• FCAT Practice, p. 257

CLASSZONE.COM
• Florida Review: Content Review and FCAT Practice

EXPLORE (the BIG idea)

Ice Power

Fill a plastic container to the top with water and seal the lid tightly. Place it in the freezer overnight. Check on your container the next morning.

Observe and Think
What happened to the container? Why?

Getting the Dirt on Soil

Remove the top and bottom of a tin can. Be careful of sharp edges. Measure and mark 2 cm from one end of the can. Insert the can 2 cm into the ground, up to the mark. Fill the can with water and time how long it takes for the can to drain. Repeat the procedure in a different location.

Observe and Think
What do you think affects how long it takes for soil to absorb water?

Internet Activity: Soil Formation

Go to **ClassZone.com** to watch how soil forms. Learn how materials break down and contribute to soil buildup over time.

Observe and Think
What do rocks and soil have in common? What do organic matter and soil have in common?

NSTA
scilinks.org
SCI LINKS

Soil Conservation **Code: MDL016**

Getting Ready to Learn

◀ CONCEPT REVIEW

- The atmosphere, hydrosphere, biosphere, and geosphere interact to shape Earth's surface.
- Natural processes form, change, break down, and re-form rocks.

◀ VOCABULARY REVIEW

hydrosphere p. 198

biosphere p. 199

equator p. 206

topography p. 212

FLORIDA REVIEW
CLASSZONE.COM

Content Review and FCAT Practice

▶ TAKING NOTES

COMBINATION NOTES

To take notes about a new concept, first make an informal outline of the information. Then make a sketch of the concept and label it so that you can study it later.

VOCABULARY STRATEGY

Place each vocabulary term at the center of a **description wheel**. On the spokes write some words explaining it.

See the Note-Taking Handbook on pages R45–R51.

SCIENCE NOTEBOOK

NOTES

Causes of Mechanical Weathering
- Ice
- Pressure Release
- Plant Roots
- Moving Water

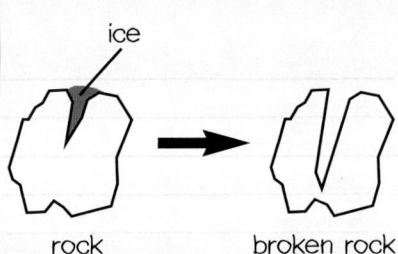

rock   broken rock

Description Wheel

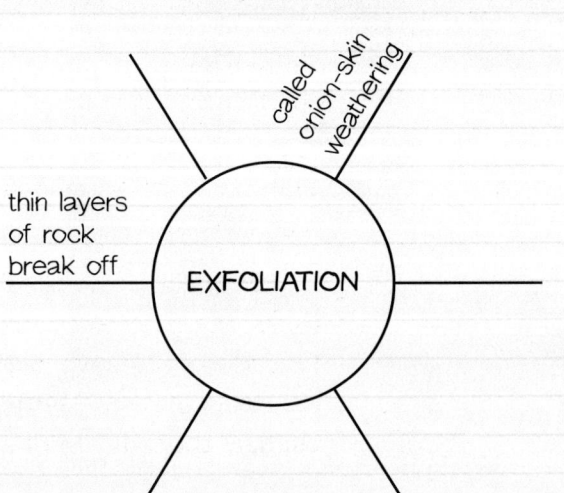

thin layers of rock break off

called onion-skin weathering

EXFOLIATION

Mechanical and chemical forces break down rocks.

FCAT VOCABULARY

weathering p. 231
chemical weathering p. 234

VOCABULARY

mechanical weathering p. 232
exfoliation p. 232
abrasion p. 232

◀ **BEFORE, you learned**

- The parts of the Earth system shape Earth's surface
- Rocks form, change, break down, and re-form through natural processes

▶ **NOW, you will learn**

- How mechanical weathering breaks down rocks
- How chemical weathering changes rocks
- What factors affect the rate at which weathering occurs

EXPLORE Mechanical Weathering

What causes rocks to break down?

PROCEDURE

1. Place a handful of rocks on a piece of dark-colored construction paper. Observe the rocks and take notes on their appearance.

2. Place the rocks in a coffee can. Put the lid on the can and shake the can forcefully for 2 minutes, holding the lid tightly shut.

3. Pour the rocks onto the construction paper. Observe them and take notes on any changes in their appearance.

MATERIALS

- coffee can with lid
- rocks
- dark-colored construction paper

WHAT DO YOU THINK?

- What happened to the rocks and why?
- What forces in nature might affect rocks in similar ways?

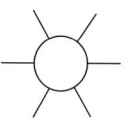

VOCABULARY
Add a description wheel for *weathering* to your notebook.

Weathering breaks rocks into smaller pieces.

Think about the tiniest rock you have ever found. How did it get so small? It didn't start out that way! Over time, natural forces break rocks into smaller and smaller pieces. If you have ever seen a concrete sidewalk or driveway that has been cracked by tree roots, you have seen this process. The same thing can happen to rocks.

Weathering is the process by which natural forces break down rocks. In this section you will read about two kinds of weathering. One kind occurs when a rock is physically broken apart—like the cracked sidewalk. Another kind occurs when a chemical reaction changes the makeup of a rock.

Mechanical weathering produces physical changes in rocks.

RESOURCE CENTER
CLASSZONE.COM

Learn more about
weathering.

READING TiP

The word *expand* means
"to increase in size
or volume."

If you smash a walnut with a hammer, you will break it into a lot of small pieces, but you will not change what it is. Even though the pieces of the walnut are no longer connected together, they are still composed of the same materials. **Mechanical weathering**—the breaking up of rocks by physical forces—works in much the same way. In this natural process, physical forces split rocks apart but do not change their composition—what they are made of. Ice wedging, pressure release, plant root growth, and abrasion can all cause mechanical weathering.

1 Ice Wedging When water freezes, it expands. When water freezes in the cracks and pores of rocks, the force of its expansion is strong enough to split the rocks apart. This process, which is called ice wedging, can break up huge boulders. Ice wedging is common in places where temperatures rise above and fall below the freezing point for water, which is 0°C (32°F).

2 Pressure Release Rock deep within Earth is under great pressure from surrounding rocks. Over time, Earth's forces can push the rock up to the surface, or the overlying rocks and sediment can wear away. In either case, the pressure inside the rock is still high, but the pressure on the surface of the rock is released. This release of pressure causes the rock to expand. As the rock expands, cracks form in it, leading to exfoliation. **Exfoliation** (ehks-FOH-lee-AY-shuhn) is a process in which layers or sheets of rock gradually break off. This process is sometimes called onion-skin weathering, because the rock surface breaks off in thin layers similar to the layers of an onion.

3 Plant Root Growth Trees, bushes, and other plants may take root in cracks in rocks. As the roots of these plants grow, they wedge open the cracks. The rock—even if it is large—can be split completely apart.

4 Abrasion Water can wear down rocks on riverbeds and along shorelines by abrasion. **Abrasion** (uh-BRAY-zhuhn) is the process of wearing down by friction, the rubbing of one object or surface against another. The force of moving water alone can wear away particles of rock. Water also causes rocks to tumble downstream. The tumbling rocks wear down as they grind against the riverbed and against each other. Ocean waves beating against a rocky shore also wear down rocks by abrasion.

 How does moving water weather rocks?

Mechanical Weathering

Ice wedging, pressure release, plant root growth, and abrasion can all break apart rocks.

① Ice Wedging

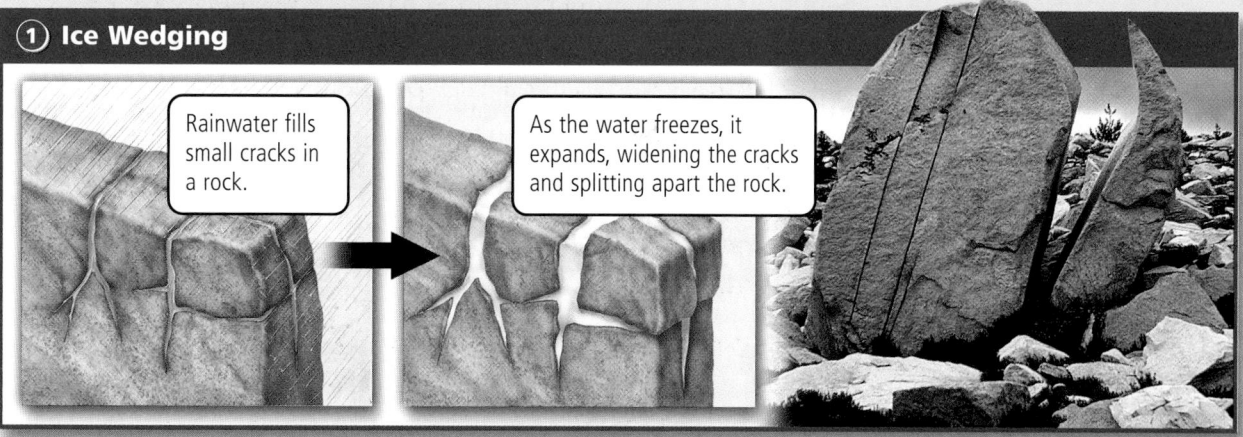

Rainwater fills small cracks in a rock.

As the water freezes, it expands, widening the cracks and splitting apart the rock.

② Pressure Release

Earth's forces can push rock that formed deep underground up to the surface.

The release of pressure causes the rock to expand and crack.

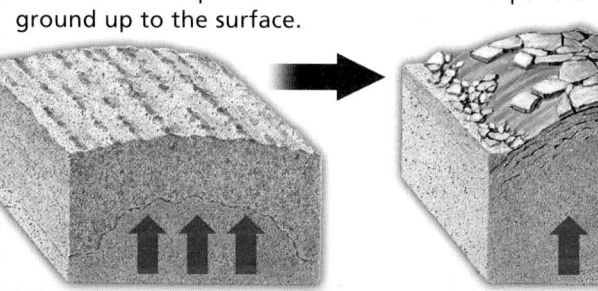

③ Plant Root Growth

When plants grow in cracks in a rock, their roots can widen the cracks and force the rock apart.

④ Abrasion

Flowing water can move rocks, causing them to rub together and wear down into rounded shapes.

READING VISUALS What evidence of mechanical weathering can you see in each photograph above?

Chemical weathering changes the mineral composition of rocks.

VISUALIZATION
CLASSZONE.COM

Watch chemical
weathering in action.

If you have seen an old rusty nail, you have witnessed the result of a chemical reaction and a chemical change. The steel in the nail contains iron. Oxygen in air and water react with the iron to form rust.

Minerals in rocks also undergo chemical changes when they react with water and air. **Chemical weathering** is the breakdown of rocks by chemical reactions that change the rocks' makeup, or composition. When minerals in rocks come into contact with air and water, some dissolve and others react and are changed into different minerals.

Dissolving

Water is the main cause of chemical weathering. Some minerals completely dissolve in ordinary water. The mineral halite, which is the same compound as table salt, dissolves in ordinary water. Many more minerals dissolve in water that is slightly acidic—like lemonade. In the atmosphere, small amounts of carbon dioxide dissolve in rainwater. The water and carbon dioxide react to form a weak acid. After falling to Earth, the rainwater moves through the soil, picking up additional

---

INVESTIGATE Chemical Weathering

What is necessary for rust to form?

PROCEDURE

1. Place a piece of steel wool in a cup filled to the top with water. Place a second piece of steel wool in a cup with a small amount of water. The water should touch but not cover the steel wool. Place a third piece in a cup with no water.

2. Allow the three cups to sit overnight. Observe the appearance of the steel wool in each container the next day.

WHAT DO YOU THINK?

- What happened to the steel wool in each cup?
- Judging by the appearance of the pieces of steel wool, what do you think is necessary for rusting to occur?

CHALLENGE Tear the steel wool that rusted most apart and compare the appearances of the inside and the outside. Why might the inside and the outside look different?

SKILL FOCUS
Identifying variables

MATERIALS
- steel wool
- 3 cups
- water

TIME
15 minutes

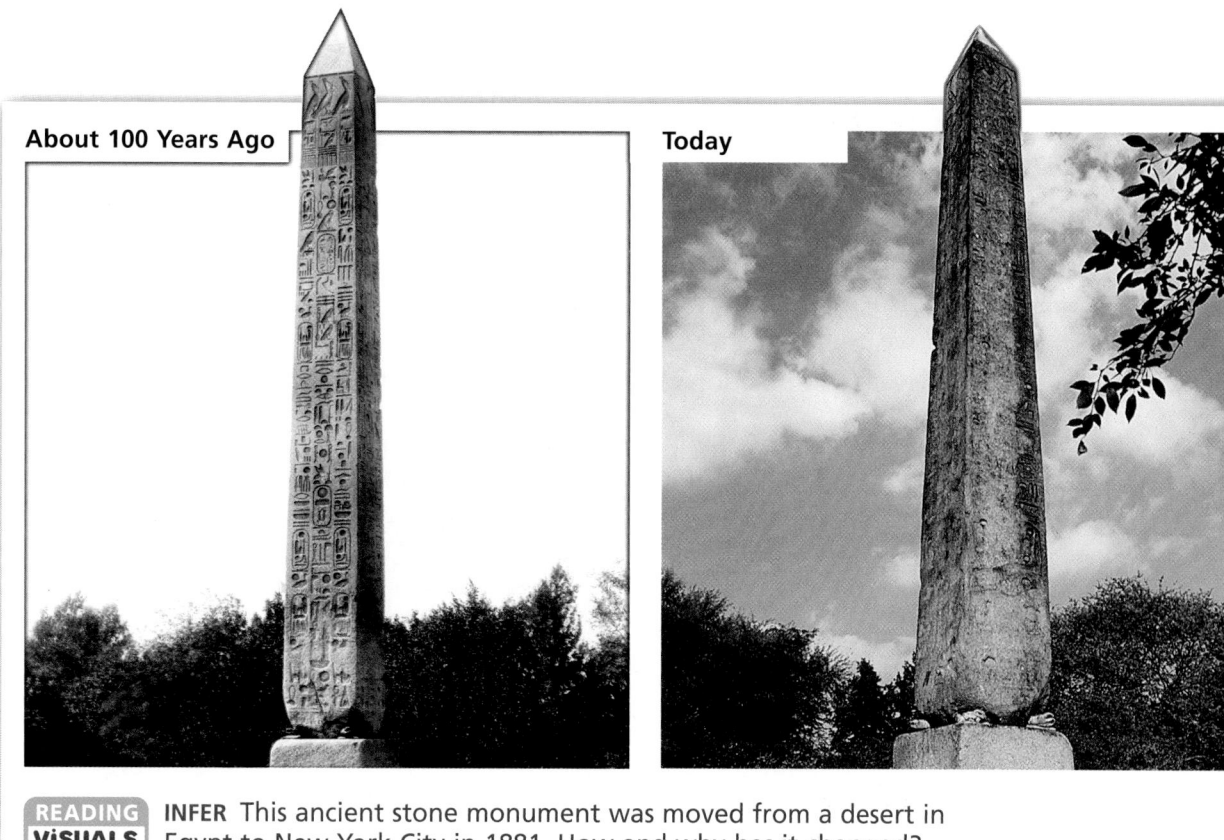

About 100 Years Ago

Today

READING VISUALS INFER This ancient stone monument was moved from a desert in Egypt to New York City in 1881. How and why has it changed?

carbon dioxide from decaying plants. The slightly acidic water breaks down minerals in rocks. In the process, the rocks may also break apart into smaller pieces.

Air pollution can make rainwater even more acidic than it is naturally. Power plants and automobiles produce gases such as sulfur dioxide and nitric oxide, which react with water vapor in the atmosphere to form acid rain. Acid rain causes rocks to weather much faster than they would naturally. The photographs above show how acid rain can damage a granite column in just a hundred years.

Rusting

The oxygen in the air is also involved in chemical weathering. Many common minerals contain iron. When these minerals dissolve in water, oxygen in the air and the water combines with the iron to produce iron oxides, or rust. The iron oxides form a coating that colors the weathered rocks like those you see in the photograph of Oak Creek Canyon in Arizona.

The rocks in Oak Creek Canyon are reddish because iron in the rocks reacted with water and air to produce iron oxides.

 CHECK YOUR READING   How is air involved in chemical weathering?

Weathering occurs at different rates.

COMBINATION NOTES
Record in your notes three factors that affect the rate at which rock weathers.

Most weathering occurs over long periods of time—hundreds, thousands, or even millions of years. It can take hundreds or thousands of years for a very hard rock to wear down only a few millimeters—a few times the thickness of your fingernail. But the rate of weathering is not the same for all rocks. Factors such as surface area, rock composition, and location influence the rate of weathering.

Surface Area The more of a rock's surface that is exposed to air and water, the faster the rock will break down. A greater surface area allows chemical weathering to affect more of a rock.

Over time, mechanical weathering breaks a rock into smaller pieces.

As a result, more of the rock's surface is exposed to chemical weathering.

Rock Composition Different kinds of rock break down at different rates. Granite, for example, breaks down much more slowly than limestone. Both of these rocks are often used for tombstones and statues.

Climate Water is needed for chemical weathering to occur, and heat speeds up chemical weathering. As a result, chemical weathering occurs faster in hot, wet regions than it does in cold, dry regions. However, mechanical weathering caused by freezing and thawing occurs more in cold regions than in hot regions.

7.1 Review

KEY CONCEPTS

1. What is weathering?
2. What are four causes of mechanical weathering?
3. How do water and air help cause chemical weathering?
4. Describe three factors that affect the rate at which weathering occurs.

CRITICAL THINKING

5. **Infer** How does mechanical weathering affect the rate of chemical weathering?
6. **Predict** Would weathering affect a marble sculpture inside a museum? Explain your answer.

◊ CHALLENGE

7. **Infer** The word *weather* is most commonly used to refer to the state of the atmosphere at a certain time. Why do you think the same word is used to refer to the breakdown of rocks?

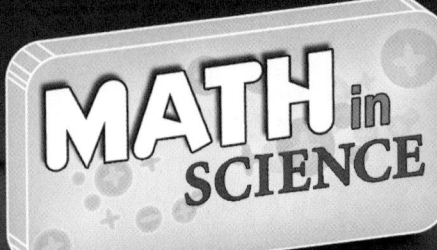

MATH TUTORIAL

CLASSZONE.COM

Click on Math Tutorial for
more help with finding
the surface areas of
rectangular prisms.

Weathering has broken apart these
rocks in the Isles of Scilly, England.

Rock Weathering

How quickly a rock weathers depends, in part, on its surface area.
The greater the surface area, the more quickly the rock weathers.
Do you think a rock will weather more quickly if you break it in half?
You can find out by using a rectangular prism to represent the rock.

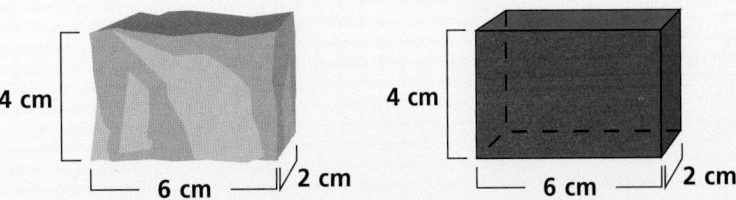

Example

To find the surface area of the prism, add the areas of its faces.

(1) Find the area of each face.

Area of top (or bottom) face: 6 cm × 2 cm = 12 cm^2
Area of front (or back) face: 6 cm × 4 cm = 24 cm^2
Area of right (or left) face: 4 cm × 2 cm = 8 cm^2

(2) Add the areas of all six faces to find the surface area.

Surface area = 12 cm^2 + 12 cm^2 + 24 cm^2 + 24 cm^2
         + 8 cm^2 + 8 cm^2
       = 88 cm^2

ANSWER The surface area of the prism is 88 cm^2.

For the rock broken in half, you can use two smaller rectangular
prisms to represent the two halves.

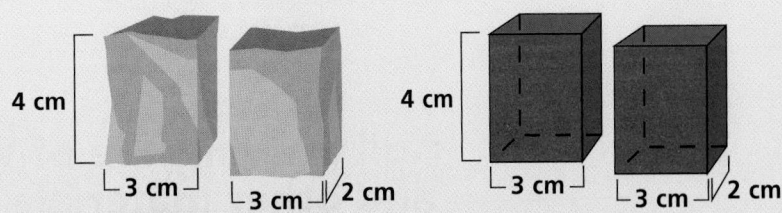

Answer the following questions.

1. What is the surface area of each of the smaller
   rectangular prisms?

2. How does the total surface area of the two smaller prisms
   compare with the surface area of the larger prism?

3. Will the rock weather more quickly in one piece or broken in half?

CHALLENGE If the two smaller prisms both broke in half, what
would be the total surface area of the resulting four prisms?

7.2 Weathering and organic processes form soil.

Sunshine State STANDARDS

SC.D.1.3.1: The student knows that mechanical and chemical activities shape and reshape the Earth's land surface by eroding rock and soil in some areas and depositing them in other areas, sometimes in seasonal layers.

SC.D.1.3.3: The student knows how conditions that exist in one system influence the conditions that exist in other systems.

SC.H.1.3.4: The student knows the ways in which plants and animals reshape the landscape.

VOCABULARY

humus p. 239
soil horizon p. 240
soil profile p. 240

BEFORE, you learned

- Weathering processes break down rocks
- Climate influences the rate of weathering

NOW, you will learn

- What soil consists of
- How climate and landforms affect a soil's characteristics
- How the activities of organisms affect a soil's characteristics
- How the properties of soil differ

EXPLORE Soil Composition

What makes soils different?

PROCEDURE

1. Spread some potting soil on a piece of white paper. Spread another type of soil on another piece of white paper.

2. Examine the two soil samples with a hand lens. Use the tweezers to look for small pieces of rock or sand, humus, and clay. Humus is brown or black, and clay is lighter in color. Record your observations.

WHAT DO YOU THINK?

- How do the two soil samples differ? How are they alike?
- What might account for the differences between the two soils?

MATERIALS

- potting soil
- local soil sample
- white paper (2 pieces)
- hand lens
- tweezers

Soil is a mixture of weathered rock particles and other materials.

Soil may not be the first thing you think of when you wake up in the morning, but it is a very important part of your everyday life. You have spent your whole life eating food grown in soil, standing on soil, and living in buildings built on soil. Soil is under your feet right now—or at least there used to be soil there before the building you are in was constructed. In this section you will learn more about the world of soil beneath your feet.

CHECK YOUR READING   Why is soil important?

Soil Composition

Soil is a mixture of four materials: weathered rock particles, organic matter, water, and air. Weathered rock particles are the main ingredient of soil. Soils differ, depending on what types of rock the rock particles came from—for example, granite or limestone.

Water and air each make up about 20 to 30 percent of a soil's volume. Organic matter makes up about 5 percent. The word *organic* (awr-GAN-ihk) means "coming from living organisms." Organic matter in soil comes from the remains and waste products of plants, animals, and other living organisms. For example, leaves that fall to a forest floor decay and become part of the soil. The decayed organic matter in soil is called **humus** (HYOO-muhs).

All soils are not the same. Different soils are made up of different ingredients and different amounts of each ingredient. In the photographs below, the black soil contains much more decayed plant material than the red soil. The black soil also contains more water. The kind of soil that forms in an area depends on a number of factors, including

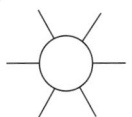

VOCABULARY
Add a description wheel for *humus* to your notebook.

- the kind of rock in the area
- the area's climate, or overall weather pattern over time
- the landforms in the area, such as mountains and valleys
- the plant cover in the area
- the animals and other organisms in the area
- time

The composition of a soil determines what you can grow in it, what you can build on it, and what happens to the rainwater that falls on it.

READING VISUALS **COMPARE AND CONTRAST** These two soils look different because they contain different ingredients. How would you describe their differences?

Soil Horizons

This soil profile in Hagerstown, Maryland, shows distinct A, B, and C horizons.

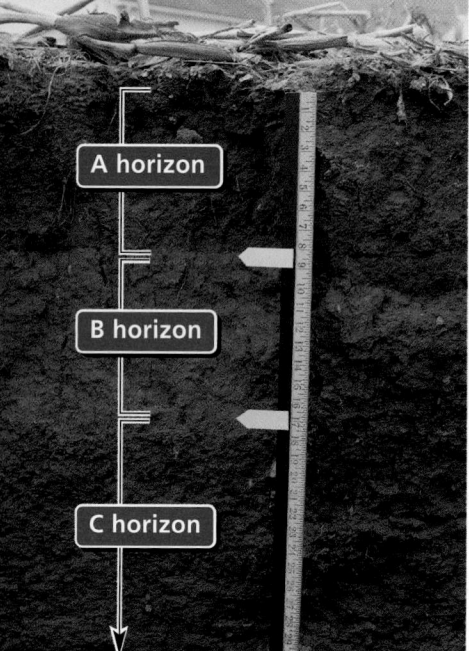

A horizon

B horizon

C horizon

If you dig a deep hole in the ground, you might notice that the deeper soil looks different. As you dig down, you will find larger rock particles that are less weathered. There is also less organic matter in deeper soil.

Soil develops in a series of horizontal layers called soil horizons. A **soil horizon** is a layer of soil with properties that differ from those of the layer above or below it. Geologists label the main horizons A, B, and C. In some places there may also be a layer of dead leaves and other organic matter at the surface of the ground.

- **The A horizon** is the upper layer of soil and is commonly called topsoil. It contains the most organic matter of the three horizons. Because of the humus the A horizon contains, it is often dark in color.

- **The B horizon** lies just below the A horizon. It has little organic matter and is usually brownish or reddish in color. It contains clay and minerals that have washed down from the A horizon.

- **The C horizon** is the deepest layer of soil. It consists of the largest and least-weathered rock particles. Its color is typically light yellowish brown.

The soil horizons in a specific location make up what geologists call a **soil profile.** Different locations can have very different soil profiles. The A horizon, for example, may be very thick in some places and very thin in others. In some areas, one or more horizons may even be missing from the profile. For example, a soil that has had only a short time to develop might be missing the B horizon.

 **CHECK YOUR READING**   What are soil horizons?

Climate and landforms affect soil.

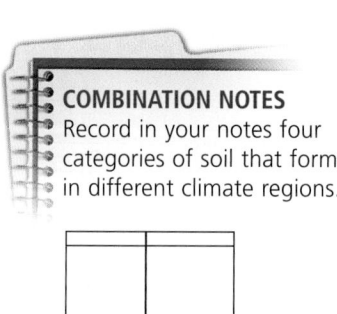

COMBINATION NOTES
Record in your notes four categories of soil that form in different climate regions.

Different kinds of soils form in different climates. The soil that forms in a hot, wet climate is different from the soil of a cold, dry climate. Climate also influences the characteristics and thickness of the soil that develops from weathered rock. Tropical, desert, temperate, and arctic soils are four types of soil that form in different climate regions.

The shape of the land also affects the development of soil. For example, mountain soils may be very different from the soils in nearby valleys. The cold climate on a mountain results in slow soil formation, and the top layer of soil continually washes down off the slopes. As a result, mountain slopes have soils with thin A horizons that cannot support large plants. The soil that washes down the slopes builds up in the surrounding valleys, so the valleys may have soils with thick A horizons that can support many plants.

World Soil Types

Different types of soils form in different climates.

Tropical Soils

Tropical soils form in warm, rainy regions. Heavy rains wash away minerals, leaving only a thin surface layer of humus. Tropical soils are not suitable for growing most crops.

Desert Soils

Desert soils form in dry regions. These soils are shallow and contain little organic matter. Because of the low rainfall, chemical weathering and soil formation occur very slowly in desert regions.

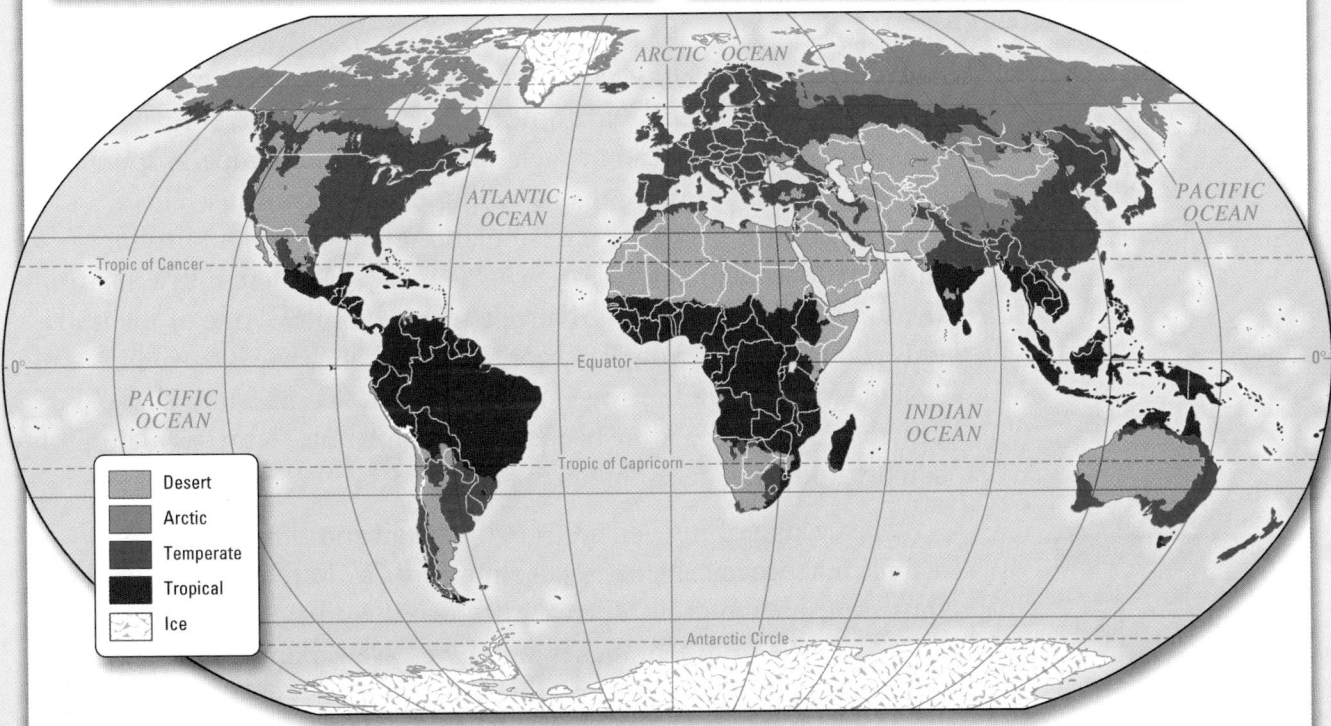

Legend:
- Desert
- Arctic
- Temperate
- Tropical
- Ice

Temperate Soils

Temperate soils form in regions with moderate rainfall and temperatures. Some temperate soils are dark-colored, rich in organic matter and minerals, and good for growing crops.

Arctic Soils

Arctic soils form in cold, dry regions where chemical weathering is slow. They typically do not have well-developed horizons. Arctic soils contain a lot of rock fragments.

The activities of organisms affect soil.

COMBINATION NOTES
Record in your notes three types of organisms that affect soil characteristics.

READING TiP

A decomposer is an organism that decomposes, or breaks down, dead plants and animals.

FLORIDA
Content Review

Plants, microorganisms, and animals are living things that reshape the landscape, as you learned in grade 6.

Under the ground beneath your feet is a whole world of life forms that are going about their daily activities. The living organisms in a soil have a huge impact on the soil's characteristics. In fact, without them, the soil would not be able to support the wide variety of plants that people depend on to live. The organisms that affect the characteristics of soils include plants, microorganisms (MY-kroh-AWR-guh-NIHZ-uhmz), and animals.

Plants, such as trees and grasses, provide most of the organic matter that gets broken down to form humus. Trees add to the organic matter in soil as they lose their branches and leaves. Trees and other plants also contribute to humus when they die and decompose, or break down.

 **CHECK YOUR READING** How are plants and humus related?

Microorganisms include decomposers such as bacteria and fungi (FUHN-jy). The prefix *micro-* means "very small." Microorganisms are so small that they can be seen only with a microscope. A spoonful of soil may contain more than a million microorganisms! These microorganisms decompose dead plants and animals and produce nutrients that plants need to grow. Plants absorb these nutrients from the soil through their roots. Nitrogen, for example, is one of the nutrients plants need to grow. Microorganisms change the nitrogen in dead organic matter—and nitrogen in the air—into compounds that plants can absorb and use. Some bacteria also contribute to the formation of soil by producing acids that break down rocks.

The cycling of nutrients through the soil and through plants is a continual process. Plants absorb nutrients from the soil and use those nutrients to grow. Then they return the nutrients to the soil when they die or lose branches and leaves. New plants then absorb the nutrients from the soil and start the cycle over again.

Animals such as earthworms, ants, termites, mice, gophers, moles, and prairie dogs all make their homes in the soil. All of these animals loosen and mix the soil as they tunnel through it. They create spaces in the soil, thereby adding to its air content and improving its ability to absorb and drain water. Burrowing animals also bring partly weathered rock particles to the surface of the ground, where they become exposed to more weathering. Just like plants, animals return nutrients to the soil when their bodies decompose after death.

CHECK YOUR READING How do animals affect soil? Name at least three ways.

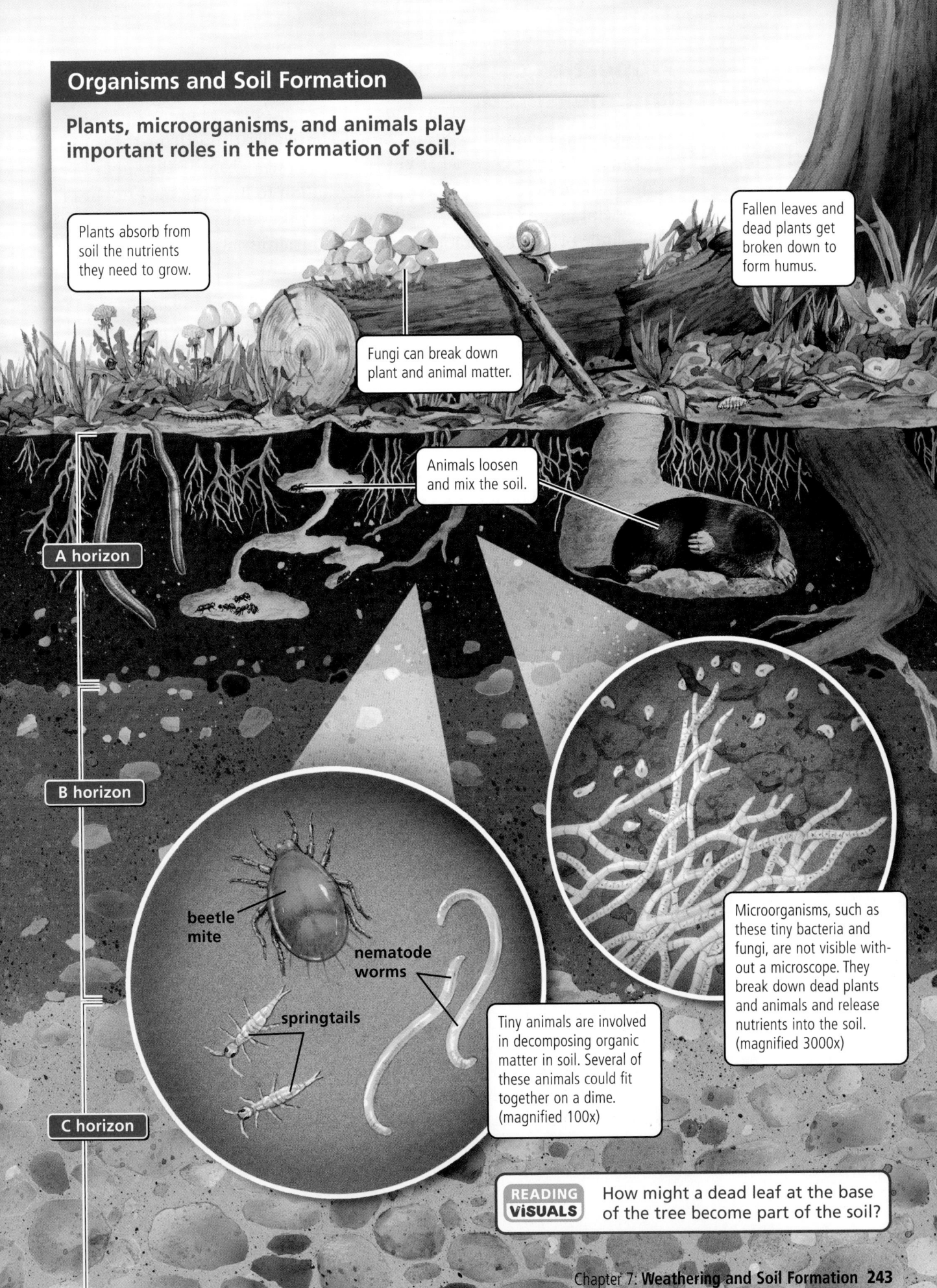

Organisms and Soil Formation

Plants, microorganisms, and animals play important roles in the formation of soil.

Plants absorb from soil the nutrients they need to grow.

Fungi can break down plant and animal matter.

Fallen leaves and dead plants get broken down to form humus.

Animals loosen and mix the soil.

A horizon

B horizon

C horizon

beetle mite

nematode worms

springtails

Tiny animals are involved in decomposing organic matter in soil. Several of these animals could fit together on a dime. (magnified 100x)

Microorganisms, such as these tiny bacteria and fungi, are not visible without a microscope. They break down dead plants and animals and release nutrients into the soil. (magnified 3000x)

READING VISUALS How might a dead leaf at the base of the tree become part of the soil?

Properties of soil can be observed and measured.

Observations and tests of soil samples reveal what nutrients the soils contain and therefore what kinds of plants will grow best in them. Farmers and gardeners use this information to improve the growth of crops and other plants. Soil scientists study many soil properties, including texture, color, pore space, and chemistry.

Texture

The texture of a soil is determined by the size of the weathered rock particles it contains. Soil scientists classify the rock particles in soils into three categories, on the basis of size: sand, silt, and clay. Sand particles are the largest and can be seen without a microscope. Silt particles are smaller than sand particles—too small to be seen without a microscope. Clay particles are the smallest. Most soils contain a mixture of sand, silt, and clay. The texture of a soil influences how easily air and water move through the soil.

Soil Texture

The texture of a soil is determined by the amounts of sand, silt, and clay it contains.

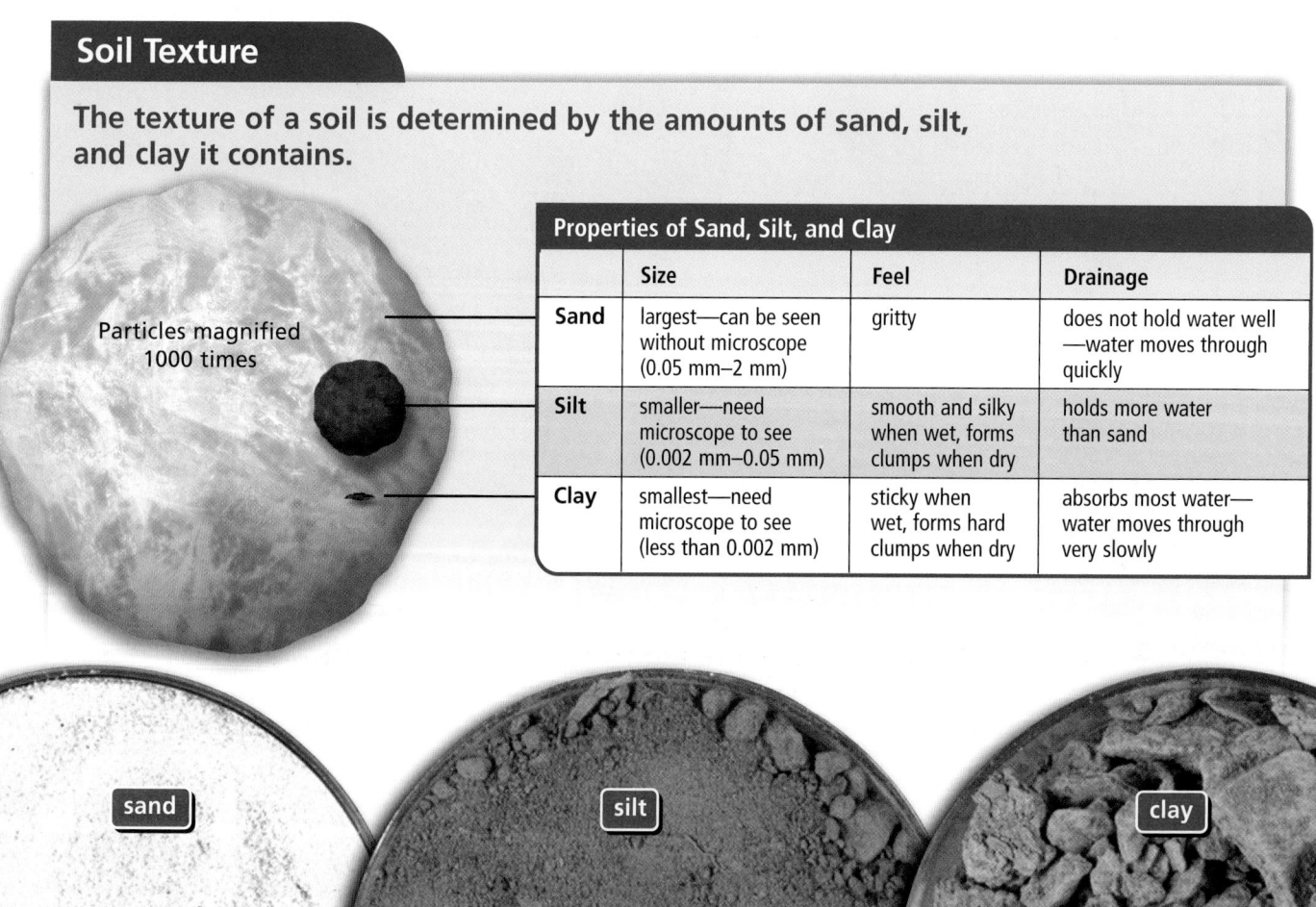

Particles magnified 1000 times

Properties of Sand, Silt, and Clay			
	Size	**Feel**	**Drainage**
Sand	largest—can be seen without microscope (0.05 mm–2 mm)	gritty	does not hold water well —water moves through quickly
Silt	smaller—need microscope to see (0.002 mm–0.05 mm)	smooth and silky when wet, forms clumps when dry	holds more water than sand
Clay	smallest—need microscope to see (less than 0.002 mm)	sticky when wet, forms hard clumps when dry	absorbs most water— water moves through very slowly

sand

silt

clay

Color

The color of a soil is a clue to its other properties. Soil colors include red, brown, yellow, green, black, and even white. Most soil colors come from iron compounds and humus. Iron gives soil a reddish color. Soils with a high humus content are usually black or brown. Besides indicating the content of a soil, color may also be a clue to how well water moves through the soil—that is, how well the soil drains. Bright-colored soils, for instance, drain well.

RESOURCE CENTER
CLASSZONE.COM

Investigate soil.

Pore Space

Pore space refers to the spaces between soil particles. Water and air move through the pore spaces in a soil. Plant roots need both water and air to grow. Soils range from about 25 to 60 percent pore space. An ideal soil for growing plants has 50 percent of its volume as pore space, with half of the pore space occupied by air and half by water.

This gardener is adding lime to the soil to make it less acidic.

Chemistry

Plants absorb the nutrients they need from the water in soil. These nutrients may come from the minerals or the organic matter in the soil. To be available to plant roots, the nutrients must be dissolved in water. How well nutrients dissolve in the water in soil depends on the water's pH, which is a measure of acidity. Farmers may apply lime to make soil less acidic. To make soil more acidic, an acid may be applied.

 CHECK YOUR READING   How does soil acidity affect whether the nutrients in soil are available to plants?

7.2 Review

KEY CONCEPTS

1. What are the main ingredients of soil?

2. How do climate and landforms affect soils' characteristics?

3. How do the activities of organisms affect the characteristics of soil?

4. Describe four properties of soil.

CRITICAL THINKING

5. **Compare and Contrast** How would a soil containing a lot of sand differ from a soil with a lot of clay?

6. **Infer** Which would you expect to be more fertile, the soil on hilly land or the soil on a plain? Why?

CHALLENGE

7. **Synthesize** What kinds of roots might you expect to find on plants that grow in arctic soils? Why?

CHAPTER INVESTIGATION

Testing Soil

OVERVIEW AND PURPOSE Soil is necessary for life. Whether a soil is suitable for farming or construction, and whether it absorbs water when it rains, depends on the particular properties of that soil. In this investigation you will
- test a soil sample to measure several soil properties
- identify the properties of your soil sample

▶ Procedure

PORE-SPACE TEST

1. Measure 200 mL of the dried soil sample in a graduated cylinder. Pour it into the jar.

2. Rinse the graduated cylinder, then fill it with 200 mL of water. Slowly pour the water into the jar until the soil is so soaked that any additional water would pool on top.

3. Record the amount of water remaining in the graduated cylinder. Then determine by subtraction the amount you added to the soil sample. Make a soil properties chart in your **Science Notebook** and record this number in it.

4. Discard the wet soil according to your teacher's instructions, and rinse the jar.

pH TEST AND DRAINAGE TEST

5. Cut off the top of a plastic bottle and use a rubber band to attach a piece of window screening over its mouth. Place the bottle top, mouth down, into the jar.

6. Use the graduated cylinder to measure 200 mL of soil, and pour the soil into the inverted bottle top.

7. Rinse the graduated cylinder, and fill it with 100 mL of water. Test the water's pH, using a pH test strip. Record the result in the "before" space in your soil properties chart.

8. Pour the water into the soil. Measure the amount of time it takes for the first drips to fall into the jar. Record the result in your soil properties chart.

MATERIALS
- dried soil sample
- 250 mL graduated cylinder
- 1 qt jar, with lid
- water
- 2 L plastic bottle
- scissors
- window screening
- rubber band
- pH test strips
- clock with second hand
- *for Challenge:* Texture Flow Chart

top of plastic bottle

jar

step 5

window screening

9 Once the water stops dripping, remove the bottle top. Use a new pH strip to measure the pH of the water in the jar. Record this measurement in the "after" space in your soil properties chart and note any differences in the appearance of the water before and after its filtering through the soil.

10 Discard the wet soil according to your teacher's instructions, and rinse the jar.

PARTICLE-TYPE TEST

11 Add water to the jar until it is two-thirds full. Pour in soil until the water level rises to the top of the jar, then replace the lid. Shake the jar, and set it to rest undisturbed on a countertop overnight.

12 The next day, observe the different soil layers. The sample should have separated into sand (on the bottom), silt (in the middle), and clay (on the top). Measure the height of each layer, as well as the overall height of the three layers. Record your measurements in your soil properties chart.

13 Use the following formula to calculate the percentage of each kind of particle in the sample:

$$\frac{\text{height of layer}}{\text{total height of all layers}} \times 100$$

Record your results and all calculations in your soil properties chart.

▶ Observe and Analyze   Write It Up

1. **RECORD** Complete your soil properties chart.

2. **IDENTIFY** How did steps 1–3 test your soil sample's pore space?

3. **IDENTIFY** How did steps 5–9 test your soil sample's drainage rate?

▶ Conclude   Write It Up

1. **EVALUATE** In step 3 you measured the amount of space between the soil particles in your sample. In step 8 you measured how quickly water passed through your sample. Are these two properties related? Explain your answer.

2. **EVALUATE** Would packing down or loosening up your soil sample change any of the properties you tested? Explain your answer.

3. **INTERPRET** What happened to the pH of the water that passed through the soil? Why do you think that happened?

4. **ANALYZE** Look at the percentages of sand, silt, and clay in your sample. How do the percentages help to explain the properties you observed and measured?

▶ INVESTIGATE Further

CHALLENGE Soil texture depends on the size of the weathered rock particles the soil contains. Use the Texture Flow Chart to determine the texture of your soil sample.

Testing Soil
Observe and Analyze
Table 1. Soil Properties Chart

Property	Result	Notes and Calculations
Pore space	— mL water added	
pH	before: pH = — after: pH = —	
Drainage	— seconds	
Particle type	height of sand = — cm height of silt = — cm height of clay = — cm total height = — cm	

Conclude

7.3 Human activities affect soil.

Sunshine State STANDARDS

SC.D.1.3.1: The student knows that mechanical and chemical activities shape and reshape the Earth's land surface by eroding rock and soil in some areas and depositing them in other areas, sometimes in seasonal layers.

SC.G.2.3.1: The student knows that some resources are renewable and others are nonrenewable.

SC.H.1.3.4: The student knows the ways in which plants and animals reshape the landscape.

VOCABULARY
desertification p. 249

BEFORE, you learned

- Soils consist mainly of weathered rock and organic matter
- Soils vary, depending on climate
- Organisms affect the characteristics of soil
- Soil properties can be measured

NOW, you will learn

- Why soil is a necessary resource
- How people's use of land affects soil
- How people can conserve soil

THINK ABOUT

How does land use affect soil?

Look outside for evidence of ways that people have affected the soil. Make a list of all the things that you can see or think of. Use your list to make a two-column table with the headings "Activity" and "Effects."

Soil is a necessary resource.

Soil helps sustain life on Earth—including your life. You already know that soil supports the growth of plants, which in turn supply food for animals. Therefore, soil provides you with nearly all the food you eat. But that's not all. Many other items you use, such as cotton clothing and medicines, come from plants. Lumber in your home comes from trees. Even the oxygen you breathe comes from plants.

Besides supporting the growth of plants, soil plays other life-sustaining roles. Soil helps purify, or clean, water as it drains through the ground and into rivers, lakes, and oceans. Decomposers in soil also help recycle nutrients by breaking down the remains of plants and animals, releasing nutrients that living plants use to grow. In addition, soil provides a home for a variety of living things, from tiny one-celled organisms to small mammals.

CHECK YOUR READING   Why is soil a necessary resource?

Land-use practices can harm soil.

The way people use land can affect the levels of nutrients and pollution in soil. Any activity that exposes soil to wind and rain can lead to soil loss. Farming, construction and development, and mining are among the main activities that impact soil resources.

Farming

Farming is very important to society because almost all of the world's food is grown on farms. Over the 10,000 years humans have been farming, people have continually improved their farming methods. However, farming has some harmful effects and can lead to soil loss.

Farmers often add nutrients to soil in the form of organic or artificial fertilizers to make their crops grow better. However, some fertilizers can make it difficult for microorganisms in the soil to produce nutrients naturally. Fertilizers also add to water pollution when rainwater draining from fields carries the excess nutrients to rivers, lakes, and oceans.

Over time, many farming practices lead to the loss of soil. All over the world, farmers clear trees and other plants and plow up the soil to plant crops. Without its natural plant cover, the soil is more exposed to rain and wind and is therefore more likely to get washed or blown away. American farmers lose about five metric tons of soil for each metric ton of grain they produce. In many other parts of the world, the losses are even higher.

Another problem is overgrazing. Overgrazing occurs when farm animals eat large amounts of the land cover. Overgrazing destroys natural vegetation and causes the soil to wash or blow away more easily. In many dry regions of the world, overgrazing and the clearing of land for farming have led to desertification. **Desertification** (dih-ZUR-tuh-fih-KAY-shuhn) is the expansion of desert conditions in areas where the natural plant cover has been destroyed.

COMBINATION NOTES
Remember to take notes about how farming affects soil.

FLORIDA
Content Review

Farming is an example of how humans impact the ecosystems, as you learned in grade 6.

Exposed soil can be blown away by wind or washed away by rain.

The top of this hill in San Bernardino County, California, was cleared for a housing development. A house will be built on each flat plot of land.

Construction and Development

To make roads, houses, shopping malls, and other buildings, people need to dig up the soil. Some of the soil at construction sites washes or blows away because its protective plant cover has been removed. The soil that is washed or blown away ends up in nearby low-lying areas, in rivers and streams, or in downstream lakes or reservoirs. This soil can cause problems by making rivers and lakes muddy and harming the organisms that live in them. The buildup of soil on riverbeds raises the level of the rivers and may cause flooding. The soil can also fill up lakes and reservoirs.

Mining

Some methods of mining cause soil loss. For example, the digging of strip mines and open-pit mines involves the removal of plants and soil from the surface of the ground.

By exposing rocks and minerals to the air and to rainwater, these forms of mining speed up the rate of chemical weathering. In mining operations that expose sulfide minerals, the increased chemical weathering causes a type of pollution known as acid drainage. Abandoned mines can fill with rainwater. Sulfide minerals react with the air and the water to produce sulfuric acid. Then the acid water drains from the mines, polluting the soil in surrounding areas.

CHECK YOUR READING How do some methods of mining affect the soil?

To make this open-pit mine in Cananea, Mexico, plants and soil were removed from the surface of the ground.

Soil can be protected and conserved.

Soil conservation is very important, because soil can be difficult or impossible to replace once it has been lost. Soil takes a very long time to form. A soil with well-developed horizons may take hundreds of thousands of years to form! Most soil conservation methods are designed to hold soil in place and keep it fertile. Below are descriptions of a few of the many soil conservation methods that are used by farmers around the world.

Crop rotation is the practice of planting different crops on the same field in different years or growing seasons. Grain crops, such as wheat, use up a lot of the nitrogen—a necessary plant nutrient—in the soil. The roots of bean crops, such as soybeans, contain bacteria that restore nitrogen to the soil. By rotating these crops, farmers can help maintain soil fertility.

Conservation tillage includes several methods of reducing the number of times fields are tilled, or plowed, in a year. The less soil is disturbed by plowing, the less likely it is to be washed or blown away. In one method of conservation tillage, fields are not plowed at all. The remains of harvested crops are simply left on the fields to cover and protect the soil. New seeds are planted in narrow bands of soil.

INVESTIGATE Soil Conservation

How can you model Earth's soil with an apple?

PROCEDURE

1. Fill in a row of the Apple Chart as you complete each step.
2. Cut the apple into quarters. Set aside three of the quarters.
3. Cut the remaining quarter in half. Set aside one of these pieces.
4. Cut the remaining piece from step 3 into four pieces. Set aside three of them.
5. Peel the skin off the remaining piece from step 4.

WHAT DO YOU THINK?

- How does the amount of fertile soil on Earth compare with what you expected?
- Do you think that the amount of fertile soil on Earth is increasing or decreasing? Explain your answer.

CHALLENGE Invent a method of soil conservation other than the ones you have read about. How would your method help keep soil in place?

SKILL FOCUS
Making models

MATERIALS
- Apple Chart
- apple
- plastic knife

TIME
20 minutes

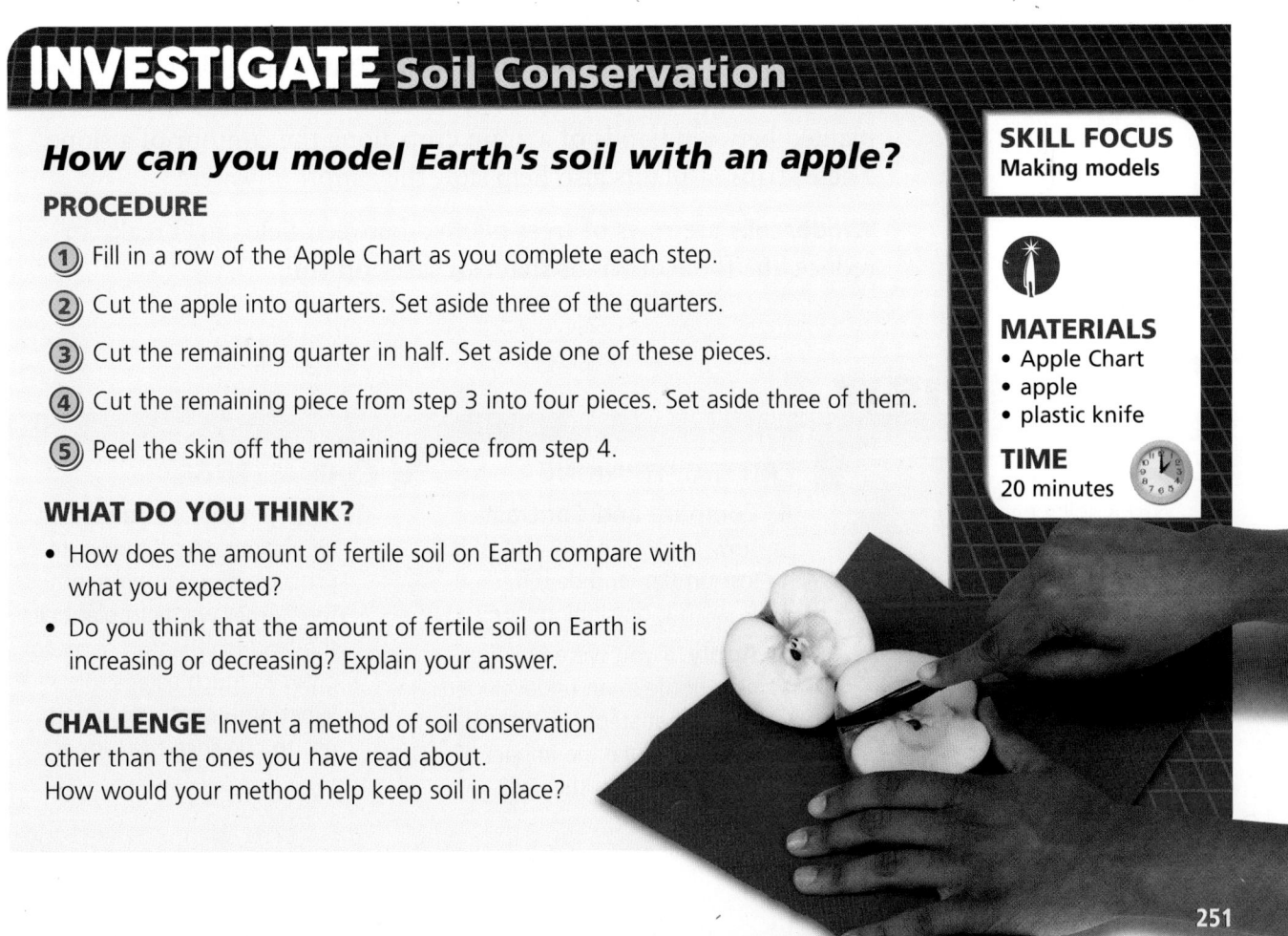

251

Terracing

Contour Plowing

COMPARE Both terracing and contour plowing are soil conservation methods used on sloping land. How does each method help conserve soil?

Terraces are flat, steplike areas built on a hillside to hold rainwater and prevent it from running downhill. Crops are planted on the flat tops of the terraces.

Contour plowing is the practice of plowing along the curves, or contours, of a slope. Contour plowing helps channel rainwater so that it does not run straight downhill, carrying away soil with it. A soil conservation method called strip-cropping is often combined with contour plowing. Strips of grasses, shrubs, or other plants are planted between bands of a grain crop along the contour of a slope. These strips of plants also help slow the runoff of water.

Windbreaks are rows of trees planted between fields to "break," or reduce, the force of winds that can carry off soil.

7.3 Review

KEY CONCEPTS

1. Why is soil a necessary resource?

2. How do land-use practices in farming, construction and development, and mining affect soil?

3. Describe at least three methods of soil conservation.

CRITICAL THINKING

4. **Compare and Contrast** How might the problem of soil loss on flat land be different from that on sloping land?

5. **Apply** If you were building a new home in an undeveloped area, what steps would you take to reduce the impact of construction on the soil?

○ CHALLENGE

6. **Apply** You have advised an inexperienced farmer to practice strip-cropping, but the farmer wants to plant all the land in wheat in order to grow as much as possible. What argument would you use to convince the farmer?

LANDSCAPE ARCHITECT

Soil, Water, and Architecture

Landscape architects design the landscapes around buildings and in parks. For example, they decide where to build sidewalks and where to place benches. Since flowing water can wash away soil, they try to control how water moves. They select plants, modify the slope of the land, and install drainage systems that will control the water. The plan below was used to build the park shown in the photographs.

Existing Plants

Large oak trees were already growing on the land. The trees were left in place to provide shade and help protect the soil.

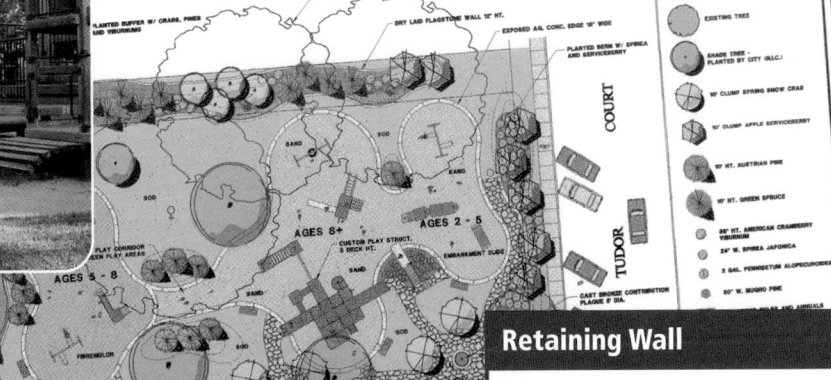

Retaining Wall

The landscape architect added mounds of soil planted with bushes to help divide the inside of the park from the roads around it. Stone walls hold the soil of the mounds in place. Without the walls, the soil would wash down onto the walkways.

Plan for New Park

A landscape architect used a computer program to draw this plan for a park. The program is designed to make the plan look as if it were drawn by hand.

EXPLORE

1. ANALYZE Examine the soil, drainage, plants, and other elements of the landscape of a park or the area around a building. Describe any areas where soil may wash away.

2. CHALLENGE Design a landscape surrounding a new school, stadium, or other building. Draw a sketch and add notes to explain your choices of locations for trees, sidewalks, and other features.

Chapter Review

the BIG idea

Natural forces break rocks apart and form soil, which supports life.

FLORIDA REVIEW
CLASSZONE.COM

Content Review and
FCAT Practice

KEY CONCEPTS SUMMARY

1 **Mechanical and chemical forces break down rocks.**

Over time, **mechanical weathering** breaks a rock into smaller pieces.

Chemical weathering affects exposed rock surfaces.

VOCABULARY
weathering p. 231
mechanical weathering p. 232
exfoliation p. 232
abrasion p. 232
chemical weathering p. 234

2 **Weathering and organic processes form soil.**

Soil has measurable properties, such as color, texture, pore space, and chemistry.

Soil is a mixture of weathered rock, organic matter, water, and air.

Plants, microorganisms, and animals affect soil characteristics.

VOCABULARY
humus p. 239
soil horizon p. 240
soil profile p. 240

3 **Human activities affect soil.**

Soil is essential to life and takes a long time to form. It is difficult or impossible to replace soil that has been lost.

Soil Loss

Farming, construction and development, and mining are three human activities that affect soil.

Soil Conservation

Soil conservation practices help keep soil from blowing or washing away.

VOCABULARY
desertification p. 249

Reviewing Vocabulary

Copy the three-column chart below. Complete the chart for each term. The first one has been done for you.

Term	Definition	Example
EXAMPLE chemical weathering	the breakdown of rocks by chemical reactions that change the rocks' mineral composition	Iron reacts with air and water to form iron oxides or rust.
1. mechanical weathering		
2. abrasion		
3. exfoliation		
4. desertification		

Reviewing Key Concepts

Multiple Choice *Choose the letter of the best answer.*

5. The force of expanding water in the cracks and pores of a rock is an example of
   - **a.** chemical weathering
   - **b.** mechanical weathering
   - **c.** oxidation
   - **d.** desertification

6. The breakdown of a rock by acidic water is an example of
   - **a.** chemical weathering
   - **b.** mechanical weathering
   - **c.** oxidation
   - **d.** desertification

7. Soil is a mixture of what four materials?
   - **a.** granite, limestone, nitrogen, and air
   - **b.** plant roots, iron oxides, water, and air
   - **c.** rock particles, plant roots, humus, and nitrogen
   - **d.** rock particles, humus, water, and air

8. What is the main component of soil?
   - **a.** humus
   - **b.** water
   - **c.** air
   - **d.** rock particles

9. What is humus?
   - **a.** the decomposed rock particles in soil
   - **b.** the decomposed organic matter in soil
   - **c.** the material that makes up the B horizon
   - **d.** the material that makes up the C horizon

10. Three factors that affect the rate of weathering are
    - **a.** microorganisms, plants, and animals
    - **b.** weather, landforms, and rainfall
    - **c.** surface area, rock composition, and climate
    - **d.** texture, color, and pore space

11. Microorganisms affect the quality of soil by
    - **a.** decomposing organic matter
    - **b.** creating tunnels
    - **c.** absorbing water
    - **d.** increasing mechanical weathering

12. The movement of air and water through a soil is influenced most by the soil's
    - **a.** color and chemistry
    - **b.** texture and pore space
    - **c.** pH and nitrogen content
    - **d.** microorganisms

13. Contour plowing, strip-cropping, and terracing are conservation methods designed to reduce the
    - **a.** runoff of water
    - **b.** activity of microorganisms
    - **c.** acidity of soil
    - **d.** pore space of soil

Short Response *Write a short response to each question.*

14. How do farming, construction and development, and mining affect soil?

15. How do ice wedging, pressure release, plant root growth, and abrasion cause mechanical weathering?

16. How do air and water cause chemical weathering?

Thinking Critically

Use the photograph to answer the next three questions.

17. APPLY Make a sketch of the soil profile above, labeling the A, B, and C horizons.

18. OBSERVE What does the color of the top layer indicate about this soil?

19. APPLY Which part of the profile is most affected by chemical and mechanical weathering? Why?

20. APPLY Suppose that you own gently sloping farmland. Describe the methods that you would use to hold the soil in place and maintain its fertility.

21. SYNTHESIZE Describe the composition, color, texture, and amount of pore space of a soil that would be good for growing crops.

22. COMPARE AND CONTRAST How does mechanical weathering differ from chemical weathering? How are the two processes similar?

23. PREDICT What effect will the continued growth of the world's population likely have on soil resources?

24. ANALYZE Soil loss is a problem all over the world. Where might lost soil end up?

25. ANALYZE Can lost soil be replaced? Explain.

26. ANALYZE Copy the concept map below and fill it in with the following terms and phrases.

acidic water	chemical weathering
damaged statue	exfoliation
mechanical weathering	moving water
oxygen and water	pressure release
rounded rocks	rust

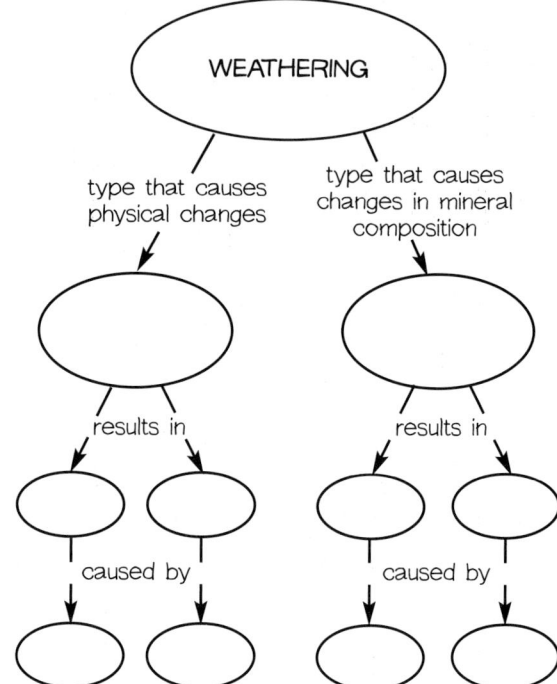

27. ANALYZE Add to the concept map to show the three factors that affect the rate of weathering.

the BIG idea

28. MODEL Draw a diagram that shows an example of a natural force breaking rocks apart to form soil that supports life.

29. SYNTHESIZE A cycle is a series of events or actions that repeats regularly. Describe a cycle that involves soil and living things.

UNIT PROJECTS

If you need to create graphs or other visuals for your project, be sure you have grid paper, poster board, markers, or other supplies.

Analyzing a Table

The table indicates some of the characteristics of four soil samples. Use the table to answer the questions below.

FCAT TiP

When answering multiple-choice questions, read all of the answer choices before you decide on the correct one.

Sample	Color	Ability to Hold Water	Percentage of Pore Space	Percentage of Humus
1	black	average	50%	9%
2	yellowish brown	low	70%	3%
3	reddish brown	average	60%	3%
4	very red	average to low	65%	2%

MULTIPLE CHOICE

1. Soils that contain a lot of sand do not hold water very well. Which sample probably contains the most sand?

    A. 1   **C.** 3

    B. 2   **D.** 4

2. Iron gives soil a reddish color. Which sample probably contains the most iron?

    F. 1   **H.** 3

    G. 2   **I.** 4

3. Crops grow best in soils with about half of their volume consisting of pore space. Which soil has an ideal amount of pore space for growing crops?

    A. 1   **C.** 3

    B. 2   **D.** 4

SHORT RESPONSE

4. Identify which soil color might indicate a high level of organic matter and explain why.

5. Explain how pore space is related to soil's ability to hold water.

EXTENDED RESPONSE

Answer the two questions below in detail. Include some of the terms shown in the word box. In your answers, underline each term you use.

abrasion	moving water
chemical weathering	plant roots
ice	rusting
mechanical weathering	

6. Jolene is comparing a rock from a riverbed and a rock from deep underground. One is very smooth. The other has very sharp edges. Explain which rock was probably found in each location.

7. In a museum, Hank sees two iron knives that were made in the early 1800s. One has spent 200 years on the top of a fortress wall. The other one has been stored in the museum for 200 years. Why might the two knives look different?

CHAPTER 8

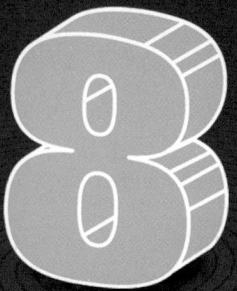

Erosion and Deposition

the **BIG** idea

Water, wind, and ice shape Earth's surface.

How can ice carve a valley?

Key Concepts

SECTION 1
Forces wear down and build up Earth's surface.
Learn how natural forces shape and change the land.

SECTION 2
Moving water shapes land.
Learn about the effects of water moving over land and underground.

SECTION 3
Waves and wind shape land.
Discover how waves and wind affect land.

SECTION 4
Glaciers carve land and move sediments.
Learn about the effect of ice moving over land.

FCAT Practice

Prepare and practice for the FCAT
- Section Reviews, pp. 265, 271, 279, 286
- Chapter Review, pp. 288–290
- FCAT Practice, p. 291

CLASSZONE.COM
- Florida Review: Content Review and FCAT Practice

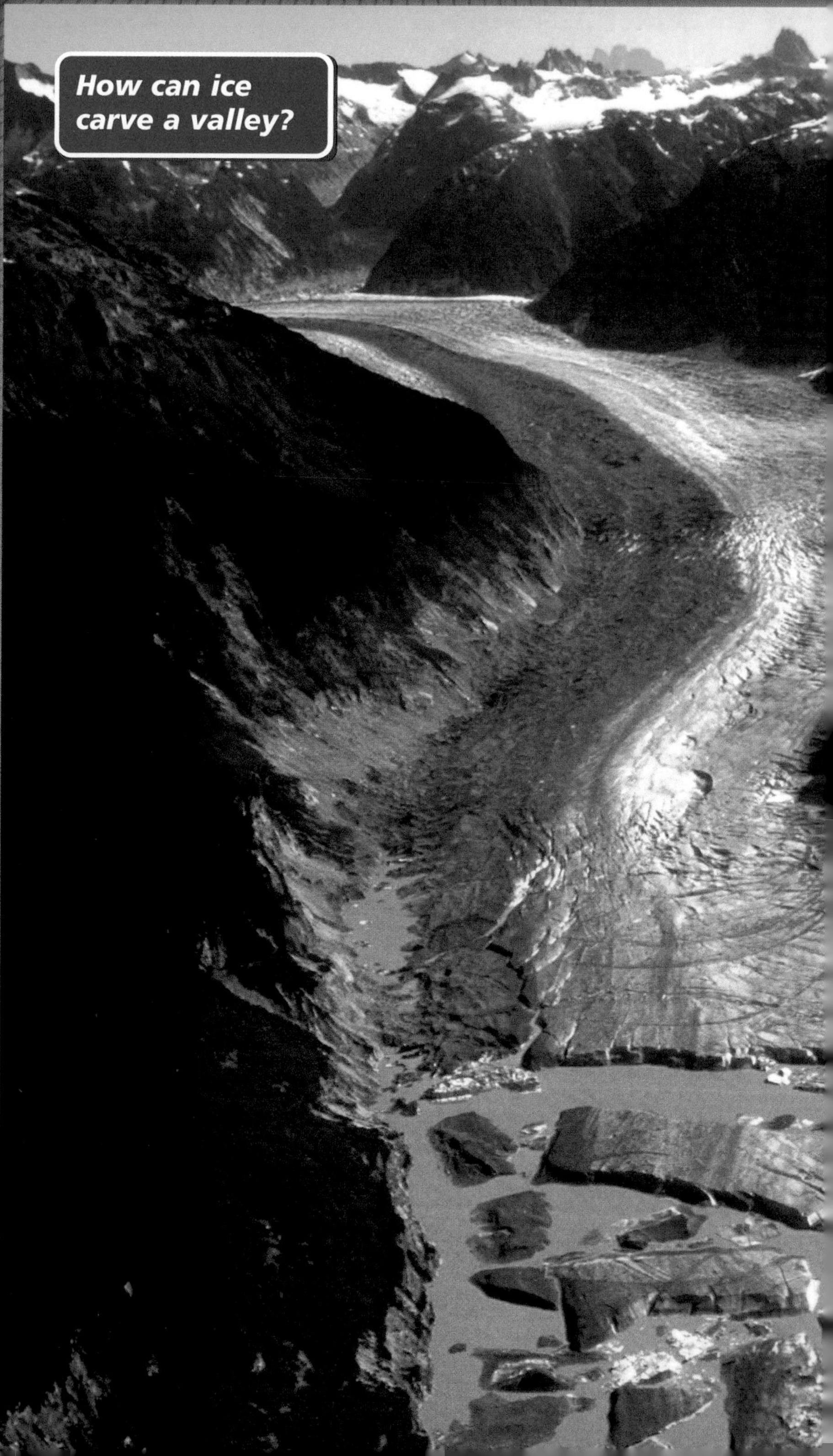

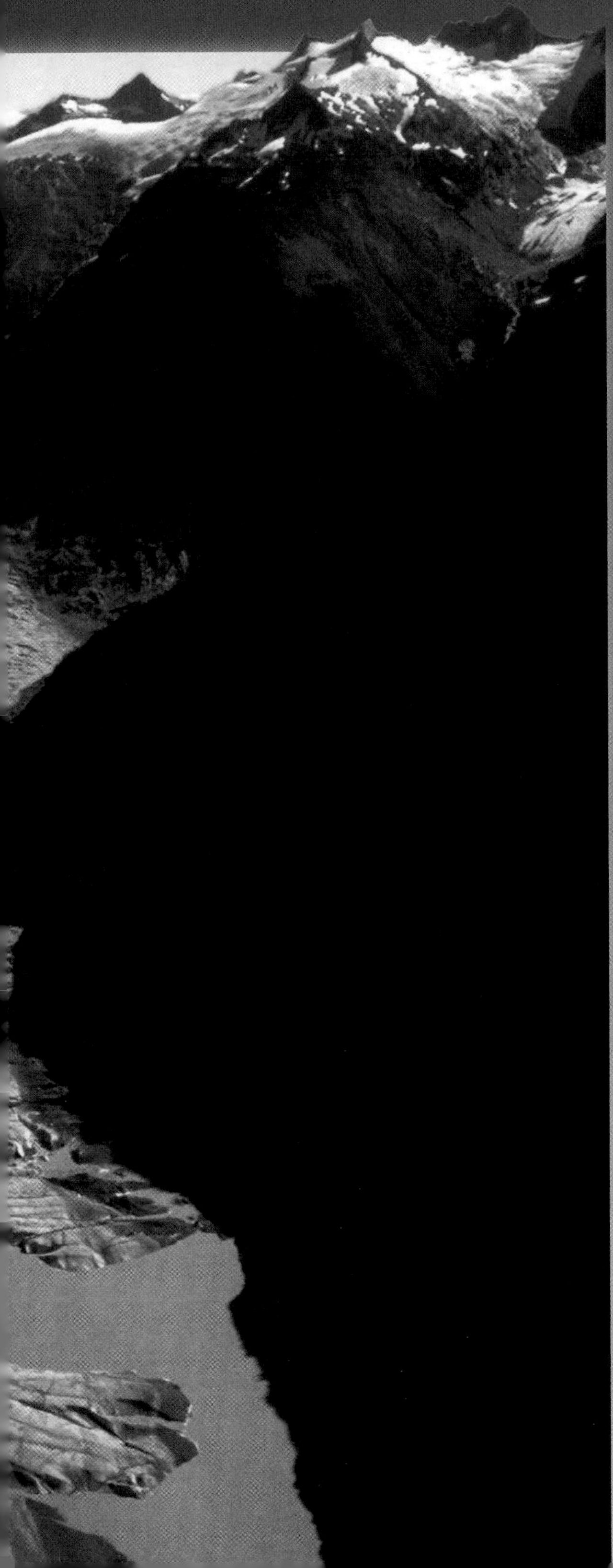

EXPLORE (the BIG idea)

Where Has Water Been?

Think about what water does when it falls and flows on the ground. Go outside your school or home and look at the ground and pavement carefully. Look in dry places for evidence of where water has been.

Observe and Think What evidence did you find? How does it show that water was in a place that is now dry?

How Do Waves Shape Land?

Pile a mixture of sand and gravel on one side of a pie tin to make a "beach." Slowly add water away from the beach until the tin is about one-third full. Use your hand to make waves in the tin and observe what happens.

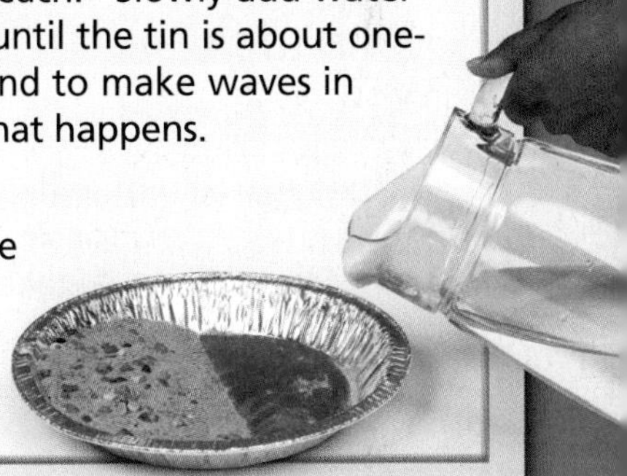

Observe and Think
What happened to the beach? How did the waves affect the sand and gravel?

Internet Activity: Wind Erosion

Go to **ClassZone.com** to learn about one type of wind erosion. See how wind can form an arch in rock.

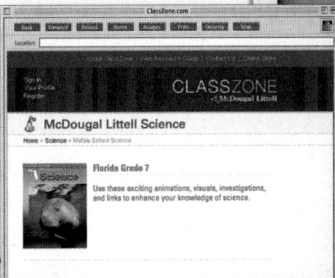

Observe and Think
How long do you think it would take for wind to form an arch?

Wind Erosion **Code: MDL017**

Getting Ready to Learn

◐ CONCEPT REVIEW

- Weathering breaks down rocks.
- Water and ice are agents of weathering.
- Soil contains weathered rock and organic material.

◐ VOCABULARY REVIEW

weathering p. 231

abrasion p. 232

humus p. 239

FLORIDA REVIEW
CLASSZONE.COM

Content Review and FCAT Practice

▶ TAKING NOTES

MAIN IDEA WEB

Write each new blue heading in the center box. In the boxes around it, take notes about important terms and details that relate to the main idea.

VOCABULARY STRATEGY

Write each new vocabulary term in the center of a **four-square** diagram. Write notes in the squares around each term. Include a definition, some characteristics, and some examples of the term. If possible, write some things that are not examples of the term.

See the Note-Taking Handbook on pages R45–R51.

SCIENCE NOTEBOOK

Main Idea Web

| Gravity pulls material downward. | Mass wasting is the downhill movement of rock and soil. |

Gravity can move large amounts of rock and soil.

| Mudflows contain debris and water. | Slumps and creep are common forms of mass movement. |

Definition	Characteristics
process in which weathered particles are picked up and moved	gravity is important part; wind and ice are agents

EROSION

Examples	Nonexamples
mass wasting, mudflow, slump, creep	longshore current, humus

8.1

KEY CONCEPT

Forces wear down and build up Earth's surface.

Sunshine State STANDARDS

SC.D.1.3.1: The student knows that mechanical and chemical activities shape and reshape the Earth's land surface by eroding rock and soil in some areas and depositing them in other areas, sometimes in seasonal layers.

FCAT VOCABULARY
erosion p. 261
deposition p. 261

VOCABULARY
mass wasting p. 263

BEFORE, you learned

• Weathering breaks rocks apart
• Weathering forms soil

NOW, you will learn

• How erosion moves and deposits rock and soil
• How gravity causes movement of large amounts of rock and soil

---

THINK ABOUT

How did natural forces shape this landform?

This valley in Iceland was formed by the action of water. How long might it have taken to form? Where did the material that once filled the valley go?

Natural forces move and deposit sediments.

The valley in the photograph was formed by the movement of water. The water flowed over the land and carried away weathered rock and soil, shaping a valley where the water flows. In this section you will learn about the processes that shape landscapes.

The process in which weathered particles are picked up and moved from one place to another is called **erosion** (ih-ROH-zhuhn). Erosion has a constant impact on Earth's surface. Over millions of years, it wears down mountains by removing byproducts of weathering and depositing them elsewhere. The part of the erosion process in which sediment is placed in a new location, or deposited, is called **deposition** (DEHP-uh-ZIHSH-uhn).

The force of gravity is an important part of erosion and deposition. Gravity causes water to move downward, carrying and depositing sediment as it flows. Gravity can pull huge masses of ice slowly down mountain valleys. And gravity causes dust carried by the wind to fall to Earth.

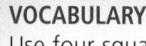

VOCABULARY
Use four square diagrams to take notes about the terms *erosion* and *deposition*.

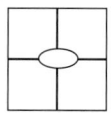

Erosion of weathered rock by the movement of water, wind, and ice occurs in three major ways:

- **Water** Rainwater and water from melting snow flow down sloping land, carrying rock and soil particles. The water makes its way to a river, which then carries the sediment along. The sediment gets deposited on the river's bottom, banks, or flood-plain, or near its mouth. Waves in oceans and lakes also carry sediment and deposit it to form beaches and other features.

- **Wind** Strong winds lift tiny particles of dust and carry them long distances. When the wind dies down, the particles drop to the ground. Wind can also push larger particles of sand along the ground.

- **Ice** As ice moves slowly downhill, it transports rock and soil particles that are embedded in it.

CHECK YOUR READING What are the three major ways in which erosion moves sediment?

INVESTIGATE Erosion

How does the effect of rainwater on sloping land differ from its effect on flat land?

DESIGN — YOUR OWN — EXPERIMENT

Streams are one of the main agents of erosion on Earth. Design an experiment to show the effect that rainwater has on sloping land.

PROCEDURE

1. Figure out how to use the soil, water, and trays to test the effects of rainwater on sloping land and on flat land.

2. Write up your procedure.

3. Carry out your experiment.

WHAT DO YOU THINK?

- What were the results of your experiment? Did it work? Why or why not?
- What were the variables in your experiment?
- What does your experiment demonstrate about erosion and running water?

CHALLENGE How would you design an experiment to demonstrate the relationship between floods and erosion?

SKILL FOCUS
Designing experiments

MATERIALS
- soil
- 2 large trays
- pitcher of water

TIME
25 minutes

Gravity can move large amounts of rock and soil.

Along the California coast many homes are built atop beautiful cliffs, backed by mountains and looking out to the sea. These homes may seem like great places to live. They are, however, in a risky location.

The California coast region and other mountainous areas have many landslides. A landslide is one type of **mass wasting**—the downhill movements of masses of rock and soil.

In mass wasting, gravity pulls material downward. A triggering event, such as heavy rain or an earthquake, might loosen the rock and soil. As the material becomes looser, it gives way to the pull of gravity and moves downward.

Mass wasting can occur suddenly or gradually. It can involve tons of rock sliding down a steep mountain slope or moving little by little down a gentle hillside. One way to classify an occurrence of mass wasting is by the type of material that is moved and the speed of the movement. A sudden, fast movement of rock and soil is called a landslide. Movements of rock are described as slides or falls. Movement of mud or soil is described as a mudflow.

FLORIDA
Content Preview

You know that gravity is a force; you'll learn more about gravity in grade 8.

VOCABULARY
Be sure to make a four-square diagram for *mass wasting* in your notebook.

Mass Wasting of Rock

Mass wasting of rock includes rockfalls and rockslides:

- In a rockfall, individual blocks of rock drop suddenly and fall freely down a cliff or steep mountainside. Weathering can break a block of rock from a cliff or mountainside. The expansion of water that freezes in a crack, for example, can loosen a block of rock.

- In a rockslide, a large mass of rock slides as a unit down a slope. A rockslide can reach a speed of a hundred kilometers per hour. Rockslides can be triggered by earthquakes.

Mass wasting of rock often takes place in high mountains. In some places, rocks can fall or slide onto roads. You might also see evidence of rockfalls and rockslides at the base of steep cliffs, where piles of rock slope outward.

Rockslides, such as this one in California, can drop huge amounts of rock onto highways.

Mudflows in 1999 in Venezuela happened very quickly and took as many as 30,000 lives.

Learn more about mudflows.

Mudflow

Sometimes a mountain slope collapses. Then a mixture of rock, soil, and plants—called debris (duh-BREE)—falls or slides down. Like mass wasting of rock, mass movements of debris are common in high mountains with steep slopes.

A major type of mass wasting of debris is a mudflow. A mudflow consists of debris with a large amount of water. Mudflows often happen in mountain canyons and valleys after heavy rains. The soil becomes so heavy with water that the slope can no longer hold it in place. The mixture of soil, water, and debris flows downward, picking up sediment as it rushes down. When it reaches a valley, it spreads in a thin sheet over the land.

Mudflows also occur on active volcanoes. In 1985, a huge mudflow destroyed the town of Armero, Colombia, and killed more than 20,000 people. When a volcano erupted there, the heat caused ice and snow near the top of the volcano to melt, releasing a large amount of water that mixed with ash from the volcano. The mixture of ash and water rushed down the volcano and picked up debris. It formed gigantic mudflows that poured into all the surrounding valleys.

Mount St. Helens, a volcanic mountain in the state of Washington, is a place where large mudflows have occurred. During an eruption in 1980, some mudflows from the volcano traveled more than 90 kilometers (56 mi) from the mountain.

 What causes a mudflow to occur?

In this example of slump, at Mesa Verde National Park in Colorado, a huge mass of rock and soil moved downward.

Slumps and Creep

Slumps and creep are two other main types of mass wasting on hilly land. These forms of mass wasting can be much less dramatic than rockslides or mudflows. But they are the types of mass movement that you are most likely to see evidence of.

264

A slump is a slide of loose debris that moves as a single unit. Slumps can occur along roads and highways where construction has made slopes unstable. They can cover sections of highway with debris. Like other types of mass movement, slumps can be triggered by heavy rain.

The slowest form of mass movement of soil or debris is creep. The soil or debris moves at a rate of about 1 to 10 millimeters a year—a rate too slow to actually be seen. But evidence of creep can be seen on hillsides that have old fences or telephone poles. The fences or poles may lean downward, or some may be out of line. They have been moved by the creeping soil. The soil closer to the surface moves faster than the soil farther down, which causes the fences or poles to lean.

Originally, the fence posts stand vertically in the ground.

Over many years, the soil holding the posts slowly shifts downhill, and the posts lean.

Even the slight slope of this land in Alberta, Canada, caused these posts to tilt because of creep.

Creep can affect buildings as well. The weight of a heavy mass of soil moving slowly downhill can be great enough to crack a building's walls. Creep affects all hillsides covered with soil, but its rate varies. The wetter the soil, the faster it will creep downhill.

8.1 Review

KEY CONCEPTS

1. How does erosion change landscapes?

2. Describe why weathering is important in erosion.

3. How can gravity move large amounts of rock and soil?

CRITICAL THINKING

4. **Compare and Contrast** What is the main difference between erosion and mass wasting?

5. **Infer** What force and what cause can contribute to both erosion and mass wasting?

⬤ CHALLENGE

6. **Rank** Which of the four locations would be the best and worst places to build a house? Rank the four locations and explain your reasoning.

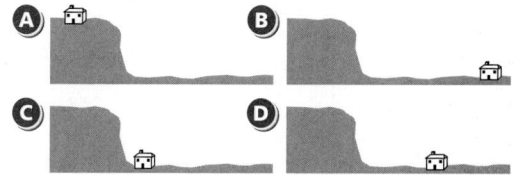

KEY CONCEPT

Moving water shapes land.

Sunshine State STANDARDS

SC.D.1.3.1: The student knows that mechanical and chemical activities shape and reshape the Earth's land surface by eroding rock and soil in some areas and depositing them in other areas, sometimes in seasonal layers.

VOCABULARY

drainage basin p. 267
divide p. 267
floodplain p. 268
alluvial fan p. 269
delta p. 269
sinkhole p. 271

BEFORE, you learned

- Erosion is the movement of rock and soil
- Gravity causes mass movements of rock and soil

NOW, you will learn

- How moving water shapes Earth's surface
- How water moving underground forms caves and other features

---

EXPLORE Divides

How do divides work?

PROCEDURE

1. Fold the sheet of paper in thirds and tape it as shown to make a "ridge."

2. Drop the paper clips one at a time directly on top of the ridge from a height of about 30 cm. Observe what happens and record your observations.

WHAT DO YOU THINK?

How might the paper clips be similar to water falling on a ridge?

MATERIALS
- sheet of paper
- tape
- paper clips

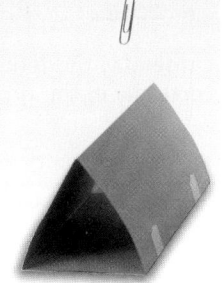

Streams shape Earth's surface.

If you look at a river or stream, you may be able to notice something about the land around it. The land is higher than the river. If a river is running through a steep valley, you can easily see that the river is the low point. But even in very flat places, the land is sloping down to the river, which is itself running downhill in a low path through the land.

Running water is the major force shaping the landscape over most of Earth. From the broad, flat land around the lower Mississippi River to the steep mountain valleys of the Himalayas, water running downhill changes the land. Running water shapes a variety of landforms by moving sediment in the processes of erosion and deposition. In this section, you will learn how water flows on land in systems of streams and rivers and how water shapes and changes landscapes. You also will learn that water can even carve out new features underground.

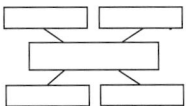

MAIN IDEA WEB

As you read, write each blue heading in a central box and record important details in boxes around it.

Drainage Basins and Divides

When water falls or ice melts on a slope, some of the water soaks into the ground and some of it flows down the slope in thin sheets. But within a short distance this water becomes part of a channel that forms a stream. A stream is any body of water—large or small—that flows down a slope along a channel.

Streams flow into one another to form complex drainage systems, with small streams flowing into larger ones. The area of land in which water drains into a stream system is called a **drainage basin.** In most drainage basins, the water eventually drains into a lake or an ocean. For example, in the Mississippi River drainage basin, water flows into the Mississippi, and then drains into the Gulf of Mexico, which is part of the ocean.

Drainage basins are separated by ridges called divides, which are like continuous lines of high land. A **divide** is a ridge from which water drains to one side or the other. Divides can run along high mountains. On flatter ground, a divide can simply be the highest line of land and can be hard to see.

Divides are the borders of drainage basins. A basin can be just a few kilometers wide or can drain water from a large portion of a continent. The Continental Divide runs from Alaska to Mexico. Most water that falls west of the Continental Divide ends up draining into the Pacific Ocean. Most water that falls east of it drains into the Gulf of Mexico and Atlantic Ocean.

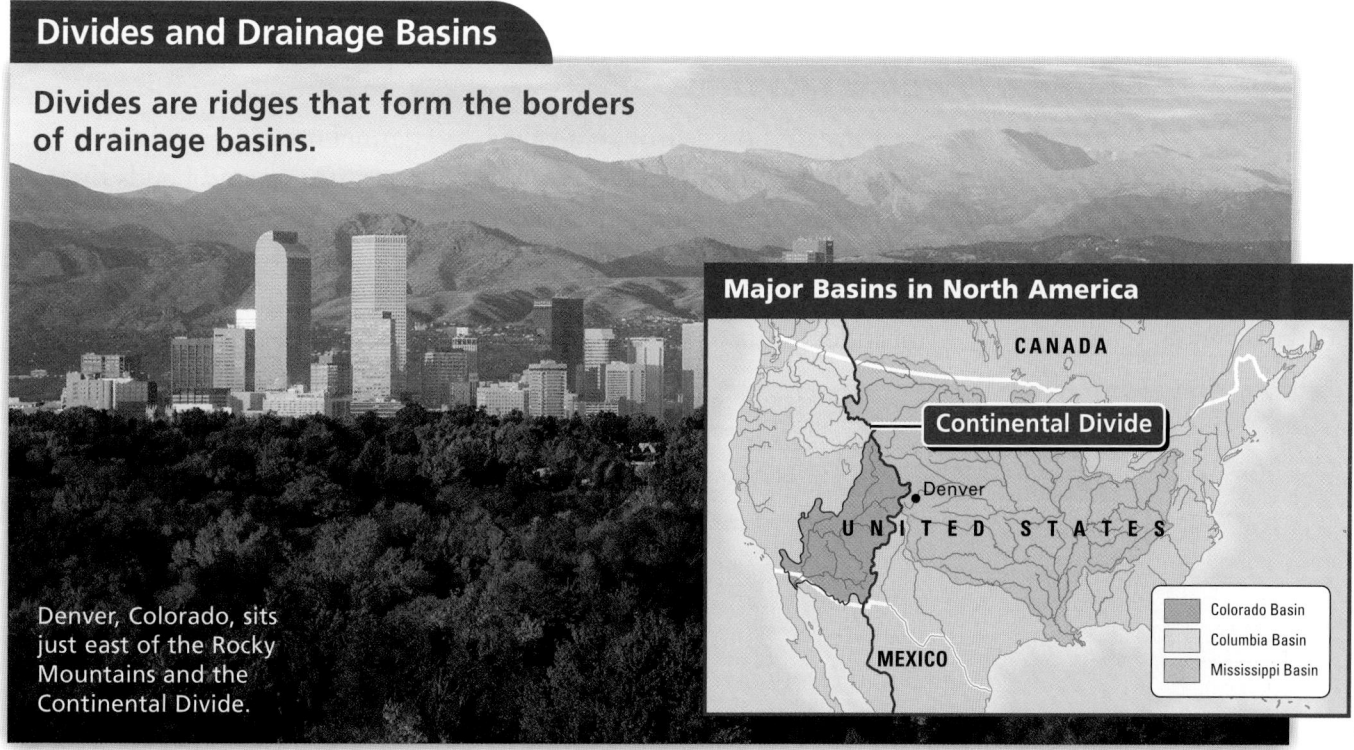

Divides and Drainage Basins

Divides are ridges that form the borders of drainage basins.

Denver, Colorado, sits just east of the Rocky Mountains and the Continental Divide.

Major Basins in North America

CANADA

Continental Divide

Denver

UNITED STATES

MEXICO

Colorado Basin
Columbia Basin
Mississippi Basin

Downtown Davenport, Iowa, sits in the flood-plain of the Mississippi River and was covered with water when the river flooded in 1993.

Valleys and Floodplains

As streams flow and carry sediment from the surface of the land, they form valleys. In high mountains, streams often cut V-shaped valleys that are narrow and steep walled. In lower areas, streams may form broad valleys that include floodplains. A **floodplain** is an area of land on either side of a stream that is underwater when the stream floods. The floodplain of a large river may be many kilometers wide.

When a stream floods, it deposits much of the sediment that it carries onto its floodplain. This sediment can make the floodplain very fertile—or able to support a lot of plant growth. In the United States, the floodplains of the Mississippi River are some of the best places for growing crops.

RESOURCE CENTER
CLASSZONE.COM

Find out more about rivers and erosion.

CHECK YOUR READING Why is fertile land often found on flat land around rivers?

Stream Channels

As a stream flows through a valley, its channel may run straight in some parts and curve around in other parts. Curves and bends that form a twisting, looping pattern in a stream channel are called mean-ders (mee-AN-duhrz). The moving water erodes the outside banks and deposits sediment along the inside banks. Over many years, meanders shift position.

During a flood, the stream may cut a new channel that bypasses a meander. The cut-off meander forms a crescent-shaped lake, which is called an oxbow lake. This term comes from the name of a U-shaped piece of wood that fits under the neck of an ox and is attached to its yoke.

The meanders of this river and oxbow lakes formed as the river deposited sediment and changed course.

oxbow lakes

meanders

Alluvial Fans and Deltas

Besides shaping valleys and forming oxbow lakes, streams also create landforms called alluvial fans and deltas. Both of these landforms are formed by the deposition of sediment.

An **alluvial fan** (uh-LOO-vee-uhl) is a fan-shaped deposit of sediment at the base of a mountain. It forms where a stream leaves a steep valley and enters a flatter plain. The stream slows down and spreads out on the flatter ground. As it slows down, it can carry less sediment. The slower-moving water drops some of its sediment, leaving it at the base of the slope.

A **delta** is an area of land formed by the buildup of sediment at the end, or mouth, of a river. When a river enters the ocean, the river's water slows down, and the river drops much of its sediment. This sediment gradually builds up to form a plain. Like alluvial fans, deltas tend to be fan-shaped. Over a very long time, a river may build up its delta far out into the sea. A large river, such as the Mississippi, can build up a huge delta. Like many other large rivers on Earth, the Mississippi has been building up its delta out into the sea for many thousands of years.

This alluvial fan was formed by a stream flowing into the Jago River in Alaska.

From Divide to Delta

On their path to the ocean, streams and rivers slow down and flatten out.

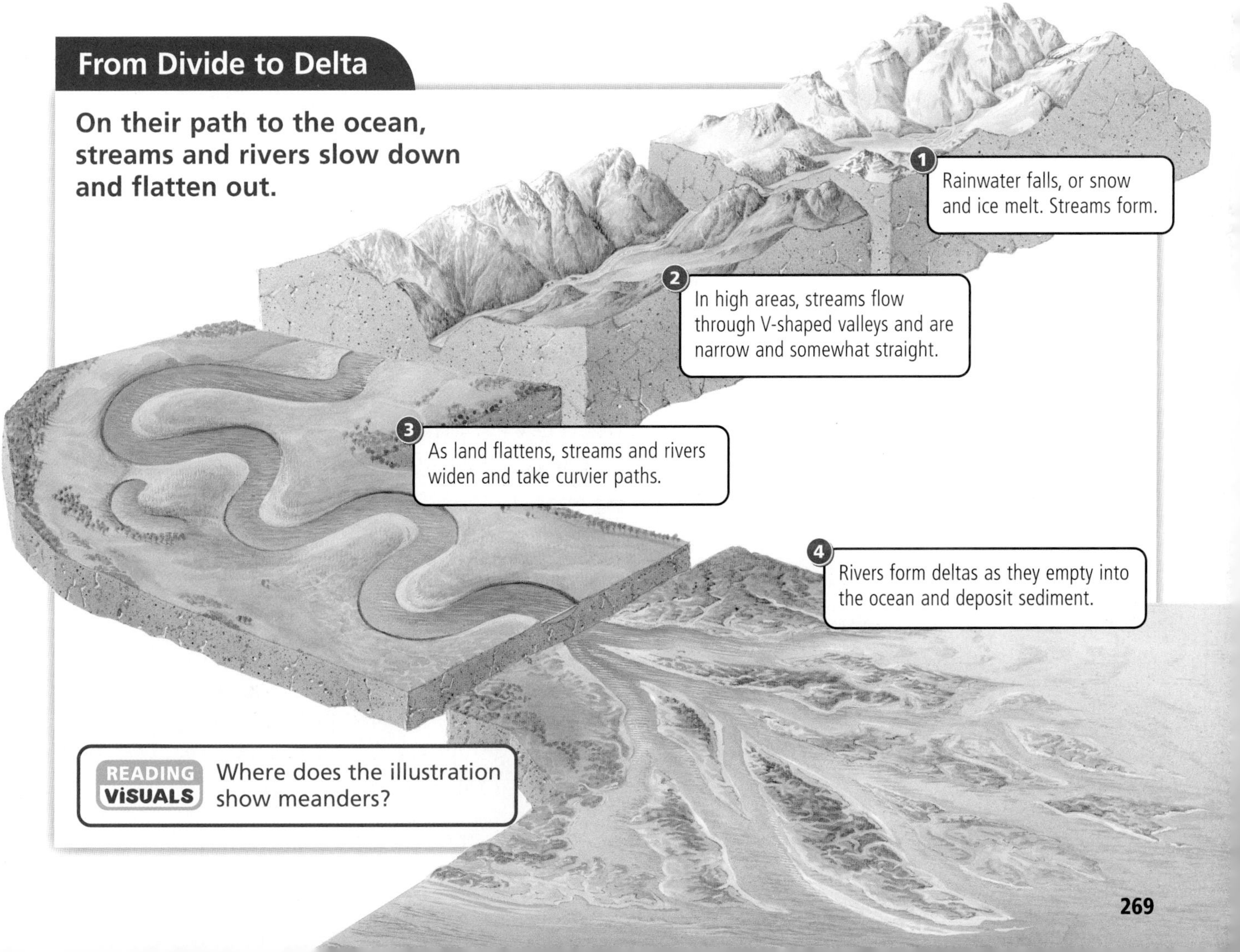

1. Rainwater falls, or snow and ice melt. Streams form.

2. In high areas, streams flow through V-shaped valleys and are narrow and somewhat straight.

3. As land flattens, streams and rivers widen and take curvier paths.

4. Rivers form deltas as they empty into the ocean and deposit sediment.

READING VISUALS Where does the illustration show meanders?

269

Water moving underground forms caverns.

Not all rainwater runs off the land and flows into surface streams. Some of it evaporates, some is absorbed by plants, and some soaks into the ground and becomes groundwater. At a certain depth below the surface, the spaces in soil and rock become completely filled with water. The top of this water-filled region is called the water table. The water below the water table is called groundwater.

The water table is at different distances below the surface in different places. Its level also can change over time in the same location, depending on changes in rainfall. Below the water table, groundwater flows slowly through underground beds of rock and soil, where it causes erosion to take place.

You have read that chemicals in water and air can break down rock. As you read in Chapter 7, rainwater is slightly acidic. This acidic water can dissolve certain rocks, such as limestone. In some areas, where the underground rock consists of limestone, the groundwater can dissolve some of the limestone and carry it away. Over time, this

VISUALIZATION
CLASSZONE.COM

Observe the process of cave formation.

Cavern Formation

Caves form as water underground dissolves limestone, leaving open spaces.

1 Rainwater enters the ground.

2 Acid in the rainwater causes limestone to dissolve, leaving open spaces, or caves.

3 Depending on the location of groundwater, caves can be hollow or filled with water.

This sinkhole took down a large part of a parking lot in Atlanta, Georgia.

process produces open spaces, or caves. Large caves are called caverns. If the water table drops, a cavern may fill with air.

Some caverns have huge networks of rooms and passageways. Mammoth Cave in Kentucky, for example, is part of a cavern system that has more than 560 kilometers (about 350 mi) of explored passageways. Within the cavern are lakes and streams.

A surface feature that often occurs in areas with caverns is a sinkhole. A **sinkhole** is a basin that forms when the roof of a cave becomes so thin that it suddenly falls in. Sometimes it falls in because water that supported the roof has drained away. Landscapes with many sinkholes can be found in southern Indiana, south central Kentucky, and central Tennessee. In Florida, the collapse of shallow underground caverns has produced large sinkholes that have destroyed whole city blocks.

 **CHECK YOUR READING** Why do caverns form in areas with limestone?

8.2 Review

KEY CONCEPTS

1. What is the difference between a drainage basin and a divide?

2. How do streams change as they flow from mountains down to plains?

3. How do caverns form?

CRITICAL THINKING

4. **Sequence** Draw a cartoon with three panels showing how a sinkhole forms.

5. **Compare and Contrast** Make a Venn diagram to compare and contrast alluvial fans and deltas.

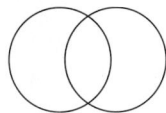

○ CHALLENGE

6. **Apply** During a flood, a river drops the largest pieces of its sediment on the floodplain close to its normal channel. Explain why. (**Hint:** Think about the speed of the water.)

CHAPTER INVESTIGATION

Creating Stream Features

OVERVIEW AND PURPOSE A view from the sky reveals that a large river twists and bends in its channel. But as quiet as it might appear, the river constantly digs and dumps Earth materials along its way. This erosion and deposition causes twists and curves called meanders, and forms a delta at the river's mouth. In this investigation you will

- create a "river" in a stream table to observe the creation of meanders and deltas
- identify the processes of erosion and deposition

▶ Problem

How does moving water create meanders and deltas?

▶ Procedure

1. Arrange the stream table on a counter so that it drains into a sink or bucket. If possible, place a sieve beneath the outlet hose to keep sand out of the drain. You can attach the inlet hose to a faucet if you have a proper adapter. Or you can gently pour water in with a pitcher or use a recirculating pump and a bucket.

2. Place wood blocks beneath the inlet end of the stream table so that the table tilts toward the outlet at about a 20 degree angle. Fill the upper two-thirds of the stream table nearly to the top with sand. Pack the sand a bit, and level the surface with the edge of a ruler. The empty bottom third of the stream table represents the lake or bay into which the river flows.

3. Using the end of the ruler, dig a gently curving trench halfway through the thickness of the sand from its upper to its lower end.

MATERIALS

- stream table, with hose attachment or recirculating pump
- sieve (optional)
- wood blocks
- sand
- ruler
- water
- sink with drain
- pitcher (optional)
- bucket (optional)

4. Direct a gentle flow of tap water into the upper end of the trench. Increase the flow slightly when the water begins to move through the trench. You may have to try this several times before you find the proper rate of flow to soak the sand and fill the stream channel. Avoid adding so much water that it pools at the top before moving into the channel. You can also change the stream table's tilt.

5. Once you are successful in creating a river, observe its shape and any movement of the sand. Continue until the top part of the sand is completely washed away and your river falls apart. Scrape the sand back into place with the ruler and repeat the procedure until you thoroughly understand the stream and sand movements.

Observe and Analyze

1. **RECORD** Diagram your stream-table setup, and make a series of drawings showing changes in your river over time. Be sure to label the river's features, as well as areas of erosion and deposition. Be sure to diagram the behavior of the sand at the river's mouth.

2. **RECORD** Write a record of the development of your river from start to finish. Include details such as the degree of tilt you used, your method of introducing water into the stream table, and features you observed forming.

Conclude

1. **EVALUATE** How do you explain the buildup of sand at the mouth of your river? Use the words *speed*, *erosion*, and *deposition* in your answer. Did the slope of the stream change over time?

2. **INTERPRET** Where in your stream table did you observe erosion occurring? Deposition? What features did each process form?

3. **INFER** What might have occurred if you had increased the amount or speed of the water flowing into your river?

4. **IDENTIFY LIMITS** In what ways was your setup a simplified version of what would actually occur on Earth? Describe the ways in which an actual stream would be more complex.

5. **APPLY** Drawing on what you observed in this investigation, make two statements that relate the age of a stream to (1) the extent of its meanders and (2) to the size of its delta or alluvial fan.

▶ INVESTIGATE Further

CHALLENGE Revise this activity to test a problem statement about a specific stream feature. You could choose to vary the stream's slope, speed, or volume to test the changes' effects on meanders and deltas, for example. Or you could vary the sediment size and observe the movements of each size. Write a hypothesis and design an experimental procedure. Identify the independent and dependent variables.

Creating stream features
Observe and Analyze
1. Before adding water

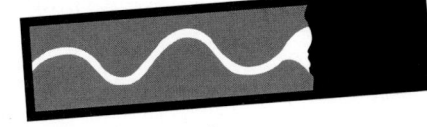

2. After one minute

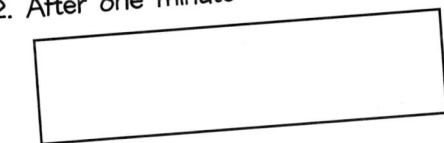

8.3 Waves and wind shape land.

Sunshine State STANDARDS

SC.D.1.3.1: The student knows that mechanical and chemical activities shape and reshape the Earth's land surface by eroding rock and soil in some areas and depositing them in other areas, sometimes in seasonal layers.

VOCABULARY

longshore drift p. 275
longshore current p. 275
sandbar p. 276
barrier island p. 276
dune p. 277
loess p. 278

BEFORE, you learned

- Stream systems shape Earth's surface
- Groundwater creates caverns and sinkholes

NOW, you will learn

- How waves and currents shape shorelines
- How wind shapes land

THINK ABOUT

How did these pillars of rock form?

The rock formations in this photograph stand along the shoreline near the small town of Port Campbell, Australia. What natural force created these isolated stone pillars? What evidence of this force can you see in the photograph?

Waves and currents shape shorelines.

MAIN IDEA WEB
Remember to organize your notes in a web as you read.

The stone pillars, or sea stacks, in the photograph above are a major tourist attraction in Port Campbell National Park. They were formed by the movement of water. The constant action of waves breaking against the cliffs slowly wore them away, leaving behind pillarlike formations. Waves continue to wear down the pillars and cliffs at the rate of about two centimeters (one inch) a year. In the years to come, the waves will likely wear away the stone pillars completely.

The force of waves, powered by wind, can wear away rock and move thousands of tons of sand on beaches. The force of wind itself can change the look of the land. Moving air can pick up sand particles and move them around to build up dunes. Wind can also carry huge amounts of fine sediment thousands of kilometers.

In this section, you'll read more about how waves and wind shape shorelines and a variety of other landforms.

Shorelines

Some shorelines, like the one near Port Campbell, Australia, are made up of steep, rock cliffs. As waves crash against the rock, they wear away the bottom of the cliffs. Eventually, parts of the cliffs above break away and fall into the water, where they are worn down and carried away by the water.

While high, rocky coasts get worn away, low coastlines often get built up. As you read earlier, when a stream flows into an ocean or a lake, it deposits its sediment near its mouth. This sediment mixes with the sediment formed by waves beating against the coast. Waves and currents move this sediment along the shore, building up beaches. Two terms are used to describe the movement of sediment and water along a shore: *longshore drift* and *longshore current*.

- **Longshore drift** is the zigzag movement of sand along a beach. Waves formed by wind blowing across the water far from shore may hit a shoreline at an angle. These angled waves carry sand up onto the shore, and then gravity pulls the water and sand directly back into the water. The sand gradually moves down the beach. The illustration below shows longshore drift.

- A **longshore current** is movement of water along a shore as waves strike the shore at an angle. The direction of the longshore current can change from day to day as the direction of the waves striking the shore changes.

Longshore drift moves large amounts of sand along beaches. It can cause a beach to shrink at one location and grow at another.

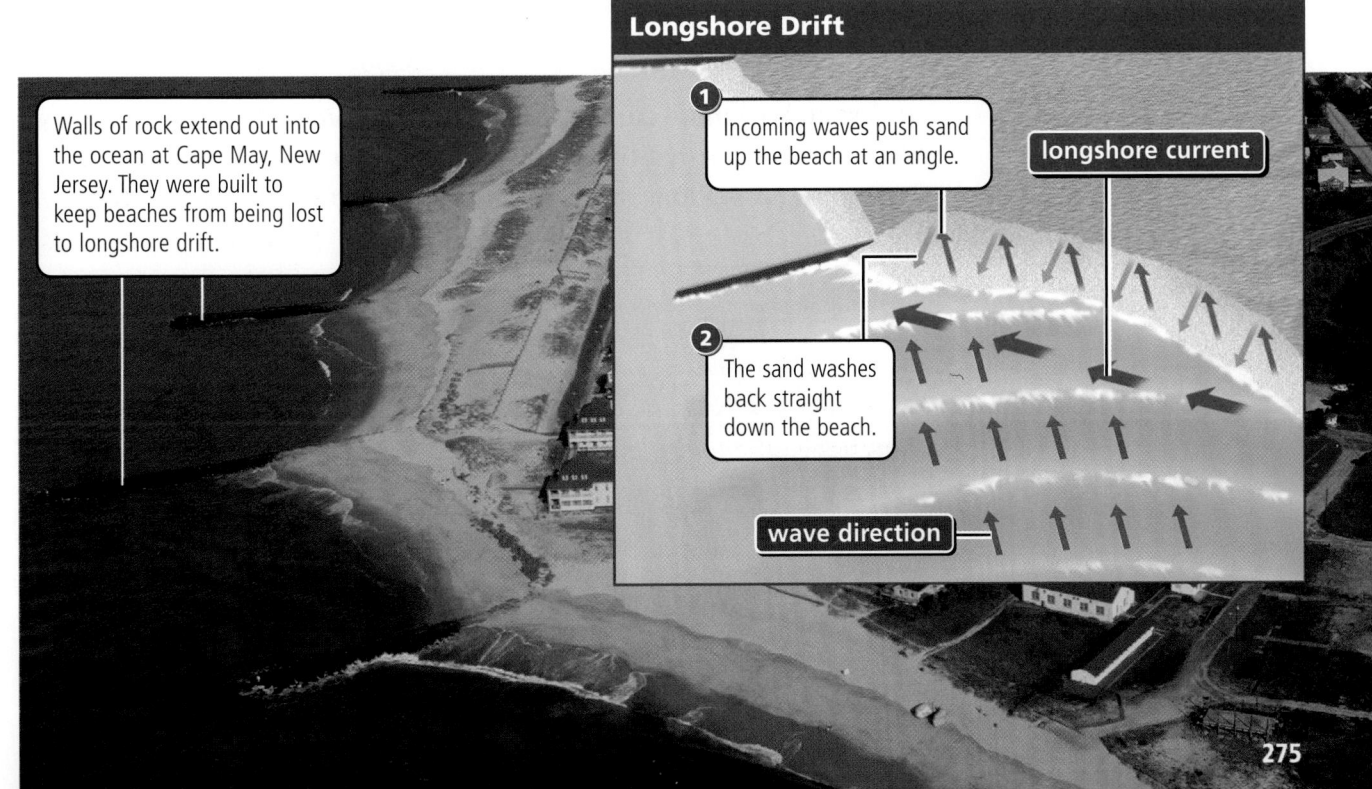

Walls of rock extend out into the ocean at Cape May, New Jersey. They were built to keep beaches from being lost to longshore drift.

Longshore Drift

1 Incoming waves push sand up the beach at an angle.

longshore current

2 The sand washes back straight down the beach.

wave direction

INVESTIGATE Longshore Drift

How does sand move along a beach?

PROCEDURE

① Prop up a book as shown.

② Hold a coin with your finger against the bottom right corner of the book.

③ Gently flick the coin up the slope of the book at an angle. The coin should slide back down the book and fall off the bottom. If necessary, readjust the angle of the book and the strength with which you are flicking the coin.

④ Repeat step 3 several times. Observe the path the coin takes. Record your observations. Include a diagram that shows the general path the coin takes as it slides up and down the book.

WHAT DO YOU THINK?

• What path did the coin take on its way up? On its way down?
• In this model of longshore drift, what represents the beach, what represents the sand, and what represents a wave?

CHALLENGE In this model, in which direction will the longshore current move? How could you change the model to change the direction of the current?

Sandbars and Barrier Islands

As they transport sand, ocean waves and currents shape a variety of coastal landforms. Longshore currents, for example, often deposit sand along shorelines. The sand builds up to form sandbars. A **sandbar** is a ridge of sand built up by the action of waves and currents. A sandbar that has built up above the water's surface and is joined to the land at one end is called a spit. The tip of Cape Cod, Massachusetts, is a spit.

Strong longshore currents that mostly move in one direction may produce sandbars that build up over time into barrier islands. A **barrier island** is a long, narrow island that develops parallel to a coast.

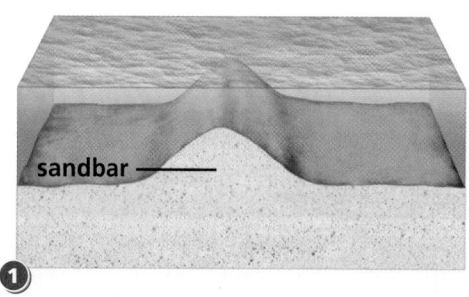

① Waves and currents move and build up sand deposits to form a sandbar under the water surface.

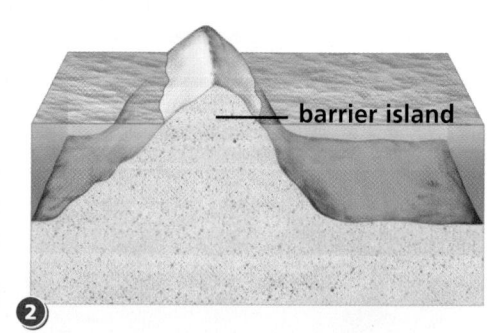

② As more sand is deposited, the sandbar rises above the surface to become a barrier island.

This lighthouse on a barrier island in North Carolina had to be moved because of beach erosion. The photograph shows the lighthouse before it was moved.

A barrier island gets its name from the fact that it forms a barrier between the ocean waves and the shore of the mainland. As a barrier island builds up, grasses, bushes, and trees begin to grow on it.

Barrier islands are common along gently sloping coasts around the world. They occur along the coasts of New Jersey and North Carolina and along the coastline of the Gulf of Mexico. Padre Island in Texas is a barrier island about 180 kilometers (110 mi) in length.

Barrier islands constantly change shape. Hurricanes or other storms can speed up the change. During large storms, waves can surge across the land, carrying away huge amounts of sediment and depositing it elsewhere. Houses on beaches can be destroyed in storms.

 **CHECK YOUR READING** How and where do barrier islands form?

Wind shapes land.

At Indiana Dunes National Lakeshore, not far from the skyscrapers of Chicago, you can tumble or slide down huge sand dunes. First-time visitors to the Indiana dunes find it hard to believe that sand formations like these can be found so far from a desert or an ocean. What created this long stretch of dune land along the southern shore of Lake Michigan? The answer: wind. A **dune** is a mound of sand built up by wind.

Like water, wind has the power to transport and deposit sediment. Although wind is a less powerful force of erosion than moving water, it can still shape landforms, especially in dry regions and in areas that have few or no plants to hold soil in place. Wind can build up dunes, deposit layers of dust, or make a land surface as hard as pavement.

Wind makes sand particles build up and tumble down, causing a dune to migrate, or move.

These hills of sand are at the Great Sand Dunes National Monument in Colorado.

Dune Formation

Even a light breeze can carry dust. A moderate wind can roll and slide grains of sand along a beach or desert, creating ripples. Only a strong wind, however, can actually pick up and carry sand particles. When the wind dies down or hits something—such as a cliff or a hill—it drops the sand. Over time, the deposits of sand build up to create dunes.

Some dunes start out as ripples that grow larger. Others form as wind-carried sand settles around a rock, log, or other obstacle. In climates with enough rainfall, plants begin to grow on dunes a short distance from beaches.

Dunes form only where there are strong winds and a constant supply of loose sand. They can be found on the inland side of beaches of oceans and large lakes, on the sandy floodplains of large rivers, and in sandy deserts.

Dunes can form in a variety of sizes and shapes. They can reach heights of up to 300 meters (about 1000 ft). Some dunes are curved; others are long, straight ridges; still others are mound-shaped hills. A dune usually has a gentle slope on the side that faces the wind and a steeper slope on the side sheltered from the wind.

Loess

Besides forming dunes, wind also changes the soil over large regions of Earth by depositing dust. A strong windstorm can move millions of tons of dust. As the wind dies down, the dust drops to the ground. Deposits of fine wind-blown sediment are called **loess** (LOH-uhs).

In some regions, deposits of loess have built up over thousands and even millions of years. Loess is a valuable resource because it forms good soil for growing crops.

This loess deposit in Iowa built up over many thousands of years.

Loess covers about 10 percent of the land surface of Earth. China has especially large deposits of loess, covering hundreds of thousands of square kilometers. Some of the deposits are more than 300 meters (about 1000 ft) thick. Such thick deposits take a long time to develop. Some of the loess deposits in China are 2 million years old. Winds blowing over the deserts and dry regions of central Asia carried the dust that formed these deposits.

Parts of east central Europe and the Mississippi Valley in the United States also contain significant loess deposits. In the central United States, loess deposits are between 8 and 30 meters (25 and 100 ft) thick.

Desert Pavement

Not only does wind shape land surfaces by depositing dust; it also shapes land surfaces by removing dust. When wind blows away all the smallest particles from a mixture of sand, silt, and gravel, it leaves behind just a layer of stones and gravel. This stony surface is called desert pavement because it looks like a cobblestone pavement. The coarse gravel and rocks are too large to be picked up by wind.

Desert pavement is made up of particles too large to be picked up by wind.

 **CHECK YOUR READING** How are both loess and desert pavement formed by wind?

 **Review**

KEY CONCEPTS

1. What kinds of landforms do longshore drift and longshore currents produce?

2. How do dunes form?

3. How does loess form, and why is it important?

CRITICAL THINKING

4. **Identify Cause and Effect** Is longshore drift the cause or effect of a longshore current? Explain.

5. **Predict** What effect would a barrier island have on the shoreline of the mainland?

CHALLENGE

6. **Hypothesize** The south and east shores of Lake Michigan have large areas of sand dunes, but the north and west shores do not. Write a hypothesis that explains why. You might want to use a map and draw the shape of Lake Michigan to explain.

Life on Dunes

Sand dunes are a difficult environment for most organisms. For example, few plants can gather enough nutrition from sand to grow quickly. However, any plant that grows slowly is likely to be buried by the shifting sand. Plants and animals that thrive on dunes generally have unusual traits that help them survive in dune conditions.

The leaves of American beach grass contain silica, the main component of sand. The leaves are therefore very tough. Why is this important on a dune?

American Beach Grass

Among the first plants to grow on new coastal dunes is American beach grass. It grows faster as sand begins to bury it, and it can grow up to 1 meter (more than 3 ft) per year. Its large root system—reaching down as much as 3 meters (about 10 ft)—helps it gather food and water. The roots also help hold sand in place. As the grass's roots make the dunes stable, other plants can begin to grow there.

Sand Food

One of the most unusual plants in desert dunes is called sand food. It is one of the few plants that cannot convert sunlight into energy it can use. Instead, its long underground stem grabs onto the root of another plant and sucks food from it. Most of the plant is the stem. Sand food plants may be more than 2 meters (almost 7 ft) long.

In spring, sand food produces a small head of purple flowers that barely comes out of the ground. How does growing mostly underground help sand food survive?

Fowler's Toad

Fowler's toad is one of the animals that can live in coastal dunes. During the day, sunlight can make the top layer of the sand very hot and dry. These toads dig down into the sand, where they are safe, cool, and moist. They are most active at night.

Fowler's toads have a brownish or greenish color that makes them hard to see against a sandy background. How would this help protect them from animals that want to eat them?

EXPLORE

1. **GENERALIZE** Dune plants often have long roots. Propose an explanation for this.

2. **CHALLENGE** Use library or Internet resources to learn about another plant or animal that lives on dunes. Describe how it has adapted to the conditions in which it lives.

Glaciers carve land and move sediments.

Sunshine State STANDARDS

SC.D.1.3.1: The student knows that mechanical and chemical activities shape and reshape the Earth's land surface by eroding rock and soil in some areas and depositing them in other areas, sometimes in seasonal layers.

BEFORE, you learned

- Running water shapes landscapes
- Wind changes landforms

NOW, you will learn

- How moving ice erodes land
- How moving ice deposits sediment and changes landforms

VOCABULARY

glacier p. 281
till p. 284
moraine p. 284
kettle lake p. 285

EXPLORE Glaciers

How do glaciers affect land?

PROCEDURE

1. Flatten the clay on top of a paper towel.
2. Drag the ice cube across the clay as shown. Record your observations.
3. Leave the ice cube to melt on top of the clay.

WHAT DO YOU THINK?

- What happened when you dragged the ice cube across the clay?
- What happened to the sand and gravel in the ice cube as it melted?

MATERIALS

- modeling clay
- paper towel
- ice cube containing sand and gravel

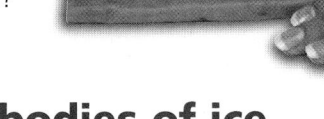

VOCABULARY
Remember to add a four square diagram for *glacier* to your notebook.

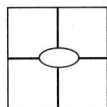

Glaciers are moving bodies of ice.

You might not think of ice as something that moves. But think about what happens to an ice cube on a table. The cube begins to melt, makes a small puddle, and may slide a little. The water under the cube makes the table surface slippery, which allows the ice cube to slide.

A similar process happens on a much larger scale with glaciers. A **glacier** is a large mass of ice that moves over land. A glacier forms in a cold region when more snow falls than melts each year. As the snow builds up, its weight presses the snow on the bottom into ice. On a mountain, the weight of a heavy mass of ice causes it to flow downward, usually slowly. On flatter land, the ice spreads out as a sheet. As glaciers form, move, and melt away, they shape landscapes.

Extent of Glaciers

Glaciers can exist only in places where it is cold enough for water to stay frozen year round. Glaciers are found in mountain ranges all over the world and in land regions near the north and south poles.

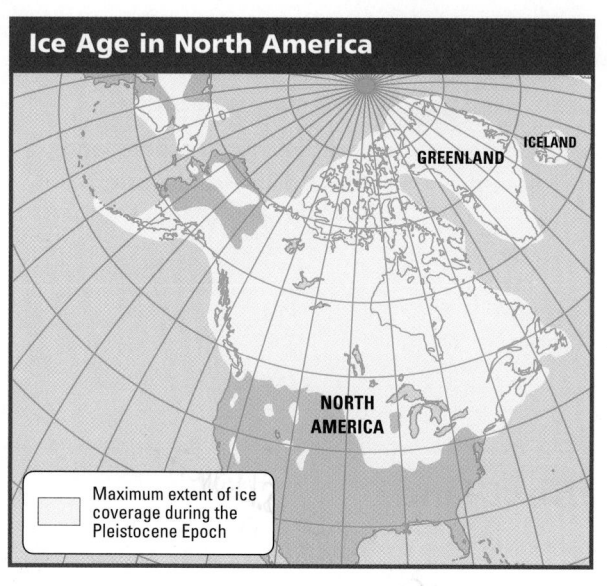

Ice Age in North America

ICELAND
GREENLAND

NORTH
AMERICA

Maximum extent of ice coverage during the Pleistocene Epoch

Today, glaciers cover about 10 percent of Earth's land surface. However, the amount of land surface covered by glaciers has varied greatly over Earth's history. Glaciers have expanded during long cold periods called ice ages and have disappeared during long warm periods. About 30,000 years ago—during the last major ice age—glaciers extended across the northern parts of North America and Eurasia. They covered nearly 30 percent of the present land surface of Earth.

There are two major types of glaciers: alpine glaciers and continental glaciers.

RESOURCE CENTER
CLASSZONE.COM

Learn more about the movement and effects of glaciers.

Alpine Glaciers

Alpine glaciers, also called valley glaciers, form in mountains and flow down through valleys. As these glaciers move, they cause erosion, breaking up rock and carrying and pushing away the resulting sediment. Over time, an alpine glacier can change a V-shaped mountain valley into a U-shaped valley with a wider, flatter bottom.

Some glaciers extend all the way down into the lower land at the bases of mountains. At an alpine glacier's lower end, where temperatures are warmer, melting can occur. The melting glacier drops sediment, and streams flowing from the glacier carry some of the sediment away. If an alpine glacier flows into the ocean, big blocks may break off and become icebergs.

Continental Glaciers

Continental glaciers, also called ice sheets, are much larger than alpine glaciers. They can cover entire continents, including all but the highest mountain peaks. An ice sheet covered most of Canada and the northern United States during the last ice age. This ice sheet melted and shrank about 10,000 years ago.

Today, ice sheets cover most of Greenland and Antarctica. Each of these glaciers is shaped like a wide dome over the land. The ice on Antarctica is as much as 4500 meters (15,000 ft) thick.

 CHECK YOUR READING What are the two major types of glaciers and where do they form?

Types of Glaciers and Movement

A glacier is a large mass of ice that moves over land.

Alpine Glaciers

A glacier, such as this one in Alaska, changes the landscape as it moves down a mountain valley.

Continental Glaciers

Huge sheets of ice cover the continent of Antarctica and other land regions.

Glacier Movement

Gravity causes the ice in a glacier to move downhill. Two different processes cause glaciers to move: flowing and sliding.

Flowing The ice near the surface of a glacier is brittle, and cracks often form in it. However, deep inside a glacier, ice does not break as easily because it is under great pressure from the weight of the ice above it. Instead of breaking, ice inside a glacier flows like toothpaste being squeezed in its tube.

As a glacier moves, it breaks up rock and pushes and carries sediment.

Sliding The weight of a glacier and heat from Earth cause ice at the bottom of a glacier to melt. A layer of water forms under the glacier. The glacier slides along on this layer of water just as an ice cube might slide on a countertop.

READING VISUALS In the illustration, why are cracks shown near the surface of the glacier and not at the bottom?

abrasion

A moving glacier left visible abrasion lines on this rock.

Glaciers deposit large amounts of sediment.

As glaciers have melted and retreated, they have shaped the landscapes of many places on Earth. As a glacier moves or expands, it transports a vast amount of sediment—a mix of boulders, small rocks, sand, and clay. It acts like a plow, pushing rock and soil and plucking out big blocks of rock. As a glacier moves over rock, it scratches and scrapes the rock in a process called abrasion. Abrasion leaves visible grooves on rock surfaces.

Moraines

When glaciers expand and advance and then melt and retreat, they affect both the land underneath them and the land around them. A glacier pushes huge amounts of sediment to its sides and front. When the glacier retreats, the deposits of sediment remain as visible evidence that ice once moved through. The sediment left directly on the ground surface by a retreating glacier is called **till.**

A deposit of till left behind by a retreating glacier is called a **moraine** (muh-RAYN). The ridges of till deposited at the sides of a glacier are called lateral moraines. The till that marks the farthest advance of a glacier forms a deposit called an end moraine. Moraines formed by continental glaciers, such as those in North America during the ice age, can be huge—many kilometers long.

The blanket of till that a glacier deposits along its bottom is called a ground moraine. Rock deposits from glaciers can often be identified as till because the till rocks are different, in type or age, from the rock that was present before the glacier formed.

A glacier scooped out this valley in California and left behind lateral moraines.

○ CHECK YOUR READING Draw a sketch of a glacier and label where lateral, end, and ground moraines would form.

Lateral moraines

Lakes

Besides ridges, hills, and blankets of till, melting glaciers also leave behind depressions of various sizes that can become lakes. Landscapes shaped by glaciers are often dotted with small kettle lakes as well as larger lakes. A **kettle lake** is a bowl-shaped depression that was formed by a block of ice from a glacier and then became filled with water.

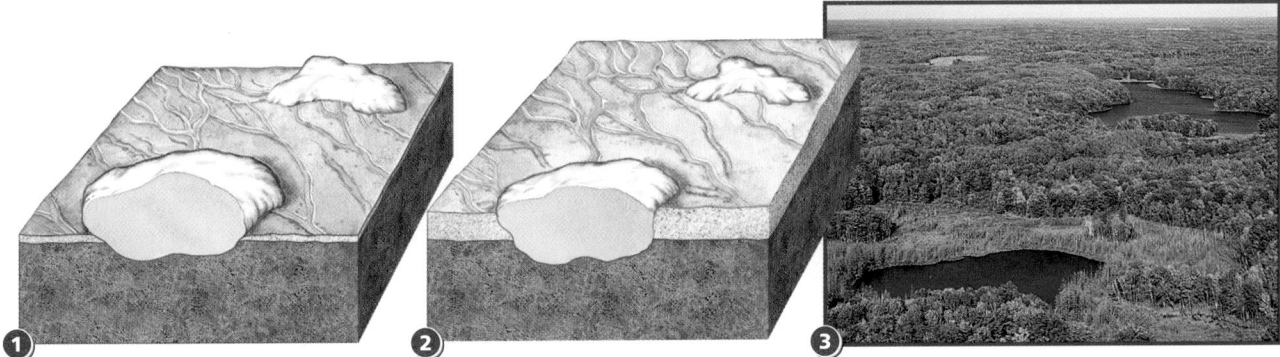

① As a glacier moves away, it leaves huge blocks of ice.

② Over time, sediment builds up around the ice.

③ The ice melts, leaving behind bowls that become kettle lakes. These lakes are in Wisconsin.

The last ice sheet in North America formed many kettle lakes in some regions. Kettle lakes are common in Michigan, Wisconsin, and Minnesota.

INVESTIGATE Kettle Lake Formation

How do kettle lakes form?

DESIGN — YOUR OWN —

Kettle lakes form when sediment builds up around blocks of ice left behind by a retreating glacier. Use what you know about kettle lake formation to design a model of the process.

PROCEDURE

① Use the tray, the ice cubes, and the other materials to model how sediment builds up around ice blocks.

② Write a description of the process you used to make your model.

WHAT DO YOU THINK?

- Describe how your model worked. What did you do first? What happened next?
- Did your model accurately represent the formation of kettle lakes? Did it work? Why or why not?
- What were the limitations of your model? Are there any aspects of kettle lake formation that are not represented? If so, what are they?

SKILL FOCUS
Designing models

MATERIALS
- shallow tray
- ice cubes
- modeling clay
- sand
- gravel
- water

TIME
30 minutes

Great Lakes Formation

① 14,000 Years Ago

ICE

The ice sheet covering a land of river valleys began to retreat.

② 7000 Years Ago

ICE

Water filled the bowls carved out by the ice.

③ Today

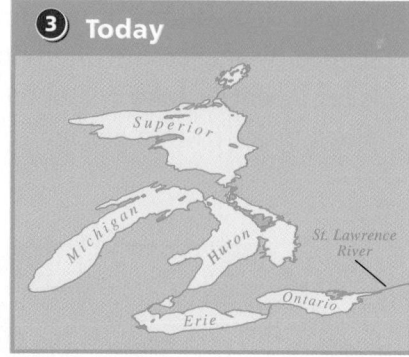

Superior
Michigan
Huron
St. Lawrence River
Erie
Ontario

The Great Lakes contain 20 percent of the world's fresh lake water.

Many large lakes are the result of ice ages. In some places, lakes formed after glaciers in valleys melted and left behind moraines that dammed the valleys. Many of these lakes are long and narrow, like the Finger Lakes in New York, which are named for their slender shape.

The Great Lakes were formed thousands of years ago as an ice sheet moved over the land and then melted. A million years ago, the region of the Great Lakes had many river valleys. The ice sheet gouged out large depressions in the land and left piles of rock and debris that blocked water from draining out. In some areas, where the deepest Great Lakes are now, the enormous weight of the glacier actually caused the land to sink as much as one kilometer.

The ice sheet started to melt about 14,000 years ago. By about 7000 years ago, it had melted past what would become Lake Erie and Lake Ontario, the lakes farthest to the east.

CHECK YOUR READING What are two ways the ice sheet formed the Great Lakes?

8.4 Review

KEY CONCEPTS

1. Describe the two processes that cause glaciers to move.

2. What are the two major types of glaciers, and where are they found?

3. Describe the land features left behind by glaciers that have melted and shrunk.

CRITICAL THINKING

4. **Compare and Contrast** Identify two ways in which the erosion effects of glaciers differ from those of rivers.

5. **Predict** How would glaciers be affected by changes in climate, such as global warming and global cooling?

⚠ CHALLENGE

6. **Infer** Regions near the equator are generally the warmest on Earth. However, in one small area of Africa, there are glaciers close to the equator. Form a hypothesis to explain why these glaciers exist.

MATH in SCIENCE

 MATH TUTORIAL

CLASSZONE.COM

Click on Math Tutorial for more help with making line graphs.

Snow Line Elevation and Latitude

Glaciers form above the snow line, the lowest elevation at which there is permanent snow in the summer. The snow line elevation depends on temperature and precipitation. In the hot tropics the snow line is high in the mountains, while at the poles it is near sea level. The table shows the snow line elevations at different locations on Earth. The latitude of each location indicates how far the location is from the equator; the latitude of the equator is 0 degrees, and the latitude of the North Pole is 90 degrees.

Location	Latitude (degrees north)	Snow Line Elevation (meters)
North Pole	90	0
Juneau, Alaska	58	1050
Glacier National Park	49	2600
Sierra Nevada	37	3725
Himalayas (East Nepal)	28	5103
Ecuador	0	4788

Follow the steps below to make a line graph of the data.

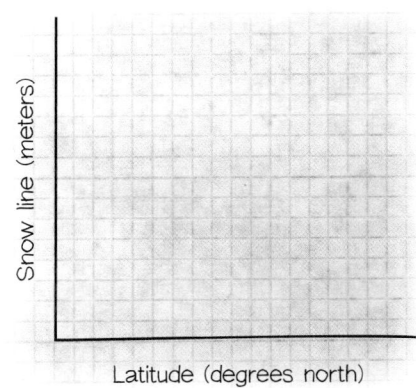

(1) On a sheet of graph paper, draw and label axes. Put latitude on the horizontal axis and snow line elevation on the vertical axis.

(2) Choose and mark a scale for each axis.

(3) Graph each point.

(4) Draw line segments to connect the points.

Use your graph to answer the following questions.

1. Mount Kenya is very close to the equator. Estimate the snow line elevation on Mount Kenya.

2. Mount Rainier is at 47 degrees north latitude and is 4389 meters tall. Can there be glaciers on Mount Rainier? If so, estimate the elevation above which the glaciers form.

3. Mount Washington in New Hampshire is at 45 degrees north latitude and is 1917 meters tall. Can there be glaciers on Mount Washington? If so, estimate their lowest elevation.

CHALLENGE Temperatures are hotter at the equator than at 28 degrees north latitude. Why is the snow line lower at the equator in Ecuador? (**Hint:** The answer involves precipitation.)

Chapter Review

the BIG idea

Water, wind, and ice shape Earth's surface.

◀ KEY CONCEPTS SUMMARY

1 **Forces wear down and build up Earth's surface.**

Water, wind, and ice move sediment in the process called **erosion**. The placement of sediment in a new location is **deposition**, part of the erosion process.

VOCABULARY
erosion p. 261
deposition p. 261
mass wasting p. 263

2 **Moving water shapes land.**

Water drains from land in **drainage basins,** which are separated by **divides.** As water flows over land and underground, it moves sediment and changes land features.

VOCABULARY
drainage basin p. 267
divide p. 267
floodplain p. 268
alluvial fan p. 269
delta p. 269
sinkhole p. 271

3 **Waves and wind shape land.**

The action of water moves sand and builds up new landforms, such as **sandbars** and **barrier islands.** Wind forms **dunes.**

VOCABULARY
longshore drift p. 275
longshore current p. 275
sandbar p. 276
barrier island p. 276
dune p. 277
loess p. 278

4 **Glaciers carve land and move sediments.**

Glaciers are large bodies of ice that change landscapes as they move.

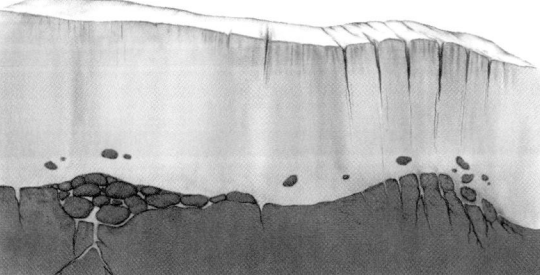

VOCABULARY
glacier p. 281
till p. 284
moraine p. 284
kettle lake p. 285

Reviewing Vocabulary

Copy and complete the chart below. Explain how each landscape feature is formed.

Feature	How It Forms
EXAMPLE delta	A river deposits sediment as it enters the ocean.
1. alluvial fan	
2. sinkhole	
3. sandbar	
4. barrier island	
5. dune	
6. loess	
7. moraine	
8. kettle lake	

Reviewing Key Concepts

Multiple Choice *Choose the letter of the best answer.*

9. The first stage in the erosion process is
   a. deposition
   b. mass wasting
   c. drainage
   d. weathering

10. The main natural force responsible for mass movements of rocks and debris is
    a. rainwater   c. gravity
    b. wind   d. fire

11. A sinkhole is formed by the collapse of
    a. an alluvial fan
    b. a cavern
    c. a moraine
    d. a kettle lake

12. Rivers transport sediment to
    a. drainage basins
    b. oceans and lakes
    c. the water table
    d. moraines

13. Drainage basins are separated by a
    a. moraine   c. tributary
    b. divide   d. barrier island

14. In high mountains, a valley carved by a stream has the shape of a
    a. U   c. plate
    b. crescent   d. V

15. An oxbow lake is formed by the cutting off of a
    a. meander   c. sinkhole
    b. drainage basin   d. glacier

16. Sandbars, spits, and barrier islands can all be built up by
    a. glaciers   c. wind
    b. ocean waves   d. mass wasting

17. A dune is a sand mound built up primarily by
    a. gravity   c. glaciers
    b. running water   d. wind

18. Strong winds can transport large quantities of
    a. gravel   c. dry sand
    b. wet sand   d. clay

19. A mountain valley carved by a glacier has the shape of a
    a. U   c. bowl
    b. crescent   d. V

Short Response *Write a short response to each question.*

20. How is deposition part of the erosion process?

21. How can rainwater in the Rocky Mountains end up in the ocean?

22. What is the effect of a longshore current on a beach?

23. Why is a mass movement of mud called a flow?

24. What visual evidence is a sign of creep?

25. What is the connection between icebergs and glaciers?

Thinking Critically

This photograph shows two glaciers joining to form one (A). Make a sketch of the glaciers to answer the next three questions.

26. **APPLY** Place an arrow to show in which direction the main glacier (A) is moving.

27. **ANALYZE** Mark the places where you think till would be found.

28. **APPLY** Mark the location of a lateral moraine.

29. **ANALYZE** Why does the main glacier not have an end moraine?

30. **COMPARE AND CONTRAST** Compare the main glacier valley in the photograph with the valley at the far right (B). How are the valleys different? Explain why they might be different.

31. **APPLY** In exploring an area of land, what clues would you look for to determine whether glaciers were once there?

32. **COMPARE AND CONTRAST** How is a deposit of till from a glacier similar to a river delta? How is it different?

33. **EVALUATE** If you were growing crops on a field near a slow-moving, curvy river, what would an advantage of the field's location be? What might be a disadvantage?

34. **COMPARE AND CONTRAST** How are mudflows and mass wasting of rock similar? How are they different? Include references to speed and types of material in your answer.

35. **INFER** If the wind usually blows from west to east over a large area of land, and the wind usually slows down over the eastern half of the area, where would you be likely to find loess in the area? Explain your answer.

36. **APPLY** If you were considering a location for a house and were concerned about creep, what two factors about the land would you consider?

37. **SYNTHESIZE** Describe how the processes of erosion and deposition are involved in the formation of kettle lakes.

the **BIG** idea

38. **SYNTHESIZE** Describe how snow falling onto the Continental Divide in the Rocky Mountains can be part of the process of erosion and deposition. Include the words *divide, glacier, stream,* and *ocean* in your answer.

39. **PROVIDE EXAMPLES** Choose three examples of erosion processes—one each from Sections 8.2, 8.3, and 8.4. Explain how gravity is involved in each of these processes.

UNIT PROJECTS

Check your schedule for your unit project. How are you doing? Be sure that you've placed data or notes from your research in your project folder.

Analyzing a Diagram

Use the diagram to answer the questions below.

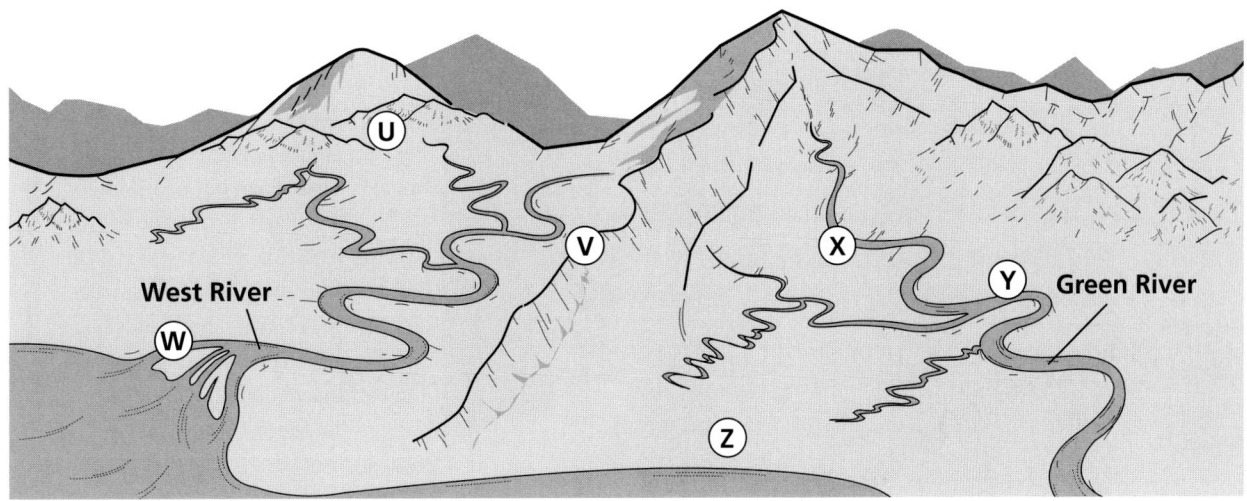

West River

Green River

MULTIPLE CHOICE

1. Where would a glacier be most likely to form?

A. U   **C.** W

B. V   **D.** X

2. Where is a divide?

F. U   **H.** X

G. V   **I.** Y

3. Where is a delta?

A. U   **C.** W

B. V   **D.** Z

4. Which process could move sediment from point U to point W?

F. weathering   **H.** deposition

G. erosion   **I.** drifting

SHORT RESPONSE

5. Study point W on the diagram and explain why sediment has built up there.

6. Compare points X and Y on the diagram. Decide at which point the river would move faster and explain why.

FCAT TiP

When answering multiple-choice questions based on a diagram, try using the diagram to answer each question before you look at the answer choices.

EXTENDED RESPONSE

Answer the two questions below in detail. Include some of the terms shown in the word box. In your answers, underline each term you use.

ocean waves	currents	barrier island
grass	glaciers	kettle lakes

7. Each year, Clark and his family visit the ocean. Clark notices that a sandbar near the coast is slightly larger each year. Predict what will happen if this trend continues.

8. Annika often goes fishing at one of several small, round lakes that are within 20 miles of her house in Minnesota. How might these lakes have formed?

TIMELINES in Science

HISTORY OF THE EARTH SYSTEM

Systems of air, water, rocks, and living organisms have developed on Earth during the planet's 4.6 billion years of history. More and more scientists have become curious about how these parts of Earth work together. Today, scientists think of these individual systems as part of one large Earth system.

The timeline shows a few events in the history of the Earth system. Scientists have developed special tools and procedures to study this history. The boxes below the timeline show how technology has led to new knowledge about the Earth system and how that knowledge has been applied.

4.6 BYA

Earth Forms in New Solar System
The Sun and nine planets, one of which is Earth, form out of a cloud of gas and dust. Earth forms and grows larger as particles collide with it. While Earth is still young, a slightly smaller object smashes into it and sends huge amounts of material flying into space. Some of this material forms a new object—the Moon.

EVENTS

5 BYA

Billion Years Ago

APPLICATIONS AND TECHNOLOGY

TECHNOLOGY

Measuring Age of Solar System
In 1956, Clair C. Patterson published his estimate that the solar system was 4.55 billion years old. Previously, scientists had learned how to use radioactive elements present in rocks to measure their ages. Patterson used this technology to determine the ages of meteorites that were formed along with the solar system and later fell to Earth. Since 1956, scientists have studied more samples and used new technologies. These studies have generally confirmed Patterson's estimate.

This iron meteorite fell in Siberia in 1947. Data from such meteorites are clues to how and when the solar system formed.

4.4 BYA

Earth Gains Atmosphere, Ocean

Earth's atmosphere forms as volcanoes release gases, including water vapor. Though some gases escape into space, Earth's gravity holds most of them close to the planet. The atmosphere contains no free oxygen. As Earth starts to cool, the water vapor becomes water droplets and falls as rain. Oceans begin to form.

3.5 BYA

Organisms Affect Earth System

Tiny organisms use energy from sunlight to make their food, giving off oxygen as a waste product. The oxygen combines with other gases and with minerals. It may be another billion years before free oxygen starts to build up in the atmosphere.

1.8 BYA

First Supercontinent Forms

All of Earth's continents come together to form one huge supercontinent. The continents and ocean basins are still moving and changing. This supercontinent will break apart in the future. New supercontinents will form and break apart as time goes on.

4 BYA   **3** BYA   **2** BYA   **1** BYA

APPLICATION

Measuring Ozone Levels

In 1924, scientists developed the first instrument to measure ozone, the Dobson spectrophotometer. Ozone is a molecule that consists of three oxygen atoms. In the 1970s, scientists realized that levels of ozone in the upper atmosphere were falling. Countries have taken action to preserve the ozone layer, which protects organisms—including humans—from dangerous ultraviolet radiation. Today, computers process ozone data as they are collected and make them quickly available to researchers around the world.

A Dobson spectrophotometer measures the total amount of ozone in the atmosphere above it.

600 MYA
New Animals Appear

The first multi-celled animals appear in the ocean. Some types of these animals are fastened to the sea floor and get food from particles in water flowing past them. Worms are the most complex type of animals to appear so far.

480 MYA
Plants Appear on Land

The earliest plants appear. These plants, perhaps similar to mosses, join the lichens that already live on land. Through photosynthesis, plants and lichens decrease the amount of carbon dioxide in the air and increase the amount of oxygen. These changes may lead to the eventual development of large, complex animals.

200 MYA
Atlantic Ocean Forms

Earth's continents, which have been combined into the supercontinent Pangaea, start to separate. As what are now the continents of North America and Africa spread apart, the Atlantic Ocean forms.

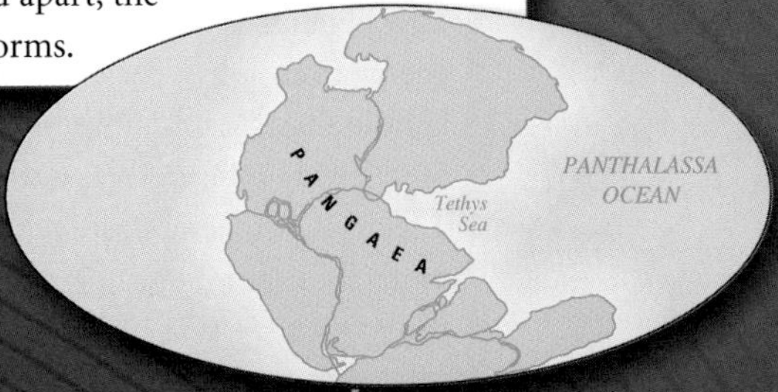

PANGAEA
Tethys Sea
PANTHALASSA OCEAN

| 800 MYA | 600 MYA | 400 MYA | 200 MYA |

Million Years Ago

TECHNOLOGY

Ocean-Floor Core Samples

In the 1960s, scientists began drilling holes into the sea floor to collect long cores, or columns, of sediment and rock. The cores give clues about Earth's climate, geology, and forms of life for millions of years.

The research ship *JOIDES Resolution* has a drilling rig built into it. Equipment attached to the rig is lowered to the sea floor to collect core samples.

12,000 years ago
Earth Emerges from Ice—Again

Earth's temperature warms slightly. Kilometers-thick ice sheets that formed during the latest of Earth's many ice ages start to melt. Forests and grasslands expand. Sea level rises about 100 meters (330 ft), and the ocean floods the edges of the continents.

1972
New View of Earth

Harrison "Jack" Schmitt, an astronaut traveling 24,000 kilometers (15,000 mi) above Earth, takes a photograph. It is the first to show Earth fully lit by the Sun, and the image is sometimes called the Blue Marble. It helps people see the planet as one system.

RESOURCE CENTER
CLASSZONE.COM

Learn more about the Earth system.

100 MYA   **Today**

APPLICATION

International Space Station

The International Space Station has laboratories in which scientists study Earth, the solar system, and the universe. Also, scientists are doing research to better understand the effects of very low gravity on people. This work is part of an effort to develop the life-support systems needed for people to remain in space a long time. Eventually it might aid in the further exploration of space by humans.

INTO THE FUTURE

In almost every area of life, from music to food to sports, the world has become more connected. Science is no exception. In the past century, scientists have begun to monitor the ozone layer. They have realized that the processes that cause continents to change positions also cause earthquakes and volcanic eruptions to occur.

Changes in technology are likely to help scientists increase their understanding of the Earth system. For example, instruments on artificial satellites measure changes in clouds, ocean life, and land temperatures. These types of data help scientists understand how changes in one part of Earth affect other parts.

ACTIVITIES

Taking a Core Sample

Add layers of damp sand of different colors to a paper cup. Switch cups with a partner. Press a clear straw through the sand, put your finger over the top of the straw, and pull the straw out. Determine the order in which your partner added the sand layers. How would you know if there was a layer of sand that did not go across the entire cup?

Writing About Science

Imagine you are living in microgravity like the astronauts on the International Space Station. Write a detailed description of two hours of your day.

CHAPTER
9 Natural Resources

the BIG idea

Society depends on natural resources for energy and materials.

Key Concepts

SECTION

1 Natural resources support human activity.
Learn about the costs and benefits of using natural resources to obtain energy and to make products.

SECTION

2 Resources can be conserved and recycled.
Learn about efforts to conserve and recycle natural resources.

SECTION

3 Energy comes from other natural resources.
Learn how nuclear power and renewable resources can provide energy to the world.

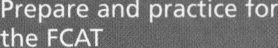
FCAT Practice

Prepare and practice for the FCAT
• Section Reviews, pp. 306, 311, 321
• Chapter Review, pp. 324–326
• FCAT Practice, p. 327

CLASSZONE.COM
• Florida Review: Content Review and FCAT Practice

How do people obtain energy from Earth's resources?

EXPLORE (the BIG idea)

Sunlight as an Energy Source

Tape black paper around two plastic cups. Half fill the cups with water. Fasten plastic wrap over each top with rubber bands. Place one cup in sunlight and one cup in shade. Wait half an hour. Remove the plastic wrap. Place a thermometer in each cup to measure the water temperature.

Observe and Think
What happened to the water temperature in each cup? How do you think people might use sunlight as a source of energy?

Saving Water as You Brush

Time how long it takes you to brush your teeth. Then set aside a bucket or large container and a measuring cup. Close the sink's drain; run the water for the same length of time you brushed your teeth. How many cups of water can you bail out of the sink?

Observe and Think
Estimate how much water you could save in a week by turning the water off as you brush.

Internet Activity: Resources

Go to **ClassZone.com** to learn more about natural resources and energy.

Observe and Think
What are the most important natural resources in your state?

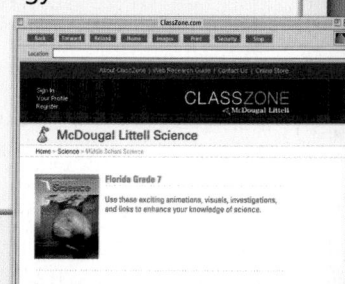

NSTA
scilinks.org
SCi LINKS

Nonrenewable Resources **Code: MDL056**

Getting Ready to Learn

CONCEPT REVIEW

- Soil is a necessary resource.
- Forces wear down and build up Earth's surface.
- The same forces that have changed Earth in the past are still at work today.

VOCABULARY REVIEW

erosion p. 261

deposition p. 261

See Glossary for definitions.

geosphere, glacier

FLORIDA REVIEW
CLASSZONE.COM

Content Review and FCAT Practice

TAKING NOTES

CHOOSE YOUR OWN STRATEGY

As you read, take notes, using one or more of the strategies from earlier chapters—**main idea and detail notes, combination notes,** or **main idea web.** Mix and match these strategies, or use an entirely different one.

VOCABULARY STRATEGY

Write each new vocabulary term in the center of a **four-square** diagram. Write notes in the squares around the term. Include a definition, some characteristics, and some examples. If possible, write some things that are not examples.

See the Note-Taking Handbook on pages R45–R51.

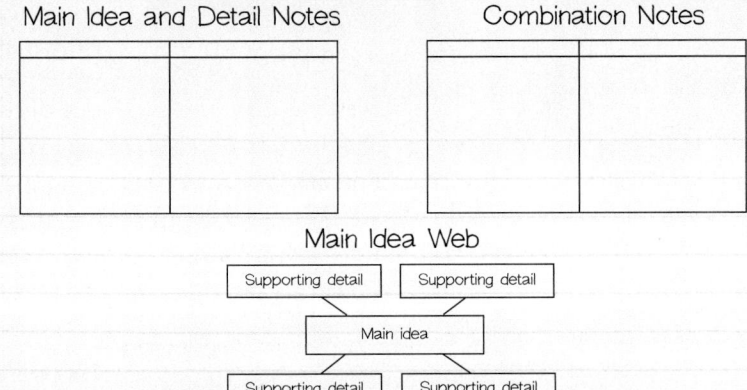

SCIENCE NOTEBOOK

Main Idea and Detail Notes

Combination Notes

Main Idea Web

Supporting detail — Supporting detail — Main idea — Supporting detail — Supporting detail

Definition	Characteristics
a natural resource that can be replaced by nature in a fairly short time	
Examples wind, plant waste, wood	Non-examples coal, natural gas, oil

RENEWABLE RESOURCE

KEY CONCEPT

Natural resources support human activity.

Sunshine State STANDARDS

SC.B.1.3.1: The student identifies forms of energy and explains that they can be measured and compared.

SC.B.2.3.2: The student knows that most of the energy used today is derived from burning stored energy collected by organisms millions of years ago (e.g., nonrenewable fossil fuels).

SC.G.2.3.1: The student knows that some resources are renewable and others are nonrenewable.

FCAT VOCABULARY

renewable resource p. 300
nonrenewable resource p. 300
fossil fuel p. 302

VOCABULARY

natural resource p. 299

VOCABULARY
Use a four-square diagram for the term *natural resource* in your notebook.

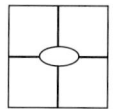

BEFORE, you learned

- The parts of the Earth system shape Earth's surface
- Life on Earth, including human life, depends on soil as a resource
- Forces change Earth's surface by wearing it down and building it up

NOW, you will learn

- What makes a natural resource renewable or nonrenewable
- About benefits and costs of using fossil fuels
- How people use natural resources in modern life

THINK ABOUT

What resources do you need the most?

Think about all the products you use at school and at home—clothing, books, video games, CDs, backpacks, and other items.

Which ones do you use the most often? What materials are these products made of? Plastic? Cloth? Metal? What would you lose if one of these materials, such as plastic, vanished from Earth overnight?

Natural resources provide materials and energy.

For thousands of years, people have used natural resources to make tools, build cities, heat their homes, and in general make their lives more comfortable. A **natural resource** is any energy source, organism, or substance found in nature that people use.

The four parts of the Earth system—atmosphere, hydrosphere, biosphere, and geosphere—provide all the materials needed to sustain human life. The atmosphere, for instance, provides the air you breathe and the rain that helps living things grow. The hydrosphere contains all of Earth's waters in rivers, lakes, oceans, and underground. The biosphere and the geosphere are sources of food, fuel, clothing, and shelter.

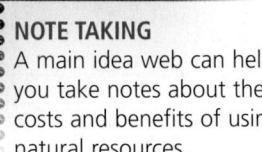

NOTE TAKING
A main idea web can help you take notes about the costs and benefits of using natural resources.

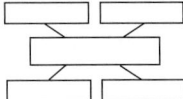

However, people also know that there are costs as well as benefits in using natural resources. For example, burning coal produces heat but also releases smoke that pollutes the air. When forests are cut down, the soil beneath is exposed to the air. Wind and rain can strip away valuable topsoil, making it harder for new trees to grow. The soil can choke streams and rivers and kill fish and other animals living in the waters. As you can see, using resources from one part of Earth's system affects all the other parts.

People are also concerned about saving natural resources. Some resources, such as the water in a river or the wind used to turn a windmill, are constantly being replaced. But others, such as oil, take millions of years to form. If these resources are used faster than they are replaced, they will run out. Today people are more aware of which resources are renewable and which are nonrenewable.

 Summarize the costs and benefits of using natural resources.

Renewable Resources

The charts on page 301 list some of the most common resources people use in modern life. As you might have guessed, sunlight, wind, water, and trees and other plants are renewable. A **renewable resource** is a natural resource that can be replaced in nature at about the same rate it is used.

For example, a lumber company might plant a new tree for each mature tree it cuts down. Over time, the forest will continue to have the same number of trees. However, if the trees are cut down faster than they can be replaced, even a renewable resource will run out.

Nonrenewable Resources

A **nonrenewable resource** is a natural resource that exists in a fixed amount or that is used up faster than it can be replaced in nature. This means the supply of any nonrenewable resource is limited. In general, all resources produced by geologic forces—coal, natural gas, oil, uranium—are nonrenewable. These resources form over millions of years.

Today people are using coal, oil, and natural gas much faster than they are forming in nature. As a result, these resources are becoming more scarce and expensive. Many countries realize that they must conserve their nonrenewable resources. Some, like the United States, are developing alternative energy sources, such as solar and wind energy.

 Compare and contrast renewable and nonrenewable resources.

Natural Resources

Natural resources can be classified as renewable and nonrenewable resources.

Renewable Resources

Resource	Common Uses
Sunlight	power for solar cells and batteries, heating of homes and businesses, and generating electricity
Wind	power to move windmills that pump water, grind grain, and generate electricity
Water	power to generate electricity, transportation with boats and ships, drinking and washing
Trees and other plants	materials for furniture, clothing, fuel, dyes, medicines, paper, cardboard, and generating electricity
Animal waste	material for fuels

Nonrenewable Resources

Resource	Common Uses
Coal	fuel to generate electricity, chemicals for medicines and consumer products
Oil	fuel for cars, airplanes, and trucks; fuel for heating and generating electricity; chemicals for plastics, synthetic fabrics, medicines, grease, and wax
Natural gas	fuel for heating, cooking, and generating electricity
Uranium	fuel to generate electricity
Minerals and rocks	materials for coins, jewelry, building, computer chips, lasers, household products, paint, and dyes

READING VISUALS Read the common uses of each resource. Which of these resources are used to generate electricity?

Fossil fuels supply most of society's energy.

When you turn on the air conditioner, a computer, or a microwave oven, you may use energy from fossil fuels. Millions of people depend on these fuels—coal, oil, and natural gas—for electricity, heat, and fuel.

A **fossil fuel** is a nonrenewable energy source formed from ancient plants and animals buried in Earth's crust for millions of years. The energy in such a fuel represents a form of stored sunlight, since ancient organisms depended on the sun. The buried organisms form layers at the bottom of oceans, ponds, and swamps. Over a long time, this material is compressed and pushed deeper into Earth's crust. High heat and pressure change it chemically into coal, oil, and natural gas.

CHECK YOUR READING Explain how fossil fuels are formed from ancient organisms.

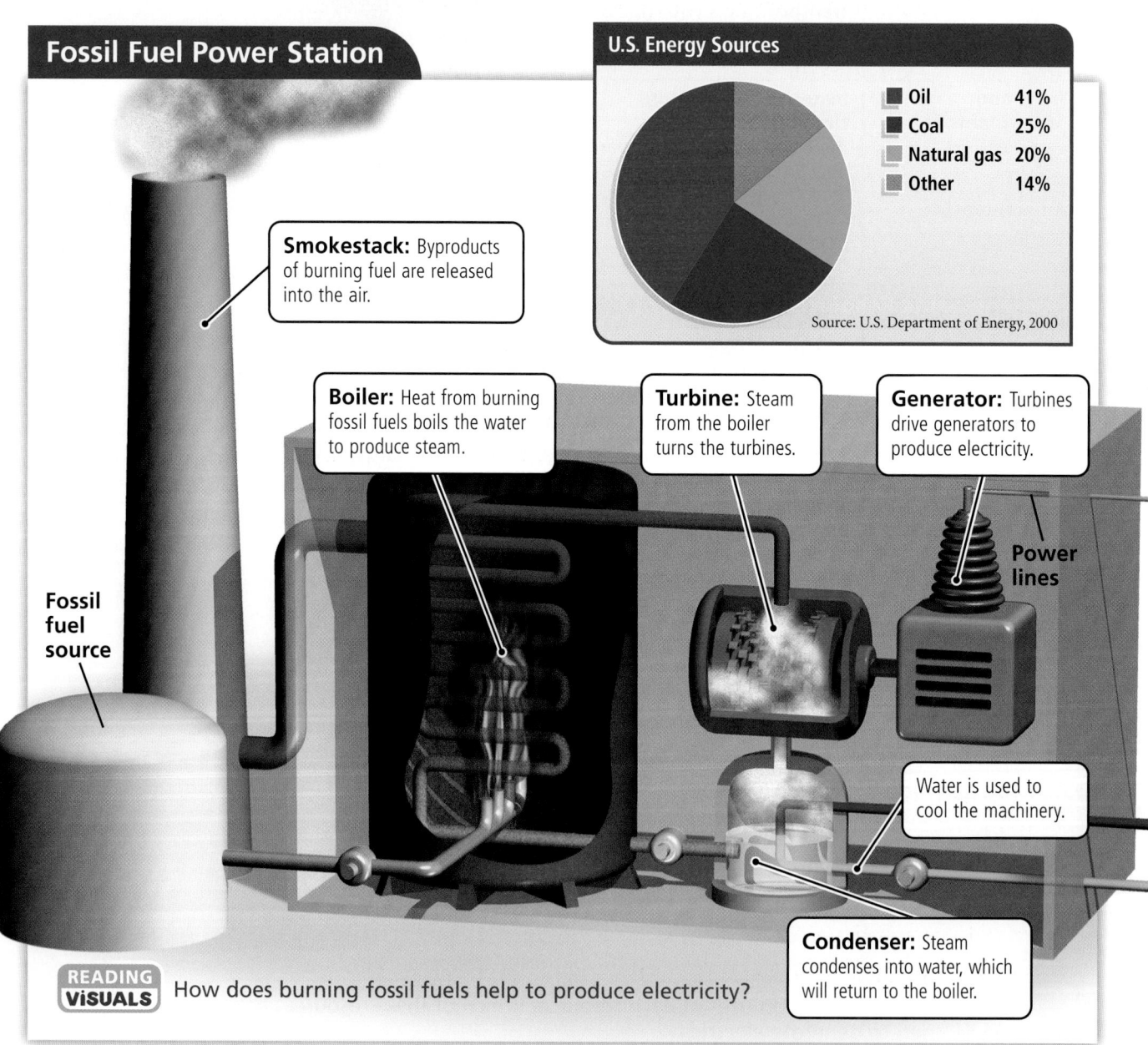

Fossil Fuel Power Station

Smokestack: Byproducts of burning fuel are released into the air.

U.S. Energy Sources

■ Oil	41%
■ Coal	25%
■ Natural gas	20%
■ Other	14%

Source: U.S. Department of Energy, 2000

Boiler: Heat from burning fossil fuels boils the water to produce steam.

Turbine: Steam from the boiler turns the turbines.

Generator: Turbines drive generators to produce electricity.

Power lines

Fossil fuel source

Water is used to cool the machinery.

Condenser: Steam condenses into water, which will return to the boiler.

READING VISUALS How does burning fossil fuels help to produce electricity?

Fossil fuels burn easily and produce a lot of heat. They are used to run most of the power plants that generate electricity. As shown in the diagram on page 302, heat from a burning fuel is used to change water into steam. The steam turns a turbine. The turbine drives a generator to produce electricity, which is carried through power lines to towns and cities. Electricity runs nearly everything in modern life, from giant factories to the smallest light in your home.

But these resources also harm the environment. Burning fossil fuels produces excess carbon dioxide, harmful acids, and other forms of pollution. Most of this pollution comes from power plants and fossil fuels burned by cars and other vehicles.

READING TiP

Turbine is based on the Latin *turbo,* which means "spinning top." *Generator* is based on the Latin *generāre,* which means "to produce."

Coal

Coal is a solid fossil fuel formed underground from buried and decayed plant material. As shown below, heat and pressure determine the type of coal formed. The hardest coal makes the best energy source. It burns hotter and much cleaner than softer coals. At one time, coal was the main source of energy in the United States.

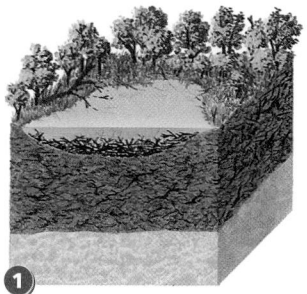 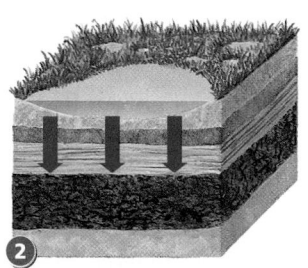 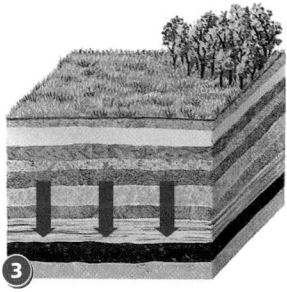 

① Swamp plants decay and are compressed to form peat.

② Sediments bury the peat, and rising pressure and heat change it into soft coal.

③ Over millions of years, increasing pressure and heat form harder coal.

④ It takes the longest time and the greatest heat and pressure to form the hardest coal.

The world's largest coal deposits are in the United States, Russia, and China. People use surface mining and deep mining to obtain coal. In surface mines, overlying rock is stripped away to expose the coal. In deep mines, miners must go underground to dig out the coal. Most of the world's coal is used to fuel power plants and to run factories that produce steel and cement.

When burned as a fuel, however, coal produces byproducts that pollute air and water. Also, surface mining can destroy entire landscapes. Coal dust in deep mines damages miners' lungs. Yet reducing pollution, restoring landscapes, and protecting miners cost millions of dollars. Society faces a difficult choice—keep the cost of energy low or raise the price to protect the environment and human health.

 CHECK YOUR READING   What is the main use of coal?

Oil and Natural Gas

READING TiP

Non- is a Latin prefix meaning "not." Porous rock is full of tiny cracks or holes. Therefore, *nonporous* rock is rock that does not have tiny cracks or holes.

Most oil and natural gas is trapped underground in porous rock. Heat and pressure can push the oil and natural gas upward until they reach a layer of nonporous rock, where they collect. As shown in the illustration below, wells can be drilled through the nonporous rock to bring the oil and natural gas to the surface. Major oil and natural gas deposits are found under the oceans as well as on land.

 **CHECK YOUR READING** How is oil removed from layers of rock?

Recovered oil is transported by ships, trucks, and pipelines from the wells to refineries. Refineries use heat to break down the oil into its different parts. Each part is used to make different products, from gasoline and jet fuel to cleaning supplies and plastics. Oil and natural gas burn at high temperatures, releasing energy. They are easily transported, which makes them ideal fuels to heat homes and to power vehicles.

There are costs in using oil. When ships that transport oil are damaged, they can spill millions of gallons into the environment. These spills pollute coastlines and waterways, killing many plants and animals. Cleaning up these spills costs governments millions of dollars each year. Even after the cleanup, some of the oil will remain in the environment for years.

Air pollution is another problem. Waste products from the burning of gasoline, jet fuels, and diesel fuels react with sunlight to produce smog—a foglike layer of air pollution. Some countries have passed clean air laws to reduce this pollution. Yet smog continues to be a problem in most large cities.

 **CHECK YOUR READING** What are the benefits and costs of using oil?

Oil and Natural Gas Wells

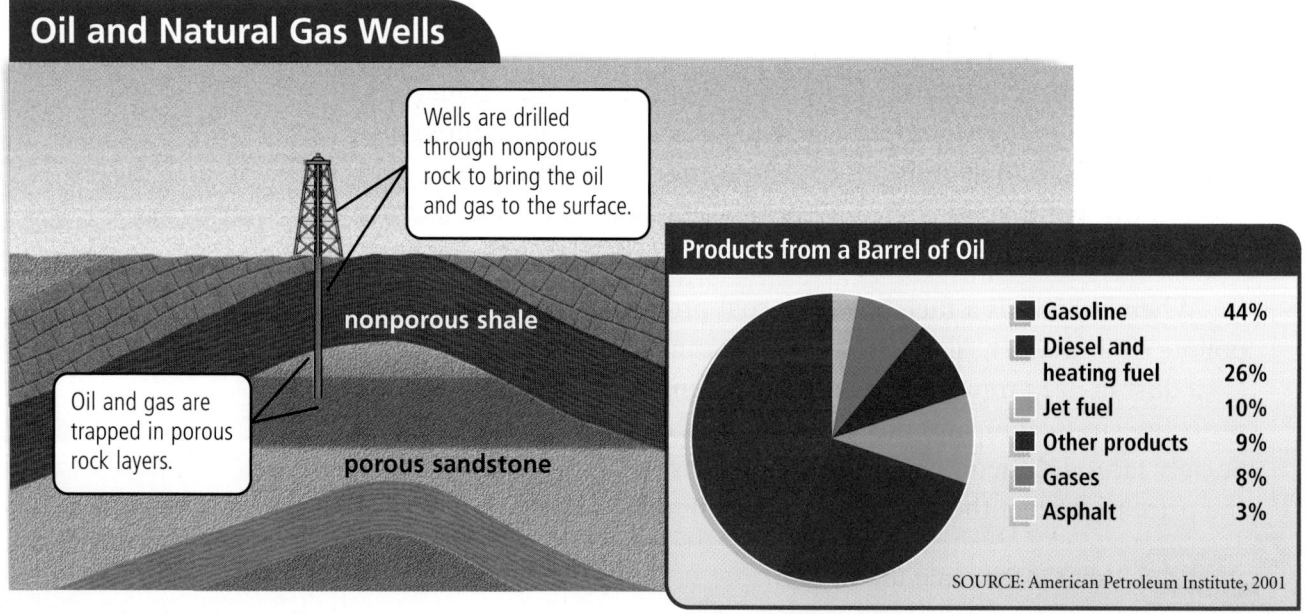

Wells are drilled through nonporous rock to bring the oil and gas to the surface.

nonporous shale

Oil and gas are trapped in porous rock layers.

porous sandstone

Products from a Barrel of Oil

■ Gasoline	44%
■ Diesel and heating fuel	26%
■ Jet fuel	10%
■ Other products	9%
■ Gases	8%
■ Asphalt	3%

SOURCE: American Petroleum Institute, 2001

INVESTIGATE Fossil Fuels

Why does an oil spill do so much harm?

PROCEDURE

1. Fill the pan about halfway with water. Using an eyedropper, carefully add 10 drops of oil in the middle of the pan. Rock the pan gently.

2. Observe what happens to the drops of oil over the next 2 min. Record your observations in your **Science Notebook.**

3. Place the plastic-foam ball in the oil slick, wait a few seconds, then carefully lift the ball out again. Examine it and record your observations.

WHAT DO YOU THINK?

- What happened when the drops of oil came in contact with the water?
- What might happen to an animal that swims through spilled oil?

CHALLENGE Think of a way to clean up the oil slick on the water. Discuss your ideas with your teacher before you test your cleaning method.

SKILL FOCUS
Modeling

MATERIALS
- water
- vegetable oil
- large pan (at least 22 cm)
- plastic-foam ball (about 5 cm)
- eyedropper

TIME
20 minutes

Fossil fuels, minerals, and plants supply materials for modern products.

Many of the products you use come from fossil fuels. For example, oil is broken down into different chemicals used to make plastics. Plastic materials can be easily shaped, colored, and formed. They are used in electronic and computer equipment, in packaging, in cars and airplanes, and in such personal items as your shoes, toothbrush, and comb.

Minerals are found in cars and airplanes, tools, wires, computer chips, and probably your chair. Minerals such as limestone, gypsum, sand, and salt are used to make building materials and cement. In the United States, it takes 9,720 kilograms (20,000 lbs) of minerals every year to make the products used by just one person.

Plants are used to make another large group of products. For centuries people have used wood to build homes and to make furniture, household utensils, and different types of paper. Plants are also rich sources of dyes, fibers, and medicines. The plant indigo, for example, has been used to dye fabrics since Roman times.

These products benefit people's lives in many important ways, but they also have drawbacks. Fossil fuels must be burned to generate power for the factories and businesses that produce these products.

Consumer Products

Thousands of everyday products are made from natural resources.

Fossil Fuels

Fossil fuels are used to make thousands of products from aspirin to zippers. For example, oil-based plastics are used to make this motocross rider's safety helmet, suit, gloves, and boots. Gasoline powers the motorbike.

Minerals and Rocks

The U.S. Treasury uses zinc, copper, and nickel to mint over 14 billion coins a year. Gold and silver are used in special coins.

Trees and Other Plants

Each year, the United States produces about 400 billion square feet of corrugated cardboard used to make boxes of all sizes.

Factory waste can pollute air, water, and soil. Even making computer chips can be a problem. So much water is needed to clean the chips during manufacture that local water supplies may be reduced.

To maintain modern life and to protect the planet, people must use natural resources wisely. In the next section you will read about ways for every person to conserve resources and reduce pollution.

9.1 Review

KEY CONCEPTS

1. Define *renewable resource* and *nonrenewable resource*. Give four examples of each type of resource.

2. List three advantages and three disadvantages of using fossil fuels.

3. In what ways are natural resources used to make people's lives more comfortable?

CRITICAL THINKING

4. **Infer** Why do you think people are willing to accept the costs as well as the benefits of using fossil fuels?

5. **Predict** If supplies of coal, oil, and natural gas ran out tomorrow, what are some of the ways your life would change?

⬤ CHALLENGE

6. **Apply** Suppose you are lost in the woods, miles from any city or town. You have some dried food and matches but no other supplies. What natural resources might you use to survive until you are found?

Got Oil Spills? Call in the Microbes!

You have seen the photographs. A beautiful coastline is fouled by dark, sticky oil. The oil slick coats birds and other animals the same dark color. Hundreds of experts and volunteers appear with buckets, chemicals, shovels, and brooms to clean up the mess.

But did you know that seawater and the world's beaches contain their own natural cleanup crews? These crews consist of tiny microbes that digest oil and other waste products and turn them into gases such as carbon dioxide.

Nature's Disposal Units Do a Great Job . . .

Scientists learned how effective oil-digesting microbes are during the 1989 *Exxon Valdez* oil spill in Alaska. Since then, cleanup crews have been using bacteria and other microbes to help clean up oil spills around the world. Scientists find that areas treated with microbes recover faster than areas treated with chemicals.

. . . But It Is Not All That Simple

Cleaning up oil spills is not as simple as watching millions of microbes munch their way through the mess. Scientists have had to solve a few problems.

- **Problem:** Microbes cannot multiply fast enough to handle a large oil spill. **Solution:** Add nutrients to help them multiply faster.

- **Problem:** There are not enough of the right types of microbes to digest oil. **Solution:** Grow the desired microbes in a laboratory, and add them into the polluted area.

- **Problem:** There is not enough oxygen in the water for all the microbes. **Solution:** Pump in more oxygen to help them work.

Who would have imagined that a partnership between people and microbes would be the best way to clean up oil spills?

Above is the oil-eating microbe *Pseudomonas fluorescens,* magnified 17,300 times. Millions of microbes like this swim in the water layer that surrounds soil particles. They digest oil clinging to the particles.

This otter swam through a spill and was covered in black, sticky oil. Animals who try to clean their fur will swallow the oil, which is poisonous.

EXPLORE

1. **COLLECT DATA** Go to the EPA Web site to learn how the agency uses microbes to clean up different types of pollution. Look under the word *bioremediation,* which means "the correction of a problem through biological means."

2. **CHALLENGE** Do research on bioremediation and find out whether there are any drawbacks to using microbes to clean up pollution.

 **RESOURCE CENTER**
CLASSZONE.COM
Read about microbes that eat pollutants for lunch.

9.2 Resources can be conserved and recycled.

Sunshine State STANDARDS

SC.D.2.3.1: The student understands that quality of life is relevant to personal experience.

SC.H.3.3.4: The student knows that technological design should require taking into account constraints such as natural laws, the properties of the materials used, and economic, political, social, ethical, and aesthetic values.

◁ BEFORE, you learned

- Natural resources are either renewable or nonrenewable
- Fossil fuels are used to supply most of society's energy and products, but at a cost to the environment

▷ NOW, you will learn

- How conservation can help people to reduce waste and reuse natural resources
- How recycling can help people to recover and extend natural resources

FCAT VOCABULARY
conservation p. 309

VOCABULARY
recycling p. 310

EXPLORE Energy Use

What is your EQ (energy quotient)?

PROCEDURE

1. Think about the electrical appliances you use every day at home (TV, computer, room lights, microwave, hair curler, hair dryer). Draw a usage chart like the one in the photo.

2. Estimate the number of hours you use each item every day. Add up all the hours in each column.

3. Multiply the total of each column by 2.5 kilowatts. This is your energy quotient.

WHAT DO YOU THINK?

- Which item(s) do you use the most? How much of the use is necessary?
- What ways can you think of to conserve electricity each day?

MATERIALS
- paper
- pen or pencil
- calculator

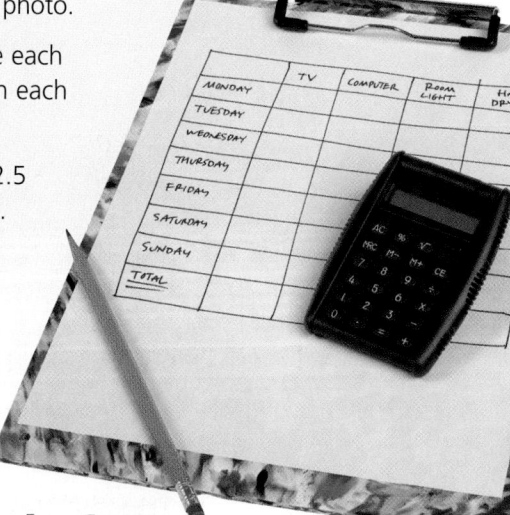

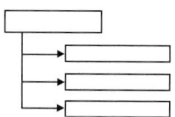

Conservation involves reducing waste and reusing natural resources.

In the 1960s, each person in the United States produced 1.2 kilograms (2.7 lb) of trash a day. Today, that number has doubled. All together, the nation's households produce nearly 180 million tons of trash each year! Over half of this amount is buried in landfills.

Conservation programs can be used to extend natural resources, to protect human health, and to slow the growing mountain of trash. Read on to find out how much your efforts count.

Conservation means protecting, restoring, and managing natural resources so that they last as long as possible. Conserving resources can also reduce the amount of pollution released into the air, water, and soil. There are two ways every person can help: reducing and reusing.

VOCABULARY
Add a four-square diagram for the term *conservation* in your notebook.

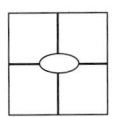

Reduce You can reduce waste at the source, whether the source is a local retail store or your own home. Here are a few suggestions:

- When choosing between two similar products, choose the one with less packaging. Product packaging is a major source of paper and plastic waste.
- When brushing your teeth or washing your face, turn the water off until you are ready to rinse. You can save 8 to 23 liters (2 to 6 gal.) of water a day, or 2920 to 8395 liters (730 to 2190 gal.) per year.
- When eating in a restaurant or cafeteria, use only the napkins and ketchup and mustard packets that you really need. The less you throw away, the less garbage will be buried in a landfill.
- Where possible, use energy-efficient light bulbs in your home. Turn off lights and appliances when you are not using them.

Reuse Many products can be used more than once. Reusable products and containers conserve materials and resources. Here are some things that you can do:

- Refill plastic water bottles instead of buying new bottles.
- Donate old clothes and other items instead of throwing them away.
- Rinse and reuse plastic sandwich and storage bags.
- Cut the top off a half-gallon container to make a watering can.

Reducing Waste

You can reduce paper and plastic waste by choosing products with the least packaging.

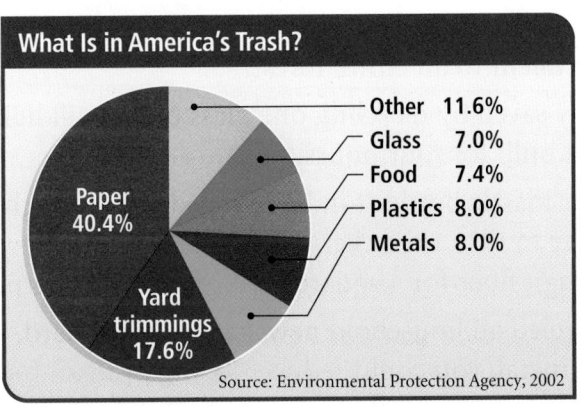

What Is in America's Trash?

Other 11.6%
Glass 7.0%
Food 7.4%
Plastics 8.0%
Metals 8.0%
Paper 40.4%
Yard trimmings 17.6%

Source: Environmental Protection Agency, 2002

This 1.9 liter (64 fl oz) carton has 1088 sq cm of packaging.

Eight travel-size containers provide 1.9 liters (64 fl oz) but have 2720 sq cm of packaging.

How can you tell which bulb wastes less energy?

The more heat a light bulb gives off, the more energy it wastes. Use what you know about how to measure the temperature of an object to design an experiment that confirms which type of light bulb wastes less energy.

DESIGN
— YOUR OWN —
EXPERIMENT

SKILL FOCUS
Designing experiments

MATERIALS
• 2 table lamps
• incandescent light bulb
• fluorescent light bulb
• 2 thermometers
• pen or pencil

PROCEDURE

1. Figure out how you are going to test which light bulb—incandescent or fluorescent—wastes less energy.

2. Write up your procedure.

3. Conduct your experiment and record your results.

WHAT DO YOU THINK?

• What were the variables in your experiment?

• What were the results of your experiment?

• How does your experiment demonstrate which light bulb is less wasteful?

Recycling involves recovering and extending natural resources.

Did you know that recycling one aluminum can saves enough energy to run a television set for three hours? **Recycling** involves recovering materials that people usually throw away. Some common materials you can recycle are glass, aluminum cans, certain plastics, paper, scrap iron, and such metals as gold, copper, and silver. Here are a few statistics that might encourage you to recycle:

With every item you recycle, you help to recover and extend limited resources.

• Recycling 90 percent of the newspapers printed in the United States on just one Sunday would save 500,000 trees, equivalent to an entire forest.

• The energy saved by recycling one glass bottle will light a 100-watt bulb for four hours.

• Five 2-liter plastic bottles can be recycled into enough plastic fiber to fill a ski jacket. Thirty-six bottles will make enough fiber for a square yard of synthetic carpet.

• If you recycled all household newspapers, cardboard, glass, and metal, you could reduce the use of fossil fuels. It takes less energy to make products from recycled materials than to make new products.

Recycled: 500 kilograms (1,102 lb) of cans, glass, plastic, and paper

Buried in landfill: 2500 kilograms (5,512 lb) of garbage

The average family of four generates about 3,000 kilograms (6614 lb) of trash per year. Recycling is catching on, but there is still a long way to go.

It is important to remember that not every item can be recycled or reused. In the photograph above, for instance, only about one-fifth of the family's trash is being recycled. Even some types of plastic and glass items must be thrown away because they cannot be recovered. All the trash in the family's plastic bags will be buried in landfills. You can see why it is important to recycle the items you can and to avoid using items that cannot be recycled.

Recycling is only part of the solution to our resource problems. It takes time, energy, and money to collect waste materials, sort them, remove what can be used, and form new objects. Even with these limitations, however, recycling can help extend available resources and protect human health and the environment.

 **CHECK YOUR READING** What are some of the benefits and drawbacks of recycling?

9.2 Review

KEY CONCEPTS

1. Give examples of ways people can reduce waste and conserve natural resources.

2. Explain how recycling can help people recover and extend natural resources.

3. What are some of the limitations of conservation and recycling programs?

CRITICAL THINKING

4. **Evaluate** How can conserving or recycling materials help protect the environment?

5. **Calculate** Your city pays $115 per ton to bury an average of 13 tons of garbage a month in a landfill. A recycling program could reduce that number to 8 tons a month. How much would the city save in landfill fees per month? per year?

⬥ CHALLENGE

6. **Synthesize** Work with a group of classmates to list some of the ways in which you could conserve and recycle resources in your home and at school. Create a graphic—such as a poster or advertisement—to present your ideas to the rest of the class.

Gas Mileage

An automobile engineer ran tests on new cars to determine their gas mileage in miles per gallon. Her results were in decimals. You can compare two decimals by looking at their place values to determine which is greater.

MATH TUTORIAL
CLASSZONE.COM

Click on Math Tutorial for more help with comparing decimals.

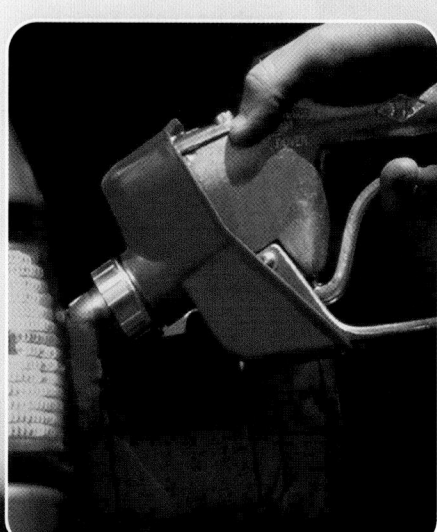

Steps for comparing decimals

(1) Write the decimals in a column, lining up the decimal points.

(2) If necessary, write zeros to the right of one decimal so that both decimals have the same number of decimal places.

(3) Compare the place values from left to right.

Examples

Example A
For two mid-size sedans, she calculated the following mileages:

The tens digits are the same.
The ones digits are the same.

Car A: 28.450 mi/gal
Car B: 28.502 mi/gal

The tenths digits are different: 5 > 4.

ANSWER:
28.450 mi/gal < 28.502 mi/gal

Example B
For two sport utility vehicles (SUVs), she calculated the following mileages:

The tens digits are the same.
The ones digits are the same.

SUV A: 12.94 mi/gal
SUV B: 12.90 mi/gal

The tenths digits are the same.
The hundredths digits are different: 4 > 0.

ANSWER:
12.94 mi/gal > 12.90 mi/gal

Copy each statement and complete it with <, >, or =.

1. 34.75 mi/gal ___ 34.56 mi/gal

2. 50.5 mi/gal ___ 50.50 mi/gal

3. 52.309 mi/gal ___ 52.311 mi/gal

4. 26.115 mi/gal ___ 26.106 mi/gal

5. 41.75 mi/gal ___ 41.750 mi/gal

CHALLENGE Find a value of n that makes the following statement true:
38.0894 mi/gal > n > 38.08925 mi/gal

KEY CONCEPT
9.3 Energy comes from other natural resources.

Sunshine State STANDARDS

SC.B.1.3.1: The student identifies forms of energy and explains that they can be measured and compared.

SC.B.1.3.3: The student knows the various forms in which energy comes to Earth from the Sun (e.g., visible light, infrared, and microwave).

SC.G.2.3.1: The student knows that some resources are renewable and others are nonrenewable.

VOCABULARY
nuclear fission p. 313
hydroelectric energy p. 316
solar cell p. 317
geothermal energy p. 318
biomass p. 320
hydrogen fuel cell p. 320

BEFORE, you learned

- Conservation helps people reduce waste and reuse natural resources
- Recycling helps people recover and extend natural resources

NOW, you will learn

- About the benefits and costs of nuclear power
- How renewable resources are used to generate energy

EXPLORE Nuclear Energy

How can you model splitting atoms?

PROCEDURE

① Work in a small group for this activity. Draw a large circle on a piece of paper. Set the paper on the floor or on a countertop.

② Put a handful of marbles in the circle (see the photograph). Imagine the circle is an atom and the marbles are particles in its nucleus.

③ Take turns shooting one marble into the others. Put the marbles back in the circle after each shot. Record your observations.

MATERIALS
- marbles
- large piece of paper
- pen or marker

WHAT DO YOU THINK?
- How many marbles were moved by each shot?
- What does this activity suggest will happen when the center of an atom is struck?

NOTE TAKING
As you read this section, pick a note-taking strategy that will help you list the benefits and limits of each type of energy source.

Nuclear power is used to produce electricity.

Fossil fuels are the most commonly used sources of energy, but they are not the only ones. The United States and many other countries use nuclear power to produce electricity. In the United States, nuclear power plants generate about 10 percent of the total energy used.

You learned that in fossil fuel power plants, water is boiled to make steam that turns a turbine, which drives a generator. In a nuclear power plant, the same process happens. However, the source of energy used to heat the water is nuclear fission. In the process of **nuclear fission,** the nucleus of a radioactive atom is split, forming lighter elements and releasing a huge amount of energy.

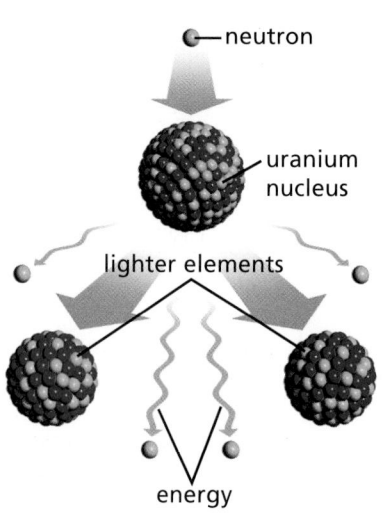

A uranium nucleus splits, forming lighter elements and releasing neutrons and a great deal of energy.

neutron

uranium nucleus

lighter elements

energy

Nuclear power plants use uranium atoms as fuel. When a uranium nucleus splits, it forms two smaller nuclei. It also releases two or three neutrons and a large amount of energy in the form of light and heat. The neutrons split other uranium nuclei in a process called a chain reaction. This process is similar to shooting one marble into a group of marbles. Every marble that is hit will strike others nearby.

The power-plant diagram below shows the reactor vessel where the chain reaction takes place. Control rods are used to limit the reaction to provide a safe amount of energy. The chain reaction creates enough heat to produce steam in the reactor vessel. The steam heats a coiled pipe, which is used to boil water in the heat exchanger.

Steam from the exchanger turns the turbines, which drive the generators that produce electricity. The steam condenses into water and is pumped back into the heat exchanger. Water from the cooling tower keeps the equipment from overheating. As you can see, nuclear power plants require an abundant water supply to produce steam and to stay cool.

Nuclear Power Plant

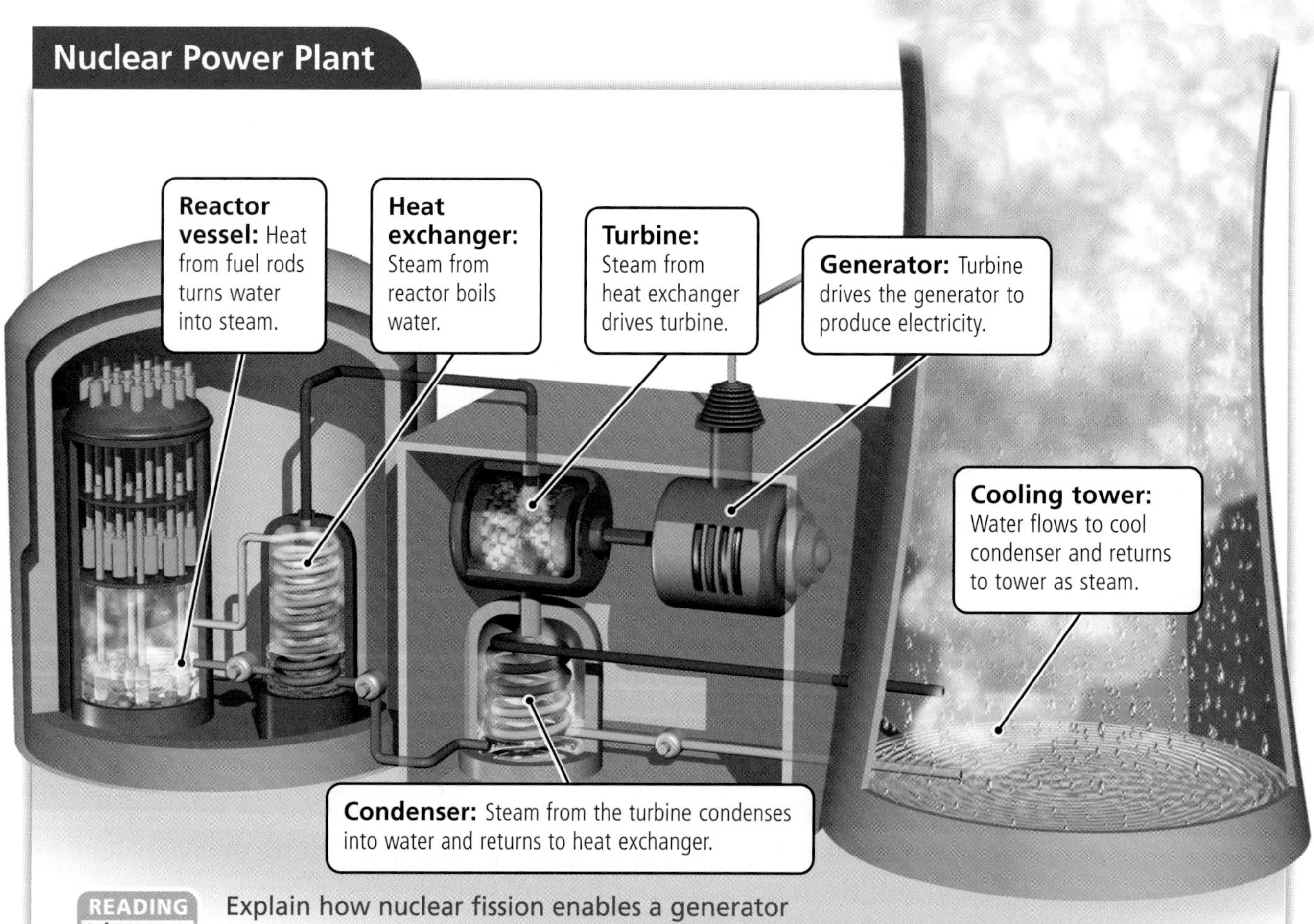

Reactor vessel: Heat from fuel rods turns water into steam.

Heat exchanger: Steam from reactor boils water.

Turbine: Steam from heat exchanger drives turbine.

Generator: Turbine drives the generator to produce electricity.

Cooling tower: Water flows to cool condenser and returns to tower as steam.

Condenser: Steam from the turbine condenses into water and returns to heat exchanger.

READING VISUALS Explain how nuclear fission enables a generator to produce electricity.

cooling towers

reactor buildings

turbine buildings

water source

Splitting just one atom of uranium releases 20 million times more energy than does burning one molecule of natural gas. However, nuclear fission also produces radioactive waste. Radioactivity is a form of energy that can cause death and disease if living things are exposed to it long enough. Nuclear waste from a power plant will remain radioactive for thousands of years. Countries that use nuclear energy face the challenge of storing this waste safely. The storage sites must keep any radioactivity from escaping until the waste material becomes harmless.

A nuclear power plant usually has three main sections: reactor buildings, turbine buildings, and cooling towers.

SIMULATION
CLASSZONE.COM

Explore how a nuclear power plant produces energy.

 CHECK YOUR READING   Explain how fission is used to generate energy.

Renewable resources are used to produce electricity and fuel.

Moving water, wind, Earth's internal heat, sunlight, living matter, and hydrogen are all sources of renewable energy. Unlike fossil fuels, many of these sources of energy are in unlimited supply. They usually produce electricity or fuel with little or no pollution. Using these clean energy sources helps preserve the environment and protect human health.

So far, however, these resources cannot produce enough energy to pay for the cost of developing them on a large scale. As a result, renewable resources provide only a small percentage of the energy used in the world. In the United States, only about 6 percent of the total energy used comes from these resources.

Scientists and engineers must improve the necessary technologies before renewable resources can supply clean energy to more of the world's people. Imagine if everyone's car ran on hydrogen and produced only water as a byproduct. Or think of solar panels generating enough electricity to light a major city. These visions could come true in your lifetime.

CHECK YOUR READING   What makes renewable resources attractive as energy sources?

Hydroelectric Energy

RESOURCE CENTER
CLASSZONE.COM

Learn more about the benefits and costs of renewable energy resources.

Hydroelectric energy is electricity produced by moving water. If you have ever stood near a waterfall or even just turned on a faucet, you have felt the force of moving water. People can use flowing water to generate electricity.

In most cases, a dam is built across a large river, blocking the river's flow and creating an artificial lake, or reservoir. As the illustration below shows, water from the lake enters the dam through intake gates and flows down a tunnel. The fast flowing water turns turbines that drive generators, which produce electricity. Because hydroelectric power does not burn any fuel, it produces no pollution. Dams in the United States generate enough electricity to save 500 million barrels of oil a year.

However, building dams poses problems for the environment. By flooding land to create reservoirs, dams destroy wildlife habitats. In some rivers, such as the Snake and Columbia rivers in the United States, dams interfere with the annual migration of salmon and other fish. Also, areas near the end of the river may receive less water than before, making it harder to raise crops and livestock.

Areas with large rivers can use their power to produce electricity. The dam in the photo was built on the Yukon River in Alaska.

Hydroelectric Dam

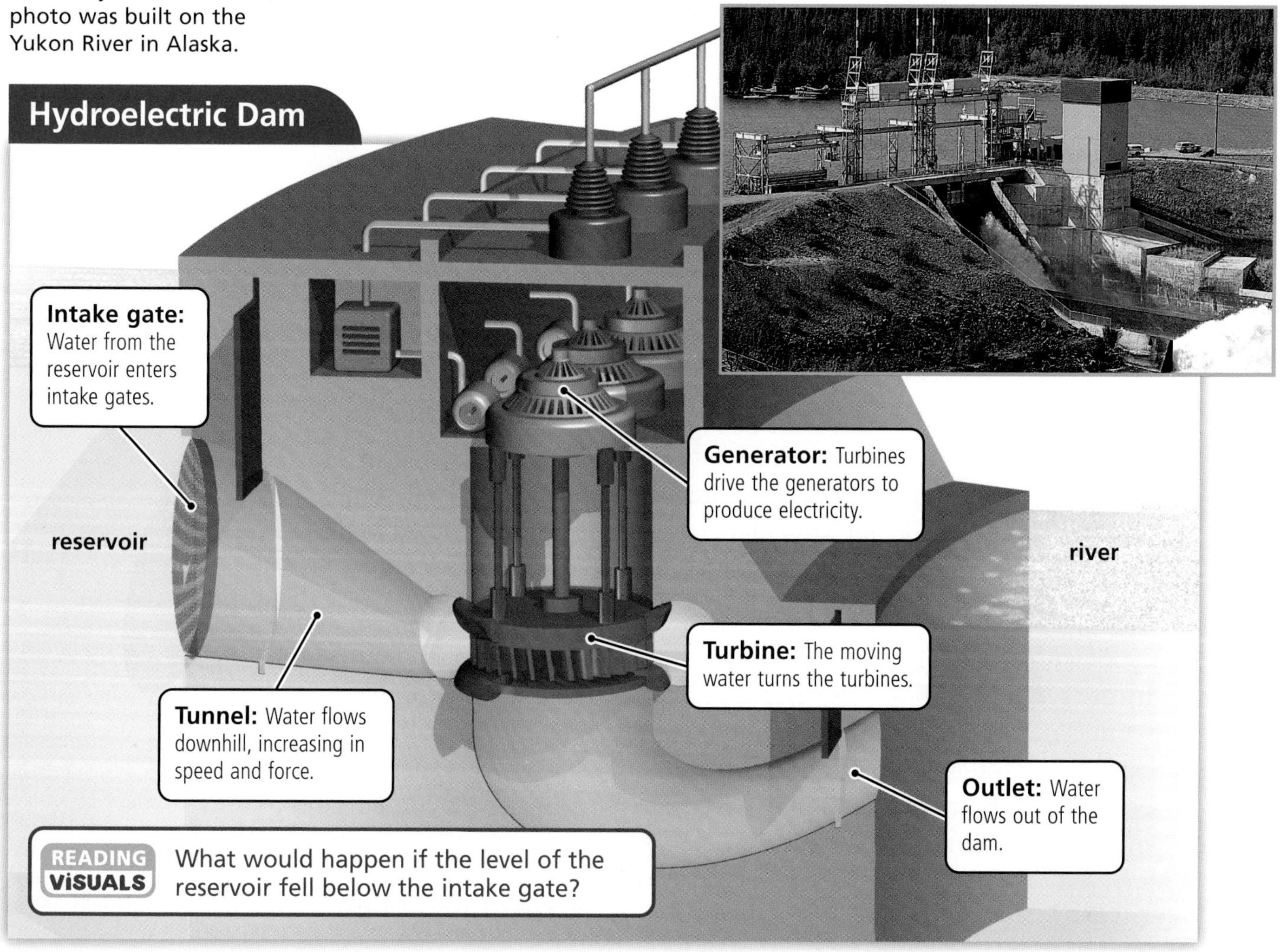

Intake gate: Water from the reservoir enters intake gates.

reservoir

Tunnel: Water flows downhill, increasing in speed and force.

Generator: Turbines drive the generators to produce electricity.

Turbine: The moving water turns the turbines.

river

Outlet: Water flows out of the dam.

READING VISUALS What would happen if the level of the reservoir fell below the intake gate?

Solar Energy

Only a small fraction of the sun's energy falls on Earth. Yet even this amount is huge. Every day enough energy from the sun strikes the United States to supply all the nation's energy needs for one and a half years. The problem is how to use this abundant resource to produce electricity.

In an effort to solve the problem, scientists developed solar cells. A **solar cell** is a specially constructed sandwich of silicon and other materials that converts light energy to electricity. As shown in the diagram below, when sunlight strikes the cell, electrons move from the lower to the upper layer, producing an electric current. Individual solar cells can power small appliances, such as calculators and lights.

Solar cells can be wired together in solar panels, which provide heat and electricity for homes and businesses. Solar panels are also used to power some spacecraft and space stations once they are in orbit. To meet the energy needs of some cities, hundreds or even thousands of solar panels are built into large structures called arrays. Many western cities like Barstow, California, receive part of their electricity from solar arrays.

Sunlight is an unlimited source of clean energy. But current methods of collecting sunlight are expensive and somewhat inefficient. As solar technology improves, sunlight is likely to become an important energy source for the world.

VOCABULARY
Add a four-square diagram for the term *solar cell* in your notebook.

READING TiP
Array refers to an arrangement of objects in rows and columns.

CHECK YOUR READING How can people use sunlight to produce electricity?

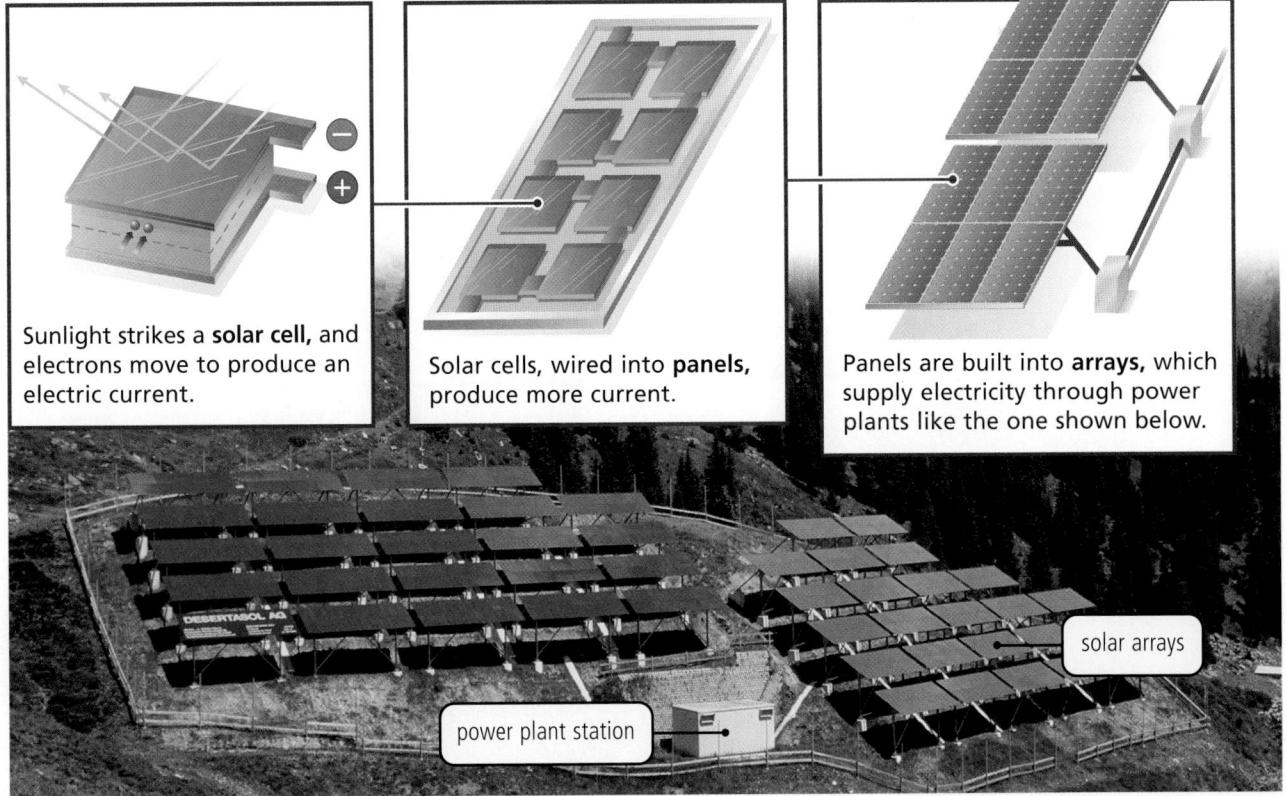

Sunlight strikes a **solar cell,** and electrons move to produce an electric current.

Solar cells, wired into **panels,** produce more current.

Panels are built into **arrays,** which supply electricity through power plants like the one shown below.

solar arrays

power plant station

Geothermal Energy

READING TIP

Geothermal combines the Greek prefix *geo-*, meaning "earth," and the Greek word *thermē*, meaning "heat."

Imagine tapping into Earth's heat to obtain electricity for your home. In some places, that is exactly what people do. They use **geothermal energy**, or energy produced by heat within Earth's crust.

Geothermal energy comes from underground water that is heated by hot rock. The illustration below shows how hot water is piped from a well into a power plant. This superheated water enters a flash tank and produces enough steam to run turbines, which power generators. Excess water is then pumped back into the ground. Some plants also pipe hot water into homes and businesses for heating.

In the United States, geothermal energy provides electricity for nearly 3.5 million homes. Other major geothermal power plants are in New Zealand and Iceland.

Geothermal energy is clean and renewable. So far, its use is limited to areas where hot water is fairly close to the surface. However, some companies are experimenting with pumping cold water into underground areas of hot rock found in all parts of Earth's crust. The rock heats the water, which is then pumped back to the surface and used

In Iceland, geothermal power plants like the one in the photograph supply nearly all of the country's electricity.

Geothermal Power Plant

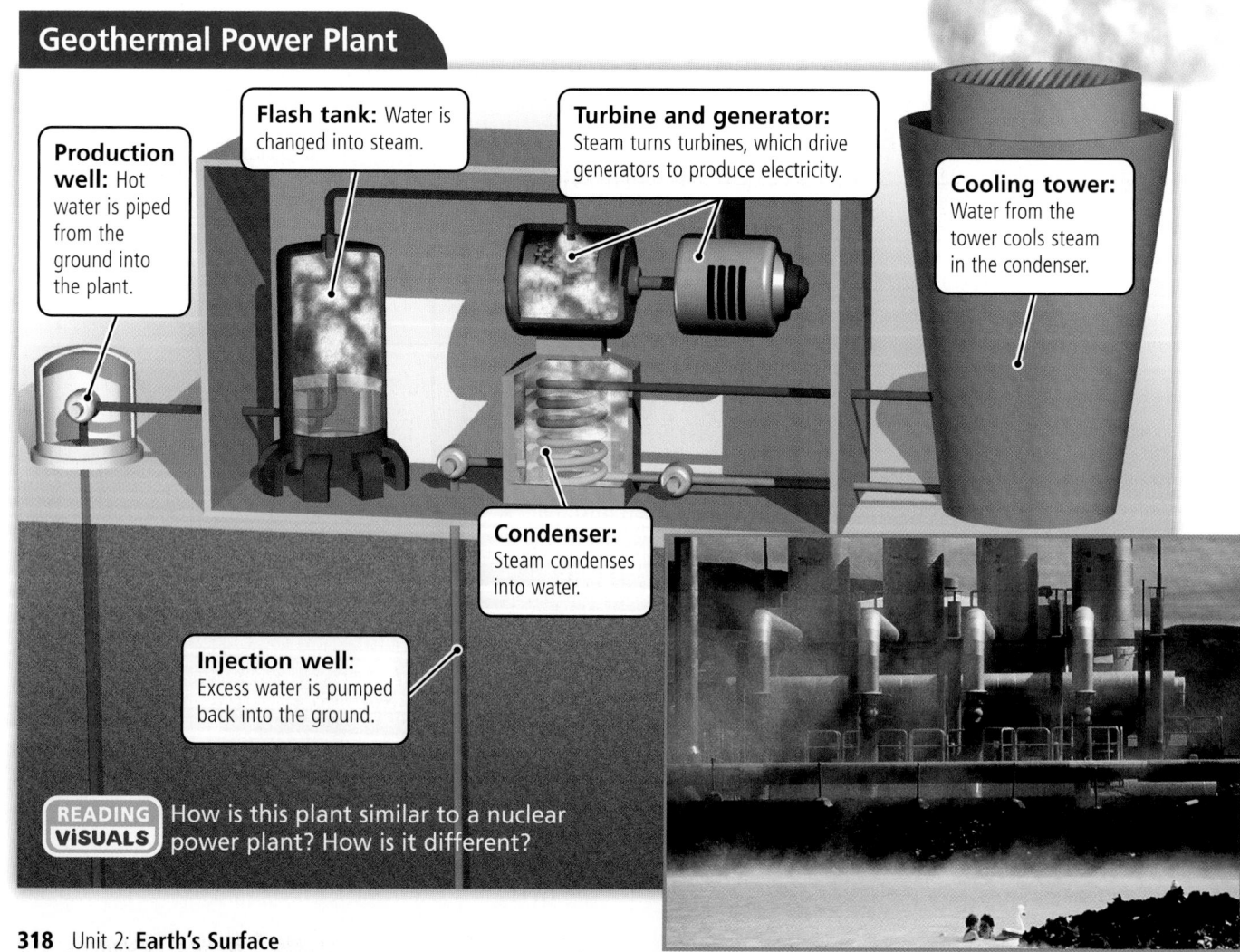

Production well: Hot water is piped from the ground into the plant.

Flash tank: Water is changed into steam.

Turbine and generator: Steam turns turbines, which drive generators to produce electricity.

Cooling tower: Water from the tower cools steam in the condenser.

Condenser: Steam condenses into water.

Injection well: Excess water is pumped back into the ground.

READING VISUALS How is this plant similar to a nuclear power plant? How is it different?

to generate electricity. This new technique may allow more countries to make use of geothermal energy.

 **CHECK YOUR READING** What is the source of geothermal energy?

Wind Energy

For thousands of years, people have captured the tremendous energy of wind to move ships, grind grain, and pump water from underground. Today, people also use wind energy—from the force of moving air—to generate electricity.

The modern windmill is made of metal and plastic and can stand as tall as a 40-story building. The blades act as a turbine, turning a set of gears that drives the generator. The amount of electricity a windmill produces depends on the speed and angle of the wind across its blades. The faster the blades turn, the more power the windmill produces.

To supply electricity to an area, hundreds of windmills are built on a "wind farm." Wind farms, like the one in the photograph below, are already producing electricity in California, Hawaii, New Hampshire, and several other states. Other countries, such as Denmark and Germany, also use wind farms to supply electricity to some of their cities.

Although wind energy is clean and renewable, it has certain drawbacks. It depends on steady, strong winds blowing most of the time, which are found only in a few places. Wind farms take up a great deal of land, and the turning blades can be noisy. There is also a limit to how much power each windmill can produce. However, in the future, wind farms may become more productive and more widely used.

REMINDER
The generator is the part that produces the electric current, whether it is driven by turbines or gears.

FLORIDA Content Review
Keep in mind that useful energy is lost as heat energy in every energy conversion, as you learned in grade 6.

CHECK YOUR READING What factor determines how much electricity a windmill produces?

The blades turn the gears, which drive the generator to produce electricity. The controller points the windmill's head into the wind to keep the blades turning rapidly.

Biomass Energy

Biomass is organic matter, such as plant and animal waste, that can be used as fuel. The U.S. Department of Energy works with state and local groups to find ways of converting biomass materials into energy sources.

This wood-burning biomass plant sends electrical energy at a rate of 21 million watts to the San Francisco Bay area. Wood waste products are collected from farms and industries as fuel for the plant.

Each year biomass power stations in the United States burn about 60 million tons of wood and other plant material to generate 37 billion kilowatt hours of electricity. That is more electricity than the state of Colorado uses in an entire year. Small biomass stations are used in rural areas to supply power to farms and towns. Fast-growing trees, grasses, and other crops can be planted to supply a renewable energy source that is cheaper than fossil fuels.

Some plant and animal waste can be converted into liquid fuels. The sugar and starch in corn and potatoes, for example, are made into a liquid fuel called ethanol. Ethanol can be added to gasoline to form gasohol. This fuel can power small cars, farm machinery, and buses. A liquid fuel made from animal waste is used for heating and cooking in many rural areas around the world.

Although biomass is a renewable resource, certain problems limit its use. Burning wood and crops can release as much carbon dioxide into the air as burning fossil fuels does. Biomass crops take up land that could be used to raise food. Also, plant fuels such as ethanol are still too expensive to produce on a large scale. For now, biomass materials provide only a small part of the world's energy.

 **CHECK YOUR READING** What are the advantages and disadvantages of biomass fuels?

Hydrogen Fuel Cells

VISUALIZATION
CLASSZONE.COM

Watch a hydrogen fuel cell in action.

Scientists are also exploring the use of hydrogen gas as a renewable energy source. Hydrogen is the simplest atom, made up of one proton—the nucleus—and one electron. Scientists have found ways to separate hydrogen from water and from fossil fuels. It is a flammable gas and must be handled with care

Hydrogen is used in a **hydrogen fuel cell,** a device that produces electricity by separating hydrogen into protons and electrons. The diagram on page 321 shows hydrogen fuel entering on one side of the cell while oxygen from the air enters on the other side. Once in the cell, electrons flow out of the cell through wires, forming an electric current that powers the motor. The protons pass through a membrane and combine with oxygen to form water as a byproduct.

Hydrogen fuel cells are used to supply electrical energy on spacecraft and space stations. Fuel-cell buses are being tested in several countries.

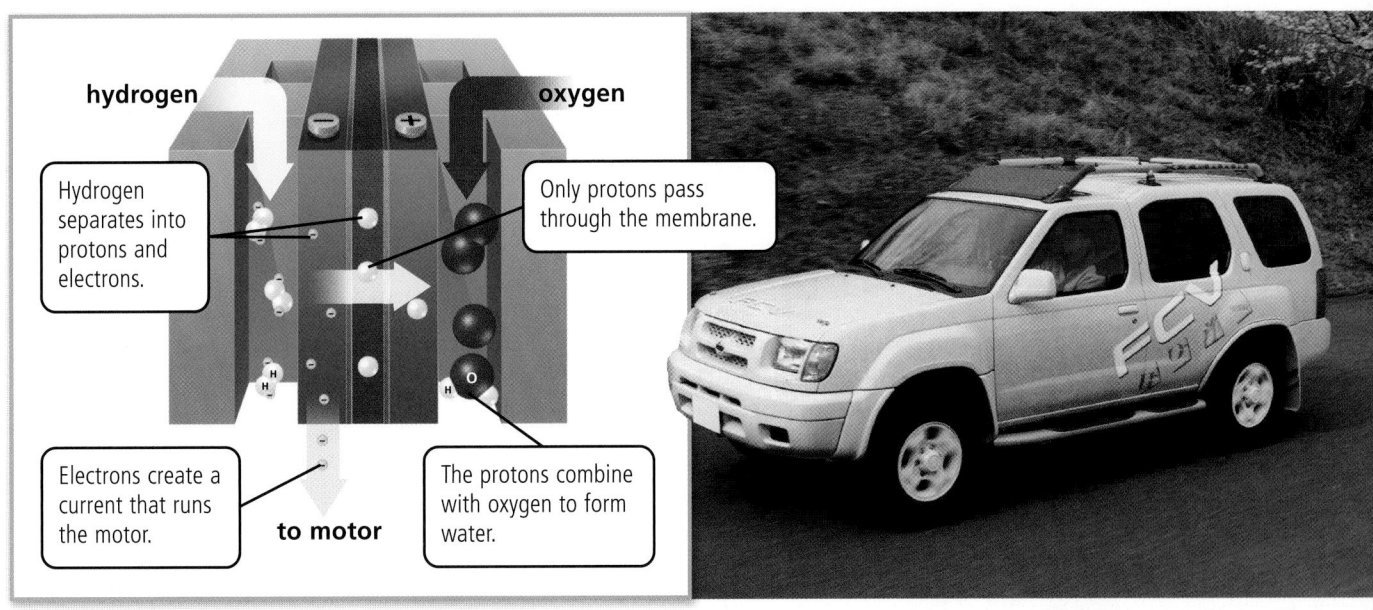

hydrogen
oxygen

Hydrogen separates into protons and electrons.

Only protons pass through the membrane.

Electrons create a current that runs the motor.

to motor

The protons combine with oxygen to form water.

A storage tank in the back of this SUV holds hydrogen fuel. Electrical energy from fuel cells powers the motor and a backup battery.

Also, some fuel-cell cars are now available to the public. Storage tanks in these vehicles carry hydrogen fuel for the cells.

Fuel-cell technology holds great promise for the future. Hydrogen is a clean source of energy, producing only water and heat as byproducts. If every vehicle in the world were powered by hydrogen, the level of air pollution would drop sharply.

However, hydrogen fuel cells are still too expensive to produce in large numbers. Separating hydrogen from water or from fossil fuels takes a great deal of energy, time, and money. Also, there are only a few fueling stations to supply cars and other vehicles that run on hydrogen. The U.S. Department of Energy is working with the automotive industry and other industries to solve these problems.

CHECK YOUR READING Why is hydrogen considered a promising alternative energy source?

9.3 Review

KEY CONCEPTS

1. List the main advantages and disadvantages of nuclear energy as a power source.

2. Describe the advantages of using sunlight, water, and Earth's heat energy to produce electrical power.

3. What are some factors that limit the use of biomass, wind, and hydrogen as energy sources?

CRITICAL THINKING

4. **Evaluate** Do you think people would use a clean, renewable fuel that cost twice as much as gasoline? Explain.

5. **Calculate** One acre of corn yields 20 gallons of ethanol. A bus gets 20 miles per gallon and travels 9000 miles in one year. How many acres of corn are needed to fuel the bus for a year?

CHALLENGE

6. **Synthesize** Review the energy sources discussed in this section. Then think of ways in which one or more of them could be used to supply electricity to a house in Florida and a house in Alaska. Which energy sources would be suitable in each environment? Describe your ideas in writing, or make sketches of the houses.

CHAPTER INVESTIGATION

Wind Power

OVERVIEW AND PURPOSE Early windmills were used mainly to pump water and grind flour. In this lab, you will use what you have learned about renewable resources to
- build a model windmill and use it to lift a small weight
- improve its performance by increasing the strength of the wind source

▶ Problem

Write It Up

What effect will increasing the wind strength have on the lifting power of a model windmill?

▶ Hypothesize

Write It Up

After completing step 8 of the procedure, write a hypothesis to explain what you think will happen in the next two sets of trials. Your hypothesis should take the form of an "If . . . , then . . . , because . . ." statement.

▶ Procedure

MATERIALS
- half of a file folder
- metric ruler
- quarter
- scissors
- paper punch
- brass paper fastener
- drinking straw
- pushpin
- masking tape
- small paper clip
- pint carton
- 30 cm of string
- clock or stopwatch
- small desktop fan

1. Make a data table in your **Science Notebook,** like the one on page 323.

2. Cut a 15 cm square from a manila file folder. With a ruler, draw lines from the corners toward the center, forming an X. Where the lines cross, use a quarter to draw a circle. Cut inward along the lines from the four corners, stopping at the small circle. Punch a hole in each corner and in the center of the circle.

15 cm

step 2

3. Bend the cardboard to align the holes. Push a brass paper fastener through the holes toward the back of the pinwheel. Do not flatten the metal strips of the fastener.

4. Use a pushpin to poke a hole through a straw, about 4 cm from the end. Then push the metal strips through the hole and flatten them at right angles to the straw. Fold the tip of the straw over and tape it to the rest of the straw.

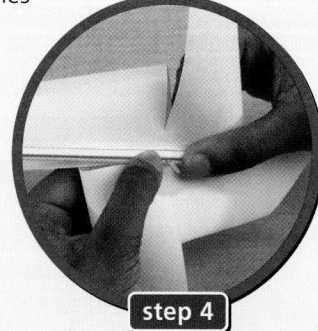

step 4

5. Cut the spout portion off the top of the pint carton. Punch two holes on opposite sides of the carton. Make sure the holes line up and are large enough for the straw to turn easily.

6. Slide the straw through the holes. Tape the string to the end of the straw. Tie a small paper clip (weight) to the other end of the string.

7. Test the model by blowing on the blades. Describe what happens to the weight.

step 6

8. Run three trials of the lifting power of the model windmill as you blow on the blades. Keep the amount of force you use constant. Have a classmate use a stopwatch or clock with a second hand to time the trials. Record the results in your data table. Average your results.

9. Vary the strength of the wind by using a desktop fan at different speeds to turn the windmill's blades. Remember to record your hypothesis explaining what you think will happen in the next two sets of trials.

▶ Observe and Analyze

Write It Up

1. **MODEL** Draw a picture of the completed windmill. What happens to the weight when the blades turn?

2. **IDENTIFY VARIABLES** What method did you use to increase the wind strength? Add a sketch of this method to your picture to illustrate the experimental procedure.

3. **RECORD OBSERVATIONS** Make sure your data table is completed.

4. **COMPARE** How did the average times it took to raise the weight at different wind strengths differ?

▶ Conclude

Write It Up

1. **INTERPRET** Answer the question posed under "problem" on page 322.

2. **ANALYZE** Did your results support your hypothesis?

3. **IDENTIFY LIMITS** What limitations or sources of error could have affected your experimental results?

4. **APPLY** Wind-powered turbines are used to generate electricity in some parts of the country. What might limit the usefulness of wind power as an energy source?

▶ INVESTIGATE Further

CHALLENGE How you can get your model windmill to do more work? You might try different weights, or you might build a larger windmill and compare it with your original. Create a new data table. Use a bar graph to compare different weights and wind strengths. How much wind power is needed to lift the additional weight?

Wind Power

Problem

Hypothesize

Observe and Analyze

Table 1. Time to Lift Weight

Wind Force Used	Trial Number	Time (sec)
Student powered	1	
	2	
	3	
	Average	
Fan on low speed	1	
	2	
	3	
	Average	
Fan on high speed	1	
	2	
	3	
	Average	

Conclude

Chapter Review

the BIG idea

Society depends on natural resources for energy and materials.

FLORIDA REVIEW
CLASSZONE.COM

Content Review and
FCAT Practice

◀ KEY CONCEPTS SUMMARY

1 **Natural resources support human activity.**

Renewable Resources
• Sunlight
• Wind
• Water
• Trees, other plants
• Plant and animal waste

Energy

Examples of Products
• Lumber
• Paper
• Clothing

Nonrenewable Resources
• Coal
• Oil, natural gas
• Uranium
• Minerals, rocks

Examples of Products
• Fuels
• Plastics
• Electronic goods

VOCABULARY
natural resource p. 299
renewable resource
  p. 300
nonrenewable
  resource p. 300
fossil fuel p. 302

---

2 **Resources can be conserved and recycled.**

People can **conserve** natural resources by reducing waste at the source and reusing products.

Recycling helps people recover materials, reduce the use of fossil fuels, and protect the environment and human health.

VOCABULARY
conservation p. 309
recycling p. 310

---

3 **Energy comes from other natural resources.**

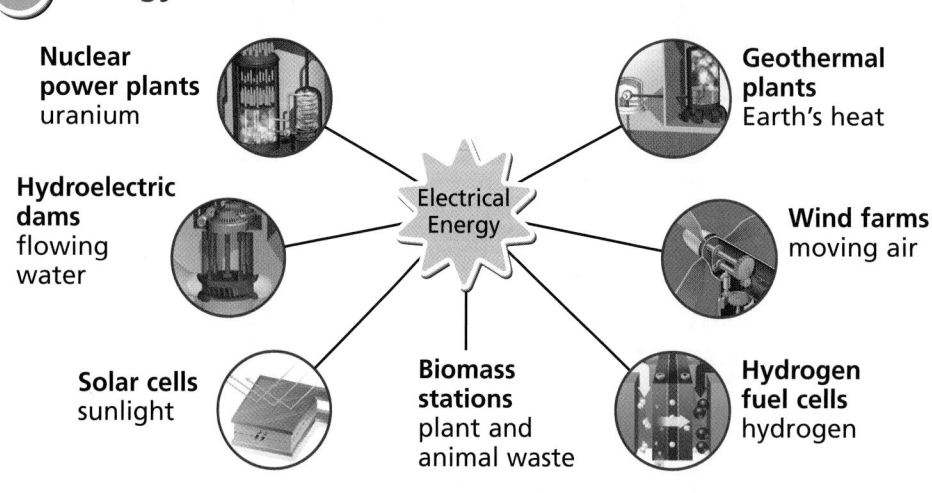

Nuclear power plants
uranium

Hydroelectric dams
flowing water

Solar cells
sunlight

Biomass stations
plant and animal waste

Electrical Energy

Geothermal plants
Earth's heat

Wind farms
moving air

Hydrogen fuel cells
hydrogen

VOCABULARY
nuclear fission p. 313
hydroelectric energy
  p. 316
solar cell p. 317
geothermal energy
  p. 318
biomass p. 320
hydrogen fuel cell
  p. 320

Reviewing Vocabulary

Copy the chart below, and write each word's definition. Use the meaning of the underlined word part to help you.

Word	Meaning of Part	Definition
1. Natural resource	to rise again	
2. Renewable resource	to refresh	
3. Nonrenewable resource	not to refresh	
4. Fossil fuel	material that burns	
5. Nuclear energy	nut or kernel	
6. Geothermal energy	heat	

Reviewing Key Concepts

Multiple Choice *Choose the letter of the best answer.*

7. What makes wind a renewable resource?
- **a.** no pollution
- **b.** varied speeds
- **c.** no waste products
- **d.** unlimited supply

8. Which of the following is a nonrenewable resource?
- **a.** trees
- **b.** oil
- **c.** sunlight
- **d.** geothermal energy

9. Fossil fuels provide most of the energy used in the United States because they
- **a.** are found everywhere in the world
- **b.** have no harmful byproducts
- **c.** are easy to transport and burn
- **d.** can be quickly replaced in nature

10. Which part of a power plant actually produces electricity?
- **a.** boiler
- **b.** generator
- **c.** turbine
- **d.** power lines

11. Which of the following is not a problem associated with the use of fossil fuels?
- **a.** air pollution
- **b.** explosions
- **c.** limited supply
- **d.** radiation

12. Which category of products is the most dependent on oil?
- **a.** pottery
- **b.** coins
- **c.** plastics
- **d.** paper

13. How do nuclear power plants generate the heat energy to turn water into steam?
- **a.** by drawing hot water from Earth's crust
- **b.** by producing an electric current
- **c.** by turning a turbine
- **d.** by splitting uranium atoms

14. Hydroelectric energy is produced by using the force of
- **a.** wind
- **b.** sunlight
- **c.** moving water
- **d.** living matter

15. Solar cells produce which of the following?
- **a.** heat energy
- **b.** steam
- **c.** radiation
- **d.** electricity

16. What limits the use of biomass liquid fuels?
- **a.** not enough plant material
- **b.** too expensive to mass-produce
- **c.** not enough energy generated
- **d.** too many harmful byproducts

17. Hydrogen fuel cells produce electricity when
- **a.** electrons from hydrogen leave the cell
- **b.** hydrogen is separated from fossil fuels
- **c.** protons from hydrogen combine with oxygen
- **d.** hydrogen fuel flows into the cell

Short Response *Write a short response to each question.*

18. Why is it important to find renewable sources of energy?

19. Why is conservation of natural resources important?

20. How can recycling help reduce the use of fossil fuels?

Thinking Critically

Use the circle graphs below to answer the following questions.

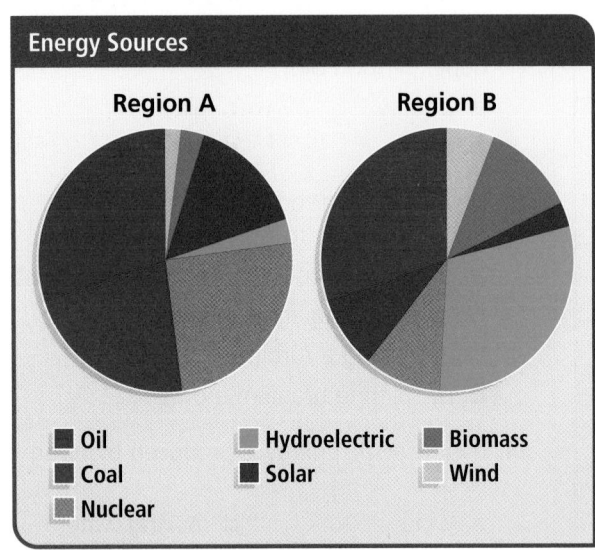

Energy Sources

Region A   Region B

■ Oil   ■ Hydroelectric   ■ Biomass
■ Coal   ■ Solar   ■ Wind
■ Nuclear

21. INTERPRET Which colors represent nonrenewable resources and which ones represent renewable resources?

22. CALCULATE Fossil fuels and nuclear energy together represent about what percentage of the total energy resources in region A? in region B?

23. PREDICT If the price of nonrenewable energy sources rises sharply, which region is likely to be affected more? Why?

24. DRAW CONCLUSIONS What might be one reason that region A uses a greater percentage of fossil fuels and nuclear energy than region B does?

25. INFER Look at the renewable energy sources used in each region. What can you infer about the climate in region A compared with the climate in region B?

26. IDENTIFY CAUSES Why might region B use so much more hydroelectric energy?

27. SYNTHESIZE Region C gets half of its electrical energy from fossil fuels. The region has only 100 days of clear sunlight a year but has abundant plant crops and strong, steady winds. Draw a circle graph for region C, showing the percentage of fossil fuels and the percentage of each renewable energy source the region might use. Explain your choices.

Charting Information

Copy and fill in this chart.

Type of Energy	Produces Energy From	Byproducts
28. uranium		radioactive waste
29. fossil fuel	burning oil, coal	
30.	moving air	none
31. river		
32. sunlight		
33.	burning wood	carbon dioxide
34. hydrogen		

the BIG idea

35. APPLY Look again at the photograph on pages 296–297. Reread the question on the photograph. Now that you have finished the chapter, what would you add to or change about your answer?

36. SYNTHESIZE Imagine that you are a scientist or engineer who is developing a new energy source. What characteristics would you want your energy source to have? List your choices in order of importance, with the most important first—for instance, nonpolluting, inexpensive to mass-produce, and so on.

37. APPLY If you were in charge of your town or city, what measures would you take to conserve natural resources?

UNIT PROJECTS

Evaluate all the data, results, and information in your project folder. Prepare to present your project. Be ready to answer questions posed by your classmates about your results.

Analyzing a Graph

This graph shows what happens to fuels consumed for energy in the United States. Some of this energy is used and some is lost as heat. Use the graph to answer the questions below.

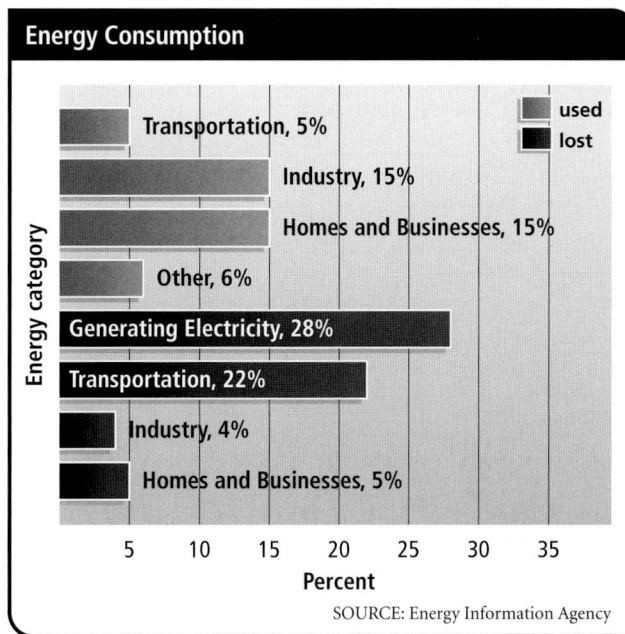

Energy Consumption

used
lost

Transportation, 5%
Industry, 15%
Homes and Businesses, 15%
Other, 6%
Generating Electricity, 28%
Transportation, 22%
Industry, 4%
Homes and Businesses, 5%

Energy category

5   10   15   20   25   30   35
Percent

SOURCE: Energy Information Agency

FCAT TiP

When answering questions based on a bar graph, be sure to read the title of the graph, the key, and all labels. This will help you understand what the graph is trying to show.

GRIDDED RESPONSE

1. What percent of energy is used for transportation and energy?

2. What is the total amount of energy used and lost in industry?

MULTIPLE CHOICE

3. What is the largest category of lost energy?
   A. transportation
   B. homes and businesses
   C. generating electricity
   D. industry

4. Which category would include energy used to heat a grocery store?
   F. used in homes and businesses
   G. used in industry
   H. used in transportation
   I. used in other ways

5. If cars burned fuel more efficiently, which category would probably be smaller?
   A. used in homes and businesses
   B. used in other ways
   C. lost in transportation
   D. lost in industry

6. Which statement is true about energy used and lost in transportation?
   F. The amount lost is greater than the amount used.
   G. The amount used is greater than the amount lost.
   H. The amounts used and lost are about the same.
   I. The amounts used and lost are very low in comparison with the other categories.

EXTENDED RESPONSE
Answer the two questions below in detail. Include some of the terms in the word box. In your answers, underline each term you use.

reusing	recycling	conserve	extends
electricity	hot water	factories	

7. Explain the difference between reusing and recycling products. How does each activity help reduce the use of natural resources?

8. Give three or more examples of ways in which people in the United States use or rely on energy resources every day.

Electricity and Magnetism

magnet

ATTRACT

magnetic field

Contents Overview

Frontiers in Science
Electronics in Music   330

Florida Connection
Animatronics   334

Timelines in Science
The Story of Electronics   404

Chapter 10 Electricity   338

Chapter 11 Circuits and Electronics   372

Chapter 12 Magnetism   408

Electronics in Music

How are
electronics changing
the way we make
and listen to music?

SCIENTIFIC
AMERICAN
FRONTIERS

View the video segment
"Toy Symphony" to learn
about some creative new
ways in which music
and electronics can be
combined.

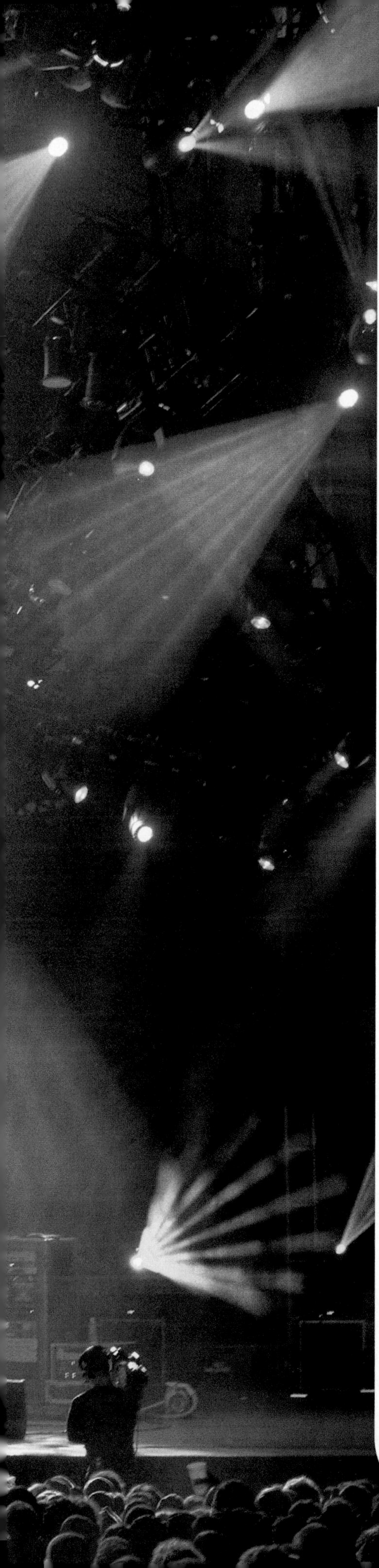

The quality of amplified sound waves can be controlled using electronics. Controls on this soundboard are adjusted in preparation for an outdoor concert.

Catching a Sound Wave

Everyone knows that music and electronics go together. If you want to hear music, you turn on a radio or TV, choose a CD or DVD to play, or listen to a computer file downloaded in MP3. All of these formats use electronics to record, play, and amplify music. Some of the most recent developments in music also use electronics to produce the music in the first place. For example, the orchestral music playing in the background of the last blockbuster movie you saw may not have been played by an orchestra at all. It may have been produced electronically on a computer.

Music consists of sound, and sound is a wave. Inside your TV or stereo equipment, electronic circuits represent sound waves as analog signals or digital signals. In analog recordings a peak in the original sound wave corresponds to a peak in the current. Radio and TV broadcasts are usually analog signals. The sound wave is converted to electromagnetic waves sent out through the air. Your radio or TV set receives these waves and converts them back to a sound wave.

In digital sound recordings the system samples the incoming sound wave at frequent intervals of time, such as 44,100 times per second. The system measures the height of each wave and assigns it a number. The numbers form a digital signal. This information can then be stored and transmitted. The playback electronics, such as CD players and DVD players, convert the signal back to a sound wave for you to hear.

Digital Devices

In a compact disc (CD), the numbers representing the sound wave are coded into a series of microscopic pits in a long spiral track burned into the plastic of the CD. A laser beam scans the track and reads the pits, converting the data back into numbers. This information is then converted into sound waves by an electronic circuit in the CD player. CDs can store up to 74 minutes of music because the pits are only a few millionths of a meter in size. Digital videodiscs (DVDs) often have several layers, each with a separate data track, and use even smaller tracks and pits than CDs use. As a result, a DVD can store seven times as much information as a CD.

The amount of computer space needed to represent a song in normal digital format is too large to store very many songs on a single device. However, the development of a compression program called MP3 decreases the size of a typical song to one-tenth its original size. This enables you to buy and download a song from the Internet in minutes instead of hours and store files on your computer or MP3 player without taking up too much space.

MP3 players store digital files that are compressed in size.

Making Music

These advances in recording and playing music enables you to listen to music, whatever your taste in music happens to be. Electronic technology also allows you to change the music or even generate your own music, as shown in the video. Recording engineers used to work with large electronic consoles with hundreds of switches in order to blend different singers and background

View the "Toy Symphony" segment of your *Scientific American Frontiers* video to learn how electronic devices allow people to interact with music in new ways.

IN THIS SCENE FROM THE VIDEO ▶
Kids play with Beatbugs at MIT's Media Lab.

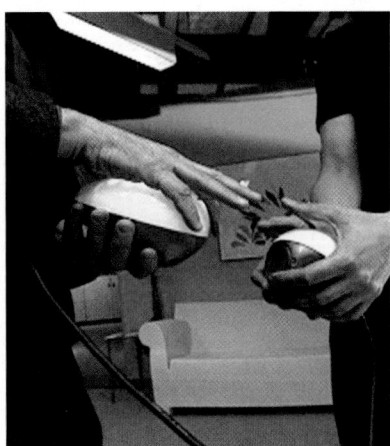

PLAYING WITH SOUNDS At the Massachusetts Institute of Technology (MIT) Media Lab, Tod Machover and his colleagues have invented several new musical instruments that are based on electronics. One such invention is the hyperviolin, demonstrated by concert violinist Joshua Bell. As Joshua plays the violin, a computer registers the movements of the bow and produces new and different sounds from the movements. Other musical electronic devices in the lab are designed to allow someone with little or no experience with an instrument to play and compose music.

With Beatbugs—small interactive devices—kids can play music and collaborate with others. They can also compose and edit their own music. Using new computer software, a ten-year-old boy was able to compose an entire symphony played by the German Symphony Orchestra.

Home recording studios are possible because of new electronic technology.

instruments or to add special effects such as echoes or distortion. Now this can all be done on a laptop computer, using the Musical Instrument Digital Interface (MIDI).

MIDI technology is an advancement in digital technology. Whereas CD, DVD, and MP3 files represent the sound waves themselves, MIDI files represent the instructions for another device—such as an electronic instrument—to play the music. With MIDI, you can connect an electronic keyboard directly to a computer and compose and edit your own music, layer in the sounds of different instruments, and dub in special effects. Once you understand how to use electronics to produce the sound waves you want, you can become your own favorite band.

UNANSWERED Questions

Every year, scientists develop new technologies affecting the way we produce and listen to music. As advances in music technology are made, new question arise.

- Are there electronic sounds that no one has heard before?
- How will the development of music technology affect who is producing music?
- What type of devices will people be using to listen to music in 50 years?

UNIT PROJECTS

As you study this unit, work alone or with a group on one of these projects.

Multimedia Presentation

Put together an informative presentation that explains how electric guitars work.

- Gather information about electric guitars. Learn how they use both electricity and magnetism.
- Give a presentation that uses mixed media, such as a computer slide show, model, poster, or tape recording.

Build a Radio

Build a working radio from simple materials.

- Using books or the Internet, find instructions for building a simple crystal radio.
- Collect the materials and assemble the radio. Modify the design of the radio to improve it.
- Demonstrate the radio to the class and explain how it works.

Design an Invention

Design an electronic invention.

- Select a purpose for your invention, such as a toy, a fan, or a burglar alarm. Write a paragraph that explains the purpose of your invention.
- Draw a sketch of your design and modify it if necessary.
- Make a pamphlet to advertise your invention. If possible, build the invention and include photographs of it in the pamphlet.

CAREER CENTER
CLASSZONE.COM

Learn more about careers in music and computer science.

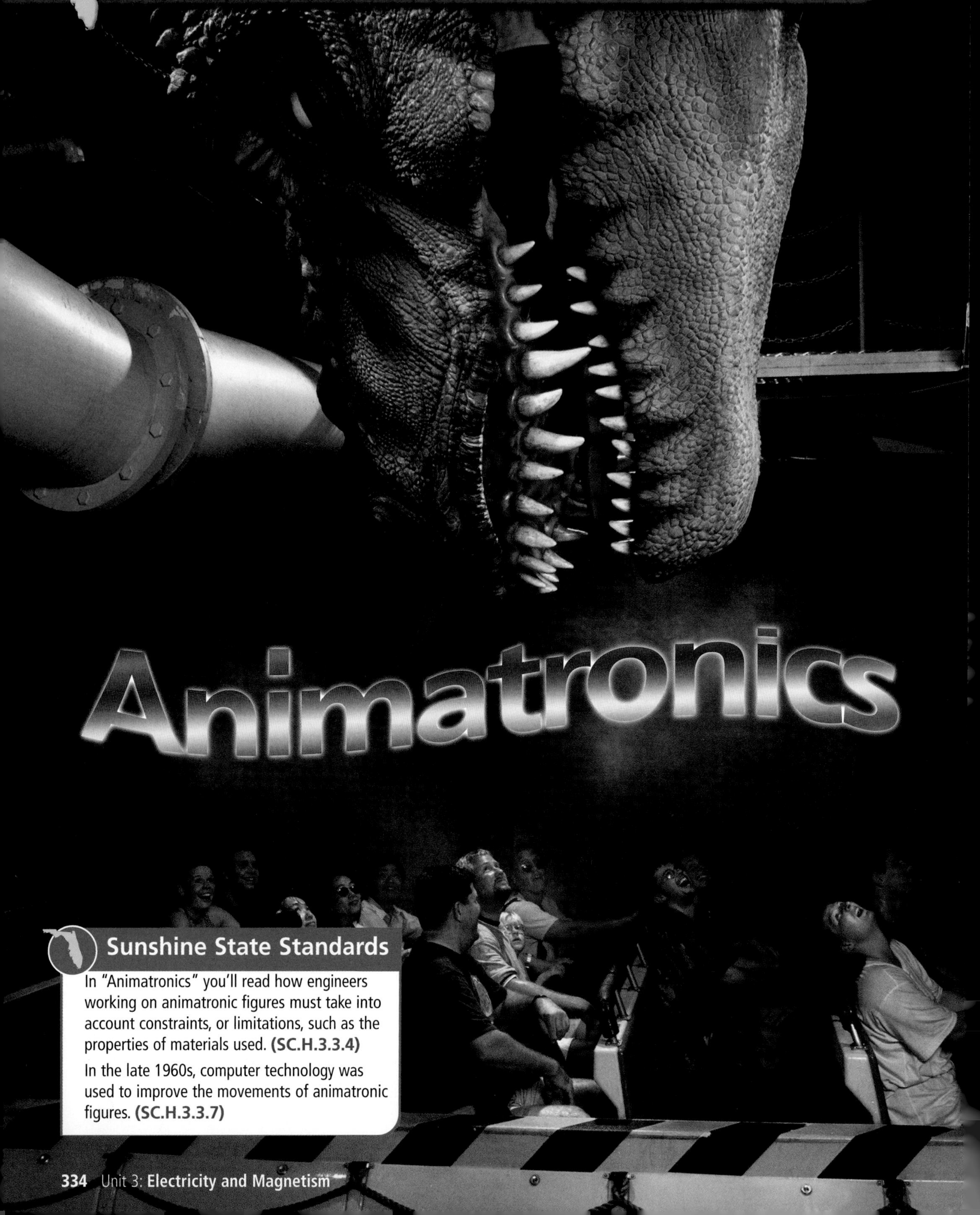

Animatronics

Sunshine State Standards

In "Animatronics" you'll read how engineers working on animatronic figures must take into account constraints, or limitations, such as the properties of materials used. **(SC.H.3.3.4)**

In the late 1960s, computer technology was used to improve the movements of animatronic figures. **(SC.H.3.3.7)**

Animatronic figures, such as these at Disney World in Orlando, entertain visitors at theme parks across the country.

A Wild Time in Florida!

Consider these experiences you can have in Florida:

- A monstrous dinosaur towers over you as a speeding asteroid threatens to wipe out life on Earth.
- A pleasant boat ride turns into an escape from the terrifying jaws of a giant great white shark.
- You find yourself in the middle of a battle among dangerous pirates over stolen treasure in a Caribbean port in the 1700s.
- You travel in a time machine to witness events of the past and future.

How is this possible? Of course, all of these experiences occur at Florida's theme parks. A theme park is an amusement park in which the attractions have a central idea, such as the world in the future. The people and creatures described above are all products of animatronics. Animatronics is a technology that uses electronics to make mechanical puppets move, or to animate them.

These mechanical puppets are run by an internal computer program or remotely controlled by a technician. The technology is sometimes called audio-animatronics because the figures move in time with a soundtrack. Voices, music, sound effects, animation, and other elements are combined to give a lifelike appearance to the three-dimensional figures.

Is It a Robot? How is an animatronic figure different from a robot? In general, robots are built to do a job—often a job that is too repetitive or dangerous for a human to do easily. Animatronic figures are usually designed for entertainment. You might think of them as giant remote-controlled toys. They are meant to look like real animals or people—or, in some cases, aliens or other fanciful creatures. Most robots, on the other hand, do not need to look like living beings. They are designed to be functional.

Economic Impact A large part of Florida's economy is based on tourism. The state's warm weather and many beaches bring visitors from around the world. Theme parks are a huge part of Florida's tourist industry. Walt Disney World, located in Orlando, is a large theme park and resort that draws tourists to Florida. Another is Universal Studios Florida, also in Orlando. Other theme parks dot the state, such as Busch Gardens in Tampa, Weeki Wachee Spring in Weeki Wachee, and SeaWorld Orlando. Theme parks also help the economy by providing jobs for many Floridians.

A number of theme parks include animatronics as part of their most popular attractions. Animatronic figures can also be seen in movies, in museums, in theme restaurants, and in traveling exhibits at malls and schools. How are these lifelike figures created?

History of Animatronics

Audio-animatronics development began around 50 years ago. Its purpose was to give lifelike movement to three-dimensional figures for the Disneyland theme park in California. The first project was called the Dancing Man. Engineers began by filming a man doing a dance. This film was used as a model for the movements of a mechanical dancer. The figure was made to imitate the dance moves through the use of cables and metal cams, or shaped wheels mounted on rotating shafts. The movements were jerky and limited, but it was a start.

In 1963 the Enchanted Tiki Room opened at Disneyland. The attraction featured 250 talking, singing, and dancing mechanical birds that were operated using digital controls. How were these creatures able to move?

- Tones were first recorded onto audiotape.
- When played, the tones caused a piece of metal to vibrate. This vibration closed a circuit, operating a relay that sent a pulse of electrical energy to the figure's internal mechanism.
- The pulse caused a pneumatic valve to operate, resulting in the desired action, such as moving a bird's beak.

Pneumatic valves are operated by air pressure. But air pressure provided only enough energy to perform simple actions. This was fine for the Tiki Room, but Disney's engineers were beginning to work on human figures. They needed a better system to imitate complicated human movements.

Hydraulics, or the use of fluids to transmit force, allowed for a wider range of movement and increased power. Movements were still jerky, however. Raising a human figure's arm, for example, requires many small actions to appear lifelike. One way of achieving lifelike motion was to have an operator wear a control harness. As the human operator moved, so did the animatronic figure. This process took a lot of time and hard work. Again, a better system was needed.

In 1969 Disney engineers turned to computer technology. They first recorded descriptions of movements onto a computer disk. Animators then manipulated a figure's actions using knobs on a control board. In the late 1980s, the Disney company developed a technology that enables movements to be more fluid and realistic. However, it still takes about eight hours of programming time to animate one second of movement.

Animatronics Today

Early animatronics engineers had to work within specific constraints, or limits. The most basic constraints were time and money. Another constraint was the limited technology of the early 1960s. Today, animatronics engineers work with more-advanced technology, but the constraints they face remain nearly unchanged. They need to create a figure that looks realistic and doesn't wear out. The figure must move in time to its soundtrack. Its controls must be hidden, and it must operate safely.

A complicated motorized puppet can take a team of engineers, designers, and artists up to two years to complete. Most large animatronic figures are produced following several basic steps.

SPOTLIGHT ON Lincoln Speaks

You may have seen the Hall of Presidents at Disney World. Forty-two presidents of the United States are represented as animatronic figures. They move, they speak, they delight visitors.

In the early 1960s, Disney engineers created the first full-size three-dimensional figure, Abraham Lincoln. First, they designed and built Lincoln's head. This took about a year. The face was made from a copy of an original cast of Lincoln's face made in 1860. It was the first time the engineers had tried to copy human movements: talking, smiling, blinking, raising eyebrows. They used solenoids, coils with insulated wire wound around them. Electric current traveled through a solenoid to a "slug" that controlled the position of a facial feature. Only two positions were available for each movement—for example, eyes open or shut, eyebrows raised or lowered.

The Lincoln figure was completed for the 1964 New York World's Fair. The "Great Moments with Mr. Lincoln" exhibit was in the State of Illinois Pavilion. The figure had a wide range of motions and expressions. Lincoln could pick up a glass, put his hands behind his back, and shrug. The final model was controlled by a combination of hydraulics and pneumatics. There were 16 air lines to control the head, 10 air lines for the hands, and 14 hydraulic lines for the body.

A worker checks out the hydraulic system on an animatronic dinosaur.

1. **Sketch It on Paper** An artist makes a sketch of the desired figure. If the figure is an animal, the artist might work closely with a biologist or other expert. For dinosaurs, artists consult with paleontologists, specialists in prehistoric forms of life. For a human figure, the artist might videotape a person performing various actions. After numerous sketches are analyzed and revised, the artist makes a final detailed drawing.

2. **Build a Miniature Model** A small-scale model called a maquette (ma-KEHT) is made, based on the artist's drawing. The model may be made of clay or another moldable material. The maquette allows the engineers to think about all three dimensions of the figure.

3. **Build a Life-Size Model** Based on the maquette, a full-size sculpture is made. Sometimes these are made by hand. For very large animatronic figures, such as dinosaurs, 3-D digitizers may be used to make laser scans of cross sections. Many cross sections are combined to create a computer model of the maquette. This computer model is used to make a life-size model of the figure out of hard foam chunks.

4. **Build the Mechanical Systems** This step usually takes the most time. Engineers design and build the inner workings of the figure. This may be a relatively simple gear system or a complicated hydraulic or computer system. The electronic controls for moving the figure are built. There may be mechanisms to control eyeballs, eyebrows, whiskers, arms, legs, and much more.

5. **Assemble the Parts** At this stage, all of the parts have been created. Now it's time to put the frame together and attach the electronic components to it. The skin, created from a mold of the life-size sculpture, is put in place over the frame. To make skin look realistic when the figure moves, bungee cords are sometimes attached inside the figure to work like tendons in the body. The outside of the figure is painted or covered with fur. Wigs, clothing, and eyeglasses are added to human figures, as appropriate.

6. **Test and Work Through Problems** At every step in the process, parts are checked and tested. But once the figure has been assembled, it's time to make the figure move. It may take months of testing and refining movements until they appear realistic.

ASKING Questions

- What other questions do you have about animatronics?

- What questions do you have about how mechanical puppets are created?

 RESOURCE CENTER

Visit **ClassZone.com** for more information on animatronics.

WRITING ABOUT SCIENCE

Write a proposal for an animatronic figure you would like to create.

Writing Tips

Plan, draft, and revise your writing using the tips below.

- Skim the article to review facts about animatronics and how figures are designed, assembled, and tested.

- Think of a figure that would appeal to others. What actions should the figure be able to perform? What constraints should you consider?

- Develop a clear statement of the purpose for your mechanical puppet.

10 Electricity

the BIG idea

Moving electric charges transfer energy.

What keeps this dragon glowing brightly?

Key Concepts

SECTION

1 Materials can become electrically charged.
Learn how the movement of electrons builds static charges and how static charges are used in technology.

SECTION

2 Charges can move from one place to another.
Learn what factors control the movement of charges.

SECTION

3 Electric current is a flow of charge.
Learn how electric current is measured and how it can be produced.

FCAT Practice

Prepare and practice for the FCAT
• Section Reviews, pp. 348, 357, 366
• Chapter Review, pp. 368–370
• FCAT Practice, p. 371

CLASSZONE.COM
• Florida Review: Content Review and FCAT Practice

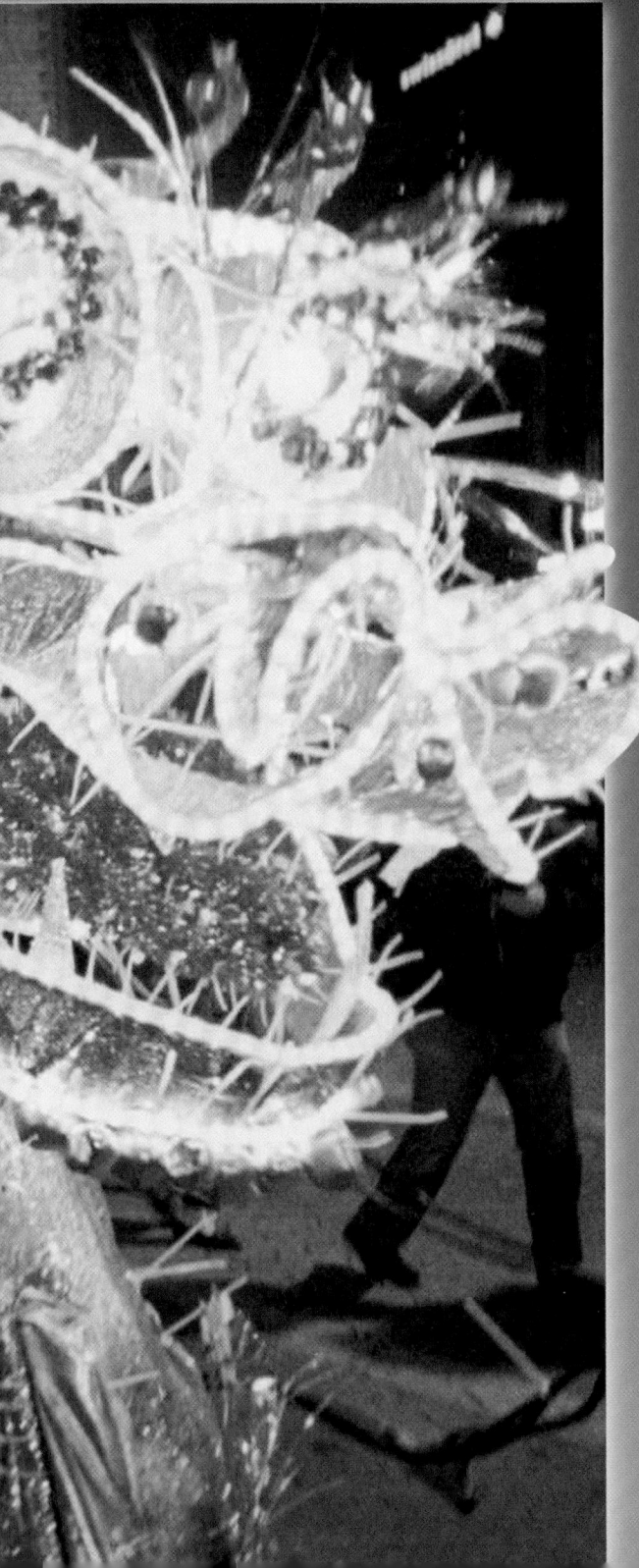

EXPLORE (the BIG idea)

How Do the Pieces of Tape Interact?

Cut three strips of tape. Press two onto your shirt. Peel them off and hold them close to each other, without touching. Observe. Hold one of them close to the third strip. Observe.

Observe and Think
How did the strips of tape behave in each case? Can you think of an explanation?

Why Does the Water React Differently?

Open a faucet just enough to let flow a thin stream of water. Run a comb through your hair a few times, and then hold it near the stream of water. Observe the behavior of the water. Touch the comb to the stream of water briefly and then hold it near the stream again.

Observe and Think How did the interaction of the comb and the stream change after you touched the comb to the water?

Internet Activity: Static Electricity

Go to **ClassZone.com** to learn more about materials and static electricity.

Observe and Think What role does the type of material play in static electricity?

NSTA
scilinks.org
SCiLINKS

Electricity **Code: MDL065**

Getting Ready to Learn

◀ CONCEPT REVIEW

- Matter is made of particles too small to see.
- Energy and matter can move from one place to another.
- Electromagnetic energy is one form of energy.

◀ VOCABULARY REVIEW

See Glossary for definitions.

atom

electron

joule

proton

FLORIDA REVIEW
CLASSZONE.COM

Content Review and FCAT Practice

▶ TAKING NOTES

COMBINATION NOTES

To take notes about a new concept, first make an informal outline of the information. Then make a sketch of the concept and label it so you can study it later.

VOCABULARY STRATEGY

Write each new vocabulary term in the center of a **four square** diagram. Write notes in the squares around each term. Include a definition, some characteristics, and some examples of the term. If possible, write some things that are not examples of the term.

See the Note-Taking Handbook on pages R45–R51.

SCIENCE NOTEBOOK

NOTES
How static charges are built
- Contact
- Induction
- Charge polarization

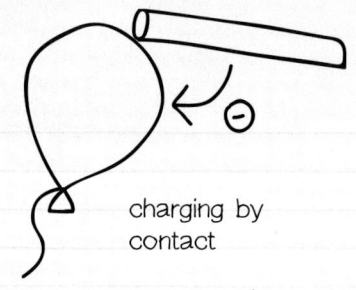

charging by contact

Definition	Characteristics
imbalance of charge in material	results from movement of electrons; affected by type of material

STATIC CHARGE

Examples	Nonexample
clinging laundry, doorknob shock, lightning	electricity from an electrical outlet

10.1 Materials can become electrically charged.

Sunshine State STANDARDS

SC.A.2.3.1: The student describes and compares the properties of particles and waves.

SC.H.3.3.4: The student knows that technological design should require taking into account constraints such as natural laws, the properties of the materials used, and economic, political, social, ethical, and aesthetic values.

VOCABULARY
electric charge p. 342
electric field p. 342
static charge p. 343
induction p. 345

BEFORE, you learned

- Atoms are made up of particles called protons, neutrons, and electrons
- Protons and electrons are electrically charged

NOW, you will learn

- How charged particles behave
- How electric charges build up in materials
- How static electricity is used in technology

EXPLORE Static Electricity

How can materials interact electrically?

PROCEDURE

1. Hold the newspaper strips firmly together at one end and let the free ends hang down. Observe the strips.

2. Put the plastic bag over your other hand, like a mitten. Slide the plastic down the entire length of the strips and then let go. Repeat several times.

3. Notice how the strips of paper are hanging. Describe what you observe.

MATERIALS
- 2 strips of newspaper
- plastic bag

WHAT DO YOU THINK?
- How did the strips behave before step 2? How did they behave after step 2?
- How might you explain your observations?

Electric charge is a property of matter.

You are already familiar with electricity, static electricity, and magnetism. You know electricity as the source of power for many appliances, including lights, tools, and computers. Static electricity is what makes clothes stick together when they come out of a dryer and gives you a shock when you touch a metal doorknob on a dry, winter day. Magnetism can hold an invitation or report card on the door of your refrigerator.

You may not know, however, that electricity, static electricity, and magnetism are all related. All three are the result of a single property of matter—electric charge.

COMBINATION NOTES
As you read this section, write down important ideas about electric charge and static charges. Make sketches to help you remember these concepts.

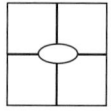
The smallest unit of a material that still has the characteristics of that material is an atom or a molecule. A molecule is two or more atoms bonded together. Most of an atom's mass is concentrated in the nucleus at the center of the atom. The nucleus contains particles called protons and neutrons. Much smaller particles called electrons move at high speeds outside the nucleus.

Protons and electrons have electric charges. **Electric charge** is a property that allows an object to exert an electric force on another object without touching it. Recall that a force is a push or a pull. The space around a particle through which an electric charge can exert this force is called an **electric field.** The strength of the field is greater near the particle and weaker farther away.

All protons have a positive charge (+), and all electrons have a negative charge (−). Normally, an atom has an equal number of protons and electrons, so their charges balance each other, and the overall charge on the atom is neutral.

Particles with the same type of charge—positive or negative—are said to have like charges, and particles with different charges have unlike charges. Particles with like charges repel each other, that is, they push each other away. Particles with unlike charges attract each other, or pull on each other.

Electric Charge

Charged particles exert forces on each other through their electric fields.

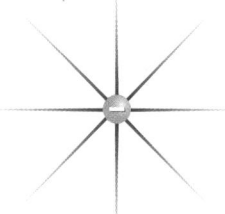

Charged Particles
Electric charge can be either negative or positive.

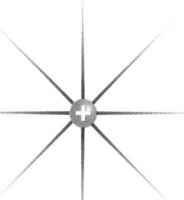

The balloon and the cat's fur have unlike charges, so they attract each other.

① Attraction

Particles with unlike charges attract—pull on each other.

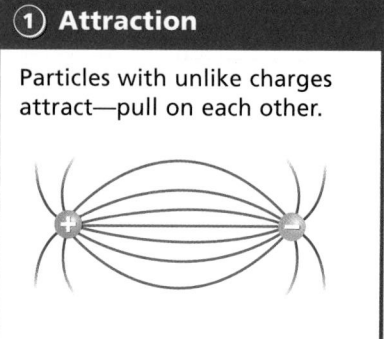

② Repulsion

Particles with like charges repel—push each other away.

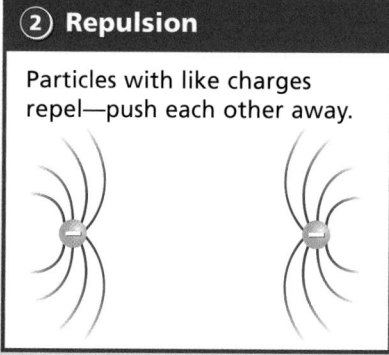

⊖ = electron

⊕ = proton

— = lines of force

READING VISUALS How do the force lines change when particles attract?

Static charges are caused by the movement of electrons.

You have read that protons and electrons have electric charges. Objects and materials can also have charges. A **static charge** is a buildup of electric charge in an object caused by the presence of many particles with the same charge. Ordinarily, the atoms that make up a material have a balance of protons and electrons. A material develops a static charge—or becomes charged—when it contains more of one type of charged particle than another.

If there are more protons than electrons in a material, the material has a positive charge. If there are more electrons than protons in a material, it has a negative charge. The amount of the charge depends on how many more electrons or protons there are. The total number of unbalanced positive or negative charges in an object is the net charge of the object. Net charge is measured in coulombs (KOO-LAHMZ). One coulomb is equivalent to more than 10^{19} electrons or protons.

Electrons can move easily from one atom to another. Protons cannot. For this reason, charges in materials usually result from the movement of electrons. The movement of electrons through a material is called conduction. If electrons move from one atom to another, the atom they move to develops a negative charge. The atom they move away from develops a positive charge. Atoms with either a positive or a negative charge are called ions.

A static charge can build up in an uncharged material when it touches or comes near a charged material. Static charges also build up when some types of uncharged materials come into contact with each other.

READING TiP

The word *static* comes from the Greek word *statos*, which means "standing."

REMINDER

10^{19} is the same as 1 followed by 19 zeros.

Charging by Contact

When two uncharged objects made of certain materials—such as rubber and glass—touch each other, electrons move from one material to the other. This process is called charging by contact. It can be demonstrated by a balloon and a glass rod, as shown below.

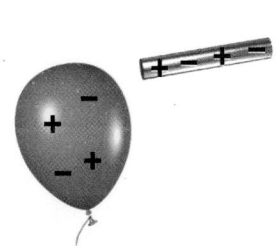

① At first, a balloon and a glass rod each have balanced, neutral charges.

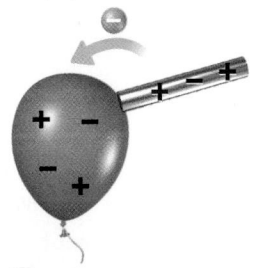

② When they touch, electrons move from the rod to the balloon.

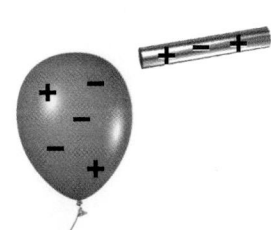

③ Afterwards, the balloon has a negative charge, and the rod has a positive charge.

metal globe

connection to globe

conveyor belt

source of electrons

As the sphere takes on a negative charge, electrons spread out over this student's skin and hair. Because her hairs all have the same charge, they repel one another.

A Van de Graaff generator is a device that builds up a strong static charge through contact. This device is shown at left. At the bottom of the device, a rubber conveyer belt rubs against a metal brush and picks up electrons. At the top, the belt rubs against metal connected to the sphere, transferring electrons to the sphere. As more and more electrons accumulate on the sphere, the sphere takes on a strong negative charge. In the photograph, the student touches the sphere as it is being charged. Some of the electrons spread across her arm to her head. The strands of her hair, which then all have a negative charge, repel one another.

CHECK YOUR READING How can a Van de Graaff generator make a person's hair stand on end?

How Materials Affect Static Charging

Charging by contact occurs when one material's electrons are attracted to another material more than they are attracted to their own. Scientists have determined from experience which materials are likely to give up or to accept electrons. For example, glass gives up electrons to wool. Wool accepts electrons from glass, but gives up electrons to rubber. The list at left indicates how some materials interact. Each material tends to give up electrons to anything below it on the list and to accept electrons from anything above it. The farther away two materials are from each other on the list, the stronger the interaction.

When you walk across a carpet, your body can become either positively or negatively charged. The type of charge depends on what materials the carpet and your shoes are made of. If you walk in shoes with rubber soles across a wool carpet, you will probably become negatively charged, because wool gives up electrons to rubber. But if you walk in wool slippers across a rubber mat, you will probably become positively charged.

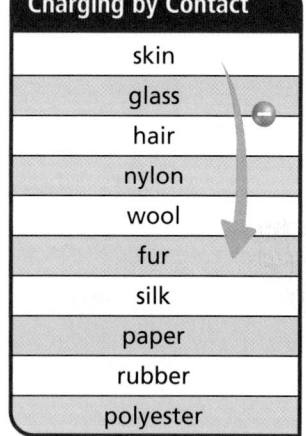

Charging by Contact
skin
glass
hair
nylon
wool
fur
silk
paper
rubber
polyester

Materials higher on the list tend to give up electrons to materials lower on the list.

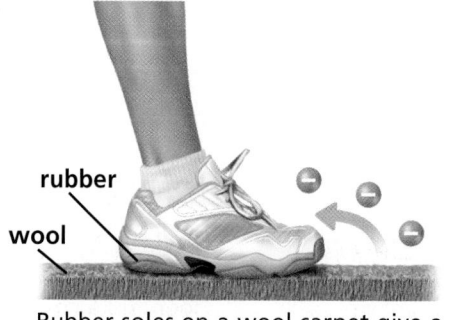

rubber

wool

Rubber soles on a wool carpet give a person a negative charge.

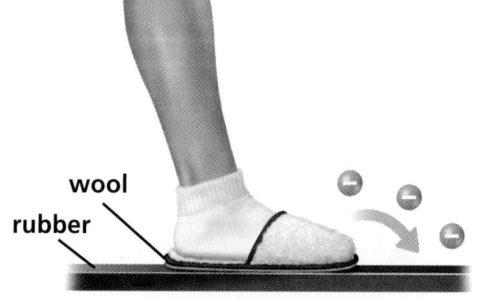

wool

rubber

Wool slippers on a rubber mat give a person a positive charge.

Charging by Induction

Charging can occur even when materials are not touching if one of the materials already has a charge. Remember that charged particles push and pull each other through their electric fields without touching. The pushing and pulling can cause a charge to build in another material. The first charge is said to induce the second charge. The buildup of a charge without direct contact is called **induction.**

READING **TiP**

Induce and *induction* both contain the Latin root *ducere,* which means "to lead."

Induction can produce a temporary static charge. Consider what happens when a glass rod with a negative charge is brought near a balloon, as shown below. The unbalanced electrons in the rod repel the electrons in the material of the balloon. Many electrons move to the side of the balloon that is farthest away from the rod. The side of the balloon that has more electrons becomes negatively charged. The side of the balloon with fewer electrons becomes positively charged. When the rod moves away, the electrons spread out evenly once again.

1 At first, the rod has a negative charge and the balloon has a balanced charge.

2 When the rod comes close to the balloon, electrons in the balloon move away from the rod.

3 When the rod moves away, electrons in the balloon spread out evenly as before.

If the electrons cannot return to their original distribution, however, induction can leave an object with a stable static charge. For example, if a negatively charged rod approaches two balloons that are touching each other, electrons will move to the balloon farther from the rod. If the balloons are then separated, preventing the electrons from moving again, the balloon with more electrons will have a negative charge and the one with fewer electrons will have a positive charge. When the rod is taken away, the balloons keep their new charges.

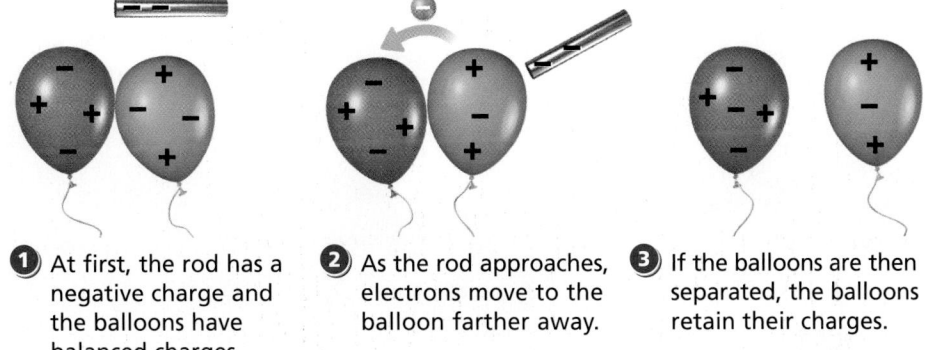

1 At first, the rod has a negative charge and the balloons have balanced charges.

2 As the rod approaches, electrons move to the balloon farther away.

3 If the balloons are then separated, the balloons retain their charges.

Charge Polarization

Induction can build a charge by changing the position of electrons, even when electrons do not move between atoms. Have you ever charged a balloon by rubbing it on your head, and then stuck the balloon to a wall? When you bring the balloon close to the wall, the balloon's negative charge pushes against the electrons in the wall. If the electrons cannot easily move away from their atoms, the negative charges within the atoms may shift to the side away from the balloon. When this happens, the atoms are said to be polarized. The surface of the wall becomes positively charged, and the negatively charged balloon sticks to it.

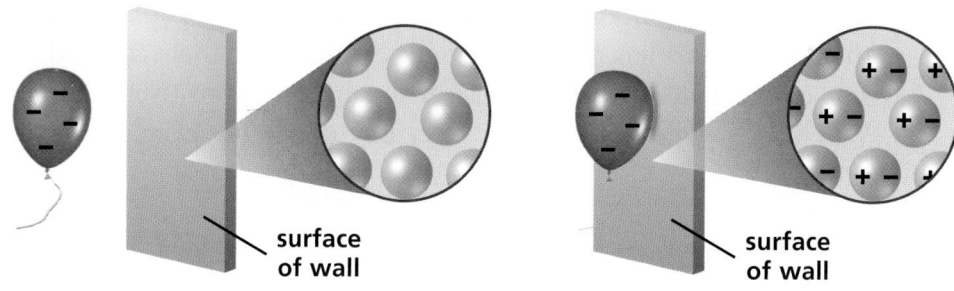

1 Before the charged balloon comes near the wall, the atoms in the surface of the wall are not polarized.

2 As the balloon nears the wall, atoms in the surface of the wall become polarized and attract the balloon.

INVESTIGATE Making a Static Detector

How can you detect a static electric charge?

PROCEDURE

1 Straighten one end of the paper clip and insert it through the hole in the cup. Use clay to hold the paper clip in place. Stick the ball of foil onto the straight end. Hang both foil strips from the hook end.

2 Give the balloon a static charge by rubbing it over your hair. Slowly bring the balloon near the ball of foil without letting them touch. Observe what happens to the foil strips inside the cup.

WHAT DO YOU THINK?

- What happened to the strips hanging inside the cup when the charged balloon came near the ball of foil?

- How can you explain what you observed?

CHALLENGE Suppose the balloon had the opposite charge of the one you gave it. What would happen to the strips if you brought the balloon near the ball of foil? Explain your answer.

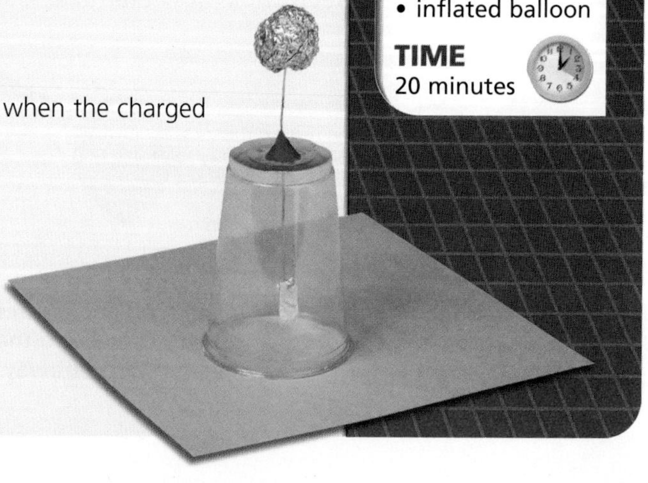

SKILL FOCUS
Inferring

MATERIALS
- metal paper clip
- clear plastic cup with hole
- modeling clay
- ball of foil
- 2 strips of foil
- inflated balloon

TIME
20 minutes

Technology uses static electricity.

Static charges can be useful in technology. An example is the photocopy machine. Photocopiers run on electricity that comes to them through wires from the power plant. But static charges play an important role in how they work.

How a Photocopier Works

A photocopier uses static charges to make copies.

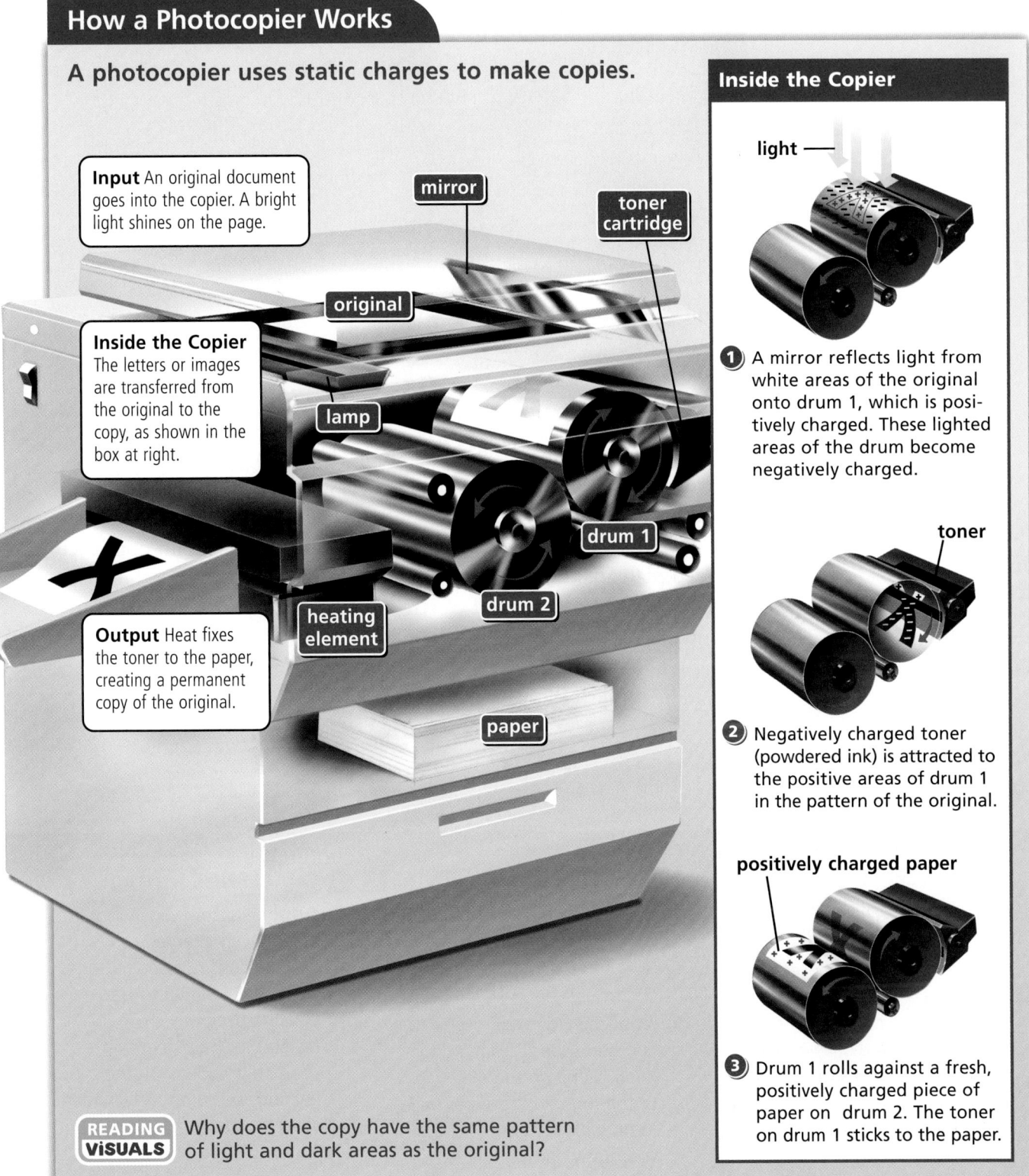

Input An original document goes into the copier. A bright light shines on the page.

Inside the Copier The letters or images are transferred from the original to the copy, as shown in the box at right.

Output Heat fixes the toner to the paper, creating a permanent copy of the original.

mirror

toner cartridge

original

lamp

drum 1

drum 2

heating element

paper

Inside the Copier

light

1 A mirror reflects light from white areas of the original onto drum 1, which is positively charged. These lighted areas of the drum become negatively charged.

toner

2 Negatively charged toner (powdered ink) is attracted to the positive areas of drum 1 in the pattern of the original.

positively charged paper

3 Drum 1 rolls against a fresh, positively charged piece of paper on drum 2. The toner on drum 1 sticks to the paper.

READING VISUALS Why does the copy have the same pattern of light and dark areas as the original?

Static electricity is also used in making cars. When new cars are painted, the paint is given an electric charge and then sprayed onto the car in a fine mist. The tiny droplets of paint stick to the car more firmly than they would without the charge. This process results in a coat of paint that is very even and smooth.

Another example of the use of static electricity in technology is a device called an electrostatic air filter. This device cleans air inside buildings with the help of static charges. The filter gives a static charge to pollen, dust, germs, and other particles in the air. Then an oppositely charged plate inside the filter attracts these particles, pulling them out of the air. Larger versions of electrostatic filters are used to remove pollutants from industrial smokestacks.

 How can static charges help clean air?

 **Review**

KEY CONCEPTS

1. How do a positive and a negative particle interact?

2. Describe how the movement of electrons between two objects with balanced charges could cause the buildup of electric charge in both objects.

3. Describe one technological use of static electricity.

CRITICAL THINKING

4. **Infer** A sock and a shirt from the dryer stick together. What does this tell you about the charges on the sock and shirt?

5. **Analyze** You walk over a rug and get a shock from a door-knob. What do the materials of the rug and the shoes have to do with the type of charge your body had?

CHALLENGE

6. **Apply** Assume you start with a negatively charged rod and two balloons. Describe a series of steps you could take to create a positively charged balloon, pick up negatively charged powder with the balloon, and drop the powder from the balloon.

Electric Eels

An electric eel is a slow-moving fish with no teeth and poor eyesight. It lives in the murky waters of muddy rivers in South America. Instead of the senses that most animals use—vision, hearing, smell, and touch—an electric eel uses electricity to find its next meal. Since the fish that it eats often can swim much faster than the eel, it also uses electricity to catch its prey.

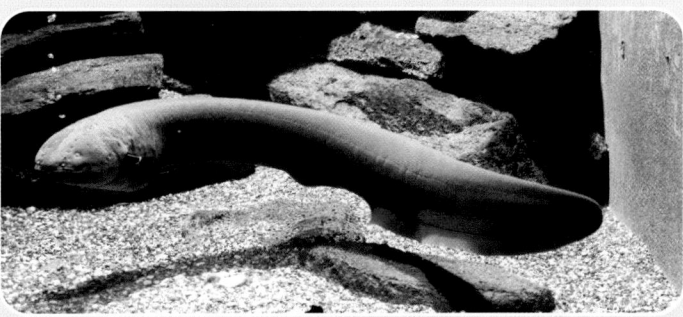

Electric Sense

An electric eel actually has three pairs of electric organs in its body. Two of them build electric charge for stunning prey and for self-defense. The third electric organ builds a smaller charge that helps in finding prey. The charge produces an electric field around the eel. Special sense organs on its body detect small changes in the electric field caused by nearby fish and other animals.

Shocking Organs

The electric eel builds an electric charge with a series of thousands of cells called electrocytes. Every cell in the series has a positive end and a negative end. Each electrocyte builds only a small charge. However, when all of the cells combine their charge, they can produce about five times as much electricity as a standard electrical outlet in a house. The charge is strong enough to paralyze or kill a human. Typically, though, the charge is used to stun or kill small fish, which the eel then swallows whole. Electric charge can also be used to scare away predators.

EXPLORE

1. **INFER** Electric eels live for 10 to 20 years, developing a stronger shock as they grow older. What could account for this increase in electric charge?

2. **CHALLENGE** Sharks and other animals use electricity also. Use the library or Internet to find out how.

An electric eel (Electrophorus electricus) can deliver a jolt five times as powerful as an electrical outlet.

10.2 Charges can move from one place to another.

Sunshine State STANDARDS

SC.A.2.3.1: The student describes and compares the properties of particles and waves.

SC.B.1.3.1: The student identifies forms of energy and explains that they can be measured and compared.

VOCABULARY

electric potential p. 351
volt p. 351
conductor p. 354
insulator p. 354
resistance p. 355
ohm p. 355
grounding p. 357

BEFORE, you learned

- Static charges are built up by the separation of electrons from protons
- Materials affect how static charges are built
- Energy is the ability to cause change

NOW, you will learn

- How charges move
- How charges store energy
- How differences in materials affect the movement of charges

---

EXPLORE Static Discharge

How can you observe electrical energy?

PROCEDURE

① Rub the balloon against the wool cloth several times to give the balloon a static charge.

② Slowly bring the balloon toward the middle part of the fluorescent bulb until a spark jumps between them.

WHAT DO YOU THINK?

- What happened in the fluorescent bulb when the spark jumped?
- How might you explain this observation?

MATERIALS

- inflated balloon
- wool cloth
- fluorescent light bulb

Static charges have potential energy.

You have read how a static charge is built up in an object such as a balloon. Once it is built up, the charge can stay where it is indefinitely. However, the charge can also move to a new location. The movement of a static charge out of an object is known as static discharge. When a charge moves, it transfers energy that can be used to do work.

What causes a charge to move is the same thing that builds up a charge in the first place—that is, the force of attraction or repulsion between charged particles. For example, suppose an object with a negative charge touches an object with a positive charge. The attraction of the unbalanced electrons in the first object to the unbalanced protons in the second object can cause the electrons to move to the second object.

> **REMINDER**
> Energy can be either kinetic (energy of motion) or potential (stored energy). Energy is measured in joules.

 **CHECK YOUR READING** What can cause a charge to move?

Electric Potential Energy

Potential energy is stored energy an object may have because of its position. Water in a tower has gravitational potential energy because it is high above the ground. The kinetic energy—energy of motion—used to lift the water to the top of the tower is stored as potential energy. If you open a pipe below the tower, the water moves downward and its potential energy is converted back into kinetic energy.

Similarly, electric potential energy is the energy a charged particle has due to its position in an electric field. Because like charges repel, for example, it takes energy to push a charged particle closer to another particle with a like charge. That energy is stored as the electric potential energy of the first particle. When the particle is free to move again, it quickly moves away, and its electric potential energy is converted back into kinetic energy.

When water moves downward out of a tower and some of its potential energy is converted into kinetic energy, its potential energy decreases. Similarly, when a charged particle moves away from a particle with a like charge, its electric potential energy decreases. The water and the particle both move from a state of higher potential energy to one of lower potential energy.

Electric Potential

To push a charged particle closer to another particle with the same charge takes a certain amount of energy. To push two particles into the same position near that particle takes twice as much energy, and the two particles together have twice as much electric potential energy as the single particle. Although the amount of potential energy is higher, the amount of energy per unit charge at that position stays the same. **Electric potential** is the amount of electric potential energy per unit charge at a certain position in an electric field.

Electric potential is measured in units called volts, and voltage is another term for electric potential. A potential of one **volt** is equal to one joule of energy per coulomb of charge.

Just as water will not flow between two towers of the same height, a charge will not move between two positions with the same electric potential. For a charge to move, there must be a difference in potential between the two positions.

Like water in a tower, a static charge has potential energy. Just as gravity moves water down the supply pipe attached under the tank, the electric potential energy of a charge moves the charge along an electrical pathway.

Charge Movement

When water moves from a higher to a lower position, some of its potential energy is used to move it. Along the way, some of its potential energy can be used to do other work, such as turning a water wheel. Similarly, when a charge moves, some of its electric potential energy is used in moving the charge and some of it can be used to do other work. For example, moving an electric charge through a material can cause the material to heat up, as in a burner on an electric stove.

You can see how a moving charge transfers energy when you get a shock from static electricity. As you walk across a rug, a charge builds up on your body. Once the charge is built up, it cannot move until you come in contact with something else. When you reach out to touch a doorknob, the charge has a path to follow. The electric potential energy of the charge moves the charge from you to the doorknob.

Why do you get a shock? Recall that the force of attraction or repulsion between charged particles is stronger when they are close together. As your hand gets closer to the doorknob, the electric potential of the static charge increases. At a certain point, the difference in electric potential between you and the doorknob is great enough to move the charge through the air to the doorknob. As the charge moves, some of its potential energy is changed into the heat, light, and sound of a spark.

 **CHECK YOUR READING** What two factors determine whether a static charge will move?

Lightning

 **RESOURCE CENTER**
CLASSZONE.COM

Find out more about lightning and lightning safety.

The shock you get from a doorknob is a small-scale version of lightning. Lightning is a high-energy static discharge. This static electricity is caused by storm clouds. Lightning comes from the electric potential of millions of volts, which releases large amounts of energy in the form of light, heat, and sound. As you read about how lightning forms, follow the steps in the illustration on page 353.

❶ **Charge Separation** Particles of moisture inside a cloud collide with the air and with each other, causing the particles to become electrically charged. Wind and gravity separate charges, carrying the heavier, negatively charged particles to the bottom of the cloud and the lighter, positively charged particles to the top of the cloud.

❷ **Charge Buildup** Through induction, the negatively charged particles at the bottom of the cloud repel electrons in the ground, causing the surface of the ground to build up a positive charge.

❸ **Static Discharge** When the electric potential, or voltage, created by the difference in charges is large enough, the negative charge moves from the cloud to the ground. The energy released by the discharge produces the flash of lightning and the sound of thunder.

How Lightning Forms

Lightning is a type of static discharge. Storm clouds may develop very large charges, each with an electric potential of millions of volts.

① Charge Separation

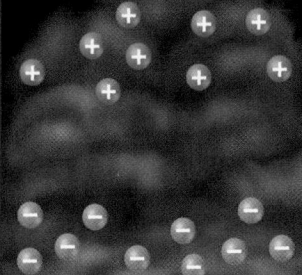

Collisions between particles in storm clouds separate charges. Negatively charged particles collect at the bottom of the cloud.

② Charge Buildup

The negatively charged bottom part of the cloud induces a positive charge in the surface of the ground.

③ Static Discharge

The charge jumps through the air to the ground. Energy released by the discharge causes thunder and lightning.

READING VISUALS How is lightning like the shock you can get from a doorknob? How is it different?

Materials affect charge movement.

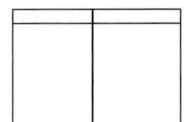

COMBINATION NOTES
Make notes on the different ways materials can affect charge movement. Use sketches to help explain the concepts.

After you walk across a carpet, a charge on your skin has no place to go until you touch or come very close to something. That is because an electric charge cannot move easily through air. However, a charge can move easily through the metal of a doorknob.

Conductors and Insulators

A material that allows an electric charge to pass through it easily is called a **conductor.** Metals such as iron, steel, copper, and aluminum are good conductors. Most wire used to carry a charge is made of copper, which conducts very well.

A material that does not easily allow a charge to pass through it is called an **insulator.** Plastic and rubber are good insulators. Many types of electric wire are covered with plastic, which insulates well. The plastic allows a charge to be conducted from one end of the wire to the other, but not through the sides of the wire. Insulators are also important in electrical safety, because they keep charges away from the body.

CHECK YOUR READING What is the difference between a conductor and an insulator?

INVESTIGATE Conductors and Insulators

What materials conduct electricity?

PROCEDURE

1. Use tape to connect the battery, wires, and bulb holder as shown in the photograph. Make sure that the wires connected to the battery stay in full contact with the metal parts on either end. Test the bulb and the battery by touching the free ends of wire together. The bulb should light up.

2. Test each object in turn by touching it simultaneously with both free ends of wire. Make sure the ends of wire do not touch each other.

WHAT DO YOU THINK?

- Which objects allowed the light bulb to light up when the wires touched them? Which did not?

- How can you explain the difference between the two groups of objects?

CHALLENGE Do any of the materials you tested seem to conduct a charge better than other conductors? How could you use the setup you have to compare the degree of conducting ability of materials?

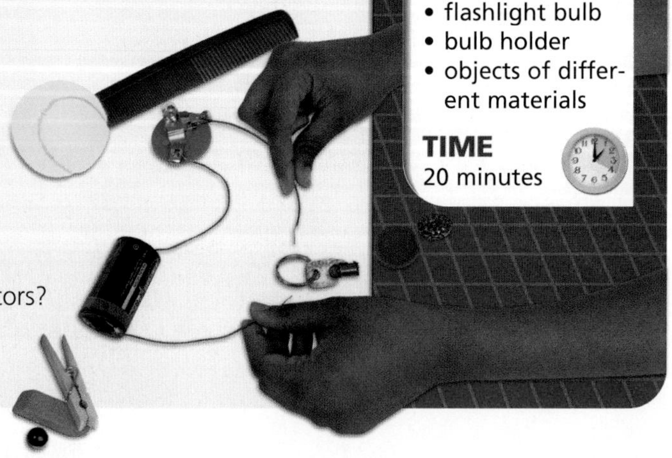

SKILL FOCUS
Interpreting data

MATERIALS
- D cell (battery)
- 3 pieces of low-voltage wire
- duct tape
- flashlight bulb
- bulb holder
- objects of different materials

TIME
20 minutes

Electrons can move freely in a material with low resistance, such as the copper wire in these power lines. Electrons cannot move freely in a material with high resistance, such as the ceramic insulator this worker is putting in place or his safety gloves.

Resistance

Think about the difference between walking through air and walking through waist-deep water. The water resists your movement more than the air, so you have to work harder to walk. If you walked waist-deep in mud, you would have to work even harder.

Materials resist the movement of a charge in different amounts. Electrical **resistance** is the property of a material that determines how easily a charge can move through it. Electrical resistance is measured in units called **ohms.** The symbol for ohms is the Greek letter *omega* (Ω).

Most materials have some resistance. A good conductor such as copper, though, has low resistance. A good insulator, such as plastic or wood, has high resistance.

Like a thick drink in a straw, an electric charge moves more easily through a short, wide pathway than a long, narrow one.

Resistance depends on the amount and shape of the material as well as on the type of material itself. A wire that is thin has more resistance than a wire that is thick. Think of how you have to work harder to drink through a narrow straw than a wide one. A wire that is long has more resistance than a wire that is short. Again, think of how much harder it is to drink through a long straw than a short one.

○ CHECK YOUR READING — What three factors affect how much resistance an object has?

By taking advantage of resistance, we can use an electric charge to do work. When a moving charge overcomes resistance, some of the charge's electrical energy changes into other forms of energy, such as light and heat. For example, the filament of a light bulb is often made of tungsten, a material with high resistance. When electricity moves through the tungsten, the filament gives off light, which is useful. However, the bulb also gives off heat. Because light bulbs are not usually used to produce heat, we think of the heat they produce as wasted energy.

A three-way light bulb has two filaments, each with a different level of resistance. The one with higher resistance produces brighter light. Both together give the brightest setting.

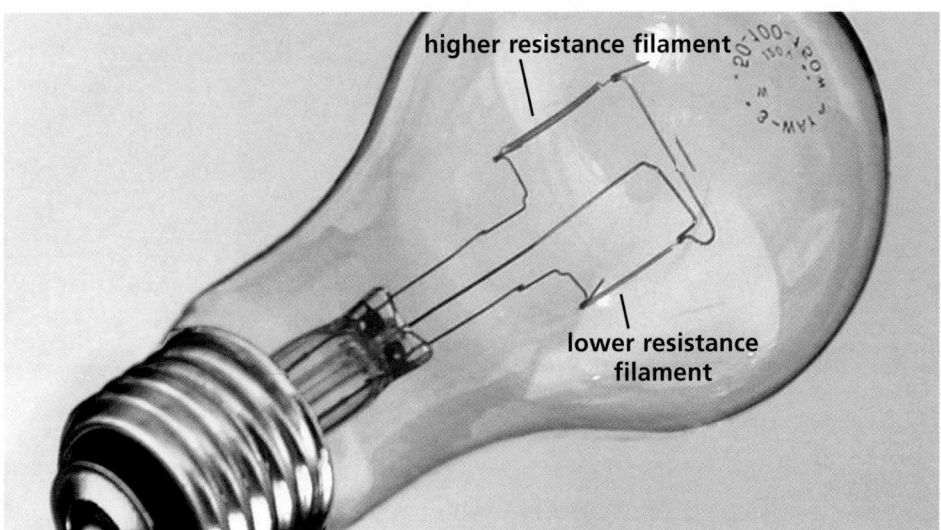

higher resistance filament

lower resistance filament

A material with low resistance is one that a charge can flow through with little loss of energy. Materials move electricity more efficiently when they have low resistances. Such materials waste less energy, so more is available to do work at the other end. That is why copper is used for electrical wiring. Even copper has some resistance, however, and using it wastes some energy.

Superconductors

Scientists have known for many years that some materials have practically no resistance at extremely low temperatures. Such materials are called superconductors, because they conduct even better than good conductors like copper. Superconductors have many uses. They can be used in power lines to increase efficiency and conserve energy, and in high-speed trains to reduce friction. Engineers are also testing superconducting materials for use in computers and other electronic devices. Superconductors would make computers work faster and might also be used to make better motors and generators.

Because superconductors must be kept extremely cold, they have not always been practical. Scientists are solving this problem by developing superconductors that will work at higher temperatures.

 **CHECK YOUR READING** How much resistance does a superconducting material have?

Grounding

If a charge can pass through two different materials, it will pass through the one with the lower resistance. This is the principle behind an important electrical safety procedure—grounding. **Grounding** means providing a harmless, low-resistance path—a ground—for electricity to follow. In many cases, this path actually leads into the ground, that is, into the Earth.

Grounding is used to protect buildings from damage by lightning. Most buildings have some type of lightning rod, which is made from a material that is a good conductor. The rod is placed high up, so that it is closer to the lightning charge. The rod is connected to a conductor cable, and the cable is attached to a copper pole, which is driven into the ground.

Because of the rod's low resistance, lightning will strike the rod before it will strike the roof, where it might have caused a fire. Lightning hits the rod and passes harmlessly through the cable into the ground.

Grounding provides a path for electric current to travel into the ground, which can absorb the charge and make it harmless. The charge soon spreads out so that its voltage in any particular spot is low.

 **CHECK YOUR READING** What is a ground cable?

① Lightning strikes the lightning rod, because the rod is the path of least resistance.

② The rod conducts the charge to a conductor cable, which has low resistance.

③ The ground wire conducts the charge into the ground, where it spreads out and becomes harmless.

10.2 Review

KEY CONCEPTS

1. Explain what happens when you get a static electric shock as you touch a doorknob.
2. What is electric potential?
3. What three factors affect how much electrical resistance an object has?
4. How can a lightning rod protect a building from fire?

CRITICAL THINKING

5. **Infer** Object A has a positive charge. After Object A touches Object B, A still has a positive charge and the same amount of charge. What can you infer about the charge of B?
6. **Analyze** Why do lightning rods work better if they are placed high up, closer to the lightning charge?

○ CHALLENGE

7. **Apply** Could the same material be used as both a conductor and an insulator? Explain your answer.

CHAPTER INVESTIGATION

Lightning

OVERVIEW AND PURPOSE Lightning is a form of static discharge. During storms, electric charges build up within clouds. Lightning occurs when these charges move. In this experiment, you will

- model the buildup of charges that can occur during a storm
- model a lightning strike
- use a ground to control the path of discharge

▶ Procedure

1. Draw a data table like the one on the sample notebook page.

2. Firmly press a lump of clay onto the inside bottom of one aluminum pan (A) to make a handle. Press another lump onto the underside of the other pan (B) as shown.

step 2
B
A

3. Place the foam plate upside down on a flat surface. Without touching the plate with your bare skin, rub the bottom of the plate vigorously with the wool cloth for 1–2 minutes.

step 3

4. Pick up aluminum pan A by the handle and hold it about 5 cm above the foam plate. Drop the pan so that it rests centered on top of the foam plate as shown. Be careful not to touch the pan or the plate.

5. Make the room as dark as possible. Slowly lower aluminum pan B over the rim of the first pan until they touch. Describe what occurs and where, in your notebook.

step 4

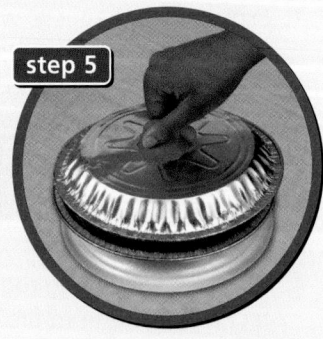
step 5

MATERIALS
- modeling clay
- 2 aluminum pie pans
- foam plate
- wool cloth
- paper clip

6. Repeat steps 3–5 two more times, recording your observations in your notebook.

7. Open the paper clip partway, as shown. Repeat steps 3–4. Then, instead of using the second aluminum pan, slowly bring the pointed end of the paper clip toward the rim of the first pan until they touch. Record your observations.

step 7

8. Repeat step 7 two more times, touching the paper clip to the aluminum pan in different places.

▶ Observe and Analyze | Write It Up

1. **RECORD OBSERVATIONS** Be sure your data table is complete. Draw pictures to show how the procedure varied between steps 5–6 and steps 7–8.

2. **ANALYZE** What did you observe in step 5 when the two aluminum pans touched? What do you think caused this to occur?

3. **COMPARE** How were your observations when you touched the aluminum pan with the paper clip different from those you made when you touched it with the other pan? How can you explain the difference?

▶ Conclude | Write It Up

1. **ANALYZE** Use the observations recorded in your data table to answer the following question: When you used the paper clip, why were you able to control the point at which the static discharge occurred?

2. **INFER** What charges did the foam plate and aluminum pan have before you began the experiment? after you dropped the pan on the plate? after you touched the pan with the paper clip?

3. **IDENTIFY VARIABLES** What variables and controls affected the outcome of your experiment?

4. **IDENTIFY LIMITS** What limitations or sources of error could have affected your results?

5. **APPLY** In your experiment, what corresponds to storm clouds and lightning? How did the paper clip work like a lightning rod?

▶ INVESTIGATE Further

CHALLENGE Where did the charge go when you touched the pie pan with the paper clip? Write a hypothesis to explain what happens in this situation and design an experiment to test your hypothesis.

Lightning
Observe and Analyze
Table 1. Observations of Static Discharge

Trial	Observations
With second aluminum pan	
1	
2	
3	
With paper clip	
4	
5	
6	

Conclude

10.3 Electric current is a flow of charge.

Sunshine State STANDARDS

SC.B.1.3.1: The student identifies forms of energy and explains that they can be measured and compared.

BEFORE, you learned

- Charges move from higher to lower potential
- Materials can act as conductors or insulators
- Materials have different levels of resistance

NOW, you will learn

- About electric current
- How current is related to voltage and resistance
- About different types of electric power cells

VOCABULARY

electric current p. 360
ampere p. 361
Ohm's law p. 361
electric cell p. 363

EXPLORE Current

How does resistance affect the flow of charge?

PROCEDURE

1. Tape the pencil lead flat on the posterboard.

2. Connect the wires, cell, bulb, and bulb holder as shown in the photograph.

3. Hold the wire ends against the pencil lead about a centimeter apart from each other. Observe the bulb.

4. Keeping the wire ends in contact with the lead, slowly move them apart. As you move the wire ends apart, observe the bulb.

WHAT DO YOU THINK?

- What happened to the bulb as you moved the wire ends apart?
- How might you explain your observation?

MATERIALS

- pencil lead
- posterboard
- electrical tape
- 3 lengths of wire
- D cell battery
- flashlight bulb
- bulb holder

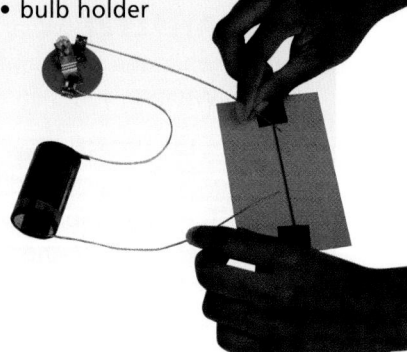

Electric charge can flow continuously.

VOCABULARY
Don't forget to make a four square diagram for the term *electric current*.

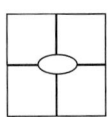

Static charges cannot make your television play. For that you need a different type of electricity. You have learned that a static charge contains a specific, limited amount of charge. You have also learned that a static charge can move and always moves from higher to lower potential. However, suppose that, instead of one charge, an electrical pathway received a continuous supply of charge and the difference in potential between the two ends of the pathway stayed the same. Then, you would have a continuous flow of charge. Another name for a flow of charge is **electric current.** Electric current is the form of electricity used to supply energy in homes, schools, and other buildings.

Current, Voltage, and Resistance

Electric current obeys the same rules as moving static charges. Charge can flow only if it has a path to follow, that is, a material to conduct it. Also, charge can flow only from a point of higher potential to one of lower potential. However, one concept that does not apply to a moving static charge applies to current. Charge that flows steadily has a certain rate of flow. This rate can be measured. The standard unit of measure for current is the **ampere,** or amp. An amp is the amount of charge that flows past a given point per unit of time. One amp equals one coulomb per second. The number of amps—or amperage—of a flowing charge is determined by both voltage and resistance.

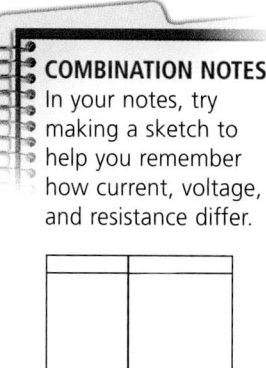

COMBINATION NOTES In your notes, try making a sketch to help you remember how current, voltage, and resistance differ.

Electric current, or amperage, can be compared to the flow of water through a pipe. Electric potential, or voltage, is like pressure pushing the water through the pipe. Resistance, or ohms, is like the diameter of the pipe, which controls how much water can flow through. Water pressure and pipe size together determine the rate of water flow. Similarly, voltage and resistance together determine the rate of flow of electric charge.

How Potential Affects Current

Current increases with potential, just as water flow increases with water pressure.

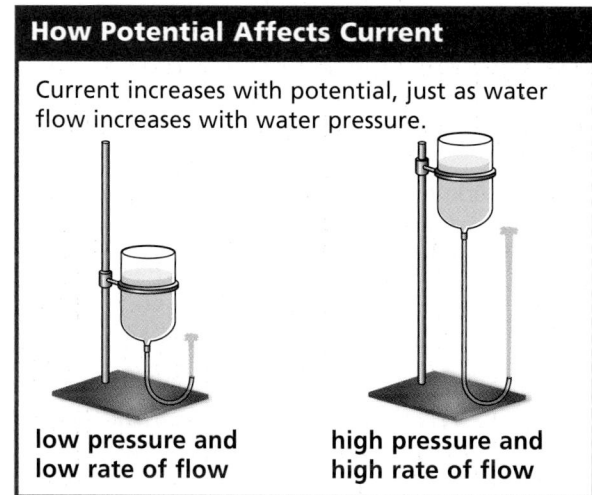

low pressure and low rate of flow

high pressure and high rate of flow

How Resistance Affects Current

Current decreases as resistance increases, just as water flow decreases as resistance to flow increases.

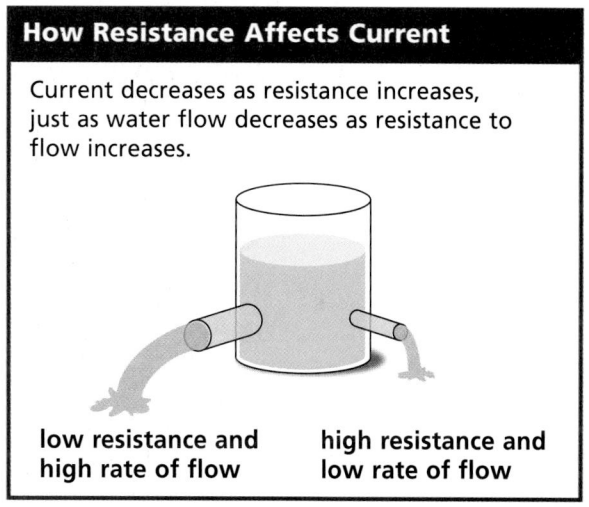

low resistance and high rate of flow

high resistance and low rate of flow

Ohm's Law

You now have three important measurements for the study of electricity: volts, ohms, and amps. The scientist for whom the ohm is named discovered a mathematical relationship among these three measurements. The relationship, called **Ohm's law,** is expressed in the formula below.

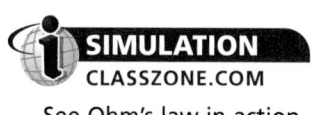

SIMULATION
CLASSZONE.COM

See Ohm's law in action.

$$\text{Current} = \frac{\text{Voltage}}{\text{Resistance}} \qquad I = \frac{V}{R}$$

I is current measured in amps (A), V is voltage measured in volts (V), and R is resistance measured in ohms (Ω).

CHECK YOUR READING What two values do you need to know to calculate the amperage of electric current?

You have read that current is affected by both voltage and resistance. Using Ohm's law, you can calculate exactly how much it is affected and determine the exact amount of current in amps. Use the formula for current to solve the sample problem below.

Calculating Current

Sample Problem

What is the current in an electrical pathway with an electric potential of 120 volts and a resistance of 60 ohms?

What do you know?	voltage = 120 V, resistance = 60 Ω
What do you want to find out?	current
Write the formula:	$I = \dfrac{V}{R}$
Substitute into the formula:	$I = \dfrac{120 \text{ V}}{60 \ \Omega}$
Calculate and simplify:	$I = 2$ A
Check that your units agree:	Unit is amps. Unit of current is amps. Units agree.
Answer:	2 A

Practice the Math

1. What is the current in an electrical pathway in which the voltage is 220 V and the resistance is 55 Ω?
2. An electrical pathway has a voltage of 12 volts and a resistance of 24 ohms. What is the current?

READING TiP

The terms *voltmeter, ohmmeter, ammeter,* and *multimeter* are all made by adding a prefix to the word *meter*.

Measuring Electricity

Volts, ohms, and amps can all be measured using specific electrical instruments. Volts can be measured with a voltmeter. Ohms can be measured with an ohmmeter. Amps can be measured with an ammeter. These three instruments are often combined in a single electrical instrument called a multimeter.

To use a multimeter, set the dial on the type of unit you wish to measure. For example, the multimeter in the photograph is being used to test the voltage of a 9-volt battery. The dial is set on volts in the 0–20 range. The meter shows that the battery's charge has an electric potential of more than 9 volts, which means that the battery is good. A dead battery would have a lower voltage.

CHECK YOUR READING What does an ohmmeter measure?

How can you produce electric current?

PROCEDURE

1 Insert the paper clip and the penny into the lemon, as shown in the photograph. The penny and paper clip should go about 3 cm into the lemon. They should be close, but not touching.

2 On the multimeter, go to the DC volts (V⎓) section of the dial and select the 0–2000 millivolt range (2000 m).

3 Touch one of the leads of the multimeter to the paper clip. Touch the other lead to the penny. Observe what is shown on the display of the multimeter.

WHAT DO YOU THINK?

• What did you observe on the display of the multimeter?

• How can you explain the reading on the multimeter?

CHALLENGE Repeat this experiment using different combinations of fruits or vegetables and metal objects. Which combinations work best?

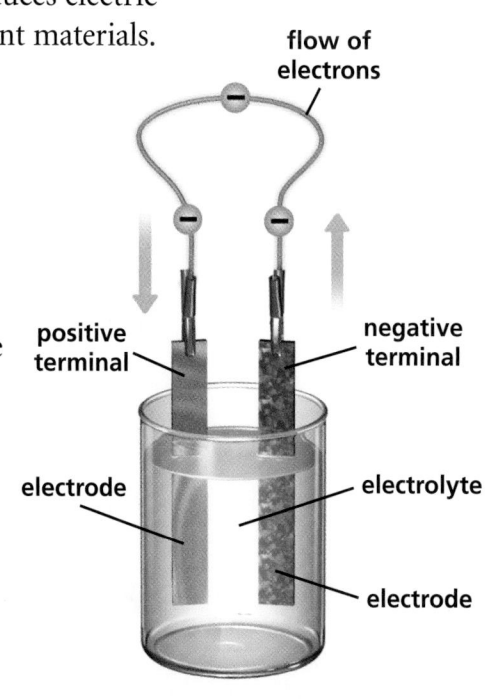

Electric cells supply electric current.

Electric current can be used in many ways. Two basic types of device have been developed for producing current. One type produces electric current using magnets. You will learn more about this technology in Chapter 12. The other type is the **electric cell,** which produces electric current using the chemical or physical properties of different materials.

Electrochemical Cells

An electrochemical cell is an electric cell that produces current by means of chemical reactions. As you can see in the diagram, an electrochemical cell contains two strips made of different materials. The strips are called electrodes. The electrodes are suspended in a third material called the electrolyte, which interacts chemically with the electrodes to separate charges and produce a flow of electrons from the negative terminal to the positive terminal.

Batteries are made using electrochemical cells. Technically, a battery is two or more cells connected to each other. However, single cells, such as C cells and D cells, are often referred to as batteries.

flow of electrons

positive terminal

negative terminal

electrode

electrolyte

electrode

Primary Cells The electrochemical cell shown on page 363 is called a wet cell, because the electrolyte is a liquid. Most household batteries in use today have a solid paste electrolyte and so are called dry cells. Both wet cells and dry cells are primary cells. Primary cells produce electric current through chemical reactions that continue until one or more of the chemicals is used up.

The primary cell on page 365 is a typical zinc-carbon dry cell. It has a negative electrode made of zinc. The zinc electrode is made in the shape of a can and has a terminal—in this case, a wide disk of exposed metal—on the bottom of the cell. The positive electrode consists of a carbon rod and particles of carbon and manganese dioxide. The particles are suspended in an electrolyte paste. The positive electrode has a terminal—a smaller disk of exposed metal—at the top of the rod. A paper separator prevents the two electrodes from coming into contact inside the cell.

When the two terminals of the cell are connected—for example, when you turn on a flashlight—a chemical reaction between the zinc and the electrolyte produces electrons and positive zinc ions. The electrons flow through the wires connecting the cell to the flashlight bulb, causing the bulb to light up. The electrons then travel through the carbon rod and combine with the manganese dioxide. When the zinc and manganese dioxide stop reacting, the cell dies.

CHECK YOUR READING Why are most household batteries called dry cells?

Storage Cells Some batteries produce current through chemical reactions that can be reversed inside the battery. These batteries are called storage cells, secondary cells, or rechargeable batteries. A car battery like the lead-acid battery shown on page 365 is rechargeable. The battery has a negative electrode of lead and a positive electrode of lead peroxide. As the battery produces current, both electrodes change chemically into lead sulfate, and the electrolyte changes into water.

When storage cells are producing current, they are said to be discharging. Whenever a car engine is started, the battery discharges to operate the ignition motor. A car's battery can also be used when the car is not running to operate the lights or other appliances. If the battery is used too long in discharge mode, it will run down completely.

While a car is running, however, the battery is continually being charged. A device called an alternator, which is run by the car's engine, produces current. When electrons flow into the battery in the reverse direction from discharging, the chemical reactions that produce current are reversed. The ability of the battery to produce current is renewed.

CHECK YOUR READING What kind of battery can be charged by reversing chemical reactions?

Batteries

Both primary cells and storage cells produce electricity through chemical reactions.

Flashlights use **primary cells.**

Car batteries and cell phones use **storage cells.**

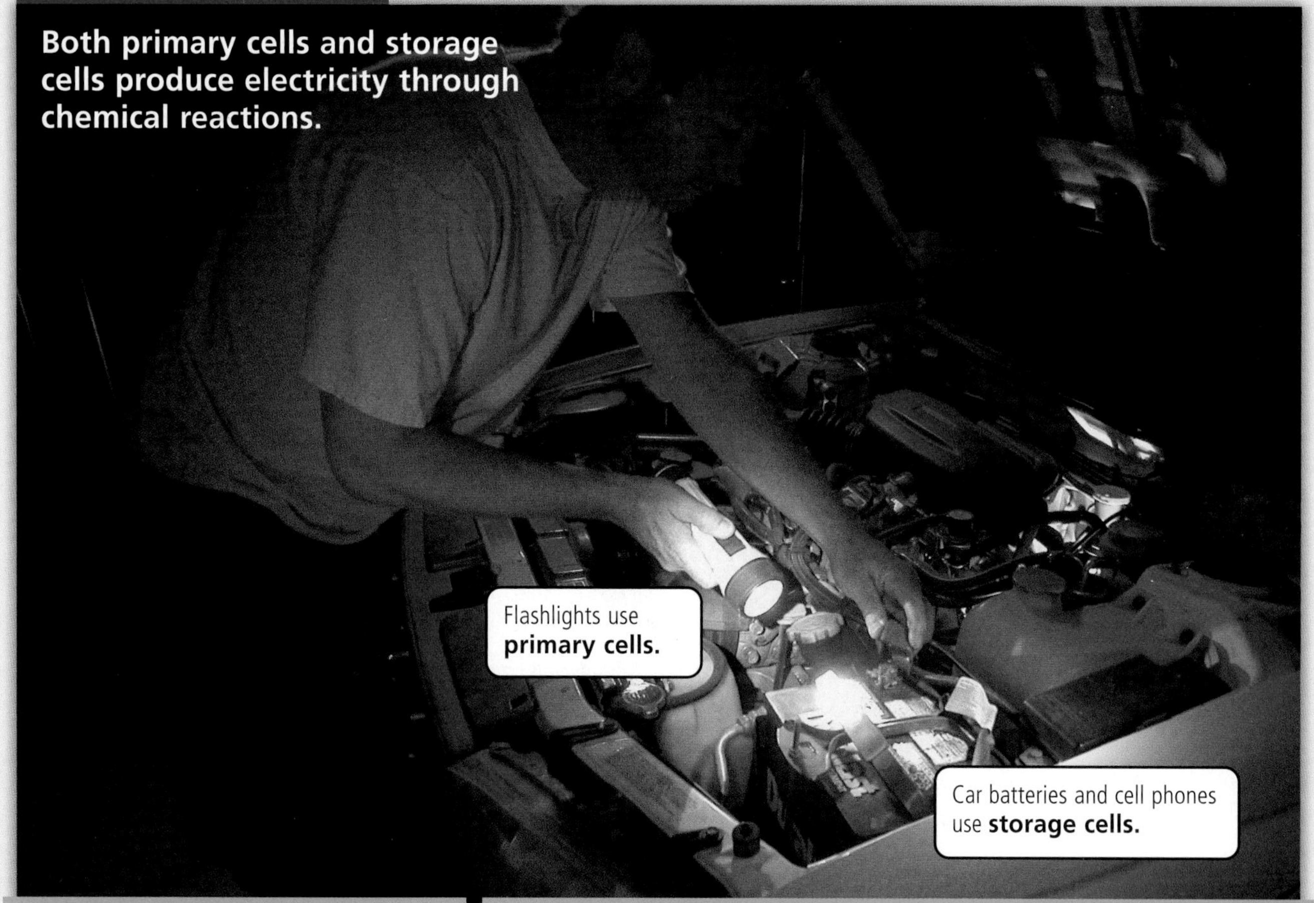

Primary Cell

Primary cells produce electric current through chemical reactions. The reactions continue until the chemicals are used up.

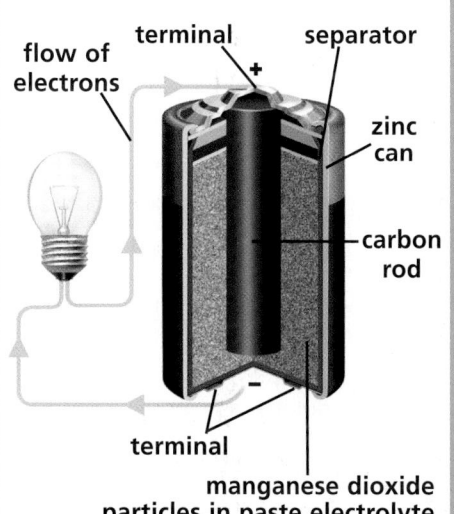

flow of electrons

terminal

separator

+

zinc can

carbon rod

terminal

manganese dioxide particles in paste electrolyte

Storage Cell

1 Discharging Storage cells produce current through chemical reactions that can be reversed in the battery.

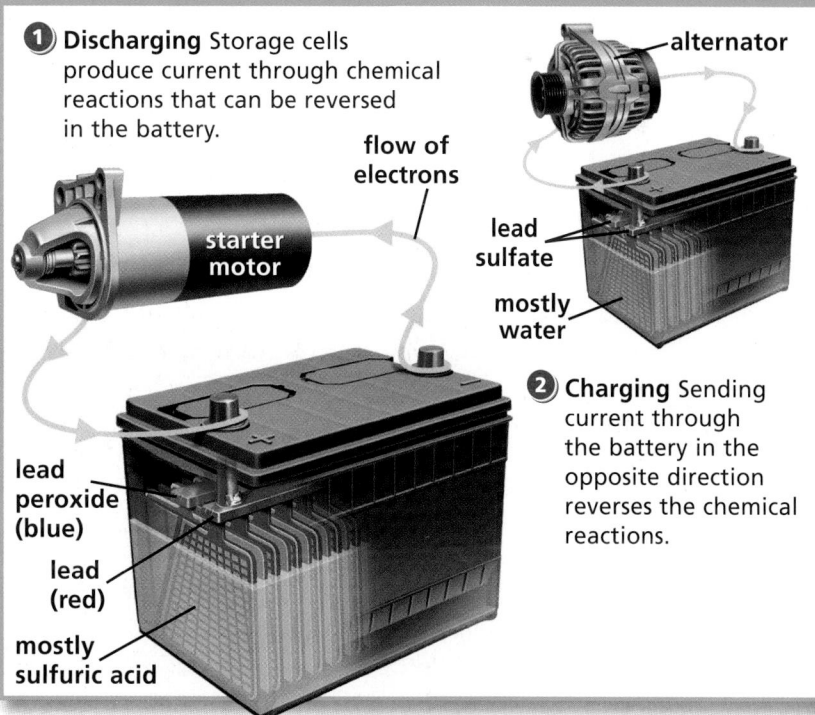

flow of electrons

alternator

starter motor

lead sulfate

mostly water

2 Charging Sending current through the battery in the opposite direction reverses the chemical reactions.

lead peroxide (blue)

lead (red)

mostly sulfuric acid

READING VISUALS In which direction do electrons flow when a storage cell is being charged?

READING TIP

The word *solar* comes from the Latin word *sol,* which means the Sun.

Solar Cells

Some materials, such as silicon, can absorb energy from the Sun or other sources of light and then give off electrons, producing electric current. Electric cells made from such materials are called solar cells.

Solar cells are often used to make streetlights come on automatically at night. Current from the cell operates a switch that keeps the lights turned off. When it gets dark, the current stops, the switch closes, and the streetlights come on.

This NASA research aircraft is powered only by the solar cells on its upper surface.

Many houses and other buildings now get at least some of their power from solar cells. Sunlight provides an unlimited source of free, environmentally safe energy. However, it is not always easy or cheap to use that energy. It must be collected and stored because solar cells do not work at night or when sunlight is blocked by clouds or buildings.

CHECK YOUR READING Where do solar cells get their energy?

10.3 Review

KEY CONCEPTS

1. How is electric current different from a static charge that moves?

2. How can Ohm's law be used to calculate the electrical resistance of a piece of wire?

3. How do rechargeable batteries work differently from nonrechargeable ones?

CRITICAL THINKING

4. **Infer** Electrical outlets in a house maintain a steady voltage, even when the amount of resistance on them changes. How is this possible?

5. **Analyze** Why don't solar cells eventually run down as electrochemical cells do?

CHALLENGE

6. **Apply** Several kinds of electric cells are discussed in this section. Which do you think would be the most practical source of electrical energy on a long trek through the desert? Explain your reasoning.

MATH in SCIENCE

MATH TUTORIAL
CLASSZONE.COM

Click on Math Tutorial for more help with equations.

A volume control works by changing the amount of resistance to the flow of current.

Which Formula Is Best?

A rock band needs an amplifier, and an amplifier needs a volume control. A volume control works by controlling the amount of resistance in an electrical pathway. When resistance goes down, the current—and the volume—go up. Ohm's law expresses the relationship among voltage *(V)*, resistance *(R)*, and amperage *(I)*. If you know the values of two variables, you can use Ohm's law to find the third. The law can be written in three ways, depending on which variable you wish to find.

$$I = \frac{V}{R} \qquad R = \frac{V}{I} \qquad V = IR$$

A simple way to remember these three versions of the formula is to use the pyramid diagram below. Cover up the variable you are looking for. The visible part of the diagram will give you the correct formula to use.

```
      /\
     /V \
    /----\
   / I | R \
  /----------\
```

Example

What is the voltage of a battery that produces a current of 1 amp through a wire with a resistance of 9 ohms?

(1) You want to find voltage, so cover up the *V* in the pyramid diagram. To find *V*, the correct formula to use is *V = IR*.

(2) Insert the known values into the formula. $V = 1\,A \cdot 9\,\Omega$

(3) Solve the equation to find the missing variable. $1 \cdot 9 = 9$

ANSWER 9 volts

Answer the following questions.

1. What is the voltage of a battery that sends 3 amps of current through a wire with a resistance of 4 ohms?

2. What is the resistance of a wire in which the current is 2 amps if the battery producing the current has a voltage of 220 volts?

3. What is the amperage of a current at 120 volts through a wire with a resistance of 5 ohms?

CHALLENGE Dimmer switches also work by varying resistance. A club owner likes the way the lights look at 1/3 normal current. The normal current is 15 amps. The voltage is constant at 110 V. How much resistance will he need?

10 Chapter Review

the BIG idea

Moving electric charges transfer energy.

KEY CONCEPTS SUMMARY

1 **Materials can become electrically charged.**

Electric charge is a property of matter.

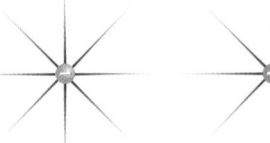

Electrons have a   Protons have a
negative charge.   positive charge.

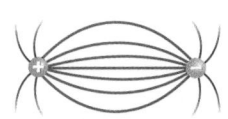

Unlike charges
attract.

Like charges repel.

Static charges are caused by the movement of electrons, resulting in an imbalance of positive and negative charges.

VOCABULARY
electric charge p. 342
electric field p. 342
static charge p. 343
induction p. 345

---

2 **Charges can move from one place to another.**

Charge movement is affected by
• electric potential, measured in volts
• resistance, measured in ohms

A conductor has low resistance.

An insulator has high resistance.

A ground is the path of least resistance.

VOCABULARY
electric potential p. 351
volt p. 351
conductor p. 354
insulator p. 354
resistance p. 355
ohm p. 355
grounding p. 357

---

3 **Electric current is a flow of charge.**

Electric current is measured in amperes, or amps.

Ohm's law states that current equals voltage divided by resistance.

Electrochemical cells produce electric current through chemical reactions.

VOCABULARY
electric current p. 360
ampere p. 361
Ohm's law p. 361
electric cell p. 363

Reviewing Vocabulary

Copy the chart below, and write each term's definition. Use the meanings of the underlined roots to help you.

Word	Root	Definition
EXAMPLE current	to run	continuous flow of charge
1. static charge	standing	
2. induction	into + to lead	
3. electric cell	chamber	
4. conductor	with + to lead	
5. insulator	island	
6. resistance	to stop	
7. electric potential	power	
8. grounding	surface of Earth	

Write a vocabulary term to match each clue.

9. In honor of scientist Alessandro Volta (1745–1827)

10. In honor of the scientist who discovered the relationship among voltage, resistance, and current

11. The amount of charge that flows past a given point in a unit of time.

Reviewing Key Concepts

Multiple Choice *Choose the letter of the best answer.*

12. An electric charge is a
 a. kind of liquid
 b. reversible chemical reaction
 c. type of matter
 d. force acting at a distance

13. A static charge is different from electric current in that a static charge
 a. never moves
 b. can either move or not move
 c. moves only when resistance is low enough
 d. moves only when voltage is high enough

14. Charging by induction means charging
 a. with battery power
 b. by direct contact
 c. at a distance
 d. using solar power

15. Electric potential describes
 a. the electric potential energy per unit charge
 b. the electric kinetic energy per unit charge
 c. whether an electric charge is positive or negative
 d. how an electric charge is affected by gravity

16. A superconductor is a material that, when very cold, has no
 a. amperage
 b. resistance
 c. electric charge
 d. electric potential

17. Ohm's law says that when resistance goes up, current
 a. increases
 b. decreases
 c. stays the same
 d. matches voltage

18. Electrochemical cells include
 a. all materials that build up a charge
 b. primary cells and storage cells
 c. batteries and solar cells
 d. storage cells and lightning rods

Short Response *Write a short response to each question.*

19. What determines whether a charge you get when walking across a rug is positive or negative?

20. What is the difference between resistance and insulation?

21. What is one disadvantage of solar cells?

Thinking Critically

Use the diagram of an electrochemical cell below to answer the next three questions.

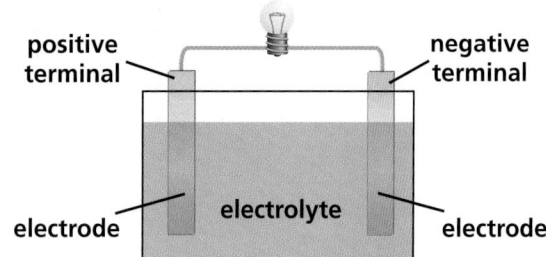

22. ANALYZE In which direction do electrons flow between the two terminals?

23. PREDICT What changes will occur in the cell as it discharges?

24. ANALYZE What determines whether the cell is rechargeable or not?

Use the graph below to answer the next three questions.

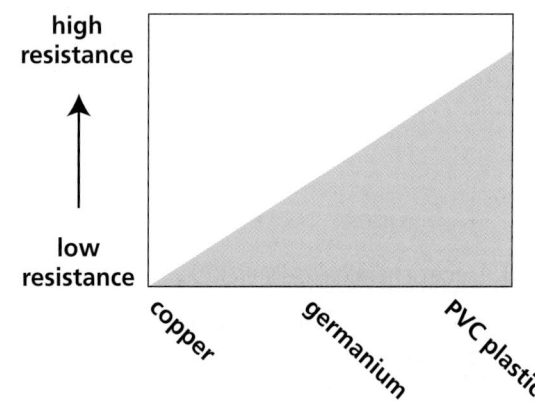

25. INFER Which material could you probably use as an insulator?

26. INFER Which material could be used in a lightning rod?

27. APPLY Materials that conduct electrons under some—but not all—conditions are known as semiconductors. Which material is probably a semiconductor?

Using Math in Science

Use the formula for Ohm's law to answer the next four questions.

$$I = \frac{V}{R}$$

28. An electrical pathway has a voltage of 240 volts and a current of 10 amperes. What is the resistance?

29. A 240-volt air conditioner has a resistance of 8 ohms. What is the current?

30. An electrical pathway has a current of 1.2 amperes and resistance of 40 ohms. What is the voltage?

31. An electrical pathway has a voltage of 400 volts and resistance of 2000 ohms. What is the current?

the BIG idea

32. INFER Look back at the photograph on pages 338 and 339. Based on what you have learned in this chapter, describe what you think is happening to keep the dragon lit.

33. COMPARE AND CONTRAST Draw two simple diagrams to compare and contrast static charges and electric current. Add labels and captions to make your comparison clear. Then write a paragraph summarizing the comparison.

UNIT PROJECTS

If you are doing a unit project, make a folder for your project. Include in your folder a list of the resources you will need, the date on which the project is due, and a schedule to keep track of your progress. Begin gathering data.

Interpreting Diagrams

Use the illustration below to answer the following questions. Assume that the balloons start off with no net charge.

> **FCAT TiP**
>
> When answering multiple-choice questions, try to answer the question before you look at the possible answers. This will help you eliminate incorrect answers.

MULTIPLE CHOICE

1. What will happen if a negatively charged rod is brought near one of the balloons without touching it?

A. The balloons will move toward each other.

B. The balloons will move away from each other.

C. Electrons on the balloons will move toward the rod.

D. Electrons on the balloons will move away from the rod.

2. What will happen if a positively charged rod is brought near one of the balloons without touching it?

F. The balloons will move toward each other.

G. The balloons will move away from each other.

H. Electrons on the balloons will move toward the rod.

I. Electrons on the balloons will move away from the rod.

3. In the previous question, the effect of the rod on the balloons is an example of which of the following?

A. charging by contact

B. charge polarization

C. induction

D. conduction

4. What will happen if a negatively charged rod is brought near one of the balloons, then taken away, and the balloons are then separated?

F. The balloon farthest from the rod will become positively charged.

G. The balloon farthest from the rod will become negatively charged.

H. Both balloons will become positively charged.

I. Both balloons will have no net charge.

SHORT RESPONSE

5. A negatively charged rod is brought near one of the balloons. The balloons are then separated. Determine what would happen and explain why.

6. Explain what will happen if you rub one balloon in your hair to charge it and then move it close to the other balloon.

EXTENDED RESPONSE

Answer the two questions below in detail. Include some of the terms from the word box. Underline each term that you use in your answers.

charge separation	recharging	resistance
source of current	static charge	induce

7. Describe the events leading up to and including a bolt of lightning striking Earth from a storm cloud.

8. Explain the advantages and disadvantages of storage cells over other types of electric cells.

CHAPTER

11 Circuits and Electronics

the **BIG** idea

Circuits control the flow of electric charge.

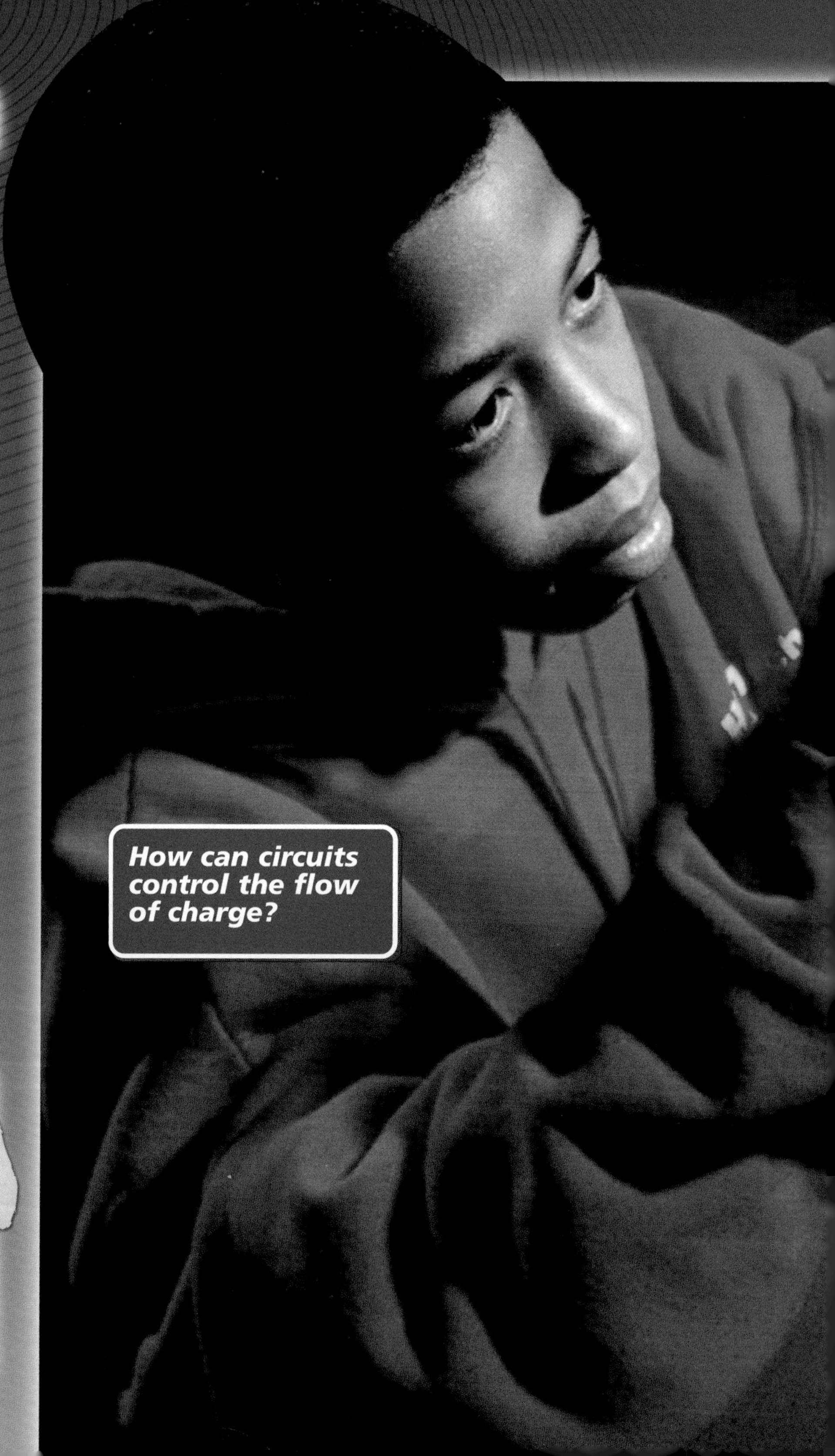

Key Concepts

SECTION

1 Charge needs a continuous path to flow.
Learn how circuits are used to control the flow of charge.

SECTION

2 Circuits make electric current useful.
Learn about series circuits and parallel circuits.

SECTION

3 Electronic technology is based on circuits.
Learn about computers and other electronic devices.

How can circuits control the flow of charge?

FCAT Practice

Prepare and practice for the FCAT
- Section Reviews, pp. 381, 387, 397
- Chapter Review, pp. 400–402
- FCAT Practice, p. 403

CLASSZONE.COM
- Florida Review: Content Review and FCAT Practice

EXPLORE (the BIG idea)

Will the Flashlight Still Work?

Experiment with a flashlight to find out if it will work in any of the following arrangements: with one of the batteries facing the wrong way, with a piece of paper between the batteries, or with one battery removed. In each case, switch on the flashlight and observe.

Observe and Think
When did the flashlight work? Why do you think it worked or did not work in each case?

What's Inside a Calculator?

Use a small screwdriver to open a simple calculator. Look at the circuit board inside.

Observe and Think How do you think the metal lines relate to the buttons on the front of the calculator? to the display? What is the source of electrical energy? How is it connected to the rest of the circuit?

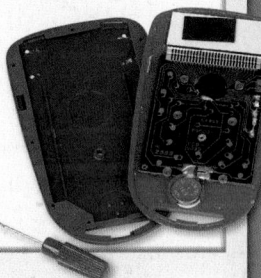

Internet Activity: Circuits

Go to **ClassZone.com** to build a virtual circuit. See if you can complete the circuit and light the bulb.

Observe and Think
What parts are necessary to light the bulb? What happened when you opened the switch? closed the switch?

NSTA
scilinks.org
SCI LINKS

Electronic Circuits **Code: MDL066**

Getting Ready to Learn

◀ CONCEPT REVIEW

- Energy can change from one form to another.
- Energy can move from one place to another.
- Current is the flow of charge through a conductor.

◀ VOCABULARY REVIEW

electric potential p. 350

conductor p. 354

resistance p. 355

electric current p. 360

ampere p. 361

FLORIDA REVIEW
CLASSZONE.COM

Content Review and FCAT Practice

▶ TAKING NOTES

OUTLINE

As you read, copy the headings on your paper in the form of an outline. Then add notes in your own words that summarize what you read.

VOCABULARY STRATEGY

Write each new vocabulary term in the center of a **frame game** diagram. Decide what information to frame it with. Use examples, descriptions, parts, sentences that use the term in context, or pictures. You can change the frame to fit each term.

See the Note-Taking Handbook on pages R45–R51.

SCIENCE NOTEBOOK

I. ELECTRIC CHARGE FLOWS IN A LOOP.
   A. THE PARTS OF A CIRCUIT
      1. voltage source
      2. connection
      3. electrical device
      4. switch

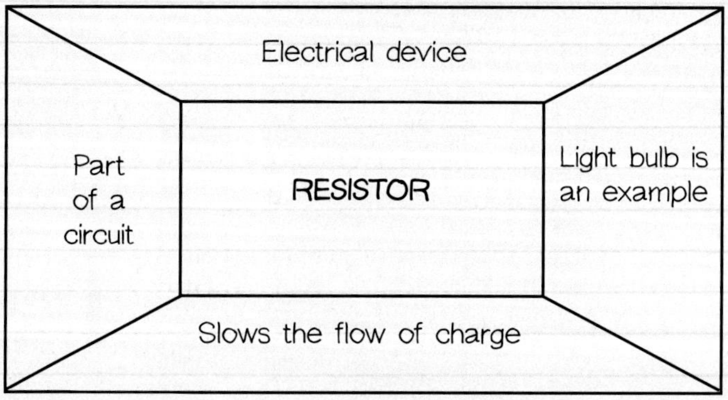

	Electrical device	
Part of a circuit	**RESISTOR**	Light bulb is an example
	Slows the flow of charge	

11.1

Charge needs a continuous path to flow.

Sunshine State STANDARDS

SC.B.1.3.1: The student identifies forms of energy and explains that they can be measured and compared.

SC.H.1.3.3: The student knows that science disciplines differ from one another in topic, techniques, and outcomes but that they share a common purpose, philosophy, and enterprise.

FCAT VOCABULARY
circuit p. 375

VOCABULARY
resistor p. 376
short circuit p. 378

BEFORE, you learned

- Current is the flow of charge
- Voltage is a measure of electric potential
- Materials affect the movement of charge

NOW, you will learn

- About the parts of a circuit
- How a circuit functions
- How safety devices stop current

EXPLORE Circuits

How can you light the bulb?

PROCEDURE

1. Tape one end of a strip of foil to the negative terminal, or the flat end, of the battery. Tape the other end of the foil to the tip at the base of the light bulb, as shown.

2. Tape the second strip of foil to the positive terminal, or the raised end, of the battery.

3. Find a way to make the bulb light.

WHAT DO YOU THINK?

- How did you make the bulb light?
- Can you find other arrangements that make the bulb light?

MATERIALS

- 2 strips of aluminum foil
- electrical tape
- D cell (battery)
- light bulb

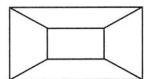

VOCABULARY
Use a frame game diagram to record the term *circuit* in your notebook.

Electric charge flows in a loop.

In the last chapter, you read that current is electric charge that flows from one place to another. Charge does not flow continuously through a material unless the material forms a closed path, or loop. A **circuit** is a closed path through which a continuous charge can flow. The path is provided by a low-resistance material, or conductor, usually wire. Circuits are designed to do specific jobs, such as light a bulb.

Circuits can be found all around you and serve many different purposes. In this chapter, you will read about simple circuits, such as the ones in flashlights, and more complex circuits, such as the ones that run toys, cameras, computers, and more.

 How are circuits related to current?

The Parts of a Circuit

The illustration below shows a simple circuit. Circuits typically contain the following parts. Some circuits contain many of each part.

REMINDER

Remember, a battery consists of two or more cells.

1 Voltage Source The voltage source in a circuit provides the electric potential for charge to flow through the circuit. Batteries are often the voltage sources in a circuit. A power plant may also be a voltage source. When you plug an appliance into an outlet, a circuit is formed that goes all the way to a power plant and back.

2 Conductor A circuit must be a closed path in order for charge to flow. That means that there must be a conductor, such as wire, that forms a connection from the voltage source to the electrical device and back.

3 Switch A switch is a part of a circuit designed to break the closed path of charge. When a switch is open, it produces a gap in the circuit so that the charge cannot flow.

4 Electrical Device An electrical device is any part of the circuit that changes electrical energy into another form of energy. A **resistor** is an electrical device that slows the flow of charge in a circuit. When the charge is slowed, some energy is converted to light or heat. A light bulb is an example of a resistor.

Circuit Parts

The parts of a basic circuit include a voltage source, conductor, switch, and one or more electrical devices.

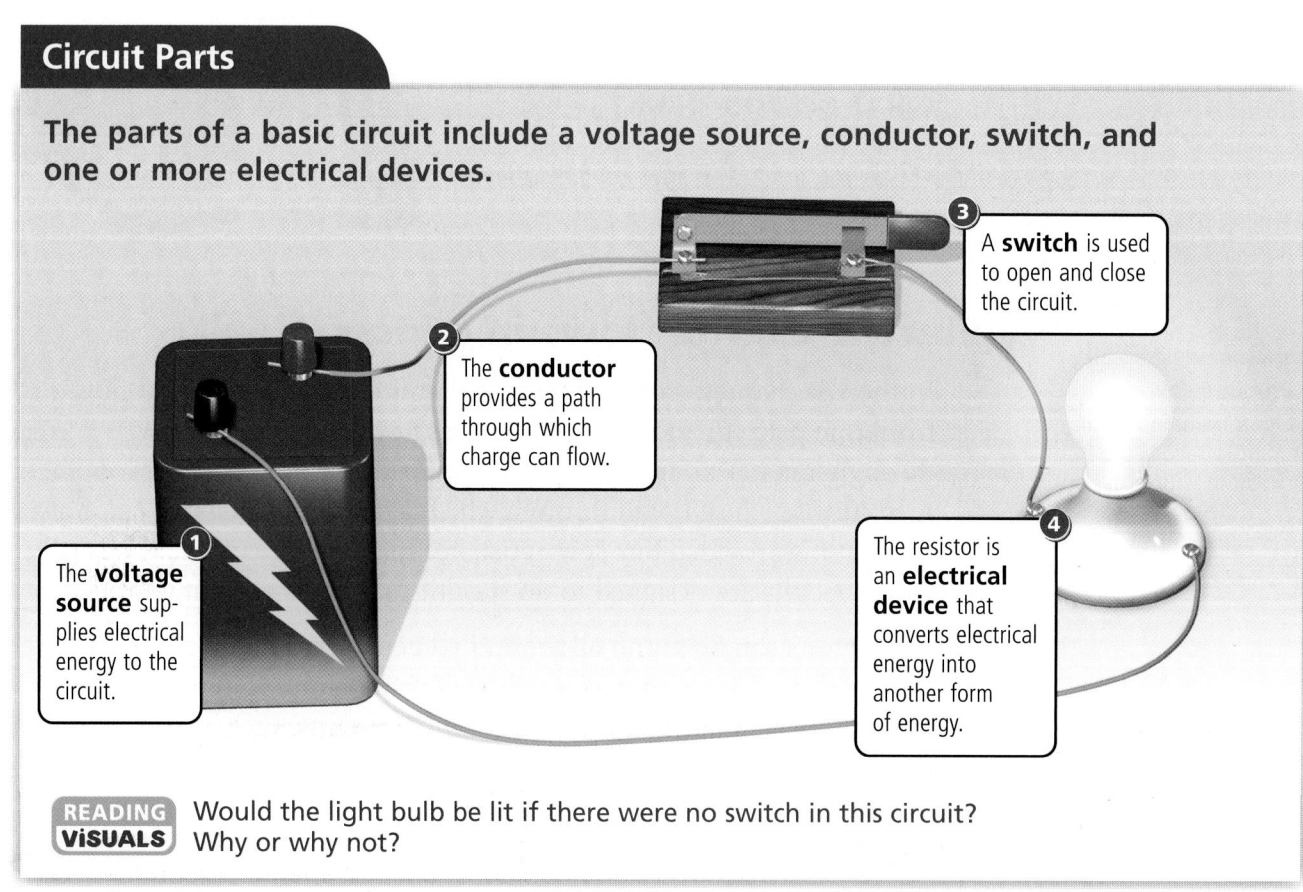

3 A **switch** is used to open and close the circuit.

2 The **conductor** provides a path through which charge can flow.

1 The **voltage source** supplies electrical energy to the circuit.

4 The resistor is an **electrical device** that converts electrical energy into another form of energy.

READING VISUALS Would the light bulb be lit if there were no switch in this circuit? Why or why not?

Open and Closed Circuits

Current in a circuit is similar to water running through a hose. The flow of charge differs from the flow of water in an important way, however. The water does not require a closed path to flow. If you cut the hose, the water continues to flow. If you cut a wire, the charge stops flowing.

Batteries have connections at both ends so that charge can follow a closed path to and from the battery. The cords that you see on appliances might look like single cords but actually contain at least two wires. The wires connect the device to a power plant and back to make a closed path.

Switches work by opening and closing the circuit. A switch that is on closes the circuit and allows charge to flow through the electrical devices. A switch that is off opens the circuit and stops the current.

REMINDER
Current requires a closed loop.

CHECK YOUR READING How are switches used to control the flow of charge through a circuit?

Standard symbols are used to represent the parts of a circuit. Some common symbols are shown in the circuit diagrams below. The diagrams represent the circuit shown on page 376 with the switch in both open and closed positions. Electricians and architects use diagrams such as these to plan the wiring of a building.

Circuit Diagrams

Symbols are used to represent the parts of a circuit. The circuit diagrams below show the circuit from page 376 in both an open and closed position.

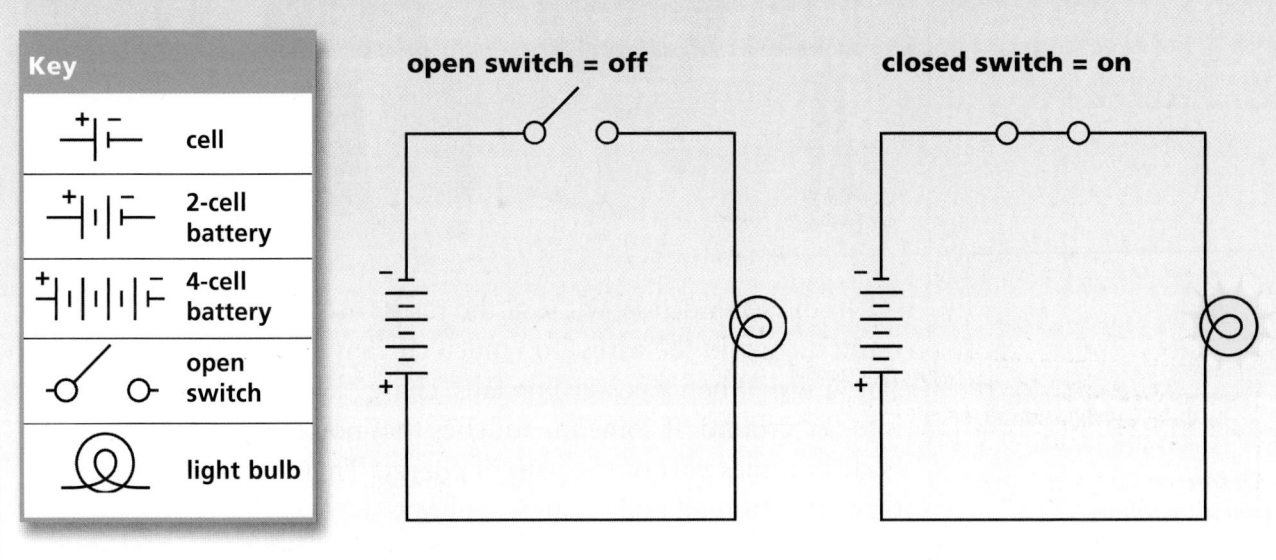

Key	
⊣⊢	cell
⊣⊦	2-cell battery
⊣⊦⊦⊦	4-cell battery
⚬/⚬	open switch
⊗	light bulb

open switch = off

closed switch = on

READING VISUALS Would charge flow through the circuit diagrammed on the left? Why or why not?

Current follows the path of least resistance.

OUTLINE
Add this heading to your outline, along with supporting ideas.

I. Main idea
  A. Supporting idea
    1. Detail
    2. Detail
  B. Supporting idea

Since current can follow only a closed path, why are damaged cords so dangerous? And why are people warned to stay away from fallen power lines? Although current follows a closed path, the path does not have to be made of wire. A person can become a part of the circuit, too. Charge flowing through a person is dangerous and sometimes deadly.

Current follows the path of least resistance. Materials with low resistance, such as certain metals, are good conductors. Charge will flow through a copper wire but not the plastic coating that covers it because copper is a good conductor and plastic is not. Water is also a good conductor when mixed with salt from a person's skin. That is why it is dangerous to use electrical devices near water.

Short Circuits

A **short circuit** is an unintended path connecting one part of a circuit with another. The current in a short circuit follows a closed path, but the path is not the one it was intended to follow. The illustration below shows a functioning circuit and a short circuit.

①Functioning Circuit The charge flows through one wire, through the light bulb, and then back through the second wire to the outlet.

②Short Circuit The cord has been damaged and the two wires inside have formed a connection. Now the path of least resistance is through one wire and back through the second wire.

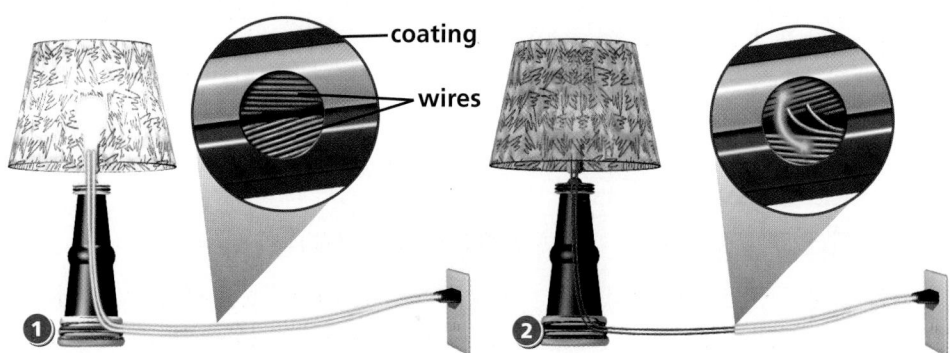

coating

wires

In the second case, without the resistance from the lamp, there is more current in the wires. Too much current can overheat the wires and start a fire. When a power line falls, charge flows along the wire and into the ground. If someone touches that power line, the person's body becomes part of the path of charge. That much charge flowing through a human body is almost always deadly.

RESOURCE CENTER
CLASSZONE.COM

Explore resources on electrical safety.

CHECK YOUR READING   Why are short circuits dangerous?

Grounding a Circuit

Recall that when lightning strikes a lightning rod, charge flows into the ground through a highly conductive metal rod rather than through a person or a building. In other words, the current follows the path of least resistance. The third prong on some electrical plugs performs a similar function. A circuit that connects stray current safely to the ground is known as a grounded circuit. Because the third prong grounds the circuit, it is sometimes called the ground.

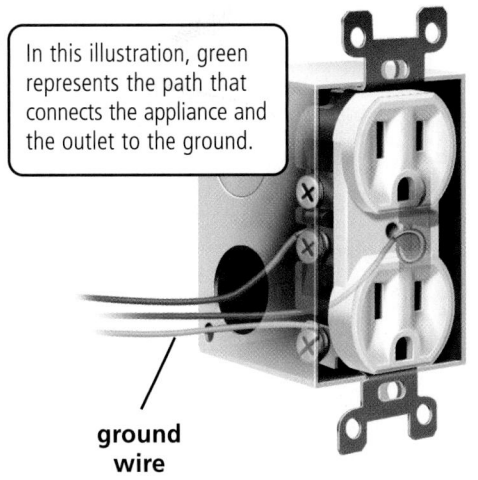

In this illustration, green represents the path that connects the appliance and the outlet to the ground.

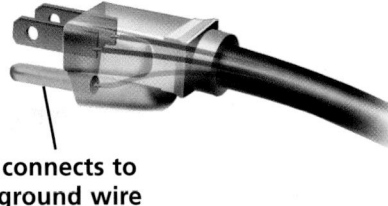

Orange is used in this illustration to represent the path that connects the appliance's circuit to a power source and back.

ground wire

connects to ground wire

Normally, charge flows through one prong, along a wire to an appliance, then back along a second wire to the second prong. If there is a short circuit, the charge might flow dangerously to the outside of the shell of the appliance. If there is a ground wire, the current will flow along the third wire and safely into the ground, along either a buried rod or a cold water pipe.

 **CHECK YOUR READING** What is the purpose of a ground wire?

Safety devices control current.

Suppose your living room wiring consists of a circuit that supplies current to a television and several lights. One hot evening, you turn on an air conditioner in the living room window. The wires that supply current to the room are suddenly carrying more current than before. The lights in the room become dim. Too much current in a circuit is dangerous. How do you know if there is too much current in a wire?

Fortunately, people have been using electric current for over a hundred years. An understanding of how charge flows has led to the development of safety devices. These safety devices are built into circuits to prevent dangerous situations from occurring.

How Fuses Work

new fuse

blown fuse

If you turn on an air conditioner in a room full of other electrical appliances that are already on, the circuit could overheat. But if the circuit contains a fuse, the fuse will automatically shut off the current. A fuse is a safety device that opens a circuit when there is too much current in it. Fuses are typically found in older homes and buildings. They are also found in cars and electrical appliances like air conditioners.

A fuse consists of a thin strip of metal that is inserted into the circuit. The charge in the closed circuit flows through the fuse. If too much charge flows through the fuse, the metal strip melts. When the strip has melted and the circuit is open, the fuse is blown. The photographs on the left show a new fuse and a blown fuse. As you can see, charge cannot flow across the melted strip. It has broken the circuit and stopped the current.

How much current is too much? That varies. The electrician who installs a circuit knows how much current the wiring can handle. He or she uses that knowledge to choose the right kind of fuse. Fuses are measured in amperes, or amps. Remember that amperage is a measure of current. If a fuse has blown, it must be replaced with a fuse of the same amperage. But a fuse should be replaced only after the problem that caused it to blow has been fixed.

INVESTIGATE Fuses

How can you stop a current?
PROCEDURE

1. Use the alligator clips to clip one end of each wire to the steel wool strand.

2. Place the steel wool strand in the jar. Tape the wires to the sides of the jar.

3. Clip the free end of one wire to the negative terminal of the battery.

4. What do you predict will happen when you complete the circuit? Clip the free end of the remaining wire to the positive terminal of the battery and observe the steel wool strand.

WHAT DO YOU THINK?
- What did you observe when you completed the circuit? Why did that happen?
- How can you stop the current?

CHALLENGE How is the setup in this activity similar to a fuse that would be found in a home circuit? How does it differ?

SKILL FOCUS
Making Models

MATERIALS
- 2 pieces of insulated wire with alligator clips
- single strand of steel wool
- glass jar
- tape
- 6 V battery

TIME
15 minutes

Other Safety Devices

Most modern homes do not use fuses. Instead, they use safety devices called circuit breakers. Circuit breakers, unlike fuses, do not have to be replaced every time they open the circuit. Like fuses, circuit breakers automatically open the circuit when too much charge flows through it. If the circuit becomes overloaded or there is a short circuit, the wire and the breaker grow hot. That makes a piece of metal inside the breaker expand. As it expands, it presses against a switch. The switch is then flipped to the off position and the current is stopped. Once the problem is solved, power can be restored manually by simply flipping the switch back. The illustration on the right shows a circuit breaker.

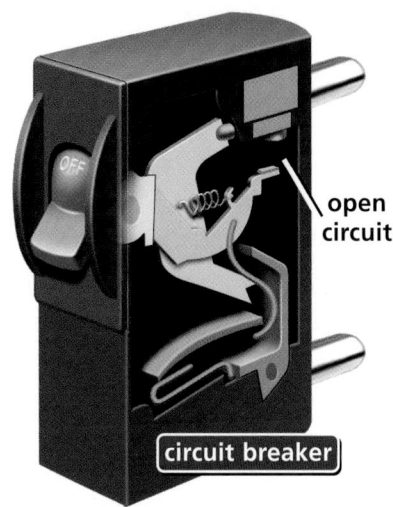

open circuit

circuit breaker

CHECK YOUR READING How are circuit breakers similar to fuses?

The photograph at the bottom right shows another safety device—a ground-fault circuit interrupter (GFCI) outlet. Sometimes a little current leaks out of an outlet or an appliance. Often it is so small you do not notice it. But if you happen to have wet hands, touching even a small current can be very dangerous.

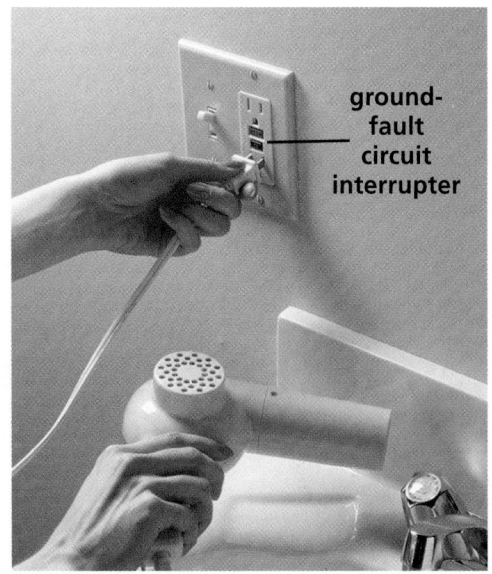

ground-fault circuit interrupter

GFCI outlets are required in places where exposure to water is common, such as in kitchens and bathrooms. A tiny circuit inside the GFCI outlet monitors the current going out and coming in. If some of the current starts to flow through an unintended path, there will be less current coming in to the GFCI. If that happens, a circuit breaker inside the GFCI outlet opens the circuit and stops the current. To close the circuit again, you push "Reset."

11.1 Review

KEY CONCEPTS

1. Describe three parts of a circuit and explain what each part does.

2. Explain the function of a ground wire.

3. What do fuses and circuit breakers have in common?

CRITICAL THINKING

4. **Apply** Suppose you have built a circuit for a class project. You are using a flat piece of wood for its base. How could you make a switch out of a paperclip and two nails?

5. **Communicate** Draw a diagram of a short circuit. Use the symbols for the parts of a circuit.

△ CHALLENGE

6. **Evaluate** A fuse in a home has blown and the owner wants to replace it with a fuse that can carry more current. Why might the owner's decision lead to a dangerous situation?

SCIENCE on the JOB

ELECTRICIAN

The Science of Electrical Work

Electricians are the professionals who know how to control and modify electrical installations safely. They are the people who install the wiring and fixtures that deliver current to the appliances in your home. They also inspect equipment and wiring to locate and correct problems. High-voltage current can cause injuries, or even death, if not handled correctly. The electrician uses science to build and repair electrical systems safely.

Choosing the Wire

Different types and thicknesses of wire have different amounts of resistance and can carry different amounts of current without overheating. The electrician knows which type of wire is suitable for each application.

Installing Safety Devices

Circuit breakers shut off a circuit when the wires carry too much current. This safety device protects the wires from overheating. The electrician chooses circuit breakers with the appropriate amperage for each circuit.

Using Circuit Diagrams

Circuit diagrams are used to map all of the circuits in a project. The electrician determines how many electrical devices each one will contain and knows how much energy those devices will use.

EXPLORE

1. **INFER** Look around the room you're in for electrical outlets. Why do you think each one is located where it is? Do you think they all connect appliances to the same circuit? Explain how this is possible.

2. **CHALLENGE** Suppose you are planning the wiring for the lighting in a room. Draw a diagram of the room's layout and indicate where the wires, lighting fixtures, and switches will be located.

11.2 Circuits make electric current useful.

BEFORE, you learned

- Charge flows in a closed circuit
- Circuits have a voltage source, conductor, and one or more electrical devices
- Current follows the path of least resistance

NOW, you will learn

- How circuits are designed for specific purposes
- How a series circuit differs from a parallel circuit
- How electrical appliances use circuits

THINK ABOUT

How does it work?

You know what a telephone does. But did you ever stop to think about how the circuits and other electrical parts inside of it work together to make it happen?

This photo shows an old telephone that has been taken apart to reveal its circuits. As you can see, there are a lot of different parts. Each one has a function. Pick two or three of the parts. What do you think each part does? How do you think it works? How might it relate to the other parts inside the telephone?

Circuits are constructed for specific purposes.

OUTLINE
Remember to include this heading in your outline.

I. Main idea
  A. Supporting idea
    1. Detail
    2. Detail
  B. Supporting idea

How many things around you right now use electric current? Current is used to transfer energy to so many things because it is easy to store, distribute, and turn off and on. Each device that uses current is a part of at least one circuit—the circuit that supplies its voltage.

Most electrical appliances have many circuits inside of them that are designed to carry out specific functions. Those circuits may be designed to light bulbs, move motor parts, or calculate. Each of those circuits may have thousands—or even millions—of parts. The functions that a circuit can perform depend on how those parts are set up within the circuit.

CHECK YOUR READING Why is the design of a circuit important?

Circuits can have multiple paths.

Even a simple circuit can contain several parts. When you flip the light switch in your classroom, how many different lights go on? If you count each light bulb or each fluorescent tube, there might be as many as ten or twelve light bulbs. There is more than one way those light bulbs could be connected in one circuit. Next, you will read about two simple ways that circuits can be constructed.

Series Circuits

READING **TiP**

The word *series* means a number of things arranged one after another.

A **series circuit** is a circuit in which current follows a single path. That means that all of the parts in a series circuit are part of the same path. The photograph and diagram below show a series circuit. The charge coming from the D cell flows first through one light bulb, and then through the next one.

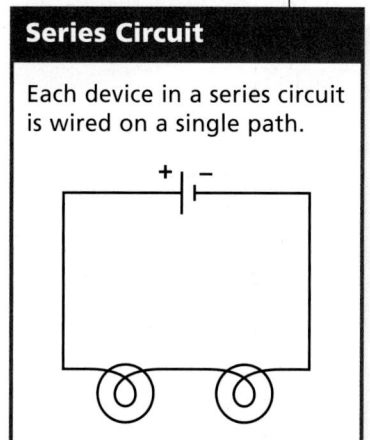

Series Circuit

Each device in a series circuit is wired on a single path.

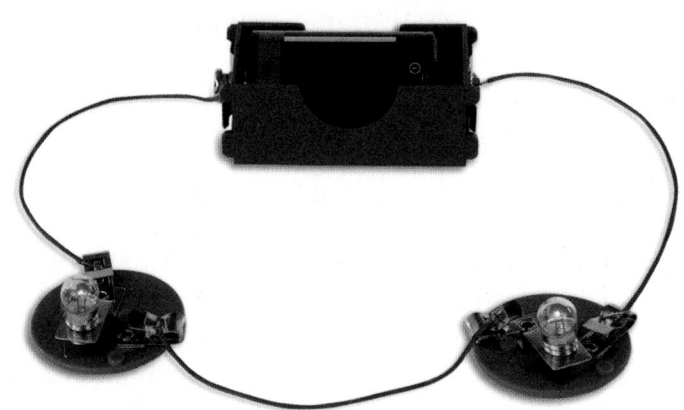

A series circuit uses a minimal amount of wire. However, a disadvantage of a series circuit is that all of the elements must be in working order for the circuit to function. If one of the light bulbs burns out, the circuit will be broken and the other bulb will be dark, too. Series circuits have another disadvantage. Light bulbs and other resistors convert some energy into heat and light. The more light bulbs that are added to a series circuit, the less current there is available, and the dimmer all of the bulbs become.

 **CHECK YOUR READING** Give two disadvantages of a series circuit.

If voltage sources are arranged in series, the voltages will add together. Sometimes batteries are arranged in series to add voltage to a circuit. For example, the circuits in flashlights are usually series circuits. The charge flows through one battery, through the next, through the bulb, and back to the first battery. The flashlight is brighter than it would be if its circuit contained only a single battery.

Parallel Circuits

A **parallel circuit** is a circuit in which current follows more than one path. Each path is called a branch. The current divides among all possible branches, so that the voltage is the same across each branch. The photograph and diagram below show a simple parallel circuit.

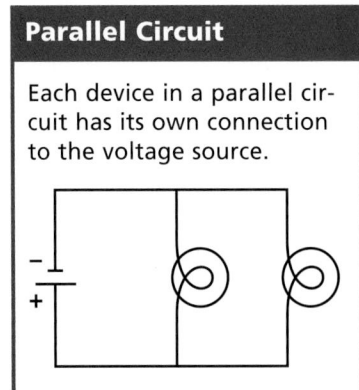

Parallel Circuit

Each device in a parallel circuit has its own connection to the voltage source.

Parallel circuits require more wire than do series circuits. On the other hand, there is more than one path on which the charge may flow. If one bulb burns out, the other bulb will continue to glow. As you add more and more light bulbs to a series circuit, each bulb in the circuit grows dimmer and dimmer. Because each bulb you add in a parallel circuit has its own branch to the power source, the bulbs burn at their brightest.

A flashlight contains batteries wired in a series circuit. Batteries can be wired in parallel, too. If the two positive terminals are connected to each other and the two negative terminals are connected to each other, charge will flow from both batteries. Adding batteries in parallel will not increase the voltage supplied to the circuit, but the batteries will last longer.

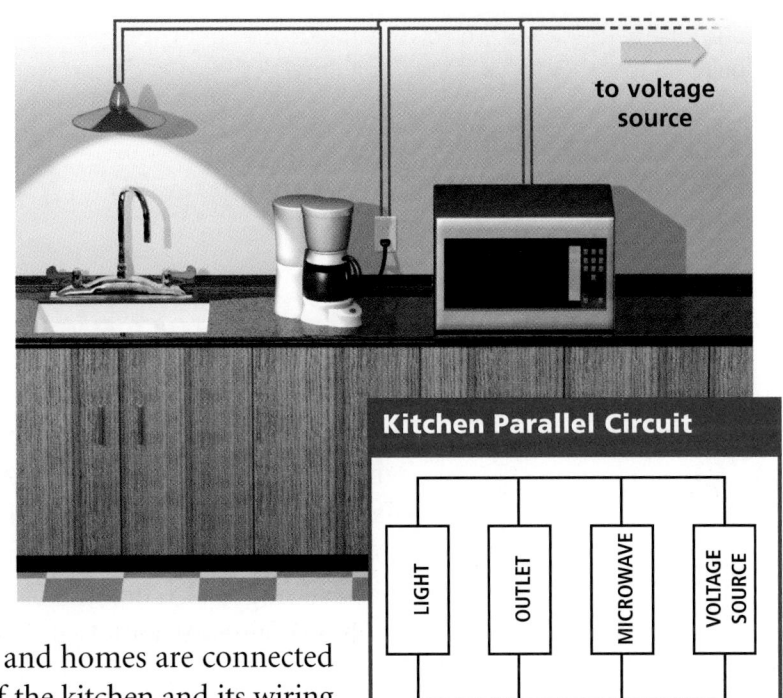

The circuits in most businesses and homes are connected in parallel. Look at the illustration of the kitchen and its wiring. This is a parallel circuit, so even if one electrical device is switched off, the others can still be used. The circuits within many electrical devices are combinations of series circuits and parallel circuits. For example, a parallel circuit may have branches that contain several elements arranged in series.

 **CHECK YOUR READING** Why are the circuits in buildings and homes arranged in parallel?

INVESTIGATE Circuits

How can you produce brighter light?

PROCEDURE

1. Clip one end of a wire to the light bulb and the other end to the negative terminal of one battery to form a connection.

2. Use another wire to connect the positive terminal of the battery with the negative terminal of a second battery, as shown in the photograph.

3. Use a third wire to connect the positive terminal of the second battery to the light bulb. Observe the light bulb.

4. Remove the wires. Find a way to reconnect the wires to produce the other type of circuit.

WHAT DO YOU THINK?

- Which circuit produced brighter light? What type of circuit was it?
- Why did the light bulb glow brighter in that circuit?

CHALLENGE Suppose you wanted to construct a new circuit consisting of four light bulbs and only one battery. How would you arrange the light bulbs so that they glow at their brightest? Your answer should be in the form of either a diagram or a sketch of the circuit.

SKILL FOCUS
Inferring

MATERIALS
- 4 insulated wires with alligator clips
- small light bulb in a holder
- 2 batteries in holders

TIME
15 minutes

Circuits convert electrical energy into other forms of energy.

We use electrical energy to do many things besides lighting a string of light bulbs. For example, a circuit in a space heater converts electrical energy into heat. A circuit in a fan converts electrical energy into motion. A circuit in a bell converts electrical energy into sound. That bell might also be on a circuit that makes it ring at certain times, letting you know when class is over.

Branches, switches, and other elements in circuits allow for such control of current that our calculators and computers can use circuits to calculate and process information for us. All of these things are possible because voltage is electric potential that can be converted into energy in a circuit.

FLORIDA
Content Review

Remember that no energy conversion is 100% efficient, as you learned in grade 6. Some energy is lost to heat and cannot be recovered.

CHECK YOUR READING Name three types of energy that electrical energy can be converted into.

A toaster is an example of an electrical appliance containing a circuit that converts energy from one form to another. In a toaster, electrical energy is converted into heat. Voltage is supplied to the toaster by plugging it into a wall outlet, which completes the circuit from a power plant. The outlet is wired in parallel with other outlets, so the appliance will always be connected to the same amount of voltage.

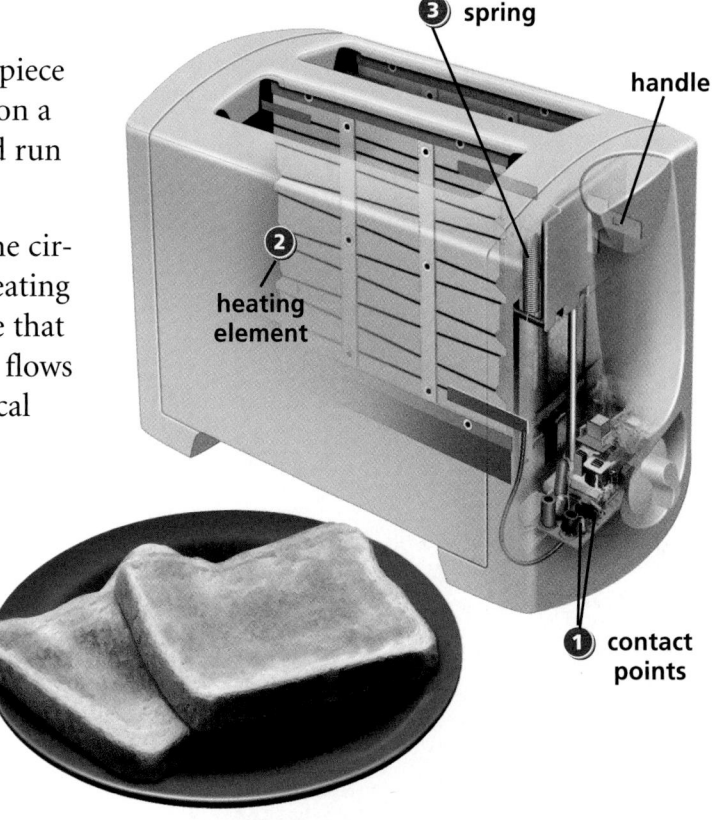

3 spring

handle

1 When you push the handle down, a piece of metal connects to contact points on a circuit board that act as a switch and run current through the circuit.

2 Charge flows through a resistor in the circuit called a heating element. The heating element is made up of a type of wire that has a very high resistance. As charge flows through the heating element, electrical energy is converted into heat.

2 heating element

3 The holder in the toaster is loaded onto a timed spring. After a certain amount of time passes, the spring is released, the toast pops up, and the circuit is opened. The toaster shuts off automatically, and your toast is done.

1 contact points

 **CHECK YOUR READING** Summarize the way a circuit in a toaster works. (Remember that a summary includes only the most important information.)

11.2 Review

KEY CONCEPTS

1. Explain how a circuit can perform a specific function.

2. How are series circuits and parallel circuits similar? How do they differ?

3. Describe three electrical appliances that use circuits to convert electrical energy into other forms of energy.

CRITICAL THINKING

4. **Analyze** Why are the batteries of flashlights often arranged in series and not in parallel?

5. **Infer** You walk past a string of small lights around a window frame. Only two of the bulbs are burned out. What can you tell about the string of lights?

△ CHALLENGE

6. **Apply** Explain how the circuit in a space heater converts electrical energy into heat. Draw a diagram of the circuit, using the standard symbols for circuit diagrams.

MATH in SCIENCE

MATH TUTORIAL
CLASSZONE.COM

Click on Math Tutorial for more help with percents and proportions.

The many lights in this spectacular display in Kobe, Japan, produce a large voltage drop. The appropriate type of wire must be used to supply its current.

Voltage Drop

A voltage drop occurs when current passes through a wire or an electrical device. The higher the resistance of a wire, the greater the voltage drop. Too much voltage drop can cause the device to overheat.

The National Electric Code—a document of guidelines for electricians—states that the voltage drop across a wire should be no more than 5 percent of the voltage from the voltage source. To find 5 percent of a number, you can set up the calculation as a proportion.

Example

The lighting in a hotel includes many fixtures that will be arranged on long wires. The electrician needs to know the maximum voltage drop allowed in order to choose the proper wire. The circuit will use a voltage source of 120 V. What is 5% of 120?

(1) Write the problem as a proportion.

$$\frac{\text{voltage drop}}{\text{voltage}} = \frac{\text{percent}}{100}$$

(2) Substitute.

$$\frac{\text{voltage drop}}{120} = \frac{5}{100}$$

(3) Calculate and simplify.

$$\frac{\text{voltage drop}}{\cancel{120}} \cdot \cancel{120} = \frac{5}{100} \cdot 120$$

$$\text{voltage drop} = 6$$

ANSWER The maximum voltage drop in the wire is 6 V.

Use the proportion to answer the following questions.

1. If the voltage source is increased to 277 V, what is the maximum voltage drop in the wire?

2. To be on the safe side, the electrician decided to find a wire with a voltage drop that is 3 percent of the voltage from the voltage source. What is the voltage drop in the wire?

CHALLENGE A student wants to hang a string of lights outside and connect it to an extension cord. The voltage drop across the extension cord is 3.1 V. The outlet supplies 240 V. Does the voltage drop in the extension cord meet the code guidelines?

Electronic technology is based on circuits.

VOCABULARY

electronic p. 389
binary code p. 390
digital p. 390
analog p. 392
computer p. 393

◁ BEFORE, you learned

- Charge flows in a closed loop
- Circuits are designed for specific purposes
- Electrical appliances use circuits

▷ NOW, you will learn

- How information can be coded
- How computer circuits use digital information
- How computers work

EXPLORE Codes

How can information be coded?

PROCEDURE

① Write the numbers 1 to 26 in your notebook. Below each number, write a letter of the alphabet. This will serve as your key.

② On a separate piece of paper, write the name of the street you live on using numbers instead of words. For each letter of the word, use the number that is directly above it on your key.

③ Exchange messages with a partner and use your key to decode your partner's information.

MATERIALS
- notebook
- small piece of paper

WHAT DO YOU THINK?
- How can information be coded?
- Under what types of circumstances would information need to be coded?

Electronics use coded information.

A code is a system of symbols used to send a message. Language is a code, for example. The symbols used in written language are lines and shapes. The words on this page represent meanings coded into the form of letters. As you read, your brain decodes the lines and shapes that make up each word, and you understand the message that is encoded.

An **electronic** device is a device that uses electric current to represent coded information. In electronics, the signals are variations in the current. Examples of electronic devices include computers, calculators, CD players, game systems, and more.

RESOURCE CENTER
CLASSZONE.COM

Find out more about electronics.

 **CHECK YOUR READING** Describe the signals used in electronic devices.

Binary Code

The English alphabet contains only 26 letters, yet there is no limit to the number of messages that can be expressed with it. That is because the message is conveyed not only by the letters that are chosen but also by the order in which they are placed.

Many electronic devices use a coding system with only two choices, as compared with the 26 in the alphabet. A coding system consisting of two choices is a **binary code.** As with a language, complex messages can be sent using binary code. In electronics, the two choices are whether an electric current is on or off. Switches in electronic circuits turn the current on and off. The result is a message represented in pulses of current.

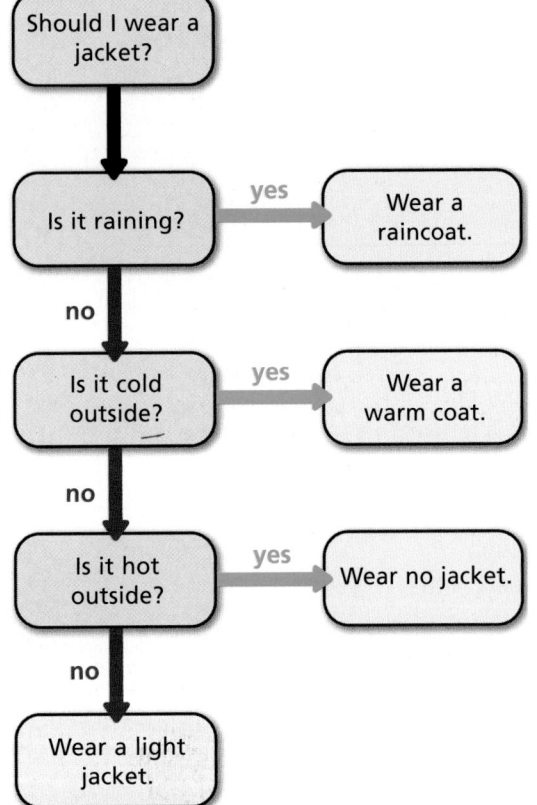

It may be hard to imagine how something as complex as a computer game can be expressed with pulses of current. But it is a matter of breaking down information into smaller and smaller steps. You may have played the game 20 questions. In that game, you receive a message by asking someone only yes-or-no questions. The player answering the questions conveys the message only in *yes's* and *no's,* a binary code.

The diagram on the left shows how a decision-making process can be written in simple steps. The diagram is similar to a computer program, which tells a computer what to do. Each step of the process has been broken down into a binary question. If you determine exactly what you mean by *cold* and *hot,* then anyone using this program—or even a computer—would arrive at the same conclusion for a given set of conditions.

CHECK YOUR READING How can a process be broken down into simple steps?

Digital Information

You can think of the yes-or-no choices in a binary system as being represented by the numbers 0 and 1. Information that is represented as numbers, or digits, is called **digital** information. In electronics, a circuit that is off is represented by 0, and a circuit that is on is represented by 1.

Digital information is represented in long streams of digits. Each 0 or 1 is also known as a bit, which is short for *binary dig*it. A group of 8 bits is known as a byte. You might have heard the term *gigabyte* in reference to the amount of information that can be stored on a computer. One gigabyte is equal to about 1 billion bytes. That's 8 billion 0s and 1s!

Computers, digital cameras, CD players, DVD players, and other devices use digital information. Digital information is used in electronic devices more and more. There are at least two reasons for this:

- Digital information can be copied many times without losing its quality. The 1s are always copied as 1s, and the 0s are always copied as 0s.

- Digital information can be processed, or worked with, on computers.

For example, a photograph taken on a digital camera can be input to a computer in the form of digital information. Once the photograph is on a computer, the user can modify it, copy it, store it, and send it.

Many portable devices such as game systems and MP3 players can also be used with computers. Because computers and the devices use the same type of information, computers can be used to add games, music, and other programs to the devices. The photograph at right of a watch shows an example of a portable device that uses digital information.

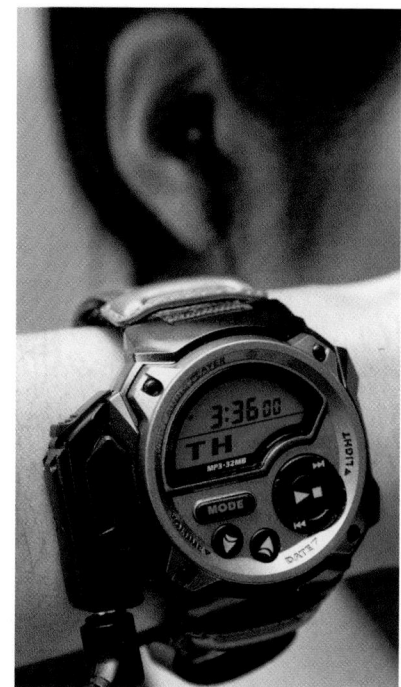

This watch also functions as an MP3 player—it can store songs as digital files.

 **CHECK YOUR READING** Why is digital information often used in electronic devices?

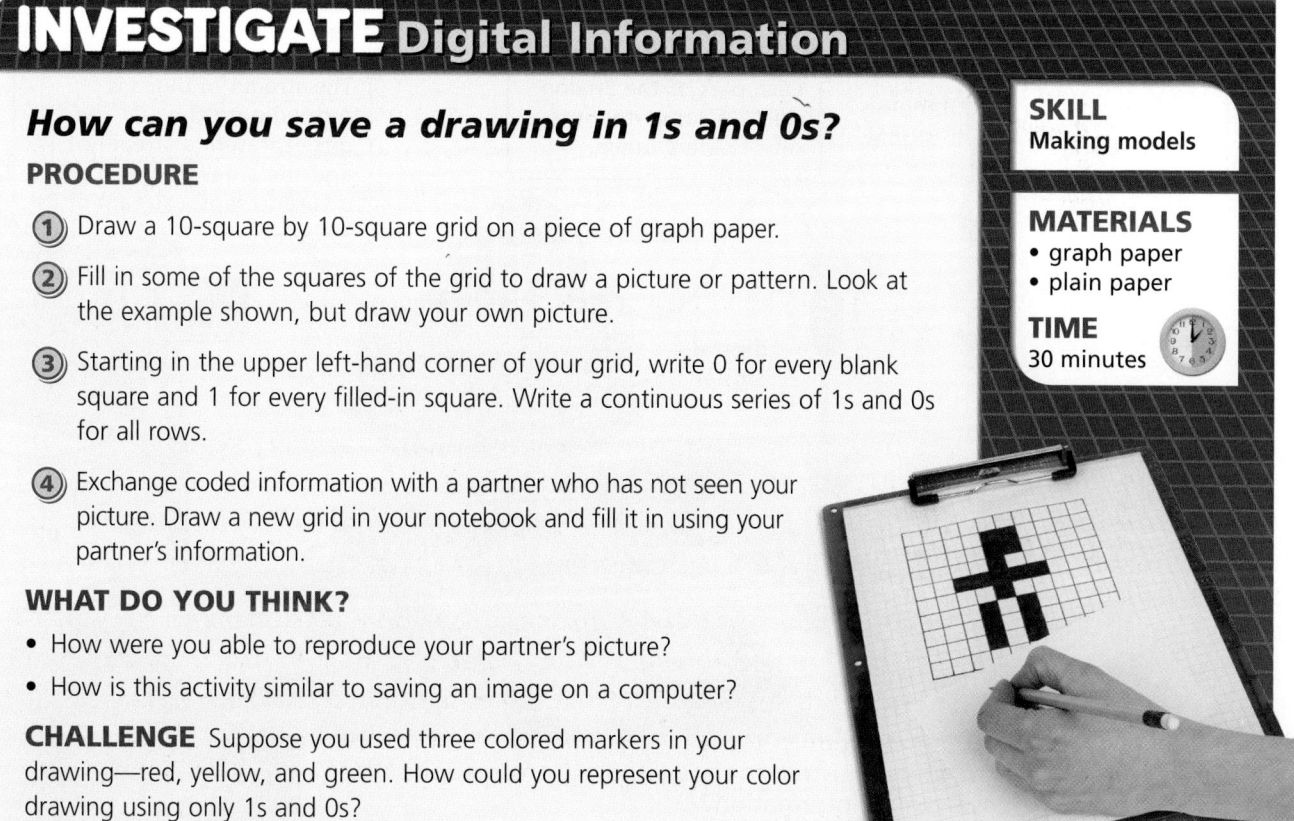

INVESTIGATE Digital Information

How can you save a drawing in 1s and 0s?

PROCEDURE

1. Draw a 10-square by 10-square grid on a piece of graph paper.

2. Fill in some of the squares of the grid to draw a picture or pattern. Look at the example shown, but draw your own picture.

3. Starting in the upper left-hand corner of your grid, write 0 for every blank square and 1 for every filled-in square. Write a continuous series of 1s and 0s for all rows.

4. Exchange coded information with a partner who has not seen your picture. Draw a new grid in your notebook and fill it in using your partner's information.

WHAT DO YOU THINK?

- How were you able to reproduce your partner's picture?
- How is this activity similar to saving an image on a computer?

CHALLENGE Suppose you used three colored markers in your drawing—red, yellow, and green. How could you represent your color drawing using only 1s and 0s?

SKILL
Making models

MATERIALS
- graph paper
- plain paper

TIME
30 minutes

Analog to Digital

Some electronic devices use a system of coding electric current that differs from the digital code. Those electronics use analog information. **Analog** information is information that is represented in a continuous but varying form.

For example, a microphone records sound waves as analog information. The analog signal that is produced varies in strength as the sound wave varies in strength, as shown below. In order for the signal to be burned onto a CD, it is converted into digital information.

① The sound waves are recorded in the microphone as an analog electrical signal.

② The signal is sent through a computer circuit that measures, or samples, each part of the wave. The signal is sampled many thousands of times every second.

③ Each measurement of the wave is converted into a stream of digits. Microscopic pits representing the stream of digits are burned onto the CD. A stereo converts the signal from digital back to analog form, making it possible for people to hear what was recorded.

Analog and Digital Signals

Sound is recorded as an analog signal and converted to digital information for storage on a CD.

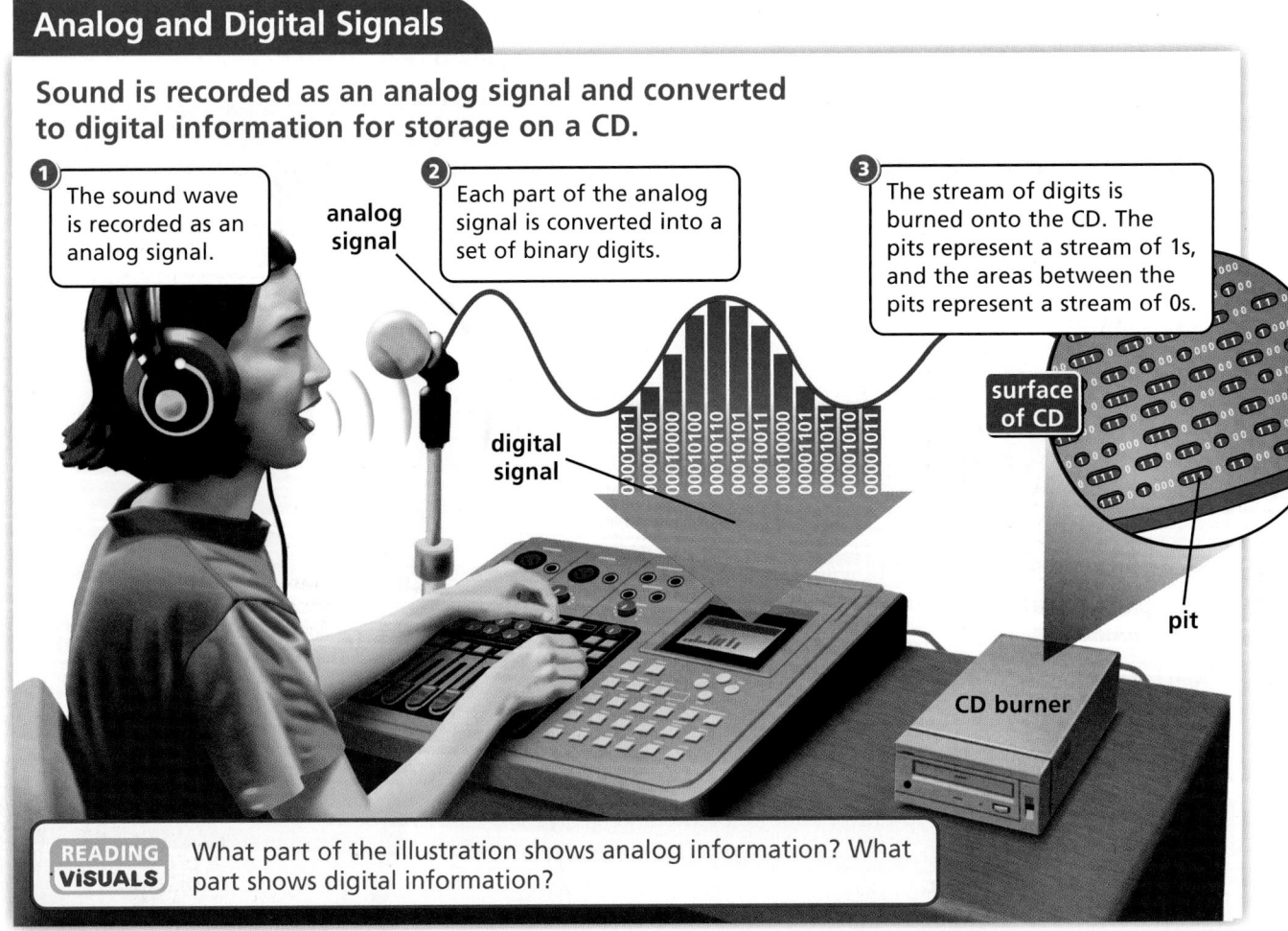

① The sound wave is recorded as an analog signal.

analog signal

② Each part of the analog signal is converted into a set of binary digits.

digital signal

③ The stream of digits is burned onto the CD. The pits represent a stream of 1s, and the areas between the pits represent a stream of 0s.

surface of CD

pit

CD burner

READING VISUALS What part of the illustration shows analog information? What part shows digital information?

Computer circuits process digital information.

A **computer** is an electronic device that processes digital information. Computers have been important in science and industry for a long time. Scientists use computers to gather, store, process, and share scientific data. As computers continue to get faster, smaller, and less expensive, they are turning up in many places.

Suppose you get a ride to the store. If the car you're riding in is a newer car, it probably has a computer inside it. At the store, you buy a battery, and the clerk records the sale on a register that is connected to a computer. You put the battery in your camera and take a picture, and the camera has a computer inside it.

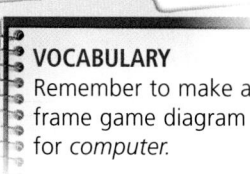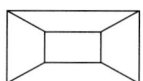
Integrated Circuits

The first digital computer weighed 30 tons and took up a whole room. After 60 years of development, computers the size of a postage stamp are able to complete the same tasks in less time. New technology in computer circuits has led to very small and powerful computers.

Computers process information on circuits that contain many switches, branches, and other elements that allow for a very fine control of current. An integrated circuit is a miniature electronic circuit. Tiny switches, called transistors, in these circuits turn off and on rapidly, signaling the stream of digits that represent information. Over a million of these switches may be on one small integrated circuit!

> **CHECK YOUR READING** How do integrated circuits signal digital information?

Most integrated circuits are made from silicon, an element that is very abundant in Earth's crust. When silicon is treated with certain chemicals, it becomes a good semiconductor. A semiconductor is a material that is more conductive than an insulator but less conductive than a conductor. Silicon is a useful material in computers because the flow of current in it can be finely controlled.

Microscopic circuits are etched onto treated silicon with chemicals or lasers. Transistors and other circuit parts are constructed layer by layer on the silicon. A small, complex circuit on a single piece of silicon is known as a silicon chip, or microchip.

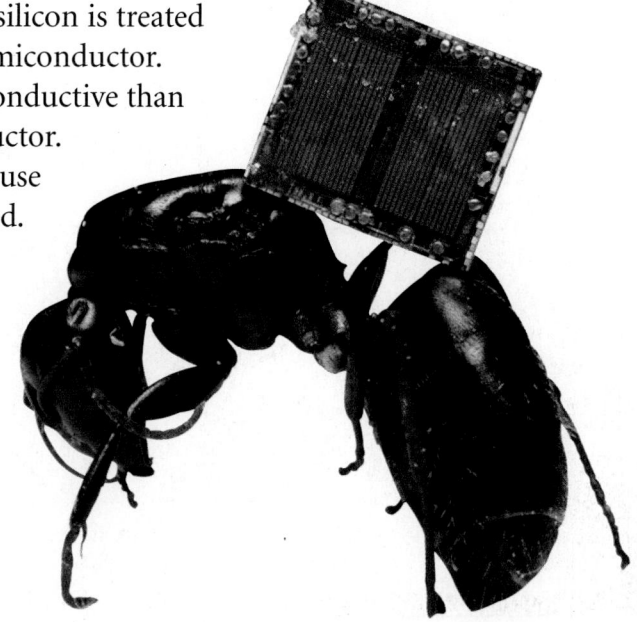

This integrated circuit is smaller than the common ant, *Camponotus pennsylvanicus,* which ranges in length from 6 to 17 mm.

Personal Computers

OUTLINE
Use an outline to take notes about personal computers.

I. Main idea
   A. Supporting idea
      1. Detail
      2. Detail
   B. Supporting idea

When you think of a computer, you probably think of a monitor, mouse, and keyboard—a personal computer (PC). All of the physical parts of a computer and its accessories are together known as hardware. Software refers to the instructions, or programs, and languages that control the hardware. The hardware, software, and user of a computer all work together to complete tasks.

 **CHECK YOUR READING** What is the difference between hardware and software?

Computers have two kinds of memory. As the user is working, information is saved on the computer's random-access memory, or RAM. RAM is a computer's short-term memory. Most computers have enough RAM to store billions of bits. Another type of memory is called read-only memory, or ROM. ROM is a computer's long-term memory, containing the programs to start and run the computer. ROM can save information even after a computer is turned off.

The illustration below shows how a photograph is scanned, modified, and printed using a personal computer. The steps fall into four main functions—input, storage, processing, and output.

How a PC Works

Digital information can move through input, processing, storage, and output devices.

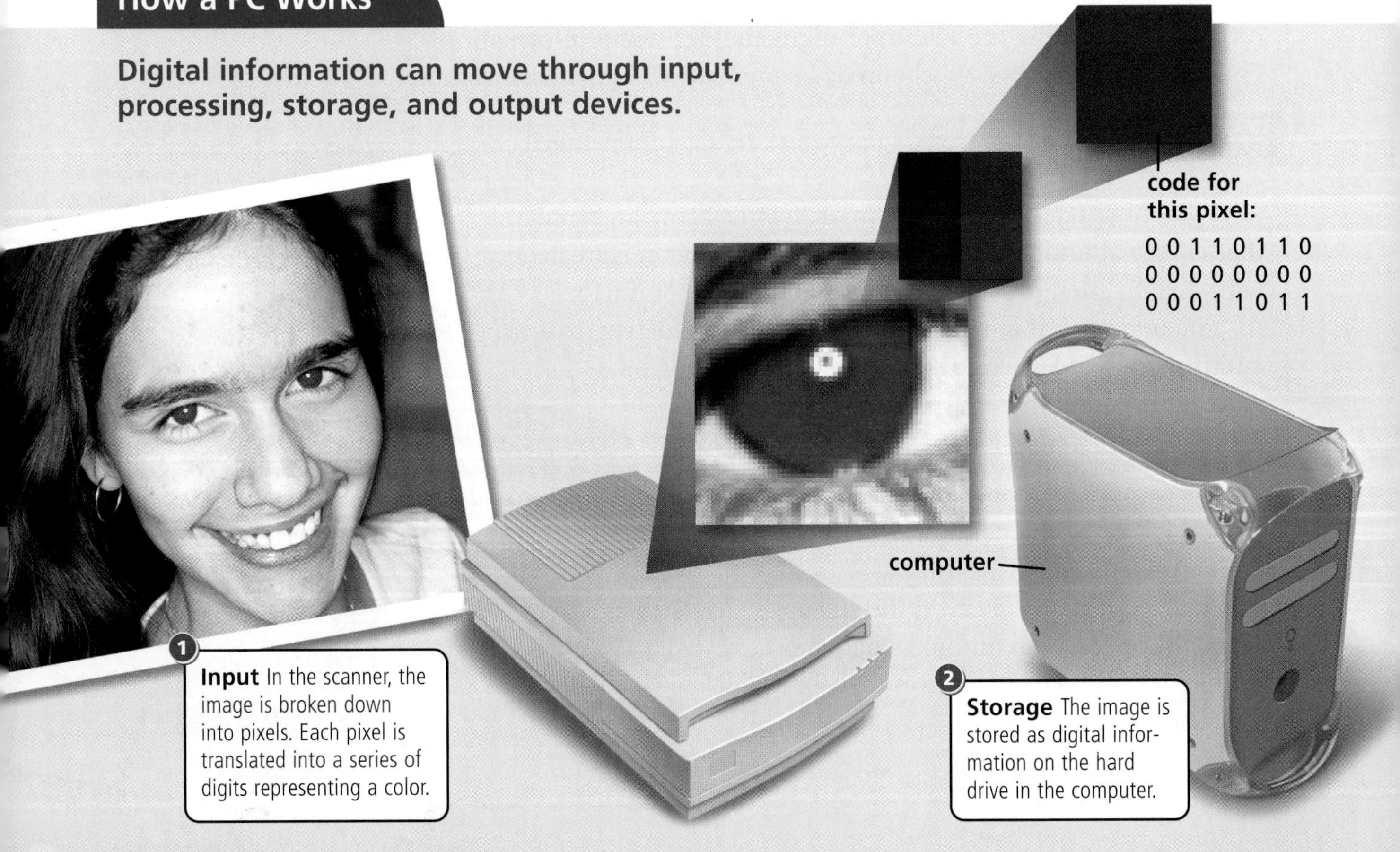

code for this pixel:
0 0 1 1 0 1 1 0
0 0 0 0 0 0 0 0
0 0 0 1 1 0 1 1

computer

① **Input** In the scanner, the image is broken down into pixels. Each pixel is translated into a series of digits representing a color.

② **Storage** The image is stored as digital information on the hard drive in the computer.

① Input The user scans the photograph on a scanner. Each small area, or pixel, of the photograph is converted into a stream of digits. The digital information representing the photograph is sent to the main computer circuit, which is called the central processing unit, or CPU.

② Storage The user saves the photograph on a magnetic storage device called the hard drive. Small areas of the hard drive are magnetized in one of two directions. The magnetized areas oriented in one direction represent 1s, and the areas oriented in the opposite direction represent 0s, as a way to store the digital information.

③ Processing The photograph is converted back into pixels on the monitor, or screen, for the user to see. The computer below has a software program installed for altering photographs. The user adds more input to the computer with the mouse and the keyboard to improve the photograph.

④ Output The user sends the improved photograph to a printer. The printer converts the digital information back to pixels, and the photograph is printed.

VISUALIZATION
CLASSZONE.COM

See how hard drives store information.

CHECK YOUR READING During which one of the four main computer functions is information converted into digital information?

---

monitor

printer

④ Output Digital information is translated back into pixels and the photograph is printed.

③ Processing The image is altered using software on the computer.

READING VISUALS How has the photograph of the girl been altered on the computer?

Computers can be linked with other computers.

You may have been at a computer lab or a library and had to wait for a printer to print something for you. Offices, libraries, and schools often have several computers that are all connected to the same printer. A group of computers that are linked together is known as a network. Computers can also be linked with other computers to share information. The largest network of computers is the Internet.

The Origin of the Internet

People have been using computer networks to share information on university campuses and military bases for decades. The computers within those networks were connected over telephone systems from one location to another. But those networks behaved like a series circuit. If the link to one computer was broken, the whole network of links went down.

The network that we now call the Internet is different. The United States Department of Defense formed the Internet by linking computers on college campuses across the country. Many extra links were formed, producing a huge web of connected computers. That way, if some links are broken, others still work.

 **CHECK YOUR READING** How does the Internet differ from earlier networks?

The Internet Today

The Internet now spans the world. E-mail uses the Internet. E-mail has added to the ways in which people can "meet," communicate, conduct business, and share stories. The Internet can also be used to work on tasks that require massive computing power. For example, millions of computers linked together, along with their combined information, might one day be used to develop a cure for cancer or model the workings of a human mind.

This map shows a representation of Internet traffic in the early 1990s. A map of Internet traffic now would be even more full of lines.

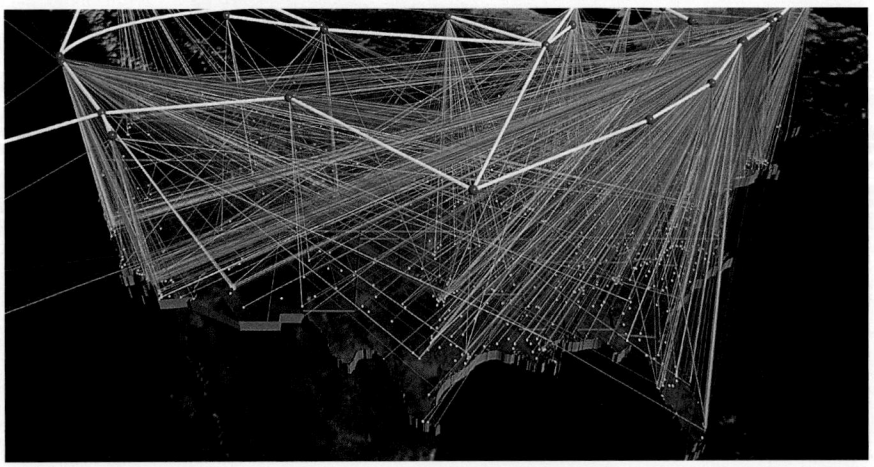

When you think of the Internet, you might think of the World Wide Web, or the Web. The Web consists of all of the information that can be accessed on the Internet. This information is stored on millions of host computers all over the world. The files that you locate are called Web pages. Each Web page has an address that begins with *www*, which stands for World Wide Web. The system allows you to search or surf through all of the information that is available on it. You might use the Web to research a project. Millions of people use the Web every day to find information, to shop, or for entertainment.

You may have heard of the Bronze Age or the Iron Age in your history class. Digital information and the Internet have had such a strong impact on the way we do things that some people refer to the era we live in as the Information Age.

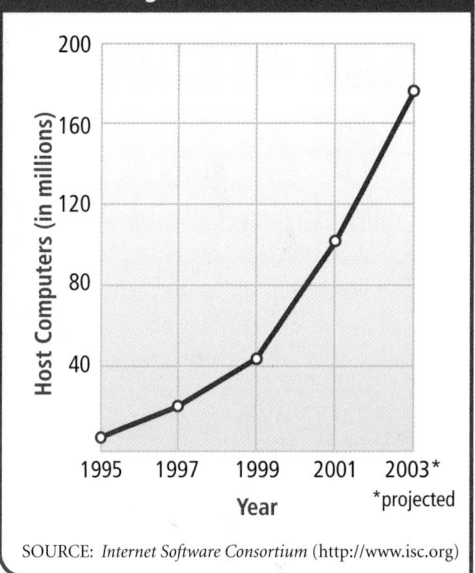

Internet Usage

SOURCE: *Internet Software Consortium* (http://www.isc.org)

11.3 Review

KEY CONCEPTS

1. Describe an example of coded information.

2. What is digital information? Give three examples of devices that use digital information.

3. Give an example of each of the following in terms of computers: input, storage, processing, and output.

CRITICAL THINKING

4. **Compare** Morse code uses a signal of dots and dashes to convey messages. How is Morse code similar to digital code?

5. **Infer** The word *integrated* means "brought together to form a whole." How does that definition apply to an integrated circuit?

▲ CHALLENGE

6. **Predict** Computers as we know them did not exist 50 years ago, and now they are used for many purposes. How do you think people will use computers 50 years from now? Write a paragraph describing what you think the computers of the future will be like and how they will be used.

CHAPTER INVESTIGATION

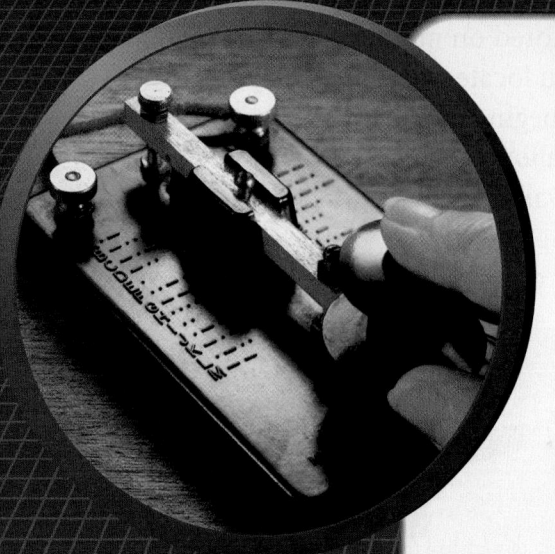

Design an Electronic Communication Device

OVERVIEW AND PURPOSE

The telegraph was one of the first inventions to demonstrate that machines could be used to communicate over long distances. In a telegraph, messages are sent as electrical signals along a wire from a sending device to a receiver.

Like modern computers, the telegraph uses a binary code. The code is called Morse code—a combination of short and long signals—to stand for letters and symbols. In this lab, you will use what you have learned about circuits to

- design a battery-powered device that uses Morse code
- build and test your design

DESIGN —YOUR OWN—

▶ Problem

A toy company has contracted you to design and build a new product for kids. They want a communication device that is similar to a telegraph. Kids will use the device to communicate with each other in Morse code. The company's market research has shown that parents do not like noisy toys, so the company wants a device that uses light rather than sound as a signal.

▶ Procedure

1. Brainstorm ideas for a communication device that can use Morse code. Look at the available materials and think how you could make a circuit that contains a light bulb and a switch.

2. Describe your proposed design and/or draw a sketch of it in your **Science Notebook.** Include a list of the materials that you would need to build it.

MATERIALS
- 2 batteries
- light bulb in holder
- piece of copper wire
- 2 wire leads with alligator clips
- 2 craft sticks
- toothpick
- paper clip
- piece of cardboard
- clothespin
- aluminum foil
- rubber band
- scissors
- tape
- wire cutters
- Morse Code Chart

3 Show your design to a team member. Consider the constraints of each of your designs, such as what materials are available, the complexity of the design, and the time available.

4 Choose one idea or combine two ideas into a final design to test with your group. Build a sample version of your device, called a prototype.

5 Test your device by writing a short question. Translate the question into Morse code. Make long and short flashes of light on your device to send your message. Another person on your team should write down the message received in Morse code, translate the message, and send an answer.

6 Complete at least two trials. Each time, record the question in English, the question in code, the answer in code, and the answer in English.

7 Write a brief evaluation of how well the signal worked. Use the following criteria for your evaluation for each trial.

- What errors, if any, occurred while you were sending the signal?
- What errors, if any, occurred while you were receiving the signal?
- Did the translated answer make sense? Why or why not?

▶ Observe and Analyze Write It Up

1. **MODEL** Draw a sketch of your final design. Label the parts. Next to your sketch, draw a circuit diagram of your device.

2. **INFER** How do the parts of your circuit allow you to control the flow of current?

3. **COMPARE** How is the signal that is used in your system similar to the digital information used by computers to process information? How does the signal differ?

4. **APPLY** A small sheet of instructions will be packaged with the device. Write a paragraph for the user that explains how to use it. Keep in mind that the user will probably be a child.

▶ Conclude  Write It Up

1. **EVALUATE** What problems, if any, did you encounter when testing your device? How might you improve upon the design?

2. **IDENTIFY LIMITS** What are the limitations of your design? You might consider its estimated costs, where and how kids will be able to use it, and the chances of the device breaking.

3. **APPLY** How might you modify your design so that it could be used by someone with limited vision?

4. **SYNTHESIZE** Write down the steps that you have used to develop this new product. Your first step was to brainstorm an idea.

▶ INVESTIGATE Further

CHALLENGE Design another system of communication that uses your own code. The signal should be in the form of flags. Make a table that lists what the signals mean and write instructions that explain how to use the system to communicate.

Design an Electronic Communication Device
Observe and Analyze
Table 1. Prototype Testing

	Trial 1	Trial 2
Question (English)		
Question (code)		
Answer (code)		
Answer (English)		
Evaluation		

Conclude

Chapter Review

FLORIDA REVIEW
CLASSZONE.COM

Content Review and
FCAT Practice

the BIG idea

Circuits control the flow of electric charge.

KEY CONCEPTS SUMMARY

1 Charge needs a continuous path to flow.

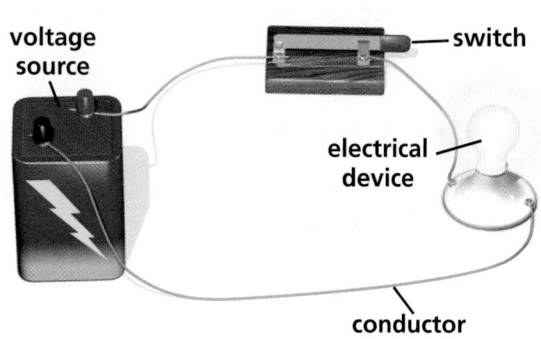

Charge flows in a closed path. Circuits provide a closed path for current. Circuit parts include voltage sources, switches, conductors, and electrical devices such as resistors.

VOCABULARY
circuit p. 375
resistor p. 376
short circuit p. 378

2 Circuits make electric current useful.

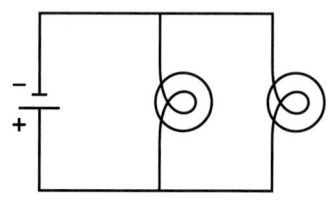

Each device in a **series circuit** is wired on a single path.

Each device in a **parallel circuit** has its own connection to the voltage source.

VOCABULARY
series circuit p. 384
parallel circuit p. 385

3 Electronic technology is based on circuits.

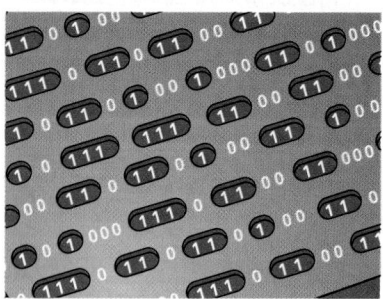

Electronic devices use electrical signals to represent coded information. Computers process information in digital code which uses 1s and 0s to represent the information.

VOCABULARY
electronic p. 389
binary code p. 390
digital p. 390
analog p. 392
computer p. 393

Reviewing Vocabulary

Draw a Venn diagram for each of the term pairs below. Write the terms above the circles. In the center, write characteristics that the terms have in common. In the outer circles write the ways in which they differ. A sample diagram has been completed for you.

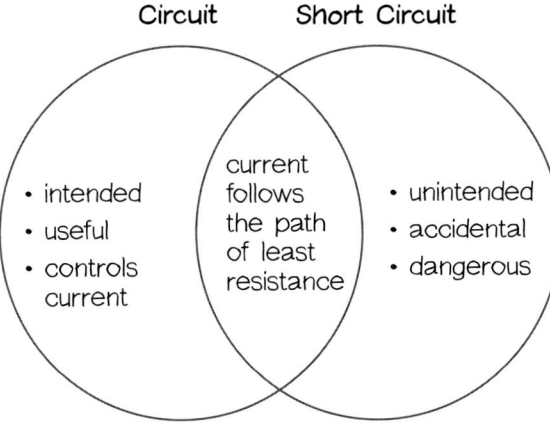

Circuit   Short Circuit

- intended
- useful
- controls current

current follows the path of least resistance

- unintended
- accidental
- dangerous

1. resistor; switch

2. series circuit; parallel circuit

3. digital; analog

4. digital; binary code

5. electronic; computer

Reviewing Key Concepts

Multiple Choice *Choose the letter of the best answer.*

6. Current always follows
   a. a path made of wire
   b. a path containing an electrical device
   c. a closed path
   d. an open circuit

7. When you open a switch in a circuit, you
   a. form a closed path for current
   b. reverse the current
   c. turn off its electrical devices
   d. turn on its electrical devices

8. Which one of the following parts of a circuit changes electrical energy into another form of energy?
   a. resistor
   b. conductor
   c. base
   d. voltage source

9. A circuit breaker is a safety device that
   a. must be replaced after each use
   b. has a wire that melts
   c. supplies voltage to a circuit
   d. stops the current

10. What happens when more than one voltage source is added to a circuit in series?
   a. The voltages are added together.
   b. The voltages cancel each other out.
   c. The voltages are multiplied together.
   d. The voltage of each source decreases.

11. Which of the following is an electronic device?
   a. flashlight
   b. calculator
   c. lamp
   d. electric fan

12. Which word describes the code used in digital technology?
   a. binary
   b. analog
   c. alphabetical
   d. Morse

13. Computers process information that has been
   a. broken down into simple steps
   b. converted into heat
   c. represented as a wave
   d. coded as an analog signal

Short Response *Write a short response to each question.*

14. How can hardware, software, and the user of a computer work together to complete a task?

15. Describe three parts of a personal computer and explain the main function of each.

Thinking Critically

Use the illustrations below to answer the next two questions.

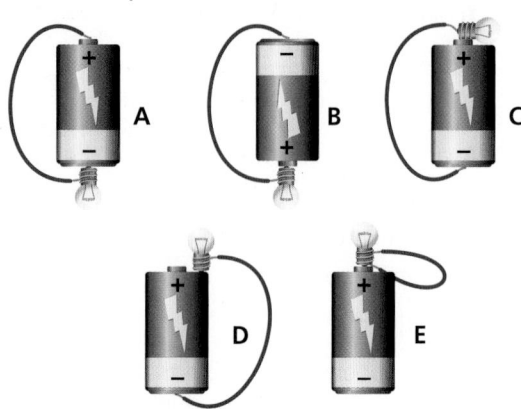

16. PREDICT In which arrangement(s) above will the light bulb glow? For each arrangement in which you think the bulb will not glow, explain your reasoning.

17. APPLY Which arrangement could be used as a battery tester? List the materials that you would use to make a battery tester.

Use the diagram below to answer the next five questions.

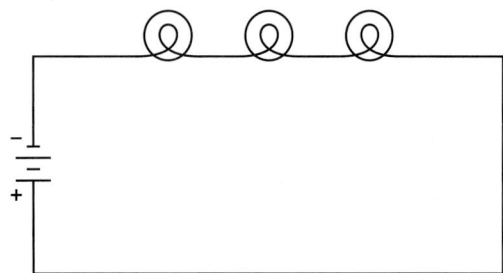

18. Is this a series circuit or a parallel circuit?

19. Explain what would happen if you unscrewed one of the bulbs in the circuit.

20. Explain what would happen if you wired three more bulbs into the circuit.

21. Draw and label a diagram of the same elements wired in the other type of circuit. Does your sketch involve more or fewer pieces of wire? How many?

22. Imagine you want to install a switch into your circuit. Where would you add the switch? Explain your answer.

23. ANALYZE Look for a pattern in the digital codes below, representing the numbers 1–10. What is the code for the number 11? How do you know?

0001; 0010; 0011; 0100; 0101; 0110; 0111; 1000; 1001; 1010

24. APPLY A computer circuit contains millions of switches that use temperature-dependent materials to operate lights, sounds, and a fan. How many different types of energy is current converted to in the computer circuit? Explain.

25. ANALYZE A music recording studio makes a copy of a CD that is itself a copy of another CD. Explain why the quality of the copied CDs is the same as the original CD.

26. INFER A new watch can be programmed to perform specific tasks. Describe what type of circuit the watch might contain.

27. SYNTHESIZE Explain how the Internet is like a worldwide parallel circuit.

the BIG idea

28. ANALYZE Look back at the photograph on pages 372–373. Think about the answer you gave to the question. How has your understanding of circuits changed?

29. SYNTHESIZE Explain how the following statement relates to electric circuits: "Energy can change from one form to another and can move from one place to another."

30. SUMMARIZE Write a paragraph summarizing how circuits control current. Using the heading at the top of page 375 as your topic sentence. Then give an example from each red and blue heading on pages 375–377.

UNIT PROJECTS

If you need to do an experiment for your unit project, gather the materials. Be sure to allow enough time to observe results before the project is due.

Interpreting Diagrams

The four circuit diagrams below use the standard symbols for the parts of a circuit.

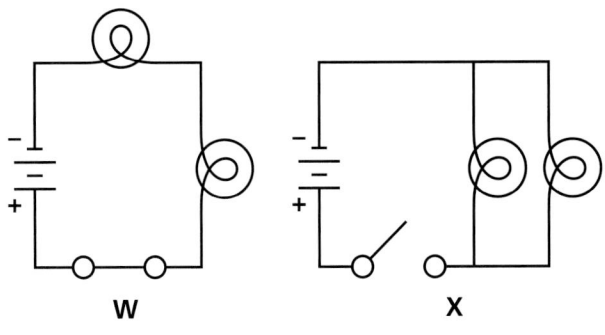

W   X

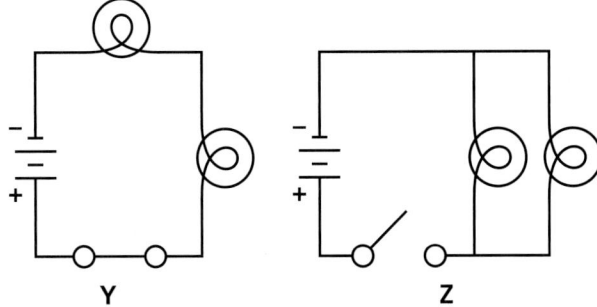

Y   Z

> **FCAT TiP**
>
> When answering multiple-choice questions based on several diagrams, compare and contrast the diagrams to see how the information they provide is similar and different.

Study the diagrams and answer the questions that follow.

MULTIPLE CHOICE

1. Which diagram shows a series circuit, with one voltage source and two light bulbs?
   - **A.** W
   - **B.** X
   - **C.** Y
   - **D.** Z

2. Which diagram shows a parallel circuit powered by a battery, with three light bulbs?
   - **F.** W
   - **G.** X
   - **H.** Y
   - **I.** Z

3. The light bulbs in these diagrams limit the flow of charge and give off heat and light. Under which category of circuit parts do light bulbs belong?
   - **A.** switches
   - **B.** conductors
   - **C.** resistors
   - **D.** voltage sources

4. In which diagram would the light bulbs be dark?
   - **F.** W
   - **G.** X
   - **H.** Y
   - **I.** Z

SHORT RESPONSE

5. Study circuit diagrams W and Y. Pretend that all the light bulbs and voltage sources are equal. Describe how the light from the bulbs in diagram Y would compare with the light from the bulbs in diagram W.

EXTENDED RESPONSE

Answer the two questions below in detail. Include some of the terms from the word box. Underline each term you use in your answer.

| flow of charge | electric current | binary code |
| open circuit | digital | signal |

6. What are two types of safety devices designed to control electric current and prevent dangerous accidents? How does each work?

7. Explain how an electronic circuit differs from an electric circuit. What role do electronic circuits play in computer operations?

TIMELINES in Science

THE STORY OF ELECTRONICS

Inventions such as the battery, the dynamo, and the motor created a revolution in the production and use of electrical energy. Think of how many tools and appliances that people depend on every day run on electric current. Try to imagine not using electricity in any form for an entire day.

The use of electricity as an energy source only begins the story of how electricity has changed our lives. Parts of the story are shown on this timeline. Research in electronics has given us not only electrical versions of machines that already existed but also entirely new technologies.

These technologies include computers. Electricity is used as a signal inside computers to code and transmit information. Electricity can even mimic some of the processes of logical reasoning and decision making, giving computers the power to solve problems.

600 B.C.

Thales Studies Static Electricity
Greek philosopher-scientist Thales of Miletus discovers that when he rubs amber with wool or fur, the amber attracts feathers and straw. The Greek word for amber, *elektron*, is the origin of the word *electricity*.

EVENTS

640 B.C.	620 B.C.	600 B.C.	A.D. 1740

APPLICATIONS AND TECHNOLOGY

APPLICATION

Leyden Jar

In 1745 German inventor Ewald Georg von Kleist invented a device that would store a static charge. The device, called a Leyden jar, was a glass container filled with water. A wire ran from the outside of the jar through the cork into the water. The Leyden jar was the first capacitor, an electronic component that stores and releases charges. Capacitors have been key to the development of computers.

1752
Franklin Invents Lightning Rod

To test his hypothesis that lightning is caused by static electric charges, U.S. inventor Ben Franklin flies a kite during a thunderstorm. A metal key hangs from the kite strings. Sparks jump from the key to Franklin's knuckle, showing that the key has a static charge. On the basis of this experiment, Franklin invents the lightning rod.

1800
Volta Invents Battery

Italian scientist Alessandro Volta creates the first battery by stacking round plates of metal separated by disks soaked in salt water. Volta's discovery refutes the competing belief that electricity must be created by living beings.

1776
Bassi Gives Physics a Boost

Italian scholar Laura Bassi, one of the first women to hold a chair at a major European university, is named professor of experimental physics. Bassi uses her position to establish one of the world's first electrical laboratories.

1760   1780   1800   1820   1840

TECHNOLOGY
The Difference Engine

Around 1822 British mathematician Charles Babbage developed the first prototype of a machine that could perform calculations mechanically. Babbage's "difference engine" used disks connected to rods with hand cranks to calculate mathematical tables. Babbage's invention came more than 100 years before the modern computer.

1879
Edison Improves Dynamo

To help bring electric lights to the streets of New York City, U.S. inventor Thomas Edison develops an improved dynamo, or generator. Edison's dynamo, known as a long-legged Mary Ann, operates at about twice the efficiency of previous models.

1904
Vacuum Tube Makes Debut

British inventor Ambrose Fleming modifies a light bulb to create an electronic vacuum tube. Fleming's tube, which he calls a valve, allows current to flow in one direction but not the other and can be used to detect weak radio signals.

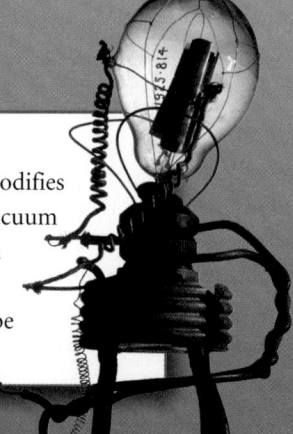

1947
Transistor Invented

A transistor—a tiny electronic switch made out of a solid material called a semiconductor—is introduced to regulate the flow of electricity. Transistors, which do not produce excess heat and never burn out, can replace the vacuum tube in electronic circuitry and can be used to make smaller, cheaper, and more powerful computers.

1860	1880	1900	1920	1940

APPLICATION

First Electronic Digital Computer

Electronic Numerical Integrator and Computer (ENIAC) was the first digital computer. It was completed and installed in 1944 at the Moore School of Electrical Engineering at the University of Pennsylvania. Weighing more than 30 tons, ENIAC contained 19,000 vacuum tubes, 70,000 resistors, and 6000 switches, and it used almost 200 kilowatts of electric power. ENIAC could perform 5000 additions per second.

1958

Chip Inventors Think Small

Jack Kilby, a U.S. electrical engineer, conceives the idea of making an entire circuit out of a single piece of germanium. The integrated circuit, or "computer chip," is born. This invention enables computers and other electronic devices to be made much smaller than before.

2001

Scientists Shrink Circuits to Atomic Level

Researchers succeed in building a logic circuit, a kind of transistor the size of a single molecule. The molecule, a tube of carbon atoms called a carbon nanotube, can be as small as 10 atoms across—500 times smaller than previous transistors. Computer chips, which currently contain over 40 million transistors, could hold hundreds of millions or even billions of nanotube transistors.

 RESOURCE CENTER
CLASSZONE.COM

Explore current research in electronics and computers.

1960   1980   2000

INTO THE FUTURE

Electronic computer components have become steadily smaller and more efficient over the years. However, the basic mechanism of a computer— a switch that can be either on or off depending on whether an electric charge is present—has remained the same. These switches represent the 1s and 0s, or the "bits," of binary code.

Quantum computing is based on an entirely new way of representing information. In quantum physics, individual subatomic particles can be described in terms of three states rather than just two. Quantum bits, or "qubits," can carry much more information than the binary bits of ordinary computers. Using qubits, quantum computers could be both smaller and faster than binary computers and perform operations not possible with current technology.

Quantum computing is possible in theory, but the development of hardware that can process qubits is just beginning. Scientists are currently looking for ways to put the theory into practice and to build computers that will make current models look as bulky and as slow as ENIAC.

ACTIVITIES

Reliving History

Make a Leyden jar capacitor. Line the inside of a jar with aluminum foil. Stop the jar with clay. Insert a copper wire through the plug so that one end touches the foil and the other sticks out of the jar about 2 centimeters.

To test for a voltage difference between the wire and the glass, touch one end of a multimeter to the exposed wire and the other end to the glass. Run a comb through your hair several times and touch it to the wire. Test the voltage difference again.

Writing About Science

Learn more about the current state of electronic circuit miniaturization. Write up the results of your research in the form of a magazine article.

TECHNOLOGY

Miniaturization

Miniaturization has led to an explosion of computer technology. As circuits have shrunk, allowing more components in less space, computers have become smaller and more powerful. They have also become easier to integrate with other technologies, such as telecommunications. When not being used for a phone call, this cell phone can be used to connect to the Internet, to access e-mail, and even to play computer games.

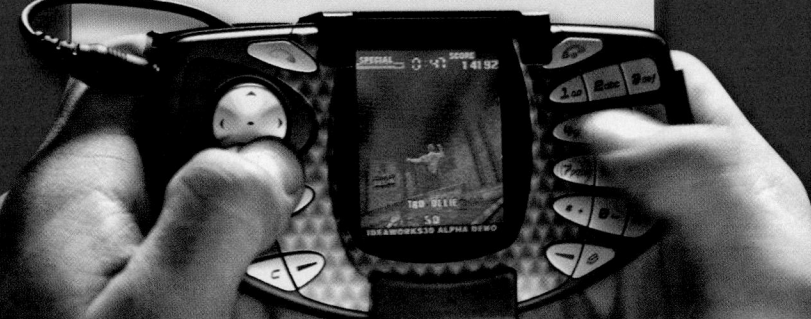

12 Magnetism

the **BIG** idea

Current can produce magnetism, and magnetism can produce current.

Key Concepts

SECTION
Magnetism is a force that acts at a distance.
Learn how magnets exert forces.

SECTION
Current can produce magnetism.
Learn about electromagnets and their uses.

SECTION
Magnetism can produce current.
Learn how magnetism can produce an electric current.

SECTION
Generators supply electrical energy.
Learn how generators are used in the production of electrical energy.

FCAT Practice

Prepare and practice for the FCAT
• Section Reviews, pp. 418, 426, 431, 438
• Chapter Review, pp. 440–442
• FCAT Practice, p. 443

CLASSZONE.COM
• Florida Review: Content Review and FCAT Practice

EXPLORE (the BIG idea)

Is It Magnetic?

Experiment with a magnet and several objects made of different materials.

Observe and Think
Which objects are attracted to the magnet? Why do you think the magnet attracts some objects and not others?

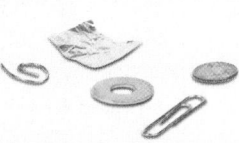

How Can You Make a Chain?

Hang a paper clip on the end of a magnet. Then hang a second paper clip by touching it to the end of the first paper clip. Add more paper clips to make a chain.

Observe and Think How many paper clips did you add? What held the chain together?

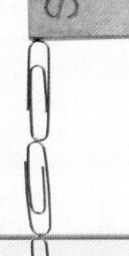

What force is acting on this compass needle?

Internet Activity: Electromagnets

Go to **ClassZone.com** to work with a virtual electromagnet. Explore how current and magnetism are related.

Observe and Think
What happens when you increase the voltage?

NSTA scilinks.org SCiLINKS

Electromagnetism **Code: MDL067**

Getting Ready to Learn

◀ CONCEPT REVIEW

- Energy can change from one form to another.
- A force is a push or a pull.

◀ VOCABULARY REVIEW

electric current p. 360

circuit p. 375

kinetic energy *See Glossary.*

FLORIDA REVIEW
CLASSZONE.COM

Content Review and FCAT Practice

▶ TAKING NOTES

MAIN IDEA WEB

Write each new blue heading in a box. Then write notes in boxes around the center box that give important terms and details about that blue heading.

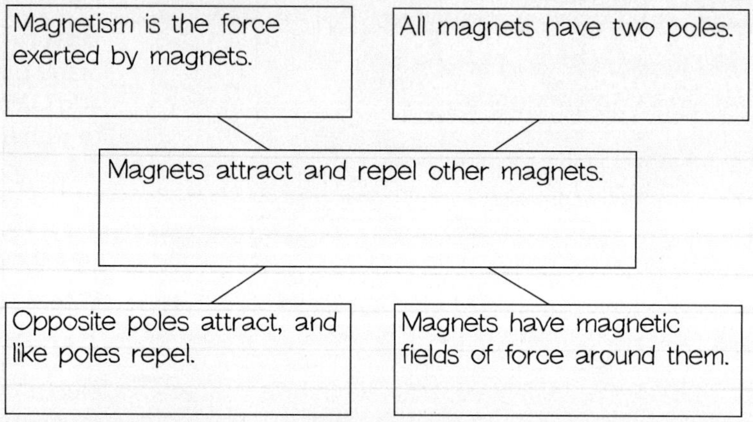

VOCABULARY STRATEGY

Place each vocabulary term at the center of a **description wheel** diagram. As you read about the term, write some words describing it on the spokes.

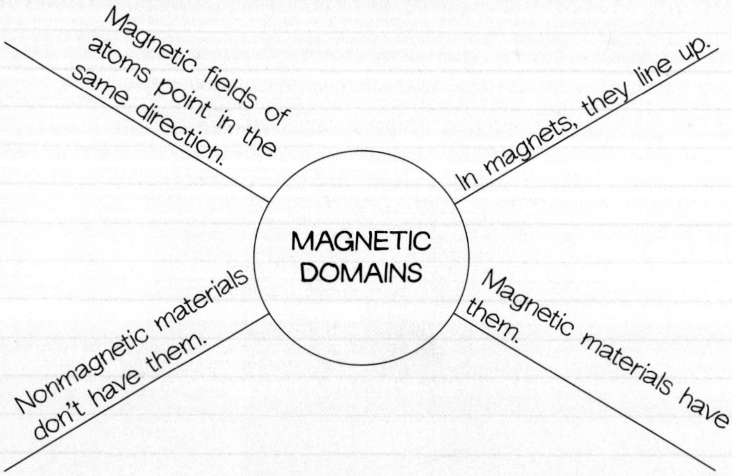

See the Note-Taking Handbook on pages R45–R51.

SCIENCE NOTEBOOK

Magnetism is the force exerted by magnets.

All magnets have two poles.

Magnets attract and repel other magnets.

Opposite poles attract, and like poles repel.

Magnets have magnetic fields of force around them.

Magnetic fields of atoms point in the same direction.

In magnets, they line up.

MAGNETIC DOMAINS

Nonmagnetic materials don't have them.

Magnetic materials have them.

KEY CONCEPT

Magnetism is a force that acts at a distance.

12.1

Sunshine State STANDARDS

SC.C.2.3.1: The student knows that many forces (e.g., gravitational, electrical, and magnetic) act at a distance (e.g., without contact).

◀ BEFORE, you learned

- A force is a push or pull
- Some forces act at a distance
- Atoms contain charged particles

▶ NOW, you will learn

- How magnets attract and repel other magnets
- What makes some materials magnetic
- Why a magnetic field surrounds Earth

FCAT VOCABULARY

magnetic field p. 413

VOCABULARY

magnet p. 411
magnetism p. 412
magnetic pole p. 412
magnetic domain p. 414

EXPLORE Magnetism

How do magnets behave?

PROCEDURE

1. Clamp the clothespin on the dowel so that it makes a stand for the magnets, as shown.

2. Place the three magnets on the dowel. If there is a space between pairs of magnets, measure and record the distance between them.

3. Remove the top magnet, turn it over, and replace it on the dowel. Record your observations. Experiment with different arrangements of the magnets and record your observations.

WHAT DO YOU THINK?

- How did the arrangement of the magnets affect their behavior?
- What evidence indicates that magnets exert a force?

MATERIALS

- clothespin
- wooden dowel
- 3 disk magnets
- ruler

Magnets attract and repel other magnets.

Suppose you get home from school and open the refrigerator to get some milk. As you close the door, it swings freely until it suddenly seems to close by itself. There is a magnet inside the refrigerator door that pulls it shut. A **magnet** is an object that attracts certain other materials, particularly iron and steel.

There may be quite a few magnets in your kitchen. Some are obvious, like the seal of the refrigerator and the magnets that hold notes to its door. Other magnets run the motor in a blender, provide energy in a microwave oven, operate the speakers in a radio on the counter, and make a doorbell ring.

VOCABULARY
Make a description wheel for the term *magnet*.

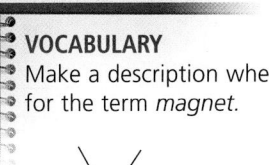

Magnetism

The force exerted by a magnet is called **magnetism.** The push or pull of magnetism can act at a distance, which means that the magnet does not have to touch an object to exert a force on it. When you close the refrigerator, you feel the pull before the magnet actually touches the metal frame. There are other forces that act at a distance, including gravity and static electricity. Later you will read how the force of magnetism is related to electricity. In fact, magnetism is the result of a moving electric charge.

The train is pushed up by magnets beneath it and pulled forward by magnets ahead of it.

You may be familiar with magnets attracting, or pulling, metal objects toward them. Magnets can also repel, or push away, objects. The train in the photograph at the left is called a maglev train. The word *maglev* is short for *mag*netic *lev*itation, or lifting up. As you can see in the diagram, the train does not touch the track. Magnetism pushes the entire train up and pulls it forward. Maglev trains can move as fast as 480 kilometers per hour (300 mi/h).

CHECK YOUR READING How can a train operate without touching the track?

Magnetic Poles

RESOURCE CENTER
CLASSZONE.COM

Find out more about magnetism.

FLORIDA
Content Preview

Like EM waves, magnetism is a force that acts at a distance. You will learn more about forces in Grade 8.

The force of magnetism is not evenly distributed throughout a magnet. **Magnetic poles** are the parts of a magnet where the magnetism is the strongest. Every magnet has two magnetic poles. If a bar magnet is suspended so that it can swing freely, one pole of the magnet always points toward the north. That end of the magnet is known as the north-seeking pole, or north pole. The other end of the magnet is called the south pole. Many magnets are marked with an *N* and an *S* to indicate the poles.

As with electric charges, opposite poles of a magnet attract and like poles—or poles that are the same—repel, or push each other away. Every magnet has both a north pole and a south pole. A horseshoe magnet is like a bar magnet that has been bent into the shape of a *U*. It has a pole at each of its ends. If you break a bar magnet between the two poles, the result is two smaller magnets, each of which has a north pole and a south pole. No matter how many times you break a magnet, the result is smaller magnets.

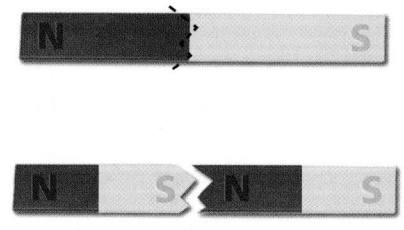

Magnetic Fields

You have read that magnetism is a force that can act at a distance. However magnets cannot exert a force on an object that is too far away. A **magnetic field** is the region around a magnet in which the magnet exerts force. If a piece of iron is within the magnetic field of a magnet, it will be pulled toward the magnet. Many small pieces of iron, called iron filings, are used to show the magnetic field around a magnet. The iron filings form a pattern of lines called magnetic field lines.

READING TiP

Thin red lines in the illustrations below indicate the magnetic field.

The Magnetic Field Around a Magnet

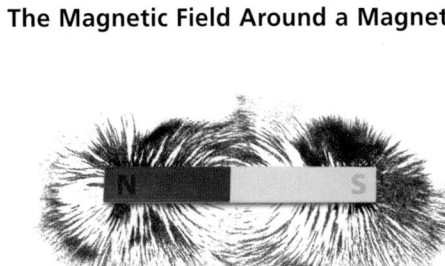
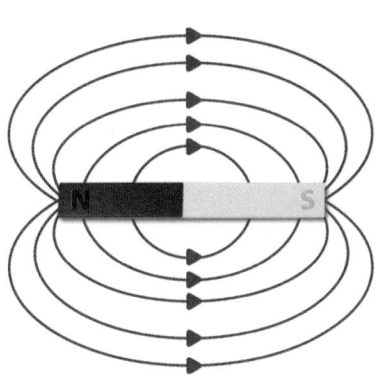
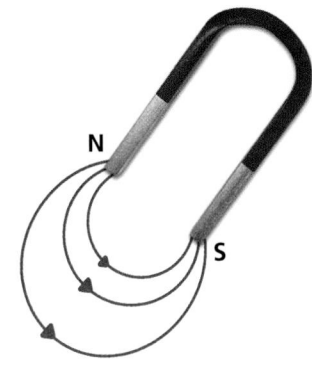

The arrangement of the magnetic field lines depends on the shape of the magnet, but the lines always extend from one pole to the other pole. The magnetic field lines are always shown as starting from the north pole and ending at the south pole. In the illustrations above, you can see that the lines are closest together near the magnets' poles. That is where the force is strongest. The force is weaker farther away from the magnet.

 CHECK YOUR READING   Where is the magnetic field of a magnet the strongest?

What happens to the magnetic fields of two magnets when the magnets are brought together? As you can see below, each magnet has an effect on the field of the other magnet. If the magnets are held so that the north pole of one magnet is close to the south pole of the other, the magnetic field lines extend from one magnet to the other. The magnets pull together. On the other hand, if both north poles or both south poles of two magnets are brought near one another, the magnets repel. It is very difficult to push like poles of strong magnets together because magnetic repulsion pushes them apart.

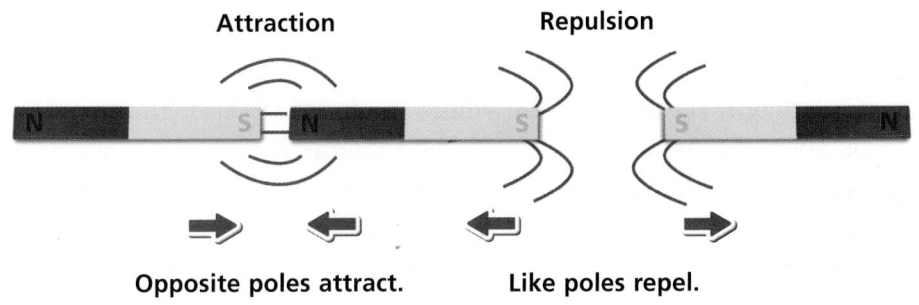

Opposite poles attract.   Like poles repel.

Some materials are magnetic.

Some magnets occur naturally. Lodestone is a type of mineral that is a natural magnet and formed the earliest magnets that people used. The term *magnet* comes from the name *Magnesia,* a region of Greece where lodestone was discovered. Magnets can also be made from materials that contain certain metallic elements, such as iron.

If you have ever tried picking up different types of objects with a magnet, you have seen that some materials are affected by the magnet and other materials are not. Iron, nickel, cobalt, and a few other metals have properties that make them magnetic. Other materials, such as wood, cannot be made into magnets and are not affected by magnets. Whether a material is magnetic or not depends on its atoms—the particles that make up all matter.

You read in Chapter 10 that the protons and electrons of an atom have electric fields. Every atom also has a weak magnetic field, produced by the electron's motion around a nucleus. In addition, each electron spins around its axis, an imaginary line through its center. The spinning motion of the electrons in magnetic materials increases the strength of the magnetic field around each atom. The magnetic effect of one electron is usually cancelled by another electron that spins in the opposite direction.

Inside Magnetic Materials

The illustration on page 415 shows how magnets and the materials they affect differ from other materials.

READING TiP

The red arrows in the illustration on page 415 are tiny magnetic fields.

❶ In a material that is not magnetic, such as wood, the magnetic fields of the atoms are weak and point in different directions. The magnetic fields cancel each other out. As a result, the overall material is not magnetic and could not be made into a magnet.

❷ In a material that is magnetic, such as iron, the magnetic fields of a group of atoms align, or point in the same direction. A **magnetic domain** is a group of atoms whose magnetic fields are aligned. The domains of a magnetic material are not themselves aligned, so their fields cancel one another out. Magnetic materials are pulled by magnets and can be made into magnets.

❸ A magnet is a material in which the magnetic domains are all aligned. The material is said to be magnetized.

CHECK YOUR READING How do magnets differ from materials that are not magnetic?

How Magnets Differ from Other Materials

Magnets, and the materials they attract, contain small regions called magnetic domains. In a magnet, the domains are aligned.

Nonmagnetic Materials

Magnet

Magnetic Materials

① Nonmagnetic Materials

Some materials, like wood, are not magnetic. The tiny magnetic fields of their spinning electrons point in different directions and cancel each other out.

② Magnetic Materials

magnetic domain

Other materials, like iron, are magnetic. Magnetic materials have magnetic domains, but the fields of the domains point in different directions.

③ Magnets

When a material is magnetized, the magnetic fields of all the domains point in the same direction.

READING VISUALS Do the paper clips in this photograph contain magnetic domains? Why or why not?

Temporary and Permanent Magnets

If you bring a magnet near a paper clip that contains iron, the paper clip is pulled toward the magnet. As the magnet nears the paper clip, the domains within the paper clip are attracted to the magnet's nearest pole. As a result, the domains within the paper clip become aligned. The paper clip develops its own magnetic field.

You can make a chain of paper clips that connect to one another through these magnetic fields. However, if you remove the magnet, the chain falls apart. The paper clips are temporary magnets, and their domains return to a random arrangement when the stronger magnetic field is removed.

Placing magnetic materials in very strong magnetic fields makes permanent magnets, such as the ones you use in the experiments in this chapter. You can make a permanent magnet by repeatedly stroking a piece of magnetic material in the same direction with a strong magnet. This action aligns the domains. However, if you drop a permanent magnet, or expose it to high temperatures, some of the domains can be shaken out of alignment, weakening its magnetism.

 How can you make a permanent magnet?

Earth is a magnet.

People discovered long ago that when a piece of lodestone was allowed to turn freely, one end always pointed toward the north. Hundreds of years ago, sailors used lodestone in the first compasses for navigation. A compass works because Earth itself is a large magnet. A compass is simply a magnet that is suspended so that it can turn freely. The magnetic field of the compass needle aligns itself with the much larger magnetic field of Earth.

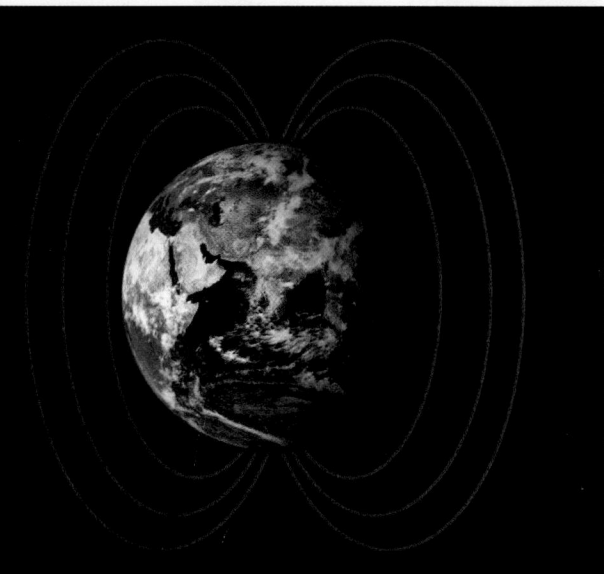

Earth's Magnetic Field

The magnetic field around Earth acts as if there were a large bar magnet that runs through Earth's axis. Earth's axis is the imaginary line through the center of Earth around which it rotates. The source of the magnetic field that surrounds Earth is the motion of its core, which is composed mostly of iron and nickel. Charged particles flow within the core. Scientists have proposed several explanations of how that motion produces the magnetic field, but the process is not yet completely understood.

 What is the source of Earth's magnetic field?

INVESTIGATE Earth's Magnetic Field

What moves a compass needle?

PROCEDURE

1. Gently place the aluminum foil on the water so that it floats.

2. Rub one pole of the magnet along the needle, from one end of the needle to the other. Lift up the magnet and repeat. Do this about 25 times, rubbing in the same direction each time. Place the magnet far away from your set-up.

3. Gently place the needle on the floating foil to act as a compass.

4. Turn the foil so that the needle points in a different direction. Observe what happens when you release the foil.

WHAT DO YOU THINK?

- What direction did the needle move when you placed it in the bowl?
- What moved the compass's needle?

CHALLENGE How could you use your compass to answer a question of your own about magnetism?

MATERIALS
- small square of aluminum foil
- bowl of water
- strong magnet
- sewing needle

TIME
15 minutes

Earth's magnetic field affects all the magnetic materials around you. Even the cans of food in your cupboard are slightly magnetized by this field. Hold a compass close to the bottom of a can and observe what happens. The magnetic domains in the metal can have aligned and produced a weak magnetic field. If you twist the can and check it again several days later, you can observe the effect of the domains changing their alignment.

Sailors learned many centuries ago that the compass does not point exactly toward the North Pole of Earth's axis. Rather, the compass magnet is currently attracted to an area 966 kilometers (600 mi) from the end of the axis of rotation. This area is known as the magnetic north pole. Interestingly, the magnetic poles of Earth can reverse, so that the magnetic north pole becomes the magnetic south pole. This has happened at least 400 times over the last 330 million years. The most recent reversal was about 780,000 years ago.

The evidence that the magnetic north and south poles reverse is found in rocks in which the minerals contain iron. The iron in the minerals lines up with Earth's magnetic field as the rock forms. Once the rock is formed, the domains remain in place. The evidence for the reversing magnetic field is shown in layers of rocks on the ocean floor, where the domains are arranged in opposite directions.

FLORIDA
Content Preview

Earth's magnetic field changes are recorded on the ocean floor, as you will read about in grade 8.

Magnetism and the Atmosphere

A constant stream of charged particles is released by reactions inside the Sun. These particles could be damaging to living cells if they reached the surface of Earth. One important effect of Earth's magnetic field is that it turns aside, or deflects, the flow of the charged particles.

Observers view a beautiful display of Northern Lights in Alaska.

Many of the particles are deflected toward the magnetic poles, where Earth's magnetic field lines are closest together. As the particles approach Earth, they react with oxygen and nitrogen in Earth's atmosphere. These interactions can be seen at night as vast, moving sheets of color—red, blue, green or violet—that can fill the whole sky. These displays are known as the Northern Lights or the Southern Lights.

CHECK YOUR READING Why do the Northern Lights and the Southern Lights occur near Earth's magnetic poles?

12.1 Review

KEY CONCEPTS

1. What force causes magnets to attract or repel one another?

2. Why are some materials magnetic and not others?

3. Describe three similarities between Earth and a bar magnet.

CRITICAL THINKING

4. **Apply** A needle is picked up by a magnet. What can you say about the needle's atoms?

5. **Infer** The Northern Lights can form into lines in the sky. What do you think causes this effect?

CHALLENGE

6. **Infer** Hundreds of years ago sailors observed that as they traveled farther north, their compass needle tended to point toward the ground as well as toward the north. What can you conclude about the magnet inside Earth from this observation?

Can Magnets Heal People?

Many people believe that a magnetic field can relieve pain and cure injuries or illnesses. They point out that human blood cells contain iron and that magnets attract iron.

▶ Claims

Here are some claims from advertisements and published scientific experiments.

a. In an advertisement, a person reported back pain that went away overnight when a magnetic pad was taped to his back.

b. In an advertisement, a person used magnets to treat a painful bruise. The pain reportedly stopped soon after the magnet was applied.

c. In a research project, people who had recovered from polio, but still had severe pain, rated the amount of pain they experienced. People who used magnets reported slightly more pain relief than those who used fake magnets that looked like the real magnets.

d. A research project studied people with severe muscle pain. Patients who slept on magnetic pads for six months reported slightly less pain than those who slept on nonmagnetic pads or no pads.

e. A research project studied people with pain in their heels, placing magnets in their shoes. About sixty percent of people with real magnets reported improvements. About sixty percent of people with fake magnets also reported improvements.

▶ Controls

Scientists use control groups to determine whether a change was a result of the experimental variable or some other cause. A control group is the same as an experimental group in every way except for the variable that is tested. For each of the above cases, was a control used? If not, can you think of some other explanation for the result?

▶ Evaluating Conclusions

On Your Own Evaluate each claim or report separately. Based on all the evidence, can you conclude that magnets are useful for relieving pain? What further evidence would help you decide?

As a Group Find advertisements for companies that sell magnets for medical use. Do they provide information about how their tests were conducted and how you can contact the doctors or scientists involved?

CHALLENGE Design an experiment, with controls, that would show whether or not magnets are useful for relieving pain.

Some people believe that pads containing magnets, such as these, can relieve pain.

KEY CONCEPT

Current can produce magnetism.

Sunshine State STANDARDS

SC.C.2.3.1: The student knows that many forces (e.g., gravitational, electrical, and magnetic) act at a distance (e.g., without contact).

SC.H.3.3.4: The student knows that technological design should require taking into account constraints such as natural laws, the properties of the materials used, and economic, political, social, ethical, and aesthetic values.

VOCABULARY

electromagnetism p. 421
electromagnet p. 422

◁ BEFORE, you learned

- Electric current is the flow of charge
- Magnetism is a force exerted by magnets
- Magnets attract or repel other magnets

▷ NOW, you will learn

- How an electric current can produce a magnetic field
- How electromagnets are used
- How motors use electromagnets

EXPLORE Magnetism from Electric Current

What is the source of magnetism?

PROCEDURE

1. Tape one end of the wire to the battery.

2. Place the compass on the table. Place the wire so that it is lying beside the compass, parallel to the needle of the compass. Record your observations.

3. Briefly touch the free end of the wire to the other end of the battery. Record your observations.

4. Turn the battery around and tape the other end to the wire. Repeat steps 2 and 3.

WHAT DO YOU THINK?

- What did you observe?
- What is the relationship between the direction of the battery and the direction of the compass needle?

MATERIALS

- electrical tape
- copper wire
- AA cell (battery)
- compass

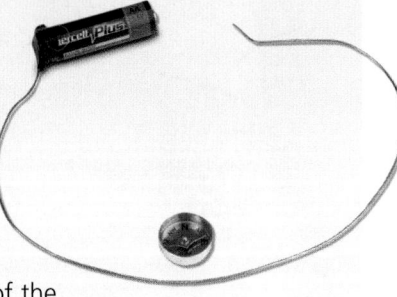

An electric current produces a magnetic field.

REMINDER

Current is the flow of electrons through a conductor.

Like many discoveries, the discovery that electric current is related to magnetism was unexpected. In the 1800s, a Danish physicist named Hans Christian Oersted (UR-stehd) was teaching a physics class. Oersted used a battery and wire to demonstrate some properties of electricity. He noticed that as an electric charge passed through the wire, the needle of a nearby compass moved.

When he turned the current off, the needle returned to its original direction. After more experiments, Oersted confirmed that there is a relationship between magnetism and electricity. He discovered that an electric current produces a magnetic field.

Electromagnetism

The relationship between electric current and magnetism plays an important role in many modern technologies. **Electromagnetism** is magnetism that results from an electric current. When a charged particle such as an electron moves, it produces a magnetic field. Because an electric current generally consists of moving electrons, a current in a wire produces a magnetic field. In fact, the wire acts as a magnet. Increasing the amount of current in the wire increases the strength of the magnetic field.

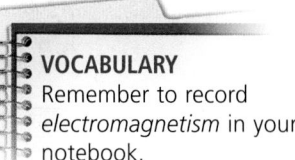
VOCABULARY
Remember to record *electromagnetism* in your notebook.

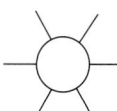

You have seen how magnetic field lines can be drawn around a magnet. The magnetic field lines around a wire are usually illustrated as a series of circles. The magnetic field of a wire actually forms the shape of a tube around the wire. The

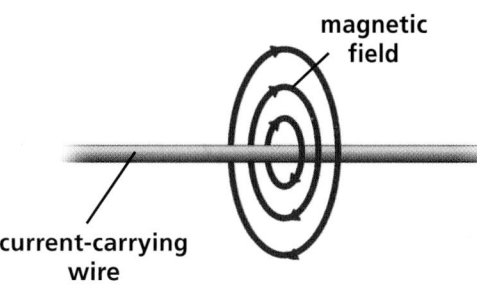

magnetic field

current-carrying wire

direction of the current determines the direction of the magnetic field. If the direction of the electric current is reversed, the magnetic field still exists in circles around the wire, but is reversed.

If the wire is shaped into a loop, the magnetism becomes concentrated inside the loop. The field is much stronger in the middle of the loop than it is around a straight wire. If you wind the wire into a coil, the magnetic force becomes stronger with each additional turn of wire as the magnetic field becomes more concentrated.

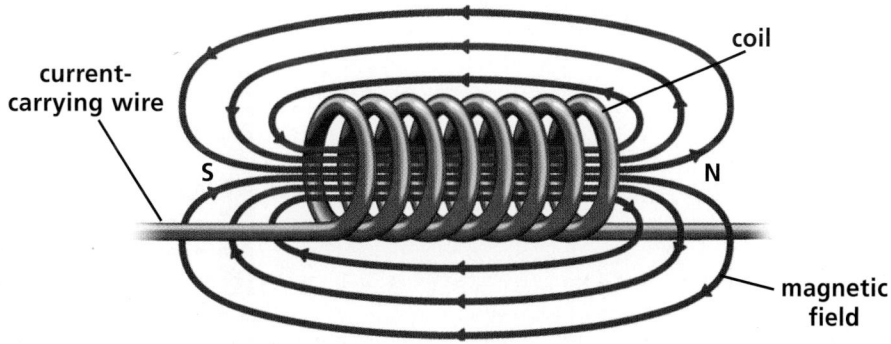

current-carrying wire

coil

S   N

magnetic field

A coil of wire with charge flowing through it has a magnetic field that is similar to the magnetic field of a bar magnet. Inside the coil, the field flows in one direction, forming a north pole at one end. The flow outside the coil returns to the south pole. The direction of the electric current in the wire determines which end of the coil becomes the north pole.

 **CHECK YOUR READING**   How is a coil of wire that carries a current similar to a bar magnet?

Making an Electromagnet

Recall that a piece of iron in a strong magnetic field becomes a magnet itself. An **electromagnet** is a magnet made by placing a piece of iron or steel inside a coil of wire. As long as the coil carries a current, the metal acts as a magnet and increases the magnetic field of the coil. But when the current is turned off, the magnetic domains in the metal become random again and the magnetic field disappears.

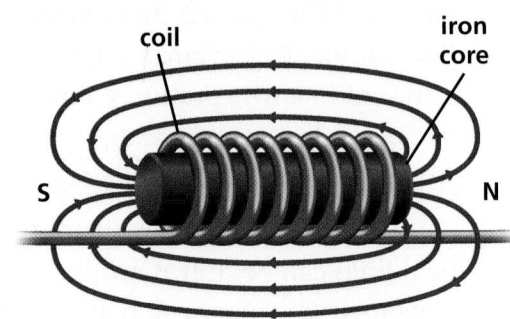

By increasing the number of loops in the coil, you can increase the strength of the electromagnet. Electromagnets exert a much more powerful magnetic field than a coil of wire without a metal core. They can also be much stronger than the strongest permanent magnets made of metal alone. You can increase the field strength of an electromagnet by adding more coils or a stronger current. Some of the most powerful magnets in the world are huge electromagnets that are used in scientific instruments.

CHECK YOUR READING How can you increase the strength of an electromagnet?

INVESTIGATE Electromagnets

How can you make an electromagnet?

PROCEDURE

(1) Starting about 25 cm from one end of the wire, wrap the wire in tight coils around the nail. The coils should cover the nail from the head almost to the point.

(2) Tape the two batteries together as shown. Tape one end of the wire to a free battery terminal.

(3) Touch the point of the nail to a paper clip and record your observations.

(4) Connect the other end of the wire to the other battery terminal. Again touch the point of the nail to a paper clip. Disconnect the wire from the battery. Record your observations.

WHAT DO YOU THINK?
- What did you observe?
- Did you make an electromagnet? How do you know?

CHALLENGE Do you think the result would be different if you used an aluminum nail instead of an iron nail? Why?

SKILL FOCUS
Observing

MATERIALS
- insulated wire
- large iron nail
- 2 D cells
- electrical tape
- paper clip

TIME
20 minutes

Uses of Electromagnets

Because electromagnets can be turned on and off, they have more uses than permanent magnets. The photograph below shows a powerful electromagnet on a crane. While the electric charge flows through the coils of the magnet, it lifts hundreds of cans at a recycling plant. When the crane operator turns off the current, the magnetic field disappears and the cans drop from the crane.

A permanent magnet would not be nearly as useful for this purpose. Although you could use a large permanent magnet to lift the cans, it would be hard to remove them from the magnet.

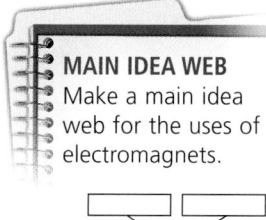
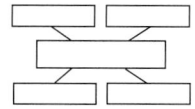

This powerful electromagnet can be turned on and off to collect and move cans at a recycling plant.

wire supplying electric current

electromagnet

You use an electromagnet every time you store information on a computer. The computer hard drive contains disks that have billions of tiny magnetic domains in them. When you save a file, a tiny electromagnet in the computer is activated. The magnetic field of the electromagnet changes the orientation of the small magnetic domains. The small magnets store your file in a form that can be read later by the computer. A similar system is used to store information on magnetic tape of an audiocassette or videocassette. Sound and pictures are stored on the tape by the arrangement of magnets embedded in the plastic film.

Magnetic information is often stored on credit cards and cash cards. A black strip on the back of the card contains information about the account number and passwords. The cards can be damaged if they are frequently exposed to magnetic fields. For example, cards should not be stored with their strips facing each other, or near a magnetic clasp on a purse or wallet. These magnetic fields can change the arrangement of the tiny magnetic domains on the card and erase the stored information.

Motors use electromagnets.

Because magnetism is a force, magnets can be used to move things. Electric motors convert the energy of an electric current into motion by taking advantage of the interaction between current and magnetism.

There are hundreds of devices that contain electric motors. Examples include power tools, electrical kitchen appliances, and the small fans in a computer. Almost anything with moving parts that uses current has an electric motor.

Motors

VISUALIZATION
CLASSZONE.COM

See a motor in motion.

Page 425 shows how a simple motor works. The photograph at the top of the page shows a motor that turns the blades of a fan. The illustration in the middle of the page shows the main parts of a simple motor. Although they may look different from each other, all motors have similar parts and work in a similar way. The main parts of an electrical motor include a voltage source, a shaft, an electromagnet, and at least one additional magnet. The shaft of the motor turns other parts of the device.

Recall that an electromagnet consists of a coil of wire with current flowing through it. Find the electromagnet in the illustration on page 425. The electromagnet is placed between the poles of another magnet.

When current from the voltage source flows through the coil, a magnetic field is produced around the electromagnet. The poles of the magnet interact with the poles of the electromagnet, causing the motor to turn.

❶ The poles of the magnet push on the like poles of the electromagnet, causing the electromagnet to turn.

❷ As the motor turns, the opposite poles pull on each other.

FLORIDA
Content Review

Notice how simple machines, which you read about in grade 6, are combined to create complicated machines.

❸ When the poles of the electromagnet line up with the opposite poles of the magnet, a part of the motor called the commutator reverses the polarity of the electromagnet. Now, the poles push on each other again and the motor continues to turn.

The illustration of the motor on page 425 is simplified so that you can see all of the parts. If you saw the inside of an actual motor, it might look like the illustration on the left. Notice that the wire is coiled many times. The electromagnet in a strong motor may coil hundreds of times. The more coils, the stronger the motor.

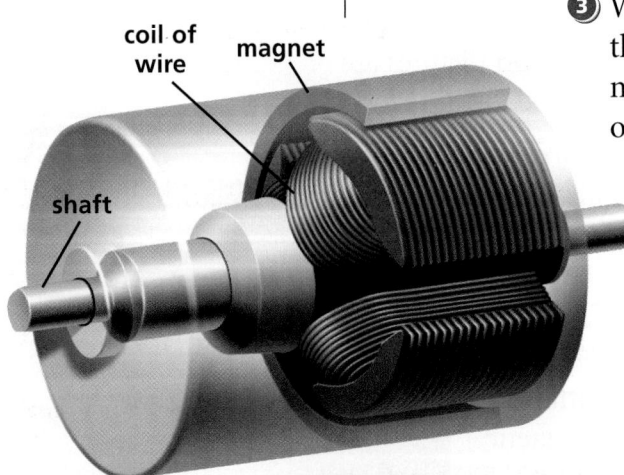

coil of wire   magnet

shaft

CHECK YOUR READING   What causes the electromagnet in a motor to turn?

How a Motor Works

Although motors may look different from each other, they all have similar parts and work in a similar way.

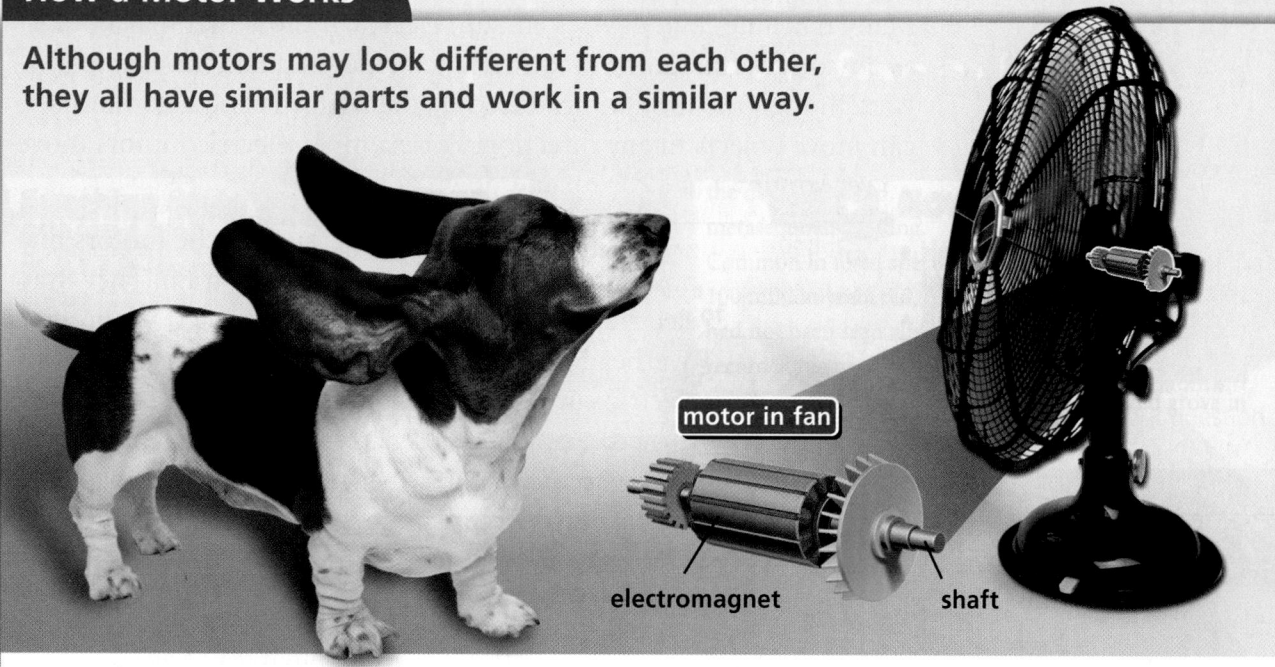

motor in fan

electromagnet   shaft

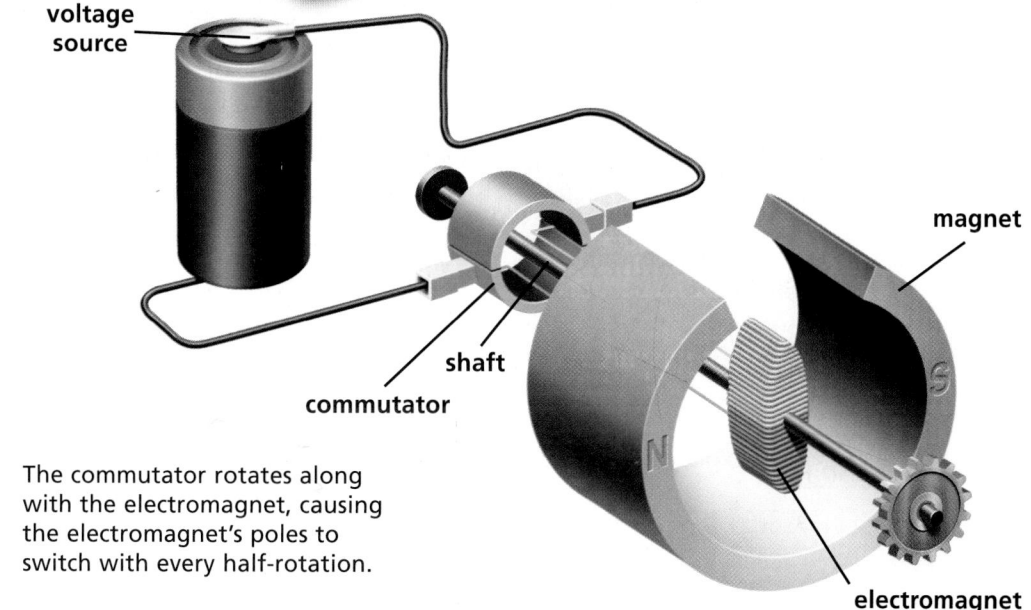

voltage source

magnet

shaft

commutator

electromagnet

The commutator rotates along with the electromagnet, causing the electromagnet's poles to switch with every half-rotation.

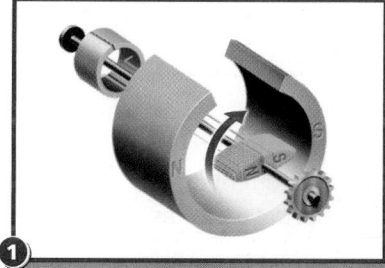

1 Like poles of the magnets push on each other.

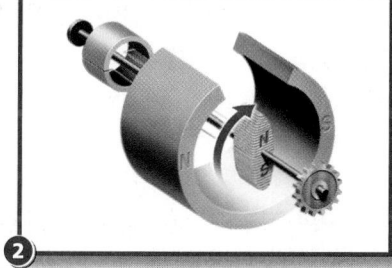

2 As the motor turns, opposite poles attract.

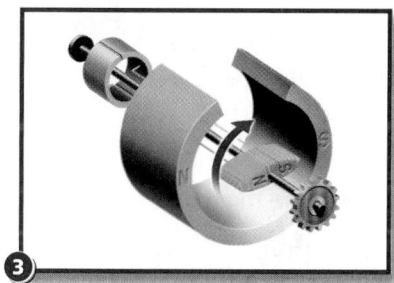

3 The electromagnet's poles are switched, and like poles again repel.

 **READING VISUALS**   Would a motor work without an electromagnet? Why or why not?

Uses of Motors

Many machines and devices contain electric motors that may not be as obvious as the motor that turns the blades of a fan, for example. Even though the motion produced by the motor is circular, motors can move objects in any direction. For example, electric motors move power windows in a car up and down.

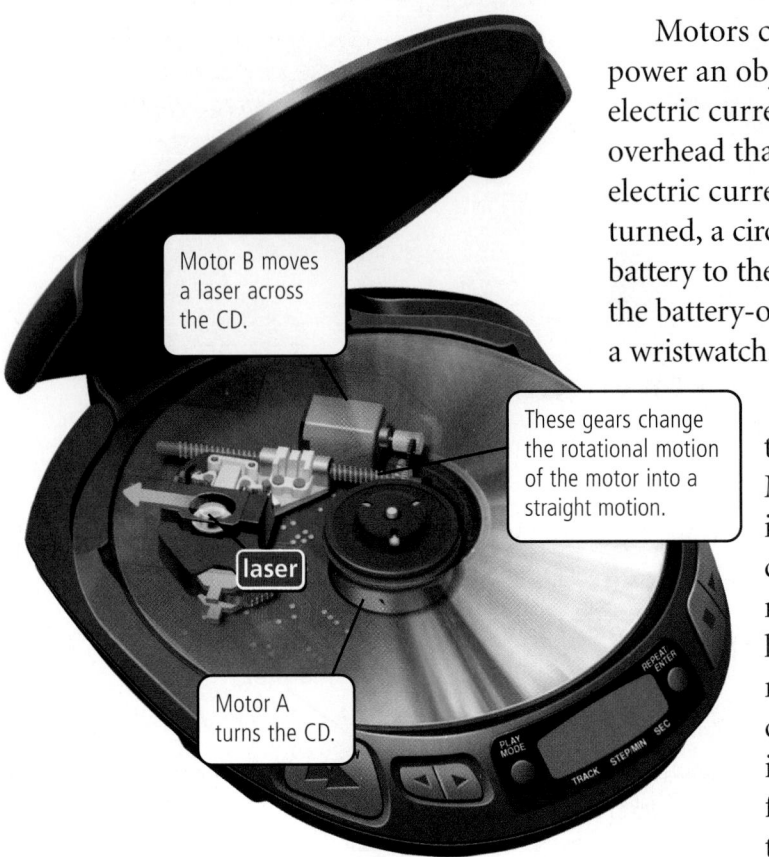

Motor B moves a laser across the CD.

These gears change the rotational motion of the motor into a straight motion.

laser

Motor A turns the CD.

Motors can be very large, such as the motors that power an object as large as a subway train. They draw electric current from a third rail on the track or wires overhead that carry electric current. A car uses an electric current to start the engine. When the key is turned, a circuit is closed, producing a current from the battery to the motor. Other motors are very small, like the battery-operated motors that move the hands of a wristwatch.

The illustration on the left shows the two small motors in a portable CD player. Motor A causes the CD to spin. Motor B is connected to a set of gears. The gears convert the rotational motion of the motor into a straight-line motion, or linear motion. As the CD spins, a laser moves straight across the CD from the center outward. The laser reads the information on the CD. The motion from Motor B moves the laser across the CD.

CHECK YOUR READING Explain the function served by each motor in a CD player.

12.2 Review

KEY CONCEPTS

1. Explain how electric current and magnetism are related.

2. Describe three uses of electromagnets.

3. Explain how electrical energy is converted to motion in a motor.

CRITICAL THINKING

4. **Contrast** How does an electromagnet differ from a permanent magnet?

5. **Apply** Provide examples of two things in your home that use electric motors, and explain why they are easier to use because of the motors.

⬤ CHALLENGE

6. **Infer** Why is it necessary to change the direction of the current in the coil of an electric motor as it turns?

KEY CONCEPT

12.3 Magnetism can produce current.

Sunshine State STANDARDS

SC.B.1.3.1: The student identifies forms of energy and explains that they can be measured and compared.

SC.H.3.3.4: The student knows that technological design should require taking into account constraints such as natural laws, the properties of the materials used, and economic, political, social, ethical, and aesthetic values.

BEFORE, you learned

- Magnetism is a force exerted by magnets
- Electric current can produce a magnetic field
- Electromagnets can make objects move

NOW, you will learn

- How a magnetic field can produce an electric current
- How a generator converts energy
- How direct current and alternating current differ

VOCABULARY

generator p. 428
direct current p. 429
alternating current p. 429
transformer p. 431

> ### EXPLORE Energy Conversion
>
> #### How can a motor produce current?
>
> **PROCEDURE**
>
> 1. Touch the wires on the motor to the battery terminals to see how the motor operates.
> 2. Connect the wires to the light bulb.
> 3. Roll the shaft, or the movable part of the motor, between your fingers. Observe the light bulb.
> 4. Now spin the shaft rapidly. Record your observations.
>
> **MATERIALS**
> - small motor
> - AA cell (battery)
> - light bulb in holder
>
>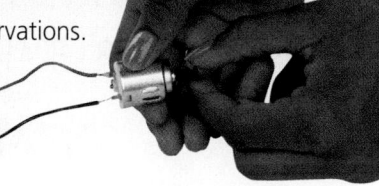
>
> **WHAT DO YOU THINK?**
> - How did you produce current?
> - What effect did your motion have on the amount of light produced?

Magnets are used to generate an electric current.

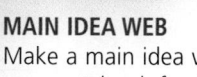
MAIN IDEA WEB
Make a main idea web in your notebook for this heading.

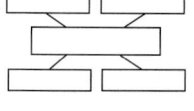

In the 1830s, about ten years after Oersted discovered that an electric current produces magnetism, physicists observed the reverse effect—a moving magnetic field induces an electric current. When a magnet moves inside a coiled wire that is in a circuit, an electric current is generated in the wire.

It is often easier to generate an electric current by moving a wire inside a magnetic field. Whether it is the magnet or the wire that moves, the effect is the same. Current is generated as long as the wire crosses the magnetic field lines.

 **CHECK YOUR READING** What must happen for a magnetic field to produce an electric current?

Generating an Electric Current

A **generator** is a device that converts the energy of motion, or kinetic energy, into electrical energy. A generator is similar to a motor in reverse. If you manually turn the shaft of a motor that contains a magnet, you can produce electric current.

The illustration below shows a portable generator that provides electrical energy to charge a cell phone in an emergency. The generator produces current as you turn the handle. Because it does not need to be plugged in, the generator can be used wherever and whenever it is needed to recharge a phone. The energy is supplied by the person turning the handle.

1 As the handle is turned, it rotates a series of gears. The gears turn the shaft of the generator.

2 The rotation of the shaft causes coils of wire to rotate within a magnetic field.

3 As the coils of the wire cross the magnetic field line, electric current is generated. The current recharges the battery of the cell phone.

CHECK YOUR READING What is the source of energy for a cell phone generator?

How a Cell Phone Generator Works

An emergency cell phone charger uses a generator to produce electric current.

1 Turning the handle provides kinetic energy to the generator, making the gears rotate.

2 The turning motion rotates coils of wire inside a magnet. This rotation produces electric current.

3 Electric current recharges the phone's battery.

gears

copper wire

generator

shaft

magnet

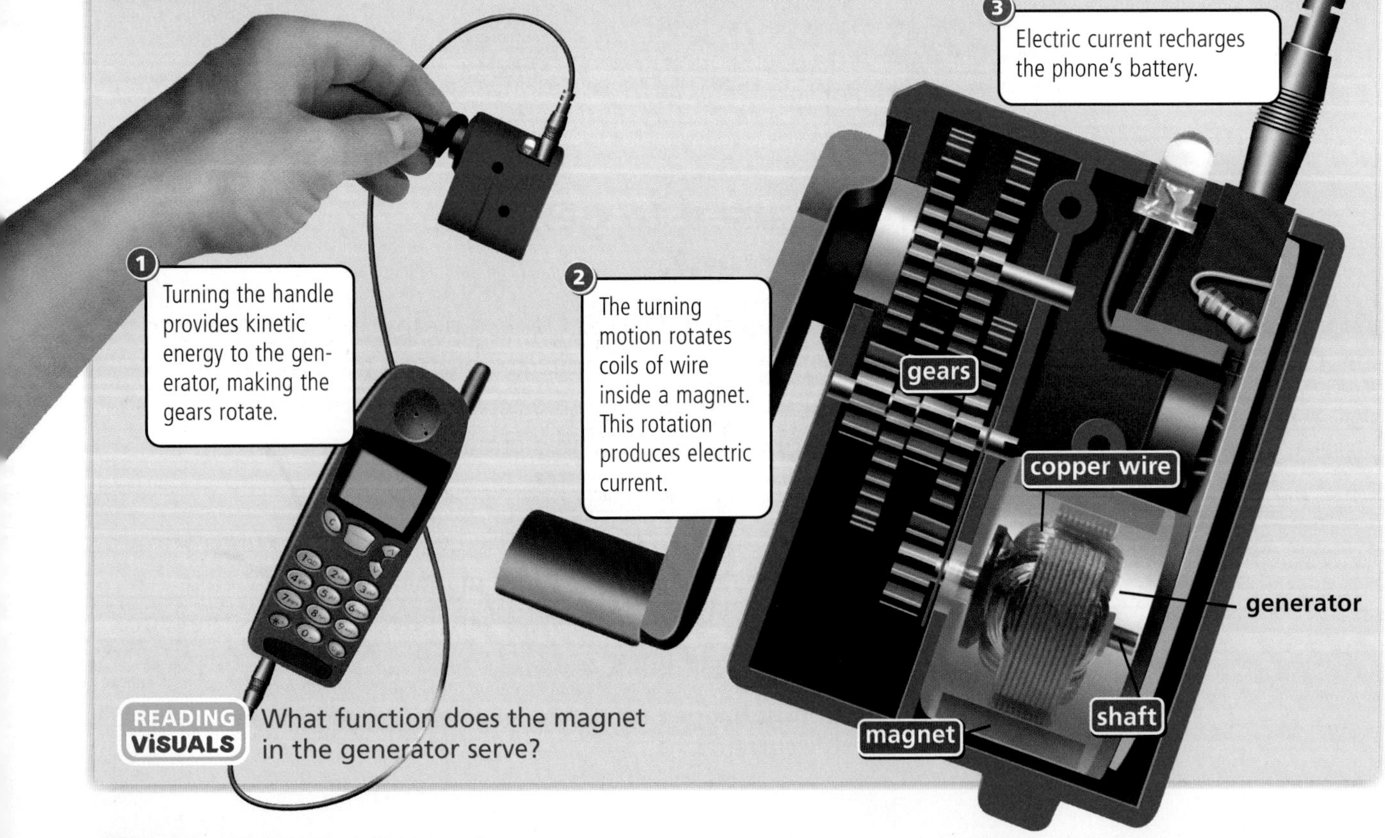

READING VISUALS What function does the magnet in the generator serve?

Direct and Alternating Currents

Think about how current flows in all of the circuits that you have studied so far. Electrons flow from one end of a battery or generator, through the circuit, and eventually back to the battery or generator. Electrons that flow in one direction produce one of two types of current.

- A **direct current** (DC) is electric charge that flows in one direction only. Direct current is produced by batteries and by DC generators such as the cell phone generator.

- An **alternating current** (AC) is a flow of electric charge that reverses direction at regular intervals. The current that enters your home and school is an alternating current.

CHECK YOUR READING What is the difference between direct current and alternating current?

Direct currents and alternating currents are produced by different generators. In an AC generator, the direction in which charge flows depends upon the direction in which the magnet moves in relation to the coil. Because generators use a rotating electromagnet, the poles of the electromagnet alternate between moving toward and moving away from the magnet. The result is a current that reverses with each half-rotation of the coil.

The illustration on the right shows a simple DC generator. DC generators are very similar to AC generators. The main difference is that DC generators have a commutator that causes the current to flow in only one direction.

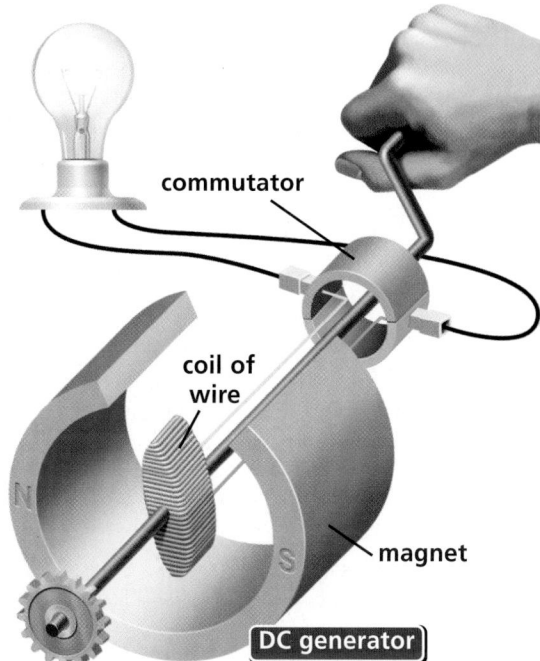

commutator

coil of wire

N

S

magnet

DC generator

Many things in your home can work with either direct or alternating currents. In light bulbs, for instance, the resistance to motion of the electrons in the filament makes the filament glow. It doesn't matter in which direction the current is moving.

Some appliances can use only direct current. The black box that is on the plug of some devices is an AC–DC converter. AC–DC converters change the alternating current to direct current. For example, laptop computers use converters like the one shown in the photograph on the right. In a desktop computer, the converter is part of the power supply unit.

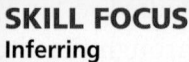

INVESTIGATE Electric Current

How can you identify the current?

PROCEDURE

(1) Wrap the wire tightly around the middle of the compass 10–15 times. Leave about 30 cm of wire free at each end. Tape the wire to the back of the compass to keep it in place.

(2) Sand the ends of the wire with sandpaper to expose about 2 cm of copper on each end. Arrange the compass on your desk so that the needle is parallel to, or lined up with, the coil. This will serve as your current detector.

(3) Tape one end of the wire to one terminal of the battery. Touch the other end of the wire to the other battery terminal. Record your observations.

(4) Observe the current detector as you tap the end of the wire to the battery terminal at a steady pace. Speed up or slow down your tapping until the needle of the compass alternates back and forth. Record your observations.

WHAT DO YOU THINK?

• What did you observe?

• What type of current did you detect in step 3? in step 4? How did you identify the type of current?

CHALLENGE How is this setup similar to an AC generator?

SKILL FOCUS
Inferring

MATERIALS
• piece of wire
• compass
• ruler
• tape
• sandpaper
• D cell (battery)

TIME
15 minutes

The energy that powers a car comes from burning gasoline, but the car also contains many devices that use electrical energy. Some of them are familiar—the headlights, turn signals, radio, power windows, and door locks. Others may be less familiar, such as the spark plugs that ignite the gasoline, the fuel and oil pumps that move fluids in the engine, and the air conditioner.

A car's engine includes a generator to provide current to its electrical devices. As the engine runs, it converts gasoline to kinetic energy. Some of that energy is transferred to the generator by a belt attached to its shaft. Inside the generator, a complex coil of copper wires turns in a magnetic field, generating a current that operates the electrical devices of the car.

The generator also recharges the battery, so that power is available when the engine is not running. Because the generator in most cars supplies alternating current, a car generator is usually called an alternator.

 What function does a generator in a car serve?

Magnets are used to control voltage.

A **transformer** is a device that increases or decreases voltage. Transformers use magnetism to control the amount of voltage. A transformer consists of two coils of wire that are wrapped around an iron ring.

An alternating current from the voltage source in the first coil produces a magnetic field. The iron ring becomes an electromagnet. Because the current alternates, the magnetic field is constantly changing. The second coil is therefore within a changing magnetic field. Current is generated in the second coil. If the two coils have the same number of loops, the voltage in the second coil will be the same as the voltage in the first coil.

A change in the voltage is caused when the two coils have different numbers of loops. If the second coil has fewer loops than the first, as in the illustration, the voltage is decreased. This is called a step-down transformer. On the other hand, if the second coil has more loops than the first, the voltage in the second circuit will be higher than the original voltage. This transformer is called a step-up transformer.

Step-Down Transformer

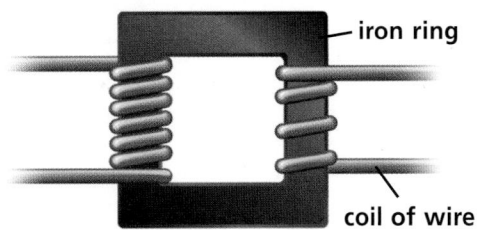

iron ring

coil of wire

Transformers are used in the distribution of current. Current is sent over power lines from power plants at a very high voltage. Step-down transformers on utility poles, such as the one pictured on the right, reduce the voltage available for use in homes. Sending current at high voltages minimizes the amount of energy lost to resistance along the way.

12.3 Review

KEY CONCEPTS

1. What is necessary for a magnetic field to produce an electric current?

2. Explain how electric generators convert kinetic energy into electrical energy.

3. Compare and contrast the ways in which direct current and alternating current are generated.

CRITICAL THINKING

4. **Apply** Many radios can be operated either by plugging them into the wall or by using batteries. How can a radio use either source of current?

5. **Draw Conclusions** Suppose that all of the electrical devices in a car stop working. Explain what the problem might be.

△ CHALLENGE

6. **Apply** European power companies deliver current at 220 V. Draw the design for a step-down transformer that would let you operate a CD player made to work at 110 V in France.

CHAPTER INVESTIGATION

Build a Speaker

OVERVIEW AND PURPOSE Speakers are found on TVs, computers, telephones, stereos, amplifiers, and other devices. Inside a speaker, magnetism and electric current interact to produce sound. The current produces a magnetic field that acts on another magnet and causes vibrations. The vibrations produce sound waves. In this lab, you will
- construct a speaker
- determine how the strength of the magnet affects the speaker's volume

▶ Problem

How does the strength of the magnet used to make a speaker affect the loudness of sound produced by the speaker?

▶ Hypothesize

Write a hypothesis that explains how you expect the strength of a magnet to affect the loudness of sound produced by the speaker, and why. Your hypothesis should be in the form of an "If . . . , then . . . , because . . ." statement.

▶ Procedure

1. Make a data table similar to the one shown on the sample notebook page.

2. Test the strength of each magnet by measuring the distance at which a paper clip will move to the magnet, as shown. Record the measurements in your **Science Notebook.**

   step 2

3. Starting about 6 cm from the end of the wire, wrap the wire around the marker 50 times to make a coil.

MATERIALS
- 3 magnets of different strengths
- paper clip
- ruler
- piece of wire
- marker
- cup
- masking tape
- 2 wire leads with alligator clips
- stereo system

4. Carefully slide the coil off the marker. Wrap the ends of the wire around the coil to keep it in the shape of a circle, as shown.

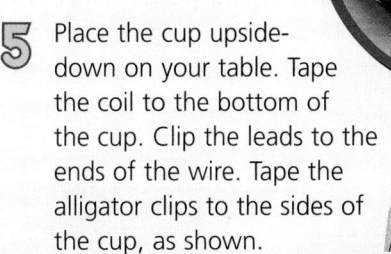
step 4

5. Place the cup upside-down on your table. Tape the coil to the bottom of the cup. Clip the leads to the ends of the wire. Tape the alligator clips to the sides of the cup, as shown.

coil

step 5

6. Take turns attaching the alligator clips to the stereo as instructed by your teacher. Place each magnet on the table near the stereo. Test the speaker by holding the cup directly over each magnet and listening. Record your observations.

Observe and Analyze
Write It Up

1. **RECORD OBSERVATIONS** Be sure to record your observations in the data table.

2. **INFER** Why is the coil of wire held near the magnet?

3. **APPLY** The diaphragm on a speaker vibrates to produce sound. What part of your stereo is the diaphragm?

4. **IDENTIFY** What was the independent variable in this experiment? What was the dependent variable?

▶ Conclude

Write It Up

1. **INTERPRET** Which magnet produced the loudest noise when used with your speaker? Answer the question posed in the problem.

2. **ANALYZE** Compare your results with your hypothesis. Did your results support your hypothesis?

3. **IDENTIFY LIMITS** Describe possible limitations or sources of error in the procedure or any places where errors might have occurred.

4. **APPLY** You have built a simple version of a real speaker. Apply what you have learned in this lab to explain how a real speaker might work.

▶ INVESTIGATE Further

CHALLENGE In what ways might you vary the design of the speaker to improve its functioning? Review the procedure to identify variables that might be changed to improve the speaker. Choose one variable and design an experiment to test that variable.

Build a Speaker

Problem How does the strength of the magnet used to make a speaker affect the loudness of sound produced by the speaker?

Hypothesize

Observe and Analyze

Table 1. Strength of Magnet and Loudness of Sound

Magnet	Strength (paper clip distance)	Observations
1		
2		
3		

Conclude

12.4 Generators supply electrical energy.

Sunshine State STANDARDS

SC.B.1.3.1: The student identifies forms of energy and explains that they can be measured and compared.

BEFORE, you learned

- Magnetism is a force exerted by magnets
- A moving magnetic field can generate an electric current in a conductor
- Generators use magnetism to produce current

NOW, you will learn

- How power plants generate electrical energy
- How electric power is measured
- How energy usage is calculated

VOCABULARY

electric power p. 434
watt p. 436
kilowatt p. 436
kilowatt-hour p. 437

THINK ABOUT

How can falling water generate electrical energy?

This photograph shows the Hoover Dam on the Nevada/Arizona border, which holds back a large lake, almost 600 feet deep, on the Colorado River. It took thousands of workers nearly five years to build the dam, and it cost millions of dollars. One of the main purposes of the Hoover Dam is the generation of current. Think about what you have read about generators. How could the energy of falling water be used to generate current?

Generators provide most of the world's electrical energy.

VOCABULARY
Use a description wheel to take notes about *electrical power.*

The tremendous energy produced by falling water provides the turning motion for large generators at a power plant. The power plant at the Hoover Dam supplies energy to more than a million people.

Other sources of energy at power plants include steam from burning fossil fuels, nuclear reactions, wind, solar heating, and ocean tides. Each source provides the energy of motion to the generators, producing electrical energy. **Electric power** is the rate at which electrical energy is generated from another source of energy.

 **CHECK YOUR READING** What do power plants that use water, steam, and wind all have in common?

How does the power plant convert the energy of motion into electrical energy? Very large generators in the plant hold powerful electromagnets surrounded by massive coils of copper wire. The illustration below shows how the energy from water falling from the reservoir to the river far below a dam is converted to electrical energy.

RESOURCE CENTER
CLASSZONE.COM

Find out more about dams that generate current.

1 As the water falls from the reservoir, its kinetic energy increases and it flows very fast. The falling stream of water turns a fan-like device, called a turbine, which is connected to the generator's shaft.

2 The rotation of the shaft turns powerful electromagnets that are surrounded by the coil of copper wires. The coil is connected to a step-up transformer that sends high-voltage current to power lines.

3 Far from the plant, step-down transformers reduce the voltage so that current can be sent through smaller lines to neighborhoods. Another transformer reduces the voltage to the level needed to operate lights and appliances.

How Electrical Power Is Generated

Power plants use generators to convert kinetic energy into electrical energy.

step-up transformers

step-down transformers

shaft

turbine

1 **Falling water** provides energy to turn the turbine of the generator.

2 The **shaft** turns a powerful electromagnet within a coil of wire, generating electrical current.

3 Current is sent along power lines at a high voltage. The voltage level is adjusted by transformers.

READING VISUALS How is kinetic energy turned into electrical energy in a power plant?

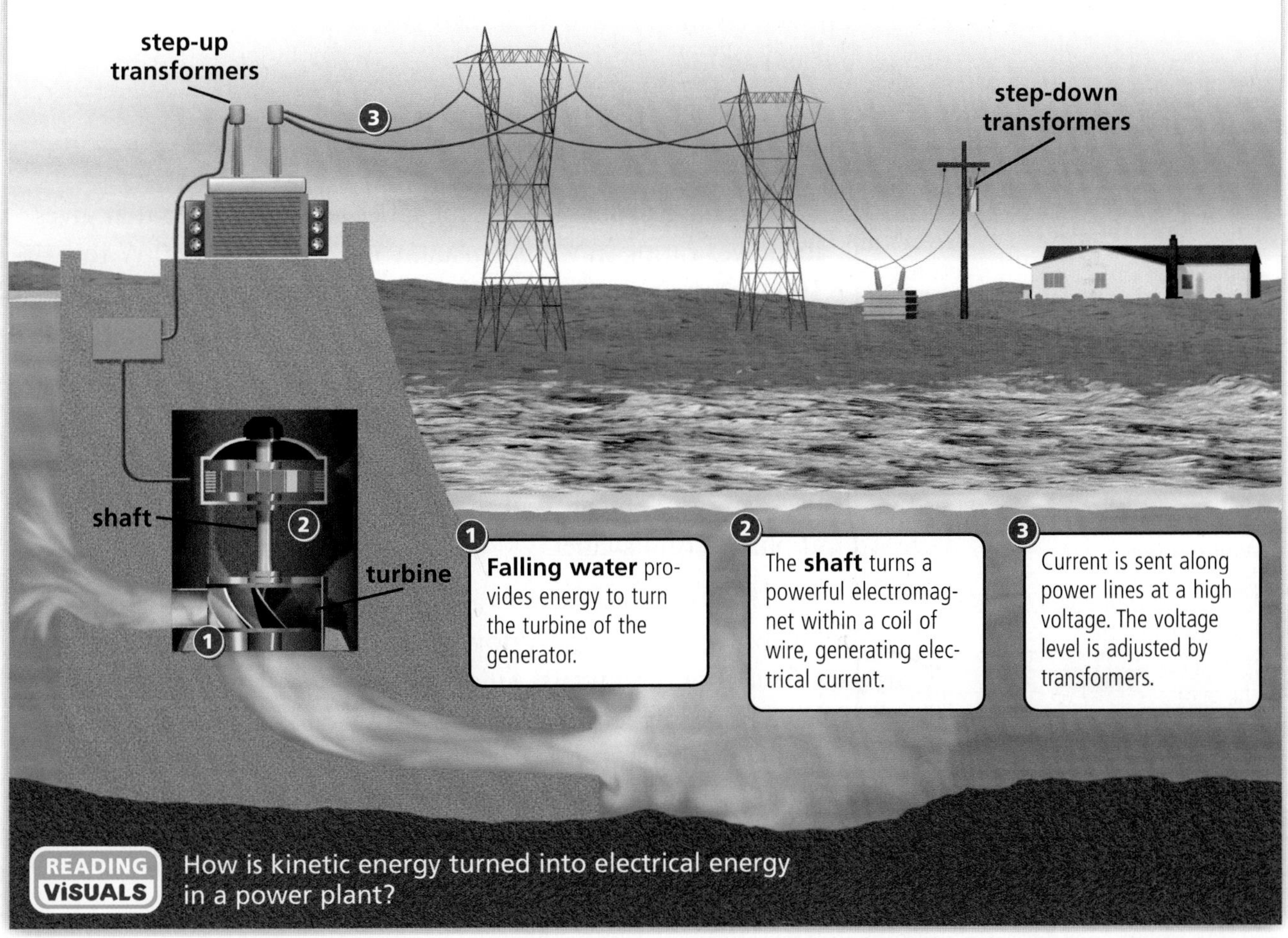

Electric power can be measured.

You have read that electric power is the rate at which electrical energy is generated from another source of energy. Power also refers to the rate at which an appliance converts electrical energy back into another form of energy, such as light, heat, or sound.

RESOURCE CENTER
CLASSZONE.COM

Learn more about
energy use and
conservation.

In order to provide electrical energy to homes and factories, power companies need to know the rate at which energy is needed. Power can be measured so that companies can determine how much energy is used and where it is used. This information is used to figure out how much to charge customers, and it is used to determine whether more electrical energy needs to be generated. To provide energy to an average home, a power plant needs to burn about four tons of coal each year.

Watts and Kilowatts

The unit of measurement for power is the **watt** (W). Watts measure the rate at which energy is used by an electrical appliance. For instance, a light bulb converts energy to light and heat. The power rating of the bulb, or of any device that consumes electrical energy, depends on both the voltage and the current. The formula for finding power, in watts, from voltage and current, is shown below. The letter I stands for current.

$$\textbf{Electric Power} = \textbf{Voltage} \cdot \textbf{Current}$$
$$P = VI$$

You have probably seen the label on a light bulb that gives its power rating in watts—usually in the range of 40 W to 100 W. A brighter bulb converts energy at a higher rate than one with a lower power rating.

The chart at the left shows typical power ratings, in watts, for some appliances that you might have in your home. The exact power rating depends on how each brand of appliance uses energy. You can find the actual power rating for an appliance on its label.

The combined power rating in a building is likely to be a fairly large number. A **kilowatt** (kW) is a unit of power equal to one thousand watts. All of the appliances in a room may have a combined power rating of several kilowatts, but all appliances are not in use all of the time. That is why energy is usually calculated based on how long the appliances are in use.

 **CHECK YOUR READING** Explain what kilowatts are used to measure.

Typical Power Ratings

Appliance	Watts
DVD player	20
Radio	20
Video game system	25
Electric blanket	60
Light bulb	75
Stereo system	100
Window fan	100
Television	110
Computer	120
Computer monitor	150
Refrigerator	700
Air conditioner	1000
Microwave oven	1000
Hair dryer	1200
Clothes dryer	3000

INVESTIGATE Power

How would you use your electrical energy?

PROCEDURE

1. On a sheet of graph paper, outline a box that is 10 squares long by 18 squares wide. The box represents a room that is wired to power a total of 1800 W. Each square represents 10 W of power.

2. From the chart on page 436, choose appliances that you want in your room. Using colored pencils, fill in the appropriate number of boxes for each appliance.

3. All of the items that you choose must fit within the total power available, represented by the 180 squares.

WHAT DO YOU THINK?

- How did you decide to use your electrical energy?
- Could you provide enough energy to operate everything you wanted at one time?

CHALLENGE During the summer, power companies sometimes cannot produce enough energy for the demand. Why do you think that happens?

SKILL FOCUS
Making models

MATERIALS
- graph paper
- colored pencils

TIME
30 minutes

Calculating Energy Use

The electric bill for your energy usage is calculated based on the rate at which energy is used, or the power, and the amount of time it is used at that rate. Total energy used by an appliance is determined by multiplying its power consumption by the amount of time that it is used.

$$\text{Energy used} = \text{Power} \cdot \text{time}$$

$$E = Pt$$

The kilowatt-hour is the unit of measurement for energy usage. A **kilowatt-hour** (kWh) is equal to one kilowatt of power for a one-hour period. Buildings usually have meters that measure how many kilowatt-hours of energy have been used. The meters display four or five small dials in a row, as shown in the photograph on the right. Each dial represents a different place value—ones, tens, hundreds, or thousands. For example, the meter in the photograph shows that the customer has used close to 9000 kWh of energy—8933 kWh, to be exact. To find how much energy was used in one month, the last month's reading is subtracted from this total.

To determine the number of kilowatt-hours of energy used by an appliance, find its wattage on the chart on page 436 or from the label. Then, substitute it into the formula along with the number of hours it was in use. Solve the sample problems below.

Finding Energy Used

> **Sample Problem**

How much energy is used to dry clothes in a 3 kW dryer for 30 minutes?

What do you know?	Power = 3.0 kW, time = 0.5 hr
What do you want to find out?	Energy used
Write the formula:	$E = Pt$
Substitute into the formula:	$E = 3.0 \text{ kW} \cdot 0.5 \text{ hr}$
Calculate and simplify:	$E = 1.5 \text{ kWh}$
Check that your units agree:	Unit is kWh. Unit for energy used is kWh. Units agree.
Answer:	1.5 kWh

> **Practice the Math**

1. All of the appliances in a computer lab are in use for 6 hours every day and together use 3.3 kW. How much energy has been used in 1 day?
2. How much energy is used when a 1.2 kW hair dyer is in use for 0.2 hr?

Energy prices vary, but you can estimate the cost of using an electrical appliance by using a value of about 8 cents/kWh. You can calculate how much energy you can save by turning off the lights or television when you are not using them. Although the number may seem small, try multiplying your savings over the course of a month or year.

12.4 Review

KEY CONCEPTS

1. How do power plants generate electrical energy from kinetic energy?
2. Explain what watts measure.
3. How is energy use determined?

CRITICAL THINKING

4. **Apply** Think about reducing energy usage in your home. What changes would make the largest difference in the amount of energy used?
5. **Calculate** How much energy is used if a 3000 W clothes dryer is used for 4 hours?

◓ CHALLENGE

6. **Calculate** An electric bill for an apartment shows 396 kWh of energy used over one month. The appliances in the apartment have a total power rating of 2.2 kW. How many hours were the appliances in use?

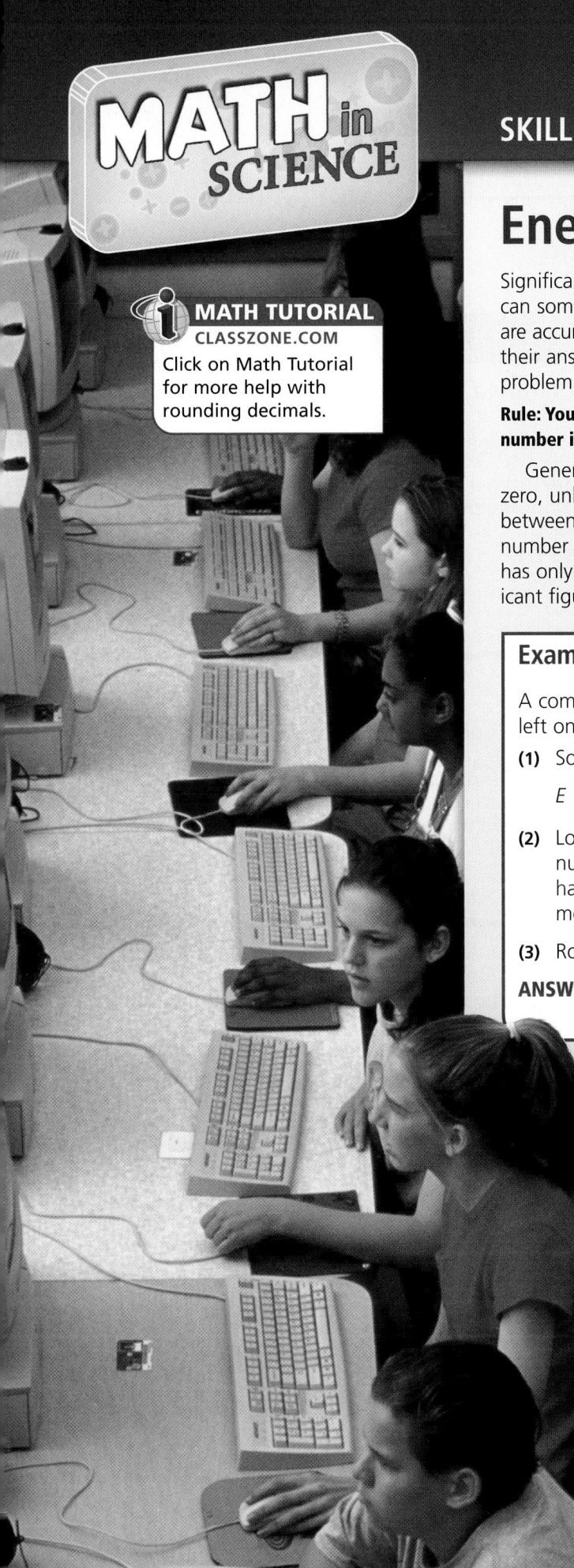

MATH in SCIENCE

MATH TUTORIAL
CLASSZONE.COM
Click on Math Tutorial for more help with rounding decimals.

Energy Calculations

Significant figures are meaningful digits in a number. Calculations can sometimes produce answers with more significant figures than are accurately known. Scientists use rules to determine how to round their answers. The rule for writing an answer to a multiplication problem is shown below.

Rule: Your answer may show only as many significant figures as the number in the problem with the fewest significant figures.

Generally, a significant figure is any digit shown except for a zero, unless the zero is contained between two nonzero digits or between a nonzero digit and a decimal point. For example, the number 40.3 has three significant figures, but the number 5.90 has only two significant figures. The number 0.034 has three significant figures, and the number 0.8 has only one significant figure.

Example

A computer uses 6.5 kWh of energy per day. If the computer is left on all the time, how much energy does it use in a year?

(1) Solve the problem.

$$E = 6.5 \; \frac{kWh}{day} \cdot 365 \; \frac{days}{year} = 2372.5 \; \frac{kWh}{year}$$

(2) Look at the number with the fewest significant figures. The number 6.5 has two significant figures, and the number 365 has three significant figures. Therefore, the answer is only meaningful to two significant figures.

(3) Round the answer to two significant figures.

ANSWER $E = 2400 \; \dfrac{kWh}{year}$

Answer the following questions. Write your answers using the significant figure rule for multiplication.

1. How much energy is used in a year by a computer that uses 1.7 kWh/day?

2. An energy-efficient computer uses 0.72 kWh/day. How much energy does it use in a week?

3. How much energy is used in one year if a 0.27 kW computer is on for 3 hours/day? (**Hint:** Use the formula $E = Pt$.)

CHALLENGE The energy usage of a computer is measured to be 0.058030 kWh. How many significant figures does this measurement have?

12 Chapter Review

Current can produce magnetism, and magnetism can produce current.

FLORIDA REVIEW
CLASSZONE.COM

Content Review and
FCAT Practice

KEY CONCEPTS SUMMARY

1 Magnetism is a force that acts at a distance.

magnetic poles

magnetic field lines

Opposite poles attract.

All magnets have a north and south pole. The like poles of two magnets repel each other and the opposite poles attract.

VOCABULARY
magnet p. 411
magnetism p. 412
magnetic pole p. 412
magnetic field p. 413
magnetic domain p. 414

2 Current can produce magnetism.

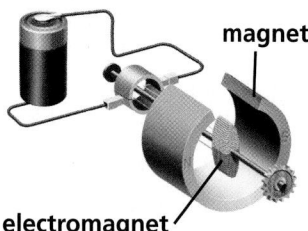

motor

magnet

electromagnet

A magnet that is produced by electric current is called an electromagnet. Motors use electromagnets to convert electrical energy into the energy of motion.

VOCABULARY
electromagnetism p. 421
electromagnet p. 422

3 Magnetism can produce current.

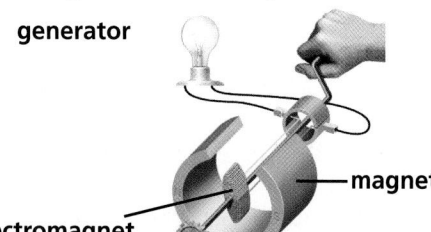

generator

magnet

electromagnet

Magnetism can be used to produce electric current. In a generator the energy of motion is converted into electrical energy.

VOCABULARY
generator p. 428
direct current p. 429
alternating current p. 429
transformer p. 431

4 Generators supply electrical energy.

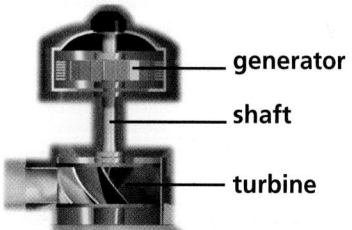

generator

shaft

turbine

Generators at power plants use large magnets to produce electric current, supplying electrical energy to homes and businesses.

VOCABULARY
electric power p. 434
watt p. 436
kilowatt p. 436
kilowatt-hour p. 437

Reviewing Vocabulary

Draw a cluster diagram for each of the terms below. Write the vocabulary term in the center circle. In another circle, write the definition of the term in your own words. Add other circles that give examples or characteristics of the term. A sample diagram is completed for you.

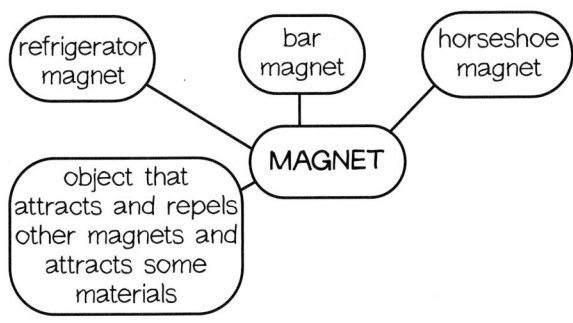

1. magnetism
2. magnetic pole
3. magnetic field
4. magnetic domain
5. electromagnet
6. generator
7. direct current
8. alternating current
9. transformer
10. electric power
11. watt
12. kilowatt-hour

Reviewing Key Concepts

Multiple Choice *Choose the letter of the best answer.*

13. Magnetic field lines flow from a magnet's
    a. north pole to south pole
    b. south pole to north pole
    c. center to the outside
    d. outside to the center

14. Which of the following is characteristic of magnetic materials?
    a. Their atoms are all aligned.
    b. Their atoms are arranged in magnetic domains.
    c. They are all nonmetals.
    d. They are all made of lodestone.

15. The Earth's magnetic field helps to protect living things from
    a. ultraviolet light
    b. meteors
    c. the Northern Lights
    d. charged particles

16. To produce a magnetic field around a copper wire, you have to
    a. place it in Earth's magnetic field
    b. run a current through it
    c. supply kinetic energy to it
    d. place it near a strong magnet

17. An electric current is produced when a wire is
    a. stationary in a magnetic field
    b. moving in a magnetic field
    c. placed between the poles of a magnet
    d. coiled around a magnet

18. In a generator, kinetic energy is converted into
    a. light energy
    b. chemical energy
    c. electrical energy
    d. nuclear energy

19. In an AC circuit, the current moves
    a. back and forth
    b. from one end of a generator to the other
    c. from one end of a battery to the other
    d. in one direction

20. What is the function of the turbine in a power plant?
    a. to increase the voltage
    b. to convert DC to AC
    c. to cool the steam
    d. to turn the coil or magnet

21. The two factors needed to measure usage of electrical energy in a building are
    a. power and time
    b. power and voltage
    c. voltage and time
    d. current and voltage

Thinking Critically

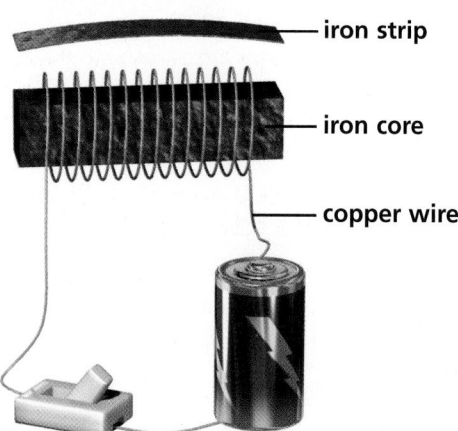

iron strip

iron core

copper wire

Refer to the device in the illustration above to answer the next three questions.

22. APPLY What will happen when the switch is closed?

23. PREDICT What effect will switching the direction of the current have on the operation of the device?

24. CONTRAST If the iron strip is replaced with a thin magnet, how would that affect the answers to the previous two questions?

25. APPLY Coal is burned at a power plant to produce steam. The rising steam turns a turbine. Describe how the motion of the turbine produces current at the plant.

26. CONNECT List three things that you use in your everyday life that would not exist without the discovery of electromagnetism.

27. APPLY A radio for use during power outages works when you crank a handle. How is the radio powered? How can it keep operating even after you stop turning the crank?

28. HYPOTHESIZE Use your understanding of magnetic materials and the source of Earth's magnetic field to form a hypothesis about the difference between Earth and the Moon that accounts for the fact that the Moon does not have a magnetic field.

Using Math in Science

Some electric bills include a bar graph of energy usage similar to the one shown below. Use the information provided in the graph to answer the next four questions.

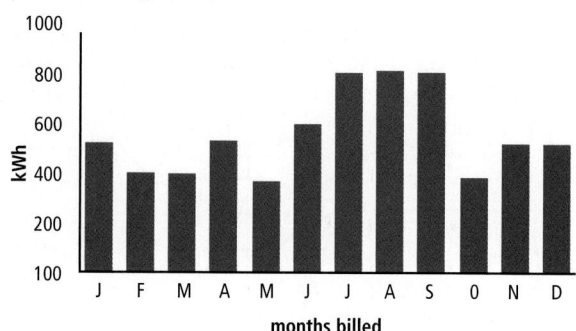

12-Month Usage (kWh)

months billed

29. The first bar in the graph shows energy usage for the month of January. About how much energy, in kWh, was used in January?

30. If the appliances in the building have a combined power rating of 2 kW, how many hours were they in use during the month of March? (**Hint:** Use the formula $E = Pt$.)

31. The cost of energy was 8 cents per kWh. How much was charged for energy usage in May?

32. The most energy is used when the air conditioner is on. During which three months was the air conditioner on?

the BIG idea

33. ANALYZE Look back at pages 408–409. Think about the answer you gave to the question about the large photograph. How has your understanding of magnetism changed? Give examples.

34. SUMMARIZE Write a paragraph summarizing the first three pages of this chapter. Use the heading at the top of page 411 as your topic sentence. Explain each red and blue heading.

UNIT PROJECTS

Evaluate all the data, results, and information from your project folder. Prepare to present your project.

Analyzing Tables

The table below lists some major advances in the understanding of electromagnetism.

> **FCAT TiP**
>
> When reading a table, be sure to match the information in the left-hand column with the correct information in the right-hand column. This will help you find the information you need when answering a question based on the table.

Scientist	Year	Advance
William Gilbert	1600	proposes distinction between magnetism and static electricity
Pieter van Musschenbroek	1745	develops Leyden jar, which stores electric charge
Benjamin Franklin	1752	shows that lightning is a form of electricity
Charles Augustin de Coulomb	1785	proves mathematically that, for electricity and magnetism, force changes with distance
Alessandro Volta	1800	invents battery, first device to generate a continuous current
Hans Christian Oersted	1820	announces he had used electric current to produce magnetic effects
André Marie Ampère	1820	shows that wires carrying current attract and repel each other, just like magnets
Georg Simon Ohm	1827	studies how well different wires conduct electric current
Michael Faraday	1831	produces electricity with a magnet; invents first electric generator

Use the table to answer the following questions.

MULTIPLE CHOICE

1. Which scientist first produced a device that allowed experimenters to hold an electric charge for later use?

A. Coulomb   **C.** Ohm

B. Franklin   **D.** van Musschenbroek

2. Which scientist developed the first device that could be used to provide a steady source of current to other devices?

F. Ampère   **H.** Volta

G. Faraday   **I.** Gilbert

3. Which scientist had the first experimental evidence that current could produce magnetism?

A. Gilbert

B. Faraday

C. van Musschenbroek

D. Oersted

SHORT RESPONSE

4. Use the table to explain why Coulomb's work was important.

EXTENDED RESPONSE

Answer the two questions below in detail.

5. How are electromagnets produced? How can the strength of these devices be increased? How can electromagnets be used in ways that permanent magnets cannot?

6. Alix chats online for an average of about an hour a day 6 days a week. Her computer has a power rating of 270 watts. She has a hair dryer with a power rating of 1200 watts. She uses it twice a week for about 15 minutes at a time. Which device is likely to use more power over the course of a year? Why?

Life Over Time

classification

FOSSIL

species

preserved remains

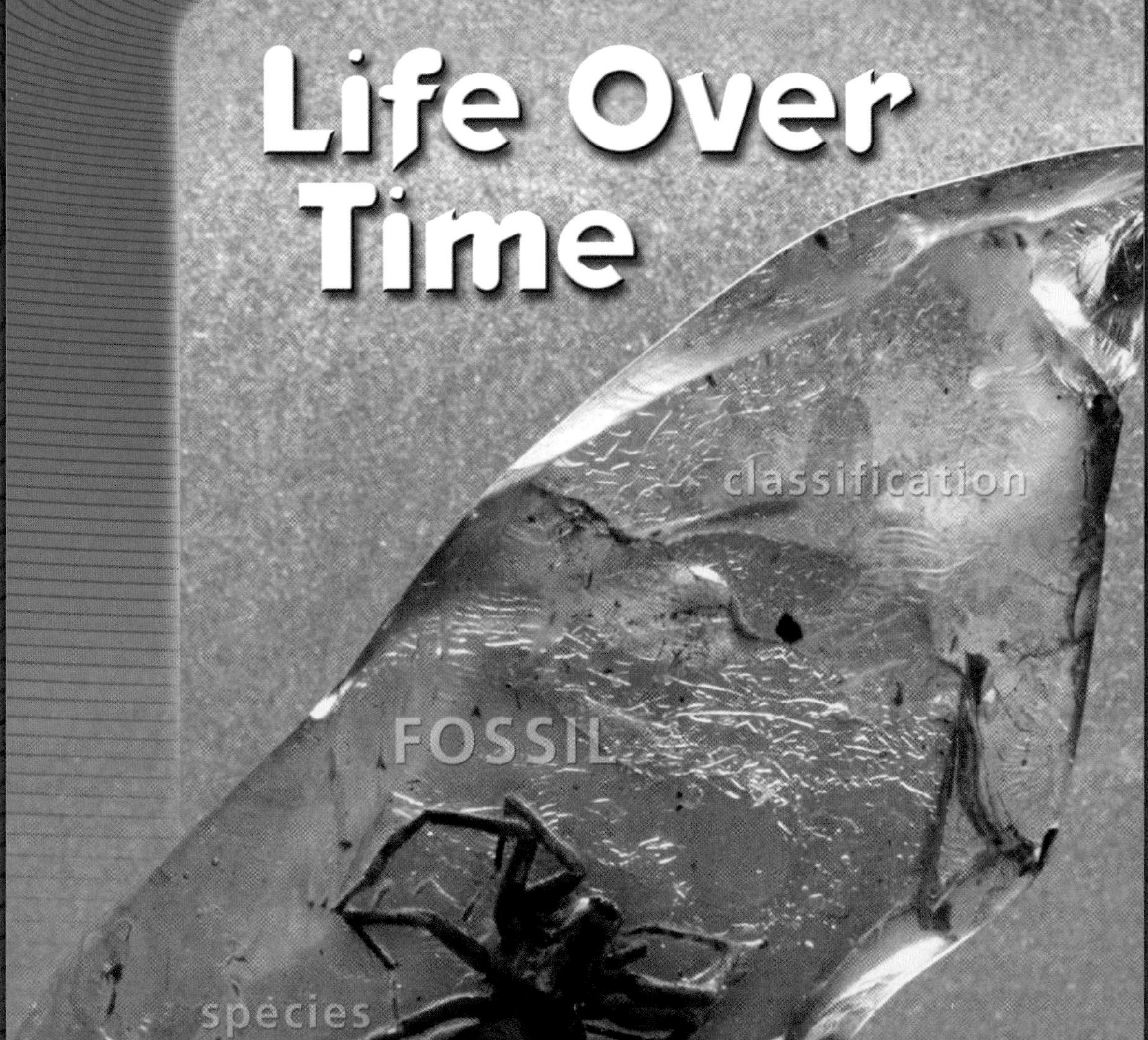

Contents Overview

Frontiers in Science
Life by Degrees   446

Florida Connection
The Ultimate Fish   450

Timelines in Science
Life Unearthed   520

Chapter 13 Views of Earth's Past   454

Chapter 14 The History of
Life on Earth   486

Chapter 15 Population Dynamics   524

Life By Degrees

What happens when Earth's climate changes? Scientists are studying how climate change has influenced the evolution of life on Earth.

SCIENTIFIC AMERICAN FRONTIERS

Learn about how climate change affected life on Earth. See the video "Noah's Snowball."

Climate and Life

Throughout its history, Earth's climate has changed many times. Often the changes are gradual. They may seem small. However, an average global temperature change of just a few degrees can have a large impact on climate. Small changes in climate then cause big changes for plants and animals.

Before there were humans to record events, Earth recorded its changes in its rocks and fossils. For example, scientists get a sense for Earth's climate at different times in the distant past by looking at fossils, the remains and traces of living things. If scientists find fossils of tropical plants in places near the arctic circle, then they may conclude that the climate in those places was different in the past.

Scientists have found that warmer climates lead to a greater diversity of organisms. One researcher examined fossils of tiny organisms called phytoplankton (FY-toh-PLANK-tuhn). During cooler climate periods, there were fewer types of phytoplankton than during warmer periods. The same is true for other organisms. Peter Wilf and Conrad Labandeira studied fossil plants. They were especially interested in the marks they found on the plants. The marks were left by plant-eating animals who bit the leaves. The warmer the climate was, the more types of plants there were—and the more kinds of animals were eating the plants.

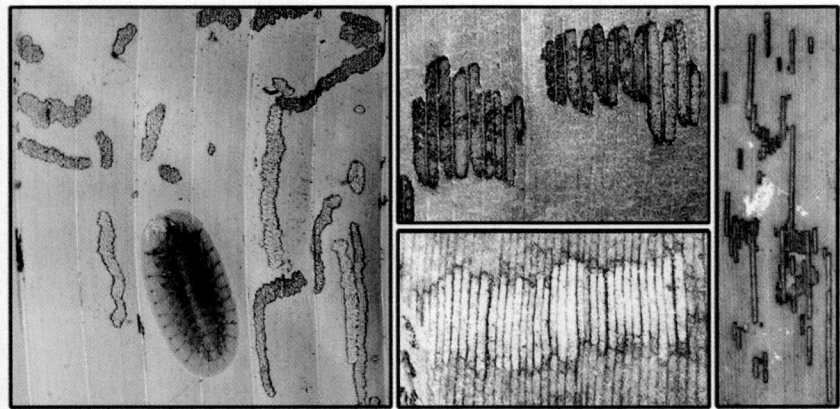

SOURCE: Images © 2000 AAAS

The chew marks of the hispine beetle larva on living ginger in Panama (left) look similar to fossilized chew marks found in Wyoming (three photos right).

Before and after photographs of the sky show that distinct bands appeared due to dust and ash from the 1991 volcanic eruption of Mt. Pinatubo.

Mass Extinction

Several times in Earth's past, many kinds of animals and plants have disappeared in a relatively short time. These events are called mass extinctions. While we don't know for sure what causes them, most scientists think climate change plays a role in mass extinctions.

The largest mass extinction in Earth's history happened at the end of the Permian (PER-mee-uhn) Period about 248 million years ago. Scientists estimate that 90–95 percent of animal species that lived in the water died out. About three quarters of the vertebrates, or animals with backbones, living on land died out too.

Turn of Events

What caused this extinction? Using fossils, scientists have concluded that Earth's climate became cooler. Material from erupting volcanoes may have blocked sunlight long enough to cool the Earth. The cool temperatures and lack of sunlight may have killed plants and animals.

Scientist Peter Ward has been studying the Permian extinction. He looked at ancient African rivers and found evidence that rivers had became clogged with soil. Plants normally holding soil in place may have been wiped out, causing the soil on the riverbanks to loosen. The plant extinction would also have led to animal extinction.

SCIENTIFIC AMERICAN FRONTIERS

View the "Noah's Snowball" segment of your *Scientific American Frontiers* video to learn about another theory of how climate change affected life on Earth.

IN THIS SCENE FROM THE VIDEO ⊙ Fossil hunters examine evidence of early life in China.

DEEP FREEZE Can you imagine what Earth would be like if it were completely covered in ice? Geologists Paul Hoffman and Dan Schrag suggest Earth was frozen solid until about 600 million years ago. They think Earth's climate changed by just a few degrees, but it was enough to make the ice caps cover the planet. The only life that survived was bacteria that were kept warm by volcanoes. And it was the volcanoes that changed the climate again, say Hoffman and Schrag. Suddenly eruptions melted the ice. Ocean levels rose. The scientists think this change might have taken only a hundred years. Not everyone agrees with the snowball hypothesis, but it could explain why new forms of life began to appear.

What Hit Them?

Not all scientists agree about what caused the Permian extinction. If an asteroid hit Earth, it would push massive amounts of dirt and dust into the air. This could block sunlight and create a cooler climate. An increase in volcanic eruptions is another possible cause.

The most famous extinction of all took place at the end of the Cretaceous Period. The extended winter that may have followed a meteor impact caused many large land animals—including dinosaurs—to become extinct.

In a new climate some species thrive and survive. They spread out and, over time, evolve to fill empty niches or unique roles in the environment. For example, before the Cretaceous extinction, the only mammals were small. After the dinosaurs became extinct, large mammals could fill the roles of large plant-eaters and meat-eaters.

Even today, climate change continues. Earth's average temperature rose about half a degree Celsius in the twentieth century. Studying how past climate changes shaped life helps scientists predict how it may affect us in the future.

A large plant-eating mammal, *Chalicotherium grande*, roamed Asia millions of years ago.

UNANSWERED Questions

Scientists have learned a lot about climate change and mass extinctions by studying fossils. There are many questions still to be answered.

• What caused changes in Earth's climate?

• What else might have caused mass extinctions?

• How might climate change affect life on Earth in the future?

UNIT PROJECTS

As you study this unit, work alone or with a group on one of the projects listed below. Use the bulleted steps to guide your project.

Museum Display

What organisms survived the Permian extinction? What organisms went extinct?

• Create a museum display using art and text.

• Use visuals to show the organisms and the modern relatives that have close connections to them.

Design a Robot

Often, scientists design robots to study dangerous or distant locations.

• Design an artificial robot that would be well-adapted to survive an event that causes a mass extinction.

• Explain why the design would help the robot remain in operation.

Species over Time

Find out more about species that have gone extinct during recorded history.

• Choose one species that is now extinct.

• Present a timeline giving a history of that species.

• Describe what some of its ancestors and surviving related organisms are.

• Describe when it was last seen. Include some of the possible reasons for why it died out.

CAREER CENTER
CLASSZONE.COM

Learn more about careers in paleontology.

THE ULTIMATE FISH

One of the fiercest sharks, the great white, has been spotted off Florida beaches.

Sunshine State Standards

In "The Ultimate Fish" you will learn how human activity may knowingly or unknowingly affect an ecosystem. (SC.G.2.3.4)

You also will learn how biological adaptation in structure, behavior, or function can enhance reproduction in sharks' environment. (SC.G.1.3.2)

There are over 350 species of shark. New species are still being discovered.

An Undeserved Reputation

Sharks have gotten a bad reputation. Many people think all sharks do is swim around beaches looking for victims to attack. When a shark attack occurs, however, it probably was an accident. In the murky waters around many beaches, sharks have difficulty distinguishing objects. Most likely, the shark mistook a person's arm or leg for one of its more common foods. As marine biologist Chris Koch of the South Florida Science Museum has pointed out, sharks are actually "apologizing by letting go." The problem is that the apology is coming from jaws loaded with razor-sharp teeth. It's easy to see why many people think the apology is not too sincere.

One tragedy of shark attacks is that they are the only news most people ever hear about sharks. Most people don't hear about all the amazing things sharks can show us. Everything a shark does is geared toward giving it the best chance of survival in its habitat. Scientists are trying to learn more about these survival mechanisms and determine ways that human beings can use them. For those who live in areas where there are sharks, it's important to know more of the facts about them. Sharks may very well one day prove to be our greatest animal friends.

The Facts on Sharks

Sharks, along with skates, rays, and chimaeras, belong to a class of fish known as chondrichthyes. A few of the more common species of shark around Florida are the bull, dusky, silky, spinner, and nurse sharks. All these sharks have different appearances, diets, and habits. Some of the characteristics shared by all sharks are listed below.

Cartilage Skeletons A shark's "bones" are not bones at all but a tough, flexible material called cartilage. You too have cartilage between your bones and in your nose.

Denticles and Gills A shark's skin is covered with toothlike structures called denticles. Shark skin is so rough that it is sometimes used as an abrasive, similar to sandpaper. Some sharks can have as many as seven gill slits on either side of their body.

Size Of the more than 350 known species of shark, the largest is the whale shark, which can grow up to 15 meters (49 ft) long. The smallest is the dwarf shark, which rarely exceeds 17 centimeters (6 in) long.

Normally, shark attacks on humans are mistakes. Sharks have difficulty seeing in murky waters and can sometimes mistake humans for their regular food.

Swimming Sharks are great swimmers. They move at an average speed of about one meter (3 ft) per second. Sharks swim constantly to keep water running over their gills to get oxygen. Although they are fast swimmers, sharks become immobile if upside down, and only a few will jump out of the water. The great white shark is the only shark species that is known to stick its head out of the water to look around.

Teeth Sharks have incredibly sharp teeth. When a shark loses a tooth, another moves in quickly to replace it. The teeth of many sharks have jagged sides, like a kitchen knife. The shark's teeth are perfect for feasting on the stingrays, squids, and crustaceans that make up its diet.

Smell and Other Senses Almost two-thirds of a shark's brain is dedicated to the sense of smell. As it swims, a shark's nostrils filter water and detect particles in it. Using their sense of smell, sharks can locate prey hundreds of meters away.

Sharks also have special organs that give them the unique ability to detect the electric fields around other organisms. A shark's electroreceptors sense the electric fields produced by an organism's heartbeat or muscle movement. This gives the shark the ability to locate prey that might be buried under the sand. Larger sharks can sense an organism's electric field from about a meter away. Smaller sharks can detect the field from about 15 cm (6 in.) away.

Solitary Creatures Sharks generally don't like to stick around each other. Usually, the only time you see two sharks together is if they're competing for the same source of food. Sharks can become vicious when it comes to their food, biting wildly at it to get every bit. One shark will even eat another shark if it gets in the way.

SPOTLIGHT ON Shark Products

People have hunted sharks for many reasons. A few of these reasons are listed below.

Food Soup prepared from the dorsal fins of certain sharks is a delicacy in China. Shark meat can be found in many fish markets and is becoming increasingly popular. In some parts of the world, plentiful shark meat could be a source of protein for undernourished people.

Oils For centuries, shark-liver oil was considered an all-purpose medicine, able to cure anything from arthritis to coughs. It also was used to tan leather and preserve wood. A single liver from the basking shark found off Florida's eastern coast can yield anywhere from 80 to 600 gallons of oil. This oil was used extensively as a lighting fuel until petroleum products became widely available. Today, shark-liver oil is still a good source of many vitamins, especially vitamin A.

Clothing Clothes designers have turned the skins of the dusky, blacktip, and nurse sharks into high-fashion items such as boots, belts, and wallets. Chemical treatment removes the scales from the skin, which, when stretched and dried, is far more

durable than cowhide. Shagreen is sharkskin that hasn't had its scales removed. It is very abrasive and is often used for polishing wood.

Jewelry The place where you're most likely to spy a remnant of a former shark is hanging around a person's neck or from an earlobe. Shark teeth make interesting jewelry pieces. The Maori people of New Zealand so prize the teeth of the mako shark that they have created a market for them.

The Mote Marine Laboratory in Sarasota, Florida is one of the world's leading shark research centers. Some sharks, like the one in this photograph, are kept in large tanks for close observation.

What Sharks Can Show Us

Relatives of today's sharks were swimming in the oceans 400 million years ago. This means sharks were around when dinosaurs lived on Earth. Sharks are amazing survivors. They may be the closest thing Earth has to a perfectly adapted living creature. It is precisely for this reason that sharks are of so much interest to scientists.

One place where sharks are being studied is at the Center for Shark Research at Sarasota's Mote Marine Laboratory. There, scientists are studying everything from the shark populations in different regions to the movement patterns and feeding mechanisms of different shark species. Although scientists know pretty well what sharks do to survive, they are trying to uncover more about how these adaptations work and why they have made sharks such great survivors. Following are just two of the adaptations scientists are studying.

Live Birth Although some sharks do lay eggs like most fish, many sharks give birth to live young, like mammals. Marine biologists are convinced that live birth must have given these sharks some kind of survival advantage. Understanding exactly what that advantage is may help biologists understand how other forms of life on Earth developed as they did.

Fighting Disease Sharks don't get sick very often. Diseases like cancer, which affect many living things, are very rare in the shark world. Scientists are investigating claims that shark cartilage placed in wounds makes them heal more quickly. Hope is high that shark cartilage will be found to stop the growth of tumors and strengthen the immune system.

But the shark's very success at surviving has given it what it managed to avoid having for millennia—a predator, humans. Sharks are hunted for food, clothing, and other products. The fishing industry also depletes many of sharks' natural prey, and in turn hurts the shark population. Although sharks can be dangerous, we can't afford to lose them. Losing them could disrupt the delicate balance of the ocean ecosystem as well as an animal friend that could help all life on Earth survive.

ASKING Questions

- What other questions do you have about sharks?

- What questions do you have about how sharks' environment has or hasn't changed?

RESOURCE CENTER

Visit **ClassZone.com** for more information on sharks.

WRITING ABOUT SCIENCE

You're listening to a news report about a shark attack, and you hear the family member of a victim yell, "All sharks should be destroyed!" Use facts from the article to write a speech explaining why destroying all sharks would be bad for people.

Writing Tips

Plan, draft, and revise your writing using the tips below.

- Identify the reasons for the person's reaction.

- List reasons from this article that show sharks are good for people.

- Make sure each fact you list supports your argument.

- Order your reasons from least to most important.

Views of Earth's Past

the BIG idea

Rocks, fossils, and other types of natural evidence tell Earth's story.

Key Concepts

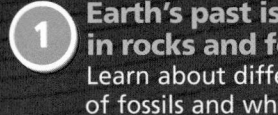

SECTION
1 **Earth's past is revealed in rocks and fossils.**
Learn about different kinds of fossils and what they tell about Earth's past.

SECTION
2 **Rocks provide a timeline for Earth.**
Learn how information from rocks tells about Earth's past.

SECTION
3 **The geologic time scale shows Earth's past.**
Learn about 4.6 billion years of Earth's history.

FCAT Practice

Prepare and practice for the FCAT
- Section Reviews, pp. 463, 471, 479
- Chapter Review, pp. 482–484
- FCAT Practice, p. 485

CLASSZONE.COM
- Florida Review: Content Review and FCAT Practice

What does this footprint tell you about the animal that left it?

How Do You Know What Happened?

Observe an area around your neighborhood to find evidence of a past event. For example, you might see tracks from tires or a stump from a tree. Record your observations.

Observe and Think
What evidence did you find? What does the evidence suggest about the past?

How Long Has That Been There?

Look inside a cabinet or refrigerator and choose one item to investigate. See if you can tell where the item was made, where it was purchased, how long it has been in the cabinet or refrigerator, and when it was last used.

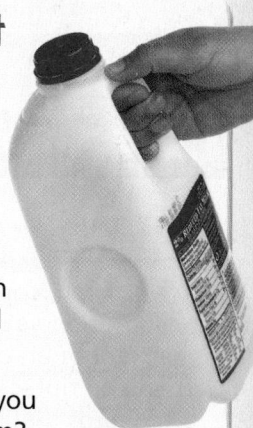

Observe and Think How did you figure out the history of the item?

Internet Activity: Earth's History

Go to **ClassZone.com** to discover how scientists pieced together information to figure out the story of the dinosaurs.

Observe and Think
What kinds of evidence did scientists use?

NSTA
scilinks.org
SC*LINKS*

Earth's Story Code: MDL055

Getting Ready to Learn

◄ CONCEPT REVIEW

- The parts of the Earth system interact to shape Earth's surface.
- Natural processes form, change, break down, and re-form rocks.
- Glaciers carve land and move sediments.

◄ VOCABULARY REVIEW

system p. 197

weathering p. 231

erosion p. 261

glacier p. 281

FLORIDA REVIEW
CLASSZONE.COM

Content Review and FCAT Practice

▶ TAKING NOTES

OUTLINE

As you read, copy the headings on your paper in the form of an outline. Then add notes in your own words that summarize what you read.

VOCABULARY STRATEGY

Place each vocabulary term at the center of a **description wheel**. On the spokes write words explaining it.

See the Note-Taking Handbook on pages R45–R51.

SCIENCE NOTEBOOK

I. Earth's past is revealed in rocks and fossils.

  A. Rocks, fossils, and original remains give clues about the past.

    1. Original Remains

      a.

      b.

      c.

    2. Fossil Formation

      a.

      b.

      c.

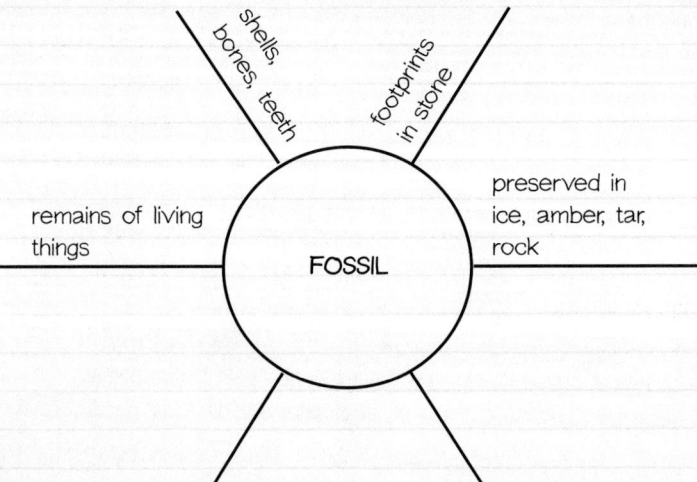

13.1 Earth's past is revealed in rocks and fossils.

◀ **BEFORE, you learned**

- Weathering processes break down rocks
- Climate influences the rate of weathering
- Water, wind, waves, and current shape landforms

▶ **NOW, you will learn**

- How different kinds of fossils show traces of life from Earth's past
- How ice cores and tree rings reveal conditions and changes in the environment

🔵 **FCAT VOCABULARY**
fossil p. 457

VOCABULARY
original remains p. 458
ice core p. 463

EXPLORE Rocks

What can we learn from a rock?

PROCEDURE

① Use a hand lens to examine the rock sample.

② Make a sketch of any shapes you see in the rock.

WHAT DO YOU THINK?

- What do you think those shapes are?
- How did they get there?

MATERIALS
- rock sample
- hand lens
- paper and pencil

OUTLINE
Remember to take notes on this section in outline form.

I. Main idea
  A. Supporting idea
    1. Detail
    2. Detail
  B. Supporting idea

Rocks, fossils, and original remains give clues about the past.

You have read about mountain formation, earthquakes, and other ways in which Earth changes over time. Scientists have learned about these changes—even changes that happened long ago—by studying rocks, fossils, and other natural evidence. Two hundred million years ago, for example, huge dinosaurs walked on Earth. These giant reptiles were a major form of animal life on the planet for millions of years. Then, about 65 million years ago, the dinosaurs became extinct, or died out. What happened?

To solve the mystery of why dinosaurs disappeared, scientists look for clues. Fossils, for example, are important clues about past events. **Fossils** are traces or remains of living things from long ago. Dinosaur bones and footprints preserved in stone are examples of fossils.

Using fossils and other natural evidence, scientists have formed a theory about why the dinosaurs disappeared. They now think that some major event, such as the crashing of one or more giant asteroids into Earth, led to rapid changes that caused the dinosaurs to become extinct.

Fossils also tell us about organisms, such as dinosaurs, that are now extinct. Even though no one has ever seen a dinosaur, people have some idea about what dinosaurs looked like and how they behaved because of fossils.

Fossils exist in many different forms. Most fossils are hardened animal remains such as shells, bones, and teeth. Minerals replace the remains, forming a fossil of the hard skeletal body parts. Other fossils are impressions or other evidence of an organism preserved in rock. Sometimes, an actual organism—or part of an organism—can be preserved and become a fossil.

Original Remains

Fossils that are the actual bodies or body parts of organisms are called **original remains.** Usually, soft parts of dead animals and plants decay and disappear. But soft parts can become fossil evidence if they are sealed in a substance that keeps out air and tiny organisms. Original remains are found in places where conditions prevent the decomposition, or breakdown, that normally occurs. Original remains are important because they give direct evidence of forms of life that lived long ago.

1 Ice Ice is one of the best preservers of the remains of prehistoric life. Huge ice fields in Siberia and Alaska contain the bodies of 10,000-year-old mammoths and prehistoric rhinos, with bones, muscle, skin, and even hair still in place. The ice preserved the animals after they died.

2 Amber Another natural substance that preserves the remains of some living things is amber. Amber forms from resin, a sticky substance inside trees that flows like syrup and protects the tree by trapping insects. If the tree gets buried after it dies, the resin can harden into amber. Amber can contain the remains of insects and other small organisms.

3 Tar The original remains of animals have also been found in places where there were pools of tar—a thick, oily liquid. Saber-toothed cats and other animals were trapped in the tar and preserved.

Original Remains

1 Ice

This frozen mammoth body was found in Siberia.

2 Amber

These insects, which are related to flies and mosquitoes, were trapped and preserved in amber 40 million years ago.

3 Tar

This skull of a saber-toothed cat, found in the La Brea Tar Pits in California, was preserved in the tar for 10,000 to 40,000 years.

Fossil Formation

VISUALIZATION
CLASSZONE.COM
Explore how fossils form.

Conditions have to be just right for a fossil to form in rock. The organism or trace of the organism must be preserved before it decomposes or disappears. Usually, the soft parts of an organism decay too quickly to be preserved in rock. For that reason, many rock fossils reveal traces or shapes of only the hard parts of animals or plants. Hard parts, such as shells, bones, teeth, and stems or tree trunks, decompose slowly, so they are more likely to be preserved as fossil evidence. Most organisms that lived in the past died and decomposed without leaving any traces. An organism that has no hard parts, such as a mushroom or a slug, rarely leaves fossil evidence.

Rock fossils form in sedimentary rock. Sedimentary rock forms from layers of sediment, such as sand or mud. Sometimes, the sediment builds up around animal and plant remains, which can leave fossils in the rock. If sedimentary rocks are changed by heat or pressure, their fossils can be destroyed. Igneous rocks never contain fossils. The heat of the molten rock—from which igneous rock cools—destroys any traces of plants or animals.

CHECK YOUR READING Why do rock fossils form in sedimentary rock rather than in igneous rock?

Theropod Fossil

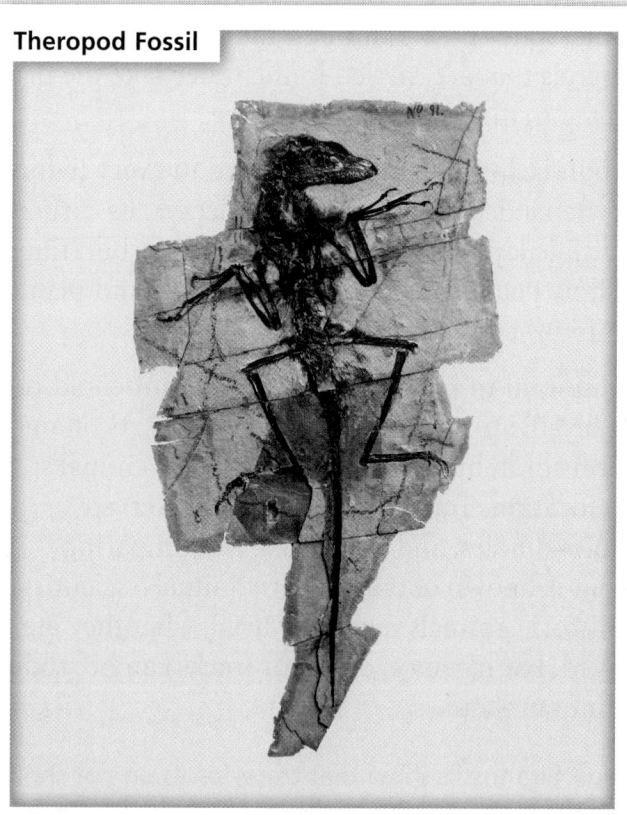

Artist's Drawing of Theropod

CHINA

This 130-million-year-old skeleton of a small theropod dinosaur, found between two slabs of rock in China, contains well-preserved featherlike structures. The fossil is about a meter (3 ft) long.

Fossils in Rocks

If an organism is covered by or buried in sediment, it may become a fossil as the sediments become rock. Many rock fossils are actual body parts, such as bones or teeth, that were buried in sediment and then replaced by minerals and turned to stone.

Some fossils are not original remains or actual body parts that have turned to stone. Instead, these fossils are impressions or traces made of rock and provide indirect evidence that the organisms were there, just as a shoeprint can reveal much about the shoe that made it. Rocks can contain detailed shapes or prints of plants, animals, and even organisms too small to see without a microscope. Fossils in rock include molds and casts, petrified wood, carbon films, and trace fossils.

1 Molds and Casts Some fossils that form in sedimentary rock are mold fossils. A mold is a visible shape that was left after an animal or plant was buried in sediment and then decayed away. In some cases, a hollow mold later becomes filled with minerals, producing a cast fossil. The cast fossil is a solid model in the shape of the organism. If you think of the mold as a shoeprint, the cast would be what would result if sand filled the print and hardened into stone.

2 Petrified Wood The stone fossil of a tree is called petrified wood. In certain conditions, a fallen tree can become covered with sediments. Over time, water passes through the sediments and into the tree's cells. Minerals that are carried in the water take the place of the cells, producing a stone likeness of the tree.

3 Carbon Films Carbon is an element that is found in every living thing. Sometimes when a dead plant or animal decays, its carbon is left behind as a visible layer. This image is called a carbon film. Carbon films can show details of soft parts of animals and plants that are rarely seen in other fossils.

4 Trace Fossils Do you want to know how fast a dinosaur could run? Trace fossils might be able to tell you. These are not parts of an animal or impressions of it, but rather evidence of an animal's presence in a given location. Trace fossils include preserved footprints, trails, animal holes, and even feces. By comparing these clues with what is known about modern animals, scientists can learn how prehistoric animals may have lived, what they ate, and how they behaved. For instance, dinosaur tracks can be studied to learn how fast dinosaurs ran.

RESOURCE CENTER
CLASSZONE.COM
Learn more about fossils.

These ancient logs in the Painted Desert Wilderness in Arizona have been preserved as petrified wood for around 225 million years. Minerals replaced the wood to make the stone logs.

CHECK YOUR READING What do carbon film fossils show that trace fossils do not show?

Fossils in Rocks

Rock fossils show shapes and traces of past life.

① Molds and Casts

A mold and cast are formed in the steps below.

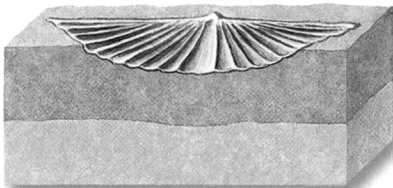

An organism dies and falls into soft sediment.

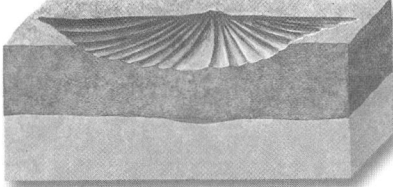

Over time, the sediment becomes rock and the organism decays, leaving a mold.

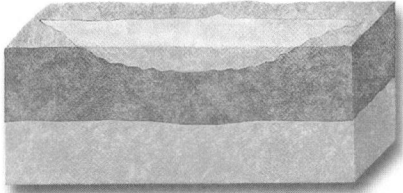

Minerals fill the mold and make a cast of the organism.

② Petrified Wood

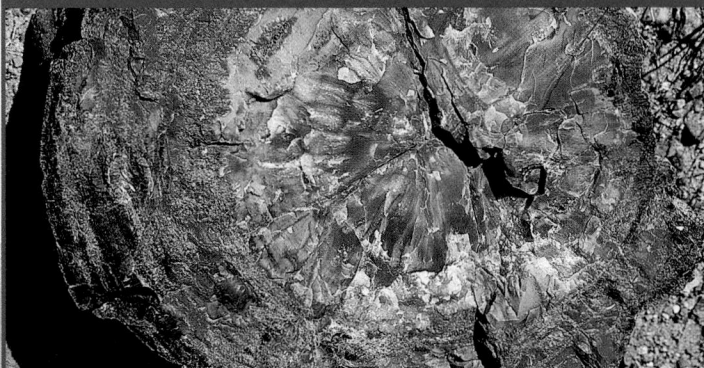

In this close-up, you can see the minerals that replaced the wood, forming petrified wood.

③ Carbon Films

This carbon film of a moth is about 10 million years old. Carbon films are especially useful because they can show details of the soft parts of organisms.

④ Trace Fossils

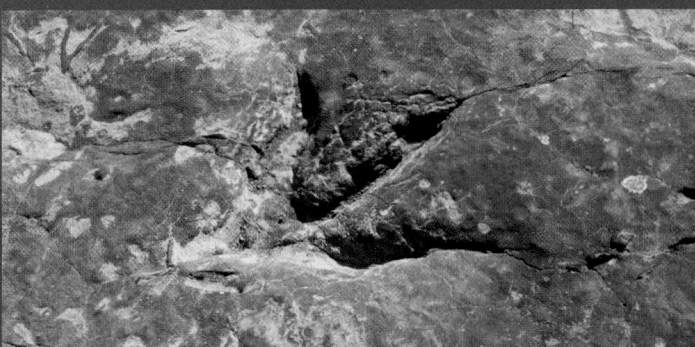

A trace fossil, such as this footprint of a dinosaur in rock, can provide important information about where an animal lived and how it walked and ran.

READING VISUALS What is similar about mold-and-cast fossils and petrified wood?

Fossils and other natural evidence show changes in life and the environment.

Fossils reveal that Earth has undergone many changes over billions of years. Scientists study fossils to learn what organisms and animals once lived in places where the fossils were found. Today the land around the South Pole is mostly covered by ice, but fossils show that crocodiles, dinosaurs, and palm trees once lived on that land. The land was once much closer to the equator.

The earliest fossils are of tiny one-celled organisms that lived in an environment without oxygen. Three billion years ago, humans or the land animals we know today could not have breathed the air on Earth. Fossils also record the disappearance of many species.

Tree Rings

The rings in tree trunks are also a tool for studying the past. The width of tree rings varies, depending on how much the tree grows in various years. In dry years, a tree does not grow very much and the rings for those years are thin. A thick ring is a sign of a good year for growth, with enough rainfall. By analyzing the tree rings of many old trees, scientists can develop an accurate history of overall weather patterns over time.

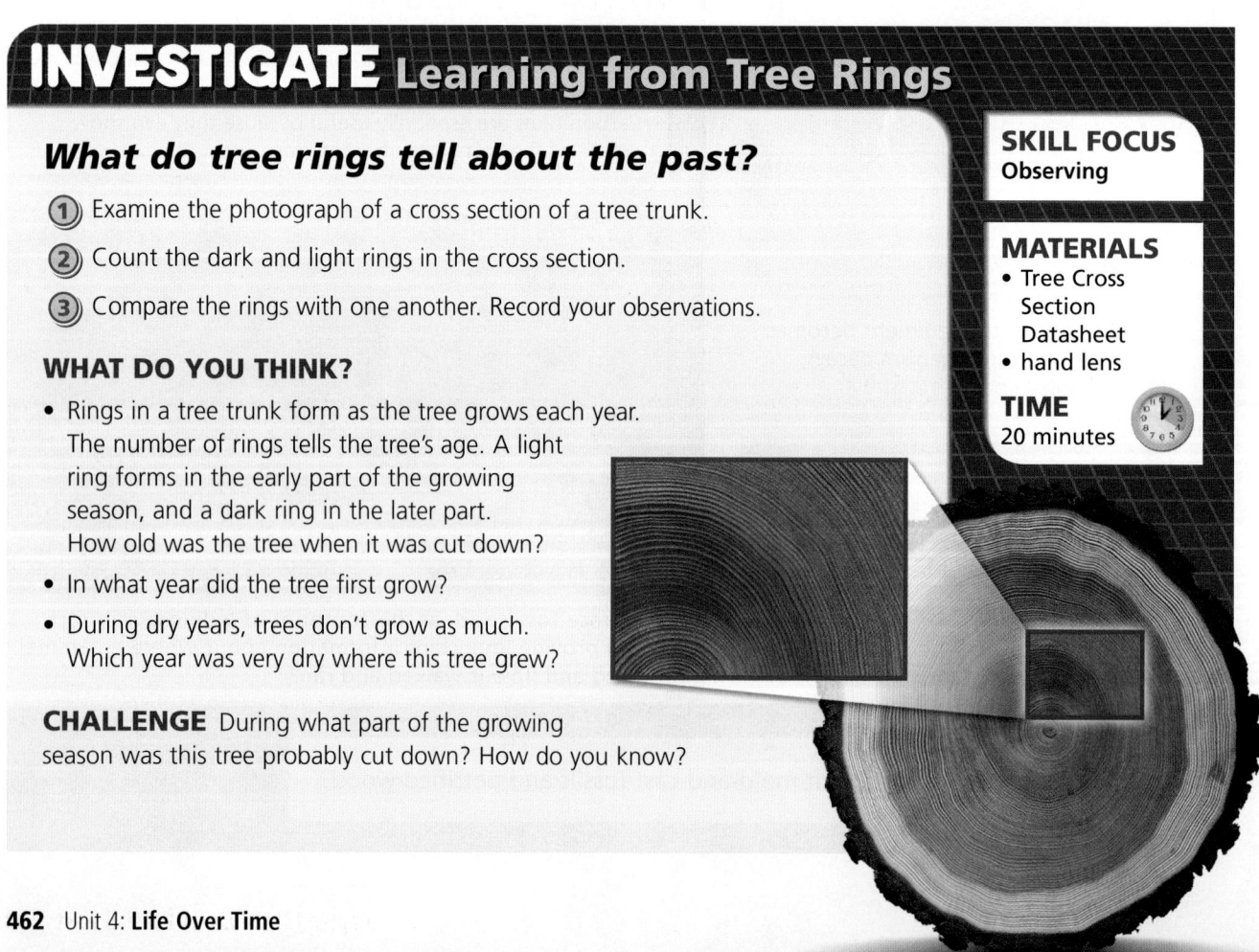

INVESTIGATE Learning from Tree Rings

What do tree rings tell about the past?

① Examine the photograph of a cross section of a tree trunk.

② Count the dark and light rings in the cross section.

③ Compare the rings with one another. Record your observations.

WHAT DO YOU THINK?

- Rings in a tree trunk form as the tree grows each year. The number of rings tells the tree's age. A light ring forms in the early part of the growing season, and a dark ring in the later part. How old was the tree when it was cut down?

- In what year did the tree first grow?

- During dry years, trees don't grow as much. Which year was very dry where this tree grew?

CHALLENGE During what part of the growing season was this tree probably cut down? How do you know?

SKILL FOCUS
Observing

MATERIALS
- Tree Cross Section Datasheet
- hand lens

TIME
20 minutes

These scientists are removing an ice core from a thick ice sheet in Antarctica. Ice at the bottom end is oldest.

Scientists study tiny specks of dirt in the ice, looking for signs of past microscopic organisms.

Ice Cores

In Greenland and Antarctica, snowfall has built up gigantic layers of ice that can be much deeper than the height of skyscrapers and as much as 530,000 years old at the bottom. Scientists drill into the ice and remove ice cores for study. An **ice core** is a tubular sample that shows the layers of snow and ice that have built up over thousands of years. The layers serve as a vertical timeline of part of Earth's past.

Scientists analyze air trapped in the ice to learn how the atmosphere has changed. Increases in dust or ash in the ice show when major volcanic eruptions occurred somewhere on Earth. Differences in the air content at different levels of the ice indicate how much temperatures went up and down, showing how long ice ages and warm periods lasted. This information can help scientists understand how Earth's climate might be changing now and how it might change in the future.

 **CHECK YOUR READING** How does an ice core provide information about Earth's history?

13.1 Review

KEY CONCEPTS

1. What can rock fossils and original remains show about Earth's past?

2. Why do rock fossils form in sedimentary rock and not in igneous rock?

3. How do tree rings and ice cores help scientists understand how Earth has changed over time?

CRITICAL THINKING

4. **Infer** If you uncovered fossils of tropical fish and palm trees, what could you say about the environment at the time the fossils formed?

5. **Synthesize** Why might ancient lake and sea beds be rich sources of fossils?

⬤ CHALLENGE

6. **Rank** Which evidence—a fossil, a tree ring, or an ice core—would be most helpful to a historian studying how the Pilgrims grew food at Plymouth Colony in 1620? Explain your reasoning.

Could *T. Rex* Win a Race?

If you want to know how fast a dinosaur ran, study a chicken. Two scientists, John Hutchinson and Mariano Garcia, did just that. They wanted to know if *Tyrannosaurus rex* was actually as fast on its feet as some people said it was.

To find the answer, the scientists worked to figure out how strong the dinosaur's legs were. What they needed to know was how much muscle the giant dinosaur had in its legs. Yet they couldn't study *T. rex's* muscle mass directly, because there are no complete remains of dinosaur muscle, just bones. This is where the chicken comes in.

Fossils and Fowls

The bone fossils of dinosaurs suggest that birds and dinosaurs have some similarities. Using the chicken as a model for *T. rex,* the scientists found that a chicken needs at least one-tenth of its body mass to be leg muscle. They measured chickens and found they have even more than that, about one-fifth.

The scientists used a computer program to learn if a chicken the size of a 5900 kilogram (10,000 lb) *T. rex* would be able to run. The computer model showed that a chicken that size would need 90 percent of its body mass in its legs to run fast. By connecting their knowledge of dinosaur fossils and chickens, the two scientists showed that *T. rex* was not a fast runner.

Still, the giant dinosaur was not exactly a slowpoke. The scientists also calculated that with its 2.5 meter (8 ft) legs *T. rex* could travel at a rate of about 24 kilometers per hour (15 mi/h). For many people, that's running speed.

EXPLORE

1. **SYNTHESIZE** Based on what you have read, what might be the relationship between the size of an animal and its speed?

2. **DRAW CONCLUSIONS** Why do you think some scientists think that *T. rex,* a meat eater, mostly ate animals already dead instead of live prey?

13.2

KEY CONCEPT
Rocks provide a timeline for Earth.

Sunshine State STANDARDS

SC.D.1.3.1: The student knows that mechanical and chemical activities shape and reshape the Earth's land surface by eroding rock and soil in some areas and depositing them in other areas, sometimes in seasonal layers.

SC.D.1.3.2: The student knows that over the whole Earth, organisms are growing, dying, and decaying as new organisms are produced by the old ones.

BEFORE, you learned

- Fossils contain information about the past
- Fossils, ice cores, and tree rings record conditions and changes in the environment

NOW, you will learn

- What the relative ages of rock layers reveal about Earth
- How index fossils are used to determine the ages of rock layers
- How the absolute ages of rocks are determined

THINK ABOUT

How old are these bicycles?

You might not know exactly when each of the bicycles shown was made, but you can probably tell which is the oldest. How could you arrange these bikes in order of their ages without knowing how old each is?

VOCABULARY
relative age p. 465
index fossil p. 467
absolute age p. 469
half-life p. 469

Layers of sedimentary rocks show relative age.

Fossils are clues in the story of Earth's past. But for the story to make sense, the clues need to be arranged in order. **Relative age** is the age of an event or object in relation to other events or objects. You probably know relative ages for many things in your life. For example, if a friend tells you she has an older brother and a younger brother, you know the relative ages of her brothers even if you don't know their exact ages.

Until the beginning of the 1900s, geologists didn't have a way to determine the exact ages of objects that existed in Earth's past. Instead, they reconstructed Earth's story based on the relative ages of different clues. Today there are still many parts of Earth's history that cannot be given exact ages. Determining relative age continues to be an important way of piecing together the puzzle of Earth's past.

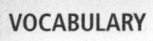
VOCABULARY
Add a description wheel for *relative age* to your notebook.

Sedimentary rock layers contain information about the relative ages of events and objects in Earth's history. As you read earlier, sedimentary rocks form from the sediments that fall to the bottom of lakes, rivers, and seas. Over time, the sediments pile up to form horizontal layers of sedimentary rocks. The bottom layer of rock forms first, which means it is oldest. Each layer above that is younger, and the top layer is youngest of all. This ordering is relative because you cannot be sure exactly when each layer formed, only that each layer is younger then the one below it.

When horizontal layers of sedimentary rock are undisturbed, the youngest layer is always on top, as shown in the photograph on the left below. But over millions of years, the movement of tectonic plates can disturb rock layers. A whole set of layers can get turned on its side. Rock layers can get bent, or even folded over, like taco shells that begin as flat tortillas. If a set of rock layers has been disturbed, the youngest layer may no longer be on top. One way scientists determine the original order is to compare the disturbed rock layers with a similar but undisturbed stack of layers.

CHECK YOUR READING When might the youngest layer in a set of sedimentary rock layers not be on top?

Rock Layers

Undisturbed Layers

younger

older

Because sedimentary rock forms in layers, the oldest layer of undisturbed sedimentary rock will be on the bottom and the youngest on top.

Disturbed Layers

older

younger

If the rock layers are bent, they may no longer be in order from oldest to youngest.

READING VISUALS Where are the youngest layers in each photo?

Igneous Rock and Sedimentary Layers

Sedimentary rock layers can also be disturbed by igneous rock. Molten rock from within Earth can force its way up through the layers above it, cooling and forming igneous rock. Because the sedimentary rock layers have to be present before the molten rock cuts through them, the igneous rock must be younger than the layers it cuts through.

VISUALIZATION
CLASSZONE.COM

Watch molten rock cut through layers of sedimentary rock.

1 Over time, sand and silt form horizontal layers of sedimentary rock.

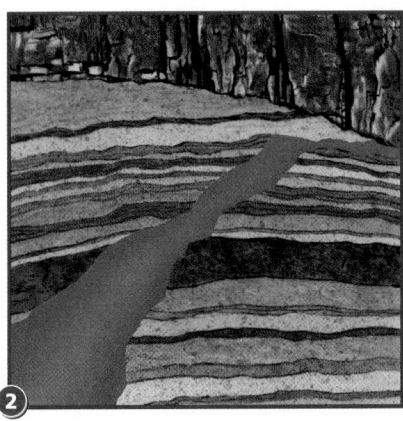

2 Deep underground, molten rock cuts through the sedimentary rock layers.

3 A river gradually wears away the rock, exposing the younger igneous rock.

If the molten rock erupts and flows onto the surface, it forms a layer of igneous rock on top of the layers of sedimentary rock. Over time, more sedimentary rock layers may form on top of the igneous rock. The igneous rock layer is younger than the sedimentary layers under it and older than the sedimentary layers that form on top of it.

 **CHECK YOUR READING** Why is igneous rock always younger than any rock it cuts through?

Index Fossils

Fossils contained within sedimentary rock can offer clues about the age of the rock. An organism that was fossilized in rock must have lived during the same time span in which the rock formed. Using information from rocks and other natural evidence, scientists have determined when specific fossilized organisms existed. If people know how long ago a fossilized organism lived, then they can figure out the age of the rock in which the fossil was found.

Fossils of organisms that were common, that lived in many areas, and that existed only during specific spans of time are called **index fossils.** These characteristics of index fossils make them especially useful for figuring out when rock layers formed.

This rock contains the index fossil *Arnioceras semicostatum,* an organism that lived between 206 million and 144 million years ago.

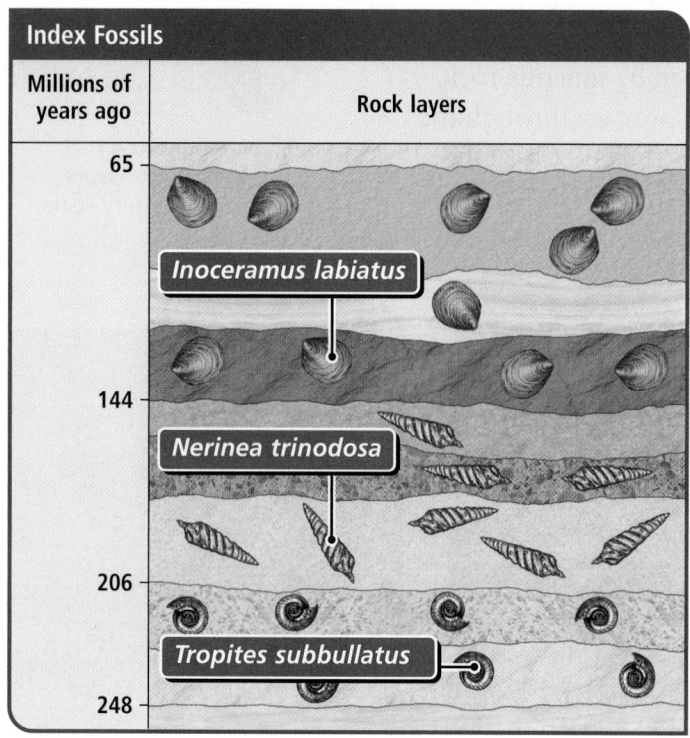

Index Fossils

Millions of years ago	Rock layers
65	*Inoceramus labiatus*
144	*Nerinea trinodosa*
206	
248	*Tropites subbullatus*

Index fossils can be used to estimate the ages of the rocks in which they are found.

The mollusk *Inoceramus labiatus,* for example, is a kind of sea animal that appeared 144 million years ago and went extinct 65 million years ago. So, if you find a rock that contains a fossil of this mollusk, the rock must be between 144 million and 65 million years old because this mollusk lived during that time span.

The chart shows a cross section of rock layers in which *Inoceramus labiatus* and two other index fossils are found. *Nerinea trinodosa* is a kind of sea animal that lived between 206 million and 144 million years ago. *Tropites subbullatus* is a kind of sea animal that lived between 248 million and 206 million years ago.

Remember that one characteristic of index fossils is that they are widespread— they are found in many different parts of the world. Because they are widespread, index fossils can be used to compare the ages of rock layers in different parts of the world.

INVESTIGATE Relative and Absolute Age

How can newspapers model rock layers?

PROCEDURE

1. Have one person in your group arrange the newspapers in a pile with the oldest newspaper on the bottom and the newest on top.

2. After the newspapers are stacked, place one pencil between two newspapers and the other pencil between two different newspapers. Use the model to answer the questions below.

WHAT DO YOU THINK?

- If the newspapers were really placed on the stack on the days they were published, which pencil has probably been there longer?

- Look at the dates on the newspapers. Now what can you say about when the pencils were placed on the stack?

CHALLENGE How does what you could tell about the "ages" of the pencils before looking at the dates differ from what you could tell after looking?

SKILL FOCUS
Making models

MATERIALS
- 5 or more newspapers with different dates
- 2 pencils

TIME
20 minutes

Radioactive dating can show absolute age.

Think again about the friend who tells you that she has two brothers, one older than she is and one younger. You know the order in which they were born—that is, their relative ages. The older brother, however, might be 1 year older or 20 years older. The exact age of the younger brother is also still a mystery. To find out how much older or younger your friend's brothers are, you need to know their actual ages. The actual age of an event or object is called its **absolute age.**

 **CHECK YOUR READING** What is the difference between relative age and absolute age? Use an example in your explanation.

Half-Life

Because scientists can't ask a rock its age, they have had to find a different way of determining the absolute ages of rocks. The solution lies in the smallest unit of matter, the atom. Atoms make up everything on Earth, including you and rocks. The atoms of many chemical elements exist in various forms. Some of these forms are unstable and break down over time into another form. This breakdown—called radioactivity—is a very useful clock because a particular unstable form of an element always breaks down at the same rate into the same other form.

The rate of change of a radioactive element is measured in half-lives. A **half-life** is the length of time it takes for half of the atoms in a sample of a radioactive element to change from an unstable form into another form. Different elements have different half-lives, ranging from fractions of a second to billions of years.

Just as a ruler is not a very useful tool for measuring the distance between planets, elements with very short half-lives are not very useful for measuring the ages of rocks. Instead, elements with half-lives of millions to billions of years are used to date rocks. For example, uranium 235 has a half-life of 704 million years. Uranium 235 is an unstable element found in some igneous rocks. Over time, uranium 235 breaks down into lead 207. Using information from radioactive dating of rocks, scientists estimate that Earth is around 4.6 billion years old.

Over time, a radioactive element breaks down at a constant rate into another form.

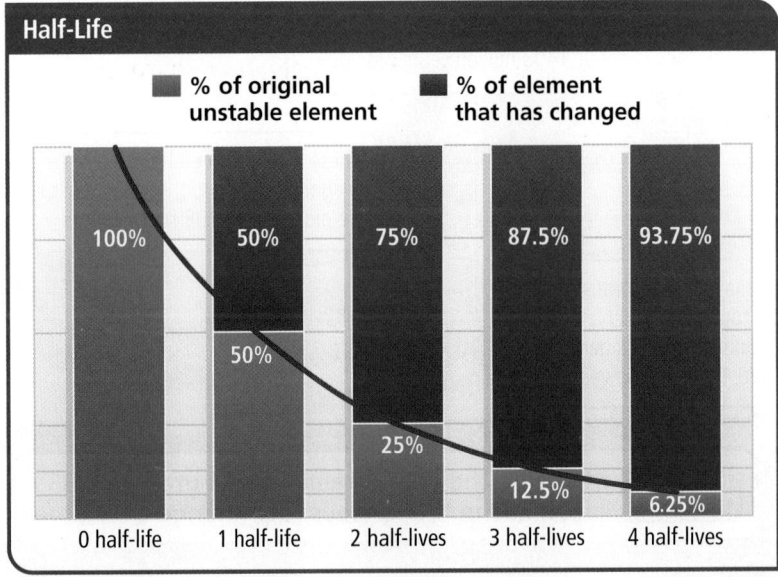

Half-Life

■ % of original unstable element   ■ % of element that has changed

0 half-life	1 half-life	2 half-lives	3 half-lives	4 half-lives
100%	50% / 50%	75% / 25%	87.5% / 12.5%	93.75% / 6.25%

Radioactive Breakdown and Dating Rock Layers

Igneous rocks contain radioactive elements that break down over time. This breakdown can be used to tell the ages of the rocks.

① 1408 Million Years Ago

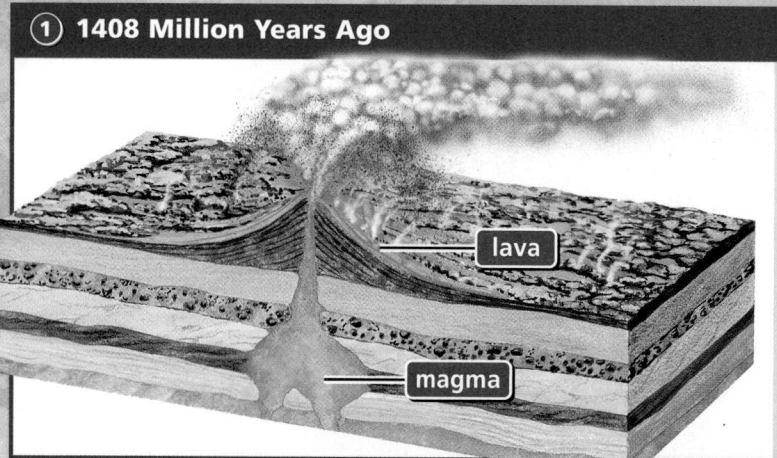

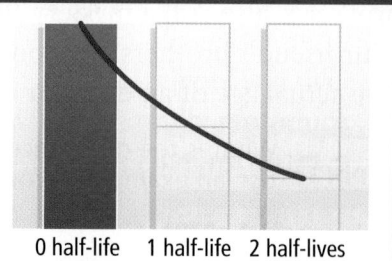

0 half-life   1 half-life   2 half-lives

When magma first hardens into rock, it contains some uranium 235 and no lead 207.

② 704 Million Years Ago

Over time, the rock formed by the volcano wore away and new sedimentary rock layers formed.

igneous rock

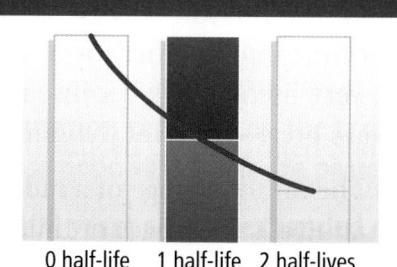

0 half-life   1 half-life   2 half-lives

After 704 million years, or one half-life, half of the uranium 235 in the igneous rock has broken down into lead 207.

③ Today

Radioactive dating shows that this igneous rock is about 1408 million years old.

These layers formed before the magma cut through, so they must be older than 1408 million years.

The layers that formed on top of the igneous rock must be younger than 1408 million years.

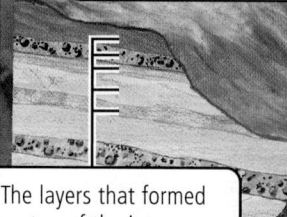

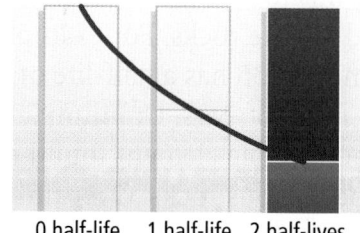

0 half-life   1 half-life   2 half-lives

After 1408 million years, or 2 half-lives, only one-fourth of the uranium 235 in the igneous rock remains.

READING VISUALS How do the relative amounts of uranium 235 and lead 207 in the igneous rock change over time?

Radioactive dating works best with igneous rocks. Sedimentary rocks are formed from material that came from other rocks. For this reason, any measurements would show when the original rocks were formed, not when the sedimentary rock itself formed.

Just as uranium 235 can be used to date igneous rocks, carbon 14 can be used to find the ages of the remains of some things that were once alive. Carbon 14 is an unstable form of carbon, an element found in all living things. Carbon 14 has a half-life of 5730 years. It is useful for dating objects between about 100 and 70,000 years old, such as the wood from an ancient tool or the remains of an animal from the Ice Age.

RESOURCE CENTER
CLASSZONE.COM

Find out more about how scientists date rocks.

Using Absolute and Relative Age

Scientists must piece together information from all methods of determining age to figure out the story of Earth's past.

- Radioactive dating of igneous rocks reveals their absolute age.
- Interpreting layers of sedimentary rock shows the relative order of events.
- Fossils help to sort out the sedimentary record.

You have read that it is not possible to date sedimentary rocks with radioactivity directly. Geologists, however, can date any igneous rock that might have cut through or formed a layer between sedimentary layers. Then, using the absolute age of the igneous rock, geologists can estimate the ages of nearby sedimentary layers.

CHECK YOUR READING   How might the absolute age of an igneous rock layer help scientists to determine the ages of nearby sedimentary rock layers?

13.2 Review

KEY CONCEPTS

1. What can you tell from undisturbed rock layers? Discuss the concept of relative age in your answer.

2. How can index fossils help scientists determine the ages of rock layers?

3. What property of radioactive elements makes them useful for determining absolute age?

CRITICAL THINKING

4. **Provide Examples** What are some things in your life for which you know only their relative ages?

5. **Apply** In your daily life are there index events (like index fossils) that tell you approximate times even when you can't see a clock? What are they?

○ CHALLENGE

6. **Apply** A rock contains a radioactive element with a half-life of 100 million years. Tests show that the element in the rock has gone through three half-lives. How old is the rock?

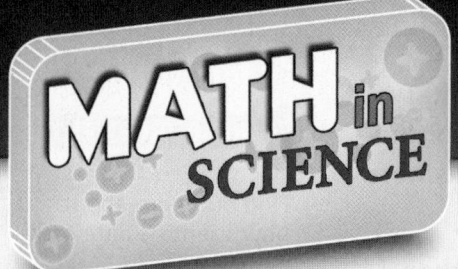

SKILL: INTERPRETING GRAPHS

Dating Mammoth Bones

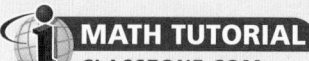

MATH TUTORIAL

CLASSZONE.COM

Click on Math Tutorial for more help with reading line graphs and multiplying whole numbers.

Mammoths were close relatives of today's elephants. Mammoths lived earlier in the Cenozoic era and are now extinct.

Imagine that scientists find an ancient lakebed with hundreds of well-preserved mammoth bones in it. They are able to measure the amount of carbon 14 that remains in the bones. Carbon 14 has a half-life of approximately 5700 years. How could you use the half-life of carbon 14 to determine how old the bones are?

Example

Mammoth bone A has $\frac{1}{4}$ of its original carbon 14. How old is mammoth bone A? Use the half-life of carbon 14 and the graph below.

(1) Find $\frac{1}{4}$ on the vertical axis and follow the line out to the red curved line.

(2) Then follow the line down to the horizontal axis to determine that the carbon 14 in the bone has been through 2 half-lives.

(3) 5700 × 2 = 11,400

    ↑   ↑

years per   number of
half-life   half-lives

ANSWER Bone A is 11,400 years old.

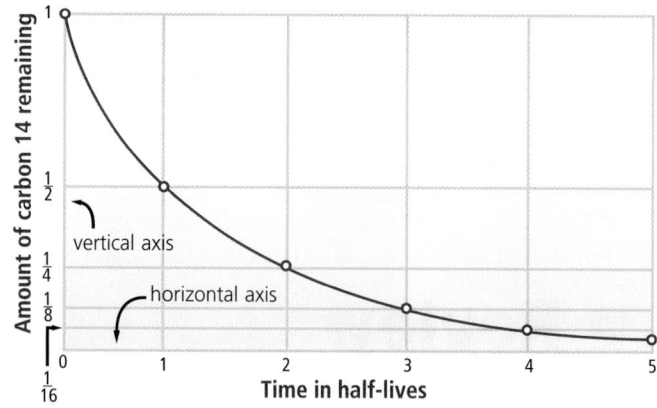

Half-Lives

Answer the following questions.

1. Mammoth bone B has $\frac{1}{8}$ of its original carbon 14. How old is mammoth bone B?

2. Mammoth bone C has $\frac{1}{16}$ of its original carbon 14. How old is mammoth bone C?

CHALLENGE Mammoth bone D is 28,500 years old. What fraction of the original carbon 14 remains in bone D?

KEY CONCEPT

13.3 The geologic time scale shows Earth's past.

Sunshine State STANDARDS

SC.D.1.3.2: The student knows that over the whole Earth, organisms are growing, dying, and decaying as new organisms are produced by the old ones.

SC.D.1.3.5: The student understands concepts of time and size relating to the interaction of Earth's processes (e.g., lightning striking in a split second as opposed to the shifting of the Earth's plates altering the landscape, distance between atoms measured in Angstrom units as opposed to distance between stars measured in light-years).

SC.H.1.3.6: The student recognizes the scientific contributions that are made by individuals of diverse backgrounds, interests, talents, and motivations.

BEFORE, you learned

- Rocks and fossils give clues about life on Earth
- Layers of sedimentary rocks show relative ages
- Radioactive dating of igneous rocks gives absolute ages

NOW, you will learn

- That Earth is always changing and has always changed in the past
- How the geologic time scale describes Earth's history

VOCABULARY

uniformitarianism p. 474
geologic time scale p. 475

EXPLORE Time Scales

How do you make a time scale of your year?

PROCEDURE

1. Divide your paper into three columns.

2. In the last column, list six to ten events in the school year in the order they will happen. For example, you may include a particular soccer game or a play.

3. In the middle column, organize those events into larger time periods, such as soccer season, rehearsal week, or whatever you choose.

4. In the first column, organize those time periods into even larger ones.

MATERIALS
- pen
- sheet of paper

WHAT DO YOU THINK?
How does putting events into categories help you to see the relationship among events?

OUTLINE
Remember to start an outline in your notebook for this section.

I. Main idea
  A. Supporting idea
    1. Detail
    2. Detail
  B. Supporting idea

Earth is constantly changing.

In the late 1700s a Scottish geologist named James Hutton began to question some of the ideas that were then common about Earth and how Earth changes. He found fossils and saw them as evidence of life forms that no longer existed. He also noticed that different types of fossilized creatures were found in different layers of rocks. Based on his observations of rocks and other natural evidence, Hutton came up with a new theory to explain the story told in the rocks. He was the first to present a hypothesis about Earth's changing over time.

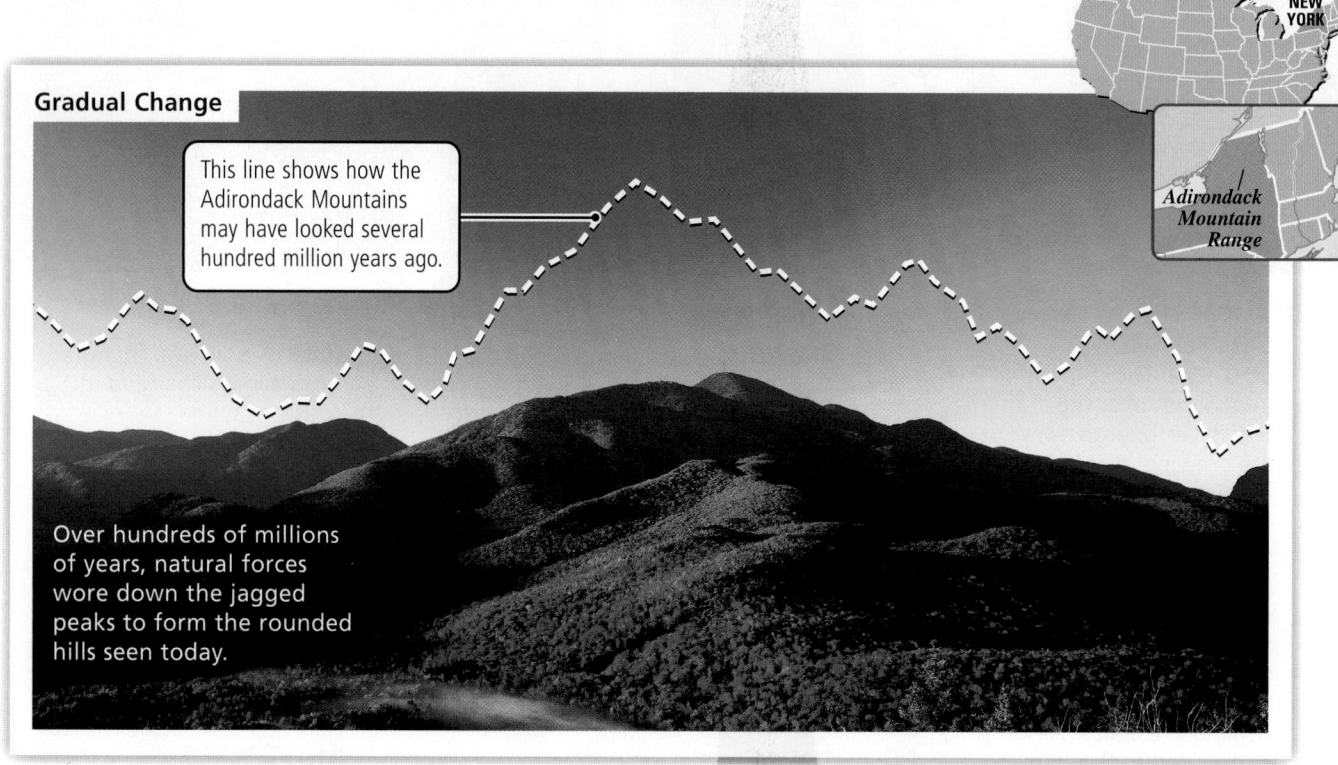

Gradual Change

This line shows how the Adirondack Mountains may have looked several hundred million years ago.

Over hundreds of millions of years, natural forces wore down the jagged peaks to form the rounded hills seen today.

NEW YORK

Adirondack Mountain Range

READING TIP

To remember what *uniformitarianism* means, think of the word *uniform*, which means "same."

Hutton recognized that Earth is a constantly changing place. Wind, water, heat, and cold break down rocks. Other processes, such as volcanic eruptions and the building up of sediment, continue to form new rock. Earth's interior is constantly churning with powerful forces that move, fold, raise, and swallow the surface of the planet.

The same processes that changed Earth in the past continue to occur today. A billion years ago a river would have carried particles of rock just as a river does today. Similarly, volcanoes in the past would have erupted just as volcanoes do today. Hutton's theory of **uniformitarianism** (YOO-nuh-fawr-mih-TAIR-ee-uh-nihz-uhm) is the idea that

- Earth is an always-changing place
- the same forces of change at work today were at work in the past

Although this idea may seem simple, it is very important. The theory of uniformitarianism is the basis of modern geology.

Some changes on Earth are gradual. Mountains form and are worn down over many millions of years. Climate and the amount of ice on land can change over hundreds or thousands of years. Other changes are fast. A volcanic eruption, an earthquake, or a flood can cause huge changes over a period of minutes or days. Fast or slow, Earth is always changing.

CHECK YOUR READING What was the new idea that Hutton had about Earth? Describe the idea in your own words.

Fast Change

WASHINGTON

Mount St. Helens

READING ViSUALS **COMPARE AND CONTRAST** These photos show Mount St. Helens before and after it erupted in 1980. What rapid changes occurred during the eruption?

The geologic time scale divides Earth's history.

From a person's point of view, 4.6 billion years is a tremendous amount of time. To help make sense of it, scientists have organized Earth's history in a chart called the geologic time scale. The **geologic time scale** divides Earth's history into intervals of time defined by major events or changes on Earth.

Scientists use information from fossils and radioactive dating to figure out what happened over the 4.6 billion years of Earth's history. The oldest evidence of life is from about 3.8 billion years ago, but life may be even older. Organisms with more than one cell appeared around 1 billion years ago, and modern humans appeared only 100,000 years ago.

Imagine Earth's history compressed into one year. If Earth forms on January 1, the first life we have evidence for appears in the beginning of March. Life with more than one cell appears months later, in the middle of October. Humans do not show up until 11 minutes before midnight on the last day of the year, and they do not understand how old Earth is until about a second before midnight.

first humans

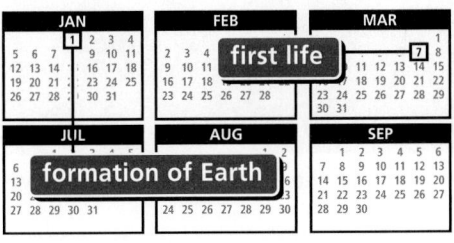

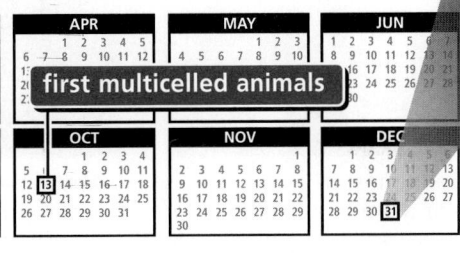

If Earth's history is compared to a calendar year, humans appear just before midnight on December 31.

READING TiP

As you read, find the eons, eras, and periods on the chart below.

Divisions of Geologic Time

The geologic time scale is divided into eons, eras, periods, and epochs (EHP-uhks). Unlike divisions of time such as days or minutes, the divisions of the geologic time scale have no fixed lengths. Instead, they are based on changes or events recorded in rocks and fossils.

Eon The largest unit of time is an eon. Earth's 4.6-billion-year history is divided into four eons.

Era Eons may be divided into eras. The most recent eon is divided into three eras: the Paleozoic, the Mesozoic, and the Cenozoic.

Period Each era is subdivided into a number of periods.

Epoch The periods of the Cenozoic, the most recent era, are further divided into epochs.

Geologic Time Scale

The geologic time scale divides Earth's history into eons, eras, periods, and epochs.

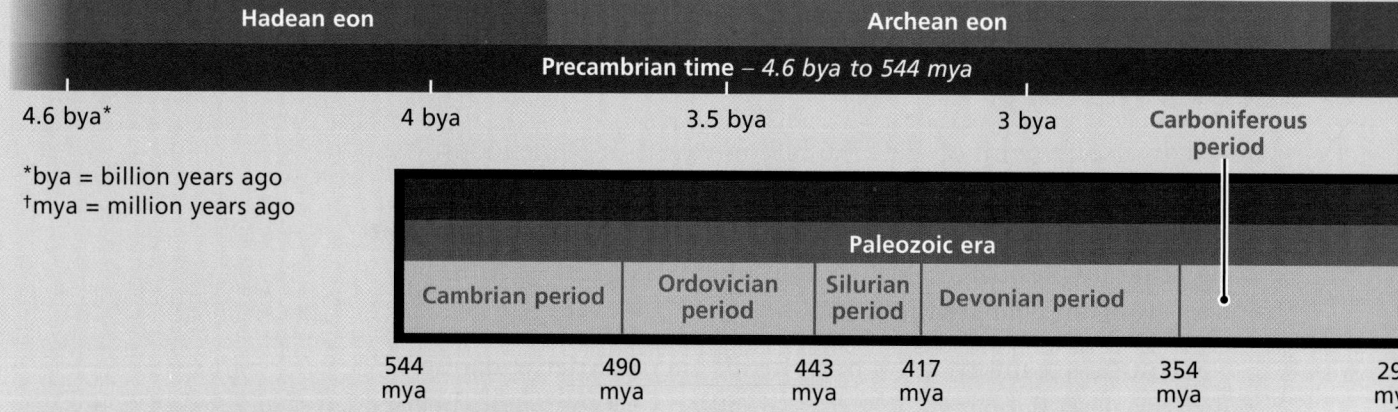

Hadean eon			Archean eon	

Precambrian time – 4.6 bya to 544 mya

4.6 bya*   4 bya   3.5 bya   3 bya   Carboniferous period

*bya = billion years ago
†mya = million years ago

Paleozoic era				
Cambrian period	Ordovician period	Silurian period	Devonian period	

544 mya   490 mya   443 mya   417 mya   354 mya   29• my•

Precambrian Time at 3.6 Billion Years Ago

For nearly 4 billion years, during most of Precambrian time, no plants or animals existed.

Paleozoic Era at 544 Million Years Ago

At the beginning of the Paleozoic era, all life lived in the oceans.

The Hadean, Archean, and Proterozoic eons together are called Precambrian time and make up almost 90 percent of Earth's history. The fossil record for Precambrian time consists mostly of tiny organisms that cannot be seen without a microscope. Other early forms of life had soft bodies that rarely formed into fossils.

The Phanerozoic eon stretches from the end of Precambrian time to the present. Because so many more changes are recorded in the fossil record of this eon, it is further divided into smaller units of time. The smaller time divisions relate to how long certain conditions and life forms on Earth lasted and how quickly they changed or became extinct.

**FLORIDA
Content Preview**

Notice how changes on Earth's surface over time affected the kinds of animals and plants that lived at the time as you will learn in Chapter 14.

 **CHECK YOUR READING** What part of geologic time makes up most of Earth's history?

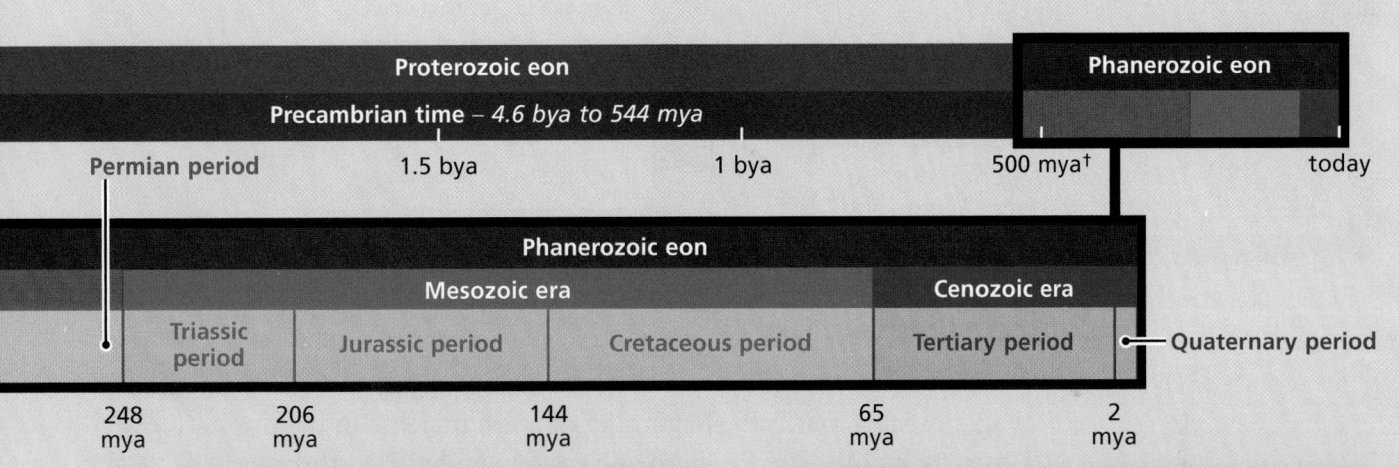

Proterozoic eon			Phanerozoic eon
Precambrian time – 4.6 bya to 544 mya			

| Permian period | 1.5 bya | 1 bya | 500 mya† | today |

Phanerozoic eon				
Mesozoic era			Cenozoic era	
Triassic period	Jurassic period	Cretaceous period	Tertiary period	Quaternary period

| 248 mya | 206 mya | 144 mya | 65 mya | 2 mya |

Mesozoic Era at 195 to 65 Million Years Ago

During the Mesozoic era, dinosaurs lived along with the first mammals, birds, and flowering plants.

Cenozoic Era at Present Day

The first humans appeared in the later part of the Cenozoic era, which continues today.

Rock Layers in the Grand Canyon

Rock layers offer clues about conditions on Earth when the layers formed.

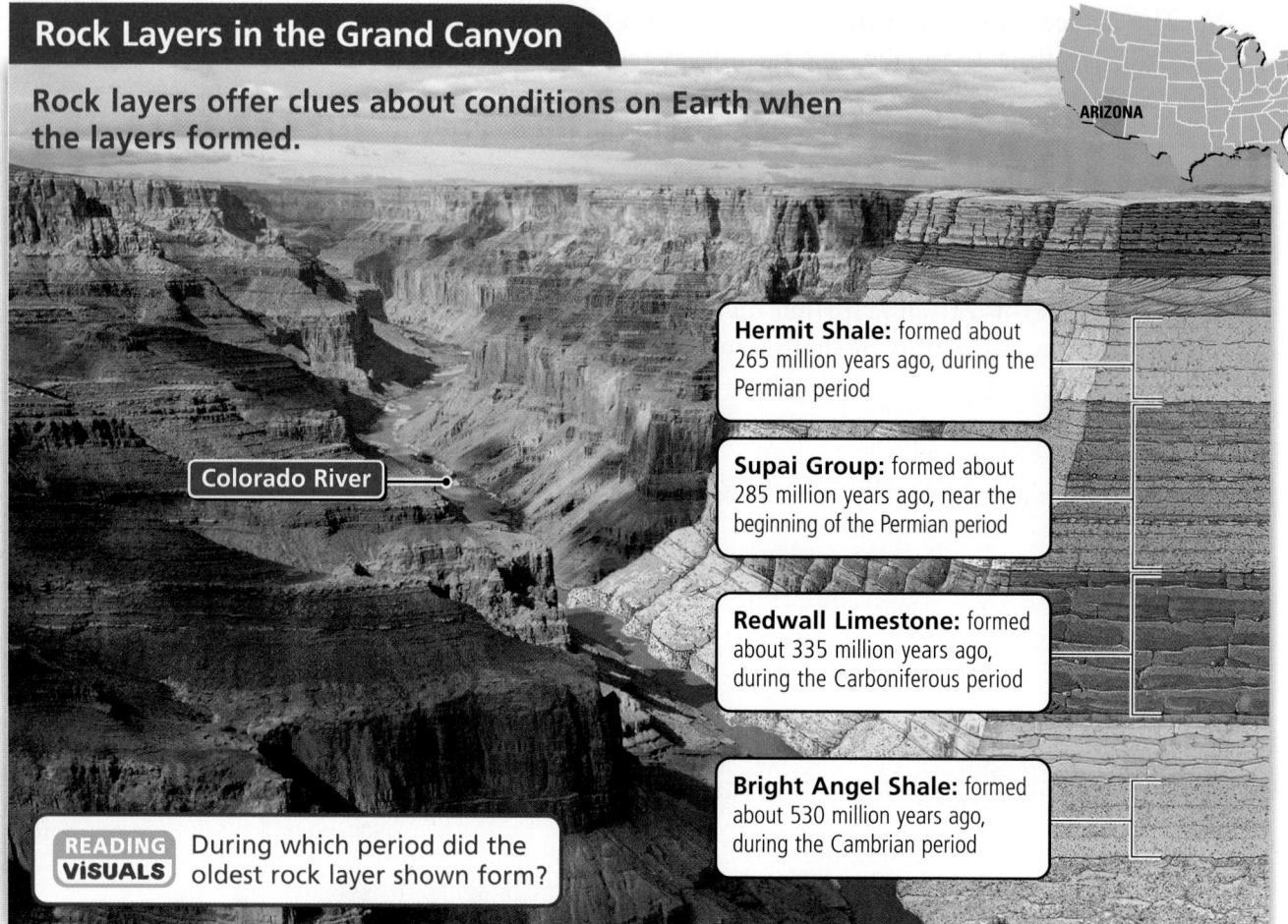

ARIZONA

Colorado River

Hermit Shale: formed about 265 million years ago, during the Permian period

Supai Group: formed about 285 million years ago, near the beginning of the Permian period

Redwall Limestone: formed about 335 million years ago, during the Carboniferous period

Bright Angel Shale: formed about 530 million years ago, during the Cambrian period

READING VISUALS During which period did the oldest rock layer shown form?

Phanerozoic Eon

The most recent eon, the Phanerozoic, began around 544 million years ago. Its start marks the beginning of a fast increase in the diversity, or variety, of life. The Phanerozoic eon is divided into three eras:

- the Paleozoic, whose name means "ancient life"
- the Mesozoic, whose name means "middle life"
- the Cenozoic, whose name means "recent life"

The Paleozoic era is the first era of the Phanerozoic eon. At the start of the Paleozoic, all life lived in the ocean. Fish, the first animals with backbones, developed during this time. Toward the end of this era, life moved onto land. Reptiles, insects, and ferns were common. A mass extinction occurred at the end of the Paleozoic era, 248 million years ago. A mass extinction is when many different life forms all die out, or become extinct, at once. The cause of this extinction is not completely understood.

The Mesozoic era spans the next 183 million years and is best known for the dinosaurs that ruled Earth. Mammals, birds, and flowering plants also first appeared during the Mesozoic. For some of this time, parts of North America were covered by a vast sea. The end of the

READING TiP

As you read, find each era in the geologic time scale on pages 476–477.

Mesozoic marks the end of the dinosaurs and many other animals in another mass extinction. This extinction may have been caused by one or more giant asteroids that slammed into Earth, throwing huge amounts of dust into the air. The dust blocked the sunlight, causing plants to die and, along with them, many animals.

The Cenozoic era, the most recent era, began 65 million years ago and continues today. The Cenozoic is often called the Age of Mammals because it marks the time when mammals became a main category of life on Earth.

Around 22,000 years ago, early humans used mammoth bones as building materials. This reconstruction shows what a bone hut may have looked like.

The Cenozoic era is divided into two periods: the Tertiary and the Quaternary. The Quaternary period stretches from about 2 million years ago to the present. Most of the Quaternary has been a series of ice ages, with much of Europe, North America, and Asia covered in thick sheets of ice. Mammoths, saber-toothed cats, and other giant mammals were common during the first part of the Quaternary. Fossils of the first modern humans are also from this period; they are about 100,000 years old.

As the amount of ice on land shrank and grew, the ocean levels rose and fell. When the ocean levels fell, exposed land served as natural bridges that connected continents previously separated by water. The land bridges allowed humans and other animals to spread around the planet. It now seems that the end of Quaternary may be defined by the rise of human civilization.

CHECK YOUR READING How did falling ocean levels lead to the spread of humans and other animals on Earth?

13.3 Review

KEY CONCEPTS

1. Describe the concept of uniformitarianism.
2. What does the geologic time scale measure?
3. What was life like on Earth for most of its history?

CRITICAL THINKING

4. **Apply** What period, era, and eon do you live in?
5. **Evaluate** Some cartoons have shown early humans keeping dinosaurs as pets. From what you know about Earth's history, is this possible? Why or why not?

⬤ CHALLENGE

6. **Infer** How might the geologic time scale be different if the event that caused the mass extinction 65 million years ago had never occurred?

CHAPTER INVESTIGATION

Geologic Time

OVERVIEW AND PURPOSE Geologists use information from rocks, fossils, and other natural evidence to piece together the history of Earth. The geologic time scale organizes Earth's history into intervals of time called eons, eras, periods, and epochs. In this investigation you will

- construct a model of the geologic time scale
- place fossil organisms and geologic events in the correct sequence on the timeline

▶ Procedure

1. Complete the geologic time scale conversion chart. Use the conversion 1 mm = 1 million years to change the number of years for each eon, era, period, and epoch on the chart into metric measurements (millimeters, centimeters, and meters).

2. Lay the adding-machine paper out in front of you. At the far right end of the strip write "TODAY" lengthwise along the edge.

3. Starting from the TODAY mark, measure back 4.6 meters, or 4600 million years. Label this point "AGE OF EARTH." Cut off excess paper.

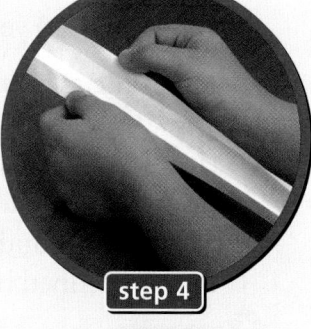
step 4

4. Fold the paper in half lengthwise and then fold it in half lengthwise again. Unfold the paper. The creases should divide your paper into four rows.

5. At the far left end of the strip, label each of the four rows as shown.

step 5

6. Using the numbers from your chart, measure each eon. Start each measurement from the TODAY line and measure back in time. For example, the Archean eon started 3800 million years ago, so measure back 3.8 meters from today. Mark that distance and write "ARCHEAN EON." Do the same for the other eons.

step 6

ARCHEAN EON
3800 million years ago (3.8 meters)

AGE OF EARTH   TODAY

MATERIALS
- geologic time scale conversion chart
- adding-machine paper 5 meters long
- scissors
- colored markers, pens, or pencils
- metric tape measure or meter stick
- sticky notes

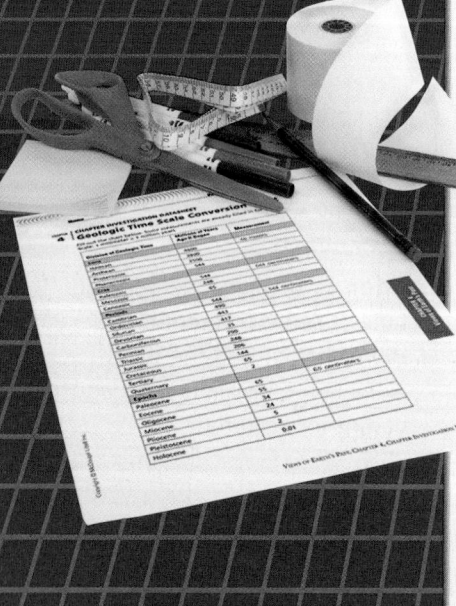

7 Repeat step 6 to measure and label the eras, periods, and epochs.

8 After all the eons, eras, periods, and epochs are measured and labeled, use the same measuring technique to add the fossils and events from the table below.

Table 1. Important Events in Earth's History

Fossils and Events	Time (millions of years ago)
First trilobite	554
First mammal	210
Greatest mass extinction	248
First green algae	1000
Early humans	2
Extinction of dinosaurs	65
First life forms	3800
Flowering plants	130

9 Draw pictures of the fossils and events or write the names of the fossils and events on the timeline. If you do not have space to write directly on the timeline, write on sticky notes and then place the sticky notes at the correct positions on the timeline.

▶ Observe and Analyze   Write It Up

1. COMPARE AND CONTRAST The time from 4.6 billion years ago up until the beginning of the Phanerozoic eon is called Precambrian time. Find the part of your timeline that represents Precambrian time. How does Precambrian time compare in length with the rest of the geologic time scale?

2. COMPARE AND CONTRAST The Cenozoic era is the most recent era, and it includes the present. How does the Cenozoic era compare in length with the other eras?

3. INTERPRET Where on the timeline are the two major extinction events?

4. INFER What does the location of the two major extinction events suggest about how geologists divided the time scale into smaller units?

▶ Conclude   Write It Up

1. INTERPRET Where are most of the life forms that you placed on your time line grouped?

2. INFER Judging by the locations of most of the life forms on your timeline, why do you think the shortest era on the timeline—the Cenozoic era—has been divided into so many smaller divisions?

3 EVALUATE What limitations or difficulties did you experience in constructing or interpreting this model of the geologic time scale?

4. APPLY Think about the relationships among fossils, rock layers, and the geologic time scale. Why do you think the geologists who first constructed the geologic time scale found it difficult to divide the first three eons into smaller time divisions?

▶ INVESTIGATE Further

CHALLENGE Choose several more events or life forms mentioned in the chapter. For each, find either an absolute date or a relative date that will allow you to place it in the correct position in the geologic sequence. Draw or label these new items on your timeline. What new patterns or connections did adding these events or life forms to the timeline reveal?

Geologic Time Scale Conversion Chart

Division of Geologic Time	Millions of Years Ago It Began	Measurement
Eons		4.6 meters
Hadean	4600	
Archean	3800	
Proterozoic	2500	
Phanerozoic	544	
Eras	544	

13 Chapter Review

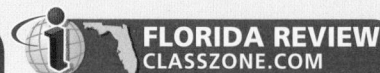

the BIG idea

Rocks, fossils, and other types of natural evidence tell Earth's story.

FLORIDA REVIEW
CLASSZONE.COM
Content Review and FCAT Practice

KEY CONCEPTS SUMMARY

1 Earth's past is revealed in rocks and fossils.

Fossils are traces or remnants of past life. Many fossils are found in rock. Rocks, fossils, and other natural evidence provide information about how Earth and life on Earth have changed over time.

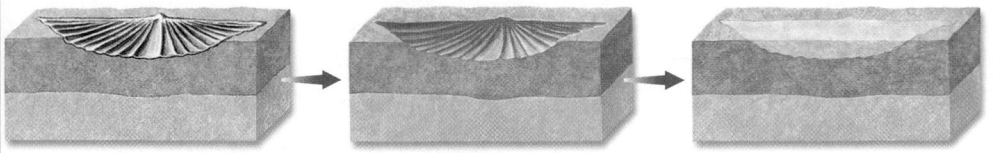

A cast fossil is formed when minerals take the shape of a decayed organism.

VOCABULARY
fossil p. 457
original remains p. 458
ice core p. 463

2 Rocks provide a timeline for Earth.

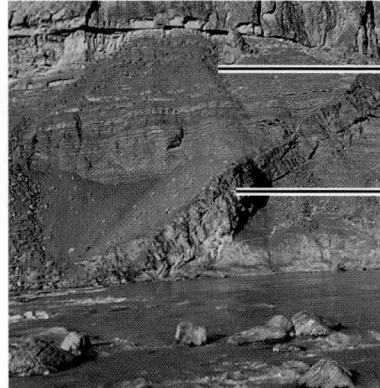

Sedimentary rock layers show the order in which rocks formed. The order of the layers is used to determine the **relative ages** of fossils found in the rock.

Radioactive dating can be used to determine the **absolute age** of igneous rock.

Scientists combine information about the relative and absolute ages of rocks and fossils to construct a timeline of Earth.

VOCABULARY
relative age p. 465
index fossil p. 467
absolute age p. 469
half-life p. 469

3 The geologic time scale shows Earth's past.

The **geologic time scale** divides Earth's history into eons, eras, periods, and epochs. The divisions are based on major changes or events that occurred in Earth's history.

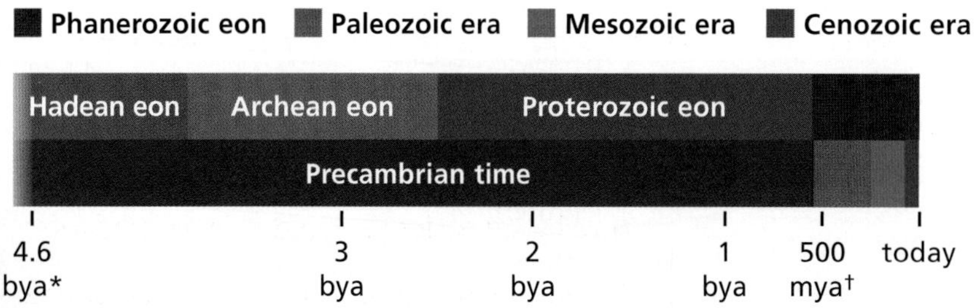

Phanerozoic eon
Paleozoic era
Mesozoic era
Cenozoic era
Hadean eon
Archean eon
Proterozoic eon
Precambrian time
4.6 bya*
3 bya
2 bya
1 bya
500 mya†
today

*bya = billion years ago †mya = million years ago

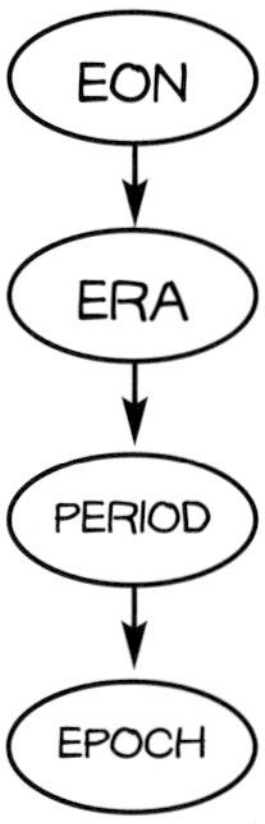

EON
ERA
PERIOD
EPOCH

VOCABULARY
uniformitarianism p. 474
geologic time scale p. 475

Vocabulary

Make a concept definition map for each of the vocabulary terms listed below. Write the term in the center box. Fill in the other boxes by answering the questions. A sample is shown below.

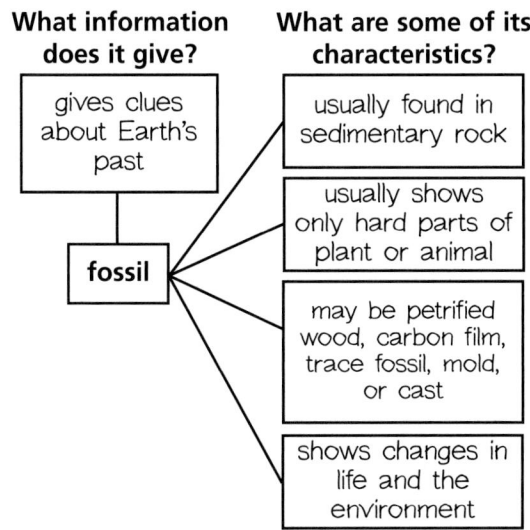

What information does it give?

gives clues about Earth's past

fossil

What are some of its characteristics?

usually found in sedimentary rock

usually shows only hard parts of plant or animal

may be petrified wood, carbon film, trace fossil, mold, or cast

shows changes in life and the environment

1. index fossil

2. ice core

3. original remains

Reviewing Key Concepts

Multiple Choice *Choose the letter of the best answer.*

4. Which of the following might show evidence of a year with low rainfall?
   a. tree rings   **c.** original remains
   b. index fossils   **d.** sedimentary rock

5. In which time span did dinosaurs live?
   a. Cenozoic era   **c.** Paleozoic era
   b. Mesozoic era   **d.** Precambrian time

6. Half-life is a measurement of
   a. fossil age
   b. radioactive breakdown
   c. cold climates
   d. relative age

7. What is the age of Earth?
   a. 570 million years   **c.** 4.6 billion years
   b. 1.1 billion years   **d.** 9.5 billion years

8. What was the earliest form of life?
   a. a fish   **c.** a one-celled organism
   b. a fern   **d.** a reptile

9. Which statement best describes the theory of uniformitarianism?
   a. Earth continues to change as it always has.
   b. Earth is changing, but not as quickly as it used to.
   c. Earth is changing, but faster than it used to.
   d. Earth is no longer changing.

10. How does petrified wood form?
   a. A log falls into water that freezes.
   b. Sedimentary rock forms over a log.
   c. Igneous rock covers a log and heats it.
   d. Water seeps through a log, replacing its cells with minerals.

11. A cast fossil is formed from
   a. igneous rock   **c.** amber
   b. a mold   **d.** wood

12. Which of these substances best preserves soft parts of an organism?
   a. sedimentary rock   **c.** amber
   b. igneous rock   **d.** air

13. Which part of an ancient reptile would you expect to see in a rock fossil?
   a. eye   **c.** heart
   b. bone   **d.** muscle

14. Which type of fossil would be most likely to show the complete outline of a leaf?
   a. petrified wood   **c.** cast fossil
   b. carbon film   **d.** trace fossil

Short Response *Write a short response to each question.*

15. Why are no fossils found in igneous rocks?

16. Why is radioactive dating not useful for determining the ages of sedimentary rocks?

Chapter 13: **Views of Earth's Past** 483

Thinking Critically

APPLY *Refer to the illustration below to answer the next four questions.*

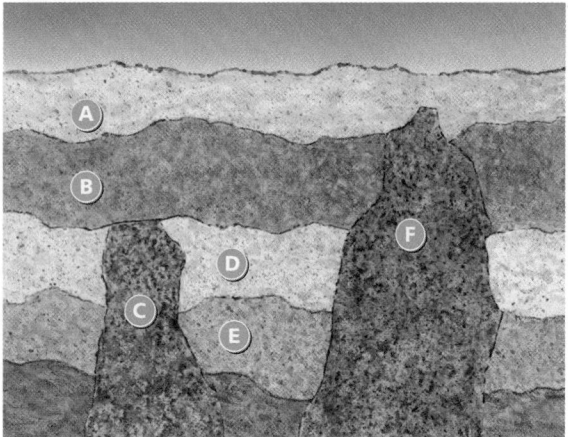

The illustration above is a side view of formations of sedimentary and igneous rock. *C* and *F* are igneous rock.

17. For which of the labeled rock formations could the absolute age be determined? Why?

18. Which of the labeled rock formations is the youngest? How do you know?

19. Which rock is younger, *C* or *D?* Why?

20. Which of the labeled rock layers is the oldest? Why?

21. INFER Why do you think the Hadean, Archean, and Proterozoic eons are not divided into eras, periods, or epochs?

22. COMPARE AND CONTRAST How is the geologic time scale like a calendar? How is it different?

23. CONNECT Copy the concept map below. Use the geologic time scale on pages 476–477 to complete the map.

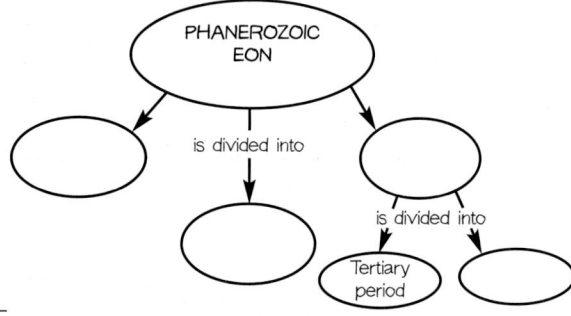

24. APPLY AND GRAPH Copy the graph below on your paper. Plot a point on the graph above each of the half-life numbers to show what percentage of the original unstable element remains. Note that the first point has been placed on the graph to show that all of the original element remains at the beginning, when no half-lives have passed.

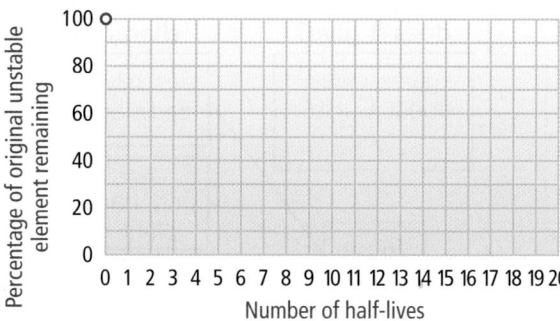

the BIG idea

25. SYNTHESIZE Look at the geologic time scale and think about the major events in the history of Earth and the changes in life forms that it shows. How do rocks, fossils, and other natural evidence tell Earth's story?

26. PREDICT What do you think will remain as evidence of today's world 100,000 years from now? How will the types of evidence differ from those that remain from 100,000 years ago?

UNIT PROJECTS

If you are doing a unit project, make a folder for your project. Include in your folder a list of the resources you will need, the date on which the project is due, and a schedule to keep track of your progress. Begin gathering data.

Analyzing a Diagram

This diagram shows a cross section of rock layers. All of the layers are sedimentary, except for the area marked as igneous. Use the diagram to answer the questions below.

> **FCAT TiP**
>
> When answering questions based on a diagram, try to answer the question using the diagram before you look at the answer choices. This will help you eliminate wrong answers.

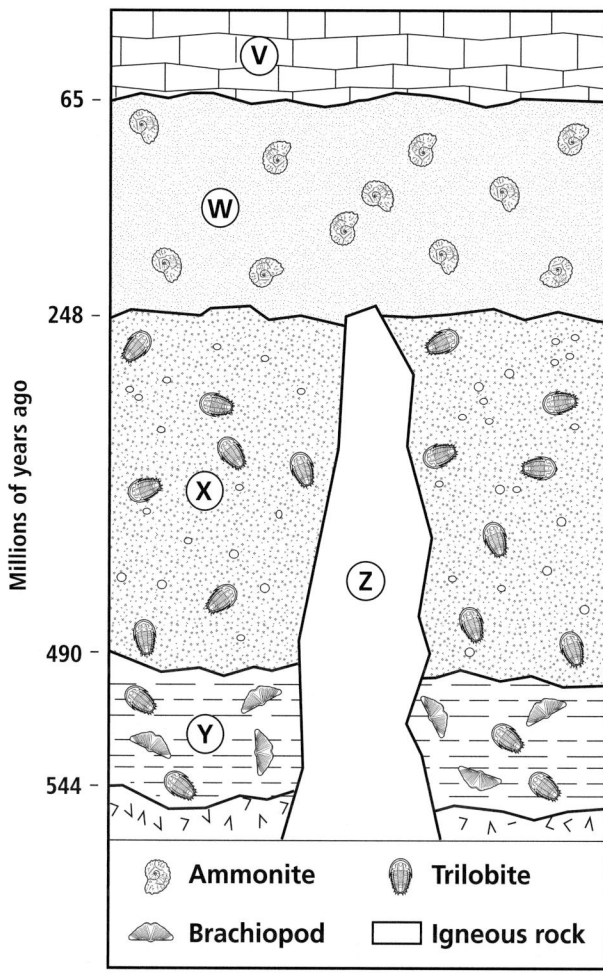

Millions of years ago

65 —
248 —
490 —
544 —

V

W

X

Z

Y

| 🐚 Ammonite | 🐛 Trilobite |
| 🦪 Brachiopod | ☐ Igneous rock |

4. Which fossils are most common in the rock that is 500 million years old?

  F. brachiopods   **H.** ammonites

  G. trilobites   **I.** theropods

5. What is the best estimate of the age of rock Z?

  A. less than 300 million years old

  B. 300 million years old

  C. more than 300 million years old

  D. more than 544 million years old

6. Which point shows where a fossil that is 500 million years old would most likely be found?

  F. V   **H.** X

  G. W   **I.** Y

EXTENDED RESPONSE
Answer the two questions below in detail.
Include some of the terms shown in the word box.
In your answers, underline each term you use.

index fossils	original remains	igneous rock
layers	folded	bent
ice core	tree ring	trilobite

7. Azeem is part of a team of scientists studying the natural history of a region. What types of natural evidence might he and his team look for? Why?

8. In studying fossils found in her community, Yvette noticed a pattern in their ages. People found older fossils close to the surface and younger fossils at greater depths. Explain why that might be.

SHORT RESPONSE

1. Explain why there are no fossils in the igneous rock.

2. What is the youngest rock layer in the diagram? Explain.

MULTIPLE CHOICE

3. When did trilobites live on Earth?

  A. within the last 65 million years

  B. between 65 million years ago and 248 million years ago

  C. between 248 million years ago and 544 million years ago

  D. more than 544 million years ago

CHAPTER 14

The History of Life on Earth

the **BIG** idea

Living things, like Earth itself, change over time.

Key Concepts

SECTION

1 Earth has been home to living things for about 3.8 billion years.
Learn how fossils help explain the development of life on Earth.

SECTION

2 Species change over time.
Learn how species develop and change.

SECTION

3 Many types of evidence support evolution.
Learn about the evidence scientists use to support evolution.

FCAT Practice

Prepare and practice for the FCAT
• Section Reviews, pp. 495, 505, 514
• Chapter Review, pp. 516–518
• FCAT Practice, p. 519

CLASSZONE.COM
• Florida Review: Content Review and FCAT Practice

How do scientists learn about the history of life on Earth?

What Can Rocks Show About Earth's History?

Look closely at two rocks from different places or at the two rocks below. What are the characteristics of each rock? Can you see evidence of living things in one of them?

Observe and Think
How could the evidence you gathered from your observations help you describe Earth's history?

Which One of These Things Is Not Like the Others?

Observe a handful of beans. Measure the length of each bean, observe the color, and note how many seeds are in each bean.

Observe and Think
What variety do you observe in the beans?

Investigate Activity: Matching Finch Beaks

Go to **ClassZone.com** to match different finch beaks with the foods they eat. Learn how each type of beak functions.

Observe and Think
Can you think of any other beak types birds may have and how they relate to the food they eat?

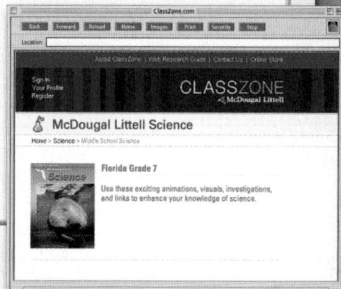

NSTA scilinks.org **SCi LINKS**
The Fossil Record **Code: MDL036**

Getting Ready to Learn

CONCEPT REVIEW

- Earth was formed over 4 billion years ago.
- Living things interact with their environment.

VOCABULARY REVIEW

See Glossary for definitions.

original remains p. 458

relative age p. 465

absolute age p. 469

geologic time scale p. 475

FLORIDA REVIEW
CLASSZONE.COM

Content Review and FCAT Practice

TAKING NOTES

MAIN IDEA AND DETAILS

Make a two-column chart. Write the main ideas, such as those in the blue headings, in the column on the left. Write details about each of those main ideas in the column on the right.

VOCABULARY STRATEGY

Write each new vocabulary term in the center of a **frame game** diagram. Decide what information to frame it with. Use examples, descriptions, and parts of sentences that use the term in context or pictures. You can change the frame to fit each item.

See the Note-Taking Handbook on pages R45–R51.

SCIENCE NOTEBOOK

MAIN IDEAS	DETAILS
1. Fossils provide evidence of earlier life	1. Bones, prints, minerals 1. Relative dating compares fossils 1. Absolute dating uses the level of radioactivity

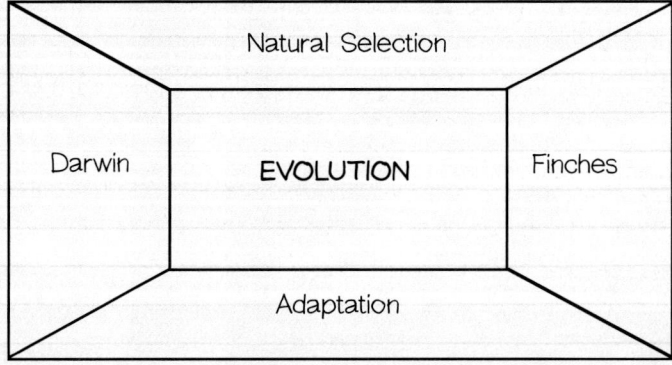

Natural Selection

Darwin   **EVOLUTION**   Finches

Adaptation

KEY CONCEPT

Earth has been home to living things for about 3.8 billion years.

Sunshine State STANDARDS

SC.D.1.3.2: The student knows that over the whole Earth, organisms are growing, dying, and decaying as new organisms are produced by the old ones.

SC.D.1.3.3: The student knows how conditions that exist in one system influence the conditions that exist in other systems.

SC.F.1.3.2: The student knows that the structural basis of most organisms is the cell and most organisms are single cells, while some, including humans, are multicellular.

 FCAT VOCABULARY
fossil p. 489

VOCABULARY
unicellular organism
  p. 492
multicellular
  organism p. 493
mass extinction p. 494

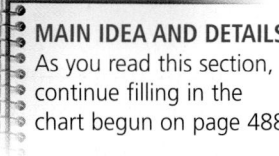

MAIN IDEA AND DETAILS
As you read this section, continue filling in the chart begun on page 488.

◀ **BEFORE, you learned**

• Living things are diverse
• Living things share common characteristics
• A species is a group of living things that can breed with one another

▶ **NOW, you will learn**

• How scientists use fossils to learn about the history of life
• About patterns in the fossil record
• About mass extinctions

EXPLORE Fossils

What can you infer from the marks an object leaves behind?

PROCEDURE

① Press a layer of clay into the petri dish.

② Choose a small object and press it into the clay to make an imprint of your object.

③ Remove the object carefully and trade your imprint with a classmate.

MATERIALS
• clay
• petri dish
• small object

WHAT DO YOU THINK?
• What object made the imprint?
• What do your observations indicate to you about how the imprint was formed?

Fossils provide evidence of earlier life.

Imagine watching a movie about the history of life on Earth. The beginning of the movie is set 3.8 billion years ago. At that time, the ocean would have been the setting. All living things lived in the sea. The end of the movie would show Earth today—a planet that is home to millions of species living on land as well as in water and air.

Of course, learning about the history of life isn't as easy as watching a movie. Modern ideas about life's history involve careful observation of the available evidence. Much of this evidence is provided by fossils. **Fossils** are the remains of organisms preserved in the earth. Fossils provide a glimpse of a very long story. In some ways, observing a fossil is like hitting the pause button on your video machine or looking at a snapshot of another time.

Fossils

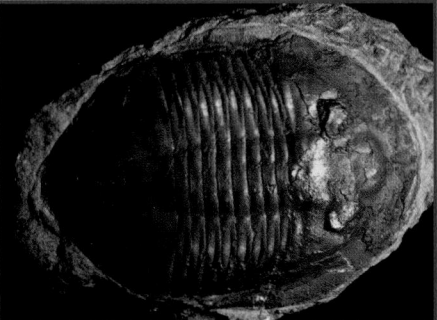

Bones, such as this jawbone, are a common type of fossil.

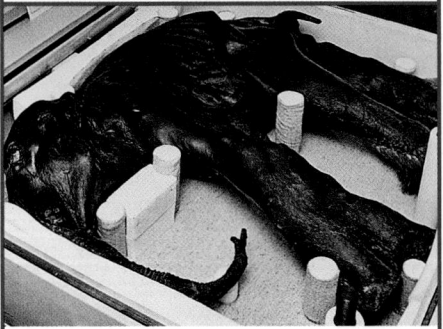

This fossil trilobite formed as minerals replaced the remains of the organism.

The preserved remains of ancient mammals, like the woolly mammoth, are rare.

VISUALIZATION
CLASSZONE.COM

Explore how a fossil can form.

Types of Fossils

You may have learned that fossils are the imprints or remains of once-living things. Most fossils are hard body parts such as bone. Perhaps you have seen displays of dinosaur skeletons in museums. These displays include fossil bones, such as the jawbone to the left. Other fossils form when minerals replace the remains of organisms or parts of organisms. The trilobite fossil shown in the middle photograph is an example of this type of fossil. Fossils also include prints made by organisms.

Very rarely, people find fossils that are the original remains of entire organisms. Explorers have found the frozen bodies of animals called woolly mammoths that lived about 10,000 years ago. The bodies of insects can be preserved in sap from plants.

Finding the Age of Fossils

How can scientists tell that the first organisms lived in oceans, or that dinosaurs lived on land and that they disappeared 65 million years ago? These questions and others can be addressed by determining the age of fossils. There are two approaches to dating fossils—relative dating and absolute dating. In relative dating, one fossil is compared with another fossil. The relative age tells you whether a fossil formed before or after another fossil.

The places where fossils are discovered provide information about their relative ages. Much of Earth's crust is rock, and rock forms over long periods of time. Understanding when and how rock forms gives scientists information about the sequence of events in Earth's history.

Materials such as sand and mud may settle to the bottom of a body of water. Over many millions of years, layers harden into rock. Shells and other remains of organisms can be trapped in those layers, forming fossils. Newer fossils are usually found in the top layers of rock, while older fossils are in the lower layers.

The absolute age of a fossil tells you when it was formed. To find the absolute age, scientists study the radioactive elements found in rocks and fossils. Some of these elements, such as uranium, decay at a very precise rate into more stable elements, such as lead. Thus, by measuring the amount of uranium and the amount of lead in an object, scientists can determine the object's age. The more lead it has, the older it is.

CHECK YOUR READING What are the two ways scientists can determine the age of fossils?

How do scientists interpret fossil evidence?

PROCEDURE

(1) Individually examine each of your group's puzzle pieces. Consider the shape and size of each piece.

(2) Arrange the pieces so that they fit together in the best possible way.

(3) On the basis of your pieces, try to interpret what the overall puzzle picture may be.

(4) Combine your puzzle pieces with another group's. Repeat steps 2 and 3.

WHAT DO YOU THINK?

- How did your interpretation of the puzzle picture change once you had more pieces to work with?
- Explain whether the gaps in the puzzle picture influenced your interpretation.
- Was it easier or more difficult to study the record with more "scientists" in your group?

CHALLENGE Brainstorm other ways scientists could learn about early life on Earth.

SKILL FOCUS
Analyzing

MATERIALS
puzzle pieces

TIME
15 minutes

Assembling the Fossil Record

By combining absolute dating with relative dating, scientists can estimate the age of most fossils. The information about the fossils found in a particular location is called the fossil record. By assembling a fossil record, scientists can identify the periods of time during which different species lived and died. Scientists have used the fossil record to develop an overview of Earth's history.

READING TIP

A species is a group of organisms with similar characteristics that can interbreed.

Information from fossils helps scientists and artists describe wooly mammoths.

More complex organisms developed over time.

One of the most striking patterns that scientists find when they study the fossil record involves the development of more complex organisms. Below you will see how scientists have reconstructed the history of a modern city to show how life has developed over time. Recall that the first organisms were made up of single cells. Most organisms living today are single-celled. However, more and more species have developed more and more complex cells and structures over time.

Unicellular Organisms

Unicellular organisms are organisms made up of a single cell. The organisms in the ocean 3.8 billion years ago were made of simple, single cells. Some of these organisms are responsible for the oxygen that now makes up our atmosphere. The early atmosphere did not contain as much oxygen as it now does. As the atmosphere changed, so did life on Earth.

Different types of single cells developed over time. Over millions of years the cells of organisms became more complex. Today, there are different species of life that include organisms made up of many cells.

Reconstructing the Past

Digging deep into the city of Denver, scientists have been able to reconstruct the ancient past.

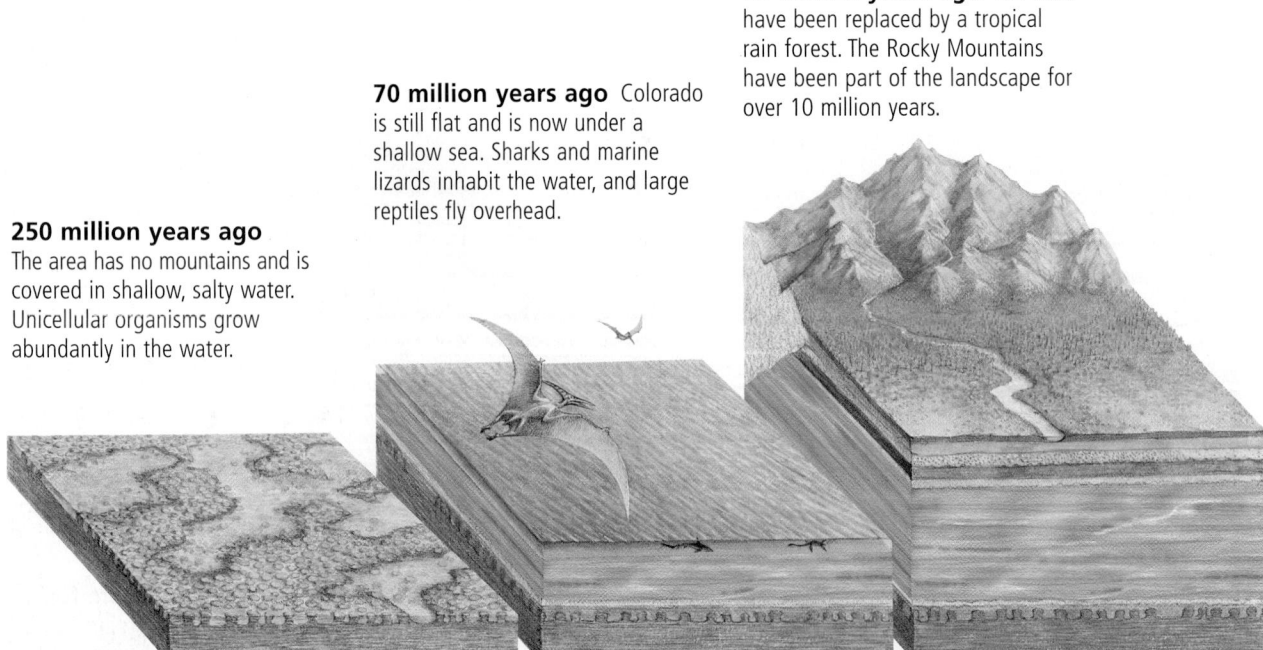

55 million years ago The seas have been replaced by a tropical rain forest. The Rocky Mountains have been part of the landscape for over 10 million years.

70 million years ago Colorado is still flat and is now under a shallow sea. Sharks and marine lizards inhabit the water, and large reptiles fly overhead.

250 million years ago The area has no mountains and is covered in shallow, salty water. Unicellular organisms grow abundantly in the water.

Multicellular Organisms

Around 1.2 billion years ago, organisms made up of many cells began to live in Earth's oceans. **Multicellular organisms** are living things made up of many cells. Individual cells within multicellular organisms often perform specific tasks. For example, some cells may capture energy. Other cells might store materials. Still others might carry materials from one part of the organism to another. The most complex species of multicellular organisms have cells that are organized into tissues, organs, and systems.

Recall that all organisms have similar needs for energy, water, materials, and living space. For almost 3 billion years, these needs were met only in oceans. According to fossil records, the earliest multicellular organisms were tiny seaweeds. The earliest animals were similar to today's jellyfish.

Scientists learn about early life by studying different layers of rock

 Explain how unicellular and multicellular organisms differ.

Life on Land

Consider the importance of water. Without it, you and most other living things would not be able to live. About 500 million years ago, the first multicellular organisms moved from water to land.

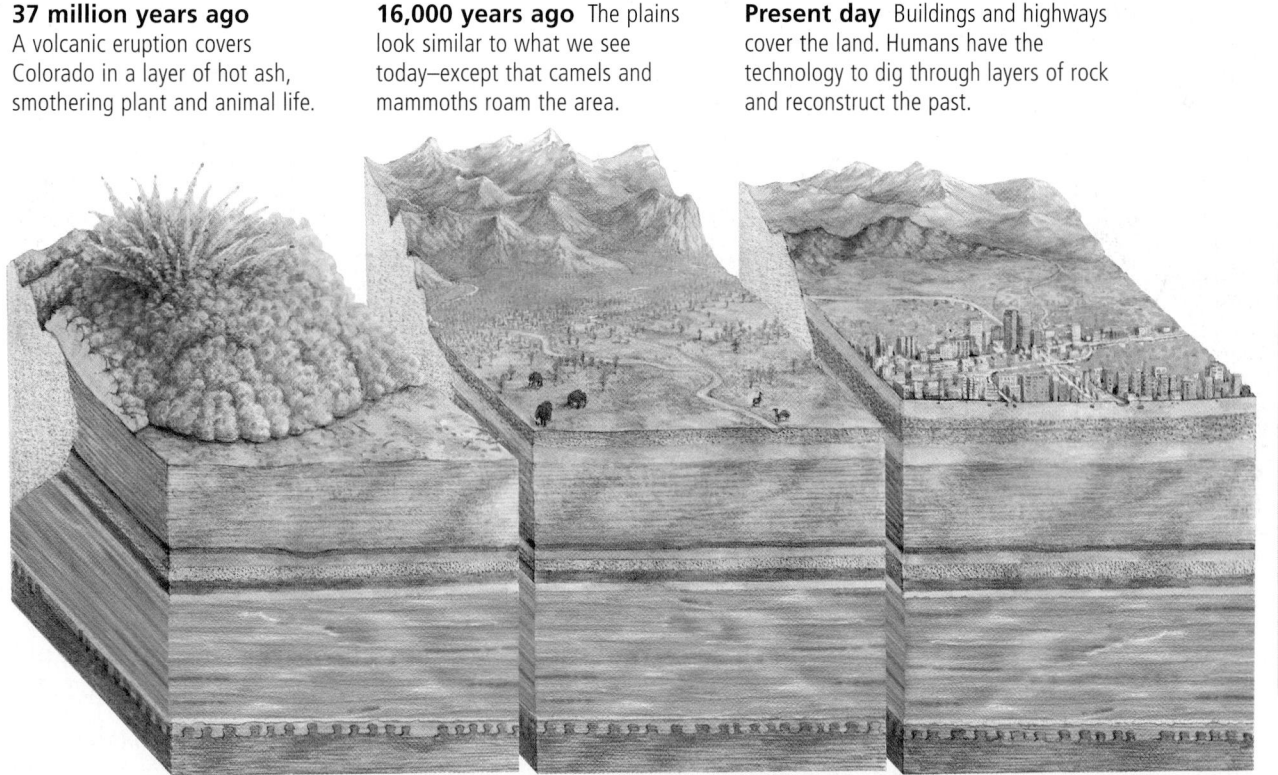

37 million years ago A volcanic eruption covers Colorado in a layer of hot ash, smothering plant and animal life.

16,000 years ago The plains look similar to what we see today—except that camels and mammoths roam the area.

Present day Buildings and highways cover the land. Humans have the technology to dig through layers of rock and reconstruct the past.

RESOURCE CENTER
CLASSZONE.COM

Find out more about mass extinctions.

In order to survive, these living things needed structures to help them get water. The first land-dwelling organisms were simple plants and fungi. Plants were able to obtain water from the soil through structures called roots. Fungi absorbed water from plants as well as from the soil. Insects were also probably among the first living things to inhabit land. Plants provided insects with food and shelter. After insects, animals such as amphibians and reptiles began living on land. They were followed by birds and mammals.

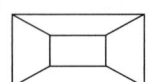

VOCABULARY
Remember to make a frame game for the term *mass extinction.*

Earth's history includes mass extinctions.

About 10,000 years ago, the last woolly mammoth died without any offspring. At that time, the species became extinct, which means it disappeared. The only way that we know that some species, such as woolly mammoths, ever existed is through the fossil record. During Earth's history, there have been several periods when huge numbers of species have died or become extinct in a very short time. These events are called **mass extinctions.**

Although the fossil record shows a pattern of mass extinctions, two of these extinctions are particularly interesting. These are the Permian Extinction and the Cretaceous Extinction. The causes of these mass extinctions are not fully known.

Permian Extinction

About 250 million years ago, approximately 90 percent of the species living in the ocean became extinct. At the same time, many land-dwelling animals disappeared. Scientists who have studied Earth's history think that Earth's landmasses joined together, forming one enormous continent. This event would have changed the climate on land and the conditions within Earth's waters.

The largest mass extinction, the Permian Extinction, affected many different living things but it was the most devastating to organisms that lived in oceans.

Cretaceous Extinction

Fossils show that around 140 million years ago, animals called dinosaurs lived all over the planet. However, the fossil record for dinosaurs ends about 65 million years ago. At the same time, more than half of the other species living on Earth became extinct.

How do scientists explain the extinction of so many species? One possibility is that a very large meteorite from space collided with Earth. The collision and its aftereffects wiped out most of the existing species. The remains of such a collision, the Chicxulub crater, can be found off the coast of Mexico. The computer graphic on page 495 shows the area of impact.

Chicxulub Crater

Scientists think the impact of a meteorite off the coast of Mexico caused the Cretaceous extinction.

110 mi

The meteorite left a 200 km-wide crater off the Yucatán peninsula in Mexico.

Fragments from the meteorite have been found in the area.

The pattern in the fossil record shows that mass extinctions were followed by periods during which increasing numbers of new species developed. There may be a connection between the extinction of one species and the development of new species. For example, the extinction of dinosaurs may have made it possible for new species of mammals to develop.

CHECK YOUR READING What do scientists think caused the most recent mass extinction?

14.1 Review

KEY CONCEPTS

1. How do fossils help scientists understand the history of life?

2. How do scientists know that the first organisms were simple, unicellular organisms?

3. What is extinction? Give an example of a mass extinction and its results.

CRITICAL THINKING

4. **Synthesize** How do absolute dating and relative dating help scientists assemble a fossil record for an area?

5. **Sequence** Draw a timeline showing the sequence of three major events in the history of life. Include the following terms on your timeline: *unicellular, multicellular, ocean, land.*

⬤ CHALLENGE

6. **Predict** Using the Denver reconstruction as your model, explain how you would reconstruct the history of the environment in your town.

SKILL: USING PROPORTIONS

MATH TUTORIAL
CLASSZONE.COM

Click on Math Tutorial for more help writing and solving proportions.

This fossil is very similar to the modern snail shown above.

A Span of Time

The history of planet Earth spans from the present to about 5 billion years back. By comparison, the history of life on the planet spans about 4/5 of that time. Such a comparison is called a proportion.

Example

To compare time spans in the history of Earth, you could make a meter-long timeline. Follow these steps:

(1) Measure and cut a piece of paper longer than 1 meter. Draw a straight line that is 1 meter long on your paper.

(2) Mark "0" at the far left to show the present day. Mark "5,000,000,000" at the right to show 5 billion years.

(3) Mark each centimeter along the line with a short stroke.

(4) Make a longer stroke at every 10 pencil marks. Your 5-billion-year span is now divided into 500-million-year sections. Each section is 1/10 in proportion to the total.

```
|---+---+---+---+---+---+---+---+---+---|
0                                        5,000,000,000
```

Label the timeline by answering the questions below.

1. Each short pencil stroke, or tick, represents 1/100 of the total span. How many years will each centimeter represent?

2. Each of the 10 long pencil marks should have its own label for the amount of time before the present day. The label for the first long pencil mark should be "500 million years." What numbers should label the others?

3. What fractions of the total span do the numbers in Question 2 represent?

CHALLENGE Copy and complete the table.

Event	Years Before Present Time	Number of cm from 0	Fraction of Total Time Span
Life appears on Earth.	3,800,000,000		
Multicellular life appears.	1,500,000,000		
First animals appear on land.	420,000,000		

14.2 Species change over time.

FCAT VOCABULARY
adaptation p. 502

VOCABULARY
evolution p. 497
natural selection p. 501
speciation p. 504

BEFORE, you learned
- Fossils are evidence of earlier life
- More complex organisms have developed over time
- Mass extinctions contributed to the development of Earth's history

NOW, you will learn
- About early ideas and observations on evolution
- How Darwin developed his theory of natural selection
- How new species arise from older species

THINK ABOUT

How have telephones changed over time?

Today people across the world can communicate in many different ways. One of the most common ways is over the telephone. Looking at the two pictures, can you describe how this form of communication has changed over time?

Scientists explore the concept of evolution.

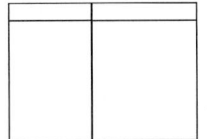

MAIN IDEA AND DETAILS
Make a chart for the main idea *scientists explore the concept of evolution.* Include details about scientists' observations.

In a general sense, evolution involves a change over time. You could say that the way humans communicate has evolved. Certainly telephones have changed over time. The first telephones were the size of a shoebox. Today a telephone can fit in the palm of your hand and can send images as well as sound.

In biology, **evolution** refers to the process though which species change over time. The change results from a change in the genetic material of an organism and is passed from one generation to the next.

CHECK YOUR READING   What is evolution?

Early Ideas

READING TiP

The word *acquire* comes from the root meaning "to add to." Acquired traits are those that are "added" after an organism is born.

In the early 1800s, a French scientist named Jean Baptiste de Lamarck was the first scientist to propose a model of how life evolves. He became convinced that the fossil record showed that species had changed over time. He proposed an explanation for evolution based on the idea that an individual organism can acquire a new trait during its lifetime and then pass that trait on to its offspring. For example, Lamarck suggested that when giraffes stretched their necks to reach the leaves of tall trees, they passed the result of this stretching—a longer neck—to the next generation. Lamarck was a highly respected scientist, but he was unable to provide any evidence to support his idea.

CHECK YOUR READING How did Lamarck explain the process of evolution?

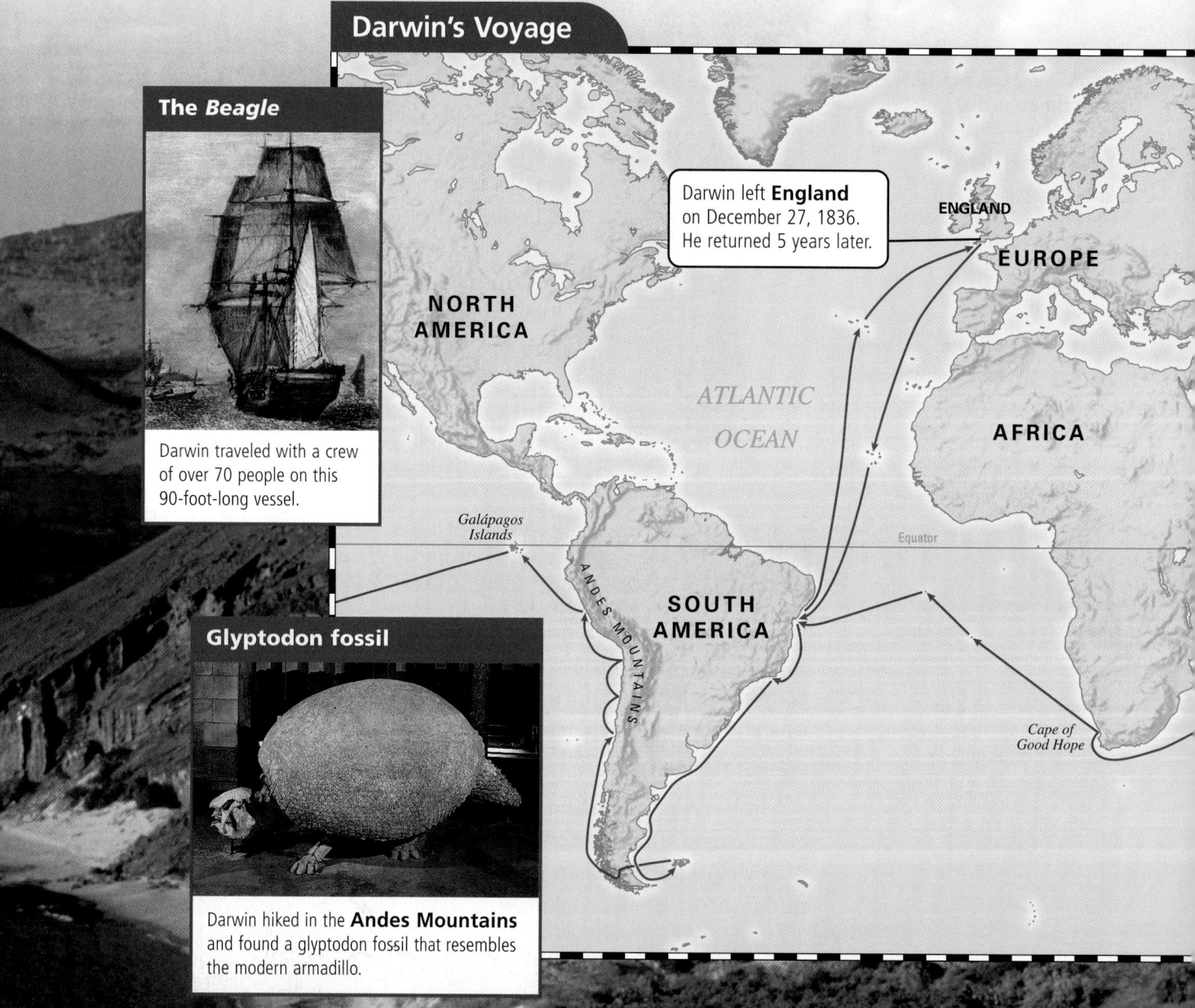

Darwin's Voyage

The *Beagle*

Darwin traveled with a crew of over 70 people on this 90-foot-long vessel.

Darwin left **England** on December 27, 1836. He returned 5 years later.

NORTH AMERICA

ENGLAND

EUROPE

ATLANTIC OCEAN

AFRICA

Galápagos Islands

Equator

ANDES MOUNTAINS

SOUTH AMERICA

Cape of Good Hope

Glyptodon fossil

Darwin hiked in the **Andes Mountains** and found a glyptodon fossil that resembles the modern armadillo.

Darwin's Observations

About 50 years after Lamarck, the British naturalist Charles Darwin published what would become the basis of the modern theory of evolution. As a young adult, Darwin spent 5 years as a naturalist aboard the *Beagle,* a ship in the British navy. The map below shows the route Darwin traveled. As he sailed along the coast of South America, he studied rock formations and collected fossils. He also began to compare the new animals he was seeing with ones from his own country.

The differences he saw in animals became more obvious when he visited the Galápagos Islands, a chain of volcanic islands about 950 kilometers (600 mi) off the South American coast. On the 498 Galápagos Islands, plants and animals not only differed from those he saw on the mainland, but some differed from island to island.

Darwin was only 20 in 1831 when he joined H.M.S. *Beagle.*

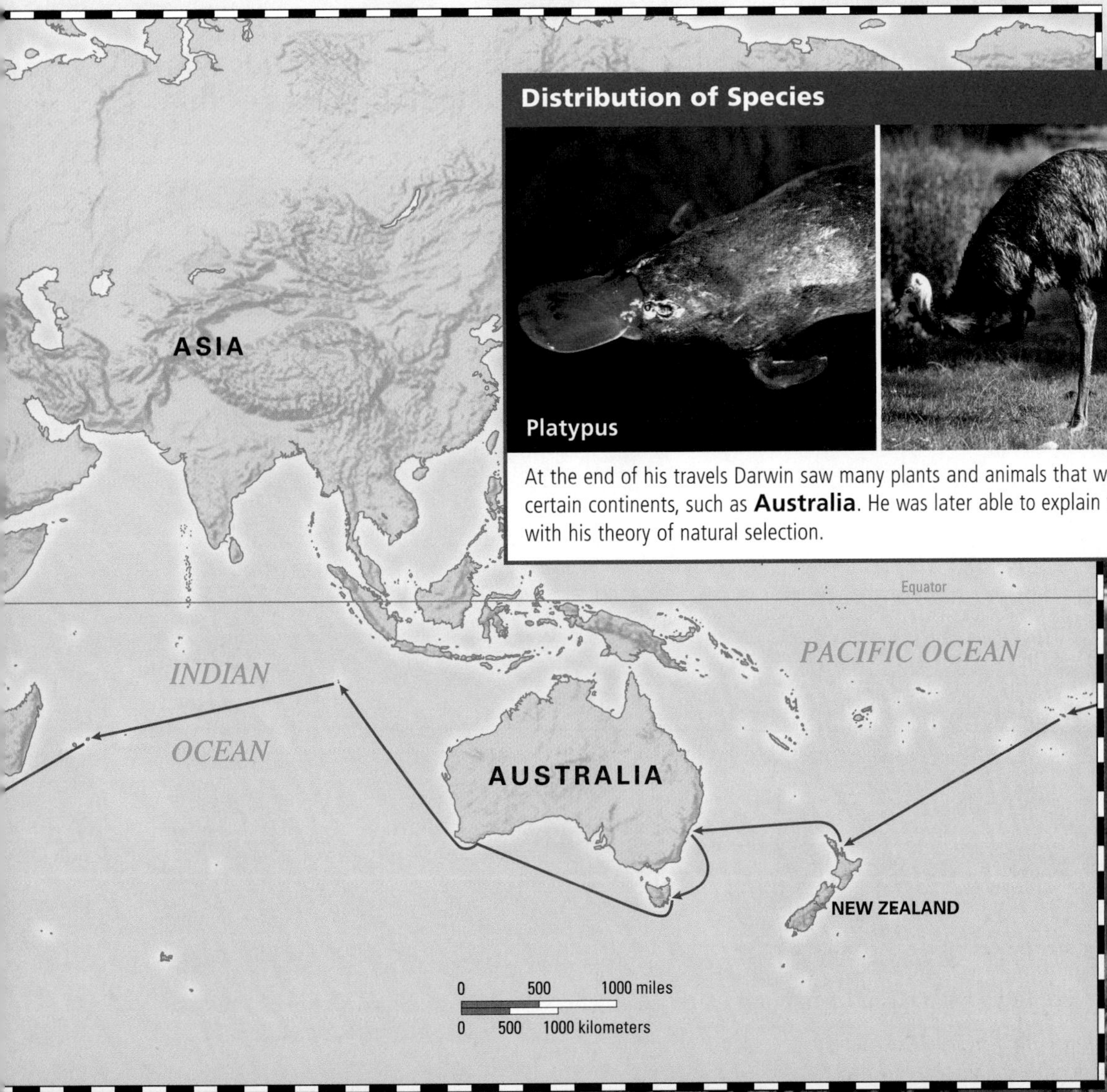

Distribution of Species

Platypus

Emu

At the end of his travels Darwin saw many plants and animals that were specific to certain continents, such as **Australia**. He was later able to explain this pattern with his theory of natural selection.

ASIA

INDIAN

OCEAN

PACIFIC OCEAN

Equator

AUSTRALIA

NEW ZEALAND

0   500   1000 miles

0   500   1000 kilometers

Darwin observed several types of tortoises on the islands. Tortoises with short necks were living in damp areas with abundant plant life that grew close to the ground. Longer-necked tortoises were living in dry areas with cacti. He considered whether the length of their necks made it possible for the tortoises to live in different environments.

Darwin also found many different types of birds called finches living on the islands. Some finches were common in the treetops, while others lived in the lower shrubs of a neighboring island. Among the different islands he noticed a variety of beak shapes and sizes. Some finches had heavy, short beaks useful for pecking trees or seeds, while others had small, thin beaks that could be used for capturing insects. These observations caused Darwin to wonder if the birds had evolved from similar species.

Darwin's Finches

On the Galápagos Islands, Darwin observed similar-looking birds with very different beaks. These birds are closely related finch species that are suited to different habitats on the island.

Woodpecker Finch

Vegetarian Finch

The woodpecker finch is able to hold a twig in its long pointed beak, which it uses to pull the larvas of insects from a tree. The vegetarian finch has a curved beak, ideal for taking large berries from a branch.

Large Ground Finch

Cactus Finch

The large ground finch has a large beak that it uses to crack open the hard shells of the seeds it feeds on. The cactus finch has a narrow beak that it uses to cut into a cactus and eat the tissue inside.

Natural selection explains how living things evolve.

After Darwin returned home to England in 1836, he spent several years analyzing the observations and specimens he had collected on his voyage. He struggled to develop an explanation that would account for the amazing diversity of species he saw and for the relationships between them. By 1844 he had developed a hypothesis based in part on an insight from one of his hobbies—breeding pigeons.

Darwin knew from personal experience that breeders can produce new varieties of an animal over time. The process breeders use is called artificial selection. For example, breeders produce a new breed of dog by selecting dogs that have certain desired traits and then allowing only those individuals to mate. From the resulting litters, they again selectively breed only the individual dogs with the desired traits. By repeating this process generation after generation, a new breed is produced.

RESOURCE CENTER
CLASSZONE.COM

Learn more about natural selection.

 **CHECK YOUR READING** What is artificial selection?

Artificial Selection

Cairne   Airedale   Tibetan

COMPARE AND CONTRAST These dogs are all terriers, but they have been bred through artificial selection to show very specific traits. How are the dogs similar? How are they different?

Darwin's insight was that a similar process might be going on in nature. He proposed that, through a process he called **natural selection,** members of a species that are best suited to their environment survive and reproduce at a higher rate than other members of the species. Darwin based this idea on a few key principles. These are overproduction, variation, adaptation, and selection.

Overproduction

Take a look at how Darwin's ideas are useful for the study of salmon. When a plant or an animal reproduces, it usually makes more offspring than the environment can support, as you can see in the diagram on page 503. A female salmon may lay several thousand fertile eggs, but not all of them will hatch. Only a few hundred of the salmon that hatch from the eggs will survive disease and avoid fish-eating predators. Several dozen of these survivors will live to adulthood. An even smaller number will successfully reproduce.

Variation

READING **TiP**

As you read about the principles of natural selection, refer to the diagrams on page 503.

Within a species there are natural differences, or variations, in traits. For example, if you looked very closely at thousands of salmon, you might see slight differences among individuals. Some might have larger fins. Others might have distinct patterns of spots on their scales. Many of the differences among individuals result from differences in the genetic material of the fish.

Sometimes the genetic material itself changes, causing a new variation to come about. A change in the genetic material is referred to as a mutation. As the fish with the new variation reproduces, the trait gets passed on to its offspring. Therefore, genetic variations are passed on from one generation to the next.

Adaptation

Sometimes a mutation occurs that makes an individual better able to survive than other members of the group. An **adaptation** is any inherited trait that gives an organism an advantage in its particular environment. For example, a slight change in the shape of a tail fin may increase a fish's chance of survival by helping it swim faster and avoid predators.

Selection

Darwin reasoned that individual organisms with a particular adaptation are most likely to survive long enough to reproduce. As a result, the adaptation becomes more common in the next generation of offspring. As this process repeats from generation to generation, more members of a species show the adaptation. Consider the shape of the salmon. If a change in the tail fin makes the salmon better able to move upstream and lay eggs, scientists say this trait has been selected for in this environment. In other words, the species is evolving through natural selection.

Natural Selection

Certain traits become more common in a group of organisms through the process of natural selection.

Overproduction

adult salmon

eggs

A fish may lay hundreds of eggs, but only a small number will survive to reach adulthood.

Variation

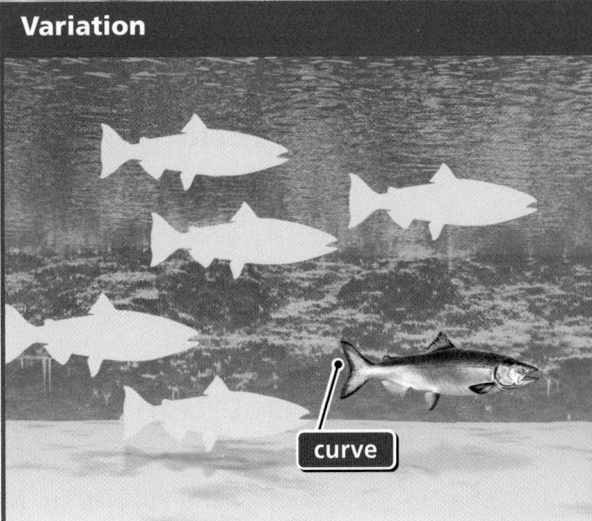

curve

A mutation may cause a slight curve to develop in a fish's tail.

Adaptation

The fish with the curved tail is able to swim more quickly and so escapes predators. The fish reproduces.

Selection

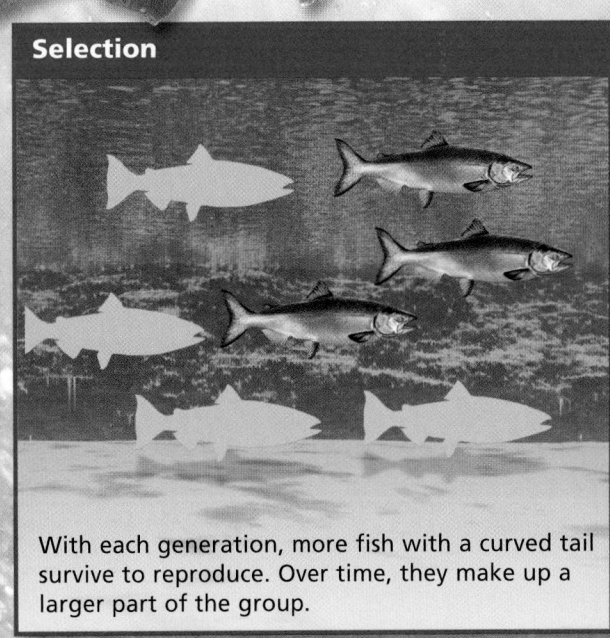

With each generation, more fish with a curved tail survive to reproduce. Over time, they make up a larger part of the group.

READING VISUALS How does natural selection occur for an individual salmon?

New species develop from earlier species.

Darwin's personal observations and the work of another scientist, Alfred Wallace, led Darwin to write about this new concept of evolution. In 1859, after more than twenty years of work, Darwin published his ideas in his book *On the Origin of Species.* This work led the way for our modern understanding of how new species arise.

Speciation

Speciation is the evolution of new species from an existing species. Speciation may occur when the environment changes dramatically, or when the environment changes gradually. The Galápagos finch populations Darwin studied showed evidence of speciation.

Isolation

Darwin's trip to the Galápagos Islands showed him an important point about speciation. Many new species had evolved after populations were separated from the mainland and were not able to breed with their mainland relatives. Darwin reasoned that isolation of populations by geographical or other barriers could contribute to the process of speciation. A species of fish called cichlids shows how a physical barrier contributes to speciation.

Speciation

In this African lake, new species of cichlids have evolved.

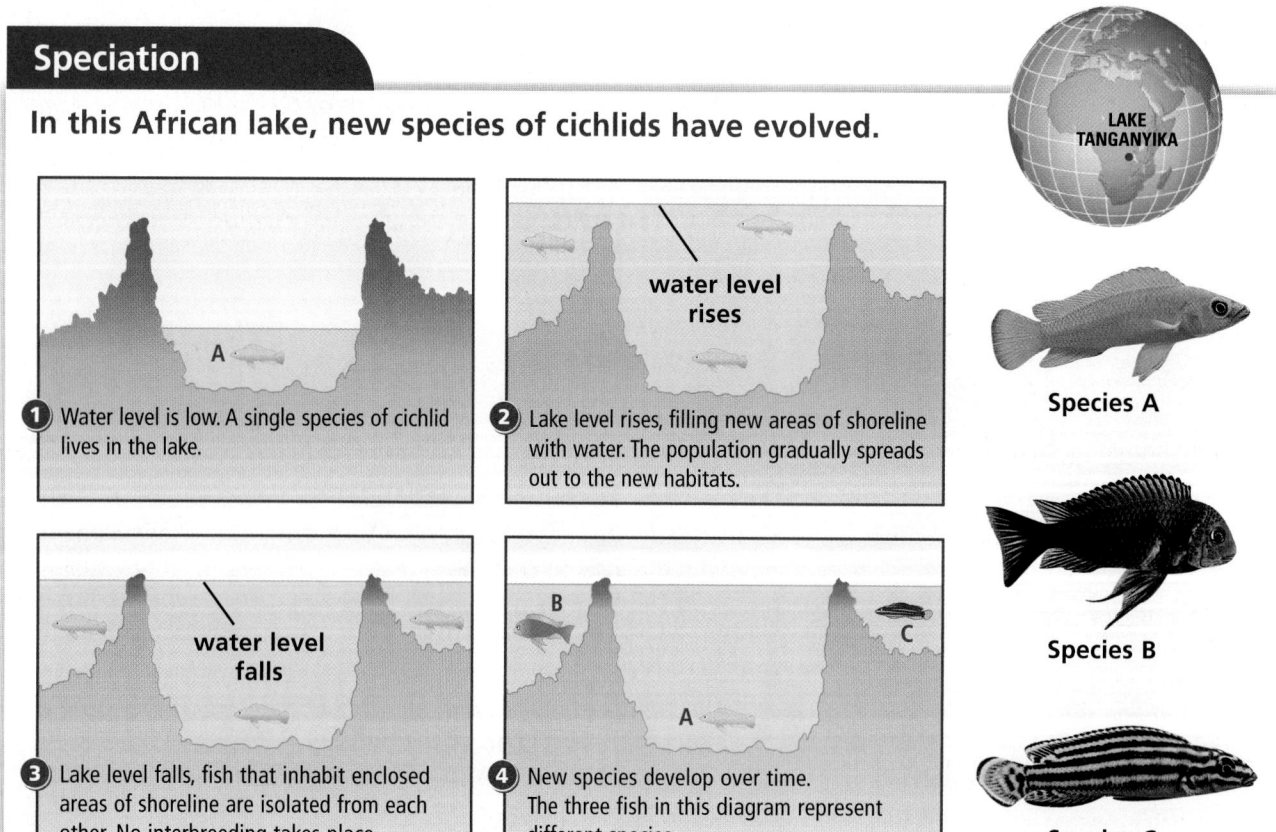

LAKE TANGANYIKA

1. Water level is low. A single species of cichlid lives in the lake.

2. Lake level rises, filling new areas of shoreline with water. The population gradually spreads out to the new habitats.

water level rises

3. Lake level falls, fish that inhabit enclosed areas of shoreline are isolated from each other. No interbreeding takes place.

water level falls

4. New species develop over time. The three fish in this diagram represent different species.

Species A

Species B

Species C

In Lake Tanganyika, one of the largest lakes in the world, there are over 150 species of cichlids. Members of one particular genus, *Tropheus*, originally lived along the rocky shore and couldn't cross the open water. The climate and geology of the area caused the lake's water level to rise and fall many times over thousands of years. As the water level changed, a new, rocky habitat was formed, and some populations of cichlids became isolated from each other.

The isolated populations were unable to interact with each other because they couldn't cross open waters. As a result, genetic differences began to add up in these populations. The cichlid populations now represent distinct species. They have developed unique characteristics and cannot breed with each other. See the diagram on page 504.

Today scientists understand that isolation is essential to speciation. For a species to separate, two populations must be prevented from reproducing with each other. A geographic boundary like an ocean or mountain range can result in isolation. Two populations of a species can also be isolated if they feed on different things or reproduce at different times of the year.

As the cichlids in Lake Tanganyika show, the mutations in one isolated group may differ from another. Two or more populations may evolve differently from each other. The result is speciation, which has contributed to the biodiversity on Earth.

The Rocky Mountains are an example of a barrier that can isolate populations.

CHECK YOUR READING What is a key factor that can lead to speciation?

14.2 Review

KEY CONCEPTS

1. How did Lamarck's ideas differ from Darwin's?
2. What did Darwin observe in the finch populations that supported his idea of natural selection?
3. Explain how isolation helps speciation.

CRITICAL THINKING

4. **Hypothesize** Two species of grasses are separated by a tall mountain range. A third species of grass shares some characteristics with each of the other two species. It inhabits a small valley, surrounded on all sides by mountains. Form a hypothesis for the origin of the third species.

○ CHALLENGE

5. **Predict** The Arctic hare lives in snow-covered mountains in Canada. The hare is hunted by foxes, wolves, and owls. Which trait is more likely to be inherited by new generations of hares: white fur or black fur?

CHAPTER INVESTIGATION

Modeling Natural Selection

OVERVIEW AND PURPOSE Organisms that are best adapted to their environment tend to survive and reproduce. In this lab you will
- play a game that models the effect of natural selection in an environment
- determine what happens to a group of organisms as a result of natural selection

▶ Question

Write It Up

As you read the steps to the game, think about what makes a population successful in an environment. How will the game model natural selection?

▶ Procedure

1 Make a game board like the one shown below. In your **Science Notebook** make a table like the one on page 507 to record your data.

	1	2	3	4
1				
2				
3				
4				

MATERIALS
- pair of number cubes
- 16 red paper clips
- 16 blue paper clips
- 16 yellow paper clips

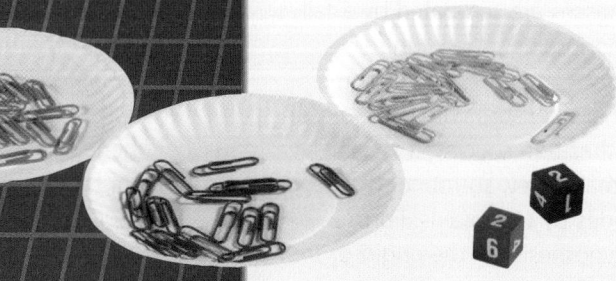

2 Count out 10 red paper clips, 4 blue paper clips, and 2 yellow paper clips. Randomly place the paper clips on the board. Keep the rest of the paper clips in a reserve pile.

3 Each color represents a different population of a single species. The board represents the environment. Roll the number cubes to determine which paper clips "live," or remain on the board, and which paper clips "die," or are removed from the board. Predict which color paper clip you think will be the last remaining color. Write down your prediction.

4 Roll the number cubes to determine which square, or part of the environment, will be affected. For example, 2,3 indicates the paper clip in column 2, row 3. If the numbers 5 or 6 come up, roll again until you have a number between 1 and 4 for each cube.

5 Now roll one cube to see what will happen to the paper clip or organism in that square. Use the chart below to determine if the paper clip "lives" or "dies." If the paper clip lives, repeat steps 4 and 5 until one paper clip dies, or is removed from the board. In your table, record which colors live and die.

Red	Remove if you roll a 1, 2, 3, 4, or 5.
Blue	Remove if you roll a 1, 2, or 3.
Yellow	Remove if you roll a 1 or 2.

6 Now that a paper clip has been removed, you need to see what population will reproduce to fill that space. Roll both cubes to choose another square. The color of the paper clip in that square represents the population that will "reproduce." Pick the same color paper clip from your reserve pile and place it on the empty square. All squares on the board should always have a paper clip.

7 Continue playing the game by repeating steps 4–6 until all the paper clips on the board are the same color.

Observe and Analyze

1. **OBSERVE** Which color paper clip filled the board at the end of the game?

2. **PREDICT** Compare the results with your prediction. Do the results support your prediction?

Conclude

1. **INFER** What does the random selection by rolling both number cubes represent? Explain.

2. **INFER** If the individual paper clips represent different members of a single species, then what might the different colors represent?

3. **LIMITATIONS** What problems or sources of error exist in this model? Give examples.

4. **APPLY** How does this game model natural selection?

▶ INVESTIGATE Further

CHALLENGE Occasionally mutations occur in a population that can either help or damage the population's chance of survival. Add another step to the game that would account for mutations.

Modeling Natural Selection

Table 1. Patterns in a Population

Paper Clip Color	Live	Die

14.3

Many types of evidence support evolution.

Sunshine State STANDARDS

SC.H.1.3.2: The student knows that the study of the events that led scientists to discoveries can provide information about the inquiry process and its effects.

◁ BEFORE, you learned

- Natural selection explains part of the process of evolution
- New species develop from earlier species

▷ NOW, you will learn

- How scientists develop theories
- About the evidence Darwin used to support evolution
- About additional evidence most scientists use today

FCAT VOCABULARY

gene p. 513

VOCABULARY

ancestor p. 509
vestigial organ p.510

EXPLORE Evidence

How can observations supply evidence?

PROCEDURE

① Consider the following statement: It rained last night.

② Look at the following observations and determine which pieces of evidence support the statement.
- There are puddles on the ground.
- The weather report says there will be scattered showers today.
- Your sister tells you there was a rain delay during last night's tennis match.

MATERIALS
- paper
- pencil

WHAT DO YOU THINK?
- What other observations can you come up with that would supply evidence for the first statement?
- Could any of the evidence be misleading?

Observations provide evidence for theories.

MAIN IDEA AND DETAILS
Don't forget to make a chart of details supporting the main idea that observations provide evidence for theories. Include a definition of *theory* in your chart.

In this chapter, you've learned about important observations that scientists have used to understand the history of living things. These observations provided Darwin with information he used to describe his ideas about evolution.

Darwin, like all good scientists, was skeptical about his observations and conclusions. Although the historic trip on the *Beagle* took place between 1831 and 1836, Darwin didn't publish the book explaining his theory until 1859. In order to understand the importance of Darwin's work, it is also important to understand the meaning of the term *theory*.

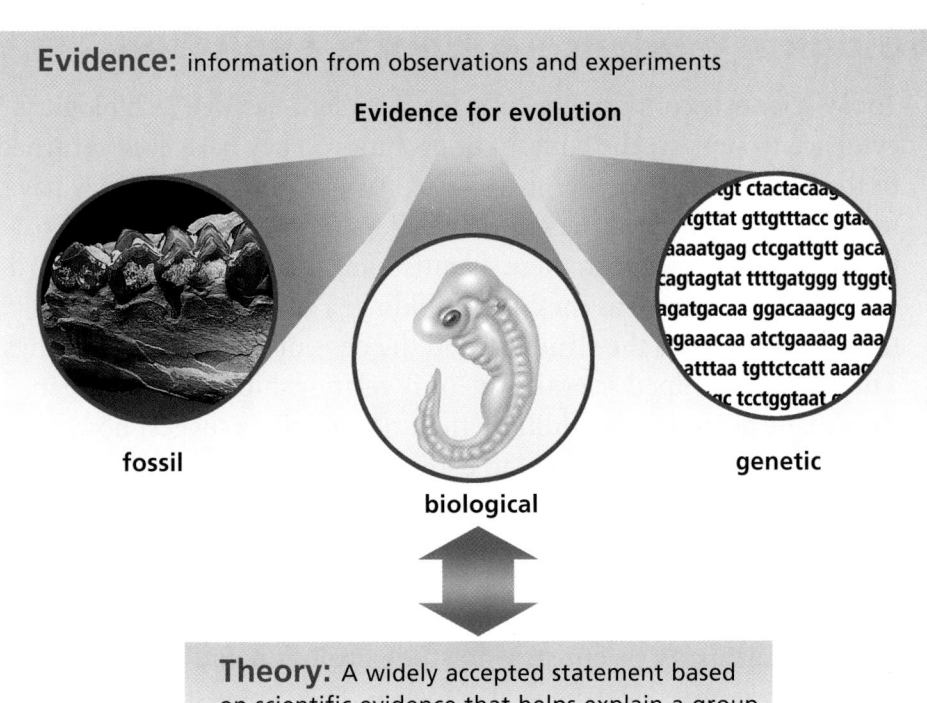

Evidence: information from observations and experiments

Evidence for evolution

fossil

biological

genetic

RESOURCE CENTER
CLASSZONE.COM

Examine evidence to support evolution.

Theory: A widely accepted statement based on scientific evidence that helps explain a group of facts

A scientific theory is a statement based on observation and experiment. If continued observation and experiment support the statement, it may become widely accepted. A theory that has been widely accepted is used to explain and predict natural phenomena. The chart above will help give you an idea of how a theory works and what evidence has been used to support evolution and the theory of natural selection.

CHECK YOUR READING   How do scientists support theories?

Fossil evidence supports evolution.

You have read that Darwin collected many specimens of fossils on his trip. These specimens provided evidence that species existing in the past were very similar to species living during Darwin's time. For example, the fossil of an extinct animal called the glyptodon resembles the modern armadillo, an animal found today in South America.

The geographic information about many fossils provides evidence that two species with a common ancestor can develop differently in different locations. An **ancestor** is an early form of an organism from which later forms descend. The idea of common ancestors is important to the theory of natural selection and to the evidence that supports the theory. Scientists comparing modern plants and modern algae to fossil algae can tell that they all share a common ancestor.

CHECK YOUR READING   What is a common ancestor?

Biological evidence supports evolution.

Today scientists continue to study fossil evidence as well as biological evidence to support the concept of evolution. They have even returned to the Galápagos to further investigate Darwin's work. What they have found gives strength to the theory he proposed nearly 150 years ago. Returning year after year, these scientists are able to follow and record evolutionary changes as they are unfolding. The biological evidence they study includes the structure and the development of living things. This work has helped scientists identify relationships between organisms that exist today. In addition, their observations suggest how modern organisms are related to earlier species.

Similarities in Structure

Evidence for evolution can be observed within the physical structures of adult organisms. Scientists who study evolution and development consider two types of structural evidence. They are vestigial (veh-STIHJ-ee-uhl) organs and similar structures with different functions.

 **CHECK YOUR READING** What are two types of structural evidence?

READING TiP

The root of the word vestigial means "footprint." A vestige refers to visible evidence that is left behind—such as a footprint.

Vestigial organs are physical structures that were fully developed and functional in an ancestral group of organisms but are reduced and unused in the later species. In the bodies of whales there are small leg bones that are vestigial. The skeletons of snakes also have traces of leglike structures that are not used. These vestigial organs help researchers see how some modern organisms are related to ancestors that had similar structures.

Similar structures with different functions Scientists studying the anatomy of living things have also noticed that many different species share similar structures. But these structures are used differently by each species. For example, lizards, bats, and manatees have forelimbs that have a similar bone structure. As you can see from the diagram on page 511, there is one short bone and one long bone that go from a shoulder structure to a wrist structure. But obviously, a lizard, a bat, and a manatee use this structure in different ways.

This similarity in structure indicates that these organisms shared a common ancestor. The process of natural selection caused the variations in form and function that can be observed today. These organisms lived in different environments and so were under different pressures. For lizards the environment was land, for bats it was the air, and for manatees the water. The environment influenced the selection of traits.

Biological Evidence for Evolution

Scientists learn about common ancestors by looking at physical structures.

Vestigial Structures

The small, leglike bones in modern whales indicate that an early ancestor may have had legs.

Ambulocetus, an extinct whalelike animal with four legs

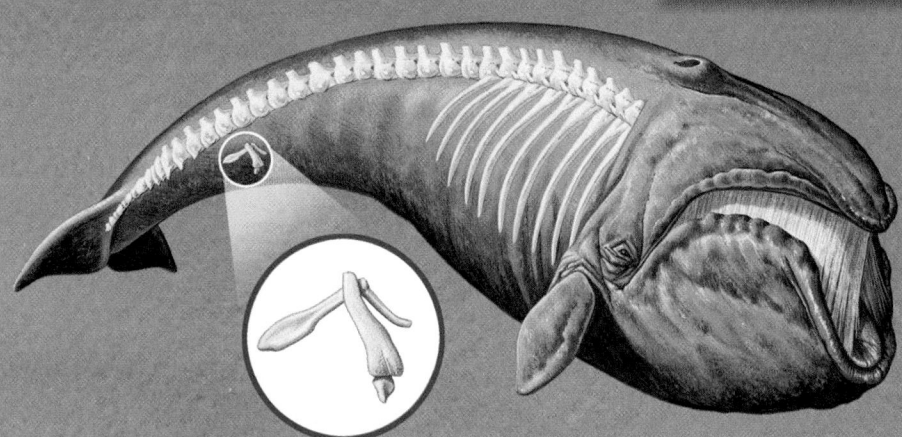

modern whale

Similar Structures, Different Functions

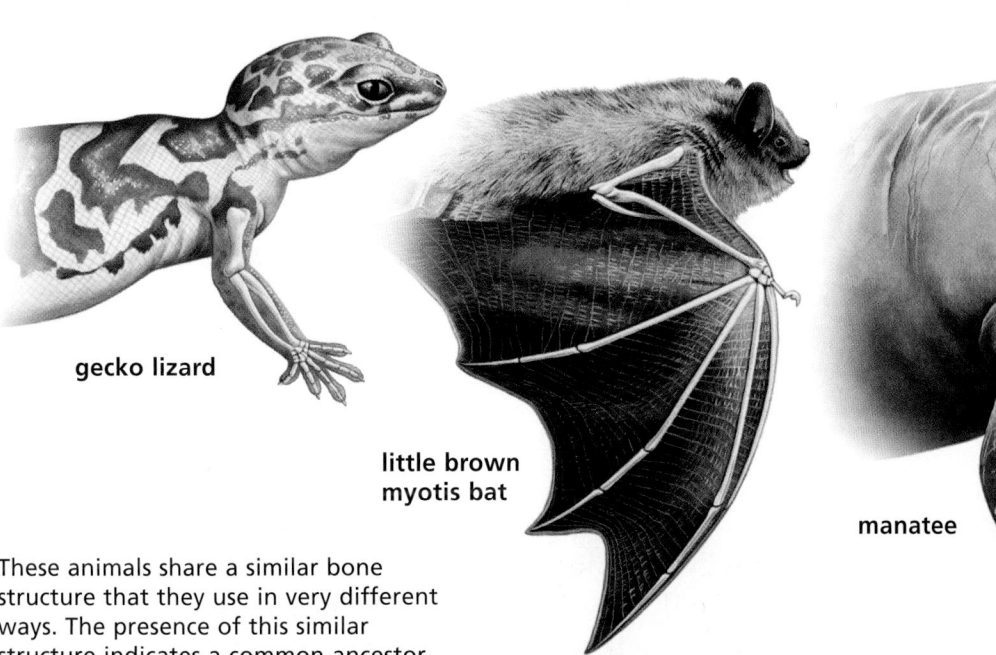

gecko lizard

little brown myotis bat

manatee

These animals share a similar bone structure that they use in very different ways. The presence of this similar structure indicates a common ancestor.

Similarities in Development

READING TiP

As you read about the development of a chicken, rabbit, and salamander, study the diagram below.

Scientists in the 1700s were fascinated by the fact that various animals looked similar in their earliest stages of life. They noted that as the organisms developed, they became less and less alike. Today's scientists continue to compare the developmental stages of different species.

The adult stages of many species do not look similar. For example, a rabbit does not look anything like a chicken. However, study reveals that the early life stages of a chicken and a rabbit are similar. An organism that is in an early stage of development is called an embryo.

In the diagram below, notice the development of three different species: a chicken, a rabbit, and a salamander. In the early stages of development, the embryos of all three organisms look similar. As they continue to develop, they begin to take on distinct characteristics. The chicken has a structure that starts to resemble a beak. The salamander begins to look as if it is adapted for life near water. In their adult stages, these three species no longer look similar.

Similarities in Development

The study of embryos shows that animals that appear to be very different as adults are similar during early development.

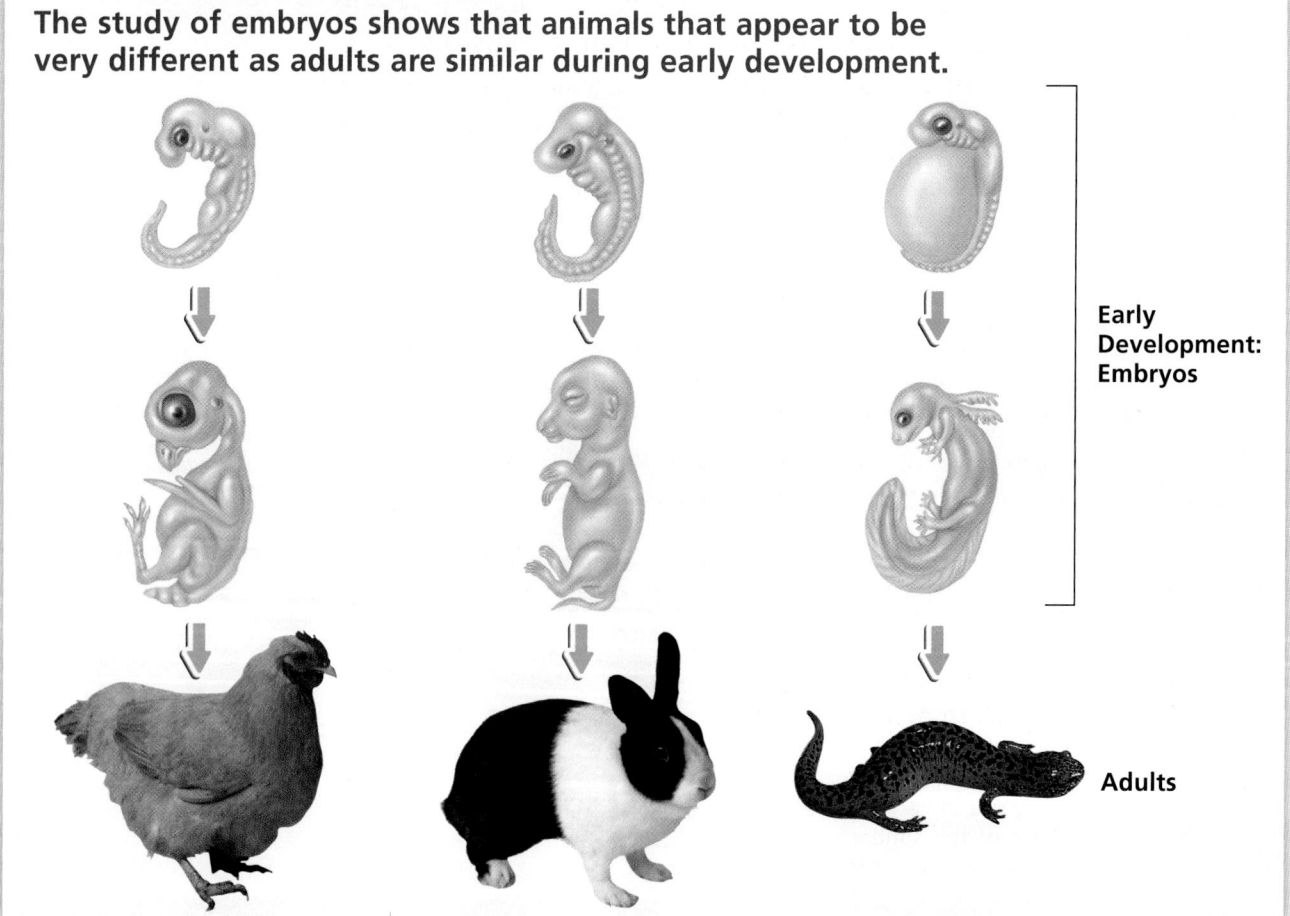

Early Development: Embryos

Adults

INVESTIGATE Genes

How can a sequence communicate information?

PROCEDURE

① From your pile of letters (A, D, E, R), spell out the word RED.

② Working with a partner, use the letters to spell two more words having three letters.

WHAT DO YOU THINK?

How does rearranging the letters change the meaning of the words?

CHALLENGE Cut out words from a newspaper. Arrange these words to form different phrases. How do these phrases communicate different messages?

SKILL FOCUS
Sequencing

MATERIALS
letter cards

TIME
20 minutes

Genetic evidence supports evolution.

The key to understanding how traits are passed from one generation to the next lies in the study of DNA, the genetic material found in all organisms. DNA contains the information all organisms need to grow and to maintain themselves. When organisms reproduce, they pass on their genetic material to their offspring.

DNA contains a code that a cell uses to put together all the materials it needs to function properly. The code is made up of four different chemical subunits called bases. The bases are symbolized by the four letters A, T, C, and G. Located within DNA are individual genes. A **gene** is a segment of DNA that relates to a specific trait or function of an organism. Each gene has a particular sequence of bases. The cell takes this sequence and translates it into the chemicals and structures the organism needs.

VOCABULARY
Remember to make a frame game for *gene*.

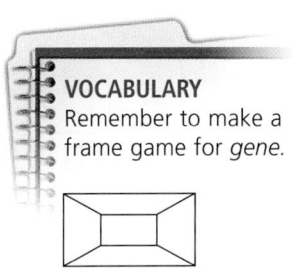

Scientists studying genes have identified a gene called the clock gene in many mammals. This particular gene relates to the function of sleeping and waking. As scientists learn more they can identify patterns of behavior in different organisms. The chart on page 514 compares the DNA sequence of part of the clock gene in both humans and mice.

 **CHECK YOUR READING** What is a gene?

Comparing Genes

Humans and mice look very different, but the DNA that makes up their genes is surprisingly similar.

DNA Sequence

clock gene sequence begins here

Human	gtacaaatgt	ctactacaag	acgaaaacgt	agtatgttat	gttgtttacc	gtaagctgta
Mouse	gtacaaatgt	ctaccacaag	acgaaaacat	aatgtgttat	ggtgtttacc	gtaagctgta
Human	gtaaaatgag	ctcgattgtt	gacagagatg	acagtagtat	ttttgatggg	ttggtggaag
Mouse	gtaaaatgag	ctcaattgtt	gacagagatg	acagtagtat	ttttgatgga	ttggtggaag
Human	aagatgacaa	ggacaaagcg	aaaagagtat	ctagaaacaa	atctgaaaag	aaacgtagag
Mouse	aagatgacaa	ggacaaagca	aaaagagtat	ctagaaacaa	atcagaaaag	aaacgtagag
Human	atcaatttaa	tgttctcatt	aaagaactgg	gatccatgct	tcctggtaat	gctagaaaga
Mouse	atcagttcaa	tgtcctcatt	aaggagctgg	ggtctatgct	tcctggtaac	gcgagaaaga

The bar shows where the mouse and human DNA are different.

The letters represent different subunits of DNA.

FLORIDA
Content Preview

Scientists have learned a great deal about human DNA, which you will study in grade 8.

Scientists can tell how closely organisms are related by comparing their DNA. The more matches there are in the sequence of bases between two organisms, the more closely related they are. For example, almost all the genes found in a mouse are also found in a human. Even though the two organisms appear so different, much of the functioning of their cells is similar.

14.3 Review

KEY CONCEPTS

1. Describe in your own words how scientists use the word *theory*.

2. What type of evidence did Darwin use to support his theory of evolution?

3. Identify three different types of evidence that today's scientists use to support the theory of evolution.

CRITICAL THINKING

4. **Analyze** Describe three characteristics of a scientific theory. Explain how Darwin's theory of evolution is an example of a scientific theory.

⬥ CHALLENGE

5. **Predict** If you were looking at the sequence within the genes of two species, how would you predict that the two species are related?

How Did the Deep-Sea Angler Get Its Glow?

A fish that uses a fishing pole to catch food might seem odd. However, anglerfish do just that. The fish have a modified spine that extends from their head, almost like a fishing pole. At the end is a small piece of tissue that is similar in shape to a small worm. The tissue functions like a lure that a fisherman uses to catch fish. The anglerfish wiggles its "lure" to attract prey. If the prey fish moves in close enough, the anglerfish opens its mouth and swallows the prey whole. The "fishing poles" of abyssal anglerfish, anglerfish that live in the deep sea, have an interesting adaptation. The "lure" actually glows in the dark—it is bioluminescent.

▶ Observations

From laboratory research and field studies, scientists made these observations.

> There are more than 200 species of anglerfish. Many of these live in deep water.
>
> Shallow-water species do not have glow-in-the-dark "lures."
>
> Only female abyssal anglerfish have a "pole." They do not have pelvic fins and are not strong swimmers.
>
> Other deep-sea organisms, including bacteria, jellyfish, even some squid, are bioluminescent.

▶ Hypotheses

Consider these hypotheses.

> The ancestors of abyssal anglerfish lived in shallow waters. Some of these fish drifted into deep waters. A bioluminescent lure helped some survive.
>
> Light does not reach down to the bottom of the deep sea. Bioluminescence provides an advantage for the anglerfish because it makes its lure noticeable.
>
> A bioluminescent lure is more valuable to a female abyssal anglerfish than the ability to swim.

▶ Evaluate Each Hypothesis

On Your Own For each hypothesis, think about whether all the observations support it. Some facts may rule out some hypotheses. Others may support them.

As a Group Decide which hypothesis is the most reasonable. Discuss your thinking and conclusions in a small group and see if the group can agree.

FLORIDA REVIEW
CLASSZONE.COM

Content Review and
FCAT Practice

the **BIG** idea

Living things, like Earth itself, change over time.

KEY CONCEPTS SUMMARY

1 Earth has been home to living things for about 3.8 billion years.

Fossil records inform humans about the development of life on Earth. Information from fossils can help scientists reconstruct Earth's history.

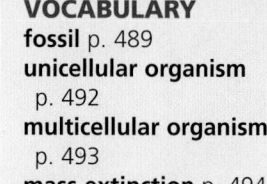

VOCABULARY
fossil p. 489
unicellular organism p. 492
multicellular organism p. 493
mass extinction p. 494

2 Species change over time.

Darwin's theory of natural selection explains evolution.

Four principles of natural selection
• overproduction
• variation
• adaptation
• selection

The beak of this cactus finch provides an example of an adaptation.

VOCABULARY
evolution p. 497
natural selection p. 501
adaptation p. 502
speciation p. 504

3 Many types of evidence support evolution.

Three different types of evidence provide a bigger picture of evolution

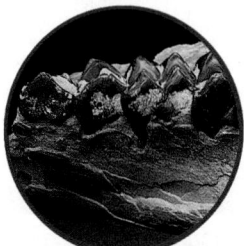

fossil

biological

genetic

VOCABULARY
ancestor p. 509
vestigial organ p. 510
gene p. 513

Reviewing Vocabulary

Draw a triangle for each of the terms below. On the wide bottom of the triangle, write the term and your own definition of it. Above that, write a sentence in which you use the term correctly. At the top of the triangle, draw a small picture to show what the term looks like.

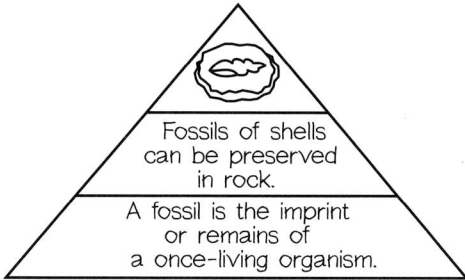

Fossils of shells can be preserved in rock.

A fossil is the imprint or remains of a once-living organism.

1. unicellular organism

2. multicellular organism

3. adaptation

4. vestigial structure

Reviewing Key Concepts

Multiple Choice *Choose the letter of the best answer.*

5. Which is *not* part of the fossil record?
   a. fossil bones
   b. preserved remains
   c. living unicellular organisms
   d. imprints

6. Whether a fossil formed before or after another fossil is described by its
   a. relative age
   b. absolute age
   c. fossil record
   d. radioactive age

7. The earliest multicellular organisms were
   a. jellyfish
   b. simple plants
   c. fungi
   d. tiny seaweeds

8. Which is a possible explanation for mass extinctions?
   a. Earth had no water.
   b. A meteorite collided with Earth.
   c. The continents separated.
   d. Woolly mammoths left no offspring.

9. Darwin's theory that species develop new traits and change over time is known as
   a. natural selection   **c.** speciation
   b. evolution   **d.** adaptation

10. Which describes Lamarck's explanation for changes in the fossil record?
   a. Species best suited to their environments survive better than others.
   b. Variation within a species can be passed on to offspring.
   c. Acquired traits are passed on from one generation to another.
   d. Giraffes adapted to their environment.

11. A slight change in a rabbit's ability to hear its predators better and help it survive is
   a. an adaptation
   b. a vestigial structure
   c. an aquired trait
   d. an isolation

12. Which is necessary for speciation to occur?
   a. adaptation
   b. mass extinction
   c. isolation
   d. acquired traits

13. Which of the following statements explain why the theory of evolution is widely accepted by the scientific community?
   a. It has been proven by experiments.
   b. The fossil record is complete.
   c. It is supported by genetic evidence.
   d. Lamarck's theory was correct.

14. Genetic evidence is based on the study of
   a. embryonic development
   b. mutations
   c. common ancestors
   d. DNA sequences

15. Genetic information that cells use to control the production of new cells is located in

a. embryos

b. genes

c. the environment

d. vestigial structures

Short Response *Write a short response to each question.*

16. Describe how the relative age of a fossil is determined by studying layers of rock.

17. Explain the difference between artificial selection and natural selection.

18. How does common ancestry between two species support evolution?

Thinking Critically

19. COMMUNICATE What have scientists learned about past life on Earth from the fossil record?

20. PROVIDE EXAMPLES Explain the principle of overproduction. Give an example.

21. SYNTHESIZE How might the mass extinction of dinosaurs enable many new species of mammals to develop?

22. EVALUATE How would natural selection have led to the development of giraffes with long necks as opposed to giraffes with short necks?

23. PROVIDE EXAMPLES How are variation and adaptations related to natural selection? Give an example.

24. PREDICT In Africa's Lake Tanganyika different populations of cichlids became isolated from each other. Based on what you already learned, predict how the changing water level helped the cichlid population to change. How do you think the development of new cichlid species affected other living things in the lake?

25. ANALYZE How is geographic isolation related to the formation of a new species?

26. EVALUATE Pandas were once considered to be closely related to raccoons and red pandas because of their physical similarities. Today, scientists have learned that pandas are more closely related to bears than to raccoons and red pandas. What evidence might scientists have used to draw this conclusion? Explain.

27. INFER What does the presence of similar structures in two organisms—such as a dolphin's flipper and a lizard's forelimb—indicate?

the BIG idea

28. INFER Look again at the picture on pages 486–487. Now that you have finished the chapter, how would you change or add details to your answer to the question on the photograph?

29. SYNTHESIZE The beaks of hummingbirds are adapted to fit into long, thin flowers. Hummingbirds can feed on the nectar inside the flower. Write an explanation for this adaptation that Lamarck might have proposed. Then write an explanation for this adaptation based on Darwin's ideas. Use the terms acquired traits and natural selection in your answer.

UNIT PROJECTS

Check your schedule for your unit project. How are you doing? Be sure that you've placed data or notes from your research in your project folder.

Interpreting Diagrams

This diagram shows how groups of carnivores are related to one another. Each Y in the diagram indicates a common ancestor.

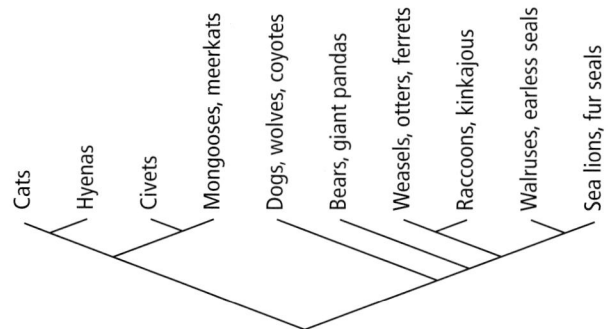

Cats | Hyenas | Civets | Mongooses, meerkats | Dogs, wolves, coyotes | Bears, giant pandas | Weasels, otters, ferrets | Raccoons, kinkajous | Walruses, earless seals | Sea lions, fur seals

FCAT TiP

If you don't know the answer to a short-response question, finish the rest of the test first and then come back to it. Other questions on the test may help you recall information that you can use to answer the short-response question.

Use the diagram to answer the questions below.

MULTIPLE CHOICE

1. Hyenas are most closely related to which group?

   A. cats   **C.** mongooses and meerkats
   B. civets   **D.** raccoons and kinkajous

2. Weasels, otters, and ferrets are most closely related to which group?

   F. bears and giant pandas
   G. sea lions and fur seals
   H. raccoons and kinkajous
   I. mongooses and meerkats

3. Sea lions and fur seals share their closest ancestor with which group?

   A. walruses and earless seals
   B. raccoons and kinkajous
   C. mongooses and muskrats
   D. civets

4. Which statement is true based on the information in the diagram?

   F. Dogs, wolves, and coyotes do not have a common ancestor with any of the groups.
   G. Raccoons are more closely related to weasels than they are to giant pandas.
   H. None of the groups shown in the diagram have a common ancestor.
   I. Mongooses and meerkats are the same as civets.

SHORT RESPONSE

5. Study the diagram and determine whether or not wolves, hyenas, cats, and ferrets all have a common ancestor. Explain your answer.

6. Each branch indicates where species separated from each other. Describe what this means.

EXTENDED RESPONSE

7. A scientist has discovered a new type of animal in the tundra area near the North Pole. Write a paragraph describing the type of evidence the scientist might use to classify the animal by its evolutionary history in the chart shown. Use these terms in your paragraph. Underline each term in your answer.

embryo	DNA sequences
vestigial structures	common ancestor

8. Write a paragraph in which you describe the traits of one of the animals named in the diagram. Choose several traits and describe how these traits might help the animal survive. Then describe how these might have been the result of adaptations and natural selection.

TIMELINES in Science

LIFE Unearthed

How do scientists know about life on Earth millions of years ago? They dig, scratch, and hunt. The best clues they find are hidden in layers of rock. The rock-locked clues, called fossils, are traces or remains of living things from long ago. Some fossils show the actual bodies of organisms, while others, such as footprints, reveal behavior.

Before 1820, most fossil finds revealed the bodies of ocean life. Then large bones of lizardlike walking animals began turning up, and pictures of a new "terrible lizard," or dinosaur, took shape. Later, discoveries of tracks and nests showed behaviors such as flocking and caring for young. Even today, discoveries of "living fossils," modern relatives of prehistoric species, have offered us a rare glimpse of the activity of early life.

1824

Giant Lizards from Fragments

William Buckland describes *Megalosaurus*, a giant crocodilelike animal he studies from only a few bits of jaw, teeth, ribs, pelvis, and one leg. A year later Gideon Mantell assembles *Iguanodon*, a similar animal, from fossil bones.

EVENTS

| 1800 | 1810 | 1820 |

APPLICATIONS AND TECHNOLOGY

TECHNOLOGY

Removing Fossils with Care

The technology for removing fossils from rock beds has not changed much since the 1820s. Collectors still work by hand with hammers, chisels, trowels, dental picks, and sieves. Gideon Mantell used these when he chiseled out *Iguanodon* bones embedded in one large rock called the "Mantle piece."

Fossil hunters also use hand lenses and microscopes. Sometimes a protective layer is built up with glue, varnish, or another finish. For larger samples, a plaster cast often supports the fossil. Most fossils are packed using a technology found in any kitchen—a sealable plastic bag.

1909
Burgess Shale Shows Soft Bodies

In the Burgess Pass of the Canadian Rocky Mountains, Charles Walcott finds fossils preserved in shale, a soft rock that preserves lacelike details such as the soft tissues of the Marella. The glimpse of life 505 million years ago is the earliest yet seen.

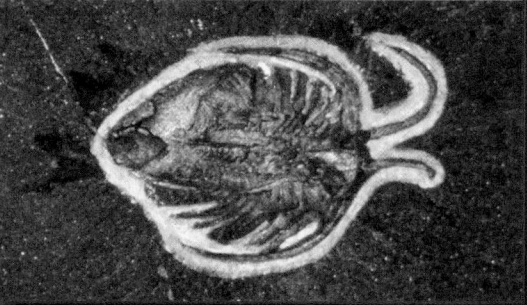

1944
New Dawn for the Dawn Redwood

Beside a small temple, a Chinese scientist discovers the dawn redwood, or metasequoia, growing. Common in fossil specimens 100 million years old, the tree had not been seen alive in recorded history. The 1944 find starts a search, and in 1948, scientists find a small wild grove in China as well.

1938
African Fisherman Hauls in History

A South African fisherman pulls up a five-foot fish he has never seen. He calls the local museum, whose curator, a naturalist, has also never seen the species. To her surprise, biologists identify it as a coelacanth, a prehistoric fish thought to be extinct for more than 50 million years.

| 1900 | 1910 | 1920 | 1930 | 1940 |

APPLICATION

Protecting Fossils and Dig Sites

The United States Antiquities Act of 1906 preserves and protects historic and prehistoric sites. The act requires collectors to have a permit to dig for or to pick up fossils on public lands such as national parks. It also requires that any major find be publicly and permanently preserved in a museum.

The United Nations also now designates World Heritage sites. For example, the original Burgess Shale find in Yoho National Park in Canada is now protected by international law. Since 1906, many states and provinces in Canada have enacted their own laws about land rights and the excavation and transport of fossils.

1974
"Lucy" and Upright Kin Found

Digging in Ethiopia, Donald Johanson finds an almost complete hominid skeleton. He names the fossil "Lucy," after a Beatles song. Lucy is over 3 million years old, is three and one-half feet tall, and has an upright stance or posture. A year later, Johanson's crew finds "The First Family," a group of 13 skeletons of the same species as Lucy.

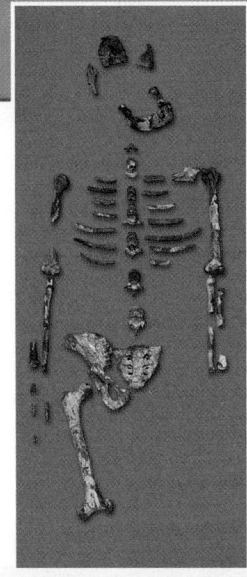

1990
Largest Tyrannosaurus, *"Sue"*

Out on a walk with her dog in the South Dakota bad-lands, amateur fossil hunter Sue Hendrickson discovers three huge bones jutting out of a cliff. Hendrickson finds the largest and most complete *T. rex* skeleton yet. The 67-million-year-old "Sue" is now on display in the Field Museum in Chicago, Illinois.

1953
Piltdown Man No Neanderthal

Scientists once applauded the discovery in 1912 of a "Neanderthal skull" in the Piltdown gravel pit, but a few had their doubts. In 1953, radioactive potassium dating proves the Piltdown man to be nothing more than the jaw of an orangutan placed beside human skull fragments.

1950   1960   1970   1980   1990

TECHNOLOGY

How Old Is a Fossil?

Before 1947, scientists used a method of fossil dating called relative dating. They assigned a date to a fossil according to the rock layer in which it was found. The deeper, or older, the layer, the older the fossil.

The discovery of radiometric dating in 1947 marked the first time a fossil's date could be pinpointed. Organic matter decays at a constant rate. So, by measuring the rate of decay, you can tell the age of the matter. Radiocarbon 14 is used to tell the age of a fossil that is less than 10,000 years old. Since most fossils are older than that, scientists use other methods.

Potassium-argon decays more slowly than carbon. It is a more common method of dating. All types of fossil dating have margins of error, or limits to accuracy.

1993

Oldest Fossils Are Too Small to See

Fossils discovered up to this point date back about 550 million years, to the dawn of the Cambrian Period. J. William Schopf identifies fossils of microorganisms scientifically dated to 3.4 billion years ago. This startling find near Australia's Marble Bar opens up a vast period of time and once again reshapes theories about life's beginnings.

 RESOURCE CENTER
CLASSZONE.COM
Discover more about the latest fossil and living-fossil finds.

2000

TECHNOLOGY

Fossil Classification and DNA

There are many ways to classify fossils. Scientists look at bone structure, body posture, evidence of behavior, and environment. Microscopes are used to identify organisms too small for the eye to see. Study of DNA molecules helps to identify species when soft tissues remain intact, such as in fossils formed in amber or crystallized tree sap. In 1985, polymerase chain reaction (PCR) became the simplest method to study the DNA extracted from fossils. In PCR, parts of DNA can be copied billions of times in a few hours.

INTO THE FUTURE

Technology is sure to play a role in future fossil finds. Scientists can communicate via laptop computers and satellites, which allow the public to follow excavations as they occur.

Computer modeling helps scientists determine what incomplete skeletons looked like. It also helps them determine how dinosaurs and other living things once moved. Fossil finds can be combined with digitized information about modern living organisms and about environmental conditions. The model can test hypotheses or even help to formulate them.

Another area of technology that may become increasingly applied to fossils is DNA testing to identify and help date fossils. This is more complicated in fossilized bone, as the genetic material can be fragmented. But with time, scientists may discover new techniques to extract better genetic information. DNA is also the basis for cloning, which as yet can only be applied to living organisms. Perhaps in the future it can be applied to preserved remains.

ACTIVITIES

Writing About Science: Film Script

Write your own version of the story of life on Earth. Include drawings, photographs, or video clips to illustrate your story.

Reliving History

Think about the equipment archaeologists and paleontologists use on excavations. Think about their goals. Write a proposal to a local university or museum asking them to fund your excavation.

Population Dynamics

the **BIG** idea

Populations are shaped by interactions between organisms and the environment.

Key Concepts

SECTION
1 **Populations have many characteristics.**
Learn about the stages and factors that all populations have in common.

SECTION
2 **Populations respond to pressures.**
Learn how change can affect populations.

SECTION
3 **Human populations have unique responses to change.**
Learn how the responses of human populations are different from responses of other populations.

This image was created by combining satellite shots of parts of Earth. What does it suggest about Earth's populations?

FCAT Practice

Prepare and practice for the FCAT
- Section Reviews, pp. 534, 542, 551
- Chapter Review, pp. 554–556
- FCAT Practice, p. 557

CLASSZONE.COM
- Florida Review: Content Review and FCAT Practice

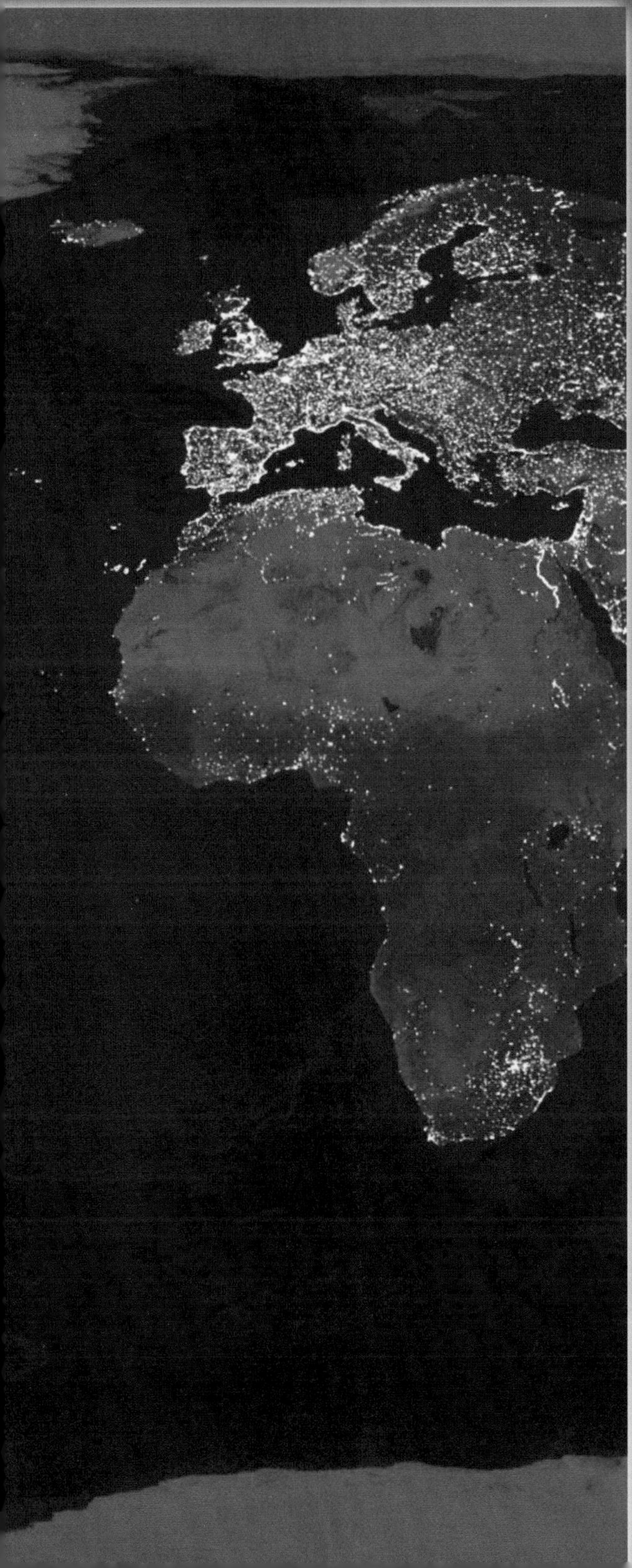

EXPLORE (the BIG idea)

How Does Population Grow?

For every three human births there is one death. Use a bucket and water to represent the human population. For every 3 cups of water you add to the bucket, take away one cup.

Observe and Think
How did the water level rise—quickly, slowly, or steadily?

How Do Populations Differ?

Put about 40 marbles in a bowl. Remove any 10 marbles from the bowl and put them in another dish. Each dish of marbles represents a population.

Observe and Think
How would a chance event such as a fire affect these two populations differently?

Internet Activity: Population Dynamics

Go to **ClassZone.com** to learn more about the factors that describe a population. Find out how change in each of the factors can affect the population.

Observe and Think
How would a change in one factor affect the dynamics of a population?

NSTA
scilinks.org
SCi LINKS

Limiting Factors **Code: MDL038**

Getting Ready to Learn

◀ CONCEPT REVIEW

- Living things change over time.
- Species adapt to their environment or become extinct.

◀ VOCABULARY REVIEW

See Glossary for definition.

species

FLORIDA REVIEW
CLASSZONE.COM

Content Review and FCAT Practice

▶ TAKING NOTES

CHOOSE YOUR OWN STRATEGY

Take notes using one or more strategies from earlier chapters—**main idea and details** or **outline.** You can also use other note-taking strategies that you might already know.

VOCABULARY STRATEGY

Think about a vocabulary term as a **magnet word** diagram. Write the other terms or ideas related to that term around it.

See the Note-Taking Handbook on pages R45–R51.

SCIENCE NOTEBOOK

Main Idea and Details

I. Main idea
  A. Supporting idea
    1. Detail
    2. Detail
  B. Supporting idea

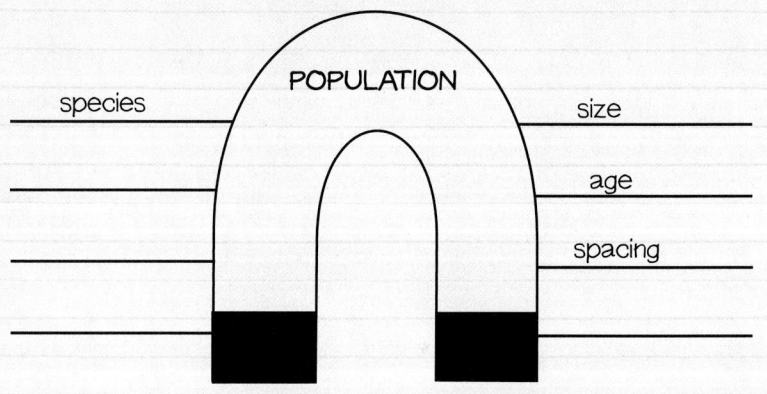

species   POPULATION   size

age

spacing

Populations have many characteristics.

Sunshine State STANDARDS

SC.G.2.3.3: The student knows that a brief change in the limited resources of an ecosystem may alter the size of a population or the average size of individual organisms and that long-term change may result in the elimination of animal and plant populations inhabiting the Earth.

SC.H.2.3.1: The student recognizes that patterns exist within and across systems.

VOCABULARY

population dynamics p. 527

carrying capacity p. 528

population size p. 530

population density p. 531

BEFORE, you learned

- Species change over time
- Evolution is a process of change
- A habitat is an area that provides organisms with resources

NOW, you will learn

- About stages in population dynamics
- About variables that define a population
- About changes that affect populations

THINK ABOUT

How fast can a population grow?

How big can a population grow? Suppose you started with a pair of fruit flies. That single pair can produce 200 eggs. In three weeks, each pair from that batch could produce 200 flies of its own—producing up to 20,000 flies. Assume all eggs hatch—an event highly unlikely in the real world. After three weeks, 2 million fruit flies would be buzzing around the area. After just 17 generations, given ideal conditions (for the fruit fly, that is), the mass of fruit flies would exceed the mass of planet Earth.

CHOOSE YOUR OWN STRATEGY

Begin taking notes on the three stages of populations. Use a strategy from an earlier chapter or one that you already know.

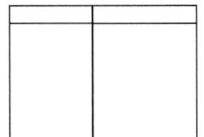

Populations go through three stages.

Look closely at the fruit flies above. As a group of the same species living together in a particular area, they represent a population. The particular area in which a scientist studies a population may be as large as a mountain range or as small as a puddle. Scientists study how populations of organisms change as they interact with each other and the environment. Over time, the number of individuals in a population changes by increasing or decreasing. **Population dynamics** is the study of why populations change and what causes them to change. In this chapter you will learn about some of the important observations scientists have made about populations.

 **CHECK YOUR READING** What is population dynamics?

One species of iguana may have several populations living on different islands. As a result, these iguana populations don't interact with each other. Yet there may be other populations of iguanas living on the islands made up of a different species.

Growth, Stability, and Decline

READING **TiP**

As you read about growth, stability, and decline, refer to the explanations on the graph.

As different as populations may be—whether cacti, finches, dragonflies, or iguanas—all populations go through the same three stages of change: growth, stability, and decline.

All living things need resources such as water, energy, and living space. Populations get their resources from the environment. However, the area a population occupies can support only so many individuals. **Carrying capacity** is the maximum number of individuals an ecosystem can support.

When a habitat contains enough resources to meet the needs of a population, the population grows rapidly. This growth stage of a population tends to be brief. On a graph, it looks like a sharp rise. The growth stage is followed by a period of stability, when the size of a population remains constant. For most populations, the stability stage is the longest stage of a population's existence. The stability stage is often followed by a decline in population size.

Population Change

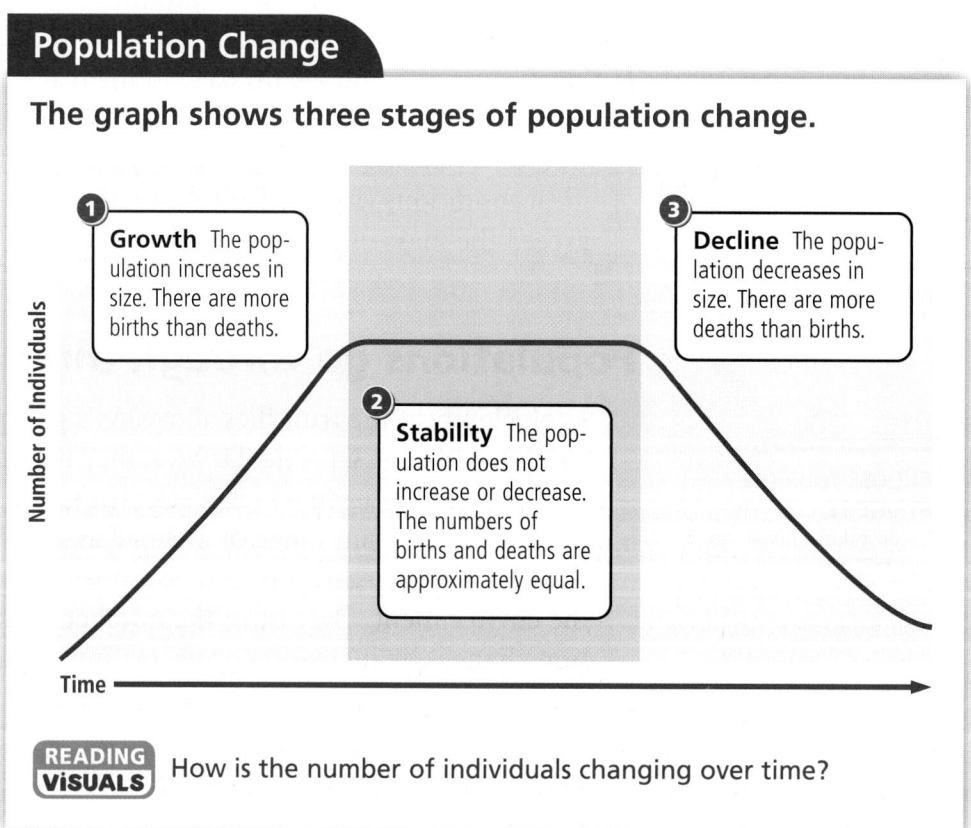

The graph shows three stages of population change.

1 Growth The population increases in size. There are more births than deaths.

2 Stability The population does not increase or decrease. The numbers of births and deaths are approximately equal.

3 Decline The population decreases in size. There are more deaths than births.

Number of Individuals

Time

READING **VISUALS** How is the number of individuals changing over time?

During the growth stage, populations can increase according to two general patterns. One pattern is rapid growth, which increases at a greater and greater rate. Another pattern is gradual growth, which increases at a fairly steady rate. The two graphs below show the two different types of growth.

Population Growth

The graphs show two patterns of population growth.

Rapid Growth

Number of individuals

Time

Gradual Growth

Number of individuals

Time

Darwin's Observations of Population Growth

In Chapter 14 you read about the observations and conclusions made by the naturalist Charles Darwin. In his book *On the Origin of Species* Darwin included important observations about population growth.

 REMINDER

A species that is no longer living is considered extinct.

- All populations are able to grow rapidly.
- Populations tend to remain constant in size.
- There are limits to natural resources.
- Within a given population there is genetic variation.

Darwin recognized that organisms in most species have the ability to produce more than two surviving offspring. He knew that if there were no limits to growth, then populations would grow rapidly. However, Darwin also observed that in the real world there are natural limits to growth, so populations tend to stabilize. In order for a species to continue, individuals must be replaced as they die. This means that, on average, one member of a population must produce one surviving offspring. If the birth rate doesn't match the death rate, a population can decline until it becomes extinct.

Four characteristics define a population.

When scientists think about population dynamics, they consider four major characteristics. These characteristics include population size, population density, population spacing, and age structure.

Population Size

Population size is the number of individuals in a population at a given time. Even when the population size appears to be stable over time, changes can occur from year to year or from place to place. Population size varies from one habitat to another. It also varies within a single habitat.

An area where the summers are hot and the winters are cold is a good place to observe how population size might change at different times of year. For example, the population sizes of many insects change within a year. Mosquitoes that are all around you on warm summer evenings are nowhere in sight when the temperatures fall below freezing.

The size of plant populations can also change during the year. In the spring and summer you can see flowering plants across the deserts, woods, and mountains of North America. However, by fall and early winter, when there is less rainfall and temperatures drop, many of these plants die. Below is a picture of a southwestern desert in full bloom. During the springtime months of March through May, many deserts in the United States experience a change. There is a period of rapid growth as a variety of wildflowers begins to bloom.

When there is little rainfall, a desert seems empty. After a rain, there is a brief time when plants bloom.

The availability of resources, such as water, increases plant growth. By summer the change in season brings higher temperatures and less rainfall. As a result, desert wildflowers experience a rapid decline in their population size.

 What are two factors that affect population size?

Population Density

Population density is a measure of the number of individuals in a certain space at a particular time. Population density is related to population size. If a population's size increases and all of the individuals remain in the same area, then population density increases, too. There are more individuals living in the same amount of space. If the size of a population in a particular area decreases, density also decreases. Some species, such as bumblebees or mice, live in populations with high densities. Other species, such as blue herons or wolves, live in populations with low densities.

 What is the difference between low density and high density?

Population Density

Density can change over time and over the entire area of the population.

Low Density

Herons are usually found alone or in pairs in marshy areas. Herons are an example of a low-density population.

High Density

Bees in a beehive are an example of a high-density population—many individuals are packed into a small area.

READING VISUALS COMPARE How does the number of herons in an area compare with the number of bees?

The distribution of a population across a large geographic area is its range. Within that range, population density may vary. For example, there may be more grasshoppers in the middle of a prairie than there are at the edges. The population density tends to be higher where more resources are available. Habitats located in the middle of a population range tend to have a greater population density than habitats located at the edges.

 **CHECK YOUR READING** How might population density vary within a range?

Population Spacing

Take a look around you as you walk through a local park. You might notice many flowers growing in open, sunny spots but few beneath the shade of large trees. The pattern in which the flowers grow is an example of population spacing. Scientists have observed three distinct patterns of spacing: clumped, uniform, and random.

In clumped spacing, individuals form small groups within a habitat. Animals like elephants clump because of their social nature. Clumping can also result from the way resources are distributed throughout a habitat. Salamanders that prefer moist, rotten logs may be clumped where logs have fallen in their habitat.

Population Spacing

Population spacing describes how individuals arrange themselves within a population.

Clumped

Individuals that clump themselves often gather around resources.

Uniform

Individuals that are uniformly arranged often compete for resources.

Random

Random patterns are rare and occur without regard to other individuals.

 **READING VISUALS** Compare and contrast the way populations are spaced.

Some individuals live at a distance from each other. These individuals are uniformly spaced. Many plants that grow too close together become evenly spaced as individuals die out. Uniform spacing can protect saguaro cacti from competing for important resources in the desert. Individuals that aren't uniform or clumped space themselves randomly. Dandelions, for instance, grow no matter where other dandelions are growing.

Age Structure

Scientists divide a population into three groups based on age.

- postreproductive: organisms can no longer reproduce
- reproductive: organisms capable of reproduction
- prereproductive: organisms not yet able to reproduce

The age structure of a population affects how much it can grow. On the graph below, the postreproductive age range for humans is over 45, reproductive is 14 to 44 years of age, and prereproductive is 0 to 14.

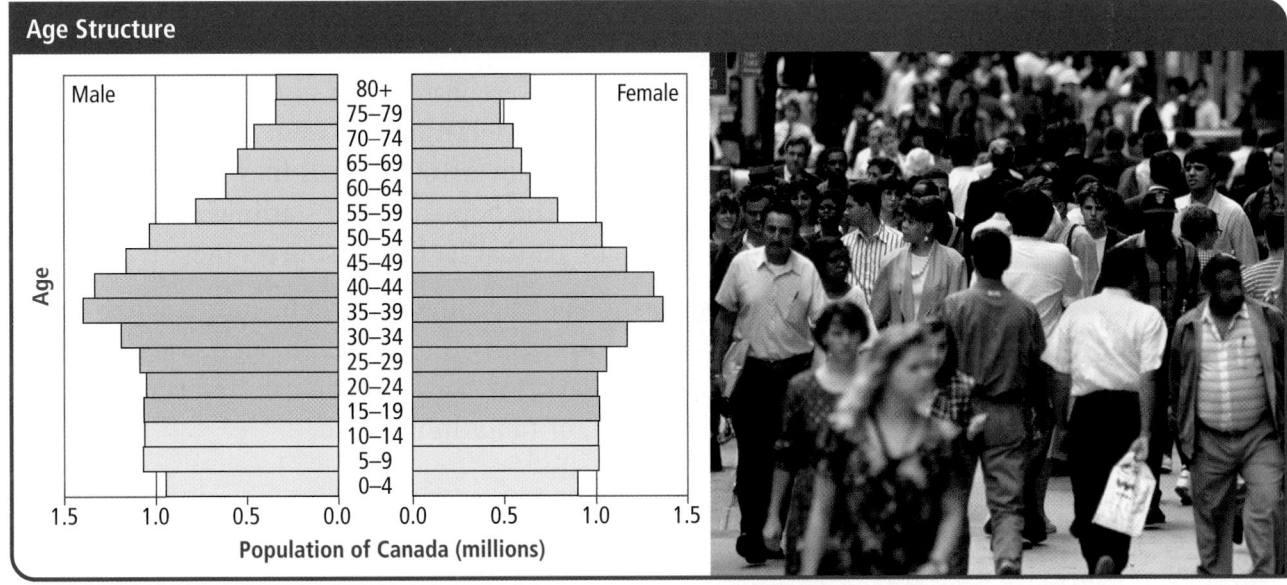

Scientists can predict population change.

Scientists use these four factors—size, density, spacing, and age structure—to describe a population and to predict how it might change over time. Sometimes a population changes when a particular factor changes.

A population can change in response to its surroundings. Suppose a population of frogs is living in a pond where the water becomes saltier. Only those frogs that can survive in an environment with more salt will survive. Thus the population size of frogs will probably decrease as a result of the changing conditions. By looking at population size, scientists can predict how changes affect the population.

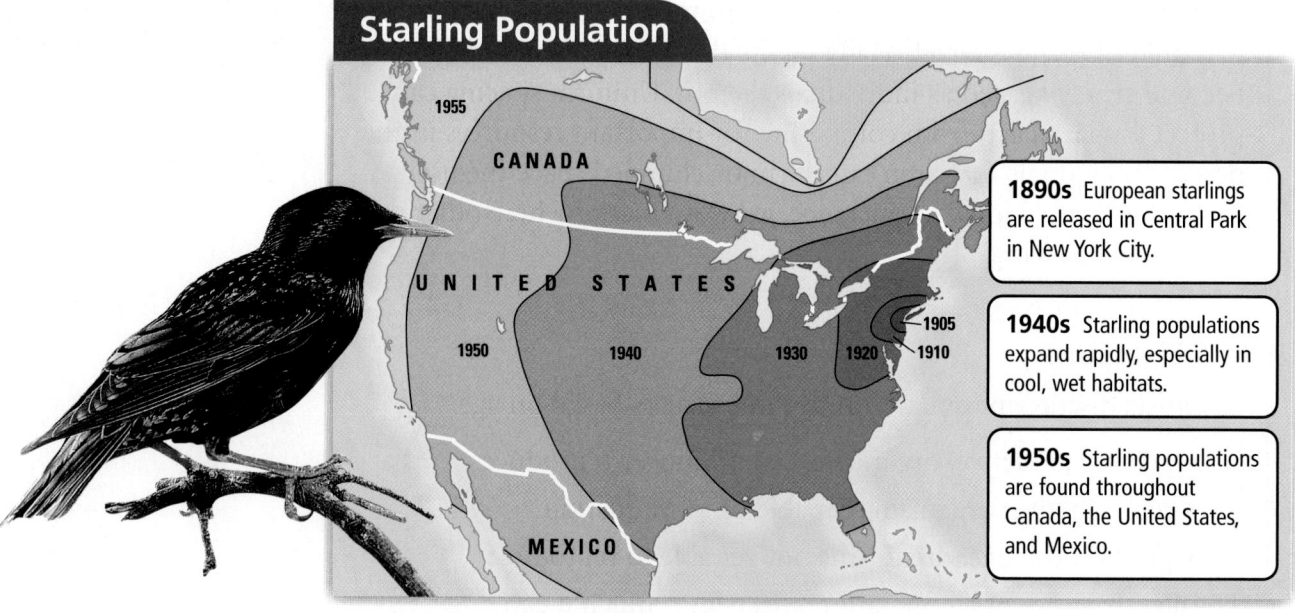

Starling Population

1955

CANADA

1890s European starlings are released in Central Park in New York City.

UNITED STATES

1905
1940s Starling populations expand rapidly, especially in cool, wet habitats.

1950   1940   1930   1920   1910

1950s Starling populations are found throughout Canada, the United States, and Mexico.

MEXICO

Scientists can also predict change by looking at the distribution of population. The story of the European starling provides a dramatic example of how the movement of organisms into or out of an area affects a population.

In 1890, the first starlings were introduced to the United States in New York City's Central Park. Their numbers went from 60 individuals to about 200 million in just over 100 years as they expanded on the North American continent. The population of starlings rose as starlings moved into new habitats that had the resources they needed.

Today large populations of starlings can still be found across the North American continent. Even within a given habitat, the population can vary. In Central Park, for example, you can find starlings in clumps, uniformly spaced, or randomly spaced.

VISUALIZATION
CLASSZONE.COM

Watch how a change in the environment can affect a population.

15.1 Review

KEY CONCEPTS

1. Describe the three stages of population growth.

2. Make a chart showing the four factors that affect population dynamics and an example of each.

3. Give an example of how a shift in age distribution can affect population growth.

CRITICAL THINKING

4. **Apply** Choose a population in your neighborhood. Describe its population spacing. Is it clumped, uniformly spaced, or randomly spaced?

5. **Compare/Contrast** How is population size related to population density? Your answer should mention area.

⬤ CHALLENGE

6. **Predict** Explain how a heavy thunderstorm might affect the population density of birds living in the area.

Making Sense of Samples

In a pond study, a biologist takes samples of water from four locations in one pond every three months. Using a microscope, she examines the samples and calculates the protist population for each location. The data table shows the number of protists found per milliliter in each sample of pond water.

Data Table: Number of protists per milliliter (mL) of pond water				
Location	Fall	Winter	Spring	Summer
Under the pier	150	50	120	410
Among the water lilies	200	80	180	500
Shallow area	220	90	200	360
Deepest area	80	60	100	390
Seasonal Average				

Example

Suppose you want to find the average number of protists per milliliter of pond water for that fall.

Step 1. Find the sum of all the data given above for "Fall."

Step 2. Divide this total by the number of data entries for "Fall."

Step 3. Round to nearest whole number.

```
  150
  200
  220
+  80
  650
```

$650 \div 4 = 162.5$

$162.5 \rightarrow 163$

ANSWER 163 protists per mL of pond water

For each season or location give the average number of protists.

1. Winter

2. Spring

3. Summer

4. Under the pier

5. Among the water lilies

6. Shallow area

7. Deepest area

8. Whole pond, yearlong

CHALLENGE Suppose the biologist only took samples from three areas in the pond. Which missing area would throw off the averages the most?

15.2 Populations respond to pressures.

Sunshine State STANDARDS

SC.G.1.3.2: The student knows that biological adaptations include changes in structures, behaviors, or physiology that enhance reproductive success in a particular environment.

SC.G.2.3.3: The student knows that a brief change in the limited resources of an ecosystem may alter the size of a population or the average size of individual organisms and that long-term change may result in the elimination of animal and plant populations inhabiting the Earth.

BEFORE, you learned

- Four characteristics are used to describe a population
- Scientists study these four characteristics to predict population change

NOW, you will learn

- About limits to population growth
- How population density affects limiting factors
- About two reproductive strategies found within populations

VOCABULARY

immigration p. 537
emigration p. 537
limiting factor p. 538
opportunist p. 541
competitor p. 542

CHOOSE YOUR OWN STRATEGY

Use a strategy from an earlier chapter or one of your own to take notes on the main idea: *Population growth is limited.*

EXPLORE Population Density

How does population density vary?

PROCEDURE

① Choose three different locations in your school where you can observe how many people enter and leave an area during a specific time period.

② Position three people at each location a counter, a timekeeper, and a recorder.

③ Count the number of people who pass through the area for at least 2 minutes. Record the number.

④ Compare your data with the data collected by other groups.

WHAT DO YOU THINK?

- Where was the number of people the highest? the lowest?
- Explain what may have affected population density at each location.

MATERIALS
- stopwatch
- notebook

Population growth is limited.

No population can grow forever. Every population has a limit to its growth. For example, the cockroach has been around for more than 300 million years. This insect has outlived the dinosaurs and may persist long after humans have become extinct. Yet even if cockroaches became the only species on the planet, several factors would limit their population size.

Birth, Death, Immigration, and Emigration

When scientists study how a population changes, they must consider four things: birth, death, immigration, and emigration. There is even a simple formula to help scientists track population change.

Population change = (birth + immigration) − (death + emigration)

It is too simple to say that a high birth rate means population growth, or that many deaths mean population decline. **Immigration** is the movement of individuals into a population. For example, if a strong wind blows the seeds of a plant from one area into another, the new plant would be said to immigrate into the new area. Immigration can increase a population or help stabilize a declining population. Birth and immigration introduce individuals into a population.

Emigration is the movement of individuals out of a population. If resources become scarce within a habitat, some of the individuals might move to areas with greater supplies. Others may even die. Death and emigration remove individuals from a population.

⬛ **CHECK YOUR READING** List two factors that lead to population growth and two that lead to population decline.

Consider, for example, a flock of seagulls that flies inland during a storm. They stop at a city dump, where food is plentiful. These incoming seagulls become part of the seagull population that is already living at the dump. A raccoon population living in the same area has been eating the seagulls' eggs, causing the number of seagull births to decrease. If enough seagulls immigrate to the dump, the seagull population would increase, making up for the decrease in births. Immigration would help keep the population stable. The seagull population would also increase if part of the raccoon population moved away.

Limiting Factors

When a population is growing at a rapid rate, the birth rate is much higher than the death rate. That means that more individuals are being born than are dying during a particular time period. There are plenty of resources available, and the population size is increasing rapidly. Eventually, however, the population will stop growing, because a habitat can support only a limited number of organisms.

A **limiting factor** is a factor that prevents the continuing growth of a population in an ecosystem. Abiotic, or nonliving, limiting factors include air, light, and water. Other limiting factors can be living things, such as other organisms in the same population or individuals belonging to different species within the same area.

 What are two limiting factors?

Competition can occur between different populations sharing the same habitat. Competition can also occur among individuals of the same population. Suppose, for example, that a population of deer in a forest preserve were to increase, either through births or immigration. Population density at the forest preserve would go up. More and more deer in that area would be competing for the same amount of food.

Density-Dependent Factors

Density-dependent factors have a greater effect on populations with many individuals in a small area.

Factors may include
- Competition
- Disease
- Parasitism
- Predation

Effects of Population Density

In the situation described above, the seagull population could decrease as a result of competition for food. Competition is an example of a density-dependent factor—that is, a limiting factor that affects a population when density is high. Disease is another density-dependent factor. The more crowded an area becomes, the easier it is for disease to spread, so more individuals are affected. If population density is low, there is less contact between individuals, which means that disease will spread more slowly. Density-dependent factors have a greater effect on the population as it grows. They can bring a population under control, because they apply more pressure to a growing population.

There are also density-independent factors. These limiting factors have the same effect on a population, whether it has a high density or a low density. Freezing temperatures could be considered a density-independent factor. A freeze might kill all of the flowering plants in an area, whether or not the population density is high. A natural event such as a wildfire is another example of a density-independent factor. When a wildfire occurs in a forest, it can wipe out an entire ecosystem.

 **CHECK YOUR READING** How are limiting factors that are density-dependent different from limiting factors that are density-independent?

Density-Independent Factors

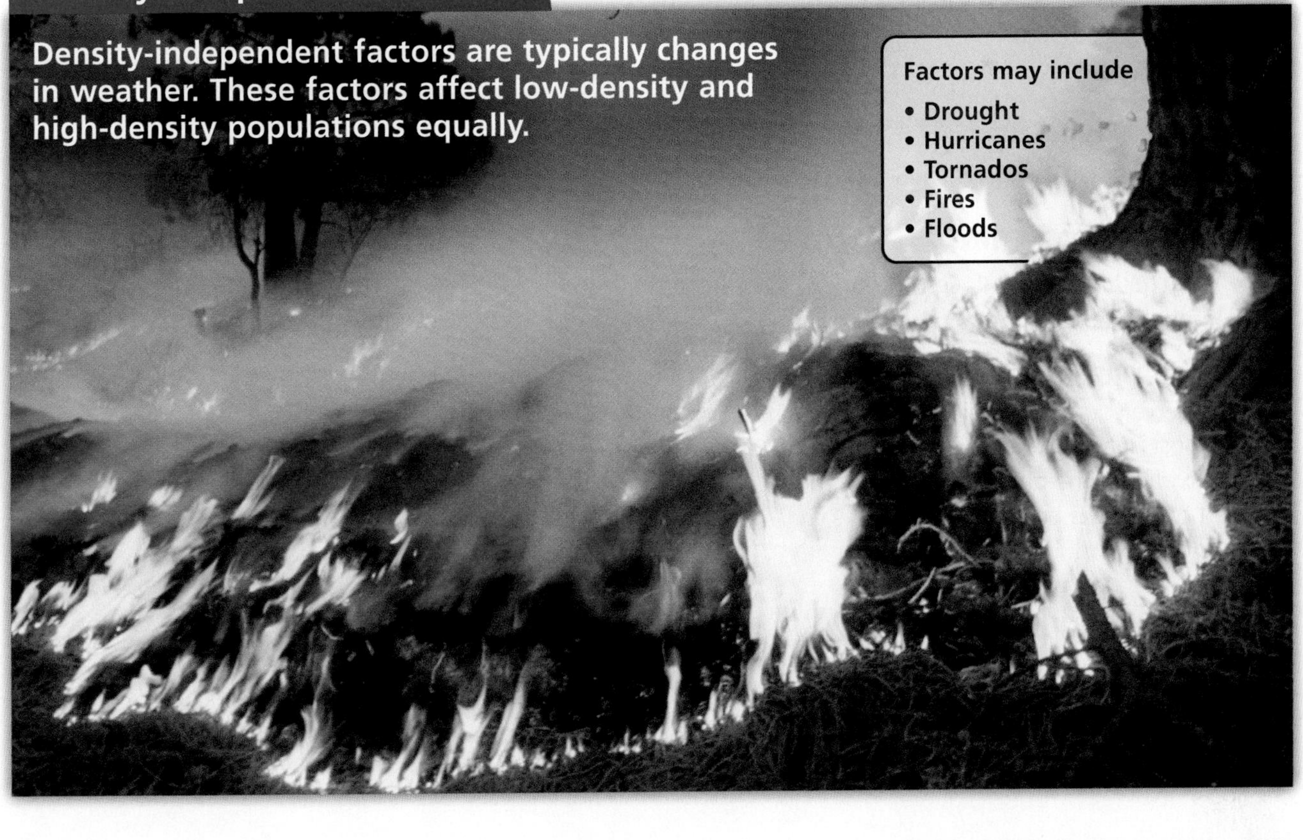

Density-independent factors are typically changes in weather. These factors affect low-density and high-density populations equally.

Factors may include
- Drought
- Hurricanes
- Tornados
- Fires
- Floods

Limiting factors include nonliving factors in the environment and natural events such as earthquakes, fires, and storms. During times of drought, there may not be enough food to meet the needs of all the organisms in an area. The quality of the food declines as well. For example, a lack of water may cause a population of trees to produce fewer pieces of fruit, and the fruit itself may be smaller. If there is little food available, a condition called famine arises. If the famine is severe, and if death rates exceed birth rates, then the population size will fall dramatically.

CHECK YOUR READING How do limiting factors affect populations? Remember: a summary includes only the most important information.

Limiting factors affect human populations as well. However, humans have found different ways to help overcome many of these limits. In Section 15.3 you will read about how the human response to limits differs from that of other biological populations.

INVESTIGATE Limiting Factors

What limiting factors determine plant growth?

Using the materials below, design an experiment to test how limiting factors such as sunlight or water can determine how well a plant population will grow.

PROCEDURE

(1) Decide how to use the beans, soil, and water.

(2) Write up your experimental procedure. Include any safety tips.

WHAT DO YOU THINK?

• What variables did you use in your experiment?

• What evidence do you expect to see to support the goal of your experiment?

CHALLENGE Conduct your experiment. Be sure to observe your beans daily and note which ones are most healthy. Make a chart and record your observations. The beans should grow for at least two weeks before you make your conclusion.

SKILL FOCUS
Designing experiments

MATERIALS
• 6 paper cups
• potting soil
• beans
• water

TIME
20 minutes

Populations have distinct reproductive survival strategies.

Although reproduction of offspring is not necessary for the survival of an individual organism, it is necessary for the survival of a species. Scientists studying populations observe patterns in the reproductive strategies used among species. There are two main strategies that many species use. There are also many species whose strategies fit somewhere in between.

FLORIDA
Content Preview
Species reproduce either asexually or sexually. Read more about this on page 817.

Strategies of Opportunists

Opportunists are species that reproduce rapidly if their population falls below carrying capacity. They share many characteristics, including a short life span and the ability to reproduce large quantities of offspring. Their population size tends to change often, and opportunists live across many areas. Opportunists include algae, dandelions, bacteria, and insects. These species can reproduce and move across an area quickly. In addition, they can adapt quickly to environmental changes. Populations of opportunists often grow rapidly.

VOCABULARY
Remember to make a word magnet for the term *opportunist*. Include examples in your diagram.

Opportunists

Pine trees are opportunists that can spread across an area quickly.

Pine cones release huge amounts of pollen into the air.

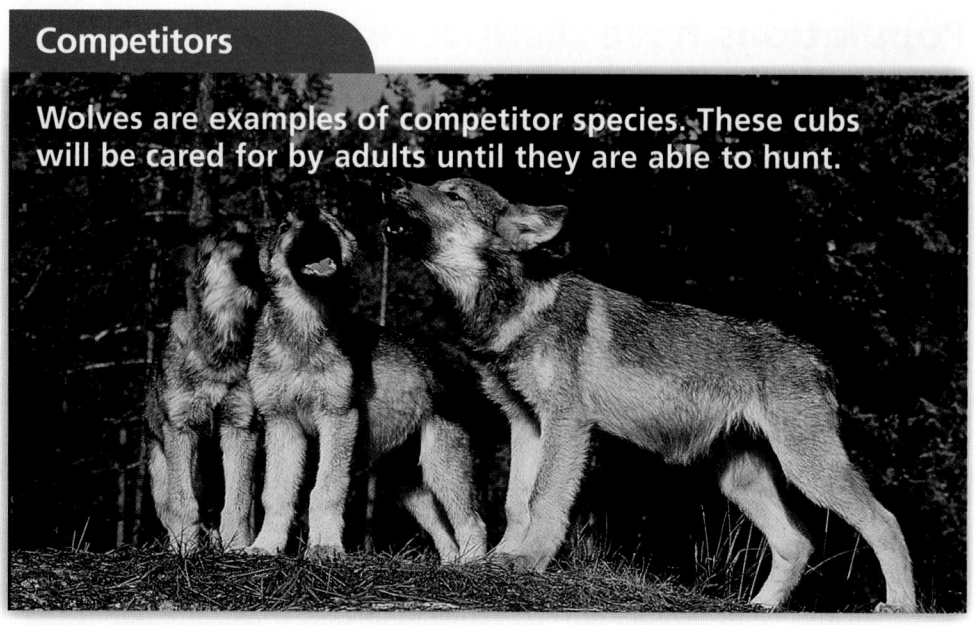

Competitors

Wolves are examples of competitor species. These cubs will be cared for by adults until they are able to hunt.

Strategies of Competitors

You might be familiar with the term *competitor* as meaning an organism that struggles with another to get resources. Scientists who study population growth use the term *competitor* in another way. **Competitors** are species with adaptations that allow them to remain at or near their carrying capacity for long periods of time. Competitors have many characteristics that differ from those of opportunists.

Species that have a competitive reproductive strategy often live longer and have fewer offspring. Elephants and saguaro cacti are two examples of competitors. The offspring of competitors take longer to develop than those of opportunists. Also, animals with this strategy tend to take care of their young for a longer period of time. Competitors are not distributed across areas as widely as opportunists, but greater numbers of their offspring survive to reproductive age.

15.2 Review

KEY CONCEPTS

1. What four factors do scientists consider when they measure population change?

2. Give two examples of density-dependent factors and two examples of density-independent factors.

3. Other than life span, how do opportunists and competitors differ?

CRITICAL THINKING

4. **Analyze** Why would it be a mistake to predict population growth based on birth rate alone?

5. **Apply** Give an example of a factor that limits a population near you.

⬤ CHALLENGE

6. **Synthesize** There has been an oil spill along a waterway famous for its populations of seals, dolphins, and sea birds. Six months later, all populations show a decline. Explain what factors might have caused such a change and whether the oil spill was a density-dependent or density-independent factor or both.

SCIENCE on the JOB

Density

If there are too few fish of a particular species in one area, it is best to leave them and look for a place with greater population density. By using the most suitable gear, the captain avoids killing or injuring fish and other animals that shouldn't be part of the catch.

Studying the Schools

There's a lot more to catching fish than putting a net or a line into the ocean. More and more these days, finding fish means looking at the big and changing picture of fish populations. Once you start fishing, you need to know when to stop fishing, as well as how to protect the other organisms in the ocean environment.

Distribution

Some fish live alone, and some live in big groups, called schools. Some, called ground fish, stay on the bottom, while others swim near the surface. One way to see the distribution of fish is with sonar. An image made from sonar shows that a school of hake swims at a depth of about 320 meters (1050 ft).

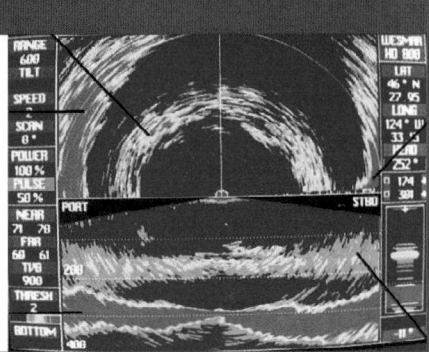

Partners in Research

Many boat captains set up partnerships with researchers to study fish and to help them to thrive. Sonar equipment is a tool shared by scientists and commercial fishers. Images are made by sending sound waves through the water and receiving the patterns of sound waves that bounce, or echo, back.

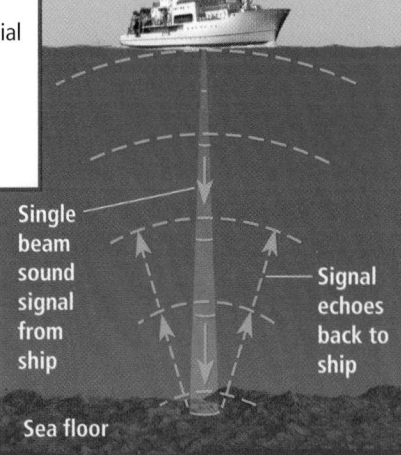

Single beam sound signal from ship

Signal echoes back to ship

Sea floor

EXPLORE

1. **INFER** Boat captains talk to each other about how many fish they catch and where and when they catch them. What are three reasons why this would be important?

2. **CHALLENGE** Suppose a fishing boat captain overfishes an organism that is a source of food for another organism. Describe what may happen to the other organism.

15.3

KEY CONCEPT

Human populations have unique responses to change.

Sunshine State STANDARDS

SC.G.1.3.2: The student knows that biological adaptations include changes in structures, behaviors, or physiology that enhance reproductive success in a particular environment.

SC.G.2.3.3: The student knows that a brief change in the limited resources of an ecosystem may alter the size of a population or the average size of individual organisms and that long-term change may result in the elimination of animal and plant populations inhabiting the Earth.

SC.G.2.3.4: The student understands that humans are a part of an ecosystem and their activities may deliberately or inadvertently alter the equilibrium in ecosystems.

VOCABULARY
pollution p. 550

CHOOSE YOUR OWN STRATEGY
Begin taking notes on the differences between human populations and populations of other species.

BEFORE, you learned

• Over time, all populations stop growing
• All populations are affected by limiting factors
• Reproductive strategies include opportunism and competition

NOW, you will learn

• How human populations differ from other populations
• How humans adapt to the environment
• How human populations affect the environment

EXPLORE Population Change

How can you predict human population growth?

PROCEDURE

① Copy the graph on the right. The graph shows population growth expected in the United States with an increase in both birth and death rates and with steady immigration.

② The graph shows a medium rate of growth. Draw another line to show what low population growth might look like. Label it.

③ Explain the patterns of birth rates, death rates, and immigration that might be likely to result in low population growth.

WHAT DO YOU THINK?

• How would the projected U.S. population size change if there were no immigration?
• How might an increase in immigration affect expected birth rates?

MATERIALS
• graph paper
• colored pencils

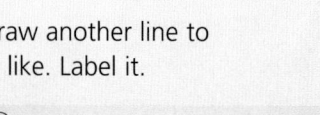

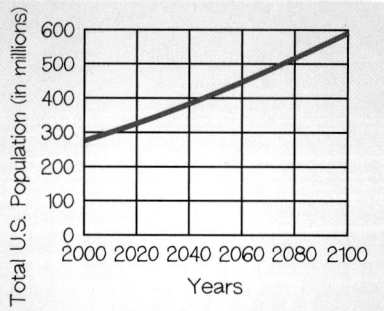

Human populations differ from populations of other species.

Humans are not the fastest or the largest organisms on Earth. They must get food from other organisms. Humans have a limited sense of smell, and the vision of a human is inferior to that of a hawk. However, the human population now dominates our planet. Why? Humans are able to shape their environment. Humans are also able to determine their own biological reproduction. Because humans can control many factors that limit growth, Earth's carrying capacity for humans has increased. Two key factors that have increased Earth's carrying capacity for humans are habitat expansion and technology.

Habitat Expansion

Individuals who study the history of ancient peoples know that populations of humans have spread throughout the world. Discoveries of ancient human tools and skeletons indicate that the first human populations lived on the continent now known as Africa. Over time, human populations have spread over nearly the entire planet.

The word *habitat* refers to a place where an organism can live. Humans have expanded their habitats, and thus the population has grown. Humans can survive in many different environments by adding air conditioning or heat to regulate indoor temperature. They can design and build shelters that protect them from harsh environments.

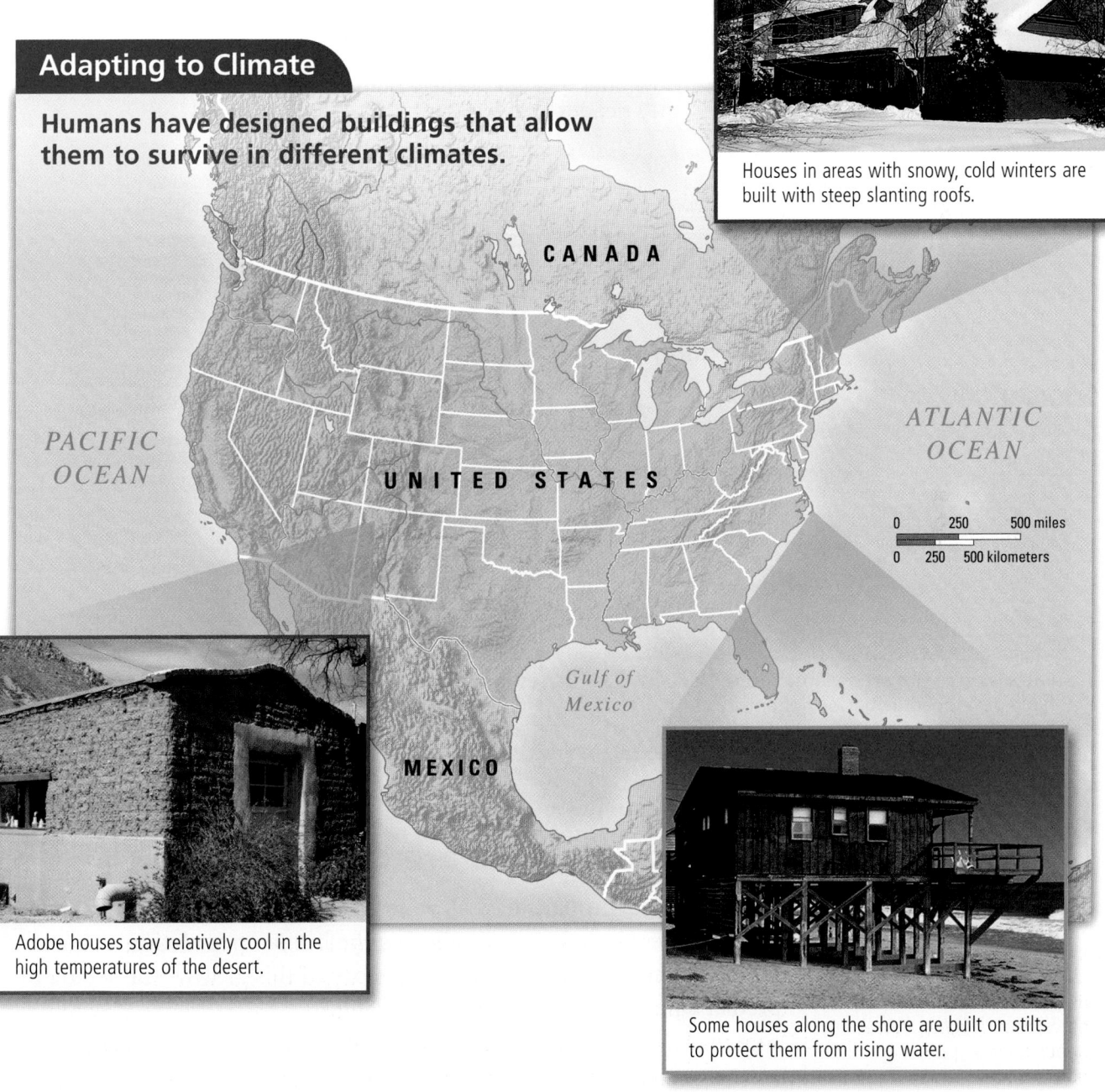

Adapting to Climate

Humans have designed buildings that allow them to survive in different climates.

Houses in areas with snowy, cold winters are built with steep slanting roofs.

Adobe houses stay relatively cool in the high temperatures of the desert.

Some houses along the shore are built on stilts to protect them from rising water.

Technology

Limited resources and environmental conditions such as climate do not affect human population growth the way they do the growth of other biological populations. Humans have found ways to fit themselves into almost every climate by altering their clothing, shelter, diet, and means of transportation.

Scientific discoveries and the advances of technology—such as improved sanitation and medical care—have increased the standard of living and the life expectancy of many humans. Important goods such as food and shelter are manufactured and shipped around the world. Water, which is a limited resource, can be transported through pipes and dams to irrigate fields or reach normally dry areas. Water can also be purified for drinking or treated before it is released back into the environment.

 CHECK YOUR READING   How does technology help humans get resources they need for survival?

Technology

Transporting Water

Food is often grown on large farms. Humans have developed irrigation systems to carry water to the fields.

Purifying Water

Water that has been used by humans contains wastes that can be removed at large watertreatment plants.

Human populations are growing.

As you've read, humans have developed solutions to many limits on growth. These solutions have allowed the human population to grow rapidly. Scientists are studying the history of this growth and trying to predict whether it will continue or change.

History of Human Population Growth

RESOURCE CENTER
CLASSZONE.COM

Learn more about world-wide human population growth.

Until about 300 years ago, the human population grew slowly. Disease, climate, and the availability of resources limited population size. Most offspring did not survive to adulthood. Even though birthrates were high, death rates were also high.

Notice the human population on the graph below. Many historical events have affected its growth. For example, the development of agriculture provided humans with a more stable food source. This in turn helped support human population growth. Today, populations across many parts of the world are increasing rapidly. Scientists identify three conditions that allow for rapid growth: the availability of resources, lack of predators, and survival of offspring to reproductive age. As these conditions change, so does the population.

Population Projections

To help prepare for the future, scientists make predictions called population projections. Population projections forecast how a population will change, based on its present size and age structure. Population projections provide a picture of what the future might look like. Using population projections, government agencies, resource managers, and economists can plan to meet the future needs of a population.

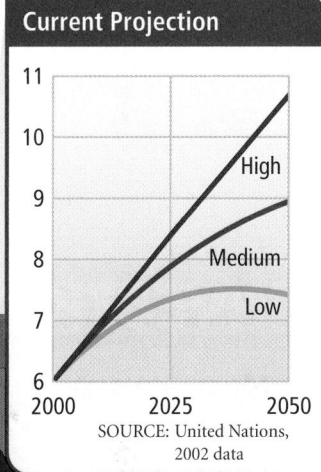

Current Projection

SOURCE: United Nations, 2002 data

The blowout of the graph shows three projections for the human population size. Experts disagree about the rate at which the population will grow.

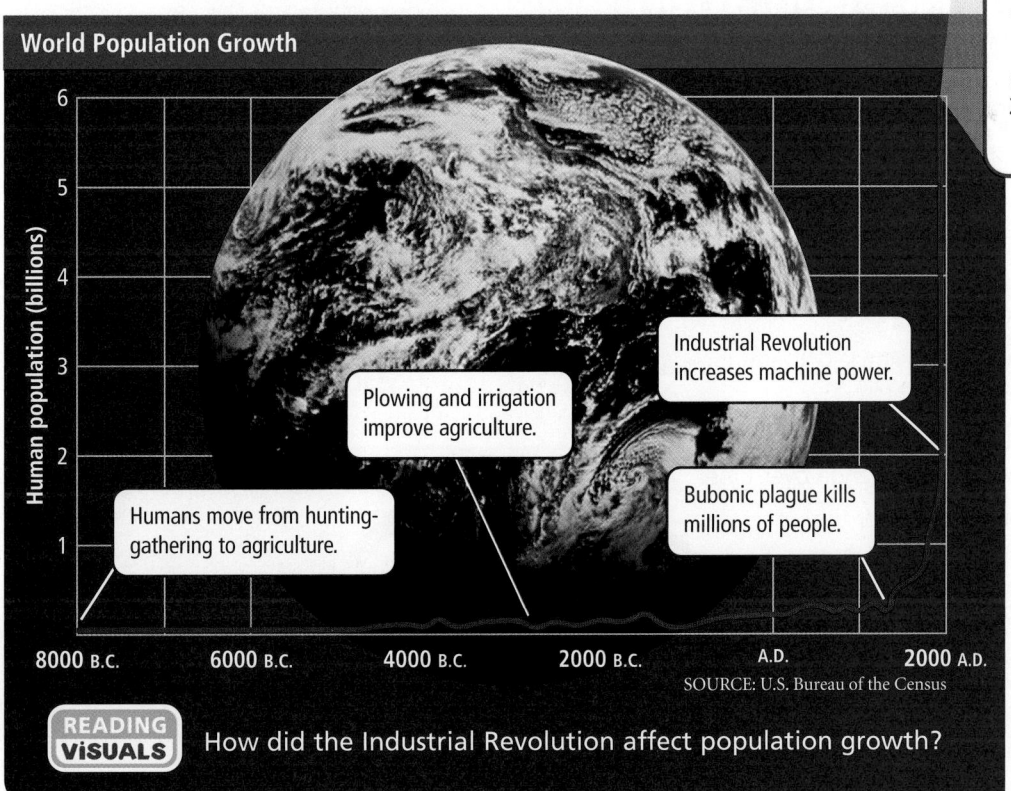

World Population Growth

Humans move from hunting-gathering to agriculture.

Plowing and irrigation improve agriculture.

Industrial Revolution increases machine power.

Bubonic plague kills millions of people.

Human population (billions)

8000 B.C.   6000 B.C.   4000 B.C.   2000 B.C.   A.D.   2000 A.D.

SOURCE: U.S. Bureau of the Census

READING VISUALS How did the Industrial Revolution affect population growth?

In addition to population size and age structure, scientists making population projections consider other factors. These factors include the ages of individuals having children. The average number of offspring produced by an individual also affects projections. In addition, life expectancy and health in a particular population affect population growth.

The factors affecting population growth vary from society to society. The human population in the African country Botswana provides an example of how disease and health can affect population growth.

In some African countries, death rates due to HIV/AIDS have lowered population projections for the year 2015 by almost 18 percent. Botswana's population will decline, because more than 30 percent of adults are infected with HIV/AIDS. So many people in Botswana have already died of HIV/AIDS that the average life expectancy has dropped from 63 years of age in the late 1980s to 32 years in 2003. Consider the impact this will have on the population's age structure. Because many people who die from HIV/AIDS are in their reproductive years, the long-term effects on population growth will be significant.

CHECK YOUR READING What factors do scientists consider when they make population projections?

INVESTIGATE Population

How can you graph population growth data for your area?

PROCEDURE

1. Use local population data taken from each census over five decades.

2. On graph paper, mark off five decades along the *x*–axis. Make a *y*–axis to show population size.

3. Plot the census information for each decade as a line graph.

WHAT DO YOU THINK?

• How did the local population change over time?

• What do you think accounted for the change?

CHALLENGE Based on the trend you see so far, how might the population change in the future? Use another color to extend the line on your graph to project population change over the next five decades. Explain why you think the population will change as you have predicted.

SKILL FOCUS
Graphing data

MATERIALS
• graph paper
• census data
• 2 colored pencils

TIME
30 minutes

Human population growth affects the environment.

You have read that extinction of species is a part of the history of life on Earth. The ways a population uses and disposes of resources have a great impact on local and global environments. As the human population continues to grow and use more resources, it contributes to the decline and extinction of other populations.

Some scientists estimate that over 99 percent of the species that have ever existed on Earth are now extinct. Most of these species vanished long before humans came on the scene. However, some experts are concerned that human activity is causing other species to become extinct at a much higher rate than they would naturally. Human populations put pressure on the environment in many ways, including

- introduction of new species
- pollution
- overfishing

FLORIDA
Content Review

Pollution, overfishing, and introduction of new species are other ways that humans impact ecosystems, which you learned about in grade 6.

RESOURCE CENTER
CLASSZONE.COM

Find out more on introduced species in the United States.

Introduction of New Species

Travelers have introduced new species to areas both on purpose and by accident. Many species introduced to an area provide benefits, such as food or beauty. Some species, however, cause harm to ecosystems. One example of an introduced species is the zebra mussel. An ocean vessel accidentally released zebra mussels from Europe into the Great Lakes region of the United States. With no natural predators that consume them, the mussels have reproduced quickly, invading all of the Great Lakes, the Mississippi River, and the Hudson River. The mussels compete with native species for food and affect water quality, endangering the ecosystem.

Kudzu is another introduced species. In the 1930s, kudzu was used in the southeastern United States to keep soil from being washed away. The plants, which have beautiful purple flowers, were imported from Japan. Starch made from kudzu is also a popular ingredient in some Asian recipes. However, populations of the kudzu vines planted in the United States have grown too far and too fast. Kudzu grows as much as 0.3 meters (about a foot) per day, killing trees and other plants living in the same area.

The kudzu plant, though at one time considered beautiful, is threatening other species.

Pollution

While human activities might cause some populations to decline, they can also cause other populations to grow. Sometimes this population growth causes pollution and habitat disturbance. **Pollution** is the addition of harmful substances to the environment. One example of such an activity is large-scale hog farming.

Human demands for pork combined with a growing human population have caused the hog farming industry to expand. Between 1987 and 2001, the hog population in North Carolina grew from 2.6 million to 10 million. These 10 million hogs produced more than 50,000 tons of waste each day. Wastes from large populations of hogs affect water supplies, soil, and air quality.

Pollution has also affected the Salton Sea in southeastern California. The growing demand for goods and agriculture has led to chemical dumping from industries and pesticide runoff from nearby farms. The rivers that run into the lake carry high levels of harmful chemicals such as DDT. Local birds that live and feed in this area have weakened shells that cannot support baby birds. Pollution has also caused fish to become deformed.

Large-scale hog farms affect water, soil, and air quality.

Pollution

The Salton Sea in California is surrounded by farm fields and industries that contribute to pollution.

Used water from irrigation drains into the Salton Sea.

Overfishing

Fish and crustaceans such as shrimp and lobsters have long been an important food source for many people. In the 1900s, the techniques and equipment that fishers used allowed them to catch so many fish that fish populations began to decrease. As the human population has continued to grow, so has the demand for fish. However, if fish do not survive long enough in the wild, they do not have the chance to reproduce. Many species have been so overfished that their populations may not recover.

Lobster fishing in particular has supported coastal communities in the northeastern United States for generations. But the demand for this food source has caused populations to decline. Areas that fishers trapped for years may now have only a small population of lobsters. And the lobsters fishers are catching may not be as large as those from earlier decades.

In order to help lobster populations recover, laws have been enforced to protect their life cycle and reproduction. Today, people who trap lobsters are required to release females with eggs. They are also allowed to keep only mature lobsters. Younger lobsters are returned to the waters to mature and reproduce. Efforts like these help protect the lobster population and secure the jobs of fishers by helping fish populations remain stable.

Fishers harvesting lobster measure the tails of the animals they catch. A lobster that is too small is returned to the sea to allow it to grow.

  Describe how overfishing would affect resources.

15.3 Review

KEY CONCEPTS

1. What factors—other than birth, death, immigration, and emigration—must scientists consider when making projections of human population?

2. Give an example of how Earth's carrying capacity for humans has increased.

3. What are three ways that humans affect other populations?

CRITICAL THINKING

4. **Infer** Consider the effect of HIV/AIDS on Botswana's human population. How might age structure affect Botswana's population growth?

5. **Analyze** Do you think it is possible to predict the maximum number of humans that Earth can support? Why or why not?

CHALLENGE

6. **Apply** Identify a challenge faced by the human population in your state. Explain how the challenge is related to pollution, introduction of new species, habitat disturbance, or overfishing.

CHAPTER INVESTIGATION

Sustainable Resource Management

OVERVIEW AND PURPOSE Wood is a renewable resource, but the demand for wood is continuing to grow worldwide. Humans are harvesting trees more quickly than trees have the ability to grow and replace themselves. The result is a forest in decline. In this activity you will
- model what happens when trees are harvested to meet the needs of a growing population
- calculate the rate at which the population of a renewable resource declines

▶ Question

Write It Up

How can people meet the ongoing human demand for wood without using all the trees? You will use the increasing human demand for wood to determine how overuse of a resource might affect a population. What would you like to discover about resource management? Write a question that begins with *Which, How, Why, When,* or *What.*

▶ Procedure

MATERIALS
- coffee can with 120 craft sticks
- bundle of 32 craft sticks
- stopwatch

1. Copy the data table on page 553 into your **Science Notebook.**

2. In your group of classmates, decide who will fill each of the following roles: forest, timer, forest manager, harvester/record keeper.

3. **Forest:** Get a coffee can of 120 craft sticks. These sticks represent the available tree supply.

4. **Timer:** Sound off each 15-second interval and each minute.

5 **Forest Manager:** Get 32 sticks from the teacher. You will add 1 new tree every 15 seconds by putting a stick in the coffee can.

6 **Harvester:** At the end of the first minute, cut down 1 tree by removing 1 stick from the coffee can. At the end of the second minute, cut down 2 trees; at the end of the third, cut down 4 trees. At the end of each additional minute cut down twice as many trees as you did before. This represents the doubling of the demand for trees based on human population growth.

▶ Observe and Analyze
Write It Up

1. **CALCULATE** At the end of each minute, add 4 trees, but subtract twice as many trees as you subtracted the minute before.

2. **RECORD AND CALCULATE** Complete the chart. How many trees are left in the forest after 8 minutes of harvesting?

▶ Conclude

1. **INFER** What effect does increasing human population growth have on forests?

2. **EVALUATE** Was the forest always shrinking?

3. **EVALUATE** How does this investigation help you to answer or change your question about resource management?

4. **IDENTIFY LIMITS** What aspects of this investigation fail to model the natural habitat?

5. **APPLY** What other renewable resources need sustainable management?

▶ INVESTIGATE Further

CHALLENGE Explain how you could use the data gathered in this investigation to develop methods of sustainable resource management.

Sustainable Resource Management

Table 1. Rate of Harvest

Minutes	Number of Trees at Start of Minute	Number of New Trees	Number of Trees Harvested	Number of Trees at End of Minute
1	120	+4	−1	123
2				
3				
4				
5				
6				
7				
8				

FLORIDA REVIEW
CLASSZONE.COM

Content Review and
FCAT Practice

the **BIG** idea

Populations are shaped by interactions between organisms and the environment.

KEY CONCEPTS SUMMARY

1 **Populations have many characteristics.**

- Populations go through three stages:
  growth
  stability
  decline

- Four characteristics define a population:
  size
  density
  spacing
  age structure

- Scientists can predict population changes.

VOCABULARY
population dynamics
p. 527
carrying capacity
p. 528
population size
p. 530
population density
p. 531

2 **Populations respond to pressures.**

Populations change as they respond to pressures from limiting factors.

Two types of limiting factors are density dependent and density independent.

VOCABULARY
immigration p. 537
emigration p. 537
limiting factor p. 538
opportunist p. 541
competitor p. 542

3 **Human populations have unique responses to change.**

Humans can control many factors that limit most biological populations.

VOCABULARY
pollution p. 550

Reviewing Vocabulary

Describe how the vocabulary terms in the following pairs are related to each other. Explain the relationship in a one- or two-sentence answer. Underline each vocabulary term in your answers.

1. population dynamics and carrying capacity

2. immigration and emigration

3. limiting factor and population density

4. opportunists and competitors

Reviewing Key Concepts

Multiple Choice *Choose the letter of the best answer.*

5. The study of changes in a population over time and the factors that affect these changes is called population
   - **a.** stability
   - **b.** dynamics
   - **c.** spacing
   - **d.** density

6. A population that has reached its maximum size in a given area is said to have reached its
   - **a.** population range
   - **b.** gradual growth
   - **c.** carrying capacity
   - **d.** population projection

7. Assuming there is no immigration or emigration, a population size will remain constant if
   - **a.** the birth rate equals the death rate
   - **b.** the birth rate exceeds the death rate
   - **c.** the death rate exceeds the birth rate
   - **d.** the birth rate increases constantly

8. Distinct patterns in a population such as clumped, uniform, or random populations are examples of population
   - **a.** density
   - **b.** spacing
   - **c.** growth
   - **d.** dynamics

9. Which factors affect the size and growth of a population?
   - **a.** number of births and deaths
   - **b.** emigration and immigration
   - **c.** competition between populations
   - **d.** all of the above

10. A limiting factor that depends on the size of the population in a given area is a
    - **a.** density-dependent factor
    - **b.** density-independent factor
    - **c.** reproduction survival strategy
    - **d.** carrying capacity

11. Density-independent limiting factors include
    - **a.** predators
    - **b.** parasites
    - **c.** floods
    - **d.** competition

12. Which are abiotic factors in an environment?
    - **a.** disease and parasites
    - **b.** air, light, and water
    - **c.** pollution and overfishing
    - **d.** competition and predators

13. Which is an example of competition for resources?
    - **a.** individuals in a population feeding on the same food sources
    - **b.** movement of seagulls into a population of other seagulls
    - **c.** an increase in the population of raccoons in a particular environment at a steady rate
    - **d.** a population of fruit trees producing less fruit because of drought

14. Two factors that have increased Earth's carrying capacity for humans are habitat expansion, and
    - **a.** habitat disturbance
    - **b.** strategies of competitors
    - **c.** strategies of opportunists
    - **d.** technology

Short Response *Write a short response to each question.*

15. What factors might affect the density of a population?

16. What is the age structure of a population?

17. Describe three factors that account for the rapid growth of the human population during the past 500 years.

Thinking Critically

18. ANALYZE Under what conditions does gradual growth in a population occur?

19. COMMUNICATE Describe four observations that Darwin made about population growth.

20. PREDICT The graph below shows the exponential growth rate of a colony of unicellular organisms. If the population continues to grow at the same rate during the next 2 hours, what will the population be after 10 hours? Explain your answer.

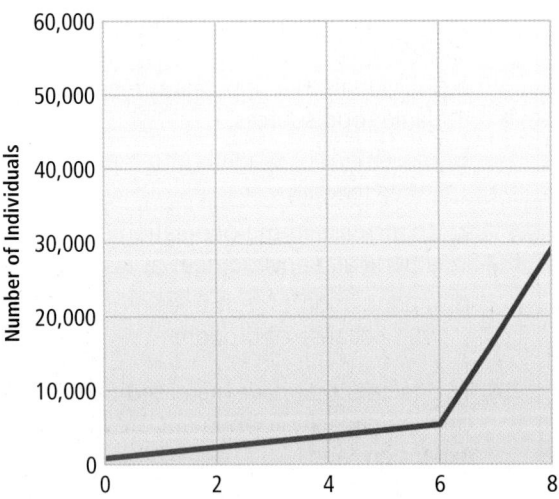

21. PREDICT In a certain population 35 percent of the individuals are under the age of 20. What predictions might you make about the size of the population in 10 years?

22. PROVIDE EXAMPLES What limiting factors might cause the carrying capacity of a population to change? Provide at least three examples. Describe how the population might change.

23. SYNTHESIZE What is an example of a density-independent factor that has affected a human population? Describe how this factor changed the population.

24. INFER Wolves are the natural predators of moose. Both populations are found on an island in the middle of Lake Superior. During one season, the population of moose increased dramatically. What could have caused the increase in the moose population?

25. EVALUATE Why do you suppose that the growth rate of human populations differs dramatically in different countries?

26. SYNTHESIZE Human activity has resulted in the decline of many populations of other species. Choose one example of how humans have put pressure on species around the world and describe ways that humans can avoid causing continued decreases in these populations.

the BIG idea

27. INFER Look again at the picture on pages 524–525. Now that you have finished the chapter, how would you change or add details to your answer to the question on the photograph?

28. SUMMARIZE Write one or more paragraphs describing the factors that affect population size, density, and age structure. Use the following terms in your descriptions.

immigration	density-dependent factors
emigration	density-independent factors
limiting factors	

UNIT PROJECTS

Evaluate all the data, results, and information from your project folder. Prepare to prepare to present your project. Be ready to answer questions posed by your classmates about your results.

FCAT Practice

Analyzing Data

The graph below is an example of a population growth curve.

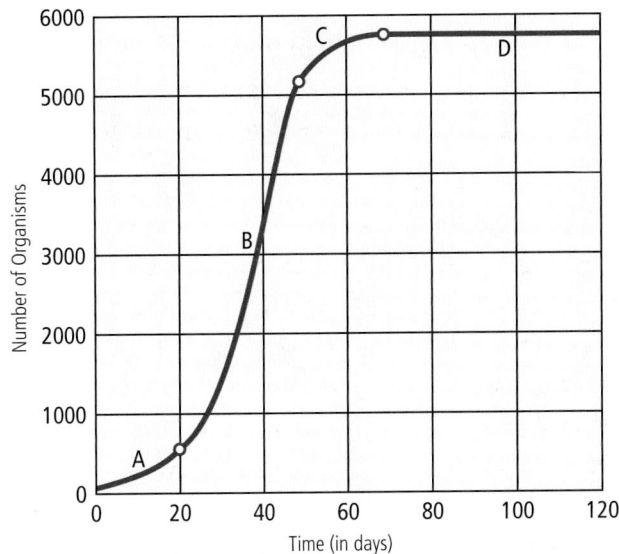

FCAT TiP

When you use a line graph to estimate an answer, use the assigned numbers on the *x*-axis and *y*-axis to help you make a good estimate.

Use the graph to answer the questions below.

SHORT RESPONSE

1. Describe how to determine the value of the point at the end of interval C.

2. Explain how to find the appropriate rate of increase in population growth per day for interval B.

MULTIPLE CHOICE

3. What does the time interval marked D represent?

  A. Population is decreasing.

  B. Carrying capacity has been reached.

  C. Birth rates exceed death rates.

  D. Population is growing.

4. Estimate the increase in the number of organisms during the time span represented by interval A.

  F. 150

  G. 300

  H. 550

  I. 900

5. During which time interval do limiting factors in a population begin to have an effect on the rate of population growth?

  A. interval A only

  B. interval B only

  C. interval C only

  D. interval C and interval D

6. What conclusion can you draw from the information in the graph?

  F. Density-dependent factors have had no effect on the population shown on the graph.

  G. The graph indicates an absence of disease and a supply of unlimited resources.

  H. Resources have become more available, so the population continues to increase exponentially.

  I. As resources become less available, the population growth rate slows or stops.

EXTENDED RESPONSE

7. Predict how the graph shown above would change if available resources steadily decreased during the interval from 120 days to 160 days. What factors did you consider when making your prediction?

8. Choose a population of organisms in your area. Describe the limiting factors that may affect the growth of that population. Make sure you include both density-dependent and density-independent factors in your discussion.

Chapter 15: **Population Dynamics** 557

Human Biology

joint

tissue

HUMAN
(Homo sapiens)

skeletal
system

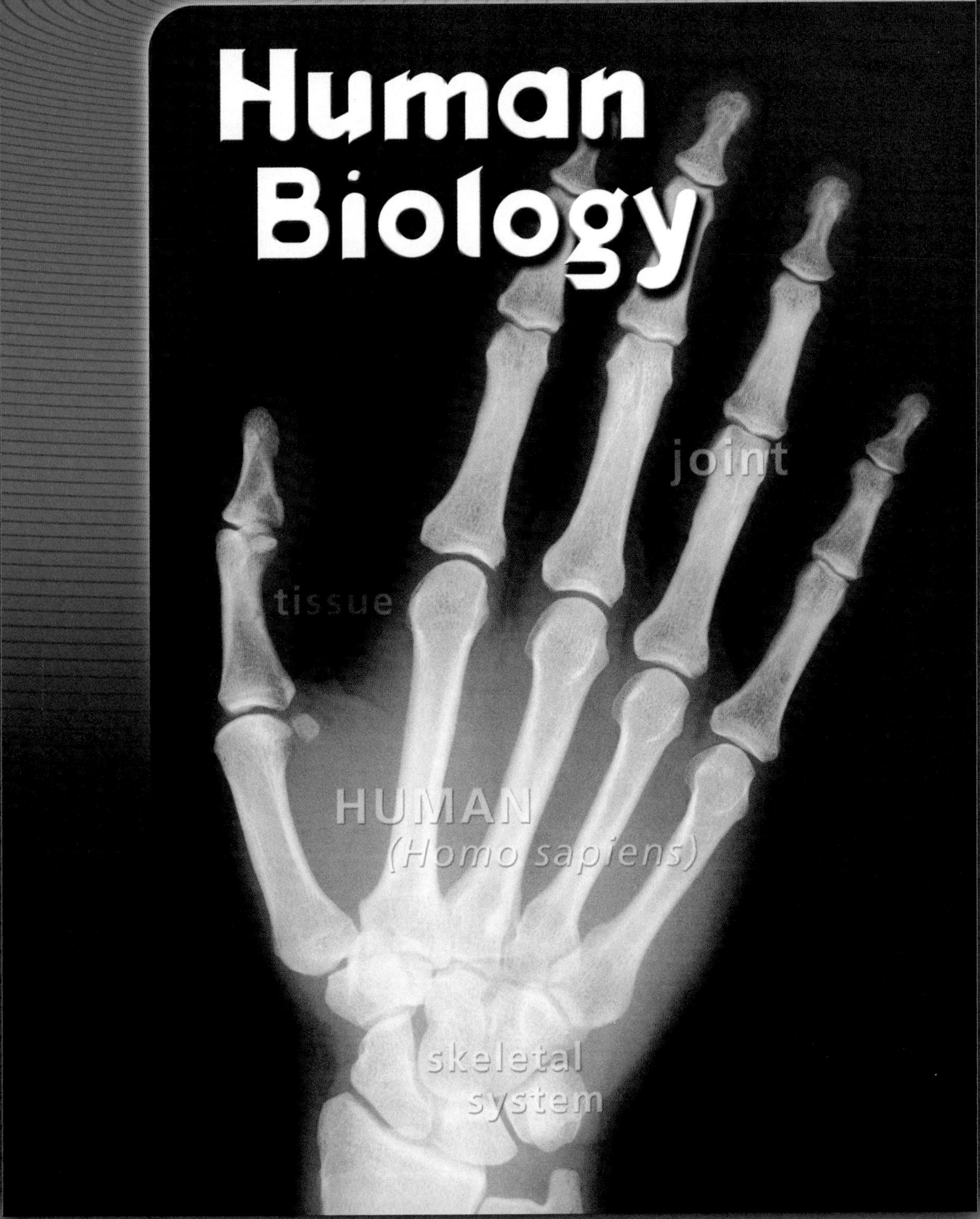

Contents Overview

Frontiers in Science
Surprising Senses   560

Florida Connection
A Place in the Sun   564

Timelines in Science
Seeing Inside the Body   624

Chapter 16 Systems, Support,
and Movement   568

Chapter 17 Absorption, Digestion,
and Exchange   596

Chapter 18 Transport and
Protection   628

Surprising Senses

SCIENTIFIC
AMERICAN
FRONTIERS

Learn more about how the
brain and senses work.
See the video "Sight of
Touch."

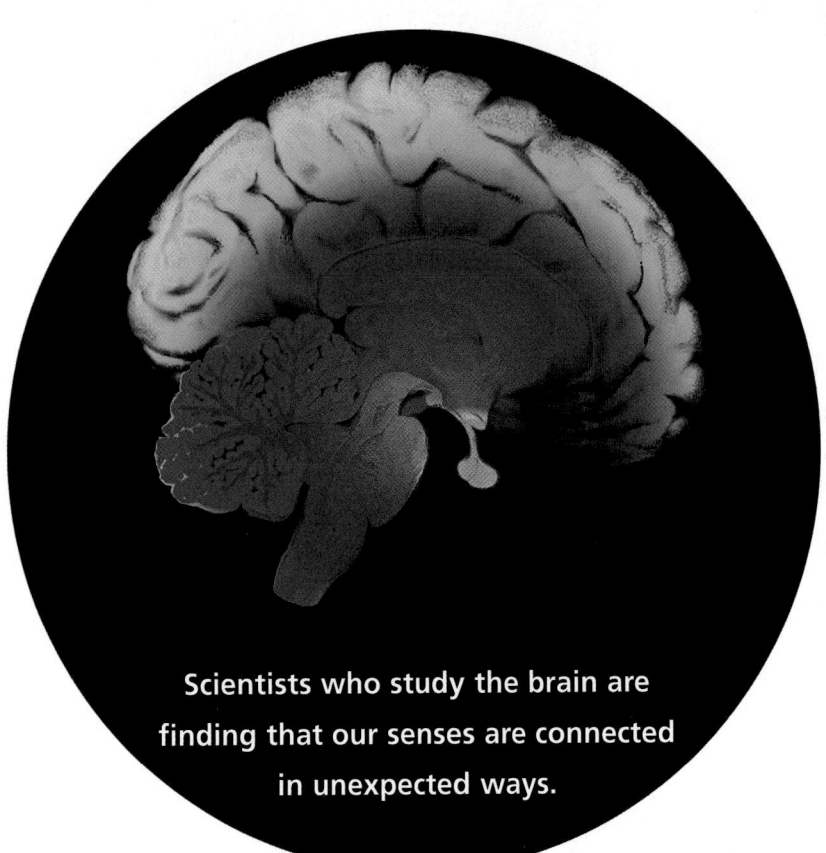

Scientists who study the brain are finding that our senses are connected in unexpected ways.

Senses and the Brain

One of the great mysteries still unsolved in science is what happens inside the brain. What is a thought? How is it formed? Where is it stored? How do our senses shape our thoughts? There are far more questions than answers. One way to approach questions about the brain is to study brain activity at times when the body is performing different functions.

Most advanced brain functions happen in the part of the brain called the cerebral cortex (suh-REE-bruhl KOR-tehks). That's where the brain interprets information from the senses. The cerebral cortex has many specialized areas. Each area controls one type of brain activity. Scientists are mapping these areas. At first, they studied people with brain injuries. A person with an injury to one area might not be able to speak. Someone with a different injury might have trouble seeing or hearing. Scientists mapped the areas in which damage seemed to cause each kind of problem.

Now scientists have even more tools to study the brain. One tool is called functional magnetic resonance imaging, or FMRI. Scientists put a person into a machine that uses radio waves to produce images of the person's brain. Scientists then ask the person to do specific activities, such as looking at pictures of faces or listening for specific sounds. The FMRI images show what parts of the person's brain are most active during each activity.

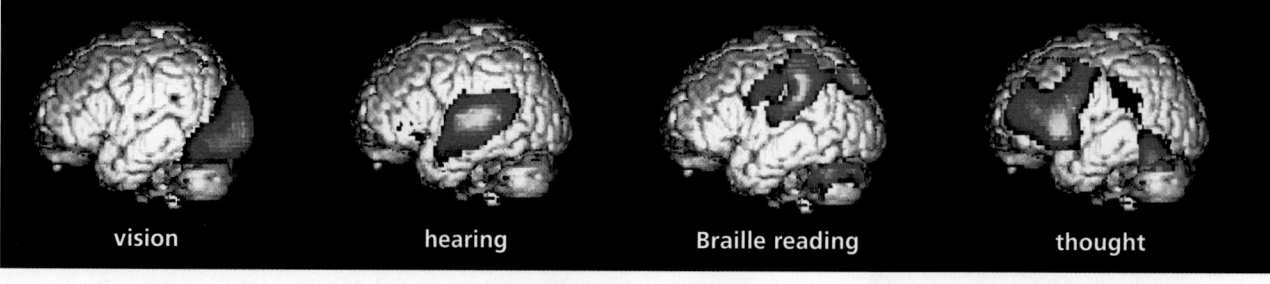

The PET scans show areas of the brain active during particular tasks. Braille is a textured alphabet read by the fingers. Braille reading activates areas associated with touch, vision, hearing, and thought.

Double Duty

Using FMRI and other tools, scientists have identified the parts of the cerebral cortex that are responsible for each of the senses. The vision area is located at the back of the brain. The smell, taste, touch, and hearing areas are all close together in the middle part of the brain.

People don't usually use just one sense at a time. Scientists have found some unexpected connections. In one study, Marisa Taylor-Clarke poked the arms of some volunteers with either one or two pins. Then she asked them how many pins they felt. Taylor-Clarke found that people who looked at their arms before the test did better than those who didn't. FMRI showed that the part of their brains responsible for touch was also more active when they used their sense of sight.

These connections in the brain show up even when one sense doesn't work. Many people who have hearing impairments read lips to understand what other people are saying. Scientists using FMRI discovered that these people use the part of the brain normally used for hearing to help them understand what they see. This is even true for people who have never been able to hear.

Scrambled Senses

Some people have more connections between their senses than most people have. They may look at numbers and see colors, or associate smells with shapes. Some even get a taste in their mouths when they touch something. All these are examples of synesthesia (sin-uhs-THEE-zhuh). About 1 in 200 people have some kind of synesthesia.

SCIENTIFIC AMERICAN FRONTIERS

View the "Sight of Touch" segment of your *Scientific American Frontiers* video to learn about another example of connections between the senses.

IN THIS SCENE FROM THE VIDEO ▶ Michelle, a research subject, reads Braille with her fingers after wearing a blindfold for three days.

SEEING BY TOUCHING Many blind people read using Braille, a system of raised dots used to represent letters. Some, such as Braille proofreader Gil Busch, can read Braille at astonishing speeds. Scientist Alvaro Pascual-Leone used MRI to study Gil's brain. The visual area of Gil's brain was active while he read Braille.

Gil has been blind since birth, so his brain has had a long time to adjust. Pascual-Leone wanted to know whether the brain could rewire itself in a shorter time. He asked volunteer Michelle Geronimo to wear a blindfold for a week. During that time, she learned to read Braille and experienced the world as a blind person does. At the end of the week, Pascual-Leone was able to demonstrate that Michelle's brain had rewired itself, too. Her visual center was active when she read Braille.

FMRI has made it possible for scientists to learn more about synesthesia. One group of scientists studied people who saw colors when they heard words. FMRI showed that the visual areas of their brains were active along with the hearing areas. (For most people, only the hearing area would be active.)

But why does synesthesia happen? Some scientists think that people with synesthesia have more connections between areas of their brains. Every person has extra connections when they're born, but most people lose many of them in childhood. Perhaps people with synesthesia keep theirs. Another theory suggests that their brains are "cross-wired," so information goes in unusual directions.

Some people with synesthesia see this colorful pattern when they hear a dog bark.

As scientists explore synesthesia and other connections between the senses, they learn more about how the parts of the brain work together. The human body is complex. And the brain, along with the rest of the nervous system, has yet to be fully understood.

?UNANSWERED Questions

Scientists have learned a lot about how senses are connected. Their research leads to new questions.

- How does information move between different areas of the brain?
- How and why does the brain rewire itself?
- How does cross-wired sensing (synesthesia) happen?

UNIT PROJECTS

As you study this unit, work alone or in a group on one of the projects below.

Your Body System

Create one or several models showing important body systems.

- Draw the outline of your own body on a large piece of craft paper.
- Use reference materials to help you place everything correctly. Label each part.

The Brain: "Then and Now"

Compare and contrast past and present understandings of the brain.

- One understanding is that each part of the brain is responsible for different body functions. This understanding has changed over time.
- Research the history of this idea.
- Prepare diagrams of then and now. Share your presentation.

Design an Experiment

Design an experiment that will test one of the senses. You should first identify a problem question you want to explore.

- The experiment may include a written introduction, materials procedure, and a plan for recording and presenting outcomes.
- Prepare a blank written experiment datasheet for your classmates to use.

CAREER CENTER
CLASSZONE.COM

Learn more about careers in neurobiology.

A Place in the SUN

Sunshine State Standards

In "A Place in the Sun" you will learn about the various forms of energy that come to Earth from the Sun. **(SC.B.1.3.3)**

The Sunshine State

In 2004 four Florida beaches received rankings among the top ten of America's best beaches. The beaches were rated for such things as sand quality, the length of hiking trails, and family-friendly atmospheres. When most people think of beaches, however, they think of only one thing: lying in the sun. Florida beaches draw millions of tourists each year because they are ideal spots for sun-bathing. These tourists bring money into the state's economy, and the tourism industry creates numerous jobs for Florida citizens. The intensity of the Sun's rays also makes Florida a rich agricultural region, ideal for growing sugar cane, citrus fruits, and vegetables. Sunshine, indeed, is one of Florida's top commodities.

Sunup to Sundown

Not so long ago, a dark tan was considered a sign of good health. Why shouldn't it have been? Don't plants grow toward the Sun and most animals apparently desire to lie in the Sun? Today, however, a lot of evidence indicates that even moderate exposure to sunlight can pose serious health risks, such as an increased rate of skin cancer. Many doctors urge the use of sunblock even in winter or in climates where the Sun's rays are not intense.

The health risks from sunlight come from the ultraviolet (UV) rays the Sun emits. These rays not only tan the skin but may also damage the chromosomes in skin cells. The effects may take years to discover.

Luckily, much of the Sun's harmful UV radiation is blocked by a region in the atmosphere called the ozone layer. Pollution from industry and other human activities, however, has done noticeable damage to the ozone layer, allowing more and more UV radiation to come through. We now seem to have a very awkward relationship with the Sun: We depend on its energy for our warmth, food, and existence, yet too much of it may be hazardous to our health.

UV Index		
Exposure Category	UVI Range	
Low	<2	No protection needed
Moderate	3 to 5	Protection: shirt, hat, sunscreen at midday
High	6 to 7	
Very High	8 to 10	Avoid outdoors at midday. Seek shade. Shirt, hat, and sunscreen are a must.
Extreme	11 +	

The UV Index was developed by the National Weather Service and the Environmental Protection Agency. It helps prevent overexposure to sunlight.

The concern for overexposure to UV radiation has led some weather reports to include reference to a UV Index (UVI) number. The higher the UVI number, the more intense the UV radiation is at Earth's surface.

The Good Sun

While dark tanning is never advisable, many doctors think everyone needs some exposure to the Sun to maintain the proper levels of vitamin D in the body. Vitamin D regulates the blood's ability to absorb calcium, and, thereby, the body's ability to make new bone. The same UV radiation that causes tanning and skin cancer also triggers chemical reactions in the body that produce vitamin D. Without the Sun, we might have difficulty obtaining the vitamin D we need. Children and older people especially need adequate amounts of vitamin D to maintain strong bones.

Much evidence also indicates that exposure to the Sun helps keep people in a better mood. Sunlight simply feels good on the skin. Many people generally prefer sunny to cloudy days and do whatever they can to spend time outside when the Sun is shining. Before retreating to live in caves, we need to think critically about our relationship with the Sun. What might happen to us if we get too little sunlight? How do we know how much sunlight is enough?

Shine On

There is no doubt that too much exposure to UV radiation can cause long-term damage to the skin. UV radiation, however, has the important biological function of producing the necessary vitamin D the body may not get in the diet. Vitamin D has many and supposed benefits for the body such as the following:

- **Prevention of Rickets** Lack of vitamin D in the blood leads to lack of calcium in the bones. This can result in abnormal bone growth and a condition known as rickets. Vitamin D is added to milk particularly to combat rickets.

- **Prevention of Diabetes** Unusually low vitamin D levels lead to reduced insulin secretion and slow the body's ability to use insulin.

- **Defense Against Heart Disease** Higher vitamin D levels are believed to decrease the chance of heart attack.

- **Prevention of High Blood Pressure** Low levels of vitamin D can lead to high blood pressure.

- **Maintenance of Muscle Strength** Vitamin D has been linked to muscle strength.

- **Treatment of Skin Conditions** UV rays have been used to treat skin conditions like psoriasis, a condition characterized by itchy, reddish skin.

- **Defense Against Multiple Sclerosis** Statistics appear to indicate that cases of multiple sclerosis increase in areas of higher latitude, which get less direct sunlight. Researchers believe the cause is the decreased level of vitamin D.

Another indication of the Sun's benefits may be seen in a condition in some people who don't get enough sunlight. The symptoms of this condition, called Seasonal Affective Disorder (SAD), include irritability, depression, and sleep problems. Instances of SAD are particularly intense in northern-latitude areas, like Alaska, where night

SPOTLIGHT ON UVA Versus UVB: What's the Difference?

UV radiation refers to a range of wavelengths in the electromagnetic spectrum from about 400 to 100 nanometers. Longer-wavelength UV radiation is called UVA radiation, and shorter-wavelength UV radiation is called UVB radiation. UVB radiation tans and burns skin and can cause skin cancer. UVA radiation, however, may be even more dangerous.

Sunblocks receive ratings based on the amount of UV radiation they shield the skin from. The higher the Sun Protection Factor (SPF) number of the lotion, the greater the amount of harmful UV radiation the lotion supposedly blocks. Some sunscreen manufacturers use more specific labeling about the types of UV radiation they block. The problem is that most sunblocks do a fine job at blocking out the shorter-wavelength UVB radiation, but often don't block out the longer-wavelength UVA radiation.

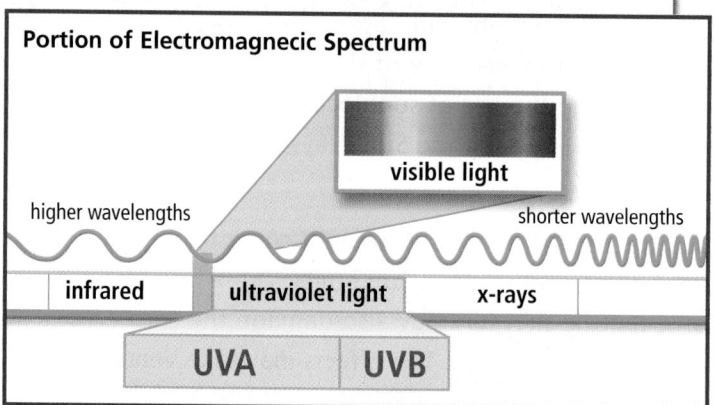

Portion of Electromagnetic Spectrum

visible light

higher wavelengths   shorter wavelengths

infrared   ultraviolet light   x-rays

UVA   UVB

Simply using sunblock, therefore, may not be enough to protect you from the Sun's harmful effects. To ensure your brand of sunblock gives you adequate protection from all ultraviolet radiation, make sure it offers "broad–spectrum protection." These sunscreens provide the best protection. Scientists worldwide are still looking for a standard for UVA protection.

Many with SAD find that special lights help them feel better.

can last for months. Think how it would be if it were always night. How would you know when to go to bed? when to get up?

Treating SAD may be as easy as turning on the lights—or more precisely, a special kind of light. Most lighting used indoors (both fluorescent and incandescent) only emits wavelengths in a very narrow region of the visible spectrum. Manufacturers of so-called "full-spectrum" lights, however, claim their lights are specially designed to produce wavelengths in all regions of the visible spectrum. Not only do these lights make objects appear more natural, but they also reduce glare that can cause headaches. Many people feel these lights improve heart rate, oxygen intake, and blood pressure and find they are successful at alleviating many symptoms of SAD.

Keep Your Head in the Clouds

Despite all the perceived health benefits, no doctor advises spending the whole day at the beach unprotected by sunblock, no matter how resistant to burning you feel your skin may be. Every sunbather must also keep in mind that the Sun's intensity is not the same everywhere; direct sunlight in one region may not be as strong as in another region. Where you get your sunlight is just as important as how long you spend in sunlight.

Luckily, getting the recommended amount of vitamin D from sunlight is not that difficult. In the United States, doctors recommend 5 micromilligrams per day for infants over six months through age 51. This increases to 10 micromilligrams for

ages 52 to 71, and 15 micromilligrams from 72 years on up. Estimates vary, but many doctors feel that 10 minutes of direct exposure per week, without sunblock, should be about all one needs. Again, you must consider how intense the sunlight is where you are and how dark your skin is. The Sun's rays need a longer time to penetrate darker skin. So before heading off to the beach in search of a healthy life, be sure you understand how much sunlight your body can safely accept, and do not exceed that limit.

 ASKING Questions

• What other things would you like to know about the positive effects of the Sun?

• What other things would you like to know about ultraviolet radiation?

RESOURCE CENTER
Visit ClassZone.com for more information the effects of sunlight.

WRITING ABOUT SCIENCE

A friend of yours is very concerned about the potential dangers of the Sun's radiation. The friend will not step outside without wearing long sleeves, a hat, pants and several coats of sunblock. In a letter, convince this friend that completely avoiding the Sun is probably not the best idea.

Writing Tip

Plan, draft, and revise your writing using the tips below.

• Reread the article.

• Make a note of the advantages and disadvantages of exposure to the Sun.

• Decide in what order you will present your points.

• Revise your letter to make it more convincing.

CHAPTER

16 Systems, Support, and Movement

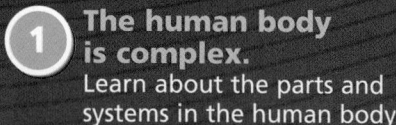

The human body is made up of systems that work together to perform necessary functions.

Key Concepts

SECTION

(1) The human body is complex.
Learn about the parts and systems in the human body.

SECTION

(2) The skeletal system provides support and protection.
Learn how the skeletal system is organized and what it does.

SECTION

(3) The muscular system makes movement possible.
Learn about the different types of muscles and how they work.

FCAT Practice

Prepare and practice for the FCAT
• Section Reviews, pp. 574, 582, 589
• Chapter Review, pp. 592–594
• FCAT Practice, p. 595

CLASSZONE.COM
• Florida Review: Content Review and FCAT Practice

What systems make it possible for this racer to move so fast?

EXPLORE (the BIG idea)

How Many Bones Are in Your Hand?

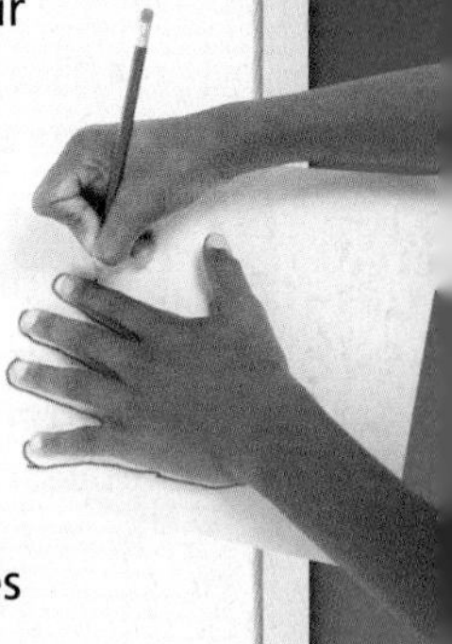

Use a pencil to trace an outline of your hand on a piece of paper. Feel the bones in your fingers and the palm of your hand. At points where you can bend your fingers and hand, draw a circle. Each circle represents a joint where two bones meet. Draw lines to represent the bones in your hand.

Observe and Think How many bones did you find? How many joints?

How Does It Move?

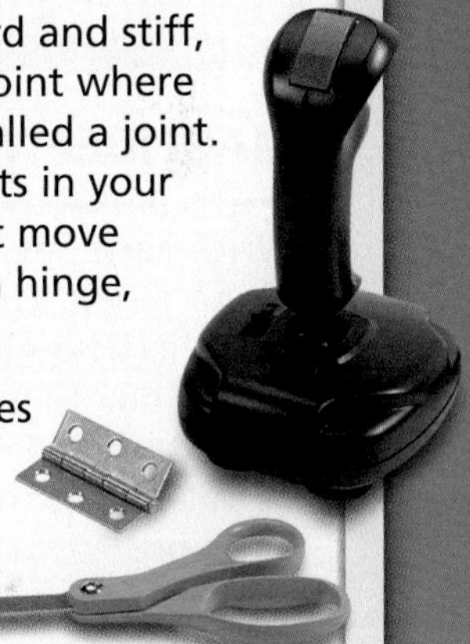

The bones in your body are hard and stiff, yet they move smoothly. The point where two bones meet and move is called a joint. There are probably many objects in your home that have hard parts that move against each other: a joystick, a hinge, a pair of scissors.

Observe and Think What types of movement are possible when two hard objects are attached to each other? What parts of your body produce similar movements?

Internet Activity: The Human Body

Go to **ClassZone.com** to explore the different systems in the human body.

Observe and Think How are the systems in the middle of the body different from those that extend to the outer parts of the body?

NSTA
scilinks.org
SCLINKS

Tissues and Organs **Code: MDL044**

Getting Ready to Learn

◁ CONCEPT REVIEW

- The cell is the basic unit of living things.
- Systems are made up of inter-acting parts that share matter and energy.
- In multicellular organisms cells work together to support life.

◁ VOCABULARY REVIEW

See Glossary for definitions.

cell
system

FLORIDA REVIEW
CLASSZONE.COM

Content Review and FCAT Practice

▶ TAKING NOTES

MAIN IDEA WEB

Write each new blue heading in a box. Then write notes in boxes around the center box that give important terms and details about that blue heading.

VOCABULARY STRATEGY

Write each new vocabulary term in the center of a **four square** diagram. Write notes in the squares around each term. Include a definition, some features, and some examples of the term. If possible, write some things that are not examples of the term.

See the Note-Taking Handbook on pages R45–R51.

SCIENCE NOTEBOOK

The cell is the basic unit of living things.	Tissues are groups of similar cells that function together.

The body has cells, tissues, and organs.

Organs are groups of tissues working together.	

Definition	Features
Group of cells that work together	A level of organization in the body

TISSUE

Examples	Nonexamples
connective tissue, like bone	individual bone cells

KEY CONCEPT

16.1 The human body is complex.

Sunshine State STANDARDS

SC.F.1.3.2: The student knows that the structural basis of most organisms is the cell and most organisms are single cells, while some, including humans, are multicellular.

SC.H.1.3.6: The student recognizes the scientific contributions that are made by individuals of diverse backgrounds, interests, talents, and motivations.

BEFORE, you learned

- All living things are made of cells
- All living things need energy
- Living things meet their needs through interactions with the environment

NOW, you will learn

- About the organization of the human body
- About different types of tissues
- About the functions of organ systems

FCAT VOCABULARY
tissue p. 572
organ p. 573

VOCABULARY
organ system p. 574
homeostasis p. 574

 THINK ABOUT

How is the human body like a city?

A city is made up of many parts that perform different functions. Buildings provide places to live and work. Transportation systems move people around. Electrical energy provides light and heat. Similarly, the human body is made of several systems. The skeletal system, like the framework of a building, provides support. The digestive system works with the respiratory system to provide energy and materials. What other systems in your body can you compare to a system in the city?

The body has cells, tissues, and organs.

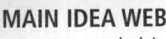

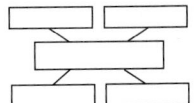

MAIN IDEA WEB
As you read this section, complete the main idea web begun on page 570.

Your body is made of many parts that work together as a system to help you grow and stay healthy. The basic level of organization in your body is the cell. Next come tissues, then individual organs, and then systems that are made up of organs. The highest level of organization is the organism itself. You can think of the body as having five levels of organization: cells, tissues, organs, organ systems, and the organism. Although these levels seem separate from one another, they all work together.

 **CHECK YOUR READING** What are five levels of organization in your body?

INVESTIGATE Systems

How do the systems in your body interact?

PROCEDURE

① Work with other classmates to make a list of everyday activities.

② Discuss how your body responds to each task. Record your ideas.

③ Identify and count the systems in your body that you think are used to perform the task.

④ Have someone from your group make a chart of the different activities.

WHAT DO YOU THINK?

• Which systems did you name, and how did they work together to perform each activity?

• When you are asleep, what activities does your body perform?

CHALLENGE How could you make an experiment that would test your predictions?

SKILL FOCUS
Predicting

MATERIALS
large sheet of paper

TIME
20 minutes

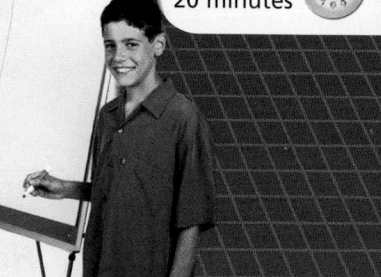

Cells

The cell is the basic unit of life. Cells make up all living things. Some organisms, such as bacteria, are made of only a single cell. In these organisms the single cell performs all of the tasks necessary for survival. That individual cell captures and releases energy, uses materials, and grows. In more complex organisms, such as humans and many other animals and plants, cells are specialized. Specialized cells perform specific jobs. A red blood cell, for example, carries oxygen from the lungs throughout the body.

Tissues

A **tissue** is a group of similar cells that work together to perform a particular function. Think of a tissue as a brick wall and the cells within it as the individual bricks. Taken together, the bricks form something larger and more functional. But just as the bricks need to be placed in a certain way to form the wall, cells must be organized in a tissue.

CHECK YOUR READING How are cells related to tissues?

The human body contains several types of tissues. These tissues are classified into four main groups according to their function: epithelial tissue, nerve tissue, muscle tissue, and connective tissue.

FLORIDA Content Review

Notice that humans have cells, tissues, organs, and organ systems like those of multicellular organisms that you studied in grade 6.

- Epithelial (ehp-uh-THEE-lee-uhl) tissue functions as a boundary. It covers all of the inner and outer surfaces of your body. Each of your internal organs is covered with a layer of epithelial tissue.

- Nerve tissue functions as a messaging system. Cells in nerve tissue carry electrical impulses between your brain and the various parts of your body in response to changing conditions.

- Muscle tissue functions in movement. Movement results when muscle cells contract, or shorten, and then relax. In some cases, such as throwing a ball, you control the movement. In other cases, such as the beating of your heart, the movement occurs without conscious control.

- Connective tissue functions to hold parts of the body together, providing support, protection, strength, padding, and insulation. Tendons and ligaments are connective tissues that hold bones and muscles together. Bone itself is another connective tissue. It supports and protects the soft parts of your body.

Organs

Groups of different tissues make up organs. An **organ** is a structure that is made up of two or more types of tissue that work together to carry out a function in the body. For example, the heart that pumps blood around your body contains all four types of tissues. As in cells and tissues, the structure of an organ relates to its function. The stomach's bag-shaped structure and strong muscular walls make it suited for breaking down food. The walls of the heart are also muscular, allowing it to function as a pump.

Levels of Organization

The human body can be studied at different levels of organization.

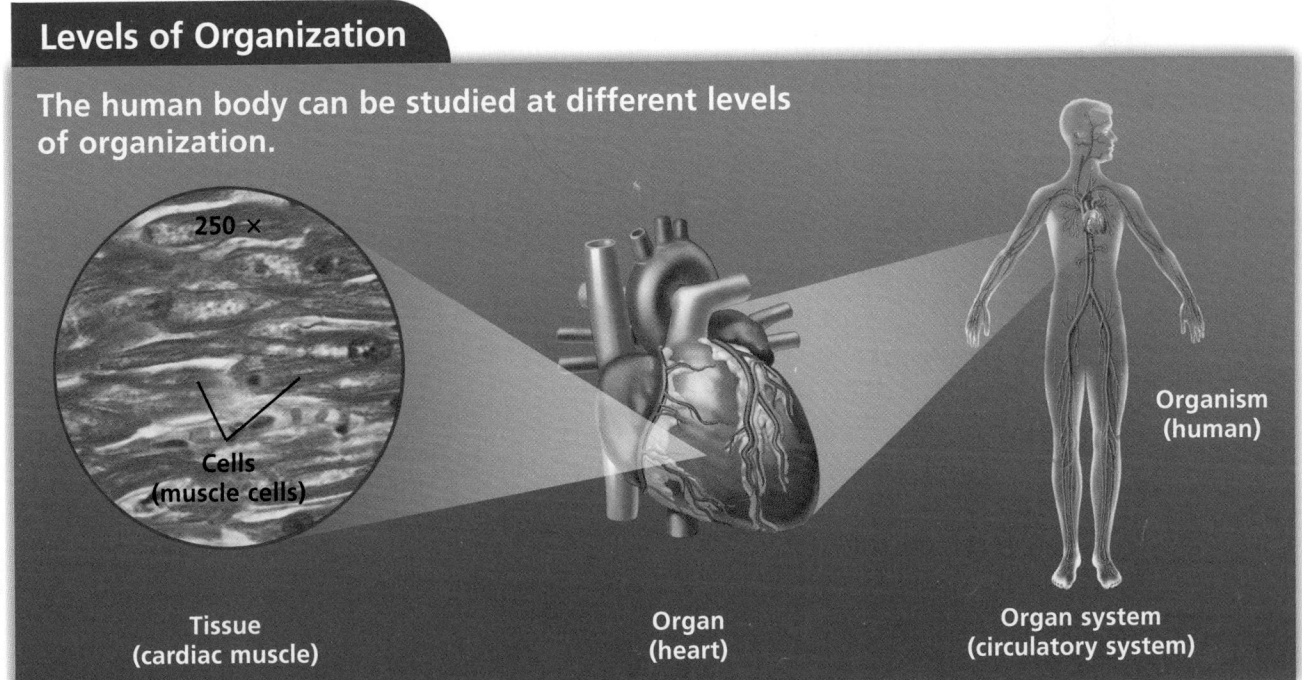

250 ×

Cells (muscle cells)

Tissue (cardiac muscle)

Organ (heart)

Organ system (circulatory system)

Organism (human)

Organ Systems

An **organ system** is a group of organs that together perform a function that helps the body meet its needs for energy and materials. For example, your stomach, mouth, throat, large and small intestines, liver, and pancreas are all part of the organ system called the digestive system. The body is made up of many organ systems. In this unit, you will read about these systems. They include the skeletal, muscular, respiratory, digestive, urinary, circulatory, immune, nervous, and reproductive systems. Together, these systems allow the human organism to grow, reproduce, and maintain life.

The body's systems interact with one another.

READING TiP

The word *homeostasis* contains two word roots. *Homeo* comes from a root meaning "same." *Stasis* comes from a root meaning "stand still" or "stay."

The ability of your body to maintain internal conditions is called **homeostasis** (HOH-mee-oh-STAY-sihs). Your body is constantly regulating such things as your body temperature, the amount of sugar in your blood, even your posture. The processes that take place in your body occur within a particular set of conditions.

The body's many levels of organization, from cells to organ systems, work constantly to maintain the balance needed for the survival of the organism. For example, on a hot day, you may sweat. Sweating keeps the temperature inside your body constant, even though the temperature of your surroundings changes.

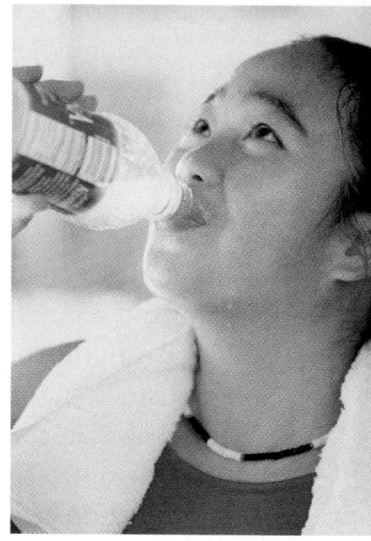

INFER This student is drinking water after exercising. Why is it important to drink fluids after you sweat?

16.1 Review

KEY CONCEPTS

1. Draw a diagram that shows the relationship among cells, tissues, organs, and organ systems.

2. Make a chart of the four basic tissue groups that includes names, functions, and examples.

3. Identify three functions performed by organ systems.

CRITICAL THINKING

4. **Apply** How does drinking water after you sweat help maintain homeostasis?

5. **Compare and Contrast** Compare and contrast the four basic tissue groups. How would all four types of tissue be involved in a simple activity, like raising your hand?

⬥ CHALLENGE

6. **Apply** Describe an object, such as a car, that can be used as a model of the human body. Explain how the parts of the model relate to the body.

What Does the Body Need to Survive?

In 1914, Ernest Shackleton and 27 men set sail for Antarctica. Their goal was to cross the continent by foot and sled. The crew never set foot on Antarctica. Instead, the winter sea froze around their ship, crushing it until it sank. They were stranded on floating ice, over 100 miles from land. How long could they survive? How would their bodies respond? What would they need to stay alive?

You can make inferences in answer to any of these questions. First you need to recall what you know. Then you need new evidence. What was available to the explorers? Did they save supplies from their ship? What resources existed in the environment?

▶ Prior Knowledge

- The human body needs air, water, and food.
- The human body needs to maintain its temperature. The body can be harmed if it loses too much heat.

▶ Observations

Several of Shackleton's explorers kept diaries. From the diaries we know the following:

- The crew hunted seals and penguins for fresh meat.
- The temperature was usually below freezing.
- Tents and overturned lifeboats sheltered the crew from the wind.
- Their clothes were made of thick fabric and animal skins and furs.
- They melted snow and ice in order to have fresh water.

▶ Make Inferences

On Your Own Describe how the explorers met each of the needs of the human body.

As a Group How long do you think these 28 men could have survived these conditions? Use evidence and inferences in your answer.

CHALLENGE How might survival needs differ for sailors shipwrecked in the tropics compared to the Antarctic?

RESOURCE CENTER
CLASSZONE.COM

Learn more about Shackleton's expedition.

The skeletal system provides support and protection.

Sunshine State STANDARDS

SC.F.1.3.2: The student knows that the structural basis of most organisms is the cell and most organisms are single cells, while some, including humans, are multicellular.

BEFORE, you learned

- The body is made of cells, tissues, organs, and systems
- Cells, tissues, organs, and organ systems work together
- Systems in the body interact

NOW, you will learn

- About different types of bone tissue
- How the human skeleton is organized
- How joints allow movement

VOCABULARY

skeletal system p. 576
compact bone p. 577
spongy bone p. 577
axial skeleton p. 578
appendicular skeleton p. 578

EXPLORE Levers

How can a bone act as a lever?

PROCEDURE

1. A lever is a stiff rod that pivots about a fixed point. Hold the bag in your hand and keep your arm straight, like a lever. Move the bag up and down.

2. Move the handles of the bag over your elbow. Again hold your arm straight and move the bag up and down.

3. Now move the bag to the top of your arm and repeat the procedure.

WHAT DO YOU THINK?

- At which position is it easiest to move the bag?
- At which position does the bag move the farthest?
- How does the position of a load affect the action of a lever?

MATERIALS
sports bag

Bones are living tissue.

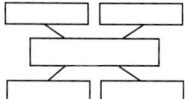

MAIN IDEA WEB
Make a web of the important terms and details about the main idea: *Bones are living tissue.*

Every movement of the human body is possible because of the interaction of muscles with the **skeletal system.** Made up of a strong connective tissue called bone, the skeletal system serves as the anchor for all of the body's movement, provides support, and protects soft organs inside the body. Bones can be classified as long bones, short bones, irregular bones, and flat bones. Long bones are found in the arms and legs. Short bones are found in the feet and hands. Irregular bones are found in the spine. Flat bones are found in the ribs and skull.

You might think that bones are completely solid and made up of dead tissue. They actually are made of both hard and soft materials.

Like your heart or skin, bones are living tissue. Bones are not completely solid, either; they have spaces inside. The spaces allow blood carrying nutrients to travel throughout the bones. Because bones have spaces, they weigh much less than they would if they were solid.

RESOURCE CENTER
CLASSZONE.COM
Explore the skeletal system.

Two Types of Bone Tissue

Every bone is made of two types of bone tissue: compact bone and spongy bone. The hard compact bone surrounds the soft spongy bone. Each individual bone cell lies within a bony web. This web is made up mostly of minerals containing calcium.

Compact Bone Surrounding the spongy, inner layer of the bone is a hard layer called **compact bone.** Compact bone functions as the basic supportive tissue of the body, the part of the body you call the skeleton. The outer layer of compact bone is very hard and tough. It covers the outside of most bones.

Spongy Bone Inside the bone, the calcium network is less dense. This tissue is called **spongy bone.** Spongy bone is strong but lightweight. It makes up most of the short, flat, and irregular bones found in your body. It also makes up the ends of long bones.

Marrow and Blood Cells

Within the spongy bone tissue is marrow, the part of the bone that produces blood cells. The new blood cells travel from the marrow into the blood vessels that run throughout the bone. The blood brings nutrients to the bone cells and carries waste materials away.

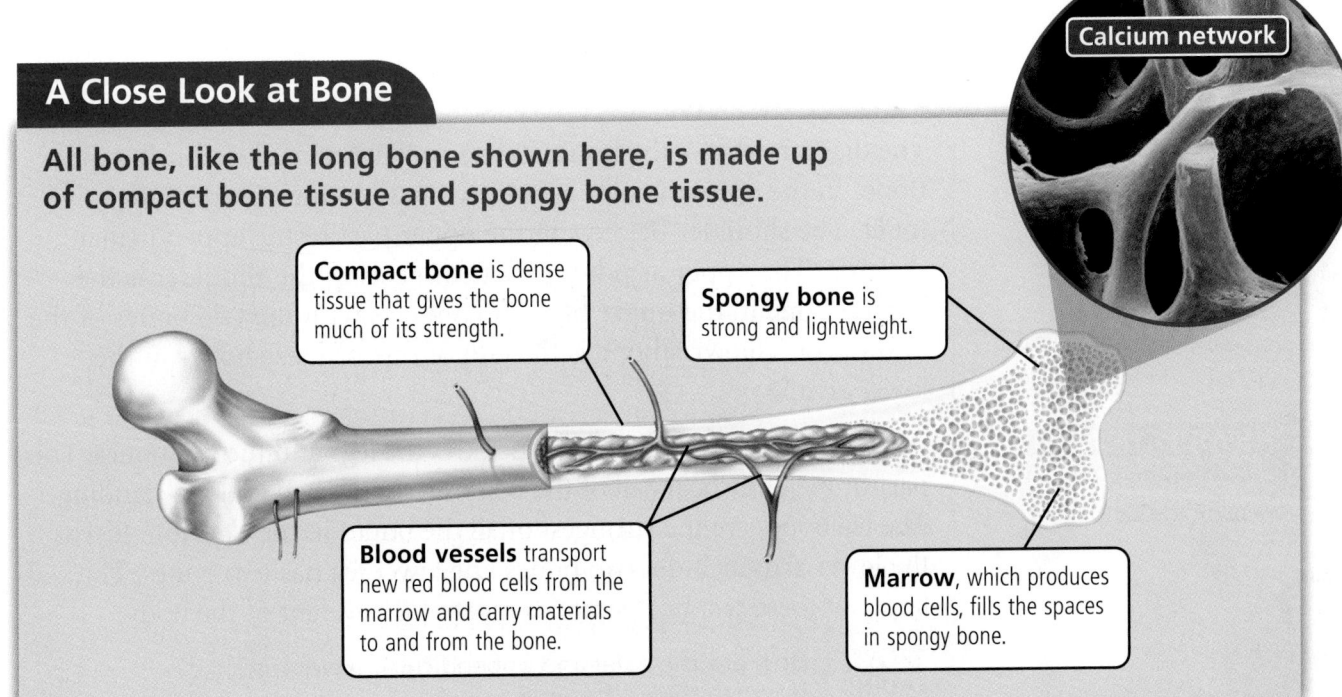

A Close Look at Bone

All bone, like the long bone shown here, is made up of compact bone tissue and spongy bone tissue.

Compact bone is dense tissue that gives the bone much of its strength.

Spongy bone is strong and lightweight.

Calcium network

Blood vessels transport new red blood cells from the marrow and carry materials to and from the bone.

Marrow, which produces blood cells, fills the spaces in spongy bone.

The skeleton is the body's framework.

Like the frame of a building, the skeleton provides the body's shape. The skeleton also works with other systems to allow movement. Scientists have identified two main divisions in the skeleton. These are the axial (AK-see-uhl) skeleton, which is the central part of the skeleton, and the appendicular (AP-uhn-DIHK-yuh-luhr) skeleton. Bones in the appendicular skeleton are attached to the axial skeleton. The diagram on page 579 labels some of the important bones in your skeleton.

VOCABULARY
Remember to add four squares for *axial skeleton* and *appendicular skeleton* to your notebook.

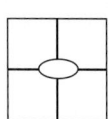

The Axial Skeleton

Imagine a line straight down your back. You can think of that line as an axis. Sitting, standing, and twisting are some of the motions that turn around the axis. The **axial skeleton** is the part of the skeleton that forms the axis. It provides support and protection. In the diagram, parts of the axial skeleton are colored in red.

The axial skeleton includes the skull, or the cranium (KRAY-nee-uhm). The major function of the cranium is protection of the brain. Most of the bones in the cranium do not move. The skull connects to the spinal column in a way that allows the head to move up and down as well as right and left.

Your spinal column makes up the main portion of the axial skeleton. The spinal column is made up of many bones called vertebrae. The many bones allow flexibility. If you run your finger along your back you will feel the vertebrae. Another set of bones belonging to the axial skeleton are the rib bones. The ribs function to protect the soft internal organs, such as the heart and lungs.

The Appendicular Skeleton

The diagram shows the bones in the appendicular skeleton in yellow. Bones in the **appendicular skeleton** function mainly to allow movement. The shoulder belongs to the upper part of the appendicular skeleton. The upper arm bone that connects to the shoulder is the longest bone in the upper body. It connects with the two bones of the lower arm. The wristbone is the end of one of these bones in the lower arm.

The lower part of the body includes the legs and the hip bones. This part of the body bears all of the body's weight when you are standing. The leg bones are the strongest of all the bones in the skeleton. Just as the lower arm includes two bones, the lower leg has two bones. The larger of these two bones carries most of the weight of the body.

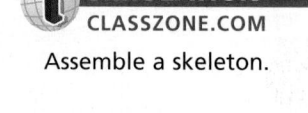

SIMULATION
CLASSZONE.COM

Assemble a skeleton.

CHECK YOUR
READING
How are the axial and appendicular skeletons alike? How are they different?

The Skeletal System

The skeletal system interacts with other body systems to allow this soccer player to stand, run, and kick.

- ■ axial skeleton
- ▫ appendicular skeleton

The **skull** protects the brain.

The lower jaw is the only bone in the skull that can move.

Twelve pairs of **ribs** protect the lungs and heart.

The shoulder blade is called the **scapula**.

The **vertebrae** of the spinal column protect the spinal cord and support the cranium and other bones.

The upper arm bone is called the **humerus**.

The lower arm bones are the **ulna** and **radius**.

The many bones in the wrist and the hand allow the hand to perform a great variety of activities.

The upper leg bone, called the **femur**, is the longest bone in the body.

The kneecap is called the **patella**.

The lower leg bones are called the **tibia** and the **fibula**.

There are 26 bones in the ankle and the foot.

READING VISUALS The word *appendicular* has the same root as the word *append*, which means to attach. How do you think this word applies to the appendicular skeleton?

The skeleton changes as the body develops and ages.

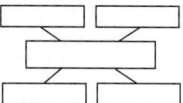
You will remember that bones are living tissue. During infancy and childhood, bones grow as the rest of the body grows. Bones become harder as they stop growing. In adulthood, bones continue to change.

Infancy The skull of a newborn is made up of several bones that have spaces between them. As the brain grows, the skull also grows. During the growth of the skull, the spaces between the bones close.

Childhood Bone growth occurs at areas called growth plates. These growth plates are made of cartilage, a firm, flexible connective tissue. The length and shape of bones is determined by growth plates. Long bones grow at the ends of the bone surrounding growth plates.

Adolescence At the end of adolescence (AD-uhl-EHS-uhns) bones stop growing. The growth plate is the last portion of the bone to become hard. Once growth plates become hard, arms and legs stop growing and the skull plates fuse.

Adulthood Even after bones stop growing, they go through cycles in which old bone is broken down and new bone is formed. As people age, more bone is broken down than is formed. This can lead to a decrease in bone mass, which causes a decrease in bone density. The strength of bones depends upon their density. As people age, their bone density may decrease. Bones that are less dense may break more easily. Many doctors recommend that adults over a certain age get regular bone density tests.

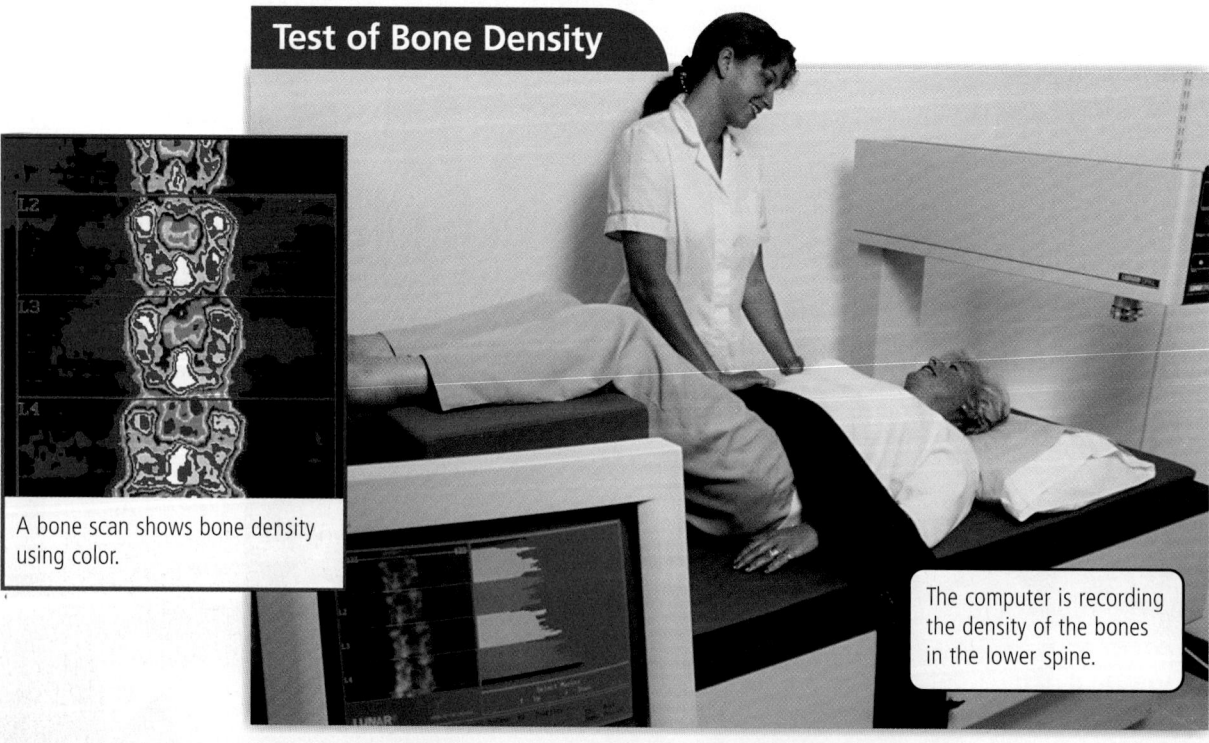

Test of Bone Density

A bone scan shows bone density using color.

The computer is recording the density of the bones in the lower spine.

Joints connect parts of the skeletal system.

A joint is a place at which two parts of the skeletal system meet. There are three types of joints: immovable, slightly movable, and freely movable.

Immovable and Slightly Movable Joints An immovable joint locks bones together like puzzle pieces. The bones of your skull are connected by immovable joints. Slightly movable joints are able to flex slightly. Your ribs are connected to your sternum by slightly movable joints.

Freely Movable Joints Freely movable joints allow your body to bend and to move. Tissues called ligaments hold the bones together at movable joints. Other structures inside the joint cushion the bones and keep them from rubbing together. The entire joint also is surrounded by connective tissue.

Movable joints can be classified by the type of movement they produce. Think about the movement of your arm when you eat an apple. Your arm moves up, then down, changing the angle between your upper and lower arms. This is angular movement. The joint that produces this movement is called a hinge joint.

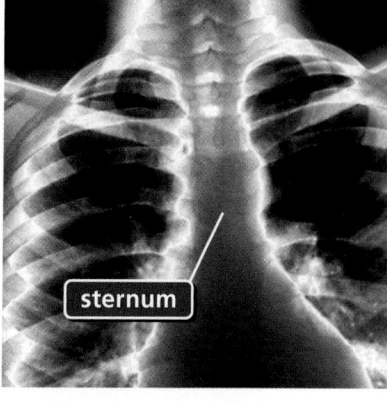

The sternum is an example of a slightly movable joint.

INVESTIGATE Movable Joints

How can you move at joints?

PROCEDURE

1. Perform several activities that involve your joints. Twist at the waist. Bend from your waist to one side. Reach into the air with one arm. Open and close your mouth. Push a book across your desk. Lift the book.

2. Record each activity and write a note describing the motion that you feel at each joint.

3. Try to see how many different ways you can move at joints.

WHAT DO YOU THINK?

- How was the motion you felt similar for each activity? How was it different?

- Based on your observations, identify two or more ways that joints move.

CHALLENGE Draw a diagram showing how you think each joint moves. How might you classify different types of joints based upon the way they move?

SKILL FOCUS
Observing

MATERIALS
book

TIME
20 minutes

The joints in the elbow and hip allow different types of movement.

Angular movement (elbow)

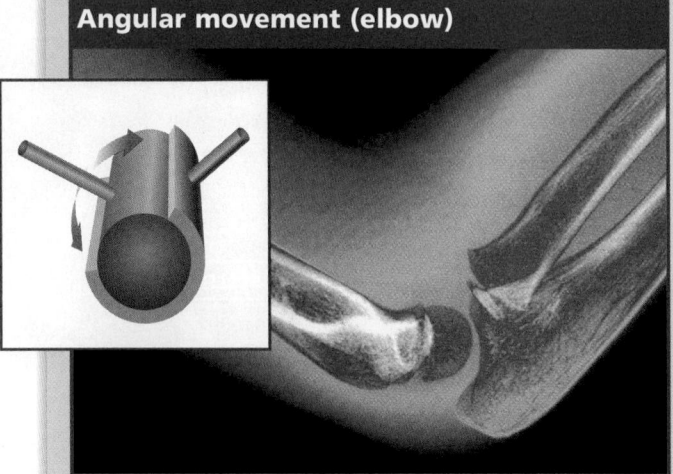

Rotational movement (hip)

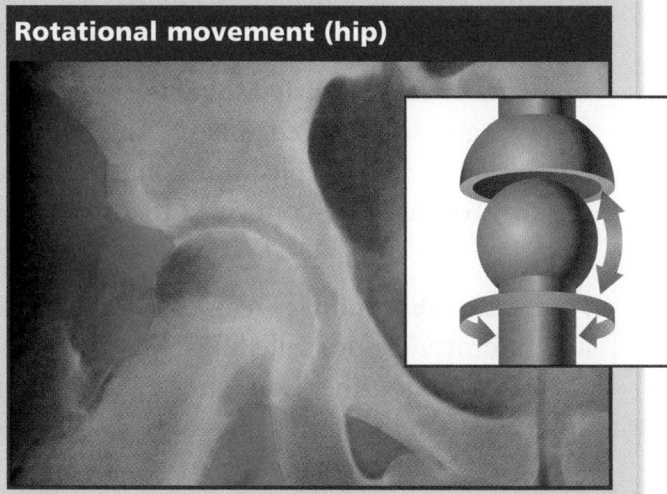

READING VISUALS **INFER** How do the structure and shape of each joint allow bones to move?

Your arm can also rotate from side to side, as it does when you turn a doorknob. Rotational movement like this is produced by a pivot joint in the elbow. You can also rotate your arm in a circle, like the motion of a softball pitcher winding up and releasing a ball. The joint in the shoulder that produces this type of rotational movement is called a ball-and-socket joint.

Joints also produce gliding movement. All joints glide, that is, one bone slides back and forth across another. In some cases, as with the joints in your backbone, a small gliding movement is the only movement the joint produces.

16.2 Review

KEY CONCEPTS

1. What are the functions of the two types of bone tissue?

2. What are the main divisions of the human skeleton?

3. Name three types of movement produced by movable joints and give an example of each.

CRITICAL THINKING

4. **Infer** What function do immovable joints in the skull perform? Think about the different stages of development in the human body.

5. **Analyze** Which type of movable joint allows the most movement? How does the joint's shape and structure contribute to this?

⚠ CHALLENGE

6. **Classify** The joints in your hand and wrist produce three different types of movement. Using your own wrist, classify the joint movement of the fingers, palm, and wrist. Support your answer.

MATH in SCIENCE

 MATH TUTORIAL
CLASSZONE.COM

Click on Math Tutorial
for more help with
unit rates.

Rates of Production

Where do red blood cells come from? They are produced inside bone marrow at the center of long bones. An average of about 200 billion red blood cells per day are produced by a healthy adult. When a person produces too few red blood cells, a condition called anemia may occur. Doctors study rates of blood cell production to diagnose and treat anemia.

A rate is a ratio that compares two quantities of different units. The number of cells produced per 24 hours is an example of a rate.

Example

A healthy adult produces red blood cells at a rate greater than 166 billion cells per 24 hours. Suppose a man's body produces 8 billion red blood cells per 1 hour. Would he be considered anemic?

(1) Write the two rates as fractions.

$$\frac{8}{1} \qquad \frac{166}{24}$$

(2) Simplify the fractions, so that the denominators are both 1. To simplify, divide the numerator by the denominator.

$$\frac{8}{1} \qquad \frac{6.9}{1}$$

(3) Compare the two whole numbers.
Is the first number $<$, $>$, or $=$ to the second number?

$$8 \qquad > \qquad 6.9$$

ANSWER The rate is greater than 6.9. The patient is not anemic.

Compare the following rates to see if they indicate that a person is anemic or normal.

1. For women, a normal rate is about 178 billion red blood cells per day. A certain woman produces 6 billion red blood cells per hour. Is her rate low or healthy?

2. Suppose a different woman produces 150 million (not billion) red blood cells per minute. How does that rate compare to 178 billion cells per day? Is it $<$, $>$, or $=$ to it?

3. Suppose a certain man is producing 135 million red blood cells per minute. Is that rate low or healthy?

CHALLENGE In the example above of a man producing 166 billion cells per day, calculate the percentage by which the rate would need to increase to bring it up to the average count of 200 billion per day.

16.3 The muscular system makes movement possible.

Sunshine State STANDARDS

SC.F.1.3.1: The student understands that living things are composed of major systems that function in reproduction, growth, maintenance, and regulation.

SC.F.1.3.7: The student knows that behavior is a response to the envi-ronment and influences growth, development, maintenance, and reproduction.

VOCABULARY

muscular system p. 585
skeletal muscle p. 586
voluntary muscle p. 586
smooth muscle p. 586
involuntary muscle p. 586
cardiac muscle p. 586

BEFORE, you learned

- There are different types of bone tissue
- The human skeleton has two separate divisions
- Joints function in several different ways

NOW, you will learn

- About the functions of muscles
- About the different types of muscles and how they work
- How muscles grow and heal

EXPLORE Muscles

How do muscles change as you move?

PROCEDURE

1. Sit on a chair with your feet on the floor.
2. Place your hand around your leg. Straighten one leg as shown in the photograph.
3. Repeat step 2 several times.

WHAT DO YOU THINK?

- How did your muscles change during the activity?
- Record your observations.
- What questions do you have about the muscular system?

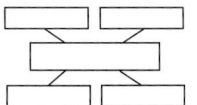

MAIN IDEA WEB
Make a web for the main idea: *Muscles perform important functions.*

Muscles perform important functions.

Every movement of your body—from the beating of your heart, to the movement of food down your throat, to the blinking of your eyes—occurs because of muscles. Some movements are under your control, and other movements seem to happen automatically. However, mus-cles do more than produce movement. They perform other functions as well. Keeping body temperature stable and maintaining posture are two additional functions of muscles.

 What are three functions that muscles perform?

Movement

RESOURCE CENTER
CLASSZONE.COM

Discover more about muscles.

The **muscular system** works with the skeletal system to allow movement. Like all muscles, the muscles that produce movement are made up of individual cells called muscle fibers. These fibers contract and relax.

Most of the muscles involved in moving the body work in pairs. As they contract, muscles shorten, pulling against bones. It may surprise you to know that muscles do not push. Rather, a muscle on one side of a bone pulls in one direction, while another muscle relaxes. Muscles are attached to bones by stretchy connective tissue.

Maintaining Body Temperature

Earlier you read that processes within the body require certain conditions, such as temperature and the right amount of water and other materials. The balance of conditions is called homeostasis. One of the functions of the muscular system is related to homeostasis. Muscles function to maintain body temperature.

When muscles contract, they release heat. Without this heat from muscle contraction, the body could not maintain its normal temperature. You may have observed the way your muscles affect your body temperature when you shiver. The quick muscle contractions that occur when you shiver release heat and raise your body temperature.

 **CHECK YOUR READING** How do muscles help maintain homeostasis?

Maintaining Posture

Have you ever noticed that you stand up straight without thinking about it, even though gravity is pulling your body down? Most muscles in your body are always a little bit contracted. This tension, or muscle tone, is present even when you are sleeping. The muscles that maintain posture relax completely only when you are unconscious.

Try standing on the balls of your feet for a few moments, or on one leg. When you are trying to balance or hold one position for any length of time, you can feel different muscles contracting and relaxing. Your muscles make constant adjustments to keep you sitting or standing upright. You don't have to think about these tiny adjustments; they happen automatically.

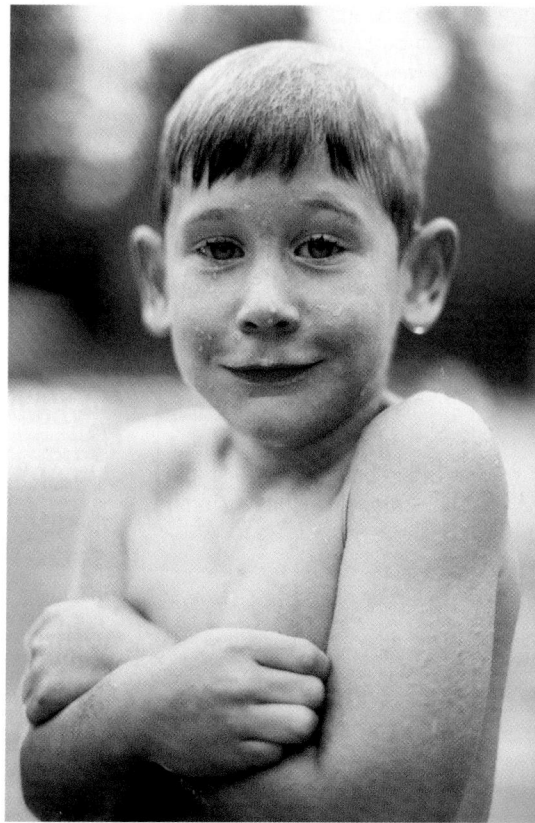

Muscles contract during shivering, raising body temperature.

Your body has different types of muscle.

Your body has three types of muscle. All three types of muscle tissue share certain characteristics. For example, each type of muscle contracts and relaxes. Yet all three muscle types have different functions, and different types of muscle are found in different locations.

Skeletal Muscle

The muscles that are attached to your skeleton are called **skeletal muscles.** Skeletal muscle performs voluntary movement— that is, movement that you choose to make. Because they are involved in voluntary movement, skeletal muscles are also called **voluntary muscles.**

Skeletal muscle, like all muscle, is made of long fibers. The fibers are made up of many smaller bundles, as a piece of yarn is made up of strands of wool. One type of bundle allows your muscles to move slowly. Those muscles are called slow-twitch muscles. Another type of bundle allows your muscles to move quickly. These are called fast-twitch muscles. If you were a sprinter, you would want to develop your fast-twitch muscles. If you were a long distance runner, you would develop your slow-twitch muscles.

 **CHECK YOUR READING** What does it mean that skeletal muscles are voluntary muscles?

READING TiP
The root of the word *voluntary* comes from the Latin root *vol-,* meaning "wish." In the word *involuntary* the prefix *in-* suggests the meaning "unwished for." *Involuntary movement* means movement you can't control.

Smooth Muscle

Smooth muscle is found inside some organs, such as the intestines and the stomach. Smooth muscles perform automatic movement and are called **involuntary muscles.** In other words, smooth muscles work without your knowing it. You have no control over their movement. For example, smooth muscles line your stomach wall and push food through your digestive system. Smooth muscle fibers are not as long as skeletal muscle fibers. Also, unlike skeletal muscles, smooth muscles are not fast-twitch. Smooth muscles contract slowly.

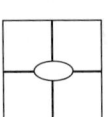 **VOCABULARY**
Remember to add four squares for *involuntary muscles* and *voluntary muscles* to your notebook. Note differences in the two diagrams.

Cardiac Muscle

Your heart is made of **cardiac muscle.** Like smooth muscle, cardiac muscle moves without conscious control. Each cardiac muscle cell has a branched shape. The cells of the heart connect in a chain. These chains form webs of layered tissue that allow cardiac cells to contract together and make the heart beat. Just like the smooth muscle cells, the cardiac muscle cells contract slowly, except in emergencies.

 **CHECK YOUR READING** Compare and contrast the three types of muscle described: skeletal, smooth, and cardiac.

Muscle Tissue

The marchers in this band are using all three different types of muscle tissue.

250×

Cardiac muscle allows the hearts of the band members to pump blood as they march to the beat of the music.

150×

Smooth muscle in the air passages of the lungs allows the band members to breathe as they play their instruments.

360×

Skeletal muscle moves the legs of these marchers.

READING VISUALS Which movements of these band members are voluntary, and which are involuntary?

Skeletal muscles and tendons allow bones to move.

Skeletal muscles are attached to your bones by strong tissues called tendons. The tendons on the end of the muscle attach firmly to the bone. As the fibers in a muscle contract, they shorten and pull the tendon. The tendon, in turn, pulls the bone and makes it move.

You can feel your muscles moving your bones. Place your left arm, stretched out flat, in front of you on a table. Place the fingers of your right hand just above your left elbow. Bend your elbow and raise and lower your left arm. You are contracting your biceps. Can you feel the muscle pull on the tendon?

The dancers in the photograph are using many sets of muscles. The diagrams show how muscles and tendons work together to move bones. Muscles are shown in red. Notice how each muscle crosses a joint. Most skeletal muscles do. One end of the muscle attaches to one bone, crosses a joint, then attaches to a second bone. As the muscle contracts, it pulls on both bones. This pulling produces movement—in the case of these dancers, very exciting movement.

tendon
muscle relaxes
muscle contracts
bones
tendons

Skeletal muscles contract by shortening and pulling the tendon.

tendon
muscle contracts
muscle relaxes
bones
tendons

Muscle fibers can return to their original length after being shortened.

Muscles grow and heal.

Developing Muscles An infant's muscles cannot do very much. A baby cannot lift its head, because the neck muscles are not strong enough to support it. For the first few months of life, a baby needs extra support, until the neck muscles grow strong and can hold up the baby's head.

The rest of the skeletal muscles also have to develop and strengthen. During infancy and childhood and into adolescence, humans develop muscular coordination and become more graceful in their movements. Coordination reaches its natural peak in adolescence but can be further improved by additional training.

Exercise and Muscles When you exercise regularly, your muscles may get bigger. Muscles increase in size with some types of exercise, because their cells reproduce more rapidly in response to the increased activity. Exercise also stimulates growth of individual muscle cells, making them larger.

Stretching your muscles before exercise helps prevent injury.

You may have experienced sore muscles during or after exercising. During exercise, chemicals can build up in the muscles and make them cramp or ache. The muscle soreness you feel a day or so after exercise is caused by damage to the muscle fibers. The muscle fibers have been overstretched or torn. Such injuries take time to heal, because the body must remove injured cells, and new ones must form.

16.3 Review

KEY CONCEPTS

1. What are the three main functions of the muscular system?

2. Make a rough outline of a human body and label places where you could find each of the three types of muscles.

3. Explain why you may be sore after exercise.

CRITICAL THINKING

4. **Apply** You are exercising and you begin to feel hot. Explain what is happening in your muscles.

5. **Analyze** Describe what happens in your neck muscles when you nod your head.

CHALLENGE

6. **Infer** The digestive system breaks down food and transports materials. How are the short length and slow movement of smooth muscle tissues in the stomach and intestines related to the functions of these organs?

CHAPTER INVESTIGATION

A Closer Look at Muscles

OVERVIEW AND PURPOSE You use the muscles in your body to do a variety of things. Walking, talking, reading the words on this page, and scratching your head are all actions that require muscles. How do your muscles interact with your bones? In this investigation you will

- examine chicken wings to see how the muscles and the bones interact
- compare the movement of the chicken wing with the movement of your own bones and muscles

▶ Problem

What are some characteristics of muscles?

▶ Hypothesize

Write a hypothesis to propose how muscles interact with bones. Your hypothesis should take the form of an "If . . . , then . . . , because . . ." statement.

▶ Procedure

MATERIALS
- uncooked chicken wing and leg (soaked in bleach)
- paper towels
- dissection tray
- scissors

1. Make a data table like the one shown on the sample notebook page. Put on your protective gloves. Be sure you are wearing gloves whenever you touch the chicken.

2. Obtain a chicken wing from your teacher. Rinse it in water and pat dry with a paper towel. Place it in the tray.

3. Extend the wing. In your notebook, draw a diagram of the extended wing. Be sure to include any visible external structures. Label the following on your diagram: lower limb, upper joint, and the wing tip.

step 3

4. Use scissors to remove the skin. Use caution so that you cut only through the skin. Peel back the skin and any fat so you can examine the muscles.

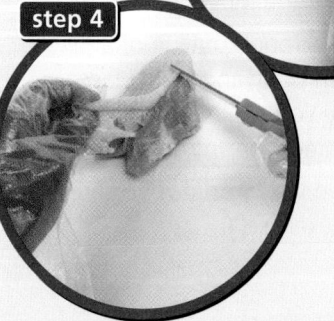
step 4

5. The muscles are the pink tissues that extend from one end of the bone to the other. Locate these in the upper wing and observe the way they move when you move the wing. Record your observations in your notebook.

6. Repeat this procedure for the muscles in the lower wing. In your notebook, draw a diagram of the muscles in the chicken wing.

7. There are also tendons in the chicken wing. These are the shiny white tissues at the end of the muscles. Add the tendons to your diagram.

8. Dispose of the chicken wing and parts according to your teacher's instructions. **Be sure to wash your hands well.**

▶ Observe and Analyze

1. **RECORD** Write a brief description of how the bones and muscles work together to allow movement.

2. **EVALUATE** What difficulties, if any, did you encounter in carrying out this experiment?

▶ Conclude

1. **INTERPRET** How does the chicken wing move when you bend it at the joint?

2. **OBSERVE** What happens when you pull on one of the wing muscles?

3. **COMPARE** Using your diagram of the chicken wing as an example, locate the same muscle groups in your own arm. How do they react when you bend your elbow?

4. **APPLY** What role do the tendons play in the movement of the muscles or bones?

▶ INVESTIGATE Further

CHALLENGE Using scissors, carefully remove the muscles and the tendons from the bones. Next find the ligaments, which are located between the bones. Add these to your diagram. Describe how you think ligaments function.

A Closer Look at Muscles

Problem What are some characteristics of muscles?

Table 1. Observations

Draw your diagrams	Write your observations
Extended wing	Muscles in the upper wing
Muscles in the wing	Muscles in the lower wing

FLORIDA REVIEW
CLASSZONE.COM

Content Review and
FCAT Practice

the BIG idea

The human body is made up of systems that work together to perform necessary functions.

◀ KEY CONCEPTS SUMMARY

① The human body is complex.

You can think of the body as having five levels of organization: cells, tissues, organs, organ systems, and the whole organism itself. The different systems of the human body work together to maintain homeostasis.

Cells ① (cardiac muscle cells)

Tissue ② (cardiac muscle)   **Organ** ③ (heart)   **Organ system** ④ (circulatory system)   ⑤ **Organism** (human)

VOCABULARY
tissue p. 572
organ p. 573
organ system p. 574
homeostasis p. 574

② The skeletal system provides support and protection.

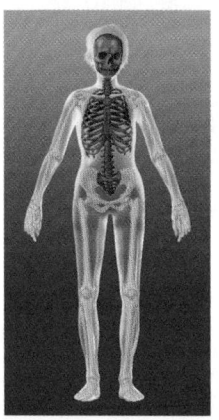

Bones are living tissue. The skeleton is the body's framework and has two main divisions, the **axial skeleton** and the **appendicular skeleton**. Bones come together at joints.

VOCABULARY
skeletal system p. 576
compact bone p. 577
spongy bone p. 577
axial skeleton p. 578
appendicular skeleton p. 578

③ The muscular system makes movement possible.

Types of muscle	Function
skeletal muscle, voluntary	moves bones, maintains posture, maintains body temperature
smooth muscle, involuntary	moves internal organs, such as the intestines
cardiac muscle, involuntary	pumps blood throughout the body

VOCABULARY
muscular system p. 585
skeletal muscle p. 586
voluntary muscle 586
smooth muscle p. 586
involuntary muscle p. 586
cardiac muscle p. 586

Reviewing Vocabulary

In one or two sentences describe how the vocabulary terms in each of the following pairs of words are related. Underline each vocabulary term in your answer.

1. cells, tissues

2. organs, organ systems

3. axial skeleton, appendicular skeleton

4. skeletal muscle, voluntary muscle

5. smooth muscle, involuntary muscle

6. compact bone, spongy bone

Reviewing Key Concepts

Multiple Choice *Choose the letter of the best answer.*

7. Which type of tissue carries electrical impulses from your brain?
   a. epithelial tissue
   b. muscle tissue
   c. nerve tissue
   d connective tissue

8. Connective tissue functions to provide
   a. support and strength
   b. messaging system
   c. movement
   d. heart muscle

9. Bone cells lie within a network made of
   a. tendons
   b. calcium
   c. marrow
   d. joints

10. The marrow produces
    a. spongy bone
    b. red blood cells
    c. compact bone
    d. calcium

11. Which bones are part of the axial skeleton?
    a. skull, shoulder blades, arm bones
    b. skull, spinal column, leg bones
    c. shoulder blades, spinal column, and hip bones
    d. skull, spinal column, ribs

12. Bones of the skeleton connect to each other at
    a. tendons
    b. ligaments
    c. joints
    d. muscles

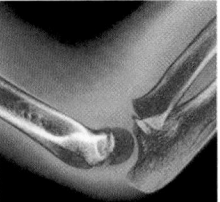

13. How do muscles contribute to homeostasis?
    a. They keep parts of the body together.
    b. They control the amount of water in the body.
    c. They help you move.
    d. They produce heat when they contract.

14. Cardiac muscle is found in the
    a. heart
    b. stomach
    c. intestines
    d. arms and legs

15. The stomach is made up of
    a. cardiac muscle
    b. skeletal muscle
    c. smooth muscle
    d. voluntary muscle

Short Response *Write a short response to each question.*

16. What is the difference between spongy bone and compact bone?

17. The root word *homeo* means "same," and the root word *stasis* means "to stay." How do these root words relate to the definition of *homeostasis*?

18. Hold the upper part of one arm between your elbow and shoulder with your opposite hand. Feel the muscles there. What happens to those muscles as you bend your arm?

Thinking Critically

19. PROVIDE EXAMPLES What are the levels of organization of the human body from simple to most complex? Give an example of each.

20. CLASSIFY There are four types of tissue in the human body: epithelial, nerve, muscle, and connective. How would you classify blood? Explain your reasoning.

21. CONNECT A clam shell is made of a calcium compound. The material is hard, providing protection to the soft body of a clam. It is also lightweight. Describe three ways in which the human skeleton is similar to a seashell. What is one important way in which it is different?

Use the diagram below to answer the next two questions

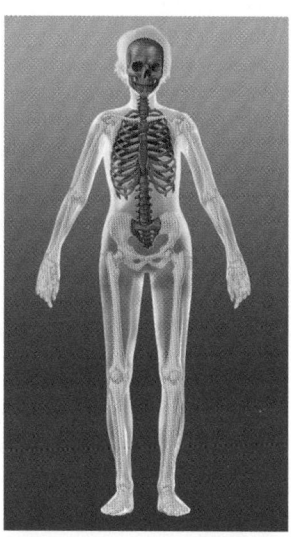

22. SYNTHESIZE Identify the types of joints that hold together the bones of the skull and sternum. How do these types of joints relate to the function of the skull and sternum?

23. SYNTHESIZE The human skeleton has two main divisions. Which skeleton do the arms and legs belong to? How do the joints that connect the arms to the shoulders and the legs to the hips relate to the function of this skeleton?

24. COMPARE AND CONTRAST How is the skeletal system of your body like the framework of a house or building? How is it different?

25. SUMMARIZE Describe three important functions of the skeleton.

26. APPLY The joints in the human body can be described as producing three types of movement. Relate these three types of movement to the action of brushing your teeth.

27. COMPARE AND CONTRAST When you stand, the muscles in your legs help to keep you balanced. Some of the muscles on both sides of your leg bones contract. How does this differ from how the muscles behave when you start to walk?

28. INFER Muscles are tissues that are made up of many muscle fibers. A muscle fiber can either be relaxed or contracted. Some movements you do require very little effort, like picking up a piece of paper. Others require a lot of effort, like picking up a book bag. How do you think a muscle produces the effort needed for a small task compared with a big task?

the BIG idea

29. INFER Look again at the picture on pages 568–569. Now that you have finished the chapter, how would you change or add details to your answer to the question on the photograph?

30. SUMMARIZE Write a paragraph explaining how skeletal muscles, bones, and joints work together to allow the body to move and be flexible. Underline the terms in your paragraph.

UNIT PROJECTS

If you are doing a unit project, make a folder for your project. Include in your folder a list of resources you will need, the date on which the project is due, and a schedule to track your progress. Begin gathering data.

Interpreting Diagrams

The action of a muscle pulling on a bone can be compared to a simple machine called a lever. A lever is a rod that moves about a fixed point called the fulcrum. Effort at one end of the rod can move a load at the other end. In the human body, a muscle supplies the effort needed to move a bone—the lever. The joint is the fulcrum, and the load is the weight of the body part being moved. There are three types of levers, which are classified according to the position of the fulcrum, the effort, and the load.

Read the text and study the diagrams, and then choose the best answer for the questions that follow.

> **FCAT TIP**
>
> Before answering questions based on a diagram, read the diagram's labels carefully. They will help you understand what the diagram is showing.

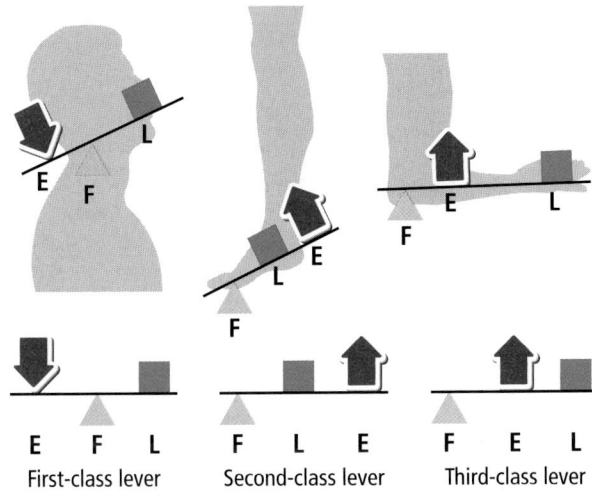

E   F   L
First-class lever

F   L   E
Second-class lever

F   E   L
Third-class lever

MULTIPLE CHOICE

1. Which of the following is true in a first-class lever?

   A. The load is at end of the lever opposite the fulcrum.

   B. The load is between the effort and the fulcrum.

   C. The fulcrum is between the load and the effort.

   D. The effort and load are on the same side.

2. What is true of all levers?

   F. The fulcrum must be located at the center of a lever.

   G. The force of the load and effort point in the same direction.

   H. The load and effort are on the same side of the fulcrum.

   I. The lever exerts a force in a direction opposite that of the load.

3. The fulcrum represents what structure in the human body?

   A. a joint   **C.** a muscle

   B. a bone   **D.** a tendon

SHORT RESPONSE

4. Describe where the effort, load, and fulcrum are in the lever formed by your leg when you run.

5. The diagram shows three types of levers. Which type of lever do you think is most common in the body? Give examples.

EXTENDED RESPONSE

6. Suppose you had a heavy box to lift. Your first thought might be to bend over, stretch out your arms, and grab the box. Your body would be acting as a simple machine. Identify the type of lever this is and the parts of this machine.

7. A doctor would advise you not to lift a heavy object, like a box, simply by bending over and picking it up. That action puts too much strain on your back. It is better to bend your knees, hold the box close to your body, and then lift. How does this way of lifting change how you are using your body?

17 Absorption, Digestion, and Exchange

the BIG idea

Systems in the body obtain and process materials and remove waste.

> **What materials does your body need to function properly?**

Key Concepts

SECTION

1 **The respiratory system gets oxygen and removes carbon dioxide.**
Learn how the respiratory system functions.

SECTION

2 **The digestive system breaks down food.**
Learn how the digestive system provides cells with necessary materials.

SECTION

3 **The urinary system removes waste materials.**
Learn how the urinary system removes wastes.

FCAT Practice

Prepare and practice for the FCAT
- Section Reviews, pp. 605, 612, 617
- Chapter Review, pp. 620–622
- FCAT Practice, p. 623

CLASSZONE.COM
- Florida Review: Content Review and FCAT Practice

EXPLORE (the BIG idea)

Mirror, Mirror

Hold a small hand mirror in front of your mouth. Slowly exhale onto the surface of the mirror. What do you see? Exhale a few more times onto the mirror, observing the interaction of your breath with the cool surface of the mirror.

Observe and Think What did you see on the surface of the mirror? What does this tell you about the content of the air that you exhale?

Water Everywhere

Keep track of how much liquid you drink in a 24-hour period of time. Do not include carbonated or caffeinated beverages. Water, juice, and milk can count. Add up the number of ounces of liquid you drink in that period of time.

Observe and Think How many ounces did you drink in one day? Do you drink fluids only when you feel thirsty?

Internet Activity: Lung Movement

Go to **ClassZone.com** to watch a visualization of lung and diaphragm movement during respiration. Observe how movements of the diaphragm and other muscles affect the lungs.

Observe and Think How do the diaphragm and lungs move during inhalation? during exhalation? Why do movements of the diaphragm cause the lungs to move?

NSTA
scilinks.org
SCLINKS

Digestion Code: MDL045

Getting Ready to Learn

◀ CONCEPT REVIEW

- Cells make up tissues, and tissues make up organs.
- The body's systems interact.
- The body's systems work to maintain internal conditions.

◀ VOCABULARY REVIEW

homeostasis p. 574

smooth muscle p. 586

energy *See Glossary.*

FLORIDA REVIEW
CLASSZONE.COM

Content Review and FCAT Practice

▶ TAKING NOTES

OUTLINE

As you read, copy the blue headings on your paper in the form of an outline. Then add notes in your own words that summarize what you read.

VOCABULARY STRATEGY

Think about a vocabulary term as a **magnet word** diagram. Write the other terms or ideas related to that term around it.

See the Note-Taking Handbook on pages R45–R51.

SCIENCE NOTEBOOK

THE RESPIRATORY SYSTEM GETS OXYGEN AND REMOVES CARBON DIOXIDE.

   A. Your body needs oxygen.

      1. Oxygen is used to release energy

      2. Oxygen is in air you breathe

   B. Structures in the respiratory system function together

      1. nose, throat, trachea

      2. lungs

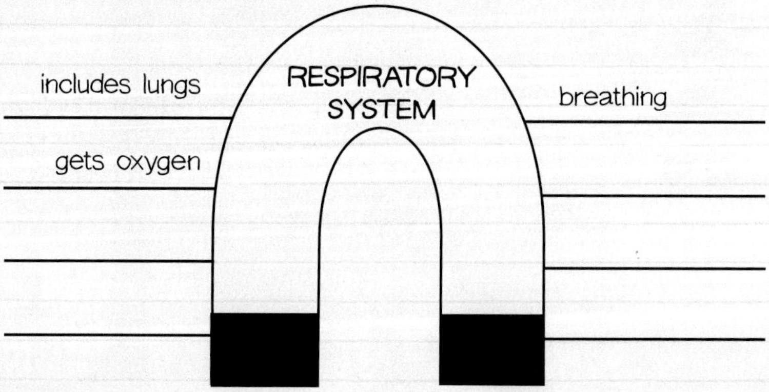

includes lungs   **RESPIRATORY SYSTEM**   breathing

gets oxygen

The respiratory system gets oxygen and removes carbon dioxide.

Sunshine State STANDARDS

SC.G.1.3.4: The student knows that the interactions of organisms with each other and with the non-living parts of their environments result in the flow of energy and the cycling of matter throughout the system.

VOCABULARY

respiratory system p. 599
cellular respiration p. 601

BEFORE, you learned

• Cells, tissues, organs, and organ systems work together
• Organ systems provide for the body's needs
• Organ systems are important to the body's survival

NOW, you will learn

• About the structures of the respiratory system that function to exchange gases
• About the process of cellular respiration
• About other functions of the respiratory system

EXPLORE Breathing

How do your ribs move when you breathe?

PROCEDURE

① Place your hands on your ribs.

② Breathe in and out several times, focusing on what happens when you inhale and exhale.

③ Record your observations in your notebook.

WHAT DO YOU THINK?
• What movement did you observe?
• Think about your observations. What questions do you have as a result of your observations?

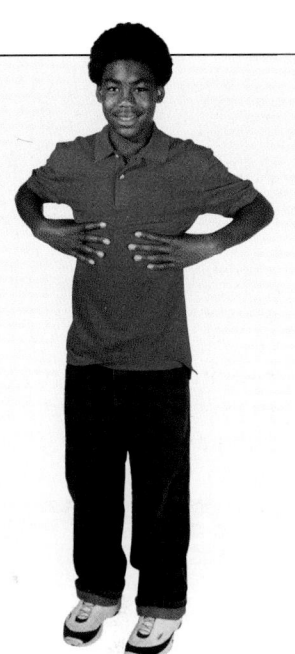

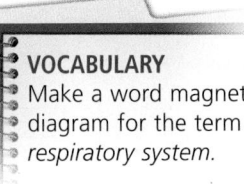

VOCABULARY
Make a word magnet diagram for the term *respiratory system*.

Your body needs oxygen.

During the day, you eat and drink only a few times, but you breathe thousands of times. In fact, breathing is a sign of life. The body is able to store food and liquid, but it is unable to store very much oxygen. The **respiratory system** is the body system that functions to get oxygen from the environment and remove carbon dioxide and other waste products from your body. The respiratory system interacts with the environment and with other body systems.

The continuous process of moving and using oxygen involves mechanical movement and chemical reactions. Air is transported into your lungs by mechanical movements, and oxygen is used during chemical reactions that release energy in your cells.

 **CHECK YOUR READING** What are the two main functions of your respiratory system?

Exchanging Oxygen and Carbon Dioxide

Like almost all living things, the human body needs oxygen to survive. Without oxygen, cells in the body die quickly. How does the oxygen you need get to your cells? Oxygen, along with other gases, enters the body when you inhale. Oxygen is then transported to cells throughout the body by red blood cells.

The air that you breathe contains only about 20 percent oxygen and less than 1 percent carbon dioxide. Almost 80 percent of air is nitrogen gas. The air that you exhale contains more carbon dioxide and less oxygen than the air that you inhale. It's important that you exhale carbon dioxide because high levels of it will damage, even destroy, cells.

In cells and tissues, proper levels of both oxygen and carbon dioxide are essential. Recall that systems in the body work together to maintain homeostasis. If levels of oxygen or carbon dioxide change, your nervous system signals the need to breathe faster or slower.

The photograph shows how someone underwater maintains proper levels of carbon dioxide and oxygen. The scuba diver needs to inhale oxygen from a tank. She removes carbon dioxide wastes with other gases when she exhales into the water. The bubbles you see in the water are formed when she exhales.

CHECK YOUR READING What gases are in the air that you breathe?

Gas Exchange

This scuba diver breathes the same mixture of gases present in air.

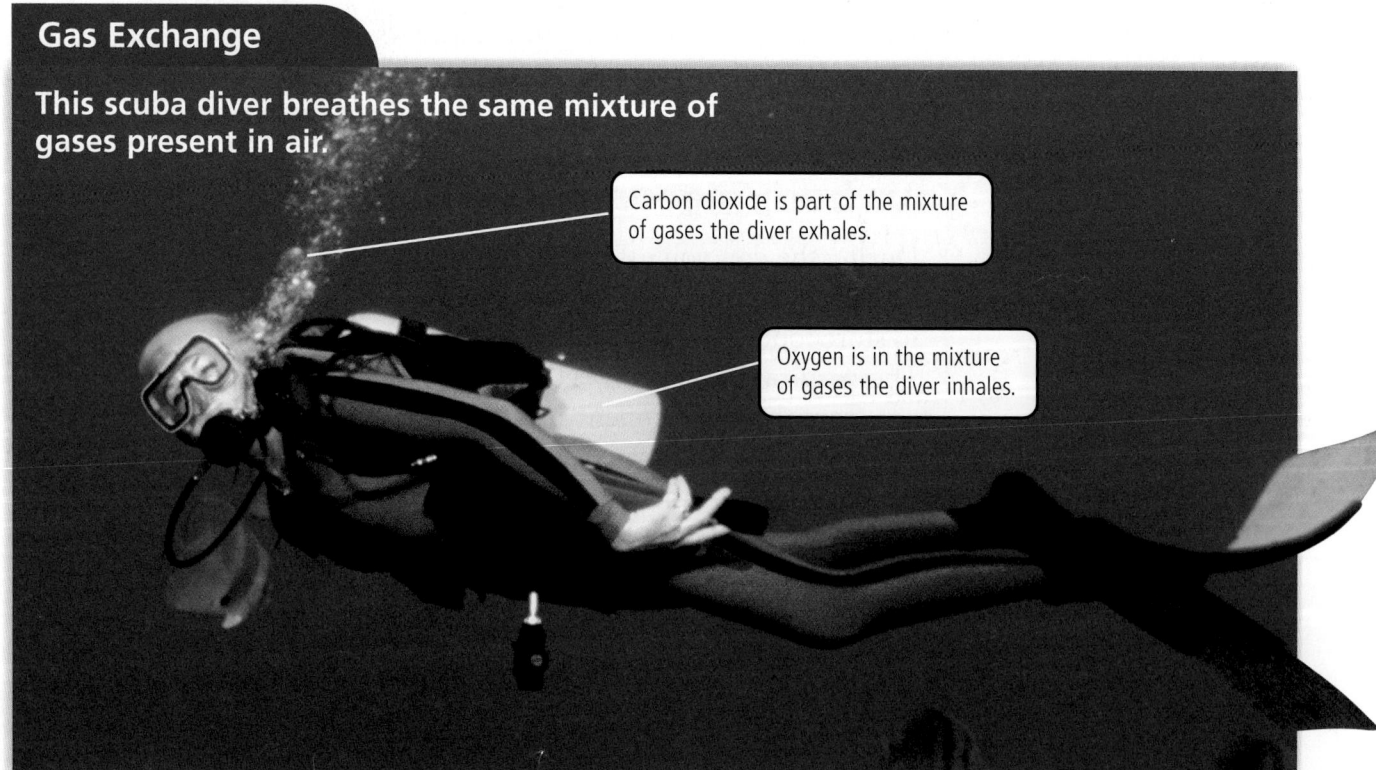

Carbon dioxide is part of the mixture of gases the diver exhales.

Oxygen is in the mixture of gases the diver inhales.

INVESTIGATE Lungs

How does air move in and out of lungs?

PROCEDURE

① Create a model of your lungs as shown. Insert an uninflated balloon into the top of the plastic bottle. While squeezing the bottle to force out some air, stretch the end of the balloon over the lip of the bottle. The balloon should still be open to the outside air. Tape the balloon in place with duct tape to make a tight seal

② Release the bottle so that it expands back to its normal shape. Observe what happens to the balloon. Squeeze and release the bottle several times while observing the balloon. Record your observations.

WHAT DO YOU THINK?

• Describe, in words, what happens when you squeeze and release the bottle.

• How do you think your lungs move when you inhale? when you exhale?

CHALLENGE Design an addition to your model that could represent a muscle called the diaphragm. What materials do you need? How would this work? Your teacher may be able to provide additional materials so you can test your model. Be sure to come up with a comprehensive list of materials as well as a specific diagram.

SKILL FOCUS
Making Models

MATERIALS
• one medium balloon
• 1-L clear plastic bottle with labels removed
• duct tape

TIME

15 minutes

Cellular Respiration

Inside your cells, a process called **cellular respiration** uses oxygen in chemical reactions that release energy. The respiratory system works with the digestive and circulatory systems to make cellular respiration possible. Cellular respiration requires glucose, or sugars, which you get from food, in addition to oxygen, which you get from breathing. These materials are transported to every cell in your body through blood vessels. You will learn more about the digestive and circulatory systems later in this unit.

During cellular respiration, your cells use oxygen and glucose to release energy. Carbon dioxide is a waste product of the process. Carbon dioxide must be removed from cells.

 What three body systems are involved in cellular respiration?

VOCABULARY
Add a magnet diagram for *cellular respiration* to your notebook.

FLORIDA
Content Review

Cellular respiration takes place in all cells—not just human cells—as you learned in grade 6.

Structures in the respiratory system function together.

OUTLINE

Add *Structures in the respiratory system function together* to your outline. Be sure to include the six respiratory structures in your outline.

I. Main idea
  A. Supporting idea
    1. Detail
    2. Detail
  B. Supporting idea

The respiratory system is made up of many structures that allow you to move air in and out of your body, communicate, and keep out harmful materials.

Nose, Throat, and Trachea When you inhale, air enters your body through your nose or mouth. Inside your nose, tiny hairs called cilia filter dirt and other particles out of the air. Mucus, a sticky liquid in your nasal cavity, also helps filter air by trapping particles such as dirt and pollen as air passes by. The nasal cavity warms the air slightly before it moves down your throat toward a tubelike structure called the windpipe, or trachea (TRAY-kee-uh). A structure called the epiglottis (EHP-ih-GLAHT-ihs) keeps air from entering your stomach.

Lungs The lungs are two large organs located on either side of your heart. When you inhale, air enters the throat, passes through the trachea, and moves into the lungs through structures called bronchial tubes. Bronchial tubes branch throughout the lungs into smaller and smaller tubes. At the ends of the smallest tubes, air enters tiny air sacs called alveoli. The walls of the alveoli are only one cell thick. In fact, one page in this book is much thicker than the walls of the alveoli. Oxygen passes from inside the alveoli through the thin walls and diffuses into the blood. At the same time, carbon dioxide waste passes from the blood into the alveoli.

 Through which structures does oxygen move into the lungs?

Ribs and Diaphragm If you put your hands on your ribs and take a deep breath, you can feel your ribs expand. The rib cage encloses a space inside your body called the thoracic (thuh-RAS-ihk) cavity. Some ribs are connected by cartilage to the breastbone or to each other, which makes the rib cage flexible. This flexibility allows the rib cage to expand when you breathe and make room for the lungs to expand and fill with air.

A large muscle called the diaphragm (DY-uh-FRAM) stretches across the floor of the thoracic cavity. When you inhale, your diaphragm contracts and pulls downward, which makes the thoracic cavity expand. This movement causes the lungs to push downward, filling the extra space. At the same time, other muscles draw the ribs outward and expand the lungs. Air rushes into the lungs, and inhalation is complete. When the diaphragm and other muscles relax, the process reverses and you exhale.

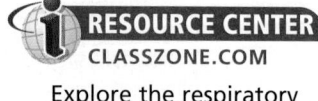
RESOURCE CENTER
CLASSZONE.COM

Explore the respiratory system.

 Describe how the diaphragm and the rib cage move.

Respiratory System

The structures in the respiratory system allow this flutist to play music.

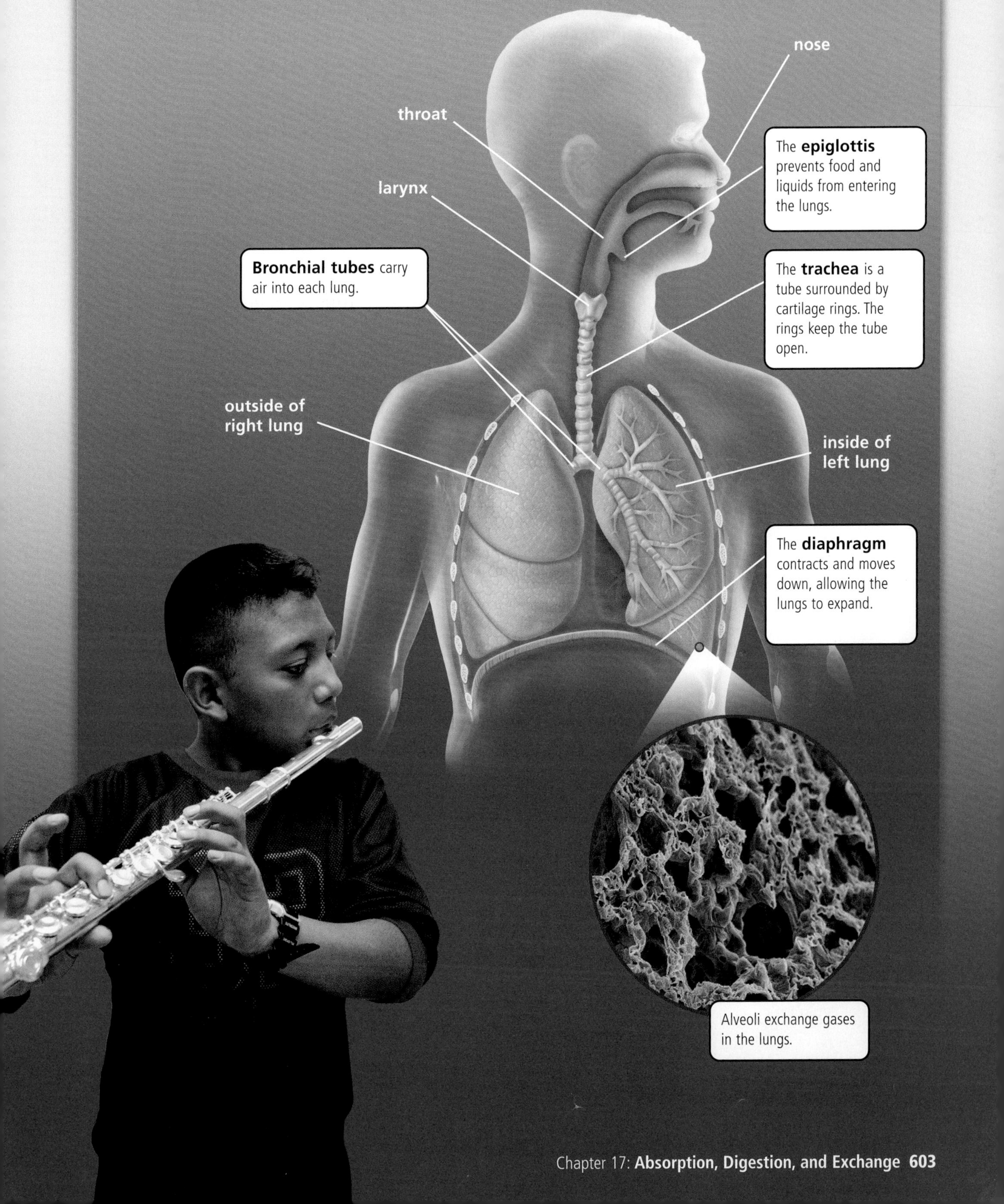

nose

throat

larynx

The **epiglottis** prevents food and liquids from entering the lungs.

Bronchial tubes carry air into each lung.

The **trachea** is a tube surrounded by cartilage rings. The rings keep the tube open.

outside of right lung

inside of left lung

The **diaphragm** contracts and moves down, allowing the lungs to expand.

Alveoli exchange gases in the lungs.

The respiratory system is also involved in other activities.

In addition to providing oxygen and removing carbon dioxide, the respiratory system is involved in other activities of the body. Speaking and singing, along with actions such as sneezing, can be explained in terms of how the parts of the respiratory system work together.

Speech and Other Respiratory Movements

If you place your hand on your throat and hum softly, you can feel your vocal cords vibrating. Air moving over your vocal cords allows you to produce sound, and the muscles in your throat, mouth, cheeks, and lips allow you to form sound into words. The vocal cords are folds of tissue in the larynx. The larynx, sometimes called the voice box, is a two-inch, tube-shaped organ about the length of your thumb, located in the neck, at the top of the trachea. When you speak, the vocal cords become tight, squeeze together, and force air from the lungs to move between them. The air causes the vocal cords to vibrate and produce sound.

How Speech Works

Sound is formed by structures in the respiratory system.

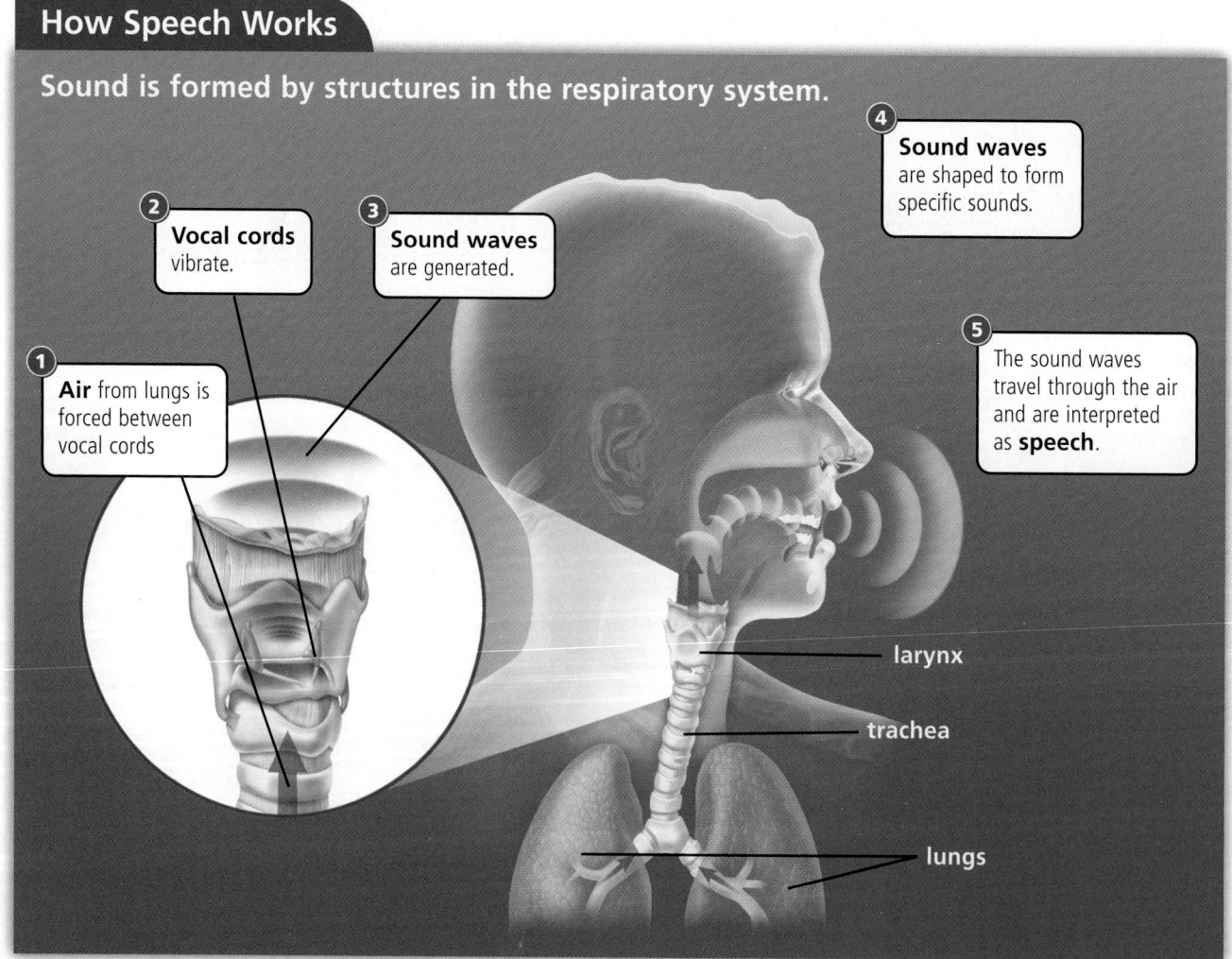

4. **Sound waves** are shaped to form specific sounds.

2. **Vocal cords** vibrate.

3. **Sound waves** are generated.

5. The sound waves travel through the air and are interpreted as **speech**.

1. **Air** from lungs is forced between vocal cords

larynx

trachea

lungs

Some movements of the respiratory system allow you to clear particles out of your nose and throat or to express emotion. The respiratory system is involved when you cough or sneeze. Sighing, yawning, laughing, and crying also involve the respiratory system.

Sighing and yawning both involve taking deep breaths. A sigh is a long breath followed by a shorter exhalation. A yawn is a long breath taken through a wide-open mouth. Laughing and crying are movements that are very similar to each other. In fact, sometimes it's difficult to see the difference between laughing and crying.

The respiratory system also allows you to hiccup. A hiccup is a sudden inhalation that makes the diaphragm contract. Several systems are involved when you hiccup. Air rushes into the throat, causing the diaphragm to contract. When the diaphragm contracts, the air passageway between the vocal cords closes. The closing of this passageway produces the sound of the hiccup. Hiccups can be caused by eating too fast, sudden temperature changes, and stress.

Water Removal

Hiccups, coughs, yawns, and all other respiratory movements, including speaking and breathing, release water from your body into the environment. Water is lost through sweat, urine, and exhalations of air. When it is cold enough outside, you can see your breath in the air. That is because the water vapor you exhale condenses into larger droplets when it moves from your warm body to the cold air.

Water leaves your body through your breath every time you exhale.

17.1 Review

KEY CONCEPTS

1. How is oxygen used by your body's cells?

2. What are the structures in the respiratory system and what do they do?

3. In addition to breathing, what functions does the respiratory system perform?

CRITICAL THINKING

4. **Sequence** List in order the steps that occur when you exhale.

5. **Compare and Contrast** How is the air you inhale different from the air you exhale?

⚠ CHALLENGE

6. **Hypothesize** Why do you think a person breathes more quickly when exercising?

Breathing and Yoga

If you're reading this, you must be breathing. Are you thinking about how you are breathing? Yoga instructors help their students learn deep, slow breathing. The practice of yoga uses an understanding of the respiratory system as a tool for healthy exercise.

nostrils

Nostril Breathing

An important aspect of breathing is removing wastes from the body:

• Yoga instructors teach students to inhale through the nostrils and exhale through the mouth.
• The nostrils filter dust and other particles, keeping dirt out of the lungs.
• The nostrils also warm the air as it enters the body.

Abdominal Breathing

Yoga instructors tell students to slowly expand and release the diaphragm:

• The diaphragm is a muscle below the lungs.
• When the muscle contracts, air enters into the lungs.
• When it relaxes, air is pushed out of the lungs.

lungs

diaphragm muscle

Full Lung Breathing

Yoga instructors help students breathe in slowly so that first the abdomen expands, then the rib cage area, and finally the upper chest by the shoulders. When students exhale, they collapse the diaphragm, then release the chest, and lastly relax the shoulders.

EXPLORE

1. **APPLY** Try one of the three breathing methods described. Start by taking a few slow deep breaths; then try the yoga breathing. Count to 4 as you inhale, and to 4 again breathing out. How do you feel after each breath?

2. **CHALLENGE** Choose one of the breathing methods above. Describe what happens to air each time you inhale and exhale. Draw or write your answer.

17.2 The digestive system breaks down food.

Sunshine State STANDARDS

SC.F.1.3.1: The student understands that living things are composed of major systems that function in reproduction, growth, maintenance, and regulation.

BEFORE, you learned

- The respiratory system takes in oxygen and expels waste
- Oxygen is necessary for cellular respiration
- The respiratory system is involved in speech and water removal

NOW, you will learn

- About the role of digestion in providing energy and materials
- About the chemical and mechanical process of digestion
- How materials change as they move through the digestive system

VOCABULARY

nutrient p. 607
digestion p. 608
digestive system p. 608
peristalsis p. 608

EXPLORE Digestion

How does the digestive system break down fat?

PROCEDURE

① Using a dropper, place 5 mL of water into a test tube. Add 5 mL of vegetable oil. Seal the test tube with a screw-on top. Shake the test tube for 10 seconds, then place it in a test tube stand. Record your observations.

② Drop 5 mL of dish detergent into the test tube. Seal the tube. Shake the test tube for 10 seconds, then place in the stand. Observe the mixture for 2 minutes. Record your observations.

MATERIALS

- water
- graduated cylinders
- test tube with cap
- vegetable oil
- test tube stand
- liquid dish detergent

WHAT DO YOU THINK?

- What effect does detergent have on the mixture of oil and water?
- How do you think your digestive system might break down fat?

The body needs energy and materials.

OUTLINE

Remember to add *The body needs energy and materials* to your outline.

I. Main idea
  A. Supporting idea
    1. Detail
    2. Detail
  B. Supporting idea

After not eating for a while, have you ever noticed how little energy you have to do the simplest things? You need food to provide energy for your body. You also need materials from food. Most of what you need comes from nutrients within food. **Nutrients** are important substances that enable the body to move, grow, and maintain homeostasis. Proteins, carbohydrates, fats, and water are some of the nutrients your body needs.

You might not think of water as a nutrient, but it is necessary for all living things. More than half of your body is made up of water.

Protein is another essential nutrient; it is the material that the body uses for growth and repair. Cells in your body—such as those composing muscles, bones, and skin—are built of proteins. Carbohydrates are nutrients that provide cells with energy. Carbohydrates make up cellulose, which helps move materials through the digestive system. Another nutrient, fat, stores energy.

Before your body can use these nutrients, they must be broken into smaller substances. **Digestion** is the process of breaking down food into usable materials. Your digestive system transforms the energy and materials in food into forms your body can use.

The digestive system moves and breaks down food.

VISUALIZATION
CLASSZONE.COM

Observe the process of peristalsis.

Your **digestive system** performs the complex jobs of moving and breaking down food. Material is moved through the digestive system by wavelike contractions of smooth muscles. This muscular action is called **peristalsis** (PEHR-ih-STAWL-sihs). Mucous glands throughout the system keep the material moist so it can be moved easily, and the muscles contract to push the material along. The muscles move food along in much the same way as you move toothpaste from the bottom of the tube with your thumbs. The body has complicated ways of moving food, and it also has complicated ways of breaking down food. The digestive system processes food in two ways: physically and chemically.

Peristalsis

The process of peristalsis moves food from the esophagus and into the stomach.

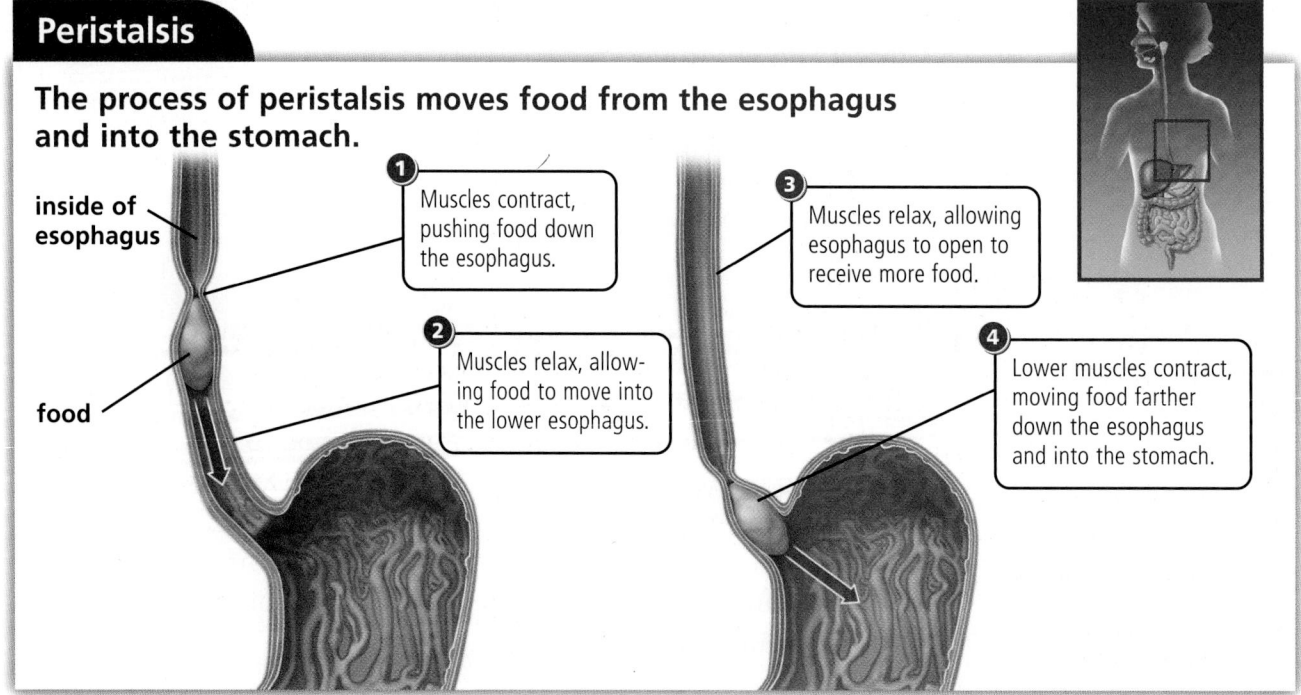

inside of esophagus

food

1 Muscles contract, pushing food down the esophagus.

2 Muscles relax, allowing food to move into the lower esophagus.

3 Muscles relax, allowing esophagus to open to receive more food.

4 Lower muscles contract, moving food farther down the esophagus and into the stomach.

INVESTIGATE Chemical Digestion

How does saliva affect starch?

PROCEDURE

1. Cut two slices of the same thickness from the center of a potato. Lay the slices on a plate or tray.

2. Using a dropper, add 15 drops of solution A to one potato slice. Add 15 drops of water to the other potato slice. Observe both potato slices for several minutes. Record your observations.

WHAT DO YOU THINK?

- What evidence did you see that starch is being broken down?
- How would you identify the substance left by the breakdown of starch?
- What is the purpose of the water in this activity?

CHALLENGE How could you change your experiment to model mechanical digestion? What structures in your mouth mechanically break down food?

SKILL FOCUS
Making Models

MATERIALS
- cooked potato slices
- droppers
- solution A
- water

TIME
25 minutes

Mechanical Digestion

Physical changes, which are sometimes called mechanical changes, break food into smaller pieces. You chew your food with your teeth so you are able to swallow it. Infants without teeth need an adult to cut up or mash food for them. They need soft food that they can swallow without chewing. Your stomach also breaks down food mechanically by mashing and pounding it during peristalsis.

Chemical Digestion

Chemical changes actually change food into different substances. For example, chewing a cracker produces a physical change—the cracker is broken into small pieces. At the same time, liquid in the mouth called saliva produces a chemical change—starches in the cracker are changed to sugars. If you chew a cracker, you may notice that after you have chewed it for a few seconds, it begins to taste sweet. The change in taste is a sign of a chemical reaction.

VOCABULARY
Don't forget to add magnet word diagrams for *digestion, digestive system,* and *peristalsis* to your notebook.

 What are the two types of changes that take place during digestion?

Materials are broken down as they move through the digestive tract.

The digestive system contains several organs. Food travels through organs in the digestive tract: the mouth, esophagus, stomach, small intestine, and large intestine. Other organs, such as the pancreas, liver, and gall bladder, release chemicals that are necessary for chemical digestion. The diagram on page 611 shows the major parts of the entire digestive system.

READING TiP

As you read about the digestive tract, look at the structures on page 611.

Mouth and Esophagus Both mechanical and chemical digestion begin in the mouth. The teeth break food into small pieces. The lips and tongue position food so that you can chew. When food is in your mouth, salivary glands in your mouth release saliva, which softens the food and begins chemical digestion. The tongue pushes the food to the back of the mouth and down the throat while swallowing.

 What part does the mouth play in digestion?

When you swallow, your tongue pushes food down into your throat. Food then travels down the esophagus to the stomach. The muscle contractions of peristalsis move solid food from the throat to the stomach in about eight seconds. Liquid foods take about two seconds.

Stomach Strong muscles in the stomach further mix and mash food particles. The stomach also uses chemicals to break down food. Some of the chemicals made by the stomach are acids. These acids are so strong that they could eat through the stomach itself. To prevent this, the cells of the stomach's lining are replaced about every three days, and the stomach lining is coated with mucus.

Villi allow broken-down nutrients to be absorbed into your bloodstream.

Small Intestine Partially digested food moves from the stomach to the small intestine. There, chemicals released by the pancreas, liver, and gallbladder break down nutrients. Most of the nutrients broken down in digestion are absorbed in the small intestine. Structures called villi are found throughout the small intestine. These structures contain folds that absorb nutrients from proteins, carbohydrates, and fats. Once absorbed by the villi, nutrients are transported by the circulatory system around the body. You will read more about the circulatory system in Chapter 18.

Large Intestine In the large intestine, water and some other nutrients are absorbed from the digested material. Most of the solid material then remaining is waste material, which is compacted and stored. Eventually it is eliminated through the rectum.

 Where in your digestive system does mechanical digestion occur?

Digestive System

As food moves through the digestive tract, structures of the digestive system break it down and absorb necessary materials.

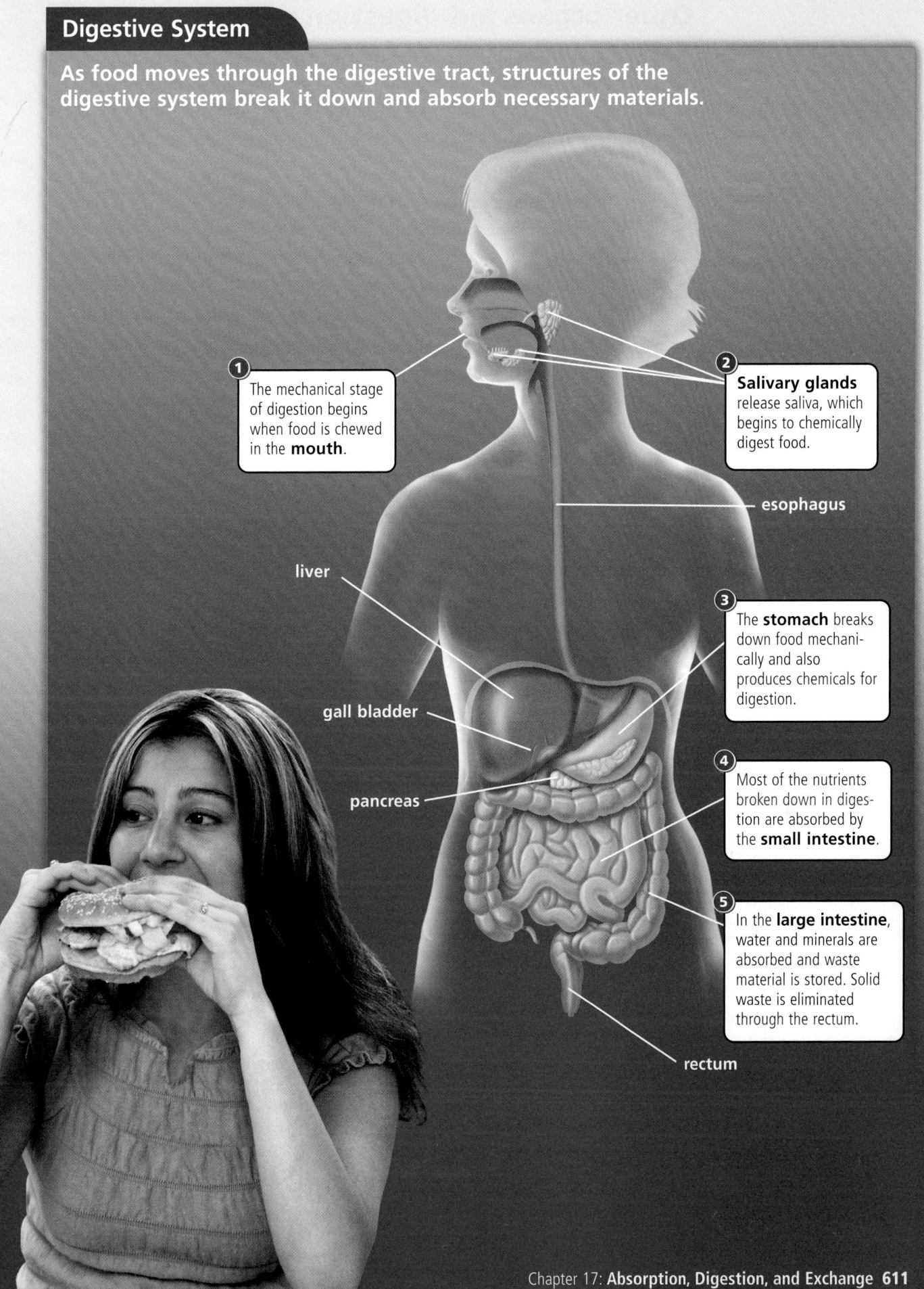

1 The mechanical stage of digestion begins when food is chewed in the **mouth**.

2 **Salivary glands** release saliva, which begins to chemically digest food.

esophagus

liver

gall bladder

pancreas

3 The **stomach** breaks down food mechanically and also produces chemicals for digestion.

4 Most of the nutrients broken down in digestion are absorbed by the **small intestine**.

5 In the **large intestine**, water and minerals are absorbed and waste material is stored. Solid waste is eliminated through the rectum.

rectum

Other organs aid digestion and absorption.

The digestive organs not in the digestive tract—the liver, gallbladder, and pancreas—also play crucial roles in your body. Although food does not move through them, all three of these organs aid in chemical digestion by producing or concentrating important chemicals.

Liver The liver—the largest internal organ of the body—is located in your abdomen, just above your stomach. Although you can survive losing a portion of your liver, it is an important organ. The liver filters blood, cleansing it of harmful substances, and stores unneeded nutrients for later use in the body. It produces a golden yellow substance called bile, which is able to break down fats, much like the way soap breaks down oils. The liver also breaks down medicines and produces important proteins, such as those that help clot blood if you get a cut.

Gallbladder The gallbladder is a tiny pear-shaped sac connected to the liver. Bile produced in the liver is stored and concentrated in the gallbladder. The bile is then secreted into the small intestine.

Pancreas Located between the stomach and the small intestine, the pancreas produces chemicals that are needed as materials move between the two. The pancreas quickly lowers the acidity in the small intestine and breaks down proteins, fats, and starch. The chemicals produced by the pancreas are extremely important for digesting and absorbing food substances. Without these chemicals, you could die of starvation, even with plenty of food in your system. Your body would not be able to process and use the food for energy without the pancreas.

 How does the pancreas aid in digestion?

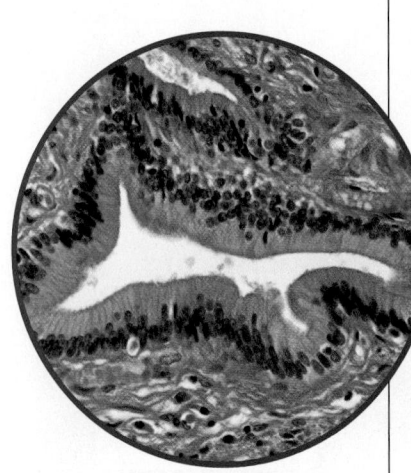

Bile is transferred from the liver to the gallbladder and small intestines through the bile duct.

17.2 Review

KEY CONCEPTS

1. List three of the functions of the digestive system.

2. Give one example each of mechanical digestion and chemical digestion.

3. How does your stomach process food?

CRITICAL THINKING

4. **Apply** Does an antacid deal with mechanical or chemical digestion?

5. **Apply** You have just swallowed a bite of apple. Describe what happens as the apple moves through your digestive system. Include information about what happens to the material in the apple.

CHALLENGE

6. **Compare and Contrast** Describe the roles of the large and the small intestines. How are they similar? How are they different?

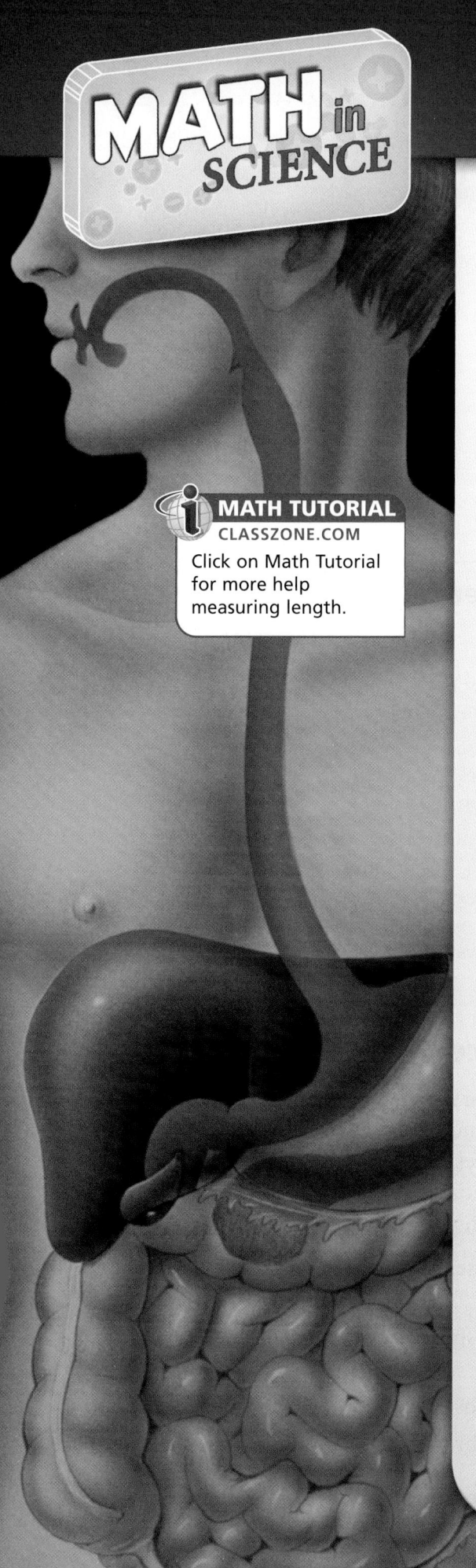

SKILL: CHOOSING UNITS OF LENGTH

Internal Measurement

It wouldn't be useful if someone told you the length of your tongue in meters, or the length of a tooth in centimeters. To be meaningful, these measurements must be given in appropriate units.

MATH TUTORIAL
CLASSZONE.COM
Click on Math Tutorial for more help measuring length.

Example

Your esophagus is about the length of your forearm. Choose the appropriate units to measure its length. Would meters, centimeters, or millimeters be most appropriate?

(1) Look at your arm from your wrist to your elbow. It is about the same as a rolling pin. You don't need to measure your forearm to see that a meter would be too large a unit. One meter is about the height of a lab table.

(2) Look at the ruler in the picture. Compare your arm to the centimeters shown and the millimeters.

(3) You can measure your arm with either unit, but if you wiggle a bit, the count of millimeters is thrown off.

ANSWER Centimeters are the most appropriate units.

Answer the following questions.

1. If you uncoiled a human intestine, its length would be about equal to that of 2 cars parked end to end. What would be appropriate units to use to measure that?

2. What units would you use to measure the length of your tongue? The length of a tooth?

3. The large intestine is actually shorter than the small intestine. The small intestine is about the length of a small bus, and the large is about as long as a car's back seat. Tell the units you would choose for each. Explain why.

CHALLENGE Your stomach when empty is about the size of your clenched fist. To measure its volume (the space it takes up), what units would you use?

The ruler shows 20 centimeters (cm). There are 10 millimeters (mm) in each centimeter.

1 cm

17.3

The urinary system removes waste materials.

Sunshine State STANDARDS

SC.F.1.3.1: The student understands that living things are composed of major systems that function in reproduction, growth, maintenance, and regulation.

SC.H.1.3.2: The student knows that the study of the events that led scientists to discoveries can provide information about the inquiry process and its effects.

◀ BEFORE, you learned

- The digestive system breaks down food
- Organs in the digestive system have different roles

▶ NOW, you will learn

- How different body systems remove different types of waste
- Why the kidneys are important organs
- About the role of the kidneys in homeostasis

VOCABULARY

urinary system p. 615
urine p. 615

EXPLORE Waste Removal

How does the skin get rid of body waste?

PROCEDURE

① Place a plastic bag over the hand you do not use for writing and tape it loosely around your wrist.

② Leave the bag on for five minutes. Write down the changes you see in conditions within the bag.

WHAT DO YOU THINK?

- What do you see happen to the bag?
- How does what you observe help explain the body's method of waste removal?

MATERIALS

- plastic bag
- tape
- stopwatch

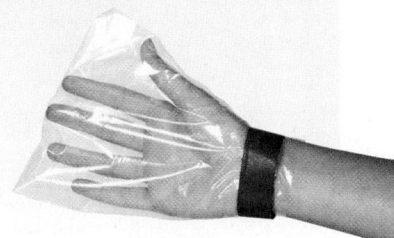

Life processes produce wastes.

OUTLINE

Add *Life processes produce wastes* to your outline. Include four ways the body disposes of waste products.

I. Main idea
   A. Supporting idea
     1. Detail
     2. Detail
   B. Supporting idea

You have read that the respiratory system and the digestive system provide the body with energy and materials necessary for important processes. During these processes, waste materials are produced. The removal of these wastes is essential for the continuing function of body systems. Several systems in your body remove wastes.

- The urinary system disposes of liquid waste products removed from the blood.
- The respiratory system disposes of water vapor and waste gases from the blood.
- The digestive system disposes of solid waste products from food.
- The skin releases wastes through sweat glands.

 **CHECK YOUR READING** What are four ways the body disposes of waste products?

The urinary system removes waste from the blood.

If you have observed an aquarium, you have seen a filter at work. Water moves through the filter, which removes waste materials from the water. Just as the filter in a fish tank removes wastes from the water, structures in your urinary system filter wastes from your blood.

As shown in the diagram, the **urinary system** contains several structures. The kidneys are two organs located high up and toward the rear of the abdomen, one on each side of the spine. Kidneys function much as the filter in the fish tank does. In fact, the kidneys are often called the body's filters. Materials travel in your blood to the kidneys. There, some substances are removed, and others are returned to the blood.

After the kidneys filter chemical waste from the blood, the liquid travels down two tubes called ureters (yu-REE-tuhrz). The ureters bring the waste to the bladder, a storage sac with a wall of smooth muscle. The lower neck of the bladder leads into the urethra, a tube that carries the liquid waste outside the body. Voluntary muscles at one end of the bladder allow a person to hold the urethra closed until he or she is ready to release the muscles. At that time, the bladder contracts and sends the liquid waste, or **urine,** out of the body.

> **VOCABULARY**
> Add a magnet diagram for *urinary system* to your notebook. Include in your diagram information about how kidneys function.

Urinary System

The urinary system transports wastes out of the body.

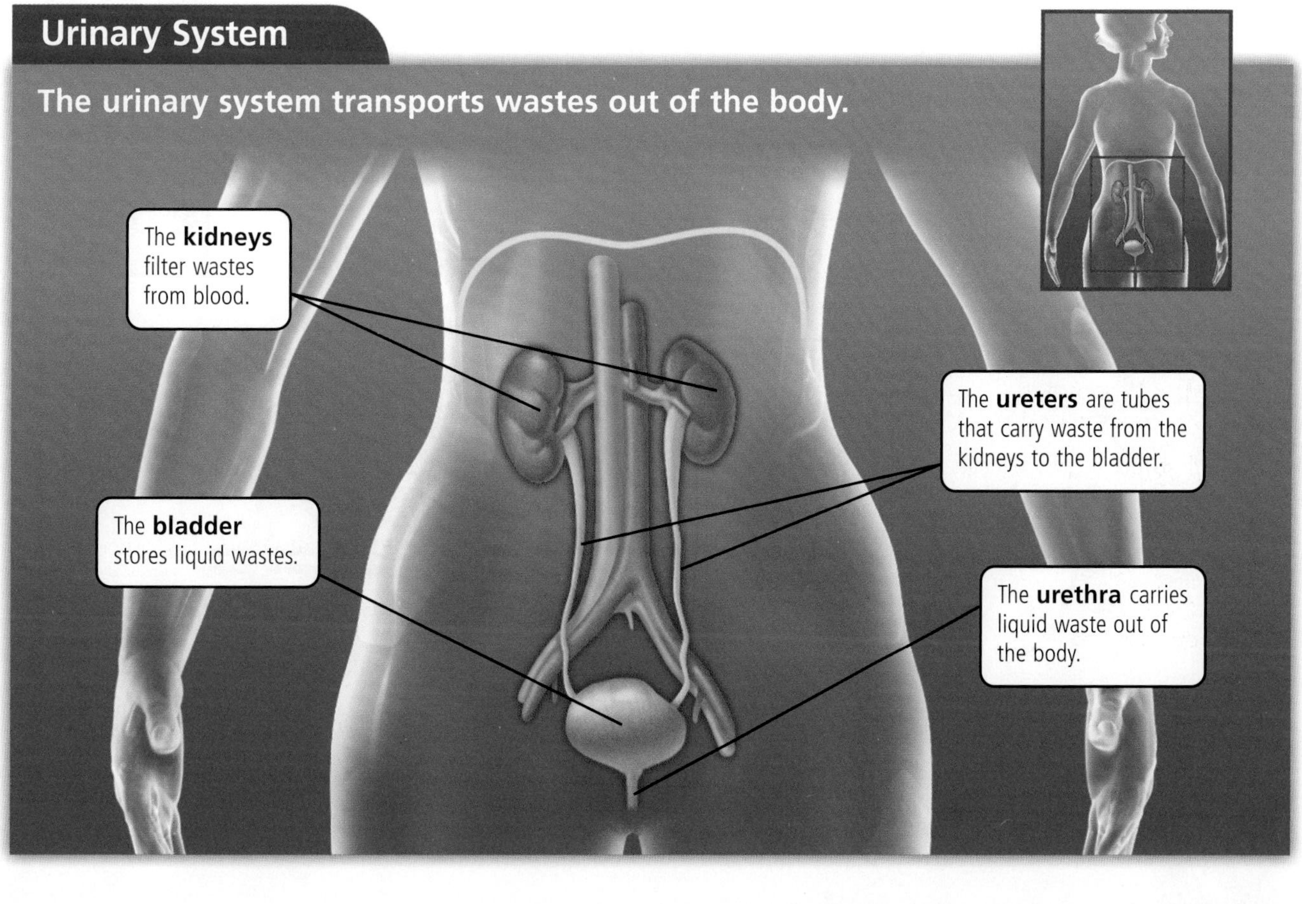

The **kidneys** filter wastes from blood.

The **ureters** are tubes that carry waste from the kidneys to the bladder.

The **bladder** stores liquid wastes.

The **urethra** carries liquid waste out of the body.

The kidneys act as filters.

RESOURCE CENTER
CLASSZONE.COM

Find out more about the urinary system.

At any moment, about one quarter of the blood leaving your heart is headed toward your kidneys to be filtered. The kidneys, which are about as long as your index finger—only 10 centimeters (3.9 in.) long—filter all the blood in your body many times a day.

The Nephron

Inside each kidney are approximately one million looping tubes called nephrons. The nephron regulates the makeup of the blood.

1 Fluid is filtered from the blood into the nephron through a structure called the glomerulus (gloh-MEHR-yuh-luhs). Filtered blood leaves the glomerulus and circulates around the tubes that make up the nephron.

2 As the filtered fluid passes through the nephron, some nutrients are absorbed back into the blood surrounding the tubes. Some water is also filtered out in the glomerulus, but most water is returned to the blood.

3 Waste products travel to the end of the nephron into the collecting duct. The remaining liquid, now called urine, passes out of the kidney and into the ureters.

Kidney Function

Kidneys filter waste materials out of the blood.

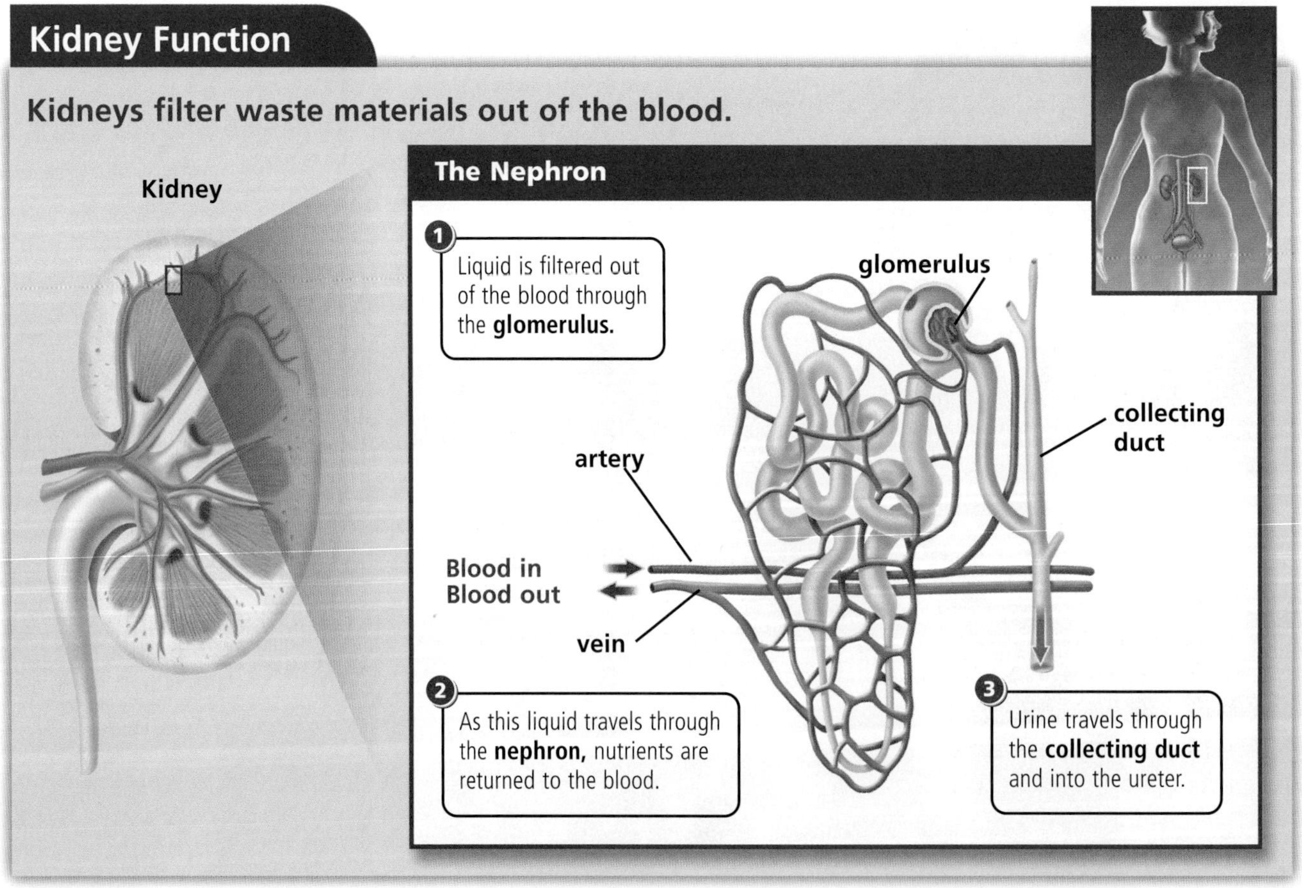

Kidney

The Nephron

1 Liquid is filtered out of the blood through the **glomerulus**.

glomerulus

collecting duct

artery

Blood in
Blood out

vein

2 As this liquid travels through the **nephron**, nutrients are returned to the blood.

3 Urine travels through the **collecting duct** and into the ureter.

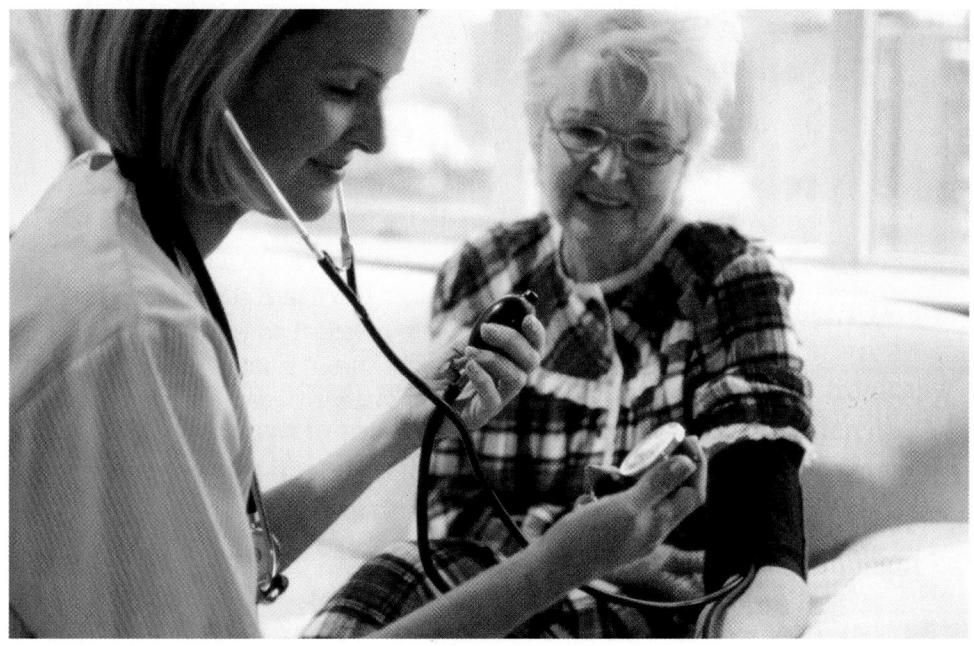

The amount of water in your body affects your blood pressure. Excess water increases blood pressure.

Water Balance

The kidneys not only remove wastes from blood, they also regulate the amount of water in the body. You read in Chapter 16 about the importance of homeostasis—a stable environment within your body. The amount of water in your cells affects homeostasis. If your body contains too much water, parts of your body may swell. Having too little water interferes with cell processes.

About one liter of water leaves the body every day. The kidneys control the amount of water that leaves the body in urine. Depending on how much water your body uses, the kidneys produce urine with more or less water.

 CHECK YOUR READING How do your kidneys regulate the amount of water in your body?

17.3 Review

KEY CONCEPTS

1. Describe the four organ systems that remove waste and explain how each removes waste.

2. Describe the function of four organs in the urinary system.

3. Describe homeostasis and explain why the kidneys are important to homeostasis.

CRITICAL THINKING

4. **Connect** Make a word web with the term *kidney* in the center. Add details about kidney function to the web.

◔ CHALLENGE

5. **Synthesize** Explain why you may become thirsty on a hot day. Include the term *homeostasis* in your explanation.

CHAPTER INVESTIGATION

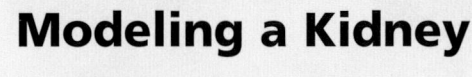

Modeling a Kidney

OVERVIEW AND PURPOSE Your kidneys are your body's filters. Every 20 to 30 minutes, every drop of your blood passes through the kidneys and is filtered. What types of materials are filtered by the kidneys? In this investigation you will
- model the filtering process of the kidneys
- determine what types of materials are filtered by your kidneys

▶ Problem

What types of materials can be removed from the blood by the kidneys?

▶ Hypothesize

Write a hypothesis to explain how substances are filtered out of the blood by the kidneys. Your hypothesis should take the form of an "If . . . , then . . . , because . . ." statement.

▶ Procedure

MATERIALS
- fine filter paper
- small funnel
- graduated cylinder
- 100 mL beaker
- solution A
- solution B
- solution C
- salinity test strips
- glucose test strips
- protein test strips

1. Make a data table like the one shown on the sample notebook page. Fold the filter paper as shown. Place the filter paper in the funnel, and place the funnel in the graduated cylinder.

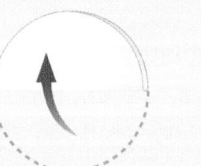

2. Pour 20 mL of solution A into a beaker. Test the solution for salt concentration using a test strip for salinity. Record the results in your notebook. Slowly pour the solution into the funnel. Wait for it all to drip through the filter paper.

step 2

3 Test the filtered liquid for salt concentration again. Record the results.

4 Repeat steps 1, 2, and 3 for solution B using glucose test strips. Record the results in your notebook.

5 Repeat steps 1, 2, and 3 for solution C using protein test strips. Record the results in your notebook.

step 5

Write It Up

▶ Observe and Analyze

Write It Up

1. **RECORD** Be sure your data table is complete.

2. **OBSERVE** What substances were present in solutions A, B, and C?

3. **IDENTIFY VARIABLES** Identify the variables and constants in the experiment. List them in your notebook.

▶ Conclude

Write It Up

1. **COMPARE AND CONTRAST** In what ways does your model function like a kidney? How is your model not like a kidney?

2. **INTERPRET** Which materials were able to pass through the filter and which could not?

3. **INFER** What materials end up in the urine? How might materials be filtered out of the blood but not appear in the urine?

4. **APPLY** How could a filtering device be useful in your body?

▶ INVESTIGATE Further

CHALLENGE Your blood contains many chemicals. Some of these chemicals are waste products, but some are in the blood to be transported to different parts of the body. What other substances are filtered out of the blood by the kidneys? Which of the filtered substances are normally present in the urine? Use a variety of reference materials to research the chemicals found in urine. Revise your experiment to test the ability of your model kidney to filter other substances.

Modeling a Kidney

Table 1. Test-strip results

	Before filtering	After filtering
Solution A		
Solution B		
Solution C		

the **BIG** idea

Systems in the body obtain and process materials and remove waste.

FLORIDA REVIEW
CLASSZONE.COM

Content Review and
FCAT Practice

◀ KEY CONCEPTS SUMMARY

1 The respiratory system gets oxygen and removes carbon dioxide.

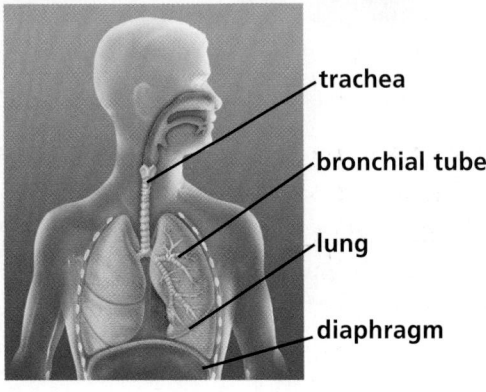

- trachea
- bronchial tube
- lung
- diaphragm

- Your body needs oxygen
- Structures in the respiratory system function together
- Your respiratory system is involved in other functions

VOCABULARY
respiratory system
p. 599
cellular respiration
p. 601

2 The digestive system breaks down food.

Structure	Function
Mouth	chemical and mechanical digestion
Esophagus	movement of food by peristalsis from mouth to stomach
Stomach	chemical and mechanical digestion; absorption of broken-down nutrients
Small intestine	chemical digestion; absorption of broken-down nutrients
Large intestine	absorption of water and broken-down nutrients, elimination of wastes

VOCABULARY
nutrient p. 607
digestion p. 608
digestive system
p. 608
peristalsis p. 608

3 The urinary system removes waste materials.

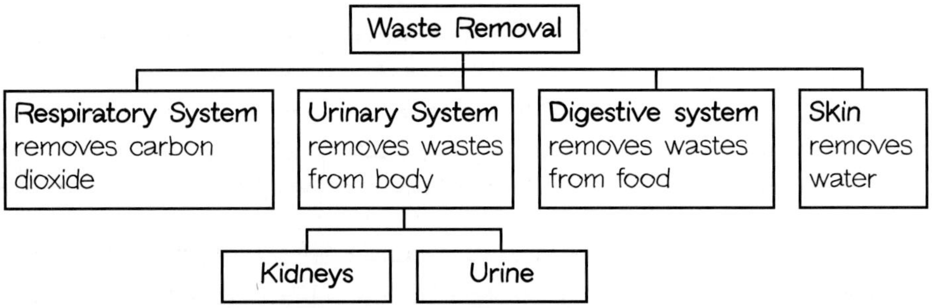

Waste Removal

| Respiratory System removes carbon dioxide | Urinary System removes wastes from body | Digestive system removes wastes from food | Skin removes water |

Kidneys — Urine

VOCABULARY
urinary system p. 615
urine p. 615

Reviewing Vocabulary

Copy the chart below and write the definition for each word. Use the meaning of the word's root to help you.

Word	Root Meaning	Definition
EXAMPLE: rib cage	to arch over	bones enclosing the internal organs of the body
1. respiration	to breathe	
2. nutrient	to nourish	
3. digestion	to separate	
4. peristalsis	to wrap around	

Reviewing Key Concepts

Multiple Choice *Choose the letter of the best answer.*

5. Which system brings oxygen into your body and removes carbon dioxide?
   a. digestive system
   b. urinary system
   c. respiratory system
   d. muscular system

6. Which body structure in the throat keeps air from entering the stomach?
   a. trachea
   b. epiglottis
   c. lungs
   d. alveoli

7. Oxygen and carbon dioxide are exchanged through structures in the lungs called
   a. bronchial tubes
   b. alveoli
   c. cartilage
   d. villi

8. Carbon dioxide is a waste product that is formed during which process?
   a. cellular respiration
   b. peristalsis
   c. urination
   d. circulation

9. Carbohydrates are nutrients that
   a. make up most of the human body
   b. make up cell membranes
   c. enable cells to grow and repair themselves
   d. are broken down for energy

10. Which is *not* a function of the digestive system?
   a. absorb water from food
   b. absorb nutrients from food
   c. filter wastes from blood
   d. break down food

11. Which is an example of a physical change?
   a. teeth grind cracker into smaller pieces
   b. liquids in mouth change starches to sugars
   c. bile breaks down fats
   d. stomach breaks down proteins

12. Where in the digestive system is most water absorbed?
   a. kidneys
   b. stomach
   c. large intestine
   d. esophagus

13. Chemical waste is filtered from the blood in which structure?
   a. alveoli
   b. kidney
   c. stomach
   d. villi

14. The kidneys control the amount of
   a. oxygen that enters the blood
   b. blood cells that leave the body
   c. urine that is absorbed by the body
   d. water that leaves the body

Short Response *Write a short response to each question.*

15. Draw a sketch that shows how the thoracic cavity changes as the diaphragm contracts and pulls downward.

16. What are two products that are released into the body as a result of cellular respiration?

17. Through which organs does food pass as it travels through the digestive system?

18. What is the function of the urinary system?

Thinking Critically

19. **SUMMARIZE** Describe how gas exchange takes place inside the lungs.

20. **SYNTHESIZE** Summarize what happens during cellular respiration. Explain how the digestive system and the respiratory system are involved.

21. **ANALYZE** When there is a lot of dust or pollen in the air, people may cough and sneeze. What function of the respiratory system is involved?

22. **INFER** When you exhale onto a glass surface, the surface becomes cloudy with a thin film of moisture. Explain why this happens.

23. **COMPARE AND CONTRAST** Where does mechanical digestion take place? How is it different from chemical digestion?

24. **PREDICT** People with stomach disease often have their entire stomachs removed and are able to live normally. Explain how this is possible. Would a person be able to live normally without the small intestine? Explain your answer.

25. **APPLY** An athlete drinks a liter of water before a basketball game and continues to drink water during the game. Describe how the athlete's body is able to maintain homeostasis during the course of the game.

26. **INTERPRET** Use the diagram of the nephron shown below to describe what happens to the blood as it travels through the vessels surrounding the nephron.

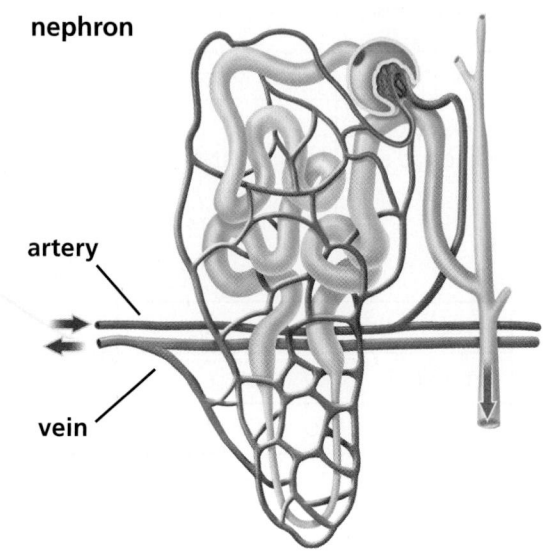

nephron

artery

vein

the BIG idea

27. **INFER** Look again at the picture on pages 596–597. Now that you have finished the chapter, how would you change or add details to your answer to the question on the photograph?

28. **SYNTHESIZE** Write a paragraph explaining how the respiratory system, the digestive system, and the urinary system work together with the circulatory system to eliminate waste materials from the body. Underline these terms in your paragraph.

UNIT PROJECTS

Check your schedule for your unit project. How are you doing? Be sure that you've placed data or notes from your research in your project folder.

FCAT Practice

Analyzing Data

The bar graph below shows respiration rates.

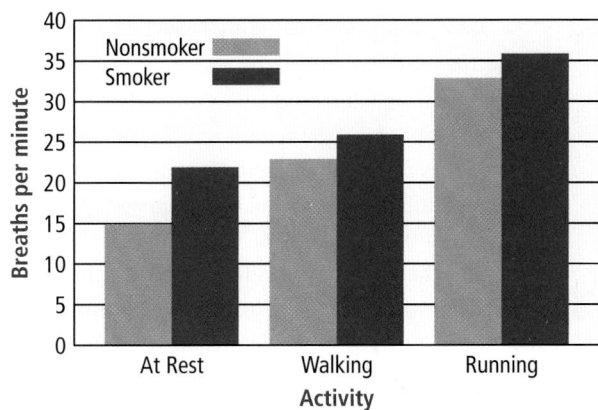

Use the graph to answer the questions below.

GRIDDED RESPONSE

1. How many breaths per minute did a smoker take while running?

2. How many more breaths per minute did a smoker take while running compared with a nonsmoker?

MULTIPLE CHOICE

3. What is the best title for this graph?
   - **A.** Respiration Rates of Smokers and Nonsmokers
   - **B.** Cigarettes Smoked During Exercise
   - **C.** Activities Performed by Smokers and Nonsmokers
   - **D.** Blood Pressure Levels of Smokers and Nonsmokers

4. How many breaths per minute were taken by a nonsmoker at rest?
   - **F.** 15 breaths per minute
   - **G.** 22 breaths per minute
   - **H.** 26 breaths per minute
   - **I.** 33 breaths per minute

5. For the nonsmokers, by how much did the respiration rate increase between resting and running?
   - **A.** 15 breaths per minute
   - **B.** 18 breaths per minute
   - **C.** 23 breaths per minute
   - **D.** 33 breaths per minute

FCAT TiP

When you use a bar graph to answer a gridded-response question that asks you to estimate a number, use the lines and numbers provided for you on the graph as a base from which to make your estimation.

6. Which statement is *not* true?
   - **F.** The nonsmoker at rest took more breaths per minute than the smoker at rest.
   - **G.** The nonsmoker took more breaths per minute while running rather than while walking.
   - **H.** The smoker took more breaths per minute than the nonsmoker while walking.
   - **I.** The nonsmoker took fewer breaths per minute than the smoker while running.

7. Which statement is the most logical conclusion to draw from the data in the chart?
   - **A.** Smoking has no effect on respiration rate.
   - **B.** Increased activity has no effect on respiration rate.
   - **C.** There is no difference in the respiration rates between the smoker and the nonsmoker.
   - **D.** Smoking and activity both cause an increase in respiration rate.

EXTENDED RESPONSE

8. Tar, which is a harmful substance found in tobacco smoke, coats the lining of the lungs over time. Based on the information in the graph and what you know about the respiratory system, write a paragraph describing how smoking cigarettes affects the functioning of the respiratory system.

9. Ads for cigarettes and other tobacco products have been banned from television. However, they still appear in newspapers and magazines. These ads make tobacco use look glamorous and exciting. Using your knowledge of the respiratory system, design an ad that discourages the use of tobacco products. Create a slogan that will help people remember how tobacco affects the health of the respiratory system.

TIMELINES in Science

SEEING INSIDE the Body

What began as a chance accident in a darkened room was only the beginning. Today, technology allows people to produce clear and complete pictures of the human body. From X-rays to ultrasound to the latest computerized scans, accidental discoveries have enabled us to study and diagnose the inner workings of the human body.

Being able to see inside the body without cutting it open would have seemed unthinkable in the early 1890s. But within a year of the discovery of the X-ray in 1895, doctors were using technology to see through flesh to bones. In the time since then, techniques for making images have advanced to allow doctors to see soft tissue, muscle, and even to see how body systems work in real time. Many modern imaging techniques employ X-ray technology, while others employ sound waves or magnetic fields.

1895

Accidental X-Ray Shows Bones

Working alone in a darkened lab to study electric currents passing through vacuum tubes, William Conrad Roentgen sees a mysterious light. He puts his hand between the tubes and a screen, and an image appears on the screen—a skeletal hand! He names his discovery the X-ray, since the images are produced by rays behaving like none known before them. Roentgen uses photographic paper to take the first X-ray picture, his wife's hand.

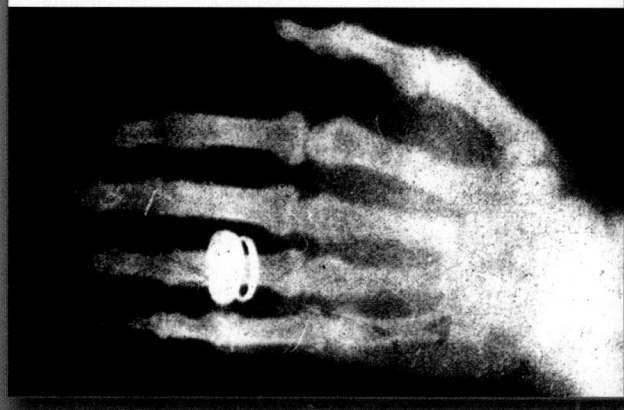

EVENTS

1880   1890

APPLICATIONS AND TECHNOLOGY

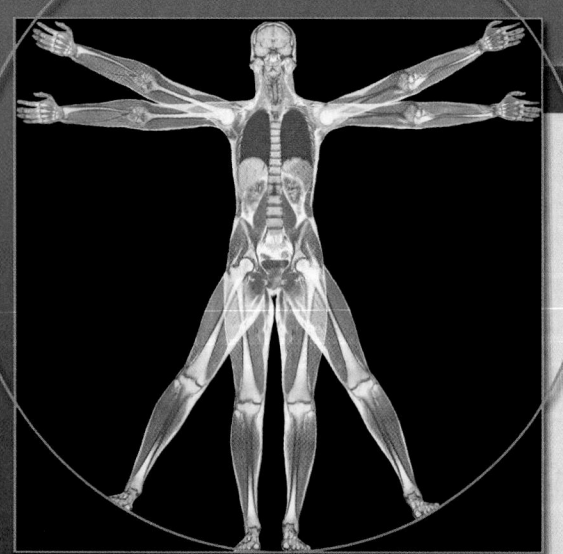

APPLICATION

Doctor Detectives

Within a year of Roentgen's discovery, X-rays were used in medicine for examining patients. By the 1920s, their use was wide-spread. Modern day X-ray tubes are based on the design of William Coolidge. Around 1913, Coolidge developed a new X-ray tube which, unlike the old gas tube, provides consistent exposure and quality. X-ray imaging changed the practice of medicine by allowing doctors to look inside the body without using surgery. Today, X-ray images, and other technologies, like the MRI used to produce the image at the left, show bones, organs, and tissues.

1914–1918
Radiologists in the Trenches
In World War I field hospitals, French physicians use X-ray technology to quickly diagnose war injuries. Marie Curie trains the majority of the female X-ray technicians. Following the war, doctors return to their practices with new expertise.

1898
Radioactivity
Building on the work of Henri Becquerel, who in 1897 discovers "rays" from uranium, physicist Marie Curie discovers radioactivity. She wins a Nobel Prize in Chemistry in 1911 for her work in radiology.

1955
See-Through Smile
X-ray images of the entire jaw and teeth allow dentist to check the roots of teeth and wisdom teeth growing below the gum line.

1900   **1910**   **1950**

APPLICATION
Better Dental Work
Throughout the 1940s and 1950s dentists began to use X-rays. Photographing teeth with an X-ray allows cavities or decay to show up as dark spots on a white tooth. Photographing below the gum line shows dentists the pattern of growth of new teeth. By 1955, dentists could take a panoramic X-ray, one which shows the entire jaw. In the early years of dental X-rays, little was known about the dangers of radiation. Today, dentists cover a patient with a lead apron to protect them from harmful rays.

1976

New Scans Show Blood Vessels

The first computerized tomography (CT) systems scan only the head, but whole-body scanners follow by 1976. With the CT scan, doctors see clear details of blood vessels, bones, and soft organs. Instead of sending out a single X-ray, a CT scan sends several beams from different angles. Then a computer joins the images, as shown in this image of a heart.

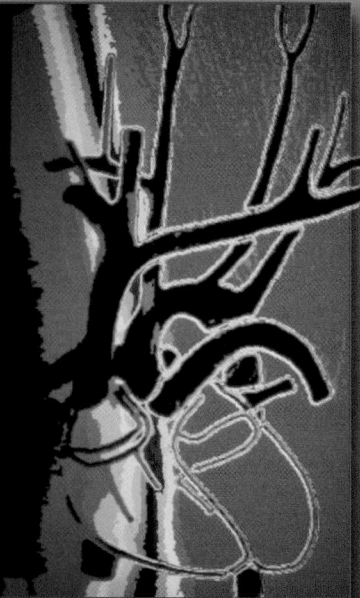

1977

Minus the X-ray

Doctors Raymond Damadian, Larry Minkoff, and Michael Goldsmith, develop the first magnetic resonance imaging (MRI). They nick-name the new machine "The Indomitable," as everyone told them it couldn't be done. MRI allows doctors to "see" soft tissue, like the knee below, in sharp detail without the use of X-rays.

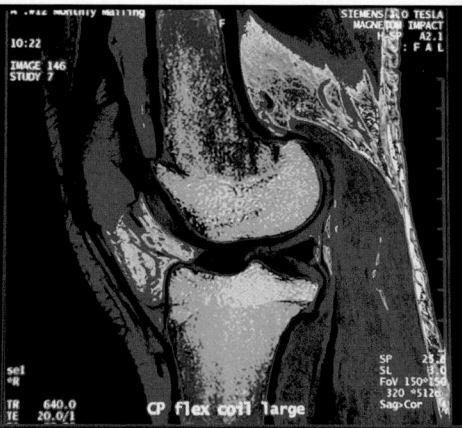

1973

PET Shows What's Working

The first positron emission tomography machine is called PET Scanner 1. It uses small doses of radioactive dye which travel through a patient's bloodstream. A PET scan then shows the distribution of the dye.

1960   1970   1980

TECHNOLOGY

Ultrasound: Moving Images in Real Time

Since the late 1950s, Ian Donald's team in Scotland had been viewing internal organs on a TV monitor using vibrations faster than sound. In 1961, while examining a female patient, Donald noticed a developing embryo. Following the discovery, ultrasound imaging became widely used to monitor the growth and health of fetuses. Ultrasound captures images in real-time, showing movement of internal tissues and organs. Ultrasound uses high frequency sound waves to create images of organs or structures inside the body. Sound waves are bounced back from organs, and a computer converts the sound waves into moving images on a television monitor.

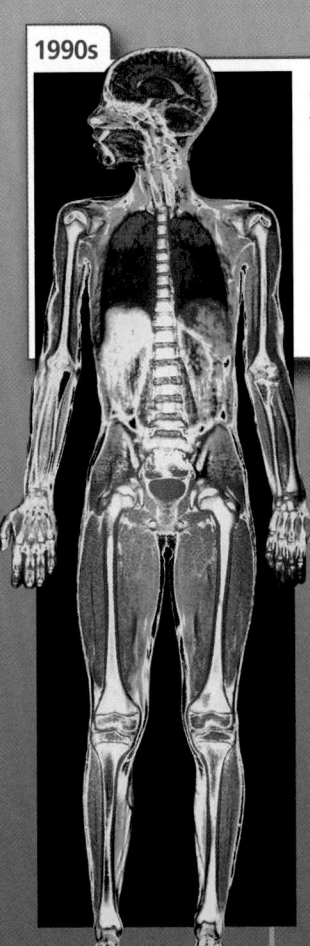

1990s

Filmless Images

With digital imaging, everything from X-rays to MRIs is now filmless. Data move directly into 3-D computer programs and shared databases.

2003

Multi-Slice CT

By 2003, 8- and 16-slice CT scanners offer detail and speed. A multi-slice scanner reduces exam time from 45 minutes to under 10 seconds.

RESOURCE CENTER
CLASSZONE.COM

Find more on advances in medical imaging.

1990   **2000**

INTO THE FUTURE

Although discovered over 100 years ago X-rays are certain to remain a key tool of health workers for many years. What will be different in the future? Dentists have begun the trend to stop using film images, and rely on digital X-rays instead. In the future, all scans may be viewed and stored on computers. Going digital allows doctors across the globe to share images quickly by email.

Magnetic resonance imaging has only been in widespread use for about 20 years. Look for increased brain mapping—ability to scan the brain during a certain task. The greater the collective data on brain-mapping, the better scientists will understand how the brain works. To produce such an image requires thousands of patients and trillions of bytes of computer memory.

Also look for increased speed and mobile MRI scanners, which will be used in emergency rooms and doctor's offices to quickly assess internal damage after an accident or injury.

TECHNOLOGY

3-D Images and Brain Surgery

In operating rooms, surgeons are beginning to use another type of 3-D ultrasound known as interventional MRI. They watch 3-D images in real time and observe details of tissues while they operate. These integrated technologies now allow scientists to conduct entirely new types of studies. For example, 3-D brain images of many patients with one disease—can now be integrated into a composite image of a "typical" brain of someone with that disease.

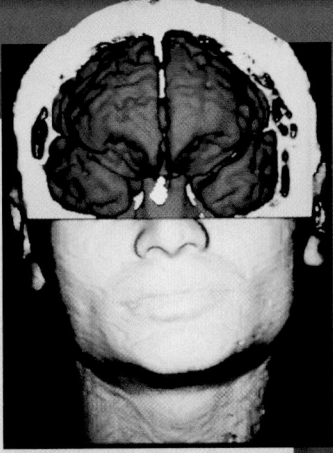

ACTIVITIES

Writing About Science: Brochure

Make a chart of the different types of medical imaging used to diagnose one body system. Include an explanation of how the technique works and list the pros and cons of using it.

Reliving History

X-rays use radioactivity which can be dangerous. You can use visible light to shine through thin materials that you don't normally see through. Try using a flashlight to illuminate a leaf. Discuss or draw what you see.

CHAPTER

Transport and Protection

the BIG idea

Systems function to transport materials and to defend and protect the body.

> **Red blood cells travel through a blood vessel. How do you think blood carries materials around your body?**

Key Concepts

SECTION 1
The circulatory system transports materials.
Learn how materials move through blood vessels.

SECTION 2
The immune system defends the body.
Learn about the body's defenses and responses to foreign materials.

SECTION 3
The integumentary system shields the body.
Learn about the structure of skin and how it protects the body.

FCAT Practice

Prepare and practice for the FCAT
- Section Reviews, pp. 637, 647, 654
- Chapter Review, pp. 656–658
- FCAT Practice, p. 659

CLASSZONE.COM
- Florida Review: Content Review and FCAT Practice

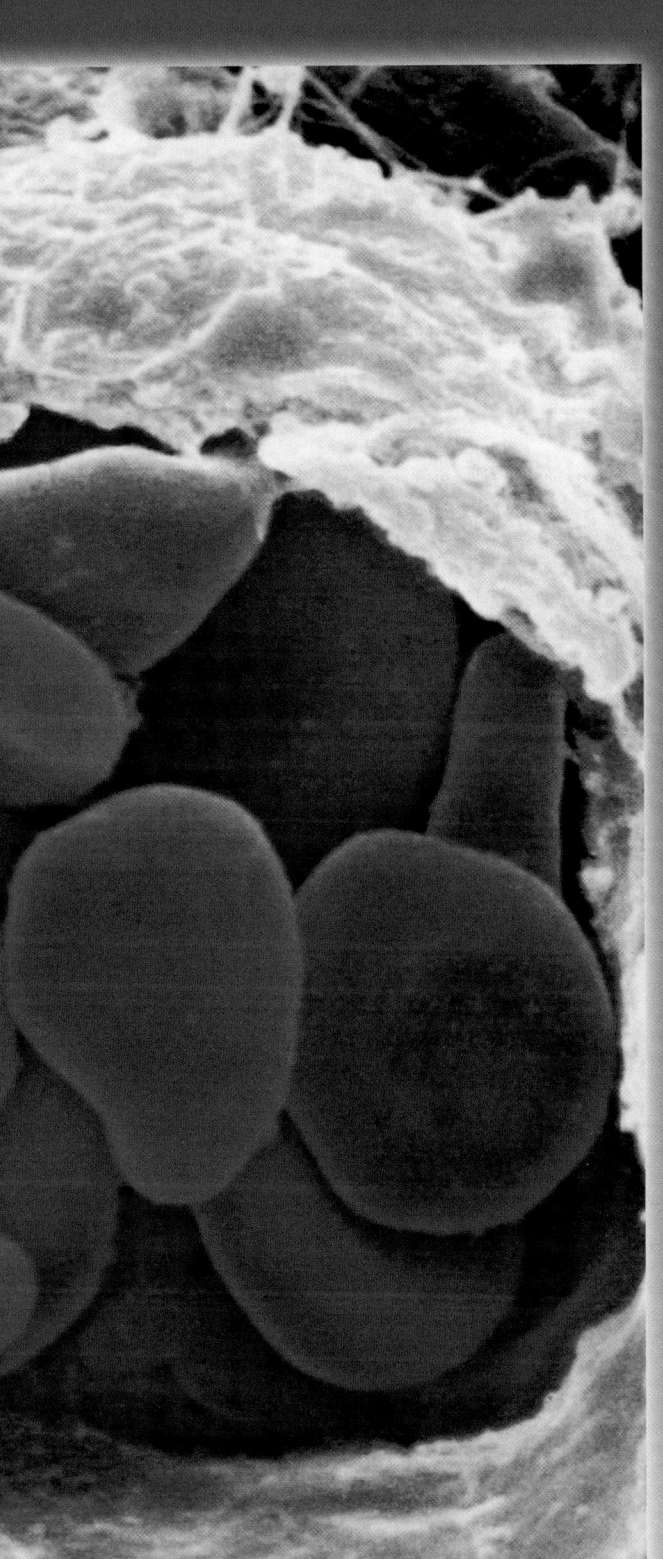

Blood Pressure

Fill a small, round balloon halfway full with air. Tie off the end. Gently squeeze the balloon in your hand. Release the pressure. Squeeze again.

Observe and Think As you squeeze your hand, what happens to the air in the balloon? What happens as you release the pressure?

Wet Fingers

Dip your finger into a cup of room-temperature water. Then hold the finger up in the air and note how it feels.

Observe and Think How does your finger feel now compared with the way it felt before you dipped it?

Internet Activity: Heart Pumping

Go to **ClassZone.com** to learn about how the heart pumps blood. See how the circulatory system interacts with the respiratory system.

Observe and Think Where does the blood go after it leaves the right side of the heart? the left side of the heart?

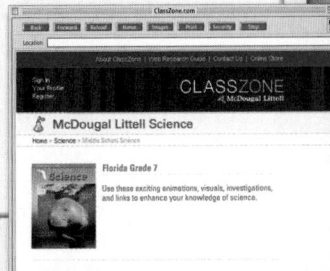

NSTA
scilinks.org

SCiLINKS

Immune System **Code: MDL046**

Getting Ready to Learn

CONCEPT REVIEW

- The body's systems interact.
- The body's systems work to maintain internal conditions.
- The digestive system breaks down food.
- The respiratory system gets oxygen and removes carbon dioxide.

VOCABULARY REVIEW

organ p. 573

organ system p. 574

homeostasis p. 574

nutrient p. 607

FLORIDA REVIEW
CLASSZONE.COM

Content Review and FCAT Practice

▶ TAKING NOTES

MAIN IDEA AND DETAIL NOTES

Make a two-column chart. Write the main ideas, such as those in the blue headings, in the column on the left. Write details about each of those main heads in the column on the right.

VOCABULARY STRATEGY

Write each new vocabulary term in the center of a **frame game** diagram. Decide what information to frame it with. Use examples, descriptions, parts, sentences that use the term in context, or pictures. You can change the frame to fit each term.

See the Note-Taking Handbook on pages R45–R51.

SCIENCE NOTEBOOK

MAIN IDEAS	DETAIL NOTES
1. The circulatory system works with other body systems.	1. Transports materials from digestive and respiratory systems to cells
	2. Blood is fluid that carries materials and wastes
	3. Blood is always moving through the body
	4. Blood delivers oxygen and takes away carbon dioxide

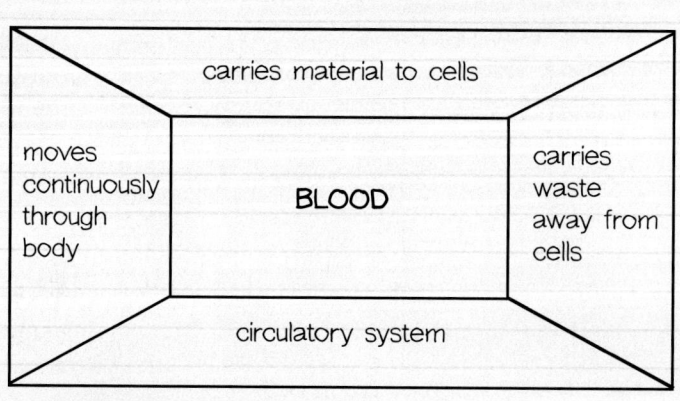

carries material to cells

moves continuously through body

BLOOD

carries waste away from cells

circulatory system

18.1 The circulatory system transports materials.

Sunshine State STANDARDS

SC.F.1.3.1: The student understands that living things are composed of major systems that function in reproduction, growth, maintenance, and regulation.

SC.H.1.3.5: The student knows that a change in one or more variables may alter the outcome of an investigation.

VOCABULARY

circulatory system p. 631
blood p. 631
red blood cell p. 633
artery p. 635
vein p. 635
capillary p. 635

BEFORE, you learned

- The urinary system removes waste
- The kidneys play a role in homeostasis

NOW, you will learn

- How different structures of the circulatory system work together
- About the structure and function of blood
- What blood pressure is and why it is important

EXPLORE The Circulatory System

How fast does your heart beat?

PROCEDURE

1. Hold out your left hand with your palm facing up.

2. Place the first two fingers of your right hand on your left wrist below your thumb. Move your fingertips slightly until you can feel your pulse.

3. Use the stopwatch to determine how many times your heart beats in one minute.

WHAT DO YOU THINK?
- How many times did your heart beat?
- What do you think you would find if you took your pulse after exercising?

MATERIALS
stopwatch

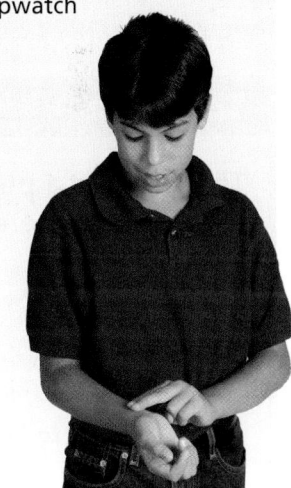

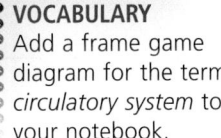

VOCABULARY
Add a frame game diagram for the term *circulatory system* to your notebook.

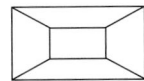

The circulatory system works with other body systems.

You have read that the systems in your body provide materials and energy. The digestive system breaks down food and nutrients, and the respiratory system provides the oxygen that cells need to release energy. Another system, called the **circulatory system,** transports materials from the digestive and the respiratory systems to the cells.

Materials and wastes are carried in a fluid called **blood**. Blood moves continuously through the body, delivering oxygen and other materials to cells and removing carbon dioxide and other wastes from cells.

Structures in the circulatory system function together.

RESOURCE CENTER
CLASSZONE.COM

Find out more about the circulatory system.

In order to provide the essential nutrients and other materials that your cells need, your blood must keep moving through your body. The circulatory system, which is made up of the heart and blood vessels, allows blood to flow to all parts of the body. The circulatory system works with other systems to provide the body with this continuous flow of life-giving blood.

The Heart

The heart is the organ that pushes blood throughout the circulatory system. The human heart actually functions as two pumps—one pump on the right side and one on the left side. The right side of the heart pumps blood to the lungs to receive oxygen, and the left side pumps blood to the entire body. The lungs receive oxygen when you inhale and remove carbon dioxide when you exhale. Inside the lungs, the respiratory system interacts with the circulatory system.

The Heart

The heart is a pump moving blood throughout the entire body.

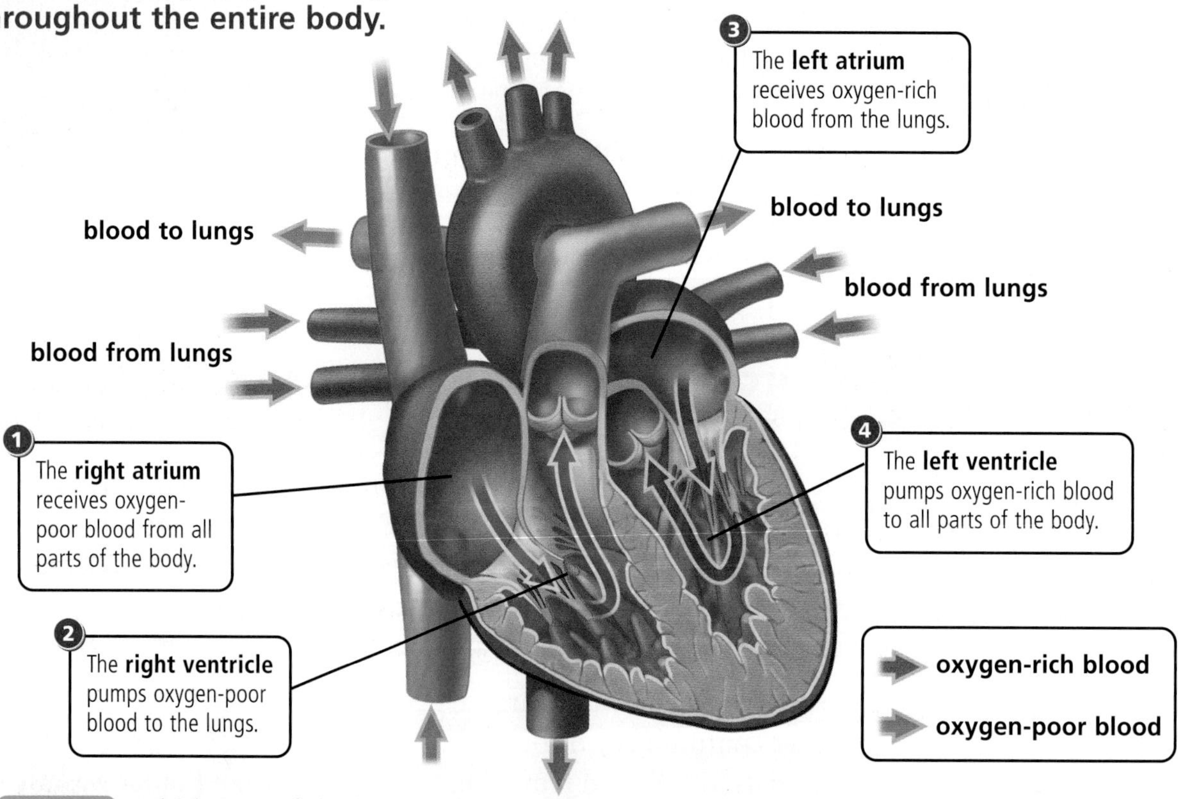

blood to lungs

blood from lungs

blood to lungs

blood from lungs

3 The **left atrium** receives oxygen-rich blood from the lungs.

1 The **right atrium** receives oxygen-poor blood from all parts of the body.

4 The **left ventricle** pumps oxygen-rich blood to all parts of the body.

2 The **right ventricle** pumps oxygen-poor blood to the lungs.

➡ **oxygen-rich blood**

➡ **oxygen-poor blood**

READING VISUALS Which part of the heart pumps oxygen-poor blood to the lungs? Which part of the heart pumps oxygen-rich blood to the body?

Each side of the heart is divided into two areas called chambers. Oxygen-poor blood, which is blood from the body with less oxygen, flows to the right side of your heart, into a filling chamber called the right atrium. With each heartbeat, blood flows from the right atrium into a pumping chamber, the right ventricle, and then into the lungs. There the blood releases carbon dioxide waste and absorbs oxygen.

After picking up oxygen, blood is pushed back to the heart, filling another chamber, which is called the left atrium. Blood moves from the left atrium to the left ventricle, a pumping chamber, and again begins its trip out to the rest of the body. Both oxygen-poor blood and oxygen-rich blood are red. However, oxygen-rich blood is a much brighter and lighter shade of red than is oxygen-poor blood. The diagram on page 632 shows oxygen-poor blood in blue, so that you can tell where in the circulatory system oxygen-poor and oxygen-rich blood are found.

 **CHECK YOUR READING** Summarize the way blood moves through the heart. Remember, a summary contains only the most important information.

Blood

The oxygen that your cells need in order to release energy must be present in blood to travel through your body. Blood is a tissue made up of plasma, red blood cells, white blood cells, and platelets. About 60 percent of blood is plasma, a fluid that contains proteins, glucose, hormones, gases, and other substances dissolved in water.

White blood cells help your body fight infection by attacking disease-causing organisms. **Red blood cells** are more numerous than white blood cells and have a different function. They pick up oxygen in the lungs and transport it throughout the body. As red blood cells travel through the circulatory system, they deliver oxygen to other cells.

Platelets are large cell fragments that help form blood clots when a blood vessel is injured. You know what a blood clot is if you've observed a cut or a scrape. The scab that forms around a cut or scrape is made of clotted blood. After an injury such as a cut, platelets nearby begin to enlarge and become sticky. They stick to the injured area of the blood vessels and release chemicals that result in blood clotting. Blood clotting keeps blood vessels from losing too much blood.

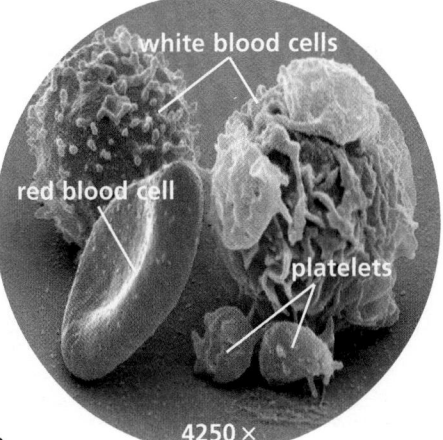

Blood is made mostly of plasma, which transports red blood cells, white blood cells, and platelets.

 **CHECK YOUR READING** What are the four components that make up blood?

Circulatory System

The circulatory system allows blood to flow continuously throughout the body. The runner depends on a constant flow of oxygen-rich blood to fuel his cells.

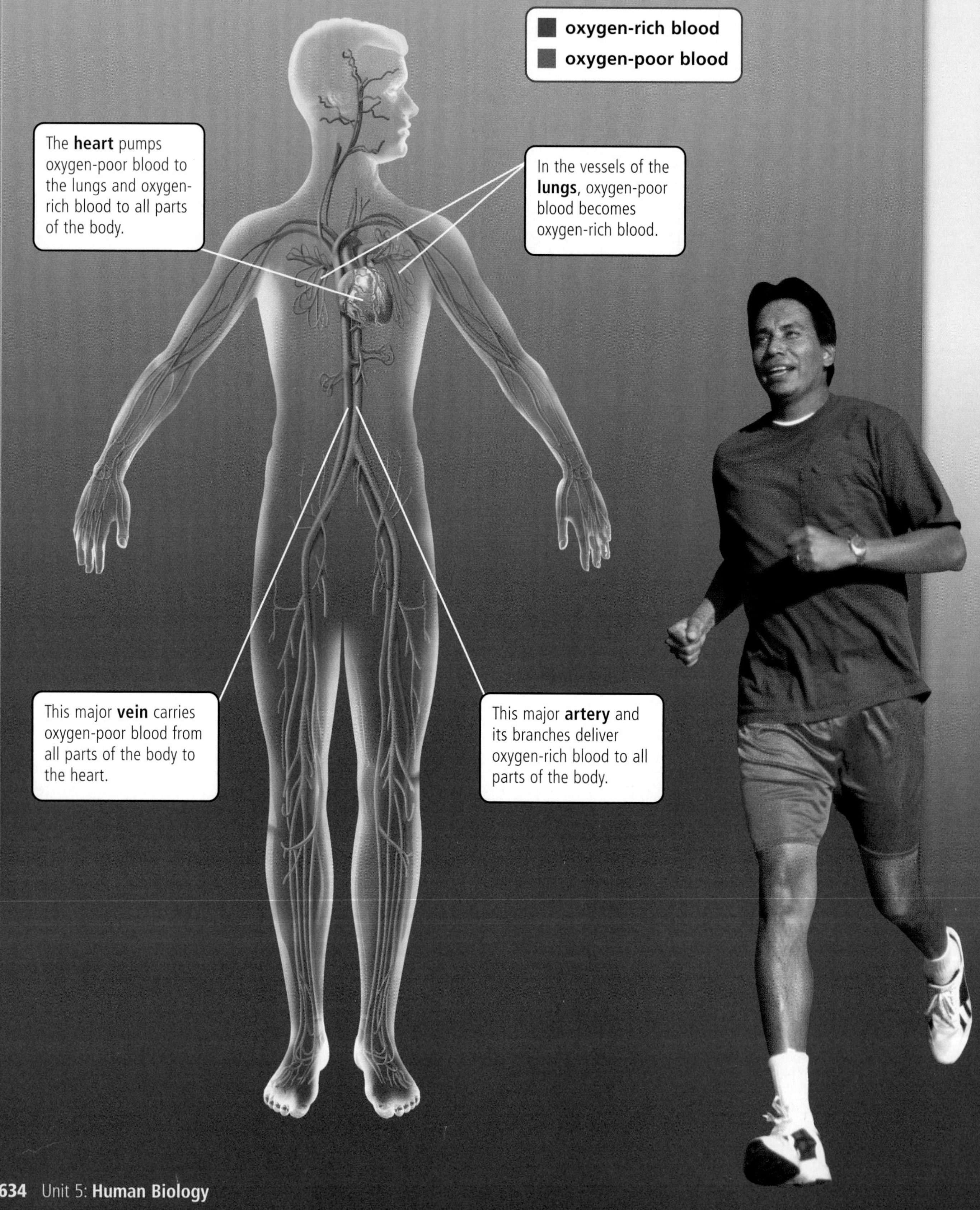

■ oxygen-rich blood
■ oxygen-poor blood

The **heart** pumps oxygen-poor blood to the lungs and oxygen-rich blood to all parts of the body.

In the vessels of the **lungs**, oxygen-poor blood becomes oxygen-rich blood.

This major **vein** carries oxygen-poor blood from all parts of the body to the heart.

This major **artery** and its branches deliver oxygen-rich blood to all parts of the body.

As blood travels through blood vessels, some fluid is lost. This fluid, called lymph, is collected in lymph vessels and returned to veins and arteries. As you will read in the next section, lymph and lymph vessels are associated with your immune system. Sometimes scientists refer to the lymph and lymph vessels as the lymphatic system. The lymphatic system helps you fight disease.

Blood Vessels

Blood moves through a network of structures called blood vessels. Blood vessels are tube-shaped structures that are similar to flexible drinking straws. The structure of blood vessels suits them for particular functions. **Arteries**, which are the vessels that take blood away from the heart, have strong walls. An artery wall is thick and elastic and can handle the tremendous force produced when the heart pumps. **Veins** are blood vessels that carry blood back to the heart. The walls of veins are thinner than those of arteries. However, veins are generally of greater diameter than are arteries.

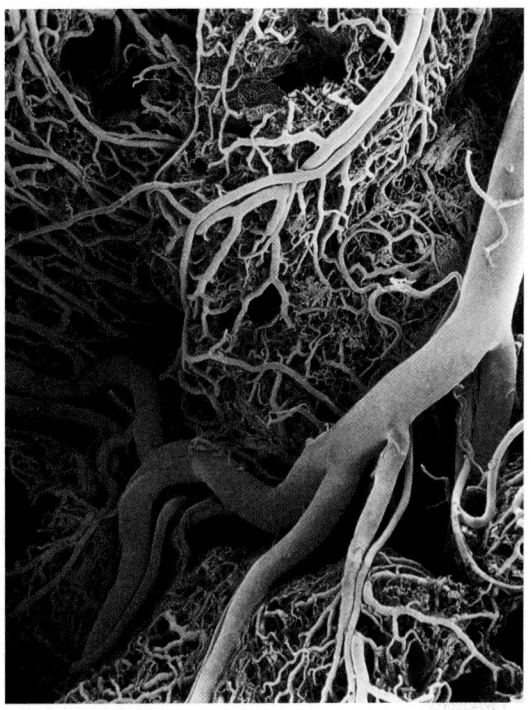

Arteries, capillaries, and veins form a complex web to carry blood to all the cells in the body (30×).

Most arteries carry oxygen-rich blood away from the heart, and most veins carry oxygen-poor blood back to the heart. However, the pulmonary blood vessels are exceptions. Oxygen-poor blood travels through the two pulmonary arteries, one of which goes to each lung. The two pulmonary veins carry oxygen-rich blood from the lungs to the heart.

Veins and arteries branch off into very narrow blood vessels called capillaries. **Capillaries** connect arteries with veins. Through capillaries materials are exchanged between blood and tissues. Oxygen and materials from nutrients move from the blood in the arteries to the body's tissues through tiny openings in the capillary walls. Waste materials and carbon dioxide move from the tissues' cells through the capillary walls and into the blood in the veins.

 CHECK YOUR READING   Compare and contrast arteries, veins, and capillaries.

Blood exerts pressure on blood vessels.

As you have read, the contractions of the heart push blood through blood vessels. The force produced when the heart contracts travels through the blood, putting pressure on the blood vessels. This force is called blood pressure. Compare a vessel to a plastic bag filled with water.

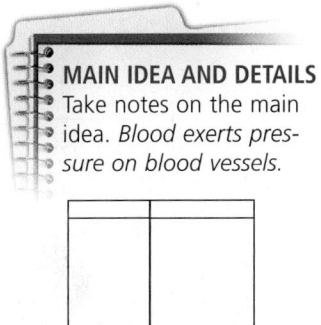

MAIN IDEA AND DETAILS
Take notes on the main idea. *Blood exerts pressure on blood vessels.*

If you push down at the center of the bag, you can see the water push out against the sides of the bag.

The heart pushes blood in a similar way, exerting pressure on the arteries, veins, and capillaries in the circulatory system. It is important to maintain healthy blood pressure so that materials in blood get to all parts of your body. If blood pressure is too low, some of the cells will not get oxygen and other materials. On the other hand, if blood pressure is too high, the force may weaken the blood vessels and require the heart to work harder to push blood through the blood vessels. High blood pressure is a serious medical condition, but it can be treated.

The circulatory system can be considered as two smaller systems: one, the pulmonary system, moves blood to the lungs; the other, the systemic system, moves blood to the rest of the body. Blood pressure is measured in the systemic part of the circulatory system.

You can think of blood pressure as the pressure that blood exerts on the walls of your arteries at all times. Health professionals measure blood pressure indirectly with a device called a sphygmomanometer (SFIHG-moh-muh-NAHM-ih-tuhr).

Blood pressure is expressed with two numbers—one number over another number. The first number refers to the pressure in the arteries when the heart contracts. The second number refers to the pressure in the arteries when the heart relaxes and receives blood from the veins.

Blood Pressure

Blood pressure allows materials to travel to all parts of your body.

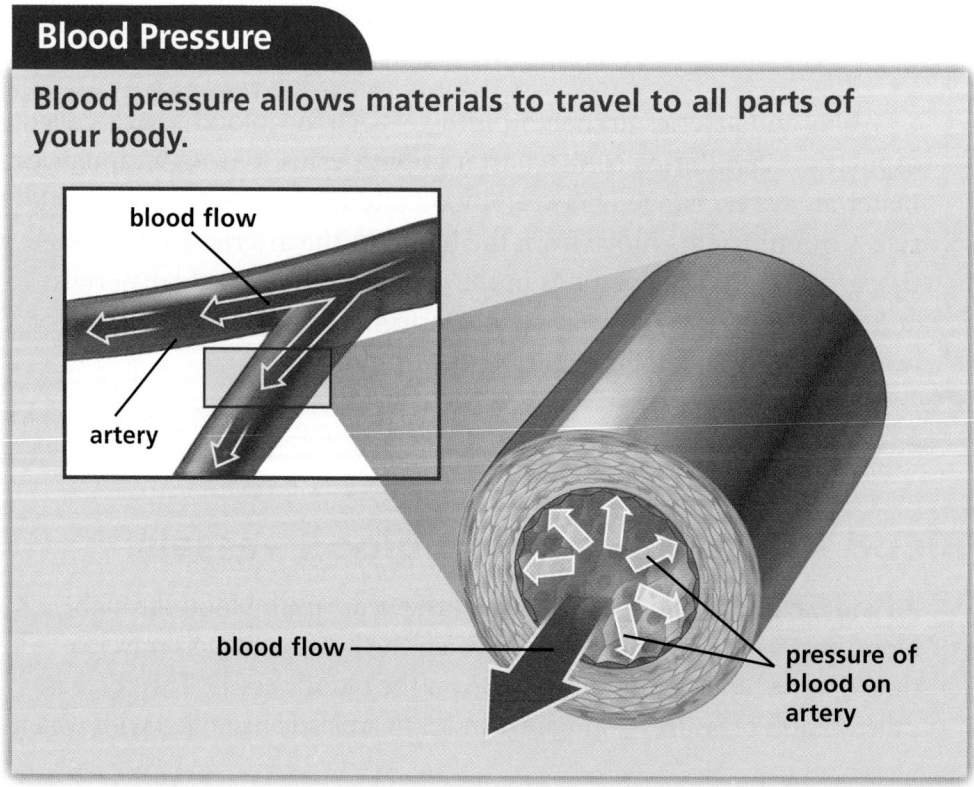

blood flow

artery

blood flow

pressure of blood on artery

There are four different blood types.

Each red blood cell has special proteins on its surface. One group of surface proteins determines blood type. There are two blood-type proteins, A and B. A person whose blood cells have the A proteins has type A blood. One with cells having B proteins has type B blood. Some people have both proteins—type AB blood. Other people have neither protein, a type of blood referred to as type O.

Maybe you, or someone you know, has had a blood transfusion, a procedure in which one person receives blood donated by another. Knowing blood type is important for transfusions. As you will learn in the next section, the body has structures that protect it from unknown substances. They are part of an immune system that recognizes and protects cells and molecules that are "self" from those that are unrecognized, or "nonself." The body attacks unrecognized substances, including those in donated blood.

The blood used for transfusions is usually the same type as the blood type of the receiver, but sometimes other blood types are used. The diagram shows which blood types are compatible. Because the cells in type O blood have neither protein, the immune system of someone with A, B, or AB blood will not attack O blood cells. A person with type O blood, however, cannot receive any other blood type because that person's immune system would attack A or B surface proteins.

 **CHECK YOUR READING** Why is it important to know your blood type?

Blood Type Compatibility		
Blood Type	**Can Donate Blood To**	**Can Receive Blood From**
A	A, AB	A, O
B	B, AB	B, O
AB	AB	A, B, AB, O
O	A, B, AB, O	O

People can donate blood to others.

 **RESOURCE CENTER**
CLASSZONE.COM

Learn more about blood types.

18.1 Review

KEY CONCEPTS

1. What are the functions of the two sides of the heart?
2. What is the primary function of red blood cells?
3. Why can both high and low blood pressure be a problem?

CRITICAL THINKING

4. **Apply** List three examples of the circulatory system working with another system in your body.
5. **Compare and Contrast** Explain why blood pressure is expressed with two numbers.

⬥ CHALLENGE

6. **Identify Cause and Effect** You can feel the speed at which your heart is pumping by pressing two fingers to the inside of your wrist. This is your pulse. If you run for a few minutes, your pulse rate is faster for a little while, then it slows down again. Why did your pulse rate speed up and slow down?

CHAPTER INVESTIGATION

Heart Rate and Exercise

OVERVIEW AND PURPOSE In this activity, you will calculate your resting, maximum, and target heart rates. Then you will examine the effect of exercise on heart rate. Before you begin, read through the entire investigation.

▶ Procedure

1. Make a data table like the one shown on the sample notebook page.

2. Measure your resting heart rate. Find the pulse in the artery of your neck, just below and in front of the bottom of your ear, with the first two fingers of one hand. Do not use your thumb to measure pulse since the thumb has a pulse of its own. Once you have found the pulse, count the beats for 30 seconds and multiply the result by 2. The number you get is your resting heart rate in beats per minute. Record this number in your notebook.

step 2

3. Calculate your maximum heart rate by subtracting your age from 220. Record this number in your notebook. Your target heart rate should be 60 to 75 percent of your maximum heart rate. Calculate and record this range in your notebook.

4. Someone who is very athletic or has been exercising regularly for 6 months or more can safely exercise up to 85 percent of his or her maximum heart rate. Calculate and record this rate in your notebook.

5. Observe how quickly you reach your target heart rate during exercise. Begin by running in place at an intensity that makes you breathe harder but does not make you breathless. As with any exercise, remember that if you experience difficulty breathing, dizziness, or chest discomfort, stop exercising immediately.

step 5

MATERIALS
- notebook
- stopwatch
- calculator
- graph paper

6. Every 2 minutes, measure your heart rate for 10 seconds. Multiply this number by 6 to find your heart rate in beats per minute and record it in your notebook. Try to exercise for a total of 10 minutes. After you stop exercising, continue recording your heart rate every 2 minutes until it returns to the resting rate you measured in step 2.

▶ Observe and Analyze
Write It Up

1. **GRAPH DATA** Make a line graph of your heart rate during and after the exercise. Graph the values in beats per minute versus time in minutes. Your graph should start at your resting heart rate and continue until your heart rate has returned to its resting rate. Using a colored pencil, shade in the area that represents your target heart-rate range.

2. **ANALYZE DATA** How many minutes of exercising were needed for you to reach your target heart rate of 60 to 75 percent of maximum? Did your heart rate go over your target range?

3. **INTERPRET DATA** How many minutes after you stopped exercising did it take for your heart rate to return to its resting rate? Why do you think your heart rate did not return to its resting rate immediately after you stopped exercising?

▶ Conclude

Write It Up

1. **INFER** Why do you think that heart rate increases during exercise?

2. **IDENTIFY** What other body systems are affected when the heart rate increases?

3. **PREDICT** Why do you think that target heart rate changes with age?

4. **CLASSIFY** Create a table comparing the intensity of different types of exercise, such as walking, skating, bicycling, weight lifting, and any others you might enjoy.

▶ INVESTIGATE Further

CHALLENGE Determine how other exercises affect your heart rate. Repeat this investigation by performing one or two of the other exercises from your table. Present your data, with a graph, to the class.

Heart Rate and Exercise

Resting heart rate:

Maximum heart rate:

Target heart rate (60-75% of maximum):

Target heart rate (85% of maximum):

Table 1. Heart Rate During and After Exercise

Time (minutes)	0	2	4	6	8	10	12	14	16	18	20
Heart rate (beats per minute)											

KEY CONCEPT

18.2 The immune system defends the body.

Sunshine State STANDARDS

SC.C.1.3.1: The student understands that living things are composed of major systems that function in reproduction, growth, maintenance, and regulation.

BEFORE, you learned

• The circulatory system works with other systems to fuel the body cells

• Structures in the circulatory system work together

• Blood pressure allows materials to reach all parts of the body

NOW, you will learn

• How foreign material enters the body

• How the immune system responds to foreign material

• Ways that the body can become immune to a disease

VOCABULARY

pathogen p. 640

immune system p. 641

antibody p. 641

antigen p. 644

immunity p. 646

vaccine p. 646

antibiotic p. 647

EXPLORE Membranes

How does the body keep foreign particles out?

PROCEDURE

① Place a white cloth into a sandwich bag and seal it. Fill a bowl with water and stir in several drops of food coloring.

② Submerge the sandwich bag in the water. After five minutes, remove the bag and note the condition of the cloth.

③ Puncture the bag with a pin. Put the bag back in the water for five minutes. Remove the bag and note the condition of the cloth.

WHAT DO YOU THINK?

• How does a puncture in the bag affect its ability to protect the cloth?

MATERIALS

• white cloth
• zippered sandwich bag
• large bowl
• water
• food coloring
• small pin

Many systems defend the body from harmful materials.

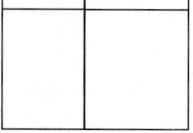

MAIN IDEA AND DETAILS Add the main idea *Many systems defend the body from harmful materials* to your chart along with detail notes.

You might not realize it, but you come into contact with harmful substances constantly. Because your body has ways to defend itself, you don't even notice. One of the body's best defenses is to keep foreign materials from entering in the first place. The integumentary (ihn-TEHG-yu-MEHN-tuh-ree), respiratory, and digestive systems are the first line of defense against **pathogens,** or disease-causing agents. Pathogens can enter through your skin, the air you breathe, and even the food you eat or liquids you drink.

CHECK YOUR READING Which systems are your first line of defense against pathogens?

Integumentary System Defenses Most of the time, your skin functions as a barrier between you and the outside world. The physical barrier the skin forms is just one obstacle for pathogens and other foreign materials. The growth of pathogens on your eyes can be slowed by substances contained in tears. The millions of bacteria cells that live on the skin can also kill pathogens. A common way pathogens can enter the body is through a cut. The circulatory system is then able to help defend the body because blood contains cells that respond to foreign materials.

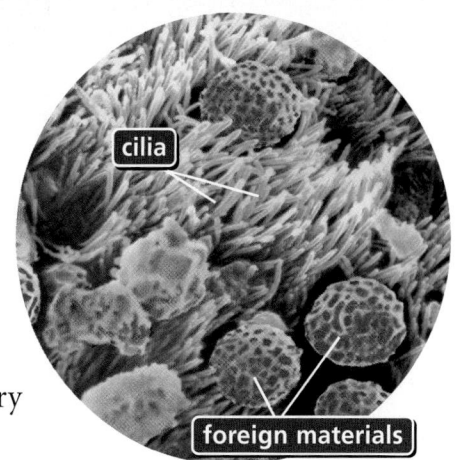

Cilia are hairlike protrusions that trap materials entering your respiratory system (600×).

Respiratory System Defenses Sneezing and coughing are two ways the respiratory system defends the body from harmful substances. Cilia and mucus also protect the body. Cilia are tiny, hairlike protrusions in the nose and the lungs that trap dust particles present in the air. Mucus is a thick and slippery substance found in the nose, throat, and lungs. Like the cilia, mucus traps dirt and other particles. Mucus contains substances similar to those in tears that can slow the growth of pathogens.

Digestive System Defenses Some foreign materials manage to enter your digestive system, but many are destroyed by saliva, mucus, enzymes, and stomach acids. Saliva in your mouth helps kill bacteria. Mucus protects the digestive organs by coating them. Pathogens can also be destroyed by enzymes produced in the liver and pancreas or by the acids in the stomach.

The immune system has response structures.

Sometimes foreign materials manage to get past the first line of defense. When this happens, the body relies on the **immune system** to respond. This system functions in several ways:

- Tissues in the bone marrow, the thymus gland, the spleen, and the lymph nodes produce white blood cells, which are specialized cells that function to destroy foreign organisms.

- Some white blood cells produce a nonspecific response to injury or infection.

- Some white blood cells produce proteins called **antibodies,** which are part of a specific immune response to foreign materials.

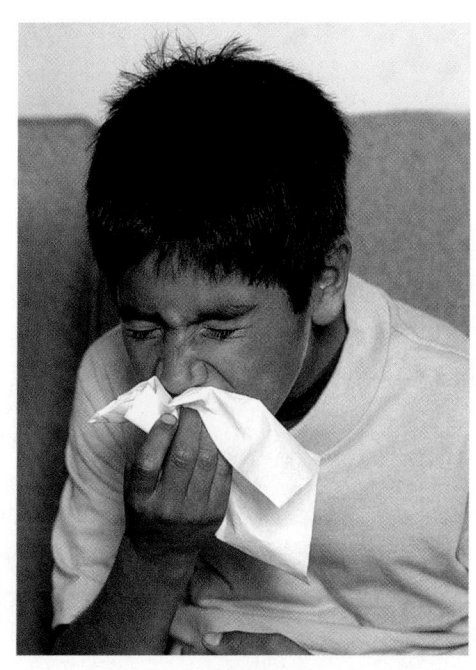

Sneezing helps to expel foreign substances from the body.

White Blood Cells

The immune system has specialized cells called white blood cells that recognize foreign materials in the body and respond. The number of white blood cells in the blood can increase during an immune response. These cells travel through the circulatory system and the lymphatic system to an injured or infected area of the body. White blood cells leave the blood vessels and travel into the damaged tissue, where the immune response takes place.

The Lymphatic System

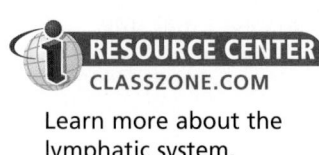

RESOURCE CENTER
CLASSZONE.COM

Learn more about the lymphatic system.

The lymphatic system transports pathogen-fighting white blood cells throughout the body, much as the circulatory system does. The lymphatic system carries lymph, and the circulatory system carries blood. Both fluids transport similar materials, such as white blood cells.

Lymph is the fluid left in the tissues by the circulatory system. It moves through lymph vessels, which are similar to veins. However, the lymphatic system has no pump like the heart to move fluid. Lymph drifts through the lymph vessels when your skeletal muscles contract or when your body changes position. As it moves, it passes through lymph nodes, which filter out pathogens and store white blood cells and antibodies. Because lymph nodes filter out pathogens, infections are often fought in your lymph nodes, causing them to swell when you get sick.

CHECK YOUR READING How does the lymphatic system help the immune system?

The immune system responds to attack.

Certain illnesses can cause symptoms such as coughing, sneezing, and fever. These symptoms make you uncomfortable when you are sick. But in fact, most symptoms are the result of the immune system's response to foreign materials in the body.

The immune system responds in two ways. The white blood cells that first respond to the site of injury or infection attack foreign materials in a nonspecific response. Some of these cells attack foreign materials and produce chemicals that help other white blood cells work better. The second part of the response is very specific to the types of pathogens invading the body. These white blood cells produce antibodies specific to each pathogen and provide your body with immunity.

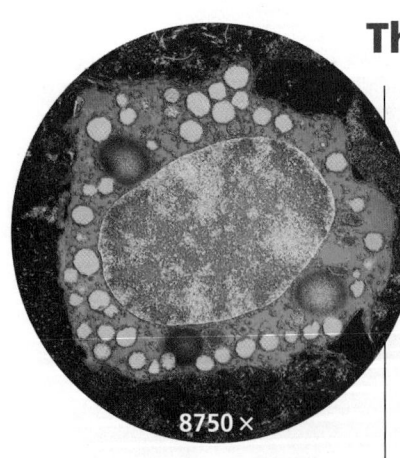

8750 ×

The mast cell above is an important part of the immune system.

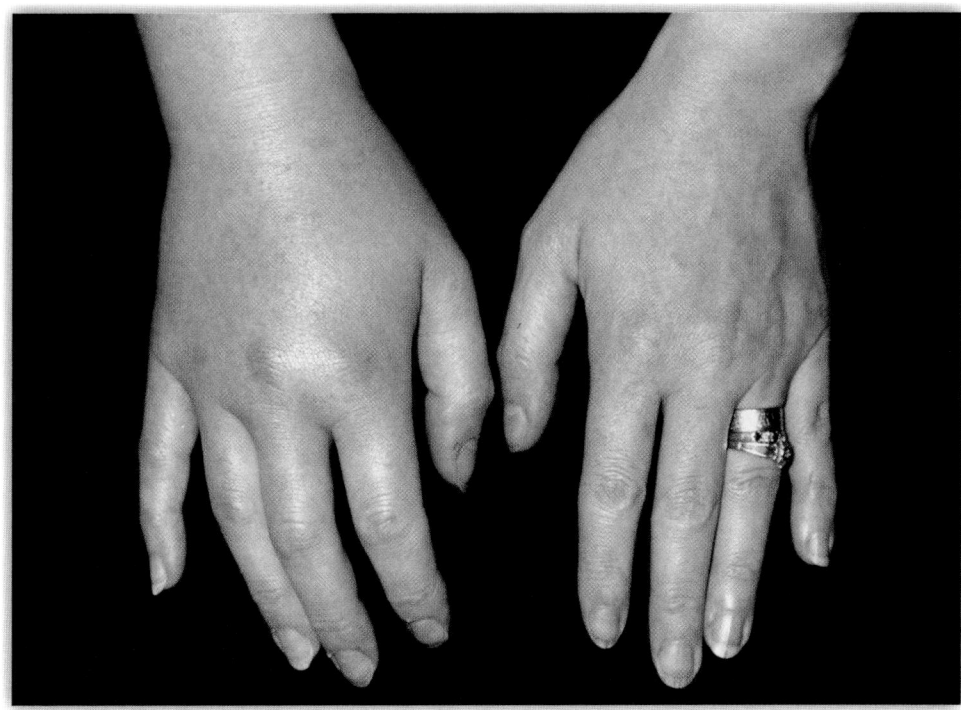

Wasp stings cause an immediate immune response. The area of the sting swells up and increases in temperature while your body battles the injury.

Nonspecific Response

Swelling, redness, and heat are some of the symptoms that tell you that a cut or scrape has become infected by foreign materials. They are all signs of inflammation, your body's first defense reaction against injuries and infections.

When tissue becomes irritated or damaged, it releases large amounts of histamine (HIHS-tuh-meen). Histamine raises the temperature of the tissues and increases blood flow to the area. Increased blood flow, which makes the injured area appear red, allows antibodies and white blood cells to arrive more quickly for battle. Higher temperatures improve the speed and power of white blood cells. Some pathogens cannot tolerate heat, so they grow weaker. The swelling caused by the production of histamine can be a small price to pay for this chemical's important work.

When a foreign material affects more than one area of your body, many tissues produce histamine. As a result, the temperature of your whole body rises. Any temperature above 37 degrees Celsius (98.6°F) is considered a fever, but only temperatures hot enough to damage tissues are dangerous. Trying to lower a high fever with medication is advisable in order to avoid tissue damage. When you have a small fever, lowering your body temperature might make you more comfortable, but it will not affect how long you stay sick.

 What causes a fever when you are sick?

Specific Response

Specific immune responses differ from nonspecific responses in two ways. First, specific responses are triggered by antigens. An **antigen** is a chemical marker on a cell's surface that indicates whether the cell is from your body or is a foreign material. When the body detects a foreign antigen, specific immune responses occur. Second, a specific immune response provides protection from future exposure to the same material. Three major types of white blood cells—phagocytes, T cells, and B cells—function together in a specific response.

Phagocytes and T Cells Phagocytes ingest and break down foreign materials. Small pieces of the foreign materials are incorporated into the surface of the phagocyte's cell membrane. These foreign particles contain antigens that are detected as foreign by T cells. The T cells

Immune Response

When pathogens invade the body, several types of white blood cells function together to identify and attack foreign materials.

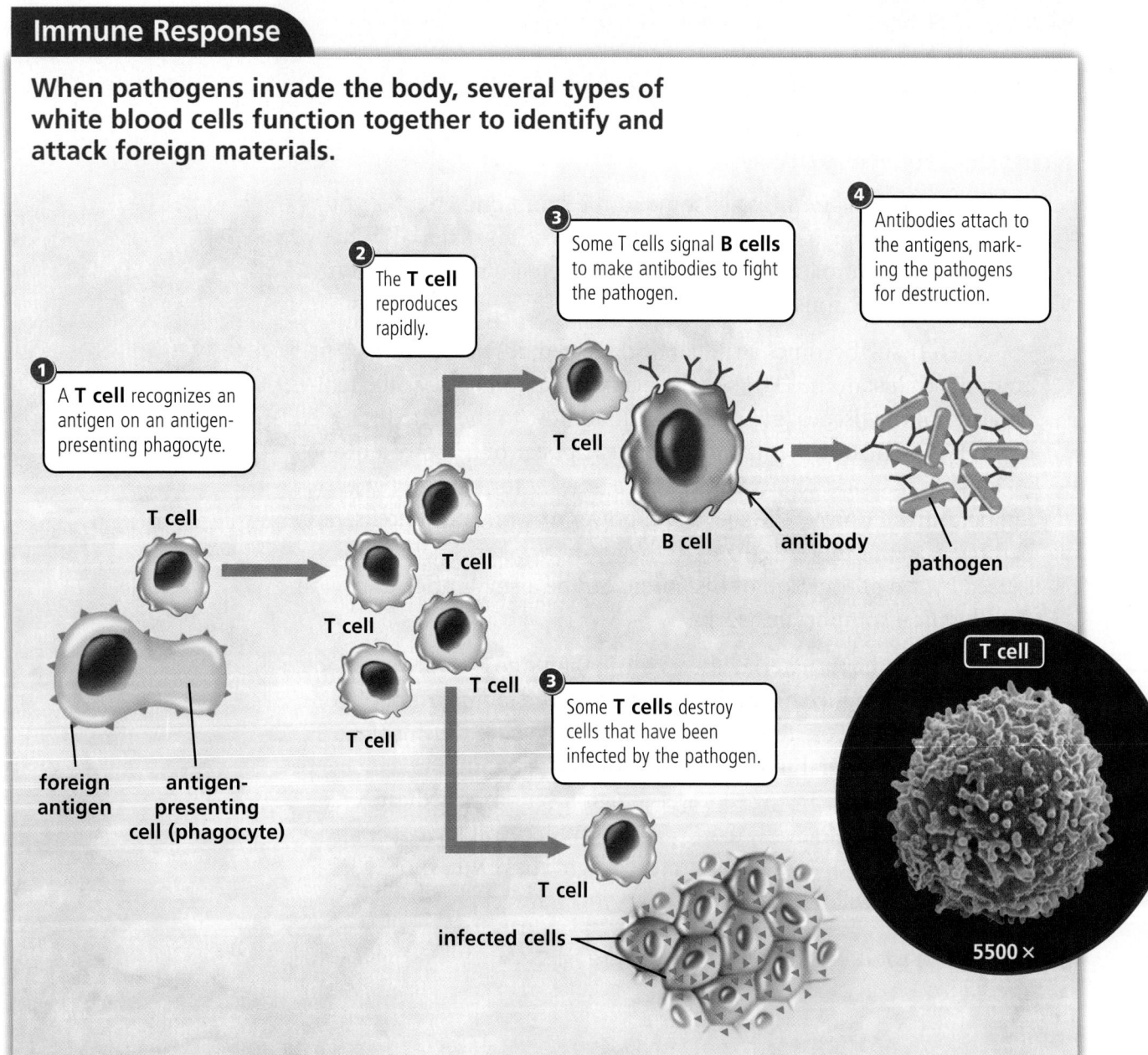

1 A **T cell** recognizes an antigen on an antigen-presenting phagocyte.

2 The **T cell** reproduces rapidly.

3 Some T cells signal **B cells** to make antibodies to fight the pathogen.

4 Antibodies attach to the antigens, marking the pathogens for destruction.

3 Some **T cells** destroy cells that have been infected by the pathogen.

T cell

T cell

T cell

T cell

T cell

T cell

T cell

B cell   antibody   pathogen

foreign antigen

antigen-presenting cell (phagocyte)

infected cells

T cell

5500×

INVESTIGATE Antibodies

How do antibodies stop pathogens from spreading?

PROCEDURE

1. Your teacher will hand out plastic lids, each labeled with the name of a different pathogen. You will see plastic containers spread throughout the room. There is one container in the room with the same label as your lid.

2. At the signal, find the plastic container with the pathogen that has the same label as your lid and wait in place for the teacher to tell you to stop. If you still haven't found the matching container when time is called, your model pathogen has spread.

3. If your pathogen has spread, write its name on the board.

WHAT DO YOU THINK?

- Which pathogens spread?
- What do you think the lid and container represent? Why?
- How do antibodies identify pathogens?

CHALLENGE Why do you think it is important for your body to identify pathogens?

SKILL FOCUS
Making models

MATERIALS
- plastic containers with lids
- masking tape

TIME
15 minutes

respond by dividing rapidly. Some types of T cells attack the materials with the foreign antigens, whereas others have different functions. Because antigens that differ from those on a person's cells and provoke an immune response are found on pathogens, the human immune system is necessary for survival in a germ-filled world.

B Cells After T cells divide, B cells that recognize the same foreign antigen are activated and divide rapidly. After several days, many of these B cells begin to produce antibodies that help destroy pathogens. Antibodies attach to the foreign antigens, marking the pathogens for killer T cells or other cells and chemicals that can destroy pathogens.

Some B cells do not make antibodies but remain in the body as a form of immune system memory. If the same pathogen enters the body again, the immune system can respond much more quickly. B cells that recognize the foreign antigen already exist, and antibodies will be produced more quickly.

 Why is it important for the body to store B cells?

Development of Immunity

After your body has destroyed a specific pathogen, B cells that fight that pathogen remain in your system. If the same pathogen were to enter your body again, your immune system would almost certainly destroy it before you became ill. This resistance to a sickness is called **immunity.**

Immunity takes two forms: passive and active. When babies are first born, they have only the immune defenses transferred to them by their mothers. They have not had the chance to develop antibodies of their own. This type of immunity is called passive immunity. Antibodies are not produced by the person's own body but given to the body from another source. Babies develop their own antibodies after a few months.

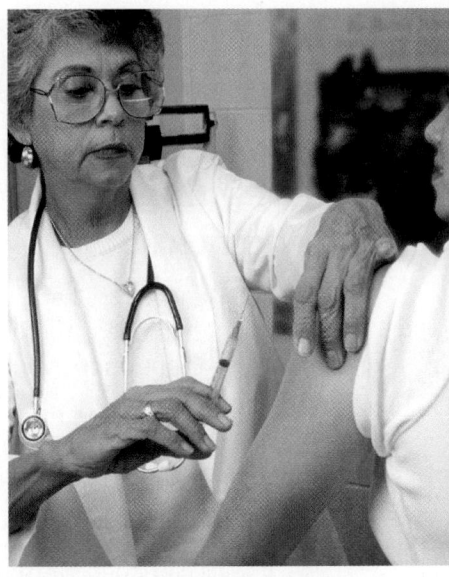

COMPARE A doctor gives a girl a vaccination. Is getting a vaccination an example of passive or active immunity?

You have active immunity whenever your body makes its own antibodies. Your body will again fight against any specific pathogen you have developed antibodies against. For example, it is most unlikely that you will get chicken pox twice.

 **CHECK YOUR READING** What is the difference between active and passive immunity?

Most diseases can be prevented or treated.

Given enough time, your immune system will fight off most diseases. However, some infections can cause significant and lasting damage before they are defeated by the body's defenses. Other infections are so strong that the immune system cannot successfully fight them. Medical advances in the prevention and treatment of diseases have reduced the risks of many serious illnesses.

Vaccination

Another way to develop an immunity is to receive a **vaccine.** Vaccines contain small amounts of weakened or dead pathogens that stimulate an immune response. Your B cells are called into action to create antibodies as if you were fighting the real illness. The pathogens are usually weakened or dead so that you will not get sick, yet they still enable your body to develop an active immunity.

Today we have vaccines for many common pathogens. Most children who are vaccinated will not get many diseases that their great grandparents, grandparents, and even parents had. Vaccinations can be administered by injection or by mouth. Babies are not the only ones who get them, either. You can be vaccinated at any age.

 **CHECK YOUR READING** Why don't vaccinations usually make you sick?

FLORIDA
Content Review

The immune system fights viruses with antibodies. Viruses are pathogens that do not usually respond to antibiotics. You learned about viruses in grade 6.

Treatment

Not all diseases can be prevented, but many of them can be treated. In some cases, treatments can only reduce the symptoms of the disease while the immune system fights the disease-causing pathogens. Other treatments attack the pathogens directly.

In some cases, treatment can only prevent further damage to body tissues by a pathogen that cannot be cured or defeated by the immune system. The way in which a disease is treated depends on what pathogen causes it. Many bacterial infections can be treated with antibiotics. **Antibiotics** are medicines that block the growth and reproduction of bacteria. You may have taken antibiotics when you have had a disease such as strep throat or an ear infection. Other types of medicine can help fight infections caused by viruses, fungi, and parasites.

Types of Pathogens	
Disease	**Pathogen**
Colds, chicken pox, hepatitis, AIDS, influenza, mumps, measles, rabies	virus
Food poisoning, strep throat, tetanus, tuberculosis, acne, ulcers, Lyme disease	bacteria
Athlete's foot, thrush, ringworm	fungus
Malaria, parasitic pneumonia, pinworm, scabies	parasites

18.2 Review

KEY CONCEPTS

1. Make a chart showing three ways that foreign material enters the body and how the immune system defends against each type of attack.

2. What are white blood cells and what is their function in the body?

3. What are two ways to develop immunity?

CRITICAL THINKING

4. **Compare and Contrast** Make a chart comparing B cells and T cells. Include an explanation of the function of antibodies.

5. **Apply** Describe how your immune system responds when you scrape your knee.

CHALLENGE

6. **Hypothesize** Explain why, even if a person recovers from a cold, that person could get a cold again.

Pollen Counts

MATH TUTORIAL
CLASSZONE.COM
Click on Math Tutorial for more help making line graphs.

Every year, sometime between July and October, in nearly every state in the United States, the air will fill with ragweed pollen. For a person who has a pollen allergy, these months blur with tears. Linn County, Iowa, takes weekly counts of ragweed and non-ragweed pollen.

Weekly Pollen Counts, Linn County, Iowa										
	Jul. 29	Aug. 5	Aug. 12	Aug. 19	Aug. 26	Sept. 2	Sept. 9	Sept. 16	Sept. 23	Sept. 30	Oct. 7
Ragweed (Grain/m^3)	0	9	10	250	130	240	140	25	20	75	0
Non-Ragweed (Grain/m^3)	10	45	15	50	100	50	40	10	20	25	0

Example

A line graph of the data will show the pattern of increase and decrease of ragweed pollen in the air.

(1) Begin with a quadrant with horizontal and vertical axes.

(2) Mark the weekly dates at even intervals on the horizontal axis.

(3) Starting at 0 on the vertical axis, mark even intervals of 50 units.

(4) Graph each point. Connect the points with line segments.

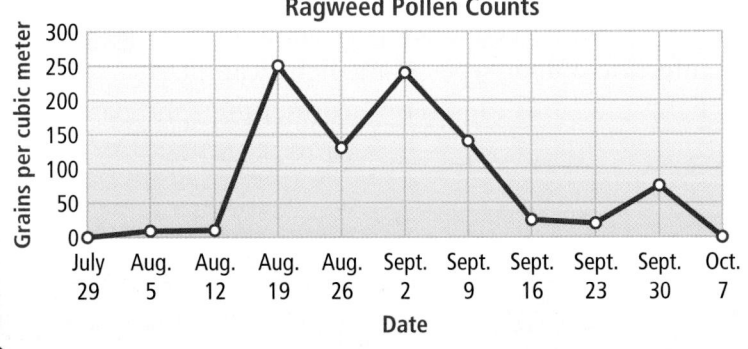

Complete and present your graph as directed below.

1. Use graph paper to make your own line graph of the non-ragweed pollen in Linn County.

2. Write some questions that can be answered by comparing the two graphs. Trade questions with a partner.

3. Which weeks have the highest pollen counts in Linn County?

CHALLENGE Try making a double line graph combining both sets of data in one graph.

The pollen of *Ambrosia artemisiifolia* (common ragweed) sets off a sneeze.

KEY CONCEPT

The integumentary system shields the body.

Sunshine State STANDARDS

SC.F.1.3.1: The student understands that living things are composed of major systems that function in reproduction, growth, maintenance, and regulation.

SC.H.3.3.4: The student knows that technological design should require taking into account constraints such as natural laws, the properties of the materials used, and economic, political, social, ethical, and aesthetic values.

BEFORE, you learned

• The body is defended from harmful materials
• Response structures fight disease
• The immune system responds in many ways to illness

NOW, you will learn

• About the functions of the skin
• How the skin helps protect the body
• How the skin grows and heals

VOCABULARY

integumentary system p. 649

epidermis p. 650

dermis p. 650

EXPLORE The Skin

What are the functions of skin?

PROCEDURE

1. Using a vegetable peeler, remove the skin from an apple. Take notes on the characteristics of the apple's peeled surface. Include observations on its color, moisture level, and texture.

2. Place the apple on a dry surface. After fifteen minutes, note any changes in its characteristics.

WHAT DO YOU THINK?

• What is the function of an apple's skin? What does it prevent?
• What does this experiment suggest about how skin might function in the human body?

MATERIALS

• vegetable peeler
• apple

Skin performs important functions.

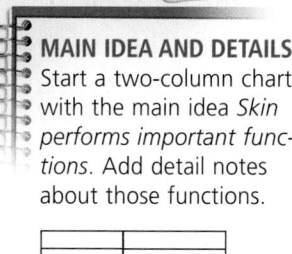

MAIN IDEA AND DETAILS
Start a two-column chart with the main idea *Skin performs important functions*. Add detail notes about those functions.

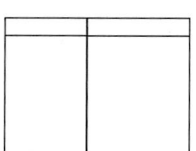

Just as an apple's skin protects the fruit inside, your skin protects the rest of your body. Made up of flat sheets of cells, your skin protects the inside of your body from harmful materials outside. The skin is part of your body's **integumentary system** (ihn-TEHG-yu-MEHN-tuh-ree), which also includes your hair and nails.

Your skin fulfills several vital functions:

• Skin repels water.
• Skin guards against infection.
• Skin helps maintain homeostasis.
• Skin senses the environment.

When you look at your hand, you only see the outer layer of skin. The skin has many structures to protect your body.

sensory receptor

nerve

oil gland

hair

blood vessels

pores

muscle

sweat gland

Epidermis: tough, protective outer layer

Dermis: strong, elastic inner layer

Fatty tissue: temperature protection and energy storage

The structure of skin is complex.

Have you ever looked closely at your skin? Your skin is more complex than it might at first seem. It does more than just cover your body. The skin is made up of many structures, which perform many different jobs.

Dermis and Epidermis

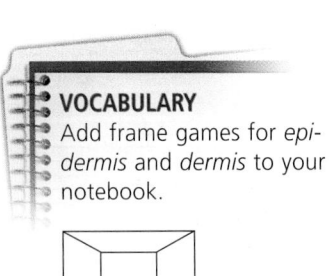

As you can see in the diagram above, human skin is composed of two layers: an outer layer, called the **epidermis,** and an inner layer, called the **dermis.** The cells of the epidermis contain many protein fibers that give the skin tough, protective qualities. These cells are formed in the deepest part of the epidermis. Skin cells move upward slowly as new cells form below them. Above new cells, older cells rub off. The surface cells in the epidermis are dead but form a thick, waterproof layer about 30 cells deep.

The dermis, the inner layer of skin, is made of tissue that is strong and elastic. The structure of the dermis allows it to change shape instead of tear when it moves against surfaces. The dermis is rich in blood vessels, which supply oxygen and nutrients to the skin's living cells. Just beneath the dermis lies a layer of fatty tissue. This layer protects the body from extremes in temperature, and it stores energy for future use. Also in the dermis are structures that have special functions, including sweat and oil glands, hair, nails, and sensory receptors.

Sweat and Oil Glands

Deep within the dermis are structures that help maintain your body's internal environment. Sweat glands help control body temperature, and oil glands protect the skin by keeping it moist. Both types of glands open to the surface through tiny openings in the skin called pores. Pores allow important substances to pass to the skin's surface. Pores can become clogged with dirt and oil. Keeping the skin clean can prevent blockages.

Sweat glands, which are present almost everywhere on the body's surface, help maintain homeostasis. When you become too warm, the sweat glands secrete sweat, a fluid that is 99% water. This fluid travels from the sweat glands, through the pores, and onto the skin's surface. You probably know already about evaporation. Evaporation is the process by which a liquid becomes a gas. During evaporation, heat is released. Thus, sweating cools the skin's surface and the body.

Like sweat glands, oil glands are present almost everywhere on the body. They secrete an oil that moistens skin and hair and keeps them from becoming dry. Skin oils add flexibility and provide part, but not all, of the skin's waterproofing.

RESOURCE CENTER
CLASSZONE.COM
Explore the structure of skin.

 **CHECK YOUR READING** What are the functions of oil glands?

INVESTIGATE Skin Protection

How does oil protect your skin?

PROCEDURE

1. Rub a cotton ball dampened with alcohol across one of your palms. Alcohol removes the oil from the surface of your skin.

2. Drip a couple of drops of water onto the palm with alcohol. Observe what happens. Record your observations.

3. Drip a couple of drops of water onto your other palm. Observe what happens. Record your observations.

WHAT DO YOU THINK?

- Compare the observations for each palm.
- What does this investigation suggest about the importance of oil and oil glands?

CHALLENGE Predict what might happen to your skin if you removed every trace of oil several times a day.

SKILL FOCUS
Observing

MATERIALS
- cotton ball
- rubbing alcohol
- dropper
- water

TIME
10 minutes

Hair and Nails

In addition to your skin, your integumentary system includes your hair and nails. Many cells in your hair and nails are actually dead but continue to perform important functions.

The hair on your head helps your body in many ways. When you are outside, it shields your head from the Sun. In cold weather, it traps heat close to your head to keep you warmer. Your body hair works the same way, but it is much less effective at protecting your skin and keeping you warm.

Fingernails and toenails protect the tips of the fingers and toes from injury. Both are made of epidermal cells that are thick and tough. They grow from the nail bed, which continues to manufacture cells as the cells that form the nail bond together and grow.

CHECK YOUR READING What are the functions of hair and nails?

145 ×

Hair

220 ×

Nails

Your hair and nails are made of dead cells, which continue to protect you.

Sensory Receptors

How does your body know when you are touching something too hot or too cold? You get that information from sensory receptors attached to the nerves. These receptors are actually part of the nervous system, but they are located in your skin. Your skin contains receptors that sense heat, cold, pain, touch, and pressure. These sensors help protect the body. For example, temperature receptors sense when an object is hot. If it is too hot and you touch it, pain receptors send signals to your brain telling you that you have been burned.

CHECK YOUR READING What are the five types of sensory receptors in skin?

The skin grows and heals.

As a person grows, skin also grows. As you have noticed if you have ever had a bruise or a cut, your skin is capable of healing. Skin can often repair itself after injury or illness.

Growth

As your bones grow, you get taller. As your muscles develop, your arms and legs become thicker. Through all your body's growth and change, your skin has to grow, too.

Most of the growth of your skin occurs at the base of the epidermis, just above the dermis. The cells there grow and divide to form new cells, constantly replacing older epidermal cells as they die and are brushed off during daily activity. Cells are lost from the skin's surface all the time: every 2 to 4 weeks, your skin surface is entirely new. In fact, a percentage of household dust is actually dead skin cells.

Healing Skin

Small injuries to the skin heal by themselves over time.

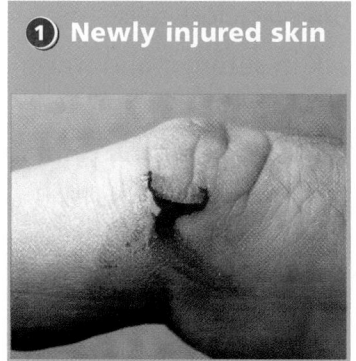

1 Newly injured skin

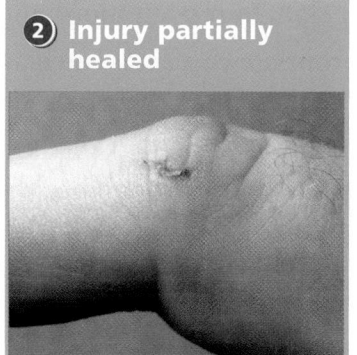

2 Injury partially healed

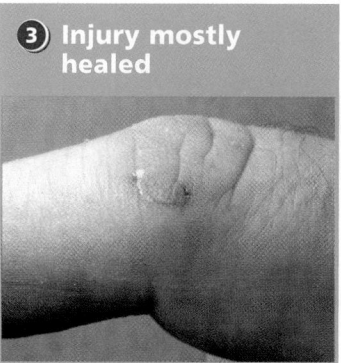

3 Injury mostly healed

READING VISUALS How do you think small injuries to the skin heal?

Injuries and Healing

You have probably experienced some injuries to your skin, such as blisters, burns, cuts, and bruises. Most such injuries result from the skin's contact with the outside world, such as a concrete sidewalk. In simple injuries, the skin can usually repair itself.

Burns can be serious injuries. They can be caused by heat, electricity, radiation, or certain chemicals. In mild cases—those of first-degree burns—skin merely becomes red, and the burn heals in a day or two. In severe cases—those of second-degree and third-degree burns—the body loses fluids, and death can result from fluid loss, infection, and other complications.

VISUALIZATION
CLASSZONE.COM

Explore how the skin heals.

Sunburns are usually minor first-degree burns, but that does not mean they cannot be serious. Rays from the Sun can burn and blister the skin much as a hot object can. Repeated burning can increase the chance of skin cancer. Specialized cells in the skin make a pigment that absorbs the Sun's ultraviolet rays and helps prevent tissue damage. These cells produce more of the skin pigment melanin when exposed to the Sun. The amount of melanin in your skin determines how dark your skin is.

Severe cold can damage skin as well. Skin exposed to cold weather can get frostbite, a condition in which the cells are damaged by freezing. Mild frostbite often heals just as well as a minor cut. In extreme cases, frostbitten limbs become diseased and have to be amputated.

 **CHECK YOUR READING** What types of weather can damage your skin?

Protection

Your skin is constantly losing old cells and gaining new cells. Although your skin is always changing, it is still important to take care of it.

- Good nutrition supplies materials the skin uses to maintain and repair itself. By drinking water, you help your body, and thus your skin, to remain moist and able to replace lost cells.

- Appropriate coverings, such as sunblock in summer and warm clothes in winter, can protect the skin from weather damage.

- Skin also needs to be kept clean. Many harmful bacteria cannot enter the body through healthy skin, but they should be washed off regularly. This prevents them from multiplying and then entering the body through small cuts or scrapes.

Wearing sunblock when you are outside protects your skin from harmful rays from the Sun.

18.3 Review

KEY CONCEPTS

1. List four functions of the skin.

2. How do the epidermis and dermis protect the body?

3. Make your own diagram with *How skin grows and repairs itself* at the center. Around the center, write at least five facts about skin growth and healing.

CRITICAL THINKING

4. **Apply** Give three examples from everyday life of sensory receptors in your skin reacting to changes in your environment.

5. **Connect** Describe a situation in which sensory receptors could be critical to survival.

CHALLENGE

6. **Infer** Exposure to sunlight may increase the number of freckles on a person's skin. Explain the connection between sunlight, melanin, and freckles.

A spray-on polymer creates an artificial outer skin to help heal surface wounds on an arm.

Artificial Skin

Skin acts like a barrier, keeping our insides in and infections out. Nobody can survive without skin. But when a large amount of skin is severely damaged, the body cannot work fast enough to replace it. In some cases there isn't enough undamaged skin left on the body for transplanting. Using skin from another person risks introducing infections or rejection by the body. The answer? Artificial skin.

Here's the Skinny

To make artificial skin, scientists start with cells in a tiny skin sample. Cells from infants are used because infant skin-cell molecules are still developing, and scientists can manipulate the molecules to avoid transplant rejection. The cells from just one small sample of skin can be grown into enough artificial skin to cover 15 basketball courts. Before artificial skin, badly burned victims didn't have much chance to live. Today, 96 out of 100 burn victims survive.

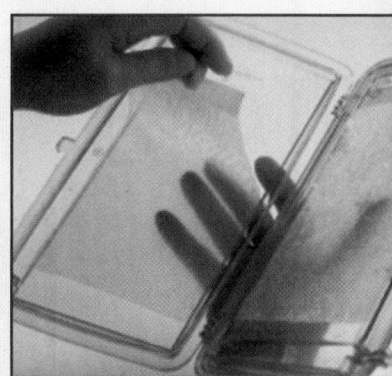

A surgeon lifts a layer of artificial skin. The skin is so thin, a newspaper could be read behind it.

What's Next?

- Scientists are hoping to be able to grow organs using this technology. Someday artificially grown livers, kidneys, and hearts may take the place of transplants and mechanical devices.

- A self-repairing plastic skin that knits itself back together when cracked has been developed. It may someday be used to create organs or even self-repairing rocket and spacecraft parts.

- Artificial polymer "skin" for robots is being developed to help robots do delicate work such as microsurgery or space exploration.

Robot designer David Hanson has developed the K-bot, a lifelike face that uses 24 motors to create expressions.

EXPLORE

1. **COMPARE AND CONTRAST** Detail the advantages and disadvantages of skin transplanted from another place on the body and artificial skin.

2. **CHALLENGE** Artificial skin is being considered for applications beyond those originally envisioned. Research and present a new potential application.

the BIG idea

Systems function to transport materials and to defend and protect the body.

KEY CONCEPTS SUMMARY

1 **The circulatory system transports materials.**

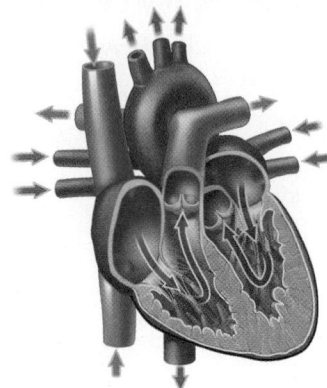

The heart, blood vessels, and blood of the circulatory system work together to transport materials from the digestive and respiratory systems to all cells. The blood exerts pressure on the walls of the blood vessels as the heart keeps the blood moving through the body.

VOCABULARY
circulatory system p. 631
blood p. 631
red blood cell p. 633
artery p. 635
vein p. 635
capillary p. 635

2 **The immune system defends the body.**

The immune system defends the body from pathogens. White blood cells identify and attack pathogens that find their way inside the body. The immune system responds to attack with inflammation, fever, and development of immunity.

Types of Pathogens	
Disease	Pathogen
colds, chicken pox, hepatitis, AIDS, influenza, mumps, measles, rabies	virus
food poisoning, strep throat, tetanus, tuberculosis, acne, ulcers, Lyme disease	bacteria
athlete's foot, thrush, ring worm	fungus
malaria, parasitic pneumonia, pinworm, scabies	parasites

VOCABULARY
pathogen p. 640
immune system p. 641
antibody p. 641
antigen p. 644
immunity p. 646
vaccine p. 646
antibiotic p. 647

3 **The integumentary system shields the body.**

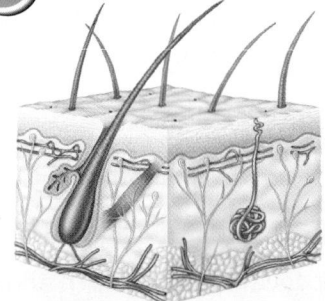

The skin protects the body from harmful materials in the environment, and allows you to sense temperature, pain, touch, and pressure. In most cases the skin is able to heal itself after injury.

VOCABULARY
integumentary system p. 649
epidermis p. 650
dermis p. 650

Draw a word triangle for each of the terms below. Write a term and its definition in the bottom section. In the middle section, write a sentence in which you use the term correctly. In the top section, draw a small picture to illustrate the term.

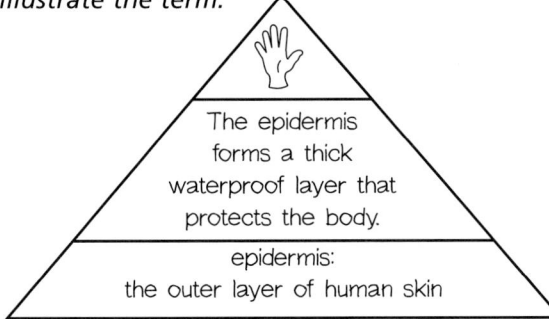

The epidermis forms a thick waterproof layer that protects the body.

epidermis: the outer layer of human skin

1. capillary

2. blood

3. dermis

4. antigen

Write a sentence describing the relationship between each pair of terms.

5. pathogen, antibody

6. artery, vein

7. immunity, vaccine

Reviewing Key Concepts

Multiple Choice *Choose the letter of the best answer.*

8. Which chamber of the heart pumps oxygen-poor blood into the lungs?
 a. right atrium
 b. right ventricle
 c. left atrium
 d. left ventricle

9. Which structures carry blood back to the heart?
 a. veins   **c.** arteries
 b. capillaries   **d.** platelets

10. The structures in the blood that carry oxygen to the cells of the body are the
 a. plasma   **c.** white blood cells
 b. platelets   **d.** red blood cells

11. High blood pressure is unhealthy because it
 a. does not exert enough pressure on your arteries
 b. causes your heart to work harder
 c. does not allow enough oxygen to get to the cells in your body
 d. causes your veins to collapse

12. Which category of pathogens causes strep throat?
 a. virus   **c.** fungus
 b. bacteria   **d.** parasite

13. Which of the following is a function of white blood cells?
 a. destroying foreign organisms
 b. providing your body with nutrients
 c. carrying oxygen to the body's cells
 d. forming a blood clot

14. Which makes up the integumentary system?
 a. a network of nerves
 b. white blood cells and antibodies
 c. the brain and spinal cord
 d. the skin, hair, and nails

15. Which structure is found in the epidermis layer of the skin?
 a. pores   **c.** hair follicles
 b. sweat glands   **d.** oil glands

16. The layer of fatty tissue below the dermis protects the body from
 a. cold temperatures   **c.** sunburn
 b. bacteria   **d.** infection

Short Response *Write a short response to each question.*

17. What are platelets? Where are they found?

18. What are antibodies? Where are they found?

19. What special structures are found in the dermis layer of the skin?

Thinking Critically

20. **COMPARE AND CONTRAST** How do the functions of the atria and ventricles of the heart differ? How are they alike? Use this diagram of the heart as a guide.

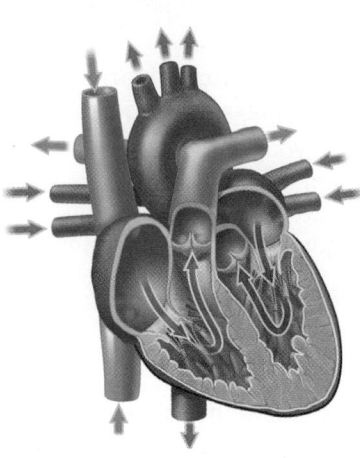

21. **APPLY** Veins have one-way valves that prevent the blood from flowing backwards. Most arteries do not have valves. Explain how these structures help the circulatory system function.

22. **PROVIDE EXAMPLES** Describe three structures in the body that help prevent harmful foreign substances from entering the body.

23. **IDENTIFY CAUSE** HIV is a virus that attacks and destroys the body's T cells. Why is a person who is infected with HIV more susceptible to infection and disease?

24. **APPLY** You fall and scrape your knee. How does the production of histamines aid the healing of this injury?

25. **ANALYZE** Describe how the structure of the epidermis helps protect the body from disease.

26. **SYNTHESIZE** Explain how sweat glands, oil glands, and hair help your body maintain homeostasis.

27. **HYPOTHESIZE** People with greater concentrations of melanin in their skin are less likely to get skin cancer than people who have lesser concentrations of melanin. Write a hypothesis explaining why this is so.

Answer the next six questions by listing the main structures and functions of the systems shown in the graphic organizer.

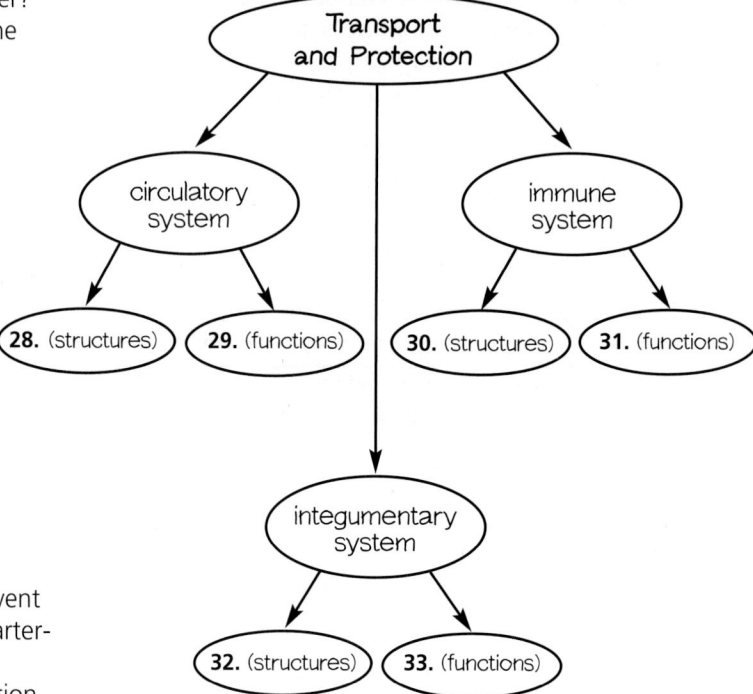

the **BIG** idea

34. **INFER** Look again at the picture on pages 628–629. Now that you have finished the chapter, how would you change or add details to your answer to the question on the photograph?

35. **SYNTHESIZE** Write a paragraph explaining how the integumentary system and the immune system work together to help your body maintain its homeostasis. Underline these terms in your paragraph.

UNIT PROJECTS

Evaluate all the data, results, and information from your project folder. Prepare to present your project. Be ready to answer questions posed by your classmates about your results.

Analyzing Data

Use the chart to answer the questions.

This chart shows the amount of time a person can stay in sunlight without burning, based on skin type and use of a sunscreen with the SPF shown.

Minimum Sun Protection Factors (SPF)

Skin Type	1 hr	2 hr	3 hr	4 hr	5 hr
Very Fair/ Sensitive	15	30	30	45	45
Fair/Sensitive	15	15	30	30	45
Fair	15	15	15	30	30
Medium	8	8	15	15	30
Dark	4	8	8	15	15

> **FCAT TiP**
>
> Always read the title of a chart and the data in the columns before you use the information to answer questions. This will help you identify the correct information you need quickly.

GRIDDED RESPONSE

1. What is the least SPF that a person with very fair skin should use while exposed to sunlight?

2. If a person with a medium skin type is exposed to sunlight for 5 hours, which SPF should be used?

MULTIPLE CHOICE

3. Which skin type requires SPF 30 for three hours of sunlight exposure?

   A. fair/sensitive   **C.** medium

   B. fair   **D.** dark

4. Based on the data in the chart, which statement is a reasonable conclusion?

   F. People with a fair skin type are less prone to UV damage than those with a dark skin type.

   G. The darker the skin type, the more SPF protection a person needs.

   H. A person with a fair skin type does not need as much SPF protection as a person with a medium skin type.

   I. If exposure to sunlight is longer, then a person needs a higher SPF for protection.

5. If a person normally burns after 10 minutes with no protection, an SPF 2 sunscreen would protect that person for 20 minutes. How long would the same person be protected with SPF 15?

   A. 1 hour   **C.** 2 hours

   B. $1\frac{1}{2}$ hours   **D.** $2\frac{1}{2}$ hours

EXTENDED RESPONSE

6. UV index levels are often broadcast with daily weather reports. A UV index of 0 to 2 indicates that it would take an average person about 60 minutes to burn. A UV index level of 10 indicates that it would take the average person about 10 minutes to burn. Write a paragraph describing some variable conditions that would affect this rate. Include both environmental as well as conditions that would apply to an individual.

7. Sun protection factors are numbers on a scale that rate the effectiveness of sunscreen. Without the use of sunscreen, UV rays from the Sun can cause sunburns. People who spend time in sunlight without protection, or who get repeated burns, are at a higher risk of developing deadly forms of skin cancer. Based on the information in the table and your knowledge of the layers of the skin, design a brochure encouraging people to protect their skin from sunlight. Include in your brochure the harmful effects on skin and ways to protect skin from harmful UV rays.

Space Science

comet

UNIVERSE

electromagnetic
radiation

telescope

Contents Overview

Frontiers in Science
Danger from the Sky   662

Florida Connection
Cape Canaveral: Step to
the Stars   666

Timelines in Science
The Story of Astronomy   736

Chapter 19 Exploring Space   670

Chapter 20 Earth, Moon,
and Sun   704

Chapter 21 Our Solar System   740

Chapter 22 Stars, Galaxies,
and the Universe   776

DANGER
from the Sky

How can astronomers find out whether a large object from space is going to strike our planet?

SCIENTIFIC AMERICAN FRONTIERS

View the video segment "Big Dish" to learn how astronomers use the largest radio telescope on Earth.

The streak of light in the photograph above was produced by a tiny particle from space burning up in Earth's atmosphere. Shown to the left is Barringer Crater in Arizona.

Collisions in Space

In the summer of 1994, telescopes all over the world were aimed at Jupiter. For the first time in history, astronomers had warning of a collision in space. Jupiter's gravity had split a comet named Shoemaker-Levy 9 into more than 20 large pieces. As the rocky objects collided with Jupiter's atmosphere, they exploded spectacularly.

Astronomers have found evidence of impacts closer to home. The craters that cover much of the Moon's surface were caused by collisions with space objects billions of years ago. In 1953 an astronomer even caught on film the bright flash of an object hitting the Moon. Other solid bodies in space also have impact craters. Little evidence of impacts remains on Earth because its surface is always changing. Fewer than 200 craters are still visible.

Earth's atmosphere protects us from collisions with small objects, which burn up in the air. However, when a large object strikes Earth, the atmosphere can spread the effects of the impact far beyond the crater. A large collision may throw dust high into the air, where it can be carried around the globe. The dust can block sunlight for months and sharply lower global temperatures.

About 65 million years ago, a large space object struck Earth. The dust from this collision can be found around the world in a layer of rock that was forming at the time. At about the same time, most species of organisms died out, including the dinosaurs. Many scientists think that the collision caused this global devastation.

The Risk of a Major Collision

When will the next space object hit Earth? A collision is probably occurring as you read this sentence. Tiny particles hit Earth's atmosphere all the time. Some of these particles have enough mass to make it through the atmosphere. Objects that reach Earth's surface are called meteorites. Most meteorites splash harmlessly into the ocean or hit unpopulated areas. Every few years a meteorite damages a home or other property. However, there is no known case of a meteorite's killing a person.

Collisions that cause widespread damage happen less often because the solar system contains fewer large objects. In 1908 a large object from space exploded above a remote region of Russia. The explosion knocked down trees across an area more than half the size of Rhode Island. Even this impact was small in comparison with major collisions that affect the entire world. Such collisions happen on average about twice every million years. Events that kill off many species occur even less often.

Tracking Asteroids

Although Earth is unlikely to have a major collision with a space object anytime soon, the danger is too great to ignore. Scientists are using telescopes to find large, rocky space objects called asteroids. After locating an asteroid, they use computer models to predict its path centuries into the future. Scientists expect that by 2008 they will have found almost all of the asteroids that could cause global devastation on Earth.

Locating objects that may threaten life on Earth is just the first step. Scientists also want to

View the "Big Dish" segment of your *Scientific American Frontiers* video to learn how astronomers are using the giant Arecibo radio telescope to explore the universe.

IN THIS SCENE FROM THE VIDEO ▶

You see a close-up of the Arecibo telescope's dome and one of its antennas.

EXPLORING ASTEROIDS An asteroid's crashing into Earth may seem like the subject of a science fiction movie. Yet asteroids pose a real danger to humans. Some asteroids could cause widespread destruction if they struck our planet.

Astronomers are tracking these asteroids to determine how close they will pass to Earth in the future.

Asteroids are too faint to be viewed clearly with optical telescopes on Earth. However, radio telescopes can provide detailed images of asteroids. Inside the dome of the Arecibo telescope is the world's most powerful radar transmitter. The transmitter can bounce a beam of radio waves off the telescope's dish to reach an asteroid millions of miles away. The telescope picks up returning signals, which are converted into images.

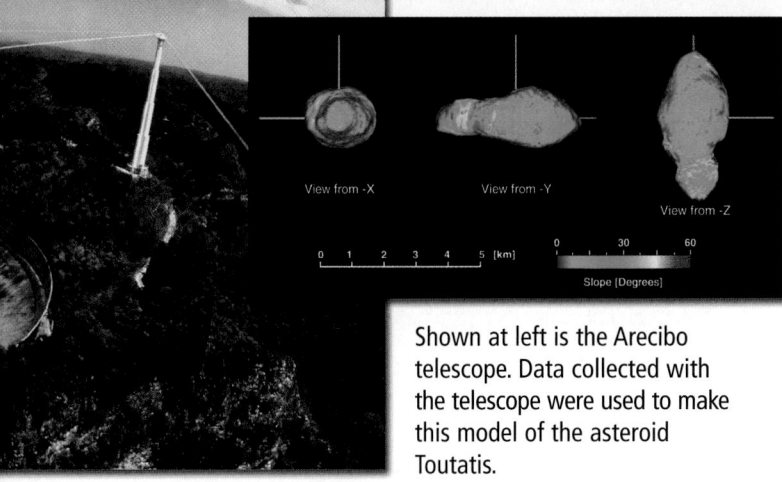

Shown at left is the Arecibo telescope. Data collected with the telescope were used to make this model of the asteroid Toutatis.

learn about the characteristics of asteroids. The Arecibo telescope in Puerto Rico is an important tool for studying asteroids. The largest radio dish in the world, it allows scientists to determine the motions and shapes of asteroids. Computer models and tests with real materials provide additional information about the mass, materials, and structure of each asteroid.

If scientists ever find an asteroid headed toward Earth, these studies may help us change the asteroid's course safely. Remember the comet that struck Jupiter in many pieces? If an asteroid broke apart before reaching Earth, pieces hitting different locations could cause even more damage than a single impact. Before using a bomb or laser to change the course of an asteroid, governments must make sure that the asteroid will not break apart. Fortunately, scientists would have decades to study a dangerous asteroid and figure out what action to take.

UNANSWERED Questions

Scientists are learning about the risk of an asteroid's colliding with Earth. The more we learn about collisions in space, the more questions we have.

- What methods can be used to change the course of an asteroid that threatens Earth?

- How can we make sure that an asteroid will not break apart because of our efforts to change its course?

- How many smaller but still dangerous objects may be headed toward Earth?

FLORIDA Connection

CAPE CANAVERAL
Step to the Stars

Sunshine State Standards

In "Step to the Stars" you'll learn how human actions can have both positive and negative effects on an ecosystem. **(SC.G.2.3.4)**

Space shuttles lift off amid some of the most diverse wildlife in the country.

Cape Canaveral is located adjacent to Merritt Island off Florida's east coast.

A Nice Place to Start

Why did the United States select Cape Canaveral, a tiny sliver of land on an island off the east central Florida coast, as the place to start the space program? It's simple: location. Cape Canaveral happens to be in a good location for launching rockets into space. The National Aeronautic and Space Administration (NASA) has centers all over the United States, but anyone who thinks of the U.S. space program most likely thinks of this cape adjacent to to Merritt Island.

The area around Cape Canaveral is a good place to launch rockets for some of the same reasons people like living in and visiting Florida—the sunshine and the ocean. Florida's sunny climate allows launches at all times of the year. Launching rockets near the ocean ensures that, in case of an accident, debris will not fall on heavily populated areas. In addition the chain of Atlantic islands to the southeast provides spots to monitor the rockets launched from the cape.

Finally, Cape Canaveral is one of the nearest points to the equator in the United States. Rockets are assisted in getting into orbit by a little push from the Earth, because Earth spins the fastest at the equator.

The Space Age

Rocket engine testing began at Cape Canaveral in the early 1950s. By the middle of that decade, scientists and engineers began to think it would be possible to use a rocket to lift artificial satellites into orbit. A satellite is any object that orbits another object in outer space. The Moon, for example, is a natural satellite of the Earth. On January 31, 1958, a rocket called the Jupiter C lifted the 14-kilogram *Explorer 1* satellite into orbit. It was a landmark day in the history of U.S. space exploration.

Explorer 1 Many things were significant about putting a satellite into orbit. While 14 kilograms may not sound like a large mass, the force needed to lift it into orbit is tremendous. Scientists could easily determine how much force was needed. Producing that force with a rocket engine was another matter. The engineers who built the rocket that lifted *Explorer 1* into space relied on the contributions of many other engineers working in many countries.

Explorer 1 detected the existence of a belt of radiation around the Earth. This was named the Van Allen Radiation Belt, after Dr. James Van Allen, who designed the experiment on the satellite that detected it. The people planning the future of space travel were very concerned about the Van Allen Belt. They didn't know whether or not the radiation might prove harmful to future human space travelers.

Vanguard 1 The second satellite successfully launched from the cape, the *Vanguard 1,* had a mass of only about 1.47 kilograms. Don't let its size fool you. *Vanguard 1* also is responsible for many significant scientific and engineering triumphs. It carried the first solar cells, or batteries, used on a satellite. These cells were recharged by exposure to solar radiation. Studying the orbit of *Vanguard 1,* scientists confirmed that the Earth wasn't a perfect sphere but had a slight bulge. These measurements suggested that there was a lot of pressure inside of the Earth. This information supported the idea that the ocean floor was spreading and the continents had drifted. *Vanguard 1* has traveled a distance equivalent to over 30 round trips to the Sun. It is expected to remain in Earth's orbit, if no dramatic changes occur, for a long time to come.

Crewed Flight Cape Canaveral has been the site of some of the greatest engineering triumphs of the last 60 years. It was the launch site for the first rocket to carry a U.S. astronaut into outer space (1961) and the first crewed mission to land on the Moon (1969). The Space Shuttle *Columbia,* the first reusable vehicle to go into Earth's orbit, was launched on April 12, 1981. Many other shuttle flights have been launched from the cape as well. Today, few months pass without some rocket taking off from Cape Canaveral.

History

Cape Canaveral was first inhabited by the Ais and the Timucuans, two native peoples of pre-colonial Florida. Evidence of these inhabitants can be found in the hundreds of middens, or mounds that mark the remains of past human settlements. The middens are typically several feet thick and contain the remains of coquina, whelk, and clam shells, indicating a largely seafood diet for the early settlers. A few middens also contain silver and gold acquired by the Native Americans from early Spanish settlers.

SPOTLIGHT ON Shuttles and Wildlife

Environmentalists began studying the effects of rocket launches on wildlife when the space program began. The noise from a launch may startle wildlife around the area, but conditions quickly appear to return to normal. There was some concern that newer rocket fuels might introduce more pollutants into the environment, but their effects also appear to be short-lived. Also, the actual rocket launching activity is confined to such a small area that the effects would probably be minimal.

Some may even argue that the existence of the Kennedy Space Center has benefited Florida's wildlife. A large part of the center is closed to the public for security reasons. This eliminates what is often the greatest threat to wildlife—human beings. The manatee population, in fact, has increased significantly since NASA has occupied the

region. The manatees discovered that boats weren't allowed into certain areas. The 69 kilometers (43 mi) of protected beach along the coast receives little sewage and industrial or agricultural fallout. The water near the cape is extremely clean.

There is a great deal of activity before a space launch. People and vehicles are constantly moving around the launch area, and this activity likely frightens the wildlife away from the area before harm can come to them. When a space shuttle lands, special crews patrol the area to ensure that no wildlife get in the way. Rumor has it that occasionally a crew will need to remove an alligator that has found the runway a nice place for sunbathing.

Cape Canaveral National Wildlife Reserve protects some unique species of plants and animals.

Ponce de Leon is credited as being the first European explorer of the region in 1513, but earlier maps showing the region in rough outline have been found. Many historians think the cape received its name almost by mistake. In Spanish, the name *Cape Canaveral* literally means "point of reeds" or "point of canes," and sailors may have called it that because they thought they saw sugar cane growing on the shore. Although sugar cane did not originally grow on the cape, a type of bamboo reed that looks a great deal like sugar cane did. Most likely, the sailors mistook the bamboo reed for sugar cane.

The shallow waters around the Florida coast caused many shipwrecks. Treasure hunters have cruised the cape in search of lost valuables.

More than Rocket Science

Cape Canaveral is more than a place for rockets. The cape has estuaries, marshes, and coastal dunes. The cape houses populations of scrub oaks, palm and oak hammocks, and pine flatwoods. It is a home for some of the state's endangered species, like manatees, wood storks, and sea turtles as well as a refuge for migratory birds.

The Merritt Island National Wildlife Refuge was established in 1963 to provide a buffer zone for NASA activities. The refuge preserves the habitat of some 1000 plant and 500 wildlife species. It offers numerous opportunities for observing one of the largest varieties of birds in the United States.

Despite determined efforts to preserve the barrier island ecosystem about the cape, it remains threatened. Plants like the Brazilian pepper (*Schinus terebinthifolius*), the Australian pine (*Casuarina equisetifolia*), and cogon grass (*Imperata cylindrica*) threaten the native plant populations. Currently, action is being taken to prevent coyotes (*Canis latrans*) from invading the region. Ask many of the cape's nearby residents, however, and they probably would say that the area's biggest pests are the hordes of mosquitoes that appear during wet periods. The mosquitoes can be a great discomfort for the people who live and work in the area.

 ASKING Questions

- What other things would you like to know about Cape Canaveral?

- What other things would you like to know about the space program?

RESOURCE CENTER

Visit **ClassZone.com** for more information on Cape Canaveral.

WRITING ABOUT SCIENCE

You work at a travel agency and are asked to write a travel brochure for Cape Canaveral. What about the cape would you emphasize? How might you try to attract different visitors?

Writing Tips

Plan, draft, and revise your writing using the tips below.

- Look through the article to find interesting facts about Cape Canaveral.

- Arrange the facts in different categories, such as "Scenery," "Historical Firsts," and so on.

- Determine what photos might best illustrate the brochure.

CHAPTER
19 Exploring Space

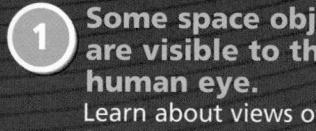

the **BIG** idea

People develop and use technology to explore and study space.

Key Concepts

SECTION

1 Some space objects are visible to the human eye.
Learn about views of space from Earth and about the arrangement of the universe.

SECTION

2 Telescopes allow us to study space from Earth.
Learn how astronomers gather information about space from different kinds of radiation.

SECTION

3 Spacecraft help us explore beyond Earth.
Learn how astronauts and instruments provide information about space.

SECTION

4 Space exploration benefits society.
Learn about the benefits of space exploration.

FCAT Practice

Prepare and practice for the FCAT
- Section Reviews, pp. 678, 683, 693, 698
- Chapter Review, pp. 700–702
- FCAT Practice, p. 703

CLASSZONE.COM
- Florida Review: Content Review and FCAT Practice

What challenges must be overcome in space exploration?

Why Does the Sun Appear to Move Around Earth?

Stand in front of a floor lamp, and turn around slowly. Notice how the lamp moves within your field of vision.

Observe and Think
Why did the lamp seem to move?

What Colors Are in Sunlight?

In bright sunlight, hold a clear plastic pen over a box. Move the pen until a rainbow pattern appears.

Observe and Think
What colors did you see? What might have caused them to appear?

Internet Activity: Universe

Go to **ClassZone.com** to simulate moving through different levels of scale in the universe.

Observe and Think How much of the universe could you see without a telescope?

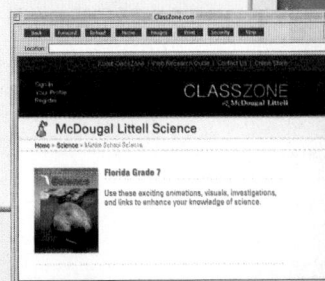

NSTA
scilinks.org
SCiLINKS

Space Probes **Code: MDL057**

Getting Ready to Learn

◀ CONCEPT REVIEW

- There are more stars in the sky than anyone can easily count.
- Telescopes magnify the appearance of distant objects in the sky.
- Once an invention exists, people are likely to think up new ways of using it.

◀ VOCABULARY REVIEW

See Glossary for definitions.

data

energy

gravity

technology

FLORIDA REVIEW
CLASSZONE.COM

Content Review and FCAT Practice

▶ TAKING NOTES

MAIN IDEA WEB

Write each new blue heading, or main idea, in the center box. In the boxes around it, take notes about important terms and details that relate to the main idea.

VOCABULARY STRATEGY

Think about a vocabulary term as a **magnet word** diagram. Write the other terms or ideas related to that term around it.

See the Note-Taking Handbook on pages R45–R51.

SCIENCE NOTEBOOK

The constellations change position in the night sky as Earth rotates.

Polaris is located straight over the North Pole.

The sky seems to turn as Earth rotates.

Polaris can help you figure out direction and location.

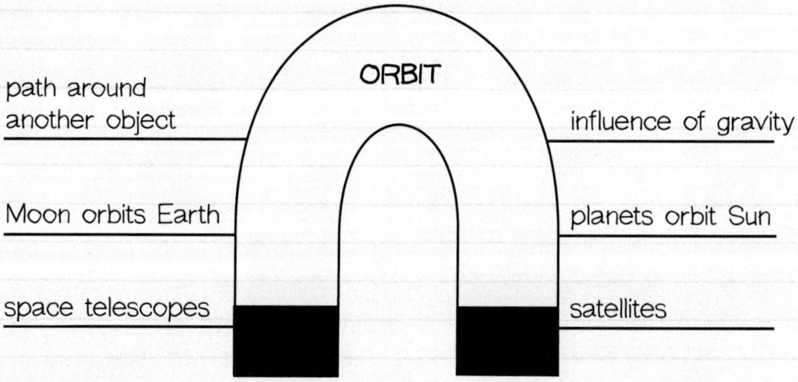

ORBIT

path around another object

influence of gravity

Moon orbits Earth

planets orbit Sun

space telescopes

satellites

KEY CONCEPT

Some space objects are visible to the human eye.

Sunshine State STANDARDS

SC.C.2.3.7: The student knows that gravity is a universal force that every mass exerts on every other mass.

SC.E.1.3.3: The student understands that our Sun is one of many stars in our galaxy.

SC.H.2.3.1: The student recognizes that patterns exist within and across systems.

FCAT VOCABULARY

solar system p. 674
galaxy p. 674
universe p. 674
constellation p. 676

VOCABULARY

orbit p. 674

◁ BEFORE, you learned

• Earth is one of nine planets that orbit the Sun
• The Moon orbits Earth
• Earth turns on its axis every 24 hours

▷ NOW, you will learn

• How the universe is arranged
• How stars form patterns in the sky
• How the motions of bodies in space appear from Earth

EXPLORE Distance

How far is the Moon from Earth?

PROCEDURE

1. Tie one end of the string around the middle of the tennis ball. The tennis ball will represent Earth.

2. Wrap the string 9.5 times around the tennis ball, and make a mark on the string at that point. Wrap the aluminum foil into a ball around the mark. The foil ball will represent the Moon.

3. Stretch out the string to put the model Moon and Earth at the right distance compared to their sizes.

MATERIALS

• tennis ball
• aluminum foil (5 cm strip)
• string (250 cm)
• felt marker

WHAT DO YOU THINK?

• How does the scale model compare with your previous idea of the distance between Earth and the Moon?
• How many Earths do you estimate would fit between Earth and the Moon?

We see patterns in the universe.

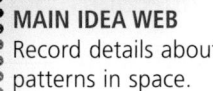
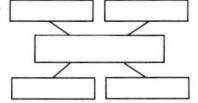

MAIN IDEA WEB
Record details about patterns in space.

For most of history, people had very limited knowledge of space. They saw planets and stars as points of light in the night sky. However, they did not know how far those bodies were from Earth or from each other. Early observers made guesses about planets and stars on the basis of their appearance and the ways they seemed to move in the sky. Different peoples around the world connected the patterns they saw in the sky with stories about imaginary beings.

Chapter 19: **Exploring Space 673**

We still have much to learn about the universe. Within the last few hundred years, however, new tools and scientific theories have greatly increased our knowledge. In this chapter you will learn about the arrangement of planets and stars. You will also learn about the ways in which astronomers explore and study space.

Arrangement of the Universe

If you look up at the sky on a clear night, you will see only a tiny fraction of the planets and stars that exist. The number of objects in the universe and the distances between them are greater than most people can imagine. Yet these objects are not spread around randomly. Gravity causes objects in space to be grouped together in different ways.

The images on page 675 show some basic structures in the universe. Like a camera lens zooming out, the images provide views of space at different levels of size.

READING **TiP**

The word *orbit* can be a noun or a verb.

1 **Earth** Our planet's diameter is about 13,000 kilometers (8000 mi). This is almost four times the diameter of the Moon, which orbits Earth. An **orbit** is the path of an object in space as it moves around another object because of gravity.

2 **Solar System** Earth and eight other major planets orbit the Sun. The Sun, the planets, and various smaller bodies make up the **solar system.** The Sun is about 100 times greater in diameter than Earth. You could fit more than 4000 bodies the size of the Sun between the Sun and the solar system's outermost planet at its average distance from the Sun. The Sun is one of countless stars in space. Astronomers have detected planets orbiting some of these other stars.

3 **The Milky Way** Our solar system and the stars you can see with your bare eyes are part of a galaxy called the Milky Way. A **galaxy** is a group of millions or billions of stars held together by their own gravity. If the solar system were the size of a penny, the Milky Way would stretch from Chicago to Dallas. Most stars in the Milky Way are so far away that our galaxy appears to us as a hazy band of light.

4 **The Universe** The **universe** is everything—space and all the matter and energy in it. The Milky Way is just one of many billions of galaxies in the universe. These galaxies extend in all directions.

Astronomers study space at each of these different levels. Some focus on planets in the solar system. Other astronomers study distant galaxies. To learn how the universe formed, astronomers even study the smallest particles that make up all matter.

CHECK YOUR READING   What is the relationship between the solar system and the Milky Way?

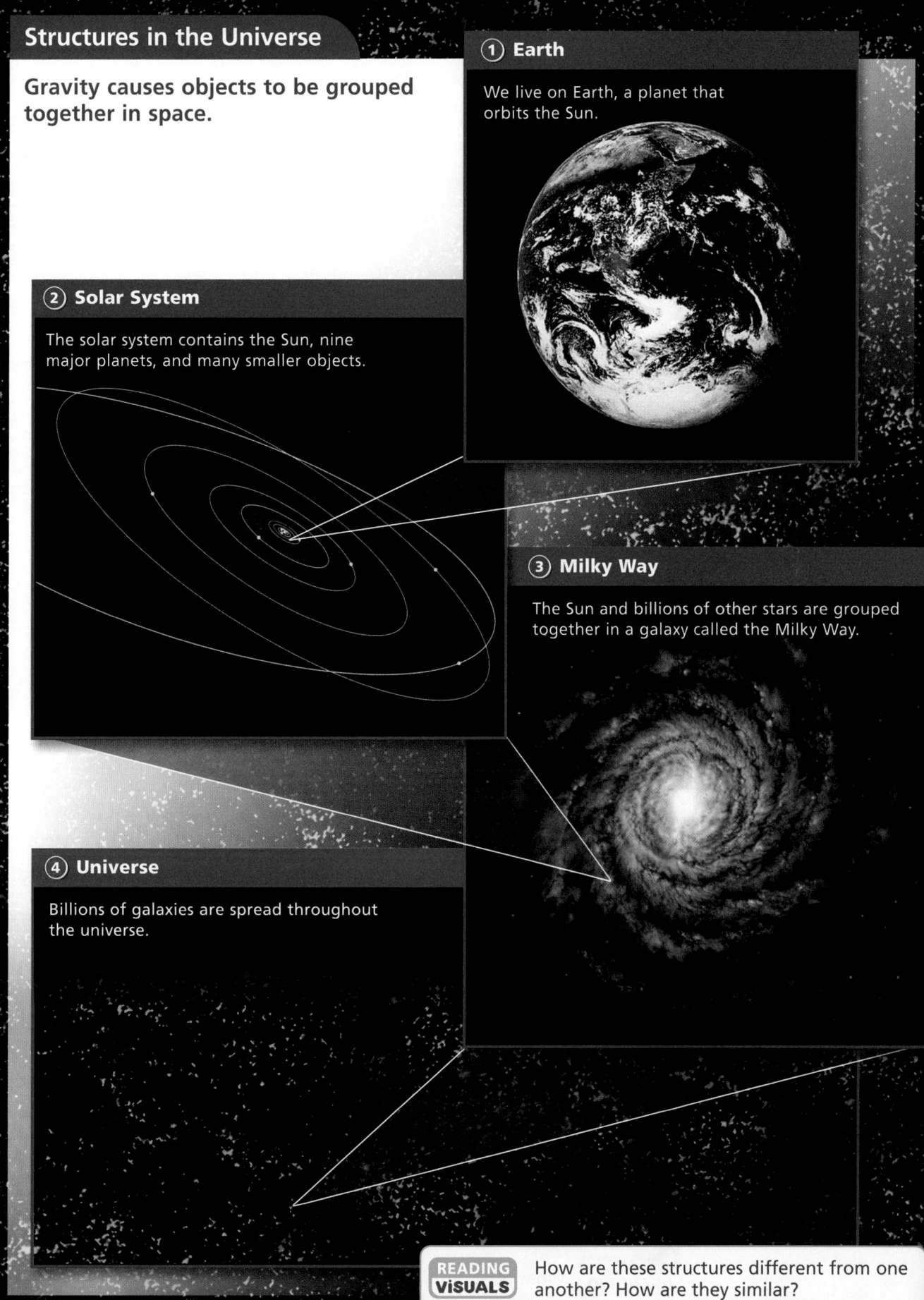

Structures in the Universe

Gravity causes objects to be grouped together in space.

① Earth

We live on Earth, a planet that orbits the Sun.

② Solar System

The solar system contains the Sun, nine major planets, and many smaller objects.

③ Milky Way

The Sun and billions of other stars are grouped together in a galaxy called the Milky Way.

④ Universe

Billions of galaxies are spread throughout the universe.

READING VISUALS How are these structures different from one another? How are they similar?

Constellation Patterns

The stars of a constellation are often far apart from one another, but they appear grouped together when viewed from Earth.

Cygnus (the Swan)

Albireo

Gienah Cygni

Delta Cygni

Sadr

Deneb

1500 light-years

1000 light-years

500 light-years

1 light-year = 9.5 trillion kilometers

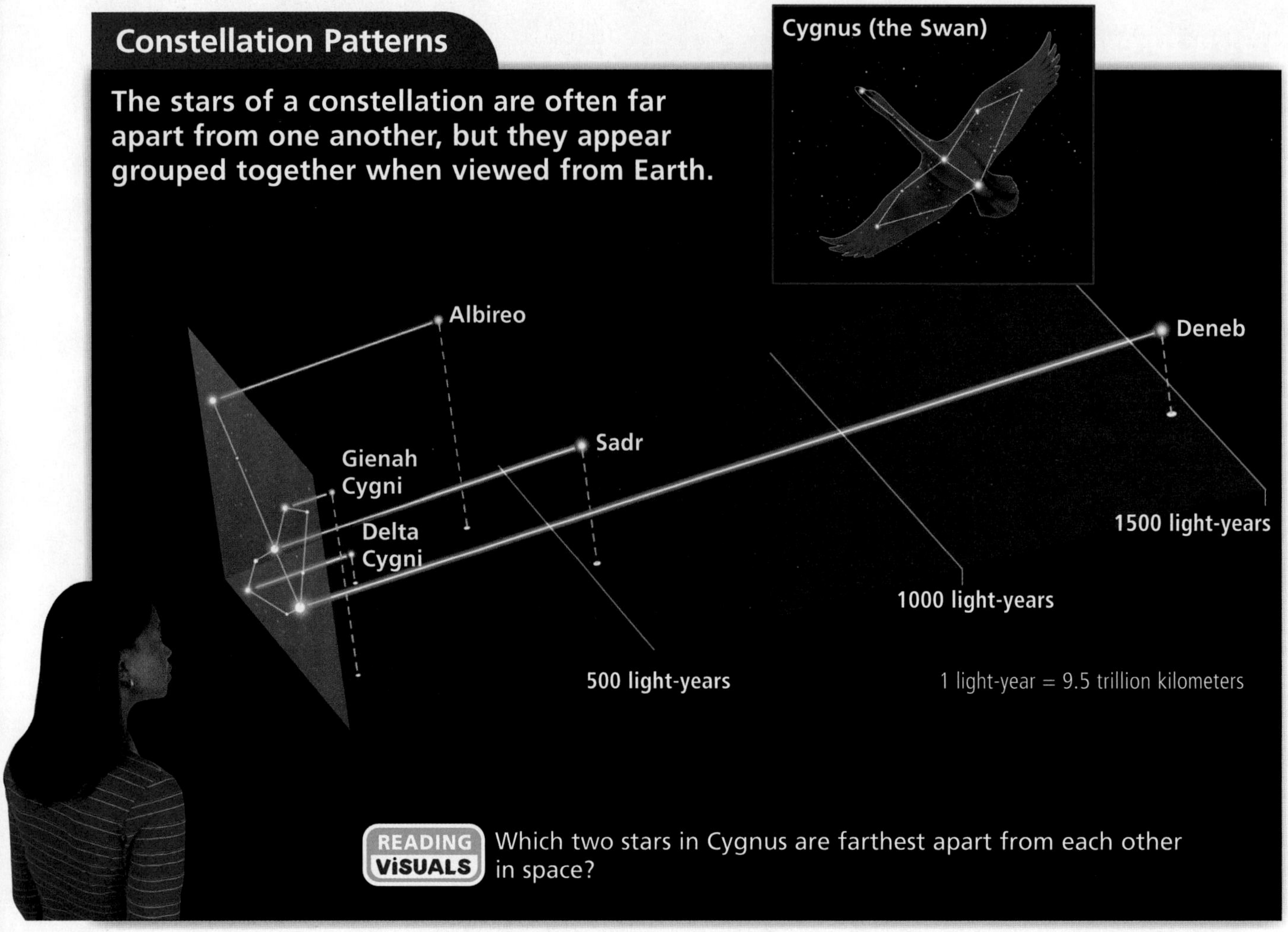

READING VISUALS Which two stars in Cygnus are farthest apart from each other in space?

VISUALIZATION
CLASSZONE.COM

View images of the night sky taken throughout the year.

Constellations

If you want to find a particular place in the United States, it helps to know the name of the state it is in. Astronomers use a similar system to describe the locations of objects in the sky. They have divided the sky into 88 areas named for the constellations.

A **constellation** is a group of stars that form a pattern in the sky. In the constellation Cygnus, for example, a group of bright stars form the shape of a flying swan. Any other objects in that area of the sky, such as galaxies, are said to be located in Cygnus, even if they are not parts of the swan pattern. The ancient Greeks named many of the constellations for animals and imaginary beings.

Unlike the planets in the solar system, the stars in a constellation are usually not really close to each other. They seem to be grouped together when viewed from Earth. But as the illustration above shows, you would not see the same pattern in the stars if you viewed them from another angle.

 **CHECK YOUR READING** What relationship exists among the stars in a constellation?

The sky seems to turn as Earth rotates.

You cannot see all of the constellations at once, because Earth blocks half of space from your view. However, you can see a parade of constellations each night as Earth rotates. As some constellations slowly come into view over the eastern horizon, others pass high in the sky above you, and still others set at the western horizon. Throughout the ages, many peoples have observed these changes and used them to help in navigation and measuring time.

If you extended the North Pole into space, it would point almost exactly to a star called Polaris, or the North Star. If you were standing at the North Pole, Polaris would be directly over your head. As Earth rotates through the night, the stars close to Polaris seem to move in circles around it. Although not the brightest star in the sky, Polaris is fairly bright and easy to find. You can use Polaris to figure out direction and location.

The stars in this image were photographed over several hours to show how they move across the night sky.

 **CHECK YOUR READING** What causes constellations to change positions during the night?

INVESTIGATE Constellation Positions

How does time of day affect the positions of constellations?

PROCEDURE

1. Cut out both diagrams on the Constellation Wheel Sheet and assemble them as shown.

2. Rotate the wheel so that the current month is aligned with 9 P.M. Observe the positions of the constellations.

3. Align the current month with other times to determine how the positions of the constellations change during the night.

WHAT DO YOU THINK?

- How do the positions of the constellations change during the night?
- In which direction does the northern sky seem to turn?

CHALLENGE Earth's rotation makes the sky seem to turn. What does the model tell you about the direction of Earth's rotation?

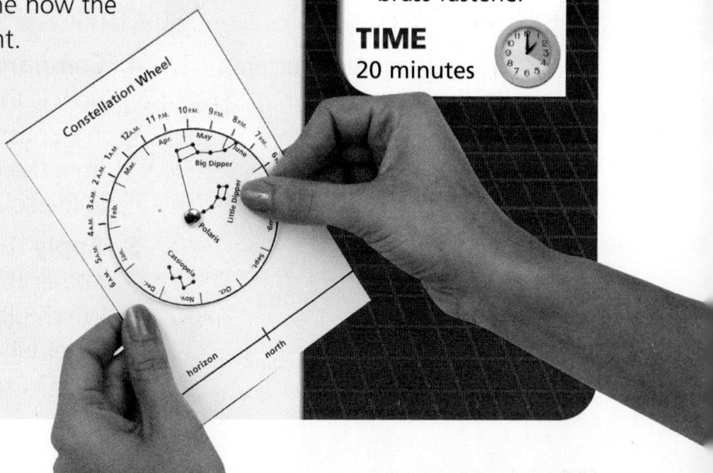

SKILL FOCUS
Analyzing

MATERIALS
- Constellation Wheel Sheet
- scissors
- brass fastener

TIME
20 minutes

The movements of planets and other nearby objects are visible from Earth.

A jet plane travels at a greater speed and altitude than a bird. Yet if a bird and a plane flew overhead at the same time, you might think that the bird was faster. You would have this impression because the farther away a moving object is from you, the less it seems to move.

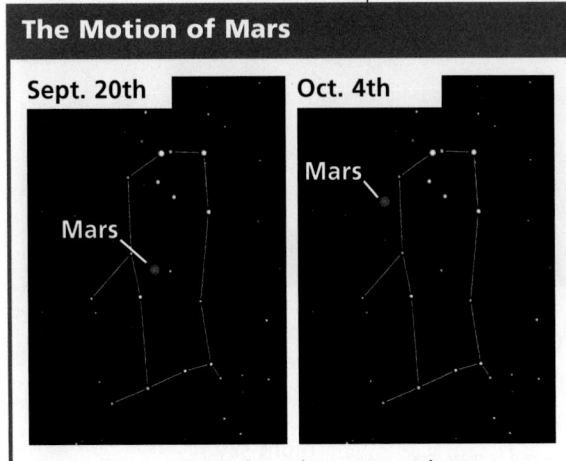

The Motion of Mars

Sept. 20th

Mars

Oct. 4th

Mars

These illustrations show how Mars changes positions in the constellation Gemini over a period of two weeks.

Stars are always moving, but they are so far away that you cannot see their movements. Observers have seen the same constellation patterns for thousands of years. Only over a much longer period does the motion of stars gradually change constellation patterns.

By contrast, the Moon moves across the star background a distance equal to its width every hour as it orbits Earth. The Moon is our closest neighbor. The planets are farther away, but you can see their gradual movements among the constellations over a period of weeks or months.

Planet comes from a Greek word that means "wanderer." Ancient Greek astronomers used this term because they noticed that planets move among the constellations. It is easiest to see the movements of Venus and Mars, the two planets closest to Earth. They change their positions in the sky from night to night.

The apparent movement of the sky led early astronomers to believe that Earth was at the center of the universe. Later astronomers discovered that Earth and the other planets orbit the Sun. The time-line on pages 736–739 introduces some of the astronomers who helped discover how planets really move in the solar system.

19.1 Review

KEY CONCEPTS

1. What are the basic structures in which objects are grouped together in space?

2. What is a constellation?

3. How does Earth's rotation affect our view of stars?

CRITICAL THINKING

4. **Compare and Contrast** How is the grouping of stars in a constellation different from the grouping of planets in the solar system?

5. **Apply** The planet Jupiter is farther than Mars from Earth. Which planet seems to move faster when viewed from Earth? Explain.

⬥ CHALLENGE

6. **Predict** Suppose that you are standing at the North Pole on a dark night. If you keep turning clockwise at the same speed as Earth's rotation, how would your movement affect your view of the stars?

19.2 Telescopes allow us to study space from Earth.

Sunshine State STANDARDS

SC.B.1.3.3: The student knows the various forms in which energy comes to Earth from the Sun.

SC.H.1.3.2: The student knows that the study of the events that led scientists to discoveries can provide information about the inquiry process and its effects.

SC.H.1.3.5: The student knows that a change in one or more variables may alter the outcome of an investigation.

BEFORE, you learned

- Objects in the universe are grouped together in different ways
- The motions of planets and other nearby objects are visible from Earth

NOW, you will learn

- About light and other forms of radiation
- How astronomers gather information about space

FCAT VOCABULARY
electromagnetic radiation
  p. 679
wavelength p. 680

VOCABULARY
spectrum p. 680
telescope p. 681

EXPLORE Distortion of Light

How can light become distorted?

PROCEDURE

(1) Place a white sheet of paper behind a glass filled with plain water. Shine a flashlight through the glass, and observe the spot of light on the paper.

(2) Pour a spoonful of salt into the water. Stir the water, and observe the spot of light.

WHAT DO YOU THINK?

- How did the spot of light change after you mixed the salt into the water?
- How could Earth's atmosphere cause similar changes in light from space?

MATERIALS

- flashlight
- glass filled with water
- sheet of white paper
- spoon
- salt

VOCABULARY
Add a magnet word diagram for *electromagnetic radiation* to your notebook.

Light and other forms of radiation carry information about space.

When you look at an object, your eyes are gathering light from that object. Visible light is a form of **electromagnetic radiation** (ih-LEHK-troh-mag-NEHT-ihk), which is energy that travels across distances as certain types of waves. There are other forms of electromagnetic radiation that you cannot see directly, such as radio waves and x-rays. Scientists have developed instruments to detect these other forms.

Electromagnetic radiation travels in all directions throughout space. Almost everything we know about the universe has come from our study of radiation. Astronomers can often learn about the size, distance, and movement of an object by studying its radiation. Radiation can also reveal what an object is made of and how it has changed.

The Electromagnetic Spectrum

The different forms of electromagnetic radiation vary in their wavelengths.

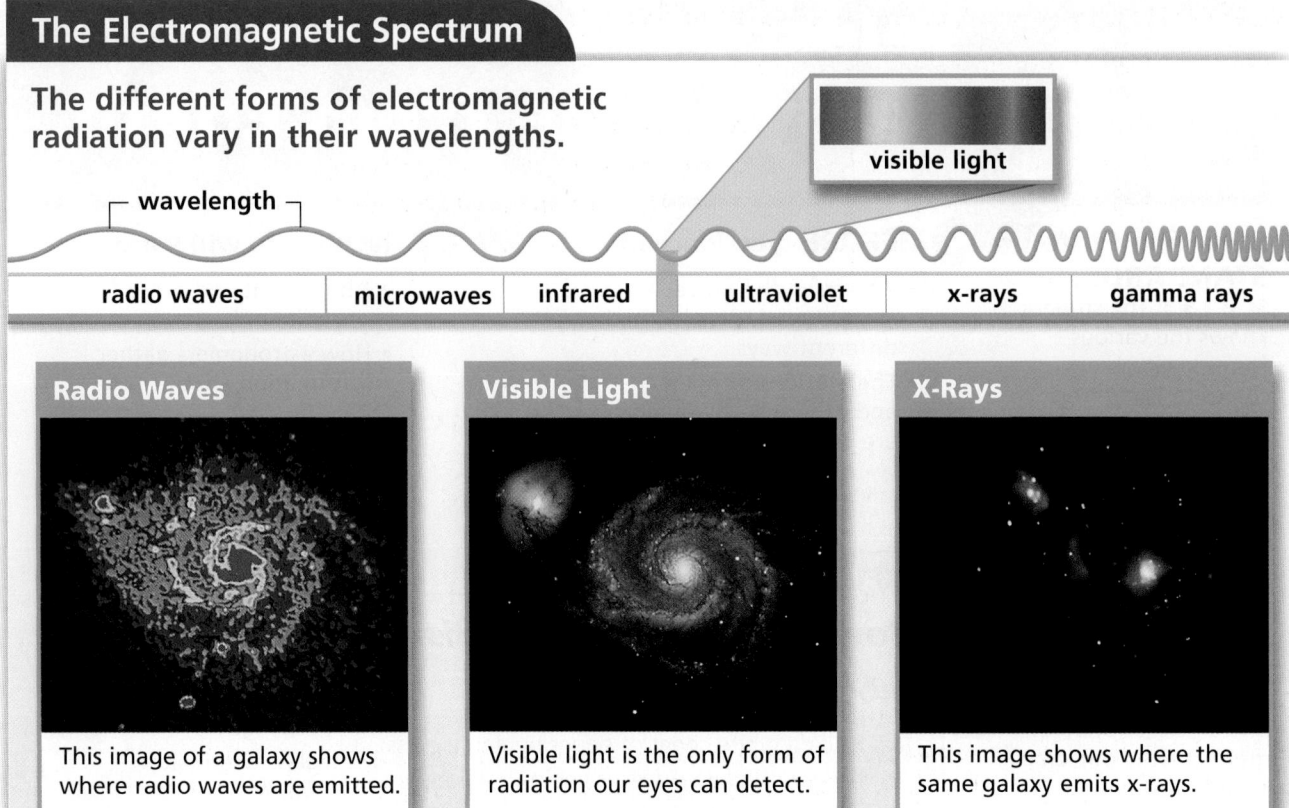

visible light

wavelength

| radio waves | microwaves | infrared | ultraviolet | x-rays | gamma rays |

Radio Waves

This image of a galaxy shows where radio waves are emitted.

Visible Light

Visible light is the only form of radiation our eyes can detect.

X-Rays

This image shows where the same galaxy emits x-rays.

READING TiP

A prism is a transparent object that is used to separate the wavelengths of light.

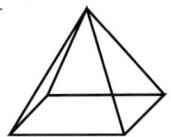

FLORIDA Content Preview

Electromagnetic waves are different from mechanical waves like ocean waves, but both carry energy. You will learn more about waves in grade 8.

If you shine a flashlight through a prism, the beam of white light will separate into a range of colors called a **spectrum** (SPEHK-truhm). The colors that make up visible light are red, orange, yellow, green, blue, indigo, and violet. These are the colors in a rainbow, which appears when light spreads out as it passes through raindrops.

In a spectrum, the colors of visible light appear in the order of their wavelengths. **Wavelength** is the distance between one wave peak and the next wave peak. Red light has the longest wavelength. Violet light has the shortest.

As you can see in the illustration above, visible light is just a tiny part of a larger spectrum called the electromagnetic spectrum. The electromagnetic spectrum includes all the forms of electromagnetic radiation. Notice that the wavelength of infrared radiation is longer than the wavelength of visible light but not as long as the wavelength of microwaves or radio waves. The wavelength of ultraviolet radiation is shorter than the wavelength of visible light but not as short as the wavelength of x-rays or gamma rays.

CHECK YOUR READING How is visible light different from other forms of electromagnetic radiation?

Astronomers use telescopes to collect information about space.

A **telescope** is a device that gathers electromagnetic radiation. If you have ever looked through a telescope, it was probably one that gathers visible light. Such telescopes provide images that are much clearer than what is seen with the naked eye. Images from other types of telescopes show radiation that your eyes cannot detect. Each form of radiation provides different information about objects in space.

Astronomers usually record images from telescopes electronically, which allows them to use computers to analyze images. Different colors or shades in an image reveal patterns of radiation. For example, in the right-hand image on page 680, the colors yellow and red indicate where the galaxy is emitting large amounts of x-rays.

Most types of telescopes gather radiation with a glass lens or a reflecting surface, such as a mirror. Larger lenses and reflecting surfaces produce brighter and more detailed images. You can magnify an image from a telescope to any size. However, enlarging an image will not bring out any more details of an object. If the image is fuzzy at a small size, it will remain fuzzy no matter how much it is enlarged.

Visible-Light, Infrared, and Ultraviolet Telescopes

There are two types of visible-light telescopes: reflecting telescopes and refracting telescopes. Reflecting telescopes can also be built to gather infrared or ultraviolet radiation.

- **Reflecting Telescope** This type of telescope has a curved mirror that gathers light. The image comes into focus in front of the mirror. Many reflecting telescopes have a second mirror that reflects the image to recording equipment or to a lens called an eyepiece.

- **Refracting Telescope** This type of telescope has an objective lens, or curved piece of glass, at one end of a long tube. The lens gathers light and focuses it to form an image near the other end of the tube. An eyepiece magnifies this image.

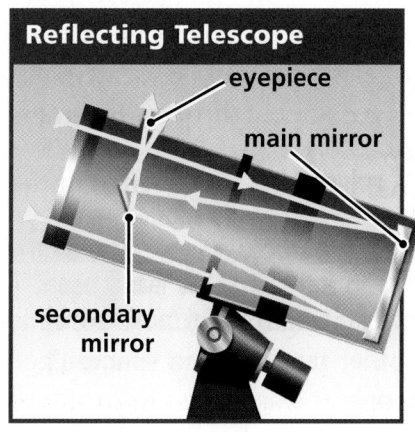

Reflecting Telescope
eyepiece
main mirror
secondary mirror

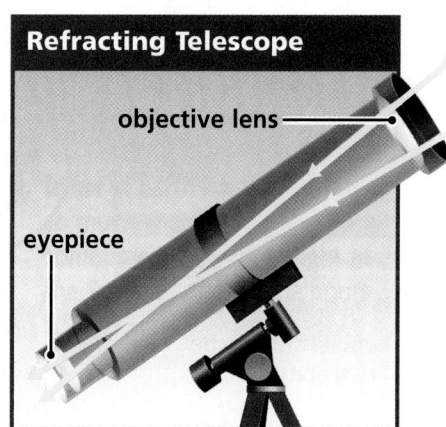

Refracting Telescope
objective lens
eyepiece

Most powerful visible-light telescopes are built on mountaintops in rural areas. Rural areas offer a much better view of the night sky than cities do, because the many electric lights in cities make dim space objects hard to see. By locating telescopes on mountaintops, astronomers reduce problems caused by Earth's atmosphere. The atmosphere interferes with light coming in from space. In fact, movements of the air are what make stars appear to twinkle. At high altitudes there is less air above the ground to interfere with light.

Radio Telescope

Radio Telescopes

Radio telescopes show where radio waves are being emitted by objects in space. A radio telescope has a curved metal surface, called a dish, that gathers radio waves and focuses them onto an antenna. The dish works in the same way as the main mirror of a reflecting telescope. Some radio telescopes have dishes made of metal mesh rather than solid metal.

Because radio waves are so long, a single radio telescope must be very large to produce useful images. To improve the quality of images, astronomers often aim a group of radio telescopes at the same object. Signals from the telescopes are combined and then converted into an image. Groups of radio telescopes, like the Very Large Array in New Mexico, can show more detail than even the largest single dish.

Signals from these radio telescopes in New Mexico can be combined to produce clearer images.

Unlike visible-light telescopes, radio telescopes are not affected by clouds or bad weather. They even work well in daylight. In addition, radio telescopes can be located at low altitudes because most radio waves pass freely through Earth's atmosphere.

 CHECK YOUR READING What is the function of the dish in a radio telescope?

 RESOURCE CENTER
CLASSZONE.COM

Find out more about telescopes.

Telescopes in Space

Many exciting images have come from the Hubble Space Telescope and other telescopes in space. The Hubble telescope is a reflecting telescope. It was placed in orbit around Earth in 1990. Astronomers operate it from the ground, although astronauts have visited it to make repairs and improvements. The telescope sends images and measurements back to Earth electronically.

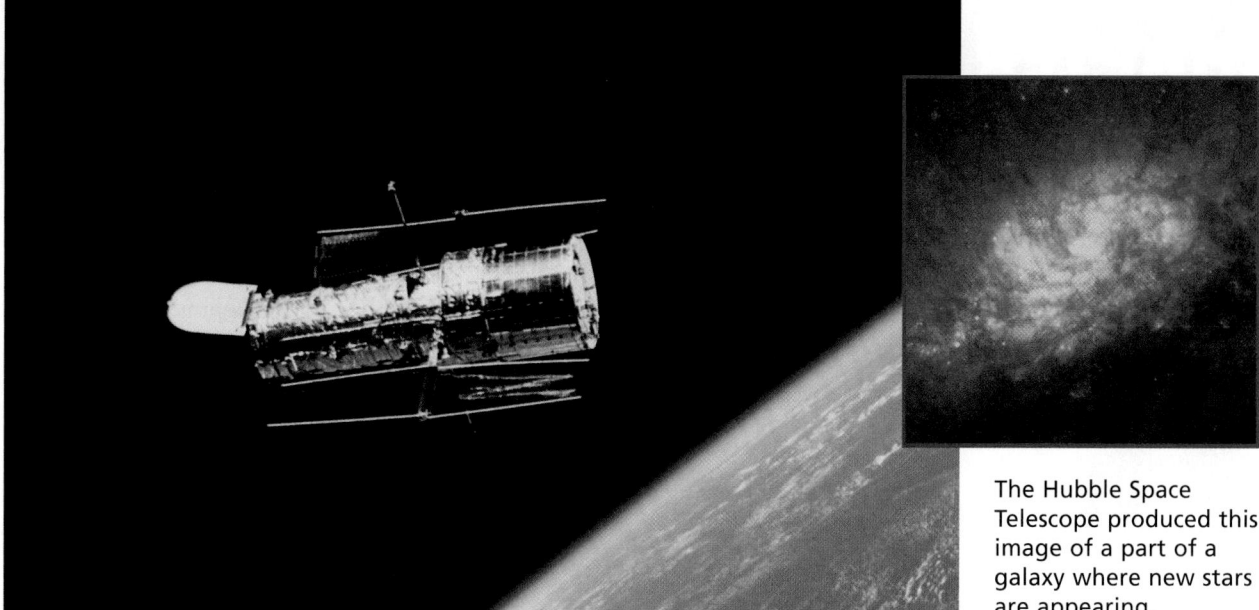

The Hubble Space Telescope produced this image of a part of a galaxy where new stars are appearing.

Because the Hubble telescope is located in space, Earth's atmosphere does not interfere with light from objects the telescope is aimed at. This lack of interference allows it to obtain clearer images than ground-based telescopes with much larger mirrors. In addition to collecting visible light, the Hubble telescope produces images of ultraviolet and infrared radiation.

The Hubble Space Telescope is part of a group of telescopes that orbit Earth. The telescopes allow astronomers to gain information from the full range of electromagnetic radiation. The Compton Gamma-Ray Observatory was sent into orbit in 1991. The Chandra X-Ray Observatory was launched eight years later. These telescopes were placed in space because Earth's atmosphere blocks most x-rays and gamma rays.

CHECK YOUR READING   Why does the Hubble telescope produce clearer images than a telescope of the same size on Earth?

19.2 Review

KEY CONCEPTS

1. How are visible light, radio waves, and other forms of electromagnetic radiation different from each other?

2. What function do mirrors serve in reflecting telescopes?

3. Why are some telescopes placed on mountains or in orbit around Earth?

CRITICAL THINKING

4. **Compare and Contrast** What are the similarities and differences between refracting telescopes and reflecting telescopes?

5. **Analyze** Why would it be difficult to build radio telescopes if they did not work well at low altitudes?

○ CHALLENGE

6. **Analyze** Why might astronomers use different types of telescopes to obtain images of the same object in space?

CHAPTER INVESTIGATION

Observing Spectra

OVERVIEW AND PURPOSE Visible light is made up of different colors that can be separated into a rainbow band called a spectrum. Astronomers gain information about the characteristics of stars by spreading their light into spectra (*spectra* is the plural form of *spectrum*). A spectroscope is a device that produces spectra. In most spectroscopes, diffraction gratings are used to separate light into different colors. The colors with the longest wavelengths appear farthest from the slit in a spectroscope. The colors with the shortest wavelengths appear closest to the slit. In this investigation you will

- build a spectroscope and observe the spectra of three different light sources
- identify ways in which the spectra of light sources differ

MATERIALS
- shoebox with lid
- ruler
- scissors
- diffraction grating
- tape
- index card
- pencils or markers in a variety of colors
- incandescent light
- fluorescent light
for Challenge:
- cellophane in several colors

▶ Procedure

1. Cut a hole measuring 3 cm by 1.5 cm in each end of a shoebox. Make sure that the holes line up.

2. On the inside of the box, tape a piece of diffraction grating over one of the holes. Handle the diffraction grating by its edges so that you do not get finger-prints on it.

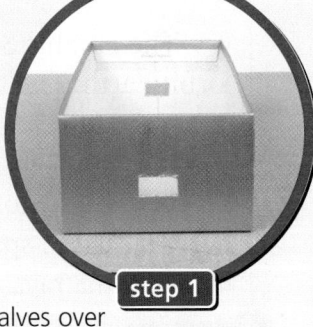

step 1

3. Cut an index card in half, and tape the halves over the outside of the other hole as shown. Leave a very narrow slit between the two halves of the index card.

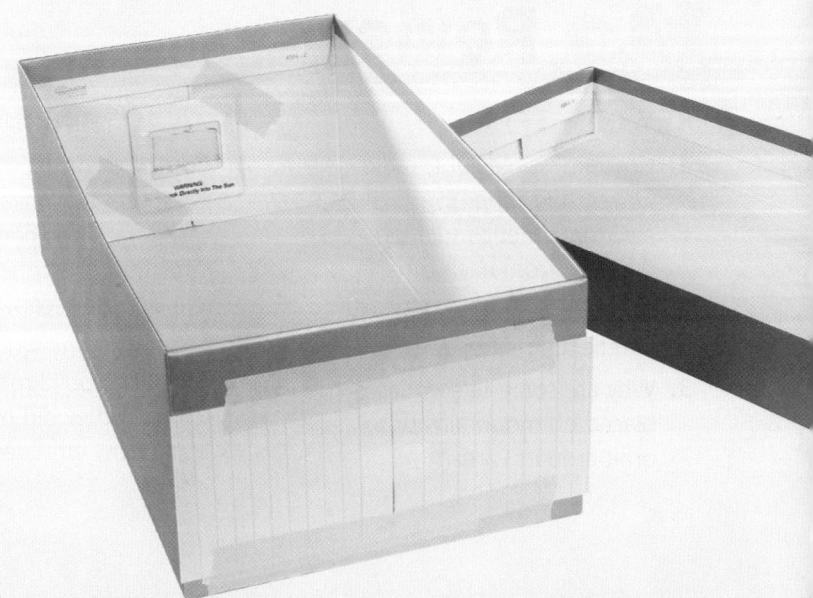

4. Put the lid on the shoebox. Then turn off the overhead lights in the classroom.

5. Look through the hole covered with the diffraction grating, aiming the spectroscope's slit at the sky through a window. **Caution:** *Never look directly at the Sun.* Observe the spectrum you see to the left of the slit.

step 5

6. Repeat step 5 while aiming the spectroscope at an incandescent light and then at a fluorescent light.

▶ Observe and Analyze
Write It Up

1. **RECORD OBSERVATIONS** For each light source, draw in your data table the spectrum you see to the left of the slit. Describe the colors and patterns in the spectrum, and label the light source.

2. **IDENTIFY LIMITS** What problems, if any, did you experience in observing the spectra? Why was it important to turn off overhead lights for this activity?

▶ Conclude
Write It Up

1. **COMPARE AND CONTRAST** How did the spectra differ from one another? Did you notice any stripes of color that were brighter or narrower than other colors in the same spectrum? Did you notice any lines or spaces separating colors?

2. **ANALYZE** The shorter the wavelength of a color, the closer it appears to the slit in a spectroscope. On the basis of your observations, which color has the shortest wavelength? Which color has the longest wavelength?

3. **INFER** How might the spectra look different if the slit at the end of the spectroscope were curved instead of a straight line?

▶ INVESTIGATE Further

CHALLENGE Cover the slit on your spectroscope with a piece of colored cellophane. Aiming the spectroscope at a fluorescent light or another light source, observe and draw the resulting spectrum. Then repeat with cellophane of other colors. List the colors that each piece of cellophane transmitted. Did these results surprise you? If so, why?

Observing Spectra
Observe and Analyze
Table 1. Spectra of Different Light Sources

Light Source	Drawing	Description

Conclude

19.3

KEY CONCEPT

Spacecraft help us explore beyond Earth.

Sunshine State STANDARDS

SC.C.2.3.7: The student knows that gravity is a universal force that every mass exerts on every other mass.

SC.H.1.3.1: The student knows that scientific knowledge is subject to modifications as new information challenges prevailing theories and as a new theory leads to looking at old observations in a new way.

BEFORE, you learned

- The motions of planets and other nearby objects are visible from Earth
- Light and other forms of radiation carry information about the universe

NOW, you will learn

- How astronauts explore space near Earth
- How different types of spacecraft are used in exploration

VOCABULARY

satellite p. 687
space station p. 688
lander p. 692
probe p. 693

EXPLORE Viewing Space Objects

How do objects appear at different distances?

PROCEDURE

1. Crumple the paper into a ball and place it on your desk.

2. Sketch the ball at the same time as another student sketches it. One of you should sketch it from a distance of 1 m. The other should sketch it from 5 m away.

WHAT DO YOU THINK?

- How do the details in the two drawings compare?
- What details might be easier to see on a planet if you were orbiting the planet?

MATERIALS
- paper
- pencils

Astronauts explore space near Earth.

Space travel requires very careful planning. Astronauts take everything necessary for survival with them, including air, water, and food. Spacecraft need powerful rockets and huge fuel tanks to lift all their weight upward against Earth's gravity. The equipment must be well designed and maintained, since any breakdown can be deadly.

Once in space, astronauts must get used to a special environment. People and objects in an orbiting spacecraft seem to float freely unless they are fastened down. This weightless condition occurs because they are falling in space at the same rate as the spacecraft. In addition, to leave their airtight cabin, astronauts must wear special protective suits. Despite these conditions, astronauts have managed to perform experiments and make important observations about space near Earth.

RESOURCE CENTER
CLASSZONE.COM

Learn more about space exploration.

Moon Missions

For about a decade, much of space exploration was focused on a race to the Moon. This race was driven by rivalry between the United States and the Soviet Union, which included Russia. In 1957 the Soviet Union launched the first artificial satellite to orbit Earth. A **satellite** is an object that orbits a more massive object. The Soviet Union also sent the first human into space in 1961. Although the United States lagged behind in these early efforts, it succeeded in sending the first humans to the Moon.

Preparation Many steps had to be taken before astronauts from the United States could visit the Moon. The National Aeronautics and Space Administration (NASA) sent spacecraft without crews to the Moon to find out whether it was possible to land on its surface. NASA also sent astronauts into space to practice important procedures.

Landings The NASA program to reach the Moon was called Apollo. During early Apollo missions, astronauts tested spacecraft and flew them into orbit around the Moon. On July 20, 1969, crew members from *Apollo 11* became the first humans to walk on the Moon's surface. NASA achieved five more Moon landings between 1969 and 1972. During this period, the Soviet Union sent spacecraft without crews to get samples of the Moon's surface.

Scientific Results The Apollo program helped scientists learn about the Moon's surface and interior. Much of the information came from 380 kilograms (weighing 840 lb) of rock and soil that astronauts brought back to Earth. These samples are still being studied.

Powerful booster rockets were used to launch the Apollo spacecraft. Beginning with *Apollo 15*, astronauts rode in lunar roving vehicles to explore greater areas of the Moon's surface.

Orbiting Earth

VOCABULARY
Add a magnet word diagram for *space station* to your notebook.

A **space station** is a satellite in which people can live and work for long periods. The United States and the Soviet Union launched the first space stations in the early 1970s. After the breakup of the Soviet Union in 1991, the Russian space agency and NASA began to act as partners rather than rivals. Russian and U. S. astronauts carried out joint missions aboard *Mir* (meer), the Russian space station.

The *Mir* missions helped prepare for the International Space Station (ISS). The United States, Russia, and 15 other nations are working together to build the ISS. When completed, it will cover an area about as large as two football fields. The ISS is too large to launch into space in one piece. Instead, sections of the space station are being launched separately and assembled in orbit over a period of years.

Construction of the ISS began in 1998. The first three-member crew arrived at the station in 2000. In addition to constructing the station, crew members make observations of Earth and perform experiments. Some experiments are much more effective when they are performed in space, where gravity affects them differently. For example, scientists can grow cell tissue more easily in space than they can on Earth. Research on cell tissue grown in space may increase our understanding of cancer and other diseases.

International Space Station

Each section of the space station has a specific function.

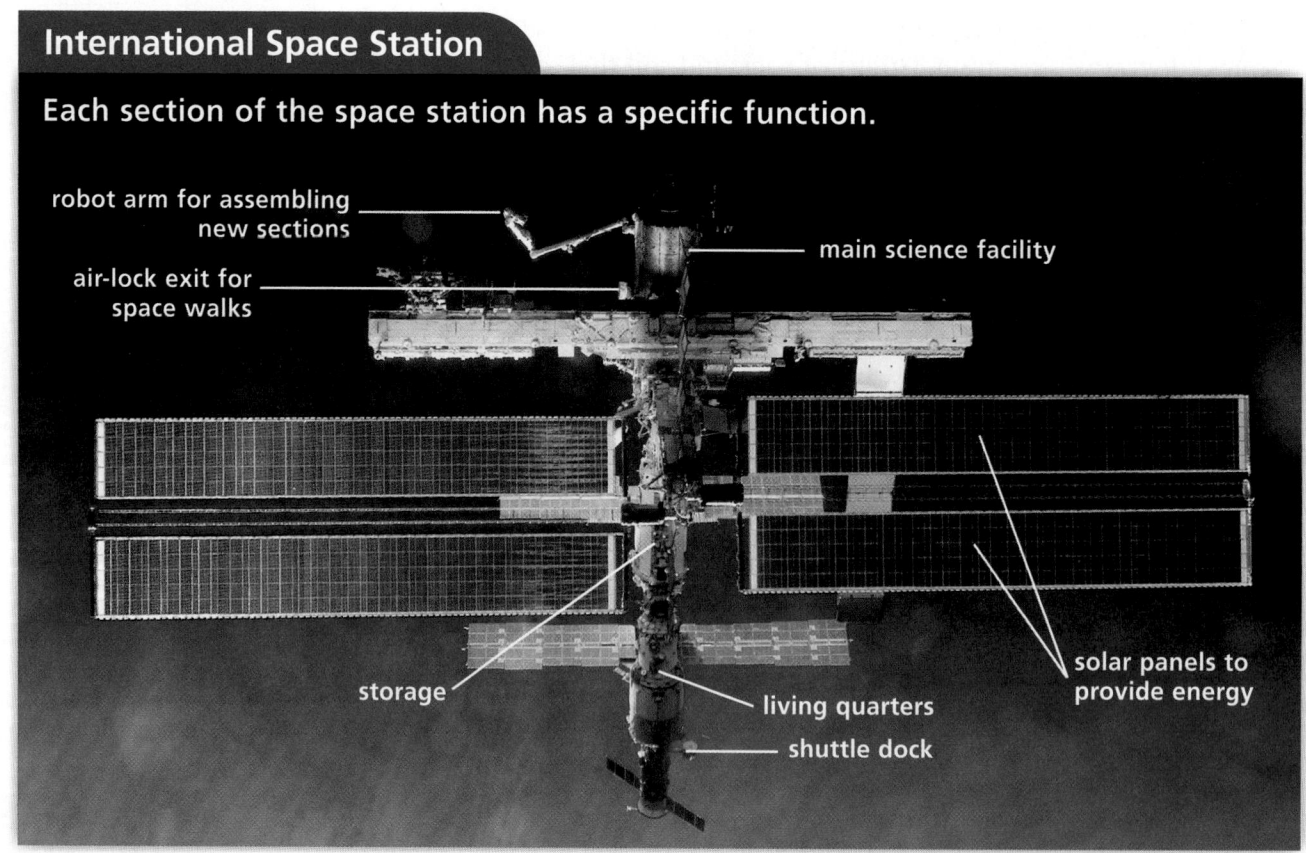

robot arm for assembling new sections

air-lock exit for space walks

main science facility

storage

living quarters

shuttle dock

solar panels to provide energy

Research and technological advances from the space station may lay the groundwork for new space exploration. ISS crew members study how living in space affects the human body over long periods. This research may provide useful information for future efforts to send astronauts to other planets.

Most crews have flown to the ISS aboard space shuttles. Unlike earlier spacecraft, a space shuttle can be used again and again. At the end of a mission, it reenters Earth's atmosphere and glides down to a runway. The large cargo bay of a space shuttle can carry satellites, equipment, and laboratories.

NASA has launched space shuttles more than 100 times since 1981. Space shuttles are much more sophisticated than the Apollo spacecraft that carried astronauts to the Moon. However, space travel remains a dangerous activity.

Two booster rockets and an external fuel tank are needed to lift a space shuttle into orbit.

CHECK YOUR READING Why might some researchers choose to perform experiments aboard a space station rather than on Earth?

INVESTIGATE Launch Planning

How does Earth's rotation affect launches of spacecraft?

PROCEDURE

1. Tightly wad 14 sheets of paper into balls, and place the balls in a small bucket.

2. Stand 1.5 m away from a large bucket placed on a desk. Try tossing 7 balls into the bucket.

3. While turning slowly, try tossing the remaining 7 balls into the bucket.

WHAT DO YOU THINK?

- How much more difficult was it to toss the paper balls into the bucket while you were turning than when you were standing still?

- Why does Earth's rotation make launching rockets into space more complicated?

CHALLENGE How would you design an experiment to show the variables involved in a launch from Earth toward another rotating body in space, such as the Moon?

SKILL FOCUS
Identifying variables

MATERIALS
- paper
- small bucket
- large bucket

TIME
10 minutes

Spacecraft carry instruments to other worlds.

Currently, we cannot send humans to other planets. One obstacle is that such a trip would take years. A spacecraft would need to carry enough air, water, and other supplies needed for survival on the long journey. Another obstacle is the harsh conditions on other planets, such as extreme heat and cold. Some planets do not even have surfaces to land on.

Because of these obstacles, most research in space is accomplished through the use of spacecraft without crews aboard. These missions pose no risk to human life and are less expensive than missions involving astronauts. The spacecraft carry instruments that test the compositions and characteristics of planets. Data and images are sent back to Earth as radio signals. Onboard computers and radio signals from Earth guide the spacecraft.

Spacecraft have visited all the major planets in our solar system except Pluto. NASA has also sent spacecraft to other bodies in space, such as comets and moons. Scientists and engineers have designed different types of spacecraft to carry out these missions.

 **CHECK YOUR READING** What questions do you still have about space exploration?

Flybys

The first stage in space exploration is to send out a spacecraft that passes one or more planets or other bodies in space without orbiting them. Such missions are called flybys. After a flyby spacecraft leaves Earth's orbit, controllers on Earth can use the spacecraft's small rockets to adjust its direction. Flyby missions may last for decades. However, because a spacecraft flies by planets quickly, it can collect data and images from a particular planet only for a brief period.

As a flyby spacecraft passes a planet, the planet's gravity can be used to change the spacecraft's speed or direction. During the flyby of the planet, the spacecraft can gain enough energy to propel it to another planet more quickly. This method allowed *Voyager 2* to fly past Saturn, Uranus, and Neptune, even though the spacecraft left Earth with only enough energy to reach Jupiter.

Many complex mathematical calculations are needed for a flyby mission to be successful. Experts must take into account Earth's rotation and the positions of the planets that the spacecraft will pass. The period of time when a spacecraft can be launched is called a launch window.

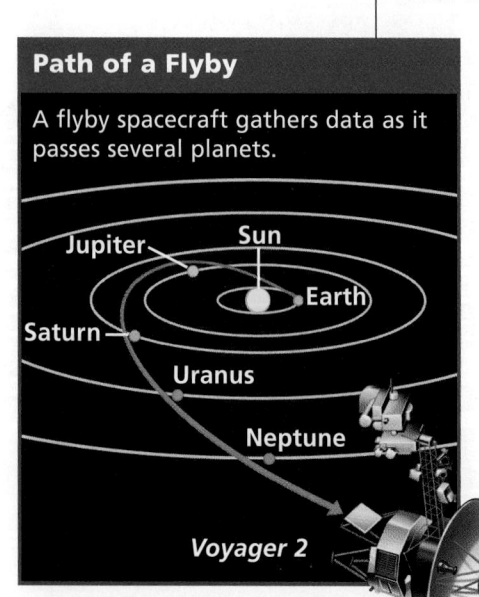

Path of a Flyby

A flyby spacecraft gathers data as it passes several planets.

Jupiter
Sun
Earth
Saturn
Uranus
Neptune

Voyager 2

Orbiters

The second stage in space exploration is to study a planet over a long period of time. Spacecraft designed to accomplish this task are called orbiters. As an orbiter approaches its target planet, rocket engines are fired to slow the spacecraft down. The spacecraft then goes into orbit around the planet.

In an orbiter mission, a spacecraft orbits a planet for several months to several years. Since an orbiter remains near a planet for a much longer period of time than a flyby spacecraft, it can view most or all of the planet's surface. An orbiter can also keep track of changes that occur over time, such as changes in weather and volcanic activity.

▼ REMINDER

Remember that objects orbit, or move around, other objects in space because of the influence of gravity.

Orbiters allow astronomers to create detailed maps of planets. Most orbiters have cameras to photograph planet surfaces. Orbiters may also carry other instruments, such as a device for determining the altitudes of surface features or one for measuring temperatures in different regions.

Some orbiters are designed to explore moons or other bodies in space instead of planets. It is also possible to send a spacecraft to orbit a planet and later move it into orbit around one of the planet's moons.

⬥ CHECK YOUR READING   What is the main difference between a flyby spacecraft and an orbiter?

How an Orbiter Provides Data

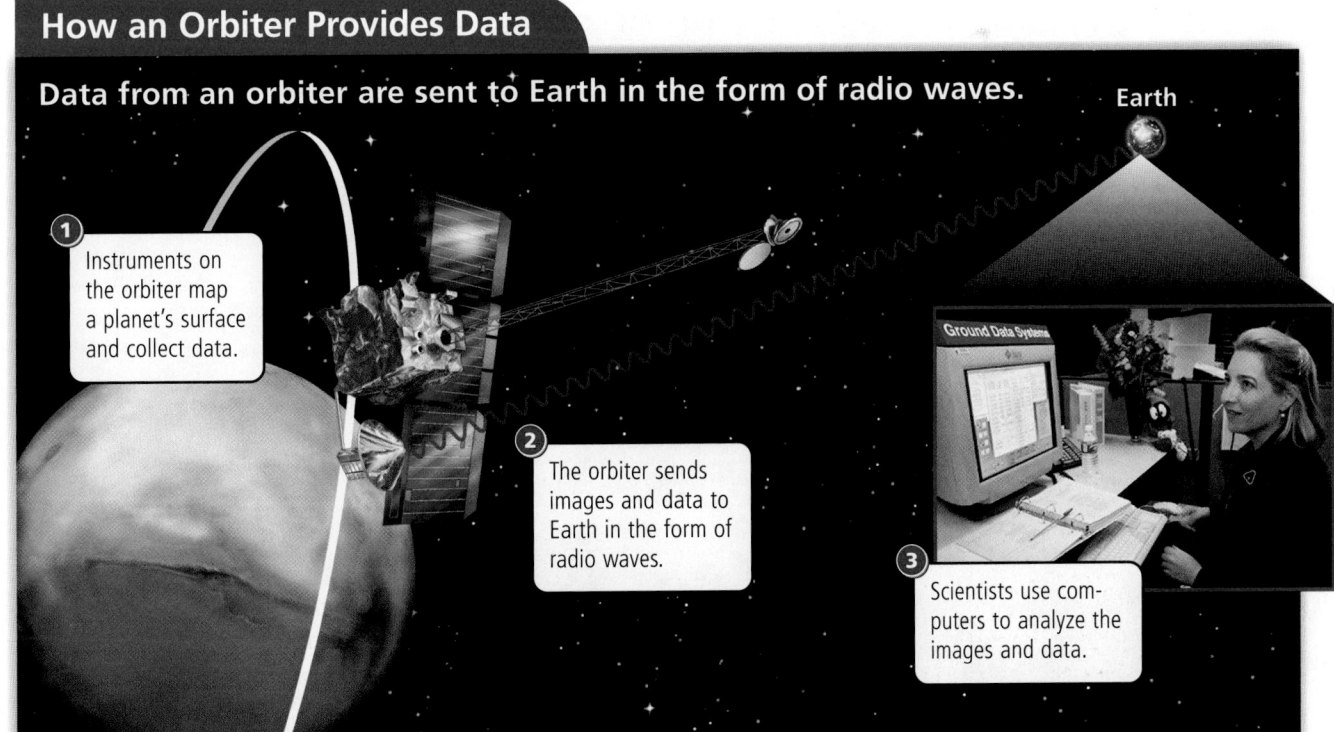

Data from an orbiter are sent to Earth in the form of radio waves.

Earth

1 Instruments on the orbiter map a planet's surface and collect data.

2 The orbiter sends images and data to Earth in the form of radio waves.

Ground Data Systems

3 Scientists use computers to analyze the images and data.

Landers and Probes

The third stage in space exploration is to land instruments on a planet or to send instruments through its atmosphere. Such a mission can tell us more about the features and properties of a planet. It can also provide clues to what the planet was like in the past.

A **lander** is a craft designed to land on a planet's surface. After a lander touches down, controllers on Earth can send it commands to collect data. Landers have been placed successfully on the Moon, Venus, and Mars. Some have operated for months or years at a time.

The images taken by a lander are more detailed than those taken by an orbiter. In addition to providing close-up views of a planet's surface, a lander can measure properties of the planet's atmosphere and surface. A lander may have a mechanical arm for gathering soil and rock samples. It may also contain a small vehicle called a rover, which can explore beyond the landing site.

1 The spacecraft slows down as it moves through the atmosphere.

Landing Sequence

Parachutes and air bags can be used to slow a lander as it descends to a planet's surface.

2 A parachute opens, and the lander is lowered from the spacecraft. Air bags are inflated shortly before landing.

3 The lander bounces on the surface and rolls to a stop.

4 The air bags are deflated and pulled back.

5 A rover from the lander begins to move across the surface.

One of the most successful space missions was that of *Mars Pathfinder,* which landed on Mars in 1997. *Mars Pathfinder* and its rover sent back thousands of photographs. These images provided evidence that water once flowed over the surface of Mars. Unfortunately, another lander, sent two years later, failed to work after it reached Mars.

Some spacecraft are designed to work only for a short time before they are destroyed by conditions on a planet. The term **probe** is often used to describe a spacecraft that drops into a planet's atmosphere. As the probe travels through the atmosphere, its instruments identify gases and measure properties such as pressure and temperature. Probes are especially important for exploring the deep atmospheres of giant planets, such as Jupiter.

 What is the difference between a probe and a lander?

Combining Missions

A lander or a probe can work in combination with an orbiter. For example, in 1995 the orbiter *Galileo* released a probe into Jupiter's atmosphere as it began orbiting the planet. The probe sent data back to the orbiter for nearly an hour before it was destroyed. The orbiter passed the data on to Earth. *Galileo* continued to orbit Jupiter for eight years.

Future space missions may involve even more complex combinations of spacecraft. Planners hope to send groups of landers to collect soil and rock samples from the surface of Mars. A rocket will carry these samples to an orbiter. The orbiter will then bring the samples to Earth for study.

19.3 Review

KEY CONCEPTS

1. Why are space stations important for scientific research?
2. How is information sent between Earth and a spacecraft?
3. What are the three main stages in exploring a planet?

CRITICAL THINKING

4. **Analyze** Why is most space exploration accomplished with spacecraft that do not have astronauts on board?
5. **Infer** Why is it important to map a planet's surface before planning a lander mission?

○ CHALLENGE

6. **Predict** Early space exploration was influenced by political events, such as the rivalry between the United States and the Soviet Union. What circumstances on Earth might interfere with future space missions?

MATH in SCIENCE

MATH TUTORIAL
CLASSZONE.COM
Click on Math Tutorial for more help with powers and exponents.

SKILL: USING EXPONENTS

Distances in Space

Astronomers often deal with very large numbers. For example, the planet Venus is about 100 million kilometers from the Sun. Written out, 100 million is 100,000,000. To use fewer zeros and to make the number easier to write and read, you could write 100 million as 10^8, which is the same value in exponent form.

Example

PROBLEM Write 1000 km, using an exponent.

To find the exponent of a number, you can write the number as a product. For example,

$$1000 \text{ km} = 10 \times 10 \times 10 \text{ km}$$

This product has 3 factors of 10. When whole numbers other than zero are multiplied together, each number is a factor of the product. To write a product that has a repeated factor, you can use an exponent. The exponent is the number of times the factor is repeated. With factors of 10, you can also determine the exponent by counting the zeros in the given number.

There are 3 zeros in 1000.　　The factor 10 is repeated 3 times.

$$1000 = 10 \times 10 \times 10$$

ANSWER The exponent form of 1000 km is 10^3 km.

Write each distance, using an exponent.

1. 10,000 km

2. 1,000,000 km

3. 100,000,000,000 km

4. 10,000,000,000,000 km

5. 100,000,000,000,000,000 km

6. 10 km

CHALLENGE The galaxy shown on this page is about 10^{18} kilometers across. Write the value of 10^{18} without using an exponent.

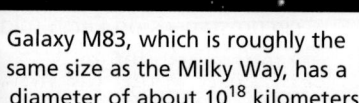

Galaxy M83, which is roughly the same size as the Milky Way, has a diameter of about 10^{18} kilometers.

19.4 Space exploration benefits society.

Sunshine State STANDARDS

SC.H.1.3.3: The student knows that science disciplines differ from one another in topic, techniques, and outcomes but that they share a common purpose, philosophy, and enterprise.

SC.H.3.3.6: The student knows that no matter who does science and mathematics or invents things, or when or where they do it, the knowledge and technology that result can eventually become available to everyone.

VOCABULARY
impact crater p. 696

BEFORE, you learned

- Light and other radiation carry information about space
- Astronauts explore space near Earth

NOW, you will learn

- How space exploration has helped us to learn more about Earth
- How space technology is used on Earth

THINK ABOUT

How does Earth look from space?

This photograph of Earth over the Moon was taken by the crew of *Apollo 8*. The Apollo missions provided the first images of our planet as a whole. What do you think we can learn about Earth from photographs taken from space?

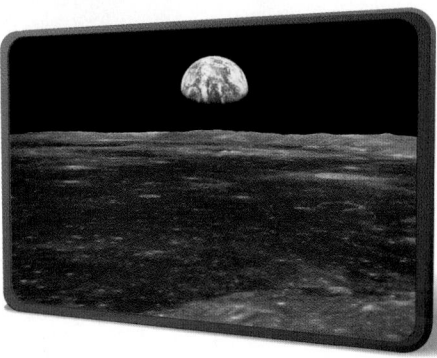

Space exploration has given us new viewpoints.

Space exploration enriches us in many ways. Throughout history, the study of stars and planets has inspired new ideas. As we meet the challenges of space exploration, we gain valuable technology. Space exploration is also an exciting adventure.

Space science has advanced knowledge in other scientific fields, such as physics. For example, observations of the Moon and other bodies in space helped scientists understand how gravity works. Scientists figured out that the same force that causes an object to fall to the ground causes the Moon to orbit Earth.

Finally, the study of other worlds can teach us about our own. Earth has changed considerably since its formation. By comparing Earth with different worlds, scientists can learn more about the history of Earth's surface features and atmosphere.

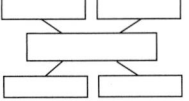

MAIN IDEA WEB
Record in your notes important information that space exploration has provided about Earth.

CHECK YOUR READING Identify some benefits of space exploration.

Formation of a Crater

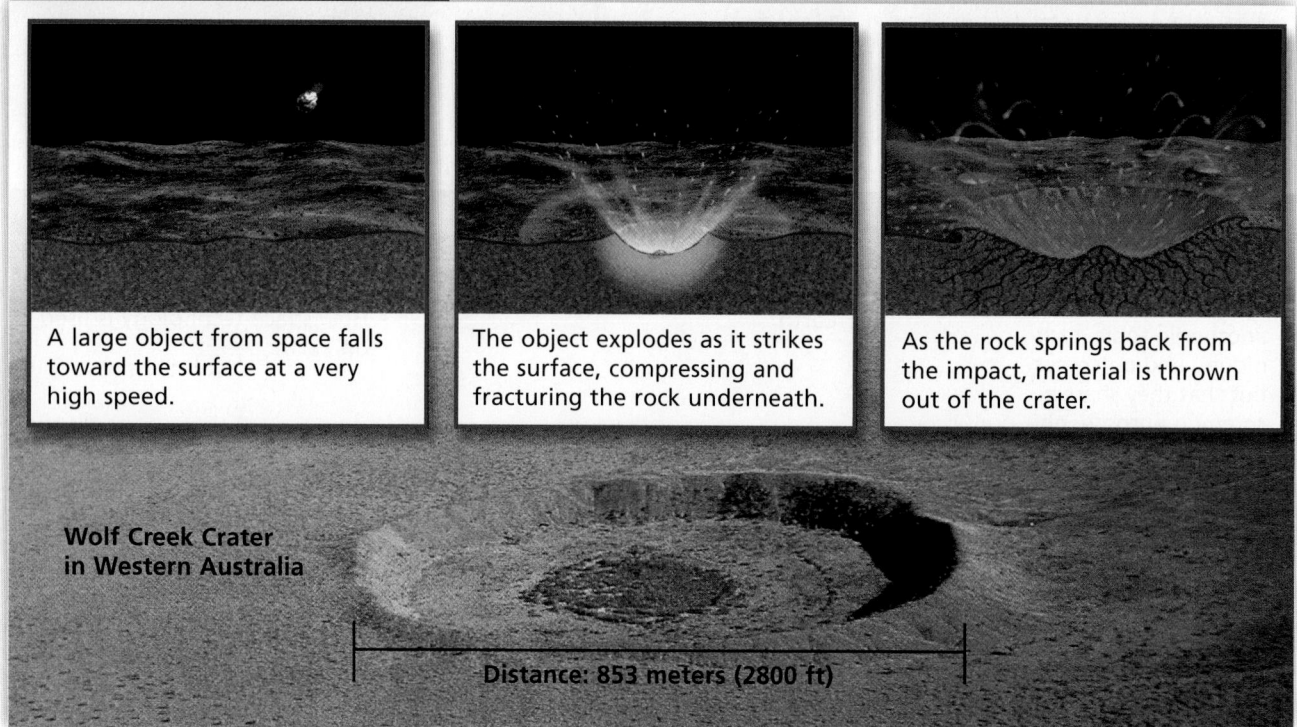

A large object from space falls toward the surface at a very high speed.

The object explodes as it strikes the surface, compressing and fracturing the rock underneath.

As the rock springs back from the impact, material is thrown out of the crater.

Wolf Creek Crater in Western Australia

Distance: 853 meters (2800 ft)

Surface Features

Exploration of other worlds has helped us learn about the impacts of space objects. When an object strikes the surface of a larger object in space, it explodes and leaves behind a round pit called an **impact crater.** The illustration above shows how an impact crater forms.

Earth has little evidence of impacts because its surface is constantly being worn down by wind and water and altered by forces beneath the surface. However, impact craters remain on the Moon, Mercury, and many other bodies that have no wind or liquid water.

Atmosphere

We are also learning about Earth's atmosphere from space exploration. Earth's temperature allows liquid water to remain on the surface. Mars and Venus, the planets closest to Earth, have no liquid water on their surfaces. By comparing Earth with those planets, we can see how liquid water has affected the development of Earth's atmosphere.

Another area of study involves the energy Earth receives from the Sun. Many scientists think that small changes visible on the Sun's surface can affect weather on Earth. These changes may have caused periods of cooling in Earth's atmosphere.

 **CHECK YOUR READING** What have scientists learned about Earth's past from studying bodies in space?

INVESTIGATE Weathering

How does weather affect evidence of impacts on Earth?

PROCEDURE

1. Fill a shoebox lid halfway with sand, and smooth the surface with a ruler.

2. Create three craters by dropping a golf ball into the sand from a height of 70 cm. Remove the ball carefully. Leave the lid inside the classroom.

3. Repeat steps 1 and 2 outdoors, leaving the lid in an area where it will be exposed to the weather.

4. Check both lids after 24 hours. Observe changes in each one.

WHAT DO YOU THINK?

- How did the craters in the sand that you left outdoors differ in appearance from the craters in the sand that remained inside?

- What aspect of weather caused any differences you observed?

CHALLENGE What natural processes besides weather can affect evidence of impacts from space objects on Earth?

Space technology has practical uses.

Space exploration has done more than increase our knowledge. It has also provided us with technology that makes life on Earth easier. Each day you probably benefit from some material or product that was developed for the space program.

Satellite Views of Earth

One of the most important benefits of space exploration has been the development of satellite technology. Satellites collect data from every region of our planet. The data are sent to receivers on Earth and converted into images. Scientists have learned from the space program how to enhance such images to gain more information.

Weather satellites show conditions throughout Earth's atmosphere. Images and data from weather satellites have greatly improved weather forecasting. Scientists can now provide warnings of dangerous storms long before they strike populated areas.

Other satellites collect images of Earth's surface to show how it is being changed by natural events and human activity. Satellite data are also used for wildlife preservation, conservation of natural resources, and mapping.

Technology Spinoffs

Have you ever come up with a new way to use something that was designed for a different purpose? NASA often creates advanced technology to meet the special demands of space travel. Many spinoffs of technology from the space program can be found in homes, offices, schools, and hospitals.

NASA designers helped develop a system that allows this boy to communicate by using eye movements.

Everything on a spacecraft must be as small and lightweight as possible because the heavier a spacecraft is, the more difficult it is to launch. Design techniques developed to meet this need have improved devices used on Earth, such as tools for diagnosing diseases and devices that help people overcome disabilities.

Materials and parts on a spacecraft have to endure harsh conditions, such as extreme heat and cold. Many new homes and buildings contain fire-resistant materials developed for the space program. Firefighters wear protective suits made from fabric originally used in space suits. NASA has also helped design devices that allow firefighters to avoid injury from inhaling smoke.

Humans need a safe environment in spacecraft and space stations. NASA has developed systems for purifying air, water, and food. These systems now help protect people on Earth as well as in space.

19.4 Review

KEY CONCEPTS

1. How has space exploration helped us learn about impacts of space objects on Earth?

2. How do satellites provide images of Earth's surface and atmosphere?

3. Give two examples of technology we use on Earth that is a result of space exploration.

CRITICAL THINKING

4. **Infer** Hurricanes form in the middle of the ocean. Why would satellites be useful in tracking hurricanes?

5. **Apply** What space-technology spinoffs might be used in a school?

⬤ CHALLENGE

6. **Predict** It takes over a year for a spacecraft to reach Mars and return to Earth. If astronauts ever travel to Mars, they will need a spacecraft that can recycle air and water. How might such technology be adapted for use on Earth?

How Earth's Gravity Affects Plants

One of the most important issues in biology is understanding how plants grow. By applying the results of research on this issue, American farmers now grow twice as much food as they did 50 years ago.

One aspect of plant growth is the direction in which plants grow. After a plant sprouts from a seed, some of its cells form a shoot that grows upward. Other cells grow downward, becoming roots. How does this happen? Biologists think that plants usually respond to signals from the Sun and from the force of gravity.

Gravity and Plant Growth

To test the importance of sunlight, biologists can grow plants in the dark on Earth. Testing the impact of gravity, though, is more difficult. In 1997, a space shuttle carried moss plants into space. The plants grew for two weeks in microgravity, an environment in which objects are almost weightless. When the shuttle returned the plants to Earth, biologists studied how they had grown.

Prediction

Biologists had predicted that the moss would grow randomly. They expected that without signals from sunlight or the force of gravity, the moss would grow in no particular pattern.

Results

The biologists were surprised by what they saw. The moss had not grown randomly. Instead, the plants had spread out in a clear pattern. Each plant had formed a clockwise spiral.

Significance

The moss experiment may be important for future space exploration. Can plants provide the food and oxygen that astronauts will need on long voyages to other planets? Experiments with moss are among the first steps in finding out.

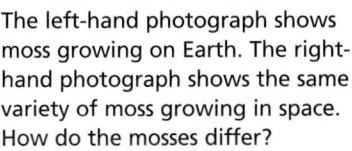

The left-hand photograph shows moss growing on Earth. The right-hand photograph shows the same variety of moss growing in space. How do the mosses differ?

EXPLORE

1. **PROVIDE EXAMPLES** Make a list of other spiral formations that occur in nature. Discuss why spirals may be common.

2. **CHALLENGE** Use library or Internet resources to learn about other experiments that test the effects of microgravity on plants and seeds.

FLORIDA REVIEW
CLASSZONE.COM

Content Review and
FCAT Practice

the BIG idea

People develop and use technology to explore and study space.

◀ KEY CONCEPTS SUMMARY

1 Some space objects are visible to the human eye.

- Gravity causes objects in space to be grouped together in different ways.
- Stars form patterns in the sky.
- The sky seems to turn as Earth rotates.

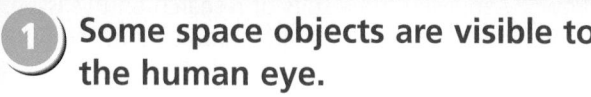

VOCABULARY
orbit p. 674
solar system p. 674
galaxy p. 674
universe p. 674
constellation p. 676

2 Telescopes allow us to study space from Earth.

Each form of electromagnetic radiation provides different information about objects in space. Astronomers use different types of telescopes to gather visible light and other forms of radiation.

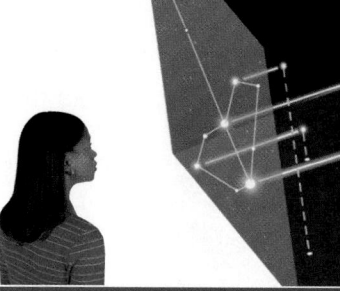

VOCABULARY
electromagnetic radiation p. 679
spectrum p. 680
wavelength p. 680
telescope p. 681

3 Spacecraft help us explore beyond Earth.

Astronauts can explore space near Earth. Spacecraft without crews carry instruments to other worlds. A flyby mission usually provides data from several bodies in space. Orbiters, landers, and probes gather data from one planet or body.

VOCABULARY
satellite p. 687
space station p. 688
lander p. 692
probe p. 693

4 Space exploration benefits society.

Space exploration has taught us about Earth's development. It has also provided technology that has important uses on Earth.

VOCABULARY
impact crater p. 696

Reviewing Vocabulary

Write a definition of each word. Use the meaning of the underlined word part to help you.

Word	Root Meaning	Definition
EXAMPLE satellite	person of lesser rank	an object that orbits a more massive object
1. orbit	circle	
2. solar system	Sun	
3. universe	one	
4. constellation	star	
5. electro-magnetic radiation	to emit rays	
6. spectrum	to look at	
7. probe	test	
8. impact crater	bowl	

Reviewing Key Concepts

Multiple Choice *Choose the letter of the best answer.*

9. Stars in a galaxy are held together by
   a. light
   b. radiation
   c. gravity
   d. satellites

10. Astronomers use constellations to
   a. locate objects in the sky
   b. calculate the distances of objects
   c. calculate the masses of objects
   d. classify spectra

11. Stars rise and set in the night sky because
   a. Earth orbits the Sun
   b. Earth rotates
   c. the North Pole points toward Polaris
   d. the stars are moving in space

12. In the electromagnetic spectrum, different forms of radiation are arranged according to their
   a. colors
   b. distances
   c. wavelengths
   d. sizes

13. Astronomers often locate telescopes on mountains to
   a. lessen the interference of Earth's atmosphere
   b. save money on land
   c. keep their discoveries secret
   d. get closer to space objects

14. A reflecting telescope gathers light with a
   a. lens
   b. eyepiece
   c. refractor
   d. mirror

15. What was the goal of the Apollo program?
   a. to view Earth from space
   b. to explore the Sun
   c. to explore the Moon
   d. to explore other planets

16. Which type of mission produces detailed maps of a planet?
   a. flyby
   b. orbiter
   c. lander
   d. probe

17. What causes an impact crater to form on a planet's surface?
   a. Gravity pulls soil and rock downward.
   b. Wind and water wear away the surface.
   c. Forces beneath the surface push upward.
   d. An object from space strikes the surface.

Short Response *Write a short response to each question.*

18. Why is it easier to see the motions of planets than to see the motions of stars?

19. How do astronomers obtain most of their information about space?

20. How does the size of a telescope's main lens or mirror affect its performance?

21. Why have lightweight materials been developed for space travel?

Thinking Critically

Copy the Venn diagram below, and use it to help you answer the next two questions.

Reflecting Telescope   Radio Dish

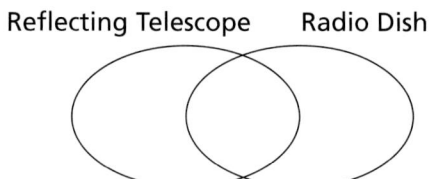

22. COMPARE AND CONTRAST Fill in the Venn diagram to show similarities and differences between a reflecting telescope and a radio dish.

23. APPLY Suppose that you live in an area that has frequent storms. Which would be more suitable for your location, a reflecting telescope or a radio dish? Explain.

24. COMPARE AND CONTRAST What are the similarities and differences between visible light and radio waves?

25. HYPOTHESIZE Many of the constellations named by ancient peoples are now hard to see from populated areas. Why might it have been easier to see them hundreds or thousands of years ago?

26. ANALYZE What may be the advantages of electronically recording an image from a telescope instead of looking at the object directly through the telescope's eyepiece?

27. SYNTHESIZE Suppose it became possible to send astronauts to explore a nearby planet. What concerns would need to be taken into account before deciding whether to send a spacecraft with astronauts or a spacecraft with no crew aboard?

28. COMPARE AND CONTRAST Compare and contrast the development of the International Space Station with the Apollo missions to the Moon.

29. ANALYZE If you were designing a medical device to be implanted in a patient's body, why might you seek help from designers of space technology?

30. EVALUATE Do you think that the United States should continue to maintain its own space program, or should it combine its space program with the programs of other nations? Explain.

31. SEQUENCE Astronomers have learned that some stars other than the Sun have planets orbiting them. Imagine that you are planning a program to explore one of these planet systems. Copy the chart below. Use the chart to identify stages in the exploration of the system and to describe what would occur during each stage.

Stage of Exploration	Description

the BIG idea

32. PROVIDE EXAMPLES Look again at the photograph on pages 670–671. Now that you have finished the chapter, how would you change your response to the question on the photograph?

33. EVALUATE In the United States billions of dollars are spent each year on space exploration. Do you think that this expense is justified? Why or why not?

UNIT PROJECTS

If you are doing a unit project, make a folder for your project. Include in your folder a list of the resources you will need, the date on which the project is due, and a schedule to track your progress. Begin gathering data.

Analyzing a Star Map

Use the star map to answer the questions below.

MULTIPLE CHOICE

1. Constellations are represented on the map as which of the following?

A. dots surrounded by planets

B. dots grouped in a spiral pattern

C. dots connected by lines

D. dots scattered in a random pattern

2. How would a map showing the same portion of the sky two hours later compare with the map above?

F. Almost all the space objects would have changed position noticeably.

G. No space objects would have changed position.

H. Only the moon would have changed position.

I. Only the planets would have changed position.

3. Why would the map for two hours later be different from this map?

A. The Moon is rotating on its axis.

B. Earth is rotating on its axis.

C. The solar system is part of the Milky Way.

D. The planets move in relation to the stars.

4. Which statement best describes the location of the stars shown on the map?

F. They are outside the solar system but within the Milky Way galaxy.

G. They are within the solar system.

H. They are outside the Milky Way galaxy but within the universe.

I. They are outside the universe.

SHORT RESPONSE

5. The stars in the constellation Draco form the shape of a dragon. Can you infer that the stars in Draco are close together? Why or why not?

6. A map showing the same portion of the sky exactly one year later would look very similar to this map. What would probably be different? Explain your answer.

EXTENDED RESPONSE
Answer the two questions below in detail.

7. What is the relationship between Earth, our solar system, the Milky Way, and the universe?

8. What do visible-light telescopes and radio telescopes have in common? How are they different?

 20 Earth, Moon, and Sun

the **BIG** idea

Earth and the Moon move in predictable ways as they orbit the Sun.

Key Concepts

SECTION

1 **Earth rotates on a tilted axis and orbits the Sun.** Learn what causes day and night and why there are seasons.

SECTION

2 **The Moon is Earth's natural satellite.** Learn about the structure and motion of Earth's Moon.

SECTION

3 **Positions of the Sun and Moon affect Earth.** Learn about phases of the Moon, eclipses, and tides.

FCAT Practice

Prepare and practice for the FCAT
- Section Reviews, pp. 713, 721, 730
- Chapter Review, pp. 732–734
- FCAT Practice, p. 735

CLASSZONE.COM
- Florida Review: Content Review and FCAT Practice

What would you see if you looked at the Moon with a telescope?

How Do Shadows Move?

Place a small sticky note on a window that sunlight shines through. At several different times of day, sketch the location of the note's shadow in the room.

Observe and Think
Does the shadow move in a clockwise or counterclockwise direction? Does the shadow's distance from the window change?

What Makes the Moon Bright?

On a day when you see the Moon in the sky, compare it with a round object. Hold the object in line with the Moon. Make sure that your hand does not block the sunlight. Notice the part of the object that is bright.

Observe and Think
How does the sunlight on the object compare with the light on the Moon?

Internet Activity: Seasons

Go to **ClassZone.com** to explore seasons. Find out how sunlight affects the temperature in different places at different times of year.

Observe and Think
Does the picture show Earth in June or in December?

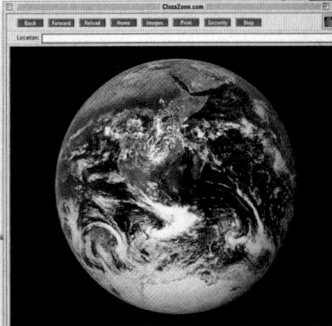

NSTA
scilinks.org
SCI LINKS

The Moon Code: MDL058

Getting Ready to Learn

◀ CONCEPT REVIEW

- The sky seems to turn as Earth rotates.
- The motions of nearby space objects are visible from Earth.
- Light and other radiation carry information about space.

◀ VOCABULARY REVIEW

orbit p. 674
electromagnetic radiation p. 679
satellite p. 687
See Glossary for definitions.
force, gravity, mass

FLORIDA REVIEW
CLASSZONE.COM

Content Review and FCAT Practice

▶ TAKING NOTES

COMBINATION NOTES

To take notes about a new concept, first make an informal outline of the information. Then make a sketch of the concept and label it so you can study it later.

VOCABULARY STRATEGY

Write each new vocabulary term in the center of a **frame game** diagram. Decide what information to frame the term with. Use examples, descriptions, pictures, or sentences in which the term is used in context. You can change the frame to fit each term.

See the Note-Taking Handbook on pages R45–R51.

SCIENCE NOTEBOOK

NOTES

Earth turns.
- It turns on an imaginary axis.
  - Poles are ends of axis.
  - Equator is halfway.
- Rotation takes 24 hours.
- Sun shines on one side only.
  - Light side is daytime.
  - Dark side is night.

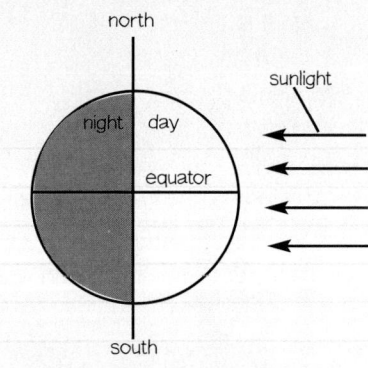

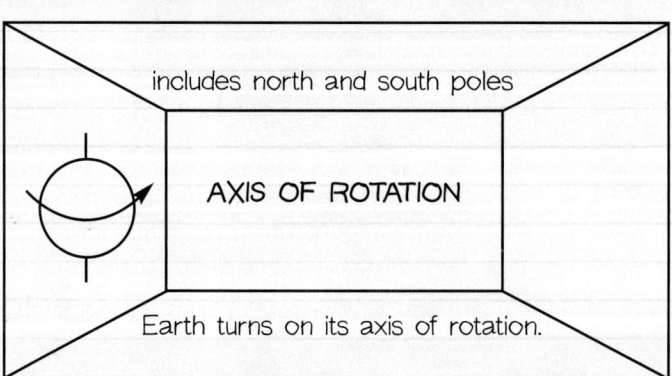

includes north and south poles

AXIS OF ROTATION

Earth turns on its axis of rotation.

KEY CONCEPT
Earth rotates on a tilted axis and orbits the Sun.

VOCABULARY

axis of rotation p. 708
revolution p. 709
season p. 710
equinox p. 710
solstice p. 710

◀ BEFORE, you learned

- Stars seem to rise, cross the sky, and set because Earth turns
- The Sun is very large and far from Earth
- Earth orbits the Sun

▶ NOW, you will learn

- Why Earth has day and night
- How the changing angles of sunlight produce seasons

EXPLORE Time Zones

What time is it in Iceland right now?

PROCEDURE

① Find your location and Iceland on the map. Identify the time zone of each.

② Count the number of hours between your location and Iceland. Add or subtract that number of hours from the time on your clock.

MATERIAL
time zone map

WHAT DO YOU THINK?

- By how much is Iceland's time earlier or later than yours?
- Why are clocks set to different times?

Earth's rotation causes day and night.

When astronauts explored the Moon, they felt the Moon's gravity pulling them down. Their usual "down"—Earth—was up in the Moon's sky.

As you read this book, it is easy to tell which way is down. But is down in the same direction for a person on the other side of Earth? If you both pointed down, you would be pointing toward each other. Earth's gravity pulls objects toward the center of Earth. No matter where you stand on Earth, the direction of down will be toward Earth's center. There is no bottom or top. Up is out toward space, and down is toward the center of the planet.

As Earth turns, so do you. You keep the same position with respect to what is below your feet, but the view above your head changes.

 **CHECK YOUR READING** In what direction does gravity pull objects near Earth?

The globe and the flat map show the progress of daylight across Earth in two ways. This location is experiencing sunrise.

noon

night moves westward

midnight

The directions north, south, east, and west are based on the way the planet rotates, or turns. Earth rotates around an imaginary line running through its center called an **axis of rotation.** The ends of the axis are the north and south poles. Any location on the surface moves from west to east as Earth turns. If you extend your right thumb and pretend its tip is the North Pole, then your fingers curve the way Earth rotates.

At any one time, about half of Earth is in sunlight and half is dark. However, Earth turns on its axis in 24 hours, so locations move through the light and darkness in that time. When a location is in sunlight, it is daytime there. When a location is in the middle of the sunlit side, it is noon. When a location is in darkness, it is night there, and when the location is in the middle of the unlit side, it is midnight.

CHECK YOUR READING   If it is noon at one location, what time is it at a location directly on the other side of Earth?

INVESTIGATE Rotation

What causes day and night?

In this model the lamp represents the Sun, and your head represents Earth. The North Pole is at the top of your head. You will need to imagine locations on your head as if your head were a globe.

PROCEDURE

1. Face the lamp and hold your hands to your face as shown in the photograph. Your hands mark the horizon. For a person located at your nose, the Sun would be high in the sky. It would be noon.

2. Face away from the lamp. Determine what time it would be at your nose.

3. Turn to your left until you see the lamp along your left hand.

4. Continue turning to the left, through noon, until you just stop seeing the lamp.

WHAT DO YOU THINK?

• What times was it at your nose in steps 2, 3, and 4?

• When you face the lamp, what time is it at your right ear?

CHALLENGE How can a cloud be bright even when it is dark on the ground?

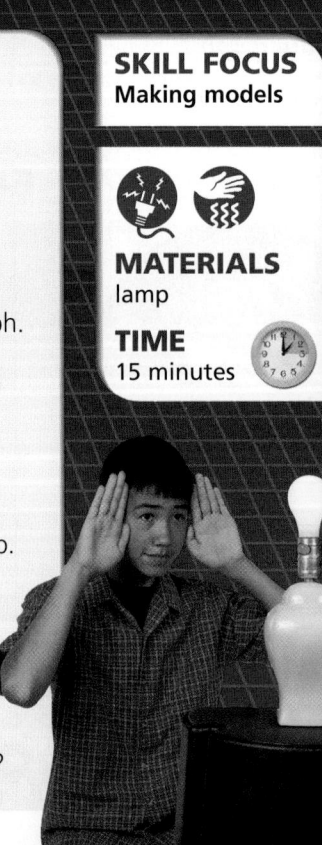

Earth's tilted axis and orbit cause seasons.

Just as gravity causes objects near Earth to be pulled toward Earth's center, it also causes Earth and other objects near the Sun to be pulled toward the Sun's center. Fortunately, Earth does not move straight into the Sun. Earth moves sideways, at nearly a right angle to the Sun's direction. Without the Sun's gravitational pull, Earth would keep moving in a straight line out into deep space. However, the Sun's pull changes Earth's path from a straight line to a round orbit about 300 million kilometers (200,000,000 mi) across.

Just as a day is the time it takes Earth to rotate once on its axis, a year is the time it takes Earth to orbit the Sun once. In astronomy, a **revolution** is the motion of one object around another. The word *revolution* can also mean the time it takes an object to go around once.

Earth's rotation and orbit do not quite line up. If they did, Earth's equator would be in the same plane as Earth's orbit, like a tiny hoop and a huge hoop lying on the same tabletop. Instead, Earth rotates at about a 23° angle, or tilt, from this lined-up position.

READING **TiP**

Use the second vowel in each word to help you remember that an object rotates on its own axis, but revolves around another object.

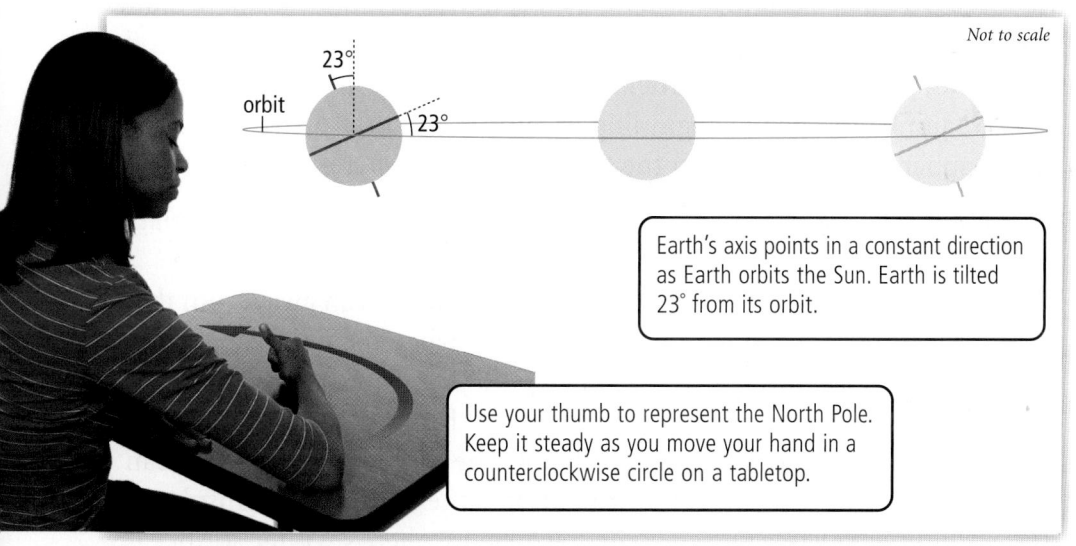

Not to scale

orbit

Earth's axis points in a constant direction as Earth orbits the Sun. Earth is tilted 23° from its orbit.

Use your thumb to represent the North Pole. Keep it steady as you move your hand in a counterclockwise circle on a tabletop.

As Earth moves, its axis always points in the same direction in space. You could model Earth's orbit by moving your right fist in a circle on a desktop. You would need to point your thumb toward your left shoulder and keep it pointing that way while moving your hand around the desktop.

Earth's orbit is not quite a perfect circle. In January, Earth is about 5 million kilometers closer to the Sun than it is in July. You may be surprised to learn that this distance makes only a tiny difference in temperatures on Earth. However, the combination of Earth's motion around the Sun with the tilt of Earth's axis does cause important changes of temperature. Turn the page to find out how.

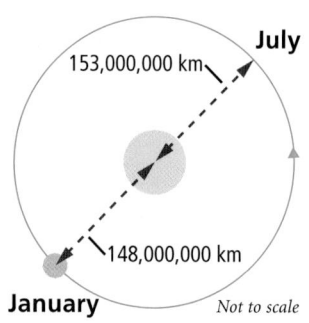

July

153,000,000 km

148,000,000 km

January *Not to scale*

Earth's orbit is almost a circle. Earth's distance from the Sun varies by only about 5,000,000 km—about 3%—during a year.

Seasonal Patterns

Most locations on Earth experience **seasons,** patterns of temperature changes and other weather trends over the course of a year. Near the equator, the temperatures are almost the same year-round. Near the poles, there are very large changes in temperatures from winter to summer. The temperature changes occur because the amount of sunlight at each location changes during the year. The changes in the amount of sunlight are due to the tilt of Earth's axis.

Look at the diagram on page 711 to see how the constant direction of Earth's tilted axis affects the pattern of sunlight on Earth at different times of the year. As Earth travels around the Sun, the area of sunlight in each hemisphere changes. At an **equinox** (EE-kwuh-NAHKS), sunlight shines equally on the northern and southern hemispheres. Half of each hemisphere is lit, and half is in darkness. As Earth moves along its orbit, the light shifts more into one hemisphere than the other. At a **solstice** (SAHL-stihs), the area of sunlight is at a maximum in one hemisphere and a minimum in the other hemisphere. Equinoxes and solstices happen on or around the 21st days of certain months of the year.

❶ **September Equinox** When Earth is in this position, sunlight shines equally on the two hemispheres. You can see in the diagram that the North Pole is at the border between light and dark. The September equinox marks the beginning of autumn in the Northern Hemisphere and of spring in the Southern Hemisphere.

❷ **December Solstice** Three months later, Earth has traveled a quarter of the way around the Sun, but its axis still points in the same direction into space. The North Pole seems to lean away from the direction of the Sun. The solstice occurs when the pole leans as far away from the Sun as it will during the year. You can see that the North Pole is in complete darkness. At the same time, the opposite is true in the Southern Hemisphere. The South Pole seems to lean toward the Sun and is in sunlight. It is the Southern Hemisphere's summer solstice and the Northern Hemisphere's winter solstice.

❸ **March Equinox** After another quarter of its orbit, Earth reaches another equinox. Half of each hemisphere is lit, and the sunlight is centered on the equator. You can see that the poles are again at the border between day and night.

❹ **June Solstice** This position is opposite the December solstice. Earth's axis still points in the same direction, but now the North Pole seems to lean toward the Sun and is in sunlight. The June solstice marks the beginning of summer in the Northern Hemisphere. In contrast, it is the winter solstice in the Southern Hemisphere.

CHECK YOUR READING   In what month does winter begin in the Southern Hemisphere?

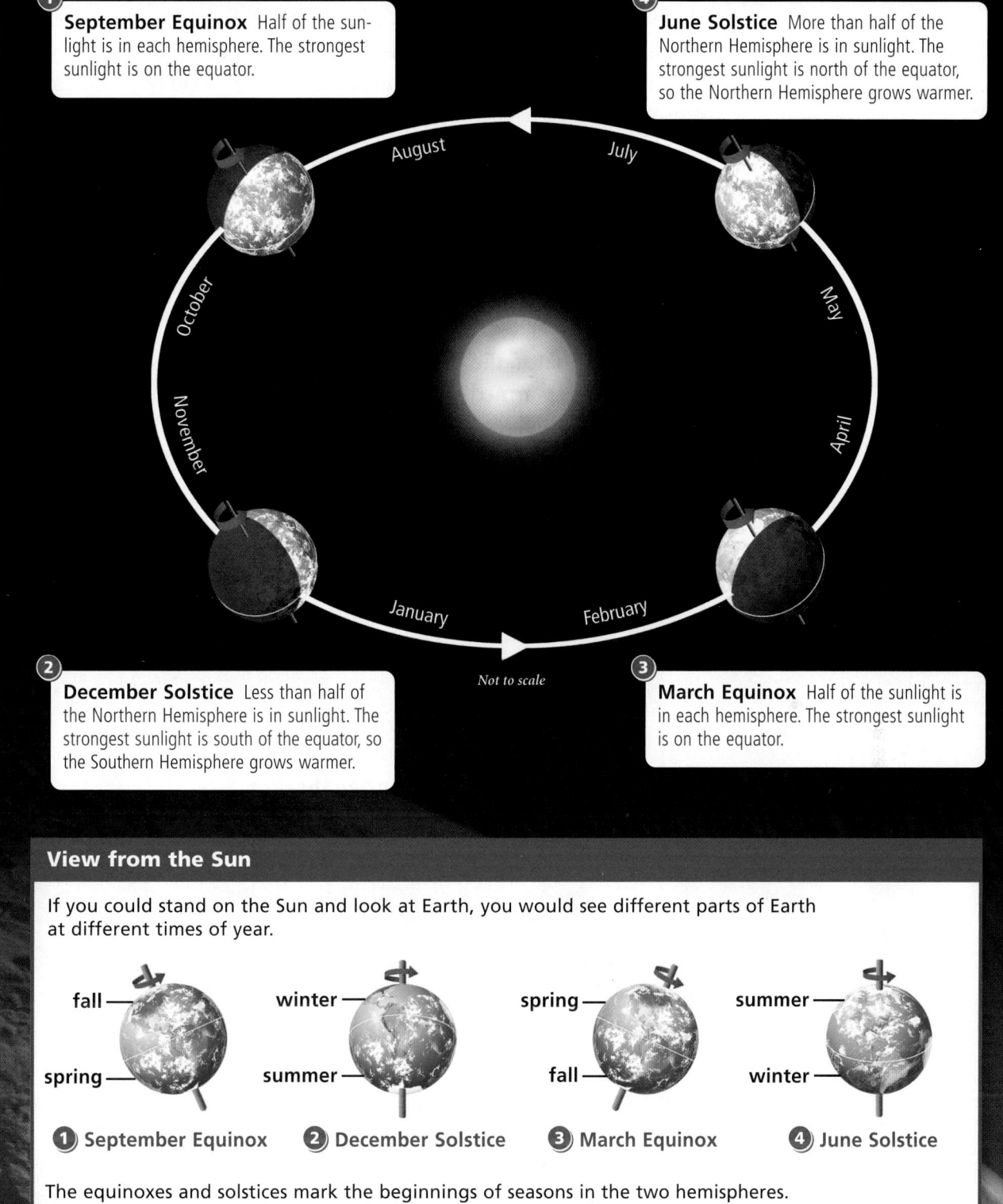

September Equinox Half of the sunlight is in each hemisphere. The strongest sunlight is on the equator.

June Solstice More than half of the Northern Hemisphere is in sunlight. The strongest sunlight is north of the equator, so the Northern Hemisphere grows warmer.

August

July

October

May

November

April

January

February

Not to scale

2 December Solstice Less than half of the Northern Hemisphere is in sunlight. The strongest sunlight is south of the equator, so the Southern Hemisphere grows warmer.

3 March Equinox Half of the sunlight is in each hemisphere. The strongest sunlight is on the equator.

View from the Sun

If you could stand on the Sun and look at Earth, you would see different parts of Earth at different times of year.

fall — spring —   **1 September Equinox**

winter — summer —   **2 December Solstice**

spring — fall —   **3 March Equinox**

summer — winter —   **4 June Solstice**

The equinoxes and solstices mark the beginnings of seasons in the two hemispheres. Warmer seasons occur when more of a hemisphere is in sunlight.

READING VISUALS Look at the poles to help you see how each hemisphere is lit. When is the South Pole completely in sunlight?

Angles of Sunlight

RESOURCE CENTER
CLASSZONE.COM

Learn more about seasons.

FLORIDA
Content Review

Notice how the angle of sunlight affects the climate of a region, which you studied in grade 6.

You have seen that seasons change as sunlight shifts between hemispheres during the year. On the ground, you notice the effects of seasons because the angle of sunlight and the length of daylight change over the year. The effects are greatest at locations far from the equator. You may have noticed that sunshine seems barely warm just before sunset, when the Sun is low in the sky. At noon the sunshine seems much hotter. The angle of light affects the temperature.

When the Sun is high in the sky, sunlight strikes the ground at close to a right angle. The energy of sunlight is concentrated. Shadows are short. You may get a sunburn quickly when the Sun is at a high angle. When the Sun is low in the sky, sunlight strikes the ground at a slant. The light is spread over a greater area, so it is less concentrated and produces long shadows. Slanted light warms the ground less.

Near the equator, the noonday Sun is almost overhead every day, so the ground is warmed strongly year-round. In the middle latitudes, the noon Sun is high in the sky only during part of the year. In winter the noon Sun is low and warms the ground less strongly.

CHECK YOUR READING How are temperatures throughout the year affected by the angles of sunlight?

Sun Height and Shadows

Winter Solstice, 12 P.M.

Winter shadows are long because sunlight is spread out. The Sun appears low in the sky even at noon.

location on Earth

Spring Equinox, 12 P.M.

Spring and fall shadows are of medium length, and the noon Sun appears higher in the sky.

Summer Solstice, 12 P.M.

Summer shadows are short because the light is concentrated in a small area. The noon Sun appears high in the sky.

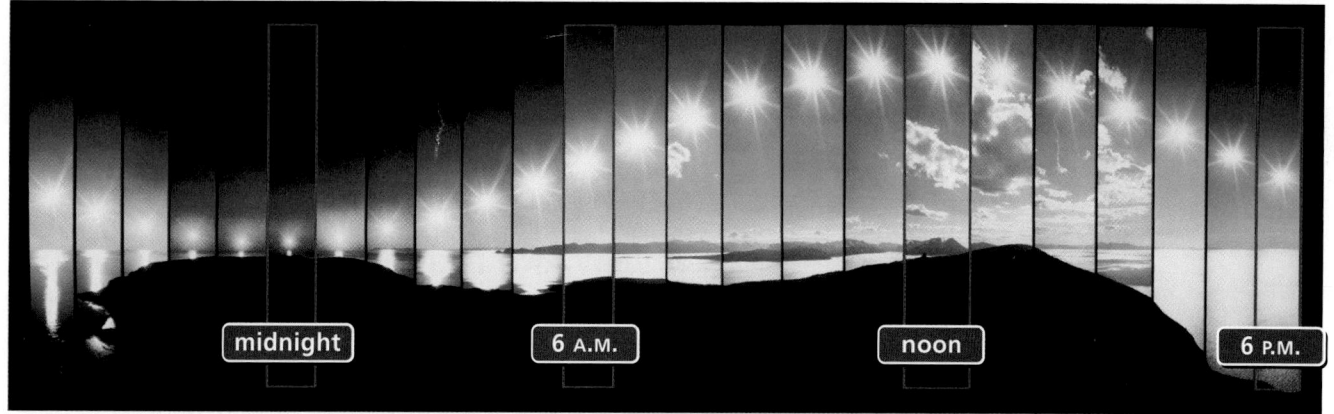

| midnight | 6 A.M. | noon | 6 P.M. |

Lengths of Days

Seasonal temperatures depend on the amount of daylight, too. In Chicago, for example, the summer Sun heats the ground for about 15 hours a day, but in winter there may be only 9 hours of sunlight each day. The farther you get from the equator, the more extreme the changes in day length become. As you near one of the poles, summer daylight may last for 20 hours or more.

Very close to the poles, the Sun does not set at all for six months at a time. It can be seen shining near the horizon at midnight. Tourists often travel far north just to experience the midnight Sun. At locations near a pole, the Sun sets on an equinox and then does not rise again for six months. Astronomers go to the South Pole in March to take advantage of the long winter night, which allows them to study objects in the sky without the interruption of daylight.

Very near the equator, the periods of daylight and darkness are almost equal year-round—each about 12 hours long. Visitors who are used to hot weather during long summer days might be surprised when a hot, sunny day ends suddenly at 6 P.M. At locations away from the equator, daylight lasts 12 hours only around the time of an equinox.

Near the pole in the summer, the Sun stays above the horizon, so there is no night. This series of photographs was taken over the course of a day.

READING TiP

Equinox means "equal night"—daylight and nighttime are equal in length.

20.1 Review

KEY CONCEPTS

1. What causes day and night?
2. What happens to Earth's axis of rotation as Earth orbits the Sun?
3. How do the areas of sunlight in the two hemispheres change over the year?

CRITICAL THINKING

4. **Apply** If you wanted to enjoy longer periods of daylight in the summertime, would you head closer to the equator or farther from it? Why?

5. **Compare and Contrast** How do the average temperatures and the seasonal changes at the equator differ from those at the poles?

⚪ CHALLENGE

6. **Infer** If Earth's axis were tilted so much that the North Pole sometimes pointed straight at the Sun, how would the hours of daylight be affected at your location?

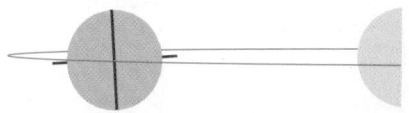

CHAPTER INVESTIGATION

Modeling Seasons

OVERVIEW AND PURPOSE Why is the weather in North America so much colder in January than in July? You might be surprised to learn that it has nothing to do with Earth's distance from the Sun. In fact, Earth is closest to the Sun in January. In this lab, you will model the cause of seasons as you
- orient a light source at different angles to a surface
- determine how the angles of sunlight at a location change as Earth orbits the Sun

▶ Problem

How does the angle of light affect the amount of solar energy a location receives at different times of year?

▶ Hypothesize

After performing step 3, write a hypothesis to explain how the angles of sunlight affect the amounts of solar energy your location receives at different times of year. Your hypothesis should take the form of an "If . . . , then . . . , because . . ." statement.

▶ Procedure

PART A

1. Mark an *X* near the center of the graph paper. Shine the flashlight onto the paper from about 30 cm straight above the X—at an angle of 90° to the surface. Observe the size of the spot of light.

2. Shine the flashlight onto the X at different angles. Keep the flashlight at the same distance. Write down what happens to the size of the spot of light as you change angles.

3. Repeat step 2, but observe just one square near the X. Write down what happens to the brightness of the light as you change the angle. The brightness shows how much energy the area receives from the flashlight.

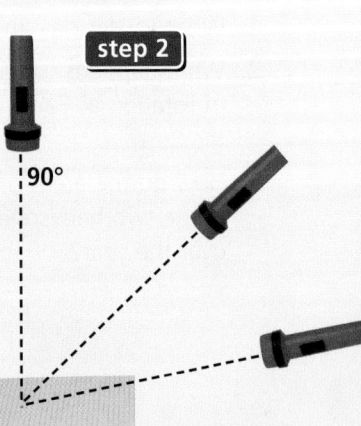
step 2
90°

4. Think about the temperatures at different times of year at your location, then write your hypothesis.

MATERIALS
- graph paper
- flashlight
- meter stick
- protractor
- globe
- stack of books
- sticky note

PART B

5 Set up the globe, books, and flashlight as shown in the photograph. Point the globe's North Pole to the right. This position represents solstice A.

solstice A

6 Find your location on the globe. Place a folded sticky note onto the globe at your location as shown in the photograph. Rotate the globe on its axis until the note faces toward the flashlight.

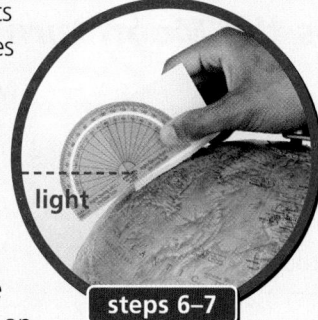
light
steps 6–7

7 The flashlight beam represents noonday sunlight at your location. Use the protractor to estimate the angle of the light on the surface.

8 Move the globe to the left side of the table and the flashlight and books to the right side of the table. Point the North Pole to the right. This position represents solstice B.

solstice B

9 Repeat step 7 for solstice B.

Observe and Analyze

Write It Up

1. RECORD Draw the setup of your materials in each part of the investigation. Organize your notes.

2. ANALYZE Describe how the angle of the flashlight in step 2 affected the area of the spot of light. Which angle concentrated the light into the smallest area?

3. EVALUATE At which angle did a square of the graph paper receive the most energy?

4. COMPARE Compare the angles of light in steps 7 and 9. In which position was the angle of light closer to 90°?

Conclude

Write It Up

1. EVALUATE How did the angle of sunlight at your location differ at the two times of year? At which position is sunlight more concentrated at your location?

2. APPLY The amount of solar energy at a location affects temperature. Which solstice—A or B—represents the summer solstice at your location?

3. INTERPRET Do your results support your hypothesis? Explain why or why not.

INVESTIGATE Further

CHALLENGE What happens in the other hemisphere at the two times of year? Use the model to find out.

Modeling Seasons

Problem How does the angle of light affect the amount of solar energy a location receives at different times of year?

Hypothesize

Observe and Analyze

Table 1. Solstices A and B

	Solstice A	Solstice B
Drawing		
Angle of light (°)		
Observations		

Conclude

KEY CONCEPT

20.2 The Moon is Earth's natural satellite.

VOCABULARY

mare p. 717

◁ BEFORE, you learned

- Earth turns as it orbits the Sun
- The day side of Earth is the part in sunlight
- The Moon is the closest body to Earth

▷ NOW, you will learn

- How the Moon moves
- What the Moon's dark-colored and light-colored features are
- About the inside structure of the Moon

EXPLORE The Moon's Motion

How much does the Moon turn?

PROCEDURE

① Draw a circle to represent the Moon's orbit with Earth at the center. The compass represents the Moon.

② Move the compass around the circle. Keep the side of the compass marked *E* always facing Earth.

③ Observe the positions of the *E* and the compass needle at several positions on the circle.

WHAT DO YOU THINK?
What does the model tell you about the Moon's motion?

MATERIALS
- paper
- magnetic compass

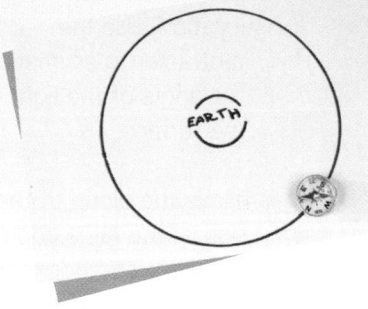

The Moon rotates as it orbits Earth.

When you look at the disk of the Moon, you may notice darker and lighter areas. Perhaps you have imagined them as features of a face or some other pattern. People around the world have told stories about the animals, people, and objects they have imagined while looking at the light and dark areas of the Moon. As you will read in this chapter, these areas tell a story to scientists as well.

The pull of gravity keeps the Moon, Earth's natural satellite, in orbit around Earth. Even though the Moon is Earth's closest neighbor in space, it is far away compared to the sizes of Earth and the Moon.

The Moon's diameter is about 1/4 Earth's diameter, and the Moon is about 30 Earth diameters away.

Earth ●━━━━━━━━━━━━━━━━━━━━━━━━━━━━━ • Moon

The distance between Earth and the Moon is roughly 380,000 kilometers (240,000 mi) —about a hundred times the distance between New York and Los Angeles. If a jet airliner could travel in space, it would take about 20 days to cover a distance that huge. Astronauts, whose spaceships traveled much faster than jets, needed about 3 days to reach the Moon.

You always see the same pattern of dark-colored and light-colored features on the Moon. Only this one side of the Moon can be seen from Earth. The reason is that the Moon, like many other moons in the solar system, always keeps one side turned toward its planet. This means that the Moon turns once on its own axis each time it orbits Earth.

 **CHECK YOUR READING** Why do you see only one side of the Moon?

Moon

The side of the Moon that constantly faces Earth has large, dark areas called maria.

Mass 1% of Earth's mass
Diameter 27% of Earth's diameter
Average distance from Earth 380,000 km
Orbits in 27.3 Earth days
Rotates in 27.3 Earth days

The Moon's craters show its history.

The half of the Moon's surface that constantly faces Earth is called the near side. The half that faces away from Earth is called the far side. Much of the Moon's surface is light-colored. Within the light-colored areas are many small, round features. There are also dark-colored features, some of which cover large areas. Much of the near side of the Moon is covered with these dark-colored features. In contrast, the far side is mostly light-colored with just a few of the darker features.

Just as on Earth, features on the Moon are given names to make it easier to discuss them. The names of the larger surface features on the Moon are in the Latin language, because centuries ago scientists from many different countries used Latin to communicate with one another. Early astronomers thought that the dark areas might be bodies of water, so they used the Latin word for "sea." Today, a dark area on the Moon is still called a lunar **mare** (MAH-ray). The plural form is *maria* (MAH-ree-uh).

The maria are not bodies of water, however. All of the features that can be seen on the Moon are different types of solid or broken rock. The Moon has no air, no oceans, no clouds, and no life.

READING TiP

Lunar means "having to do with the Moon." The word comes from *luna,* the Latin word for the Moon.

Craters and Maria

The light-colored areas of the Moon are higher—at greater altitudes—than the maria, so they are called the lunar highlands. The ground of the lunar highlands is rocky, and some places are covered with a powder made of finely broken rock.

The highlands have many round features, called impact craters, that formed when small objects from space hit the Moon's surface. Long ago, such collisions happened more often than they do today. Many impact craters marked the surfaces of the Moon, Earth, and other bodies in space. On Earth, however, most craters have been worn away by water and wind. On the dry, airless Moon, impact craters from a long time ago are still visible.

Long ago, some of the largest craters filled with molten rock, or lava, that came from beneath the Moon's surface. The lava filled the lowest areas and then cooled, forming the large, flat plains called maria. Smaller impacts have continued to occur, so the dark plains of the maria do contain some craters. Most of the large maria are on the near side of the Moon. However, the widest and deepest basin on the Moon is on the far side, near the Moon's south pole.

 **CHECK YOUR READING** How did the maria form? List the steps.

Lunar Map

Light-colored highlands and dark maria form a familiar pattern on the near side of the Moon and a very different pattern on the far side.

Near Side

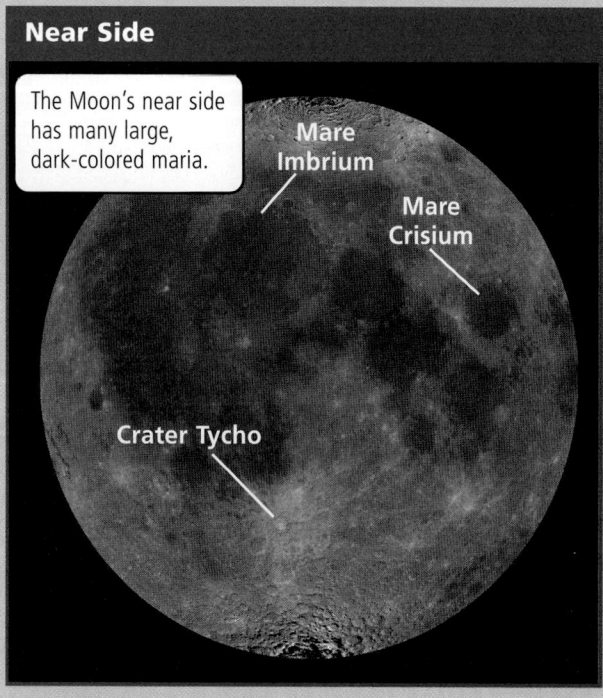

The Moon's near side has many large, dark-colored maria.

Mare Imbrium

Mare Crisium

Crater Tycho

Far Side

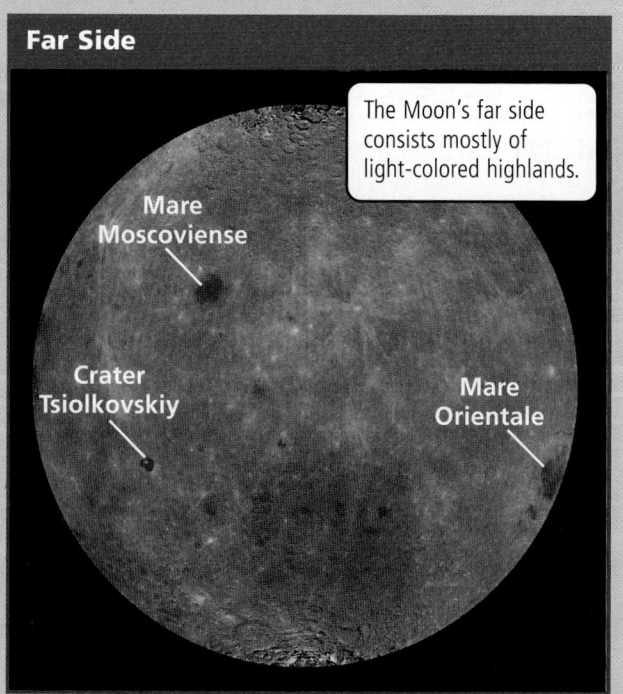

The Moon's far side consists mostly of light-colored highlands.

Mare Moscoviense

Crater Tsiolkovskiy

Mare Orientale

INVESTIGATE Moon Features

How did the Moon's features form?

In this model, you will use a paper towel to represent the Moon's surface and gelatin to represent molten rock from inside the Moon.

PROCEDURE

1. Pour about 1 cm of partly cooled liquid gelatin into the cup.

2. Hold the paper towel by bringing its corners together. Push the towel into the cup until the center of the towel touches the bottom of the cup. Open the towel slightly.

3. Place the cup in the bowl of ice, and allow the gelatin time to solidify.

WHAT DO YOU THINK?

- What part of the towel did the gelatin affect?
- When you look down into the cup, what can the smooth areas tell you about heights?

CHALLENGE Early astronomers thought there might be oceans on the Moon. How does your model lava resemble an ocean?

Moon Rocks

Moon rocks have different ages. Some of the surface rock of the Moon is about 4.5 billion years old—as old as the Moon itself. This very old rock is found in the lunar highlands. The rock in the maria is younger because it formed from lava that solidified later, 3.8–3.1 billion years ago. These two main types of rock and their broken pieces cover most of the Moon's surface. Astronauts explored the Moon and brought back samples of as many different types of material as they could.

Impacts from space objects leave craters, and they also break the surface material into smaller pieces. This breaking of material is called weathering, even though it is not caused by wind and water. Weathered material on the Moon forms a type of dry, lifeless soil. The lunar soil is more than 15 meters (50 ft) deep in some places. Impacts can also toss lunar soil into different places, compact it into new rocks, or melt it and turn it into a glassy type of rock.

The dark-colored rock that formed from lava is called basalt (buh-SAWLT). Lunar basalt is similar to the rock deep beneath Earth's oceans. The basalt of the lunar maria covers large areas but is often only a few hundred meters in depth. However, the basalt can be several kilometers deep at the center of a mare, a depth similar to that of Earth's oceans.

Almost 400 kg (weighing more than 800 lb) of Moon rocks and soil were collected and brought back to Earth by astronauts.

highland rock

basalt

The Moon has layers.

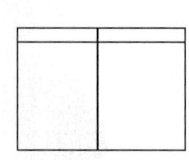
Scientists on Earth have analyzed the lunar rocks and soil to determine their ages and materials. These results told scientists a story about how the Moon changed over time. During an early stage of the Moon's history, impacts happened often and left craters of many different sizes. That stage ended about 3.8 billion years ago, and impacts have happened much less often since then. The highland rocks and soil come from the original surface and impacts. Shortly after the impacts slowed, lava flooded the low-lying areas and formed the maria. Then the flooding stopped. During the last 3 billion years, the Moon has gained new impact craters from time to time but has remained mostly unchanged.

Structure

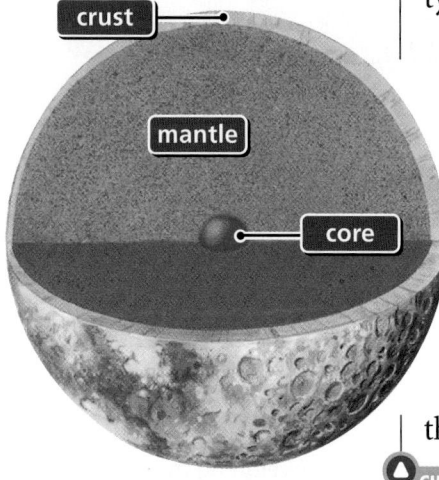

The Moon's interior resembles Earth's interior in several ways.

crust

mantle

core

Scientists have used information from lunar rocks and other measurements to figure out what is inside the Moon. Beneath its thin coating of crushed rock, the Moon has three layers—a crust, a mantle, and a core. As on Earth, the crust is the outermost layer. It averages about 70 kilometers (about 40 mi) thick and contains the least dense type of rock.

Beneath the crust is a thick mantle that makes up most of the Moon's volume. The mantle is made of dense types of rock that include the elements iron and magnesium. The basalt on the lunar surface contains these same elements, so scientists infer that the material of the basalt came from the mantle.

In the middle of the Moon is a small core, approximately 700 kilometers (400 mi) across. Although dense, it makes up only a tiny fraction of the Moon's mass. Scientists have less information about the core than the mantle because material from the core did not reach the Moon's surface. The core seems to consist of iron and other metals.

CHECK YOUR READING What are your own questions about the Moon?

Formation

Scientists develop models to help them understand their observations, such as the observed similarities and differences between Earth and the Moon. The two objects have similar structures and are made of similar materials. However, the materials are in different proportions. The Moon has more materials like Earth's crust and mantle and less material like Earth's core.

Scientists have used these facts to develop models of how the Moon formed. A widely accepted model of the Moon's origin involves a giant collision. In this model, an early version of Earth was hit by a

Formation of the Moon

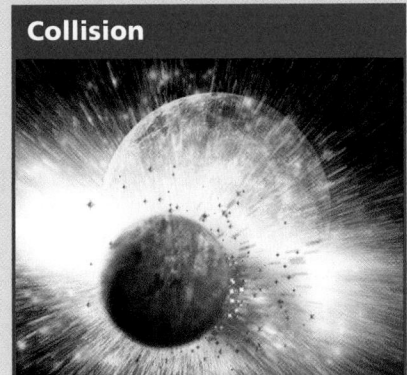

Collision

An early version of Earth is struck by a slightly smaller space body.

Re-Forming

The many pieces pull each other into orbits. Most of the material forms a new version of Earth.

Earth and Moon

The Moon forms from material that orbits the new version of Earth.

smaller space body. Much of the material from both bodies, especially the cores, combined to form a new version of Earth. The energy of the collision also threw material out, away from Earth. Bits of material from the crusts and mantles of both bodies went into orbit around the new Earth. Much of this orbiting material clumped together and became the Moon. Computer simulations of these events show that the Moon may have formed quickly—perhaps within just one year.

Evidence from fossils and rocks on Earth show that, whether the Moon formed from a giant collision or in some other way, it was once much closer to Earth than it is today. The Moon has been moving slowly away from Earth. It now moves 3.8 centimeters (1.5 in.) farther from Earth each year. However, this change is so slow that you will not notice any difference in your lifetime.

20.2 Review

KEY CONCEPTS

1. How many times does the Moon rotate on its axis during one trip around Earth?

2. What are the dark spots and the light areas on the Moon called?

3. Describe the Moon's layers.

CRITICAL THINKING

4. **Compare and Contrast** How are the Moon's dark-colored areas different from its light-colored areas?

5. **Draw Conclusions** How have the Moon rocks that astronauts brought back to Earth helped scientists understand the history of the Moon?

◔ CHALLENGE

6. **Analyze** Scientists use indirect methods to learn about the cores of Earth and the Moon. Imagine you have several Styrofoam balls, some with steel balls hidden inside. Without breaking a ball open, how might you tell whether it contains a steel ball?

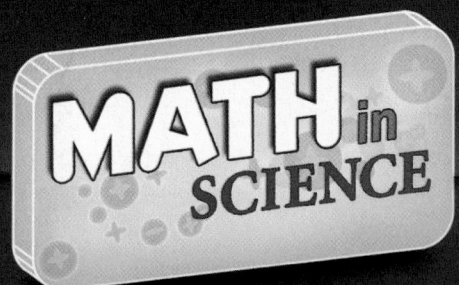

Graphing Sunlight

The location of the Moon and the Sun in the sky depend on your location on Earth and when you look. In summer, the noon Sun is at a greater angle above the horizon—closer to 90°—than it is in winter. In summer, the Sun rises earlier and sets later than in winter. Longer days and steeper angles of sunlight combine to make summer days much warmer than winter days. Plot the data for Washington, D.C. (latitude 39° N) to see the changing patterns of sunlight.

MATH TUTORIAL
CLASSZONE.COM

Click on Math Tutorial for more help with line graphs.

Washington, D.C.

Month	Sunlight Each Day (h)	Angle of Sun at Noon (°)
Jan.	9.9	31.4
Feb.	11.0	40.8
Mar.	12.2	51.6
Apr.	13.5	63.2
May	14.5	71.4
June	14.9	74.6
July	14.5	71.4
Aug.	13.5	63.0
Sept.	12.2	51.6
Oct.	11.0	40.2
Nov.	9.9	31.1
Dec.	9.5	27.7

This is a series of images of the Sun photographed at exactly the same time of day every few days over most of a year. The bottom of the photograph is from just one of the days and includes a stone circle calendar.

Example

You can make a double line graph to see patterns in the data. Use a colored pencil to label the second *y*-axis.

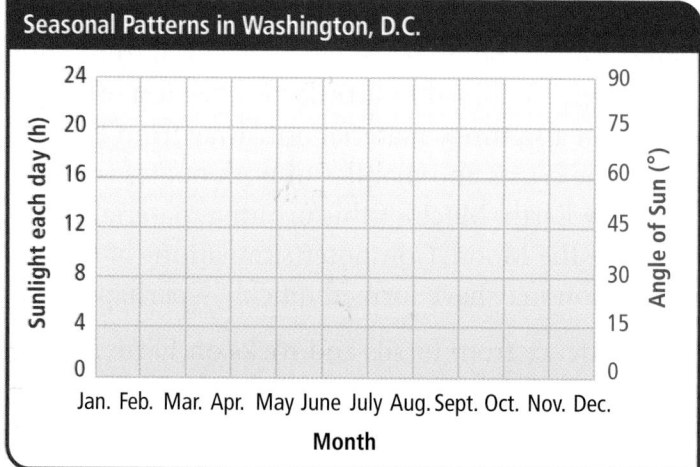

(1) Copy all three graph axes onto graph paper.

(2) Use the *y*-axis on the left to plot the data for the hours of daylight. Draw line segments to connect the points.

(3) Use the *y*-axis on the right and a colored pencil to plot the data for the angle of the Sun. Draw line segments to connect the points.

Answer the following questions.

1. During which time period do days get shorter?

2. About how many degrees higher in the sky is the noon Sun in June than in December? About how many more hours of sunlight are there each day in June than in December?

3. Does the angle of the Sun change more quickly between June and July or between September and October? How can you tell?

CHALLENGE Copy the axes again, then graph the data your teacher gives you for a location near the North Pole. Use your graphs to compare daylight patterns at the two latitudes.

KEY CONCEPT

20.3 Positions of the Sun and Moon affect Earth.

Sunshine State STANDARDS

SC.C.2.3.7: The student knows that gravity is a universal force that every mass exerts on every other mass.

SC.E.1.3.1: The student understands the vast size of our Solar System and the relationship of the planets and their satellites.

SC.H.2.3.1: The student recognizes that patterns exist within and across systems.

VOCABULARY
eclipse p. 727
umbra p. 727
penumbra p. 727

◀ **BEFORE, you learned**

- The Moon orbits Earth
- Sunlight shines on Earth and the Moon

▶ **NOW, you will learn**

- Why the Moon has phases
- What causes eclipses
- Why Earth's oceans have tides

THINK ABOUT

Have you seen the Moon in daylight?

Many people think that the Moon is visible only at night. This idea is not surprising, because the Moon is the brightest object in the sky at night. In the daytime the Moon is only as bright as a tiny, thin cloud. It is easy to miss, even in a cloudless blue sky. You can see the Moon sometimes in the daytime, sometimes at night, often at both times, and sometimes not at all. Why does the Moon sometimes disappear from view?

Phases are different views of the Moon's sunlit half.

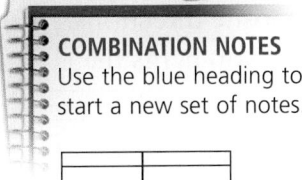

COMBINATION NOTES
Use the blue heading to start a new set of notes.

What you see as moonlight is really light from the Sun reflected by the Moon's surface. At any time, sunlight shines on half of the Moon's surface. Areas where sunlight does not reach look dark, just as the night side of Earth looks dark from space. As the Moon turns on its axis, areas on the surface move into and out of sunlight.

When you look at the Moon, you see a bright shape that is the lit part of the near side of the Moon. The unlit part is hard to see. Lunar phases are the patterns of lit and unlit portions of the Moon that you see from Earth. It takes about a month for the Moon to orbit Earth and go through all the phases.

 **CHECK YOUR READING** Why do you sometimes see only part of the near side of the Moon?

Chapter 20: **Earth, Moon, and Sun** **723**

The Moon's position in its monthly orbit determines how it appears from Earth. The diagram on page 725 shows how the positions of the Moon, the Sun, and Earth affect the shapes you see in the sky.

Waxing Moon

First Week The cycle begins with a new moon. From Earth, the Moon and the Sun are in the same direction. If you face a new moon, you face the Sun. Your face and the far side of the Moon are in sunlight. The near side of the Moon is unlit, so you do not see it. During a new moon, there appears to be no Moon.

As the Moon moves along its orbit, sunlight begins falling on the near side. You see a thin crescent shape. During the first week, the Moon keeps moving farther around, so more of the near side becomes lit. You see thicker crescents as the Moon waxes, or grows.

Second Week When half of the near side of the Moon is in sunlight, the Moon has completed one-quarter of its cycle. The phase is called the first quarter, even though you might describe the shape as a half-moon. You can see in the diagram that the Moon is 90 degrees—at a right angle—from the Sun. If you face the first-quarter moon when it is high in the sky, sunlight will shine on the right side of your head and the right side of the Moon.

You see more of the Moon as it moves along its orbit during the second week. The phase is called gibbous (GIHB-uhs) when the near side is more than half lit but not fully lit. The Moon is still waxing, so the phases during the second week are called waxing gibbous moons.

 **CHECK YOUR READING** Why does the Moon sometimes seem to have a crescent shape?

Waning Moon

Third Week Halfway through its cycle, the whole near side of the Moon is in sunlight—a full moon. You might think of it as the second quarter. Viewed from Earth, the Moon and the Sun are in opposite directions. If you face a full moon at sunset, sunlight from behind you lights the back of your head and the near side of the Moon.

As the Moon continues around during the third week, less and less of the near side is in sunlight. The Moon seems to shrink, or wane, so these phases are called waning gibbous moons.

Fourth Week When the near side is again only half in sunlight, the Moon is three-quarters of the way through its cycle. The phase is called the third quarter. The Moon is again 90 degrees from the Sun. If you face the third-quarter moon when it is high in the sky, sunlight will shine on the left side of your head and the left side of the Moon.

Lunar Phases

The appearance of the Moon depends on the positions of the Sun, Moon, and Earth.

If you could watch the Moon from high above its pole, you would always see half the Moon in sunlight and half in darkness.

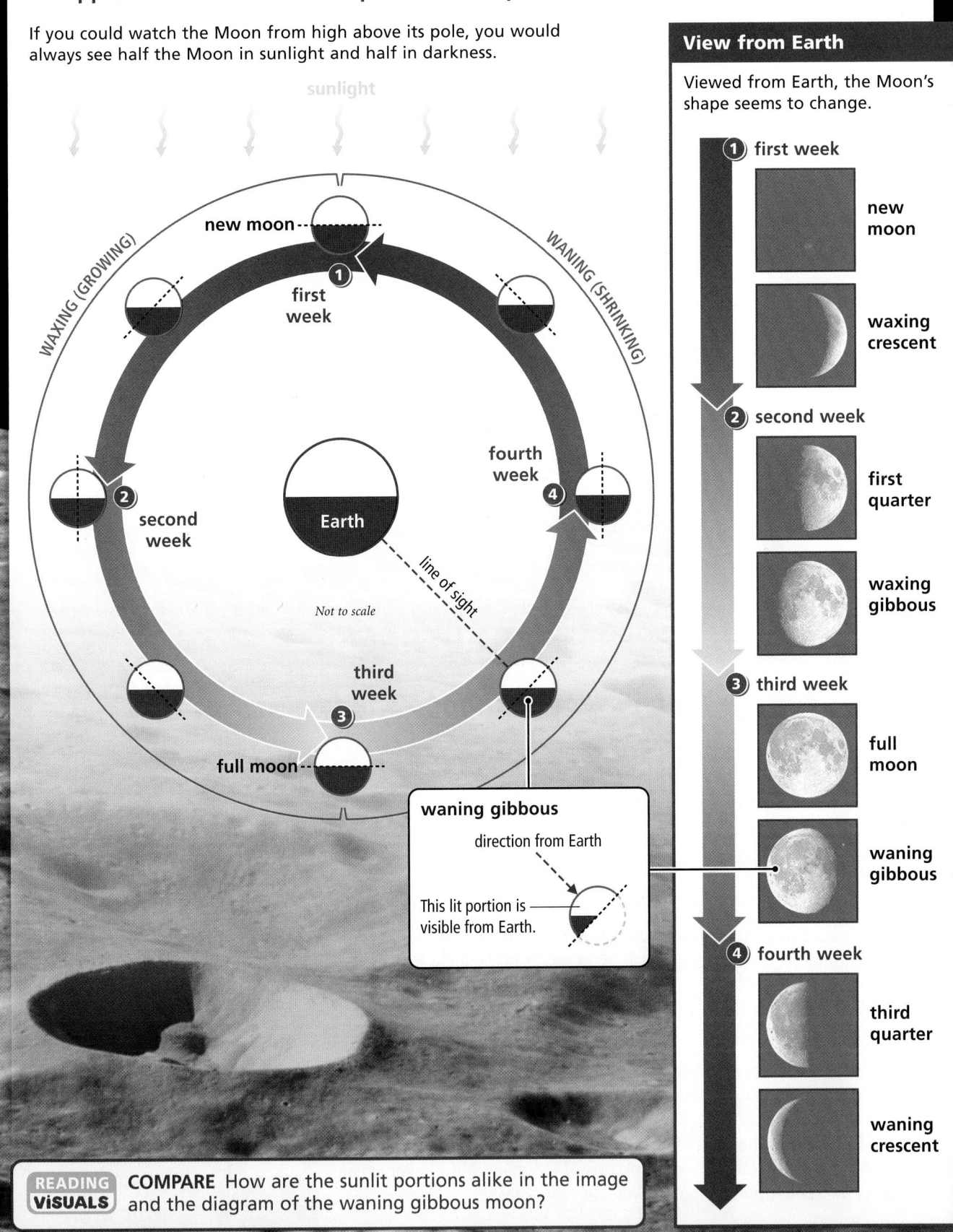

sunlight

WAXING (GROWING)

WANING (SHRINKING)

new moon

first week

Earth

line of sight

Not to scale

second week

fourth week

third week

full moon

waning gibbous

direction from Earth

This lit portion is visible from Earth.

View from Earth

Viewed from Earth, the Moon's shape seems to change.

1 first week
- new moon
- waxing crescent

2 second week
- first quarter
- waxing gibbous

3 third week
- full moon
- waning gibbous

4 fourth week
- third quarter
- waning crescent

READING VISUALS **COMPARE** How are the sunlit portions alike in the image and the diagram of the waning gibbous moon?

As the Moon continues to move around Earth during the fourth week, less and less of the near side is in sunlight. The waning crescent moon grows thinner and thinner. At the end of the fourth week, the near side is again unlit, and the new moon begins a new cycle.

Crescent and Gibbous Moons

Think through the waxing lunar phases again. The Moon waxes from new to crescent to gibbous during the first half of its cycle. Then it wanes from full to gibbous to crescent during the second half of its cycle.

The amount of the Moon that you see from Earth depends on the angle between the Moon and the Sun. When this angle is small, you see only a small amount of the Moon. Crescent moons occur when the Moon appears close to the Sun in the sky. As a result, they are visible most often in the daytime or around the time of sunrise or sunset. When the angle between the Sun and the Moon is large, you see a large amount of the Moon. Gibbous and full moons appear far from the Sun in the sky. You may see them in the daytime, but you are more likely to notice them at night.

 CHECK YOUR READING What shape does the Moon appear to be when it is at a small angle to the Sun?

INVESTIGATE Phases of the Moon

Why does the Moon seem to change shape?

SKILL FOCUS
Making models

PROCEDURE

1. Place the ball on the stick, which will act as a handle. The ball will represent the Moon, and your head will represent Earth.

2. Hold the ball toward the light, then move it to your left until you see a bright edge. Draw what you see.

3. Move the ball farther around until half of what you see is lit. Draw it.

4. Keep moving the ball around to your left until the side you see is fully lit, then half lit, then lit only a little bit. Each time, face the ball and draw it.

MATERIALS
• foam ball
• stick
• lamp

TIME
20 minutes

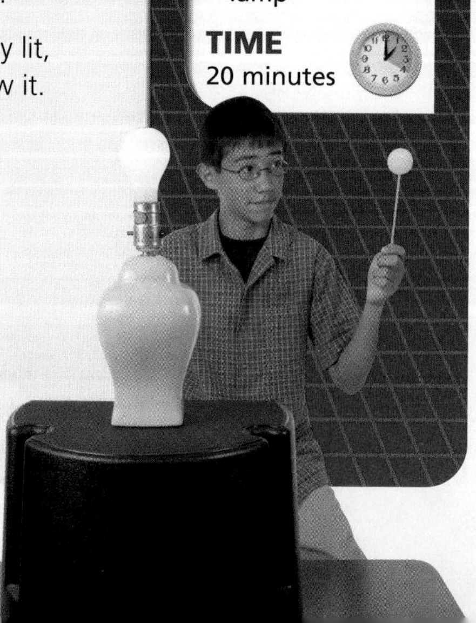

WHAT DO YOU THINK?

• In step 2, which side of the ball was lit? Explain why.

• How are your drawings like the photographs of the Moon's phases? Label each drawing with the name of the corresponding lunar phase.

CHALLENGE When the Moon is a crescent, sometimes you can dimly see the rest of the Moon if you look closely. Where might the light that makes the darker part of the Moon visible come from?

Shadows in space cause eclipses.

Sunlight streams past Earth and the Moon, lighting one side of each body. Beyond each body is a long, thin cone of darkness where no sunlight reaches—a shadow in space. The two bodies are far apart, so they usually miss each other's shadow as the Moon orbits Earth. However, if the Moon, the Sun, and Earth line up exactly, a shadow crosses Earth or the Moon. An **eclipse** occurs when a shadow makes the Sun or the Moon seem to grow dark. In a lunar eclipse, the Moon darkens. In a solar eclipse, the Sun seems to darken.

VOCABULARY
Remember to record vocabulary terms.

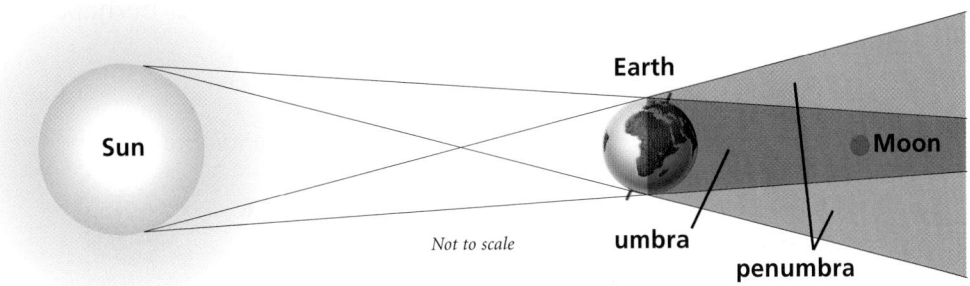

Sun

Earth

Moon

Not to scale umbra

penumbra

Lunar Eclipses

The Moon becomes dark during a lunar eclipse because it passes through Earth's shadow. There are two parts of Earth's shadow, as you can see in the diagram above. The **umbra** is the darkest part. Around it is a spreading cone of lighter shadow called the **penumbra.**

Just before a lunar eclipse, sunlight streaming past Earth produces a full moon. Then the Moon moves into Earth's penumbra and becomes slightly less bright. As the Moon moves into the umbra, Earth's dark shadow seems to creep across and cover the Moon. The entire Moon can be in darkness because the Moon is small enough to fit entirely within Earth's umbra. After an hour or more, the Moon moves slowly back into the sunlight that is streaming past Earth.

A total lunar eclipse occurs when the Moon passes completely into Earth's umbra. If the Moon misses part or all of the umbra, part of the Moon stays light and the eclipse is called a partial lunar eclipse.

Earth's shadow

The Moon starts getting dark on one side as it passes into Earth's umbra. Even when the Moon is completely within Earth's umbra, some red sunlight, bent by Earth's atmosphere, may still reach the Moon.

Solar Eclipses

In a solar eclipse, the Sun seems to darken because the Moon's shadow falls onto part of Earth. Imagine that you are in the path of a solar eclipse. At first, you see a normal day. You cannot see the dark Moon moving toward the Sun. Then part of the Sun seems to disappear as the Moon moves in front of it. You are in the Moon's penumbra. After several hours of growing darkness, the Moon covers the Sun's disk completely. The sky becomes as dark as night, and you may see constellations. In place of the Sun is a black disk—the new moon—surrounded by a pale glow. You are in the Moon's umbra, the darkest part of the shadow, experiencing a total solar eclipse. After perhaps a minute, the Sun's bright surface starts to appear again.

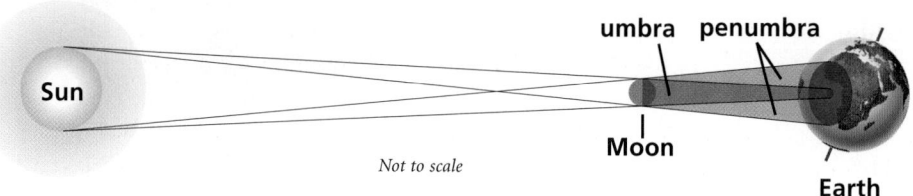

Not to scale

A solar eclipse occurs when the Moon passes directly between Earth and the Sun. As you can see in the diagram above, the side of the Moon that faces Earth is unlit, so solar eclipses occur only during new moons.

If you could watch a solar eclipse from space, it might seem more like a lunar eclipse. You would see the Moon's penumbra, with the dark umbra in the center, move across Earth's daylight side. However, the Moon is smaller than Earth, so it casts a smaller shadow. As you can see in the diagram above, the Moon's umbra covers only a fraction of Earth's surface at a time.

June 21, 2001, Eclipse

total eclipse

In this time-lapse photograph, the Sun's disk appears darker as the Moon passes in front. When the Moon is exactly in front of the Sun, the sky grows as dark as night.

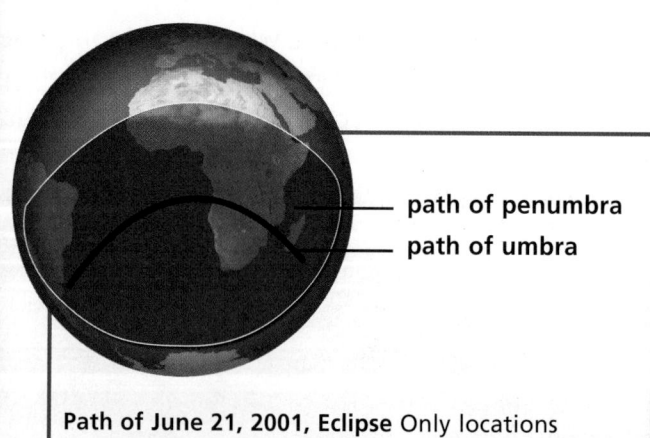

path of penumbra
path of umbra

Path of June 21, 2001, Eclipse Only locations along the thin central path of the shadow experience a total eclipse. Other locations experience a partial eclipse.

Only locations in the path of the Moon's shadow experience a solar eclipse. Some people travel thousands of miles to be in the thin path of the Moon's umbra so that they can experience a total solar eclipse. Locations near the path of the umbra get an eclipse that is less than total. If only the penumbra moves over your location, you experience a partial solar eclipse. The Moon covers just part of the Sun.

Bright light from the Sun's disk can damage your eyes if you look directly at it. The Sun is unsafe to look at even when the Moon covers most of the Sun's disk. If you have the chance to experience a solar eclipse, use a safe method to view the Sun.

COMBINATION NOTES
Remember to make notes about new ideas.

CHECK YOUR READING Where is the Moon during a solar eclipse? Find a way to remember the difference between the two types of eclipses.

The Moon's gravity causes tides on Earth.

If you have spent time near an ocean, you may have experienced the usual pattern of tides. At first, you might see dry sand that slopes down to the ocean. Then, waves creep higher and higher onto the sand. The average water level rises slowly for about 6 hours. The highest level is called high tide. Then the water level slowly drops for about 6 hours. The lowest level is called low tide. Then the water level rises and falls again. The entire pattern—two high tides and two low tides—takes a little more than 24 hours.

In areas with tides, the water generally reaches its lowest level twice a day and its highest level twice a day.

CHECK YOUR READING How many high tides do you expect per day?

Tides occur because the Moon's gravity changes the shape of Earth's oceans. The Moon pulls on different parts of Earth with different amounts of force. It pulls hardest on the side of Earth nearest it, a little less hard on the center of Earth, and even less hard on the farthest side of Earth. If Earth were flexible, it would be pulled into a football shape. Earth's crust is hard enough to resist being pulled into a different shape, but Earth's oceans do change shape.

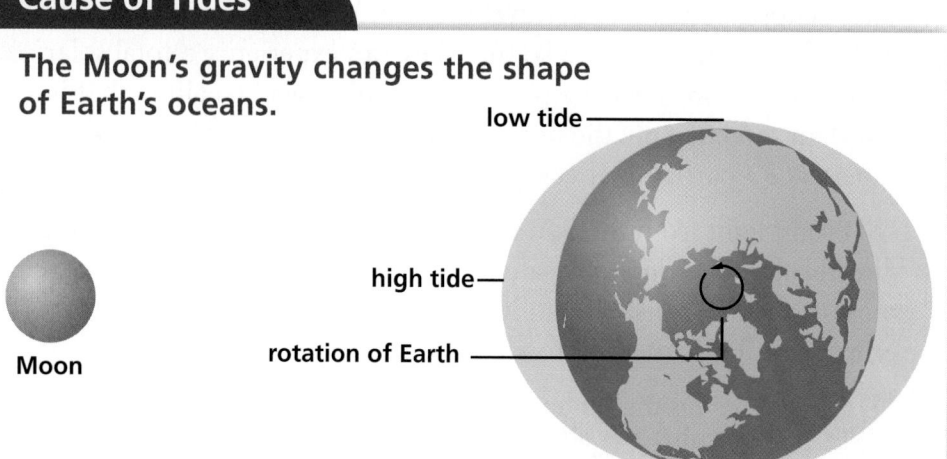

Cause of Tides

The Moon's gravity changes the shape of Earth's oceans.

Moon

low tide

high tide

rotation of Earth

Not to scale

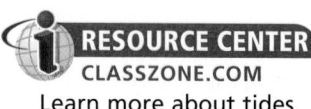
RESOURCE CENTER
CLASSZONE.COM
Learn more about tides.

FLORIDA
Content Preview

Gravity is a force of attraction between objects. You'll learn more about gravity in grade 8.

The diagram above shows what would happen if Earth were covered with a thick layer of water. The Moon's pull produces a bulge of thicker ocean water on the side of Earth nearest the Moon. Another bulge of water is produced on the side of Earth farthest from the Moon because the Moon pulls the center of Earth away from that side. The layer of water is thinnest in the middle, between the bulges.

A location moves past different thicknesses of water as Earth turns on its axis. As a result, the water level there rises and falls. The thickest water produces the highest level, which is high tide. A quarter of a rotation—6 hours—later, the location has moved to the thinnest layer of water, or low tide. Another high tide and low tide complete the cycle. Because the Moon is orbiting while Earth is turning, the cycle takes a little longer than the 24 hours in a day.

 **CHECK YOUR READING** Why does a cycle of tides take about 24 hours?

20.3 Review

KEY CONCEPTS

1. When the Moon is full, where is it in its orbit around Earth?

2. Where is the Moon in its orbit at the time of a solar eclipse?

3. If it is high tide where you are, is the tide high or low on the side of Earth directly opposite you?

CRITICAL THINKING

4. **Apply** If you were on the Moon's near side during a new moon, how much of the side of Earth facing you would be sunlit?

5. **Predict** If Earth did not turn, how would the pattern of tides be affected?

◯CHALLENGE

6. **Predict** Would we see lunar phases if the Moon did not rotate while it orbits Earth?

Astronomy in Archaeology

In order to understand how people lived and thought long ago, archaeologists study the buildings and other physical remains of ancient cultures. Archaeologists often think about what needs people had in order to figure out how they used the things they built. For example, people needed to know the time of year in order to decide when to plant crops, move to a different location for winter, or plan certain ceremonies.

Archaeologists can use their knowledge about objects in the sky to hypothesize about the purpose of an ancient structure. They can also use knowledge and models from astronomy to test their hypotheses. For example, archaeologists found some structures at Chimney Rock that were built at times of special events in the sky.

Antikythera Computer

A device with gears and dials was found in an ancient Greek shipwreck. While examining the device, a scientist noticed terms, patterns, and numbers from astronomy. These observations led him to form a hypothesis that ancient Greeks used the instrument to calculate the positions of the Sun, Moon, and other bodies in space. Gamma-ray images of the instrument's interior later supported this hypothesis.

Chimney Rock

Chimney Rock, in Colorado, is topped by two natural pillars of rock. The Moon appears to rise between the pillars under special circumstances that happen about every 18 years. Near the pillars are ruins of buildings of the Anasazi people. In order to construct the buildings and live here, the builders had to haul materials and water much farther than was usual. Some archaeologists hypothesize that the Anasazi built here in order to watch or celebrate special events in the sky.

Stonehenge

Stonehenge is an arrangement of stones in Britain. The first stones were placed there around 3100 B.C. The way that the Sun and Moon line up with the stones has led some archaeologists to think that they were designed to help people predict solstices and eclipses. Solstices tell people the time of year, so Stonehenge has sometimes been called a calendar.

path of rising Sun on solstice

Stonehenge as seen from above

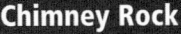

EXPLORE

1. **COMPARE** How is each archaeological example related to astronomy?

2. **CHALLENGE** Make a list of five print or television advertisements that feature the Sun or other objects in the sky. Bring in copies of the advertisements if you can. Why might the advertisers have chosen these objects?

Ruins of buildings were found on a high, narrow ridge at Chimney Rock.

20 Chapter Review

Earth and the Moon move in predictable ways as they orbit the Sun.

FLORIDA REVIEW
CLASSZONE.COM

Content Review and
FCAT Practice

◄ **KEY CONCEPTS SUMMARY**

① Earth rotates on a tilted axis and orbits the Sun.

Earth's rotation in sunlight causes day and night.

The changing angles of sunlight on Earth cause seasons.

VOCABULARY
axis of rotation p. 708
revolution p. 709
season p. 710
equinox p. 710
solstice p. 710

② The Moon is Earth's natural satellite.

Dark-colored maria formed from lava-filled craters.

Light-colored highlands are old and cratered.

The Moon's near side always faces Earth.

crust
mantle
core

VOCABULARY
mare p. 717

③ Positions of the Sun and Moon affect Earth.

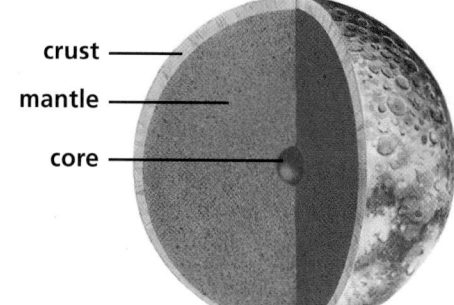

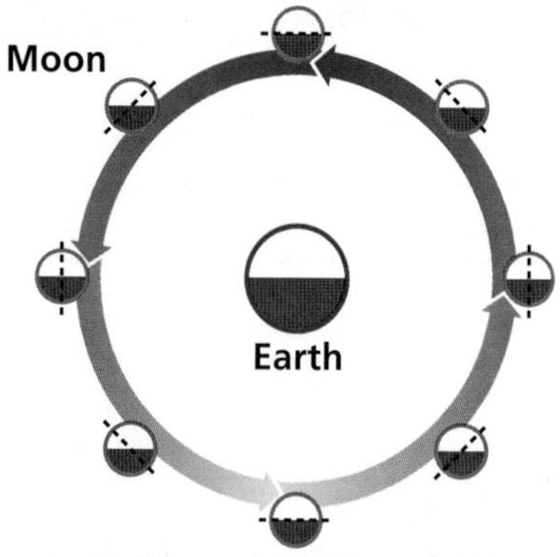

Moon

Earth

penumbra

umbra

Shadows cause eclipses.

The Moon's gravity causes tides as Earth turns.

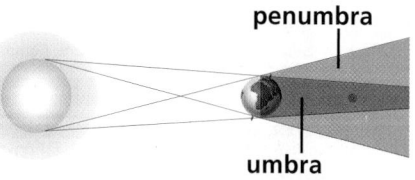

Lunar phases are different views of the Moon's sunlit half.

VOCABULARY
eclipse p. 727
umbra p. 727
penumbra p. 727

Reviewing Vocabulary

Use words and diagrams to show the relationship between the terms in each the following pairs. Underline the two terms in each answer.

1. revolution, rotation

2. revolution, season

3. solstice, equinox

4. mare, impact crater

5. eclipse, umbra

6. umbra, penumbra

Reviewing Key Concepts

Multiple Choice *Choose the letter of the best answer.*

7. How long does it take Earth to turn once on its axis of rotation?
   a. an hour   c. a month
   b. a day   d. a year

8. How long does it take Earth to orbit the Sun?
   a. an hour   c. a month
   b. a day   d. a year

9. About how long does it take the Moon to revolve once around Earth?
   a. an hour   c. a month
   b. a day   d. a year

10. Why is it hotter in summer than in winter?
    a. Earth gets closer to and farther from the Sun.
    b. Sunlight strikes the ground at higher angles.
    c. Earth turns faster in some seasons.
    d. Earth revolves around the Sun more times in some seasons.

11. The dark maria on the Moon formed from
    a. dried-up seas
    b. finely-broken rock
    c. large shadows
    d. lava-filled craters

12. The lunar highlands have more impact craters than the maria, so scientists know that the highlands
    a. are older than the maria
    b. are younger than the maria
    c. are flatter than the maria
    d. are darker than the maria

13. Why is just one side of the Moon visible from Earth?
    a. The Moon does not rotate on its axis as it orbits Earth.
    b. The Moon rotates once in the same amount of time that it orbits.
    c. Half of the Moon is always unlit by the Sun.
    d. Half of the Moon does not reflect light.

14. Why does the Moon seem to change shape from week to week?
    a. Clouds block part of the Moon.
    b. The Moon moves through Earth's shadow.
    c. The Moon is lit in different ways.
    d. Different amounts of the dark-colored side of the Moon face Earth.

15. Which words describe the different shapes that the Moon appears to be?
    a. waning and waxing
    b. waning and crescent
    c. waxing and gibbous
    d. crescent and gibbous

16. During a total eclipse of the Moon, the Moon is
    a. in Earth's umbra
    b. in Earth's penumbra
    c. between Earth and the Sun
    d. casting a shadow on Earth

Short Response *Write a short response to each question.*

17. What motion produces two high tides in a day? Explain your answer.

18. How are the structure of the Moon and the structure of Earth similar?

Thinking Critically

Use the lunar map below to answer the next four questions.

Near Side **Far Side**

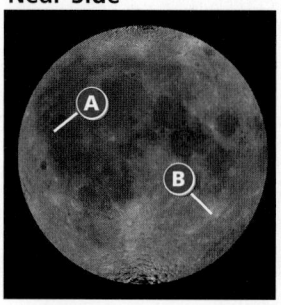 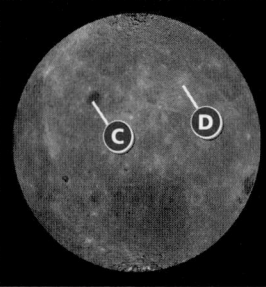

19. APPLY Which points are at higher elevations? Explain how you know.

20. COMPARE During a first-quarter moon, will point A, point B, both, or neither be in sunlight? **Hint:** Use the diagram on page 725.

21. INFER During a total lunar eclipse, which points will be in darkness?

22. INFER During a total solar eclipse, the Moon is new. Which points will be in darkness?

23. CONNECT Use your knowledge of the motions of Earth and the Moon to determine how long it takes the Moon to travel once around the Sun.

24. ANALYZE Which two parts of the Moon have important chemical elements in common? Choose from the following: core, mantle, crust, maria, highlands.

25. APPLY If it is noon for you, what time is it for someone directly on the opposite side of Earth?

26. CLASSIFY On what part or parts of Earth are winter and summer temperatures the most different from each other?

27. APPLY If it is the winter solstice in New York, what solstice or equinox is it in Sydney, Australia, in the Southern Hemisphere?

28. PREDICT If Earth stayed exactly the same distance from the Sun throughout the year, would the seasons be different? Explain what you think would happen.

29. PREDICT If Earth's axis were not tilted with respect to the orbit, would the seasons be different? Explain what you think would happen.

30. PROVIDE EXAMPLES How do the positions of the Sun and the Moon affect what people do? Give three examples of the ways that people's jobs or other activities are affected by the positions of the Sun, the Moon, or both.

31. PREDICT Which shape of the Moon are you most likely to see during the daytime? **Hint:** Compare the directions of the Sun and Moon from Earth in the diagram on page 725.

32. CLASSIFY What types of information have scientists used to make inferences about the Moon's history?

— **South Pole**

33. ANALYZE The photograph above shows the side of Earth in sunlight at a particular time. The location of the South Pole is indicated. Was the photograph taken in March, in June, in September, or in December?

the BIG idea

34. APPLY Look again at the photograph on pages 704–705. Now that you have finished the chapter, how would you change your response to the question on the photograph?

35. SYNTHESIZE If you were an astronaut in the middle of the near side of the Moon during a full moon, how would the ground around you look? How would Earth, high in your sky, look? Describe what is in sunlight and what is in darkness.

UNIT PROJECTS

If you need to do an experiment for your unit project, gather the materials. Be sure to allow enough time to observe results before the project is due.

Analyzing a Diagram

The sketches show the phases of the Moon one week apart. The diagram shows the Moon's orbit around Earth. Use the diagram and the sketches to answer the questions below.

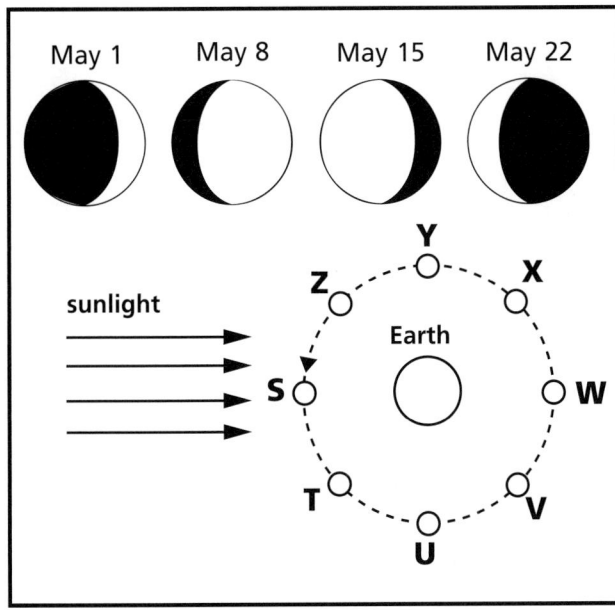

> **FCAT TiP**
>
> When answering multiple-choice questions, try to come up with the answer to the question in your head before you look at the choices. This will help you avoid being distracted by incorrect answer choices.

MULTIPLE CHOICE

1. At which letter on the diagram might a full moon occur?

   A. S   **C.** W

   B. U   **D.** X

2. Which letter on the diagram shows the position of the Moon on May 8?

   F. S   **H.** U

   G. T   **I.** V

3. Approximately when was the Moon full?

   A. May 4   **C.** May 18

   B. May 11   **D.** May 29

4. At which letter on the diagram might a solar eclipse occur?

   F. S   **H.** W

   G. V   **I.** Z

5. How much of the sunlit part of the Moon was visible from Earth on May 8?

   A. None of the sunlit part was visible.

   B. About one-quarter of the sunlit part was visible.

   C. About three-quarters of the sunlit part was visible.

   D. All of the sunlit part was visible.

SHORT RESPONSE

6. Which of these sketches show Earth's shadow on the Moon? Explain your answer.

7. Using the diagram, determine which factor is most directly responsible for determining how often a full moon appears: how quickly the Moon orbits Earth or how quickly the Moon turns on its axis. Explain your answer.

EXTENDED RESPONSE
Answer the two questions below in detail. A diagram may help you to answer.

8. The Moon was once much closer to Earth. What effect do you think that this distance had on eclipses?

9. What do you think would happen to tides on Earth if Earth stopped rotating? Why?

TIMELINES in Science

THE STORY OF ASTRONOMY

Around the year A.D. 140, an astronomer named Ptolemy wrote down his ideas about the motion of bodies in space. Ptolemy shared the view of many Greek astronomers that the Sun, the Moon, and the planets orbit Earth in perfect circles. The Greeks had observed that planets sometimes seem to reverse direction in their motion across the sky. Ptolemy explained that the backward movements are smaller orbits within the larger orbits. For 1400 years, Europeans accepted this Earth-centered model. In the mid-1500s, however, astronomers began to challenge and then reject Ptolemy's ideas.

The timeline shows a few events in the history of astronomy. Scientists have developed special tools and procedures to study objects in the sky. The boxes below the timeline show how technology has led to new knowledge about space and how that knowledge has been applied.

1543

Sun Takes Center Stage
Nicolaus Copernicus, a Polish astronomer, proposes that the planets orbit the Sun rather than Earth. His Sun-centered model shocks many because it conflicts with the traditional belief that Earth is the center of the universe.

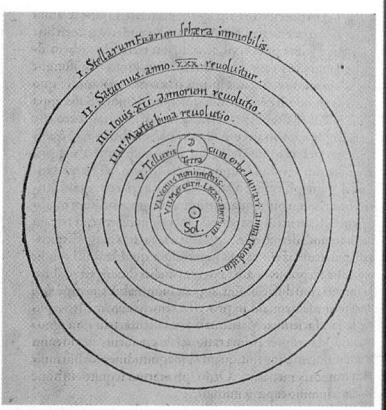

EVENTS

| 1500 | 1520 | 1540 | 1560 |

APPLICATIONS AND TECHNOLOGY

APPLICATION

Navigating by Sunlight and Starlight
For thousands of years, sailors studied the sky to find their way at sea. Because the Sun and stars move in predictable ways, sailors used them to navigate across water. During the 1400s, sailors began to use a device called a mariner's astrolabe to observe the positions of the Sun and stars. Later devices allowed sailors to make more accurate measurements.

This mariner's astrolabe was made in the 1600s.

1609
Scientist Pinpoints Planet Paths

German astronomer Johannes Kepler concludes that the orbits of planets are not circles but ellipses, or flattened circles. Kepler, formerly the assistant of Tycho Brahe, reached his conclusion by studying Brahe's careful observations of the motions of planets.

1863
Stars and Earth Share Elements

English astronomer William Huggins announces that stars are made of hydrogen and other elements found on Earth. Astronomers had traditionally believed that stars were made of a unique substance. Huggins identified the elements in stars by studying their spectra.

1687
Laws of Gravity Revealed

English scientist Isaac Newton explains that gravity causes planets to orbit the Sun. His three laws of motion explain how objects interact on Earth as well as in space.

| 1600 | 1620 | 1640 | 1660 | 1680 | 1860 |

TECHNOLOGY
Viewing Space

The telescope was probably invented in the early 1600s, when an eyeglass maker attached lenses to both ends of a tube. Soon afterward, Italian scientist Galileo Galilei copied the invention and used it to look at objects in space. Galileo's telescope allowed him to study features never seen before, such as mountains on the Moon. Most astronomers now use telescopes that gather visible light with mirrors rather than lenses. There are also special telescopes that gather other forms of electro-magnetic radiation.

1912

Cycles of Stars Are Key to Distances

Certain types of stars, called Cepheid variables, get brighter and then dimmer in a regular cycle. Astronomer Henrietta Leavitt finds that brighter stars have longer cycles. This discovery will allow the distances to these stars to be calculated.

1916

Time, Space, and Mass Are Connected

The general theory of relativity expands Newton's theory of gravitation. Albert Einstein shows that mass affects time and space. According to this theory, gravity will affect the light we receive from objects in space.

1929

Big Is Getting Bigger

Edwin Hubble has already used Cepheid variables to show that some objects in the sky are actually distant galaxies. Now he finds that galaxies are generally moving apart, at rates that increase with distance. Many astronomers conclude that the universe is expanding.

1880   1900   1920   1940   1960

TECHNOLOGY

Colliding Particles Give Details About the Start of the Universe

Scientists think that all matter and energy was in an extremely hot, dense state and then exploded rapidly in an event called the big bang. Some scientists are attempting to re-create some of the conditions that existed during the first billionth of a second after the big bang. They use devices called particle accelerators to make tiny particles move almost at the speed of light. When the particles crash into each other, they produce different types of particles and radiation. Scientists use what they learn from the particles and the radiation to develop models of conditions at the beginning of the universe.

1998

Fast Is Getting Faster

Two groups of astronomers studying exploding stars called supernovae come to the same remarkable conclusion. Not only is the universe expanding, but the rate of expansion is increasing. In the diagram below, the rate of expansion is shown by the distances between rings and between galaxies.

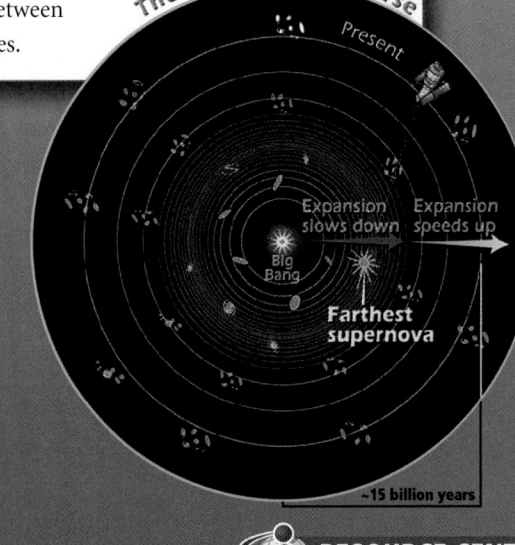

The expanding universe

Present

Expansion slows down

Expansion speeds up

Big Bang

Farthest supernova

~15 billion years

RESOURCE CENTER
CLASSZONE.COM
Learn more about current advances in astronomy.

1980   2000

TECHNOLOGY

Measuring the Big Bang

In 1965 two researchers noticed radio waves that came from all directions instead of from just one direction, like a signal from a space object. They inferred that the radiation was left over from the big bang. In 1989 and again in 2001, NASA launched spacecraft to study the radiation. Data gathered using these telescopes in space are still being used to test different models of the big bang, including the arrangement of matter in the universe. In this map of the sky, red and yellow show the areas that were hottest after the big bang.

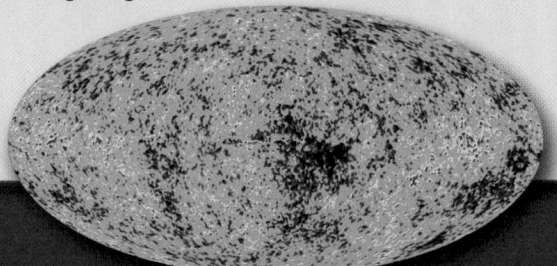

INTO THE FUTURE

Throughout history, people have learned about the universe from visible light and other radiation. New and better measurements have been made as technologies improved. Better and more complex models are filling in details that cannot be measured directly. In the future, improvements will continue. Computers, telescopes in space, and other instruments will allow astronomers to collect better data and make better models.

Some matter in the universe does not give off or reflect any detectable radiation. This is called dark matter. Astronomers infer its existence from its effects on matter that is detected. In the future, astronomers hope to determine what dark matter is, exactly where it is, and how it moves in the universe. In a similar way, astronomers will learn more about why the universe is expanding faster with time and what energy is involved in this acceleration.

ACTIVITIES

Reliving History

Some early astronomers observed the Moon in order to develop and test their ideas about space. For two weeks or more, make frequent observations of the Moon and keep your notes, sketches, and thoughts in a notebook. You might look for the Moon at a certain time each day or night or perhaps record the direction in which the Moon sets. A newspaper may list the times of moonrise and moonset for your location.

Compare your observations and thoughts with those of other students. You might also find out what people in other cultures thought of the patterns of change they saw in the Moon.

Writing About Science

Choose one of these famous astronomers and research his or her story. Write a biographical profile or an imaginary interview with that person.

Our Solar System

the **BIG** idea

Planets and other objects form a system around our Sun.

Key Concepts

SECTION

1 **Planets orbit the Sun at different distances.**
Learn about the sizes and the distances of objects in the solar system and about its formation.

SECTION

2 **The inner solar system has rocky planets.**
Learn about the processes that shape Earth and other planets.

SECTION

3 **The outer solar system has four giant planets.**
Learn about the largest planets.

SECTION

4 **Small objects are made of ice and rock.**
Learn about moons, asteroids, and comets.

FCAT Practice

Prepare and practice for the FCAT
- Section Reviews, pp. 747, 756, 763, 769
- Chapter Review, pp. 772–774
- FCAT Practice, p. 775

CLASSZONE.COM
- Florida Review: Content Review and FCAT Practice

This image shows Jupiter with one of its large moons. How big are these objects compared with Earth?

EXPLORE (the BIG idea)

How Big Is Jupiter?

Measure 1.4 mL of water (about 22 drops) into an empty 2 L bottle to represent Earth. Use a full 2 L bottle to represent Jupiter. Lift each one.

Observe and Think How big is Jupiter compared with Earth? Using this scale, you would need more than nine hundred 2 L bottles to represent the Sun. How big is the Sun compared with Jupiter?

How Round Is an Orbit?

Tie a loop 10 cm long in a piece of string. Place two thumbtacks 2 cm apart in the center of a piece of paper. Loop the string around the thumbtacks and use a pencil to draw an oval the shape of Pluto's orbit. Remove one thumbtack. The remaining thumbtack represents the Sun.

Observe and Think How would you describe the shape of this orbit? How different is it from a circle?

Internet Activity: Spacing

Go to **ClassZone.com** to take a virtual spaceflight through the solar system. Examine distances between planets as your virtual spaceship travels at a constant speed.

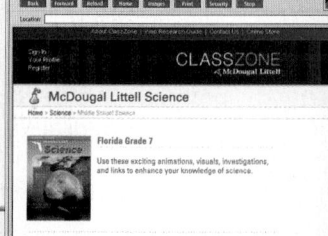

Observe and Think What do you notice about the relative distances of the planets?

NSTA
scilinks.org
SCi LINKS

The Solar System **Code: MDL059**

Getting Ready to Learn

◀ CONCEPT REVIEW

- The planets we see are much closer than the stars in constellations.
- The Sun, the planets, and smaller bodies make up the solar system.
- Scientists observe different types of electromagnetic radiation from space objects.

◀ VOCABULARY REVIEW

orbit p. 674

solar system p. 674

satellite p. 687

impact crater p. 696

axis of rotation p. 708

FLORIDA REVIEW
CLASSZONE.COM

Content Review and FCAT Practice

▶ TAKING NOTES

MAIN IDEA AND DETAILS

Make a two-column chart. Write **main ideas,** such as those in the blue headings, in the column on the left. Write **details** about each of those main ideas in the column on the right.

VOCABULARY STRATEGY

Draw a **word triangle** diagram for each new vocabulary term. In the bottom row write and define the term. In the middle row, use the term correctly in a sentence. At the top, draw a small picture to help you remember the term.

See the Note-Taking Handbook on pages R45–R51.

SCIENCE NOTEBOOK

MAIN IDEAS	DETAIL NOTES
1. Planets have different sizes and distances.	1. Objects in the solar system • Sun • planets • moons • comets and asteroids
2.	2.

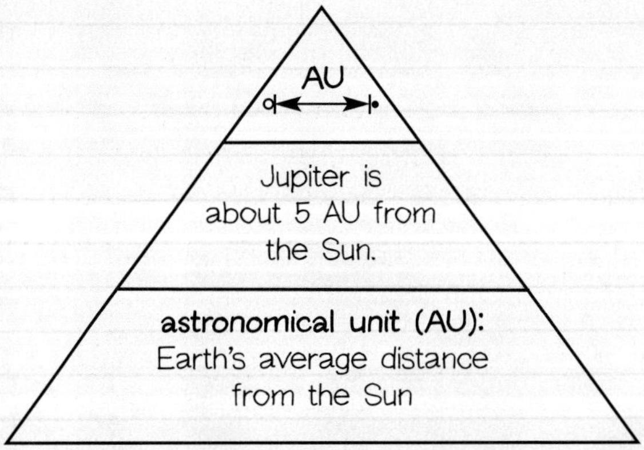

AU

Jupiter is about 5 AU from the Sun.

astronomical unit (AU): Earth's average distance from the Sun

KEY CONCEPT

Planets orbit the Sun at different distances.

VOCABULARY

astronomical unit (AU) p. 745

ellipse p. 745

BEFORE, you learned

- Earth orbits the Sun
- The Moon is Earth's natural satellite
- The Moon's features tell us about its history

NOW, you will learn

- What types of objects are in the solar system
- About sizes and distances in the solar system
- How the solar system formed

EXPLORE Planet Formation

How do planets form?

PROCEDURE

① Fill the bowl about halfway with water.

② Stir the water quickly, using a circular motion, and then remove the spoon.

③ Sprinkle wax pieces onto the swirling water.

WHAT DO YOU THINK?

- In what direction did the wax move?
- What else happened to the wax?

MATERIALS
- bowl
- water
- spoon
- wax pieces

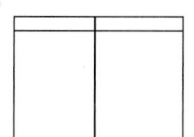

MAIN IDEA AND DETAILS
Put sizes and distances in the solar system into a chart.

Planets have different sizes and distances.

You may have seen some planets in the sky without realizing it. They are so far from Earth that they appear as tiny dots of light in the darkened sky. If you have seen something that looks like a very bright star in the western sky in the early evening, you have probably seen the planet Venus. Even if you live in a city, you may have seen Mars, Jupiter, or Saturn but thought that you were seeing a star. Mercury is much more difficult to see. You need a telescope to see three of the planets in our solar system—Uranus, Neptune, and Pluto.

Like the Moon, planets can be seen because they reflect sunlight. Planets do not give off visible light of their own. Sunlight is also reflected by moons and other objects in space, called comets and asteroids. However, these objects are usually too far away and not bright enough to see without a telescope.

 Why do planets look bright?

Objects in the Solar System

The sizes of objects in the solar system range from very small to very large.

asteroids

Sun
On this scale, the Sun is about a meter across.

Mars

Saturn

Saturn's moons

Earth

Venus

Mercury

Jupiter's moons

Neptune

Neptune's moons

Jupiter

0   20,000   40,000 kilometers

Objects smaller than about 100 kilometers are represented as dots.

Uranus's moons

Uranus

comets

Pluto

Distances of Planets

Sun   Venus   Mars   Jupiter   Saturn   Uranus

Mercury   Earth   asteroids

0   2   4 AU

Objects in the solar system have very different sizes. An asteroid may be as small as a mountain, perhaps 1/1000 Earth's diameter. In contrast, the largest planets are about 10 Earth diameters across. The Sun's diameter is about 100 times Earth's. If the planets were the sizes shown on page 744, the Sun would be about a meter across.

Distances

The distances between most objects in space are huge in comparison with the objects' diameters. If Earth and the Sun were the sizes shown on page 744, they would be more than 100 meters from each other.

Astronomers understand huge distances by comparing them with something more familiar. One **astronomical unit,** or AU, is Earth's average distance from the Sun. An AU is about 150 million kilometers (93 million mi). Mercury is less than 0.5 AU from the Sun, Jupiter is about 5 AU from the Sun, and Pluto gets nearly 50 AU from the Sun at times. You can use the diagram at the bottom of pages 744–745 to compare these distances. However, the planets are not arranged in a straight line—they move around the Sun.

You can see that the planets are spaced unevenly. The first four planets are relatively close together and close to the Sun. They define a region called the inner solar system. Farther from the Sun is the outer solar system, where the planets are much more spread out.

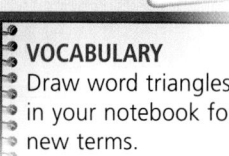

VOCABULARY
Draw word triangles in your notebook for new terms.

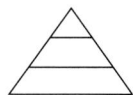

 **CHECK YOUR READING** What are the two regions of the solar system?

Orbits

More than 99 percent of all the mass in the solar system is in the Sun. The gravitational pull of this huge mass causes planets and most other objects in the solar system to move around, or orbit, the Sun.

The shape of each orbit is an **ellipse**—a flattened circle or oval. A circle is a special type of ellipse, just as a square is a special type of rectangle. Most of the planets' orbits are very nearly circles. Only one planet—Pluto—has an orbit that looks a little flattened instead of round.

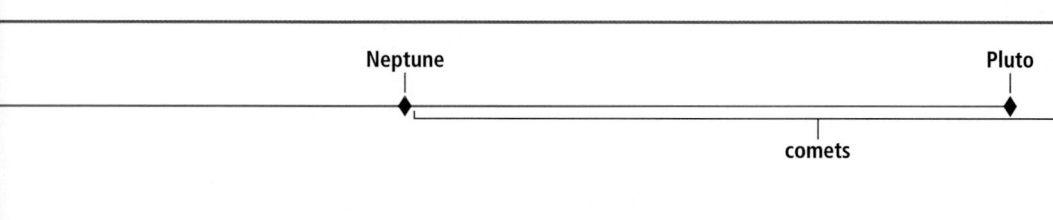

Neptune

Pluto

comets

INVESTIGATE Distances

How far apart are the planets?

PROCEDURE

1. Mark one sheet from the end of the roll of paper as the location of the Sun. Mark an *X* and write the word *Sun* with dots rather than lines.

2. Use the Distance Table data sheet to mark the distances for the rest of the solar system. Count sheets and estimate tenths of a sheet as necessary. Re-roll or fold the paper neatly.

3. Go to a space where you can unroll the paper. Compare the distances of planets as you walk along the paper and back again.

WHAT DO YOU THINK?

- How does the distance between Earth and Mars compare with the distance between Saturn and Uranus?
- How would you use the spacing to sort the planets into groups?

CHALLENGE If it took two years for the *Voyager 2* spacecraft to travel from Earth to Jupiter, about how long do you think it took for *Voyager 2* to travel from Jupiter to Neptune?

SKILL FOCUS
Using models

MATERIALS
- roll of toilet paper
- felt-tipped pen
- Distance Table

TIME
30 minutes

The solar system formed from a swirling cloud of gas and dust.

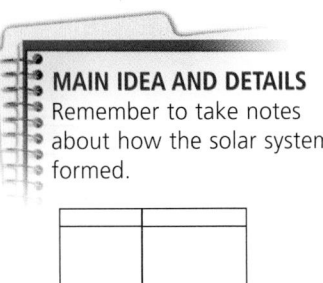

MAIN IDEA AND DETAILS
Remember to take notes about how the solar system formed.

The planets orbit the Sun in similar ways. Their paths are almost in a flat plane, like the rings of a target. They all orbit the Sun in the same direction—counterclockwise as seen from above Earth's North Pole. Most of the planets rotate on their axes in this direction, too. Many other objects in the solar system also orbit and rotate in this same direction. These similar motions have given scientists clues about how the solar system formed.

According to the best scientific model, the solar system formed out of a huge cloud of different gases and specks of dust. The cloud flattened into a disk of whirling material. Most of the mass fell to the center and became a star—the Sun. At the same time, tiny bits of dust and frozen gases in the disk stuck together into clumps. The clumps stuck together and became larger. Large clumps became planets. They moved in the same direction that the flat disk was turning.

Not all the clumps grew big enough to be called planets. However, many of these objects still orbit the Sun the same way that planets orbit. Some of the objects close to the Sun are like rocks or mountains in space and are called asteroids. Other objects, farther from the Sun, are more like enormous snowballs or icebergs. They are called comets.

Formation of the Solar System

The Sun and other objects formed out of material in a flat disk.

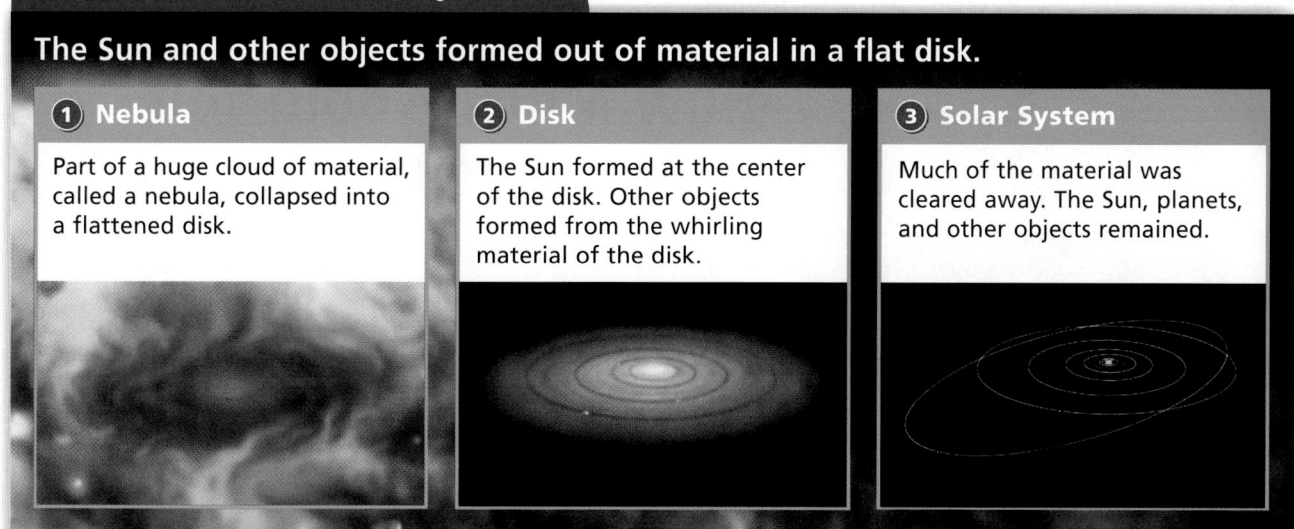

① Nebula

Part of a huge cloud of material, called a nebula, collapsed into a flattened disk.

② Disk

The Sun formed at the center of the disk. Other objects formed from the whirling material of the disk.

③ Solar System

Much of the material was cleared away. The Sun, planets, and other objects remained.

Some objects orbit planets instead of orbiting the Sun directly, so they are considered moons. You will read more about asteroids, comets, and moons in Section 21.4.

You can tell a little bit about the size of an object in space from its shape. Lumpy objects are usually much smaller than round objects. As a space object starts to form, the clumps come together from many directions and produce an uneven shape. The gravity of each part affects every other part. The pieces pull each other closer together. When an object has enough mass, this pulling becomes strong enough to make the object round. Any parts that would stick far out are pulled in toward the center until the object becomes a sphere.

CHECK YOUR READING Why do planets and large moons have a spherical shape?

21.1 Review

KEY CONCEPTS

1. What are the types of space objects in the solar system?

2. Why is the unit of measurement used for the distances of planets from the Sun different from the unit used for their sizes?

3. How did planets and other objects in the solar system form out of material in a disk?

CRITICAL THINKING

4. **Analyze** Why do the planets all orbit in one direction?

5. **Infer** Which of the two moons below has more mass? Explain why you think so.

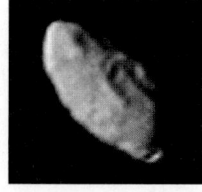 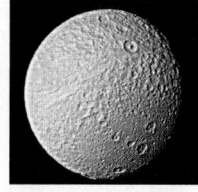

⬤ CHALLENGE

6. **Apply** Could you model all the sizes of objects in the solar system by using sports balls? Explain why or why not.

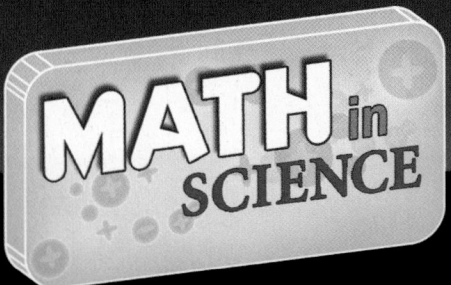

MATH TUTORIAL
CLASSZONE.COM

Click on Math Tutorial for more help with the percent equation.

How Much Would You Weigh on Other Worlds?

When astronauts walked on the Moon, they felt much lighter than they felt when they were on Earth. Neil Armstrong's total mass—about 160 kilograms with space suit and backpack—did not change. However, the Moon did not pull as hard on him as Earth did, so he weighed less on the Moon. At the surface, the Moon's gravitational pull is only 17% of Earth's gravitational pull. You can use percentages to calculate Neil Armstrong's weight on the Moon.

Example

On Earth, with his heavy space suit and backpack, Neil Armstrong weighed about 1600 newtons (360 lb). To calculate his weight on the Moon, find 17% of 1600 newtons.

"Of" means "multiply." 17% of 1600 N = 17% × 1600 N

Change the percent to a decimal fraction. = 0.17 × 1600 N

Simplify. = 272 N

ANSWER With his suit and backpack, Neil Armstrong weighed about 270 newtons on the Moon.

Use the percentages in the table to answer the following questions.

1. A backpack weighs 60 newtons (13 lb) on Earth. **(a)** How much would it weigh on Jupiter? **(b)** How much would it weigh on Jupiter's moon Io?

2. **(a)** How much would a student weighing 500 newtons (110 lb) on Earth weigh on Saturn? **(b)** on Venus?

3. On which planet or moon would you be lightest?

CHALLENGE A pencil weighs 0.3 newtons (1 oz) on Earth. How much would it weigh on the Moon? If an astronaut let go of the pencil on the Moon, would the pencil fall? Explain.

Percent of Weight on Earth	
Planet or Moon	**%**
Mercury	38
Venus	91
Earth	100
Moon (Earth)	17
Mars	38
Jupiter	236
Io (Jupiter)	18
Europa (Jupiter)	13
Ganymede (Jupiter)	15
Callisto (Jupiter)	13
Saturn	92
Titan (Saturn)	14
Uranus	89
Neptune	112
Triton (Neptune)	8.0
Pluto	6.7
Charon (Pluto)	2.8

This picture of Buzz Aldrin on the Moon was taken by Neil Armstrong, who can be seen reflected in Aldrin's helmet.

KEY CONCEPT

21.2
The inner solar system has rocky planets.

Sunshine State STANDARDS

SC.E.1.3.1: The student understands the vast size of our Solar System and the relationship of the planets and their satellites.

SC.E.1.3.2: The student knows that available data from various satellite probes show the similarities and differences among planets and their moons in the Solar System.

SC.H.1.3.2: The student knows that the study of the events that led scientists to discoveries can provide information about the inquiry process and its effects.

BEFORE, you learned

- Planets are closer together in the inner solar system than in the outer solar system
- Planets formed along with the Sun
- Gravity made planets round

NOW, you will learn

- How four processes change the surfaces of solid planets
- How atmospheres form and then affect planets
- What the planets closest to the Sun are like

VOCABULARY

terrestrial planet p. 749
tectonics p. 750
volcanism p. 750

EXPLORE Surfaces

How does a planet's mantle affect its surface?

PROCEDURE

① Dampen a paper towel and place it on top of two blocks to model a crust and a mantle.

② Move one block. Try different amounts of motion and different directions.

WHAT DO YOU THINK?

- What happened to the paper towel?
- What landforms like this have you seen?

MATERIALS

- 2 blocks
- paper towel
- newspaper

The terrestrial planets have rocky crusts.

Scientists study Earth to learn about other planets. They also study other planets to learn more about Earth. The **terrestrial planets** are Mercury, Venus, Earth, and Mars—the four planets closest to the Sun. They all have rocky crusts and dense mantles and cores. Their insides, surfaces, and atmospheres formed in similar ways and follow similar patterns. One planet—Earth—can be used as a model to understand the others. In fact, the term *terrestrial* comes from *terra*, the Latin word for Earth.

Earth

Most of Earth's rocky surface is hidden by water. More details about Earth and other planets are listed in the Appendix at the back of this book.

Mass 6×10^{24} kg
Diameter 12,800 km
Average distance from Sun 1 AU

Orbits in 365 days
Rotates in 24 hours

Processes and Surface Features

All terrestrial planets have layers. Each planet gained energy from the collisions that formed it. This energy heated and melted the planet's materials. The heaviest materials were metals, which sank to the center and formed a core. Lighter rock formed a mantle around the core. The lightest rock rose to the surface and cooled into a crust.

Four types of processes then shaped each planet's rocky crust. The processes acted to different extents on each planet, depending on how much the crust and inside of the planet cooled.

READING TiP

Compare what you read about each type of feature with the pictures and diagrams on page 751.

❶ Tectonics Earth's crust is split into large pieces called tectonic plates. These plates are moved by Earth's hot mantle. Mountains, valleys, and other features form as the plates move together, apart, or along each other. The crusts of other terrestrial planets are not split into plates but can be twisted, wrinkled up, or stretched out by the mantle. **Tectonics** is the processes of change in a crust due to the motion of hot material underneath. As a planet cools, the crust gets stiffer and the mantle may stop moving, so this process stops.

❷ Volcanism A second process, called **volcanism,** occurs when molten rock moves from a planet's hot interior onto its surface. The molten rock is called lava when it reaches the surface through an opening called a volcano. On Earth, lava often builds up into mountains. Volcanoes are found on Earth, Venus, and Mars. Lava can also flow onto large areas and cool into flat plains like the lunar maria. When the inside of a planet cools enough, no more molten rock reaches the surface.

❸ Weathering and Erosion You have read about weathering on Earth and the Moon. Weather or small impacts break down rocks. The broken material is moved by a group of processes called erosion. The material may form dunes, new layers of rock, or other features. On Earth, water is important for weathering and erosion. However, similar things happen even without water. Wind can carry sand grains that batter at rocks and form new features. Even on a planet without air, rock breaks down from being heated in the daylight and cooled at night. The material is pulled downhill by gravity.

RESOURCE CENTER
CLASSZONE.COM

Find out more about impact craters on Earth and other space objects.

❹ Impact Cratering A small object sometimes hits a planet's surface so fast that it causes an explosion. The resulting impact crater is often ten times larger than the object that produced it. On Earth, most craters have been erased by other processes. Impact craters are easier to find on other planets. If a planet or part of a planet is completely covered with impact craters, then the other processes have not changed the surface much in billions of years.

 **CHECK YOUR READING** What processes affect the surfaces of terrestrial planets?

Features of Rocky Planets

The processes that shape features on a planet's surface can be divided into four types. The features can tell you different things about the planet.

① Tectonics

A hot mantle can move and distort the crust above it.
This system of mountains and valleys on **Earth** formed as the crust was stretched.

② Volcanism

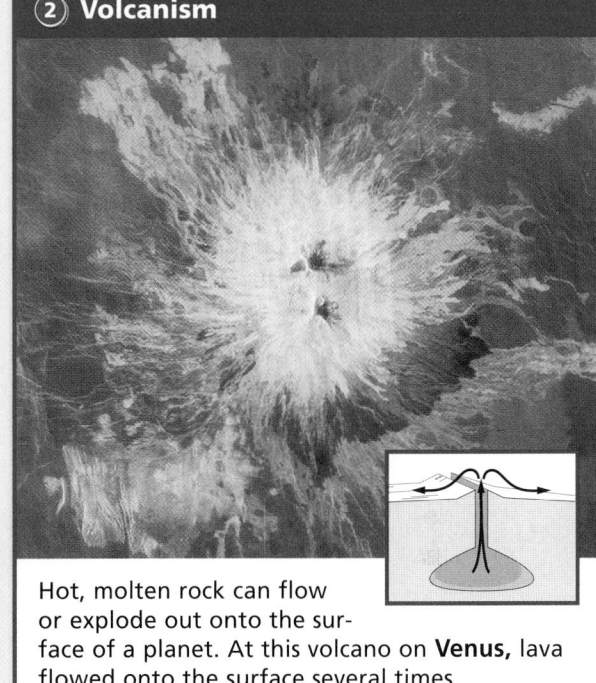

Hot, molten rock can flow or explode out onto the surface of a planet. At this volcano on **Venus,** lava flowed onto the surface several times.

③ Weathering and Erosion

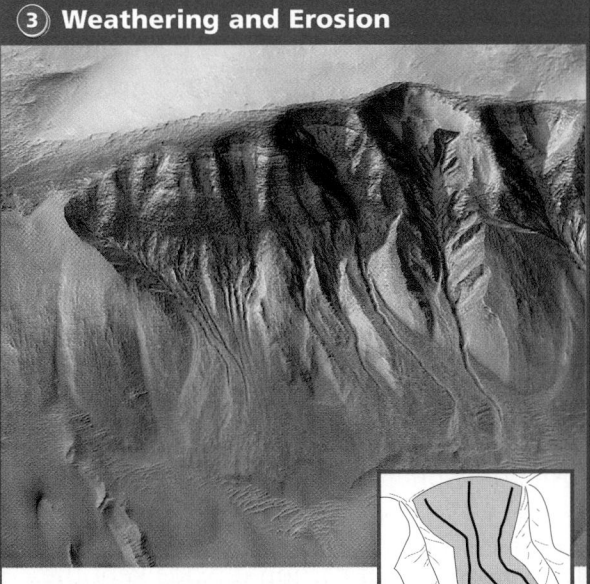

Rock can be broken down and moved. In this region of **Mars,** material broken from a cliff was moved by erosion into new slopes and dunes.

④ Impact Cratering

A small space object can hit a planet's surface and leave a crater. Because the other processes on **Mercury** are weak, newer craters can be seen on a background of older, more eroded craters.

READING VISUALS Which two processes happen because of hot material beneath the surface?

How do the layers inside of planets form?

In this model, the materials you use represent different rocks and metals that make up the solid planets.

PROCEDURE

① Put pieces of gelatin into the container until it is about one-quarter full.

② Mix in a spoonful each of sand and wax. Use the spoon to break the gelatin into small pieces as you mix. Remove the spoon.

③ Place the container in a bowl of hot tap water (about 70°C) and observe what happens as the gelatin melts.

WHAT DO YOU THINK?

• What happened to each of the materials when the gelatin melted?

• How do the results resemble the core, mantle, and crust of Earth and other planets?

CHALLENGE How might you improve this model?

SKILL FOCUS
Using models

MATERIALS
• container
• spoon
• firm gelatin
• sand
• wax pieces
• bowl of hot tap water

TIME
40 minutes

Atmospheres

Atmospheres on terrestrial planets mainly formed from gases that poured out of volcanoes. If a planet's gravity is strong enough, it pulls the gases in and keeps them near the surface. If a planet's gravity is too weak, the gases expand into outer space and are lost.

Venus, Earth, and Mars each had gravity strong enough to hold heavy gases such as carbon dioxide. However, the lightest gases—hydrogen and helium—escaped into outer space. The atmospheres of Venus and Mars are mostly carbon dioxide.

An atmosphere can move energy from warmer places to cooler places. This movement of heat energy makes temperatures more uniform between a planet's day side and its night side and between its equator and its poles. An atmosphere can also make a planet's whole surface warmer by slowing the loss of energy from the surface.

After Earth formed, its atmosphere of carbon dioxide kept the surface warm enough for water to be liquid. Oceans covered most of Earth's surface. The oceans changed the gases of the atmosphere, and living organisms caused even more changes. Earth's atmosphere is now mostly nitrogen with some oxygen.

FLORIDA
Content Review

Remember that Earth's atmosphere is like a blanket that protects Earth, as you learned in grade 6.

CHECK YOUR READING Why is the solid Earth surrounded by gases?

Craters cover the surface of Mercury.

Mercury, like the Moon, has smooth plains and many craters. The processes at work on Earth also affected Mercury.

Tectonics Long, high cliffs stretch across Mercury's surface. Scientists think that Mercury's huge core of iron shrank when it cooled long ago. The crust wrinkled up, forming cliffs, as the planet got a little smaller.

Volcanism Parts of the surface were covered with lava long ago. Large, smooth plains formed. The plains are similar to lunar maria.

Weathering and Erosion Small impacts and temperature changes have broken rock. Gravity has moved broken material downhill.

Impact Cratering Round features cover much of the surface. These craters show that the other processes have not changed Mercury's surface very much for a long time.

Mercury has the longest cycle of day and night of the terrestrial planets—three months of daylight and three months of darkness. There is no atmosphere to move energy from the hot areas to the cold areas. In the long daytime, it can get hotter than 420°C (about 800°F)—hot enough to melt lead. During the long, cold night, the temperature can drop lower than –170°C (about –280°F).

—no data

Mercury

This map of Mercury was made from many images taken by one spacecraft. The blank patches show areas that were not mapped by the spacecraft.

Mass 6% of Earth's mass

Diameter 38% of Earth's diameter

Average distance from Sun 0.39 AU

Orbits in 88 Earth days

Rotates in 59 Earth days

How is Mercury similar to the Moon?

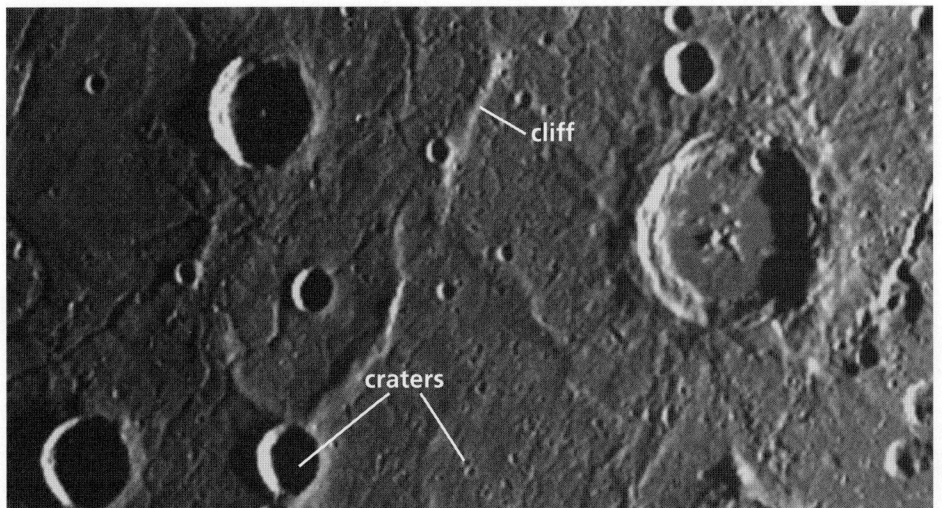

cliff

craters

Craters of all sizes cover Mercury's surface, but there are also flat lava plains and cliffs from long ago.

Volcanoes shape the surface of Venus.

The planet Venus is only a little smaller than Earth and orbits a little closer to the Sun. As a result, Venus is sometimes called Earth's sister planet. However, Venus is different from Earth in important ways.

Venus takes about eight months to turn just once on its axis. Unlike most other planets, Venus rotates and orbits in opposite directions. The rotation and orbit together produce very long days and nights—two months of daylight followed by two months of darkness.

The atmosphere of Venus is very dense. Air pressure on Venus is 90 times that on Earth. Venus's atmosphere is mostly carbon dioxide. This gas slows the loss of energy and makes the surface very hot. The ground temperature on Venus is about 470°C (about 870°F). The atmosphere of Venus moves energy around so well that the long nights are as hot as the days and the poles are as hot as the equator. In addition, there are droplets of sulfuric acid, a corrosive chemical, in the atmosphere. These droplets form thick white clouds that completely cover the planet and hide the surface.

Like Mercury, Venus is affected by the same four types of processes that change Earth's surface. Scientists think that tectonics and volcanism may still be changing Venus's surface today.

Tectonics Patterns of cracks and cliffs have formed as movements of the hot mantle have stretched, wrinkled, and twisted the surface.

Volcanism Most of the surface of Venus has been covered with lava in the last billion years or so. Volcanoes and flat lava plains are found all over the surface.

Thick clouds make it impossible to see Venus's surface in visible light. This inset shows a map of Venus that scientists made using radio waves.

Venus

Venus is nearly the size of Earth but has a thicker atmosphere and is much hotter than Earth. The surface is rocky, as you can see in the image below.

Mass 82% of Earth's mass

Diameter 95% of Earth's diameter

Average distance from Sun 0.72 AU

Orbits in 225 Earth days

Rotates in 243 Earth days

weathered and eroded rock

spacecraft

Weathering and Erosion Venus is too hot to have liquid water, and the winds do not seem to move much material. Erosion may be slower on Venus than on Earth.

Impact Cratering Round craters mark the surface here and there. Older craters have been erased by the other processes. Also, Venus's thick atmosphere protects the surface from small impacts.

 Why is Venus not covered with craters?

Erosion changes the appearance of Mars.

Mars is relatively small, with a diameter about half that of Earth. The orange color of some of the surface comes from molecules of iron and oxygen—rust. Mars has two tiny moons. They were probably once asteroids that were pulled into orbit around Mars.

Surface of Mars

The same processes that affect the other terrestrial planets affect Mars.

Tectonics Valleys and raised areas formed on Mars as the mantle moved. One huge system of valleys, called Valles Marineris, is long enough to stretch across the United States.

Volcanism Most of the northern hemisphere has smooth plains of cooled lava. Several volcanoes are higher than any mountain on Earth. The lava must have built up in the same spot for a long time, so scientists have inferred that the crust of Mars has cooled more than Earth's crust. On Earth, the tectonic plates move, so chains of smaller volcanoes form instead of single larger volcanoes.

Weathering and Erosion Fast winds carry sand that breaks down rocks. Wind and gravity move the broken material, forming new features such as sand dunes. There are also landforms that look like the results of gigantic flash floods that happened long ago.

Impact Cratering Round craters cover much of the southern hemisphere of Mars. Many craters are very old and eroded. A few impact craters on the volcanoes make scientists think that the volcanoes have not released lava for a long time.

Mars

The atmosphere of Mars is thin but causes weathering and erosion.

Mass 11% of Earth's mass
Diameter 53% of Earth's diameter
Average distance from Sun 1.5 AU
Orbits in 1.9 Earth years
Rotates in 25 hours

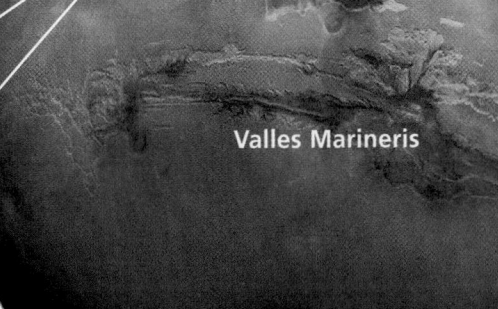

volcanoes

Valles Marineris

red dust carried by wind

distant hills

weathered and eroded rock

The sky of Mars is made red by dust that the wind picks up and carries to new places.

Gases and Water on Mars

The atmosphere of Mars is mostly carbon dioxide. The air pressure is only about 1 percent of the air pressure on Earth. The gas is not dense enough to keep the surface warm or to move much energy from cold areas to warmer areas. Therefore, temperatures may reach almost 20°C (about 60°F) in the daytime and −90°C (−130°F) at night. The large differences in temperature produce fast winds. The winds cause gigantic dust storms that sometimes cover most of the planet.

Like Earth, Mars has polar caps that grow in winter and shrink in summer. However, the changing polar caps of Mars are made mostly of frozen carbon dioxide—dry ice. The carbon dioxide of the atmosphere can also form clouds, fog, and frost on the ground.

There is no liquid water on the surface of Mars today. Any water would quickly evaporate or freeze. However, there were floods in the past, and there is still frozen water in the ground and in one polar cap. Water is important for life and will also be needed to make rocket fuel if humans are ever to make trips to Mars and back.

 CHECK YOUR READING   In what ways is Mars different from Earth?

21.2 Review

KEY CONCEPTS

1. What are the four types of processes that shape planets' surfaces? For each, give one example of a feature that the process can produce.

2. How can an atmosphere affect the temperature of a planet's surface?

3. Which terrestrial planet has the oldest, least-changing surface?

CRITICAL THINKING

4. **Compare and Contrast** Make a chart with columns for the four types of processes and for an atmosphere. Fill out a row for each planet.

5. **Apply** If a planet had a surface with craters but no other features, what could you say about the inside of the planet?

⬤ CHALLENGE

6. **Infer** Describe how a hot mantle can affect a planet's atmosphere. **Hint:** Which of the four processes is involved?

What Shapes the Surface of Mars?

Many features on Mars, when seen close up, look a lot like features found on Earth. Astronomers use their knowledge of the four types of processes that affect the terrestrial planets to hypothesize about the features on Mars. Using what you know about the processes, make your own hypotheses to explain the features in the image to the left.

▶ Results of Research

- Small objects hit the surface, producing craters.
- Volcanoes erupt, creating mountains and flows of lava.
- The mantle moves the crust, producing mountains and valleys.
- Wind, water, and gravity move material on the surface, eroding some places and building up others.

▶ Observations

- Dark, raised triangles point roughly east.
- Patterns of light stripes run mostly north-south between the dark hills.
- The features are inside a huge impact crater.

dark hills

light stripes

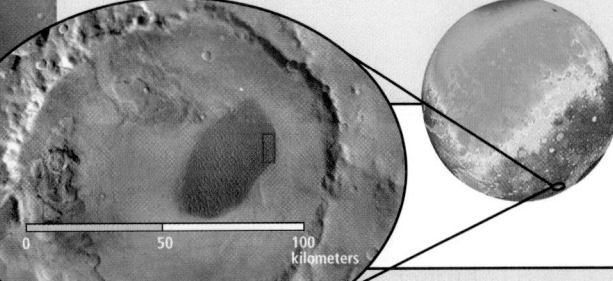

The large image shows details of the area in the red rectangle.

The black oval on the globe shows the location of the crater.

0   50   100 kilometers

0   0.5   1.0 kilometers

▶ Form a Hypothesis

On Your Own Consider one or more processes that might produce the hills and stripes seen in the image at left.

As a Group With a small group discuss possible hypotheses to explain the formation of these features. See if the group can agree on which one is most reasonable.

CHALLENGE Create a model that you can use to test your hypothesis. What will you use to represent the surface of Mars and the forces acting on it?

21.3
The outer solar system has four giant planets.

Sunshine State STANDARDS

SC.E.1.3.1: The student understands the vast size of our Solar System and the relationship of the planets and their satellites.

SC.E.1.3.2: The student knows that available data from various satellite probes show the similarities and differences among planets and their moons in the Solar System.

 **BEFORE, you learned**

- Planets formed along with the Sun
- Vast distances separate planets
- The gravity of a terrestrial planet may be strong enough to hold the heavier gases

▶ **NOW, you will learn**

- About the four giant planets in the solar system
- What the atmospheres of giant planets are like
- About the rings of giant planets

VOCABULARY
gas giant p. 758
ring p. 761

THINK ABOUT

What is Jupiter like inside?

Most of Jupiter's huge mass is hidden below layers of clouds. Scientists learn about Jupiter by studying its gravity, its magnetic field, its motions, and its radiation. Scientists also use data from other space bodies to make models, from which they make predictions. Then they observe Jupiter to test their predictions. What might it be like under Jupiter's clouds?

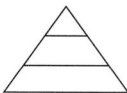

VOCABULARY
Remember to draw a word triangle when you read a new term.

The gas giants have very deep atmospheres.

You have already read about the four rocky planets in the inner solar system, close to the Sun. Beyond Mars stretches the outer solar system, where the four largest planets slowly orbit the Sun. The **gas giants**—Jupiter, Saturn, Uranus (YUR-uh-nuhs), and Neptune—are made mainly of hydrogen, helium, and other gases.

When you think of gases, you probably think of Earth's air, which is not very dense. However, the giant planets are so large and have such large amounts of these gases that they have a lot of mass. The huge gravitational force from such a large mass is enough to pull the gas particles close together and make the atmosphere very dense. Inside the giant planets, the gases become more dense than water. The outermost parts are less dense and more like Earth's atmosphere.

 Why are the gas giants dense inside?

The atmosphere of a giant planet is very deep. Imagine traveling into one. At first, the atmosphere is thin and very cold. There may be a haze of gases. A little lower is a layer of clouds that reflect sunlight, just like clouds on Earth. There are strong winds and other weather patterns. Lower down, it is warmer and there are layers of clouds of different materials. As you go farther, the atmosphere gradually becomes dense enough to call a liquid. It also gets thousands of degrees hotter as you get closer to the center of the planet. The materials around you become more and more dense until they are solid. Scientists think that each of the four gas giants has a solid core, larger than Earth, deep in its center.

Interior of a Giant Planet

Jupiter

hydrogen—gas and liquid

hydrogen—liquid metal

dense, hot core

Jupiter is a world of storms and clouds.

Jupiter is the largest planet in the solar system. It is more than 10 times larger than Earth in diameter and more than 1200 times larger in volume. A jet plane that could circle Earth in about 2 days would take 23 days to circle Jupiter. If you could weigh the planets on a cosmic scale, all the other planets put together would weigh less than half as much as Jupiter.

Jupiter is more than five times farther from the Sun than Earth is. It moves more slowly through space than Earth and has a greater distance to travel in each orbit. Jupiter takes 12 Earth years to go once around the Sun.

Even though it is big, Jupiter takes less than 10 hours to turn once on its axis. This fast rotation produces fast winds and stormy weather. Like Earth, Jupiter has bands of winds that blow eastward and westward, but Jupiter has many more bands than Earth does.

Jupiter

Jupiter's colorful stripes are produced by clouds at different levels in Jupiter's deep atmosphere.

Mass 318 Earth masses
Diameter 11 Earth diameters
Average distance from Sun 5.2 AU
Orbits in 12 Earth years
Rotates in 9.9 hours

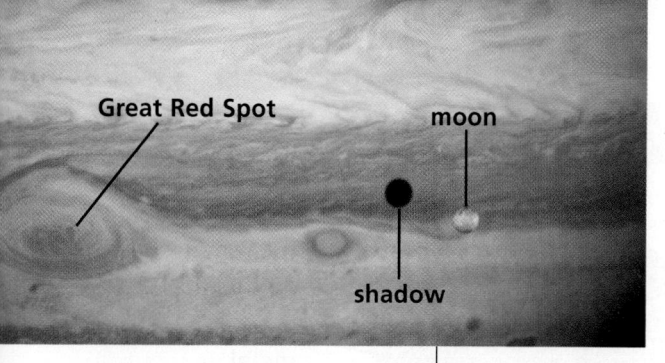

Great Red Spot

moon

shadow

This image shows one of Jupiter's moons casting a shadow on Jupiter. If you were in that shadow, you would experience a solar eclipse.

Stripes of cold clouds form along the bands. The clouds look white because they are made of crystals that reflect sunlight. The crystals in these high white clouds are frozen ammonia rather than frozen water, as on Earth. Between Jupiter's white bands of clouds, you can see down to the next layer. The lower clouds are brown or red and made of different chemicals. Sometimes there are clear patches in the brown clouds, where the next layer of bluish clouds shows through.

CHECK YOUR READING What are Jupiter's white stripes?

Storms can form between bands of winds that blow in opposite directions. Because Jupiter has no land to slow the storms, they can last for a long time. The largest of these storms is the Great Red Spot, which is twice as wide as Earth and at least 100 years old. Its clouds rise even higher than the white ammonia-ice clouds. Scientists are trying to find out which chemicals produce the spot's reddish color.

Saturn has large rings.

REMINDER

Density is the amount of mass in a given volume. An object of low density can still have a great total mass if it has a large volume.

The sixth planet from the Sun is Saturn. Saturn is only a little smaller than Jupiter, but its mass is less than one-third that of Jupiter. Because there is less mass, the gravitational pull is weaker, so the gas particles can spread out more. As a result, Saturn has a much lower density than Jupiter. The storms and stripes of clouds form deeper in Saturn's atmosphere than in Jupiter's, so the details are harder to see.

Saturn

Saturn has an average density less than that of liquid water on Earth. The diameter of Saturn's ring system is almost as great as the distance from Earth to the Moon.

Mass 95 Earth masses   **Orbits in** 29 Earth years
Diameter 9 Earth diameters   **Rotates in** 11 hours
Average distance from Sun 9.5 AU

Saturn was the first planet known to have rings. A planetary **ring** is a wide, flat zone of small particles that orbit a planet. All four gas giants have rings around their equators. Saturn's rings are made of chunks of water ice the size of a building or smaller. Larger chunks, considered to be tiny moons, orbit within the rings. Saturn's main rings are very bright. The outermost ring is three times as wide as the planet, but it is usually too faint to see. Saturn's rings have bright and dark stripes that change over time.

You can use Saturn's rings to see the planet's seasons. Like Earth's axis of rotation, Saturn's axis is tilted. The angle is 27 degrees. When the image on this page was taken, sunlight shone more on the northern hemisphere, so the north side of the rings was bright. The shadow of the rings fell on the southern hemisphere. Winter started in Saturn's northern hemisphere in May 2003 and will last more than seven Earth years. Saturn is almost ten times farther from the Sun than Earth is, so Saturn takes almost 30 Earth years to go around the Sun once.

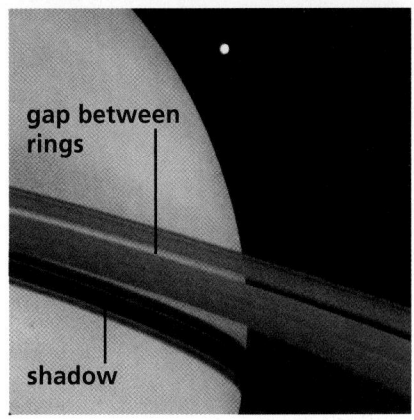

gap between rings

shadow

Sunlight shines from the upper right of this image. The rings cast shadows on Saturn's clouds.

INVESTIGATE Giant Planets

Why do Saturn's rings seem to change size?

PROCEDURE

1. Poke the stick through the plate and cut off the plate's rim. Shape the clay onto both sides of the plate to make a model of a planet with rings.

2. Model Saturn's orbit for your partner. Stand between your partner and the classroom clock. Point one end of the stick at the clock. Hold the model at the same height as your partner's eyes. Have your partner watch the model with just one eye open.

3. Move one step counterclockwise around your partner and point the stick at the clock again. Make sure the model is as high as your partner's eyes. Your partner may need to turn to see the model.

4. Continue taking steps around your partner and pointing the stick at the clock until you have moved the model all the way around your partner.

5. Switch roles with your partner and repeat steps 2, 3, and 4.

WHAT DO YOU THINK?

- How did your view of the rings change as the model planet changed position?

- How many times per orbit do the rings seem to vanish?

CHALLENGE How do Saturn's axis and orbit compare with those of Earth?

SKILL FOCUS
Observing

MATERIALS
- ice-cream stick
- disposable plate
- scissors
- clay

TIME
20 minutes

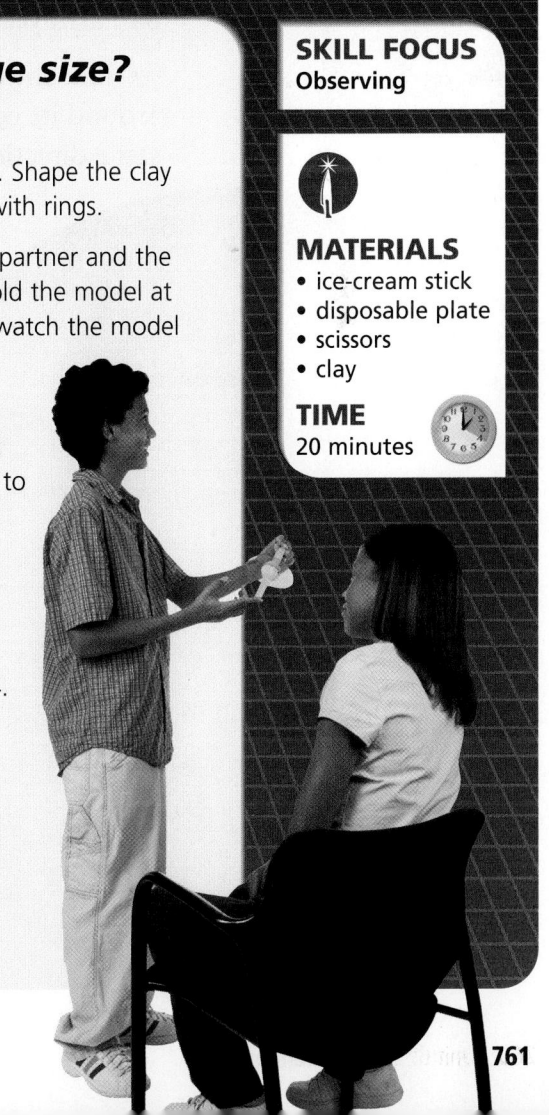

Uranus and Neptune are extremely cold.

The seventh and eighth planets from the Sun are Uranus and Neptune. These planets are similar in size—both have diameters roughly one-third that of Jupiter. Unlike Jupiter and Saturn, Uranus and Neptune are only about 15 percent hydrogen and helium. Most of the mass of each planet is made up of heavier gases, such as methane, ammonia, and water. As a result, Uranus and Neptune are more dense than Jupiter.

Uranus looks blue-green, and Neptune appears deep blue. The color comes from methane gas, which absorbs certain colors of light. Each planet has methane gas above a layer of white clouds. Sunlight passes through the gas, reflects off the clouds, then passes through the gas again on its way out. The gas absorbs the red, orange, and yellow parts of sunlight, so each planet's bluish color comes from the remaining green, blue, and violet light that passes back out of the atmosphere.

Uranus is a smooth blue-green in visible light. The small infrared image shows that the pole facing the Sun is warmer than the equator.

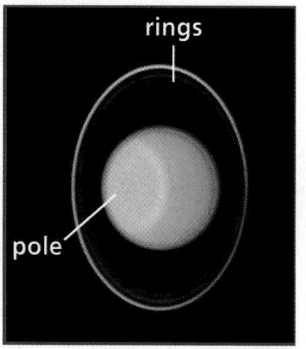

rings

pole

Uranus

Uranus is about twice Saturn's distance from the Sun. The farther a planet is from the Sun, the more slowly it moves along its orbit. The greater distance also results in a larger orbit, so it takes Uranus 84 Earth years to travel around the Sun.

Like the other gas giants, Uranus has a system of rings and moons around its equator. The ring particles and moons orbit Uranus in the same direction as the planet's spin. Unlike the other planets, Uranus has an axis of rotation that is almost in the plane of its orbit. As a result, Uranus seems to spin on its side. During a solstice, one pole of Uranus points almost straight toward the Sun.

Some scientists think that there was a large collision early in Uranus's history. The result left the planet and its system spinning at an unusual angle.

Uranus

Each pole of Uranus experiences more than 40 years of sunlight and then more than 40 years of darkness as the planet orbits the Sun.

Mass 15 Earth masses **Orbits in** 84 Earth years
Diameter 4 Earth diameters **Rotates in** 17 hours
Average distance from Sun 19 AU

Neptune

Neptune orbits about 10 AU farther from the Sun than Uranus, so you would expect it to be colder. However, Neptune has about the same outside temperature as Uranus because it is hotter inside.

Uranus is usually one smooth color, but light and dark areas often appear on Neptune. Clouds of methane ice crystals can form high enough in the atmosphere of Neptune to look white.

Storm systems can appear in darker shades of blue than the rest of the planet. One storm, seen during the flyby of the *Voyager 2* spacecraft in 1989, was named the Great Dark Spot. Unlike the huge storm on Jupiter, the Great Dark Spot did not stay at the same latitude. It moved toward Neptune's equator. The winds there may have broken up the storm. Images of Neptune obtained a few years later with the Hubble Space Telescope showed no sign of the Great Dark Spot.

CHECK YOUR READING What are the white patches often seen on Neptune?

Neptune

Neptune has a large moon that orbits in a direction opposite to Neptune's rotation. Scientists think a giant collision might have occurred in Neptune's past.

Mass 17 Earth masses
Diameter 4 Earth diameters
Average distance from Sun 30 AU
Orbits in 164 Earth years
Rotates in 16 hours

High clouds cast shadows on the layer below.

cloud

shadow

21.3 Review

KEY CONCEPTS

1. Which planet has a greater mass than all the other planets put together?

2. What do you see instead of a solid surface when you look at an image of a giant planet?

3. Which planets have rings?

CRITICAL THINKING

4. **Compare and Contrast** Why do Jupiter and Saturn show a lot of white, while Uranus and Neptune are more blue in color?

5. **Analyze** Most of Saturn is much less dense than most of Earth. Yet Saturn's mass is much greater than Earth's mass. How can this be so?

⚠ CHALLENGE

6. **Apply** If Uranus had areas of ice crystals high in its atmosphere, how would its appearance change?

KEY CONCEPT

Small objects are made of ice and rock.

Sunshine State STANDARDS

SC.C.2.3.7: The student knows that gravity is a universal force that every mass exerts on every other mass.

SC.E.1.3.1: The student understands the vast size of our Solar System and the relationship of the planets and their satellites.

SC.E.1.3.2: The student knows that available data from various satellite probes show the similarities and differences among planets and their moons in the Solar System.

VOCABULARY

asteroid p. 767
comet p. 768
meteor p. 769
meteorite p. 769

READING TiP

The name of Earth's satellite is the Moon, but the word *moon* is also used to refer to other satellites.

BEFORE, you learned

- Smaller bodies formed with the Sun and planets
- Planets in the inner solar system consist of rock and metal
- The outer solar system is cold

NOW, you will learn

- About Pluto and the moons of the giant planets
- How asteroids and comets are similar and different
- What happens when tiny objects hit Earth's atmosphere

THINK ABOUT

Do small space bodies experience erosion?

Very small bodies in space often have potato-like shapes. Some are covered with dust, boulders, and craters. Solar radiation can break down material directly or by heating and cooling a surface. Broken material can slide downhill, even on a small asteroid. What other processes do you think might act on small and medium-sized bodies in space?

Pluto and most objects in the outer solar system are made of ice and rock.

The materials in a space body depend on where it formed. The disk of material that became the solar system was cold around the outside and hottest in the center, where the Sun was forming. Far from the center, chemicals such as carbon dioxide, ammonia, and water were frozen solid. These ices became part of the material that formed bodies in the outer solar system. Bodies that formed near the center of the solar system are made mostly of rock and metal. Bodies that formed far from the center are mostly ice with some rock and a little metal.

Some of the bodies had enough mass to become rounded. Some even melted and formed cores, mantles, and crusts. Many of these bodies have mountains and valleys, volcanoes, and even winds and clouds. The processes at work on Earth also affect other space bodies.

 **CHECK YOUR READING** What do the proportions of ice, rock, and metal show about a space object?

Pluto and Charon

Many space bodies of ice and rock orbit the Sun at the distance of Neptune and beyond. Since 1992, scientists have been using sophisticated equipment to find and study these bodies. However, one body has been known since 1930. Because Pluto was discovered decades before the other objects, it is considered one of the nine major planets.

Pluto is the smallest of the nine planets. It is smaller than the Moon. Pluto's mass is less than 0.3 percent of Earth's mass, so its gravitational pull is weak. However, Pluto is round and probably has a core, mantle, and crust. Pluto also has a thin atmosphere. No spacecraft has passed close to Pluto, so scientists do not have clear images of the planet's surface.

CHECK YOUR READING Why do scientists know less about Pluto than about other planets?

Pluto's moon, Charon, has a diameter half that of Pluto and a mass about 15 percent of Pluto's. Because Pluto and Charon orbit each other, they are sometimes called a double planet. Just as the Moon always has the same side facing Earth, Pluto and Charon always keep the same sides turned toward each other.

Pluto and Charon also move together around the Sun. Pluto's path around the Sun is not as round as the orbits of the rest of the planets, so its distance from the Sun changes a lot as it orbits. Pluto gets closer to the Sun than Neptune's distance of 30 AU. At the other side of its orbit, Pluto is about 50 AU from the Sun. Pluto's orbit is at an angle with respect to Neptune's, as you can see in the diagram below, so the two paths do not cross and the planets will not collide.

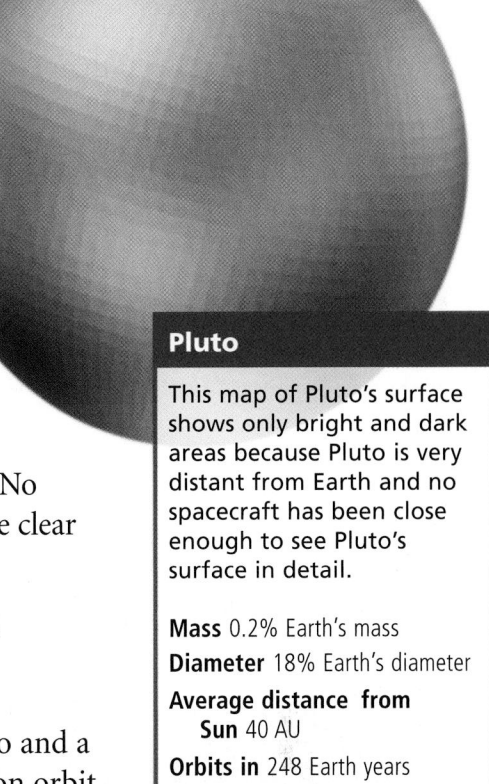

Pluto

This map of Pluto's surface shows only bright and dark areas because Pluto is very distant from Earth and no spacecraft has been close enough to see Pluto's surface in detail.

Mass 0.2% Earth's mass
Diameter 18% Earth's diameter
Average distance from Sun 40 AU
Orbits in 248 Earth years
Rotates in 6 Earth days

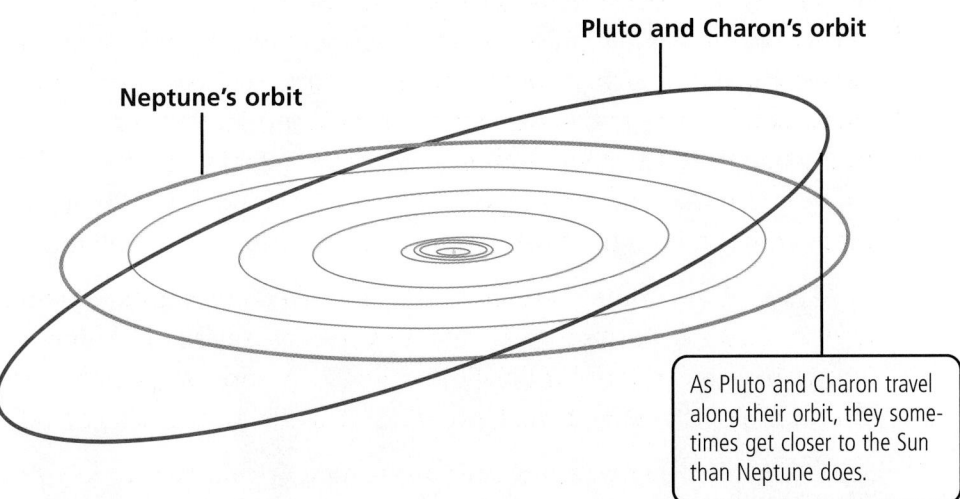

Neptune's orbit

Pluto and Charon's orbit

As Pluto and Charon travel along their orbit, they sometimes get closer to the Sun than Neptune does.

Moons of Gas Giants

RESOURCE CENTER
CLASSZONE.COM

Learn more about the different moons of giant planets.

Each giant planet has a system of moons. Six of the moons are larger than Pluto. Their features are formed by the same processes that shape the terrestrial planets. Saturn's largest moon, Titan, has a dense atmosphere of nitrogen, as Earth does, although a haze hides Titan's surface. Neptune's largest moon, Triton, has a thin atmosphere and ice volcanoes. Jupiter has four large moons—Io, Europa, Ganymede, and Callisto. Io (EYE-oh) is dotted with volcanoes, which continue to erupt, so Io has few impact craters. Europa (yu-ROH-puh) has long ridges where the crust has been pushed and pulled by the material beneath it. The outer two moons have craters over most of their surfaces.

The other moons of the gas giants are all smaller than Pluto, with diameters ranging from about 1600 kilometers (1000 mi) down to just a few kilometers. The smallest moons have irregular shapes, and some may be bodies that were captured into orbit.

CHECK YOUR READING What processes are at work on the largest moons?

Some Moons of Gas Giants

Moons in the outer solar system are shaped by the same processes that produce features on the terrestrial planets.

Saturn's moon **Titan** has a dense atmosphere of cold nitrogen gas. A thick haze hides this moon's surface.

haze

Jupiter's moon **Europa** has a crust of frozen water shaped by tectonics. Warm material below has broken the crust into many pieces.

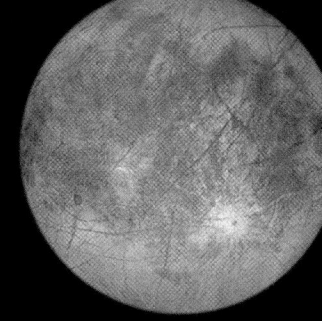

ridges

Neptune's moon **Triton** has dark streaks that show where ice volcanoes have erupted. Winds in the thin atmosphere blow material to one side of an eruption.

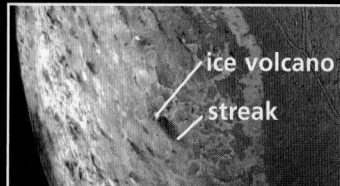

ice volcano

streak

Jupiter's moon **Io** has a surface constantly being changed by volcanoes. New material covers the surface and then changes color over time.

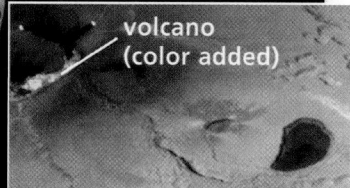

volcano (color added)

READING VISUALS Which images show volcanoes?

Asteroids and comets orbit the Sun.

Objects called asteroids and comets formed along with the Sun, planets, and moons. These objects still orbit the Sun at different distances. Most of the objects are much smaller than planets and had too little mass to become round. The objects that formed far from the Sun are made mostly of ice, with some rock and metal. The objects that formed closer to the Sun, where it was warmer, have little or no ice.

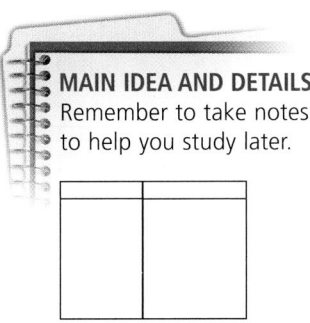

MAIN IDEA AND DETAILS
Remember to take notes to help you study later.

Asteroids

Small, solid, rocky bodies that orbit close to the Sun are called **asteroids.** They range from almost 1000 kilometers (600 mi) in diameter down to a kilometer or less. Except for the largest, their gravity is too weak to pull them into round spheres. Therefore, most asteroids have irregular shapes. Some asteroids are the broken pieces of larger, rounded asteroids.

Most asteroids have paths that keep them between the orbits of Mars and Jupiter. This huge region is called the asteroid belt, and contains more than 10,000 asteroids. However, the asteroids are so far apart that spacecraft from Earth have passed completely through the belt without danger of collision. The mass of all the asteroids put together is estimated to be less than the mass of our Moon.

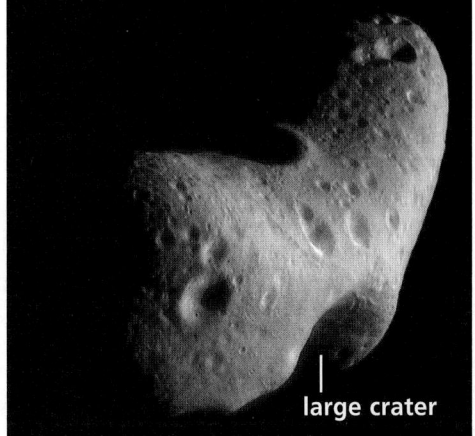
large crater

The surfaces of asteroids are covered with craters, broken rock, and dust. Even though asteroids are far apart, smaller objects do hit them from time to time. Impacts from very long ago are still visible because most asteroids are not massive enough to have formed cores, mantles, and crusts. Therefore, they do not have volcanism or tectonics to erase the craters. Most asteroids do not have atmospheres, so their surfaces change only when impacts happen or when gravity pulls material downhill.

This asteroid is small compared with a planet, but it is large compared with a person. The large crater at the bottom is about the size of a small city.

CHECK YOUR READING   Why do asteroids have craters?

Some asteroids have collided with Earth in the past. The collisions left impact craters, some of which can still be seen today. Scientists have found evidence that an asteroid 10 kilometers (6 mi) in diameter hit Earth 65 million years ago. A cloud of dust from the collision spread around the world and probably affected surface temperatures. Many forms of life, including dinosaurs, died off at about that time, and the impact may have been part or all of the reason. Today astronomers are working to study all asteroids larger than 1 kilometer (0.6 mi) in diameter to determine whether any could hit Earth.

Comets

Sometimes, a fuzzy spot appears in the night sky. It grows from night to night as it changes position against the background stars. The fuzzy spot is a cloud of material, called a coma (KOH-muh), around a small space object. An object that produces a coma is called a **comet.** A comet without its coma is a small, icy object that is difficult to see even with a powerful telescope. Scientists use the number of comets that have become visible to infer that vast numbers of comets exist.

Comets formed far from the Sun, so they are made of different ices as well as rock and some metal. Their orbits are usually more oval than the paths of planets. A comet's orbit may carry it from regions far beyond Pluto's orbit to the inner solar system.

When a comet gets close to the Sun, solar radiation warms the surface and turns some of the ice into gas. A coma forms as the gas moves outward, often carrying dust with it. High-speed particles and radiation from the Sun push this material into one or more tails that can stretch for millions of kilometers. A comet's tails point away from the Sun no matter which way the comet is moving. The coma and tails look bright because sunlight shines on them, even though they may be less dense than Earth's atmosphere.

Comets

Comets have oval orbits around the Sun. Their appearances change as they orbit.

A Comet's Orbit

coma and tails

orbit

Sun

Not to scale

A comet produces a coma as it nears the Sun. Tails grow longer and then shorter again but always point away from the Sun.

Tails Two tails are visible in this photograph of comet Hale-Bopp. When a comet is close to the Sun, its tails can be millions of kilometers long.

Nucleus Far from the Sun, a comet has little or no coma. This image shows comet Borrelly's solid part, or nucleus, which is only 8 km (5 mi) long.

READING VISUALS In what part of a comet's orbit is its tail longest?

Most comets are too faint to be noticed easily from Earth. Many years can go by between appearances of bright comets, such as the one in the photograph on page 768.

 **CHECK YOUR READING** What makes a comet visible?

Meteors and Meteorites

Earth collides constantly with particles in space. Earth orbits the Sun at about 100,000 kilometers per hour (70,000 mi/h), so these particles enter Earth's thin upper atmosphere at very high speeds. The particles and the air around them become hot enough to glow, producing brief streaks of light called **meteors.** You may be able to see a few meteors per hour on a clear, dark night. Several times during the year, Earth passes through a stream of orbiting particles left by a comet. In the resulting meteor shower, you can see many meteors per hour.

A meteor produced by a particle from a comet may last less than a second. Bits of rock or metal from asteroids may produce brighter, longer-lasting meteors. Rarely, a very bright meteor, called a fireball, lights up the sky for several seconds.

An object with greater mass, perhaps 10 grams or more, may not be destroyed by Earth's atmosphere. A **meteorite** is a space object that reaches Earth's surface. The outside of a meteorite is usually smooth from melting, but the inside may still be frozen. Most meteorites come from the asteroid belt, but a few are rocky fragments that have been blasted into space from the Moon and Mars.

This piece of iron is part of a huge meteorite. The energy of the impact melted the metal and changed its shape.

 **CHECK YOUR READING** What is the difference between a meteor and a meteorite?

21.4 Review

KEY CONCEPTS

1. How are Pluto and most moons of the gas giant planets similar?
2. List two differences between asteroids and comets.
3. What causes meteors?

CRITICAL THINKING

4. **Apply** Of the four types of processes that shape terrestrial worlds, which also shape the surfaces of moons of giant planets?
5. **Compare and Contrast** How is a comet different from a meteor?

○ CHALLENGE

6. **Predict** What do you think Pluto would look like if its orbit brought it close to the Sun?

CHAPTER INVESTIGATION

Exploring Impact Craters

DESIGN
— YOUR OWN —
EXPERIMENT

OVERVIEW AND PURPOSE Nearly 50,000 years ago, an asteroid plummeted through Earth's atmosphere and exploded near what is now Winslow, Arizona. The photograph at left shows the resulting impact crater, which is about 1.2 kilometers (0.7 mi) wide. Most of the other craters on Earth have been erased. However, some planets and most moons in the solar system have surfaces that are covered with craters. In this investigation you will

- use solid objects to make craters in a flour surface
- determine how one variable affects the resulting crater

▶ Problem

Write It Up

How does one characteristic of an impact or a colliding object affect the resulting crater?

▶ Hypothesize

Write It Up

Complete steps 1–5 before writing your problem statement and hypothesis. Once you have identified a variable to test, write a hypothesis to explain how changing this variable will affect the crater. Your hypothesis should take the form of an "If . . . , then . . . , because . . ." statement.

▶ Procedure

1. Place the container on newspapers and add flour to a depth of 2–4 cm. Stir the flour to break up any lumps, and then smooth the surface with a ruler. Sprinkle the top with colored powder.

MATERIALS
- newspapers
- container
- flour
- colored powder
- several objects
- meter stick
- ruler
- balance

2. Drop an object into the flour from waist height, then carefully remove it without disturbing the flour. Use the diagram to identify the various parts of the impact crater you made.

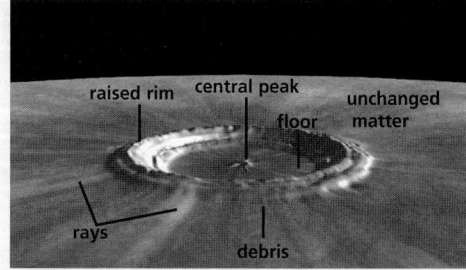

raised rim   central peak   unchanged matter
floor
rays   debris

3. To help you design your experiment, try several cratering methods. Make each new crater in a different location in the container. If your container becomes too full of craters, stir the flour, smooth it, and sprinkle on more colored powder.

4. Design an experiment to test the effects of a variable. Choose just one variable to change—the height, the size or mass of the object, or perhaps the fluffiness of the flour. Determine how much you need to change your variable in order to get results different enough to see.

5. Experiment to find some part of the crater that is affected by changing your variable, such as the depth, the size of the blanket of debris, or the number of rays. Design your experiment so that you measure the part of the crater that changes the most.

6. Write a specific problem statement by completing the question, How does _____ affect _____? Write a hypothesis to answer your problem statement.

7. Perform your experiment. Do not change any factors except your chosen variable.

8. Make several trials for each value of your variable, because there are some factors you cannot control.

9. Record measurements and other observations and make drawings as you go along.

▶ Observe and Analyze
Write It Up

1. **RECORD** Use a diagram to show how you measure the craters. Organize your data into a table. Include spaces for averages.

2. **IDENTIFY VARIABLES** List the variables and constants. The independent variable is the factor that you changed. The dependent variable is affected by this change. Use these definitions when you graph your results.

3. **CALCULATE** Determine averages by adding all of your measurements at each value of your independent variable, then dividing the sum by the number of measurements.

4. **GRAPH** Make a line graph of your average results. Place the independent variable on the horizontal axis and the dependent variable on the vertical axis. Why should you use a line graph instead of a bar graph for these data?

▶ Conclude
Write It Up

1. **ANALYZE** Answer your problem statement. Do your data support your hypothesis?

2. **EVALUATE** Did you identify a trend in your results? Is your experiment a failure if you did not identify a trend? Why or why not?

3. **IDENTIFY LIMITS** How would you modify the design of your experiment now that you have seen the results?

4. **APPLY** What do you think would happen if a colliding object hit water instead of land?

▶ INVESTIGATE Further

CHALLENGE How do the craters in this model differ from real impact craters? Design, but do not attempt, an experiment to simulate the cratering process more realistically.

Exploring Impact Craters
Problem How does _____ affect _____?
Hypothesize
Observe and Analyze
Table 1. Data and Averages

Conclude

Chapter Review

the BIG idea

Planets and other objects form a system around our Sun.

FLORIDA REVIEW
CLASSZONE.COM

Content Review and
FCAT Practice

KEY CONCEPTS SUMMARY

1 **Planets orbit the Sun at different distances.**

The planets have different sizes and distances from the Sun. The solar system formed from a disk of dust and gas. Massive objects became round.

inner solar system
| Mercury, Venus, Earth, Mars, asteroids

outer solar system
| Jupiter, Saturn, Uranus, Neptune, Pluto, comets

VOCABULARY
astronomical unit
 (AU) p. 745
ellipse p. 745

2 **The inner solar system has rocky planets.**

- The terrestrial planets are round and have layers.
- Atmospheres came from volcanoes and impacts.
- Four processes produce surface features.

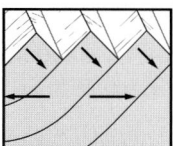
tectonics

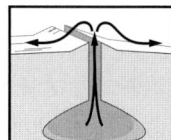
volcanism

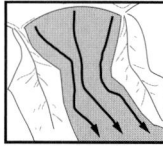
weathering
and erosion

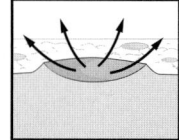
impact cratering

VOCABULARY
terrestrial planet
 p. 749
tectonics p. 750
volcanism p. 750

3 **The outer solar system has four giant planets.**

- The gas giants have very dense, deep atmospheres with layers of clouds.
- All four giant planets have ring systems.

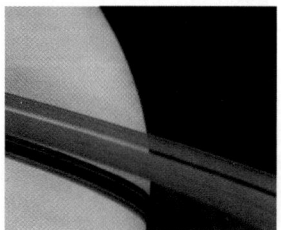
Close-up of Saturn's rings

VOCABULARY
gas giant p. 758
ring p. 761

4 **Small objects are made of ice and rock.**

- Objects in the inner solar system are rocky.
- Pluto and most other objects in the outer solar system are made of ice and rock.
- Rocky asteroids and icy comets orbit the Sun and produce tiny fragments that may become meteors.

The asteroid Eros

VOCABULARY
asteroid p. 767
comet p. 768
meteor p. 769
meteorite p. 769

Reviewing Vocabulary

Make a Venn diagram for each pair of terms. Put an important similarity in the overlapping part. Use the rest of the diagram to show an important difference.

Example:

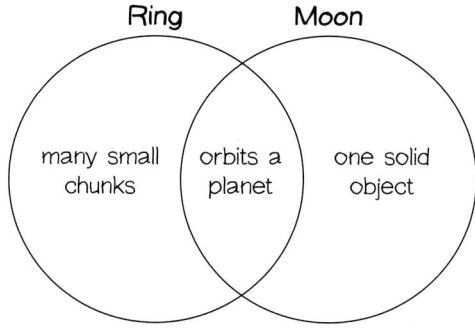

Ring   Moon

many small chunks | orbits a planet | one solid object

1. terrestrial planet, gas giant

2. volcanism, impact cratering

3. erosion, tectonics

4. asteroid, comet

5. meteor, meteorite

6. comet, meteor

Reviewing Key Concepts

Multiple Choice *Choose the letter of the best answer.*

7. Even though orbits are ellipses, what shape is a typical planet's orbit most like?
   a. a short rectangle
   b. an egg-shape with a pointy end
   c. a long, narrow oval
   d. a circle

8. How is a moon different from a planet?
   a. A moon is smaller than any planet.
   b. A moon is less massive than any planet.
   c. A moon is in orbit around a planet.
   d. A moon is unable to have an atmosphere.

9. Which of these appears in Earth's atmosphere?
   a. a moon   **c.** a meteor
   b. an asteroid   **d.** a comet

10. How did planets and other objects in the solar system form?
    a. After the Sun formed, it threw off hot pieces that spun and cooled.
    b. The Sun captured objects that formed in other places in the galaxy.
    c. Two stars collided, and the broken pieces went into orbit around the Sun.
    d. Material in a disk formed large clumps as the Sun formed in the center of the disk.

11. Which process occurs only when a small space object interacts with a larger space body?
    a. tectonics   **c.** erosion
    b. volcanism   **d.** impact cratering

12. Which processes occur because a planet or another space body is hot inside?
    a. tectonics and volcanism
    b. volcanism and erosion
    c. erosion and impact cratering
    d. impact cratering and tectonics

13. What do all four gas giants have that terrestrial planets do not have?
    a. atmospheres   **c.** moons
    b. solid surfaces   **d.** rings

14. What are the white stripes of Jupiter and the white spots of Neptune?
    a. clouds high in the atmosphere
    b. smoke from volcanoes
    c. continents and islands
    d. holes in the atmosphere

Short Response *Write a short response to each question.*

15. The solid part of a comet is small in comparison with a planet. However, sometimes a comet appears to be larger than the Sun. What makes it seem so large?

16. Why do all nine major planets orbit the Sun in the same direction?

Thinking Critically

Use the image of Jupiter's moon Ganymede to answer the next five questions.

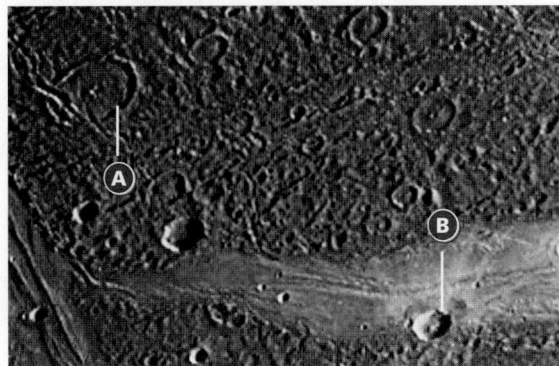

17. OBSERVE Which crater, A or B, is more eroded? Explain why you think so.

18. COMPARE AND CONTRAST Describe the differences between the surface in the upper half of the image and the long, triangular area near the bottom of the image.

19. INFER Explain which area of the surface, the smooth part or the heavily cratered part, is probably older.

20. APPLY The lighter area was produced by tectonic processes and may have been covered with molten material. What can you infer about the inside of this moon?

21. SEQUENCE A crack runs through part of crater A. Explain how you can tell whether the crack or the crater formed first. **Hint:** Think about what would have happened if the other feature had formed first.

22. PREDICT Suppose the Moon were hotter inside. How might its surface be different?

23. IDENTIFY CAUSE Mercury's surface is not as hot as Venus's, even though Mercury is closer to the Sun. In addition, the night side of Mercury gets very cold, while the night side of Venus is about as hot as the day side. Why are the temperature patterns on these two planets so different?

24. EVALUATE Would it be easier to design a lander mission for the surface of Venus or the surface of Mercury? Explain your reasoning.

25. INFER Some comets orbit in a direction opposite to that of the planets. Why might this make some scientists wonder if they formed with the rest of the solar system?

26. HYPOTHESIZE Scientists calculate the mass of a planet from the effects of its gravity on other objects, such as moons. However, Mercury and Venus have no moons. What other objects in space could have been used to determine the planets' masses?

27. COMPARE AND CONTRAST Images of Earth from space show white clouds above darker land and water. In what ways are they like and unlike images of Jupiter?

Earth　　　　**Jupiter**

28. ANALYZE Scientists sometimes use round numbers to compare quantities. For example, a scientist might say that the Sun's diameter is about 100 times Earth's diameter, even though she knows that the precise value is 109 times. Why might she use such an approximation?

the BIG idea

29. APPLY Look back at pages 740–741. Think about the answer you gave to the question about the large image of a planet and moon. How would you answer this question differently now?

30. SYNTHESIZE Ice is generally less dense than rock, which is generally less dense than metal. Use what you know about materials in the solar system to estimate whether a moon of Mars, a moon of Uranus, or the planet Mercury should be the least dense.

UNIT PROJECTS

Check your schedule for your unit project. How are you doing? Be sure that you have placed data or notes from your research in your project folder.

Interpreting a Passage

Read the following passage. Then answer the questions that follow.

Life in Extreme Environments

Could living organisms survive in the crushing, hot atmosphere of Venus? Could they thrive on a waterless asteroid or get their energy from tides in the dark ocean that might be beneath the surface of Europa? Scientists are looking for answers to these questions right here on Earth. They study extremophiles, which are life forms that can survive in extreme environments—very high or low temperatures or other difficult conditions. These environments have conditions similar to those on other planets, and those on moons, asteroids, and comets.

Scientists have found tiny organisms that grow in the scalding water of hot vents on the ocean floor, deep inside rock, and in miniature ponds within glaciers. Scientists have also found organisms that were dormant because they were frozen solid for thousands of years but that were still capable of living and growing after warming up. By studying extremophiles, scientists learn more about the conditions needed to support life.

Choose from the four environments in the box to answer the following questions.

- the dark ocean that might be underneath Europa's surface

- the flood channels on Mars, which have been dry and frozen for a long time

- the very hot, high-pressure environment of Venus

- the dry rock of an asteroid that alternately heats and cools

MULTIPLE CHOICE

1. Some organisms survive deep underwater, where photosynthesis does not occur because little or no sunlight reaches those depths. Which environment can these organisms teach about?

   A. under Europa's surface   **C.** Venus

   B. Martian flood channels   **D.** an asteroid

2. Some organisms survive in very deep cracks in rocks, where they are protected from changing temperatures. Where else might scientists look for these types of organisms?

   F. under Europa's surface   **H.** Venus

   G. Martian flood channels   **I.** an asteroid

SHORT RESPONSE

3. Where might scientists look for tiny organisms that are dormant but that might revive if given warmth and water? Explain your answer.

4. Where, outside Earth, should scientists look for tiny ponds of water within solid ice? Explain why.

EXTENDED RESPONSE
Answer the two questions in detail.

5. A class was given a sample of ordinary dormant, dry yeast that had been exposed to an extreme environment. Describe ways the students might test the yeast to see if it remained undamaged, or even survived, the conditions.

6. Imagine that scientists have found extremophiles in clouds of frozen water crystals high in Earth's atmosphere. How might this discovery affect a search for organisms on the gas giants?

CHAPTER

Stars, Galaxies, and the Universe

the **BIG** idea

Our Sun is one of billions of stars in one of billions of galaxies in the universe.

What could be present in the light and dark areas in this galaxy?

Key Concepts

SECTION

1 **The Sun is our local star.**
Learn how the Sun produces energy and about the Sun's layers and features.

SECTION

2 **Stars change over their life cycles.**
Learn how stars form and change.

SECTION

3 **Galaxies have different sizes and shapes.**
Learn how galaxies are classified.

SECTION

4 **The universe is expanding.**
Learn about the formation and expansion of the universe.

FCAT Practice

Prepare and practice for the FCAT
• Section Reviews, pp. 783, 792, 797, 803
• Chapter Review, pp. 804–806
• FCAT Practice, p. 807

CLASSZONE.COM
• Florida Review: Content Review and FCAT Practice

EXPLORE (the BIG idea)

How Can Stars Differ?

Look at the sky at night and find three stars that differ in appearance. Try to identify the locations of these stars, using the star maps in the Appendix at the back of this book.

Observe and Think
How did the characteristics of the stars differ?

How Do Galaxies Move Apart?

Blow air into a balloon until it is partially inflated. Use a felt-tip pen to make 12 dots on the round end. Then stand in front of a mirror and observe the dots as you completely inflate the balloon.

Observe and Think What caused the dots to move apart? What might cause galaxies to move apart in the universe?

Internet Activity: Galaxy Shapes

Go to **ClassZone.com** to explore the different shapes of galaxies in the universe.

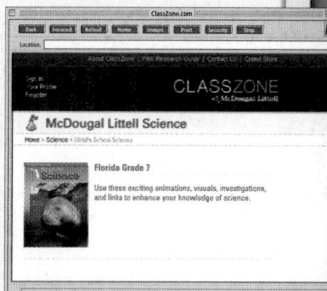

Observe and Think
How do the types of galaxies differ from one another?

NSTA
scilinks.org

The Sun Code: MDL060

Getting Ready to Learn

◀ CONCEPT REVIEW

- Electromagnetic radiation carries information about space.
- Our solar system is in the Milky Way galaxy.
- A galaxy is a group of millions or billions of stars.

◀ VOCABULARY REVIEW

solar system p. 674

galaxy p. 674

universe p. 674

electromagnetic radiation p. 679

wavelength p. 680

FLORIDA REVIEW
CLASSZONE.COM

Content Review and FCAT Practice

▶ TAKING NOTES

CHOOSE YOUR OWN STRATEGY

Take notes using one or more of the strategies from earlier chapters—**main idea web, combination notes,** or **main idea and details.** Feel free to mix and match the strategies, or use an entirely different note-taking strategy.

VOCABULARY STRATEGY

Place each vocabulary term at the center of a **description wheel** diagram. Write some words describing it on the spokes.

See the Note-Taking Handbook on pages R45–R51.

SCIENCE NOTEBOOK

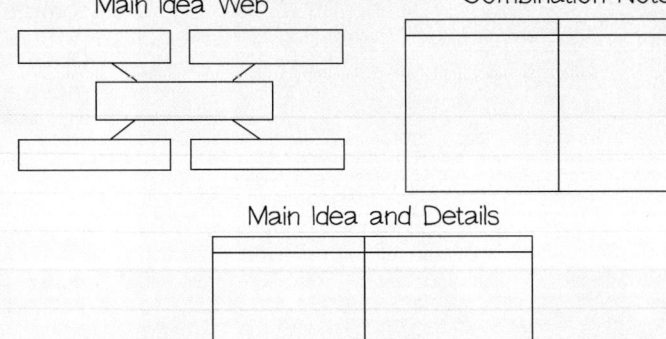

Main Idea Web

Combination Notes

Main Idea and Details

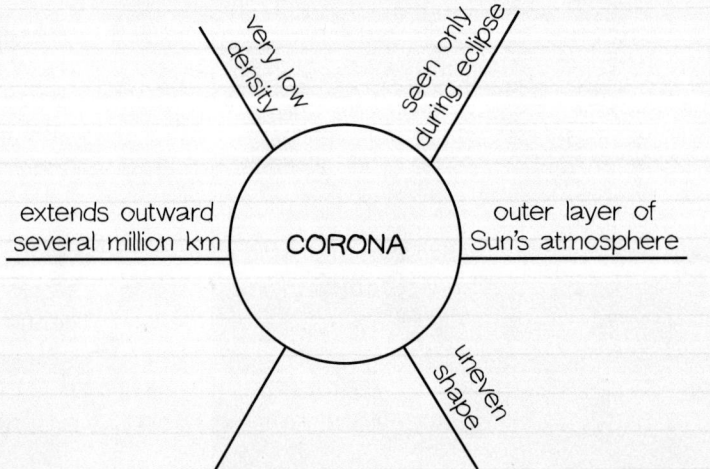

very low density

seen only during eclipse

extends outward several million km

CORONA

outer layer of Sun's atmosphere

uneven shape

22.1

KEY CONCEPT
The Sun is our local star.

FCAT VOCABULARY
convection p. 780

VOCABULARY
fusion p. 780
corona p. 780
sunspot p. 782
solar wind p. 783

BEFORE, you learned

- There are different wavelengths of electromagnetic radiation
- The Sun provides light in the solar system

NOW, you will learn

- How the Sun produces energy
- How energy flows through the Sun's layers
- About solar features and solar wind

EXPLORE Solar Atmosphere

How can blocking light reveal dim features?

PROCEDURE

① Unbend the paper clip and use it to make a tiny hole in the center of the card.

② Turn on the lamp, and briefly try to read the writing on the bulb.

③ Close one eye, and hold the card in front of your other eye. Through the hole, try to read the writing on the bulb.

WHAT DO YOU THINK?
- How did looking through the hole affect your view of the writing?
- How might a solar eclipse affect your view of the Sun's dim outermost layer?

MATERIALS
- small paper clip
- index card
- lamp with 45-watt bulb

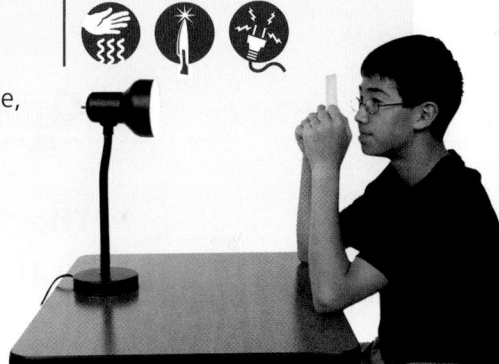

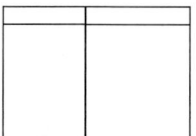

MAIN IDEA AND DETAILS
You could record information about the Sun by using a main idea and details table.

The Sun produces energy from hydrogen.

The Sun is the only star in our solar system. Astronomers have been able to study the Sun in more detail than other stars because it is much closer to Earth. As a result, they have learned a great deal about its size and composition and the way it produces energy.

The Sun is far larger than any of the planets. It contains 99.9 percent of the mass of the entire solar system. For comparison, imagine that Earth had the mass of a sparrow; then the Sun would have the mass of an elephant.

The Sun consists mostly of hydrogen gas. Energy is produced when hydrogen in the Sun's interior turns into helium. This energy is the source of light and warmth that make life possible on Earth.

Energy flows through the Sun's layers.

Although the Sun is made entirely of gas, it does have a structure. Energy produced in the center of the Sun flows out through the Sun's layers in different forms, including visible light.

The Sun's Interior

The Sun's interior generally becomes cooler and less dense as you move away from the center.

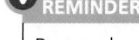 **REMINDER**

Remember that radiation is energy that travels across distances as electromagnetic waves.

1 Core The center of the Sun, called the core, is made of very dense gas. Temperatures reach about 15 million degrees Celsius. Under these extreme conditions, some hydrogen particles collide and combine to form helium in a process called **fusion.** The process releases energy that travels through the core by radiation.

2 Radiative Zone Energy from the core moves by radiation through a thick layer called the radiative zone. Although this layer is very hot and dense, conditions in the radiative zone are not extreme enough for fusion to occur.

3 Convection Zone In the convection zone, energy moves mainly by convection. **Convection** is the transfer of energy from place to place by the motion of heated gas or liquid. Rising currents of hot gas in the convection zone carry energy toward the Sun's surface.

 **CHECK YOUR READING** Where does the Sun's energy come from?

The Sun's Atmosphere

The Sun's outer layers are called its atmosphere. These layers are much less dense than the interior. The atmosphere generally becomes hotter and less dense as you move outward.

4 Photosphere Visible light moves by radiation out into space from the photosphere. It takes about eight minutes for the light to reach Earth. Since the photosphere is the layer you see in photographs of the Sun, it is often called the Sun's surface. Convection currents beneath the photosphere cause it to have a bumpy texture.

5 Chromosphere The chromosphere is the thin middle layer of the Sun's atmosphere. It gives off a pinkish light.

6 Corona The Sun's outermost layer is called the **corona.** The corona, which varies in shape, extends outward several million kilometers. Both the chromosphere and the corona are much hotter than the photosphere. However, they have such low densities that you can see their light only during a total eclipse of the Sun, when the Moon blocks the much brighter light from the photosphere.

Layers of the Sun

Energy produced by fusion in the Sun's core flows out through its layers.

prominence

(1) Energy is produced in the Sun's **core**.

(2) Energy moves by radiation through the **radiative zone.**

sunspots

(3) Currents of hot gas in the **convection zone** carry energy outward.

(4) The **photosphere** is the visible layer of the Sun.

(5) The **chromosphere** is the middle layer of the Sun's atmosphere.

(6) The **corona,** the Sun's outermost layer, has a very low density.

Energy travels by radiation and convection from the Sun's core out into space.

Corona

During a solar eclipse, the corona becomes visible because the much brighter photosphere is hidden. The corona varies in shape.

Features on the Sun

Astronomers have observed features on the Sun that vary over time. Near the Sun's surface there are regions of magnetic force called magnetic fields. These magnetic fields get twisted into different positions as the Sun rotates. Features appear on the surface in areas where strong magnetic fields are located.

Sunspots are spots on the photosphere that are cooler than surrounding areas. Although they appear dark, sunspots are actually bright. They only seem dim because the rest of the photosphere is so much brighter.

Sunspot activity follows a pattern that lasts about 11 years. At the peak of the cycle, dozens of sunspots may appear. During periods of low activity, there may not be any sunspots.

Sunspots move across the Sun's surface as it rotates. Astronomers first realized that the Sun rotates when they noticed this movement. Because the Sun is not solid, some parts rotate faster than others.

Other solar features include flares and prominences (PRAHM-uh-nuhn-sihz). Flares are eruptions of hot gas from the Sun's surface. They usually occur near sunspots. Prominences are huge loops of glowing gas that extend into the corona. They occur where magnetic fields connecting sunspots soar into the outer atmosphere.

 **CHECK YOUR READING** How are sunspots different from other areas of the photosphere?

Solar Features

Features on the Sun appear in areas where a magnetic field is strong.

Sunspots

Sunspots on the photosphere can be larger than Earth.

Prominences

Prominences can soar more than 100,000 kilometers above the photosphere.

Solar Wind

Material in the Sun's corona is continually streaming out into space. The electrically charged particles that flow out in all directions from the corona are called the **solar wind.** The solar wind extends throughout our solar system.

This circular green aurora occurred over Alaska when particles from the solar wind entered the atmosphere.

Most of the solar wind flowing toward Earth is safely guided around the planet by Earth's magnetic field. When solar-wind particles do enter the upper atmosphere, they release energy, which can produce beautiful patterns of glowing light in the sky. Such displays of light are called auroras (uh-RAWR-uhz), or the northern and southern lights. Auroras often occur near the poles.

Earth's atmosphere usually prevents charged particles from reaching the surface. However, during the peak of the sunspot cycle, flares and other kinds of solar activity release strong bursts of charged particles into the solar wind. These bursts, called magnetic storms, can disrupt electric-power delivery across large regions by causing surges in power lines. They can also interfere with radio communication.

Magnetic storms are much more harmful above the protective layers of Earth's atmosphere. Bursts of particles in the solar wind can damage or destroy orbiting satellites. The solar wind also poses a danger to astronauts during space flights.

CHECK YOUR READING   What causes auroras to form?

22.1 Review

KEY CONCEPTS

1. How does the Sun produce energy?

2. How does energy move from the Sun's core to the photosphere?

3. How does the solar wind normally affect Earth?

CRITICAL THINKING

4. **Analyze** Why is the core the only layer of the Sun where energy is produced?

5. **Compare and Contrast** Make a diagram comparing sunspots, flares, and prominences.

⬥ CHALLENGE

6. **Infer** A communications satellite stops working while in orbit, and a surge in an electric power line causes blackouts in cities across a large region. What probably happened in the Sun's atmosphere shortly before these events?

CHAPTER INVESTIGATION

Temperature, Brightness, and Color

OVERVIEW AND PURPOSE Think of the metal heating surface on a hot plate. How can you tell whether the hot plate is fully heated? Is the metal surface brighter or dimmer than when it is just starting to get warm? Does the color of the surface change as the hot plate gets hotter? You may already have an idea of how temperature, brightness, and color are related—at least when it comes to heated metal. Do the same relationships apply to electric lights? to stars? This investigation is designed to help you find out. You will

- construct a wax photometer to compare the brightnesses and colors of different light sources
- determine how the temperature of a light source affects its brightness and color

MATERIALS

- 2 paraffin blocks
- aluminum foil
- 2 rubber bands
- 2 light-bulb holders
- 2 miniature light bulbs
- 3 AA batteries
- 4 pieces of uninsulated copper wire 15 cm long
- masking tape

for Challenge:
- incandescent lamp
- dimmer switch

▶ Problem

How are brightness and color related to temperature?

▶ Hypothesize

Write a hypothesis to explain how brightness and color are related to temperature. Your hypothesis should take the form of an "If . . . , then . . . , because . . ." statement.

▶ Procedure

1. An instrument called a photometer makes it easier to compare the brightnesses and colors of different light sources. Assemble the wax photometer as shown on page 785. The aluminum foil between the wax blocks should be folded so that the shiny side faces out on both sides.

2. Hold the photometer so that you can see both blocks. Bring it to different locations in the classroom, and observe how the brightnesses and colors of the blocks change as the two sides of the photometer are exposed to different light conditions.

3. Tape a piece of copper wire to each end of a battery, and connect the wires to a light-bulb holder. The battery will provide electricity to heat up the wire inside a light bulb.

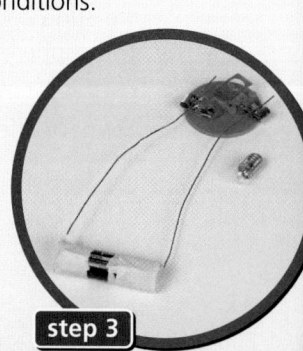

step 3

4. Tape the negative terminal, or flat end, of one battery to the positive terminal of another battery. Tape a piece of copper wire to each end, and connect the wires to a light-bulb holder. Because two batteries will provide electricity to the bulb in this holder, the wire in the bulb will be hotter than the wire in the bulb powered by one battery.

step 4

5. With the room darkened, insert a bulb into each light-bulb holder. If the bulb connected to two batteries does not light up, you may need to press the two batteries together with your fingers.

6. Place the photometer halfway between the two light bulbs. Compare the brightnesses of the two light sources. Record your observations in your **Science Notebook.**

7. Move the photometer closer to the cooler bulb until both sides of the photometer are equally bright. Compare the colors of the two light sources. Record your observations in your **Science Notebook**. To avoid draining the batteries, remove the bulbs from the holders when you have completed this step.

▶ Observe and Analyze
Write It Up

1. **RECORD OBSERVATIONS** Draw the setup of your photometer and light sources. Be sure your data table is complete with descriptions of brightness and color.

2. **IDENTIFY** Identify the variables in this experiment. List them in your **Science Notebook.**

▶ Conclude
Write It Up

1. **INTERPRET** Answer the question in the problem. Compare your results with your hypothesis.

2. **ANALYZE** How does distance affect your perception of the brightness of an object?

3. **APPLY** Judging by the results of the investigation, would you expect a red star or a yellow star to be hotter? Explain why.

▶ INVESTIGATE Further

CHALLENGE Connect an incandescent lamp to a dimmer switch. Write a procedure to show how you would use a photometer to show the relationship between the color and the temperature of the bulb as it fades from brightest to dimmest. Then carry out your procedure.

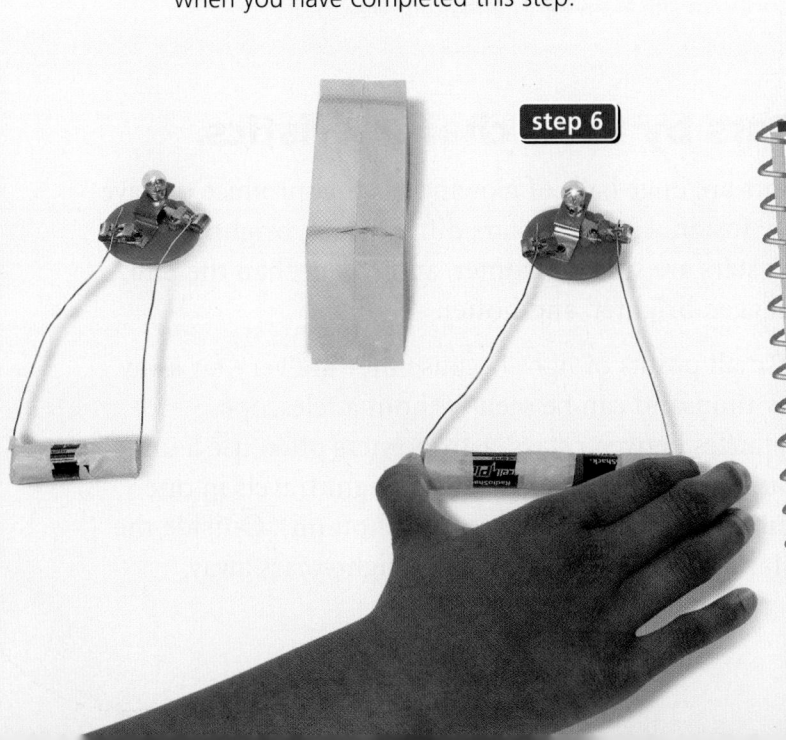

step 6

Temperature, Brightness, and Color
Observe and Analyze
Table 1. Properties of Light from Two Sources

	Cooler Bulb (one battery)	Warmer Bulb (two batteries)
Brightness		
Color		

22.2 Stars change over their life cycles.

Sunshine State STANDARDS

SC.E.1.3.3: The student understands that our Sun is one of many stars in our galaxy.

SC.E.1.3.4: The student knows that stars appear to be made of similar chemical elements, although they differ in age, size, temperature, and distance.

BEFORE, you learned

• The Sun is our local star
• The other stars are outside our solar system
• There are huge distances between objects in the universe

NOW, you will learn

• How stars are classified
• How stars form and change

VOCABULARY

light-year p. 786
parallax p. 787
nebula p. 789
main sequence p. 790
neutron star p. 790
black hole p. 790

EXPLORE Characteristics of Stars

How does distance affect brightness?

PROCEDURE

① In a darkened room, shine a flashlight onto a dark surface from 30 cm away while your partner shines a flashlight onto the surface from the same distance. Observe the two spots of light.

② Move one of the flashlights back 15 cm and then another 15 cm. Compare the two spots of light each time you move the flashlight.

MATERIALS
• 2 flashlights
• meter stick
• dark surface

WHAT DO YOU THINK?
• How did distance affect the brightness of the light on the dark surface?
• How does the distance of a star from Earth affect our view of it?

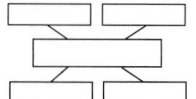

MAIN IDEA WEB
A main idea web would be a good choice for taking notes about the characteristics of stars.

We classify stars by their characteristics.

Like our Sun, all stars are huge balls of glowing gas that produce or have produced energy by fusion. However, stars differ in size, brightness, and temperature. Some stars are smaller, fainter, and cooler than the Sun. Others are much bigger, brighter, and hotter.

Stars look like small points of light because they are very far away. At most, only a few thousand can be seen without a telescope. To describe the distances between stars, astronomers often use a unit called the light-year. A **light-year** is the distance light travels in one year, which is about 9.5 trillion kilometers (6 trillion mi). Outside the solar system, the star closest to Earth is about 4 light-years away.

Brightness and Distance

If you look at stars, you will probably notice that some appear to be brighter than others. The amount of light a star gives off and its distance from Earth determine how bright it appears to an observer. A star that gives off a huge amount of light can appear faint if it is far away. On the other hand, a star that gives off much less light can appear bright if it is closer to Earth. Therefore, to determine the true brightness of a star, astronomers must measure its distance from Earth.

One way astronomers measure distance is by using **parallax,** which is the apparent shift in the position of an object when viewed from different locations. Look at an object with your right eye closed. Now quickly open it and close your left eye. The object will seem to move slightly because you are viewing it from a different angle. The same kind of shift occurs when astronomers view stars from different locations.

To measure the parallax of a star, astronomers plot the star's position in the sky from opposite sides of Earth's orbit around the Sun. They then use the apparent shift in position and the diameter of Earth's orbit to calculate the star's distance.

 **CHECK YOUR READING** What factors affect how bright a star appears from Earth?

INVESTIGATE Parallax

How does the distance of an object affect parallax?

PROCEDURE

1. Stand 1 m away from a classmate. Have the classmate hold up a meter stick at eye level.

2. With your left eye closed, hold a capped pen up close to your face. Look at the pen with your right eye, and line it up with the zero mark on the meter stick. Then open your left eye and quickly close your right eye. Observe how many centimeters the pen seems to move. Record your observation.

3. Repeat step 2 with the pen held at arm's length and then with the pen held at half your arm's length. Record your observation each time.

WHAT DO YOU THINK?

• How many centimeters did the pen appear to move each time you observed it?

• How is parallax affected when you change the distance of the pen from you?

CHALLENGE How could you use this method to estimate distances that you cannot measure directly?

SKILL FOCUS
Measuring

MATERIALS
• meter stick
• capped pen

TIME
10 minutes

Size

It is hard to get a sense of how large stars are from viewing them in the sky. Even the Sun, which is much closer than any other star, is far larger than its appearance suggests. The diameter of the Sun is about 100 times greater than that of Earth. A jet plane flying 800 kilometers per hour (500 mi/h) would travel around Earth's equator in about two days. If you could travel around the Sun's equator at the same speed, the trip would take more than seven months.

Some stars are much larger than the Sun. Giant and supergiant stars range from ten to hundreds of times larger. A supergiant called Betelgeuse (BEET-uhl-JOOZ) is more than 600 times greater in diameter than the Sun. If Betelgeuse replaced the Sun, it would fill space in our solar system well beyond Earth's orbit. Because giant and supergiant stars have such huge surface areas to give off light, they are very bright. Betelgeuse is one of the brightest stars in the sky, even though it is 522 light-years away.

There are also stars much smaller than the Sun. Stars called white dwarfs are about 100 times smaller in diameter than the Sun, or roughly the size of Earth. White dwarfs cannot be seen without a telescope.

A star the size of the Sun
Diameter = 1.4 million kilometers (900,000 mi)

White dwarf
1/100 the Sun's diameter

Giant star
10–100 times the Sun's diameter

Supergiant star
100–1000 times the Sun's diameter

Color and Temperature

If you observe stars closely, you may notice that they vary slightly in color. Most stars look white. However, a few appear slightly blue or red. The differences in color are due to differences in temperature.

You can see how temperature affects color by heating up metal. For example, if you turn on a toaster, the metal coils inside will start to glow a dull red. As they get hotter, the coils will turn a brighter orange. The illustration on page 789 shows changes in the color of a metal bar as it heats up.

Like the color of heated metal, the color of a star indicates its temperature. Astronomers group stars into classes by color and surface temperature. The chart on page 789 lists the color and temperature range of each class of star. The coolest stars are red. The hottest stars are blue-white. Our Sun—a yellow, G-class star—has a surface temperature of about 6000°C.

Stars of every class give off light that is made up of a range of colors. Astronomers can spread a star's light into a spectrum to learn about the star's composition. The colors and lines in a spectrum reveal which gases are present in the star's outer layers.

CHECK YOUR READING How does a star's temperature affect its appearance?

Color and Temperature

Objects that radiate light change color as they heat up.

Classification of Stars		
Class	Color	Surface Temperature (°C)
O	blue-white	above 25,000
B	blue-white	10,000–25,000
A	white	7500–10,000
F	yellow-white	6000–7500
G	yellow	5000–6000
K	orange	3500–5000
M	red	below 3500

Stars are classified according to their colors and temperatures. The Sun is a G-class star.

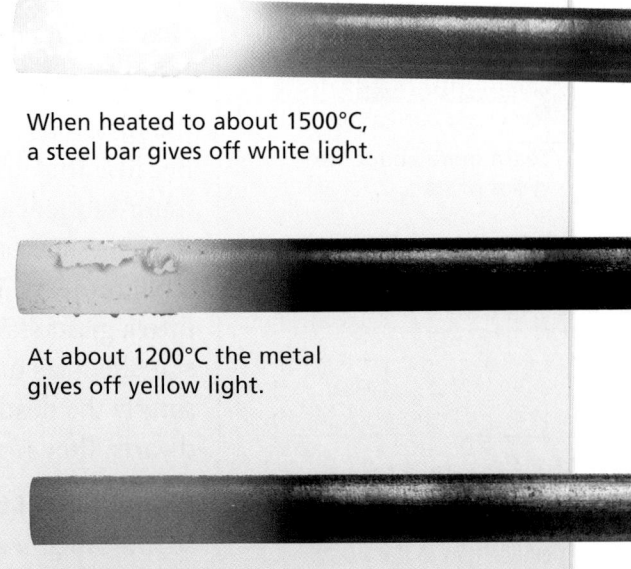

When heated to about 1500°C, a steel bar gives off white light.

At about 1200°C the metal gives off yellow light.

A steel bar glows red when heated to about 600°C.

Stars have life cycles.

Although stars last for very long periods, they are not permanent. Like living organisms, stars go through cycles of birth, maturity, and death. The life cycle of a star varies, depending on the mass of the star. Higher-mass stars develop more quickly than lower-mass stars. Toward the end of their life cycles, higher-mass stars also behave differently from lower-mass stars.

Stars form inside a cloud of gas and dust called a **nebula** (NEHB-yuh-luh). Gravity pulls gas and dust closer together in some regions of a nebula. As the matter contracts, it forms a hot, dense sphere. The sphere becomes a star if its center grows hot and dense enough for fusion to occur.

When a star dies, its matter does not disappear. Some of it may form a nebula or move into an existing one. There, the matter may eventually become part of new stars.

CHECK YOUR READING How is gravity involved in the formation of stars?

Colors have been added to this photograph of the Omega Nebula in order to bring out details.

Stages in the Life Cycles of Stars

The diagram on page 791 shows the stages that stars go through in their life cycles. Notice that the length of a cycle and the way a star changes depend on the mass of the star at its formation.

Lower-Mass Stars The stage in which stars produce energy through the fusion of hydrogen into helium is called the **main sequence.** Because they use their fuel slowly, lower-mass stars can remain in the main-sequence stage for billions of years. The Sun has been a main-sequence star for 4.6 billion years and will remain one for about another 5 billion years. When a lower-mass star runs out of hydrogen, it expands into a giant star, in which helium fuses into carbon. Over time a giant star sheds its outer layers and becomes a white dwarf. A white dwarf is simply the dead core of a giant star. Although no fusion occurs in white dwarfs, they remain hot for billions of years.

Higher-Mass Stars Stars more than eight times as massive as our Sun spend much less time in the main-sequence stage because they use their fuel rapidly. After millions of years, a higher-mass star expands to become a supergiant star. In the core of a supergiant, fusion produces heavier and heavier elements. When an iron core forms, fusion stops and gravity causes the core to collapse. Then part of the core bounces outward, and the star erupts in an explosion called a supernova.

For a brief period, a supernova can give off as much light as a galaxy. The outer layers of the exploded star shoot out into space, carrying with them heavy elements that formed inside the star. Eventually this matter may become part of new stars and planets.

RESOURCE CENTER
CLASSZONE.COM

Learn more about life cycles of stars.

FLORIDA
Content Review

Notice that in the lives of stars, as useful energy of the star system decreases, disorder in the system increases.

Neutron Stars and Black Holes

The collapsed core of a supergiant star may form an extremely dense body called a **neutron star.** Neutron stars measure only about 20 kilometers (12 mi) in diameter, but their masses are one to three times that of the Sun.

Neutron stars emit little visible light. However, they strongly emit other forms of radiation, such as x-rays. Some neutron stars emit beams of radio waves as they spin. These stars are called pulsars because they seem to pulse as the beams rotate.

Sometimes a supernova leaves behind a core with a mass more than three times that of the Sun. In such a case, the core does not end up as a neutron star. Instead, it collapses even further, forming an invisible object called a **black hole.** The gravity of a black hole is so strong that no form of radiation can escape from it.

A pulsar emits beams of radio waves as it spins rapidly. The pulsar seems to pulse as the beams rotate toward and away from Earth.

CHECK YOUR READING How do lower-mass stars differ from higher-mass stars after the main-sequence stage?

Life Cycles of Stars

A star forms inside a cloud of gas and dust called a nebula. The life cycle of a star depends on its mass.

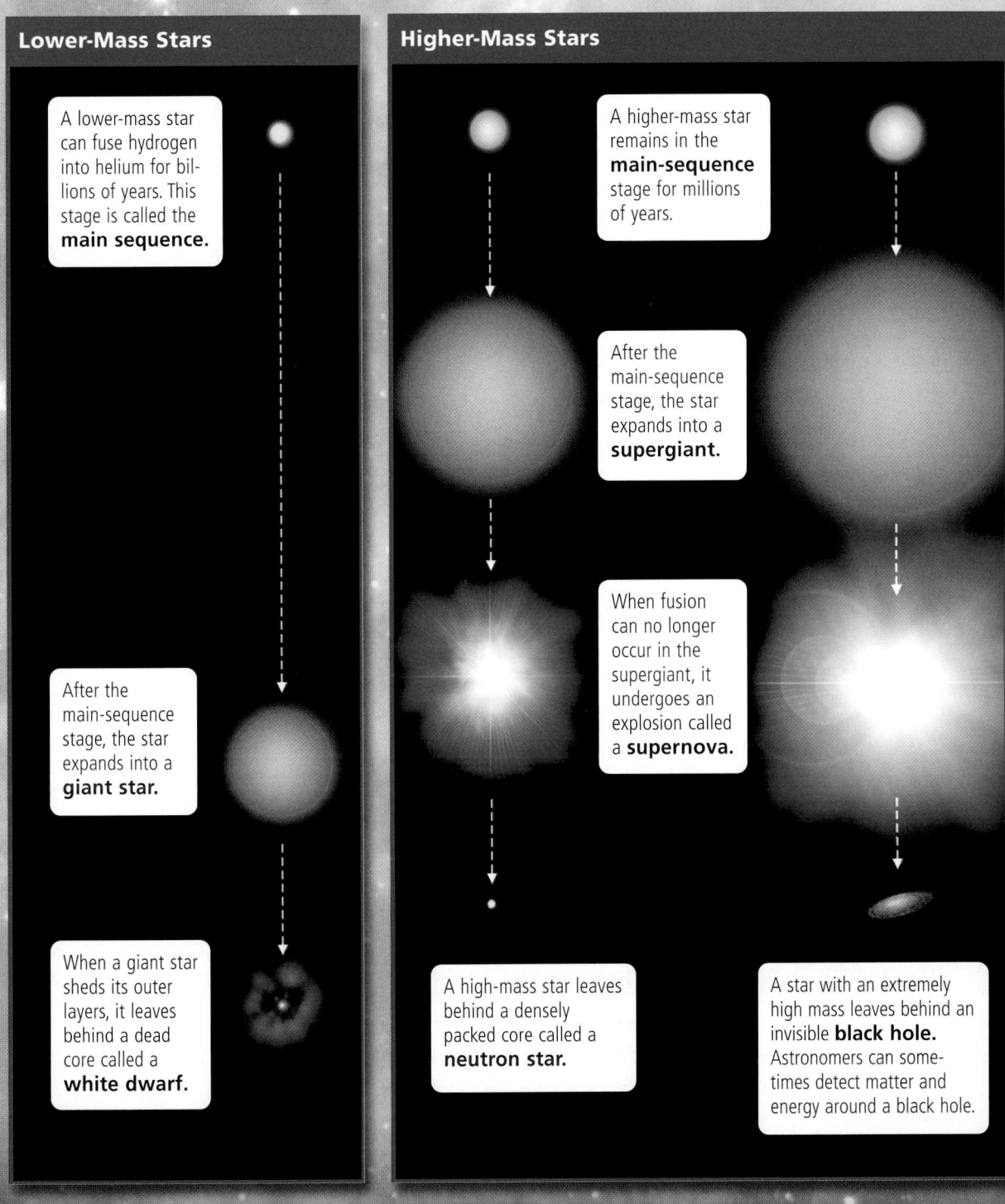

Lower-Mass Stars

A lower-mass star can fuse hydrogen into helium for billions of years. This stage is called the **main sequence.**

After the main-sequence stage, the star expands into a **giant star.**

When a giant star sheds its outer layers, it leaves behind a dead core called a **white dwarf.**

Higher-Mass Stars

A higher-mass star remains in the **main-sequence** stage for millions of years.

After the main-sequence stage, the star expands into a **supergiant.**

When fusion can no longer occur in the supergiant, it undergoes an explosion called a **supernova.**

A high-mass star leaves behind a densely packed core called a **neutron star.**

A star with an extremely high mass leaves behind an invisible **black hole.** Astronomers can sometimes detect matter and energy around a black hole.

READING VISUALS How do the stars shown in this illustration differ in the main-sequence stage of their life cycles?

Star Systems

Unlike our Sun, most stars do not exist alone. Instead, they are grouped with one or more companion stars. The stars are held together by the force of gravity between them. A binary star system consists of two stars that orbit each other. A multiple star system consists of more than two stars.

In many star systems, the stars are too close together to be seen individually. However, astronomers have developed ways of detecting such systems. For example, in a binary star system, one of the stars may orbit in front of the other when viewed from Earth. The star that orbits in front will briefly block some of the other star's light, providing a clue that more than one star is present. The illustration at right shows a binary star system that can be detected this way. Sometimes astronomers can also figure out whether a star is really a star system by studying its spectrum.

Star systems are an important source of information about star masses. Astronomers cannot measure the mass of a star directly. However, they can figure out a star's mass by observing the effect of the star's gravity on a companion star.

Binary Star System

Some binary star systems appear to dim briefly when one star orbits in front of the other and blocks some of its light.

When neither star is in front of the other, the star system appears to give off more light.

CHECK YOUR READING Why are star systems important to astronomers?

22.2 Review

KEY CONCEPTS

1. Why must astronomers figure out a star's distance to calculate its actual brightness?

2. How are color and temperature related in stars?

3. How does a star's mass affect its life cycle?

CRITICAL THINKING

4. **Analyze** Some of the brightest stars are red supergiants. How can stars with cooler red surfaces be so bright?

5. **Infer** Will the Sun eventually become a black hole? Why or why not?

⬤ CHALLENGE

6. **Infer** At what stage in the life cycle of the Sun will it be impossible for life to exist on Earth? Explain.

MATH TUTORIAL
CLASSZONE.COM
Click on Math Tutorial for more help with scatter plots.

Brightness and Temperature of Stars

A star's brightness, or luminosity, depends on the star's surface temperature and size. If two stars have the same surface temperature, the larger star will be more luminous. The Hertzsprung-Russell (H-R) diagram below is a scatter plot that shows the relative temperatures and luminosities of various stars.

Example

Describe the surface temperature and luminosity of Spica.

(1) Surface temperature: Without drawing on the graph, imagine a line extending from Spica down to the temperature axis. Spica is one of the hottest stars.

(2) Luminosity: Imagine a line extending from Spica across to the luminosity axis. Spica has a high luminosity.

ANSWER Spica is one of the hottest and most luminous stars.

Hertzsprung-Russell (H-R) Diagram

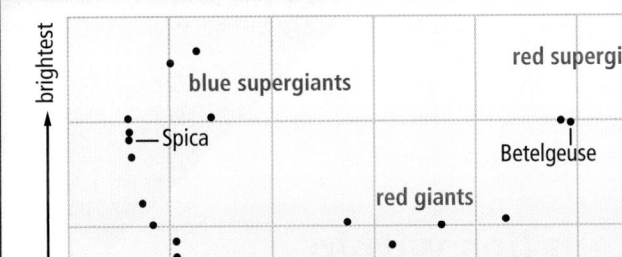

Use the diagram to answer the questions.

1. Describe the surface temperature and luminosity of Proxima Centauri.

2. Compare the surface temperature and luminosity of the Sun with the surface temperature and luminosity of Betelgeuse.

3. Compare the surface temperature and luminosity of the red dwarfs with the surface temperature and luminosity of the blue supergiants.

CHALLENGE When an old red giant star loses its outer atmosphere, all that remains is the very hot core of the star. Because the core is small, it does not give off much light. What kind of star does the red giant star become after it loses its outer atmosphere? How can you tell from the diagram?

KEY CONCEPT

22.3 Galaxies have different sizes and shapes.

Sunshine State STANDARDS

SC.E.2.3.1: The student knows that thousands of other galaxies appear to have the same elements, forces, and forms of energy found in our Solar System.

BEFORE, you learned

- Our solar system is part of a galaxy called the Milky Way
- Stars change over their life cycles

NOW, you will learn

- About the size and shape of the Milky Way
- How galaxies are classified
- About the centers of galaxies

VOCABULARY

quasar p. 797

EXPLORE The Milky Way

Why does the Milky Way look hazy?

PROCEDURE

1. Use a white gel pen to make 50 small dots close together on a piece of black paper.

2. Tape the paper to a wall, and move slowly away from it until you have difficulty seeing the individual dots.

WHAT DO YOU THINK?

- At what distance did the dots become hazy?
- Why might some of the stars in the Milky Way appear hazy from Earth?

MATERIALS

- white gel pen
- black paper
- tape

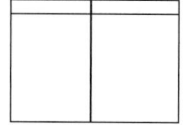

COMBINATION NOTES
You could record information about the Milky Way in a combination notes table.

Our solar system lies within the Milky Way galaxy.

The Sun lies within a galaxy called the Milky Way. Remember that a galaxy is a huge grouping of stars, gas, and dust held together by gravity. Without a telescope, you can only see nearby stars clearly. Those stars are a tiny fraction of the several hundred billion in the Milky Way.

The Milky Way is shaped like a disk with a bulge in the center. Because Earth is inside the disk, you have an edge-on view of part of the galaxy. On a dark night, the galaxy appears as a band of blended starlight. The Milky Way got its name from the hazy, or milky, appearance of this band of stars. You cannot see the center of the galaxy because it is hidden by dust.

 **CHECK YOUR READING** Why can't we see all of the Milky Way from Earth?

The Milky Way

When you look at the Milky Way, it appears as a band of hazy light.

Illustration of Side View

disk   Sun's location   bulge

The Milky Way is about 100,000 light-years in diameter.

The disk of the Milky Way measures more than 100,000 light-years in diameter. The bulge of densely packed stars at the center is located about 26,000 light-years from the Sun. A large but very faint layer of stars surrounds the disk and bulge. In addition to stars, the Milky Way contains clouds of gas and dust called nebulae.

The stars and nebulae in the Milky Way orbit the galaxy's center at very high speeds. However, the galaxy is so large that the Sun takes about 250 million years to complete one orbit.

INVESTIGATE Galaxy Shapes

How can you classify galaxies according to shape?

PROCEDURE

1. Cut out the photographs of galaxies on the Galaxy Photo Sheet.

2. Sort the galaxies into different groups according to their shapes. You may need a group for galaxies that do not fit in other groups.

WHAT DO YOU THINK?

- How many groups did you sort the galaxies into?
- Describe each group briefly, and list which galaxies you put in each group.

CHALLENGE What is the connection between the apparent shape of a galaxy and the galaxy's relationship to the viewer? **Hint:** Think about how an edge-on view of a compact disc differs from a view of it lying flat on a table.

SKILL FOCUS
Classifying

MATERIALS
- Galaxy Photo Sheet
- scissors

TIME
15 minutes

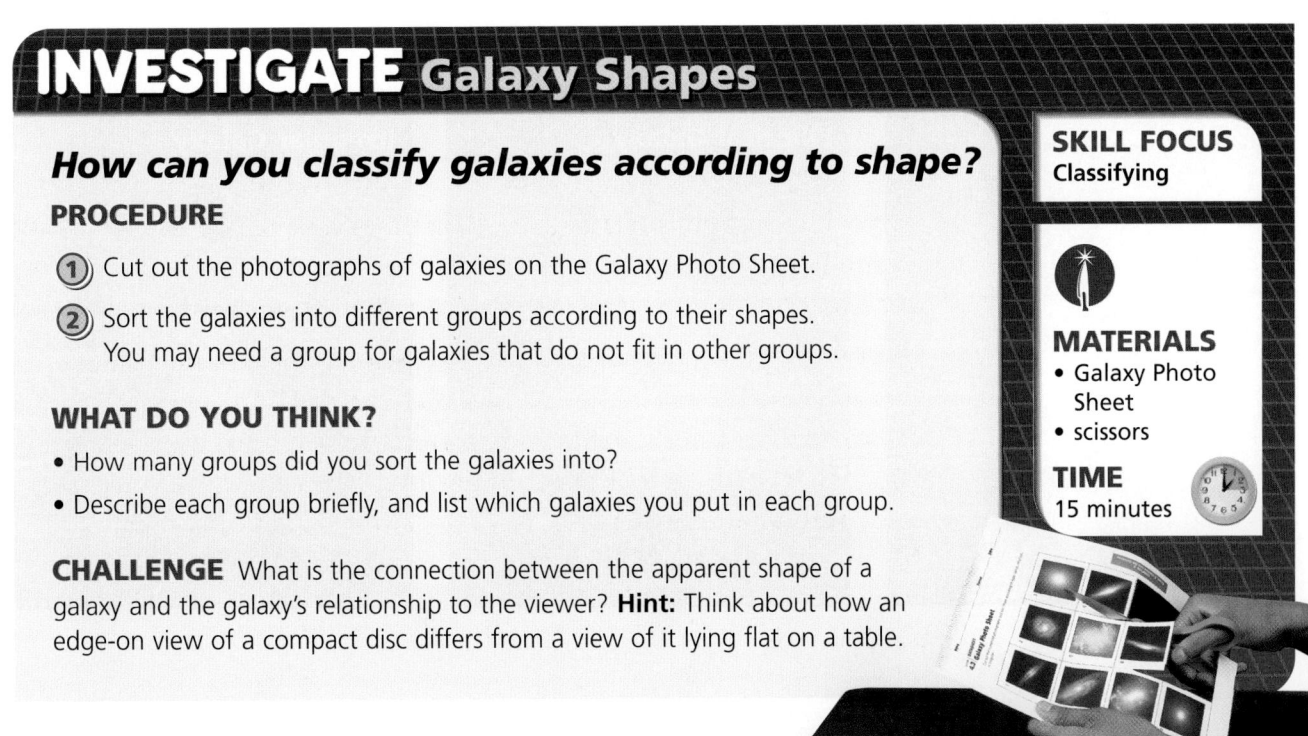

795

Galaxies vary in appearance.

RESOURCE CENTER
CLASSZONE.COM

Learn more about galaxies.

Galaxies differ greatly in size. Some contain as few as a hundred million stars, but the biggest have more than a trillion stars. Galaxies also vary in shape. Astronomers have classified galaxies into three main types based on their shape.

 What are two ways in which galaxies can differ from one another?

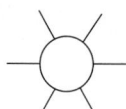

VOCABULARY
Make a description wheel for each type of galaxy in your notebook.

Types of Galaxies

The three main types of galaxies are spiral, elliptical, and irregular. Most galaxies are either spiral or elliptical.

Spiral galaxies have arms of stars, gas, and dust that curve away from the center of the galaxy in a spiral pattern. The Milky Way is a spiral galaxy. Like the Milky Way, other spiral galaxies are disk-shaped and have a central bulge. Most of the stars in the disk and the bulge are old stars. However, the dense spiral arms within the disk contain many young, bright stars.

Elliptical galaxies are shaped like spheres or eggs. Unlike spiral galaxies, elliptical galaxies have almost no dust or gas between stars, and all of their stars are old.

Irregular galaxies are faint galaxies without a definite shape. They are smaller than the other types of galaxies and have many fewer stars.

Galaxies sometimes collide with other galaxies. These collisions can cause changes in their shapes. The Extreme Science feature on page 798 describes such collisions.

Spiral Galaxy

Elliptical Galaxy

Irregular Galaxy

Centers of Galaxies

Most large galaxies seem to have supermassive black holes at their centers. The mass of a supermassive black hole can be millions or even billions of times greater than that of the Sun. At the center of the Milky Way, for example, is a black hole with a mass about three million times that of the Sun.

Like all black holes, a supermassive black hole is invisible. Astronomers can identify the presence of a black hole by the behavior of matter around it. The gravity of a supermassive black hole is so strong that it draws in a huge whirlpool of gas from nearby stars. As gases are pulled toward the black hole, they become compressed and extremely hot, so they give off very bright light. The motions of stars orbiting the black hole can also reveal its presence.

If the center of a galaxy is very bright, it may look like a star from a great distance. The very bright centers of some distant galaxies are called **quasars.** *Quasar* is a shortened form of *quasi-stellar,* which means "seeming like a star." The galaxy surrounding a quasar is often hard to see because the quasar is so much brighter than it.

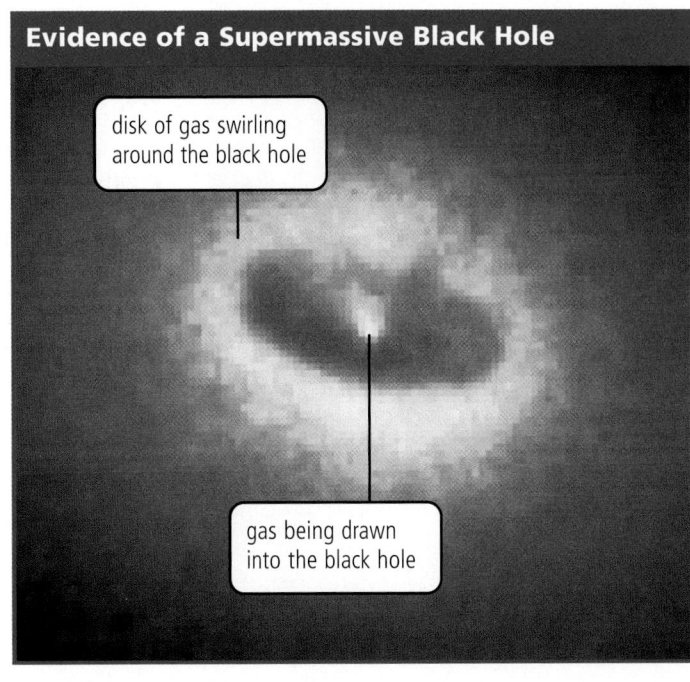

Evidence of a Supermassive Black Hole

disk of gas swirling around the black hole

gas being drawn into the black hole

CHECK YOUR READING How can astronomers detect the presence of a supermassive black hole at the center of a galaxy?

22.3 Review

KEY CONCEPTS

1. What is the shape of the Milky Way?

2. Why does the Milky Way look like a hazy band of stars in the sky?

3. What keeps the stars in galaxies from moving apart?

CRITICAL THINKING

4. **Compare and Contrast** Make a diagram showing similarities and differences among the three main types of galaxies.

5. **Infer** How might our view of the Milky Way be different if the Sun were located inside the central bulge?

CHALLENGE

6. **Predict** If two spiral galaxies collide, what might eventually happen to the supermassive black holes at their centers?

When Galaxies Collide

A small galaxy is moving through our galaxy, the Milky Way, right now!

- The small galaxy may be destroyed by the collision, but the Milky Way is not in danger.
- The same galaxy seems to have moved through the Milky Way ten times before.
- Other galaxies may also be moving through the Milky Way.

Not to Worry!

Galaxies containing many billions of stars are colliding all the time. What are the chances that their stars will crash into one another? The chances are very small, because there is so much empty space between stars.

Galactic Cannibals

When galaxies collide, a larger galaxy can "eat up" a smaller one.

- The stars of the smaller galaxy become part of the larger one.
- The collision of two spiral galaxies may form a new elliptical galaxy.

Bent Out of Shape

Sometimes galaxies pass very close to each other without actually colliding. In these near misses, gravity can produce some interesting new shapes. For example, the Tadpole Galaxy (left) has a long tail of dust and gas pulled out by the gravity of a passing galaxy.

Model Galaxies

Astronomers use computer simulations to predict how the stars and gas in galaxies are affected by a collision. To understand galaxy collisions better, they then compare the simulations with images of actual galaxies.

EXPLORE

1. **PREDICT** Draw the shape of the new galaxy that the two in the photograph on the left might form.

2. **CHALLENGE** Look at online images and simulations of galaxy collisions. Make a chart showing how these collisions can differ.

RESOURCE CENTER
CLASSZONE.COM
Find out more about galaxy collisions.

Come back in a few billion years and you may see that these two spiral galaxies have become one elliptical galaxy.

22.4

The universe is expanding.

BEFORE, you learned

- Galaxies contain millions or billions of stars
- Electromagnetic radiation carries information about space

NOW, you will learn

- How galaxies are moving apart in the universe
- What scientists are discovering about the development of the universe

VOCABULARY

Doppler effect p. 800
big bang p. 802

EXPLORE Large Numbers

How much is a billion?

PROCEDURE

1. Guess how thick a billion-page book would be. Write down your guess.

2. Count how many sheets of paper in a book add up to a millimeter in thickness. Multiply by 2 to calculate the number of pages.

3. Then divide 1 billion (1,000,000,000) by that number to determine how many millimeters thick the book would be. Divide your result by 1,000,000 to convert to kilometers.

WHAT DO YOU THINK?

- How thick would a billion-page book be?
- How close was your guess?

MATERIALS

- book
- ruler
- calculator

Galaxies are moving farther apart in the universe.

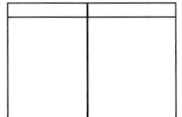

COMBINATION NOTES
You could record information about the expansion of the universe in a combination notes table.

The universe is unbelievably huge. It consists of all space, energy, and matter. The Milky Way is just one of about 100 billion galaxies. These galaxies occur in groups that together form superclusters. Between the superclusters are huge areas of nearly empty space.

Because the universe is so huge, you might think that the most distant regions of the universe are very different from space near Earth. However, by looking at the spectra of light from stars and galaxies, astronomers have determined that the same elements are found throughout the universe. Scientific observations also indicate that the same physical forces and processes operate everywhere.

Looking Back in Time

When we look far out into space, we see galaxies by the light they gave off long ago. This light has traveled millions or even billions of years before reaching telescopes on Earth. The Andromeda Galaxy, for example, is the closest large galaxy. The light of its stars takes over 2 million years to reach Earth. When we view this galaxy through a telescope, we are seeing what happened in it 2 million years ago. To see what is happening there now, we would have to wait 2 million years for the light to arrive.

As astronomers look at galaxies farther and farther away, they see how the universe looked at different times in the past. These views are like photographs in an album that show someone at various stages of life. Astronomers can see how the universe has developed over billions of years.

Light from the Andromeda Galaxy takes 2 million years to reach Earth.

CHECK YOUR READING Why can astronomers learn about the past by looking at distant galaxies?

The Motion of Galaxies

Have you ever noticed that the sound of an ambulance siren changes as it travels toward and then away from you? The pitch of the siren seems to be higher as the ambulance approaches. As the ambulance passes you and starts moving away, the pitch of the siren seems to get lower. The shifting pitch of the siren is an example of the **Doppler effect,** which is a change in the observed wavelength or frequency of a wave that occurs when the source of the wave or the observer is moving.

The Doppler effect occurs with light as well as sound. If a galaxy is moving toward Earth, the light we receive will seem compressed to shorter wavelengths. This change is called a blue shift because the light shifts toward the blue end of the spectrum. If a galaxy is moving away from Earth, the light we receive will seem stretched to longer wavelengths. This change is called a red shift because the light shifts toward the red end of the spectrum.

In the early 1900s, astronomers discovered that light from distant galaxies is stretched to longer wavelengths. This fact indicates that the galaxies are moving apart. By analyzing the spectra of galaxies, astronomers also discovered that the galaxies are moving apart faster the farther away they are. These observations led astronomers to conclude that the universe has been expanding throughout its history.

Evidence of an Expanding Universe

The Doppler effect can show how galaxies are moving in relation to Earth.

moving away

moving toward

Earth

Light from a galaxy moving away from Earth will seem stretched to longer wavelengths.

Light from a galaxy moving toward Earth will seem compressed to shorter wavelengths.

READING VISUALS What do the arrows on the light waves indicate?

The illustration of raisin-bread dough rising will help you imagine this expansion. Suppose you were a raisin. You would observe that all the other raisins are moving away from you as the dough expands. The raisins are being moved apart by the expanding dough. Furthermore, you would observe that distant raisins are moving away faster than nearby raisins. They move away faster because there is more dough expanding between you and those raisins.

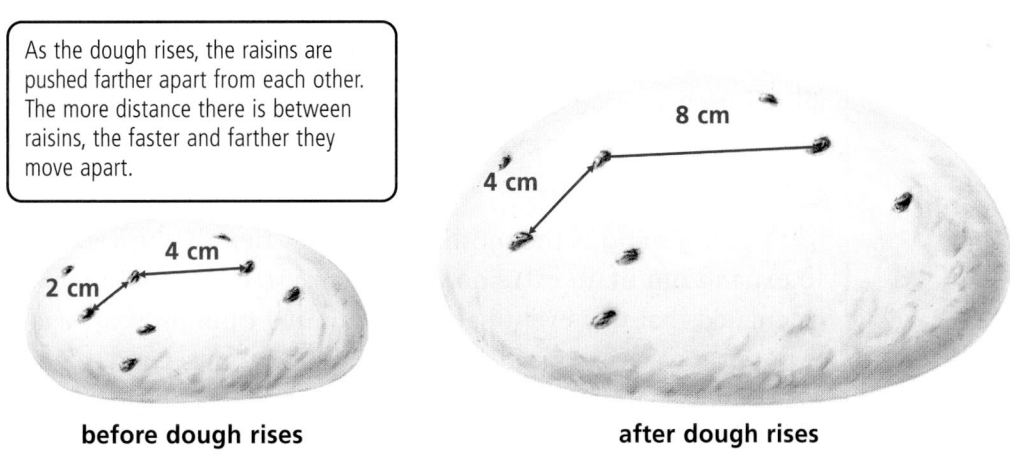

As the dough rises, the raisins are pushed farther apart from each other. The more distance there is between raisins, the faster and farther they move apart.

4 cm

8 cm

2 cm

4 cm

before dough rises

after dough rises

Like the dough that expands and moves raisins apart, space in the universe is expanding and moving galaxies apart. The universe does not expand into anything, since there is nothing outside the universe. Rather, the universe itself is expanding.

 **CHECK YOUR READING** How are galaxies moving in relation to each other?

How does the universe expand?

PROCEDURE

① Spread the cut rubber band against the ruler without stretching it. Mark off every centimeter for 6 centimeters.

② Align the first mark on the rubber band with the 1-centimeter mark on the ruler and hold it in place tightly. Stretch the rubber band so that the second mark is next to the 3-centimeter mark on the ruler.

③ Observe how many centimeters each mark has moved from its original location against the ruler.

WHAT DO YOU THINK?

• How far did each mark on the rubber band move from its original location?

• What does this activity demonstrate about the expansion of the universe?

CHALLENGE How could you calculate the rates at which the marks moved when you stretched the rubber band?

SKILL FOCUS
Measuring

MATERIALS
• thick rubber band cut open
• ballpoint pen
• ruler

TIME
20 minutes

Scientists are investigating the origin of the universe.

After astronomers learned that galaxies are moving apart, they developed new ideas about the origin of the universe. They concluded that all matter was once merged together and then the universe suddenly began to expand. The evidence for this scientific theory is so strong that almost all astronomers now accept it.

The **big bang** is the moment in time when the universe started to expand out of an extremely hot, dense state. Astronomers have calculated that this event happened about 14 billion years ago. The expansion was very rapid. In a tiny fraction of a second, the universe may have expanded from a size much smaller than a speck of dust to the size of our solar system.

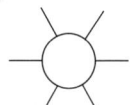

VOCABULARY
Add a description wheel for *big bang* in your notebook.

Evidence of the Big Bang

Evidence for the big bang comes from various sources. One important source of evidence is microwave radiation. Astronomers predicted in 1948 that the universe would still be filled with microwaves emitted shortly after the big bang. In 1965 researchers detected this kind of radiation streaming through space in all directions.

Besides the presence of microwave radiation and the motions of galaxies, scientists have found other evidence of the big bang by observing space. For example, images of very distant galaxies provide information about the universe's development. Additional evidence of the big bang has come from experiments and computer models.

Development of the Universe

Immediately after the big bang, the universe was incredibly dense and hot—much hotter than the core of the Sun. Matter and energy behaved very differently than they do under present conditions. As the universe rapidly expanded, it went through a series of changes.

Scientists do not fully understand what conditions were like in the early universe. However, they are gaining a clearer picture of how the universe developed. One way that scientists are learning about this development is by performing experiments in particle accelerators. These huge machines expose matter to extreme conditions.

Scientists have found that the earliest stages in the universe's development occurred in a tiny fraction of a second. However, it took about 300,000 years for the first elements to form. Stars, planets, and galaxies began to appear within the next billion years. Some evidence suggests that the first stars formed only a few hundred million years after the big bang.

This Hubble telescope image of very distant galaxies has helped scientists learn what the universe was like about 13 billion years ago.

 **CHECK YOUR READING** What happened to the universe shortly after the big bang?

22.4 Review

KEY CONCEPTS

1. How are distant regions of the universe similar to space near Earth?

2. What does the Doppler effect indicate about the motion of galaxies?

3. How do scientists explain the origin of the universe?

CRITICAL THINKING

4. **Apply** If a star 100 light-years from Earth is beginning to expand into a giant star, how long will it take for astronomers to observe this development? Explain.

5. **Analyze** Why do scientists need to perform experiments to learn about the earliest stages of the universe?

△ CHALLENGE

6. **Infer** Galaxy A and galaxy B both give off light that appears stretched to longer wavelengths. The light from galaxy B is stretched to even longer wavelengths than the light from galaxy A. What can you infer from these data?

the **BIG** idea

Our Sun is one of billions of stars in one of billions of galaxies in the universe.

 **FLORIDA REVIEW**
CLASSZONE.COM

Content Review and
FCAT Practice

◀ **KEY CONCEPTS SUMMARY**

1 The Sun is our local star.

The Sun produces energy from hydrogen. Energy flows through the Sun's layers. Features appear on the Sun's surface.

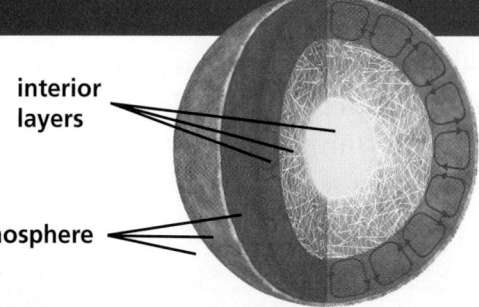

interior layers

atmosphere

VOCABULARY
fusion p. 780
convection p. 780
corona p. 780
sunspot p. 782
solar wind p. 783

2 Stars change over their life cycles.

Stars vary in brightness, size, color, and temperature. The development of a star depends on the mass of the star. Most stars are grouped with one or more companion stars.

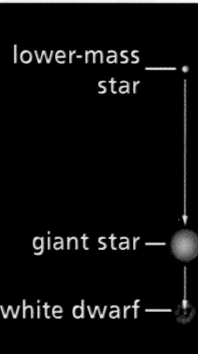

lower-mass star

giant star

white dwarf

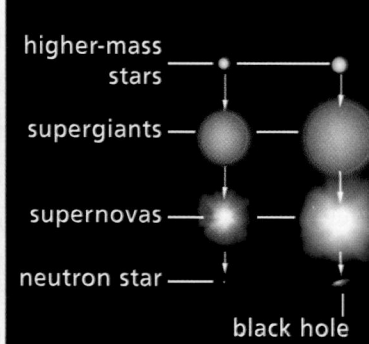

higher-mass stars

supergiants

supernovas

neutron star

black hole

VOCABULARY
light-year p. 786
parallax p. 787
nebula p. 789
main sequence p. 790
neutron star p. 790
black hole p. 790

3 Galaxies have different sizes and shapes.

Our galaxy, the Milky Way, is a spiral galaxy. Galaxies can also be elliptical or irregular. Irregular galaxies have no definite shape.

Spiral Galaxy   **Elliptical Galaxy**   **Irregular Galaxy**

VOCABULARY
quasar p. 797

4 The universe is expanding.

Galaxies are moving farther apart in the universe. Scientists are investigating the origin and development of the universe.

VOCABULARY
Doppler effect p. 800
big bang p. 802

Reviewing Vocabulary

Make a frame for each of the vocabulary words listed below. Write the word in the center. Decide what information to frame it with. Use definitions, examples, descriptions, parts, or pictures. An example is shown below.

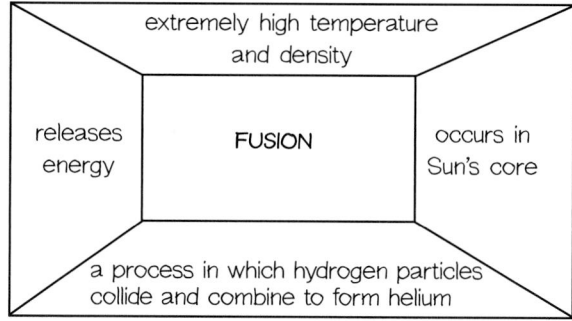

extremely high temperature and density

releases energy

FUSION

occurs in Sun's core

a process in which hydrogen particles collide and combine to form helium

1. convection
2. corona
3. sunspot
4. solar wind
5. nebula
6. black hole
7. Doppler effect
8. big bang

Reviewing Key Concepts

Multiple Choice *Choose the letter of the best answer.*

9. Which layer do you usually see in photographs of the Sun?
   a. convection zone
   b. photosphere
   c. chromosphere
   d. corona

10. Which statement is true of sunspots?
   a. They are permanent features on the Sun's surface.
   b. They are caused by solar wind.
   c. They are where fusion occurs.
   d. They are cooler than surrounding areas.

11. Which unit is usually used to describe the distances of stars?
   a. astronomical units
   b. light-years
   c. kilometers
   d. miles

12. Which example best shows the relationship between color and temperature?
   a. A rainbow forms when sunlight strikes raindrops.
   b. A flashlight beam looks red when passed through a red plastic filter.
   c. A chemical light-stick glows a yellow-green color.
   d. A metal rod in a fireplace changes in color from red to orange.

13. How do lower-mass stars differ from higher-mass stars?
   a. They develop more quickly.
   b. They develop more slowly.
   c. They end up as black holes.
   d. They have too little mass to produce energy.

14. Which term describes the Milky Way?
   a. spiral galaxy
   b. elliptical galaxy
   c. irregular galaxy
   d. quasar

15. The Doppler effect is used to determine
   a. the number of stars in a galaxy
   b. the number of galaxies in the universe
   c. the size of the universe
   d. whether a galaxy is moving toward or away from Earth

16. What is the big bang?
   a. the collision of galaxies
   b. the formation of the solar system
   c. the beginning of the universe's expansion
   d. the time when stars began to form

Short Response *Write a short response to each question.*

17. Why can't we see the Sun's corona under normal conditions?

18. How do astronomers use parallax to calculate a star's distance?

19. Where do heavy elements, such as iron, come from?

20. How can astronomers tell whether a black hole exists in the center of a galaxy?

Thinking Critically

The table below shows the distances of some galaxies and the speeds at which they are moving away from the Milky Way. Use the table to answer the next three questions.

Galaxy	Distance (million light-years)	Speed (kilometers per second)
NGC 7793	14	241
NGC 6946	22	336
NGC 2903	31	472
NGC 6744	42	663

21. COMPARE AND CONTRAST How do the speed and distance of NGC 7793 compare with the speed and distance of NGC 2903?

22. ANALYZE What general pattern do you see in these data?

23. APPLY What would you estimate to be the speed of a galaxy located 60 million light-years away? **Hint:** Notice the pattern between the first and third rows and the second and fourth rows in the chart.

24. INFER Why might the solar wind have a stronger effect on inner planets than on outer planets in the solar system?

25. PREDICT The core of a particular star consists almost entirely of helium. What will soon happen to this star?

26. ANALYZE Planets shine by reflected light. Why do some planets in our solar system appear brighter than stars, even though the stars give off their own light?

27. IDENTIFY CAUSE A star dims for a brief period every three days. What could be causing it to dim?

28. COMPARE AND CONTRAST Describe the similarities and differences between the life cycles of lower-mass stars and higher-mass stars.

29. EVALUATE If you wanted to study a neutron star, would you use a visible-light telescope or an x-ray telescope? Explain why.

30. INFER Suppose that astronomers find evidence of iron and other heavy elements in a galaxy. On the basis of this evidence, what can you assume has already occurred in that galaxy?

31. ANALYZE Why did the discovery that galaxies are moving farther apart help scientists conclude that all matter was once merged together?

32. PREDICT What changes do you predict will happen in the universe over the next 10 billion years?

33. COMPARE AND CONTRAST The photographs above show a spiral galaxy and an elliptical galaxy. What similarities and differences do you see in these two types of galaxies?

the BIG idea

34. INFER Look again at the photograph on pages 776–777. Now that you have finished the chapter, how would you change your response to the question on the photograph? What else might be present?

35. SYNTHESIZE Think of a question that you still have about the universe. What information would you need to answer the question? How might you obtain this information?

UNIT PROJECTS

Evaluate all the data, results, and information in your project folder. Prepare to present your project.

Analyzing a Chart

Use the chart and diagram to answer the following questions.

Classification of Stars

Class	Color	Surface Temperature (°C)
O	blue-white	above 25,000
B	blue-white	10,000–25,000
A	white	7500–10,000
F	yellow-white	6000–7500
G	yellow	5000–6000
K	orange	3500–5000
M	red	below 3500

FCAT TiP

When using two charts to answer questions, study both charts closely so you understand how the information presented in both charts is related.

Hertzsprung-Russell (H-R) Diagram

GRIDDED RESPONSE

1. Below what temperature are stars classed as M?

2. What is the top of the temperature range for a class G star?

MULTIPLE CHOICE

3. What would be the color of a star with a surface temperature of 8000°C?

   A. blue-white   **C.** orange

   B. white   **D.** red

4. Toward the end of their life cycles, very massive stars expand in size, and their surface temperature becomes lower. Which of the following is an example of this change?

   F. A white star becomes a blue-white star.

   G. A blue-white star becomes a red star.

   H. A red star becomes a blue-white star.

   I. A yellow star becomes a yellow-white star.

5. The H-R diagram shows the surface temperatures and luminosities, or true brightnesses, of four stars. Which of the stars is a type O?

   A. 1   **C.** 3

   B. 2   **D.** 4

6. Which two stars on the H-R diagram have the most similar surface temperatures?

   F. 1 and 2   **H.** 2 and 3

   G. 1 and 3   **I.** 3 and 4

EXTENDED RESPONSE
Answer the two questions below in detail.

7. Why is looking at a star in the night sky like seeing back into time?

8. How could you use two flashlights to demonstrate the concept that the apparent brightness of a star is affected by its distance from Earth? You can include a diagram as part of your answer.

Florida Resources

Florida Content Review/Preview

The following pages contain reviews of some of the topics you learned about in grade 6 and previews of some of the topics you will study in grade 8. They are grouped according to the strands of the Sunshine State Standards.

A. The Nature of Matter
Temperature and Heat	811
Mass and Volume	811
Waves	812
Atoms	812
Atomic Number	812
Atomic Mass Number	813

B. Energy
Potential and Kinetic Energy	813
Energy Conversions	813
Electromagnetic Waves	814
Infrared, Ultraviolet, and Visible Light	814

C. Force and Motion
Describing Motion	814
Mechanical Waves	814
Intensity of Sound Waves	814
Damage from Seismic Waves	815
Properties of Forces	815
Gravitational Force	815
Acceleration of Falling Objects	815
Simple Machines	816
Complicated Machines	816

E. Earth and Space
Estimating the Age of a Star	816

F. Processes of Life
Asexual Reproduction	817
Sexual Reproduction	817
Comparing Asexual and Sexual Reproduction	817
Life Cycle of Nonflowering Plants	818
Life Cycle of Flowering Plants	818
Life Cycle of Insects	819
Life Cycle of Amphibians	819
Life Cycle of Reptiles	819
Life Cycle of Birds	819
Life Cycle of Mammals	819

G. How Living Things Interact with Their Environment

Viruses	820
Classification	820
Ecosystems	821
Matter Cycles Through Ecosystems	821
Energy Flows Through Ecosystems	822
Food Chain and Food Webs	822

FCAT Science Reference

Formulas Required for the FCAT	823

Appendix

Topographic Map Symbols	825
Divisions of Geologic Time	826
Fossils in Rocks	828
Half-Life, Radiometric Dating	830
Seasonal Star Maps	832
Hertzsprung-Russell Diagram	837
Time Zones	838
Characteristics of Planets	839
The Periodic Table of the Elements	840

A. The Nature of Matter

TEMPERATURE AND HEAT

The particles in matter are constantly moving. In a solid, such as ice, the particles are close together and fixed in place, but they vibrate. In a liquid, the particles are close together, but they are not fixed in place. They move easily past one another. The particles in a gas are far apart and move freely and quickly.

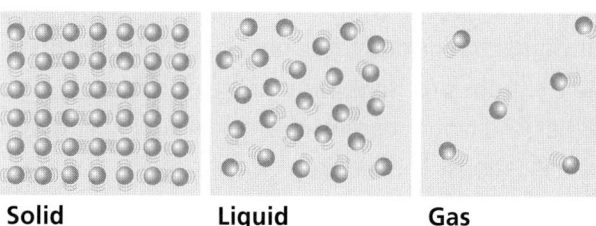

Solid   **Liquid**   **Gas**

Because the particles in matter are always moving, they have kinetic energy—the energy of motion. **Temperature** is a measure of the average kinetic energy of the particles in a substance. For example, ice has a lower temperature than liquid water because its molecules are moving more slowly. When the ice melts, its molecules begin moving past each other, and the temperature of the substance goes up. When water boils, its molecules begin moving even more quickly, and its temperature rises.

Flow of Energy in Phase Changes It takes added energy to make the molecules in a substance move more quickly, that is to raise its temperature. At some temperature that is characteristic of that substance, adding energy changes the substance from a solid to a liquid. At some higher temperature, adding energy changes the substance from a liquid to a gas. These changes are called **phase changes.**

It takes added energy to change ice to water and water to water vapor. If you put a cube of ice into a hot frying pan, for example, energy in the form of heat flows from the hot metal to the cold ice. This added energy raises the temperature of the ice until it starts to melt. It remains at the same temperature until it has all melted. At a higher temperature, the water gradually becomes water vapor. Heat energy always flows from the warmer object, such as the flame, to the cooler object, such as the pan. **Heat** is defined as the flow of energy from a warmer object to a cooler object.

> **FLORIDA**
> **Content Preview**
>
> You will learn more about temperature, heat, and the flow of energy between and within substances in grade 8.

MASS AND VOLUME

Mass is a measure of the amount of matter in an object. **Volume** is a measure of the amount of space that an object takes up. An object may be very small and still have a fair amount of mass—a golf ball is an example. Another object may be the same size but have less mass—like a Ping-Pong ball.

Two objects of the same volume may have different masses. Likewise, two objects of the same mass may have different volumes. For example, a Ping-Pong ball and a potato chip may weigh the same amount, but each takes up different amounts of space.

The relationship between mass and volume is expressed as density. Density is found with this formula:

$$\text{Density} = \frac{\text{mass}}{\text{Volume}}$$

You can always calculate the volume of an object if you know its density and its mass.

Suppose you measure and weigh 20 grams of quartz pebbles and 20 grams of iron filings. You have the same mass of each substance, but you don't know their volumes. You can see by looking at them that their volumes are not the same. Using the formula, you can determine the volumes of each substance, if you know their densities. Simply rearrange the formula and substitute the known values into it:

$$\text{Volume} = \frac{\text{Density}}{\text{mass}}$$

Another way to find the volume of each substance is to use the displacement method. Fill a graduated cylinder about half full of water. Drop in the iron filings and note the new water level. Subtract the original water level from the new water level: the difference is the volume of the iron filings. Do the same for the quartz pebbles, and you can compare their volumes.

WAVES

Recall that three measurable properties of a wave are frequency, amplitude, and wavelength. In waves like water waves, **wavelength** is a measure of the distance from one wave crest to the next. **Frequency** is a measure of how many waves pass a fixed point in a given amount of time. For waves that are traveling at the same speed, the longer the wavelength, the lower the frequency. In other words, fewer waves will pass a fixed point in a second if the waves are long than if the waves are short.

Electromagnetic waves (EM waves) include visible light as well as radio waves, microwaves, x-rays, and other waves that we cannot see. EM waves are unlike water waves in several important ways.

low frequency, long wavelength

high frequency, short wavelength

- They do not require a material medium, like water, in which to travel. They can move across a vacuum.

- In a vacuum, all EM waves travel at the same speed. Therefore, if you know the frequency of an EM wave, you know its wavelength.

Radio waves are relatively low-frequency waves with long wavelengths. X-rays have short wavelengths and high frequency. You can always determine the wavelength of an EM wave if you know its frequency, and you can determine the frequency if you know the wavelength.

FLORIDA
Content Preview

You will learn much more about the relationship between frequency and wavelength when you study EM waves in grade 8.

ATOMS

Matter is made of particles called atoms, which are too small to see with the eyes or with ordinary microscopes. Atoms are made of three types of smaller particles—protons, neutrons, and electrons. Protons carry a positive charge, and electrons carry a negative charge. The protons and neutrons make up the nucleus at the center of the atom. The nucleus contains almost all of the atom's mass.

Electrons are much smaller and less massive than protons and neutrons. They move around the nucleus at a distance. The electrons do not move in fixed orbits, but move within an electron cloud that surrounds the nucleus. It is not possible to locate the electrons precisely within the electron cloud. Rather, the cloud represents areas of probability for their locations. The electron cloud is about 10,000 times the diameter of the nucleus. Most of the atom consists of empty space.

The Atomic Model

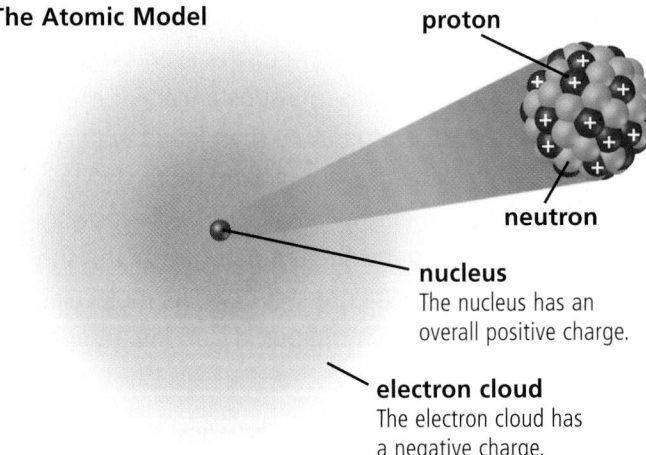

proton

neutron

nucleus
The nucleus has an overall positive charge.

electron cloud
The electron cloud has a negative charge.

ATOMIC NUMBER

The identity of an atom is determined by the number of protons in its nucleus—the **atomic number.** Every hydrogen atom has one proton, and every oxygen atom has eight protons—the atomic number of hydrogen is one, and the atomic number of oxygen is eight. Because every atom of an element has the same number of protons, every atom has the same atomic number. An atom with a different number of protons is an atom of a different substance.

ATOMIC MASS NUMBER

The **atomic mass number** is the total of the protons and the neutrons in the nucleus. While all atoms of the same element have the same number of protons, the number of neutrons in the atoms of an element varies. For example, every chlorine atom has 17 protons, but some chlorine atoms have 18 neutrons, while others have 20. Atoms of the same element that have a different number of neutrons are called **isotopes.** The atomic mass number of each isotope is different. For example, the atomic mass number of a chlorine atom with 18 neutrons and 17 protons is 35 (as shown below), and that of a chlorine atom with 20 neutrons is 37.

Chlorine-35
atomic mass number = 35

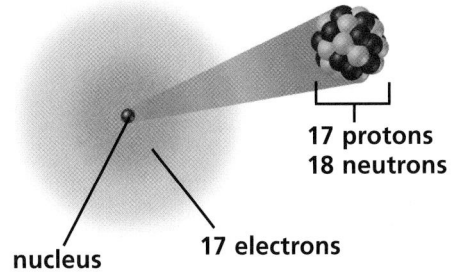

17 protons
18 neutrons

17 electrons

nucleus

FLORIDA
Content Preview

You will learn much more about the structure of the atom and the characteristics of the elements in grade 8.

B. Energy

POTENTIAL AND KINETIC ENERGY

Kinetic energy is the energy of motion. All moving objects have kinetic energy, from the smallest particle vibrating in a solid to a person walking.

Potential energy is energy that an object has because of its position or its composition. The most obvious form of potential energy is potential energy that results from gravity. A rock on the edge of a cliff has potential energy because it could fall. Other forms of potential energy are less obvious. A spring has potential energy when it is compressed, and substances have chemical potential energy because of the atoms they contain.

Potential energy can be converted into kinetic energy. For example, the gravitational potential energy of the rock on the cliff changes into the energy of motion as the rock falls. If kinetic energy is used to lift the rock up again, that kinetic energy is converted into potential energy and the rock has gravitational potential energy again. If a coiled spring is released, its potential energy is converted into the kinetic energy as it expands. The chemical potential energy in food is converted into a form that the body can use to move, that is, into kinetic energy.

ENERGY CONVERSIONS

Energy comes in many forms, including mechanical, chemical, thermal, sound, electromagnetic, and nuclear energy. Energy in one form can change into energy in another form, as when chemical energy in food is converted into the mechanical energy of running, or sound energy is converted into the vibration of the membrane in an ear.

No new energy is created in an energy conversion, and no energy is destroyed. The total amount of energy in a system remains the same, or is conserved. However, energy conversions are never 100 percent efficient. The amount of useful energy in a system does decrease, as some of the energy in every conversion is changed into forms of energy that cannot be used. Often the useful energy is lost as heat. Usually, when energy is lost as heat, the energy goes to raise the disorder of the system.

For example, a bike rider uses kinetic energy to turn the wheels of a bike, which move the bike forward. However, some of the energy the rider gives to the bike is not used to move the bike forward but is lost to friction between the various parts of the bike and between the tires and the pavement. The tires and the parts of the bike that rub together feel warm, which tells you that energy was lost as heat in the energy conversion.

FLORIDA
Content Preview

In grade 8 you will take a closer look at energy conversions, calculate potential and kinetic energy, and learn how work transfers energy.

ELECTROMAGNETIC WAVES

Energy comes to Earth from the Sun in the form of electromagnetic waves (EM waves). From the longer wavelengths to the shorter wavelengths, EM waves include radio waves, microwaves, visible light, x-rays, and gamma waves. Since all EM waves travel at the same speed—the speed of light—those waves with long wavelengths have low frequencies, and those with short wavelengths have high frequencies.

INFRARED, ULTRAVIOLET, AND VISIBLE LIGHT

On either side of visible light waves on the electro-magnetic spectrum, are waves that we cannot see but that have useful applications—infrared light and ultraviolet light. Infrared lamps are used to provide warmth in bathrooms and to keep food warm after it is cooked. Ultraviolet (UV) waves have higher energy than visible light waves and infrared waves, and they can damage skin. Sunblock and UV-protection sunglasses are designed to filter out UV waves. When used carefully, however, UV waves can be beneficial. UV light is used to sterilize surgical instruments and food by killing harmful bacteria. Some animals can see infrared and ultraviolet light. Waves in the small visible light portion of the EM spectrum are what make objects visible to us and give them their characteristic colors.

FLORIDA
Content Preview

In grade 8 you will study the electromagnetic spectrum in depth.

C. Force and Motion

DESCRIBING MOTION

Motion is a change of position over time. In order to describe the motion of an object, you need to know its position, the direction of its motion, and the speed it is going.

- The **position,** or location, of an object can be described by means of a reference point. An object is a certain distance in a certain direction from the point. For example, a school may be one kilometer (distance) north (direction) of the train station (reference point).

- You can describe the **direction** of motion by using the directions north, south, east, west, and combinations of these, as in "northeast." Or you can use local references, as in "toward the river" or "toward town."

- You can calculate **speed** if you have measurements of both distance and time. If a bike has moved ten kilometers (distance) in one hour (time), it is traveling at a speed of ten kilometers per hour, or 10 km/h.

Together, position, direction, and speed describe motion. For example, you can describe the motion of a train by saying it travels north from the station at a speed of 50 km/h.

FLORIDA
Content Preview

You will learn more about describing motion and speed in grade 8, where you will also learn about velocity and acceleration.

MECHANICAL WAVES

A wave is a disturbance in a medium. Mechanical waves—such as sound waves and the seismic waves of an earthquake—are set off by vibrations. Such waves travel through air, water, steel, glass, and many other substances including earth and rock. The disturbances spread away from the source of the wave in all directions. The waves transfer energy through the medium. Depending on the amount of energy that is transferred, the vibrations of a wave can cause damage.

INTENSITY OF SOUND WAVES

Hearing loss caused by exposure to very loud sound waves is a familiar example of damage caused by mechanical waves. The delicate hair cells in the inner ear can be damaged or destroyed by extremely intense sound waves, generally those over 90 decibels (dB). For reference, the bark of a dog is about 60 dB, the sound of a lawnmower 90 dB, and a jet plane taking off 150 dB.

FLORIDA
Content Preview

In grade 8 you will study all types of waves in depth, including sound.

DAMAGE FROM SEISMIC WAVES

Earthquakes produce three types of seismic waves. Each disturbs the medium of the ground in a different way. Primary waves travel through Earth's crust at an average speed of 5 kilometers per second. They can travel through solids, liquids, and gases. Buildings on Earth's surface are pushed and pulled as primary waves pass.

Secondary waves start at the same time as primary waves but they travel about half as fast. Secondary waves rock small buildings back and forth as they pass. They travel through rock, but not through liquids or gas.

Surface waves are seismic waves that move along Earth's surface. They make the ground roll up and down or shake from side to side. They travel more slowly than other seismic waves, and cause the most damage.

Different earthquakes have seismic waves of different magnitudes, or amounts of energy. Here is a chart that relates the magnitude of the earthquake to the damage it can cause.

Magnitude of Earthquake		Effects Near Origin
0–3.9	Very minor to minor	rarely noticed
4.0–4.9	Light	slight damage
5.0–5.9	Moderate	some structures damaged
6.0–6.9	Strong	major damage to structures
7.0–7.9	Major	some well-built structures destroyed
8.0+	Great	major to total destruction

PROPERTIES OF FORCES

A force is a push or a pull. Some forces require contact. A bat strikes a ball. A tugboat pulls a freighter. A piece of sandpaper scrapes a board. Other forces, however, do not depend on contact. They act at a distance. Forces that act at a distance include gravitational force, electrical force, and magnetic force.

GRAVITATIONAL FORCE

An object does not have to be in contact with Earth to fall toward Earth. The object and the planet Earth are drawn toward each other by the force of gravity between them. In fact, it is gravity that causes an object to have weight. The force is equally strong in both directions, but the object moves toward Earth rather than the other way around because Earth is so much more massive than any object near it.

FLORIDA Content Preview

In grade 8, you will study gravity and friction in depth.

ACCELERATION OF FALLING OBJECTS

When objects first start to fall, they don't fall at a constant speed—they accelerate. The acceleration due to Earth's gravity is 9.8 m/s^2. This means that every second an object is falling, it falls 9.8 m/s faster. In a vacuum—a space containing few or no particles of matter—objects fall at this constant rate of acceleration all the way down, until they are acted on by another force.

Unlike objects falling in a vacuum, objects falling in Earth's atmosphere encounter air resistance, or friction due to air. The falling object pushes the molecules in air out of the way. The molecules in air exert an equal and opposite force on the falling object. As the object accelerates, it pushes against the air with greater force. This increases air resistance. Eventually the force of air resistance balances the force of gravity, and the object no longer accelerates. It continues falling at a constant speed. This final maximum velocity of the falling object is called **terminal velocity.**

FLORIDA Content Preview

In grade 8 you will see how gravity and friction act on objects and how objects move in a vacuum, where there is no air.

SIMPLE MACHINES

The six simple machines are the lever, wheel and axle, pulley, inclined plane, wedge, and screw (shown below). Each of the simple machines can be used to change the size or the direction of a force, which makes it easier to do work. For example, suppose you want to lift a heavy box from the ground into the back of a truck. It is easier to push the box up a ramp (inclined plane) than it would be to climb straight up with the box. You cover more distance, but you use less force than you would otherwise.

Lever

Wheel and axle

Screw

Wedge

Pulley

Inclined plane

COMPLICATED MACHINES

Simple machines can be combined in various ways to make complicated or compound machines. The eggbeater shown below combines a lever with two wheel and axles. A wheelbarrow combines a wheel and axle with two levers, the handles. An axe combines a lever (the handle) with a wedge (the cutting blade). A crank handle on any device is a lever. The crank may turn a wheel and axle or a screw.

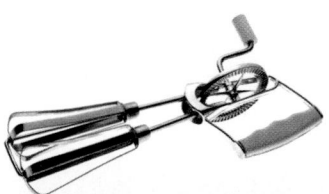

Complicated machines typically must overcome more friction than simple machines because they tend to have many moving parts. Scissors, for example, consist of two levers. They have a lower efficiency than one lever because there is friction at the point where the two levers are connected. The slanted edges of the blades are wedges. There is also friction between the blades of the scissors as they close.

By making work easier, machines save effort. The amount of effort that a simple or a complicated machine can save is called the **mechanical advantage.** The mechanical advantage of any complicated machine is equal to the products of the mechanical advantages of all the simple machines that make it up.

E. Earth and Space

ESTIMATING THE AGE OF A STAR

Astronomers study the light from stars. Color and other details help astronomers determine the stage a star is in. Astronomers can estimate the amount of fuel in a star from its mass. They can also estimate how long a star takes to use up all its fuel and move to the next stage. For example, massive blue stars use up their fuel quickly compared with less massive white or yellow stars. Because blue stars do not last long, astronomers know that blue stars that exist today must have formed relatively recently. If a group of stars formed together and contains blue stars, astronomers can infer that other stars in the group are also young. Even if a group does not include blue stars, it can be compared with other stars using the Hertzsprung-Russell diagram (shown on page 837) to estimate its age.

The light from a star also provides information about the materials that make up the star, which can help astronomers estimate the star's age. Stars can produce and release new materials during the later stages in their life cycles. Other stars can then form out of these materials. Stars with these materials are usually younger than stars without them.

F. Processes of Life

ASEXUAL REPRODUCTION

Most unicellular organisms, and a few multicellular organisms, use cell division to reproduce, in a process called asexual reproduction. In **asexual reproduction,** one organism produces one or more new organisms that are identical to itself and that live independently of it. The organism that produces the new organism or organisms is the parent. Each new organism is an offspring. The offspring produced by asexual reproduction are genetically identical to their parents.

Types of asexual reproduction include binary fission, budding, and regeneration. Cell division and reproduction are the same thing in all single-celled organisms. In **binary fission,** the parent organism splits in two, producing two separate, independent, and genetically identical offspring. Algae, some yeasts, and protozoans such as paramecium reproduce in this way.

Both unicellular and multicellular organisms can reproduce by budding. **Budding** is a process in which an organism develops tiny buds on its body. Each bud forms from the parent's cells, so the bud's genetic material is the same as the parent's. The bud grows until it forms a complete or nearly complete new organism that is genetically identical to the parent. Budding occurs in some yeast and single-celled organisms. Multicellular organisms that reproduce by budding include hydras, which are freshwater animals, and kalanchoe, a plant that produces tiny buds from the tips of its leaves.

In certain multicellular organisms, specialized cells at the site of a wound or lost limb are able to become different types of tissues. The process of new tissue growth at these sites is called **regeneration.** Regeneration can result in regrowth of body parts or in reproduction. For example, if a starfish is cut in half, each half can regenerate its missing body parts from its own cells. The result is two complete, independent, and genetically identical starfish. The growth of plants from cuttings is also a kind of asexual reproduction through regeneration.

SEXUAL REPRODUCTION

Sexual reproduction involves two parent organisms rather than one. During **sexual reproduction,** a cell containing genetic information from the mother and a cell containing genetic information from the father combine into a completely new cell, which becomes the offspring. Sexual reproduction leads to diversity because the offspring have genetic material from both parents. The DNA in the offspring is different from the DNA in either of the parents.

Two different cellular processes are involved in sexual reproduction. The first is meiosis, a special form of cell division that produces sperm cells in a male and egg cells in a female. The second process is fertilization, which occurs when a sperm cell combines with an egg cell. A fertilized egg is a single cell with DNA from both parents.

COMPARING ASEXUAL AND SEXUAL REPRODUCTION

Most reproduction in multicellular organisms is sexual reproduction. Many multicellular organisms, however, can reproduce by asexual reproduction as well. For example, a second organism can grow and break off from the first in the process of budding. Some plants, such as strawberries, reproduce by sending out shoots called runners from which new plants grow. Plants can spread quickly this way. This form of asexual reproduction allows the plant to reproduce even when conditions are not right for germination of seeds. Asexual reproduction limits the genetic diversity within a group, however, because offspring have the same genetic material as the parent.

With sexual reproduction, there is an opportunity for new combinations of characteristics to occur in the offspring. The new organisms might have survival advantages over the parents, such as the ability to process food more efficiently. The chart below compares the two methods of reproduction.

Asexual vs. Sexual Reproduction	
Asexual Reproduction	**Sexual Reproduction**
Cell division	Cell division and other processes
One parent organism	Two parent organisms
Rapid rate of reproduction	Slower rate of reproduction
Offspring have identical genetic information to parent	Offspring have genetic information from two parents

LIFE CYCLE OF NONFLOWERING PLANTS

Mosses are small, grasslike plants that live in moist, cool environments. They reproduce with spores. A **spore** is a single reproductive cell that is protected by a hard, watertight covering. Spores are small and can be transported through air without drying out. This means offspring from spores can grow in places that are distant from the parent organisms.

Within a clump of moss are both male and female reproductive structures, which produce sperm and eggs. The sperm move through a film of water to the eggs in another part of the plant. A fertilized egg grows into a stalk with a capsule on the end. Inside the capsule, the process of meiosis produces thousands of tiny spores. When the spores are released, the cycle begins again.

Ferns are seedless, vascular plants. Like mosses, ferns have a two-part life cycle. Spores grow into tiny structures close to the ground. Inside these structures both sperm and eggs are produced. The sperm fertilize the eggs. A fern plant grows from the fertilized egg. Spores are produced on the undersides of the leaves, or fronds, and these spores are released to spread through the air.

spores

spore cluster

LIFE CYCLE OF FLOWERING PLANTS

Flowering plants have seeds, and seed plants have pollen. A **pollen** grain is a small multicellular structure that holds a sperm cell. It has a hard outer covering to keep the sperm from drying out. Pollen grains can be carried from one plant to another by wind, water, and animals. The process of pollination is completed when a pollen grain attaches to the part of a plant that contains the egg and releases the sperm.

A **seed** is a young plant that is enclosed in a protective coating. Within the coating are nutrients to enable the plant to grow. A seed must be fertilized with sperm carried in the pollen; then an embryo begins to grow. The embryo can develop into a new plant.

Sometimes the male and female reproductive structures grow on the same plant and sometimes on separate male and female plants. In flowering plants, the sperm and egg cells are contained in a **flower.** Once the eggs are fertilized and the seeds form, the part of the flower that contains the seeds, the ovary, becomes the fruit.

seed

fruit

LIFE CYCLE OF INSECTS

Insects include beetles, bees, wasps, ants, butterflies, moths, and grasshoppers. All insects reproduce sexually. Females lay eggs, sometimes a great number of eggs. Insect eggs often have a hard outer covering, which protects the egg from drying out and allows hatching to be delayed until conditions are right. The life cycles of insects include a process of **metamorphosis.** A complete metamorphosis has three stages: larva, pupa, and adult. You can see all four stages of the mosquito's life cycle in the pictures below.

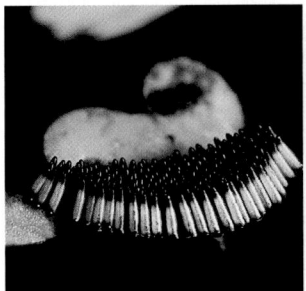

A female mosquito lays a mass of eggs on the surface of the water.

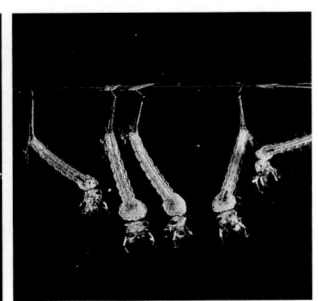

Each egg develops into a larva that swims head down, feeding on algae.

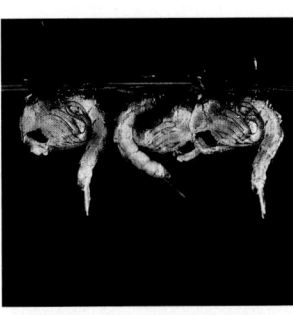

The larva develops into a pupa. Inside, the body of the insect matures.

At the adult stage, the mosquito leaves the water and flies away.

LIFE CYCLE OF AMPHIBIANS

Amphibians, such as frogs, live in moist environments and reproduce sexually. In most amphibian species, a female lays eggs in water, a male fertilizes them with sperm, and then the offspring develop and hatch on their own. Yolk inside the eggs provides developing embryos with nutrients. Like fish eggs, amphibian eggs do not have hard shells. This means developing amphibians can get water and oxygen directly from their surroundings.

When a young amphibian hatches, it is a **larva.** The larval form is very different from the mature adult. The larvae of frogs and toads are called tadpoles, and they look and behave like fish. After a few weeks, the tadpole's body starts to change, and it begins to live more like the mature animal. It leaves the water and uses its legs to move around on land. Some amphibians remain in or near water for all their lives, while others live in moist land environments as adults.

LIFE CYCLE OF REPTILES

Reptiles reproduce sexually. The egg cell of the female joins with the sperm cell of the male in the process of fertilization. After fertilization, a protective shell forms around each egg while it is still inside the female's body. The female lays her eggs on land, sometimes building or digging a nest for them. When reptiles hatch, they look like small adults.

LIFE CYCLE OF BIRDS

Birds reproduce sexually. Their reproduction process is similar to that of reptiles. After the eggs are fertilized inside the female's body, a hard shell forms around each fertilized egg. The female lays the fertilized eggs, usually in a nest. They must be kept at a constant, warm temperature in order to develop. Most birds use their body heat to keep the eggs warm, by sitting on the hard eggs. After this process, called **incubation,** the young birds hatch. They are not yet able to fly and must be cared for until they can meet their own needs.

LIFE CYCLE OF MAMMALS

Fertilization in mammals takes place inside the female. In almost every species of mammal, the offspring develop inside the female's body as well. Many mammals have a special organ called a **placenta** that transports nutrients, water, and oxygen from the mother's blood to the developing embryo. The embryo's waste materials leave through the placenta as well.

The period of development inside the mother is called **gestation.** The length of gestation varies greatly, from about 3 weeks for a mouse, to about 55 weeks for a manatee, and as long as 88 weeks for an elephant. Human gestation is 39 weeks. Mammals' bodies have special glands for producing milk, which is full of protein, fats, sugars, and other nutrients. Mothers feed their offspring this rich food.

Different species of mammals are born at varying stages of development. Most mice are helpless, blind, and have no fur at birth, while giraffes can walk soon after they are born. The length of time a young mammal needs care from an adult varies. Some seals nurse their young for less than a month before leaving them to survive on their own. Manatees nurse for a long time, and the offspring remain dependent on their mother for up to two years.

G. How Living Things Interact with Their Environment

VIRUSES

Viruses are very small microorganisms, even smaller than bacteria. They consist of genetic material contained inside a protective protein coat called a capsid. The protein coat may be a simple tube or have many layers. Viruses come in many shapes and sizes, but all viruses consist of a capsid and genetic material.

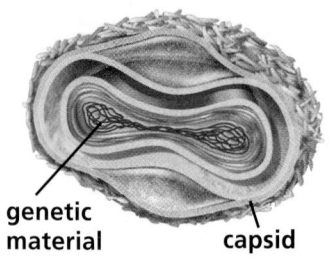

genetic material   capsid

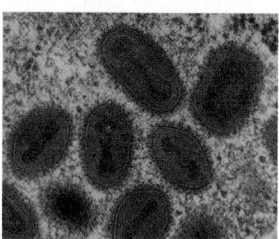

smallpox virus 65,000 x

Comparison to Living Things The ability of viruses to make copies of their genetic material is one way that viruses are similar to living things. Also, the protein coat is similar to a cell's outer membrane. But viruses do not grow, and viruses do not respond to changes in their environment. Therefore, they are not living. Unlike living things, viruses cannot reproduce by themselves. However, viruses can use materials within living cells to make copies of themselves.

Damage Caused by Viruses The virus uses the cell's material, energy, and processes. In many cases, after a virus has made many copies of itself, new viruses burst out of the host cell and destroy it. Viruses cause many different diseases in humans, including polio, smallpox, diphtheria, AIDS, influenza, chicken pox, and colds.

The treatment of diseases caused by viruses is different from the treatment of diseases caused by bacteria. Antibiotic drugs are effective against bacteria, but they do not work against viruses. Vaccines can be developed to prevent viral diseases, and they have saved many lives.

CLASSIFICATION

Suppose you find a leaf or a shell and want to know what tree or animal produced it. Taxonomists—scientists who name and classify living things—have come up with a tool to help identify an organism. A **dichotomous key** asks a series of questions that can be answered in only two ways. Your answer to each question leads you to another question with only two answers. After answering a number of such questions, you will identify the organism. An example is shown below.

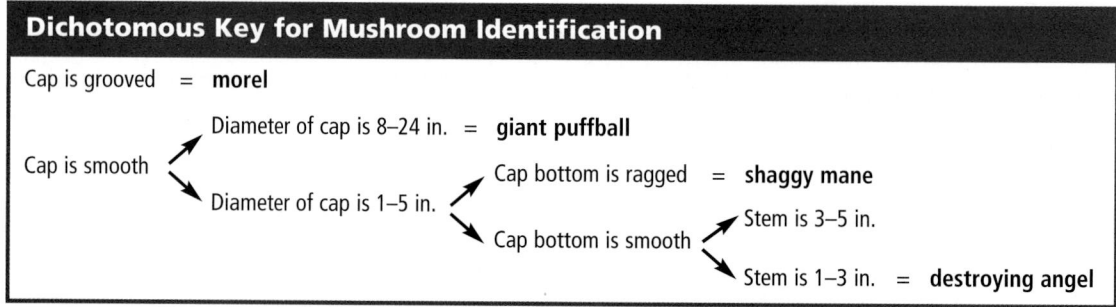

Dichotomous Key for Mushroom Identification

Cap is grooved = **morel**

Cap is smooth
- Diameter of cap is 8–24 in. = **giant puffball**
- Diameter of cap is 1–5 in.
  - Cap bottom is ragged = **shaggy mane**
  - Cap bottom is smooth
    - Stem is 3–5 in.
    - Stem is 1–3 in. = **destroying angel**

If you wanted to design a dichotomous key for the identification of a mushroom, you could begin with any trait—color, shape, size, and so on. In designing a dichotomous key, you should look for the broadest category first. Each answer to your broadest category will lead to another set of questions that has two possible answers. The key shown on the bottom of page 820 is a portion of such a key.

What mushroom is this?

The chart to identify mushrooms begins with a broad question—whether the cap is grooved or smooth. Notice that a yes answer to a question at any level may result in a positive identification or in another choice between two possibilities. For example, if the mushroom has a grooved cap, you know right away that it is a morel. Using this key to identify the mushroom pictured above, you follow this path: the cap is smooth, the diameter of the cap is 1–5 inches, and the bottom of the cap is ragged: it is a shaggy mane mushroom.

ECOSYSTEMS

Scientists use the word *ecosystem* to refer to a particular environment and all the living things that are supported by it. An ecosystem can be as small as a pond or as large as a desert. In a pond ecosystem, for example, plants grow in water, and animals feed on the plants. A variety of tiny microorganisms in the water are food for the fish and for each other. These are the living parts of the pond ecosystem, called the biotic factors. The nonliving parts, called the abiotic factors, include the air that supplies oxygen and carbon dioxide, the soil that provides nutrients, the water in the pond, and the sunlight that plants need to grow.

Temperature, light, soil, and water are important abiotic factors in all ecosystems. Changes in one of these factors can affect others. If the amount of sunlight is reduced, the temperature goes down. This could happen if a tall shade tree grew over a pond, reducing the amount of sunlight that reached the water. The strength of sunlight and the amount of sunlight available determine the kinds of plants in a land ecosystem. Different types of soil retain water differently and so affect the way that plants grow.

MATTER CYCLES THROUGH ECOSYSTEMS

A cycle is a series of events that happens over and over again. Water, carbon, and nitrogen cycle through ecosystems. As water moves through an ecosystem, it changes in physical form, moving back and forth between gas, liquid, and solid. Water in the atmosphere is usually in the form of water vapor. Water vapor condenses and falls to Earth's surface as precipitation (rain, snow, sleet, mist, or hail). Water returns to the atmosphere through evaporation.

Carbon is an element found in all living things. It is through carbon dioxide gas in the atmosphere that carbon enters the living parts of an ecosystem. Plants use carbon to produce sugar, in a process called photosynthesis. Sugars supply the energy and materials living things need to live and grow. To release the energy in food, organisms break down the carbon compounds in a process called respiration. Carbon is released and cycles back into the atmosphere as carbon dioxide.

Plants and animals cannot use nitrogen directly from the air, but plants absorb certain compounds containing nitrogen. They take in these compounds through their roots, along with water and other nutrients.

ENERGY FLOWS THROUGH ECOSYSTEMS

Because energy is continuously used by the activities of all living things, it must be continuously replaced in an ecosystem. Most of the energy in an ecosystem is originally supplied by the Sun and enters the ecosystem through photosynthesis.

Producers are organisms that capture energy and store it in food as chemical energy. Plants are the most common producers found in land ecosystems; in water ecosystems, most food is produced by bacteria and algae.

Consumers are organisms that get their energy by eating other organisms. In a meadow ecosystem, for example, animals such as antelopes and grasshoppers feed on grasses. The grasses are the producer, and the animals are the primary consumers. Primary consumers are the first link between the producers and the rest of the consumers. The wolves that eat the antelopes and the meadowlarks that eat the grasshoppers are next. They are secondary consumers. A prairie hawk that eats a meadowlark is a tertiary consumer.

FOOD CHAINS AND FOOD WEBS

A **food chain** describes the feeding relationship between a producer and a single chain of consumers in an ecosystem. The grasses, grasshopper, meadowlark, and prairie hawk make up a meadow food chain. A wetland food chain, as shown on the right, could include cattails as the producer, with caterpillars as the primary consumer, frogs as the secondary consumer, and herons as the tertiary consumer.

A **food web** is a model of the feeding relationships among many different consumers and producers in an ecosystem. It contains many overlapping and interconnected food chains. Each consumer may play several roles in the ecosystem—sometimes eating plants and sometimes eating the animals that feed on plants.

Both food chains and food webs show the flow of energy through an ecosystem starting with producers who capture energy from the Sun. Life on Earth depends on energy supplied by the Sun and cycled through various life forms.

A Wetland Food Chain

Flow of Energy
Energy flow starts at the bottom. Arrows represent energy moving from an organism that is eaten to the organism that eats it.

heron — Tertiary consumer

frog — Secondary consumer

caterpillar — Primary consumer

cattails — Producer

FCAT Science Reference

Formulas Required for the FCAT

	FORMULA		FOUND IN
Density (D)	$= \dfrac{\text{mass (g)}}{\text{Volume (cm}^3)}$	$D = \dfrac{m}{V}$	Grade 6, Chapter 3 *Properties of Matter*
Average speed ($\bar{v}$)	$= \dfrac{\text{distance}}{\text{time}}$	$\bar{v} = \dfrac{d}{t}$	Grade 6, Chapter 5 *Forces and Machines* Grade 8, Chapter 2 *Motion*
Work (W)	$=$ Force (N) $\times$ distance (m)	$W = Fd$	Grade 6, Chapter 5 *Forces and Machines* Grade 8, Chapter 5 *Work and Energy*
Percent efficiency (e)	$= \dfrac{\text{Work out (J)}}{\text{Work in (J)}} \times 100$	$\% \, e = \dfrac{W_{out}}{W_{in}} \times 100$	Grade 6, Chapter 5 *Forces and Machines*
Acceleration ($\bar{a}$)	$= \dfrac{\text{change in velocity (m/s)}}{\text{time taken for this change (s)}}$	$\bar{a} = \dfrac{v_f - v_i}{t_f - t_i}$	Grade 8, Chapter 2 *Motion*
Force in newtons (F)	$=$ mass (kg) $\times$ acceleration (m/s^2)	$F = ma$	Grade 8, Chapter 3 *Forces*
Momentum (p)	$=$ mass (kg) $\times$ velocity (m/s)	$p = mv$	Grade 8, Chapter 3 *Forces*
Wavelength (λ)	$= \dfrac{\text{velocity (m/s)}}{\text{frequency (Hz)}}$	$\lambda = \dfrac{v}{f}$	Grade 8, Chapter 10 *Waves*
Frequency in hertz (f)	$= \dfrac{\text{number of events (waves)}}{\text{time (s)}}$	$f = \dfrac{n \text{ of events}}{t}$	Grade 8, Chapter 10 *Waves* Grade 8 *Florida Review*

Units of Measure Often Used in Formulas:

Mass	Length	Time	Force	Energy	Frequency
g=gram kg=kilogram	cm=centimeter m=meter	s=second	N=newton	J=joule (newton-meter)	Hz=hertz

Appendix

Topographic Map Symbols

The U.S. Geological Survey uses the following symbols to mark human-made and natural features on all of the topographic maps the USGS produces.

Primary highway, hard surface

Secondary highway, hard surface

Light-duty road, hard or improved surface

Unimproved road

Trail

Railroad: single track

Railroad: multiple track

Bridge

Drawbridge

Tunnel

Footbridge

Overpass—Underpass

Power transmission line with located tower

Landmark line (labeled as to type) .... TELEPHONE

Dam with lock

Canal with lock

Large dam

Small dam: masonry—earth

Buildings (dwelling, place of employment, etc.)

School—Church—Cemeteries

Buildings (barn, warehouse, etc.)

Tanks; oil, water, etc. (labeled only if water)

Wells other than water (labeled as to type) ... ○ Oil   ○ Gas

U.S. mineral or location monument—Prospect

Quarry—Gravel pit

Mine shaft—Tunnel or cave entrance

Campsite—Picnic area

Located or landmark object—Windmill

Exposed wreck

Rock or coral reef

Foreshore flat

Rock: bare or awash

Benchmarks .... BM ×671   ×672

Road fork—Section corner with elevation ... 429   +58

Checked spot elevation .... × 5970

Unchecked spot elevation .... × 5970

Boundary: national

State

county, parish, municipio

civil township, precinct, town, barrio

incorporated city, village, town, hamlet

reservation, national or state

small park, cemetery, airport, etc.

land grant

Township or range line, U.S. land survey

Section line, U.S. land survey

Township line, not U.S. land survey

Section line, not U.S. land survey

Fence line or field line

Section corner: found—indicated .... +.............+

Boundary monument: land grant—other ... ▣ .... ▣

Index contour   Intermediate contour

Supplementary cont   Depression contours

Cut—Fill   Levee

Mine dump   Large wash

Dune area   Distorted surface

Sand area   Gravel beach

Glacier   Intermittent streams

Seasonal streams   Aqueduct tunnel

Water well—Spring   Falls

Rapids   Intermittent lake

Channel   Small wash

Sounding—Depth curve   10   Marsh (swamp)

Dry lake bed   Land subject to controlled flooding

Woodland   Mangrove

Submerged marsh   Scrub

Orchard   Wooded marsh

Vineyard   Many buildings

Areas revised since previous edition

Source: U.S. Geological Survey

Divisions of Geologic Time

The geologic time scale is divided into eons, eras, periods, epochs (ehp-uhks), and ages. Unlike divisions of time such as days or minutes, the divisions of the geologic time scale have no exact fixed lengths. Instead, they are based on changes or events recorded in rocks and fossils.

Eon The largest unit of time is an eon. Earth's 4.6-billion-year history is divided into four eons.

The Hadean, Archean, and Proterozoic eons together are called Precambrian time and make up almost 90 percent of Earth's history.

Geologic Time Scale

This geologic time scale shows the longest divisions of Earth's history: eons, eras, and periods.

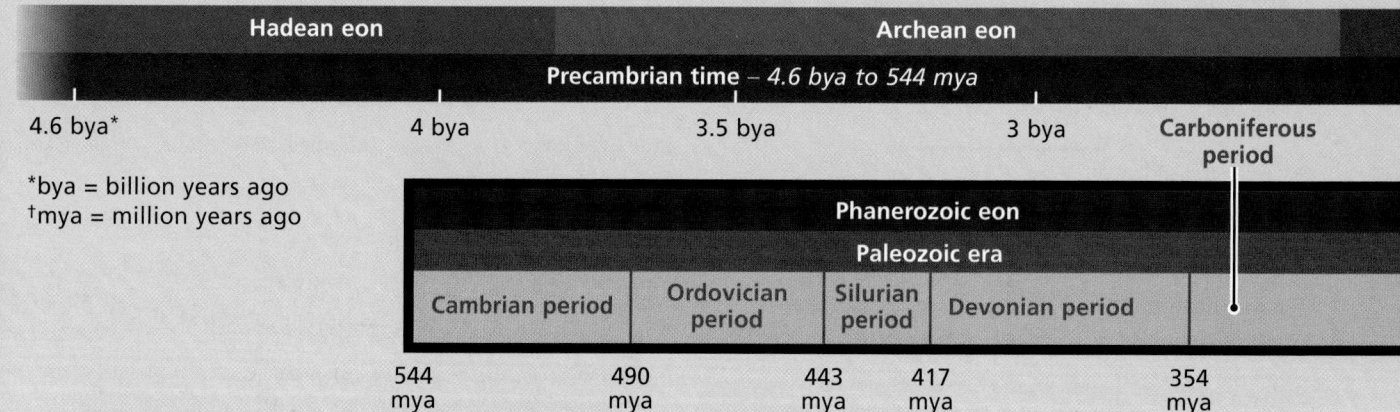

Hadean eon			Archean eon	

Precambrian time – *4.6 bya to 544 mya*

4.6 bya*   4 bya   3.5 bya   3 bya   Carboniferous period

*bya = billion years ago
†mya = million years ago

Phanerozoic eon				
Paleozoic era				
Cambrian period	Ordovician period	Silurian period	Devonian period	

544 mya   490 mya   443 mya   417 mya   354 mya

Precambrian Time at 3.6 Billion Years Ago

For nearly 4 billion years, during most of Precambrian time, no plants or animals existed.

Paleozoic Era at 544 Million Years Ago

At the beginning of the Paleozoic era, all life lived in the oceans.

APPENDIX

The fossil record for Precambrian time consists mostly of tiny organisms that cannot be seen without a microscope. Other early forms of life had soft bodies that rarely formed into fossils.

The Phanerozoic eon stretches from the end of Precambrian time to the present. Because so many more changes are recorded in the fossil record of this eon, it is further divided into smaller units of time called eras, periods, epochs, and ages.

The Phanerozoic eon is divided into three eras: the Paleozoic, the Mesozoic, and the Cenozoic. Each era is subdivided into a number of periods. The periods of the Cenozoic, the most recent era, are further divided into epochs, which are in turn further divided into ages. The smaller time divisions relate to how long certain conditions and life forms on Earth lasted and how quickly they changed or became extinct.

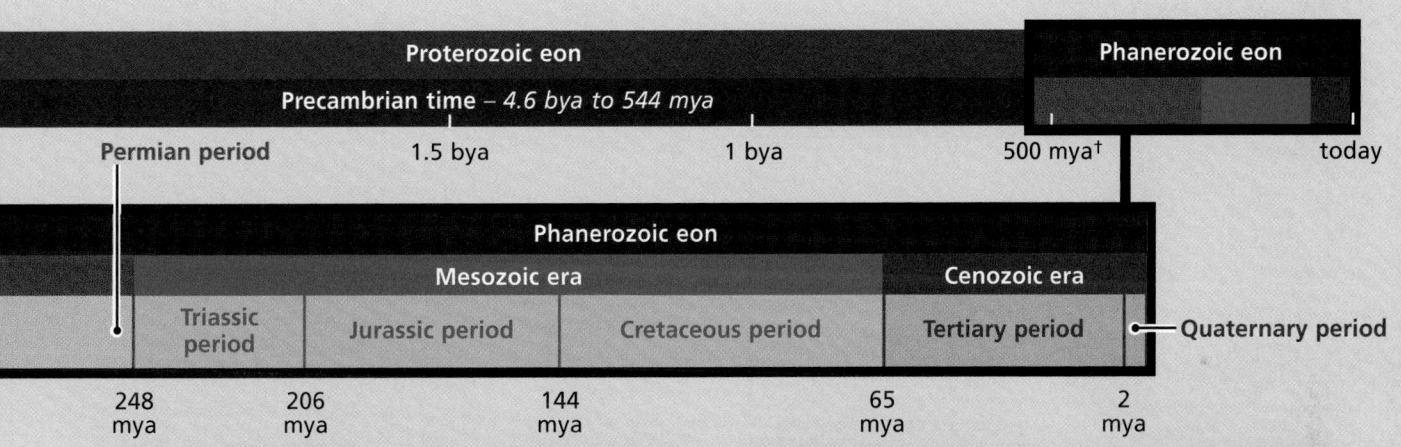

Proterozoic eon — Precambrian time – 4.6 bya to 544 mya | Phanerozoic eon

Permian period — 1.5 bya — 1 bya — 500 mya† — today

Phanerozoic eon

| Mesozoic era | | | Cenozoic era | |
| Triassic period | Jurassic period | Cretaceous period | Tertiary period | Quaternary period |

248 mya — 206 mya — 144 mya — 65 mya — 2 mya

Mesozoic Era at 195 to 65 Million Years Ago

During the Mesozoic era, dinosaurs lived along with the first mammals, birds, and flowering plants.

Cenozoic Era at Present Day

The first humans appeared in the later part of the Cenozoic era, which continues today.

Fossils in Rocks

If an organism is covered by or buried in sediment, it may become a fossil as the sediments become rock. Many rock fossils are actual body parts, such as bones or teeth, that were buried in sediment and then replaced by minerals and turned to stone. Fossils in rock include molds and casts, petrified wood, carbon films, and trace fossils.

① **Molds and Casts** Some fossils that form in sedimentary rock are mold fossils. A mold is a visible shape that was left after an animal or plant was buried in sediment and then decayed away. In some cases, a hollow mold later becomes filled with minerals, producing a cast fossil. The cast fossil is a solid model in the shape of the organism. If you think of the mold as a shoeprint, the cast would be what would result if sand filled the print and hardened into stone.

Fossils in Rocks

Rock fossils show shapes and traces of past life.

① Molds and Casts

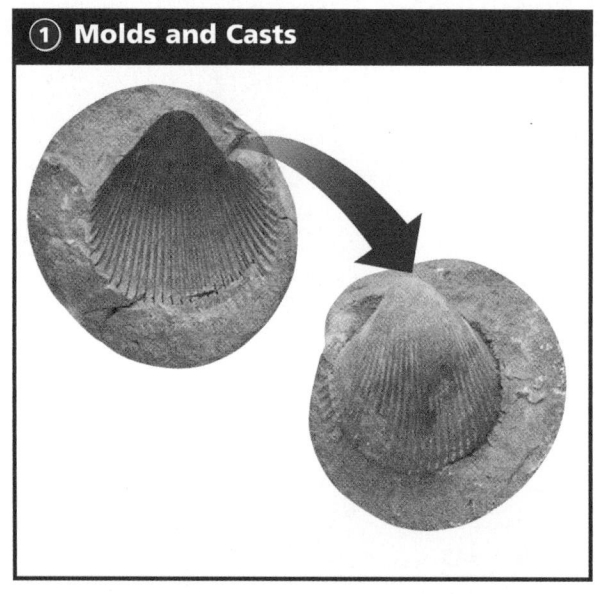

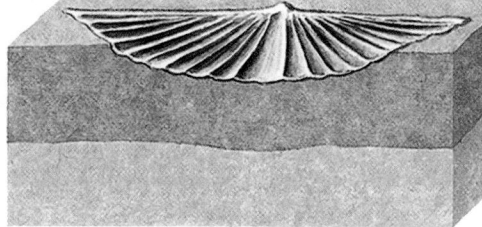

An organism dies and falls into soft sediment.

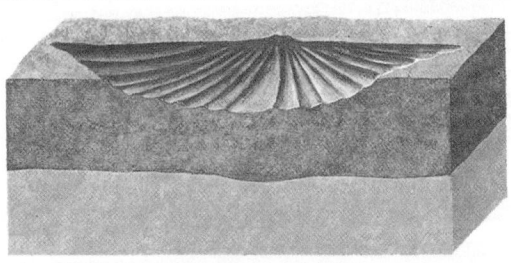

Over time, the sediment becomes rock and the organism decays, leaving a mold.

Minerals fill the mold and make a cast of the organism.

② **Petrified Wood** The stone fossil of a tree is called petrified wood. In certain conditions, a fallen tree can become covered with sediments. Over time, water passes through the sediments and into the tree's cells. Minerals that are carried in the water take the place of the cells, producing a stone likeness of the tree.

In this close-up, you can see the minerals that replaced the wood, forming petrified wood.

③ **Carbon Films** Carbon is an element that is found in every living thing. Sometimes when a dead plant or animal decays, its carbon is left behind as a visible layer. This image is called a carbon film. Carbon films can show details of soft parts of animals and plants that are rarely seen in other fossils.

This carbon film of a moth is about 10 million years old. Carbon films are especially useful because they can show details of the soft parts of organisms.

④ **Trace Fossils** Do you want to know how fast a dinosaur could run? Trace fossils might be able to tell you. These are not parts of an animal or impressions of it, but rather evidence of an animal's presence in a given location. Trace fossils include preserved footprints, trails, animal holes, and even feces. By comparing these clues with what is known about modern animals, scientists can learn how prehistoric animals may have lived, what they ate, and how they behaved.

A trace fossil, such as this footprint of a dinosaur in rock, can provide important information about where an animal lived and how it walked and ran.

Half-Life

Over time, a radioactive element breaks down at a constant rate into another form.

The rate of change of a radioactive element is measured in half-lives. A half-life is the length of time it takes for half of the atoms in a sample of a radioactive element to change from an unstable form into another form. Different elements have different half-lives, ranging from fractions of a second to billions of years.

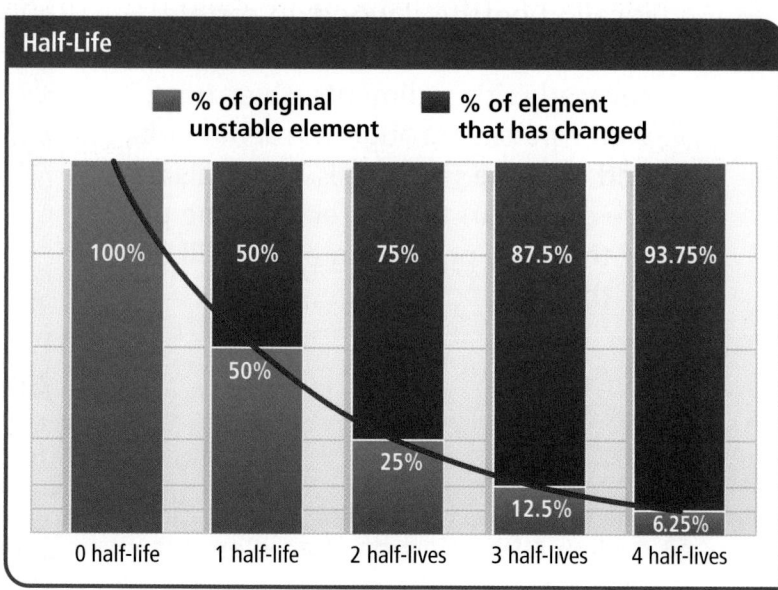

Half-Life

■ % of original unstable element   ■ % of element that has changed

0 half-life	1 half-life	2 half-lives	3 half-lives	4 half-lives
100%	50% / 50%	75% / 25%	87.5% / 12.5%	93.75% / 6.25%

Radiometric Dating

Radiometric dating works best with igneous rocks. Sedimentary rocks are formed from material that came from other rocks. For this reason, any measurements would show when the original rocks were formed, not when the sedimentary rock itself formed.

Elements with half-lives of millions to billions of years are used to date rocks.

Radioactive Breakdown and Dating Rock Layers

Igneous rocks contain radioactive elements that break down over time. This breakdown can be used to tell the ages of the rocks.

① **1408 Million Years Ago**

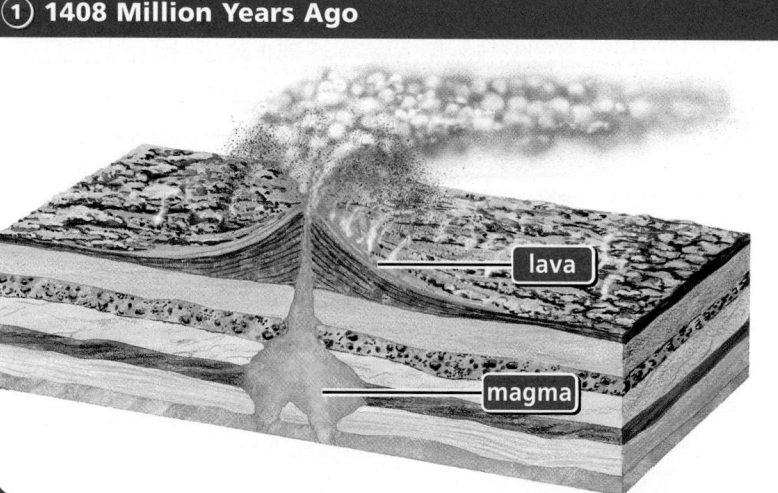

lava

magma

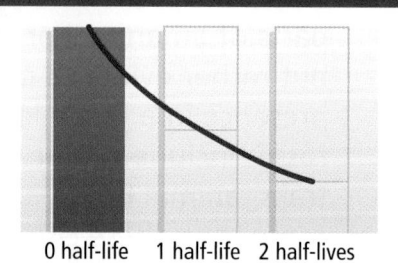

0 half-life   1 half-life   2 half-lives

When magma first hardens into rock, it contains some uranium 235 and no lead 207.

Uranium 235, an unstable element found in some igneous rocks, has a half-life of 704 million years. Over time, uranium 235 breaks down into lead 207.

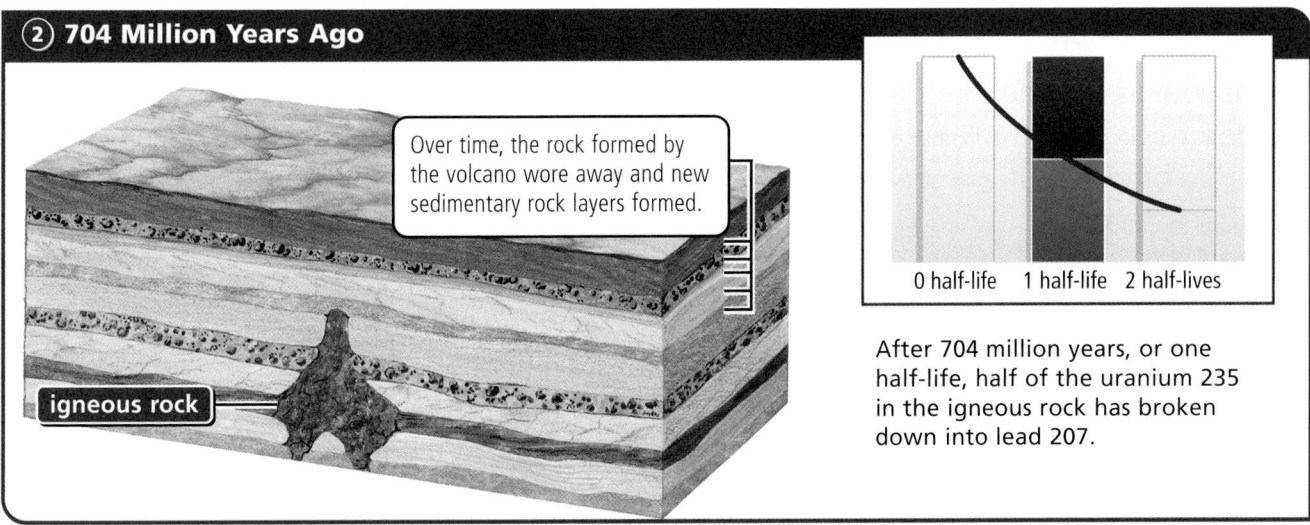

② 704 Million Years Ago

Over time, the rock formed by the volcano wore away and new sedimentary rock layers formed.

igneous rock

0 half-life   1 half-life   2 half-lives

After 704 million years, or one half-life, half of the uranium 235 in the igneous rock has broken down into lead 207.

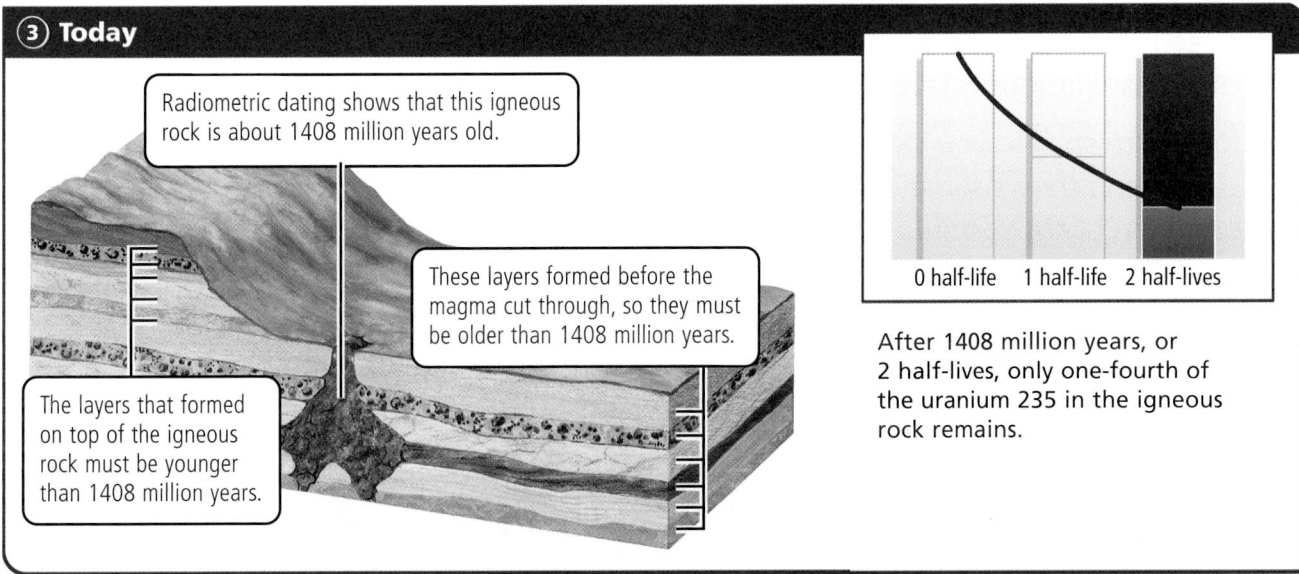

③ Today

Radiometric dating shows that this igneous rock is about 1408 million years old.

These layers formed before the magma cut through, so they must be older than 1408 million years.

The layers that formed on top of the igneous rock must be younger than 1408 million years.

0 half-life   1 half-life   2 half-lives

After 1408 million years, or 2 half-lives, only one-fourth of the uranium 235 in the igneous rock remains.

Just as uranium 235 can be used to date igneous rocks, carbon 14 can be used to find the ages of the remains of some things that were once alive. Carbon 14 is an unstable form of carbon, an element found in all living things. Carbon 14 has a half-life of 5730 years. It is useful for dating objects between about 100 and 70,000 years old, such as the wood from an ancient tool or the remains of an animal from the Ice Age.

Seasonal Star Maps

Your view of the night sky changes as Earth orbits the Sun. Some constellations appear throughout the year, but others can be seen only during certain seasons. And over the course of one night, the constellations appear to move across the sky as Earth rotates.

When you go outside to view stars, give your eyes time to adjust to the darkness. Avoid looking at bright lights. If you need to look toward a bright light, preserve your night vision in one eye by keeping it closed.

The star maps on pages 833–836 show parts of the night sky in different seasons. If you are using a flashlight to view the maps, you should attach a piece of red balloon over the lens. The balloon will dim the light and also give it a red color, which affects night vision less than other colors. The following steps will help you use the maps:

1 Stand facing north. To find this direction, use a compass or turn clockwise 90° from the location where the Sun set.

2 The top map for each season shows some constellations that appear over the northern horizon at 10 P.M. During the night, the constellations rotate in a circle around Polaris, the North Star.

3 Now turn so that you stand facing south. The bottom map for the season shows some constellations that appear over the southern horizon at 10 P.M.

WINTER SKY to the NORTH, *January 15*

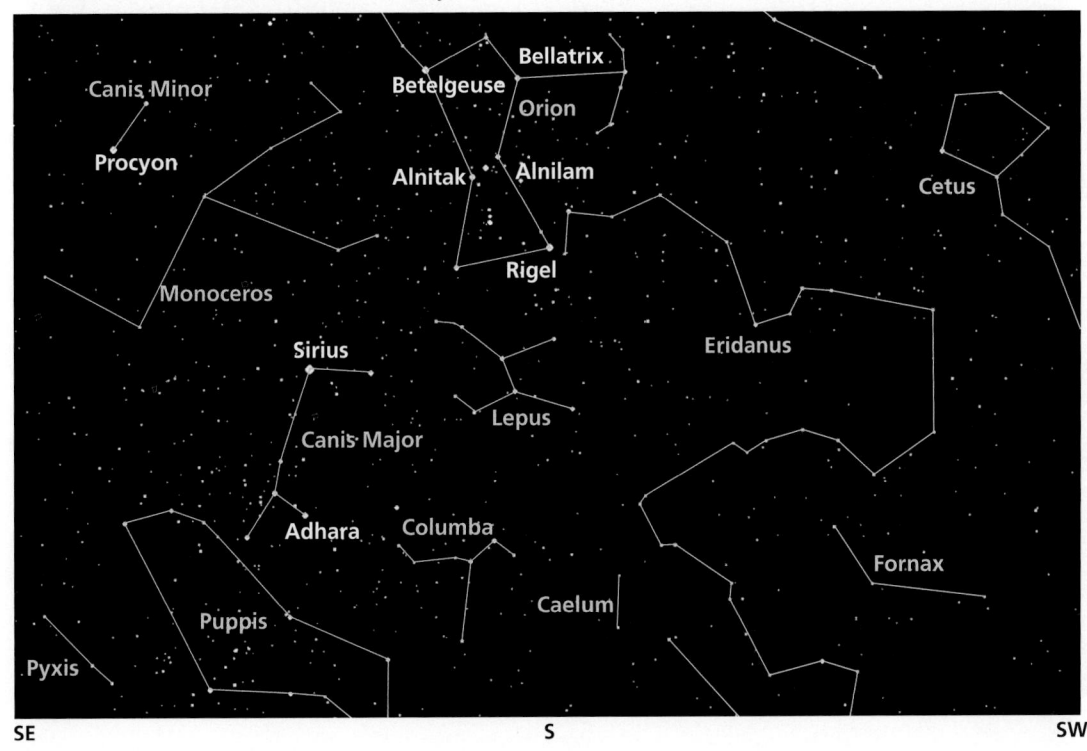

Cassiopeia

Polaris

Dubhe

Ursa Major

Cepheus

Ursa Minor

Kochab

Alioth

Lacerta

Mizar

Draco

Alkaid

Canes Venatici

Deneb

Cygnus

Eltanin

NW   N   NE

WINTER SKY to the SOUTH, *January 15*

Canis Minor

Bellatrix

Betelgeuse

Orion

Procyon

Alnitak

Alnilam

Cetus

Rigel

Monoceros

Eridanus

Sirius

Lepus

Canis Major

Adhara

Columba

Fornax

Puppis

Caelum

Pyxis

SE   S   SW

Seasonal Star Maps *continued*

SPRING SKY to the NORTH, *April 15*

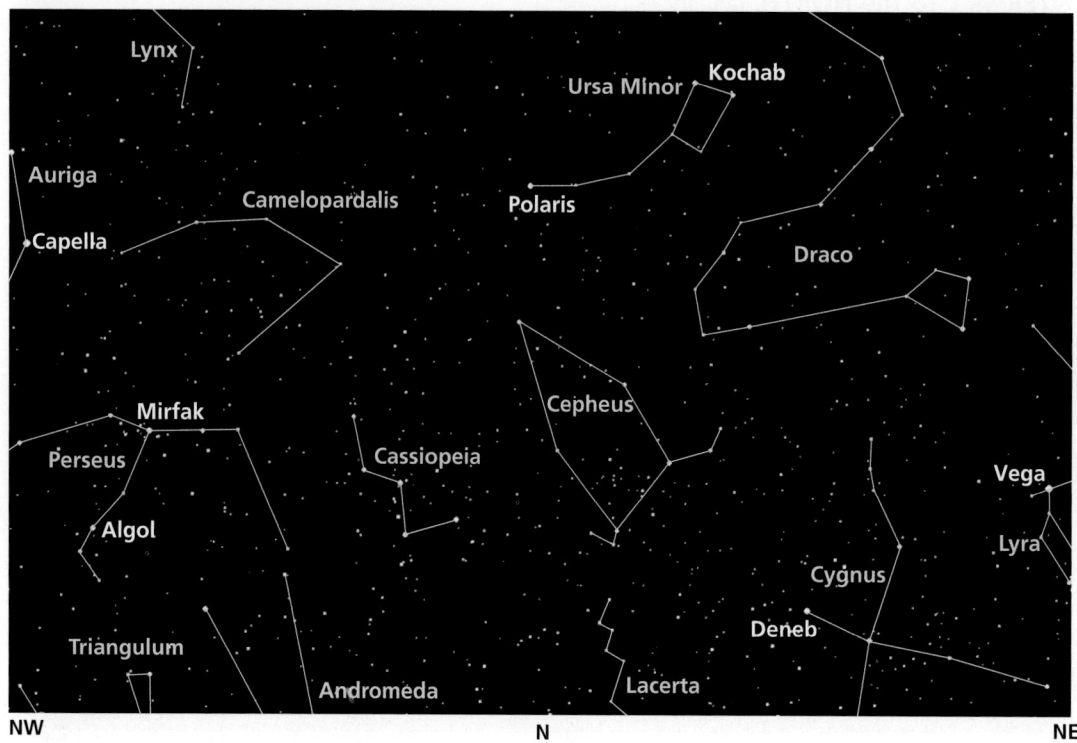

Lynx · Ursa Minor · Kochab · Auriga · Capella · Camelopardalis · Polaris · Draco · Mirfak · Perseus · Cepheus · Vega · Cassiopeia · Algol · Lyra · Cygnus · Deneb · Triangulum · Andromeda · Lacerta

NW   N   NE

SPRING SKY to the SOUTH, *April 15*

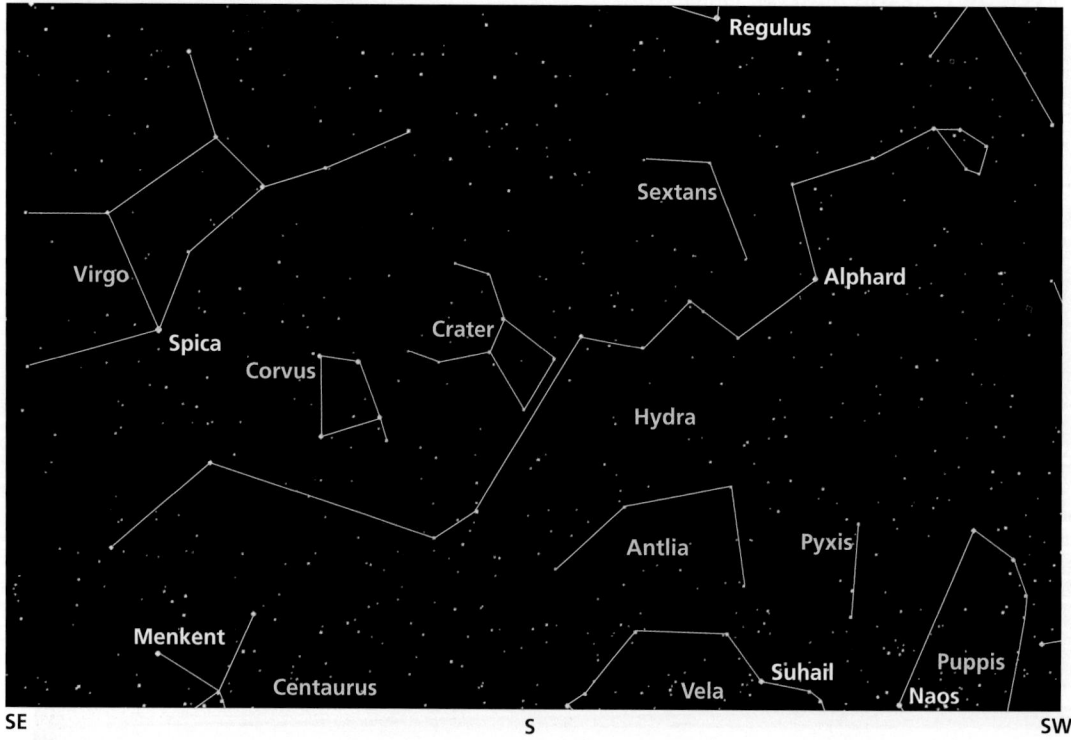

Regulus · Sextans · Virgo · Alphard · Spica · Crater · Corvus · Hydra · Antlia · Pyxis · Menkent · Centaurus · Vela · Suhail · Puppis · Naos

SE   S   SW

SUMMER SKY to the NORTH, *July 15*

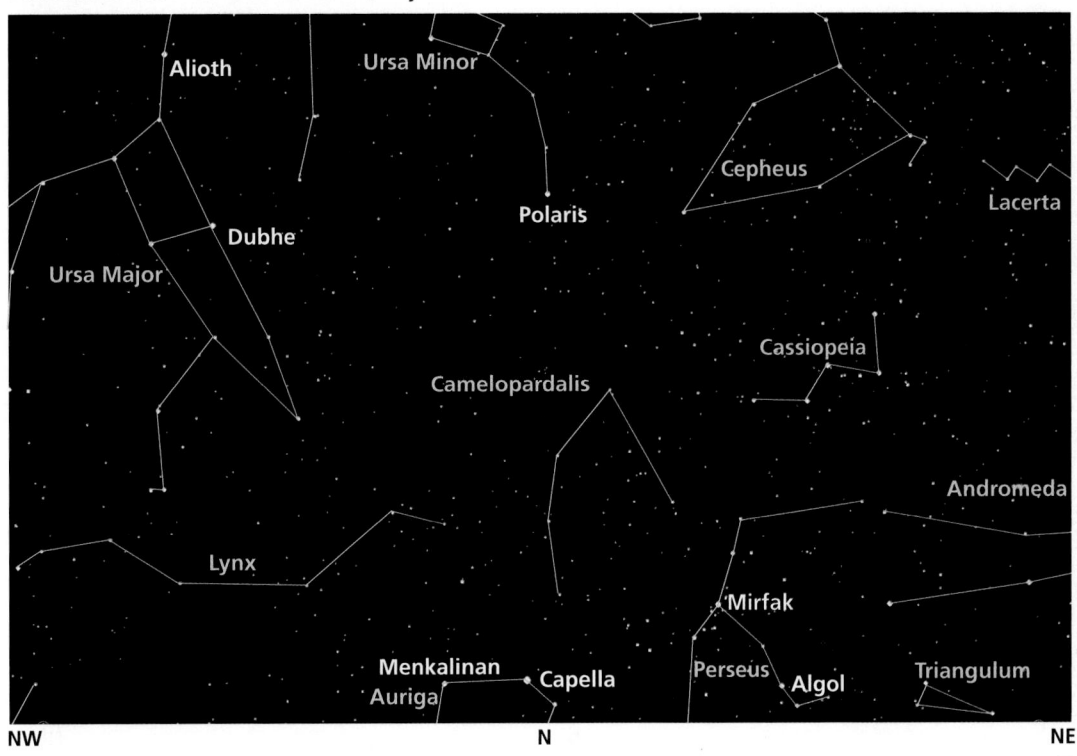

SUMMER SKY to the SOUTH, *July 15*

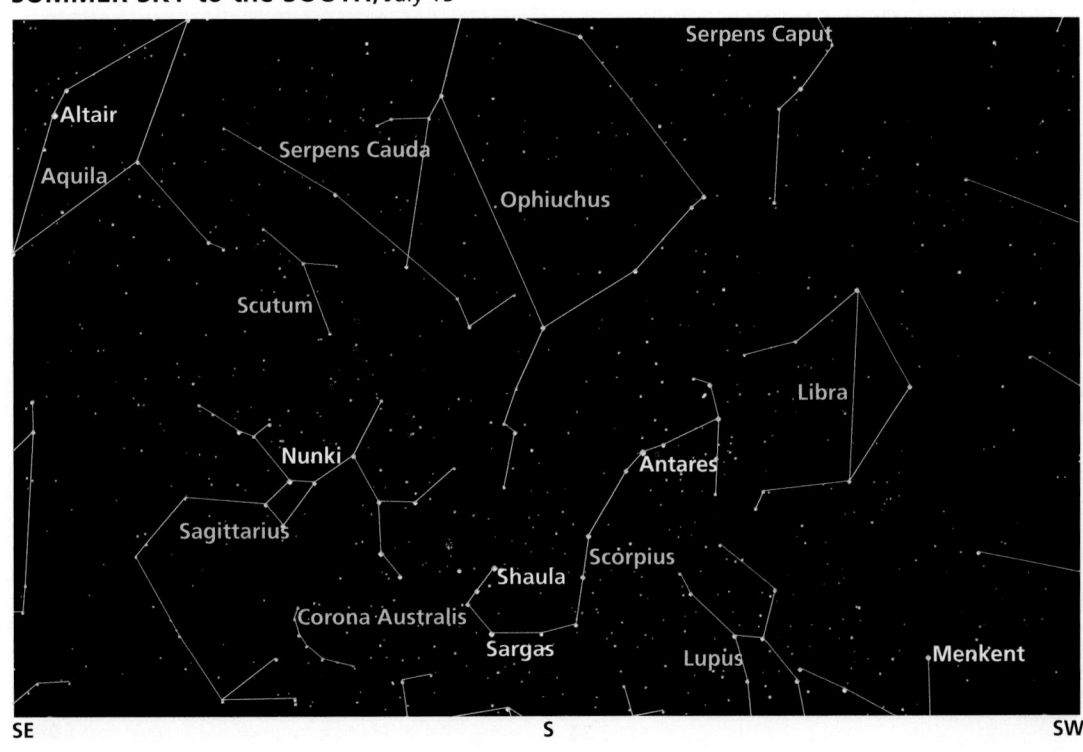

Seasonal Star Maps *continued*

AUTUMN SKY to the NORTH, *October 15*

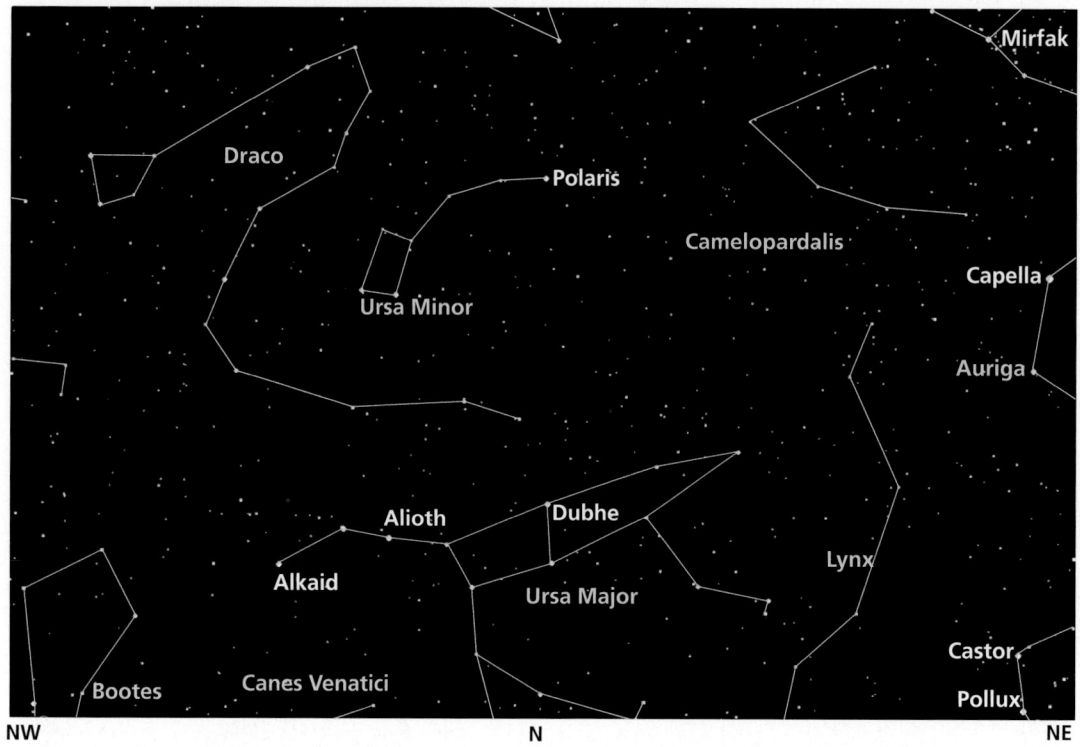

NW   N   NE

AUTUMN SKY to the SOUTH, *October 15*

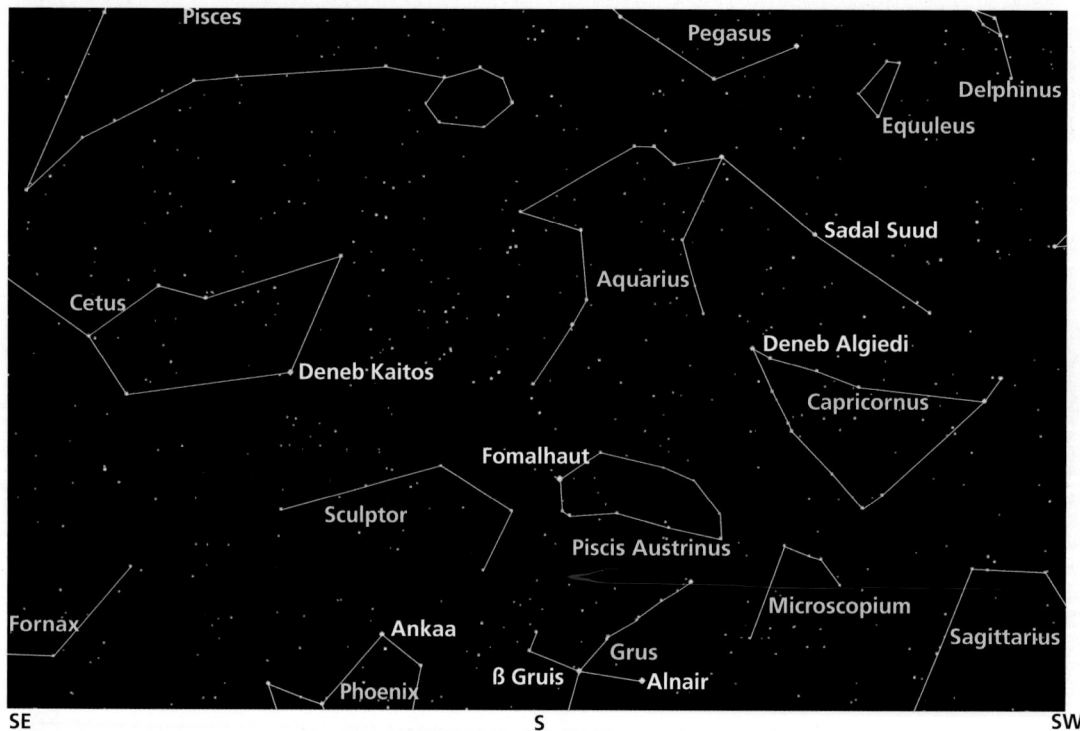

SE   S   SW

The Hertzsprung-Russell Diagram

The Hertzsprung-Russell (H-R) Diagram is a graph that shows stars plotted according to brightness and surface temperature. Most stars fall within a diagonal band called the main sequence. In the main-sequence stage of a star's life cycle, brightness is closely related to surface temperature. Red giant and red supergiant stars appear above the main sequence on the diagram. These stars are bright in relation to their surface temperatures because their huge surface areas give off a lot of light. Dim white dwarfs appear below the main sequence.

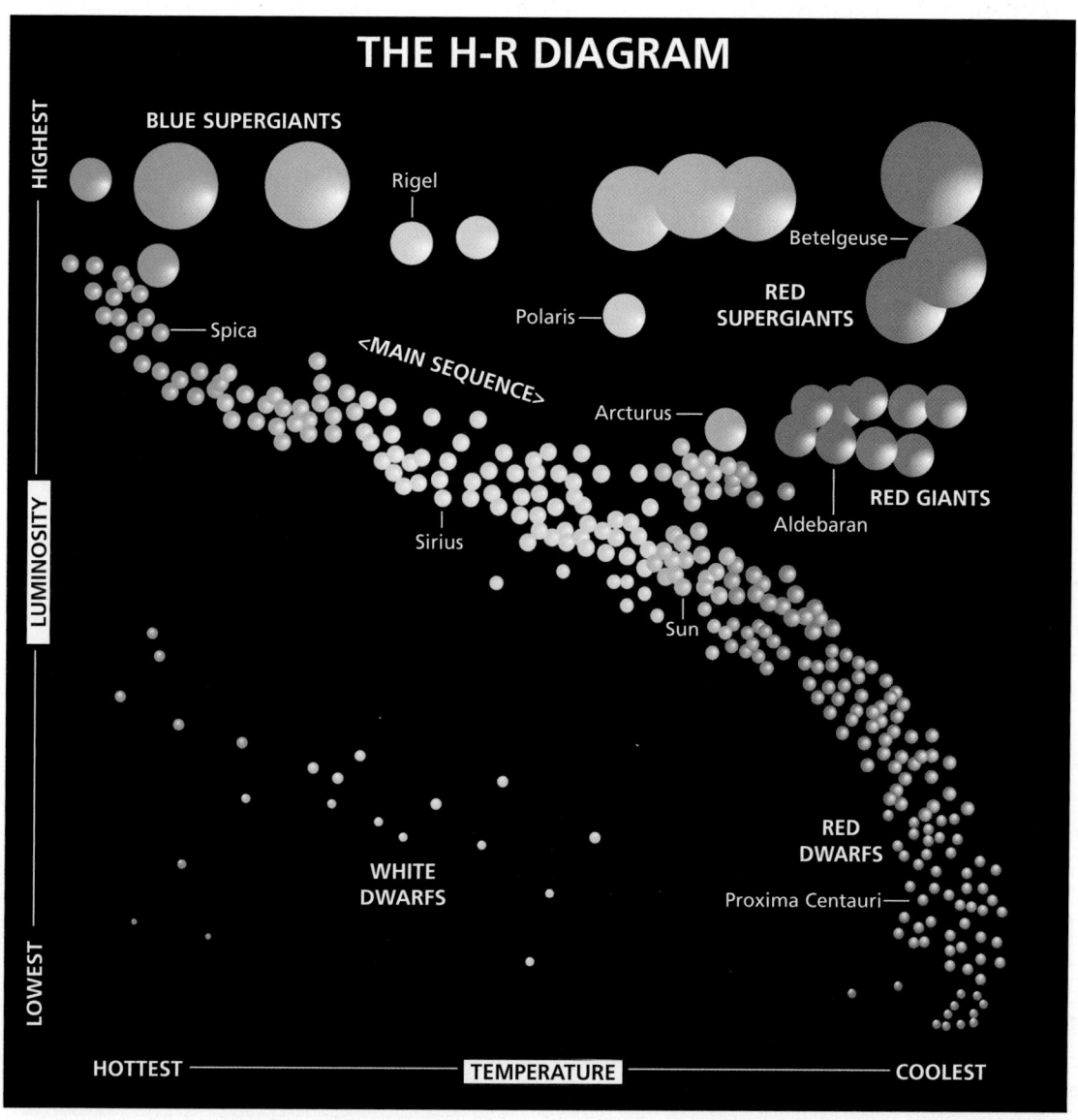

Time Zones

Because Earth rotates, noon can occur in one location at the same moment that the Sun is setting in another location. To avoid confusion in transportation and communication, officials have divided Earth into 24 time zones. Within a time zone, clocks are set to the same time of day.

Time zones are centered on lines of longitude, but instead of running straight, their boundaries often follow political boundaries. The starting point for the times zones is centered on the prime meridian (0°). The time in this zone is generally called Greenwich Mean Time (GMT), but it is also called Universal Time (UT) by astronomers and Zulu Time (Z) by meteorologists. The International Date Line is centered on 180° longitude. The calendar date to the east of this line is one day earlier than the date to the west.

In the map below, each column of color represents one time zone. The color beige shows areas that do not match standard zones. The labels at the top show the times at noon GMT. Positive and negative numbers at the bottom show the difference between the local time in the zone and Greenwich Mean Time.

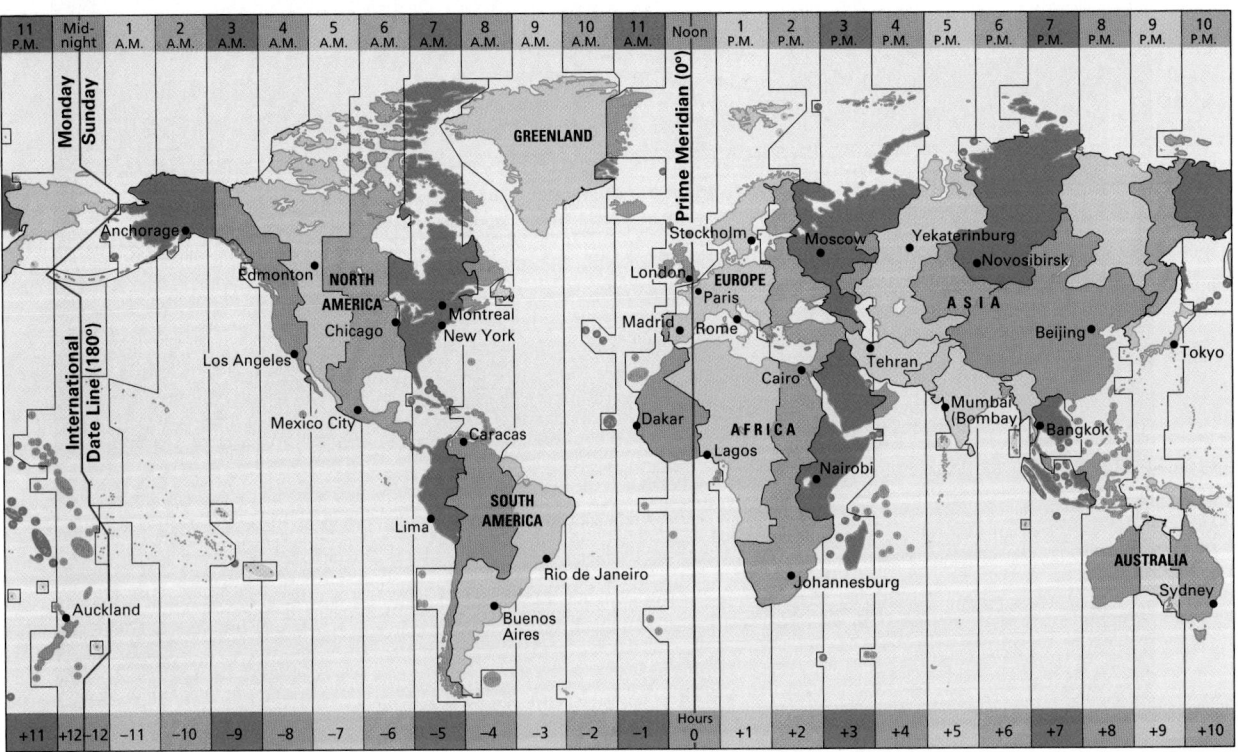

Characteristics of Planets

Some data about the planets and Earth's satellite, the Moon, are listed below. Some data, such as the tilt of Mercury and the mass of Pluto, are not known as well as other data. One astronomical unit (AU) is Earth's average distance from the Sun, or 149,597,870 kilometers. For comparison, Earth's mass is 5.97×10^{24} kilograms, and Earth's diameter is 12,756 kilometers.

Eccentricity is a measure of how flattened an ellipse is. An ellipse with an eccentricity of 0 is a circle. An ellipse with an eccentricity of 1 is completely flat.

Venus, Uranus, and Pluto rotate backward compared to Earth. If you use your left thumb as one of these planets' north pole, your fingers curve in the direction the planet turns.

Characteristics of Planets

Characteristic	Mercury	Venus	Earth	Mars	Jupiter	Saturn	Uranus	Neptune	Pluto	Moon
Mean distance from Sun (AU)	0.387	0.723	1.00	1.52	5.20	9.55	19.2	30.1	39.5	
Period of revolution (Earth years)	0.241 (88 Earth days)	0.615 (225 Earth days)	1.00	1.88	11.9	29.4	83.7	164	248	0.075 (27.3 Earth days)
Eccentricity of orbit	0.206	0.007	0.017	0.093	0.048	0.056	0.046	0.009	0.249	0.055
Diameter (Earth = 1)	0.382	0.949	1.00	0.532	11.21	9.45	4.01	3.88	0.180	0.272
Volume (Earth = 1)	0.06	0.86	1.00	0.15	1320	760	63	58	0.006	0.02
Period of rotation	58.6 Earth days	243 Earth days	23.9 hours	24.6 hours	9.93 hours	10.7 hours	17.2 hours	16.1 hours	6.39 Earth days	27.3 Earth days
Tilt of axis (°) (from perpendicular to orbit)	0.1 (approximate)	2.6	23.45	25.19	3.12	26.73	82.14	29.56	60.4	6.67
Mass (Earth = 1)	0.0553	0.815	1.00	0.107	318	95.2	14.5	17.1	0.002	0.0123
Mean density (g/cm³)	5.4	5.2	5.5	3.9	1.3	0.7	1.3	1.6	2	3.3

The Periodic Table of the Elements

Period

Each row of the periodic table is called a **period**. As read from left to right, one proton and one electron are added from one element to the next.

Group

Each column of the table is called a **group**. Elements in a group share similar properties. Groups are read from top to bottom.

1

1								
1 **H** Hydrogen 1.008								

2

2								
3 **Li** Lithium 6.941	**4** **Be** Beryllium 9.012							

3

		3	**4**	**5**	**6**	**7**	**8**	**9**
11 **Na** Sodium 22.990	**12** **Mg** Magnesium 24.305							

4

| **19**
K
Potassium
39.098 | **20**
Ca
Calcium
40.078 | **21**
Sc
Scandium
44.956 | **22**
Ti
Titanium
47.87 | **23**
V
Vanadium
50.942 | **24**
Cr
Chromium
51.996 | **25**
Mn
Manganese
54.938 | **26**
Fe
Iron
55.845 | **27**
Co
Cobalt
58.933 |

5

| **37**
Rb
Rubidium
85.468 | **38**
Sr
Strontium
87.62 | **39**
Y
Yttrium
88.906 | **40**
Zr
Zirconium
91.224 | **41**
Nb
Niobium
92.906 | **42**
Mo
Molybdenum
95.94 | **43**
Tc
Technetium
(98) | **44**
Ru
Ruthenium
101.07 | **45**
Rh
Rhodium
102.906 |

6

| **55**
Cs
Cesium
132.905 | **56**
Ba
Barium
137.327 | **57**
La
Lanthanum
138.906 | **72**
Hf
Hafnium
178.49 | **73**
Ta
Tantalum
180.95 | **74**
W
Tungsten
183.84 | **75**
Re
Rhenium
186.207 | **76**
Os
Osmium
190.23 | **77**
Ir
Iridium
192.217 |

7

| **87**
Fr
Francium
(223) | **88**
Ra
Radium
(226) | **89**
Ac
Actinium
(227) | **104**
Rf
Rutherfordium
(261) | **105**
Db
Dubnium
(262) | **106**
Sg
Seaborgium
(266) | **107**
Bh
Bohrium
(264) | **108**
Hs
Hassium
(269) | **109**
Mt
Meitnerium
(268) |

58 **Ce** Cerium 140.116	**59** **Pr** Praseodymium 140.908	**60** **Nd** Neodymium 144.24	**61** **Pm** Promethium (145)	**62** **Sm** Samarium 150.36
90 **Th** Thorium 232.038	**91** **Pa** Protactinium 231.036	**92** **U** Uranium 238.029	**93** **Np** Neptunium (237)	**94** **Pu** Plutonium (244)

 Metal   Metalloid   Nonmetal    **Fe** Solid   Hg Liquid   Gas

APPENDIX

Metals and Nonmetals

This zigzag line separates metals from nonmetals.

13	14	15	16	17	
					2 **He** Helium 4.003
5 **B** Boron 10.811	**6** **C** Carbon 12.011	**7** **N** Nitrogen 14.007	**8** **O** Oxygen 15.999	**9** **F** Fluorine 18.998	**10** **Ne** Neon 20.180
13 **Al** Aluminum 26.982	**14** **Si** Silicon 28.086	**15** **P** Phosphorus 30.974	**16** **S** Sulfur 32.066	**17** **Cl** Chlorine 35.453	**18** **Ar** Argon 39.948

10	11	12	13	14	15	16	17	18
28 **Ni** Nickel 58.69	**29** **Cu** Copper 63.546	**30** **Zn** Zinc 65.39	**31** **Ga** Gallium 69.723	**32** **Ge** Germanium 72.61	**33** **As** Arsenic 74.922	**34** **Se** Selenium 78.96	**35** **Br** Bromine 79.904	**36** **Kr** Krypton 83.80
46 **Pd** Palladium 106.42	**47** **Ag** Silver 107.868	**48** **Cd** Cadmium 112.4	**49** **In** Indium 114.818	**50** **Sn** Tin 118.710	**51** **Sb** Antimony 121.760	**52** **Te** Tellurium 127.60	**53** **I** Iodine 126.904	**54** **Xe** Xenon 131.29
78 **Pt** Platinum 195.078	**79** **Au** Gold 196.967	**80** **Hg** Mercury 200.59	**81** **Tl** Thallium 204.383	**82** **Pb** Lead 207.2	**83** **Bi** Bismuth 208.980	**84** **Po** Polonium (209)	**85** **At** Astatine (210)	**86** **Rn** Radon (222)
110 **Ds** Darmstadtium (269)	**111** **Uuu** Unununium (272)	**112** **Uub** Ununbium (277)						

Lanthanides & Actinides

The lanthanide series (elements 58–71) and actinide series (elements 90–103) are usually set apart from the rest of the periodic table.

63	64	65	66	67	68	69	70	71
Eu Europium 151.964	**Gd** Gadolinium 157.25	**Tb** Terbium 158.925	**Dy** Dysprosium 162.50	**Ho** Holmium 164.930	**Er** Erbium 167.26	**Tm** Thulium 168.934	**Yb** Ytterbium 173.04	**Lu** Lutetium 174.967

95	96	97	98	99	100	101	102	103
Am Americium (243)	**Cm** Curium (247)	**Bk** Berkelium (247)	**Cf** Californium (251)	**Es** Einsteinium (252)	**Fm** Fermium (257)	**Md** Mendelevium (258)	**No** Nobelium (259)	**Lr** Lawrencium (262)

Atomic Number
number of protons in the nucleus of the element

1
H
Hydrogen
1.008

Symbol
Each element has a symbol. The symbol's color represents the element's state at room temperature.

Name

Atomic Mass
average mass of isotopes of this element

Student Resource Handbooks

Scientific Thinking Handbook   R2

Making Observations   R2

Predicting and Hypothesizing   R3

Inferring   R4

Identifying Cause and Effect   R5

Recognizing Bias   R6

Identifying Faulty Reasoning   R7

Analyzing Statements   R8

Lab Handbook   R10

Safety Rules   R10

Using Lab Equipment   R12

The Metric System and SI Units   R20

Precision and Accuracy   R22

Making Data Tables and Graphs   R23

Designing an Experiment   R28

Math Handbook   R36

Describing a Set of Data   R36

Using Ratios, Rates, and Proportions   R38

Using Decimals, Fractions, and Percents   R39

Using Formulas   R42

Finding Areas   R43

Finding Volumes   R43

Using Significant Figures   R44

Using Scientific Notation   R44

Note-Taking Handbook   R45

Note-Taking Strategies   R45

Vocabulary Strategies   R50

Scientific Thinking Handbook

Making Observations

An **observation** is an act of noting and recording an event, characteristic, behavior, or anything else detected with an instrument or with the senses.

Observations allow you to make informed hypotheses and to gather data for experiments. Careful observations often lead to ideas for new experiments. There are two categories of observations:

- **Quantitative observations** can be expressed in numbers and include records of time, temperature, mass, distance, and volume.

- **Qualitative observations** include descriptions of sights, sounds, smells, and textures.

EXAMPLE

A student dissolved 30 grams of Epsom salts in water, poured the solution into a dish, and let the dish sit out uncovered overnight. The next day, she made the following observations of the Epsom salt crystals that grew in the dish.

> To determine the mass, the student found the mass of the dish before and after growing the crystals and then used subtraction to find the difference.

> The student measured several crystals and calculated the mean length. (To learn how to calculate the mean of a data set, see page R36.)

Table 1. Observations of Epsom Salt Crystals

Quantitative Observations	Qualitative Observations
• mass = 30 g • mean crystal length = 0.5 cm • longest crystal length = 2 cm	• Crystals are clear. • Crystals are long, thin, and rectangular. • White crust has formed around edge of dish.

> Photographs or sketches are useful for recording qualitative observations.

Epsom salt crystals

MORE ABOUT OBSERVING

- Make quantitative observations whenever possible. That way, others will know exactly what you observed and be able to compare their results with yours.

- It is always a good idea to make qualitative observations too. You never know when you might observe something unexpected.

Predicting and Hypothesizing

A **prediction** is an expectation of what will be observed or what will happen. A **hypothesis** is a tentative explanation for an observation or scientific problem that can be tested by further investigation.

EXAMPLE

Suppose you have made two paper airplanes and you wonder why one of them tends to glide farther than the other one.

1. Start by asking a question.

2. Make an educated guess. After examination, you notice that the wings of the airplane that flies farther are slightly larger than the wings of the other airplane.

3. Write a prediction based upon your educated guess, in the form of an "If . . . , then . . ." statement. Write the independent variable after the word *if*, and the dependent variable after the word *then*.

4. To make a hypothesis, explain why you think what you predicted will occur. Write the explanation after the word *because*.

1. Why does one of the paper airplanes glide farther than the other?

2. The size of an airplane's wings may affect how far the airplane will glide.

3. Prediction: If I make a paper airplane with larger wings, then the airplane will glide farther.

To read about independent and dependent variables, see page R30.

4. Hypothesis: If I make a paper airplane with larger wings, then the airplane will glide farther, because the additional surface area of the wing will produce more lift.

Notice that the part of the hypothesis after *because* adds an explanation of why the airplane will glide farther.

MORE ABOUT HYPOTHESES

• The results of an experiment cannot prove that a hypothesis is correct. Rather, the results either support or do not support the hypothesis.

• Valuable information is gained even when your hypothesis is not supported by your results. For example, it would be an important discovery to find that wing size is not related to how far an airplane glides.

• In science, a hypothesis is supported only after many scientists have conducted many experiments and produced consistent results.

Inferring

An **inference** is a logical conclusion drawn from the available evidence and prior knowledge. Inferences are often made from observations.

EXAMPLE

A student observing a set of acorns noticed something unexpected about one of them. He noticed a white, soft-bodied insect eating its way out of the acorn.

The student recorded these observations.

Observations

- There is a hole in the acorn, about 0.5 cm in diameter, where the insect crawled out.
- There is a second hole, which is about the size of a pinhole, on the other side of the acorn.
- The inside of the acorn is hollow.

Here are some inferences that can be made on the basis of the observations.

Inferences

- The insect formed from the material inside the acorn, grew to its present size, and ate its way out of the acorn.
- The insect crawled through the smaller hole, ate the inside of the acorn, grew to its present size, and ate its way out of the acorn.
- An egg was laid in the acorn through the smaller hole. The egg hatched into a larva that ate the inside of the acorn, grew to its present size, and ate its way out of the acorn.

When you make inferences, be sure to look at all of the evidence available and combine it with what you already know.

MORE ABOUT INFERENCES

Inferences depend both on observations and on the knowledge of the people making the inferences. Ancient people who did not know that organisms are produced only by similar organisms might have made an inference like the first one. A student today might look at the same observations and make the second inference. A third student might have knowledge about this particular insect and know that it is never small enough to fit through the smaller hole, leading her to the third inference.

Identifying Cause and Effect

In a **cause-and-effect relationship,** one event or characteristic is the result of another. Usually an effect follows its cause in time.

There are many examples of cause-and-effect relationships in everyday life.

Cause	Effect
Turn off a light.	Room gets dark.
Drop a glass.	Glass breaks.
Blow a whistle.	Sound is heard.

Scientists must be careful not to infer a cause-and-effect relationship just because one event happens after another event. When one event occurs after another, you cannot infer a cause-and-effect relationship on the basis of that information alone. You also cannot conclude that one event caused another if there are alternative ways to explain the second event. A scientist must demonstrate through experimentation or continued observation that an event was truly caused by another event.

EXAMPLE

Make an Observation

Suppose you have a few plants growing outside. When the weather starts getting colder, you bring one of the plants indoors. You notice that the plant you brought indoors is growing faster than the others are growing. You cannot conclude from your observation that the change in temperature was the cause of the increased plant growth, because there are alternative explanations for the observation. Some possible explanations are given below.

- The humidity indoors caused the plant to grow faster.

- The level of sunlight indoors caused the plant to grow faster.

- The indoor plant's being noticed more often and watered more often than the outdoor plants caused it to grow faster.

- The plant that was brought indoors was healthier than the other plants to begin with.

To determine which of these factors, if any, caused the indoor plant to grow faster than the outdoor plants, you would need to design and conduct an experiment.

See pages R28–R35 for information about designing experiments.

Recognizing Bias

Television, newspapers, and the Internet are full of experts claiming to have scientific evidence to back up their claims. How do you know whether the claims are really backed up by good science?

Bias is a slanted point of view, or personal prejudice. The goal of scientists is to be as objective as possible and to base their findings on facts instead of opinions. However, bias often affects the conclusions of researchers, and it is important to learn to recognize bias.

When scientific results are reported, you should consider the source of the information as well as the information itself. It is important to critically analyze the information that you see and read.

SOURCES OF BIAS

There are several ways in which a report of scientific information may be biased. Here are some questions that you can ask yourself:

1. **Who is sponsoring the research?**

   Sometimes, the results of an investigation are biased because an organization paying for the research is looking for a specific answer. This type of bias can affect how data are gathered and interpreted.

2. **Is the research sample large enough?**

   Sometimes research does not include enough data. The larger the sample size, the more likely that the results are accurate, assuming a truly random sample.

3. **In a survey, who is answering the questions?**

   The results of a survey or poll can be biased. The people taking part in the survey may have been specifically chosen because of how they would answer. They may have the same ideas or lifestyles. A survey or poll should make use of a random sample of people.

4. **Are the people who take part in a survey biased?**

   People who take part in surveys sometimes try to answer the questions the way they think the researcher wants them to answer. Also, in surveys or polls that ask for personal information, people may be unwilling to answer questions truthfully.

SCIENTIFIC BIAS

It is also important to realize that scientists have their own biases because of the types of research they do and because of their scientific viewpoints. Two scientists may look at the same set of data and come to completely different conclusions because of these biases. However, such disagreements are not necessarily bad. In fact, a critical analysis of disagreements is often responsible for moving science forward.

Identifying Faulty Reasoning

Faulty reasoning is wrong or incorrect thinking. It leads to mistakes and to wrong conclusions. Scientists are careful not to draw unreasonable conclusions from experimental data. Without such caution, the results of scientific investigations may be misleading.

EXAMPLE

Scientists try to make generalizations based on their data to explain as much about nature as possible. If only a small sample of data is looked at, however, a conclusion may be faulty. Suppose a scientist has studied the effects of the El Niño and La Niña weather patterns on flood damage in California from 1989 to 1995. The scientist organized the data in the bar graph below.

The scientist drew the following conclusions:

1. The La Niña weather pattern has no effect on flooding in California.
2. When neither weather pattern occurs, there is almost no flood damage.
3. A weak or moderate El Niño produces a small or moderate amount of flooding.
4. A strong El Niño produces a lot of flooding.

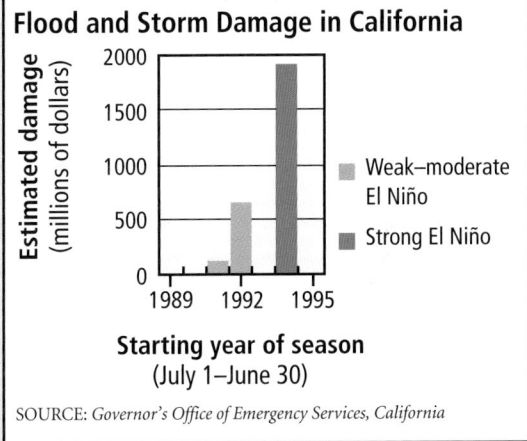

Flood and Storm Damage in California

SOURCE: *Governor's Office of Emergency Services, California*

For the six-year period of the scientist's investigation, these conclusions may seem to be reasonable. However, a six-year study of weather patterns may be too small of a sample for the conclusions to be supported. Consider the following graph, which shows information that was gathered from 1949 to 1997.

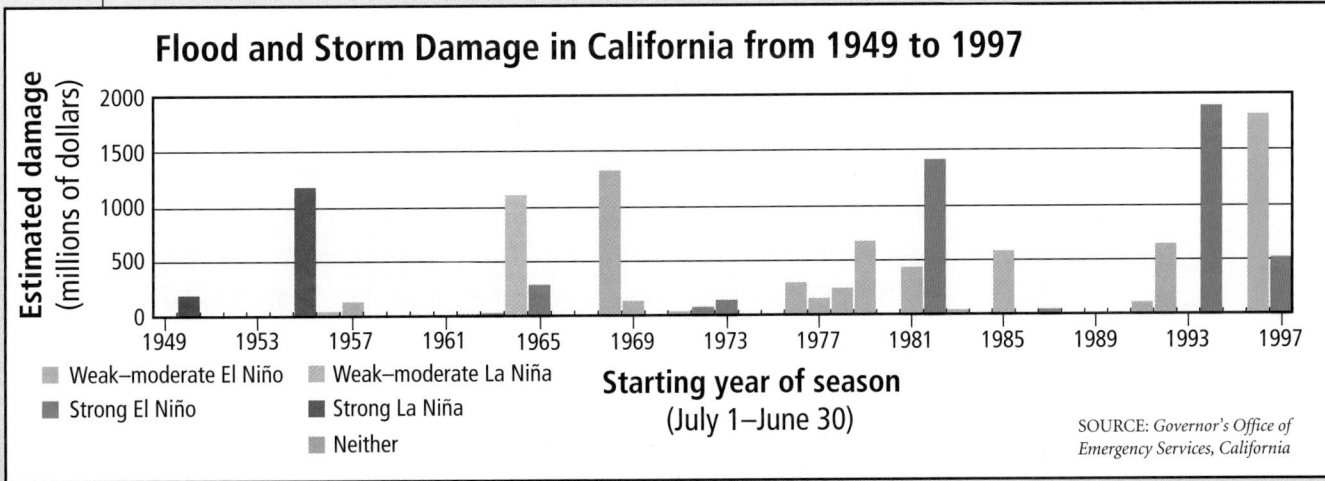

Flood and Storm Damage in California from 1949 to 1997

SOURCE: *Governor's Office of Emergency Services, California*

The only one of the conclusions that all of this information supports is number 3: a weak or moderate El Niño produces a small or moderate amount of flooding. By collecting more data, scientists can be more certain of their conclusions and can avoid faulty reasoning.

Analyzing Statements

To **analyze** a statement is to examine its parts carefully. Scientific findings are often reported through media such as television or the Internet. A report that is made public often focuses on only a small part of research. As a result, it is important to question the sources of information.

Evaluate Media Claims

To **evaluate** a statement is to judge it on the basis of criteria you've established. Sometimes evaluating means deciding whether a statement is true.

Reports of scientific research and findings in the media may be misleading or incomplete. When you are exposed to this information, you should ask yourself some questions so that you can make informed judgments about the information.

1. **Does the information come from a credible source?**

   Suppose you learn about a new product and it is stated that scientific evidence proves that the product works. A report from a respected news source may be more believable than an advertisement paid for by the product's manufacturer.

2. **How much evidence supports the claim?**

   Often, it may seem that there is new evidence every day of something in the world that either causes or cures an illness. However, information that is the result of several years of work by several different scientists is more credible than an advertisement that does not even cite the subjects of the experiment.

3. **How much information is being presented?**

   Science cannot solve all questions, and scientific experiments often have flaws. A report that discusses problems in a scientific study may be more believable than a report that addresses only positive experimental findings.

4. **Is scientific evidence being presented by a specific source?**

   Sometimes scientific findings are reported by people who are called experts or leaders in a scientific field. But if their names are not given or their scientific credentials are not reported, their statements may be less credible than those of recognized experts.

Differentiate Between Fact and Opinion

Sometimes information is presented as a fact when it may be an opinion. When scientific conclusions are reported, it is important to recognize whether they are based on solid evidence. Again, you may find it helpful to ask yourself some questions.

1. **What is the difference between a fact and an opinion?**

   A **fact** is a piece of information that can be strictly defined and proved true. An **opinion** is a statement that expresses a belief, value, or feeling. An opinion cannot be proved true or false. For example, a person's age is a fact, but if someone is asked how old they feel, it is impossible to prove the person's answer to be true or false.

2. **Can opinions be measured?**

   Yes, opinions can be measured. In fact, surveys often ask for people's opinions on a topic. But there is no way to know whether or not an opinion is the truth.

HOW TO DIFFERENTIATE FACT FROM OPINION

Human Activities and the Environment

Unfortunately, human use of fossil fuels is one of the most significant developments of the past few centuries. Humans rely on fossil fuels, a non-renewable energy resource, for more than 90 percent of their energy needs.

This careless misuse of our planet's resources has resulted in pollution, global warming, and the destruction of fragile ecosystems. For example, oil pipelines carry more than one million barrels of oil each day across tundra regions. Transporting oil across such areas can only result in oil spills that poison the land for decades.

Opinions
Notice words or phrases that express beliefs or feelings. The words *unfortunately* and *careless* show that opinions are being expressed.

Opinion
Look for statements that speculate about events. These statements are opinions, because they cannot be proved.

Facts
Statements that contain statistics tend to be facts. Writers often use facts to support their opinions.

Lab Handbook

Safety Rules

Before you work in the laboratory, read these safety rules twice. Ask your teacher to explain any rules that you do not completely understand. Refer to these rules later on if you have questions about safety in the science classroom.

Directions

- Read all directions and make sure that you understand them before starting an investigation or lab activity. If you do not understand how to do a procedure or how to use a piece of equipment, ask your teacher.
- Do not begin any investigation or touch any equipment until your teacher has told you to start.
- Never experiment on your own. If you want to try a procedure that the directions do not call for, ask your teacher for permission first.
- If you are hurt or injured in any way, tell your teacher immediately.

Dress Code

goggles

apron

gloves

- Wear goggles when
  — using glassware, sharp objects, or chemicals
  — heating an object
  — working with anything that can easily fly up into the air and hurt someone's eye
- Tie back long hair or hair that hangs in front of your eyes.
- Remove any article of clothing—such as a loose sweater or a scarf—that hangs down and may touch a flame, chemical, or piece of equipment.
- Observe all safety icons calling for the wearing of eye protection, gloves, and aprons.

Heating and Fire Safety

fire safety

heating safety

- Keep your work area neat, clean, and free of extra materials.
- Never reach over a flame or heat source.
- Point objects being heated away from you and others.
- Never heat a substance or an object in a closed container.
- Never touch an object that has been heated. If you are unsure whether something is hot, treat it as though it is. Use oven mitts, clamps, tongs, or a test-tube holder.
- Know where the fire extinguisher and fire blanket are kept in your classroom.
- Do not throw hot substances into the trash. Wait for them to cool or use the container your teacher puts out for disposal.

Electrical Safety

electrical safety

- Never use lamps or other electrical equipment with frayed cords.
- Make sure no cord is lying on the floor where someone can trip over it.
- Do not let a cord hang over the side of a counter or table so that the equipment can easily be pulled or knocked to the floor.
- Never let cords hang into sinks or other places where water can be found.
- Never try to fix electrical problems. Inform your teacher of any problems immediately.
- Unplug an electrical cord by pulling on the plug, not the cord.

Chemical Safety

chemical safety

poison

fumes

- If you spill a chemical or get one on your skin or in your eyes, tell your teacher right away.
- Never touch, taste, or sniff any chemicals in the lab. If you need to determine odor, waft. Wafting consists of holding the chemical in its container 15 centimeters (6 in.) away from your nose, and using your fingers to bring fumes from the container to your nose.
- Keep lids on all chemicals you are not using.
- Never put unused chemicals back into the original containers. Throw away extra chemicals where your teacher tells you to.
- Pour chemicals over a sink or your work area, not over the floor.
- If you get a chemical in your eye, use the eyewash right away.
- Always wash your hands after handling chemicals, plants, or soil.

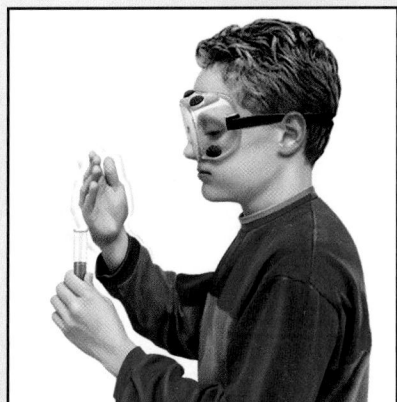

Wafting

Glassware and Sharp-Object Safety

sharp objects

- If you break glassware, tell your teacher right away.
- Do not use broken or chipped glassware. Give these to your teacher.
- Use knives and other cutting instruments carefully. Always wear eye protection and cut away from you.

Animal Safety

- Never hurt an animal.
- Touch animals only when necessary. Follow your teacher's instructions for handling animals.
- Always wash your hands after working with animals.

Cleanup

disposal

- Follow your teacher's instructions for throwing away or putting away supplies.
- Clean your work area and pick up anything that has dropped to the floor.
- Wash your hands.

Using Lab Equipment

Different experiments require different types of equipment. But even though experiments differ, the ways in which the equipment is used are the same.

Beakers

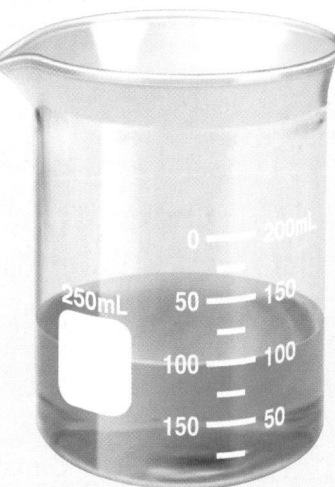

- Use beakers for holding and pouring liquids.
- Do not use a beaker to measure the volume of a liquid. Use a graduated cylinder instead. (See page R16.)
- Use a beaker that holds about twice as much liquid as you need. For example, if you need 100 milliliters of water, you should use a 200- or 250-milliliter beaker.

Test Tubes

- Use test tubes to hold small amounts of substances.
- Do not use a test tube to measure the volume of a liquid.
- Use a test tube when heating a substance over a flame. Aim the mouth of the tube away from yourself and other people.
- Liquids easily spill or splash from test tubes, so it is important to use only small amounts of liquids.

Test-Tube Holder

- Use a test-tube holder when heating a substance in a test tube.
- Use a test-tube holder if the substance in a test tube is dangerous to touch.
- Make sure the test-tube holder tightly grips the test tube so that the test tube will not slide out of the holder.
- Make sure that the test-tube holder is above the surface of the substance in the test tube so that you can observe the substance.

Test-Tube Rack

- Use a test-tube rack to organize test tubes before, during, and after an experiment.

- Use a test-tube rack to keep test tubes upright so that they do not fall over and spill their contents.

- Use a test-tube rack that is the correct size for the test tubes that you are using. If the rack is too small, a test tube may become stuck. If the rack is too large, a test tube may lean over, and some of its contents may spill or splash.

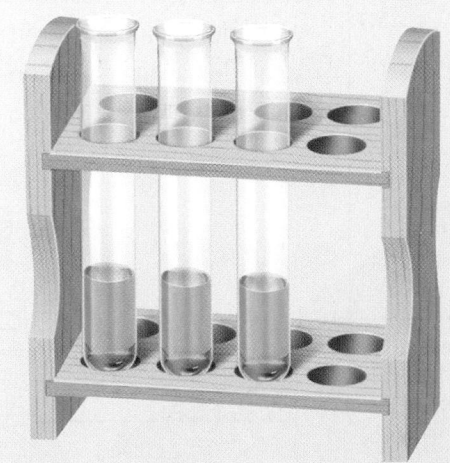

Forceps

- Use forceps when you need to pick up or hold a very small object that should not be touched with your hands.

- Do not use forceps to hold anything over a flame, because forceps are not long enough to keep your hand safely away from the flame. Plastic forceps will melt, and metal forceps will conduct heat and burn your hand.

Hot Plate

- Use a hot plate when a substance needs to be kept warmer than room temperature for a long period of time.

- Use a hot plate instead of a Bunsen burner or a candle when you need to carefully control temperature.

- Do not use a hot plate when a substance needs to be burned in an experiment.

- Always use "hot hands" safety mitts or oven mitts when handling anything that has been heated on a hot plate.

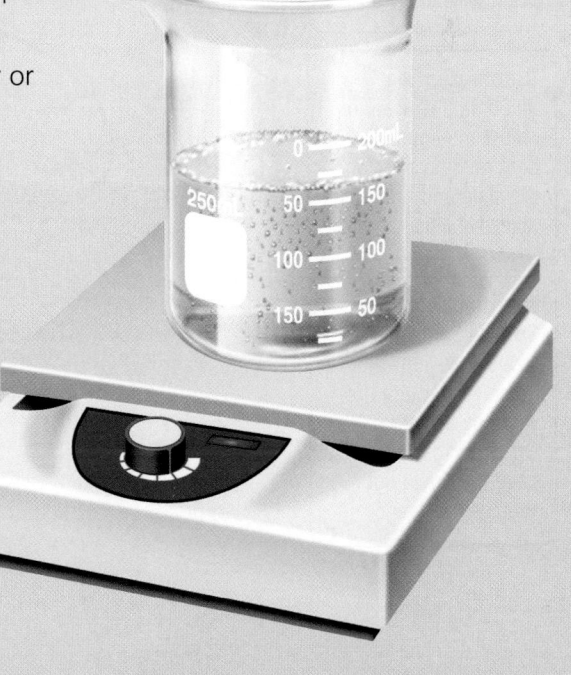

Microscope

Scientists use microscopes to see very small objects that cannot easily be seen with the eye alone. A microscope magnifies the image of an object so that small details may be observed. A microscope that you may use can magnify an object 400 times—the object will appear 400 times larger than its actual size.

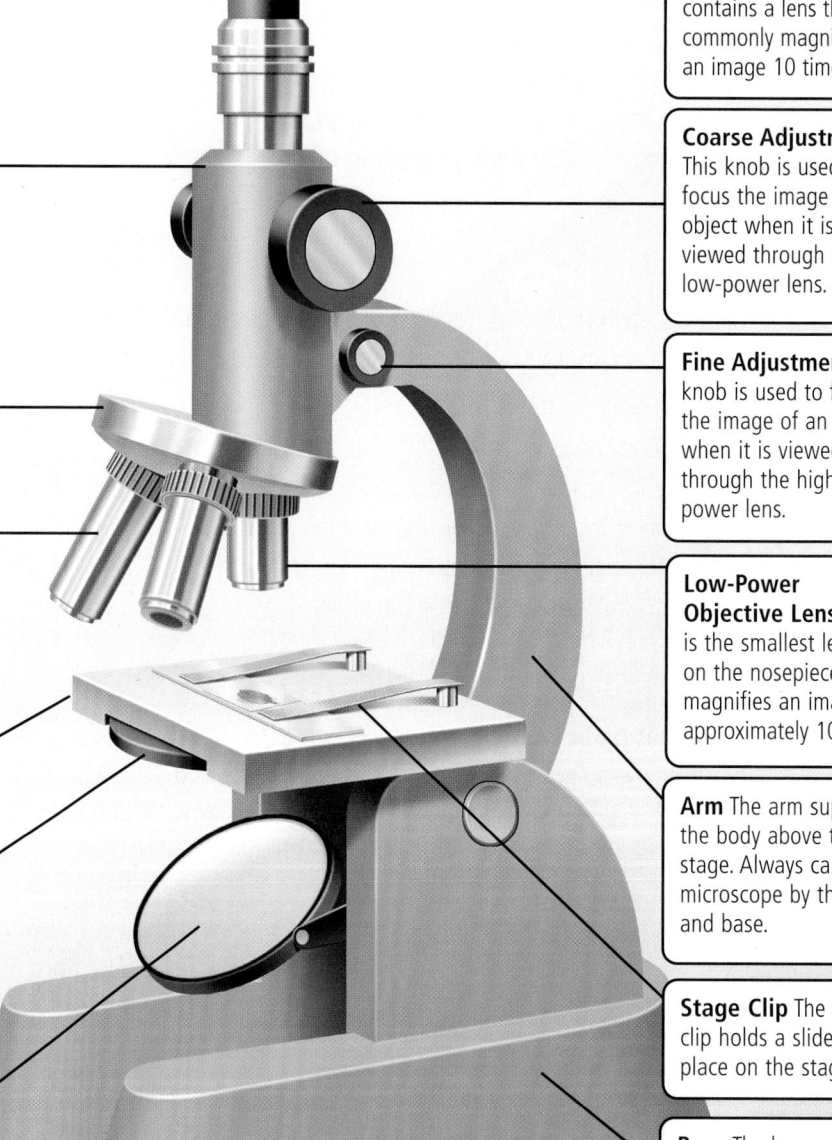

Body The body separates the lens in the eyepiece from the objective lenses below.

Nosepiece The nosepiece holds the objective lenses above the stage and rotates so that all lenses may be used.

High-Power Objective Lens This is the largest lens on the nosepiece. It magnifies an image approximately 40 times.

Stage The stage supports the object being viewed.

Diaphragm The diaphragm is used to adjust the amount of light passing through the slide and into an objective lens.

Mirror or Light Source Some microscopes use light that is reflected through the stage by a mirror. Other microscopes have their own light sources.

Eyepiece Objects are viewed through the eyepiece. The eyepiece contains a lens that commonly magnifies an image 10 times.

Coarse Adjustment This knob is used to focus the image of an object when it is viewed through the low-power lens.

Fine Adjustment This knob is used to focus the image of an object when it is viewed through the high-power lens.

Low-Power Objective Lens This is the smallest lens on the nosepiece. It magnifies an image approximately 10 times.

Arm The arm supports the body above the stage. Always carry a microscope by the arm and base.

Stage Clip The stage clip holds a slide in place on the stage.

Base The base supports the microscope.

VIEWING AN OBJECT

1. Use the coarse adjustment knob to raise the body tube.
2. Adjust the diaphragm so that you can see a bright circle of light through the eyepiece.
3. Place the object or slide on the stage. Be sure that it is centered over the hole in the stage.
4. Turn the nosepiece to click the low-power lens into place.
5. Using the coarse adjustment knob, slowly lower the lens and focus on the specimen being viewed. Be sure not to touch the slide or object with the lens.
6. When switching from the low-power lens to the high-power lens, first raise the body tube with the coarse adjustment knob so that the high-power lens will not hit the slide.
7. Turn the nosepiece to click the high-power lens into place.
8. Use the fine adjustment knob to focus on the specimen being viewed. Again, be sure not to touch the slide or object with the lens.

MAKING A SLIDE, OR WET MOUNT

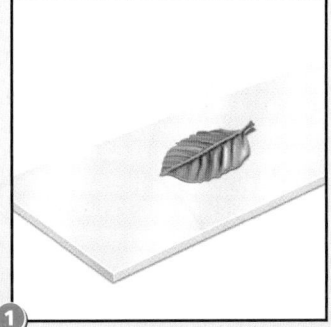

1 Place the specimen in the center of a clean slide.

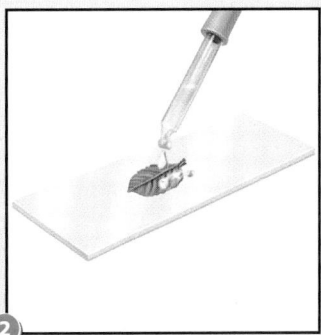

2 Place a drop of water on the specimen.

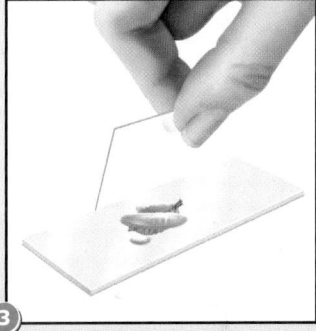

3 Place a cover slip on the slide. Put one edge of the cover slip into the drop of water and slowly lower it over the specimen.

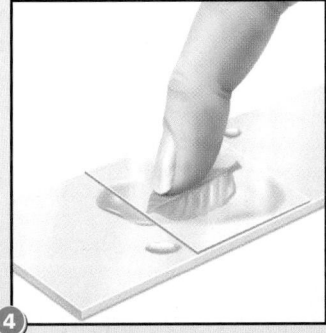

4 Remove any air bubbles from under the cover slip by gently tapping the cover slip.

5 Dry any excess water before placing the slide on the microscope stage for viewing.

Spring Scale (Force Meter)

- Use a spring scale to measure a force pulling on the scale.

- Use a spring scale to measure the force of gravity exerted on an object by Earth.

- To measure a force accurately, a spring scale must be zeroed before it is used. The scale is zeroed when no weight is attached and the indicator is positioned at zero.

- Do not attach a weight that is either too heavy or too light to a spring scale. A weight that is too heavy could break the scale or exert too great a force for the scale to measure. A weight that is too light may not exert enough force to be measured accurately.

Graduated Cylinder

- Use a graduated cylinder to measure the volume of a liquid.

- Be sure that the graduated cylinder is on a flat surface so that your measurement will be accurate.

- When reading the scale on a graduated cylinder, be sure to have your eyes at the level of the surface of the liquid.

- The surface of the liquid will be curved in the graduated cylinder. Read the volume of the liquid at the bottom of the curve, or meniscus (muh-NIHS-kuhs).

- You can use a graduated cylinder to find the volume of a solid object by measuring the increase in a liquid's level after you add the object to the cylinder.

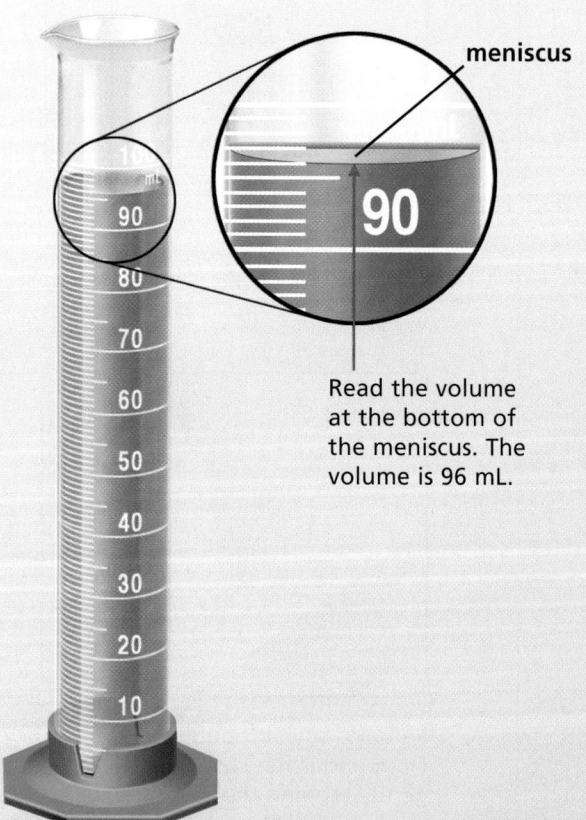

meniscus

Read the volume at the bottom of the meniscus. The volume is 96 mL.

Metric Rulers

- Use metric rulers or meter sticks to measure objects' lengths.

- Do not measure an object from the end of a metric ruler or meter stick, because the end is often imperfect. Instead, measure from the 1-centimeter mark, but remember to subtract a centimeter from the apparent measurement.

- Estimate any lengths that extend between marked units. For example, if a meter stick shows centimeters but not millimeters, you can estimate the length that an object extends between centimeter marks to measure it to the nearest millimeter.

- **Controlling Variables** If you are taking repeated measurements, always measure from the same point each time. For example, if you're measuring how high two different balls bounce when dropped from the same height, measure both bounces at the same point on the balls—either the top or the bottom. Do not measure at the top of one ball and the bottom of the other.

EXAMPLE

How to Measure a Leaf

1. Lay a ruler flat on top of the leaf so that the 1-centimeter mark lines up with one end. Make sure the ruler and the leaf do not move between the time you line them up and the time you take the measurement.

2. Look straight down on the ruler so that you can see exactly how the marks line up with the other end of the leaf.

3. Estimate the length by which the leaf extends beyond a marking. For example, the leaf below extends about halfway between the 4.2-centimeter and 4.3-centimeter marks, so the apparent measurement is about 4.25 centimeters.

4. Remember to subtract 1 centimeter from your apparent measurement, since you started at the 1-centimeter mark on the ruler and not at the end. The leaf is about 3.25 centimeters long (4.25 cm – 1 cm = 3.25 cm).

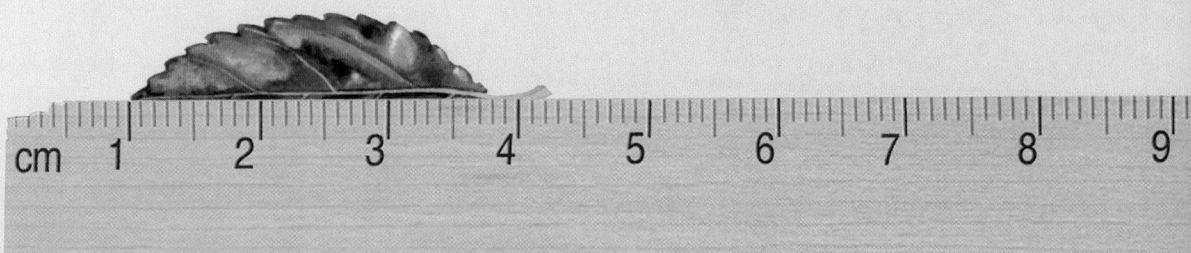

Triple-Beam Balance

This balance has a pan and three beams with sliding masses, called riders. At one end of the beams is a pointer that indicates whether the mass on the pan is equal to the masses shown on the beams.

1. Make sure the balance is zeroed before measuring the mass of an object. The balance is zeroed if the pointer is at zero when nothing is on the pan and the riders are at their zero points. Use the adjustment knob at the base of the balance to zero it.

2. Place the object to be measured on the pan.

3. Move the riders one notch at a time away from the pan. Begin with the largest rider. If moving the largest rider one notch brings the pointer below zero, begin measuring the mass of the object with the next smaller rider.

4. Change the positions of the riders until they balance the mass on the pan and the pointer is at zero. Then add the readings from the three beams to determine the mass of the object.

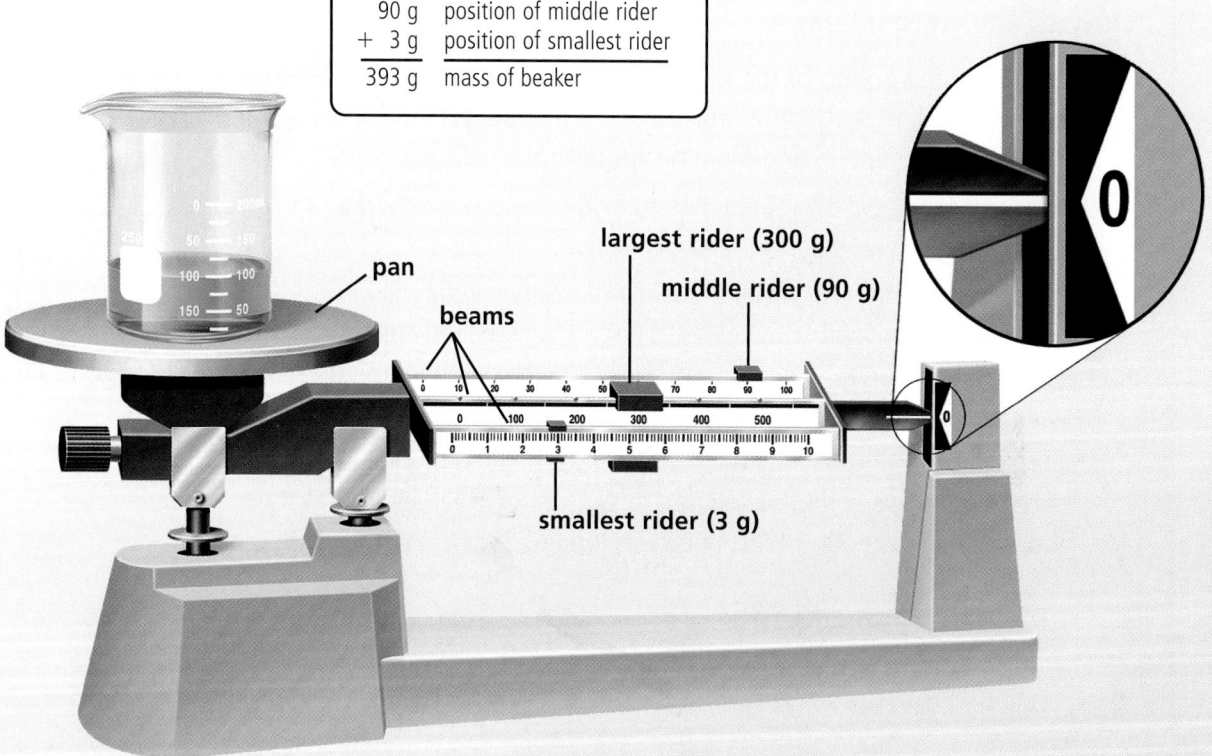

300 g	position of largest rider
90 g	position of middle rider
+ 3 g	position of smallest rider
393 g	mass of beaker

pan

beams

largest rider (300 g)

middle rider (90 g)

smallest rider (3 g)

Double-Pan Balance

This type of balance has two pans. Between the pans is a pointer that indicates whether the masses on the pans are equal.

1. Make sure the balance is zeroed before measuring the mass of an object. The balance is zeroed if the pointer is at zero when there is nothing on either of the pans. Many double-pan balances have sliding knobs that can be used to zero them.

2. Place the object to be measured on one of the pans.

3. Begin adding standard masses to the other pan. Begin with the largest standard mass. If this adds too much mass to the balance, begin measuring the mass of the object with the next smaller standard mass.

4. Add standard masses until the masses on both pans are balanced and the pointer is at zero. Then add the standard masses together to determine the mass of the object being measured.

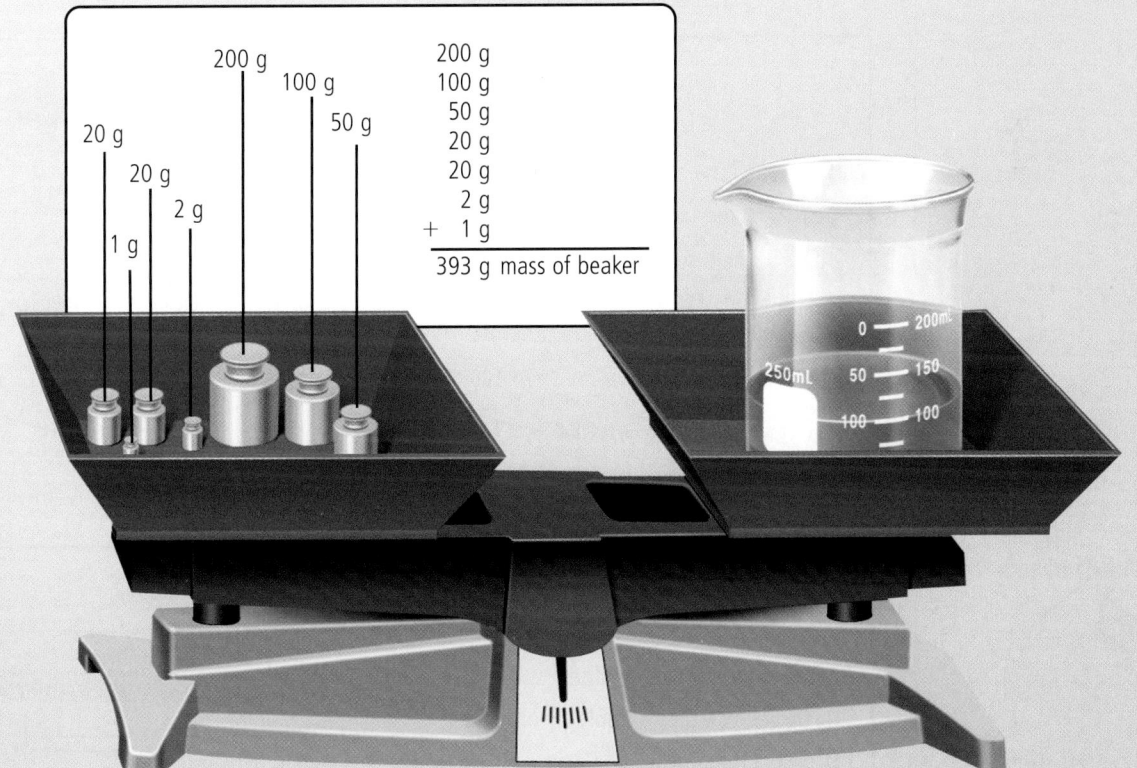

20 g
20 g
1 g
2 g
200 g
100 g
50 g

200 g	
100 g	
50 g	
20 g	
20 g	
2 g	
+ 1 g	

393 g mass of beaker

Never place chemicals or liquids directly on a pan. Instead, use the following procedure:

1. Determine the mass of an empty container, such as a beaker.

2. Pour the substance into the container, and measure the total mass of the substance and the container.

3. Subtract the mass of the empty container from the total mass to find the mass of the substance.

The Metric System and SI Units

Scientists use International System (SI) units for measurements of distance, volume, mass, and temperature. The International System is based on multiples of ten and the metric system of measurement.

Basic SI Units		
Property	**Name**	**Symbol**
length	meter	m
volume	liter	L
mass	kilogram	kg
temperature	kelvin	K

SI Prefixes		
Prefix	**Symbol**	**Multiple of 10**
kilo-	k	1000
hecto-	h	100
deca-	da	10
deci-	d	$0.1 \left(\frac{1}{10}\right)$
centi-	c	$0.01 \left(\frac{1}{100}\right)$
milli-	m	$0.001 \left(\frac{1}{1000}\right)$

Changing Metric Units

You can change from one unit to another in the metric system by multiplying or dividing by a power of 10.

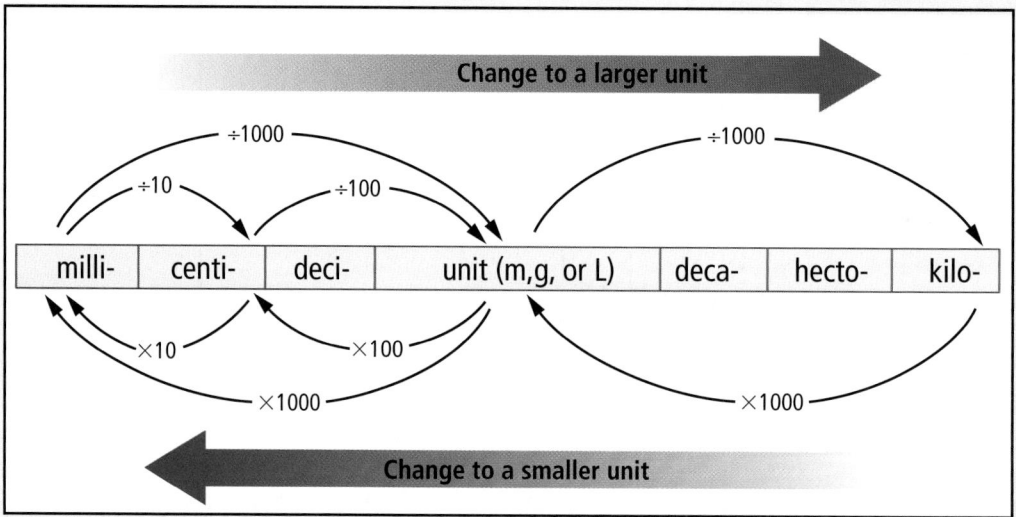

Example

Change 0.64 liters to milliliters.

(1) Decide whether to multiply or divide.

(2) Select the power of 10.

ANSWER 0.64 L = 640 mL

> Change to a smaller unit by multiplying.
> mL ← × 1000 — L
> 0.64 × 1000 = **640.**

Example

Change 23.6 grams to kilograms.

(1) Decide whether to multiply or divide.

(2) Select the power of 10.

ANSWER 23.6 g = 0.0236 kg

> Change to a larger unit by dividing.
> g — ÷ 1000 → kg
> 23.6 ÷ 1000 = **0.0236**

Temperature Conversions

Even though the kelvin is the SI base unit of temperature, the degree Celsius will be the unit you use most often in your science studies. The formulas below show the relationships between temperatures in degrees Fahrenheit (°F), degrees Celsius (°C), and kelvins (K).

$$°C = \frac{5}{9}(°F - 32)$$

$$°F = \frac{9}{5}°C + 32$$

$$K = °C + 273$$

See page R42 for help with using formulas.

Examples of Temperature Conversions

Condition	Degrees Celsius	Degrees Fahrenheit
Freezing point of water	0	32
Cool day	10	50
Mild day	20	68
Warm day	30	86
Normal body temperature	37	98.6
Very hot day	40	104
Boiling point of water	100	212

Converting Between SI and U.S. Customary Units

Use the chart below when you need to convert between SI units and U.S. customary units.

SI Unit	From SI to U.S. Customary			From U.S. Customary to SI		
Length	**When you know**	**multiply by**	**to find**	**When you know**	**multiply by**	**to find**
kilometer (km) = 1000 m	kilometers	0.62	miles	miles	1.61	kilometers
meter (m) = 100 cm	meters	3.28	feet	feet	0.3048	meters
centimeter (cm) = 10 mm	centimeters	0.39	inches	inches	2.54	centimeters
millimeter (mm) = 0.1 cm	millimeters	0.04	inches	inches	25.4	millimeters
Area	**When you know**	**multiply by**	**to find**	**When you know**	**multiply by**	**to find**
square kilometer (km²)	square kilometers	0.39	square miles	square miles	2.59	square kilometers
square meter (m²)	square meters	1.2	square yards	square yards	0.84	square meters
square centimeter (cm²)	square centimeters	0.155	square inches	square inches	6.45	square centimeters
Volume	**When you know**	**multiply by**	**to find**	**When you know**	**multiply by**	**to find**
liter (L) = 1000 mL	liters	1.06	quarts	quarts	0.95	liters
	liters	0.26	gallons	gallons	3.79	liters
	liters	4.23	cups	cups	0.24	liters
	liters	2.12	pints	pints	0.47	liters
milliliter (mL) = 0.001 L	milliliters	0.20	teaspoons	teaspoons	4.93	milliliters
	milliliters	0.07	tablespoons	tablespoons	14.79	milliliters
	milliliters	0.03	fluid ounces	fluid ounces	29.57	milliliters
Mass	**When you know**	**multiply by**	**to find**	**When you know**	**multiply by**	**to find**
kilogram (kg) = 1000 g	kilograms	2.2	pounds	pounds	0.45	kilograms
gram (g) = 1000 mg	grams	0.035	ounces	ounces	28.35	grams

Precision and Accuracy

When you do an experiment, it is important that your methods, observations, and data be both precise and accurate.

low precision

precision, but not accuracy

precision and accuracy

Precision

In science, **precision** is the exactness and consistency of measurements. For example, measurements made with a ruler that has both centimeter and millimeter markings would be more precise than measurements made with a ruler that has only centimeter markings. Another indicator of precision is the care taken to make sure that methods and observations are as exact and consistent as possible. Every time a particular experiment is done, the same procedure should be used. Precision is necessary because experiments are repeated several times and if the procedure changes, the results will change.

EXAMPLE

Suppose you are measuring temperatures over a two-week period. Your precision will be greater if you measure each temperature at the same place, at the same time of day, and with the same thermometer than if you change any of these factors from one day to the next.

Accuracy

In science, it is possible to be precise but not accurate. **Accuracy** depends on the difference between a measurement and an actual value. The smaller the difference, the more accurate the measurement.

EXAMPLE

Suppose you look at a stream and estimate that it is about 1 meter wide at a particular place. You decide to check your estimate by measuring the stream with a meter stick, and you determine that the stream is 1.32 meters wide. However, because it is hard to measure the width of a stream with a meter stick, it turns out that you didn't do a very good job. The stream is actually 1.14 meters wide. Therefore, even though your estimate was less precise than your measurement, your estimate was actually more accurate.

Making Data Tables and Graphs

Data tables and graphs are useful tools for both recording and communicating scientific data.

Making Data Tables

You can use a **data table** to organize and record the measurements that you make. Some examples of information that might be recorded in data tables are frequencies, times, and amounts.

EXAMPLE

Suppose you are investigating photosynthesis in two elodea plants. One sits in direct sunlight, and the other sits in a dimly lit room. You measure the rate of photosynthesis by counting the number of bubbles in the jar every ten minutes.

1. Title and number your data table.
2. Decide how you will organize the table into columns and rows.
3. Any units, such as seconds or degrees, should be included in column headings, not in the individual cells.

Table 1. Number of Bubbles from Elodea

Time (min)	Sunlight	Dim Light
0	0	0
10	15	5
20	25	8
30	32	7
40	41	10
50	47	9
60	42	9

> Always number and title data tables.

The data in the table above could also be organized in a different way.

Table 1. Number of Bubbles from Elodea

Light Condition	Time (min)						
	0	10	20	30	40	50	60
Sunlight	0	15	25	32	41	47	42
Dim light	0	5	8	7	10	9	9

> Put units in column heading.

Making Line Graphs

You can use a **line graph** to show a relationship between variables. Line graphs are particularly useful for showing changes in variables over time.

EXAMPLE

Suppose you are interested in graphing temperature data that you collected over the course of a day.

Table 1. Outside Temperature During the Day on March 7

	Time of Day						
	7:00 A.M.	9:00 A.M.	11:00 A.M.	1:00 P.M.	3:00 P.M.	5:00 P.M.	7:00 P.M.
Temp (°C)	8	9	11	14	12	10	6

1. Use the vertical axis of your line graph for the variable that you are measuring—temperature.

2. Choose scales for both the horizontal axis and the vertical axis of the graph. You should have two points more than you need on the vertical axis, and the horizontal axis should be long enough for all of the data points to fit.

3. Draw and label each axis.

4. Graph each value. First find the appropriate point on the scale of the horizontal axis. Imagine a line that rises vertically from that place on the scale. Then find the corresponding value on the vertical axis, and imagine a line that moves horizontally from that value. The point where these two imaginary lines intersect is where the value should be plotted.

5. Connect the points with straight lines.

Be sure to add a number and a title to your graph.

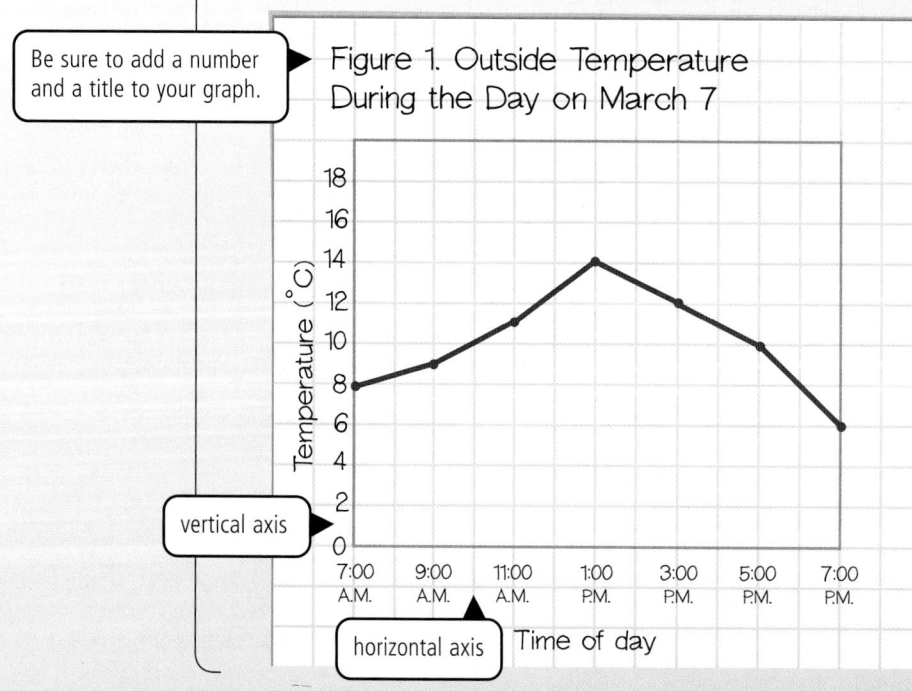

Figure 1. Outside Temperature During the Day on March 7

vertical axis

horizontal axis   Time of day

Making Circle Graphs

You can use a **circle graph,** sometimes called a pie chart, to represent data as parts of a circle. Circle graphs are used only when the data can be expressed as percentages of a whole. The entire circle shown in a circle graph is equal to 100 percent of the data.

EXAMPLE

Suppose you identified the species of each mature tree growing in a small wooded area. You organized your data in a table, but you also want to show the data in a circle graph.

1. To begin, find the total number of mature trees.

    $56 + 34 + 22 + 10 + 28 = 150$

2. To find the degree measure for each sector of the circle, write a fraction comparing the number of each tree species with the total number of trees. Then multiply the fraction by 360°.

    Oak: $\frac{56}{150} \times 360° = 134.4°$

3. Draw a circle. Use a protractor to draw the angle for each sector of the graph.

4. Color and label each sector of the graph.

5. Give the graph a number and title.

Table 1. Tree Species in Wooded Area

Species	Number of Specimens
Oak	56
Maple	34
Birch	22
Willow	10
Pine	28

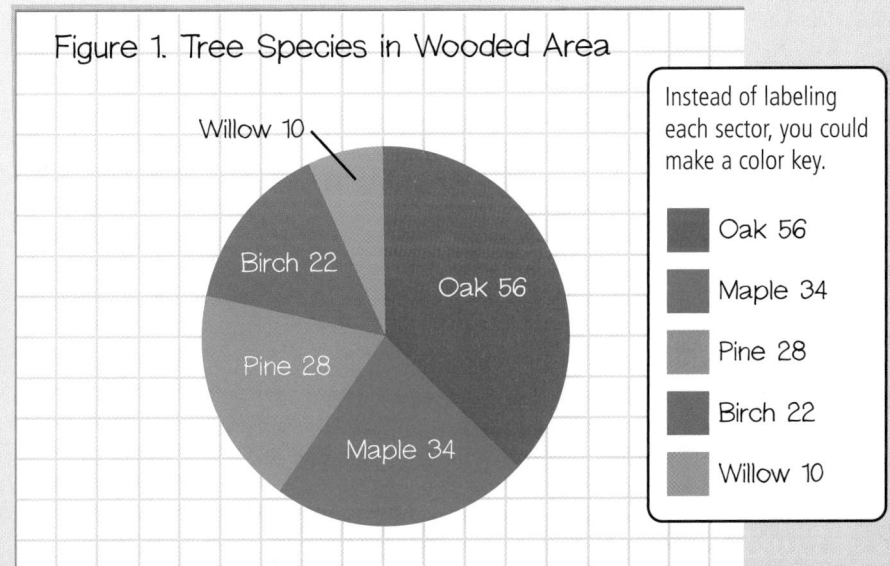

Figure 1. Tree Species in Wooded Area

Instead of labeling each sector, you could make a color key.

- Oak 56
- Maple 34
- Pine 28
- Birch 22
- Willow 10

Bar Graph

A **bar graph** is a type of graph in which the lengths of the bars are used to represent and compare data. A numerical scale is used to determine the lengths of the bars.

EXAMPLE

To determine the effect of water on seed sprouting, three cups were filled with sand, and ten seeds were planted in each. Different amounts of water were added to each cup over a three-day period.

Table 1. Effect of Water on Seed Sprouting

Daily Amount of Water (mL)	Number of Seeds That Sprouted After 3 Days in Sand
0	1
10	4
20	8

1. Choose a numerical scale. The greatest value is 8, so the end of the scale should have a value greater than 8, such as 10. Use equal increments along the scale, such as increments of 2.

2. Draw and label the axes. Mark intervals on the vertical axis according to the scale you chose.

3. Draw a bar for each data value. Use the scale to decide how long to make each bar.

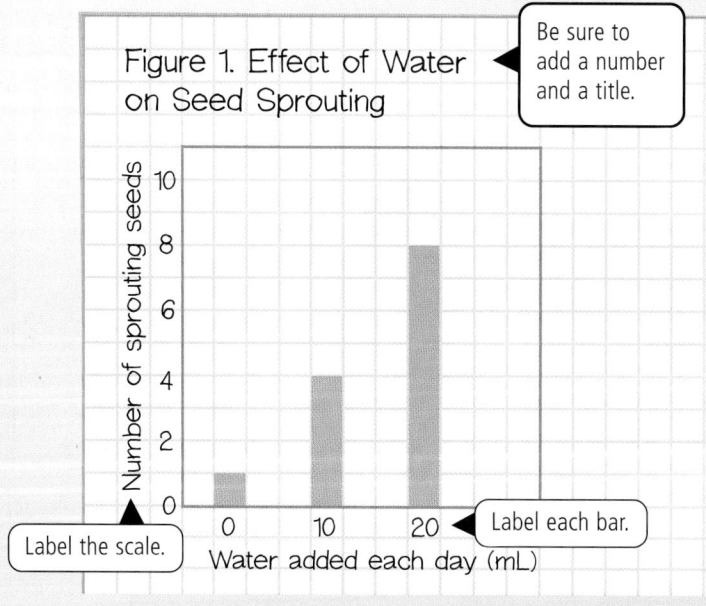

Figure 1. Effect of Water on Seed Sprouting

Be sure to add a number and a title.

Label the scale.

Label each bar.

Double Bar Graph

A **double bar graph** is a bar graph that shows two sets of data. The two bars for each measurement are drawn next to each other.

EXAMPLE

The seed-sprouting experiment was done using both sand and potting soil. The data for sand and potting soil can be plotted on one graph.

1. Draw one set of bars, using the data for sand, as shown below.

2. Draw bars for the potting-soil data next to the bars for the sand data. Shade them a different color. Add a key.

Table 2. Effect of Water and Soil on Seed Sprouting

Daily Amount of Water (mL)	Number of Seeds That Sprouted After 3 Days in Sand	Number of Seeds That Sprouted After 3 Days in Potting Soil
0	1	2
10	4	5
20	8	9

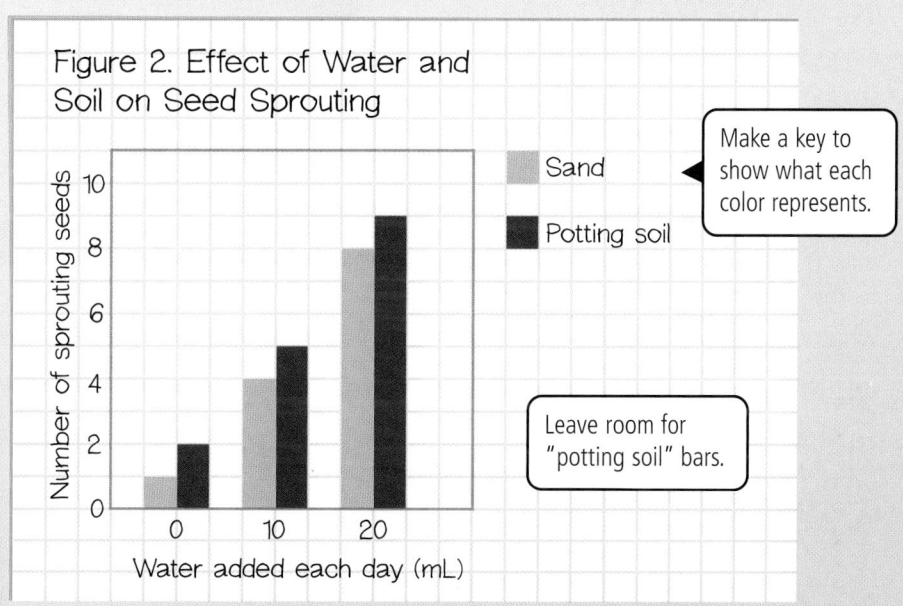

Figure 2. Effect of Water and Soil on Seed Sprouting

Make a key to show what each color represents.

Leave room for "potting soil" bars.

Designing an Experiment

Use this section when designing or conducting an experiment.

Determining a Purpose

You can find a purpose for an experiment by doing research, by examining the results of a previous experiment, or by observing the world around you. An **experiment** is an organized procedure to study something under controlled conditions.

> Don't forget to learn as much as possible about your topic before you begin.

1. Write the purpose of your experiment as a question or problem that you want to investigate.

2. Write down research questions and begin searching for information that will help you design an experiment. Consult the library, the Internet, and other people as you conduct your research.

EXAMPLE

Middle school students observed an odor near the lake by their school. They also noticed that the water on the side of the lake near the school was greener than the water on the other side of the lake. The students did some research to learn more about their observations. They discovered that the odor and green color in the lake came from algae. They also discovered that a new fertilizer was being used on a field nearby. The students inferred that the use of the fertilizer might be related to the presence of the algae and designed a controlled experiment to find out whether they were right.

Problem

How does fertilizer affect the presence of algae in a lake?

Research Questions

- Have other experiments been done on this problem? If so, what did those experiments show?
- What kind of fertilizer is used on the field? How much?
- How do algae grow?
- How do people measure algae?
- Can fertilizer and algae be used safely in a lab? How?

> **Research**
> As you research, you may find a topic that is more interesting to you than your original topic, or learn that a procedure you wanted to use is not practical or safe. It is OK to change your purpose as you research.

Writing a Hypothesis

A **hypothesis** is a tentative explanation for an observation or scientific problem that can be tested by further investigation. You can write your hypothesis in the form of an "If . . . , then . . . , because . . ." statement.

Hypothesis

If the amount of fertilizer in lake water is increased, then the amount of algae will also increase, because fertilizers provide nutrients that algae need to grow.

Hypotheses
For help with hypotheses, refer to page R3.

Determining Materials

Make a list of all the materials you will need to do your experiment. Be specific, especially if someone else is helping you obtain the materials. Try to think of everything you will need.

Materials

- 1 large jar or container
- 4 identical smaller containers
- rubber gloves that also cover the arms
- sample of fertilizer-and-water solution
- eyedropper
- clear plastic wrap
- scissors
- masking tape
- marker
- ruler

Determining Variables and Constants

EXPERIMENTAL GROUP AND CONTROL GROUP

An experiment to determine how two factors are related always has two groups—a control group and an experimental group.

1. Design an experimental group. Include as many trials as possible in the experimental group in order to obtain reliable results.

2. Design a control group that is the same as the experimental group in every way possible, except for the factor you wish to test.

> **Experimental Group:** two containers of lake water with one drop of fertilizer solution added to each
>
> **Control Group:** two containers of lake water with no fertilizer solution added

> Go back to your materials list and make sure you have enough items listed to cover both your experimental group and your control group.

VARIABLES AND CONSTANTS

Identify the variables and constants in your experiment. In a controlled experiment, a **variable** is any factor that can change. **Constants** are all of the factors that are the same in both the experimental group and the control group.

1. Read your hypothesis. The **independent variable** is the factor that you wish to test and that is manipulated or changed so that it can be tested. The independent variable is expressed in your hypothesis after the word *if*. Identify the independent variable in your laboratory report.

2. The **dependent variable** is the factor that you measure to gather results. It is expressed in your hypothesis after the word *then*. Identify the dependent variable in your laboratory report.

> **Hypothesis**
> If the amount of fertilizer in lake water is increased, then the amount of algae will also increase, because fertilizers provide nutrients that algae need to grow.

Table 1. Variables and Constants in Algae Experiment

Independent Variable	Dependent Variable	Constants
Amount of fertilizer in lake water	Amount of algae that grow	• Where the lake water is obtained • Type of container used • Light and temperature conditions where water will be stored

> Set up your experiment so that you will test only one variable.

MEASURING THE DEPENDENT VARIABLE

Before starting your experiment, you need to define how you will measure the dependent variable. An **operational definition** is a description of the one particular way in which you will measure the dependent variable.

Your operational definition is important for several reasons. First, in any experiment there are several ways in which a dependent variable can be measured. Second, the procedure of the experiment depends on how you decide to measure the dependent variable. Third, your operational definition makes it possible for other people to evaluate and build on your experiment.

EXAMPLE 1

An operational definition of a dependent variable can be qualitative. That is, your measurement of the dependent variable can simply be an observation of whether a change occurs as a result of a change in the independent variable. This type of operational definition can be thought of as a "yes or no" measurement.

Table 2. Qualitative Operational Definition of Algae Growth

Independent Variable	Dependent Variable	Operational Definition
Amount of fertilizer in lake water	Amount of algae that grow	Algae grow in lake water

A qualitative measurement of a dependent variable is often easy to make and record. However, this type of information does not provide a great deal of detail in your experimental results.

EXAMPLE 2

An operational definition of a dependent variable can be quantitative. That is, your measurement of the dependent variable can be a number that shows how much change occurs as a result of a change in the independent variable.

Table 3. Quantitative Operational Definition of Algae Growth

Independent Variable	Dependent Variable	Operational Definition
Amount of fertilizer in lake water	Amount of algae that grow	Diameter of largest algal growth (in mm)

A quantitative measurement of a dependent variable can be more difficult to make and analyze than a qualitative measurement. However, this type of data provides much more information about your experiment and is often more useful.

Writing a Procedure

Write each step of your procedure. Start each step with a verb, or action word, and keep the steps short. Your procedure should be clear enough for someone else to use as instructions for repeating your experiment.

> If necessary, go back to your materials list and add any materials that you left out.

Procedure

1. Put on your gloves. Use the large container to obtain a sample of lake water.

2. Divide the sample of lake water equally among the four smaller containers.

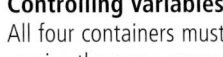

> **Controlling Variables**
> The same amount of fertilizer solution must be added to two of the four containers.

3. Use the eyedropper to add one drop of fertilizer solution to two of the containers.

4. Use the masking tape and the marker to label the containers with your initials, the date, and the identifiers "Jar 1 with Fertilizer," "Jar 2 with Fertilizer," "Jar 1 without Fertilizer," and "Jar 2 without Fertilizer."

5. Cover the containers with clear plastic wrap. Use the scissors to punch ten holes in each of the covers.

> **Controlling Variables**
> All four containers must receive the same amount of light.

6. Place all four containers on a window ledge. Make sure that they all receive the same amount of light.

7. Observe the containers every day for one week.

8. Use the ruler to measure the diameter of the largest clump of algae in each container, and record your measurements daily.

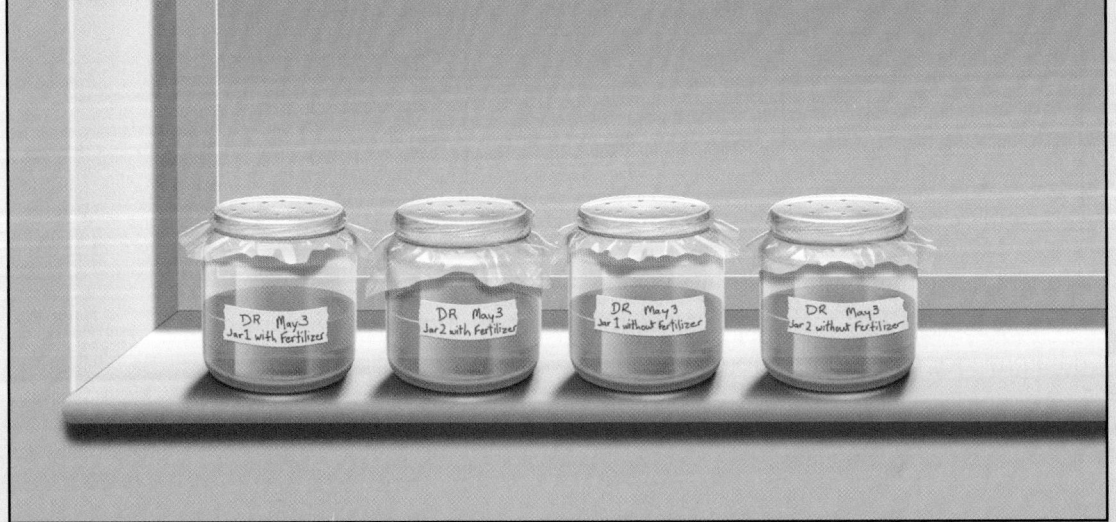

LAB HANDBOOK

Recording Observations

Once you have obtained all of your materials and your procedure has been approved, you can begin making experimental observations. Gather both quantitative and qualitative data. If something goes wrong during your procedure, make sure you record that too.

> **Observations**
> For help with making qualitative and quantitative observations, refer to page R2.

> For more examples of data tables, see page R23.

Table 4. Fertilizer and Algae Growth

Date and Time	Experimental Group		Control Group		Observations
	Jar 1 with Fertilizer (diameter of algae in mm)	Jar 2 with Fertilizer (diameter of algae in mm)	Jar 1 without Fertilizer (diameter of algae in mm)	Jar 2 without Fertilizer (diameter of algae in mm)	
5/3 4:00 P.M.	0	0	0	0	condensation in all containers
5/4 4:00 P.M.	0	3	0	0	tiny green blobs in jar 2 with fertilizer
5/5 4:15 P.M.	4	5	0	3	green blobs in jars 1 and 2 with fertilizer and jar 2 without fertilizer
5/6 4:00 P.M.	5	6	0	4	water light green in jar 2 with fertilizer
5/7 4:00 P.M.	8	10	0	6	water light green in jars 1 and 2 with fertilizer and in jar 2 without fertilizer
5/8 3:30 P.M.	10	18	0	6	cover off jar 2 with fertilizer
5/9 3:30 P.M.	14	23	0	8	drew sketches of each container

> Notice that on the sixth day, the observer found that the cover was off one of the containers. It is important to record observations of unintended factors because they might affect the results of the experiment.

> Use technology, such as a microscope, to help you make observations when possible.

Drawings of Samples Viewed Under Microscope on 5/9 at 100x

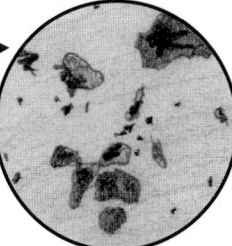
Jar 1 with Fertilizer

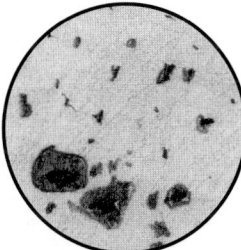
Jar 2 with Fertilizer

Jar 1 without Fertilizer

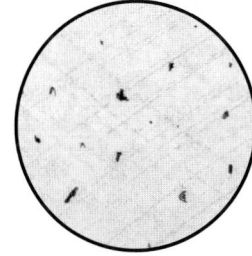
Jar 2 without Fertilizer

Summarizing Results

To summarize your data, look at all of your observations together. Look for meaningful ways to present your observations. For example, you might average your data or make a graph to look for patterns. When possible, use spread-sheet software to help you analyze and present your data. The two graphs below show the same data.

EXAMPLE 1

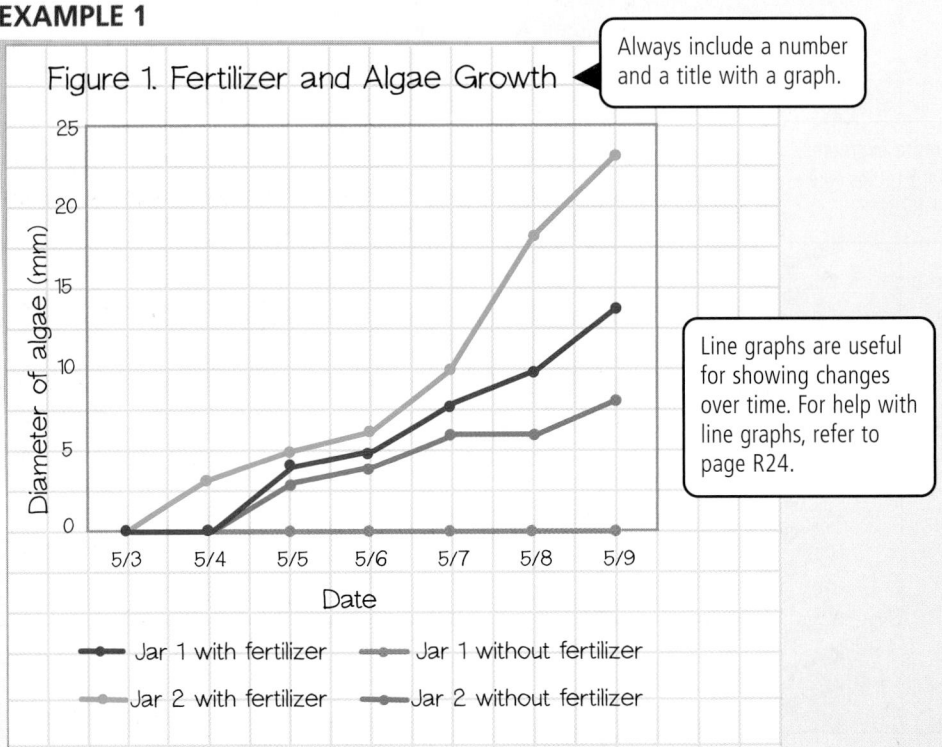

Always include a number and a title with a graph.

Line graphs are useful for showing changes over time. For help with line graphs, refer to page R24.

EXAMPLE 2

Bar graphs are useful for comparing different data sets. This bar graph has four bars for each day. Another way to present the data would be to calculate averages for the tests and the controls, and to show one test bar and one control bar for each day.

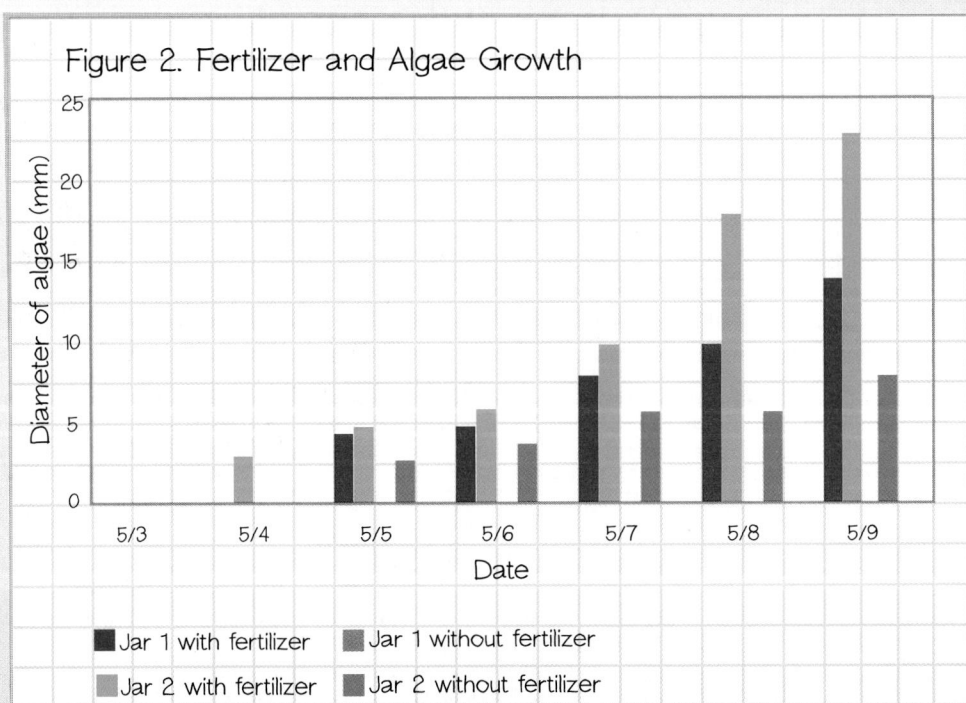

LAB HANDBOOK

Drawing Conclusions

RESULTS AND INFERENCES

To draw conclusions from your experiment, first write your results. Then compare your results with your hypothesis. Do your results support your hypothesis? Be careful not to make inferences about factors that you did not test.

> For help with making inferences, see page R4.

Results and Inferences

The results of my experiment show that more algae grew in lake water to which fertilizer had been added than in lake water to which no fertilizer had been added. My hypothesis was supported. I infer that it is possible that the growth of algae in the lake was caused by the fertilizer used on the field.

> Notice that you cannot conclude from this experiment that the presence of algae in the lake was due only to the fertilizer.

QUESTIONS FOR FURTHER RESEARCH

Write a list of questions for further research and investigation. Your ideas may lead you to new experiments and discoveries.

Questions for Further Research

- What is the connection between the amount of fertilizer and algae growth?
- How do different brands of fertilizer affect algae growth?
- How would algae growth in the lake be affected if no fertilizer were used on the field?
- How do algae affect the lake and the other life in and around it?
- How does fertilizer affect the lake and the life in and around it?
- If fertilizer is getting into the lake, how is it getting there?

Math Handbook

Describing a Set of Data

Means, medians, modes, and ranges are important math tools for describing data sets such as the following widths of fossilized clamshells.

13 mm   25 mm   14 mm   21 mm   16 mm   23 mm   14 mm

Mean

The **mean** of a data set is the sum of the values divided by the number of values.

> **Example**
>
> To find the mean of the clamshell data, add the values and then divide the sum by the number of values.
>
> $$\frac{13 \text{ mm} + 25 \text{ mm} + 14 \text{ mm} + 21 \text{ mm} + 16 \text{ mm} + 23 \text{ mm} + 14 \text{ mm}}{7} = \frac{126 \text{ mm}}{7} = 18 \text{ mm}$$
>
> **ANSWER** The mean is 18 mm.

Median

The **median** of a data set is the middle value when the values are written in numerical order. If a data set has an even number of values, the median is the mean of the two middle values.

> **Example**
>
> To find the median of the clamshell data, arrange the values in order from least to greatest. The median is the middle value.
>
> 13 mm   14 mm   14 mm   16 mm   21 mm   23 mm   25 mm
>
> **ANSWER** The median is 16 mm.

Mode

The **mode** of a data set is the value that occurs most often.

> ### Example
>
> To find the mode of the clamshell data, arrange the values in order from least to greatest and determine the value that occurs most often.
>
> 13 mm   14 mm   14 mm   16 mm   21 mm   23 mm   25 mm
>
> **ANSWER** The mode is 14 mm.

A data set can have more than one mode or no mode. For example, the following data set has modes of 2 mm and 4 mm:

2 mm   2 mm   3 mm   4 mm   4 mm

The data set below has no mode, because no value occurs more often than any other.

2 mm   3 mm   4 mm   5 mm

Range

The **range** of a data set is the difference between the greatest value and the least value.

> ### Example
>
> To find the range of the clamshell data, arrange the values in order from least to greatest.
>
> 13 mm   14 mm   14 mm   16 mm   21 mm   23 mm   25 mm
>
> Subtract the least value from the greatest value.
>
> 13 mm is the least value.
> 25 mm is the greatest value.
>
> 25 mm − 13 mm = 12 mm
>
> **ANSWER** The range is 12 mm.

Using Ratios, Rates, and Proportions

You can use ratios and rates to compare values in data sets. You can use proportions to find unknown values.

Ratios

A **ratio** uses division to compare two values. The ratio of a value a to a nonzero value b can be written as $\frac{a}{b}$.

Example

The height of one plant is 8 centimeters. The height of another plant is 6 centimeters. To find the ratio of the height of the first plant to the height of the second plant, write a fraction and simplify it.

$$\frac{8 \text{ cm}}{6 \text{ cm}} = \frac{4 \times \overset{1}{\cancel{2}}}{3 \times \underset{1}{\cancel{2}}} = \frac{4}{3}$$

ANSWER The ratio of the plant heights is $\frac{4}{3}$.

You can also write the ratio $\frac{a}{b}$ as "a to b" or as $a : b$. For example, you can write the ratio of the plant heights as "4 to 3" or as $4 : 3$.

Rates

A **rate** is a ratio of two values expressed in different units. A unit rate is a rate with a denominator of 1 unit.

Example

A plant grew 6 centimeters in 2 days. The plant's rate of growth was $\frac{6 \text{ cm}}{2 \text{ days}}$. To describe the plant's growth in centimeters per day, write a unit rate.

Divide numerator and denominator by 2: $\quad \dfrac{6 \text{ cm}}{2 \text{ days}} = \dfrac{6 \text{ cm} \div 2}{2 \text{ days} \div 2}$

> You divide 2 days by 2 to get 1 day, so divide 6 cm by 2 also.

Simplify: $\quad = \dfrac{3 \text{ cm}}{1 \text{ day}}$

ANSWER The plant's rate of growth is 3 centimeters per day.

Proportions

A **proportion** is an equation stating that two ratios are equivalent. To solve for an unknown value in a proportion, you can use cross products.

Example

If a plant grew 6 centimeters in 2 days, how many centimeters would it grow in 3 days (if its rate of growth is constant)?

$$\text{Write a proportion:} \quad \frac{6 \text{ cm}}{2 \text{ days}} = \frac{x}{3 \text{ days}}$$

$$\text{Set cross products:} \quad 6 \text{ cm} \cdot 3 = 2x$$

$$\text{Multiply 6 and 3:} \quad 18 \text{ cm} = 2x$$

$$\text{Divide each side by 2:} \quad \frac{18 \text{ cm}}{2} = \frac{2x}{2}$$

$$\text{Simplify:} \quad 9 \text{ cm} = x$$

ANSWER The plant would grow 9 centimeters in 3 days.

Using Decimals, Fractions, and Percents

Decimals, fractions, and percentages are all ways of recording and representing data.

Decimals

A **decimal** is a number that is written in the base-ten place value system, in which a decimal point separates the ones and tenths digits. The values of each place is ten times that of the place to its right.

Example

A caterpillar traveled from point A to point C along the path shown.

A   **36.9 cm**   **B**   **52.4 cm**   C

ADDING DECIMALS To find the total distance traveled by the caterpillar, add the distance from A to B and the distance from B to C. Begin by lining up the decimal points. Then add the figures as you would whole numbers and bring down the decimal point.

```
   36.9 cm
+ 52.4 cm
   89.3 cm
```

ANSWER The caterpillar traveled a total distance of 89.3 centimeters.

Example continued

SUBTRACTING DECIMALS To find how much farther the caterpillar traveled on the second leg of the journey, subtract the distance from A to B from the distance from B to C.

$$
\begin{array}{r}
52.4 \text{ cm} \\
- \ 36.9 \text{ cm} \\
\hline
15.5 \text{ cm}
\end{array}
$$

ANSWER The caterpillar traveled 15.5 centimeters farther on the second leg of the journey.

Example

A caterpillar is traveling from point D to point F along the path shown. The caterpillar travels at a speed of 9.6 centimeters per minute.

D   E   33.6 cm   F

MULTIPLYING DECIMALS You can multiply decimals as you would whole numbers. The number of decimal places in the product is equal to the sum of the number of decimal places in the factors.

For instance, suppose it takes the caterpillar 1.5 minutes to go from D to E. To find the distance from D to E, multiply the caterpillar's speed by the time it took.

> Align as shown.

$$
\begin{array}{rl}
9.6 & \quad 1 \quad \text{decimal place} \\
\times \ 1.5 & \quad + \ 1 \quad \text{decimal place} \\
\hline
480 & \\
96 \quad & \\
\hline
14.40 & \quad 2 \quad \text{decimal places}
\end{array}
$$

ANSWER The distance from D to E is 14.4 centimeters.

DIVIDING DECIMALS When you divide by a decimal, move the decimal points the same number of places in the divisor and the dividend to make the divisor a whole number.

For instance, to find the time it will take the caterpillar to travel from E to F, divide the distance from E to F by the caterpillar's speed.

$$9.6\overline{)33.6}$$

> Move each decimal point one place to the right.

$$
\begin{array}{r}
3.5 \\
96\overline{)336.} \\
\underline{288} \\
480 \\
\underline{480} \\
0
\end{array}
$$

> Line up decimal points.

ANSWER The caterpillar will travel from E to F in 3.5 minutes.

Fractions

A **fraction** is a number in the form $\frac{a}{b}$, where b is not equal to 0. A fraction is in **simplest form** if its numerator and denominator have a greatest common factor (GCF) of 1. To simplify a fraction, divide its numerator and denominator by their GCF.

Example

A caterpillar is 40 millimeters long. The head of the caterpillar is 6 millimeters long. To compare the length of the caterpillar's head with the caterpillar's total length, you can write and simplify a fraction that expresses the ratio of the two lengths.

Write the ratio of the two lengths: $\dfrac{\text{Length of head}}{\text{Total length}} = \dfrac{6 \text{ mm}}{40 \text{ mm}}$

Write numerator and denominator as products of numbers and the GCF: $= \dfrac{3 \times 2}{20 \times 2}$

Divide numerator and denominator by the GCF: $= \dfrac{3 \times \cancel{2}^{1}}{20 \times \cancel{2}_{1}}$

Simplify: $= \dfrac{3}{20}$

ANSWER In simplest form, the ratio of the lengths is $\frac{3}{20}$.

Percents

A **percent** is a ratio that compares a number to 100. The word *percent* means "per hundred" or "out of 100." The symbol for *percent* is %.

For instance, suppose 43 out of 100 caterpillars are female. You can represent this ratio as a percent, a decimal, or a fraction.

Percent	Decimal	Fraction
43%	0.43	$\frac{43}{100}$

Example

In the preceding example, the ratio of the length of the caterpillar's head to the caterpillar's total length is $\frac{3}{20}$. To write this ratio as a percent, write an equivalent fraction that has a denominator of 100.

Multiply numerator and denominator by 5: $\dfrac{3}{20} = \dfrac{3 \times 5}{20 \times 5}$

$= \dfrac{15}{100}$

Write as a percent: $= 15\%$

ANSWER The caterpillar's head represents 15 percent of its total length.

Using Formulas

A **formula** is an equation that shows the general relationship between two or more quantities.

The term *variable* is also used in science to refer to a factor that can change during an experiment.

In science, a formula often has a word form and a symbolic form. The formula below expresses Ohm's law.

Word Form

$$\text{Current} = \frac{\text{voltage}}{\text{resistance}}$$

Symbolic Form

$$I = \frac{V}{R}$$

In this formula, *I*, *V*, and *R* are variables. A mathematical **variable** is a symbol or letter that is used to represent one or more numbers.

Example

Suppose that you measure a voltage of 1.5 volts and a resistance of 15 ohms. You can use the formula for Ohm's law to find the current in amperes.

Write the formula for Ohm's law: $I = \dfrac{V}{R}$

Substitute 1.5 volts for V and 15 ohms for R: $I = \dfrac{1.5 \text{ volts}}{15 \text{ ohms}}$

Simplify: $I = 0.1$ amp

ANSWER The current is 0.1 ampere.

If you know the values of all variables but one in a formula, you can solve for the value of the unknown variable. For instance, Ohm's law can be used to find a voltage if you know the current and the resistance.

Example

Suppose that you know that a current is 0.2 amperes and the resistance is 18 ohms. Use the formula for Ohm's law to find the voltage in volts.

Write the formula for Ohm's law: $I = \dfrac{V}{R}$

Substitute 0.2 amp for I and 18 ohms for R: $0.2 \text{ amp} = \dfrac{V}{18 \text{ ohms}}$

Multiply both sides by 18 ohms: $0.2 \text{ amp} \cdot 18 \text{ ohms} = V$

Simplify: $3.6 \text{ volts} = V$

ANSWER The voltage is 3.6 volts.

Finding Areas

The area of a figure is the amount of surface the figure covers.

Area is measured in square units, such as square meters (m^2) or square centimeters (cm^2). Formulas for the areas of three common geometric figures are shown below.

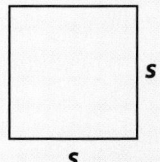

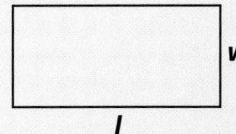

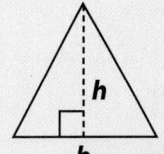

Area = (side length)^2
$A = s^2$

Area = length × width
$A = lw$

Area = $\frac{1}{2}$ × base × height
$A = \frac{1}{2} bh$

Example

Each face of a halite crystal is a square like the one shown. You can find the area of the square by using the steps below.

3 mm

3 mm

Write the formula for the area of a square:	$A = s^2$
Substitute 3 mm for s:	$= (3 \text{ mm})^2$
Simplify:	$= 9 \text{ mm}^2$

ANSWER The area of the square is 9 square millimeters.

Finding Volumes

The volume of a solid is the amount of space contained by the solid.

Volume is measured in cubic units, such as cubic meters (m^3) or cubic centimeters (cm^3). The volume of a rectangular prism is given by the formula shown below.

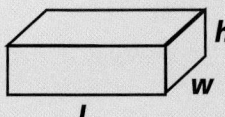

Volume = length × width × height
$V = lwh$

Example

A topaz crystal is a rectangular prism like the one shown. You can find the volume of the prism by using the steps below.

10 mm
12 mm
20 mm

Write the formula for the volume of a rectangular prism:	$V = lwh$
Substitute dimensions:	$= 20 \text{ mm} \times 12 \text{ mm} \times 10 \text{ mm}$
Simplify:	$= 2400 \text{ mm}^3$

ANSWER The volume of the rectangular prism is 2400 cubic millimeters.

Using Significant Figures

The **significant figures** in a decimal are the digits that are warranted by the accuracy of a measuring device.

When you perform a calculation with measurements, the number of significant figures to include in the result depends in part on the number of significant figures in the measurements. When you multiply or divide measurements, your answer should have only as many significant figures as the measurement with the fewest significant figures.

Example

Using a balance and a graduated cylinder filled with water, you determined that a marble has a mass of 8.0 grams and a volume of 3.5 cubic centimeters. To calculate the density of the marble, divide the mass by the volume.

Write the formula for density: $\text{Density} = \dfrac{\text{mass}}{\text{Volume}}$

Substitute measurements: $= \dfrac{8.0 \text{ g}}{3.5 \text{ cm}^3}$

Use a calculator to divide: $\approx 2.285714286 \text{ g/cm}^3$

ANSWER Because the mass and the volume have two significant figures each, give the density to two significant figures. The marble has a density of 2.3 grams per cubic centimeter.

Using Scientific Notation

Scientific notation is a shorthand way to write very large or very small numbers. For example, 73,500,000,000,000,000,000,000 kg is the mass of the Moon. In scientific notation, it is 7.35×10^{22} kg.

Example

You can convert from standard form to scientific notation.

Standard Form	Scientific Notation
720,000	7.2×10^5
5 decimal places left	Exponent is 5.
0.000291	2.91×10^{-4}
4 decimal places right	Exponent is −4.

You can convert from scientific notation to standard form.

Scientific Notation	Standard Form
4.63×10^7	46,300,000
Exponent is 7.	7 decimal places right
1.08×10^{-6}	0.00000108
Exponent is −6.	6 decimal places left

Note-Taking Handbook

Note-Taking Strategies

Taking notes as you read helps you understand the information. The notes you take can also be used as a study guide for later review. This handbook presents several ways to organize your notes.

Content Frame

1. Make a chart in which each column represents a category.
2. Give each column a heading.
3. Write details under the headings.

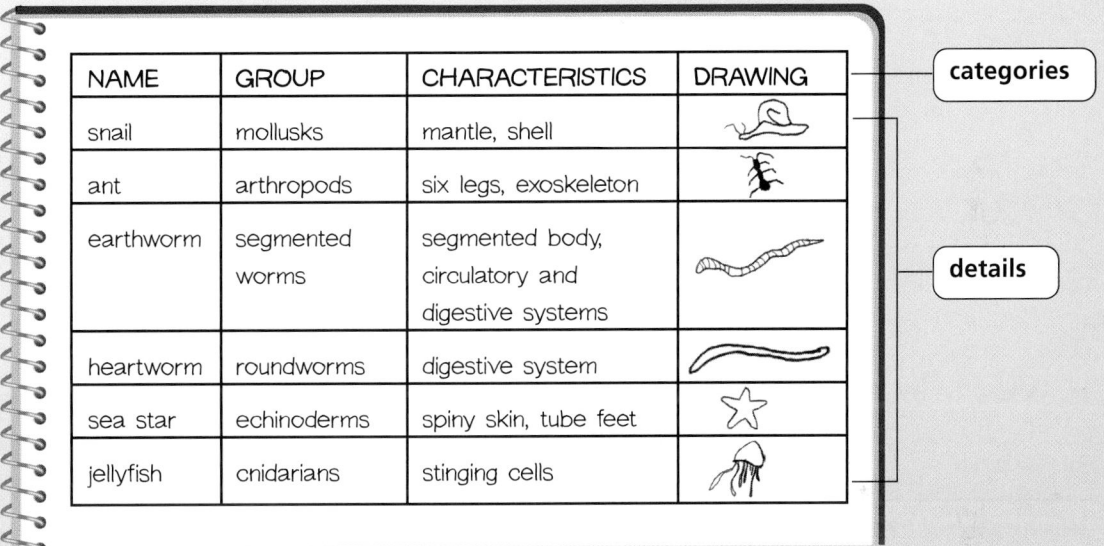

NAME	GROUP	CHARACTERISTICS	DRAWING
snail	mollusks	mantle, shell	
ant	arthropods	six legs, exoskeleton	
earthworm	segmented worms	segmented body, circulatory and digestive systems	
heartworm	roundworms	digestive system	
sea star	echinoderms	spiny skin, tube feet	
jellyfish	cnidarians	stinging cells	

categories

details

Combination Notes

1. For each new idea or concept, write an informal outline of the information.
2. Make a sketch to illustrate the concept, and label it.

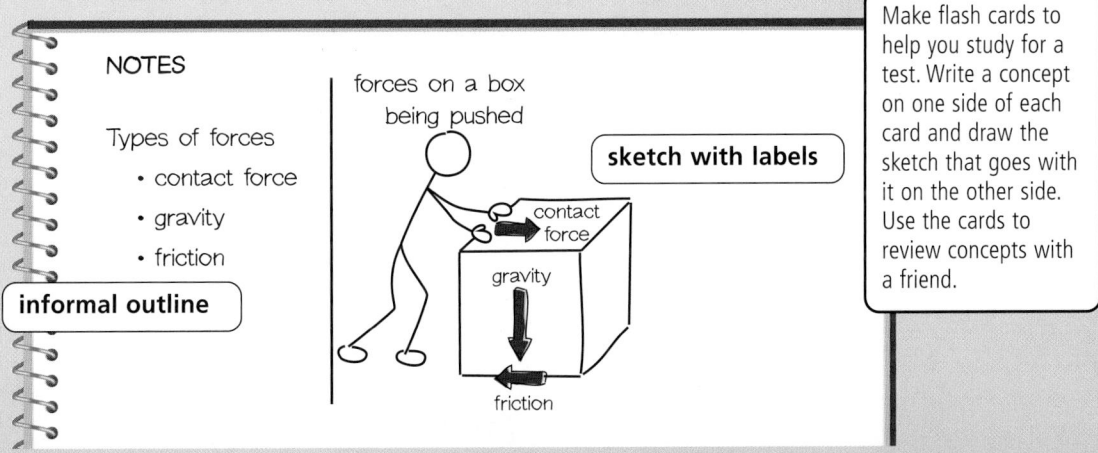

NOTES

Types of forces
- contact force
- gravity
- friction

informal outline

forces on a box being pushed

sketch with labels

contact force

gravity

friction

> Make flash cards to help you study for a test. Write a concept on one side of each card and draw the sketch that goes with it on the other side. Use the cards to review concepts with a friend.

Main Idea and Detail Notes

1. In the left-hand column of a two-column chart, list main ideas. The blue headings express main ideas throughout this textbook.

2. In the right-hand column, write details that expand on each main idea.

You can shorten the headings in your chart. Be sure to use the most important words.

When studying for tests, cover up the detail notes column with a sheet of paper. Then use each main idea to form a question—such as "How does latitude affect climate?" Answer the question, and then uncover the detail notes column to check your answer.

MAIN IDEAS	DETAIL NOTES
1. Latitude affects climate.

main idea 1 | 1. Places close to the equator are usually warmer than places close to the poles.

1. Latitude has the same effect in both hemispheres. → details about main idea 1 |
| 2. Altitude affects climate.

main idea 2 | 2. Temperature decreases with altitude.

2. Altitude can overcome the effect of latitude on temperature. → details about main idea 2 |

Main Idea Web

1. Write a main idea in a box.

2. Add boxes around it with related vocabulary terms and important details.

You can find definitions near highlighted terms.

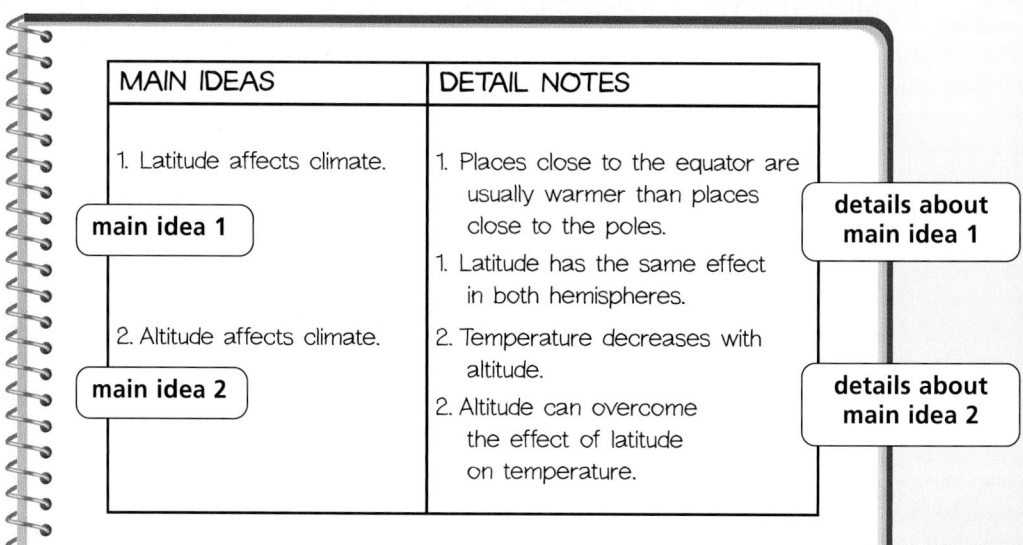

definition of *work*
Work is the use of force to move an object.

formula
Work = force · distance

main idea
Force is necessary to do work.

The joule is the unit used to measure work.
definition of *joule*

Work depends on the size of a force.
important detail

Mind Map

1. Write a main idea in the center.
2. Add details that relate to one another and to the main idea.

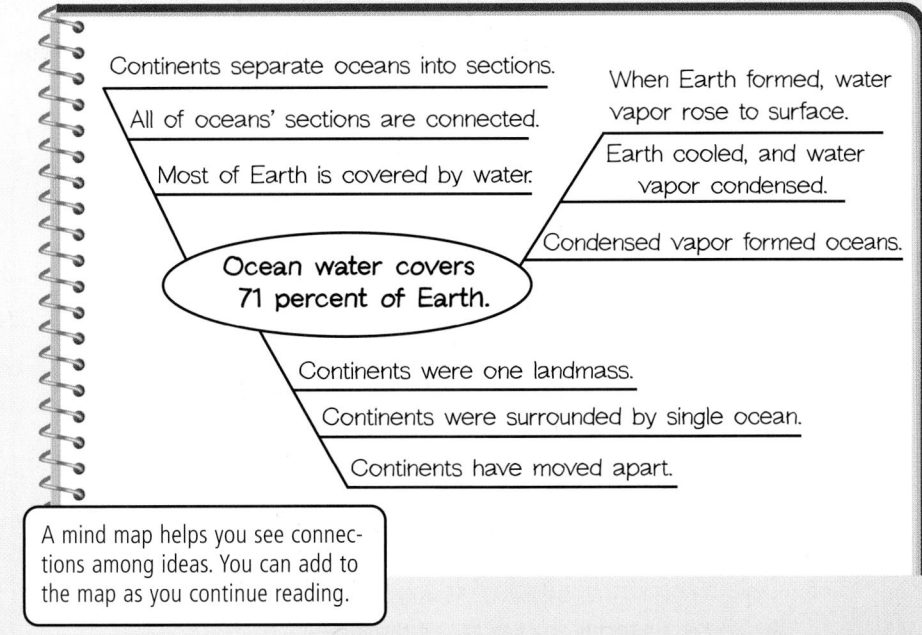

Continents separate oceans into sections.

All of oceans' sections are connected.

Most of Earth is covered by water.

When Earth formed, water vapor rose to surface.

Earth cooled, and water vapor condensed.

Condensed vapor formed oceans.

Ocean water covers 71 percent of Earth.

Continents were one landmass.

Continents were surrounded by single ocean.

Continents have moved apart.

A mind map helps you see connections among ideas. You can add to the map as you continue reading.

Supporting Main Ideas

1. Write a main idea in a box.
2. Add boxes underneath with information—such as reasons, explanations, and examples—that supports the main idea.

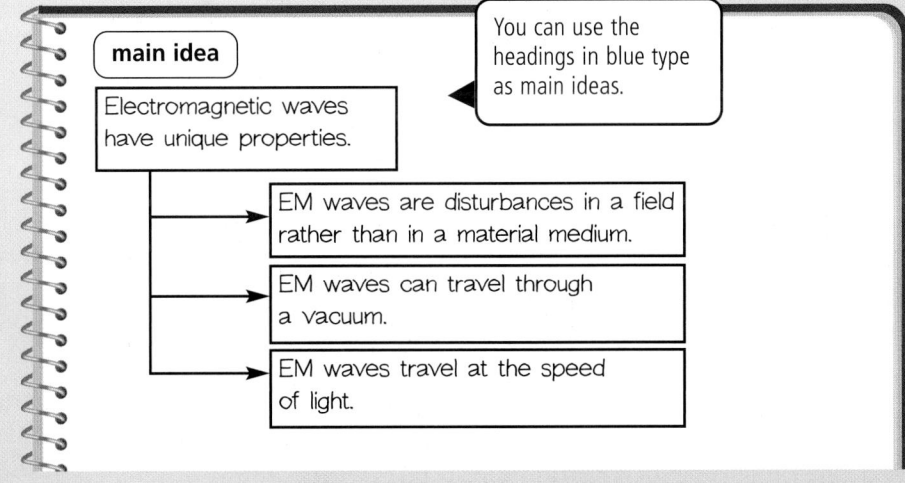

main idea

Electromagnetic waves have unique properties.

You can use the headings in blue type as main ideas.

EM waves are disturbances in a field rather than in a material medium.

EM waves can travel through a vacuum.

EM waves travel at the speed of light.

Outline

1. Copy the chapter title and headings from the book in the form of an outline.

2. Add notes that summarize in your own words what you read.

Cell Processes

1st key idea

I. Cells capture and release energy.

1st subpoint of I

A. All cells need energy.

B. Some cells capture light energy.

2nd subpoint of I

1st detail about B

   1. Process of photosynthesis

2nd detail about B

   2. Chloroplasts (site of photosynthesis)

   3. Carbon dioxide and water as raw materials

   4. Glucose and oxygen as products

C. All cells release energy.

   1. Process of cellular respiration

   2. Fermentation of sugar to carbon dioxide

   3. Bacteria that carry out fermentation

II. Cells transport materials through membranes.

A. Some materials move by diffusion.

   1. Particle movement from higher to lower concentrations

   2. Movement of water through membrane (osmosis)

B. Some transport requires energy.

   1. Active transport

   2. Examples of active transport

Correct Outline Form

Include a title.

Arrange key ideas, subpoints, and details as shown.

Indent the divisions of the outline as shown.

Use the same grammatical form for items of the same rank. For example, if A is a sentence, B must also be a sentence.

You must have at least two main ideas or subpoints. That is, every A must be followed by a B, and every 1 must be followed by a 2.

Concept Map

1. Write an important concept in a large oval.
2. Add details related to the concept in smaller ovals.
3. Write linking words on arrows that connect the ovals.

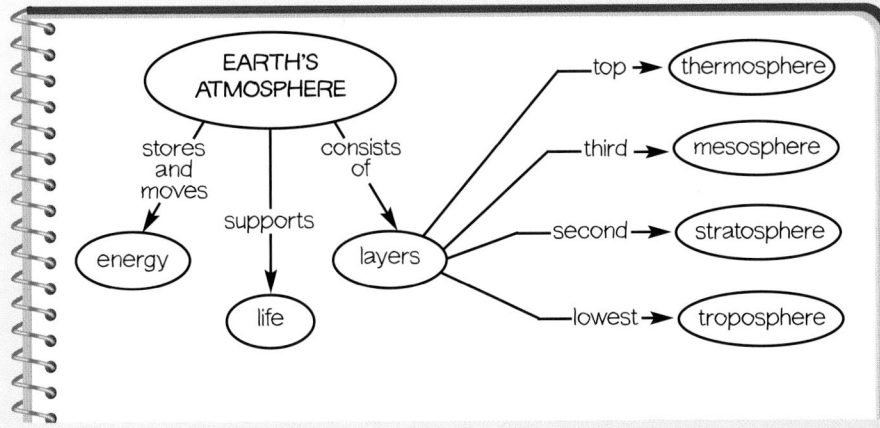

The main ideas or concepts can often be found in the blue headings. An example is "The atmosphere stores and moves energy." Use nouns from these concepts in the ovals, and use the verb or verbs on the lines.

Venn Diagram

1. Draw two overlapping circles, one for each item that you are comparing.
2. In the overlapping section, list the characteristics that are shared by both items.
3. In the outer sections, list the characteristics that are peculiar to each item.
4. Write a summary that describes the information in the Venn diagram.

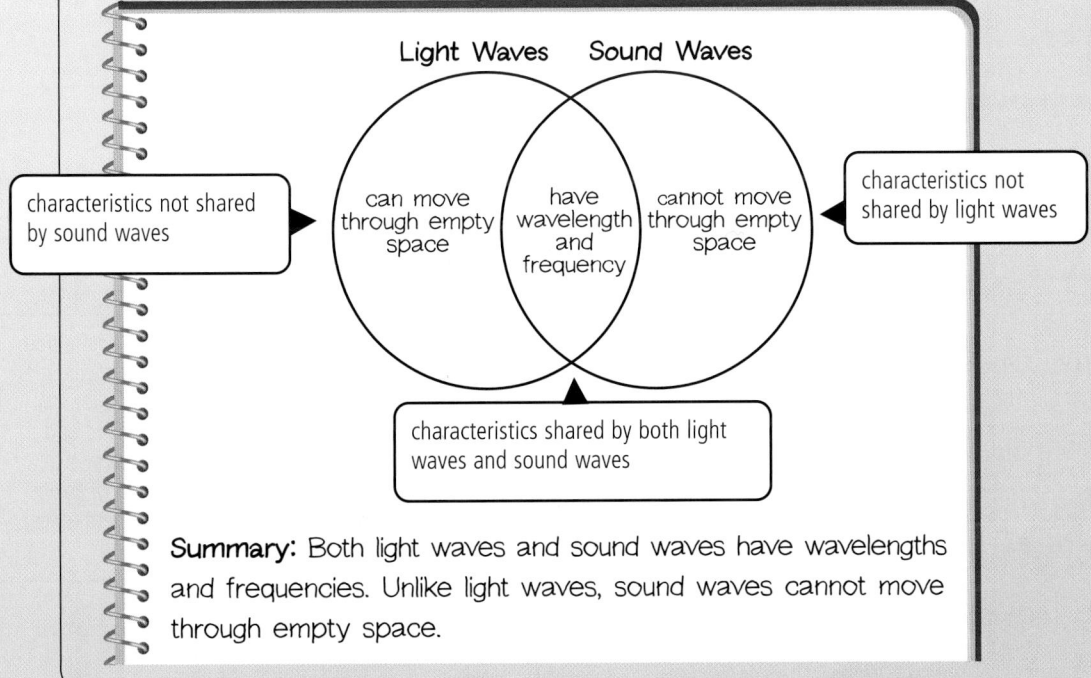

Summary: Both light waves and sound waves have wavelengths and frequencies. Unlike light waves, sound waves cannot move through empty space.

Vocabulary Strategies

Important terms are highlighted in this book. A definition of each term can be found in the sentence or paragraph where the term appears. You can also find definitions in the Glossary. Taking notes about vocabulary terms helps you understand and remember what you read.

Description Wheel

1. Write a term inside a circle.
2. Write words that describe the term on "spokes" attached to the circle.

When studying for a test with a friend, read the phrases on the spokes one at a time until your friend identifies the correct term.

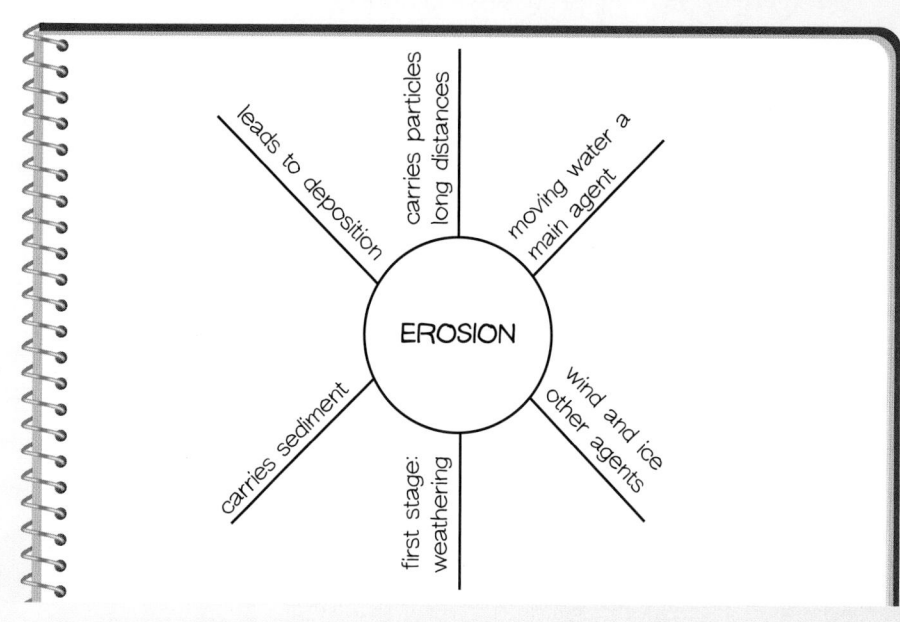

- leads to deposition
- carries particles long distances
- moving water a main agent
- wind and ice other agents
- first stage: weathering
- carries sediment

 EROSION

Four Square

1. Write a term in the center.
2. Write details in the four areas around the term.

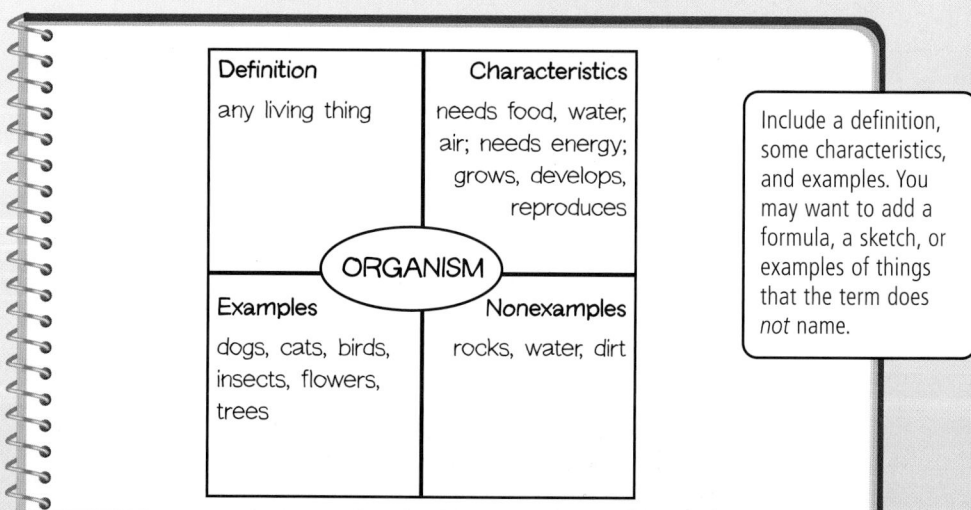

Definition	Characteristics
any living thing	needs food, water, air; needs energy; grows, develops, reproduces

ORGANISM

Examples	Nonexamples
dogs, cats, birds, insects, flowers, trees	rocks, water, dirt

Include a definition, some characteristics, and examples. You may want to add a formula, a sketch, or examples of things that the term does *not* name.

Frame Game

1. Write a term in the center.
2. Frame the term with details.

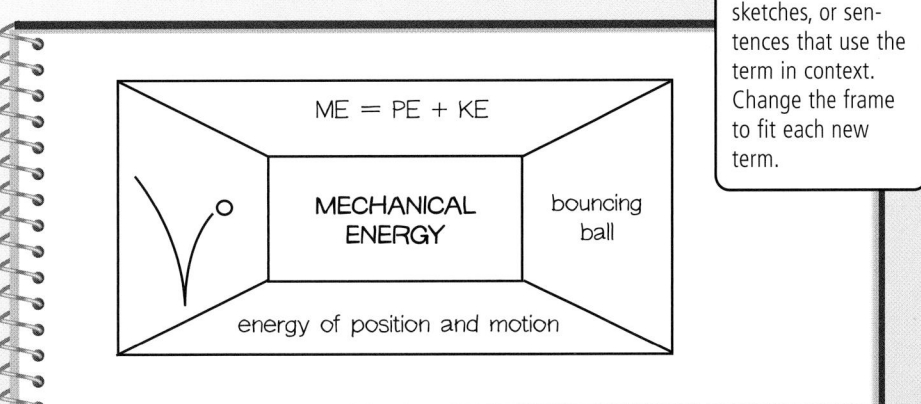

Include examples, descriptions, sketches, or sentences that use the term in context. Change the frame to fit each new term.

Magnet Word

1. Write a term on the magnet.
2. On the lines, add details related to the term.

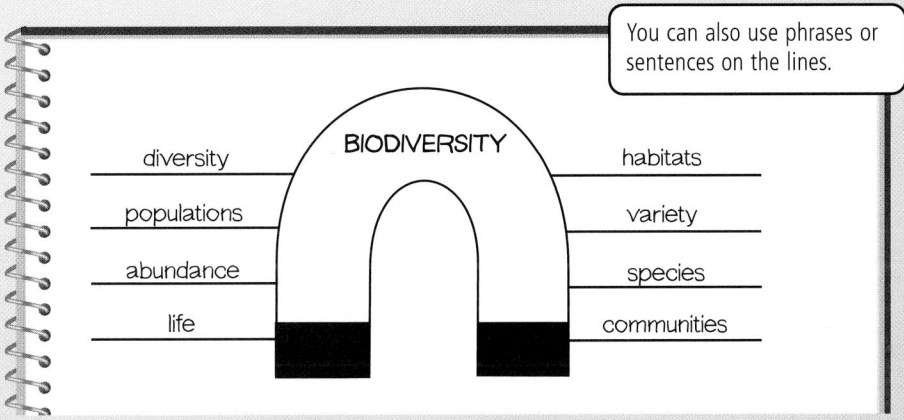

You can also use phrases or sentences on the lines.

Word Triangle

1. Write a term and its definition in the bottom section.
2. In the middle section, write a sentence in which the term is used correctly.
3. In the top section, draw a small picture to illustrate the term.

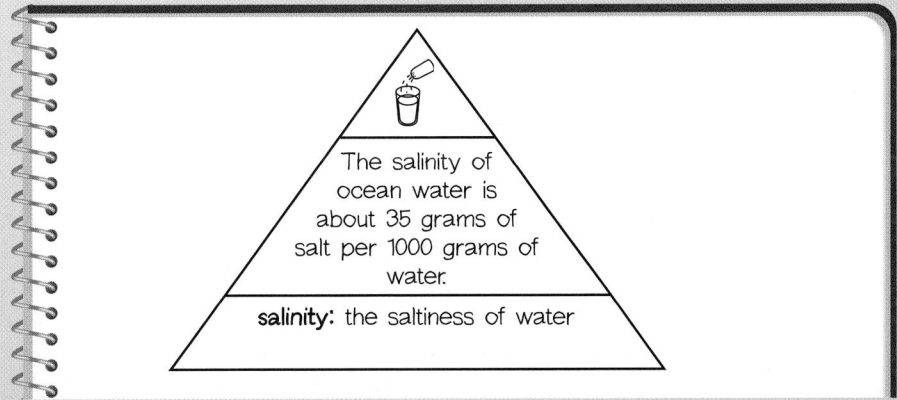

Glossary

GLOSSARY

A

abrasion (uh-BRAY-zhuhn)
The process of wearing something down by friction.
(p. 232)

> **abrasión** El proceso de desgaste de algo por efecto de
> la fricción.

absolute age
The actual age in years of an event or object. (p. 469)

> **edad absoluta** La edad real en años de un evento
> u objeto.

adaptation
A characteristic, a behavior, or any inherited trait that
makes a species able to survive and reproduce in a
particular environment. (p. 502)

> **adaptación** Una característica, un comportamiento o
> cualquier rasgo heredado que permite a una especie
> sobrevivir o reproducirse en un medio ambiente
> determinado.

alluvial fan (uh-LOO-vee-uhl)
A fan-shaped deposit of sediment at the base of a slope,
formed as water flows down the slope and spreads at the
bottom. (p. 269)

> **abanico aluvial** Un depósito de sedimentos en forma
> de abanico situado en la base de una pendiente; se
> forma cuando el agua baja por la pendiente y se
> dispersa al llegar al pie de la misma.

alternating current AC
Electric current that reverses direction at regular intervals.
(p. 429)

> **corriente alterna** Corriente eléctrica que invierte su
> dirección a intervalos regulares.

ampere amp
The unit of measurement of electric current, which is
equal to one coulomb per second. The number of amps
flowing through a circuit equals the circuit's amperage.
(p. 361)

> **amperio** La unidad de medición de la corriente
> eléctrica, la cual es igual a un culombio por segundo. El
> número de amperios fluyendo por un circuito es igual
> al amperaje del circuito.

analog
Represented by a continuous but varying quantity,
such as a wave. In electronics, analog information is
represented by a continuous but varying electrical signal.
(p. 392)

> **análogo** Que es representado por una cantidad
> variante pero continua, como una onda. En la
> electrónica, la información análoga se representa
> mediante una señal eléctrica continua pero variante.

ancestor
A distant or early form of an organism from which later
forms descend. (p. 509)

> **ancestro** Una forma distante o temprana de un
> organismo a partir de la cual descienden formas
> posteriores.

antibiotic
A medicine that can block the growth and reproduction
of bacteria. (p. 647)

> **antibiótico** Una medicina que puede impedir el
> crecimiento y la reproducción de las bacterias.

antibody
A protein produced by some white blood cells to attack
specific foreign materials. (p. 641)

> **anticuerpo** Una proteína producida por algunos
> glóbulos blancos para atacar materiales extraños
> específicos.

antigen
A particular substance that the body recognizes as foreign
and that stimulates a response. (p. 644)

> **antígeno** Una sustancia que el cuerpo reconoce come
> extraña y que causa una respuesta.

appendicular skeleton (AP-uhn-DIHK-yuh-luhr)
The bones of the skeleton that function to allow
movement, such as arm and leg bones. (p. 578)

> **esqueleto apendicular** Los huesos del esqueleto cuya
> función es permitir el movimiento, como los huesos del
> brazo y los huesos de la pierna.

aquaculture
The science and business of raising and harvesting fish in
a controlled situation. (p. 85)

> **acuacultura** La ciencia y el negocio de criar y cosechar
> peces en una situación controlada.

aquifer

An underground layer of permeable rock that contains water. (p. 66)

> **acuífero** Una capa subterránea de roca permeable que contiene agua.

artery

A blood vessel with strong walls that carries blood away from the heart. (p. 635)

> **arteria** Un vaso sanguíneo con paredes fuertes que lleva la sangre del corazón hacia otras partes del cuerpo.

artesian well

A well in which pressurized water flows upward to the surface. (p. 68)

> **pozo artesiano** Un pozo en el cual el agua bajo presión fluye hacia arriba hasta la superficie.

asteroid

A small, solid, rocky body that orbits the Sun. Most asteroids orbit in a region between Mars and Jupiter called the asteroid belt. (p. 767)

> **asteroide** Un pequeño cuerpo sólido y rocoso que orbita alrededor del Sol. La mayoría de los asteroides orbitan en una región entre Marte y Júpiter denominada cinturón de asteroides.

astronomical unit AU

Earth's average distance from the Sun, which is approximately 150 million kilometers (93 million mi). (p. 745)

> **unidad astronómica** ua La distancia promedio de la Tierra al Sol, la cual es de aproximadamente 150 millones de kilómetros (93 millones de millas).

atom

The smallest particle of an element that has the chemical properties of that element.

> **átomo** La partícula más pequeña de un elemento que tiene las propiedades químicas de ese elemento.

atmosphere (AT-muh-SFEER)

The outer layer of gases of a large body in space, such as a planet or star; the mixture of gases that surrounds the solid Earth; one of the four parts of the Earth system. (p. 198)

> **atmósfera** La capa externa de gases de un gran cuerpo que se encuentra en el espacio, como un planeta o una estrella; la mezcla de gases que rodea la Tierra sólida; una de las cuatro partes del sistema terrestre.

axial skeleton

The central part of the skeleton, which includes the cranium, the spinal column, and the ribs. (p. 578)

> **esqueleto axial** La parte central del esqueleto que incluye al cráneo, a la columna vertebral y a las costillas.

axis of rotation

An imaginary line about which a turning body, such as Earth, rotates. (p. 708)

> **eje de rotación** Una línea imaginaria alrededor de la cual gira un cuerpo, como lo hace la Tierra.

B

barrier island

A long, narrow island that develops parallel to a coast as a sandbar builds up above the water's surface. (p. 276)

> **isla barrera** Una isla larga y angosta que se desarrolla paralelamente a la costa al crecer una barra de arena hasta rebasar la superficie del agua.

black hole

The final stage of an extremely massive star, which is invisible because its gravity prevents any form of radiation from escaping. (p. 790)

> **hoyo negro** La etapa final de una estrella de enorme masa, la cual es invisible porque su gravedad evita que cualquier tipo de radiación escape.

blood

A fluid in the body that delivers oxygen and other materials to cells and removes carbon dioxide and other wastes. (p. 631)

> **sangre** Un fluido en el cuerpo que reparte oxígeno y otras sustancias a las células y elimina dióxido de carbono y otros desechos.

big bang

The moment in time when the universe started to expand out of an extremely hot, dense state, according to scientific theory. (p. 802)

> **la gran explosión** De acuerdo a la teoría científica, el momento en el tiempo en el cual el universo empezó a expandirse a partir de un estado extremadamente caliente y denso.

binary code

A coding system in which information is represented by two figures, such as 1 and 0. (p. 390)

> **código binario** Un sistema de codificación en el cual la información se representa con dos números, como el 1 y el 0.

biodiversity

The number and variety of living things found on Earth or within an ecosystem. (p. FL31)

> **biodiversidad** La cantidad y variedad de organismos vivos que se encuentran en la Tierra o dentro de un ecosistema.

biomass
Organic matter that contains stored energy from sunlight and that can be burned as fuel. (p. 320)

    biomasa Materia orgánica que contiene energía almacenada proveniente de la luz del Sol y que puede ser usada como combustible.

biosphere (BY-uh-SFEER)
All living organisms on Earth in the air, on the land, and in the waters; one of the four parts of the Earth system. (p. 199)

    biosfera Todos los organismos vivos de la Tierra, en el aire, en la tierra y en las aguas; una de las cuatro partes del sistema de la Tierra.

by-catch
The portion of animals that are caught in a net and then thrown away as unwanted. (p. 172)

    captura incidental La porción de los animales que se capturan en una red y luego se desechan como no deseados.

C

capillary
A narrow blood vessel that connects arteries with veins. (p. 635)

    capilar Un vaso sanguíneo angosto que conecta a las arterias con las venas.

cardiac muscle
The muscle that makes up the heart. (p. 586)

    músculo cardiaco El músculo del cual está compuesto el corazón.

carrying capacity
The maximum size that a population can reach in an ecosystem. (p. 528)

    capacidad de carga El tamaño máximo que una población puede alcanzar en un ecosistema.

cell
The smallest unit that is able to perform the basic functions of life. (p. FL31)

    célula La unidad más pequeña capaz de realizar las funciones básicas de la vida.

cellular respiration
A process in which cells use oxygen to release energy stored in sugars. (p. 601)

    respiración celular Un proceso en el cual las células usan oxígeno para liberar energía almacenada en las azúcares.

chemical weathering
The breakdown or decomposition of rock that takes place when minerals change through chemical processes. (p. 234)

    meteorización química La descomposición de las rocas que ocurre cuando los minerales cambian mediante procesos químicos.

circuit
A closed path through which charge can flow. (p. 375)

    circuito Una trayectoria cerrada por la cual puede fluir una carga.

circulatory system
The group of organs, consisting of the heart and blood vessels, that circulates blood through the body. (p. 631)

    sistema circulatorio El grupo de órganos, que consiste del corazón y los vasos sanguíneos, que hace circular la sangre por el cuerpo.

comet
A body that produces a coma of gas and dust; a small, icy body that orbits the Sun. (p. 768)

    cometa Un cuerpo que produce una coma de gas y polvo; un cuerpo pequeño y helado que se mueve en órbita alrededor del Sol.

compact bone
The tough, hard outer layer of a bone. (p. 577)

    hueso compacto La capa exterior, resistente y dura de un hueso.

competitor
A species characterized by a relatively longer life span, with relatively few offspring, when compared with an opportunist species. (p. 542)

    competidor Una especie caracterizada por una vida relativamente larga, con relativamente pocas crías, en comparación con una especie oportunista.

compound
A substance made up of two or more different types of atoms.

    compuesto Una sustancia formada por dos o más diferentes tipos de átomos enlazados.

computer
An electronic device that processes digital information. (p. 393)

    computadora Un aparato electrónico que procesa información digital.

condensation
The process by which a gas becomes a liquid. (p. 53)

    condensación El proceso mediante el cual un gas se convierte en un líquido.

concentration

The amount of a substance that is contained in another substance—such as dissolved sugar in water—often expressed as parts per million or parts per billion. (p. 91)

concentración La cantidad de una sustancia contenida en otra sustancia, como el azúcar disuelto en agua; a menudo se expresa como partes por millón o partes por mil millones.

conductor

1. A material that transfers energy easily. 2. A material that transfers electric charge easily. (p. 354)

conductor 1. Un material que transfiere energía fácilmente. 2. Un material que transfiere cargas eléctricas fácilmente.

conservation

The process of saving or protecting a natural resource. (p. 309)

conservación El proceso de salvar o proteger un recurso natural.

constellation

A group of stars that form a pattern in the sky. (p. 676)

constelación Un grupo de estrellas que forman un patrón en el cielo.

continental shelf

The flat or gently sloping land that lies submerged around the edges of a continent and that extends from the shoreline out to the continental slope. (p. 120)

plataforma continental La tierra plana o ligeramente inclinada que está sumergida alrededor de las orillas de un continente y que se extiende desde la costa hasta el talud continental.

contour interval

On a topographic map, the difference in elevation from one contour line to the next. (p. 214)

equidistancia entre curvas de nivel En un mapa topográfico, la diferencia en elevación de una curva de nivel a la siguiente.

contour line

A line on a topographic map that joins points of equal elevation. (p. 213)

curva de nivel Una línea en un mapa topográfico que une puntos de igual elevación.

control group

A set of experimental trials in which all variables are kept constant; used for comparison in an experiment (p. 15)

grupo control Un conjunto de pruebas experimentales en las que todas las variables permanecen constantes; que se usa para una comparación en un experimento.

convection

The transfer of energy from place to place by the motion of heated gas or liquid; in Earth's mantle, convection is thought to transfer energy by the motion of solid rock, which when under great heat and pressure can move like a liquid. (p. 780)

convección La transferencia de energía de un lugar a otro por el movimiento de un líquido o gas calentado; se piensa que en el manto terrestre la convección transfiere energía mediante el movimiento de roca sólida, la cual puede moverse como un líquido cuando está muy caliente y bajo alta presión.

coral reef

A built-up limestone deposit formed by tiny organisms called coral polyps. (p. 162)

arrecife de coral Un depósito de piedra caliza formado por diminutos organismos llamados pólipos de coral.

corona

The outer layer of the Sun's atmosphere. (p. 780)

corona La capa exterior de la atmósfera del Sol.

creative thinking

A habit of mind that involves considering new ideas for solving problems. (p. 8)

razonamiento creativo Un hábito mental en que se consideran nuevas ideas para resolver los problemas.

critical thinking

A method of analysis that depends on logic and reasoning. (p. 10)

razonamiento crítico Un método de análisis que depende de la lógica y el razonamiento.

cycle

n. A series of events or actions that repeat themselves regularly; a physical and/or chemical process in which one material continually changes locations and/or forms. Examples include the water cycle, the carbon cycle, and the rock cycle.

v. To move through a repeating series of events or actions.

ciclo *s.* Una serie de eventos o acciones que se repiten regularmente; un proceso físico y/o químico en el cual un material cambia continuamente de lugar y/o forma. Ejemplos: el ciclo del agua, el ciclo del carbono y el ciclo de las rocas.

D

dam
A structure that holds back and controls the flow of water in a river or other body of water. (p. 86)

presa Una estructura que retiene y controla el flujo de agua en un río u otro cuerpo de agua.

data
Information gathered by observation or experimentation that can be used in calculating or reasoning. *Data* is a plural word; the singular is *datum*.

datos Información reunida mediante observación o experimentación y que se puede usar para calcular o para razonar.

delta
An area of land at the end, or mouth, of a river that is formed by the buildup of sediment. (p. 269)

delta Un área de tierra al final, o en la desembocadura, de un río y que se forma por la acumulación de sedimentos.

density
A property of matter representing the mass per unit volume. (p. 116)

densidad Una propiedad de la materia que representa la masa por unidad de volumen.

dependent variable
A factor that responds to, or depends on, another factor or factors. Results usually come from the observation of one or more dependent variables. (p. 15)

variable dependiente Un factor que responde a, o depende de, otros factores. Los resultados provienen por lo general de la observación de una o más variables dependientes.

deposition (DEHP-uh-ZISH-uhn)
The process in which transported sediment is laid down. (p. 261)

sedimentación El proceso mediante el cual se deposita sedimento que ha sido transportado.

dermis
The inner layer of the skin. (p. 650)

dermis La capa interior de la piel.

desalination (de-SAL-ih-NAY-shun)
The process of removing salt from ocean water. Desalination is used to obtain fresh water. (p. 106)

desalinización El proceso de eliminar la sal del agua de mar. La desalinización se usa para obtener agua dulce.

desertification (dih-ZUR-tuh-fih-KAY-shuhn)
The expansion of desert conditions in areas where the natural plant cover has been destroyed. (p. 249)

desertificación La expansión de las condiciones desérticas en áreas donde la vegetación natural ha sido destruida.

digestion
The process of breaking down food into usable materials. (p. 608)

digestión El proceso de descomponer el alimento en sustancias utilizables.

digestive system
The structures in the body that work together to transform the energy and materials in food into forms the body can use. (p. 608)

sistema digestivo Las estructuras en el cuerpo que trabajan juntas para transformar la energía y las sustancias en el alimento a formas que el cuerpo puede usar.

digital
Represented by numbers. In electronics, digital information is represented by the numbers 1 and 0, signaled by a circuit that is either on or off. (p. 390)

digital Que es representado por números. En la electrónica, la información digital es representada por los números 1 y 0, señalados por un circuito que está encendido o apagado.

direct current DC
Electric current that flows in one direction only. (p. 429)

corriente directa Corriente eléctrica que fluye en una sola dirección.

divide
A continuous high line of land—or ridge—from which water drains to one side or the other. (pp. 57, 267)

línea divisoria de aguas Una línea continua de tierra alta, o un cerro, desde donde el agua escurre hacia un lado o hacia el otro.

Doppler effect
A change in the observed frequency of a wave, occurring when the source of the wave or the observer is moving. Changes in the frequency of light are often measured by observing changes in wavelength, whereas changes in the frequency of sound are often detected as changes in pitch. (p. 800)

efecto Doppler Un cambio en la frecuencia observada de una onda que ocurre cuando la fuente de la onda o el observador están en movimiento. Los cambios en la frecuencia de la luz a menudo se miden observando los cambios en la longitud de onda, mientras que los cambios en la frecuencia del sonido a menudo se detectan como cambios en el tono.

downwelling
The movement of water from the surface to greater depths. (p. 126)

> **sumergencia** El movimiento de agua de la superficie hacia mayores profundidades.

drainage basin
An area of land in which water drains into a stream system. The borders of a drainage basin are called divides. (pp. 57, 267)

> **cuenca tributaria** Un área de tierra en la cual el agua escurre a un sistema de corrientes. Los límites de una cuenca tributaria se denominan líneas divisorias de aguas.

drought (drowt)
A long period of abnormally low amounts of rainfall. (p. 101)

> **sequía** Un período largo con cantidades inusualmente bajas de lluvia.

dune
A mound of sand built up by wind. (p. 277)

> **duna** Un montículo de arena formado por el viento.

E

eclipse
An event during which one object in space casts a shadow onto another. On Earth, a lunar eclipse occurs when the Moon moves through Earth's shadow, and a solar eclipse occurs when the Moon's shadow crosses Earth. (p. 727)

> **eclipse** Un evento durante el cual un objeto en el espacio proyecta una sombra sobre otro. En la Tierra, un eclipse lunar ocurre cuando la Luna se mueve a través de la sombra de la Tierra, y un eclipse solar ocurre cuando la sombra de la Luna cruza la Tierra.

El Niño (ehl NEEN-yoh)
A disturbance of wind patterns and ocean currents in the Pacific Ocean that causes temporary climate changes in many parts of the world. (p. 128)

> **El Niño** Un disturbio en los patrones de viento y las corrientes oceánicas del océano Pacífico que causa cambios climáticos temporales en muchas partes del mundo.

electric cell
A device that produces electric current using the chemical or physical properties of different materials. A battery consists of two or more cells linked together. (p. 363)

> **celda eléctrica** Un aparato que produce corriente eléctrica usando las propiedades químicas o físicas de diferentes materiales. Una pila consiste de dos o más celdas conectadas.

electric charge
A property that allows one object to exert an electric force on another object without touching it. Electric charge can be positive or negative: positive charge is a property of the proton, while negative charge is a property of the electron. (p. 342)

> **carga eléctrica** Una propiedad que permite a un objeto ejercer una fuerza eléctrica sobre otro objeto sin tocarlo. La carga eléctrica puede ser positiva o negativa: la carga positiva es una propiedad del protón mientras que la carga negativa es una propiedad del electrón.

electric current
A continuous flow of electric charge, which is measured in amperes. (p. 360)

> **corriente eléctrica** Un flujo continuo de una carga eléctrica, el cual se mide en amperios.

electric field
An area surrounding a charged object, within which the object can exert an electric force on another object without touching it. (p. 342)

> **campo eléctrico** Un área que rodea un objeto con carga, dentro del cual el objeto puede ejercer una fuerza eléctrica sobre otro objeto sin tocarlo.

electric potential
The amount of potential energy per unit charge that a static charge or electric current has. Electric potential is measured in volts and is often called voltage. (p. 351)

> **potencial eléctrico** La cantidad de energía potencial por unidad de carga que tiene una carga estática o una corriente eléctrica. El potencial eléctrico se mide en voltios y a menudo se llama voltaje.

electric power
The rate at which electrical energy is generated from, or converted into, another source of energy, such as kinetic energy. (p. 434)

> **potencia eléctrica** El ritmo al cual se genera energía eléctrica a partir de, o se convierte en, otra fuente de energía, como energía cinética.

electromagnet
A magnet that consists of a piece of iron or steel inside a coil of current-carrying wire. (p. 422)

> **electroimán** Un imán que consiste de un pedazo de hierro o de acero dentro de una bobina de alambre por la cual fluye una corriente eléctrica.

electromagnetic radiation

(ih-LEHK-troh-mag-NEHT-ihk RAY-dee-AY-shuhn)
Energy that travels across distances as certain types of waves. Types of electromagnetic radiation are radio waves, microwaves, infrared radiation, visible light, ultraviolet radiation, x-rays, and gamma rays. (p. 679)

radiación electromagnética Energía que viaja a través de las distancias en forma de ciertos tipos de ondas. Las ondas de radio, las microondas, la radiación infrarroja, la luz visible, la radiación ultravioleta, los rayos X y los rayos gama son tipos de radiación electromagnética.

electromagnetism

Magnetism that results from the flow of electric charge. (p. 421)

electromagnetismo Magnetismo que resulta del flujo de una carga eléctrica.

electron

A negatively charged particle located outside an atom's nucleus. An electron is about 2000 times smaller than either a proton or neutron.

electrón Una partícula con carga negativa localizada fuera del núcleo de un átomo. Un electrón es como aproximadamente 2000 veces más pequeño que un protón o un neutrón.

electronic

adj. Operating by means of an electrical signal. An electronic device is a device that uses electric current to represent coded information. (p. 389)

n. An electronic device or system, such as a computer, calculator, CD player, or game system.

electrónico *adj.* Que opera por medio de una señal eléctrica. Un aparato electrónico es un aparato que usa corriente eléctrica para representar información codificada.

element

A substance that cannot be broken down into a simpler substance by ordinary chemical changes. An element consists of atoms of only one type. (p. FL35)

elemento Una sustancia que no puede descomponerse en otra sustancia más simple por medio de cambios químicos normales. Un elemento consta de átomos de un solo tipo.

elevation

A measure of how high something is above a reference point, such as sea level. (p. 213)

elevación Una medida de lo elevado que está algo sobre un punto de referencia, como el nivel del mar.

ellipse

An oval or flattened circle. (p. 745)

elipse Un óvalo o círculo aplanado.

emigration

In population studies, the movement of individuals out of an ecosystem. (p. 537)

emigración En estudios poblacionales, el movimiento de individuos fuera de un ecosistema.

energy

The ability to do work or to cause a change. For example, the energy of a moving bowling ball knocks over pins; energy from food allows animals to move and to grow; and energy from the Sun heats Earth's surface and atmosphere, which causes air to move. (p. FL33)

energía La capacidad para trabajar o causar un cambio. Por ejemplo, la energía de una bola de boliche en movimiento tumba los pinos; la energía proveniente de su alimento permite a los animales moverse y crecer; la energía del Sol calienta la superficie y la atmósfera de la Tierra, lo que ocasiona que el aire se mueva.

environment

Everything that surrounds a living thing. An environment is made up of both living and nonliving factors. (p. FL31)

medio ambiente Todo lo que rodea a un organismo vivo. Un medio ambiente está compuesto de factores vivos y factores sin vida.

epidermis

The outer layer of the skin. (p. 650)

epidermis La capa exterior de la piel.

equator

An imaginary east-west line around the center of Earth that divides the planet into the Northern Hemisphere and the Southern Hemisphere; a line set at 0° latitude. (p. 206)

ecuador Una línea imaginaria de este a oeste alrededor del centro de la Tierra y que divide al planeta en hemisferio norte y hemisferio sur; la línea está fijada a latitud 0°.

equinox (EE-kwuh-NAHKS)

In an orbit, a position and time in which sunlight shines equally on the Northern Hemisphere and the Southern Hemisphere; a time of year when daylight and darkness are nearly equal for most of Earth. (p. 710)

equinoccio En una órbita, la posición y el tiempo en los cuales la luz del Sol incide de la misma manera en el Hemisferio Norte y en el Hemisferio Sur; una época del año en la cual la luz del día y la oscuridad son casi iguales para la mayor parte de la Tierra.

erosion
The process in which sediment is picked up and moved from one place to another. (p. 261)

> **erosión** El proceso en el cual el sedimento es recogido y transportado de un lugar a otro.

estuary (EHS-choo-EHR-ee)
A shoreline area where fresh water from a river mixes with salt water from the ocean. (p. 156)

> **estuario** Un litoral donde se mezcla agua dulce de un río con agua salada del océano.

ethics
The rules or standards governing the conduct of a person or the members of a profession. (p. 27)

> **ética** Las reglas o normas que gobiernan la conducta de una persona o de los miembros de una profesión.

eutrophication (yoo-TRAF-ih-KAY-shun)
An increase in nutrients in a lake or pond. Eutrophication can occur naturally or as a result of pollution, and causes increased growth of algae and plants. (p. 60)

> **eutrofización** Un aumento en los nutrientes de un lago o una laguna. La eutrofización puede ocurrir de manera natural o como resultado de la contaminación y ocasiona un aumento en el crecimiento de algas y plantas.

evaporation
The process by which liquid changes into gas. (p. 53)

> **evaporación** El proceso por el cual un líquido se transforma en gas.

evolution
The process through which species change over time; can refer to the changes in a particular population or to the formation and extinction of species over the course of Earth's history. (p. 497)

> **evolución** El proceso mediante el cual las especies cambian con el tiempo; puede referirse a cambios en una población en particular o a la formación y extinción de especies en el curso de la historia de la Tierra.

exfoliation (ex-FOH-lee-AY-shuhn)
In geology, the process in which layers or sheets of rock gradually break off. (p. 232)

> **exfoliación** En geología, el proceso en el cual capas u hojas de roca se desprenden gradualmente.

experiment
An organized procedure to study something under controlled conditions.

> **experimento** Un procedimiento organizado para estudiar algo bajo condiciones controladas.

experimental group
A set of experimental trials in which the effects of changes in an independent variable is tested. (p. 15)

> **grupo experimental** Un conjunto de pruebas experimentales en las que se examinan los efectos de los cambios en una variable independiente.

extinction
The permanent disappearance of a species. (p. FL31)

> **extinción** La desaparición permanente de una especie.

F

false-color image
A computer image in which the colors are not what the human eye would see. A false-color image can assign different colors to different types of radiation coming from an object to highlight its features. (p. 220)

> **imagen de color falso** Una imagen computacional en la cual los colores no son los que el ojo humano observaría. Una imagen de color falso puede asignar diferentes colores a los diferentes tipos de radiación que provienen de un objeto para hacer destacar sus características.

floodplain
A flat area of land on either side of a stream that becomes flooded when a river overflows its banks. (p. 268)

> **planicie de inundación** Un área plana de tierra en cualquier costado de un arroyo que se inunda cuando un río se desborda.

force
A push or a pull; something that changes the motion of an object. (p. FL35)

> **fuerza** Un empuje o un jalón; algo que cambia el movimiento de un objeto.

fossil
The imprint or hardened remains of a plant or animal that lived long ago. (pp. 457, 489)

> **fósil** La huella o los restos endurecidos de una planta o un animal que vivió hace mucho tiempo.

fossil fuels
Fuels formed from the remains of prehistoric organisms that are burned for energy. (p. 302)

> **combustibles fósiles** Combustibles formados a partir de los restos de organismos prehistóricos que son consumidos para obtener energía.

fresh water
Water that is not salty and has little or no taste, color, or smell. Most lakes and rivers are made up of fresh water. (p. 51)

agua dulce Agua que no es salada y que tiene muy poco o ningún sabor, color u olor. La mayoría de los lagos y los ríos están compuestos de agua dulce.

friction
A force that resists the motion between two surfaces in contact. (p. FL35)

fricción Una fuerza que resiste el movimiento entre dos superficies en contacto.

fusion
A process in which particles of an element collide and combine to form a heavier element, such as the fusion of hydrogen into helium that occurs in the Sun's core. (p. 780)

fusión Un proceso en el cual las partículas de un elemento chocan y se combinan para formar un elemento más pesado, como la fusión de hidrógeno en helio que ocurre en el núcleo del Sol.

G

galaxy
Millions or billions of stars held together in a group by their own gravity. (p. 674)

galaxia Millones o miles de millones de estrellas unidas en un grupo por su propia gravedad.

gas giant
A large planet that consists mostly of gases in a dense form. The four large planets in the outer solar system—Jupiter, Saturn, Uranus, and Neptune—are gas giants. (p. 758)

gigante de gas Un planeta grande compuesto principalmente de gases en forma densa. Los cuatro planetas grandes en el sistema solar exterior—Júpiter, Saturno, Urano y Neptuno —son gigantes de gas.

gene
The basic unit of heredity that consists of a segment of DNA on a chromosome. (p. 513)

gen La unidad básica de herencia que consiste en un segmento de ADN en un cromosoma.

generator
A device that converts kinetic energy, or the energy of motion, into electrical energy. Generators produce electric current by rotating a magnet within a coil of wire or rotating a coil of wire within a magnetic field. (p. 428)

generador Un aparato que convierte energía cinética, o la energía del movimiento, a energía eléctrica. Los generadores producen corriente eléctrica al girar un imán dentro de una bobina de alambre o haciendo rotar una bobina de alambre dentro de un campo magnético.

geographic information systems
Computer systems that can store, arrange, and display geographic data in different types of maps. (p. 221)

sistemas de información geográfica Sistemas computarizados que pueden almacenar, organizar y mostrar datos geográficos en diferentes tipos de mapas.

geologic time scale
The summary of Earth's history, divided into intervals of time defined by major events or changes on Earth. (p. 475)

escala de tiempo geológico El resumen de la historia de la Tierra, dividido en intervalos de tiempo definidos por los principales eventos o cambios en la Tierra.

geosphere (JEE-uh-SFEER)
All the features on Earth's surface—continents, islands, and seafloor—and everything below the surface—the inner and outer core and the mantle; one of the four parts of the Earth system. (p. 200)

geosfera Todas las características de la superficie de la Tierra, es decir, continentes, islas y el fondo marino, y de todo bajo la superficie, es decir, el núcleo externo e interno y el manto; una de las cuatro partes del sistema de la Tierra.

geothermal energy
Heat energy that originates from within Earth and drives the movement of Earth's tectonic plates. Geothermal energy can be used to generate electricity. (p. 318)

energía geotérmica Energía calorífica que se origina en el interior de la Tierra y que impulsa el movimiento de las placas tectónicas de planeta. La energía geotérmica puede usarse para generar electricidad.

glacier (GLAY-shuhr)
A large mass of ice that exists year-round and moves over land. (p. 281)

glaciar Una gran masa de hielo que existe durante todo el año y se mueve sobre la tierra.

gravity
The force that objects exert on each other because of their mass. (p. FL35)

gravedad La fuerza que los objetos ejercen entre sí debido a su masa.

grounding

The creation of a harmless, low-resistance path—a ground—for electricity to follow. Grounding is an important electrical safety procedure. (p. 357)

conexión a tierra La creación de una trayectoria inofensiva, de baja resistencia—una tierra—para que la siga la electricidad. La conexión a tierra es un importante procedimiento de seguridad eléctrica.

groundwater

Water that collects and is stored underground. (p. 64)

agua subterránea Agua que se acumula y almacena bajo tierra.

H

habitat

The natural environment in which a living thing gets all that it needs to live; examples include a desert, a coral reef, and a freshwater lake. (p. 154)

hábitat El medio ambiente natural en el cual un organismo vivo consigue todo lo que requiere para vivir; ejemplos incluyen un desierto, un arrecife coralino y un lago de agua dulce.

half-life

The length of time it takes for half of the atoms in a sample of a radioactive element to change from an unstable form into another form. (p. 469)

vida media El tiempo que tardan la mitad de los átomos de una muestra de un elemento radiactivo en cambiar de una forma inestable a otra forma.

homeostasis (HOH-mee-oh-STAY-sihs)

The process by which an organism or cell maintains the internal conditions needed for health and functioning, regardless of outside conditions. (p. 574)

homeostasis El proceso mediante el cual un organismo o una célula mantienen las condiciones internas necesarias para la salud y el funcionamiento, independientemente de las condiciones externas.

humus (HYOO-muhs)

The decayed organic matter in soil. (p. 239)

humus La materia orgánica en descomposición del suelo.

hydroelectric energy

Electricity that is generated by the conversion of the energy of moving water. (p. 316)

energía hidroeléctrica Electricidad que se genera por la conversión de la energía del agua en movimiento.

hydrogen fuel cell

A device that uses hydrogen and oxygen to produce electricity. The byproducts are heat and water. (p. 320)

celda de combustible de hidrógeno Un aparato que usa hidrógeno y oxígeno para producir electricidad. Los subproductos son calor y agua.

hydrosphere (HY-druh-SFEER)

All water on Earth—in the atmosphere and in the oceans, lakes, glaciers, rivers, streams, and underground reservoirs; one of the four parts of the Earth system. (p. 198)

hidrosfera Toda el agua de la Tierra: en la atmósfera y en los océanos, lagos, glaciares, ríos, arroyos y depósitos subterráneos; una de las cuatro partes del sistema de la Tierra.

hydrothermal vent

An opening in the sea floor from which heated water rises and mixes with the ocean water above. (p. 168)

abertura hidrotermal Una salida en el fondo marino desde la cual asciende agua caliente que se mezcla con el agua del océano.

hypothesis

A tentative explanation for an observation or phenomenon. A hypothesis is used to make testable predictions. (p. 7)

hipótesis Una explicación provisional de una observación o de un fenómeno. Una hipótesis se usa para hacer predicciones que se pueden probar.

I

ice core

A tubular sample that shows the layers of snow and ice that have built up over the years. (p. 463)

núcleo de hielo Una muestra tubular que presenta las capas de nieve y hielo que se han acumulado con los años.

iceberg

A mass of floating ice that broke away from a glacier. (p. 62)

iceberg Una masa de hielo flotante que se separó de un glaciar.

immigration

In population studies, the movement of an organism into a range inhabited by individuals of the same species. (p. 537)

inmigración En estudios poblacionales, el movimiento de un organismo hacia un territorio habitado por individuos de la misma especie.

immune system
A group of organs that provides protection against disease-causing agents. (p. 641)

sistema inmune o **inmunológico** Un grupo de órganos que provee protección contra agentes que causan enfermedades.

immunity
Resistance to a disease. Immunity can result from antibodies formed in the body during a previous attack of the same illness. (p. 646)

inmunidad La resistencia a una enfermedad. La inmunidad puede resultar de anticuerpos formados en el cuerpo durante un ataque previo de la misma enfermedad.

impact crater
A round pit left behind on the surface of a planet or other body in space after a smaller object strikes the surface. (p. 696)

cráter de impacto Un pozo circular en la superficie de un planeta u otro cuerpo en el espacio que se forma cuando un objeto más pequeño golpea la superficie.

impermeable
Resistant to the passage of water. (p. 65)

impermeable Resistente al paso del agua.

independent variable
A factor that can be changed separately, or independently. An experiment usually has only one independent variable, although it may have many controlled variables and other constants. (p. 15)

variable independiente Un factor que se puede cambiar por separado o independientemente. Por lo general, un experimento sólo tiene una variable independiente aunque puede tener muchas variables controladas y otras constantes.

index fossil
A fossil of an organism that was common, lived in many areas, and existed only during a certain span of time. Index fossils are used to help determine the age of rock layers. (p. 467)

fósil indicador Un fósil de un organismo que era común, vivió en muchas áreas y existió sólo durante cierto período de tiempo. Los fósiles indicadores se usan para ayudar a determinar la edad de las capas de roca.

induction
The buildup of a static charge in an object when the object is close to, but not touching, a charged object. (p. 345)

inducción La acumulación de carga estática en un objeto cuando el objeto está cercano a, pero no en contacto con, un objeto con carga.

informed consent
An agreement to participate in an experiment based on information about the purpose, procedures, and risks involved. (p. 29)

consentimiento informado Un acuerdo para participar en un experimento basado en la información sobre el propósito, los procedimientos y los riesgos incluidos.

insulator
1. A material that does not transfer electric charge easily.
2. A material that does not transfer energy easily. (p. 354)

aislante 1. Un material que no transfiere cargas eléctricas fácilmente. **2.** Un material que no transfiere energía fácilmente.

integumentary system (ihn-TEHG-yu-MEHN-tuh-ree)
The body system that includes the skin and its associated structures. (p. 649)

sistema integumentario El sistema corporal que incluye a la piel y a sus estructuras asociadas.

interaction
The condition of acting or having an influence upon something. Living things in an ecosystem interact with both the living and nonliving parts of their environment. (p. FL31)

interacción La condición de actuar o influir sobre algo. Los organismos vivos en un ecosistema interactúan con las partes vivas y las partes sin vida de su medio ambiente.

intertidal zone (ihn-tuhr-TYD-uhl)
The narrow ocean margin between the high-tide mark and the low-tide mark. (p. 154)

zona intermareal El estrecho margen oceánico entre el límite de la marea alta y el límite de la marea baja.

involuntary muscle
A muscle that moves without conscious control. (p. 586)

músculo involuntario Un músculo que se mueve sin control consciente.

irrigation
The process of supplying water to land to grow crops. (p. 83)

irrigación El proceso de suministrar agua a las tierras de cultivo.

J

joule (jool) J
A unit used to measure energy and work. One calorie is

equal to 4.18 joules of energy; one joule of work is done when a force of one newton moves an object one meter.

julio Una unidad que se usa para medir la energía y el trabajo. Una caloría es igual a 4.18 julios de energía; se hace un joule de trabajo cuando una fuerza de un newton mueve un objeto un metro.

K

kelp forest
A large community of kelp, a type of seaweed that can attach to the ocean floor. (p. 164)

bosque de kelp Una comunidad grande de kelp, un tipo de alga marina que puede adherirse al fondo marino.

kettle lake
A bowl-shaped lake that was formed as sediment built up around a block of ice left behind by a glacier. (p. 285)

lago kettle Un lago en forma de tazón que se formó al acumularse sedimento alrededor de un bloque de hielo que quedó tras el paso de un glaciar.

kilowatt kW
A unit of measurement for power equal to 1000 watts. (p. 436)

kilovatio Una unidad de medición para la potencia equivalente a 1000 vatios.

kilowatt-hour kWh
The unit of measurement for electrical energy equal to one kilowatt of power over a one-hour period. (p. 437)

kilovatio-hora La unidad de medición de energía eléctrica igual a un kilovatio de potencia en un período de una hora.

kinetic energy
The energy of motion. A moving object has the most kinetic energy at the point where it moves the fastest.

energía cinética La energía del movimiento. Un objeto que se mueve tiene su mayor energía cinética en el punto en el cual se mueve con mayor rapidez.

L

lander
A craft designed to land on a planet's surface. (p. 692)

módulo de aterrizaje Una nave diseñada para aterrizar en la superficie de un planeta.

latitude
The distance in degrees north or south from the equator. (p. 206)

latitud La distancia en grados norte o sur a partir del ecuador.

law of conservation of energy
A law stating that no matter how energy is transferred or transformed, it continues to exist in one form or another. (p. 82)

ley de la conservación de la energía Una ley que establece que no importa cómo se transfiere o transforma la energía, toda la energía sigue presente en alguna forma u otra.

light-year
The distance light travels in one year, which is about 9.5 trillion kilometers (6 trillion mi). (p. 786)

año luz La distancia que viaja la luz en un año, la cual es de casi 9.5 billones de kilómetros (6 billones de millas).

limiting factor
A factor or condition that prevents the continuing growth of a population in an ecosystem. (p. 538)

factor limitante Un factor o una condición que impide el crecimiento continuo de una población en un ecosistema.

lock
A section of a waterway, closed off by gates, in which the water level is rasied or lowered to move ships through. (p. 86)

esclusa Una sección de un canal cerrado con compuertas, en la cual se eleva o se baja el nivel del agua para que pasen barcos.

loess (LOH-uhs)
Deposits of fine-grained, wind-blown sediment. (p. 278)

loes Depósitos de sedimento de grano fino transportado por el viento.

longitude
The distance in degrees east or west of the prime meridian. Longitude lines are numbered from 0° to 180°. (p. 207)

longitud La distancia en grados al este o al oeste del primer meridiano. Las líneas de longitud están numeradas de 0° a 180°.

longshore current
The overall direction and movement of water as waves strike the shore at an angle. (pp. 132, 275)

corriente litoral La dirección y el movimiento general del agua conforme las olas golpean la costa en ángulo.

longshore drift
The zigzag movement of sand along a beach, caused by the action of waves. (p. 275)

> **deriva litoral** El movimiento en zigzag de la arena a lo largo de una playa, ocasionado por la acción de las olas.

M

main sequence
The stage in which stars produce energy through the fusion of hydrogen into helium. (p. 790)

> **secuencia principal** La etapa en la cual las estrellas producen energía mediante la fusión de hidrógeno en helio.

magnet
An object that attracts certain other materials, particularly iron and steel. (p. 411)

> **imán** Un objeto que atrae a ciertos otros materiales, especialmente al hierro y al acero.

magnetic domain
A group of atoms whose magnetic fields align, or point in the same direction. Magnetic materials have magnetic domains, whereas nonmagnetic materials do not. (p. 414)

> **dominio magnético** Un grupo de átomos cuyos campos magnéticos se alinean, o apuntan en la misma dirección. Los materiales magnéticos tienen dominios magnéticos mientras que los materiales no magnéticos no tienen.

magnetic field
An area surrounding a magnet within which the magnet can exert a force. Magnetic fields are concentrated into a pattern of lines that extend from the magnet's north pole to its south pole. (p. 413)

> **campo magnético** Un área alrededor de un imán dentro del cual el imán puede ejercer una fuerza. Los campos magnéticos se concentran en un patrón de líneas que se extienden del polo norte del imán a su polo sur.

magnetic pole
One of two ends of a magnet where the magnetic force is the strongest. Every magnet has two poles. (p. 412)

> **polo magnético** Uno de dos extremos de un imán donde la fuerza magnética es lo más fuerte. Todos los imanes tienen dos polos.

magnetism
The force exerted by a magnet. Opposite poles of two magnets attract, or pull together, whereas like poles of two magnets repel, or push apart. (p. 412)

> **magnetismo** La fuerza que ejerce un imán. Los polos opuestos de dos imanes se atraen, o jalan hacia si, mientras que los polos iguales de dos imanes se repelen, o se empujan para alejarse uno del otro.

map legend
A chart that explains the meaning of each symbol used on a map; also called a key. (p. 205)

> **clave del mapa** Una tabla que explica el significado de cada símbolo usado en un mapa.

map scale
The comparison of distance on a map with actual distance on what the map represents, such as Earth's surface. Map scale may be expressed as a ratio, a bar scale, or equivalent units. (p. 205)

> **escala del mapa** La comparación de la distancia en un mapa con la distancia real en lo que el mapa representa, como la superficie de la Tierra. La escala del mapa puede expresarse como una azón, una barra de escala o en unidades equivalentes.

mare (MAH-ray)
A large, dark plain of solidified lava on the Moon. The plural form of *mare* is *maria* (MAH-ree-uh). (p. 717)

> **mare** Una planicie grande y oscura de lava solidificada en la Luna. El plural de *mare* es *maría*.

mass
A measure of how much matter an object is made of.

> **masa** Una medida de la cantidad de materia de la que está compuesto un objeto.

mass extinction
One of several periods in Earth's history when large numbers of species became extinct at nearly the same time. (p. 494)

> **extinción masiva** Uno de varios períodos en la historia de la Tierra cuando grandes números de especies se extinguieron casi al mismo tiempo.

mass wasting
The downhill movement of loose rock or soil. (p. 263)

> **movimiento de masa** El desplazamiento cuesta abajo de suelo o de roca suelta.

matter
Anything that has mass and volume. Matter exists ordinarily as a solid, a liquid, or a gas. (p. FL33)

> **materia** Todo lo que tiene masa y volumen. Generalmente la materia existe como sólido, líquido o gas.

mechanical weathering
The breakdown of rock into smaller pieces of the same material without any change in its composition. (p. 232)

meteorización mecánica El desmoronamiento de las rocas en pedazos más pequeños del mismo material, sin ningún cambio en su composición.

meteor
A brief streak of light produced by a small particle entering Earth's atmosphere at a high speed. (p. 769)

meteoro Un breve rayo luminoso producido por una partícula pequeña que entra a la atmósfera de la Tierra a una alta velocidad.

meteorite
A small object from outer space that passes through Earth's atmosphere and reaches the surface. (p. 769)

meteorito Un pequeño objeto del espacio exterior que pasa a través de la atmósfera de la Tierra y llega a la superficie.

model
A representation of an object or process. (p. 16)

modelo Una representación de un objeto o proceso.

molecule
A group of atoms that are held together by covalent bonds so that they move as a single unit.

molécula Un grupo de átomos que están unidos mediante enlaces covalentes de tal manera que se mueven como una sola unidad.

moraine (muh-RAYN)
A deposit of till left behind by a retreating glacier. Moraines can form along a glacier's sides and at its end. (p. 284)

morrena Un depósito de sedimentos glaciares dejado por un glaciar que retrocede. Las morrenas pueden formarse en los costados de un glaciar o en su extremo.

multicellular organism
An organism that is made up of many cells. (p. 493)

organismo multicelular Un organismo compuesto de muchas células.

muscular system
The muscles of the body that, together with the skeletal system, function to produce movement. (p. 585)

sistema muscular Los músculos del cuerpo que, junto con el sistema óseo, sirven para producir movimiento.

N

natural resource
Any type of matter or energy from Earth's environment that humans use to meet their needs. (p. 299)

recurso natural Cualquier tipo de materia o energía del medio ambiente de la Tierra que usan los humanos para satisfacer sus necesidades.

natural selection
The process through which members of a species that are best suited to their environment survive and reproduce at a higher rate than other members of the species. (p. 501)

selección natural El proceso mediante el cual los miembros de una especie que están mejor adecuados a su medio ambiente sobreviven y se reproducen a una tasa más alta que otros miembros de la especie.

neap tide
A tide of small range occurring during the first- and third-quarter phases of the Moon. (p. 139)

marea muerta Una marea de poco rango que ocurre durante las fases cuarto menguante y cuarto creciente de la Luna.

nebula (NEHB-yuh-luh)
A cloud of gas and dust in space. Stars form in nebulae. (p. 789)

nebulosa Una nube de gas y polvo en el espacio. Las estrellas se forman en las nebulosas.

neutron star
A dense core that may be left behind after a higher-mass star explodes in a supernova. (p. 790)

estrella de neutrones Un núcleo denso que puede resultar después de que una estrella de mayor masa explota en una supernova.

nonpoint-source pollution
Pollution with a source that is hard to find or scattered. (p. 94)

contaminación por fuentes difusas Contaminación de fuentes que son dispersas o difíciles de encontrar.

nonrenewable resource
A resource that exists in a fixed amount or is used up more quickly than it can be replaced in nature. (p. 300)

recurso no renovable Un recurso que existe en una cantidad fija o se consume más rápidamente de lo que puede reemplazarse en la naturaleza.

GLOSSARY

nuclear fission (FIHSH-uhn)
The process of splitting the nuclei of radioactive atoms, which releases huge amounts of energy mainly in the form of radiation and heat energy. (p. 313)

fisión nuclear El proceso de rotura de los núcleos de átomos radioactivos, el cual libera inmensas cantidades de energía, principalmente en forma de radiación y energía calorífica.

nutrient (NOO-tree-uhnt)
A substance that an organism needs to live. Examples include water, minerals, and materials that come from the breakdown of food particles. (p. 607)

nutriente Una sustancia que un organismo necesita para vivir. Ejemplos incluyen agua, minerales y sustancias que provienen de la descomposición de partículas de alimento.

ocean current
A mass of moving ocean water. (p. 124)

corriente oceánica Una masa de agua oceánica en movimiento.

ohm Ω
The unit of measurement for electrical resistance. (p. 355)

ohmio La unidad de medición para la resistencia eléctrica.

Ohm's law
The mathematical relationship among current, voltage, and resistance, expressed in the formula $I = V/R$ (current = voltage/resistance). (p. 361)

ley de Ohm La relación matemática entre la corriente, el voltaje y la resistencia, expresada en la fórmula $I = V/R$ (corriente = voltaje/resistencia).

opportunist
A species characterized by a relatively short life span, with relatively large quantities of offspring, as compared with a competitor species. (p. 541)

oportunista Una especie caracterizada por una vida relativamente corta, que produce relativamente grandes cantidades de crías, en comparación con una especie competidora.

orbit
n. The path of an object in space as it moves around another object due to gravity; for example, the Moon moves in an orbit around Earth. (p. 674)

v. To revolve around, or move in an orbit; for example, the Moon orbits Earth.

órbita *s.* La trayectoria de un objeto en el espacio a medida que se mueve alrededor de otro objeto debido a la gravedad; por ejemplo, la Luna se mueve en una órbita alrededor de la Tierra.

orbitar *v.* Girar alrededor de algo, o moverse en una órbita; por ejemplo, la Luna orbita la Tierra.

original remains
A fossil that is the actual body or body parts of an organism. (p. 458)

restos originales Un fósil que es en realidad el cuerpo o partes del cuerpo de un organismo.

organ
A structure in a plant or animal that is made up of different tissues working together to perform a particular function. (p. 573)

órgano Una estructura en una planta o en un animal compuesta de diferentes tejidos que trabajan juntos para realizar una función determinada.

organism
An individual living thing, made up of one or many cells, that is capable of growing and reproducing.

organsismo Un individuo vivo, compuesto de una o muchas células, que es capaz de crecer y reproducirse.

organ system
A group of organs that together perform a function that helps the body meet its needs for energy and materials. (p. 574)

sistema de órganos Un grupo de órganos que juntos realizan una función que ayuda al cuerpo a satisfacer sus necesidades energéticas y de materiales.

overfishing
The catching of fish at a faster rate than they can reproduce. (p. 171)

sobrepesca La captura de peces a un ritmo mayor a la que pueden reproducirse.

pathogen
An agent that causes disease. (p. 640)

patógeno Un agente que causa una enfermedad.

parallax
The apparent shift in the position of an object when viewed from different locations. (p. 787)

paralaje El cambio aparente en la posición de un objeto cuando se observa desde diferentes puntos.

parallel circuit
A circuit in which current follows more than one path. Each device that is wired in a parallel circuit has its own path to and from the voltage source. (p. 385)

circuito paralelo Un circuito en el cual la corriente sigue más de una trayectoria. Cada aparato que está conectado a un circuito paralelo tiene su propia trayectoria desde y hacia la fuente de voltaje.

penumbra
A region of lighter shadow that may surround an umbra; for example, the spreading cone of lighter shadow cast by a space object. (p. 727)

penumbra Una región de sombra más tenue que puede rodear a una umbra; por ejemplo, la sombra más tenue cónica proyectada por un objeto espacial.

peristalsis (PEHR-ih-STAWL-sihs)
Wavelike contractions of smooth muscles in the organs of the digestive tract. The contractions move food through the digestive system. (p. 608)

peristalsis Contracciones ondulares de músculos lisos en los órganos del tracto digestivo. Las contracciones mueven el alimento por el sistema digestivo.

permeable
Allowing the passage of water. (p. 64)

permeable Que permite el paso del agua.

phytoplankton (FY-toh-PLANGK-tuhn)
Microscopic floating organisms that live in water and, like plants, convert sunlight and carbon dioxide into food. (p. 166)

fitoplancton Organismos microscópicos que flotan y viven en el agua y, al igual que las , convierten la luz del Sol y el dióxido de carbono en alimento.

planet
A spherical body, larger than a comet or asteroid, that orbits the Sun, or a similar body that orbits a different star.

planeta Un cuerpo esférico, más grande que un cometa o un asteroide, que orbita alrededor del Sol, o un cuerpo similar que orbita alrededor de una estrella distinta.

point-source pollution
Pollution that enters water from a known source. (p. 94)

contaminación por fuentes puntuales Contaminación que entra al agua proveniente de una fuente conocida.

pollution
The release of harmful substances into the air, water, or land. (p. 550)

contaminación La descarga de sustancias nocivas al aire, al agua o a la tierra.

population density
A measure of the number of organisms that live in a given area. The population density of a city may be given as the number of people living in a square kilometer. (p. 531)

densidad de población Una medida de la cantidad de organismos que viven un área dada. La densidad de población de una ciudad puede expresarse como el número de personas que viven en un kilómetro cuadrado.

population dynamics
The study of the changes in the number of individuals in a population and the factors that affect those changes. (p. 527)

dinámica de población El estudio de los cambios en el número de individuos en una población y los factores que afectan a estos cambios.

population size
The number of individuals of the same species that live in a given area. (p. 530)

tamaño de la población El número de individuos de la misma especie que vive en un área determinada.

precipitation
Any type of liquid or solid water that falls to Earth's surface, such as rain, snow, or hail. (p. 53)

precipitación Cualquier tipo de agua líquida o sólida que cae a la superficie de la Tierra, como por ejemplo lluvia, nieve o granizo.

prime meridian
An imaginary north-south line that divides the planet into the Eastern Hemisphere and the Western Hemisphere. The prime meridian passes through Greenwich, England. (p. 207)

primer meridiano Una línea imaginaria de norte a sur que divide al planeta en hemisferio oriental y hemisferio occidental. El primer meridiano pasa a través de Greenwich, Inglaterra.

probe
A spacecraft that is sent into a planet's atmosphere or onto a solid surface. (p. 693)

sonda espacial Una nave espacial enviada a la atmósfera de un planeta o a una superficie sólida.

projection
A representation of Earth's curved surface on a flat map. (p. 208)

proyección Una representación de la superficie curva de la Tierra en un mapa plano.

proton
A positively charged particle located in an atom's nucleus.

protón Una partícula con carga positiva localizada en el núcleo de un átomo.

Q

qualitative
Descriptive; relating to a characteristic, quality, or trait.

cualitativo Descriptivo; relacionado con una característica, una cualidad o un rasgo.

quantitative
Expressed as a number or amount.

cuantitativo Que se expresa como un número o una cantidad.

quasar
The very bright center of a distant galaxy. (p. 797)

quásar El centro muy brillante de una galaxia distante.

R

radiation (RAY-dee-AY-shuhn)
Energy that travels across distances as certain types of waves.

radiación Energia que viaja a través de las distancias en forma de ciertos tipos de ondas.

recycling
The reusing of materials that people would otherwise throw away, such as paper, glass, plastics, and certain metals. (p. 310)

reciclaje El reutilizar los materiales que la gente de otra forma desecharía, como el papel, el vidrio, los plásticos y ciertos metales.

red blood cell
A type of blood cell that picks up oxygen in the lungs and delivers it to cells throughout the body. (p. 633)

glóbulos rojos Un tipo de célula sanguínea que toma oxígeno en los pulmones y lo transporta a células en todo el cuerpo.

relative age
The age of an event or object in relation to other events or objects. (p. 465)

edad relativa La edad de un evento u objeto en relación a otros eventos u objetos.

relief
In geology, the difference in elevation between an area's high and low points. (p. 213)

relieve En geología, la diferencia en elevación entre los puntos altos y bajos de un área.

relief map
A map that shows the differences in elevation in an area. Relief maps can show elevations through the use of contour lines, shading, colors, and, in some cases, three-dimensional materials. (p. 204)

mapa de relieve Un mapa que muestra las diferencias en elevación de un área. Los mapas de relieve pueden mostrar elevaciones mediante del uso de curvas de nivel, sombreado, colores y, en algunos casos, materiales tridimensionales.

remote sensing
A method of using scientific equipment to gather information about something from a distance. Most remote-sensing methods make use of different types of electromagnetic radiation. (p. 218)

sensoramiento remoto Un método de reunir información sobre algo a distancia usando equipo científico. La mayoría de los métodos de sensoramiento remoto hacen uso de diferentes tipos de radiación electromagnética.

renewable resource
A natural resource that can be replaced in nature at about the same rate as it is used. (p. 300)

recurso renovable Un recurso natural que puede reemplazarse en la naturaleza casi al mismo ritmo al que es utilizado.

reproducible
Capable of being produced again. Reproducible results can be obtained by different people following the same procedures.

reproducible Que puede reproducirse de nuevo. Diferentes personas pueden obtener los resultados reproducibles siguiendo el mismo procedimiento.

resistance
1. The ability of an organism to protect itself from a disease or the effects of a substance. 2. The property of a material that determines how easily a charge can move through it. Resistance is measured in ohms. (p. 355)

resistencia 1. La habilidad de un organismo para protegerse de una enfermedad o de los efectos de una sustancia. 2. La propiedad de un material que determina qué tan fácilmente puede moverse una carga a través de él. La resistencia se mide en ohmios.

resistor

An electrical device that slows the flow of charge in a circuit. (p. 376)

  resistencia Un aparato eléctrico que hace más lento el flujo de carga en un circuito.

respiratory system

A system that interacts with the environment and with other body systems to bring oxygen to the body and remove carbon dioxide. (p. 599)

  sistema respiratorio Un sistema que interactúa con el medio ambiente y con otros sistemas corporales para traer oxígeno al cuerpo y eliminar dióxido de carbono.

revolution

The motion of one body around another, such as Earth in its orbit around the Sun; the time it takes an object to go around once. (p. 709)

  revolución El movimiento de un cuerpo alrededor de otro, como la Tierra en su órbita alrededor del Sol; el tiempo que le toma a un objeto dar la vuelta una vez.

ring

In astronomy, a wide, flat zone of small particles that orbit around a planet's equator. (p. 761)

  anillo En astronomía, una zona ancha y plana de pequeñas partículas que orbitan alrededor del ecuador de un planeta.

rip current

A narrow stream of water that breaks through sandbars and drains rapidly back into deeper water. (p. 132)

  corriente de retorno Una estrecha corriente de agua que atraviesa barras de arena y drena rápidamente hacia aguas más profundas.

S

salinity (suh-LIHN-ih-tee)

The measure of the amount of dissolved salt contained in water. (p. 116)

  salinidad La medida de la cantidad de sal disuelta en el agua.

salt water

Water that contains dissolved salts and other minerals. Oceans consist of salt water. (p. 51)

  agua salada Agua que contiene sales disueltas y otros minerales. Los océanos están compuestos de agua salada.

sandbar

A ridge of sand built up by the action of waves and currents. (p. 276)

  barra de arena Una colina de arena que se forma por la acción de las olas y las corrientes.

satellite

A body that orbits a more massive body. A natural satellite is also called a moon. (p. 687)

  satélite Un cuerpo que orbita otro de mayor masa. Un satélite natural también se denomina luna.

scientific processes

The actions that make up an inquiry; these usually include asking questions, determining what is known, investigating, interpreting results, and sharing information. (p. 6)

  proceso científico Las acciones que conforman una inquisición; éstas incluyen, por lo general, hacer preguntas, determinar lo que se conoce, investigar, interpretar los resultados y compartir la información.

season

One part of a pattern of temperature changes and other weather trends over the course of a year. Astronomical seasons are defined and caused by the position of Earth's axis relative to the direction of sunlight. (p. 710)

  estación Una parte de un patrón de cambios de temperatura y otras tendencias meteorológicas en el curso de un año. Las estaciones astronómicas se definen y son causadas por la posición del eje de la Tierra en relación a la dirección de la luz del Sol.

sensor

A mechanical or electronic device that receives and responds to a signal, such as light. (p. 219)

  sensor Un dispositivo mecánico o electrónico que recibe y responde a una señal, como la luz.

septic system

A small sewage system, often for one home or business, that uses an underground tank to treat wastewater. (p. 94)

  sistema séptico Un pequeño sistema de aguas residuales, a menudo para un hogar o un negocio, que usa un tanque subterráneo para tratar las aguas de desecho.

series circuit

A circuit in which current follows a single path. Each device that is wired in a series circuit shares a path to and from the voltage source. (p. 384)

  circuito en serie Un circuito en el cual la corriente sigue una sola trayectoria. Cada aparato conectado a un circuito en serie comparte una trayectoria desde y hacia la fuente de voltaje.

sewage system
A system that collects and treats wastewater from a city or a town. (p. 93)

> **sistema de aguas residuales** Un sistema que recolecta y trata las aguas de desecho de una ciudad o población.

short circuit
An unintended and undesired path connecting one part of a circuit with another. (p. 378)

> **corto circuito** Una trayectoria no intencionada y no deseada que conecta una parte de un circuito con otra.

sinkhole
An open basin that forms when the roof of a cavern becomes so thin that it falls in. (p. 271)

> **sumidero** Una cuenca abierta que se forma cuando el techo de una caverna se vuelve tan delgado que se desploma.

skeletal muscle
A muscle that attaches to the skeleton. (p. 586)

> **músculo esquelético** Un músculo que está sujeto al esqueleto.

skeletal system
The framework of bones that supports the body, protects internal organs, and anchors all the body's movement. (p. 576)

> **sistema óseo** El armazón de huesos que sostiene al cuerpo, protege a los órganos internos y sirve de ancla para todo el movimiento del cuerpo.

skepticism
The act of doubting and questioning. A skeptic accepts only explanations that are based on evidence. (p. 9)

> **escepticismo** La acción de dudar y cuestionar. Un escéptico sólo acepta explicaciones basadas en pruebas.

slope
A measure of how steep a landform is. Slope is calculated as the change in elevation divided by the distance covered. (p. 213)

> **pendiente** Una medida de lo inclinada de una formación terrestre. La pendiente se calcula dividiendo el cambio en la elevación por la distancia recorrida.

smooth muscle
Muscle that performs involuntary movement and is found inside certain organs, such as the stomach. (p. 586)

> **músculo liso** Músculos que realizan movimiento involuntario y se encuentran dentro de ciertos órganos, como el estómago.

soil horizon
A soil layer with physical and chemical properties that differ from those of soil layers above or below it. (p. 240)

> **horizonte del suelo** Una capa del suelo con propiedades físicas y químicas que difieren de las de las capas del suelo superior e inferior a la misma.

soil profile
The soil horizons in a specific location; a cross section of soil layers that displays all soil horizons. (p. 240)

> **perfil del suelo** Los horizontes del suelo en un lugar específico; una sección transversal de las capas del suelo que muestra todos los horizontes del suelo.

solar cell
A type of technology in which light-sensitive materials convert sunlight into electrical energy. (p. 317)

> **celda solar** Un tipo de tecnología en el cual materiales sensibles a la luz convierten luz solar a energía eléctrica.

solar system
The Sun and its family of orbiting planets, moons, and other objects. (p. 674)

> **sistema solar** El Sol y su familia de planetas, lunas y otros objetos en órbita.

solar wind
A stream of electrically charged particles that flows out in all directions from the Sun's corona. (p. 783)

> **viento solar** Una corriente de partículas eléctricamente cargadas que fluye hacia fuera de la corona del Sol en todas las direcciones.

solstice (SAHL-stihs)
In an orbit, a position and time during which one hemisphere gets its maximum area of sunlight, while the other hemisphere gets its minimum amount; the time of year when days are either longest or shortest, and the angle of sunlight reaches its maximum or minimum. (p. 710)

> **solsticio** En una órbita, la posición y el tiempo durante los cuales un hemisferio obtiene su área máxima de luz del Sol, mientras que el otro hemisferio obtiene su cantidad mínima; la época del año en la cual los días son los más largos o los más cortos y el ángulo de la luz del Sol alcanza su máximo o su mínimo.

sonar (SO-nahr)
Instruments that use echolocation to locate objects underwater; acronym for "sound navigation and ranging." (p. 122)

> **sonar** Instrumentos que usan la ecolocación para localizar objetos bajo agua; acrónimo en inglés para "navegación y determinación de distancias por sonido".

space station

A satellite in which people can live and work for long periods. (p. 688)

estación espacial Un satélite en el cual la gente puede vivir y trabajar durante períodos largos.

speciation

The evolution of a new species from an existing species. (p. 504)

especiación La evolución de una nueva especie a partir de una especie existente.

species

A group of organisms so closely related that they can breed with one another and produce offspring that are able to breed. (p. FL31)

especie Un grupo de organismos que están tan estrechamente relacionados que pueden aparearse entre sí y producir crías que también pueden aparearse.

spectrum (SPEHK-truhm)

1. Radiation from a source separated into a range of wavelengths. 2. The range of colors that appears in a beam of visible light when it passes through a prism. *See also* electromagnetic radiation. (p. 680)

espectro 1. Radiación de una fuente separada en una gama de longitudes de onda. 2. La gama de colores que aparece en un haz de luz visible cuando éste pasa a través de un prisma. Ver también radiación electromagnética.

spongy bone

Strong, lightweight tissue inside a bone. (p. 577)

hueso esponjoso Tejido fuerte y de peso ligero dentro de un hueso.

spring

A flow of water from the ground at a place where the surface of the land dips below the water table. (p. 68)

manantial Un flujo de agua proveniente del suelo en un punto donde la superficie de la tierra desciende por debajo del nivel freático.

spring tide

A tide of large range occurring during the new and full moons, resulting in an extra-high tidal bulge and an extra-low tidal dip. (p. 139)

marea viva Una marea de amplio rango que ocurre durante la luna nueva y la luna llena y que resulta en una protuberancia mareal más alta de lo normal y un descenso de la marea más bajo de lo normal.

static charge

The buildup of electric charge in an object caused by the uneven distribution of charged particles. (p. 343)

carga estática La acumulación de carga eléctrica en un objeto ocasionada por la desigual distribución de partículas con carga.

sunspot

A darker spot on the photosphere of the Sun. A sunspot appears dark because it is cooler than the surrounding area. (p. 782)

mancha solar Una mancha oscura en la fotosfera del Sol. Una mancha solar se ve oscura porque es más fría que el área que la rodea.

system

A group of objects or phenomena that interact. A system can be as simple as a rope, a pulley, and a mass. It also can be as complex as the interaction of energy and matter in the four spheres of the Earth system. (p. 197)

sistema Un grupo de objetos o fenómenos que interactúan. Un sistema puede ser algo tan sencillo como una cuerda, una polea y una masa. También puede ser algo tan complejo como la interacción de la energía y la materia en las cuatro esferas del sistema de la Tierra.

T

technology

The use of scientific knowledge to solve problems or engineer new products, tools, or processes. (p. 25)

tecnología El uso de conocimientos científicos para resolver problemas o para diseñar nuevos productos, herramientas o procesos.

tectonics (tehk-TAHN-ihks)

The processes in which the motion of hot material under a crust changes the crust of a space body. Earth has a specific type of tectonics called plate tectonics. (p. 750)

tectónica Los procesos en los cuales el movimiento del material caliente bajo una corteza cambia la corteza de un cuerpo espacial. La Tierra tiene un tipo específico de tectónica denominado tectónica de placas.

telescope

A device that gather visible light or another form of electromagnetic radiation. (p. 681)

telescopio Un aparato que reúne luz visible u otra forma de radiación electromagnética.

terrestrial planet
Earth or a planet similar to Earth that has a rocky surface. The four planets in the inner solar system—Mercury, Venus, Earth, and Mars—are terrestrial planets. (p. 749)

> **planeta terrestre** La Tierra o un planeta parecido a la Tierra que tiene una superficie rocosa. Los cuatro planetas en el sistema solar interior—Mercurio, Venus, la Tierra y Marte— son planetas terrestres.

theory
In science, a set of widely accepted explanations of observations and phenomena. A theory is a well-tested explanation that is consistent with all available evidence. (p. 19)

> **teoría** En las ciencias, un conjunto de explicaciones de observaciones y fenómenos que es ampliamente aceptado. Una teoría es una explicación bien probada que es consecuente con la evidencia disponible.

tidal range
The difference in height between high tide and low tide. (p. 138)

> **rango de marea** La diferencia en altura entre la marea alta y la marea baja.

tide
The periodic rising and falling of the water level of the ocean due to the gravitational pulls of the Moon and the Sun. (p. 136)

> **marea** La subida y caída periódica del nivel del agua del océano debido a las atracciones gravitacionales de la Luna y del Sol.

till
Sediment of different sizes left directly on the ground by a melting, or retreating, glacier. (p. 284)

> **sedimentos glaciares** Sedimentos de diferentes tamaños depositados directamente en el suelo por un glaciar que se derrite o retrocede.

tissue
A group of similar cells that together perform a specific function in an organism. (p. 572)

> **tejido** Un grupo de células parecidas que juntas realizan una función específica en un organismo.

topography
All natural and human-made surface features of a particular area. (p. 212)

> **topografía** Todas las características de superficie de origen natural y humano en un área particular.

transformer
A device that uses electromagnetism to increase or decrease voltage. A transformer is often used in the distribution of current from power plants. (p. 431)

transformador Un aparato que usa electromagnetismo para aumentar o disminuir el voltaje. A menudo se usa un transformador en la distribución de corriente desde las centrales eléctricas.

turnover
The yearly rising and sinking of cold and warm water layers in a lake. (p. 59)

> **renovación** La ascensión y el hundimiento anual de las capas de agua fría y agua cálida en un lago.

U

umbra
The dark, central region of a shadow, such as the cone of complete shadow cast by an object. (p. 727)

> **umbra** La región central y oscura de una sombra, como la sombra completa cónica proyectada por un objeto.

unicellular organism
An organism that is made up of a single cell. (p. 492)

> **organismo unicelular** Un organismo compuesto de una sola célula.

uniformitarianism
(YOO-nuh-fawr-mih-TAIR-ee-uh-nihz-uhm)
A theory stating that processes shaping Earth today, such as erosion and deposition, also shaped Earth in the past, and that these processes cause large changes over geologic time. (p. 474)

> **uniformismo** Una teoría que afirma que los procesos que le dan forma a la Tierra hoy en día, como la erosión y la sedimentación, también le dieron forma a la Tierra en el pasado; además, afirma que estos procesos ocasionan grandes cambios en tiempo geológico.

universe
Space and all the matter and energy in it. (p. 674)

> **universo** El espacio y toda la materia y energía que hay dentro de él.

upwelling
The vertical movement of deep water up to the surface. (p. 126)

> **surgencia** El movimiento vertical del agua profunda a la superficie.

urinary system
A group of organs that filter waste from an organism's blood and excrete it in a liquid called urine. (p. 615)

> **sistema urinario** Un grupo de órganos que filtran desechos de la sangre de un organismo y los excretan en un líquido llamado orina.

urine
Liquid waste that is secreted by the kidneys. (p. 615)

   orina El desecho líquido que secretan los riñones.

V

vaccine
A small amount of a weakened pathogen that is introduced into the body to stimulate the production of antibodies. (p. 646)

   vacuna Una pequeña cantidad de un patógeno debilitado que se introduce al cuerpo para estimular la producción de anticuerpos.

variable
Any factor that can change in a controlled experiment, observation, or model.

   variable Cualquier factor que puede cambiar en un experimento controlado, en una observación o en un modelo.

vein
A blood vessel that carries blood back to the heart. (p. 635)

   vena Un vaso sanguíneo que lleva la sangre de regreso al corazón.

vestigial organ (veh-STIHJ-ee-uhl)
A physical structure that was fully developed and functional in an earlier group of organisms but is reduced and unused in later species. (p. 510)

   órgano vestigial Una estructura física que fue completamente desarrollada y funcional en un grupo anterior de organismos pero que está reducido y en desuso en especies posteriores.

volcanism
The process of molten material moving from a space body's hot interior onto its surface. (p. 750)

   vulcanismo El proceso del movimiento de material fundido del interior caliente de un cuerpo espacial a su superficie.

volt V
The unit of measurement for electric potential, which is equal to one joule per coulomb. The number of volts of an electric charge equals the charge's voltage. (p. 351)

   voltio La unidad de medición para el potencial eléctrico, el cual es igual a un julio por culombio. El número de voltios de una carga eléctrica es igual al voltaje de la carga.

volume
An amount of three-dimensional space, often used to describe the space that an object takes up.

volumen Una cantidad de espacio tridimensional; a menudo se usa este término para describir el espacio que ocupa un objeto.

voluntary muscle
A muscle that can be moved at will. (p. 586)

   músculo voluntario Un músculo que puede moverse a voluntad.

W, X, Y, Z

water cycle
The continuous movement of water on Earth, through its atmosphere, and in the living things on Earth. (p. 52)

   ciclo del agua El movimiento continuo de agua sobre la Tierra, por su atmósfera y dentro de los organismos vivos de la Tierra.

water table
The highest part in the ground that is saturated, or completely filled with water. (p. 65)

   nivel freático La parte más alta del suelo que está saturada, o completamente llena de agua.

watt W
The unit of measurement for power, which is equal to one joule of work done or energy transferred in one second. For example, a 75 W light bulb converts electrical energy into heat and light at a rate of 75 joules per second. (p. 436)

   vatio La unidad de medición de la potencia, el cual es igual a un julio de trabajo realizado o energía transferida en un segundo. Por ejemplo, una bombilla de 75 W convierte energía eléctrica a calor y luz a un ritmo de 75 julios por segundo.

wavelength
The distance from one wave crest to the next crest; the distance from any part of one wave to the identical part of the next wave. (p. 680)

   longitud de onda La distancia de una cresta de onda a la siguiente cresta; la distancia de cualquier parte de una onda a la parte idéntica de la siguiente onda.

weathering
The process by which natural forces break down rocks. (p. 231)

   meteorización El proceso por el cual las fuerzas naturales fragmentan las rocas.

wetland
A wet, swampy area that is often flooded with water. (p. 156)

   humedal Un área húmeda y pantanosa que a menudo está inundada de agua.

Index

Page numbers for definitions are printed in **boldface** type.
Page numbers for illustrations, maps and charts are printed in *italic* type.

A

abdominal breathing, *606*
abiotic factors, 538
abrasion, **232,** *233,* 284, *284*
absolute age, **469,** *470,* 471, 482, 490
absorption of radiation, 188
AB type blood, 637, *637*
abyssal plains, 120, *120–121*
acceleration, 815
accuracy, **R22,** R22
AC-DC converter, 429, *429*
acid drainage, 250
acid rain, 105, 235, *235*
actinides, *841*
active immunity, 646
adaptations, **FL31,** 501, **502,** 516
    change in behavior, *39,* 280, 500, *500,* 545–546, 554
    change in color, 39, 166, *500, 501,* 504–505, *504,* 515, *515*
    change in physiology, 168, 280, 349, 453, 510
    change in structure, 166, 280, *280,* 494, 499–500, *499, 500, 503,* 510, 515, *515*
    of deep-sea creatures, 166
    of electric eels, 349
    protective, *163*
    reproductive success and, 453, 541, *541,* 542, *542*
    of sharks, 451, 453
address, of Web pages, 397
adolescence, 580, 589
adulthood, 580
Africa
    first people in, 545
    food shortages in, 105
    new fish species in, 521, *521*
    speciation in, *504*
    water shortages in, 100, 102, *105*
Age of Mammals, 479
age of rocks
    absolute age, 469, *469, 470,* 471
    dating rocks, *466, 467, 468, 469, 470,* 471
    index fossils, 467–468, *467, 468*
    radioactive dating, 469, *470, 472*
    relative age, 465–468, *466, 467, 468,* 471
    sedimentary layers, 466–467, *467*
ages, geologic, 827
age structure, 533, *533,* 547, 548, 554
agriculture
    affect on soil, 249, *249,* 254
    aquaculture, 85, *85*
    changes in Earth's surface for, 201
    conservation practices of, 97, *97,* 103, 251–252, *252*
    effects on ecosystems, 45
    in Egypt, 87
    in Florida, 565
    human population growth and, *546,* 547
    irrigation, 70, 107
    pollution and, 94, *95,* 97, 249, 550, *550*
    precipitation and, 54
    research, 24
    use of water, 81, 82, 83, *83,* 101, 104
AIDS, 548
air
    gases in, 600
    ocean water and, 127
    in soil, 239, 244, 245
air bladders, 161, 166
air filter, 348
airplanes
    fishing industry and, 171
    remote imaging from, *186–187,* 187–188, *188,* 189, 218–219
    for weather forecasting, 198
air pollution
    chemical weathering and, 235, *235*
    from factories, 306
    from fossil fuels, 300, 303, 304
    ocean pollution and, *176*
    spread of, 105
air pressure, 754
Ais people, 668
Alaska, 40, *269,* 307
Aldrin, Buzz, *748*
Alexander the Great, 146, *146*
algae, *118*
    as bottom dweller, 154
    coral and, 43, 44, 162
    eutrophication and, 60, *60*
    as food source, 170
    as opportunist, 541
    pollution and, 175
allergens, 648, *648*
alluvial fan, **269,** *269*
alpine glaciers, 282, *283*
alternating current (AC), **429**
alternative energy sources, 300, *301,* 313–321
alternator, 364, 430
alveoli, 602, *603*
Alvin, 40
amber, original remains in, 458, *458*
Ambulocetus, 511
American beach grass, 280, *280*
ammeter, 362
amperage, 361–362, *361,* 380
ampere, **361**
Ampère, André, *437*
amphibians, 494, 819

amplitude, sound waves, 331
analog (information), 331, **392,** *392*
analysis, critical, **R8**
Anasazi people, 731
ancestors, **509,** 519, *519*
Andes Mountains, 204
Andromeda Galaxy, 800, *800*
anemia, 583
anemone, *163,* 164
anglerfish, 166, *167,* 515, *515*
angular movement, 581, *582*
animals. *See also* humans
    affect on soil, 242, *243*
    biomass energy, 320
    in coastal environments, 162, *162*
    of coral reef, 43
    in deep-zone ocean environments, 166
    development of, 512, *512*
    effects on Earth's surface, 201
    of estuaries, 156
    experimentation with, 28, 29
    first mammals, 478
    fossil fuels, 302
    mass extinction of, 448
    as ocean resource, 170
    in ocean waters, 118, 126, 154
    pollution and, 105, 175
    populations of, 528–534, *528, 529, 531, 532, 534,*
     536–542
    of sand dunes, 280, *280*
    satellite monitoring of, 199
    soil type and, 239
    use of water, 82, 83
    wastes as renewable resource, *301*
    water pollution and, 97, *97*
animatronics, 334–337, *334, 335, 336, 337*
Antarctica, 61, 62, 126, 282
    fossils, 462
    ice cores from, *17,* 463, *463*
antibiotics, **647**
antibodies, 637, **641,** 642, *644,* 645
antigens, 637, **644,** 644–645, *644*
antikythera computer, 731, *731*
Apollo space program, 687, 695
appendicular skeleton, **578,** 578, *579,* 592, *592*
aquaculture, **85,** *85,* 172, *172*
aquariums, 89, *89*
Aquarius, 149, *149*
aquifers, **66,** 66–68, *66, 68, 69,* 82
    depletion of, 101, 102
    filtration of water in, 13, *13*
    irrigation and, 70, 82
    sinkholes and, 192
Archaean eon, *476,* 477, 826, *826*
archeologists, *FL15,* 486–487, 731
Arctic Ocean, 126
area, calculating, R43, *R43*
Arecibo radio telescope, 664–665, *664, 665*
Argo floats, 149, *149*
armadillo, 509
Armstrong, Neil, 748, *748*
Arnioceras semicostatum, 467

arteries, *634,* **635,** 635, *635*
    blood pressure and, 635–636, *636*
artesian wells, **68,** *68, 69*
artificial selection, 501, *501*
artificial skin, 655, *655*
asexual reproduction, **817**
    compared to sexual reproduction, 817–818
asteroid belt, 767
asteroids, 449, 458, 479, *665,* **767,** *767,* 772
    distance from the Sun, *744,* 767, *772*
    formation of, 746–747, 767
    seen by reflected light, 743
    size of, *744,* 745
    tracking of, 664–665
astrolabe, 736, *736*
astronauts, 700
    Buzz Aldrin, *748*
    Neil Armstrong, 748, *748*
    conditions for, 686
    danger from solar wind, 783
    gravity and, 707
    Hubble Telescope repair, 682
    Moon missions, 687, *687, 688,* 748
    shuttle flights, 689, *689*
    space station missions, 688
    weight on Moon, 748
astronomers, 664–665, 674, 678, 681, 713
    early peoples, 731, *731*
    Moon rocks and, 719
astronomical unit (AU), **745,** 839
Aswan Dam (Egypt), 87
Atlanta, Georgia, *271*
Atlantic Ocean, 62, 115, 294, *294*
atmosphere, **FL33,** 197, **198.** *See also* pollution
    air pollution, 105, *176,* 235, *235,* 300, 303, 304, 306
    development of, 292, *292,* 293, *293*
    of Earth, 695, 752
    Earth's surface and, 201, *202*
    effect of oceans on, 40
    effects of volcanoes on, 448–449, *448*
    formation of, 293, 492
    of gas giants, 758
    Hubble Telescope and, 682–683, *683*
    interaction with winds and ocean currents, 199
    of Jupiter, 760
    knowledge of from space exploration, 695, 696
    light and, 682, 683
    magnetism and, 418, *418*
    of Mars, *756*
    of Neptune, 763
    new knowledge about, 695
    of Pluto, 765
    resources in, 299
    satellite monitoring of, 697
    of Saturn, 758–759, 760
    solar winds and, 783, *783*
    space exploration and, 696
    space objects and, 663, *663*
    of the Sun, 779, 780
    temperature control, 752
    of terrestrial planets, 752
    of Titan, 766, *766*

of Triton, 766, *766*
Uranus, 758–759, 762
on Venus, 754
volcanic eruptions and, 200
x-rays, gamma rays and, 683
atomic mass, *841*
atomic mass number, 813
atomic number, 812, *841*
atoms, 812, **FL35**
    electric charge and, 343–346, *343, 344, 345, 346*
    half-life, 469
    magnetism and, 414
    nuclear power and, 313–314, *314*
    polarized, 346
    structure of, 342, 812
atrium of heart, *632, 633*
attraction
    electrical, *342,* 350, 352, 368
    magnetic, 412, 413, *413*
A type blood, 637, *637*
audio-animatronics, 334–337
audiocassette, 423
auroras, 783, *783*
Australia, *499,* 523, *523*
automobile. *See* cars.
autumn, 710, *711,* 836
axial skeleton, **578,** 578, *579,* 592, *592*
axis of rotation, **708,** 730
    angles of sunlight and, 712–713, *712, 713*
    of Earth, 416, 417, *708*
    of Moon, 717
    of Saturn, 761
    seasons and, 709–710, *711*
    tides and, 730, *730*
    time zones and, 707–708, *708*
    of Uranus, 762

B

Babbage, Charles, 405
backbone, 582
bacteria, 572
    chemical weathering by, 242
    in coastal environments, 162
    diseases caused by, 647, *647*
    near hydrothermal vents, 168, 169
    in ocean waters, 154
    as opportunist, 541
    pathogens and, 633
    pollution and, 175
    soil formation and, 242
    survival of, 448
    water treatment and, 93, 94
Ballard, Robert, 40
bar magnets, 412, *412, 413*
barrier islands, **276,** 276–277, *276, 277,* 288
Barringer Crater (Arizona), *662–663*
basalt, 719, *719,* 720
Bassi, Laura, 405
bats, 510, *511*
batteries
    car, 364, *365*

DC current, 429
electrochemical cells, 363–364, *363, 365*
invention of, 405, *405*
in open and closed circuits, 377, *377*
in parallel circuits, 385
primary (wet) cells, 364, *365*
rechargeable (storage) batteries, 364, *365*
secondary (storage) cells, 364, *365*
in series circuits, 384
symbols for in circuits, 377, *377*
voltage source, 376, *376*
bays, 156
B cells, *644,* 645, 646
beaches, *564,* 565
Beagle, 498, 508
Beatbugs, 332, *332*
bees, 531, *531*
behaviors, *39*
Bell, Jocelyn, 8–11, *8*
Bell, Joshua, 332
Betelgeuse (star), 788, *792*
bias, 21, *21,* **R6**
big bang theory, 738, 739, *739,* **802**
bile, 612
bile duct, *612*
binary code, **390,** *390, 392, 394,* 398, 407
binary fission, 817
binary star system, 792, *792*
biodiversity, **FL31,** 448–449, 505
biological evidence, *509,* 510, *511,* 512, *512,* 516, *516*
biology, *6*
bioluminescence, 515, *515*
biomass energy, **320,** 320, *320,* 324
bioremediation, 307
biosphere, **FL33,** *185,* 197, **199,** *199,* 201, *202,* 299
biotic factors, 821
birds, *FL30,* 478, 669, 818
    estuaries and, 156
    first appearance of, 494
    lakes and ponds and, 58
    pollution and, 550
    of salt marshes, 157, *157*
birth, in sharks, 453
birth rate, 537–538, 547
bit, 390, 407
black holes, **790,** *791,* 797, *797, 804*
bladder, 615, *615*
blindness, *560–561,* 562, *562*
blood, **631,** *634,* 656
    bones and, 577
    clotting of, 612, 633
    composition of, 633, *633*
    function of, 51, 577
    kidneys and, 615
    path in circulatory system, 632–633, *632,* 635
    types of, 637, *637*
    waste removal from, 615–616, *616*
blood cells, *FL17, 583,* 633
    formation of, 577, 583
blood pressure, 566, 617, 635–636, *636,* 656
blood transfusions, 637

blood vessels, *628–629*, 631–632, *632*, 635–636, *635*, 656
  blood pressure and, 635–636, *636*
  in bones, *577*
  cellular respiration and, 601
  CT scan of, 626, *626*
  in kidneys, *616*
  in skin, 650, *650*
Blue Marble, 295, *295*
blue shift light, 800, *801*
body temperature
  exercise, 589, 638–639
  fatty tissue and, 650, *650*
  hair and, 652
  immune response and, 643
  shivering and, 585, *585*
  sweat and, 574, 650–651, *650*
bone density, 580, *580*
bone density test, 580, *580*
bone hut, *479*
bone marrow, 577, *577*, 583, 641
bones, 573, 576–577, *577*
  classification of, 576
  coral grafts for, 44
  as levers, 576, 595, *595*
  vitamin D and, 565–566, 567
Borelly (comet), *768*
bottom dwellers, 154
Brahe, Tycho, 737
Braille, 562, *562*
brain
  mapping of, 561–562, *561*, *562*
  scans of, 627, *627*
  of sharks, 452
brainstorming, 8
breathing, 599–600, *600*, 606, *606*
breeding, 501, *501*
brightness of stars, 784–785, 787, 792
bronchial tubes, 602, *603*, *620*
B type blood, 637, *637*
Buckland, William, 520
budding, **817**
buoyancy, 116, *117*
Burgess Shale, 521, *521*
burns, 653–654, 655
Busch, Gil, 562
Busch Gardens, 335
Bushnell, David, 147
butterfly fish, 44
by-catch, **172**, *172*, 180
byte, 390

C

cacti, *532*, 533, 542
calculators, 386
Callisto (moon), 766
Cambrian period, *476, 477*, 523, *523*, 826
Canada
  Burgess Shale found in, 521, *521*
  diamonds in, 188–189
  Great Lake water sales and, 105
  in ice age, 282, *282*
  icebergs near, 62
  mountain ranges of, 204
Canada Center for Remote Sensing, 189
Canadian Rocky Mountains, 204
canals, 85, 86
cancer, 170, 565, 566
capacitors, 404, *404*
capsid, 820
Cape Canaveral, *666*, 667–669, *667, 668, 669*
capillaries, **635**, 635, *635*
carbohydrates, 607
carbon, 790
  cycle, 821
carbon 14 dating, 471, 472, *472, 522*, 831
carbonate rock, 191
carbon dioxide
  in atmosphere, 198, 600
  biomass energy and, 320
  cellular respiration and, 601
  circulatory system and, 631, 632–633, 635
  forests and, 199
  fossil fuels use and, 303
  gravity and formation of atmospheres, 752
  in Mar's atmosphere, 756
  in ocean water, 118, *118*
  photosynthesis and, 166
  respiratory system and, 599–600, *600*, 602, 620
  rock weathering and, 234–235
  in Venus's atmosphere, 754
carbon films, 460, *461*, 828, 829, *829*
Carboniferous period, *476–477, 826–827*
carbon nanotube, 407
cardiac muscle, **586**, *587*, 592
carrying capacity, **528**, 544
cars
  alternator (generator), 364, *365*, 430
  battery, 364, *365*
  changes in society, 26
  computers in, 393
  electrostatic painting process, 348, *348*
  gas mileage of, 312, *312*
  hydrogen powered, *26*, 320–321, *321*
  manufacturing of, 84
  pollution from, 302–306
  starter motor, 364, *365*
  use of GPS in, 207
cartilage, 580, 602
  of sharks, 451, 453
cast fossils, 460, *461*, 482, *482*
cause-and-effect relationship, **R5**
caverns, 191, *191*, 270–271, *270*
caves, 270–271, *270*
cavities, 35
CD player, 391, 426, *426*
CDs (compact disks), 331, 332, 392, *392*
cell phone generator, 428, *428*
cells, 571, 572, *573*, 592, *592*
  delivery of nutrients and oxygen to, 635
  division, 817
  of multicellular organisms, 493

and proteins, 608
    unicellular organisms, 492
cell tissue growth, 688
cellular respiration, **601**
cellulose, 608
Cenozoic era, *472,* 476, *476, 477,* 478, 827, *827*
centers of galaxies, 797
central processing unit, *394,* 395
Cepheid variables, 738
cerebral cortex, 561–562
Chalicotherium grande, 449
Challenger expedition, 147, *147*
Chandra X-Ray Observatory, 683
change over time, 473–479, *475, 476–477, 478*
Chapter Investigations
    build a speaker, 432–433, *432*
    creating stream features, 272–273, *272*
    electronic devices, 398–399, *398*
    geologic time, 480–481, *480*
    heart rate and exercise, 638–639, *638*
    impact craters, 770–771
    kidneys, 618–619, *618*
    lightning, 358–359, *358*
    modeling natural selection, 506–507, *506*
    modeling seasons, 714–*714*
    monitoring water quality, 98–99, *98*
    muscles, 590–591
    population sampling, 178–179, *178*
    sustainable resource management, 552–553, *552*
    temperature, brightness, and color of stars,
      784–785, *784, 785*
    testing soil, 246–247, *246*
    topographic maps, 216–217, *216*
    using a filter, 22–23, *22*
    visible light spectra, 684–685, *684*
    water moving underground, 72–73
    wave movement, 134–135, *134*
    wind power, 322–323, *322*
charge
    circuits, 375–381, 383–387, *384, 385, 386,* 400
    conductors and insulators, 354
    current, *356,* 360–364, *361, 365*
    discharge of, 350–351
    grounding, 357, *357*
    ionic, 343
    movement of, 352, *353,* 354, 360–362, *361*
    particles, 342, *342,* 351
    positive and negative, 343, *343, 344, 346*
    resistance, 355–356, *355, 356*
    static, 343–348, *343, 344, 345, 346, 347, 348*
charge buildup, 343–345, *343, 344, 345*
    in lightning, 352, *353*
charged particles
    in Earth's core, 416
    electricity and, 342–343, *342,* 351–352
    electrons, 414, 421
    magnetism and, 416, 418, 421
    protons, 414
    release from Sun, 418
    solar wind, 783, *783*
charge polarization, 346, *346*
charging by contact, 343–344, *343, 344*

charging by induction, 345, *345,* 352, *353*
Charon (moon), 765, *765*
chemical digestion, 609, 610, 612
chemical disinfection, 92, *92,* 93
chemical energy, FL31
chemical pollutants, 550
    in fresh water, 94, 95, *95,* 97
    in ocean waters, 175, 176
chemical reactions, 368
    in digestion, 609
    production of electricity, 363–364, *363, 365*
    respiration and, 599, 601
    weathering and, 234–235
chemical weathering, **234,** 234–235, *235, 236,* 250,
      254, *254*
chemistry, FL34, *6,* 147, 245, *245*
chemosynthesis, 168, 169
Chicago, Illinois, *58*
Chicxulub crater, 494–495, *495*
childhood, 580, 589
Chimney Rock (Colorado), 731, *731*
China, 279, 303, 521, *521*
chlorine, 93
chondrichthyes, 451
chromosphere, 780, *781*
cichlids, 504–505, *504*
cilia, 602, 641, *641*
circuit breakers, 381, *381*
circuit diagrams, 377, *377,* 382, *384,* 385, *385,* 400,
      400, 403
circuits, *FL12, 372–373,* **375,** 375–381, 400, *400*
    in appliances, 387, *387*
    circuit breakers, 381, *381*
    closed, 377, *377*
    diagrams of, 377, *377, 384, 385, 403*
    electronic technology and, 389
    energy conversions in, 386–387
    functions of, 383
    fuses, 380, *380*
    grounding, 379, *379*
    integrated, 407, *407*
    open, 377, *377*
    parallel, 385, *385,* 400, *400*
    parts of, 376, *376*
    paths of, 378–381, *380, 381,* 384–385, *384, 385*
    safety devices, 379–381, *380, 381*
    series, 384
    short, 378, *378*
circulatory system, **631,** 656, *656*
    blood, 633–634, *633*
    blood pressure, 635–636, *636*
    blood types and, *573,* 637, *637*
    blood vessels, 634, *634, 635*
    cellular respiration and, 601
    digestion and, 610
    heart, 632–633, *632*
    immune response and, 642
    pathogens and, 641
    respiration and, 631–633
cities
    development along waterways, 82, *82*
    drinking water treatment, 90–92

wastewater treatment, 93–94
water supplies, 81, *82,* 100–101, 102
classification, 820–821
of bones, 576
of stars, 788, *789*
clay, 240, 244, *244*
climate. *See also* weather.
biodiversity and, 447–449, *504,* 505
change over time, 462–463, *462, 463,* 473–474
effect of ocean on, 40, 127–128, *128,* 199
human adaptations to, 545–546, *545*
impact on weathering, 236
mass extinction and, 448–449, *493,* 494
ocean and, 39
soil type and, 239, 240
clock gene, 513, *514*
cloning, 523
closed circuit, 377, *377*
closed systems, 197
clotting of blood, 612, 633
clouds
air pollution and, 105
of gas giants, 758
lightning formation in, 352, *353*
in Milky Way, 795
of Neptune, 763, *763*
role in water cycle, 52, 53
satellite mapping of, *194–195*
of Uranus and Neptune, 762
of Venus, 754
clown fish, *163,* 164
coal, 300, *301,* 303, *303*
coastal plains, *204*
coastline. *See* shorelines.
cobalt, 414
cod, 171
code, binary, 389, 390, *390,* 394
coelacanth, 148, *148,* 521, *521*
collapse sinkholes, 192
collecting duct, 616, *616*
collisions
formation of Moon and, 721, *721*
of galaxies, 796, 798, *798*
on Neptune, *763*
of particles, 53, 292, 738, 750
of space objects and the Moon, 18
of space objects with Earth, 663–665
Uranus and, 762
color
Chapter Investigation, 684–685, 784–785
of stars, 788, *789,* 792, *792*
temperature and, 788, *789*
visible light, 680
Colorado Plateau, 204
Colorado River, 101, 110, *110,* 316, 434, *434*
Columbia space shuttle, 668
coma, 768, *768*
comets, *661,* 743, *744–745,* 746, **768,** 768–69, *768,*
772, 772
communication, 523, 627, 698, *698*
magnetic storms and, 783
technology for, 26

commutator, 424, *425,* 429, *429*
compact bone, **577,** 577, *577*
compact disk. *See* CDs (compact disks).
companion stars, 792, *792*
comparing, 10
compass, *FL13, 408–409,* 416, 417
compass rose, 205, *205,* 211
competition, 538–539, *538*
competitors, **542,** *542*
complicated machines, 816
compression programs, 332
Compton Gamma-Ray Observatory, 683
computer chips, 407, *407*
computerized tomography systems (CT scan), 626, *626,*
627, *627*
computers, **393,** 397, 404, 428
analysis of space, 681
animatronics and, *334,* 335–337, *335, 336, 337*
circuits in, 386, 393, *393*
communication and, 523, 627
converters for, 429, *429*
effect on society, 26
electromagnets and, 423
ENIAC, 406, *406*
filmless body imaging with, 627, *627*
geographic information systems and, *221,* 222, *222*
imaging of geosphere, 200, 219
integrated circuits, 407, *407*
Internet, 396–397, *396, 397*
miniaturization, 407, *407*
modeling animal behaviors, 464
modeling big bang, 803
modeling galaxies, 798
modeling molecules, *17*
modeling Moon's formation, 720–721
modeling of asteroid paths, 664
modeling of fossils, 523
modeling the universe, 739
music and, 331–333
networks, 396–397
ozone level analysis by, 293
personal, 394–395, *394, 395*
proper disposal of, 97
prototype of, 405, *405*
quantum computing, 407
remote sensing data and, 188, 189
space exploration and, *691,* 692, *692*
superconductors and, 356
use of capacitors, 400
use of digital information, 391, 404
use of transistors, 406
worldwide use of, 25
concentration, 90, **91**
conclusions
drawing, R35
evaluating, 10, 12, 20–21, 419
condensation, **53,** 74, *74*
role in water cycle, 52–53, *53*
conduction
charging by contact, 343–344, *343, 344, 345*
charging by induction, 345
polarization, 346, *346*

conductors, **354,** 355, 368, 375, 376, *376,* 400, *400*
conic projections, 209, *209,* 210
Connecting Sciences
 earth science and life science, 280, *280,* 307, *307,* 464, *464,* 699, *699*
 physical science and earth science, 13, *13,* 141, *141*
 physical science and life science, 349, *349*
connective tissue, 573
 body temperature and, 585, *585*
 bone, 577, *577,* 585
 cartilage, 580
 joints and, 581
 ligaments, 581
consequences, 26–28
conservation, 105, **309,** 324
 of fresh water, 102–104, *102,* 105
 of natural resources, 308–311
 nonrenewable resources, 300
 satellites and, 697
 of soil, 251–252, *252*
 of wetlands, 159
conservation tillage, 251
constants, **R30**
constellations, **676,** 676–677, *676,* 678, *678, 700, 703*
 seasonal star maps, 832, *833–836*
construction, 45, 250, *250*
consumers, 822
Continental Divide, 267, *267*
continental glaciers, 61, 282, *283*
continental shelf, **120,** *120,* 173
continental slope, 120, *120*
continents
 formation of, 293
 ocean currents and, 125, *125*
 separation of, 115, 294
contour interval, *213,* **214,** *214*
contour lines, **213,** 213–215, *213, 214*
contour plowing, 252, *252*
contrasting, 10
control group, **15,** R30
controlled variables, 15
controversial results, 20–21
convection, **780**
convection zone, 780, *781*
conversion of energy, 197
 change in form, 351
 digestion and, 608
 electrical devices and, 355, 376, *376,* 384, 386–387, *387*
 electrical to kinetic, 424
 generators and, 428
 kinetic to electrical, 427–430, *428, 429,* 434–435, *434, 435*
 loss as heat, 352, 356, 376, 384
 motors and, 428
 power and, 436
 transformers and, 431, *431,* 435, *435*
conversions
 of analog and digital information, 392, *392*
 metric to U.S. units, *R20,* R21
 of sound waves, 331
 temperature, R21, *R21*

Coolidge, William, 624
Copernicus, Nicolaus, 736
copper
 as conductor, 354, 355, 356
 in fresh water, 91, *91*
coral, *42, 43,* 44, 154, 162, *163*
coral reefs, 42–45, *42, 43,* 149, **162, 162,** *163,* 164
core
 of Earth, 200, *200,* 750
 of gas giants, 759, *759*
 of the Moon, 720, *720, 732*
 of neutron stars, 790
 of the Sun, 780
 of supergiant stars, 790
 of terrestrial planets, 749–750
corona, **780,** *781,* 783
costs, 26
coughing, 641, 642
Coulomb, Charles Augustin de, *437*
coulombs, 343
Cousteau, Jacques, *148*
CPU, 395
crabs, *38–39,* 154, 157, 158, 164, 168, 169
cranium, 578, *579*
Crater Lake (Oregon), 58
craters. *See* impact craters.
creative thinking, **8**
credit cards, *423*
creep, 265, *265*
crescent moons, 724, *725,* 726
crest of waves, 130, *131*
Cretaceous Extinction, 449, 494–495
Cretaceous period, *477, 827*
critical analysis, **R8,** R8–R9
critical thinking, **10**
crop rotation, 251
crust
 of Earth, 200, *200,* 750, *751*
 of the Moon, 720, *720, 732*
 of terrestrial planets, 749–750, *751*
CT scan, 626, *626,* 627, *627*
Curie, Marie, 625, *625*
curiosity, 8
curious mind, FL28
current. *See* electric current; ocean currents.
cycles
 of nutrients, 242
 water, 52–54, *53,* 102
 of water use, 93, *93*
Cygnus, 676, *676*
cylindrical projection, 208–209, *209*

D

daily tides, 137, *137*
damage, from vibrations, 814, 815
dams, **86,** 86–88, *86, 87,* 324
 changes in Earth's surface by, 201
 hydroelectric power and, 316, *316,* 434, *434, 435, 435*
 in tidal waters, 140, *140*
dandelions, *532,* 533, 541

Danube River, 105
dark matter, 739
Darwin, Charles, *499*
   natural selection and, 499–501, 516
   and population growth, 529
   publication of book, 508
   voyage of, *498–499,* 499–500, 508
data
   analysis, 10
   collection, 7, 8–9, 15, 16, 19, 40, *184–185,* 187–189, *187, 188, 198,* 218–222, 690, 691, 692, *692*
   description of, R36–R39
   interpreting, 223, *223*
   making tables of, R23, R*23*
data tables, making, **R23**
dating rocks, 465–469, *466, 467, 468, 469, 470,* 471
dawn redwood, 521, *521*
daylight hours, 713
day-night cycle
   on Earth, 732, *732, 753*
   on Mercury, 753
   on Uranus, *762*
   on Venus, 754
daytime, 708, *708*
DDT, 550
Dead Sea, 116, *117*
death, 537, 547
December solstice, 710, *711, 712*
decibels, 814
decimals, 312, R39–R40
   adding, R39
   dividing, R40
   multiplying, R40
   subtracting, R40
decline of populations, 528, *528,* 529, 539–540, *539,* 554
decomposers, 248
decomposition, 157, 239, 242, *243*
deep biosphere, 149
deep ocean currents, 126, 142
deep water of oceans, 39–40, 119, *119*
deep-zone ocean environments, 166, *167*
deer, 538
delta, **269,** *269*
density, **116, 811**
   deep ocean currents and, 126
   of populations, 531–532, *531,* 538–540, *538, 539,* 543, *543,* 554
   of salt water, 116–117, *117*
   of surface layer of ocean, 119
density-dependent factors, 538–539, *538,* 554
density-independent factors, 539–540, *539,* 554
denticles, 451
dentists, 625, 627
Denver, Colorado, *492–493*
dependent variables, **15, R30**
   operational definition, **R30,** *R31*
deposition, **261,** 261–286
   alluvial fan, 269, *269*
   barrier islands, 276–277, *276, 277,* 288
   delta, *200,* 269, *269*
   dunes, 274, 277, 278, *278,* 280, *280,* 288

floodplain, 268, *268,* 277–278, *278*
   glaciers, *258–259,* 284–286, *284*
   loess, 278
   longshore drift and currents, 132, *132,* 142, 275, *275,* 276
   moraines, 284, *284*
   mudflow, 264, *264*
   natural forces and, 261–262
   oxbow lakes, 268, *268*
   running water and, 266
   sandbars, 132, *133,* 276, 276–277, *276,* 288
   till, 284
   waves and, 258, 262
   wind and, 277
dermis, **650,** *650*
desalination, **106,** *106,* 173
desertification, **249**
desert pavement, 279, *279*
deserts
   aquifers of, 66, 67
   dunes in, 277–278, *278,* 280
   populations of, 530, *530*
   soil of, 240, *241*
development, 45, 250, *250*
Devil's Millhopper Geological State Park, 192, *192*
Devonian period, *476, 826*
diabetes, 566
diamonds, *174, 187,* 188–189
diaphragm, 602, *603,* 606, *606, 620*
diatoms, *168*
dichotomous guide, 820–821
difference engine, 405, *405*
digestion, **608**
   mechanical and chemical, 609
digestive system, **608,** *608, 610, 611, 612,* 620
   body defenses and, 640, 641
   cellular respiration and, 601
   digestion, 571, 608–610
   muscles in, 586
   organs of, 574, 612, *612*
   peristalsis in, 608, *608*
   solid waste disposal, 614
digital camera, 391, 393
digital devices, 331, 332, 391
digital information, **390,** 390–391, *394,* 395, 400, *400*
digital music, 331
digital videodisk. *See* DVDs (digital videodisks).
dinosaurs
   extinction of, 18–19, 449, 457–458, *481,* 494, 663, 767
   fossil evidence of, *19, 459,* 460, *461,* 464, *520*
   in Mesozoic era, *477,* 478
   at South Pole, 462
   speed of *T. rex,* 464, *464*
   theropods, *459*
direct current (DC), **429**
direct high tide, *137*
direction, of motion, 814
disappearing stream, 192
discharge, 350–351, 352, *353*
   conductors and insulators, 354
   grounding, 357, *357*
   resistance, 355–356

disease
    bodies defenses against, 641–646
    fresh water and, 101, 104
    as limiting factor, 538, *538*, 539
    lymphatic system and, 635
    population and, 548
    prevention of, 646–647
    prions and, 20, *20*
    research on, 24, 25, 28
    sharks and, 452, 453
    treatment of, 647, *647*, 656, *656*
Disneyland (California), 335
Disney World (Florida), 335, 336, *336*
disorder, of system, 790, 813
dissolving (rocks), 191, *191*, 234–235, 270, *270*
distribution of population, 534, *534*, 543, *543*
diversity
    climate and, *446–447*, 447–449
    of life in Phanerozoic eon, 478
divides, 56–57, **57**, *57*, 74, **267**, *267*, 288, *288*
diving suit, 147, 199
DNA, 513–514, 523
Dobson spectrophotometer, 293, *293*
dolphins, 154, *167*, 172
Donald, Ian, 626
Doppler effect, **800**, *801*
downwelling, 41, *41*, **126**, *126*
drainage basins, 56–57, **57**, *57*, 74, **267**, *267*, 288, *288*
drill, 68, *69*
drinking water
    distribution of, *92*
    EPA Standards for Substances in Water, 91, *91*
    pollution of, 13, 92
    storage of, 13, *13*, 92
    treatment of, 13, 90–92, *92*
    water cycle and, 54
drip irrigation, 103, 107, *107*
drought, **101**, *101*, *539*, 540
dry cells, 364, *365*
dunes, 274, **277**, 280, *280*, 288
    at Cape Canaveral, 669
    on Earth, 750
    formation, 278, *278*
    on Mars, 755
    on terrestrial planets, 755
dust
    in atmosphere, 448, *448*, 449, 479, 663, 767
    coral reefs and, 45
    Milky Way and, 794
DVD player, 391
DVDs (digital videodisk), 331
dynamo, 406, *406*

E

Earth, 674, *675*, *700*, *707*, *725*, *744*, *749*
    ages of rocks, 465–469, *466*, *467*, *468*, *469*, *470*, 471, *472*, 474
    asteroid collisions, 18–19, 767, 770
    atmosphere, 198, *198*, 201, 696, 752
    biosphere, 199, *199*, 201

change over time, FL33, 200–202, 231–232, *233*, 234–236, *235*, *236*, 261–286, 292, 293, 294, 462–463, *462*, *463*, 473–479, *474*, *475*, *476–477*, *478*, 492–493, *492–493*, 752
characteristics of, *839*
color, 49
consequences of human actions on, 158–159, 164, 175–176, 201, 235, 248, *248*, 249–250, *249*, *250*, 265, 316
craters, *662–663*, 663–664, *696*, 718, 750, 767
crust, 750
density, *839*
development of atmosphere, 293, *293*
development of life on, 492–494, *492–493*, 496, *496*, 516, *516*
diameter, 674, *749*, *839*
distance from Moon, *716*, 717, *717*
distance from the Sun, *709*, *744*, 749, *772*
early life, 475, *475*, *476–477*, 477–479, *477*
effects of earthquakes on, 201, 263, 474
effects of glaciers on, 281–286, *284*, *285*, *286*
effects of hurricanes on, 277
effects of natural processes on, 129, 261–265, *263*, *264*, *265*, 266–271, *268*, *269*, *270*, *271*, 293, *293*, 474
effects of volcanoes on, 129, 200, 201, 222, 264, 448, 449, 750
erosion, 261–286, 750
first humans, 479, *479*
formation of atmosphere, 293, *293*
geographic features of, *195*
geologic time scale, 475–479, *475*, *476–477*, 480–482, *481*, *482*, *492–493*, *826–827*, 827
geosphere, *199*, 200, *200*, 201
gravity of, FL33, FL35, 752
history, 457–479
hydrosphere, 198–199, *198*, 201
ice sheets of, 61
layers of, 750
magnetic field of, 416, *416*
mapping, 187–191
mass, *749*, *839*
meteorites and, 769, *769*
Moon and, 678, 720–721, *721*
oceans, 50–51, *50*, *51*, 115, 142, 198
orbit of, 709–710, *709*, *711*, *749*, *839*
planets and, 678, *678*
position during lunar eclipse, *727*
position during new moon and full moon, 139, 142, *142*
position during solar eclipse, 728, *728*
pulsars and, 10, *10*
revolution of, 832, *839*
rotation of, 125, 677, *677*, 690, 700, 707–708, 710–713, *711*, *712*, *713*, 732, *732*, *749*, *749*, 838, *838*, *839*
satellite monitoring, 697
satellite views of, *194–195*
shaping of surface, 261–286
size of, *744*, *839*
solar wind and, 783, *783*
space exploration and, 695

space objects and, *662–663, 663–665*
stars and, 676–677, *676, 677,* 832
surface of, 201, 288, *749*
tectonics, 750, *751*
theory of formation of, 292
tides and, *139*
tilt of axis and seasonal changes, 709–710, *711,* 712–713, 732, *732*
time zones of, 838, *838*
viewed from outer space, 295, *295*
viewing and mapping, 203–210, 218–222
views of, 695, *695,* 697
water movement on, 52–54
as water planet, 49
weathering, 201, 231–232, *233,* 234–236, *235, 236,* 696, 750
wind, 696
earthquakes, FL33, 474, 815
damage caused by, 815
as density-independent factors, 540
effects on Earth's surface, 201
magnitude of, 815
mass wasting and, 263
ocean waves and, 129
studies of, 295
earth science, FL29, FL32–FL33, *6*
life science and, 280, 307, 464, 699, *699*
physical science and, 13, 141
Earth system, FL33, 292, 320
atmosphere, 197, 198, *198,* 299
biosphere, 197, **199,** *199,* 201, *202,* 299
geosphere, *185,* 197, *199,* 200, *200,* 201, 202, *202,* 261–286, 299
hydrosphere, 198, *198,* 299
studies of, 295
eccentricity, 839
eclipse, **727,** 731
on Jupiter, *760*
lunar, 727, *727*
solar, 728, *728*
ecosystems, 821–822
carrying capacity of, 528
coral reefs, *42, 43–45, 43*
effects of human activities on, 27, *27,* 44, 86–87, 94, *95*
effects of natural processes on, 45, 821–822
food chains in, 822
food webs in, 822
introduction of new species, 549, *549,* 669
sharks and, 453
eddies, 41, *41*
Edison, Thomas, 406, *406*
eels, *163,* 349, *349*
Egypt, 100, 146
Einstein, Albert, 738
elbow joint, *582*
electrical devices, 376, *376,* 383, 400, *400*
electrical energy, 338
conversion of, 383, 386–387, *387*
generation of, 434–435, *435*
electrical potential, 376

electric cells, **363,** *363*
primary (wet) cells, 364, *365*
secondary (storage) cells, 364, *365*
solar cells, 366, *366*
electric charge, **342,** *342, 353,* 360, 368
circuits, 375–381, 383–387, *384, 385, 386*
conductors and insulators, 354, 356
by contact, 343–344, *343, 344*
current, *356,* 360–364, *361, 365,* 375
eels and, 349, *349*
grounding, 357, *357*
by induction, 345, *345*
movement of, 352, *353,* 354–356, 368
polarization, 346, *346*
potential energy of, 350–351
resistance, 355–356, *356*
use in technology, 347–348
electric circuits, *372–373,* 375–381
electric current, **360,** *361,* 375, 383–387, *384, 385, 386*
alternating, 429
calculating, *62,* 361–362
compared to static charge, 360
conductors and insulators, 354
direct, 429
distribution of, 99
electric cells, 363–364, *365*
electricians and, 382, *382*
electromagnets and, 421–424, *421, 423, 424, 425, 426, 426*
electronic devices and, 389–397
generation of, *363*
grounding, 379, *379*
magnetically generated, 427–431, *428, 429*
magnetic fields from, 420, 440
Ohm's law, **361,** 361–362, *361,* 367, 368
path of, 375–378, *376, 377,* 383–385, *384, 385*
resistance, 355–356, *355, 356*
safety devices, 379–381, *380, 381*
solar cells, 366, *366*
step-down transformer, *435*
transformers and, 431, *431,* 435
voltage, electric power and, 436
electric eels, 349, *349*
electric field, **342,** *342,* 345, 349
sharks and, 452
electricians, 382, *382*
electricity, *338–339,* 368, 388. *See also* electric charge; electric current; electronics; static charge; static electricity.
biomass generated, 320, *320*
discovery of, 404
electric eels, 349, *349*
fossil fuel generated, 149, *302,* 303
Franklin's experiment, 405, *405*
generation of, 315, 427–430, *428, 429,* 434–438
geothermally generated, 318–319, *318*
magnetism and, 341, 412, 420–424, *425,* 426
nuclear generated, 86, 314, *314*
renewable resources, 315
safety, 379
solar generated, 317, *317*
tide generated, 140, *140*

transformers and, 431, *431*
water generated, 316
wind generated, 319, *319,* 322–323
electric light bulb, 356, *356*
electric potential, **351**
electric power, **434**
appliance ratings, *436*
energy use and, 436, 437–438
generation of, 434–435, *435*
measurement of, 436
transformers and, 431, *431,* 435
units of measurement for, 436
voltage, current and, 436
electrochemical cells, 363–364, *363, 365,* 368
electrocytes, 349
electrodes, 363, *363,* 364, *365*
electrolytes, *363,* 364, *365*
electromagnetic radiation, *661,* **679,** 679–681, *680,* 700
electromagnetic spectrum, 566, *566,* 680–681, *680*
electromagnetic waves, 331, 814
electromagnetism, **421,** *421*
electromagnets, **422,** *425,* 428, 434
in CD player, 426, *426*
in computers, 423
electronic devices, 423, *423*
in generators, 435, *435*
making of, 422, *422*
motors, 424–425, *425*
transformers, 431, *431,* 435, *435*
uses of, 423–426, *423, 424, 425, 426*
electronic devices, **389,** 400. *See also* computers.
CD player, 391, *391,* 426, *426*
coded information and, 331–333, 389–392, *392*
DVD player, 331, 391
music and, *330–331,* 331–333, *332, 333*
Electronic Numerical Integrator and Computer
(ENIAC), 406, *406*
electronics, 404, 406
in music, *330–331, 332, 333*
electrons, 342, 368, 414, 812
conduction, 343–346
electrochemical cells, 363, *363*
static charge and, 343
electroreceptors, 452
electrostatic air filter, 348
elements, **FL35,** 116, 799, *840–841*
elevation, **213,** *213, 214*
ellipse, **745,** 839
elliptical galaxies, 796, *796,* 804, *804*
El Niño, **128,** R7, *R7*
e-mail, 396, 627
embryo, development of, 512, *512*
emergency cell phone charger, 428, *428*
emigration, **537**
emission of radiation, 188
emu, *499*
enamel, 35
endangered habitats, 164
energy, **FL33,** *429*
biomass, 320, *320,* 324
calculating use, 437–438, *437,* 439

changes in form, FL35, 351, 363–366, *363, 365, 366*
chemical, 168, 169, 300, *301,* 302–306, 434
in closed systems, 197
convection, 780
conversion in electrical devices, 355, 384, 386–387, *387*
conversion of, FL31, 424, 428, 434–435, *434, 435,* 813
cycles of, *FL32,* FL33
electrical, 338, 376, 427–431, *428, 429,* 434–435, *434, 435, 436, 437*
electrical potential, 351
electrochemical, 363–364, *363, 365*
electromagnetic radiation, *661,* 679–680, *680,* 681, 700
fusion, 780
geothermal, 318, *318,* 324
heat transfer by oceans, 40
hydroelectric, 86, *86,* 316, *316,* 324, 434
hydrogen fuel cells, 320–321, *321,* 324
kinetic, 129, 130, 140, 141, 142, 319, *319,* 322–323, 324, 351, 427–431, *428, 429,* 434
law of conservation of, FL35
loss to heat, 319, 356, 384
measurement of, 436
as need of living things, 493
nuclear, 313–315, *314,* 324, 434
in phase changes, 811
photosynthesis and, FL31, 162, 164, 166
planet formation and, 750
potential, 350, 351
solar, 317, *317,* 324
sources of in ocean, 40, 173
stored in nutrients, 607, 608
from the Sun, 162, 164, 166, 188, 197, 300, *301,* 302, 366, *366,* 696, 779, *781,* 804, 822
of tides, 140, 141, 434
transfer in electrical circuits, 383
use of in U. S., *302*
in waves, 129, 130, 142
in wind, 319, *319,* 322–323, 324, 434
energy sources, FL33
coal, 303, *303*
fossil fuels, 302–304
nonrenewable resources, 300, *301*
in oceans, 40, 173
oil and natural gas, 304, *304*
renewable resources, 300, *301*
environment, **FL31**
effects of changes in, 447–449, 504–505, *504,* 510, 533–534, 539–540, *539*
effects of earthquakes on, 263
effects of human activities on, 60, *60,* 70, 86–88, 91, 235, 248, *248,* 249–250, *249, 250,* 254, 265, 316
effects of human population on, 549–551, *549, 550, 551*
effects of hurricanes on, 277
evidence of changes in, 462
experiments affecting, 29, 30
human adaptations to, 545, *545*
as limiting factor, 533–534, 538–540, *539*
living things' dependence upon, FL31

natural selection and, 501, 502
of ocean waters, 153
skin and, 649
in spacecraft, 686
viewing changes in, 222, *222*
environmental concerns. *See also* international aspects
of science; pollution.
conservation, 102–104, *102,* 105, 159, 251–252, *252,*
308–311, 324, 697
destruction from dams, 316
oil spills, 307, *307*
radioactive waste, 315
recycling, 96, 97, 310–311, *310, 311,* 324
soil erosion, 300
Environmental Protection Agency (EPA), 91, *91,* 176
eons, 476, *476–477,* 482, *482,* **826**
EPA. *See* Environmental Protection Agency (EPA).
epidermis, **650,** *650,* 653
epiglottis, 602, *603*
epithelial tissue, 572–573
epochs, 476, *476–477,* 482, *482,* 827
equations, R42
equator, **206,** *206*
on conic projections, *209*
length of days near, 713
on Mercator projections, 209
ocean currents and, 125
ocean temperatures near, 119, *119*
rocket launches and, 667
seasons and, 710, 712
wetlands near, 156, *158*
equinox, **710,** 711, *711,* 712, *712,* 713, *713*
eras, 476, *476–477,* 482, *482,* 827
Eros, *767, 772*
erosion, *185, 200,* **261,** 261–286, 270, 288, 772, *772*
creep, 264–265, *265*
deforestation, 300
desert pavement, 279
dissolving limestone as, 191, *191*
of Earth, 750
glaciers and, *258–259,* 282, *283,* 284–286, *285, 286*
of land, 261, *261,* 266
longshore drift and currents, 132, *132,* 142, 275,
275, 276
on Mars, 755
mass wasting, 263–265, *263*
on Mercury, *753*
mudflow, 263, 264, *264*
planet surfaces and, 750, *751*
of rock, 261–262
of shorelines, 274–277, *274, 275, 276, 277*
slumps, 264–265, *264*
on small space bodies, 764
on Venus, 755
waves, 262
esophagus, *608,* 610, *611, 620*
estuaries, **156,** *156,* 158, 669
ethanol, 320
ethics, **27,** 27–30
Europa (moon), 766, *766*
European Union, 105
eutrophication, **60,** *60*

evaluation, **R8**
hypotheses, 10, 515
media claims, R8
evaporation, **53,** 77, *77*
from basins, 57
body temperature and, 651
desalination by, 106
exploration of, 79
irrigation and, 70, 101, 107
rainwater, 270
role in water cycle, 52, 53, *53,* 54, 74, *74*
salinity and, 117, 154
salt processing and, 175, *175*
Everest, Mount, 187
evidence, 18–19, 32, R8
evidence for evolution, 529
biological, *509,* 510, *511,* 512, *512,* 516, *516*
fossils, 447, *509,* 520, *520,* 521, *521,* 522, *522,*
523, *523*
genetic, 513–514, *514*
and scientific theory, 508–509, *509, 523*
evolution, **497,** *503,* 504–505
Chapter Investigation, 506–507
Darwin's theory of, 499–505, *499, 500, 501,*
503, 504
and early organisms, 492–493
evidence supporting, 508–510, *509, 511,* 512–514,
512, 514
Lamarck's theory of, 498
mass extinction, *493,* 494
natural selection, 501, 506–510, *509, 511,* 512–514,
512, 514, 516
exercise, 589, 638–639
exfoliation, **232,** *233*
exhalation, 602
Exxon Valdez oil spill, 307
expansion of universe, 738, *738,* 739, *739,* 800–801,
801, 804, *804*
experiment, 7, 15, 28–29, **R28,** *R31. See also* labs.
conclusions, drawing, R35
controlled, R28, R30
dependent variable, measuring, R31
designing, R28–R35
determining purpose, R28
hypothesis, writing, R29
materials, determining, R29
observations, recording, R33, *R33*
procedure, writing, R32
purpose, determining, *R28*
questions for further research, R35
results, summarizing, R34
variable and constants, determining, R30
experimental group, **15,** R30
exploration of oceans, 121, *121*
exploration of space, *666,* 686–693, 765
Apollo program, 687, 695
astronauts, 686–689, *687, 688, 689*
benefits of, *638,* 695–698, *696*
Cape Canaveral and, *666,* 667–669, *667, 668*
constellations, 676–677, *676, 678, 700, 703*
Earth's atmosphere, 682–683
experiments with plants, 699, *699*

flybys, 690, *690*
galaxies, 674, *675*, 679–682, 683, *683*
Hubble Space Telescope, 682–683, *683*, 763, *803*
impact craters, 696, *696*
International Space Station (ISS), 295, *295*,
  688–689, *688*
knowledge from, 695–696, *696*, 699, *699*, 700
landers and probes, 692–693, *692*
light, 679–683, *680, 683*, 684
of Mars, 756
Milky Way, 674, 675, *675*, 794–795, *795*
Moon missions, 668, *670*, 673, 687, *687*, 692, *692*,
  696, 717, 719, *719*, 748, *748*
orbiters, 691, *691*, 693
orbits, 674, *675*, 695
other planets, 690–693
rotation of Earth, 677, *677*
satellites, 667–668
shuttles, 689, *689*
solar system, 674, *675*, 690–693, *690, 691, 692*
solar wind, 783, *783*
space shuttles, 668
space stations, 688–689, *688*
technological advances from, 697–698, *698*,
  700, *700*
telescopes, 681–683, *681, 682, 683*
unmanned missions, 690–693
Voyager 2, 690, *690*, 763
Explore
  air bladders, 161, *161*
  breathing, 599, *599*
  changes in procedures, 14, *14*
  characteristics of stars, 786, *786*
  circuits, 375, *375*
  circulatory system, 631, *631*
  codes, 389, *389*
  concentration, 90, *90*
  density, 115, *115*
  digestion, 607, *607*
  distance, 673, *673*
  distortion of light, 679, *679*
  divides, 266, *266*
  electric current, 360, *360*
  energy conversion, 427, *427*
  energy use, 308, *308*
  evidence, 508, *508*
  flow and collection of water, *56*, 64, *64*
  fossils, 489, *489*
  glaciers, 281, *281*
  large numbers, 799, *799*
  levers, 576, *576*
  magnetism, 411, *411*
  magnetism from electric current, 420, *420*
  mapping, 203, *203*
  mechanical weathering, 231, *231*
  membranes, 640, *640*
  Milky Way, 794, *794*
  Moon's motion, 716, *716*
  muscles, 584, *584*
  nuclear energy, 313, *313*
  observations and opinions, 5, *5*
  ocean currents, 124, *124*

ocean pollution, 170, *170*
planet formation, 743, *743*
population change, 544, *544*
population density, 536, *536*
rocks, 457, *457*
skin, 649, *649*
soil composition, 238, *238*
solar atmosphere, 779, *779*
static discharge, 350, *350*
static electricity, 341, *341*
surfaces, 749, *749*
time scales, 473, *473*
time zones, 707, *707*
topographic maps, 212, *212*
value of fresh water, 100, *100*
viewing space objects, 686, *686*
waste removal, 614, *614*
water collection, 56
water vapor, 49, *49*
waves, 129, *129*
Explorer 1 satellite, 667
extended-response questions (ER), FL37,
  FL50–FL51, *FL51*
extinction, **FL31**
  causes of, 448–449, 549, 663, 767
  dinosaurs, 18–19, 449, 457–458, 478, 767
  human contribution to, 550–551
  mass, 494
  woolly mammoths, 494
Extreme Science
  astronomy and the universe, 798
  extreme environment, 169
  growing new skin, 655

F

fact, **R9**
  different from opinion, R9
fall, 710, *711*
false-color images, **220**, 220, *220, 665, 754, 757, 789,*
  797
famine, 24, 540
Faraday, Michael, *437*
farming. *See* agriculture.
fast-switch muscle, 586
fats, 607
fatty tissue, 650, *650*
faulty reasoning, **R7**, R7
FCAT Practice
  analyzing a chart, 807, *807*
  analyzing a star map, 703, *703*
  analyzing data, 77, *77*, 557, *557*, 623, *623*, 659
  analyzing diagrams, 183, *183*, 227, *227*, 291, *291*,
    485, *485*, 735, *735*
  analyzing graphs, 111, *111*, 327, *327*
  analyzing tables, 35, *35*, 145, *145*, 257, *257*,
    443, *443*
  interpreting diagrams, 371, *371*, 403, *403*, 519, *519*,
    595, *595*
feeding habits, 452, 453
femur, *579*
ferns, 478

fertilization, 817
fertilizers, 87, 97, 249
    eutrophication and, 60
    pollution and, 44, *95*, 175, 176
    sinkholes and, 192
Fessenden, Reginald, 148
fever, 642, 643
fibula, *579*
fiddler crabs, 158
field work, 16, *17*, 29
Fiji Islands, *162*
filtration
    Chapter Investigation, 22–23, *22*
    of drinking water, 13, 92, *92*
    of groundwater, 67
    in nose, 602
finches, 500, *500*, 504, *516*
fires
    causes of, 31, *31*
    as density-independent factors, 539, *539*, 554
    drought and, 101
    satellite tracking of, 220, *220*
    technology and, 698
first-quarter moon, 724, *725*
fish, 154, 168, *550*
    air bladders, 166
    aquaculture, 85, *85*, 172, *172*
    in aquariums, 89
    by-catch, 172, 180
    coral reefs and, 44
    dams and, 87
    development of, 478
    estuaries and, 156
    eutrophication and, 60
    farming of, 85, *85*
    food of, 166
    glowing, 166, *167*, 515, *515*
    ladders, 87
    in lakes and ponds, 58, 59
    overfishing, 171, *171*, 178–179, 180, 551
    oxygen and, 118
    pollution and, 105, 550
    predators, 166, *167*, 180, *450*, 452, 453, *453*, 515, *515*
    reproduction, 453
    of salt marshes, 157
    sharks, *450*, 451–453, *451*, *452*, *453*
    tidal dams and, 140
    upwelling and, 126
fisheries, 85
fishing industry, 43, 162, 164, 171–172, 543, *543*, 551
fish ladders, 87
flares, 782, *782*
flashlight, *365*, 385
Fleming, Ambrose, 406
floaters, 154
flood irrigation, 83, 107, *107*
floodplain, **268**, *268*, 277–278, *278*
floods
    damage in California, R7
    dams and, 88, *88*, 474
    as density-independent factors, *539*

    erosion and, 250
    in India, 54, *54*
    on Mars, 755
Florida
    causes of fire in, 31, *31*
    desalination of sea water in, 106
    mangrove forests of, 158, *158*
    road map of, 205, *205*
    sinkholes in, 271
    tides of, 138
Florida Caverns State Park, 191, *191*
Florida Comprehensive Assessment Test. *See* FCAT Practice; Sunshine State Standards.
Florida Connections
    Animatronics, 334–337, *334, 335, 336, 337*
    Cape Canaveral: Step to the Stars, 666–669, *666, 667, 668, 669*
    Florida's Sinkholes, 190–193, *190, 191, 192, 193*
    A Place in the Sun, 564–567, *564, 565, 566, 567*
    Saving Coral, 42–45, *42, 43, 44, 45*
    The Ultimate Fish, 450–453, *450, 451, 452, 453*
Florida Current, 43
Florida Marine Research Institute, 43
flower, 818
flowering plants, 478, *481*, 818
flyby spacecraft, *690*, 700
FMRI. *See* functional magnetic resonance imaging.
food chain, 168, 169, 822
food web, 27, 162, *183*, 822
forces, **FL33**, *FL34*, **815**
    direction of, 816
    at a distance, 412, 413, 814. *See also* gravity.
    electric, 342, 424
    friction, FL35
    gravity, FL35, 53, 56, 65, *65*, 94, 137–138, *137*, 261, 263, 293, 352, 815
    hydraulics and, 336
    magnetism, 412–417, *412, 413, 414, 415, 416, 418*, 424
    size of, 816
    tidal waters as, 141
forests, 199, 295
formulas, **R42**
    area, R43, *R43*
    current, R42
    for energy use, 437–438
    Ohm's law, 361–362, 367
    for population change, 537
    for power, 436
    volume, R43, *R43*
fossil fuel power station, *302*
fossil fuels, **302**, 302–306
    air pollution from, 300, 303, 304, 306
    alternatives to, 26
    coal, *301*, 303, *303*
    energy source, 302–306
    natural gas, *301*
    nonrenewable resources, 300, *301*
    oil and natural gas, *301*, 304, *304*
    products of, *304*, 305, *306*
fossil record, 491, 495
    of Phanerozoic eon, 827

for Precambrian time, 827
fossils, *FL14, 445, 447, 454–455,* **457,** *457–462, 457, 481,* 482, **489,** *496, 522*
   carbon films, 460, *461,* 829, *829*
   classification of, 523
   dating, 465–469, *466, 467, 468, 469, 470, 472,* 490–491, 522, *522*
   at Devil's Millhopper Geological State Park, 192
   evidence in, FL31, 448, *461, 462,* 509, 516, *516,* 520, *520*
   evidence supporting evolution, 447, *509,* 520, *520,* 521, *521,* 522, *522,* 523, *523*
   formation of, 458–459, *459, 461,* 482, 490, 828–829, *828*
   index fossils, *467,* 468–469, *468*
   molds and casts, 460, *461,* 828, *828*
   one-celled organisms, 462
   original remains, 457, 458, *458*
   petrified wood, 460, *460, 461,* 829, *829*
   Phanerozoic eon, 477
   protection of, 521
   removal of, 520
   from South Pole, 462
   trace, *454–455,* 460, *461,* 829, *829*
   types of, 460, *461,* 490, *490,* 828–829
Fowler's toad, 280, *280*
fractions, 63, R41
Franklin, Benjamin, 401, *401,* 405, *405*
frequency
   of sound waves, 331
   wavelength and, 812
fresh water, **51,** *51,* 78, *78,* 84. *See also* hydrosphere.
   agriculture, 81, 83, *83,* 108
   aquaculture, 85, *85,* 108
   energy generation, 86, *86,* 108
   estuaries and, 156
   flow and collection of, 56–62, 74, *74*
   forms of, *51*
   groundwater, 64–68, *69,* 70–71
   hydroelectric power, 82
   industry, 84, *84,* 108
   limited amount of, 51
   living things and, 100, 108
   manufacturing, 82
   mining, 82
   pollution, 82
   precipitation as, 54
   quality standards for, 91, *91*
   recreation, 85, 86, 108
   as resource, 108
   shortages of, 100–106
   sources of, 50, 54, 61, 62, 90–91, 198
   support of life, 81–82, 83, 85
   transportation, 84, *84,* 86–87, *87,* 108
   treatment of, 90–91
   uses of, *78–79,* 81–88, 108
friction, **FL35,** 232, 356
Frogmen, The, 148
Frontiers in Science
   Danger from the Sky, 662–665, *662–663, 664, 665*
   Electronics in Music, 330–333, *330–331, 332, 333*
   Exploring the Water Planet, 38–41, *38–39, 40*

Life by Degrees, *446–447,* 447–449, *448, 449*
   Remote Sensing, 186–189, *186–187, 188, 189*
   Surprising Senses, 560–563, *560–561, 562, 563*
frostbite, 654
fruit flies, 527, *527*
full lung breathing, 606, *606*
full moon, 724, *725,* 727, *727*
full-spectrum lights, 567, *567*
functional magnetic resonance imaging (FMRI), 561–562, 563
fungi
   adaptations of, 494
   medicine and, 647, *647*
   soil formation and, 242, *243*
fuses, 380, *380*
fusion, **780,** 789, 790

G

Galápagos Islands
   current research at, 510
   Darwin's voyage to, *498–499,* 499–500, 504
galaxies, **674,** *675, 776–777,* 794. *See also* Milky Way.
   Andromeda Galaxy, 800, *800*
   centers, 797, *797*
   collisions of, 796, 798, *798*
   elliptical, 796, *796,* 804, *804*
   Galaxy M83, *694*
   irregular, 796, *796,* 804, *804*
   light emissions in, *680*
   Milky Way, 674, *675,* 794–795, *795*
   motion of, 738, 797, 799, 800, *801,* 804
   movement of, *738*
   quasars, 797
   shape of, 794, *794,* 796, 798, *798,* 804, *804*
   size of, 795, *795,* 796
   spiral, 796, *796,* 804, *804*
   superclusters, 799
   Tadpole Galaxy, 798, *798*
Galilei, Galileo, 737
Galileo (orbiter), 693
gall bladder, 610, *611*
gamma rays, 680, *680,* 683
Ganges River, 101
Ganymede (moon), 766
garbage, 44, 308
Garcia, Mariano, 464
gas, offshore drilling, 173, *173*
gases
   in atmosphere, 198
   in ocean water, 118, *118,* 142
   in stars' outer layers, 788
gas exchange, 600, *600,* 620
   circulatory system and, 631, 632–633, *632,* 635
   in lungs, 602, 632
gas giants (outer planets), *744,* 745, **758,** 758–763, *758, 759, 760, 761, 762, 763,* 772
   atmospheres of, 758–759, 760, 762, 763
   cores of, 759, *759*
   exploration of, 693
   gases of, 758
   gravity on, 758

INDEX

interior of, 759, *759*
Jupiter, 759–760, *759, 760*
moons of, *760,* 762, 766, *766*
Neptune, 762, 763, *763*
orbits of, *759, 760,* 762, *762, 763*
rings of, 761, *761,* 762
Saturn, 760–761, *760, 761*
temperatures, 760
Uranus, 762, *762*
weather patterns on, 759
gas mileage, 312, *312*
gasohol, 320
gears, 428, *428*
Gemini (constellation), *678*
gene, **513**
generators, 427, **428,** 440, *440*
    alternating current (AC), *428,* 429
    in cars, 430
    cell phone, 428, *428*
    direct current (DC), 429, *429*
    Edison's dynamo, 406, *406*
    hydroelectric power, 434–435, *434, 435*
    Van de Graaff, 344, *344*
genetic material
    evidence supporting evolution, *509,* 513–514,
        514, 516
    extraction from fossils, 523
    information passed from parents to offspring,
        497, 513, 817
    and natural selection, 502
geographic information systems (GIS), *218,* **221,** *221,*
    222, 222, 224
geographic time scale, 826
geography
    effect on height of tides, 138
    ocean temperatures and, 119
    speciation and, 504–505, *504, 505*
geologic time scale, **475,** 475–479, *475, 476–477,*
    480–482, *480, 481, 482, 492–493*
geology, *6*
geosphere, **FL33,** *185,* 197, *199,* **200,** *200*
    Earth's surface and, 201, 202, *202*
    resources in, 299
geothermal energy, **318,** *318,* 324
germanium, 407
Geronimo, Michelle, 562, *562*
gestation, in mammals, 819
geysers, 71, *71*
giant clams, 40, *163,* 164, 168, 169
giant stars, 788, *788,* 790, *791, 792,* 804
gibbous moon, 724, *725*
gigabyte, 390
Gilbert, William, *443*
gills, 451
glaciers, *258–259,* **281,** *283*
    alpine, 282, *283*
    continental, 61, 282, *283*
    effect on Earth's surface, 284–286, *284, 285, 286,*
        288, *288*
    extent of, *282*
    formation of, 281–282
    fresh water source, 62

lake formation by, *285,* 286, *286*
movement of, 281, 282, *283*
as part of hydrosphere, 198
types of, 61, 282, *283*
valley, 61, 282
global ocean, 50, *50,* 115–116, *116*
global positioning system (GPS), 207, *207*
globes, 203, 206–207, *206,* 224, *224*
glomerulus, 616, *616*
glucose, 601
glyptodon fossil, *198,* 509
gold, *174*
Goodall, Jane, *17*
Goosen, Hendrick, 148
Grand Canyon (Arizona), 201, *478*
granite, 236
graphs
    bar, 31, *31,* 327, *327,* 623, **R26,** *R26*
    circle, **R25,** *R25*
    double bar, 160, **R27,** *R27,* R34, *R34*
    line, 111, *111,* 287, *287,* 472, 648, *648,* 722, *722,*
        R24, *R24,* R34, *R34*
    scatter plot, 792, *792*
grasses, 157, *157,* 242
grasslands, 295
gravel, 175
gravitational potential energy, 351, *351*
gravity, FL33, **FL35,** 730, 737, 815
    of asteroids, 767
    of black holes, 790, 797
    of Earth, 707, 750, 752
    effect on light, 738
    effect on orbits, 709, 716, 745
    effect on plants, 699, *699*
    erosion and deposition and, 261, 263, 750
    flyby spacecraft and, 690
    formation of atmosphere and, 293, 752
    formation of space objects, 747, *747*
    galaxies and, 794, 798
    on gas giants, 758
    glacier movement, *283*
    groundwater and, 65, *65*
    lightning formation and, 352
    of Mars, 752
    mass wasting, 263–265
    on Mercury, 753, 765
    Moon and, 716, 748
    planetary atmospheres and, 752, 758
    on Pluto, 765
    solar systems and, *675*
    space exploration and, 695
    space objects and, 674, 700, *748*
    star formation and, 789
    between stars, 792
    star systems and, 792
    of Sun, 709, 745
    of supergiant stars, 790
    tides and, 137–138, *137,* 729–730, *729, 730,* 732
of Venus, 752
    water flow, 53, 56, 94
    weathering and erosion, 750
    weight and, 748

Great Barrier Reef (Australia), 162
Great Britain, 40, 127
Great Dark Spot, 763
Great Lakes
  canals of, 85
  formation of, 58, *58*, 286, *286*
  proposed water sales, 105
  transportation on, 84, *84*
  zebra mussel invasion, 549
Great Plains, 204, *204*
Great Red Spot, 760, *760*
Greenland, 61, 62, 209, *209*, 282, 463
Greenwich Mean Time (GMT), 838, *838*
gridded-response questions (GR), FL37, *FL37*, FL49, *FL49*
groundfault circuit interrupter (GFCI), 381, *381*
grounding, **357**, *357*, 368, 379, *379*
ground moraines, 284
groundwater, 52, **64**, 64–65, *65*, 74, *74*
  aquifers, 66–67, *66, 69*
  cavern formation, *270*
  Chapter Investigation, 72–73, *72*
  depletion of, 101
  formation of caverns, 270–271
  geysers, 71, *71*
  hot springs, 70–71, *70, 71*
  irrigation and, 70, 83
  lake water and, 58
  as part of hydrosphere, 198
  protection agreements, 105
  role in water cycle, 53
  sources of, 57, *57*
  water table, 65, *65, 66, 69*, 70, 270
  wells and springs, 68, *68, 69*, 70–71, *70, 71*
groups, on periodic table, *840*
growth, skin, 653
growth of populations, 528, *528*, 554
  Darwin's observation of, 529
  factors leading to, 538
  human, 547–548
  human impact on, 550–551
  limiting factors, 537, 538–540, *538, 539*
  predicting, 547–548
  rapid and gradual, 529, *529*
growth plates, 580
Gulf Stream, *125*, 127
gulper fish, *167*

H

habitats, **154**
  dams and, 88
  destruction of, 316
  effects of changes in, 533–534
  human adaptations of, 544–545, *545, 546*
  intertidal zone, 154
  ocean, *37*
  populations growth and, 528, 530, *530*, 532
  of salt marshes, 157
habits of scientific minds, 8–9
Hadean eon, *476*, 477, 826, *826*
hair, 649, *650*, 652, *652*

Hale-Bopp (comet), *768*
half-life, **469**, *469*, 830, *830*, 831, *831*
halite, 234
Hamburg, Germany, 207
harbors, 156
hard drive, *394*, 395, 423
hardware, 394, *394–395*, 395
hatcheries, 85
hatchet fish, *167*
hazardous waste, 175
healing, 653–654, *653*, 656
  magnets and, 419, *419*
  of skin, 653
hearing, 562, *562*
  loss, 814
heart, *573*, 632–633, *632, 634*, 656, *656*
  blood pressure and, 635–636
  cardiac muscle, 586, *587*, 592
  exercise and, 638–639
heart disease, 566
heart rate, 638–639
heat, **811**, 813
  in closed systems, 197
  electrical resistance and, 352, 356, 386, 387, *387*
  evaporation and, 77
  magnetic force and, 416
  movement of in oceans, 124
  from nuclear fission, 314
  sources of, FL33, 779
  and temperature, 811
  unevenness of and winds, 125
heat energy, 813
  from within Earth, 40
  layers of in ocean, 40
  transfer of by oceans, 40
heavy metals, *91*, 175
helium, 752, 758, 762, 779, 780, 790
Hendrickson, Sue, 522, *522*
herons, 531, *531*
Hertzsprung-Russell (HR) diagram, 792, *792, 807*, 837, *837*
Hewish, Anthony, 8–11, *8*
Heyerdahl, Thor, 124
hiccups, 605
high blood pressure, 566
higher-mass stars, 789, 790, *791, 804*
high tide, 136, *137, 138, 145*, 729, *729*, 730, *730*
  intertidal zone and, 154, *155*
high-voltage current, *382*
hinge joints, 581–582, *582, 626*
hispine beetle, 447, *447*
histamine, 643
HIV, 548
Hoffman, Paul, 448
hog farming, 550, *550*
homeostasis, **574**, 617
  breathing and, 600
  muscles and, 585
  nutrients and, 607
  skin and, 649, 650–651
homes
  conservation practices in, 103

INDEX

water pollution and, 94, *95*, 97
hominid skeleton, 522, *522*
Hood, Mount, *213*
horseshoe magnet, 412, *413*
hot springs, 70–71, *70, 71*
Hubble, Edwin, 738
Hubble Space Telescope, 682–683, *683*, 763, *803*
Huggins, William, 737
human body, 571, 575, *615, 616*
   circulatory system, 631–633, *632, 633, 634*, 635–637, *635, 636, 637*
   digestive system, 608–610, *608, 610, 611, 612*, 641
   exchange of gases in, 600, *600*
   immune system, 641–647, *641, 642, 643, 644*
   integumentary system, 641, 649–654, *650, 652, 653, 654*
   muscular system, 584–586, *585, 587*, 588–589, *588, 589*
   needs of, *FL16*, 81–82
   organization of, 571–574, *573*
   respiratory system, 599–602, *600, 603*, 604–605, *604, 605*, 641
   skeletal system, 576–578, *579*, 580–582
   survival of, 575
   urinary system, 614–617, *616*
humans. *See also* human body.
   adaptations to environment, 545–546, *545, 546*
   carrying capacity for, 544–545
   conduction of electricity, 378
   DNA compared with mice DNA, 34, *34*
   effects of activities on environment, 60, 158–159, 235, 248, 249–250, *250*, 254, 265, 565
   effects of activities on water systems, 70, 82–88, *83, 84, 85, 86, 87, 88*, 91, 94, *95*, 96, 164
   effects of technology, 546, *546*
   effects on ecosystems, 44, 45, 86–88
   effects on soil, 248–252, *248, 249*
   experimentation with, 28–29
   first appearance of, *477, 479, 481*
   health issues, 303
   impact on environment, 549–551, *549, 550, 551*
   limiting factors on populations of, 540
   population growth, *544*, 546–548, *547*, 554
   preservation efforts of, 45, 176–177, 669
   response to change, 544–548, *545, 546*
   water uses, 82–88
humerus, *579*
humus, **239**, *239*, 240, 242, 245
hurricanes, 43, 45, 277, *539*
Hutchinson, John, 464
Hutton, James, 473–474
hydraulics, 336
hydroelectric energy, **316**
hydroelectric power, 82, 316, *316*
hydroelectric power plant, 435, *435*
hydrogen, 315, 320, 758, 762, 779, 780, 790, 804
hydrogen fuel cell, **320**, 320–321, *321*, 324
hydrogen sulfide, 169
hydrosphere, *FL33, 37*, 197, **198**, 198–199, *198*. *See also* fresh water; ocean; water.
   Earth's surface and, 201, *202*
   resources in, 299

hydrothermal vents, 40, *40*, **168**, *168*, 169, *169*
hyperviolin, 332
hypotheses, **7**, 10, 18, **R3, R29**
   evaluation, 10, 515
   formation of, 757

I

ice
   breaking of rocks by, 232, *233*
   in clouds, 53
   collection of water in, *51*, 61
   comets, 768, *768*
   erosion and deposition by, 262
   glaciers, *62*, 281–286, *283*, 288
   icebergs, 63, *63*
   on lakes, 59
   ocean salinity and, 117
   original remains in, 458, *458*
   of rings of planets, 761
   rock weathering by, 232, *233*
   space objects and, 764, 765, 767
ice ages, 282, *282*, 295, 448, 479
   formation of lakes during, 58
icebergs, **62**, *62, 63*
   formation of, 62, 282
   size of, 63
   sonar and, 148
   as source of fresh water, 106
ice cores, *17*, **463**, *463*
Iceland, 261, *261*
ice sheets, 50, 62, 282, *283*
   collection of water in, 61
   melting of, 295
ice shelves, 62
ice wedging, 232, *233*
igneous rocks, *470*, 471
   fossil formation and, 459
   radioactive dating and, *470*, 830–831, *830, 831*
   in sedimentary layers, 467, *467*
Iguanodon, 520
immigration, **537**
immune response, 642–645, *643, 644*, 648, *648*
immune system, 635, **641**, 641–647, 656, *656*
   allergies and, 648, *648*
   B cells, *644*, 645, 646
   blood transfusions and, 637
   immunity and, 645–646
   inflammation and, 643
   lymph system and, 635
   mast cells, *642*
   nonspecific response, 642, 643, *644*
   other body defenses and, 640–642, *641*
   specific response, 644
   T cells, 644–645, *644*
   use of antibiotics and, 647
   vaccinations and, 646–647, *646*
   white blood cells, *583*, 633, *633*, 641–642, 644, *644*, 656
immunity, **646**, 646–647, 656
impact craters, **696**, *696*, 772, *772*
   on asteroids, 767, *767*

Chapter Investigation, 770–771
on Earth, 18–19, *662–663*, 663–664, *696*, 718, 750, 767, *770*
on Ganymede and Callisto, 766
on Io, 766, *766*
on Mars, 755
on Mercury, *751*, 753, *753*
on Moon, 18, *18*, 663, 717–718, *717*, 718, *718*
terrestrial planets and, 750
on Venus, 755
impermeable materials, **65,** *65, 66,* 74, *74*
incendiary fires, 31, *31*
inclined plane, 816
incubation, of eggs, 819
independent variables, **15, R30**
operational definition, R31, *R31*
index fossils, **467,** 467–468, *467, 468*
India, 54, *54,* 101
Indiana Dunes National Lakeshore, 277
Indian Ocean, 54, 115
indirect high tide, *137*
induction, **345,** *345*
in lightning, 352, *353*
Indus River, 101
industry
conservation practices of, 103
estuaries and, 158
fishing, 162, 164, 171–172, 551
sources of pollution, 94, *95,* 96, 550, *550*
uses of water, 82, 84, *85,* 104
infancy
bones and, 580
food and, 609
muscles and, 589
inference, 10, 575, **R4,** R35
inflammation, 643, 656
information, evaluation of, R8
Information Age, 397
informed consent, **29**
infrared radiation, 680, *680,* 814
inhalation, 602
injury, 653–654, *653,* 656
inlets, 156
inner core of Earth, 200, *200*
inner solar system, 749–756, 772, *772*
atmospheres of, 752
Earth, 749–750, *751*
formation of, 764
Mars, 755–756, *755, 756,* 757
Mercury, 753, *753*
spacing of planets, *744,* 745
Venus, 754–755, *754*
Inoceramus labiatus, 468, *468*
input, 394–395, *394*
insects, 7, *7,* 819
first appearance of, 478, 494
fossils of, 458, *458,* 490
lakes and ponds and, 58
as opportunist, 541
insulator, **354,** 355, 368, 375, 376
integrated circuits, 393, *393,* 407, *407*
integumentary system, **649,** 649–654, 656

body protection and, 640, 641
dermis and epidermis, 650–651, *650*
growth and healing, 653–654, *653*
hair and nails, 652, *652*
protection of, 654, *654*
sensory receptors, 652
skin, 650–651, *650*
sweat and oil glands, *650,* 651
temperature control and, 651
wastes and, 614
interaction, **FL31**
interior plains, *204*
international aspects of science
fossil preservation, 521
introduction of new species, 549, *549*
Law of the Sea (1994), 177
overfishing, 551, *551*
pollution, 175–177, 550, *550*
space exploration, 688, *688*
space objects and, 663–665
technological advances and, 25
water shortages, 100–106
worldwide water movement, 52–54
International Date Line, 838, *838*
International Space Station (ISS), 295, 688–689, *688*
International System (SI) units, 14, R20–R21, *R21*
Internet, 396–397, *396*
effect on society, 26
worldwide usage, 25, *397*
Internet activities
aquifers, 79
circuits, 373
Earth's history, 455
electromagnets, 409
ethics, 2, 3
galaxy shapes, 777
heart pumping, 629
human body, 569
lung movement, 597
mapping, 195
matching finch beaks, 487
ocean environments, 150
ocean floor, 113
population dynamics, 525
resources, 297
seasons, 705
soil formation, 229
spacing, 741
static electricity, 339
universe, 671
water, 47
wind erosion, 259
Internet resources, FL22
interpreting data, 222
intertidal zones, *153,* **154,** *155,* 180, *180*
interventional MRI, 627, *627*
intestines, 610, *611, 620*
Investigate. *See also* Chapter Investigations.
antibodies, 645, *645*
aquifer filtration, 67, *67*
chemical digestion, 609, *609*
chemical weathering, 234, *234*

circuits, 386, *386*
coastal environments, 156, *156*
conductors and insulators, 354, *354*
conservation, 310, *310*
constellation positions, 677, *677*
currents, 127, *127*
density, 118, *118*
digital information, 391, *391*
distances, 746, *746*
Earth's magnetic field, 414, *414*
electric cells, 363, *363*
electric charge, 346, *346*
electric current, 429, *429*
electromagnets, 422, *422*
erosion, 262, *262*
ethics, 28, *28*
floating, 165, *165*
fossil fuels, 305, *305*
fossil records, 491, *491*
fuses, 380, *380*
galaxies, 802, *802*
galaxy shapes, 795, *795*
genes, 513, *513*
giant planets, 761, *761*
icebergs, 61, *61*
kettle lake formation, 285, *285*
launch planning, 689, *689*
layers, 752, *752*
layers of geosphere, 201, *201*
limiting factors, 540, *540*
longshore drift, 276, *276*
lungs, 601, *601*
making a static detector, 346, *346*
map projections, 208, *208*
Moon features, 719, *719*
movable joints, 581, *581*
parallax, 787, *787*
phases of the Moon, 726, *726*
population, 548, *548*
power, 437, *437*
relative and absolute age, 468, *468*
rotation, 708, *708*
satellite imaging, 220, *220*
skin protection, 651, *651*
soil conservation, 251, *251*
solving problems, 9, *9*
systems, 572, *572*
tides, 138, *138*
tree rings, 462, *462*
water conservation, 103, *103*
water cycle, 52, *52*
water usage, 83, *83*
weathering, 697, *697*
investigation, 7
involuntary muscle, **586**, 586, 592
Io (moon), 766, *766*
ions, 343
iridium, 19
iron, 720, 790
    in Earth's core, 416
    magnetism and, 411, 414, 417
    rust formation and, 234, 235

in soils, 245
irregular galaxies, 796, *796*, 804, *804*
irrigation, **83**, *83*, 103, 107, *107*, 546
    groundwater and, 70
islands, volcanic, 120, *121*
isolation, 504–505, *504*
isotopes, 813

J

Jasper Ridge (California), *186–187*
jellyfish, 154, *167*
Johanson, Donald, 522
JOIDES Resolution, 294
joints, 581
    freely movable, 581
    hinge, 581, 626, *626*
    immovable, 581
    knee, 626, *626*
    slightly movable, 581, *581*, 602
June solstice, 710, *711*, 712
Jupiter, *FL19, 740–741*, 743, 759–760, *759*
    atmosphere, 758–759, 760
    characteristics of, *839*
    density, *839*
    diameter, 759, *759*, 839
    distance from the Sun, *744*, 759, *759*, *772*
    eclipse on, *760*
    exploration of, 690, 693
    gravitational pull, 758
    Great Red Spot, 760, *760*
    mass, 759, *759*, 839
    moons of, *FL19*, 760, 766, *766*
    orbit, *759*, 839
    revolution of, 759, *839*
    rotation of, 759, *759*, *839*
    Shoemaker-Levy 9 and, 663
    size of, *744*, 839
    studies of, 758, *758*
    winds, 759–760
Jurassic period, *477*, 827

K

karst topography, 191
kelp forests, 162, 164, *164*
Kepler, Johannes, 737, *737*
kettle lakes, **285**
keyboard, 395, *395*
kidneys, 615–616, *615, 616, 620*
    Chapter Investigation, 618–619
Kilby, Jack, 407
kilowatt, **436**
kilowatt-hour, **437**
kimberlite, 189
kinetic energy, 351, 386, 813
Kleist, Ewald Georg von, 404, *404*
Klingert, Karl Heinrich, 147
knee, 626, *626*
knowledge
    comparing and contrasting, 10

new evidence and, 18–19
what is known, 6, 7
Koch, Chris, 451
kudzu, 549, *549*

L

Labandeira, Conrad, 447
lab equipment, R12–R20
  beakers, R12, *R12*
  double-pan balance, R19, *R19*
  forceps, R13, *R13*
  graduated cylinder, R16, *R16*
  hot plate, R13, *R13*
  microscope, R14–R15, *R14*
  rulers, metric, R17, *R17*
  spring scale, R16, *R16*
  test-tube holder, R12, *R12*
  test-tube rack, R13, *R13*
  test tubes, R12, *R12*
  triple-beam balance, R18, *R18*
laboratory experiments, 15, *15*, 16, *17*
labs, R10–R35. *See also* experiment.
  equipment, R12–R19
  experiment design, R28–R35
  precision and accuracy, R22
  presentation of data, R23–R27
  safety, R10–R11
Lake Chad, 105, *105, 108*
lakes, 50
  collection of water in, 56, 57, 58, 267
  dunes formation around, 277–278, *278*
  erosion and, 250
  eutrophication in, 60, *60*
  flow into and out of, 58
  formation of, 58, 86, 192, 285–286, *285, 286*
  fresh water in, 51
  irrigation and, 83
  kettle, 285
  overuse of waters of, 102
  oxbow, 268, *268*
  as part of hydrosphere, 198
  ponds compared to, 58
  recreation on, 85
  role in water cycle, 52, 53
  turnover of, 59, *59*
Lamarck, Jean-Baptiste de, 498
landers, space exploration, **692**, 692–693, *692*, 700
landforms, 239, 240
landmasses, 201
landscape
  effects of human activities on, 86–87, 249–252, *249,
    250, 252*, 253, *253*, 303
  relief map of, 204, *204*
  reshaping by animals and plants, 201, 242
  reshaping by natural processes, 201, 202, *202,*
    261–265, *263, 264, 265,* 266–271, *268, 269, 270,*
    271, 288, *288*
landslides, 129, 202, *202,* 263, 264, *264*
land-use practices, 248, *248,* 249–250, *249, 250*
La Niña, R7
lantern fish, 166, *167*

lanthanides, *841*
large intestine, 610, *611, 620*
larva, 819
larynx, 604, *604*
laser beam, 332
lateral moraines, 284, *284*
latitude, **206,** 206–207, *206,* 209, *209,* 287, *287*
launch window, 690
lava
  on Earth, 750
  lunar maria and, 718, *718,* 719, 720
  on Mars, 755, 757
  on Mercury, 753
  on Venus, *751,* 754
law of conservation of energy, **FL35**
Law of the Sea (1994), 177
lead, *91,* 175, 469, 490
Leavitt, Henrietta, 738, *738*
legends, 17
Leon, Juan Ponce de, 669
levers, 816
  bones as, 576, 595, *595*
Leyden jar, 404, *404*
lichens, 294
life cycle, 29
  of amphibians, 819
  of birds, 819
  of flowering plants, 818
  of insects, 819
  of mammals, 819
  of nonflowering plants, 818
  of reptiles, 819
  of stars, 780, 789–790, *791,* 804, *804,* 816
life science, FL29, FL30–FL31, *6,* 280, 307, 464, 699
life span, 541, 542
ligaments, 573, 581
light
  Chapter Investigations, 684–685
  Doppler effect, 800
  electrically produced, 352, 356
  forms of, 679, *680*
  gamma rays, *680*
  infrared, *680*
  microwaves, *680*
  from nuclear fission, 314
  of other galaxies, 800, *800*
  in photosphere, 780
  plant growth and, 699, *699*
  radio waves, 679, *680*
  source of, 779
  telescopes and, 681
  ultraviolet, *680*
  visible, 679, *680,* 780
  x-rays, 679, *680*
light bulb, 356, *356*
lightning, 352, *353,* 358–359, *358,* 401, *401*
  fire and, 31, *31*
lightning rod, 357, *357,* 379, 401, *401*
light-year, **786**
like charges, 342, *342*
lime (in soil), 245, *245*
limestone, 191, 192, 236

limiting factors, **538**, 554
   density-dependent, 538–539, *538*
   density-independent, 539, *539*
Lincoln animatronics figure, 336, *336*
liver, 610, *611*, 641
living space, 493
living things, *FL30,* 50–51. *See also* human body.
   in coastal environments, *162,* 164–165
   diversity of, FL31
   effects of changes in environment on, 164
   evidence of evolution of, *511,* 512–514, *512 , 514*
   evolution of, 497–502, *503,* 504–505
   first appearance on Earth, *492–493,* 493–494
   in fresh water, 85
   as limiting factors of populations, 538
   mass extinctions, 448–449, 478, *493,* 494–495
   needs of, 49, 51, 81–82, 493, 528
   in ocean waters, 140
   organization of, 571–574, *573, 573*
   populations of, 527–534, *528, 529, 530, 531,*
    532, 534
   soil and, 242, 248
   Sun and, 779, 780
lizards, 510, *511*
loadstone, 414, *414,* 416
lobsters, 164, 551
lock (on waterway), **86,** *87*
loess, **278,** 278–279, *279*
logic circuit, 407
longitude, *206,* **207,** 209, *209*
   time zones and, 838, *838*
longshore currents, **132,** *132,* 142, **275,** *275,* 276
longshore drift, **275,** *275,* 276
low-mass stars, 789, 790, *791,* 804
low tide, 136, *137, 138, 145,* 729, *729,* 730, *730*
   animals in intertidal zone and, 154, *155*
Lucy, 522, *522*
luminosity, 792, *792*
lunar eclipse, 727, *727*
lunar highlands, 718, *718,* 719, 732, *732*
lunar maria, 717, *717, 718,* 719, 720, 732, *732*
lungs, 602, *603, 606, 620*
   circulatory system and, 632, 633, *634,* 635
   dust and, 641
   of Earth, 199
lymph, 635, 642
lymphatic system, 635, 641, 642
lymph nodes, 641, 642
lymph vessels, 635, 642

M

machines
   complicated, 816
   mechanical advantage of, 816
   simple, 816
Machover, Tod, 332
mad cow disease, 20
maglev train, 412, *412*
magnet, *329,* **411,** 440, *440*
   Earth as, 416–418, *416, 418*
   electric current and, 363

electromagnets, 422–424, *422*
   in generators, 428–430, *428, 429*
   healing properties of, 419, *419*
   magnetic domains of, 414, *415*
   magnetic field, 413, *413*
   materials attracted by, 414, *414*
   in motors, 424, *424, 425*
   permanent, 416, 423
   poles, 412, *412*
   temporary, 416
magnetic domain, **414,** 414, *415,* 416
magnetic field, *329,* **413,** *413,* 414, *440*
   of Earth, 416–418, *416, 418*
   electricity and, 420
   of electromagnet, 421, *421*
   solar wind and, 783
   of Sun, 782
magnetic materials, 414, *414, 415*
magnetic north pole, 417
magnetic poles, **412,** 440, *440*
   of Earth, 416, *416,* 417
   of electromagnet, 421, *421*
magnetic resonance imaging (MRI), 626, *626,* 627, *627*
magnetic storms, 783
magnetism, **412,** 412–418, *412, 413, 414, 415, 416,* 440
   atmosphere and, 417, *417*
   current and, 408
   digital information storage and, 395
   electricity and, 341, *425,* 426
   electromagnetism, 421
   produced by electric current, 420–424
   producing electric current, 427–431, 440, *440*
main sequence of stars, **790,** *791,* 837, *837*
mammals, 478, *481,* 494, 819
mammoth fossils, 458, *458, 472,* 479, 490, *491,* 494
Mammoth Mountain, *222*
manatee, *FL1,* 510, *511,* 669
mangrove forests, 156, 158, *158,* 172
Mantell, Gideon, 520
mantle
   of Earth, 200, *200,* 750
   of the Moon, 720, *720, 732*
   of terrestrial planets, 749–750, *751*
Mantle piece (fossil), 520, *520*
manufacturing
   use of water, 82, 84, *85*
   water pollution and, 94, *95,* 96
map key, 205, *205*
map legend, **205,** *205*
mapping technology
   false-color imaging, 220, *220*
   geographic information systems (GIS), 189,
    221–222, *221, 222*
   global positioning system (GPS), 207, *207*
   remote sensing devices, 187–189, *187, 188,*
    218–220
   satellite imaging, 219, *219*
maps, 203–205, *205,* 211, *211,* 212–215, 224, *224*
   Chapter Investigation, 216–217
   contour lines, 213–214, *213*
   land features, 204, *204*
   latitude and longitude, 206–207, *206*

legend, 205
Mercator projection, 208–209, *209,* 210
projections, 208–210, *209, 210*
relief, 204, *204*
scales and symbols, 205, *205*
topography, 212–215
map scale, **205,** *205,* 211, *211*
March equinox, 710, *711, 712*
mare (maria), **717,** 717–718, *717, 718,* 719, 720
Marella, 521, *521*
Mariana Trench, 120
marine ecosystems, *42,* 43–45, *43*
marine life, 118, 140
marrow, 577, *577,* 583, 641
Mars. *See also* terrestrial planets.
    atmosphere, 752, 756
    characteristics of, *839*
    crust of, 750
    density, *839*
    diameter of, 755, *755, 839*
    distance from the Sun, *744, 755, 772*
    exploration of, 692, 693
    gravity of, 752, 755
    impact cratering, 755, 757, *757*
    lava on, 755
    layers of, 750
    mass, *755, 839*
    moons of, 755
    movement of, *678*
    orbit of, *755, 839*
    polar caps, 756
    revolution of, *839*
    rotation of, *755, 839*
    as seen from Earth, 678, 743
    size of, *744, 839*
    surface of, 755, *756*
    tectonics, 755, 757, *757*
    temperatures on, 756
    volcanism, 755, *757*
    water on, 55, *55,* 756, 757
    weathering and erosion on, 55, *55, 751,* 755, *756,
        757, 757*
    wind, 755, 756, 757
marshes, 669
Mars Pathfinder, 693
mass, **811**
    of atoms, 342
    of Charon, 765
    of gas giants, *759, 760, 762*
    of Pluto, 765, *765*
    of stars, 790, 792
    of Sun, 779
    of terrestrial planets, *749, 753, 754, 755*
    time and space and, 738
mass extinction, 448–449, 478, *481, 493,* **494,** 494
mass wasting, **263,** 263–265
materials, 493
    for experiments, R29
math skills
    area, R43, *R43*
    bar graphs, 31, *31*
    data, comparing, R38–R39

decimals, 312, R39
describing a set of data, R36–R37
double bar graph, 160, *160*
exponents, 694
finding averages, 535
formulas, R42–R43
fractions, 63, R40
interpreting graphs, 472
line graphs, 287, 648, *648,* 722, *722*
mean, R36
median, R36
percents, 388, 748, R40
plotting coordinates, 123, *123*
proportions, 211, 496, R39
range, R37
rates, 583, R38
ratios, R38
scatter plot, 793, *793*
scientific notation, R44, *R44*
significant figures, 439
surface area of rectangular prism, 237
units of length, 613
variables, 367
volume, R43, *R43*
volume of rectangular prisms, 89, *89*
matter, **FL33**
    changes in form, FL35
    conservation of, FL35
    cycles of in ecosystems, FL33
    electrical charge property of, 341
    forces acting on, FL33
    in open and closed systems, 197
    properties of, 368
    smallest units of, FL35
Maury, Matthew, 147
meadows, 60, *60*
mean, **R36,** *R36*
meanders, 268, *268, 269, 272*
measurement, 14
    distance between stars, 787
    of electrical potential, 351
    electrical resistance, 355
    electric current, 361, 362, *362*
    energy use, 437, *437*
    net charge, 343
    of power used, 436–438, *436*
    using map scale, 205
mechanical advantage, 816
mechanical digestion, 609, 610
mechanical weathering, 231, *231,* **232,** *233, 236,
        254, 254*
median, **R36,** *R36*
medicine
    human population growth and, 546
    from ocean organisms, 44, *44,* 170
    from plants, 305
    sharks and, 452, 453
    from soil, 248
    technology and, 624–627, *624,* 698
Megalosaurus, 520, *520*
meiosis, 817
melanin, 654

memory (computer), 394
meniscus, R16, *R16*
Mercator projection, 208–209, *209*, 210
Mercury, 743, *744, 753. See also* terrestrial planets.
    atmosphere, 753
    characteristics of, *839*
    crust of, 750, 753
    day-night cycle, 753
    density, *839*
    diameter, *753, 839*
    distance from Sun, *744, 753, 772*
    impact craters on, 696, *751, 753, 753*
    lava plains, 753
    layers of, 750
    mass, *753, 839*
    orbit of Sun, *753, 839*
    revolution of, *839*
    rotation of, *753, 839*
    size, *744, 839*
    tectonics on, 753
    temperatures, 753
    as viewed from Earth, 743
    volcanism on, 753
    weathering and erosion on, 753
mercury (element), *91*, 175
Merritt Island National Wildlife Refuge, 669, *669*
Mesozoic era, 476, *476, 477,* 478–479, 827, *827*
Mesozoic extinction, 479
metals, *841*
metamorphosis, 819
metasequoia, 521, *521*
meteorites, 292, *292,* 494–495, *495,* 664, **769,** 769
meteors, 449, **769,** 769, 772
methane, 762, 763
metric system, 14, R20–R21
Mexico, 104, *104, 159,* 494–495, *495*
Miami Beach, Florida, 205, *205*
Michigan, Lake, *58*
microchip, 393, *393*
microorganisms
    in coastal environments, 162
    from deep biosphere, 149
    effect on soil, 242, *243*
    fossils of, 477, 523
microscope
    making a slide or wet mount, R15, *R15*
    parts of, R14, *R14*
    viewing an object, R15
microscopic organisms, fossils of, 827
microwave radiation, *680,* 802
microwaves, 680
middens, 668
Middle East, 100, 102, 173
MIDI (Musical Instrument Digital Interface), 332–333
mid-ocean ridge, 40, *121*
migration
    of osprey, 153, *153*
    of salmon, 316
    salt marshes and, 157
Milky Way, 674, *675,* 794–795, *795,* 796, 797
minerals
    fossil formation and, 460, *461,* 490, *490*

as nonrenewable resource, *301*
    in ocean waters, 40, 168, 169, 174, *174,* 180
    products of, 305, *306*
    prospecting for, 187–189
    in soil, 240
mining, *199*
    coal, 303
    destruction of soil by, 250, *250*
    effects on ecosystems, 45
    in the ocean, 149, 173
    use of water, 82, 84
Mir (space station), 688, *688*
Mississippi River
    cities built near, *82*
    dams controlling, *87*
    delta of, 269
    drainage basin, 267
    transportation on, 84
    zebra mussel invasion, 549
Mississippi Valley, 279
Missouri River, *82*
mode, **R37**
models, **16,** 16, *16, 17, 18*
molds and casts, 460, *461,* 828, *828*
molecules, 342
monitor (computer), 395, *395*
monthly tides, 139, *139*
Moon, FL35, *717, 725, 730, 732, 732, 744*
    change over time, 720
    characteristics of, *839*
    craters, 18, *18,* 663, 696
    distance from Earth, *716,* 717, *717*
    Earth and, 674
    eclipses, 727, *727, 728, 728,* 731, 732, *732*
    exploration of, *670–671,* 687, 689, 692
    far side, 717, *718*
    gibbous, 724, *725*
    gravity and, 137–139, *137,* 716, 729–730, *729, 730,*
      732, 748
    highlands, 718, *718,* 719, *732*
    layers of, 720, *720,* 732, *732*
    maria, 717, *717, 718,* 719, 720, *732*
    near side, 717, 718, *718*
    orbit of, *716, 717*
    origins of, 720–721, *721*
    phases of, 139, 723–724, *725,* 732, *732*
    position during lunar eclipse, 727, *727, 732*
    position during solar eclipse, 728, *728*
    rocks of, 719, *719,* 720
    rotation of, 678, 716, 717, *717*
    size of, *744*
    soil, 719, 720
    theory of formation of, 292
    tides and, 137–139, *137, 139,* 729–730, *729,*
      730, 732
    waning, 724, *725*
    waxing, 724, *725,* 726
    weathering, 719
moons of other planets, 743, *744,* 746–747, 760–766
moraines, **284,** *284*
moray eels, *163*
mosses, 294, 699, *699*

Mote Marine Laboratory, 453, *453*
motion, 814
motors, 424, *424, 425*, 440, *440*
mountain ranges, 204, *204*
mountains, 204, *204*
    change over time, FL33, 261, 474, *474*
    formation of, 201, *492,* 750
    on ocean floor, 120, *121,* 122, 142
    soil of, 240
    on topographic maps, *213, 214*
Mount St. Helens, 264, *475*
mouse, 395, *395*
    DNA of, 34, *34*
mouth, 604, 610, *611, 620*
movable joints, 581
movement. *See also* axis of rotation; revolution;
    rotation.
    angular, 581, *582*
    of charged particles in core of Earth, 416
    of continents, 293, 294
    of electric charge, 352, *353,* 354–356, 360–362,
    362, 368
    of electrons, 350–351
    of energy in the Sun, 780, *781*
    of galaxies, 738, *738,* 797, 799, 800, *801,* 804
    of glaciers, 281, *283*
    gliding, 582
    of heat in oceans, 124
    involuntary, 586
    of landmasses, 201
    of matter, FL33
    muscles and, 573, 584, 588, *588*
    of nutrients in lakes, 59
    of nutrients in oceans, 39, 41, 124, 126
    of oxygen in a body, 599
    of particles in waves, *131,* 134–135
    rotational, 582, *582*
    of sediment, 266, 268, 274, 275, *275*
    shark patterns, 452, 453
    speech and other respiratory movements,
    604–605, *604*
    of static charge, 350–351, 352, *353*
    voluntary, 586
    of water, 52–54, 66–67, *131*
MP3 player, 331, 332, *332,* 391, *391*
MRI, 562, 626, *626, 627*
mucous glands, 608
mucus, 602, 610, 641
mudflow, 202, *202,* 263, 264, *264*
mudskippers, 158
mudslides, 202, *202,* 263, 264, *264*
multicellular organisms, 462, 475, **493,** 493–494
    first appearance of, 294, 475
multimeter, 362, *362*
multiple-choice questions (MC), FL37, FL48
multiple sclerosis (MS), 566
multiple star system, 792
muscles, 584
    of bladder, 615
    body temperature and, 585, *585*
    cardiac, 592
    Chapter Investigation, 590–591

    development of, 589
    digestion and, 608, *608,* 610
    exercise and, 589, *589*
    involuntary, 586
    movement and, 585, 588, *588*
    posture and, 585
    skeletal, 592
    in skin, *650*
    smooth, 592
    of speech, 604, *604*
    vitamin D and, 566
    voluntary, 586
muscle tissue, 573, *573*
    cardiac, 586
    skeletal, 586
    smooth, 586
muscle tone, 585
muscular system, *568–569,* 584–585, **585,** *590*
    body temperature and, 585, *585*
    movement and, 585, 588, *588*
    posture and, 585
music, 330–333, *330–331, 332, 333,* 392, *392*
Musical Instrument Digital Interface. *See* MIDI.
Musschenbroek, Peter van, *443*
mussels, 154, *155,* 156, 168, 172
mutations, 502, 505

N

nails, 649, 652, *652*
National Aeronautics and Space Administration
    (NASA), 667–669, 687–689, 697. *See also*
    exploration of space.
    satellite images from, *195*
    study of radiation, 739, *739*
National Electric Code, 388
natural gas
    as nonrenewable resource, 300, *301*
    recovery of, 304, *304*
natural processes, FL33
    removal of salt from oceans by, 116
    reshaping the landscape, 261–265, *261, 263, 264,*
    265, 266–271, *268, 269, 270, 271,* 274–279, *274,*
    275, 276, 277, 278, 279
natural resources, **299,** 299
    availability, 300, 305
    biomass energy, 320, *320*
    conservation, 308–311
    fresh water, 81–88, *82*
    geothermal energy, 318–319, *318*
    groundwater, 67
    hydroelectric power, 82, 316, *316,* 435, *435*
    hydrogen fuel cells, 320–321, *321*
    nonrenewable resources, 300, *301*
    nuclear, 313–315, *314, 315*
    in the ocean, 40, 170–175, 180
    products of, 305
    renewable resources, 300, *301*
    satellite monitoring of, 697
    soil, 248
    solar energy, *317*
    solar system, 674

wind energy, 319, *319*
natural selection, **501,** 516. *See also* adaptations; evolution.
  Chapter Investigation, 506–507, *506*
  evidence supporting, 508–510, *509, 511,* 512–514, *512, 514*
  speciation, 504–505, *504*
natural world, 5
nature of science, FL28–FL29
navigation, 206, 208–209, 416, 736
neap tides, **139,** *139*
near-shore environments, 161–162, *163,* 164–165, *164,* 180, *180*
nebulae, *747,* **789,** *789,* 795
  negative charge, 343–348, *343, 344, 345, 346*
  in clouds, 352, *353*
nephrons, 616, *616*
Neptune, 743, 760, 762, *763*
  atmosphere of, 758–759, 762, 763
  characteristics of, *839*
  clouds, 763, *763*
  color, 762, 763
  density, *839*
  diameter, 762, *763, 839*
  distance from the Sun, *744–745,* 763, *763, 772*
  exploration of, 690
  gravitational pull, 758
  mass, *763, 839*
  moons of, 766, *766*
  orbit of, 763, *763, 839*
  revolution of, *839*
  rotation of, *763, 839*
  size, *744, 839*
  temperatures, 763
  weather, 763
  winds, 763
Nerinea trinodosa, 468, *468*
nerves, *650*
nerve tissue, 572, 573
nervous system, *600*
net charge, 343
network (computer), 396–397
neutrons, 342, 812, 813
neutron stars, **790,** *791, 804*
new moon, 724, *725,* 728, *728*
Newton, Sir Isaac, 137, 737, *737*
nickel, 414, 416
night, 708, *708,* 732, *732*
Nile River, 87
nitrogen, 600
  in atmosphere, 198
  cycle, 821
  eutrophication and, 60
  Northern Lights and, 418
  in ocean water, 118
  in soil, 242
  in Titan's atmosphere, 766
nodules, 174, *174*
noncontroversial results, 21
nonflowering plants, 818
nonmagnetic materials, 414, *415*
nonmetals, *841*

nonpoint-source pollution, **94,** *95*
nonrenewable resources, **300,** *301,* 324
  fossil fuels, 302–306
  uranium, 313–315
nonspecific immune response, 642, 643, *643*
Northern Hemisphere currents, 125, *125*
northern lights, 418, *418,* 783, *783*
North Pole
  axis of rotation and, 708
  length of days near, 713, *713*
  Polaris and, 677
  seasons and, 710
north pole (magnetic), 412, *412,* 417, 421
North Star, 677
nose, 602, *603*
nostrils, 606, *606*
note-taking strategies, R45–R49
  combination notes, 230, *230,* 298, *298,* 340, *340,* 706, *706,* 778, *778,* R45, *R45*
  concept map, R49, *R49*
  content frame, R45, *R45*
  main idea and detail notes, 48, *48,* 196, *196,* 298, *298,* 488, *488,* 526, *526,* 630, *630,* 742, *742,* 778, *778,* R46, *R46*
  main idea web, 4, *4,* 152, *152,* 260, *260,* 298, *298,* 410, *410,* 570, *570,* 672, *672,* 778, *778,* R46, *R46*
  mind map, R47, *R47*
  outline, 114, *114,* 374, *374,* 456, *456,* 525, *526,* 598, *598,* R48, *R48*
  supporting main ideas, 80, *80,* R47, *R47*
  Venn diagram, R49, *R49*
nuclear energy, 324
nuclear fission, **313,** *314*
nuclear power plants, 86, 314, *314, 315,* 316
nuclear wastes, 175
nucleus, 342
nudibranch, *163*
nutrients, 40, **607**
  circulatory system and, 632, 635
  decomposition and, 199
  digestion of, 607–610, *611*
  in estuaries, 156
  eutrophication and, 60, *60*
  movement of in lakes, 59, *59*
  movement of in oceans, 39, 41, *41,* 124, 126
  in salt marshes, 157
  skin protection and, 654
  in soil, 242, 245, 248
  upwelling and, 126

O blood type, 637, *637*
observations, 8, 14, **R2,** R4, R5
  qualitative, R2
  quantitative, R2
  recording, R33, *R33*
ocean, 37. *See also* hydrosphere.
  abyssal plains, 120, *120*
  aquaculture, 172, *172*
  atmosphere and, 127
  bouys, 149, *149,* 199

by-catch, 172, *172*
carbon dioxide, 118
Challenger expedition, 147
charting floor of, 122, *122*, 147, *147*
climate and weather and, 40
coasts of, 153–154, *155*, 156–159
connected globally, 50, *50*
continental shelf, 120, *120*
continental slope, 120, *120*
core samples of floor, 160, *160*, 294
coverage of the Earth, 50, *50*, 51, *51*, 115–116, *115*
currents, 124–128, 142, *142*, 199
deep water, 39
density, 116–117, *117*
depth, 122, *122*, 146, 147, 148
development of, *492*
dunes formation near, 277–278, *278*
ecosystems of, *42*, 43–45, *43*
eddies in, 41
effects on climate, 40
energy resources in, 40
environments of, 153–154, *155*, 156–159, *156*, *157*, *158*, 161–162, *162*, *163*, 164–166, *167*, *168*, 180
exploration of, 39–40, 146, 147, *147*, 168
first animals in, 294, *294*
first life in, 489, 493
floor of, 120, *120*, 123, 142, 147, *147*
flow of water into, 56, 267
food web, *178*
formation of, 293, *293*, 294, *294*
formation of atmosphere and, 752
gases in, 116
hydrothermal vents of, 39, 40
ice ages and, 295, 479
icebergs, 62
Internet activities, 113, 150
living resources, 170–171
mapping of, 122, *122*, 123, 142, *123*, 147
measuring depth of, 146, *146*, 147, 148
mid-ocean ridge, 40, 120, *121*
minerals and rocks in, 39, 40
mixing of water layers, 40
nonliving resources, 173–175, *173*, *174*
nutrients in, 39, 41
oil spills, *95*, 96, 176, *176*, 304, 307, *307*
overfishing, 171–172, *171*, 178–179
oxygen in, 118, 126, 175
as part of hydrosphere, 198
pollution, 175–177, *175*, *176*, *177*, 180, 550, *550*
resources in, 170–175
role in water cycle, 53, 54
salinity, 51, 116, 117, *117*, 126, 148, 154, 156
seamounts, 120, *121*
studies of, 39, 149, *198*
submarine canyons, 120, *120*
surface current, 125, *125*, 142, 199
surface layer, 119
survey of, 147, *147*
temperatures, 119, *119*, 187, 199
theory of formation, 116
tides, 136–140, *145*, 729–730, *729*, *730*
trenches, 120, *120*

volcanic islands, 120, *121*
waves, *112–113*, 129–130, *130*, *131*, 132–133
ocean currents, FL33, **124,** 124–128, *125*, 146
climate, weather and, 40, 125, 127–128
deep current, 126, *126*
downwelling, 41, *41*, 126, *126*
effect on shorelines, 132, *132*, 142, *142*, 275–277, *275*, *276*
electromagnets and, *426*
global surface, 125, *125*
longshore current, 132, *132*, 275, *275*, 276
pollution and, 176
rip, 132–133, *133*
study of, 147
surface current, 125, 199
undertows, 132, 133
upwelling, 126, *126*
ocean environments, 153
algae, 154
aquaculture, 172, *172*
bottom dwellers, 154
coastal wetlands, 156–158, *157*, *158*
coral reefs, 162, *163*, 164
deep zone, *167*
estuaries, 156, *156*
floaters, 154
humans activities and, 158–159
hydrothermal vents, 40, 168, *168*, 169, *169*
intertidal zone, 154, 155
kelp forests, 164–165, *164*
life forms in, 154, 162
mangrove forests, 158, *158*
near shore, 161–162, *162*
open ocean, 166–168, *167*, *168*
pollution of, 15, 158–159, *159*
salt marshes, 157
surface zone, 166, *167*
swimmers, 154
tidal pools, 154
wetlands, 156–159
oceanographers, 148
ocean trenches, 120, *120*, 122
ocean waves. *See* waves.
octopus, 39, *39*, 154, *163*, 164, 166
Oersted, Hans Christian, 420, *437*
offshore drilling, *FL11*, 173, *173*, 176, *180*, 296–297
offspring, 817
Ogallala Aquifer, 66, 101
Ohm, Georg Simon, *437*
ohmmeter, 362
ohms, **355,** 368
Ohm's law, **361,** 361–362, *361*, 367, *367*, 368
oil
drilling on land, 304, *304*
as nonrenewable resource, 300, *301*
offshore drilling for, 149, 173, *173*, 296–297
pollution from, 304
products from, 305
spills, *95*, 96, 176, *176*, 304, 307, *307*
transportation of, 304
oil-eating microbes, *307*
oil glands, 650–651, *650*

oil spills, *95, 96,* 176, *176,* 304, 307, *307*
oil well, *301*
Old Faithful geyser, 71
Omega Nebula, *789*
onionskin weathering, 232
On the Origin of Species (Darwin), 504, 529
open circuit, 377, *377*
open ocean environments, 166, *167,* 168
open systems, 197
operational definition, **R31**
opinion, different from fact, R9
opportunist, **541,** *541*
orange groves, *2–3,* 11, *11*
orbit, **674**
    of comets, 768, *768*
    of Earth, 709, *709*
    gravity and, 695
    of Jupiter, *759*
    of Mars, *755*
    of Mercury, *753*
    of Neptune, 763, *763*
    of planets, 746–747, *839*
    of Pluto and Charon, 765
    of Saturn, *760*
    shape of, 745, *745*
    of stars in the Milky Way, 795
    of Uranus, 762, *762*
    of Venus, *754*
orbiters, 691, *691,* 693, 700
Ordovician period, *476, 826*
organic farming, 97
organic matter, 239
organisms, 571, *573. See also* living things.
    development of, 492–493, *492–493*
    discovery of new species, 39
    effect of ocean eddies on, 41
    effect on soil, 242
    eutrophication and, 60
    first appearances of, 475, *475*
    formation of atmosphere and, 293, *293*
    in fresh water, 51, 91
    in ocean waters, 140
    organization of, 571–574, *573,* 592, *592*
    protective coloration, 39, *39*
    in salt water, 51
    water treatment and, 92, 93
organs, 571, **573,** *573,* 592, *592*
    of circulatory system, 632, *632,* 634
    of digestive system, 610, 612, *612,* 641
    of immune system, 641
    of integumentary system, 641, 649–652, *650, 652*
    multicellular organisms and, 493
    muscle tissue in, 586
    of respiratory system, 602, *603,* 632, 641
    ultrasound machines and, *626*
    of urinary system, 615, *615*
original remains, **458**
osprey, 153, *153,* 157
outer core of Earth, 200, *200*
outer solar system, *744–745,* 745, 758–763, *758, 759,*
    772, *772*
    asteroids, 767, *767*

comets, 767, 768, *768*
composition of objects in, 764
formation of bodies in, 764
Jupiter, 759–760, *759, 760*
Neptune, 762, 763, *763*
Pluto and Charon, 765, *765*
Saturn, 760–761, *760, 761*
Uranus, 762, *762*
output, 394, 395, *395*
overfishing, 44, **171,** *171,* 178–179, 180, 551
overgrazing, 249
overpopulation, 501–502, *503,* 516
oxbow lakes, 268, *268, 272*
oxygen
    in atmosphere, 198, 600
    cellular respiration and, 601
    circulatory system and, 631, 632–633, 635
    development of atmosphere and, 492
    from forests, 199
    formation of atmosphere and, 293
    in lake water, 59, *59,* 60, *60*
    as material needed by living things, FL31
    Northern Lights and, 418
    in ocean water, 118, *118,* 126, 175
    phytoplankton as source of, 166, 170
    plants and, 248
    respiratory system and, 599–600, *600,* 602, 620
    rust formation and, 234, 235
    water treatment and, 93
oysters, 158, 172, 176, *177*
ozone, 293
ozone layer, 295, 565

P

Pacific Ocean, 115, 128
pain receptors, 652
Paleozoic era, 476, *476,* 478, *826,* 827
Paleozoic extinction, 478
Panama Canal, 86
pancreas, 610, *611,* 641
Pangaea, 293, 294, *294*
panoramic x-ray, 625, *625*
paper mills, 84, *84*
parallax, **787**
parallel circuits, **385,** *385,* 400, *400*
parasites, 647, *647*
parasitism, *538*
pareuts, 817
parrotfish, 44, *163,* 164
particle accelerator, 738, *738,* 803
particle pollution, 105
particles
    in atmosphere, 198
    atoms, 414, 812
    charged, 342–343, *342,* 351–352, 416, 418, 421
    collisions of, *738*
    electrons, 342, 343–346, 363, *363,* 368, 414
    kinetic energy of, 811
    movement in waves, *131,* 134–135
    neutrons, 342, 812, 813
    protons, 342, 368, 414, 812, 813

subatomic, 407, 811, 812
Pascual-Leone, Alvaro, 562
passive immunity, 646
patella, *579*
Pathfinder, 693
pathogens, **640**, *647*, 656
    white blood cells and, 633, 640–646, *644*
patterns, FL29
patterns in structure and function, 464, *464*, 510, *511*, 512, *512*
patterns in structure and processes
    of galaxies, 796–797, *796, 797*
    of gas giants, 758–759, *759*
    of other space bodies, 764
    of planets, *751*
    of rocky inner planets, 749–750
    in the universe, 799
Patterson, Clair C., 292
Pawcatuck River estuary, *156*
Paynes Prairie State Preserve, 192
PC (personal computer), 394–395
penguins, 29, *29*
penumbra, **727**, *727*, 728, *728*, 729
percents, 388, 748, R40, R41
periodic table of elements, *840–841*, R54
periods, geologic, 476, *476–477*, 482, *482*, 827
peristalsis, **608**, *608*
permeable materials, **64**, *65*, 66, *66*, 74, *74*
Permian Extinction, 448–449, 494, *494*
Permian period, *477*, 827
personal computer, 394–395, *394–395*, *439*
pesticides, 97, 176, 550
    ingredients of, 171
    pollution and, 44, 95, *95*
petrified wood, 460, *460*, *461*, 828, 829, *829*
PET scans, *562*, 626, *626*
phagocytes, 644, *644*
Phanerozoic eon, *477*, 478–479, *826*, 827
phase changes, 811
phases of matter, 52–54, 811
phases of the Moon, 723–724, *725*, 726, 732, *732*
Phoenicians, 146
pH of soil, 245, *245*
phosphorite, *174*
phosphorus, 60
photocopier, 347, *347*
photosphere, 780, *781*, 782, *782*
photosynthesis, 162, 164, 166
physical properties
    electric charge, 341
    magnetism, 414
physical science, FL29, FL34–FL35
    earth science and, *6*, 13, 141, *141*
    unifying principles, FL35
physical states of water, 49
physics, FL34, *6*
phytoplankton, **166**, *167*, 170, 447
pigment, 654
Piltdown Man, 522
Pinatubo, Mount, *448*
pine trees, 541, *541*
pivot joints, 582, *582*

pixel, *394*, 395
placenta, 819
plains, 204, *204*
planar projections, 210, *210*
planetary rings, 761, *761*, 772
    of Saturn, 760, *760*, 761, *761*, *772*
    of Uranus, 762, *762*
planets. *See also* solar system.
    characteristics of, 839
    cores, 749–750, 759, *759*
    distances from Sun, *744–745*, 745
    doubles, 743, *744*, 745, 765, *765*, 772, *772*
    exploration of, 690–693, *690, 691, 692*
    formation of, 746–747
    gas giants (outer solar system), *744*, 745, 758–763, *758, 759, 760, 761, 762, 763*, 766, *766*, 772
    mantles of, 749–750, *751*
    moons of, *FL19*, 663, *670–671*, 674, 678, 687, 689, 692, 696, 716–724, *716, 717, 718, 719, 720, 721*, 725, 726, 727, *727*, 728, *728*, 729–730, *730*, 732, *732*, 743, *744*, 746–747, *760*, 761, *761*, 762, 765, *765*, 766, *766*
    movement of, 678
    orbits of the Sun, 695, 709–710, *709, 711*, 737, 745, *745*, 746–747, 749, *753, 754, 755*, 759, *760*, 762, *762, 763, 763*, 765, 795
    processes of surface features, 18–19, 750, *751*, 753, *753*, 754
    sizes of, *744*, 745
    solar systems and, 674
    terrestrial (inner solar system), 749–750, *749, 751*, 752–756, *753, 754, 755, 756*, 757, *757*, 764
    theory of formation of, 292
plankton, 165
plants, *264*
    biomass energy, 320
    in coastal environments, 162, *162*
    deep-zone ocean environments and, 166
    effect on soil, 242, *243*
    in estuaries, 156
    first appearance on land, 294, *294, 493*, 494
    fossil fuels, 302
    gravity and, 699, *699*
    in lakes and ponds, 58
    mass extinction of, 448
    in ocean waters, 154
    pollution and, 105
    populations of, 528–534, *528, 530, 532*, 536–542
    as producers, FL31
    products from, 248, 305, *306*
    as renewable resource, *301*
    role in water cycle, 54
    of sand dunes, 278, 280, *280*
    satellite monitoring of, 199
    soil type and, 239
    use of water, 82, 83
    weathering of rocks, 232, *233*
plasma, 633
plastics, 305
plateau, 204, *204*
platelets, 633, *633*
platypus, *499*

INDEX

Pluto, 743, *744*, 765, *765*, 772
    atmosphere of, 765
    characteristics of, *839*
    density, *839*
    diameter, *765, 839*
    distance from the Sun, *744–745, 772*
    formation of, 764
    gravity, 765
    layers of, 765
    mass, 765, *765, 839*
    moon, 765
    orbit of, 745, 765, *765, 839*
    revolution of, *839*
    rotation of, *765,* 839, *839*
    size of, *744, 839*
point-source pollution, **94,** *95*
polar icecaps, on Mars, 55, *55*
Polaris, 677
polarization, 346, *346*
polar regions
    density of water near, 126
    length of days in, 713, *713*
    of Mars, 756
    ocean currents and, 125
    on projection maps, 209, *209,* 210, *210*
    soil of, 240, *241*
poles, magnetic, **412,** *412,* 440, *440*
    of Earth, 416, *416,* 417
    of electromagnets, 421, *421*
pollen, 648, *648*
pollution, **550**
    agriculture and, 550, *550*
    of air, 235, 300, 304, 306
    from aquaculture, 172, 550, *550*
    biomass energy and, 320
    effect on coral reefs, 44, 164
    of estuaries, 159
    eutrophication and, 60
    from factories, 306
    from fossil fuels, 303, 306
    of oceans, 44, 175–176, *175,* 177, 180
    oil spills, 304
    ozone layer and, 565
    prevention of, 26, 96–97
    reduction of, 309
    sinkholes and, 192
    of soil, 249, 250
    spread of, 105
    of water, 82, 91, 94, *95,* 96–97, 105, 249, 550, *550*
polymerase chain reaction (PCR), 523
Polynesians, 146
polyps (coral), 43, *43*
ponds, 56, 58, 60, *60*
POODLE (vehicle), 148
population density, **531,** 531–532, *531,* 536–542, *537, 538, 539, 541, 542*
population dynamics, **527**
population maps, 221, *524–525*
population projections, 547–548, *547*
populations, 102, 524, 536–542, *665*
    age structure of, 533, *533*
    conditions for growth, 547, *547,* 548

Darwin's observation of, 529
    decline, 528, *528,* 529, 539–540, *539,* 554
    density, 531–532, *531,* 538
    distribution of, 534, *534*
    geographic information systems and, 221, *221*
    growth, 528, *528,* 529, *529,* 537, 538–540, *538, 539,* 554
    human effects on, 549–551, *549, 550, 551*
    of humans, 544–551, *544,* 547
    interrelationships in, 538
    limits on growth, 536–540
    predicting changes in, 533–534
    range of, 532
    of sharks, 453
    size of, 530–531
    spacing, 532–533, *532*
    stability, 528, *528,* 554
    stages of, 527–529, *528*
    studies of, 535, *535*
    survival strategies, 541–542, *541, 542,* 545–546, *545, 546*
    water supplies and, 100–102
population size, **530**
pores, 650–651, *650*
pore space, 245
Port Campbell, Australia, 274, *274,* 275
Posidonius, 146
position, 814
positive charge, 343–348, *343, 344, 345, 346*
    in clouds, 352, *353*
positron emission tomography (PET) scan, 626, *626*
posture, 585
Potassium-argon dating, 522
potential energy, 351, 813
power, 436–438
power meter, 437, *437*
power plant, 376, 435, *435,* 440
power ratings, 436, *436*
Precambrian time, *476,* 826, *826–827*
precipitation, **53,** 54, 74, *74*
    aquifers and, 70
    lake water and, 58
    role in water cycle, 52–53, *53*
precision, **R22,** *R22*
predation, *538*
predators
    coral reefs and, 44
    of deep-zone ocean environments, 166
    electric eels, 349, *349*
predictions, 10, **R3**
presentation of results, R34, *R34*
preservation, 45, 176–177, 669
pressure
    artesian wells and, 68, *68*
    in blood vessels, 635–636
    in deep ocean waters, 121, 168, 169
    hot springs and, 71
    tidal power plants and, 141
pressure release, 232, *233*
primary cells, 364, *365*
prime meridian, *206,* **207,** 838, *838*
printer, 395, *395*

prions, 20, *20*
prism, 680, *680*
probes, **693**, 700
problems, scientific, 8–9
procedure, writing, R32
processes in atmosphere, biosphere, hydrosphere,
    lithosphere, 751, 799
    reshaping by natural processes, 261–265, *263, 264,
    265,* 266–271, *268, 269, 270, 271,* 750, 751
    on terrestrial planets, 750, *751*
processing, 394, 395, *395*
producers, 822
projection, **208**, 208–210, *209, 210*
prominences, 782, *782*
properties of matter
    electric charge, 341
    magnetism, 414
proportions, 211, 496, R39
prospecting, 187–189
proteins, 607, 608
Proterozoic eon, 477, *477,* 826, *826–827*
protists, 154, 162
protons, 342, 368, 414, 812
Proxima Centauri, *792*
Prusiner, Stanley, 20–21
Ptolemy, 736
pulley, 816
pulmonary arteries, *632,* 635
pulmonary system, 636. *See also* circulatory system;
    respiratory system
pulmonary veins, *632,* 635
pulsars, 8–11, *10,* 790, *790*

Q

qualitative observations, R2, *R2*
qualitative operational definitions, R31
quality standards for water, 91, *91*
quantitative observations, R2, *R2*
quantitative operational definitions, R31
quantum computing, 407
quasars, **797**
Quaternary period, *477,* 479, *827*
qubits, 407
questions, FL28
    extended response, FL37, FL50–FL51, *FL51*
    gridded response, FL37, *FL37,* FL49, *FL49*
    multiple choice, FL37, FL48
    scientific, 8
    short response, FL37, FL50, *FL50*

R

radar, 24, *24,* 25
radiation, **FL33**, 679
    big bang, 738, 739, *739,* 802
    black hole and, 790
    electromagnetic, 679–681, *680*
    microwaves, *680*
    neutron stars, 790
    remote sensing and, 188
    small space objects and, 764, *764*
    studies of, *739*
    Sun and, 780
    Van Allen Radiation Belt, 667
radiation zone, 780, *781*
radio, 331
radioactive dating, 469, *470,* 471, 472, *472,* 482, 522,
    522, 830–831, *830*
radioactive elements, 830, *830*
radioactivity, 315, 469, 625
radiology, 625, *625, 626*
radiometric dating, 830, *830*
radio telescopes, 664–665, *664,* 682, *682*
radio waves, 679, 680, *680,* 739
    neutron stars and, 790
    pulsars and, 8–11, *8, 10,* 790
    radar and, 24, 25
    telescopes and, 682, *682*
radius, *579*
rain, 263
    aquifers and, 70
    cavern formation, 270–271, *270*
    effects on Earth's surface, 191, 201, 261–262, *263,*
    264, *264,* 265
    elements in oceans and, 116, 117
    formation of, 53
    lake water and, 58
    pollution and, 94
    rock weathering and, 234–235
    run off from, 57, *57*
    salinity and, 154
    sinkholes and, 191, *191*
    soil and, 239, 249, 250, 300
rainbow, 680, 684, 684–685, *684*
random-access memory (RAM), 394
range, **R37**
rates, 583, R38
ratios, R38
read-only memory (ROM), 394
rechargeable batteries, 364, *365*
recording engineer, 332–333, *333*
records, R33
recreation, 85, 86
rectum, 610
recycling, 96, 97, **310**, 310–311, *310, 311,* 324
red blood cells, *FL17, 583,* 628–629, **633**, 633, *633*
    blood types and, 637, *637*
red boring sponge, 44
red giant stars, 837, *837*
red shift light, 800, *801*
red supergiant stars, 837, *837*
reduction of waste, 309, *309*
reflecting telescopes, 681, *681,* 682
reflection of radiation, 188
refracting telescopes, 681, *681*
regeneration, 817
relative age, **465**, 465–466, 482, 490, 522
relativity, theory of, 738
relevance, determining, 55
relief, **213**, *213*
relief map, **204**, *204, 213*
remote operated vehicles (ROVs), 148
remote sensing, **218**

INDEX

remote sensing devices, *186–187,* 187–188, *188,* 189, 218–220, *218, 219,* 224
    false-color image, 220, *220*
renewable resources, **300,** 300, 315, 324
    biomass, 320, *320*
    falling water, 316
    geothermal energy, 318–319, *318*
    hydrogen fuel cells, 320–321, *321*
    sunlight, 317, *317*
    tides, 140
    trees, 300, *301,* 552, *552*
    water, *316*
    wind, 319, *319,* 322–323
reproduction survival strategies, 541–542, *541, 542*
reptiles, 478, 494, 819
repulsion
    electrical, *342,* 344, *344,* 350, 352, 368
    magnetic, 412, 413, *413*
research conducted in space, 688–689, 699, *699. See also* exploration of space.
reservoirs, 54, 86, 250
resistance, **355,** 355–356, *355, 356,* 368, 378
    grounding and, 357, *357*
    Ohm's law, 361–362, *361*
    transformers and, 431
resistors, **376,** *376,* 387, *387,* 400
resource centers, FL23
resources
    availability, 300, 306
    biomass energy, 320, *320*
    Chapter Investigations, 552–553
    conservation, 308–311
    geothermal energy, 318–319, *318*
    hydrogen, 320–321, *321*
    in the ocean, 170–175, 180
    populations and, 530–531, 532
    products of, *306*
    soil, 248
    water, 316, *316*
    wind energy, 319, *319,* 322–323
respiratory system, **599,** 620, *620*
    body defenses and, 641, *641*
    breathing and, 599–600, 602
    cellular respiration and, 601
    circulatory system and, 632
    cough and sneezing and, 605, 641
    exchange of gases in, 614
    function of, 571
    organs of, 602, *603*
    pathogens and, 640, 641, *641*
    speech and other respiratory movements, 604–605, *604*
    water removal and, 605, *605,* 614
    yoga and, 606, *606*
response to environment, 573
results, *R33,* R34
reuse of resources, 103, 309
revolution, **709**
rhino fossils, 458
ribs, 578, *579,* 581, 602, *603*
rickets, 566

rings, **761,** 772
    of Saturn, 760, *760,* 761, *761, 772*
    of Uranus, 762, *762*
Rio Grande, 104, *104*
rip currents, **132,** 133, *133,* 142
risks, 26
rivers, 50
    dams and locks on, 86–88, *86, 87*
    droughts and, *101*
    elements in oceans and, 116, 117
    erosion and deposition, 250, 262, 266–271
    estuaries and, 156–159, *156, 157*
    flow of water through, 56, 57, *57,* 58
    fresh water in, 51
    irrigation and, 83
    navigation, 84
    overuse of, 101, 102
    as part of hydrosphere, 198
    paths of, 268, *268, 269*
    recreation on, 85
    role in water cycle, 52, 53
    water rights, 104, *104*
road maps, 205, *205,* 221
robots, 121, 335, 655
rockets, 667, *687, 689*
rockfalls, 263
rock formations, *274*
rocks, *228–229, 454–455, 457,* 478, 482
    dating of, 465–469, *466, 467, 468, 469, 470,* 471, 490
    fossils, 457–462, *457, 458, 459, 460, 461,* 467–468, *467, 468,* 520
    ground water and, 65, 66, *66*
    igneous, 459, 467, *467, 470,* 471
    layers, 466–467, *467, 470,* 482, *482,* 485, *493*
    mass wasting of, 263, *263*
    of the Moon, 719, *719,* 720
    as nonrenewable resource, *301*
    permeability of, 65
    products of, *306*
    sedimentary, *185,* 459, 466–467, *466, 467, 470,* 471, *478,* 482, *482*
    in soil, 239, 240, 244
    on terrestrial planets, 749, 750, 755, *756*
    weathering of, *FL10,* 231–232, *233,* 234–236, *235, 236*
rockslides, 263, *263*
Rocky Mountains, 204, *204*
Roentgen, William Conrad, 624
ROM, 394
roots, 494
rotation
    of Earth, 677, *677,* 690, 710–713, *711, 712, 713,* 732, *732,* 749, 838, *838*
    of Jupiter, 759, *759*
    of Mars, *755*
    of Mercury, *753*
    of Moon, 678, 716, 717, *717*
    of Neptune, 763
    ocean currents and, 125
    of planets, 746
    of Pluto, *765*

of Saturn, *760, 761*
of the Sun, 782
tides and, 138, *730*
of Uranus, *762*
of Venus, *754*
rotational movement, 582, *582*
rovers, *687,* 692, *692, 700*
runoff, 53, 96
    conservation practices and, 252, 253
    irrigation and, 101, 107
    pollution and, 94, *95,* 176, *176,* 177, 249
Russia, 303, 664, 687–688
rusting, 232, 234, 235, *235*

S

saber-toothed cats, 458, *458,* 479
safety, R10–R11
    animal, R11
    chemical, R11, *R11*
    cleanup, R11
    directions, R10
    dress code, R10
    electrical, 379, R11
    fire, R10
    glassware, R11
    heating, R10
    icons, *R10–R11*
    in laboratory, 30, *30*
    sharp objects, R11
    during solar eclipse, 729
safety devices, 382, *382*
salinity, **116,** 116–117, *117*
    deep ocean currents and, 126
    of estuaries, 156
    sonar for measuring, 148
    variation in tidal pools, 154
saliva, 609, 610, 641
salivary glands, 610, *611*
salmon, 316, 502, *503*
    dams and, 88
    effect of ocean eddies on, 41
salt, 106, *106,* 116, *117,* 126, 142, 175
salt marshes, 156–157, *157*
Salton Sea, California, 550, *550*
salt water, **51,** *51. See also* ocean.
    desalination of, 106, *106*
    estuaries and, 156
    percentage of Earth's waters, 51
samples, R6
sand
    barrier islands, 277, *277*
    dunes, 277–278, *278*
    longshore current and, 275, *275*
    as ocean resource, 175
    sandbars, 132, *133,* 276–277, 288
    in soil, 244, *244*
sandbars, 132, *133,* **276,** 276–277, *276,* 288
sand food, 280, *280*
satellites, **687**
    development of, 697
    of early space programs, 667

fishing industry and, 171
imaging Earth's surface, 187–188, *194–195,* 200,
    218–219, *219*
for locating positions on Earth, 207
magnetic storms and, 783
for mapmaking, 204
monitoring biosphere with, 195, 199
monitoring oceans with, 128, 149, 199
ocean floor images from, 122
population mapping and, *524–525*
for studying Earth system, 295
for weather forecasting, 198, 199
saturation zone, 65, 68
Saturn, 743, *744,* 760–761, *760, 761, 772*
    atmosphere, 758–759, 760
    axis of rotation and seasons, 761
    density, 760, *839*
    diameter, 760, *839*
    distance from the Sun, *744, 760, 772*
    exploration of, 690
    gravity, 758, 760
    mass, 760, *760, 839*
    moons of, 761, 766
    orbit of, *760,* 761, *839*
    revolution of, *839*
    rings of, 760–761, *760*
    rotation of, *760, 839*
    size of, *744, 839*
Saudi Arabia, 173
scale worms, 40, *40*
scanner, *394,* 395
scapula, *579*
Schmidt, Harrison, 295
Schrag, Dan, 448
science, 32
    categories of, FL29, 6, *6*
    earth science, FL32–FL33
    life science, FL30–FL31
    nature of, FL28–FL29, 5–6
    physical science, FL34–FL35
    society, technology and, 24–30, 32
    tools of, 5–12
    unifying principles of, FL29, FL31, FL33, FL35
Science on the Job
    archeologist, 731, *731*
    electrician, 382, *382*
    farmer, 107, *107*
    fishing boat captain, 543, *543*
    landscape architect, 253, *253*
    yoga instructor, 606, *606*
Scientific American Frontiers
    All That Glitters, 188, *188*
    Big Dish, 664, *664*
    Into the Deep, 40, *40*
    Noah's Snowball, 448, *448*
    The Sight of Touch, 562, *562*
    Toy Symphony, 332, *332*
scientific bias, R6
scientific ethics, 27–30
scientific evidence, 14
scientific inquiries
    field work, 16

laboratory experiments, 15, 16
models, 16
surveys, 16
scientific notation, 694, 709–710, R44
scientific processes, FL29, **6,** 6–12
asking questions, 6, 7, 8
critical thinking, 10
determining what is known, 6, 7, 8, 11
interpreting results, 6, 7, 8, 9, 12, 18–19, 20
investigating, 6–7, 8
sharing information, 6, 7, 11, *11,* 20
scientific theory, 508–509, *509*
scientists
habits of mind, FL28, 8–10
processes used, FL29, 6–12
screw, 816
scuba divers, 43, 44, 121, 148, 600, *600*
sea fans, 45
seafood, 170, 171, 551
sea horse, *118*
seamounts, 120, *121,* 122, 142
sea otters, 164, *165, 307*
Seasonal Affective Disorder (SAD), 566–567, *567*
seasonal star maps, 832, *833–834*
seasons, **710,** *711,* 712–713, 732, *732*
angle of sunlight and, 712, *712*
changes in constellation, 832, *833–836*
Chapter investigation of, 714–715, *714*
lake turnover and, 59, *59*
length of days, 713
ocean temperatures and, 119
seasons, population size and, 530
sea stacks, 274, *274*
sea turtles, 669
sea urchins, 164
seaweed, 44, 154, *155,* 158, 164, 171, 172, 493
SeaWorld Orlando, 335
sediment, 269
barrier islands and, 277
erosion and deposition of, 261–262
glaciers and, 282, *283,* 284, *284,* 285
in lakes and ponds, 60, *60*
loess, 278–279, *279*
movement of, 266, 268, 274, 275, *275*
of ocean floor, 168
sedimentary rocks, *185,* 830, *830*
fossil formation, 459
layers, 466–467, *467, 470,* 482, *482, 493*
radioactive dating and, 471
relative age and, 465–467, *466, 467*
seed, 818
selection, 501, 502, *503,* 516
semiconductor, 393
senses, 561–562, *562*
of sharks, 452
sensor, **219**
sensory receptors, 650, *650,* 652
September equinox, 710, *711*
septic system, **94,** *94*
series circuit, **384,** *384,* 400, *400*
sewage, *95,* 175, 192
sewage system, **93,** *93*

sewage treatment plants, 93, *93,* 159
sexual reproduction, **817,** 817–820
compared to asexual reproduction, 817–818
Shackleton, Ernest, 575
shadows
angle of sunlight and, 712, *712*
eclipses, 727, *727,* 732, *732*
shaft, 424, *425,* 428, *428*
shagreen, 452
sharing information, 11, *11, 12*
shark-liver oil, 452
sharks, 450–453, *450, 451, 452, 453*
shellfish, 154, 156, 171, 551
shells, 118
shipping, 84, *84, 95*
estuaries and, 158
pollution and, *95,* 176, *176,* 177
shivering, 585, *585*
Shoemaker-Levy 9, 663
shorelines, *150–151*
environments near, 161–162, *163,* 164–165
environments of, 153
longshore currents, 132, *132*
plants of, 154
recreation on, 158
reshaping of, 275–277, *275, 276*
salt marshes and, 157
tides and, 136–140
waves and, 130
short circuit, **378,** *378*
short-response questions (SR), FL37, FL50, *FL50*
shoulder joint, 582, *582*
shrimp, 158, 166, *167,* 168, 172
significant figures, R44
silicon chip, 393, *393*
silt, 244, *244*
Silurian period, *476,* 826
simple machines, 816
singing, 604
single-celled organisms. *See* unicellular organisms.
sinkholes, *190,* 191–193, *191, 192, 193,* **271,** *271*
SI units, R20–R21, *R21*
size of populations, *530,* 554
skeletal muscle, **586,** *587,* 588, *588,* 592
skeletal system, *559,* **576,** 576–578, *579,* 580–582, 592, *592*
appendicular, 578, *579*
axial, 578, *579*
changes with time, 580, *580*
function of, 571
marrow and blood cells, 577, *577*
skepticism, FL28, **9**
skin, *620,* 656, *656*
artificial, 655, *655*
body temperature and, 651
functions of, 649
infection and, *640,* 641, 649
removal of waste, 614
of sharks, 451
structure of, 650–651, *650*
ultraviolet radiation and, 565, 566
skull, 578, *579,* 580, 581

sleet, 53
slides, making, R15, *R15*
slope, **213,** *213*
slow-switch muscles, 586
sludge, 93, 94, *94*
slumps, 192, 264–265, *264*
small intestine, *620*
smell, 452, 562
smog, 304
smooth muscle, **586,** *587,* 592
snails, 157, 158, *496*
sneezing, 604, 641, *641,* 642
snow, *70*
snow line, 287, *287*
society, science and, 24–30, 32
Society Islands, *172*
sodium chloride, 116
software, 394, 395, *395*
soil. *See also* deposition.
    agriculture, 249, *249*
    chemical weathering, 234–235, *235,* 250, 254
    chemistry, 245
    climate, 238–239, *241*
    color, 245
    composition, 238–240, *239, 241,* 244, *244,* 257
    conservation of, 251–252, *252,* 254
    decomposition and, 199. *See also* deposition.
    deforestation and, 300
    erosion. *See* erosion.
    formation of, 242, 251, 254, *254*
    functions of, 248
    groundwater and, 64, 65
    landforms, 240, *241*
    loess, 278, *279*
    mechanical weathering, 232, *233,* 237, *237*
    on the Moon, 719, 720
    organic processes, 242, *242, 243,* 248
    pore space, 245
    of salt marshes, 157
    soil horizons, 240, *240*
    testing of, 246–247, *246*
    texture, 244, *244*
    use of lime, 245
    worm action in, 201, 242
soil horizon, **240,** *240*
soil profile, **240,** *240*
soil properties
    chemistry, 245
    color, 245
    pore space, 245
    texture, 244, *244*
soil use and abuse
    agriculture, 249, *249*
    conservation practices, 251–252, *252*
    construction and development, 249, 250, *250*
    mining, 250, *250*
solar cells, **317,** *317,* 324, 366, *366*
    first use of, 668
solar eclipse, 728–729, *728,* 781
solar energy, 317, *317*
    conversion to chemical energy, FL31

solar system, **674,** *675, 744. See also* Sun; *specific planets.*
    asteroid belt, 767
    asteroids, 767, *767*
    comets, 768–769, *769*
    distances, 743, *744–745,* 745
    exploration of, 690–693, *690, 691, 692*
    formation of, 292, *292,* 746–747, *747,* 764, 772
    gas giants (outer planets), *744,* 758–763, *758, 759, 760, 761, 762, 763*
    measuring age of, 292
    meteors and meteorites, 769, *769*
    model of, *18*
    Moon, *748*
    moons of other planets, 748, 765, 766, *766*
    new ideas concerning, 18–19
    orbits, 745
    Pluto and Charon, 764–765, *765*
    size of objects in, 743, *744*
    small objects in, 764
    solar wind, 783, *783*
    Sun-centered model of, 736, *736*
    terrestrial (inner) planets, 749–756, *749, 751, 753, 754, 755, 756, 757, 757*
solar wind, **783,** 783, *783*
solstice, **710,** 731
solution sinkholes, 192
sonar, **122,** *122,* 146, 148, *148,* 543, *543*
    fishing industry and, 171
    imaging of geosphere by, 200
sound waves, 331, 432
    conversion digital information, 392, *392*
    Doppler effect, 800
    electrical devices and, 386
    movement of charge and, 352
    ultrasound machines and, 626, *626*
    vocal cords and, 604, *604*
South America, 204, *209*
Southern Hemisphere currents, 125, *125*
southern lights, 418, 783, *783*
South Pole
    axis of rotation and, 708
    fossils, 462
    ice cores from, 462, 463, *463*
    length of days near, 713, *713*
    seasons and, 710
south pole (magnetic), 412, *412,* 417, 421
Soviet Union. *See* Russia.
spacecraft, 686, 687, 690, 700, *700. See also* satellites.
    Apollo program, 686–687, *687*
    flybys, 690, *690*
    hydrogen fuel cell, 320
    landers, *687,* 692–693, *692*
    orbiters, 691, *691,* 693
    probes, 693
    rovers, *687*
    solar power, 317
    space shuttle, 689, *689*
    space station, 688, *688*
    telescopes, 682–683, *683*
space exploration. *See* exploration of space.
space objects, *663,* 696

space shuttle, 689, *689*
space stations, **688,** 688–689, *688*
   hydrogen fuel cell, 320
   solar power, 317
spacing of populations, 532–533, *532,* 554
specialized cells, 573
speciation, **504,** 504–505, *504*
species, **FL31**
   change over time, 492–495, *492–493,* **497**–505, *500,*
    501, 503, 504, 516, *516*
   discovery of extinct species, 148, *148,* 521, *521*
   distribution of, *499*
   endangered, 27, *27,* 669
   evidence of evolution of, 509–510, *511,* 512–514,
    512, 514
   evolution of, *496*
   extinction, FL31, 18–19, 448–449, 457–458, 478, 494
   introduction of new species, 533–534, *534,* 549, *549*
   new discoveries in oceans, 147, 149, 153
   survival strategies, 541–542, *541, 542*
specific immune response, 642, 644, *644*
spectroscope, 684–685
spectrum, **680,** 684–685, *684, 685,* 737, 792
speech, 604–605, *604*
speed, 814
sperm whales, *167*
SPF factors, 659
sphygnomanometer, 636, *637*
Spica (star), *792*
spinal column, 578
spiral galaxies, 796, *796,* 804, *804*
spit, 276
spleen, 641
spongy bone, **577,** 577, *577*
spores, 818
spray irrigation, 83, *83,* 103, 107, *107*
spring (season), 710, *711, 712, 834*
springs, **68,** *69, 70*
spring tide, **139,** *139*
squids, 166, *167*
stability of populations, 528, *528,* 529, 554
starfish, 154, 164
starlings, 534, *534*
stars, *678,* 700, *703,* 784–785, 816. *See also* Sun
   ages of, 816
   black holes, *804*
   brightness, 787, 792, *792,* 804, *807*
   Cepheid variables, 738
   classification of, 786, *789, 807,* 816
   color, 788, *792,* 804, *807*
   companions, 792, *792*
   composition of, 737, 788
   constellations of, 676, *676*
   distance, 787
   fusion, 780, 789, 790
   giant, supergiant and white dwarf, **788,** *788,* 790,
    791, 804
   gravity of, 789, 790, 792
   Hertzsprung-Russell (HR) diagram, *792, 792, 807,*
    816, 837, *837*
   higher-mass, 789, 790, *791, 804*
   life cycle, 780, 789–790, *791, 804, 804,* 816

   lower-mass, 789, 790, *791, 804,* 816
   mass, 792
   movement of, 677–678, *677*
   neutron stars, 790, *804*
   orbit of, 795
   pulsars, 790, *790*
   radiation, 790
   rotation of, 11
   seasonal star maps, 832, *833–836*
   size of, 788, 792
   supernovas, 790, *804*
   surface temperatures, 788, *789,* 792, *792,* 804, *807,*
    837, *837*
   systems, 792, *792*
star systems, 792, *792*
static charge, **343,** 343–348, *343, 344, 345, 346, 348*
   compared to electric current, 360
   conductors and insulators, 355, *355*
   discovery of, 401
   Franklin's experiment, 405
   grounding, 357, *357*
   industrial uses of, 347–348, *347, 348*
   movement of, 350–351, 352, *353*
   potential energy of, 350–351
   resistance, 356–357
static discharge, 350–351, 358, *358*
   conductors and insulators, 354
   grounding, 357, *357*
   lightning, 352, *353*
   resistance, 355–356
static electricity, 341
steel, 411
step-down transformer, 431, *431, 435, 435*
step-up transformer, 431, 435, *435*
sternum, 581, *581*
St. Lawrence Seaway, 85
stomach, *608,* 610, *611, 620,* 641
Stonehenge, Great Britain, 731, *731*
storage cells, 364, *365, 394, 394,* 395
storms
   El Niño and, R7, *R7*
   on Jupiter, 760, *760*
   on Neptune, 763
   on Saturn, 760
strands, FL36
stream channels, 268, *268*
streams, *269, 272*
   alluvial fan, 269
   channels, 268, *268*
   delta, 269
   erosion and deposition by, 266–271
   flow of water through, 56, 57, *57,* 58
   as part of hydrosphere, 198
   sinkholes in, 192
street map, 205, *205,* 211, *211*
subatomic particles, 407
submarine canyons, 120, *120,* 142
submarines, 121, *121,* 147, *147*
submersibles, *38–39,* 40, 199
subsidence, 192
subway train, 426
Sue (dinosaur), 522, *522*

summer, 710, *711, 712,* 713, 835
Sun, *711, 725*
    angles of light on Earth, 712, *712*
    atmosphere of, 779, 780
    atmospheric dust and, 663
    chromosphere, 780
    comets and, 768, *768*
    convection zone, 780
    core, 780, *781*
    corona, 780, 783
    day length on Earth and, 713
    days and nights, 708, *708,* 713, *713*
    daytime and, 708, *708*
    distances, 743, *744–745,* 745
    Earth's orbit and, 709–710, *709, 711*
    Earth's seasons and, 709–710, *711*
    effect on ocean temperatures, 119
    flares, 782, *782*
    formation of, 746
    fusion, 780
    gravitational pull, *745*
    gravity and, FL35
    interior, 780
    layers of, 804, *804*
    magnetic fields, 782
    magnetic storms, 783
    main sequence, 790
    Milky Way and, 794
    moonlight and, 723
    Moon phases and, 724, *725,* 726
    photosphere, 780
    photosynthesis and, FL31
    position during lunar eclipse, 727, *727*
    position during new moon and full moon, 139
    position during solar eclipse, 728, *728*
    prominences, 782, *782*
    radiation zone, 780
    role in water cycle, 53
    seasons on Earth and, **710,** *711,* 712–713, 714–715, 732, *732*
    size, 743, *744,* 788, *788*
    skin and, 654, *654*
    solar wind, 783, *783*
    as source of energy, 300, 302
    study of energy from, 696
    sunspots, 780, *782*
    surface of, 804, *804*
    temperature of, 788
    theory of formation of, 292
    tides and, 137–138, 139, *139*
    zones of, 780
sunblock, 566, 567
Sun-centered model of solar system, 736, *736*
sunlight
    angles of and seasons, 712, *712*
    in deep oceans waters, 168, 169
    in Florida, *564,* 565–567, *565*
    health benefits of, 566–567, *566*
    health risks from exposure, 565
    near-shore environments and, 162, 164
    protection from, 567

    remote sensing and, 188
    as renewable resource, *301*
    as source of energy, 300
    in surface waters of oceans, 166, *167*
    tilt of Earth's axis and, 710
Sun Protection Factor (SPF), 566
Sunshine State, *564,* 565–567, *565*
Sunshine State Benchmarks, FL36, FL37, FL38–FL47
Sunshine State Standards, FL36–FL47
    identification of in lessons, FL37
    organization of, FL36
sunspots, **782,** *782*
superclusters, 799
superconductors, 356
supercontinent, 293, 294, *294*
supergiant stars, 788, *788,* 790, *791, 792,* 804
supermassive black hole, 797, *797*
supernovas, 739, 790, *791,* 804
surface current, 125, *125,* 142, 199
surface layer of oceans
    as carrier of nutrients, 39, 41
    currents of, 125, *125*
    temperature of, 119, *119*
    waves in, 119, 129–130, *131,* 132–133
surface water, 56–62, *57*
surface-zone environments, 166, *167*
surveys, 16, *17,* R6
survival, 451, *575*
swallowing, 610
sweat, 574, *574,* 614, 651
sweat glands, 614, 650–651, *650*
swelling, 643
switches, 376, *376,* 377, *377,* 387, *387,* 400, *400,* 407
    transistors, 393, 406, *406,* 407
symbols
    for electrical circuits, 377, *377*
    on periodic table, *841*
    on topographic maps, 215, *215*
synesthesia, 562–563, *563*
systemic circulatory system, 636
systems, **197,** 493, 571, *573,* **574,** 574, 592, *592,* 813
    See also solar system.
    circulatory, *573,* 574, 631–633, *632, 633, 634, 635–637, 635, 636, 637*
    digestive, 571, 574, 608–610, *608, 610, 611, 612,* 641
    energy in, 813
    fresh water, 56–62, *57*
    growth and, 580, 589, 609, 653
    immune, 574, 641–647, *641, 642, 643, 644*
    integumentary, 641, 649–654, *650, 652, 653, 654*
    interaction of, 574, 601
    lymphatic system, 635
    maintenance, 571, 599–600, *600,* 601, 606, *606,* 608–610, 614–617, 632, 635, 640–641
    muscular, 574, 584–586, *585, 587,* 588–589, *588, 589*
    nervous, 574
    regulation, 574, *574,* 614, 649, 651
    reproductive, 574
    respiratory, 571, 574, 599–602, *600, 603,* 604–605, *604, 605,* 641

INDEX

skeletal, 574, 578, *579*, 580–582, *582*, *583*
solar system, 292, *292*, 674, *675*, 735
urinary, 574, 614–617, *615*, *616*

T

Tadpole Galaxy, 798, *798*
tagging, 29
tar, fossils in, 458, *458*
Taylor-Clarke, Marisa, 562
T cells, 644–645, *644*
tears, 641
technology, **25**, 120, *523*, 739. *See also* computers.
 ammeter, 362
 animatronics, *334*, 335–337, *335*, *336*, *337*
 artificial skin, 655, *655*
 astrolabe, 736, *736*
 batteries, 405, *405*
 capacitors, 404, *404*
 for classifying fossils, 523, *523*
 for communications, 26
 computer chips, 407, *407*
 core sampling of ocean floor, 294
 cores samples, 463, *463*
 CT systems, 626, *626*
 dams, **86**, 86–88, *86*, *87*, 140, *140*, 201, 316, 324, *434*, *434*, 435, *435*
 for dating fossils, 522, *522*
 desalination, 106
 difference engine, 405, *405*
 digital devices, 331–333
 diving suit, 146, 147
 Dobson spectrophotometer, 293, *293*
 dynamo, 406, *406*
 electric cells, 363, *363*, 364, *365*, 366, *366*
 electromagneticism and, 421
 electronics, 389–397, 404
 electrostatic air filter, 348
 electrostatic paint process, 348, *348*
 e-mail, 627
 ENIAC, 406, *406*
 false-color images, 220, *665*, *754*, *757*, *789*, *797*
 filmless body imaging, 627, *627*
 for fishing industry, 171, 551
 functional magnetic resonance imaging (FMRI), 561–562
 generators, 344, *344*, 406, *406*, 427, 428, *428*, 429, *429*, 430, 434–435, *434*, *435*, 440, *440*
 geographic information systems, 221, 221–222, *221*, *222*
 global positioning system (GPS), 207, *207*
 for human habitat expansion, 546
 human population growth and, 544
 hydrogen fuel cells, 26, *26*, 320–321, *321*, 324
 International Space Station (ISS), 295, *295*, 688–689, *688*
 Internet, 396–397
 interventional MRI, 627
 irrigation, 83, *83*, 103, 107, *107*, 546
 lightning rod, 405, *405*
 logic circuit, 407
 maglev train, 412, *412*

 for mapmaking, 204, 218–222, *219*, 224
 measuring age of solar system, 292
 for measuring ocean depth, 122, *122*, 146, 147, 148
 microscopes, *523*
 MIDI (Musical Instrument Digital Interface), 332–333, *332*, *333*
 miniaturization, 407
 motors, 424, *424*, *425*, 440, *440*
 MRI machines, 562, 626, *626*
 multimeter, 362
 nanotube, 407
 ocean buoys, 149, *149*, 199
 offshore drilling, 173, *173*
 ohmmeter, 362
 particle accelerator, 738, *738*
 PET scans, 626, *626*
 photocopier, 347, *347*
 polymerase chain reaction (PCR), 523
 radioactive dating, 469, *469*
 radiometric dating, 292, 522, *522*
 remote sensing devices, 187–189, *188*, **218**, 218–220, *218*, *219*, *220*, 224
 research aircraft, *187*
 risks and costs of, 26
 satellites, 122, 128, 149, 171, 187–188, *194–195*, 198, 199, 204, 218–220, 295
 science, society and, 25–30, *25*, *26*
 society and, 24–25
 solar cells, **317**, 317, *317*, 324, 366, *366*
 sonar, 148, 543, *543*
 from space exploration, *298*
 for space exploration, 686–693, *687*, *688*, *689*, *690*, 695, 697–698
 from space exploration, 698, *698*
 sphygmomanometer, 636
 for studying deep-sea vents, 40
 for study of biosphere, 199
 study of Earth system and, 292
 for study of hydrosphere, 199
 submarines, 147
 superconductors, 356
 telegraph, 147
 telescopes, 664, *664*, *665*, 681–683, *681*, *682*, 737, *737*, 739
 tools for fossil removal, 520, *520*
 transformers, **431**, *431*, 435, *435*
 transistors, 406, *406*
 ultrasound imaging, 626, *626*
 use of static electricity, 347–348, *347*, *348*
 vacuum tubes, 406, *406*
 voltmeter, 362, *362*
 water treatment, 92, *92*
 for weather forecasting, 198, *198*
 x-ray machines, 624, *624*, 625, *625*
tectonic plates, 466
tectonics, **750**, 750, *751*, 772, *772*
 of Earth, 750
 on Europa, 766, *766*
 on Mars, 755
 on Mercury, 753
 on Venus, 754
teeth, 35, 609, 610, 625, *625*

of sharks, 452
telegraph, 147, 398
telescopes, *FL18, 661,* 664–665, *664, 665,* **681,** 681–683,
    700, 704–705, 737, 737, 739
    Hubble Space Telescope, 682–683, *683,* 763, *803*
    light, 680–682, *681*
    radio telescopes, 664–665, *664,* 682, *682*
    reflecting telescopes, 681, *681,* 682
    refracting telescopes, 681–682, *681*
temperate zones, 240, *241*
temperature, **811**
    atmospheric dust and, 663
    body's response to, 574, 585, *585,* 650–651
    Chapter Investigation, 784–785
    in closed systems, 197
    color and, 788
    conversions, R21, *R21*
    coral reefs and, 44
    as density-independent factors, 539
    El Niño and, 128
    on gas giants, 759
    and heat, 811
    lake turnover and, 59, *59*
    magnetic force and, 416
    on Mars, 756
    on Mercury, 753
    on Neptune, *763*
    ocean currents and, 125, 126
    of ocean layers, 119, *119,* 142, *142*
    satellite mapping of, *195*
    sonar for measuring, 148
    of stars, 788, *789,* 792, *792,* 837, *837*
    study of in oceans, 147
    sunlight and, 712, 713
    variation in intertidal zones, 154
    on Venus, 753
temperature receptors, 652
tendons, 573, 588, *588*
Tennessee, 85, 271
terminal velocity, 815
terracing, 252, *252*
terrain maps, *221*
terrestrial planets, **749.** *See also* Earth; Mars; Mercury;
    Venus.
    atmospheres of, 749, 752
    cores, 749
    crusts of, 749, 750
    formation of, 750, 764
    impact cratering, 750
    mantles, 749, 750
    orbits of, *749, 753, 754, 755*
    plate tectonics, 750, *751*
    volcanism, 750, *751*
    weathering and erosion, 750
Tertiary period, *477,* 479, *827*
Texas, *104,* 138
Thales of Miletus, 404, *404*
theme parks, 335
theory, **19,** 508–509, *509*
thermocline, 119, *119*
theropod dinosaur, *459*

Think About
    changes in telephones, 497, *497*
    erosion on small space bodies, 764
    events in society, 24, *24*
    how telephones work, 383, *383*
    human body and cities, 571, *571*
    hydroelectric power generation, 434, *434*
    images of Earth, 218, *218*
    land use and soil, 248, *248*
    Moon and daylight, 723, *723*
    natural forces shaping landforms, 261, *261*
    ocean water levels, 136, *136*
    population growth, 527, *527*
    relationships in a system, 197
    relationships in a terrarium, *197*
    relative age, 465, *465*
    resources, 299, *299*
    rock formations, 274, *274*
    shoreline environments, 153, *153,* 463
    value of water, 81, *81*
    view of Earth from space, 695, *695*
third-quarter moon, 724, *725*
thoracic cavity, *603*
throat, 602, *603,* 610
thymus gland, 641
tibia, *579*
tidal dams, 140, *140*
tidal pools, 154, *155*
tidal power plants, 141, *141*
tidal range, **138,** *138,* 141
tides, **136,** 136–140, *136,* 142, *142,* 729–730, *729,*
    730, 732
    daily, 137, *137*
    direct high, *137*
    energy of, 141
    generation of electricity, 140, *140,* 141
    gravity and, 137–138, *137*
    high, 136, *137, 138, 145,* 154, *155*
    indirect high, *137*
    intertidal zone, 154, *155*
    low, 136, *137, 138, 145,* 154, *155*
    monthly, 139, *139*
    neap, **139,** *139*
    spring, **139,** *139*
    tidal pools and, 154, *155*
    timing, 139
tide tables, 139
till, **284,** *284*
Timelines in Science
    astronomy, 736–739
    Earth system, 292–295
    electronics, 404–407
    exploring the ocean, 146–149
    life unearthed, 520–523
time zones, 838, *838*
Timucuan people, 668
tin, *174*
tissues, 493, 571, **572,** 573, 576, 592, *592*
    bones, 577, *577*
    cardiac muscle, 586
    cartilage, 602

INDEX

connective, 573
epithelial, 573
of immune system, 641
muscle, 573, *573*, 584, *587*
nerve, 573
skeletal muscle, 586
smooth muscle, 586
types of, 572–573
Titan, 766, *766*
Titanic, 62
tongue, 610
tools. *See also* technology.
chimpanzees and, *17*
gathering data and, 7
for measuring electricity, 362
for observing, 14
of prospectors, 187–189, *188, 189*
for removing fossils, 520, *520*
of scientists, FL29
topographic maps, 212–215, *213, 214, 215,* 216–217, *216, 217,* 224, *224*
closed circles, *213,* 214, *214*
index contour lines, *214,* 215
symbols on, 825
topography, 191, **212,** *213*
topsoil, 240
tornadoes, *539*
touch, 562, 652
tourism, 43, 191, 335, 565
toxic waste, *91*
trace fossils, *FL14, 454–455,* 460, *461,* 828, 829, *829*
trachea, 602, *603, 604,* 620
transformers, **431,** *431,* 435, *435*
transistors, 393, 406, *406,* 407
transportation
water pollution and, *95,* 96
on waterways, 84, *84,* 86–87, *87,* 88
trash, 44, 308
treatment of water, 90–94, 108, *108,* 546, *546*
trees, 462, 552
drought and, 101
fossils of, 460, *460*
products from, 248, 305, *306*
as renewable resource, 300, *301*
rings of, 462, *462*
soil formation, 242, *243*
trenches, 120, *120,* 122
trials, 15
Triassic period, *477, 827*
trilobite fossil, *481,* 490, *490*
Triton, 766, *766*
tropical areas, 240, *241*
Tropites subbullatus, 468, *468*
troughs of waves, 130, *131*
tubeworms, 40, 168, 169, *169*
turnover, **59,** *59*
Turtle, 147, *147*
turtles, 172
Tyrannosaurus rex, 464, *464,* 522, *522*

U

ulna, *579*
ultrasound imaging, 626, *626*
ultraviolet radiation, 565, 654, *680,* 814
coral and, 44
UVA and UVB, 566, *566*
umbra, **727,** *727,* 728, *728,* 729
uncontrolled variables, 15
underground water, 52
aquifers, 13, 66 67, *66,* 69
cavern formation, *270*
Chapter Investigation of, 72–73, *72*
depletion of, 101
formation of caverns, 270–271
geysers, 71, *71*
hot springs, 70–71, *70, 71*
irrigation and, 70, 83
lake water and, 58
as part of hydrosphere, 198
pollution of, 192
protection agreements, 105
role in water cycle, 53
sources of, 57
water table, 65, *65, 66, 69,* 70, 270
undertow, 130, 133
unicellular organisms, 154, 475, *475,* **492,** *492,* 573
uniformitarianism, **474**
unifying principles
of earth science, FL33
of life science, FL31
of physical science, FL35
unintended consequences, 26–27
United Nations, 105, 177, 521
United States
aquifers of, 66, *66,* 101
coal deposits in, 303
dams in, *87*
deserts of, 530, *530*
drownings from rip currents, 133
electricity generation in, 317, 318, *320*
farming in, 83, *83*
fuel consumption, *327*
in ice age, 282, *282, 286*
loess deposits, 279
mangrove forests of, 158, *158*
minerals used in, 305
nuclear power plants in, 313
relief map of, *204*
salt marshes of, 157, *157*
seafood consumption in, 170, 171
space program of, 687–688
trash produced in, 308, *309*
water quality in, 91
water rights agreements of, 104
water use in, 102, *102, 108*
United States Antiquities Act of 1906, 521
United States Department of Defense, 396
United States Geological Survey (USGS), *215*
Unit Projects, 41, 189, 333, 449, 563, *665*
units of measurement, 14, R20–R21

ampere, 361
astronomical unit (AU), 745
centimeters, 613
changing metric to U.S., *R20, R21*
changing metric units, R20
coulombs, 343
decibels, 814
kilowatt, 436
kilowatt-hour, 437
light-year, 786
map scales, 205
meters, 613
millimeters, 613
ohms, 355
volt, 351
watts, 436
Universal Studios, 335
Universal Time (UT), 838, *838*
universe, FL33, *661, 673*–674, **674,** *675,* 803
    arrangement of, 674, *675*
    development of, 803, *803*
    expansion of, 738, *738,* 739, *739,* 800–801, *801,* 804, *804*
    looking back in time, 800, *800*
    motion of galaxies, 800
    origin, 802–803, 804
unlike charges, 342, *342*
upwelling, **126,** *126*
uranium, 300, *301,* 314, *314*
uranium 235 dating, 469, 490, *831,* 860–861
Uranus, 743, *744,* 762, *762*
    atmosphere, 758–759, 762
    axis of rotation, 762, *762*
    characteristics of, *839*
    clouds, 762
    color, 762
    density, *839*
    diameter, 762, *762, 839*
    distance from the Sun, *744,* 762, *762, 772*
    exploration of, 690
    gravitational pull, 758
    mass, 762, *762, 839*
    orbit, 762, *762, 839*
    revolution of, *839*
    rotation of, *762,* 839, *839*
    size of, *744, 839*
urban centers, 158
ureter, 615, *615*
urethra, 615, *615*
urinary system, 614–617, **615,** *615, 616, 620*
urine, **615,** 615, 616, 617, *620*
U.S. Department of Energy, 320, 321
UV index number, 565, *565*

V

vaccine, 25, *25,* **646,** 646–647, *647*
vacuum tube, 406, *406*
valley glaciers, 61, *283*
valleys, 240, 268, *269,* 750
Van Allen, James, 667
Van Allen Radiation Belt, 667

Van de Graaff generator, 344, *344*
Vanguard 1 satellite, 667
variables, 15, R29, **R30**
    controlling, R17
    dependent, R30
    independent, R30
variation, 501, 502, *503,* 516
veins, *634,* **635,** 635–636, *635*
Venezuela, *264*
ventricle of heart, *632,* 633
Venus, 678, 694, 743, *744, 754. See also* terrestrial planets.
    atmosphere of, 752, 754
    characteristics of, *839*
    craters, 755
    crust of, 750
    day-night cycle, 754
    density, *839*
    diameter, *754, 839*
    distance from the Sun, *744, 754, 772*
    exploration of, 692
    gravity of, 752
    impact cratering, 755
    layers of, 750
    mass, *754, 839*
    orbit of Sun, 754, *839*
    revolution of, *839*
    rotation of, 754, 839, *839*
    size of, *744, 839*
    surface of, *754*
    tectonics on, 754
    temperature, 755
    volcanism on, *751,* 754
    weathering and erosion, *754,* 755
vertebrae, 578, *579*
vertebrates, 448
Very Large Array, New Mexico, 682, *682*
vestigial organs, **510,** *511*
vibrations, of waves, 814
villi, 610, *610*
viruses, 820
    diseases caused by, 647, *647,* 820
visible light, 679, 680, *680,* 681, 814
    Chapter Investigation, 684–685
    neutron stars and, 790
    in photosphere, 780
    telescopes and, 681–682
visible-light telescopes, 681–682
vision, 562, *562*
vitamin D, 565–567
vocabulary strategies, R50–R51
    description wheel, 80, *80,* 152, *152,* 230, *230,* 410, *410,* 456, *456,* 778, *778,* R50, *R50*
    four square, 48, *48,* 152, *152,* 260, *260,* 298, *298,* 340, *340,* 570, *570,* R50, *R50*
    frame game, 374, *374,* 488, *488,* 630, *630,* 706, *706,* R51, *R51*
    magnet word, 4, *4,* 526, *526,* 598, *598,* 672, *672,* R51, *R51*
    word triangle, 114, *114,* 152, *152,* 196, *196,* 742, *742,* R51, *R51*

vocal cords, 604, *604*
voice box, 604, *604*
volcanic islands, 120, *121*
volcanism, **750,** 750, *751,* 772, *772*
    of Earth, 750
    on Mars, 755
    on Mercury, *753*
    on Venus, 754
volcanoes
    crater lakes, 58
    on Earth, 750
    effects on atmosphere, 200, *448,* 449
    formation of, 201
    formation of atmosphere and, 293, 752
    formation of islands, 120, *121,* 200
    formation of waves and, 129
    hot springs and, 70
    on Io, 766, *766*
    mass extinction and, 448, 449, *493*
    mid-ocean ridge as, 40
    monitoring of, 222, *222*
    mudflows and, 264, *264*
    preservation of living things, 448
    rapid changes in Earth, 474, *475, 751*
    salt and, 116
    studies of, 295
    on Triton, 766, *766*
volt, **351**
Volta, Alessandro, 405, *437*
voltage, 351
    control of, 431, *431,* 435, *435*
    current, electric power and, 436
    drops in, 388
    Ohm's law, 361–362, *361*
    resistance and, 388
    in series of batteries, 384
    source, 376, *376,* 384, 400, *400,* 424, *424, 425*
voltmeter, 362
volume, 89, *89,* **811,** R43, *R43*
voluntary muscle, **586,** 592
Voyager 2, 690, *690,* 763

W

Walcott, Charles, 521
Wallace, Alfred, 504
Walt Disney World, 335
waning gibbous moon, 724, *725*
waning moon, 724, *725*
Ward, Peter, 448
waste disposal (trash), 44, 309
waste removal (body), 614–616, *615, 616, 620*
wastewater, 93–94, 158
water. *See also* evaporation; fresh water; glaciers;
    hydrosphere; ocean; rain; salt water.
    agriculture, 81, 82, 83, *83,* 101, 104
    alluvial fans and, 269, *269*
    in atmosphere, 53, *53,* 198, 696
    caverns, 270–271, *270*
    Chapter Investigation, 72–73, *72*
    chemical weathering, 234–235, *235,* 250, 254, *254*
    condensation, 52, 53, *53,* 74, *74*
    conservation of, 102–103
    cycle of, 52–54, *53,* 74, *74,* 102, 821
    deltas, 269, *269*
    density of, 59
    divides, 56–57, *57, 74,* ·267, *267,* 288, *288*
    drainage basins, 56–57, *57, 74,* 267, *267,* 288, *288*
    drought, 101, *101, 539,* 540
    on Earth, 752
    effect on Earth's surface, 201, 288
    erosion by, 261–262, *261*
    on Europa, *766*
    floodplain, *268,* 277–278, *278*
    floods, 54, *54,* 88, *88,* 250, *539,* 755
    flow and collection of, 52–54, 56–62, 64–67, *65, 69,*
      70–71, 74
    forms of, *46–47*
    fresh, 51, *51,* 56–62
    generation of electricity, 316, *316*
    human body and, 605, *605,* 617, *617*
    hydroelectric power, 82, 316, *316,* 435, *435*
    life forms in, 51
    as limiting factor, *539,* 540
    longshore drift and currents, 132, *132,* 142, 275,
      275, 276
    on Mars, 693, 696, 756
    meanders, 268, *268, 269*
    as need of living things, *FL8,* 493, 607
    phases of, 52
    pollution, 82, 94, *95,* 96–97
    populations size and, 530–531
    precipitation, 52, 53, *53,* 54, 58, 70, 74, *74*
    quality standards, 91, *91,* 98–99, *98,* 161
    ratio of land to, 50, *50*
    ratio of salt to fresh, 51, *51*
    as renewable resource, *301*
    rock weathering by, 232, *233,* 234–235, 750
    salt, 51, *51. See also* ocean.
    shortages of, 100–106, *101,* 108, *108,* 306
    soil and, 239, 245, 248
    as source of energy, 300
    sources of, 82, *82*
    stream channels, 268, *268*
    streams, 56, 57, *57,* 58, 198, 266–271, *269*
    transportation of, 546, *546*
    treatment of, 90–94, 108, *108,* 546, *546*
    underground, 52, 53, 57, 58, 64–68, *65, 66, 68, 69,*
      70–71, *70, 71,* 74, *74,* 83, 101, 105, 198, 270–271
    as unique substance, 49
    on Venus, 696
    waves, *112–113,* 119, 129–130, *130, 131,* 132–133,
      132, 142, *142,* 154, *155,* 232, 258, 262, 274–276,
      275, 276, 277, 288, *288,* 331, 800
water-catching devices, *102*
water cycle, FL33, **52,** 52–54, *53,* 55, 74, *74,* 102
water particles, *131*
water pollution, *96,* 105, 159, 249, 550, *550*
    consequences of, 82
    eutrophication and, 60, *60*
    sources of, *95,* 96–97, *97*
water rights, 104
watershed, 57, *57*
water table, **65,** *65, 66, 69,* 70, 270

water-treatment plants, 13, 92, *92*
water use cycle, 93
water vapor, 49, 293
water wheels, 86
watt, **436**
wave height, 130, *131*
wavelength, **680**, *812*
    absorption and reflection of, 188
    blue and red shift, 800
    Doppler effect, 800
    electromagnetic radiation, 680, *680*
    and frequency, 812
    ocean, 130, *131*
waves, *FL9*, FL33, 812, *814*
    animals in intertidal zone and, 154, *155*
    Chapter Investigation, 134–135, *134*
    damage caused by, 814, 815
    deposition by, 258, 262
    Doppler effect, 800
    effect on ocean temperatures, 119
    effect on shorelines, 132, *132*, 142, 274–276, *274, 275, 276, 277*, 288, *288*
    effects on Earth's surface, 132, *132*, 142, *275*
    electromagnetic, 331
    ocean, *112–113*, 129–130, *130, 131*, 132–133, 142, *142*
    rock weathering by, 232
    seismic, 815
    sound waves, 331, 392, *392*
    studies of, 146
waxing gibbous moon, 724, *725*
waxing moon, 724, *725*
weather. *See also* climate.
    as density-independent factors, 539, 540
    El Niño and, 128
    ocean currents and, 127–128, 199
weather balloons, 198, *198*
weather forecasting
    Argo floats and, *149*
    ocean studies and, 149
    satellites and, 697
    technology for, 198
weathering, 228–229, **231**, 231–232, 254, *254*
    chemical, 234–235, *235*, 236, *236*
    of Earth, 750
    on Mars, 755
    mechanical, 231, *231*, 232, *233, 236, 263*
    on Mercury, *753*
    on the Moon, 719
    planet surfaces and, 750, *751, 772, 772*
    rates of, 236, *236*, 237, *237*
    rockfalls, 263
    soil formation, 239
    on Venus, 755
Web pages, 397
wedge, 816
Weeki Wachee Spring, 335
weight, 748
weightlessness, 686
Welland Canal, 85
wells, 67, 68, *69,* 70
    artesian, 68, *68*

wet cell, 364
wetlands, **156,** 156–159
    aquifers of, 66
    human damage to, 158–159
    pollution of, 96
wet mount, making, R15, *R15*
whales, 154, 166, *167*, 510, *511*
wheel and axel, 816
white blood cells, *583*, 633, *633*, 641–642, 656
    types of, 644, *644*
white dwarfs, 788, *788*, 790, *791, 792, 804*, 837, *837*
wildlife, 58
Wilf, Peter, 447
Willamette River, *82*
wind
    on Earth, 750
    effect on climate, 40
    effect on Earth's surface, 201, 258, 261, 262, 277–279, *278, 279*, 288
    effect on shorelines, 274, *274*
    on gas giants, *759*
    generation of electricity, 319, *319*, 322–323, *322*
    on Jupiter, 759–760
    on Mars, 756
    ocean water and, 119, 127
    as renewable resource, *301*
    rip currents and, 132, *133*
    soil and, 249, 250, 300
    as source of energy, 300
    on the Sun, 783, *783*
    surface current and, 125, 199
    on Triton (moon), *766*
    uneven heating and, FL33
    wave formation, 129–130
    weathering and, 750
windbreaks, 252
wind farms, 319, *319*, 324
windmills, 319, *319*
windpipe, 602, *603*
winter, 710, *711*, 712, *712, 833*
Winter Park sinkhole (Florida), 191, *191*
wire, 382, *382*
wolves, *FL32*, 27, *27*, 542
wood storks, 669
wooly mammoths, 458, *458, 472*, 479, 490, *491*, 494
work, 141, 355
World Food Programme, 105
World Heritage sites, 521
World Wide Web, 397
worms, 156, 164, 201, 242, *243*, 294
writing tips, 45, 193, 337, 453, 567, 669

X, Y, Z

x-rays, 627, *627*, 680, *680*, 681, 683, 790
x-ray technicians, 625, *625*
yawns, 605
year, 709
yellowfin tuna, *171*
Yellowstone National Park, 27, *27*, 70, *70*, 71, *71*
zebra mussel, 549
zooplankton, 166, *167*

Acknowledgments

Photography

Cover © Stuart Westmorland/Getty Images; **FL1** © Stuart Westmorland/Getty Images; **FL3** *left (top to bottom)* Photograph of James Trefil by Evan Cantwell; Photograph of Rita Ann Calvo by Joseph Calvo; Photograph of Linda Carnine by Amilcar Cifuentes; Photograph of Sam Miller by Samuel Miller; *right (top to bottom)* Photograph of Kenneth Cutler by Kenneth A. Cutler; Photograph of Donald Steely by Marni Stamm; Photograph of Vicky Vachon by Redfern Photographics; **FL8** © Photographer's Choice/Getty Images; **FL9** © Darrell Jones/Getty Images; **FL10** © Wendy Conway/Alamy Images; **FL11** © Richard Folwell/Photo Researchers, Inc.; **FL12** 2003 Barbara Ries; **FL13** © Philip & Karen Smith/age fotostock america, inc.; **FL14** © Louis Psihoyos/psihoyos.com; **FL15** © Richard T. Nowitz/Corbis; **FL16** © Larry Dale Gordon/Getty Images; **FL17** © Professors P.M. Motta & S. Correr/Photo Researchers, Inc.; **FL18** © Roger Ressmeyer/Corbis; **FL19** Courtesy of NASA/JPL/Caltech; **FL24, FL25** Photographs by Sharon Hoogstraten; **FL30–FL31** © Ron Sanford/Corbis; **FL32–FL33** © Tim Fitzharris/Masterfile; **FL34–FL35** © Jack Affleck/SuperStock; **2–3** © Tony Ranze/Getty Images; **6** *top left* © Roger Ressmeyer/Corbis; *top right* © MedioImages/Alamy Images; *bottom left* © Colin Cuthbert/Photo Researchers, Inc.; *bottom right* © Peter Yates/Photo Researchers, Inc.; **7** © Barbara Strnadova/Photo Researchers, Inc.; **8** © Hencoup Enterprises Ltd/Photo Researchers, Inc.; **10** J. Hester *et al.*/NASA/CXC/ASU; **11** *top* © John Gress/AP/Wide World Photos; *bottom* © Kevin Fleming/Corbis; **12** Courtesy Science Magazine. Image by T. Koropatnick; **13** *left* © Thom Lang/Corbis; *center* Illustration by Gary Hincks; **15** © James King-Holmes/Science Photo Library; **16** © Andrew Lambert Photography/Photo Researchers, Inc.; **17** *top left* © William Taufic/Corbis; *top right* © Kennan Ward/Corbis; *bottom left* © British Antarctic Survey/Photo Researchers, Inc.; *bottom right* © James King-Holmes/Photo Researchers, Inc.; **18** *left* © Corbis; *right* The Granger Collection; **19** © Michael S. Yamashita/Corbis; **20** © Alfred Pasieka/Photo Researchers, Inc.; **22** © Phil Schermeister/Corbis; **24** © Donald C. Johnson/Corbis; **25** © Ovak Arslanian/Time Life Pictures/Getty Images; **26** © Alexandra Winkler/Reuters/Corbis; **27** © Campbell William/Corbis; **29** © John Shaw/Bruce Coleman, Inc.; **30** © Jim Cummins/Corbis; **31** © Juan Silva/Getty Images; **32** *top left to right* © Colin Cuthbert/Photo Researchers, Inc.; © Roger Ressmeyer/Corbis; © William Taufic/Corbis; © Peter Yates/Photo Researchers, Inc.; *center right* AP/Wide World Photos; *center left* © Alfred Pasieka/Photo Researchers, Inc.; **34** © Klaus Guldbrandsen/Photo Researchers, Inc.; **37** © Denis Scott/Corbis; **38–39** © Ralph White/Corbis; **39** *center* © Roger Steene/imagequestmarine.com; *bottom* Wolcott Henry/National Geographic Image Collection; **40** *top* NOAA/Pacific Marine Environmental Laboratory; *bottom* © The Chedd-Angier Production Company; **41** © Orbital Imaging Corporation and processing by NASA Goddard Space Flight Center. Image provided by ORBIMAGE; **42** © Masa Ushioda/Bruce Coleman, Inc.; **43** © Peters Scoones/Photo Researchers, Inc.; **44** *left* © Susumu Nishinaga/Photo Researchers, Inc.; *right* © Secret Sea Visions/Peter Arnold, Inc.; **45** © Mote Marine Laboratory, Sarasota, Florida; **46–47** © John Lawrence/Getty Images; **47** *top* © Anderson Ross/Getty Images; *bottom* Photograph by Sharon Hoogstraten; **49, 52** Photograph by Sharon Hoogstraten; **52** © Jagdish Agarwal/Alamy Images; **55** *left, inset* AP/WideWorld Photos/NASA Jet Propulsion Laboratories; **56** Photograph by Sharon Hoogstraten; **58** *center inset* © NASA/Getty Images; *bottom* © Claver Carroll/photolibrary/PictureQuest; **60** © Bruce Heinemann/Photodisc/PictureQuest; **61** Photograph by Sharon Hoogstraten; **62** © The Image Bank/Getty Images; **63** © Ron Erwin Photography; **64, 67** Photograph by Sharon Hoogstraten; **68** Peter Essick/Aurora; **70** © Michael S. Lewis/Corbis; **71** *left, right* © Jon Arnold/Jon Arnold Images/Alamy Images; **72** *top* Peter Essick/Aurora; *bottom* Photograph by Sharon Hoogstraten; **76** Photograph by Sharon Hoogstraten; **78–79** © Photographer's Choice/Getty Images; **79** *top, bottom* Photographs by Sharon Hoogstraten; **81** AP/Wide World Photos; **82** © Charles E. Rotkin/Corbis; **83** *top* Photograph by Sharon Hoogstraten; *bottom* © Michael Andrews/Animals Animals/Earth Scenes; **84** *top* © Geoff Tompkinson/Photo Researchers; *bottom* AP/Wide World Photos; **85** © Macduff Everton/Corbis; **86** © Shubroto Chattopadhyay/Index Stock Imagery/PictureQuest; **87** © 1987 Tom Bean; **88** AP/Wide World Photos; **89** © J.C. Carton/Bruce Coleman, Inc./PictureQuest; **90** Photograph by Sharon Hoogstraten; **91** AP/Wide World Photos; **96** *left* © Brand X Pictures; *right* © Photodisc/Getty Images; **97** AP/Wide World Photos; **98** *top* © William Taufic/Corbis; *bottom left, right* Photographs by Sharon Hoogstraten; **100** © Dieter Melhorn/Alamy Images; **101** AP/Wide World Photos; **102** *top left* © Digital Vision; *top right* © Bob Melnychuk/Getty Images; *center left* © Photodisc/Getty Images; *center right* © Digital Vision; *bottom* AP/Wide World Photos; **103** Photograph by Sharon Hoogstraten; **105** NASA Goddard Space Flight Center Scientific Visualization Studio; **107** *left* © Denny Eilers/Grant Heilman Photography; *left inset* © Bob Rowan/Progressive Image/Corbis; *right* AP/WideWorld Photos; **108** *top* AP/Wide World Photos; *bottom* NASA Goddard Space Flight Center Scientific Visualization Studio; **112–113** © Darrell Jones/Getty Images; **113** *top, center* Photograph by Sharon Hoogstraten; **115** Photograph by Sharon Hoogstraten; **117** © Roger Antrobus/Corbis; **118** *top* Photograph by Sharon Hoogstraten; *bottom* © Jane Burton/Bruce Coleman, Inc.; **119** *bottom* NASA/Photo Researchers; **121** Emory Kristof/National Geographic Image Collection; **123** Walter H.F. Smith/NOAA; **124** Photograph by Sharon Hoogstraten; **125** © AFP/Corbis/NASA; **126** © Dan Gair Photographic/Index Stock Imagery/PictureQuest; **127** Photograph by Sharon Hoogstraten; **128** *left* Ron Erwin Photography; *right* © Bettmann/Corbis; **129** Photograph by Sharon Hoogstraten; **132** © C.C. Lockwood/Bruce Coleman, Inc.; **133** © Buddy Mays/Corbis; **134** *top* AP/Wide World Photos; *bottom left, right* Photographs by Sharon Hoogstraten; **136** *top, bottom* © M.H. Black/Bruce Coleman, Inc.; **138** Photograph by Sharon Hoogstraten; **141** *left* © Attar Maher/Corbis; **144** Photograph by Sharon Hoogstraten; **146** *top* NOAA/OAR/National Undersea Research Program; *bottom* NOAA; **147** *top left* NOAA/OAR/National Undersea Research Program; *top right* The Granger Collection, New York; *bottom* NOAA Central Library; **148** *top* AP/Wide

World Photos; *center* © Silva Joao/Corbis Sygma; *bottom* Alan Schietzch/ARSTI/NOAA; **149** *top* OAR/National Undersea Research Program/Fairleigh Dickinson University; *bottom* Photograph by Ben Allsup/Webb Research Corporation; **150–151** © Brandon Cole; *top right* © Maximilian Weinzierl/Alamy Images; *center right* Photograph by Sharon Hoogstraten; **153** © Eric and David Hosking/Corbis; **155** *top, bottom* © Brandon Cole; **156** *top* Photograph by Sharon Hoogstraten; *bottom* © Robert Perron; **157** © W.K. Almond/Stock Boston/PictureQuest; **158** *top* © Lee Foster/Bruce Coleman, Inc.; *right inset* © Masa Ushioda/V&W/Bruce Coleman, Inc.; **159** AP/Wide World Photos; **160** *left, inset* © Lowell Georgia/Corbis; **161** Photograph by Sharon Hoogstraten; **162, 164** © Stone/Getty Images; **165** *top* © Mark A. Johnson/Alamy; *bottom* Photograph by Sharon Hoogstraten; **167** © Norbert Wu; **168** *top* © Dr. Ken Mac Donald/Photo Researchers; *center left* © The Natural History Museum, London; *bottom* © John Burbidge/Photo Researchers; **169** *left* © B. Murton/Southampton Oceanography Centre/Photo Researchers; *inset* © NSF Oasis Project/Norbert Wu Productions; **170** Photograph by Sharon Hoogstraten; **171** © Stephen Frink Collection/Alamy Images; **172** *top* © Norbert Wu; *bottom* © Dani/Jeske/Animals Animals/Earth Scenes; **173** *bottom* Jan Stromme/Strom/Bruce Coleman, Inc.; **174** © Institute of Oceanographic Sciences/NERC/Photo Researchers; **175** *top* © James Marshall/Corbis; *bottom* © Dr. Morley Read/Photo Researchers; **176** © Simon Fraser/Photo Researchers; **177** *top left* © Richard A. Cooke/Corbis; *top right* © Dorling Kindersley; **178** *top* © Gary Bell/Alamy Images; *bottom* Photograph by Sharon Hoogstraten; **180** *bottom left* © Norbert Wu; *bottom right* Jan Stromme/Strom/Bruce Coleman, Inc.; **182** © Lawson Wood/Corbis; **185** © Per Breiehagen/Getty Images; **186–187** Courtesy of NASA/JPL/Caltech; **187** *top* Carla Thomas/NASA; *bottom* Diamonds North Resources, Ltd.; **188** *top* Carla Thomas/NASA; *bottom* © The Chedd-Angier Production Company; **189** © William Whitehurst/Corbis; **190** AP/Wide World Photos; **192** Photo courtesy of the Alachua County Library District, Gainesville, Florida; **193** © Masa Ushioda/Bruce Coleman, Inc.; **194–195** NASA; **195** *top left* © NASA; *center left* SeaWiFS Project/NASA Goddard Space Flight Center; *bottom left* National Air & Space Museum/Smithsonian Institution; *top right* Courtesy of L. Sue Baugh; *center right* Bike Map courtesy of Chicagoland Bicycle Federation. Photograph by Sharon Hoogstraten; *bottom right* NASA Goddard Space Flight Center; **197** Photograph by Sharon Hoogstraten; **198–199** NASA; **199** *bottom left* © David Parker/Photo Researchers; *bottom center* © R. Wickllund/OAR/National Undersea Research Program; **199** *bottom center* University of Victoria, Victoria, British Columbia, Canada; *bottom right* © Peter and Georgina Bowater/Stock Connection/PictureQuest; **200** © Photodisc/Getty Images; **201** Photograph by Sharon Hoogstraten; **202** © A. Ramey/PhotoEdit/PictureQuest; **203** Photograph by Sharon Hoogstraten; **204** U.S. Geological Survey; **207** © David Parker/Photo Researchers; **208** Photograph by Sharon Hoogstraten; **211** © Jerry Driendl/Getty Images; **212** Photograph by Sharon Hoogstraten; **213** *top* © Stan Osolinski/Getty Images; *bottom* U.S. Geological Survey; **214, 216** *top left* U.S. Geological Survey; *bottom left, center right, bottom right* Photographs by Sharon Hoogstraten; **218, 219** *top right* © Space Imaging; *bottom background* © Paul Morrell/Getty Images; *bottom left* National Oceanic and Atmospheric Administration/Department of Commerce; **220** *top left, top center* Eros Data Center/U.S. Geological Survey; *bottom right* Photograph by Sharon Hoogstraten; **222** Photo courtesy of John D. Rogie, 1997; **223** © Lynn Radeka/SuperStock Images; **224** *top* NASA; *lower center* U.S. Geological Survey; *bottom left, background,* © Paul Morrell/Getty Images; *bottom left* National Oceanic and Atmospheric Administration/Department of Commerce; **226** U.S. Geological Survey; **228–229** © Wendy Conway/Alamy Images; **229** *top right, center* Photographs by Sharon Hoogstraten; **231** Photograph by Sharon Hoogstraten; **233** *background* © Photodisc/Getty Images; *inset top* © Susan Rayfield/Photo Researchers; *inset center, bottom left* Photographs courtesy of Sara Christopherson; *inset bottom right* © Kirkendall-Spring Photographer; **234** Photograph by Sharon Hoogstraten; **235** *top left* © Bettmann/Corbis; *top right* © Runk/Schoenberger/Grant Heilman Photography; *bottom* © Cheyenne Rouse/Visuals Unlimited; **237** *background* © Ecoscene/Corbis; *inset* © Michael Nicholson/Corbis; **238** Photograph by Sharon Hoogstraten; **239** *left* © Joel W. Rogers/Corbis; *right* © Barry Runk/Grant Heilman Photography; **240** © Barry Runk/Grant Heilman Photography; **241** *top left* © Sally A. Morgan/Corbis; *top right* © Peter Falkner/Photo Researchers; *bottom left* © Tony Craddock/Photo Researchers; *bottom left* © Tui de Roy/Bruce Coleman, Inc.; **244** © Barry Runk/Grant Heilman Photography; **245** © Jim Strawser/Grant Heilman Photography; **246** *top left* © Larry Lefever/Grant Heilman Photography; *center right, bottom left* Photograph by Sharon Hoogstraten; **248** © Cameron Davidson/Stock Connection, Inc./Alamy Images; **249** AP/Wide World Photos; **250** *top* © Steve Strickland/Visuals Unlimited; *bottom* Betty Wald/Aurora; **251** Photograph by Sharon Hoogstraten; **252** *left* © Charles O'Rear/Corbis; *right* © Larry Lefever/Grant Heilman Photography; **253** *center inset* Courtesy of Teska Associates, Evanston. Illinois; **254** *top right* © Runk/Schoenberger/Grant Heilman Photography; *bottom* © Larry Lefever/Grant Heilman Photography; **256** © Barry Runk/Grant Heilman Photography; **258–259** © A.C. Waltham/Robert Harding Picture Library/Alamy Images; **259** *center right* Photograph by Sharon Hoogstraten; **261** © Bernhard Edmaier/Photo Researchers; **262** Photograph by Sharon Hoogstraten; **263** AP/Wide World Photos; **264** *top* Photograph by L.M. Smith, Waterways Experiment Station, U.S. Army Corps of Engineers. Courtesy, USGS; *bottom* © Thomas Rampton/Grant Heilman Photography; **265** © Troy and Mary Parlee/Alamy Images; **266** Photograph by Sharon Hoogstraten; **267** © Bill Ross/Corbis; **268** *top* © Kevin Horan/Stock Boston /PictureQuest; *bottom* © Yann Arthus-Bertrand/Corbis; **269** © 1992 Tom Bean; **270** © Charles Kennard/Stock Boston/PictureQuest; **271** © Reuters NewMedia, Inc./Corbis; **272** © Peter Bowater/Alamy Images; **274** © John and Lisa Merrill/Getty Images; **275** © Robert Perron; **276** Photograph by Sharon Hoogstraten; **277** © Tim Barnwell/Picturesque/PictureQuest; **278** © John Shaw/Bruce Coleman, Inc.; **279** *top* © 1994 Tom Bean; *right* © Goodshoot/Alamy Images; **280** *background* © Gustav Verderber/Visuals Unlimited; *inset left* © Gary Meszaros/Bruce Coleman, Inc.; *inset right* © Lee Rentz/Bruce Coleman, Inc.; **281** Photograph by Sharon Hoogstraten; **283** *left* © Bernard Edmaier/Photo Researchers; *right* © ImageState-Pictor/PictureQuest; **284** *top* © Norman Barett/Bruce Coleman, Inc.; *bottom* © Jim Wark/Airphoto; **285** *top* © 1990 Tom Bean; *bottom* Photograph by Sharon Hoogstraten; **287** © Charles W. Campbell/Corbis; **288** *top* © Bernhard Edmaier/Photo Researchers; *center* © John and Lisa Merrill/Getty Images; **290** © Tom Bean; **292** *top* © Chris Butler/Photo Researchers; *bottom* © Detlev van Ravenswaay/Photo Researchers; **293** *top* © Jim Brandenburg/Minden Pictures; *center* J.W. Schopf/University of California, Los Angeles; *bottom* Japan Meteorological Agency; **294** *top left* © Simon Fraser/Photo Researchers; *top right* © Chase Studios/Photo Researchers; *bottom* Courtesy of the Ocean Drilling Program; **295** *top* NASA Goddard Space Flight Center; *bottom* STS-113 Shuttle Crew/NASA; **296–297** © Richard Folwell/Photo Researchers; **297** *top right, center* *right* Photographs by Sharon Hoogstraten; **299** © Corbis; **301** *top* © SuperStock; *bottom* © Gunter Marx Photography/Corbis; **305** Photograph by Sharon Hoogstraten; **306** *left* Diane Moore/Icon SMI; *top right* © Corbis; *bottom right* © Photodisc/Getty Images; **307** *left* © Photolink/Photodisc/PictureQuest; *inset* © Dr. Tony Braun/Photo Researchers; **308, 309** Photograph by Sharon Hoogstraten; **310** *top* Photograph by Sharon Hoogstraten; *bottom* © David Young-Wolff/PhotoEdit; **311** José Azel/Aurora; **312** *top* © Dick Luria/Index Stock/PictureQuest; *bottom* © Johnston Images/Picturesque/PictureQuest; **313** Photograph by Sharon Hoogstraten; **315** © Steve Allen/Brand X Pictures/PictureQuest; **316** © Beth Davidow/Visuals Unlimited; **317** © Martin Bond/Photo Researchers; **318** © James Stilling/Getty Images; **319** © Lynne Ledbetter/Visuals Unlimited; **320** Andrew Carlin/Tracy Operators; **321** © California Fuel Cell Partnership; **322** *top* © M.L. Sinibald/Corbis; *bottom left, right* Photograph by Sharon Hoogstraten; **323** Photograph by Sharon Hoogstraten; **324** *top left* (1) © SuperStock; *top left* (2) © Gunter Marx Photography/Corbis; *bottom* José Azel/Aurora. **329** © Nick Koudis/Getty Images; **330–331** © PHISH 2003; **331** © Jacques M. Chenet/Corbis; **332** *top* © John Foxx/ImageState; *bottom* © The Chedd-Angier Production Company; **333** © Stuart Hughes/Corbis; **334** © Louie Psihoyos/Corbis; **335** © Joe Raedle/Getty Images; **336** © Thomas Nebbia/National Geographic Image Collection; **337** Photo Chuck Zlotnick/Courtesy of Stan Winston Studio; **338–339** AP/Wide World Photos; **339, 341** Photographs by Sharon Hoogstraten; **342** © Roger Ressmeyer/Corbis; **344** © Charles D. Winters/Photo Researchers; **346** Photograph by Sharon Hoogstraten; **348** © Maximilian Stock Ltd./Photo Researchers; **349** *left* © Ann and Rob Simpson; *right* © Patrice Ceisel/Visuals Unlimited; **350** Photograph by Sharon Hoogstraten; **351** © Steve Crise/Corbis; **353** © A & J Verkaik/Corbis; **354** Photograph by Sharon Hoogstraten; **355** *top* © Tim Wright/Corbis; *bottom* © Leland Bobb/Corbis; **356** © James D. Hooker/Lighting Equipment News (UK); **358** *top left* © Scott T. Smith; All other photographs by Sharon Hoogstraten; **359, 360, 362, 363** Photographs by Sharon Hoogstraten; **365** © Chip Simons 2003; **366** Photo Courtesy of NASA/Getty Images; **367** © Julian Hirshowitz/Corbis; **368** © James D. Hooker/Lighting Equipment News (UK); **372–373** © 2003 Barbara Ries; **373, 375** Photographs by Sharon Hoogstraten; **380** *left* © 1989 Paul Silverman/Fundamental Photographs, NYC; *right* Photograph by Sharon Hoogstraten; **381** © Creative Publishing International, Inc.; **382** *top left* © Gary Rhijnsburger/Masterfile; *center left* © Creative Publishing International, Inc.; **383, 384, 385, 386** Photographs by Sharon Hoogstraten; **388** © Robert Essel NYC/Corbis; **389** Photograph by Sharon Hoogstraten; **391** *top* AP/Wide World Photos; *bottom* Photograph by Sharon Hoogstraten; **393** © Kurt Stier/Corbis; **394, 395** © Gen Nishino/Getty Images; **396** © Donna Cox and Robert Patterson/National Center for Supercomputing Applications, University of Illinois, Urbana; **397** AP/Wide World Photos; **398** *top* © Sheila Terry/Photo Researchers; *bottom* Photograph by Sharon Hoogstraten; **404** *top* © SPL/Photo Researchers; *bottom* The Granger Collection, New York; **405** *top left* © Philadelphia Museum of Art/Corbis; *top right* © Archivo Iconografico, S.A./Corbis; *bottom* © Adam Hart-Davis/Photo Researchers; **406** *top* Science Museum/Science & Society Picture Library; *center left* © Bettmann/Corbis; *center right* © Tony Craddock/Photo Researchers; *bottom* © Bettmann/Corbis; **407** *top* © Alfred Pasieka/Photo Researchers; *bottom* AP/Wide World Photos; **408–409** © Philip & Karen Smith/age fotostock america, inc.; **409, 411** Photographs by Sharon Hoogstraten; **412** *top* © Michael S. Yamashita/Corbis; *bottom* Photograph by Sharon Hoogstraten; **413** Photographs by Sharon Hoogstraten; **414** © The Natural History Museum, London; **415** Photograph by Sharon Hoogstraten; **416** NASA; **417** Photograph by Sharon Hoogstraten; **418** © Chris Madeley/Photo Researchers; **419** © Brian Bahr/Getty Images; *inset* Courtesy of Discover Magnetics; **420, 422** Photographs by Sharon Hoogstraten; **423** *top* © George Haling/Photo Researchers; *bottom* © Dick Luria/Photo Researchers; **425** © G. K. & Vikki Hart/Getty Images; **427** Photograph by Sharon Hoogstraten; **429** © Ondrea Barbe/Corbis; **430** Photograph by Sharon Hoogstraten; **431** © Randy M. Ury/Corbis; **432** *top* © Christopher Gould/Getty Images; *bottom* Photographs by Sharon Hoogstraten; **433** Photographs by Sharon Hoogstraten; **434** Bureau of Reclamation; **436** Courtesy of General Electric; **437** *top* Photograph by Sharon Hoogstraten; *bottom* © Maya Barnes/The Image Works; **439** © Mark Richards/PhotoEdit; **440** *top* Photograph by Sharon Hoogstraten; **445** © Martin Siepman/Age Fotostock America Inc.; **446, 447** *background* © Alfredo Maiquez/Lonely Planet Images; **447** *top left* © Donald Windsor; *bottom right* Reprinted with permission from "Timing the Radiations of Leaf Beetles: Hispines on Gingers from Latest Cretaceous to Recent" Peter Wilf and Conrad C. Labandeira, SCIENCE V. 289:291-294 (2000). © 2000 AAAS.; **448** *bottom* © The Chedd-Angier Production Company; *top* Courtesy, Earth Sciences and Image Analysis, NASA-Johnson Space Center; **449** © The Natural History Museum, London; **450** © Brandon D. Cole/Bruce Coleman, Inc.; **451** *top* © Bill Curtsinger/National Geographic Image Collection; *bottom* © Jonathan Blair/Corbis; **452** © Jeffrey L. Rotman/Corbis; **453** © Mote Marine Laboratory; **454–455** © Louis Psihoyos/psihoyos.com; **455** *top right* © Digital Vision; *center right* Photograph by Sharon Hoogstraten; *bottom right* © Chris Butler/Photo Researchers; **457** Photograph by Sharon Hoogstraten; **458** *top left* Latreille-Cerpolex; *center left* © Alfred Pasteka/Photo Researchers; *bottom left* © Dominique Braud/Animals Animals; **459** *bottom left, bottom right* Courtesy, American Museum of Natural History; **460** © 2001 Tom Bean; **461** *background* © Images Ideas, Inc./PictureQuest; *top left* © Dorling Kindersley; *top right* © John Elk III; *center right* © Kaj R. Svensson/Photo Researchers; *bottom right* © Francesc Muntada/Corbis; **462** © Doug Wilson/Corbis; **463** *top left* © B & C Alexander; *top right* © Maria Stenzel/National Geographic Image Collection; **464** © Chris Butler/Photo Researchers; *inset* © Robert Dowling/Corbis; **465** *left* Courtesy of The Bicycle Museum of America; *center* © Softride, Inc.; *right* © Photodisc/Getty Images; **466** *bottom left* © Tom Bean 1993; *bottom right* © Dr. Morley Read/Photo Researchers; **467** *top right* © Asa C. Thoresen/Photo Researchers; *bottom right* © Sinclair Stammers/Photo Researchers; **468** *bottom* Photograph by Sharon Hoogstraten; **470** *background* © G. Brad Lewis/Getty Images; **472** *left* © Jonathan Blair/Corbis; *inset* AP/Wide World Photos; **473** Photograph by Sharon Hoogstraten; **474** © Sime s.a.s./eStock Photography/PictureQuest; **475** *left, right* © John Marshall Photography; **476** *bottom left* Mural by Peter Sawyer © National Museum of Natural History, Smithsonian Institution, Washington, D.C.; *bottom right* Exhibit Museum of Natural History, The University of Michigan, Ann Arbor, Michigan; **477** *bottom left* © Ludek Pesek/Photo Researchers; *bottom right* © Steve Vidler/SuperStock; **478** © Tom Bean; **479** © Sisse Brimberg/National Geographic Image Collection; **480** *top* © Jonathan Blair/Corbis; *left, right* Photographs by Sharon Hoogstraten; **482** *center left* © Asa C. Thoresen/Photo Researchers; **486, 487** © Richard T. Nowitz/Corbis; **490** *top* © Mark A. Schneider/Photo

Researchers, Inc.; *center* © Sinclair Stammers/Photo Researchers, Inc.; *bottom* © Novosti/Science Photo Library/Photo Researchers, Inc.; **491** *bottom* © Field Museum/Photo Researchers, Inc.; **493** *top* © Ken M. Johns/Photo Researchers, Inc.; **494** *bottom* © Lynette Cook/Photo Researchers, Inc.; **495** *top right* © D. Van Ravenswaay/Photo Researchers, Inc.; *bottom right* © David Parker/Photo Researchers, Inc.; *top left* © D. Van Ravenswaay/Photo Researchers, Inc.; **496** *top* © Paddy Ryan/Animals Animals; *bottom* © Layne Kennedy/Corbis; **497** *left* © Corbis-Royalty Free; **498, 499** *background* © Ralph Lee Hopkins/Lonely Planet Images; *bottom* © The Natural History Museum, London; *top* © The Granger Collection, New York; **499** *top right* © Volker Steger/Photo Researchers, Inc.; *right* © Zig Leszczynski/Animals Animals; *left* © Theo Allots/Visuals Unlimited; **500** *bottom right, top left, top right* © Tui De Roy/Minden Pictures; *bottom left* © Richard I'Anson/Lonely Planet Images; *background* © Ralph Lee Hopkins/Lonely Planet Images; **501** *right* © Hans Reinhard/Bruce Coleman, Inc.; *center, left* © Larry Allan/Bruce Coleman, Inc.; **503** *top left* © Bruce Coleman, Inc.; *background* © Paul Souders/Accent Alaska; **504** *top* © Hans Reinhard/Bruce Coleman, Inc.; *bottom, center* © Jane Burton/Bruce Coleman, Inc.; **505** © John Winnie, Jr./DRK Photo; **506** *top* © Marian Bacon/Animals Animals; **508** © Ed Degginger/Color-Pic, Inc.; **509** © Mark A. Schneider/Photo Researchers, Inc.; **511** *background* © Corbis-Royalty Free; **512** *center, left* © Photodisc/Getty Images; *right* © Mark Smith/Photo Researchers, Inc.; **514** © Photodisc/Getty Images; **515** © Norbert Wu; **516** *bottom* © Mark A. Schneider/Photo Researchers, Inc.; *top* © Tui de Roy/Bruce Coleman, Inc.; **518** © Hans Reinhard/Bruce Coleman, Inc.; **520** *bottom right* © Visuals Unlimited; *bottom left, top right* The Natural History Museum Picture Library, London; **521** *top left* American Museum of Natural History Library; *bottom right* © O. Louis Mazzatenta/National Geographic Image Collection; *center* © Peter Scoones/Photo Researchers, Inc.; *top right* © Geoff Bryant/Photo Researchers, Inc.; **522** *top left* © Science/Visuals Unlimited; *top right* © Kevin O. Mooney/Odyssey/Chicago; *center right* © Ira Block/National Geographic Image Collection; *bottom left* © James King-Holmes/Photo Researchers, Inc.; **523** *top left* © John Reader/Science Photo Library; *bottom left* © David Parker/Photo Researchers, Inc.; **524, 525** *background* NASA; **527** © David M. Phillips/Photo Researchers, Inc.; **529** *left* © Photo Researchers, Inc.; *right* © Wayne Lynch/DRK Photo; **530** *right* © Darrell Gulin/DRK Photo; *left* © Thomas Wiewandt/Corbis; **531** *left* © Stephen J. Krasemann/DRK Photo; *right* © D. Cavagnaro/DRK Photo; **532** *center* © Visuals Unlimited; *right* © Judy White/GardenPhotos.com; *left* © Betty Press/Animals Animals; **533** © Jim Sulley/The Image Works; **534** © Anthony Mercieca/Photo Researchers, Inc.; **535** *left* © Rod Planck/Photo Researchers, Inc.; *right* © Michael Abbey/Photo Researchers, Inc.; **537** © OSF/N. Rosing/Animals Animals; **538** © Tom Brakefield/Corbis; **539** © Najlah Feanny/Corbis; **541** *right* © Martha Cooper/Peter Arnold, Inc.; *bottom* © Dennis Flaherty/Photo Researchers, Inc.; **542** © Stephen J. Krasemann/DRK Photo; **543** *left* © Ted Spiegel/Corbis; *top right* © Wesmar; **545** *bottom right* © Rob Crandall/The Image Works; *bottom left* © Grant Heilman/Grant Heilman Photography; *top right* © Ed Degginger/Color-Pic, Inc.; **546** *left* © Bob Daemmrich/The Image Works; *right* © Geri Engberg/The Image Works; **547** NASA; **549** *top* © Ray Coleman/Photo Researchers, Inc.; *bottom* © John Serrao/Photo Researchers, Inc.; **550** *top* © Donald Speckler/Animals Animals; *bottom* © Janis Burger/Bruce Coleman, Inc.; **551** © Jeff Greenberg/The Image Works; **552** © Gaetano/Corbis; **554** *center* © Najlah Feanny/Corbis; *bottom* © Bob Daemmrich/The Image Works; **556** © Photo Researchers, Inc.; **557** © Wayne Lynch/DRK Photo; **559** RNHRD NHS Trust; **560–561** © Peter Byron/PhotoEdit; **561** *top right* © ISM/Phototake; **562** *top* © Wellcome Department of Cognitive Neurology/Photo Researchers, Inc., *bottom* Chedd-Angier Production Company; **563** © Myrleen Ferguson Cate/PhotoEdit; **564** © SuperStock; **567** © Najlah Feanny/Corbis; **568–569** © Chris Hamilton/Corbis; **569** *top* Frank Siteman, *bottom* Ken O'Donoghue; **571** © SuperStock; **572** Frank Siteman; **573** *left* © Martin Rotker/Phototake; **574** © SW Production/Index Stock Imagery/PictureQuest; **575** *background* © Hulton-Deutsch Collection/Corbis, *center* © Underwood & Underwood/Corbis; **576** Frank Siteman; **577** © Prof. P. Motta/Dept. of Anatomy/University "La Sapienza," Rome/Photo Researchers, Inc.; **578** © Photodisc/Getty Images; **580** *bottom* © Science Photo Library/Photo Researchers, Inc., *bottom left* © Zephyr/Photo Researchers, Inc.; **581** *top* © Zephyr/Photo Researchers, Inc., *bottom* Frank Siteman; **582** *top left* © Stock Image/SuperStock, *top right* © Science Photo Library/Photo Researchers, Inc.; **583** © Dennis Kunkel/Phototake; **584** Frank Siteman; **585** © Kevin R. Morris/Corbis; **587** *background* © Mary Kate Denny/PhotoEdit, *top* © Martin Rotker/Phototake, *left* © Triarch/Visuals Unlimited, *bottom* © Eric Grave/Phototake; **588** © Ron Frehm/AP Wide World Photos; **589** © Jeff Greenberg/PhotoEdit; **590** *top* © Gunter Marx Photography/Corbis, *bottom, all* Frank Siteman; **592** © Martin Rotker/Phototake; **593** *top* © Stock Image/SuperStock; **596–597** © Larry Dale Gordon/Getty Images; **597** *top* Frank Siteman, *bottom* Ken O'Donoghue; **599** Frank Siteman; **600** © Amos Nachoum/Corbis; **601** Ken O'Donoghue; **603** *bottom left* © Michael Newman/PhotoEdit, *bottom right* © Science Photo Library/Photo Researchers, Inc.; **605** © Kennan Harvey/Getty Images; **606** *background* © Jim Cummins/Getty Images, *center* © Steve Casimiro/Getty Images; **607** Ken O'Donoghue; **609** Ken O'Donoghue; **610** © Professors P. Motta & A. Familiari/University "La Sapienza," Rome/Photo Researchers, Inc.; **611** © David Young-Wolff/PhotoEdit; **612** © Dr. Gladden Willis/Visuals Unlimited; **613** © David Gifford/SPL/Custom Medical Stock Photo; **614** Frank Siteman; **617** © LWA-Dann Tardif/Corbis; **618** *top* © Myrleen Ferguson Cate/PhotoEdit, *bottom left* Ken O'Donoghue, *bottom right* Frank Siteman; **619** Frank Siteman; **624** *top* © Hulton Archive/Getty Images, *bottom* © Simon Fraser/Photo Researchers, Inc.; **625** *top* © Bettmann/Corbis, *center* © Underwood & Underwood/Corbis, *bottom* © George Bernard/Photo Researchers, Inc.; **626** *top left* © Collection CNRI/Phototake, *top right* © Geoff Tompkinson/Photo Researchers, Inc., *bottom* © Josh Sher/Photo Researchers, Inc.; **627** *top* © Simon Fraser/Photo Researchers, Inc., *bottom* © GJLP/Photo Researchers, Inc.; **628–629** © Professors P.M. Motta & S. Correr/Photo Researchers, Inc.; **629** *both* Frank Siteman; **631** Frank Siteman; **633** © Science Photo Library/Photo Researchers, Inc.; **634** © Myrleen Ferguson Cate/PhotoEdit; **635** © Susumu Nishinaga/Photo Researchers, Inc.; **637** © Journal-Courier/The Image Works; **638** *top left* © Michael Newman/PhotoEdit, *bottom left* Ken O'Donoghue, *center right, bottom right* Frank Siteman; **640** Frank Siteman; **641** *top* © Eddy Gray/Photo Researchers, Inc., *bottom* © Mary Kate Denny/PhotoEdit; **642** © Science Photo Library/Photo Researchers, Inc.; **643** *top* © Dr. P. Marazzi/Photo Researchers, Inc., *top right* © Dr. Jeremy Burgess/Photo Researchers, Inc.; **644** © Science Photo Library/Photo Researchers, Inc.; **645** Frank Siteman; **646** © Bob Daemmrich/The Image Works; **647** © Richard Lord/The Image Works; **648** *background* © SCIMAT/Photo Researchers, Inc., *inset* © Vision/Photo Researchers; **649** Ken O'Donoghue; **650** RMIP/Richard Haynes; **651** Frank Siteman; **652** *top inset* © Dennis Kunkel/Phototake, *bottom inset* © Andrew Syred/Photo Researchers, Inc., *center* © Photodisc/Getty Images; **653** *all* © Eric Schrempp/Photo

R120 Acknowledgments

Researchers, Inc.; **654** © The Image Bank/Getty Images; **655** *background* © James King-Holmes/Photo Researchers, Inc., *top right* © Sygma/Corbis, *bottom right* © David Hanson; **661** © David Nunuk/Photo Researchers; **662–663** © Charles O'Rear/Corbis; **663** *top right* © D. Nunuk/Photo Researchers; **664** © The Chedd-Angier Production Company; **664–665** © David Parker/Photo Researchers; **665** *top center* NASA/JPL; **666** © Bettmann/Corbis; **667** *left* © Frank Whitney/Alamy Images; **668** © Bettmann/Corbis; **669** © Jeff Greenberg/Alamy Images; **670–671** NASA; **671, 673** Photographs by Sharon Hoogstraten; **675** Johnson Space Center/NASA; **676** Photograph by Sharon Hoogstraten; **677** *top* © Roger Ressmeyer/Corbis; *bottom* Photograph by Sharon Hoogstraten; **679** Photograph by Sharon Hoogstraten; **680** *center left* Kapteyn Laboratorium/Photo Researchers; *center* National Optical Astronomy Observatories/Photo Researchers; *center right* A. Wilson (UMD) et al., CXC/NASA; **682** © Roger Ressmeyer/Corbis; **683** *top left* NASA Johnson Space Center; *top right* © STScI/NASA/Photo Researchers; **684** *top left* © ImageState-Pictor/PictureQuest; **684–685, 686** Photographs by Sharon Hoogstraten; **687** *bottom, inset* NASA; **688** Courtesy of NASA/JSC; **689** *top* NASA; *bottom* Photograph by Sharon Hoogstraten; **691** Photograph by Bill Ingalls/NASA; **694** *left, inset* Chris Butler/Photo Researchers; **695** NASA; **696** Courtesy of V.R. Sharpton University of Alaska-Fairbanks and the Lunar and Planetary Institute; **697** Photograph by Sharon Hoogstraten; **698** NASA; **699** *background* © Jan Tove Johansson/Image State-Pictor/PictureQuest; *left inset* Andy Fyon, Ontariowildflower.com (Division of Professor Beaker's Learning Labs); *right inset* NASA; **700** *top* Photograph by Sharon Hoogstraten; *center* © Roger Ressmeyer/Corbis; *bottom* NASA; **704–705** © Roger Ressmeyer/Corbis; **705** *top right, center right* Photographs by Sharon Hoogstraten; *bottom right* NASA Goddard Space Flight Center; **707** *left* NASA; *right* Photograph by Sharon Hoogstraten; **708** *top* © 2003 The Living Earth Inc.; *bottom* Photograph by Sharon Hoogstraten; **709** Photograph by Sharon Hoogstraten; **711** NASA/JSC; **713** © Arnulf Husmo/Getty Images; **714** *top* © Christian Perret/jump; *bottom left, bottom right* Photograph by Sharon Hoogstraten; **715, 716** Photographs by Sharon Hoogstraten; **717** Courtesy of NASA and the Lunar and Planetary Institute; **718** USGS Flagstaff, Arizona; **719** *top right* Photograph by Sharon Hoogstraten; *bottom right* NASA; *right inset* NASA and the Lunar and Planetary Institute; **722** Photograph by Steve Irvine; **723** © DiMaggio/Kalish/Corbis; **725** *background* Lunar Horizon View/NASA; **726** Photograph by Sharon Hoogstraten; **727** *top* © Roger Ressmeyer/Corbis; *bottom* Photograph by Jean-Francois Guay; **728** *center* NASA/Getty Images; *bottom left* © Fred Espenak; **729** *top* © Jeff Greenberg/MRP/Photo Researchers; *bottom* © 1999 Ray Coleman/Photo Researchers; **731** *top left* © Peter Duke; *right inset* © David Parker/Photo Researchers; *bottom left* Public Domain; *bottom center* Barlow Aerial Photography, Ignacio, CO; **732** *top left* © 2003 The Living Earth, Inc.; *center left* Photograph courtesy of NASA and the Lunar and Planetary Institute; **734** *left* USGS Flagstaff, Arizona; *right* NASA Goddard Space Flight Center; **736** Courtesy of Adler Planetarium & Astronomy Museum, Chicago, Illinois; **737** *top left* © Stapleton/Corbis; *center* © Science Museum/Science & Society Picture Library; *right* Provided by Roger Bell, University of Maryland, and Michael Briley, University of Wisconsin, Oshkosh; *bottom* Courtesy of Adler Planetarium & Astronomy Museum, Chicago, Illinois; **738** *top left* © Harvard College Observatory/Photo Researchers; *top right* Robert Williams and the Hubble Deep Field Team (STScI) and NASA; *bottom* © Fermi National Accelerator Laboratory/Photo Researchers; **739** *top* Ann Feild (STScI); *bottom* © NASA/Photo Researchers; **740–741** Courtesy of NASA/JPL/University of Arizona; **741** *top right, center right* Photographs by Sharon Hoogstraten; **743, 746** Photographs by Sharon Hoogstraten; **747** *left* Photo © Calvin J. Hamilton; *right* Courtesy of NASA/JPL/Caltech; **748** NASA; **749** *top* Photograph by Sharon Hoogstraten; *bottom* Johnson Space Center NASA; **751** *background* Mark Robinson/Mariner 10/NASA; *top right* NASA; *top left* © Walt Anderson/Visuals Unlimited; *bottom left* NASA/JPL/Malin Space Science Systems; **752** Photograph by Sharon Hoogstraten; **753** *top* USGS; *bottom* Courtesy of NASA/JPL/Northwestern University; **754** *top, center, bottom* NASA; **755** NASA/JSC; **756** Courtesy of NASA/JPL/Caltech; **757** *left* Courtesy of NASA/JPL/Malin Space Science Systems; *right* MAP-A-Planet/NASA; *right inset* NASA/Goddard Space Flight Center Scientific Visualization Studio; **758, 759** Courtesy of NASA/JPL/Caltech; **760** *top* Courtesy of NASA/JPL/Caltech; *bottom* Photograph by Sharon Hoogstraten; **761** *top* NASA; *bottom* NASA and the Hubble Heritage Team (STScI/AURA); **762** *top* E. Karkoschka(LPL) and NASA; *bottom* © Calvin J. Hamilton; **763** *top* Courtesy of NASA/JPL/Caltech; *center* NASA; **764** near.jhuapl.edu; **765** Hubble Space Telescope, STScI-PR96-09a/NASA; **766** *top left, inset* NASA; *bottom left* Courtesy of NASA/JPL/Caltech; *bottom left inset* NASA; *top right* © NASA/JPL/Photo Researchers; *top right inset, bottom right, bottom right inset* NASA; **767** Courtesy of NASA/JPL/Caltech; **768** *background* © 1997 Jerry Lodriguss; *right* Courtesy of NASA/JPL/Caltech; **769** Fred R. Conrad/The New York Times; **770** *top left* © James L. Amos/Corbis; *bottom left* Photograph by Sharon Hoogstraten; **771** Photograph by Sharon Hoogstraten; **772** *top* NASA; *bottom* Courtesy of NASA/JPL/Caltech; **776–777** David Malin Images/Anglo-Australian Observatory; **777** *top left* © Jerry Schad/Photo Researchers; *center left* Photograph by Sharon Hoogstraten; **779** Photograph by Sharon Hoogstraten; **781** Photograph by Jay M. Paschoff, Bryce A. Babcock, Stephan Martin, Wendy Carlos, and Daniel B. Seaton © Williams College; **782** *left* © John Chumack/Photo Researchers; *right* © NASA/Photo Researchers; **783** © Patrick J. Endres/Alaskaphotographics.com; **784** *top* © Dave Robertson/Masterfile; *left bottom, right bottom* Photographs by Sharon Hoogstraten; **785, 786, 787** Photographs by Sharon Hoogstraten; **789** *top* © Dorling Kindersley; *bottom* ESA and J. Hester (ASU), NASA; **790** J. Hester et al./NASA/CXC/ASU; **791** Hubble Heritage Team/AURA/STScI/NASA; **793** © MPIA-HD, Birkle, Slawik/Photo Researchers; **794** Photograph by Sharon Hoogstraten; **795** *top* Allan Morton/Dennis Milon/Photo Researchers; *bottom* Photograph by Sharon Hoogstraten; **796** David Malin Images /Anglo-Australian Observatory; **797** Walter Jaffe/Leiden Observatory, Holland Ford/JHU/STScI, and NASA; **798** *left* NASA and Hubble Heritage Team (STScI); *center* NASA, H. Ford (JHU), G. Illingworth (UCSC/LO), M. Clampin (STScI), G. Hartig (STScI), the ACS Science Team, and ESA; **799** Photograph by Sharon Hoogstraten; **800** © Jason Ware; **802** Photograph by Sharon Hoogstraten; **803** N. Benitez (JHU), T. Broadhurst (The Hebrew University), H. Ford (JHU), M. Clampin (STScI), G. Hartig (STScI), G. Illingworth (UCO/Lick Observatory), the AGS Science Team and ESA/NASA; **804** *top* David Malin Images/Anglo-Australian Observatory; *bottom* N. Benitez (JHU), T. Broadhurst (The Hebrew University), H. Ford (JHU), M. Clampin (STScI), G. Hartig (STScI), G. Illingworth (UCO/Lick Observatory), the AGS Science Team and ESA/NASA; **806** *left* Hubble Heritage Team (AURA/STScI/NASA); *right* Anglo-Australian Observatory/David Malin Images; **818** *left* © Dwight R. Kuhn; *right* © Sylvester Allred/Fundamental

Photographs; **819** © Dwight R. Kuhn; **820** © Hans Gelderblom/Visuals Unlimited; **826** *bottom left* Mural by Peter Sawyer © National Museum of Natural History, Smithsonian Institution, Washington, D.C.; *bottom right* Exhibit Museum of Natural History, The University of Michigan, Ann Arbor, Michigan; **827** *bottom left* © Ludek Pesek/Photo Researchers; *bottom right* © Steve Vidler/SuperStock; **828** © Dorling Kindersley; **829** *top right* © John Elk III; *center right* © Kaj R. Svensson/Photo Researchers; *bottom right* © Francesc Muntada/Corbis; **R28** © Photodisc/Getty Images.

Illustrations and Maps

Accurate Art Inc. **183, 291, 485, 770;** Ampersand Design Group **133, 382;** Argosy **317, 319, 321,** *left* **812;** Julian Baum **721 781, 791, 792, 795, 804;** Richard Bonson/Wildlife Art Ltd. **53, 59, 65, 66, 69, 74, 492, 493, 516** (*top*); Peter Bull/Wildlife Art Ltd. **92, 93, 95, 108, 276, 278, 283, 285, 468, 690, 691, 711, 712, 732, 820;** Bill Cigliano **731, 801;** Steve Cowden **131, 392, 394–395, 400, 712;** Sandra Doyle/Wildlife Art Ltd. **822;** Stephen Durke **51, 71, 87, 94, 106, 173, 343, 344, 345, 353, 357, 363, 368, 371, 376, 378, 385, 400, 435, 440, 442, 676, 678, 682,** *right* **812, 813;** Chris Forsey **17, 20, 34;** Luigi Galante **243, 254;** David Hardy **200, 675, 696, 744, 747, 759, 772;** Gary Hincks **120–121, 265, 269, 478;** Ian Jackson **155, 163, 167, 180;** Ian Jackson/Wildlife Art Ltd. **511;** Dan Maas/Maas Digital **692, 700;** Debbie Maizels **577, 588, 650, 656, 818;** Mapquest.com, Inc. **43, 50, 70, 82, 84, 85, 87, 96, 101, 104, 105, 116, 117, 125, 128, 138, 141, 153, 157, 158, 162, 172, 174, 191, 205, 206, 211, 220, 221, 222, 224, 241, 282, 286, 294, 459, 494, 495, 498, 498-499, 534, 545, 667, 728, 838;** Janos Marffy **303, 461, 480, 482, 828;** Morgan, Cain & Assoc. **117, 122, 125, 140, 173, 244;** Linda Nye **573, 592, 608, 632, 636, 656, 658;** Steve Oh/KO Studios **644;** Laurie O'Keefe **509, 512, 516** (*bottom*); Mick Posen/Wildlife Art Ltd. **503;** Precision Graphics **304, 543;** Mike Saunders **233, 236, 254;** Peter Scott/Wildlife Art Ltd. **500, 504, 516** (*center*); SlimFilms **302, 314, 316, 318;** Space.comCanada, Inc. **833–836;** Dan Stukenschneider **141, 347, 365, 379, 381, 387, 424, 425, 426, 428, 429, 440, 681, 700, 816, R11–R19, R22, R32;** Raymond Turvey **126, 130–132, 275;** Rob Wood **233, 270;** Ron Wood/Wood Ronsaville Harlin **467, 484, 720, 732;** Bart Vallecoccia **573, 579, 592, 594, 603, 604, 606, 608, 611, 615, 616, 620, 622, 634**